The **Hallmark Features**

A COMPLETE LEARNING PACKAGE

Working with a panel of experts, A. Javier Treviño thoroughly examines all aspects of social problems, offering a contemporary and authoritative introduction and focusing on the troublesome situations that are endemic to social structures and institutions. The latest data provides a strong research-based foundation for exploration of the topic.

- **"EXPERIENCING"** features in every chapter help to reveal concepts of intersectionality, exploring the interplay of race/ethnicity, class, and gender, and how their various combinations compound social inequalities.

- **"BEYOND OUR BORDER"** features encourage the reader to consider the global scope of the social problem in question and examine how the interconnectedness or transnational character of these problems impact people (often quite differently) around the world.

- **"SOCIAL CHANGE: WHAT CAN YOU DO?"** discusses how students can help solve a particular social problem through volunteer work, service learning, community activism, and other forms of civic engagement.

Experiencing Education

Race, Class, and the Gender Gap in Achievement

Whereas researchers once asked whether schools were "failing at fairness" when it came to educating girls (Sadker & Sadker, 1994), today concerns focus on the lower levels of achievement and college completion among boys and young men (DiPrete & Buchmann, 2013). When it comes to many standardized tests, GPA, high school completion, and college enrollment, girls and young women outperform their male counterparts. For example, about 85% of girls finish high school on time, while only 78% of boys do so (Stetser & Stillwell, 2014); 71% of those female high school graduates enroll in some form of postsecondary education, while only 61% of male graduates do so (Lopez & Gonzalez-Barrera, 2014). In fact, the gender gap in scores on the National Assessment of Educational Progress widens between fourth and 12th grade—something that has prompted researchers to look to social processes to explain.

Many sociologists see the gender gap in education as an issue of socialization and messages about masculinity. Yet notions of how masculinity and school success are related require an intersectional perspective: It is not a simple story about how young men understand education, but a complex story of how notions of masculinity with race and...

...that common sense and street smarts trump book smarts. According to Morris, this response emerges among white, working-class boys growing up in lower-income communities, as they begin to recognize that traditional avenues for adult male success no longer exist. Within their rural and de-industrialized communities, jobs have disappeared, and a sense of masculine identity and achievement along with them. In response, some boys reject academic success as a legitimate basis for identity and instead gain status by asserting an alternative standard of masculinity—one that emphasizes toughness, fighting, and an interest in traditionally masculine pursuits like sports, hunting, and fishing.

Similar processes are evident among black and Latino males—where the gender gap is even larger. According to both Edward Morris and Prudence Carter (2006), when black males succeed in school, they risk being labeled gay or effeminate... these are stim... bla...

respect by being *ballers* and *gangstas*, or by demonstrating cleverness and verbal skills through *clownin'* and *riffin'* (Morris, 2012). Although the responses of white and nonwhite boys parallel each other, Morris finds that black and Latino boys have additional personas available to them to reassert their masculinity.

Finally, it is important to note that the gender gap in achievement is negligible or nonexistent among middle- and upper-class boys (DiPrete & Buchmann, 2013); among the more affluent, boys— on to colleg...

▲ Members of the Bloods street gang sitting in front of their homeboy's gravesite in 1995. How did these young men assert their masculinity? Where do you suppose they are now?

Aging Beyond Our Borders

The Challenges of Aging in the Developing World

A recent article by Panruti, Liebig, and Duvvuru (2015) offers insight into the societal consequences of a rapid expansion of the aging population in India. The article includes an overview of the demographics of India's population; shows developments in research, education, and training; and concludes by addressing three emerging issues associated with aging in India.

As a country, India has the second-largest population in the world. Currently 1.2 billion, it is expected to increase to 1.4 billion by 2030. Although India's elderly population, as a percentage of the total population, is relatively small, it will continue to grow because of a continuing decrease in the overall fertility rate. As a result, the current 90 -elderly will increase to some 130

According to the authors, the emerging aging issues in India address fundamental needs of the growing elderly population. The first emerging aging issue is who is responsible for their support—the government or the family? This has become increasingly important with the trend toward a nuclear family structure rather than the traditional multigenerational family in which older members are provided care by their children.

The second emerging issue is that of health care. Specifically, health care that meets the needs of an expanding aging population. As in other countries, older citizens are in need of care for chronic health conditions that are more expensive and result in greater -v on others. In response, the -implementing the -nters

live in rural areas, the need for adequate income in old age is significant, as most do not have any form of a pension plan.

▶ **THINK ABOUT IT**

1. Which emerging aging issue should be the primary issue of the Indian government? Why?

2. As birth rates continue to decline and life expectancy increases, the older-age population will continue to increase. What other aging-related issues will become important in the near future?

3. Given that the majority of old--age Indians live in rural areas -how could they -f social

▲ An Indian street dentist installs dentures on an elderly patient at his roadside dentistry stall. Do you expect that street dentistry in India will be a booming business as the country's population ages?

SOCIAL CHANGE: WHAT CAN YOU DO?

Identify steps toward media-related social change.

Activist organizations often develop media strategies aimed at influencing, and sometimes presenting alternatives to, the narratives that circulate in the major media. Such "media activism" takes a wide variety of forms, with different organizations focused on different media-related problems, offering concerned citizens a range of different ways to get involved.

▶ Media Reform

In the early 2010s, media reform activists began seeking to restructure the U.S. media system, advocating for policies that highlight the public interest stakes in media policy, promote openness and accessibility, and emphasize the democratic role of media. Among the leading media reform organizations is Free Press (http://www.freepress.net), a national organization that "fight[s] to save the free and open internet, curb runaway media consolidation, protect press freedom, and ensure diverse voices are represented in our media." Free Press seeks to democratize the media policy-making process; engage the public in federal media policy decisions through public education campaigns; mobilize citizens to communicate directly with elected officials; and participate in policy debates in Washington, including ongoing policy research and advocacy. Students can become members of Free Press, sign up for the organization's regular e-mail updates, attend the National Conference for Media Reform, and take action by participating in one of Free Press's timely campaigns.

▶ Media Literacy

In our media-saturated society, citizens face a daily barrage of images and messages. Advocates of media literacy argue that citizens need to be equipped with the skills and experiences that will enable them to engage critically with the media they consume and to lear the fundamentals of m

focused, such as Healthy Youth Peer Education in Allentown, Pennsylvania, and the Spark Media Project in Poughkeepsie, New York. Several national media literacy organizations try to connect media literacy activists, forging links among them so they can build strategy and share resources, and develop curricula for school and community use. Among the most prominent of these organizations are the Center for Media Literacy (http://www.medialit.org), which works to help citizens "develop critical thinking and media production skills needed to live fully in the 21st century media culture," and the National Association for Media Literacy Education (http://namle.net), which seeks to "help individuals of all ages develop the habits of inquiry and skills of expression that they need to be critical thinkers, effective communicators and active citizens in today's world."

Media literacy groups around the United States are sponsored by schools and universities or run by community-based nonprofit organizations. You can become a media literacy activist by joining a group in your community, or by partnering with a local high school or elementary school to develop new media literacy activities. Either way, you will find valuable resources for media literacy education on the Center for Media Literacy's website, including the CML MediaLit Kit.

▶ Efforts to Limit Commercialism

With ads appearing almost anywhere we can imagine— from our computer screens and smart phones to inside school buses and even pieces of fruit—it is increasingly difficult to identify any commercial-free zones in contemporary society. Some media activists define the omnipresence of advertising as a growing social problem in need of a sustained response. They try to protect and promote public spaces free of constant sales pitches. So (http://www.co...

SAGE
Premium Resources

BOOST COMPREHENSION. BOLSTER ANALYSIS.

- SAGE Premium Video **INCLUDES AP NEWS CLIPS AND HIGHLIGHTS FROM THE SAGE SOCIOLOGY VIDEO COLLECTION**

- Includes short, auto-graded quizzes that **DIRECTLY FEED TO YOUR LMS GRADEBOOK**

- Premium content is **ADA COMPLIANT WITH TRANSCRIPTS**

- Comprehensive media guide helps you **QUICKLY SELECT MEANINGFUL VIDEO** tied to your course objectives

- Additional assets are available in **INTERACTIVE DATA MAPS**

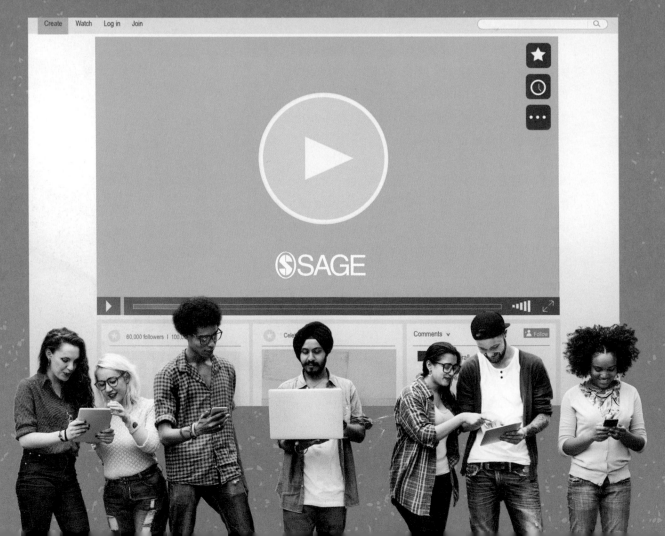

INVESTIGATING SOCIAL PROBLEMS

EDITION 2

Sara Miller McCune founded SAGE Publishing in 1965 to support the dissemination of usable knowledge and educate a global community. SAGE publishes more than 1000 journals and over 800 new books each year, spanning a wide range of subject areas. Our growing selection of library products includes archives, data, case studies and video. SAGE remains majority owned by our founder and after her lifetime will become owned by a charitable trust that secures the company's continued independence.

Los Angeles | London | New Delhi | Singapore | Washington DC | Melbourne

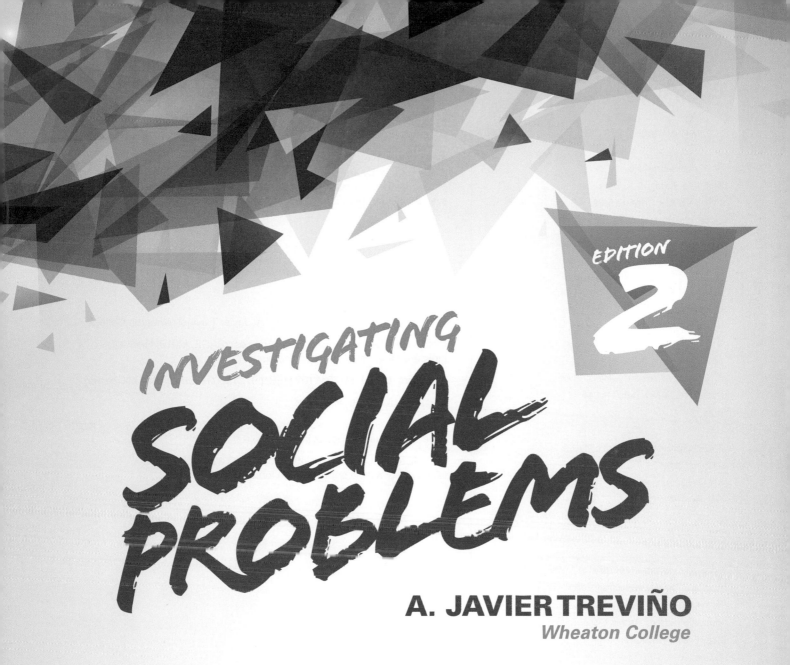

INVESTIGATING SOCIAL PROBLEMS

EDITION 2

A. JAVIER TREVIÑO
Wheaton College

CHAPTER AUTHORS

Michael M. Bell, Michael Ian Borer, Benjamin C. Hamilton, Katie Ann Hasson, Leslie Hossfeld, William Hoynes, Meg Wilkes Karraker, E. Brooke Kelly, Katharine A. Legun, Valerie Leiter, Michael Mascarenhas, Duane A. Matcha, Eileen O'Brien, Carrie B. Oser, Tyler S. Schafer, Jenny Stuber, Ori Swed, Kyle J. Thomas, Rudi Volti, Julia Waity, Elroi J. Windsor

Los Angeles | London | New Delhi
Singapore | Washington DC | Melbourne

FOR INFORMATION:

SAGE Publications, Inc.
2455 Teller Road
Thousand Oaks, California 91320
E-mail: order@sagepub.com

SAGE Publications Ltd.
1 Oliver's Yard
55 City Road
London EC1Y 1SP
United Kingdom

SAGE Publications India Pvt. Ltd.
B 1/I 1 Mohan Cooperative Industrial Area
Mathura Road, New Delhi 110 044
India

SAGE Publications Asia-Pacific Pte. Ltd.
3 Church Street
#10–04 Samsung Hub
Singapore 049483

Acquisitions Editor: Jeff Lasser
Assistant Content Development Editor: Sarah Dillard
Editorial Assistant: Adeline Wilson
Production Editor: Andrew Olson
Copy Editor: Talia Greenberg
Typesetter: C&M Digitals (P) Ltd.
Proofreader: Sally Jaskold
Indexer: Teddy Diggs
Cover Designer: Scott Van Atta
Marketing Manager: Kara Kindstrom

Library of Congress Cataloging-in-Publication Data

Names: Treviño, A. Javier, editor.

Title: Investigating social problems / A. Javier Trevino, Wheaton College.

Description: Second edition. | Los Angeles : SAGE, [2019] | Includes bibliographical references and index.

Identifiers: LCCN 2017041103 | ISBN 9781506348506 (pbk. : alk. paper)

ISBN 9781544324074 (ll.)

Subjects: LCSH: Social problems—21st century. | Social problems—Health aspects. | Equality. | Social institutions.

Classification: LCC HN18.3 .I57 2019 | DDC 306—dc23
LC record available at https://lccn.loc.gov/2017041103

18 19 20 21 22 10 9 8 7 6 5 4 3 2 1

ABOUT THE AUTHORS

1. SOCIOLOGY AND SOCIAL PROBLEMS

A. Javier Treviño is a professor of sociology at Wheaton College (Massachusetts). He is the author and editor of several books, including *The Social Thought of C. Wright Mills* (SAGE, 2012) and *The Development of Sociological Theory: Readings From the Enlightenment to the Present* (SAGE, 2017). He has served as president of the Justice Studies Association (2000–2002) and the Society for the Study of Social Problems (2010–2011). He was a Visiting Research Fellow at the University of Sussex, England (2006); a Fulbright Scholar to the Republic of Moldova (2009); and since 2014 has been a visiting professor in social and political theory at the University of Innsbruck, Austria.

2. POVERTY AND CLASS INEQUALITY

Leslie Hossfeld is a professor and head of the Department of Sociology at Mississippi State University. She has trained in rural sociology at the North Carolina State University College of Agriculture and Life Sciences. Dr. Hossfeld has extensive experience examining rural poverty and economic restructuring and has made two presentations to the U.S. Congress and one to the North Carolina legislature on job loss and rural economic decline. Dr. Hossfeld has served as cochair of the American Sociological Association Task Force on Public Sociology, vice president of Sociologists for Women in Society, and president of the Southern Sociological Society, and was appointed to the USDA Rural Growth and Opportunity Board of Advisors. She is cofounder and president of the Southeastern North Carolina Food Systems Program, Feast Down East. In 2015, she founded the Mississippi Food Insecurity Project (MFIP; www.mfip.msstate.edu), which examines food access and food insecurity in Mississippi. Dr. Hossfeld is also the associate director of the Myrlie Evers Williams Institute for the Elimination of Health Disparities.

E. Brooke Kelly is a professor of sociology at the University of North Carolina at Pembroke, where she has worked with students and community partners on numerous public sociology projects addressing poverty and food insecurity. Since her training at Michigan State University, her research has maintained a focus on social inequalities, work, and family, with a more recent focus on food insecurity. With Leslie Hossfeld and Julia Waity, she is coediting a forthcoming book on food and poverty. Dr. Kelly has served as chair of the Poverty, Class, and Inequalities Division of the Society for the Study of Social Problems and as chair of the Southern Sociological Society's Committee on Sociological Practice. Dr. Kelly has also served as a fellow and research affiliate of the Rural Policy Research Institute's Rural Poverty Center, which supported her research on rural low-income mothers' efforts to attain and maintain paid employment.

Julia Waity is an assistant professor of sociology at the University of North Carolina at Wilmington, where she studies poverty, food insecurity, and spatial inequality. She teaches courses related to her research interests, including sociology of poverty, social problems, public sociology, the community, and introduction to sociology. She received her Ph.D. from Indiana University Bloomington. She is involved with community-based research, especially with her public sociology students. She is the coeditor with Leslie Hossfeld and Brooke Kelly of a forthcoming book on food and poverty.

3. RACE AND ETHNICITY

Eileen O'Brien received her Ph.D. in sociology from the University of Florida, focusing on race relations. She is the author of several books, including *Whites Confront Racism: Antiracists and Their Paths to Action*; *White Men on Race: Power, Privilege, and the Shaping of Cultural Consciousness* (with Joe Feagin); and *The Racial Middle: Latinos and Asian Americans Living Beyond the Racial Divide*. Her upcoming and ongoing projects include interviews with Asian American participants in hip-hop culture, as well as a study of race and gender in military families.

4. GENDER

Katie Ann Hasson is the program director on genetic justice at the Center for Genetics and Society. She earned her Ph.D.

in sociology with a designated emphasis on women, gender, and sexuality at the University of California, Berkeley, and was previously an assistant professor of sociology and gender studies at the University of Southern California. Her research on gender, bodies, and science/technology/medicine has been published in *Gender & Society*, *Social Science and Medicine*, and *Social Studies of Science*.

5. SEXUALITIES

Elroi J. Windsor is an assistant professor of sociology and chair of the sociology and criminal studies department at Salem College, in Winston-Salem, North Carolina. In this role, Dr. Windsor teaches introductory and capstone sociology courses, as well as classes related to gender, sexuality, and the body and embodiment. Dr. Windsor also teaches Introduction to Women's, Gender, and Sexuality Studies classes at Wake Forest University. Dr. Windsor is in the process of coediting the fifth edition of *Sex Matters: The Sexuality & Society Reader*. As a researcher, Dr. Windsor is working on a book based on an ethnographic study with health care professionals who work with body parts, corpses, and cadavers.

6. AGING

Duane A. Matcha is a professor of sociology and director of the interdisciplinary health studies major at Siena College. He received his Ph.D. in sociology from Purdue University in West Lafayette, Indiana. He is the author of a number of books, including *Sociology of Aging: A Social Problems Perspective*, *Medical Sociology,* and *Readings in Medical Sociology*. Other books include *Health Care Systems of the Developed World: How the United States' System Remains an Outlier* and *The Sociology of Aging: An International Perspective*. He is the recipient of two Fulbright teaching scholarships to the Jagiellonian University in Krakow, Poland, and Vilnius University in Vilnius, Lithuania. In 2012, he received the Kennedy Award for Scholarship at Siena College.

7. EDUCATION

Jenny Stuber is an associate professor of sociology at the University of North Florida. She received her Ph.D. in sociology from Indiana University; she also holds degrees from Northwestern University and Brown University. Her work, which has been published in numerous books and journals, focuses on the social and cultural dimensions of social class, examining how people understand social class and utilize their class-based resources (social capital, cultural capital, economic capital) within social settings like schools and communities.

8. MEDIA

William Hoynes is a professor of sociology and former director of the Media Studies Program at Vassar College, where he teaches courses on media, culture, and social theory. He is the author of *Public Television for Sale: Media, the Market, and the Public Sphere,* and coauthor, with David Croteau, of *Media/Society: Images, Industries, and Audiences,* now in its fifth edition, and *The Business of Media: Corporate Media and the Public Interest.*

9. FAMILY

Meg Wilkes Karraker is professor emerita at the University of St. Thomas, where she taught sociology for 26 years and served as a Family Business Center Fellow and University Scholar. She is the coauthor of *Families With Futures: Family Studies Into the 21st Century;* editor of *The Other People: Interdisciplinary Perspectives on Migration;* and author of *Global Families* and *Diversity and the Common Good: Civil Society, Religion, and Catholic Sisters in a Small City.* Her current research is "Middle Class in Middle America: Families, Neighbors, and a Good Society." Karraker is the recipient of the University of St. Thomas John Ireland Presidential Award for Outstanding Achievement as a Teacher/Scholar and the American Sociological Association Hans O. Mauksch Award for Distinguished Contributions to Undergraduate Sociology.

10. WORK AND THE ECONOMY

Rudi Volti is Emeritus Professor of Sociology at Pitzer College in Claremont, California. He has been a Senior Fellow at the Smithsonian Institution and a visiting scholar at the Universities Service Centre in Hong Kong, the University of Michigan, and the Autonomous University of Barcelona. He also has served as book editor for *Transfers: Interdisciplinary Journal of Mobility Studies.* His books include *The Encyclopedia of Science, Technology and Society;* *The Engineer in History;* *An Introduction to the Sociology of Work and Occupations;* *Society and Technological Change;* *Technology Transfer and East Asian Economic Transformation;* *Cars and Culture;* and *Technology and Commercial Air Travel.*

11. CRIME

Kyle J. Thomas is an assistant professor in the Department of Criminology and Criminal Justice at the University of Missouri–St. Louis. His research interests include offender decision making, peer influence, and delinquent attitudes.

Benjamin C. Hamilton is a doctoral student in the Department of Criminology and Criminal Justice at the University of Missouri–St. Louis. His research interests include offender decision making, measurement of criminological constructs, and quantitative methodology.

12. DRUGS

Carrie B. Oser is a professor in the Sociology Department, with joint appointments in the Behavioral Science Department and the Center on Drug and Alcohol Research, at the University of Kentucky. Her research interests include health services, health disparities, HIV risk behaviors/interventions, social networks, and drug use among vulnerable populations. Dr. Oser has received numerous grants from the National Institute on Drug Abuse (NIDA) for scientific inquiry of these topics and has published over 100 peer-reviewed journal articles and book chapters.

13. HEALTH

Valerie Leiter is a professor of sociology at Simmons College, where she co-created an undergraduate liberal arts–based Public Health Program (with biologist Liz Scott). Her research focuses on disability and chronic illness. She is the author of *Their Time Has Come: Youth With Disabilities on the Cusp of Adulthood*, and coeditor of the ninth edition of *The Sociology of Health and Illness: Critical Perspectives* (with Peter Conrad).

14. THE ENVIRONMENT

Katharine A. Legun is a lecturer in environmental sociology at the University of Otago, New Zealand, and is affiliated with the Centre for Sustainability. She completed a Ph.D. from the University of Wisconsin–Madison, where she did research on patented apple varieties owned by cooperatives. Her research looks at relationships between (biological) materials, social organization, and markets. Her work has been published in *Society and Natural Resources*.

Michael M. Bell is Vilas Distinguished Achievement Professor of Community and Environmental Sociology at the University of Wisconsin–Madison. He is principally an environmental sociologist and a social theorist, focusing on dialogics, the sociology of nature, and social justice. His books include *An Invitation to Environmental Sociology*, *Country Boys: Masculinity and Rural Life*, and *Walking Toward Justice: Democratization in Rural Life*.

15. SCIENCE AND TECHNOLOGY

Michael Mascarenhas is an associate professor in the Department of Environmental Science, Policy, and Management at the University of California, Berkeley. He is the author of *Where the Waters Divide Neoliberalism, White Privilege, and Environmental Racism in Canada* (2012) and *New Humanitarianism and the Crisis of Charity: Good Intentions on the Road to Help* (2017). In over a dozen peer-review publications, he has written on water, wolves, seed-saving, standards, supermarkets, family farms, and forests. Professor Mascarenhas's scholarship examines the interconnections among contemporary neoliberal reforms, environmental change, and racial justice. This interdisciplinary body of research brings together concepts from critical race theory and environmental studies to build critical insights into the environmental race relational aspects of widespread political economy reform.

16. WAR AND TERRORISM

Ori Swed is a lecturer in the Sociology Department at the University of Texas at Austin. He earned his Ph.D. from the University of Texas, and his M.A. in history and his B.A. in history and sociology from the Hebrew University in Jerusalem. In addition, Ori is a reserve captain at the Israeli Defense Forces and a former private consultant for the hi-tech sector. Ori's main research agenda focuses on the new forms of interaction between the armed forces and nonstate actors—namely, private military companies, nongovernmental organizations, and violent nonstate actors. His work addresses recent developments in the global security field, among them the proliferation of nonstate actors in contemporary battlefields, and the repercussions of these changes. His forthcoming edited volume on the privatization of security opens the door for sociological debate and inquiry on private contractors' roles in society, politics, and the economy.

17. URBANIZATION

Michael Ian Borer is an associate professor of sociology at the University of Nevada, Las Vegas. His specializations include urban sociology, culture, and concepts of the sacred. He is the editor of *The Varieties of Urban Experience: The American City and the Practice of Culture;* the author of *Faithful to Fenway: Believing in Boston, Baseball, and America's Most Beloved Ballpark;* and coauthor of *Urban People and Places: The Sociology of Cities, Suburbs, and Towns*. His work has been published in *City & Community*, the *Journal of Popular*

Culture, Religion & American Culture, Social Psychology Quarterly, and *Symbolic Interaction*. Borer served as the 2011–2012 vice president of the Society for the Study of Symbolic Interaction.

Tyler S. Schafer is an assistant professor of sociology at California State University, Stanislaus. He specializes in urban and community sociology, culture, collective action, environmental sociology, and food justice. His research explores the intersections of these themes in local food initiatives. His work has been published in *Sociology Compass, Qualitative Sociology Review*, and the *Journal of Media and Religion*. He spent 2 years working in the UNLV Urban Sustainability Initiative and teaches undergraduate course on urban sociology, social inequalities, and food and culture.

BRIEF CONTENTS

DETAILED CONTENTS

PART III: Problems of Institutions

7. EDUCATION 152

Jenny Stuber

8. MEDIA 180

William Hoynes

9. FAMILY 208

Meg Wilkes Karraker

10. WORK AND THE ECONOMY 234

Rudi Volti

PART IV: **Problems of Health and Safety**

11. CRIME 262

Kyle J. Thomas and Benjamin C. Hamilton

PART V: Problems of Global Impact

14. THE ENVIRONMENT 340

Katharine A. Legun and Michael M. Bell

15. SCIENCE AND TECHNOLOGY 368

Michael Mascarenhas

16. WAR AND TERRORISM 396

Ori Swed

17. URBANIZATION 422

Michael Ian Borer and Tyler S. Schafer

PREFACE

"Introduction to sociology" courses and courses in "social problems" generally have a couple of things in common. First, they tend to serve as "gateway" courses that introduce students to sociology as a discipline and as a major; second, they teach students to think sociologically. But beyond that, these two kinds of courses are quite different, and the main difference has to do with the issues they cover. While general sociology courses acquaint students with fundamental concepts such as social structure and institutions, social problems courses go beyond this and focus on the troublesome situations endemic to social structures and institutions: poverty, social inequalities, crime, drug addiction, unemployment, environmental disasters, terrorism, and so on. Given the panoply of distressing, harmful, and threatening social situations and conditions—and their complexity—the study of social problems requires, indeed demands, specialized focus by experts.

Every social problems textbook currently on the market is written by one, two, or perhaps three authors who endeavor to cover a wide range of different social problems. This book is different: *It is written by a panel of 22 specialists.* As such, each chapter has been prepared by one or more scholars who specialize in that particular issue. All of them are sociologists who frame the problems in question within the sociological imagination and provide the most current theories, research, and examples. That said, this is *not* a specialized text that assumes foundational knowledge on the part of the student; rather, it is intended to service a general introductory class in social problems. Additionally, although this is an edited text, it is not a reader; every effort has been made to link themes and discussions between chapters. There is, in short, no other textbook like it. Below are descriptions of some of the other unique features of *Investigating Social Problems*.

LEARNING OBJECTIVES

Half a dozen or so learning objectives are listed at the beginning of each chapter. These alert students to the chapter's main themes and ask them to describe, explain, evaluate, or apply the information to be discussed. Each learning objective is repeated next to the first-level heading to which it corresponds, making it easier for students to keep track of the objectives as they read.

CRITICAL THINKING QUESTIONS

Interspersed throughout each chapter are critical thinking questions, flagged as "Ask Yourself." These help students apply the concepts discussed, get them to think about how the information provided relates to their everyday lives, and challenge them to think about what they would do in similar situations. In addition, all boxed features end with "Think About It" questions intended to spur classroom discussion.

OUR STORIES

Because each chapter is written by one or more sociologists who are experts in the social problem under discussion, chapter-opening "Investigating the Social Problem" boxes present the contributing authors' "stories" of how they came to be interested in their particular areas of expertise. These short biographies personalize the chapters and help the students see that real people are involved in investigating real problems.

OPENING VIGNETTES

Every chapter begins with a brief opening vignette that sets the stage for the social problem to be discussed. The vignettes are summations of current news reports, documentary films, ethnographic accounts, or trade books that vividly describe provocative scenarios to introduce students to the social problems at hand. Along with each vignette, one or more questions are posed to get students to begin thinking about the topic.

THE USES OF GENERAL AND SPECIALIZED THEORIES

This textbook, more than any other on the market, takes seriously the application of sociological theory in investigating social problems. As such, each chapter considers the social problem in question from the point of view of the *three general theoretical approaches* of structural functionalism, conflict theory, and symbolic interactionism. These provide the student with distinct ways of making sense of the complex realities of the social problem. Beyond that, each chapter also provides greater in-depth analysis by employing particular *specialized theories* that the expert author or authors have specifically chosen to use in further investigating the social problem of concern. No other textbook employs specific theories. The utilization of both general and specialized theories shows students that conceptual analysis has an important place in the investigation of social problems.

A FOCUS ON SOCIAL POLICY

As a set of official strategies intended to manage specific social problems, *social policy* is given special consideration in every chapter. Each author proposes policy recommendations for social change that arise from the three main theoretical perspectives. This demonstrates to students that theory has a practical utility in addressing social problems.

BOXED FEATURES AND THREE KEY THEMES

Every chapter underscores three key themes that are of particular importance in the study of social problems. These are set off in boxes to illustrate their significance. "Beyond Our Borders" boxes demonstrate that social problems are global in scope. These help students, first, to understand the social problems of U.S. society in relationship to social problems in other countries. Second, the contents of these boxes show students that social problems are interconnected in that they affect many countries, cultures, and people around the world. "Experiencing" boxes pertain to intersectionality; that is, the problems in question are considered in the context of how individuals experience them in reference to their interrelated statuses of social class, race/ethnicity, gender, and so on. "Researching" boxes discuss recent studies or reports on particular aspects of the social problems under discussion and present quantitative or qualitative data on the topics. The boxed features also contain critical thinking questions to help students reflect on the information covered.

GENERAL SOCIAL SURVEY EXERCISES

Near the beginning of each chapter, students are presented with a set of questions under the rubric "What Do You Think?" These questions are related to the social problem under discussion, and students are invited to give their personal responses. At the end of each chapter, data from the General Social Survey pertaining to these questions are provided under the title "What Does America Think?" These data allow students to compare the opinions and attitudes they held prior to reading the chapter with those of the general U.S. population after they have read the chapter.

PHOTOS AND OTHER VISUALS

Carefully selected photographs are strategically placed throughout the chapters. These are not merely stock photos used for visual interest; rather, they are intended to aid students in connecting personally with real-life situations. As such, all the photos are accompanied by informative captions, many of which impart the names of the real people, places, and events that are shown. This is another way in which the text reflects reality. Most of the photo captions also pose a question or questions. Other visuals include tables, figures, charts, and maps designed to help students better understand and remember the information provided in the chapter.

STUDENTS' ROLE IN SOCIAL CHANGE

After being informed about the problems that plague society, students frequently want to know what solutions are available. Indeed, they often want to know what *they* can do to make a difference. Another unique feature of this textbook is that the chapter authors provide suggestions on the opportunities available for students to involve themselves personally in practical efforts to ameliorate social problems.

GLOSSARIES

This text features marginal glossaries, offering students easy access to definitions and descriptions of concepts and other important terms and phrases. Key terms are bolded in the text on their first substantive use, and a comprehensive glossary appears at the end of the book.

CHAPTER REVIEW

Each chapter ends with a summary that encapsulates the main learning points and a set of discussion questions designed to help students review what they have learned and to foster critical thinking about the material.

ANCILLARIES

Instructor Teaching Site

http://edge.sagepub.com/trevino2e

A password-protected instructor teaching site provides one integrated source for all instructor materials, including the following key components for each chapter:

- A **test bank** offers a diverse set of test questions and answers for each chapter in the book. Multiple-choice, true/false, and short-answer/essay questions for every chapter will aid instructors in assessing students' progress and understanding.

- **PowerPoint presentations** are designed to assist with lecture and review, highlighting essential content, features, and artwork from the book.

Student Study Site

http://edge.sagepub.com/trevino2e

- Mobile-friendly **eFlaschards** reinforce understanding of key terms and concepts that have been outlined in the chapters.

- Mobile-friendly **Web quizzes** allow for independent assessment of progress made in learning course material.

- Influential **SAGE journal articles** that tie important research and scholarship to chapter concepts.

Interactive eBook

Investigating Social Problems is also available as an interactive eBook, which can be packaged free with the book or purchased separately. The interactive eBook offers links to video cases and SAGE journal articles and reference articles, as well as additional audio, video, and Web resources.

ACKNOWLEDGMENTS

A small army of highly talented staff and editors at SAGE, most of them working "behind the scenes," made my job as this text's general editor that much easier and more enjoyable. I very much appreciate their hard work and dedication to this project. I thank Jeff Lasser, Adeline Wilson, Andrew Olson, and Talia Greenberg.

Above all, I'm especially grateful to each of the authors who wrote the various chapters presented here. Simply put, without their industriousness, persistence, and expertise, the volume would not have been possible. All chapters in the second edition have been updated to include the latest research and information. New authors have revised chapters 2, 4, 5, 7, 11, 12, 13, 15, and 16. The authors of these chapters in the first edition were:

Wenda K. Bauchspies (Chapter 15)

Ryan W. Coughlan (Chapter 7)

Kathleen Currul-Dykeman (Chapter 11)

Susan Guarino-Ghezzi (Chapter 11)

Paul Joseph (Chapter 16)

Brian C. Kelly (Chapter 12)

Keith M. Kilty (Chapter 2)

Dina Perrone (Chapter 12)

Rebecca F. Plante (Chapter 5)

Robyn Ryle (Chapter 4)

Alan R. Sadovnik (Chapter 7)

Susan F. Semel (Chapter 7)

Kevin White (Chapter 13)

Thanks also to my wife, Nancy, and son, Myles, for their extraordinary patience while I spent many long hours at the computer and on the phone orchestrating the book's development.

Finally, I wish to thank all of the reviewers who contributed their many suggestions, critiques, and insights that helped make *Investigating Social Problems* a better text:

Evan Adelson, San Diego Mesa College

Brian Aldrich, Winona State University

Kristian Alexander, Zayed University

Annett Marie Allen, Troy University

Tammy L. Anderson, University of Delaware

Judith Andreasson, North Idaho College

Rebecca Bach, Duke University

Sam Elizabeth Baroni, Nova Southeastern University

Roberta Campbell, Miami University

Susan Eidson Claxton, Georgia Highlands College

Marian Colello, Bucks County Community College

Maia Cudhea, University of North Texas

Kristen De Vall, University of North Carolina Wilmington

Melanie Deffendall, Delgado Community College

Ricardo A. Dello Buono, Manhattan College

Sophia DeMasi, Mercer County Community College

Ione DeOllos, Ball State University

Andrew Dzurisin, Middlesex County College

Lois Easterday, Onondaga Community College

Kathy Edwards, Ashland Community and Technical College

Kathryn Feltey, University of Akron

Bethaney W. Ferguson, Cape Fear Community College

Sharman H. French, Capital Community College

Caren J. Frost, University of Utah

Albert Fu, Kutztown University

Brian Garavaglia, Macomb Community College

David Gauss, San Diego State University

Peggy Geddes, Trios College

Gary Gilles, Argosy University

Otis Grant, Indiana University South Bend

Lecia Gray, Belhaven University

Johnnie Griffin, Jackson State University

Stephen Groce, Western Kentucky University

William Gronfein, Indiana University–Purdue University Indianapolis

George Guay, Bridgewater State University

Gary Hamill, Lehigh Carbon Community College

Ayre J. Harris, Mountain View College

Franklin H. Harris, Roanoke Chowan Community College

Donna Haytko-Paoa, University of Hawaii Maui College

Gary Heidinger, Roane State Community College

Teresa Hibbert, University of Texas at El Paso

Sarah Hogue, Bridgewater State University

Kathryn Hovey, New Mexico State University

Hua-Lun Huang, University of Louisiana

Linda L. Jasper, Indiana University Southeast

Angela Lewellyn Jones, Elon University

Bennett Judkins, Lee University

Kyle Knight, University of Alabama in Huntsville

Rosalind Kopfstein, Western Connecticut State University

Charles Kusselow, River Valley Community College

Erma Lawson, University of North Texas

Debra LeBlanc, Bay Mills Community College

Laurie J. Linhart, Drake University

Jackie Logg, Cabrillo College

Dennis Loo, California State Polytechnic University Pomona

Steve Mabry, Cedar Valley College

Michael Macaluso, Grand Valley State University

Keith Mann, Cardinal Stritch University

Susan E. Mannon, Utah State University

Marguerite Marin, Gonzaga University

Vanessa Martinez, Holyoke Community College

Teresa Mayors, Curry College

Sheila McKinnon, HBI College

Neil McLaughlin, McMaster University

Pamela McMullin-Messier, Central Washington University

Stephanie Medley-Rath, Lake Land College

Sharon Methvin, Mt. Hood Community College

Kari Meyers, Moorpark College

Susan Nelson, University of South Alabama

Yvonne Newsome, Agnes Scott College

Erin Niclaus, Bucks County Community College

Michael J. O'Connor, Hawkeye Community College

David O'Donnell, Vermilion Community College

Josh Packard, University of Northern Colorado

Malcolm Potter, California State University Long Beach

Janice Kay Purk, Mansfield University

Susan Rahman, Santa Rose Junior College

Jean M. Raniseski, Alvin Community College

Abigail Richardson, Colorado Mesa University

Jacquelyn Robinson, Albany State University

Paulina X. Ruf, Lenoir-Rhyne University

Frank A. Salamone, Iona College

Baranda Sawyers, Lansing Community College

Luceal J. Simon, Wayne State University

Sheryl Skaggs, University of Texas at Dallas

Buffy Smith, University of St. Thomas

Stephen Soreff, Boston University

John R. Sterlacci, Broome Community College

Dennis J. Stevens, University of North Carolina Charlotte

Colin E. Suchland, St. Louis Community College

Sara C. Sutler-Cohen, Bellevue College

Susan Turner, Front Range Community College

Deidre Ann Tyler, Salt Lake Community College

Nicholas Vargas, Purdue University

Melissa D. Weise, Holyoke Community College

Bill Winders, Georgia Tech

Michael Woo, Bellevue University

Susan L. Wortmann, Nebraska Wesleyan University

Anat Yom-Tov, Haverford College

A. Javier Treviño
Norton, Massachusetts

1 SOCIOLOGY AND SOCIAL PROBLEMS

A. Javier Treviño

If you have ever spent time walking around a city, you have probably seen different kinds of street art. Some of this artwork, which includes various forms of graffiti and murals, is intended to convey socially relevant messages. What do you think the artist who painted this wall mural in Cape Town, South Africa, is saying?

Investigating Sociology and Social Problems: My Story

A. Javier Treviño

I took my first sociology course as a high school senior, and I knew I had found my calling. Although no one in my family had ever gone to college, I took both sociology courses offered at the local community college in Laredo, Texas, one of which was about social problems. My appetite whetted, I transferred to a state university to get a B.A. degree in sociology. After graduating and completing a year of substitute teaching at my former high school, I decided to get a master's degree in applied sociology, with an emphasis in social planning. Thinking this would be the end of my academic journey, I planned to work as a probation officer, a marriage counselor, or even a sociology teacher at a community college. But I soon realized I needed to know more about *theory* to gain a better understanding of the nature and causes of social problems. I enrolled in the Ph.D. sociology program at Boston College, concentrating on crime, deviance, and social control. I was fortunate to study and work with the preeminent criminologist Richard Quinney, who opened my eyes to a critical approach to the problem of crime. Since then I have looked at various issues—crime, deviance, legal matters—theoretically.

LEARNING OBJECTIVES

1.1 Describe how working-class young adults are currently experiencing their lives.

1.2 Define what constitutes a social problem.

1.3 Explain the sociological imagination.

1.4 Discuss how sociological research can be used to study social problems.

1.5 Explain the three main sociological perspectives of structural functionalism, conflict theory, and symbolic interactionism.

1.6 Evaluate how each of the three theoretical perspectives can be applied to improve our understanding of social problems.

1.7 Discuss the role of social policy in managing social problems.

1.8 Explore the role of specialized theories in sociology.

1.9 Identify ways in which service sociology can make a difference.

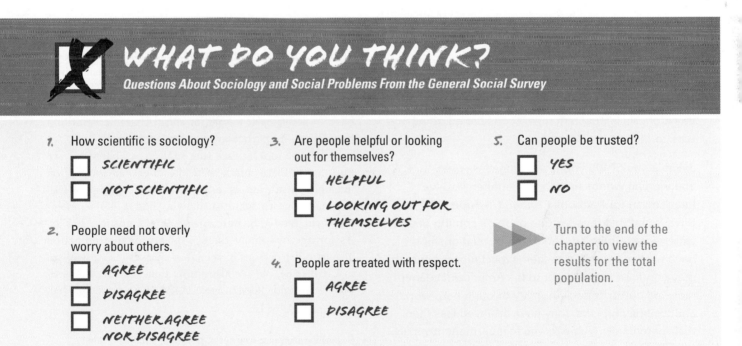

WHAT DO YOU THINK?

Questions About Sociology and Social Problems From the General Social Survey

1. How scientific is sociology?
    - [ ] SCIENTIFIC
    - [ ] NOT SCIENTIFIC

2. People need not overly worry about others.
    - [ ] AGREE
    - [ ] DISAGREE
    - [ ] NEITHER AGREE NOR DISAGREE

3. Are people helpful or looking out for themselves?
    - [ ] HELPFUL
    - [ ] LOOKING OUT FOR THEMSELVES

4. People are treated with respect.
    - [ ] AGREE
    - [ ] DISAGREE

5. Can people be trusted?
    - [ ] YES
    - [ ] NO

Turn to the end of the chapter to view the results for the total population.

SOURCE: National Opinion Research Center, University of Chicago.

SETTLING FOR LESS

 1.1 Describe how working-class young adults are currently experiencing their lives.

Jalen is a 24-year-old, single black man who works the baseball season as a night-time security guard at a local stadium. He is living in the basement of his aunt and uncle's house. After graduating high school, with no clear plans for what to do next, Jalen impulsively joined the Marine Corps. After 5 years of service, which included three tours of duty in Afghanistan, he was honorably discharged. That was a year ago. Since then, his attempts to go to college and find a stable job have been thwarted again and again.

Wanting a career in firefighting, Jalen took the civil service exam. He made the city's hiring list and enrolled at the fire academy. However, on the second day of training Jalen tested positive for marijuana and was expelled. Although he does not consider himself "book smart," he knows a college degree will get him a good job, and, because he is a veteran, the G.I. Bill will pay for his schooling. He recently enrolled in a local community college, but 2 weeks into the semester, he still doesn't have his books because he has not yet received his G.I. Bill benefits check, which he needs to buy them. To make matters worse, he owes $18,000 in credit card debt and has no way to pay it off. He is now tentatively considering going back to the Marine Corps.

Jalen is one of 100 young working-class men and women whom sociologist Jennifer M. Silva interviewed for her book *Coming Up Short* (2013). Silva found that these young people's coming-of-age experiences—with education, work, relationships—have not measured up to their expectations. Although they continue to hold tight to the American Dream of realizing upward social mobility through hard work and well-paying jobs, they have achieved less than their parents were able to and feel permanently stuck in an extended adolescence. All the milestones that had previously marked adulthood in U.S. society—owning a home, getting married, having children, finding stable employment—remain hopelessly out of reach for these working-class young people.

What is the social problem in the scenario above? Let's see.

Due to their difficult situation, these young people experience a whole range of feelings: confusion, bitterness, regret, disappointment, betrayal, hope. In their interviews with Silva about their individual life experiences, they largely blame themselves for their inadequate education, unexpected layoffs, and failed relationships. They believe they are responsible for their own fates. They feel they can't trust **social institutions**—any set of persons cooperating together for the purpose of organizing stable patterns of human activity—such as the labor market, education, marriage, and government to help them attain a sense of dignity and well-being.

But let's look at the larger picture and consider these young adults not on a case-by-case basis but as a generational **cohort**—a group of individuals of similar age within a population who share a particular experience. Now we see that in 2014, 32% of the nation's 18- to 34-year-olds—the so-called millennial generation—were living with their parents (Fry, 2016a), compared to 20% of those in the same age group in 1960. They were also delaying marriage or not marrying at all. Consider that in the early 1960s the median age at first marriage was 20 for women and 22 for men. By 2016 it had increased to almost 28 for women and 30 for men (U.S. Census Bureau, 2017).

Now, you may say that being single and living with parents is an unfortunate or undesirable situation for those twentysomethings who would rather be married and on their own, but these circumstances are not *social* problems. Fair enough. But let's also look at a situation in which many of the young people Silva interviewed found themselves, and that most of us would agree generally *is* regarded as a social problem: unemployment (the subject of Chapter 10). And let's consider unemployment on the basis of **demographic factors,** or social characteristics of a population—in particular race, age, and gender.

When we look at race (the subject of Chapter 3), we find that in 2016, black men like Jalen had the highest unemployment rate of any racial/ethnic group, 9.1%. Compare this to white men, who had a 4.4% unemployment rate (U.S. Bureau of Labor Statistics, 2017c). As for age, we know there is plenty of discrimination against older persons in the labor market (as we will see in Chapter 6), but we also know that in 2016, 8.4% of people around Jalen's age, 20–24, were unemployed,

....

Social institutions: Any set of persons, such as a family, economy, government, or religion, cooperating for the purpose of organizing stable patterns of human activity.

Cohort: Within a population, a group of individuals of similar age who share a particular experience.

Demographic factors: Social characteristics of a population, in particular those of race, age, and gender.

compared to 4.2% of people 25–54 years of age (U.S. Bureau of Labor Statistics, 2017d). Concerning gender (the subject of Chapter 4), we know that in 2015, women working full-time received 81 cents for every dollar earned by male workers (U.S. Bureau of Labor Statistics, 2016b).

But what are we to make of all these statistics? For the moment, simply this: An awful lot of U.S. adults—tens of thousands, hundreds of thousands, even millions—are in the same predicament as those young men and women, like Jalen, whom Silva interviewed. And though they may have felt alone and isolated, these young people were not the only ones experiencing such circumstances. In other words, unemployment is not only a matter of these young people's *personal* troubles; it is, in fact, a *collective* problem.

Another important issue to consider briefly now, to which we will be paying greater attention in the rest of this textbook, is that some groups of people experience social conditions—like unemployment and its related issues of discrimination in hiring and wage earning—at higher levels than do other groups. It is for this reason that sociologists look at **intersectionality**, or the ways in which several demographic factors combine to affect people's experiences. In Jalen's case, we would consider how his age (young adult), race (black), gender (male), and social class (working class) combine to shape his life.

So let's now look at the demographic factor that, in addition to age, characterized all the 100 young people with whom Silva spoke: social class (discussed in more depth in Chapter 2). A **social class** is a category of people whose experiences in life are determined by the amount of income and wealth they own and control. Remember that the young adults Silva interviewed were from a *working-class* background. No doubt you have heard and read about the various social classes that exist in U.S. society. There is no agreement, even among social scientists, on how to distinguish among social classes, much less on how many there are. But we typically hear about the *upper class* (think here about such wealthy people as Amazon.com founder Jeff Bezos and Facebook founder Mark Zuckerberg), the *middle classes* (usually referred to in the plural because there are several levels within this middle rank), and the *poor* (sometimes called the working poor, the homeless, or the indigent).

The working class, which we can place between the middle classes and the poor, generally consists of people who have a basic education (a high school diploma, vocational skills training, certification in a service occupation), modest income (earned from hourly wages), and jobs in manufacturing or the "service economy" (factory workers, truck drivers, cooks, waiters and waitresses, nurses, police officers). Thirty or so years ago, when the parents of the young men and women Silva spoke with were coming of age, young working-class adults were better able to get

▶ Dimitris Voutsinos, a Greek sound technician, drinks coffee at his home in Athens. Dimitris was fired from a radio station and has been working since then mainly in call centers. He and his unemployed wife rely on his disabled mother's pension of 750 euros. The unemployment rate in Greece remains the highest in the European Union, standing at 20.6% in August 2017.

steady jobs and maintain relatively stable lives for themselves and their families. What has happened since then to lead thousands of working-class men and women in their 20s and 30s to increasingly remain unmarried, live at home with their parents, have children out of wedlock or not have children at all, divorce, and remain unemployed or stuck in low-paying jobs? We'll address this important question in due course, but first we turn to the discipline of sociology and its examination of social problems.

ASK YOURSELF: Think of a social issue about which you and your peers have expressed concern. How do you think this issue affects other people your age but from a social class different from yours? A different race or ethnicity? Think of the ways in which you do or do not identify with the young working-class adults Jennifer Silva interviewed.

THE SOCIOLOGICAL STUDY OF SOCIAL PROBLEMS

1.2   Define what constitutes a social problem.

Intersectionality: The ways in which several demographic factors—especially social class, race, ethnicity, and gender—combine to affect people's experiences.

Social class: A category of people whose experiences in life are determined by the amount of income and wealth they own and control.

As the study of social behavior and human society, **sociology** is the field most likely to examine systematically social problems such as poverty, social discrimination (on the basis of race, ethnicity, gender, sexual identity, age), crime, drug abuse, immigration, climate change, terrorism, and more.

This textbook consists of 17 chapters on various social problems. They were written by sociologists who are experts in the social problems they discuss. While social problems may sometimes differ in their extent, and while we may research and analyze them differently, we define a **social problem** as a social condition, event, or pattern of behavior that negatively affects the well-being of a significant number of people (or a number of significant people) who believe that the condition, event, or pattern needs to be changed or ameliorated. Let's consider the various aspects of our definition, and some of their implications, in turn.

Patterns and Trends

To begin with, in discussing social problems we are talking about conditions, events, or behaviors that occur locally, nationally, or globally and cause or threaten to cause harm to all or some segment of the population. Consider the failure of U.S. schools to teach children basic literacy skills as a social *condition* that means many students (particularly poor and minority children) will not be well prepared to enter the job market, and that the United States will be less competitive in the world economy. Or consider a series of *events* like Hurricanes Harvey, Irma, and Maria, which, when they made landfall in Texas, Florida, and Puerto Rico during the summer of 2017, flooded hundreds of thousands of homes, caused hundreds of billions of dollars in property damage, and killed over 100 people. Finally, consider as a social problem a *pattern of behavior* like the increased abuse of prescription opioid pain relievers, ADHD stimulants, and anti-anxiety drugs by young adults, which in 2014 led to more than 1,700 deaths (National Institute on Drug Abuse, 2017a).

Because social problems affect large numbers of people, sociologists typically discuss them in terms of *patterns* and *trends*, and use measures of *rates* to describe how frequent and pervasive their occurrence is. For example, we've all heard about how politicians, civic leaders, religious leaders, and average citizens are concerned about the crime rates in their cities and communities. In studying rates of crime, sociologists and criminologists rely on certain **data sources**, or collections of information, like the FBI's Uniform Crime Reports (UCR; to be discussed in Chapter 11). When we look at the UCR's percentage of violent crime by U.S. region, we see that in 2015, the South had the highest rate of violent crime (murder, rape, robbery, aggravated assault) at 41.2%, compared to the Northeast region, with 14.7% (Federal Bureau of Investigation, 2015a).

Patterns and trends can be visually presented in a variety of formats, including charts, tables, and graphs. Throughout this textbook you will see data depicted in this way. Back in the 1920s and 1930s the sociologists at the University of Chicago were interested in studying the incidence and prevalence of alcoholism, suicide, mental illness, and crime and delinquency in the city. Knowing that these problems tend to be more concentrated in some areas than in others, they wanted to identify their distribution throughout Chicago. For this they used maps. One of the most common types was the *spot map*, on which the researchers plotted the locations where a particular social problem was present. For example, Figure 1.1 is a map in which the spots indicate the home addresses of 8,591 alleged male juvenile delinquents during 1927.

The Objective and Subjective Aspects of Social Problems

We will come back to the way sociologists use and produce information about social problems when they do research, but for now notice that in measuring the rate of crime—or, for that matter, of divorce, population growth, or sex

TABLE 1.1 A Ranking of Social Problems

Rank	Problem	Percentage
1	Dissatisfaction with government/Poor leadership	23
2	Race relations/Racism	10
3	Health care	9
4	Unifying the country	7
5	Immigration/Illegal aliens	6

In a Gallup public opinion poll conducted in November 2017, a random national sample of 1,000 adults was asked, "What do you think is the most important problem facing the country today?" Above are the top five results.

SOURCE: http://www.gallup.com/poll/1675/most-important-problem.aspx

....

Sociology: The study of social behavior and human society.

Social problem: A social condition, event, or pattern of behavior that negatively affects the well-being of a significant number of people (or a number of significant people) who believe that the condition, event, or pattern needs to be changed or ameliorated.

Data sources: Collections of information.

FIGURE 1.1 Example of a Spot Map

SOURCE: Originally published in *Delinquency Areas*, by Clifford R. Shaw, with the collaboration of Frederick M. Zorbaugh, Henry D. McKay, & Leonard S. Cottroll, 1929. Reprinted with permission from the University of Chicago Press.

trafficking—we are able to call attention to the **objective aspect of social problems**. In other words, data allow us to show, concretely, how much crime is really out there. Again, in looking at the UCR we can see that in 2015, 352 murders were reported in New York City compared to 333 the year before, and that there were 478 murders in Chicago in 2015, compared to 411 in 2014 (Federal Bureau of Investigation, 2015b). These statistics tell us two things in straightforward terms: First, Chicago—with one-third the population of New York—had 126 *more* murders than New York, and second, the murder rate in Chicago *went up* from one year to the next.

More complicated, however, is the **subjective aspect of social problems**. Here we are talking about what people *define* as a social problem. There is often a close link between the objective and subjective aspects of a problem. For example, people are made objectively aware (usually through official data) that the murder rate in their community has doubled over the past 5 years, and, as a consequence, they become subjectively concerned about their safety and that of their community.

But even without a direct interaction between the objective and the subjective, people can be troubled about a particular social condition, event, or pattern of behavior. Consider that, on average, over twice as many people in the United States die from injuries sustained in motor vehicle crashes as die from HIV infection: In 2014, fatalities from these two causes were 32,744 and 12,333, respectively (Centers for Disease Control and Prevention, 2016c; National Traffic Safety Administration, 2015). Yet there are far more organizations and campaigns for AIDS awareness in the United States and worldwide—such as Acting on AIDS, ACT UP, the Stop AIDS Project, and the Elton John AIDS Foundation—than there are for car crashes. No doubt there are many justifiable reasons for this disproportionate focus, but while *objectively* the problem of auto fatalities causes twice as much harm to people and society, *subjectively* people are much more concerned about the problem of AIDS. In other words, if one troubling condition is more pervasive or more detrimental than another (and even if there's factual information indicating this), that doesn't necessarily mean people will perceive the condition as more problematic.

Another subjective aspect of social problems is the *relativity* with which people identify them. First, what is viewed as a social problem in one time and place may not be viewed as a social problem in another time and place. As we will see in Chapter 6, public attitudes toward the aged have fluctuated between positive and negative over the past 200 years. Currently, politicians and policy makers worry that the rapidly growing segment of the U.S. population aged 65 and older will strain government programs like Social Security and Medicare; contrast this attitude with the past, when elderly people were more respected and were valued for their wisdom and insight. Second, relativity ensures that some segments of the population experience the social problem and others do not, or they experience it to a different extent. For

Objective aspect of social problems: Those empirical conditions or facts that point to the concreteness of social problems "out there."

Subjective aspect of social problems: The process by which people define social problems.

Steve Exum/FilmMagic/Getty Images

▶ Demonstrators attend the Women's March on January 21, 2017, in Washington, D.C. The march took place the day after Donald Trump's inauguration as president of the United States due largely to statements he had made and positions he had taken that many regarded as antiwomen or otherwise offensive. Do you think these types of protests are effective in bringing about social change?

store thefts, and drug use. Conversely, there will be fewer laws to prohibit behaviors like profiting from campaign financing, insider trading, and price-fixing. According to Quinney, definitions of crime align with the interests of those segments of society with the power to shape social policy. We will discuss the relationship between social problems and social policy shortly. But first let's consider why, once people perceive a social situation as detrimental to their well-being or that of others, they believe some sort of *action* must be taken to change or improve the situation.

Types of Action

The type of action needed to bring about large-scale *social change* is usually aimed at transforming the **social structure**, the pattern of interrelated social institutions. Such action typically includes organizing and mobilizing large numbers of people into **social movements**, which are collective efforts to realize social change in order to solve social problems. Think about how the Black Lives Matter movement, the 2017 Women's March on Washington, and the Occupy Wall Street movement, mainly through various forms of demonstration, brought attention to the issues of racial, gender, and income inequality, respectively. In order to bring about greater justice and equality for people of color, women, and the 99%, these social movements sought to change, among other things, immigration policy, women's rights, financial institutions, the police, and the political system.

example, the pervasiveness of assault rifles in U.S. society is a social problem to advocates of stricter gun laws, but not to supporters of gun ownership rights.

The subjective element of social problems is framed by a theoretical approach called **social constructionism**, which describes the social process by which people define a social problem into existence. Simply put, "social problems are what people think they are" (Spector & Kitsuse, 1987, p. 73). Throughout the chapters in this textbook you will find many of the authors taking a constructionist approach in their analyses of various social phenomena.

Returning to our definition of a social problem, we've said that a sufficient or *significant number of people* must conceptualize the condition as problematic. This means enough people—a critical mass, in fact—must be concerned about the troubling or objectionable situation to call attention to it (in the chapters to follow they are generally called *claims-makers*). Because social problems are collective in nature, large collections of people are required to define them as such.

Sociologists also acknowledge that, when it comes to deciding which conditions are problematic, some people and groups are more significant or have greater influence than others. This speaks to the issue of political *power*. For example, as criminologist Richard Quinney (1970) notes, the more the powerful segments of society—such as politicians, bankers, and corporate executives—are concerned about crime, the greater the probability that laws will be created to prohibit such behaviors as muggings,

Actions meant to *ameliorate* (from the Latin *melior*, to improve) a problematic condition are usually aimed at helping those in need. This means providing, in some cases, the material relief necessary for physical survival (money, food, clothes); in most cases, however, it means providing nonmaterial services, such as counseling (employment, parenting), dispute resolution (peace talks, mediation), education (instruction and encouragement), and professional consultation (on specific troublesome

Social constructionism: The social process by which people define a social problem into existence.

Social structure: The pattern of interrelated social institutions.

Social movements: The collective efforts of people to realize social change in order to solve social problems.

issues). People hoping to take or support these kinds of actions typically engage in community service, civic engagement, and advocacy. Think about organized forms of volunteerism and activism like AmeriCorps, the Red Cross, Big Brothers/Big Sisters, Do Something, Save the Children, Oxfam, and the United Way.

 ASK YOURSELF: What troubling situations do you see in your community (neighborhood, campus)? How do these fit, or not fit, the definition of social problems given above? Do they have both objective and subjective aspects? Explain.

THE SOCIOLOGICAL IMAGINATION

1.3 Explain the sociological imagination.

We now return to the question of what social structural changes have occurred during the past three decades to lead millions of working-class young adults like Jalen to join the military because they can't find jobs, to move back in with their parents, or to struggle to get through college, pay back their loans, and make their monthly car payments. Remember that these millennials—though they try hard to achieve the American Dream of finding stable jobs, getting married, and owning their own homes—largely blame themselves for having stopped "growing up." They feel insecure, powerless, and isolated. They feel trapped.

More than half a century ago, the American sociologist C. Wright Mills (1916–1962) wrote the following lines, which could easily be describing the lives of young working-class men and women today:

> Nowadays men [and women] often feel that their private lives are a series of traps. They sense that within their everyday worlds, they cannot overcome their troubles. . . . Underlying this sense of being trapped are seemingly impersonal changes in the very *structure* of continent-wide societies. . . . Neither *the life of an individual* nor the *history* of a society can be understood without understanding both. (Mills, 1959, p. 3; emphases added)

Mills is saying that in order to understand our personal hardships and our own individual feelings, we must be aware of the larger forces of history and of social structure. To gain this awareness, he proposes, we should use a way of thinking that he calls the sociological imagination. The **sociological imagination** is a form of self-consciousness

Fritz Goro /Time Life Pictures/Getty Images

▶ C. Wright Mills was a leading critic of U.S. society in the 1950s and made contributions to the sociological perspective known as conflict theory. Mills taught at Columbia University and wrote about the power arrangements in U.S. society in such books as *White Collar* and *The Power Elite*. His most famous book, *The Sociological Imagination*, was published in 1959.

that allows us to go beyond our immediate environments (of family, neighborhood, work) and understand the major structural transformations that have occurred and are occurring. For working-class young men and women, some of these transformations have to do with family patterns, increased inequality of income and wealth, the rise of the service economy, declining social mobility, and depressed wages. These are some of the structural changes that have occurred during the past 30 years that in many ways operate against the working-class millennials' attempts to create stable and predictable adult lives.

The sociological imagination provides us with insight into the social conditions of our lives. It helps us understand why we feel trapped and insecure, isolated and powerless. The sociological imagination helps us make the connection between *history* and *biography,* between our own society and our private lives, and become aware

Sociological imagination: A form of self-consciousness that allows us to go beyond our immediate environments of family, neighborhood, and work and understand the major structural transformations that have occurred and are occurring.

of all individuals in similar circumstances. In short, the sociological imagination allows us to *see our personal troubles as social problems*. In this way we are not only able to confront social problems, but we are also aware of the social problems' origins. We come to understand that what we see and feel as personal misfortunes (for example, our inability to achieve the milestones of adulthood) are predicaments shared by many others and difficult for any one individual to solve.

But Mills (1959, p. 150) also asserts that the "problems of [our] societies are almost inevitably problems of the world." In other words, the sociological imagination requires that we take a **global perspective**, comparing our own society to other societies in all the world's regions. When we can understand the social problems of U.S. society in relationship to social problems in other countries, we are using the sociological imagination even more broadly. You will see that, in discussing social problems, the authors of the following chapters take a global perspective. In addition, each chapter contains a "Beyond Our Borders" box featuring discussion of the problem in a global context.

Also be aware that the expert authors writing on various social problems in these chapters have all been trained in sociology. And regardless of the fact that they specialize in one or a few social problems in their research and writing, as sociologists they have several things in common. First, they employ the sociological imagination, frequently from a global perspective. Second, they rely on sociological research. Third, they make use of sociological theory.

....

ASK YOURSELF: Do people you know feel trapped in their daily lives? How or why? Explain the sociological imagination in your own words. Explain how a social problem in the United States affects other areas of the world.

....

SOCIOLOGICAL RESEARCH

1.4   Discuss how sociological research can be used to study social problems.

In discussing the *objective* aspect of social problems, we noted that sociologists look at patterns and trends in regard to police brutality, poverty, the opioid epidemic, auto fatalities, and so on. In order to identify these patterns and trends they require numerical facts, like rates, percentages, and ratios. Sometimes these facts are available in data sources such as the General Social Survey

(GSS). One of the largest sources for social scientific data in the United States, the GSS includes data on social trends, demographics, behaviors, opinions, and attitudes. GSS data are feely available over the Internet (http://www.gss.norc.org) to policy makers, researchers, government officials, students, and the general public. Other data sources from which sociologists draw numerical facts for conducting social problems research include the ones listed in Table 1.2. Often, however, sociologists need to collect their own original data firsthand. In either case, we refer to these types of data collection as **quantitative research** because they rely on the empirical investigation of social problems through statistical analysis.

When it comes to the *subjective* aspects of social problems, sociologists tend to be less interested in facts and figures and more interested in the ways people define, experience, or understand problematic situations. In order to achieve this understanding, they engage in **qualitative research**, much as Jennifer Silva did when she talked with 100 young men and women of the working class to learn about their lives and feelings. When sociologists conduct studies of social problems, they can employ several **research methods** or techniques for obtaining information. Let's look at three of these research methods.

Survey Research

For quantitative research, the method most commonly used is the **survey**, a technique in which respondents are asked to answer questions on a written questionnaire. A *questionnaire* is a set of questions a researcher presents to respondents for their answers. Questionnaires typically ask questions that measure *variables,* such as attitudes (say, political affiliation), behaviors (religious services attendance), and marriage statuses. Researchers may administer questionnaires in person or by telephone, or they can send them through the mail or use the Internet. Because it is often impractical to survey every subject in a population of interest—for example, every homeless person in a large city—the researcher selects a *sample* of subjects that represents that population. In this way the researcher tries to reach conclusions about all the

....

Global perspective: A viewpoint from which we compare our own society to other societies around the world.

Quantitative research: Research that studies social problems through statistical analysis.

Qualitative research: Research that studies how people define, experience, or understand problematic situations.

Research methods: Techniques for obtaining information.

Survey: A research method that asks respondents to answer questions on a written questionnaire.

TABLE 1.2 Some Data Sources for Social Problems Research

Data Source	Description
National Center for Education Statistics (http://nces .ed.gov)	Government agency (part of the U.S. Department of Education) that collects data on a variety of issues related to education, including academic achievement and performance, illiteracy, dropout rates, home schooling, adult learning, teacher qualifications, and public and private school comparisons
National Center for Health Statistics (http://www.cdc .gov/nchs/index .htm)	Government agency (part of the Centers for Disease Control and Prevention) responsible for collecting data from birth and death records, medical records, nutrition records, and interview surveys, as well as through direct physical exams and laboratory testing, in order to provide information to help identify and address critical health problems in the United States
The Pew Research Center (http://www .pewresearch .org)	Nonpartisan "fact tank" that provides information on social issues, public opinion, and demographic trends shaping the United States and the world
U.S. Bureau of Labor Statistics (http://www.bls .gov)	Government agency (branch of the U.S. Department of Labor) responsible for collecting data about employment, unemployment, pay and benefits, consumer spending, work productivity, workplace injuries and fatalities, and employment productivity
U.S. Census Bureau (http://www .census.gov)	Government agency (a branch of the U.S. Department of Commerce) responsible for conducting the decennial U.S. Census; serves as a leading source of data about the American people and economy

homeless people in a city by studying a smaller number of them. In other words, by measuring relationships between variables, survey research quantifies data and generalizes findings from the sample group to some larger population.

Although he employs several research methods, sociologist Steven J. Tepper (2011) relied extensively on survey research in his study examining controversies over cultural expressions. One of Tepper's hypotheses is that citizens are most likely to feel offended by certain forms of art, and will protest them, when they feel their lifestyles and values are being threatened. In other words, people will want to ban certain films, books, paintings, sculptures, clothing styles, popular music, and television programs when they have a fear or anxiety about social change. To test this hypothesis, Tepper consulted data from three national surveys that ask thousands of U.S. adults about their attitudes toward art, culture, and entertainment. He found that those most concerned about the rate of immigration into the country (an issue that relates to concerns about social change) were most likely to want to prohibit an unpopular speaker and remove an unpopular book from the library. And those who thought that "everything is changing too fast" were more likely to favor restrictions on television programming. These findings from large sample populations could have been obtained only from such large-scale surveys as the ones used by Tepper.

Participant Observation

Because qualitative researchers seek to understand the social world from the subject's point of view, they frequently employ **participant observation**, a method in which the researcher observes and studies people in their everyday settings. The researcher collects data through direct observation and in this way gains a deep understanding of and familiarity with the workings of a particular group, community, or social event. Groups and settings that sociologists observe include impoverished neighborhoods, emergency rooms, homeless shelters, religious groups, secret societies, gangs, welfare mothers, taxi drivers, and pregnant teens.

A good example of participant observation research is a study in which sociologist Nicole Gonzalez Van Cleve (2016) examined how the criminal courts in Cook County–Chicago dispensed racialized punishments to African American and Latino defendants before, during, and after they were found guilty. Van Cleve spent 9 months working as a law clerk in order to incorporate both participant and observer roles. During that time she observed open-court interactions and private plea-bargaining exchanges. She interacted with court officials and defendants—in attorney's offices, courtrooms, hallways, jails, and judge's chambers. Van Cleve learned how racial meanings become ingrained within the courthouse culture despite the procedural protections available to the defendants—most of whom were people of color. She found that the race-neutral or "colorblind" ideology espoused by the white attorneys and judges masked the

....

Participant observation: A research method that includes observing and studying people in their everyday settings.

racial divides and unequal treatment that were endemic in the criminal courts she studied. Van Cleve could not have revealed the culture of racialized justice that exists in the Cook County court system had she not spent long periods of time observing the everyday nature of the courthouse.

Interviewing

Quantitative research has the advantages of providing precise numerical data and of generalizing research findings. Qualitative research, on the other hand, has the advantage of providing in-depth information that describes complex phenomena in rich detail. One research method that may include both quantitative and qualitative elements is **interviewing**, the form of data collection in which the researcher asks respondents a series of questions. Interviews can be conducted face to face or on the phone, on a number of issues (sexual harassment, texting while driving, cutbacks to social welfare programs), and in a variety of settings (at home, on the street, on the Internet). Researchers record the subjects' responses in writing or

Carlos Chavez/Los Angeles Times/Getty Images

▶ Andrea Neal, a sociology student at Pierce College, interviews Nathan Jaffe, a retired engineer. She is attempting to find out what it means to be a senior citizen in the community. What do you think are some of the merits of conducting interviews in doing research?

by audio recording. Once recorded, the responses can be treated quantitatively when researchers assign numerical values to them, enter the values into a data analysis program, and then run various statistical commands to identify patterns across responses. Researchers can use the patterns to make comparisons between different sample groups. Interviews can also be treated qualitatively, as guided conversations that let respondents talk at length and in detail. In this case the researcher listens carefully and may ask follow-up questions. Once the responses have been recorded, the researcher can identify categories or themes across them. This helps the researcher determine which issues from the interviews are significant.

One study that relied heavily on interviews was done by sociologist Sharmila Rudrappa (2015). Wanting to find out how the phenomenon of surrogacy—when women are paid to carry and deliver babies for people who cannot conceive them biologically—was experienced and transacted, Rudrappa conducted in-depth interviews with women from India, who served as surrogate mothers. These Indian women were hired to have babies mostly by white parents in the United States and Australia. She discovered that many of the surrogate mothers experienced a great deal of ambivalence in the process of sharing children. In the interviews, some women spoke candidly about how grateful they were to become surrogates, while others told about how they had to emotionally distance themselves from the babies they were bearing. As she listened carefully to what these women had to say, Rudrappa realized they were giving new meanings to the value of babies and motherhood.

Mixed Methods

Because each method offers its own advantages, sociologists often combine quantitative and qualitative methods of research to achieve a fuller picture of the social problems they are studying. One example is Carla Shedd's (2015) research exploring how the views that inner-city youth have of themselves and the larger social world are shaped by their experiences as they go from home to school and back. Shedd relied on a University of Chicago data source that documents thousands of Chicago public school students' perceptions of social injustice, on in-depth interviews that she conducted with students in high schools with different racial compositions, and on her participant observation research of schools and local communities. By employing these various techniques, Shedd was able to show how these young people's beliefs about their economic and educational opportunities are determined by their race and place of residence.

Interviewing: A method of data collection in which the researcher asks respondents a series of questions.

Interview With Sociologist Joel Best

You have written many important books that focus on understanding how and why people become concerned with particular social problems. These include The Stupidity Epidemic: Worrying About Students, Schools, and America's Future; How Claims Spread: Cross-National Diffusion of Social Problems; *and* Images of Issues: Typifying Contemporary Social Problems. *How, in brief, do social problems emerge?*

We start thinking that something is a social problem after someone makes a claim and other folks start to pay attention. Imagine a guy standing on the sidewalk warning about invading extraterrestrials—that's a claim, but if no one responds to it, then the alien invasion doesn't become a social problem. All sorts of people can make claims: people who have been victimized, activists, experts, journalists, and so on. Typically, there is a social problems process: the original claim attracts attention, which leads to media coverage that brings the topic to a wider audience, which in turn affects public opinion, and that leads to policy makers trying to establish some way of dealing with the troubling condition. In my view, it is not the nature of a social condition that makes something a social problem; rather, social problems emerge through this process

of collective definition. If people don't define something as a social problem, then it isn't one.

You have also written several books on how questionable statistics influence how we think about social problems. These include Damned Lies and Statistics; More Damned Lies and Statistics; *and* Stat-Spotting: A Field Guide to Identifying Dubious Data. *How can we deal with statistics and other data intended to influence how we think about social problems?*

Social problems can be big and messy. We need statistics to understand them. At the same time, we need to realize statistics about social problems may come from people who worry more about the problem than the accuracy of their numbers. "This is a big problem," they reason, "and here's a big number, so it must be about right." This doesn't mean they're trying to spread false numbers, just that they may not be thinking carefully about the statistics they use. Therefore, it is important that we think critically about the social problems statistics we hear. In particular, when you encounter a statistic that seems particularly alarming, it's a good idea to take a deep breath and start asking some questions. Who did the counting? What did they count? How did they count it,

and why? Statistics may be accurate, but sometimes we discover that a figure is little more than a guess.

In the conference talk that you gave as president of the Society for the Study of Social Problems, you ended by saying that you believe in the value of the sociological perspective. What value does sociology have for understanding social problems?

Sociology is like a pair of glasses: Put them on and you'll see the world differently. Our common-sense reasoning tells us that of course the world is the way it is, while everyday explanations for people's behavior tend to emphasize personality traits. In contrast, sociology teaches us to look for the ways people affect one another, for the patterns in social life. It encourages us to stop taking things for granted, to question why our lives take the forms they do. Psychologists tend to focus on the behavior of individuals, just as economists try to understand life in terms of rational choices. Each of these perspectives can be illuminating when we ask some sorts of questions. Sociology offers another, distinctive perspective. I find the questions it can answer particularly interesting, and that's why I became a sociologist.

SOURCE: Author interview conducted April 7, 2017.

In each of the chapters to follow you will find a "Researching" box feature that discusses a study or two done on a particular social problem, including information on methods and results.

ASK YOURSELF: Think of a social problem you would like to research. Which of the three research methods discussed above do you think is best suited for your purposes? Why?

THREE SOCIOLOGICAL THEORIES

1.5 Explain the three main sociological perspectives of structural functionalism, conflict theory, and symbolic interactionism.

Once researchers have collected the information they need—whether through data sources, surveys, participant observation, interviewing, or other research methods—they must then *make sociological sense* of that information. In other words, they need to manage the data in a way that tells them something new or different about the social issue under consideration. In order to do this, they use **theory**, a collection of related concepts.

Concepts are ideas sociologists have about some aspect of the social world. They tend to be articulated as terms—words or phrases that make up the vocabulary of sociology. So far in this chapter, we have used and defined several sociological concepts, including "social institution," "social class," "social problem," "social constructionism," and "social structure." Throughout this textbook you will meet many concepts, introduced in boldface green type. These terms are defined at the bottom of the page, and the Glossary at the end of the book provides a comprehensive listing of these concepts and their definitions.

Concepts are also the building blocks of theory, and in this sense a theory is an attempt to articulate the relationship between concepts. Sociologists, for example, may want to examine the connection between certain types of social structure and certain types of social problems. Thus, they may pose such questions as the following: Does the kind of economic institution we have contribute to high

▶ Talcott Parsons was the leading American sociological theorist during the middle decades of the 20th century and did much to advance the theoretical perspective known as structural functionalism. Parsons, who taught at Harvard University, was most interested in knowing what contributes to order in society. His books include *The Social System* and *Toward a General Theory of Action*.

levels of poverty? How does our political system prevent us from providing adequate health care to everyone? Why do some communities have higher rates of violent crime than others? Or sociologists may want to analyze the relationship between social problems and certain behaviors and attitudes. In that case they might ask questions like these: How might sexist attitudes prevent the country from maximizing the numbers of scientists and engineers it produces? Why do students in some countries have uniformly high scores on math, science, and literacy exams, while in the United States there are large gaps in performance between the highest-scoring and the lowest-scoring students?

While sociology encompasses many theories, there are three main theories with which all sociologists, regardless of their specialty areas, are familiar: structural functionalism, conflict theory, and symbolic interactionism. Because they are very broad theories they are sometimes called **paradigms**, or theoretical perspectives. Let's get familiar with each of these in turn before we look at how policy makers can apply them to addressing social problems.

Structural Functionalism

Structural functionalism (or functionalism) is the sociological theory that considers how various social phenomena function, or work in a positive way, to maintain unity and order in society. The theory of structural functionalism dates back to the beginnings of sociology, and some of its ideas can be traced to several 19th-century sociologists, including Herbert Spencer.

Herbert Spencer (1820–1903) viewed society as an organism, which is to say as an integrated *system* made up of different social institutions, all working together to keep it going. Just as the human body (a biological organism) has many organs (the heart, brain, liver, kidneys, and so on), all of which are necessary for its survival, so too does society need the various institutions of the economy, the government, the family, religion, and so on to keep it orderly and cohesive. Each institution works in different ways to benefit society. For example, some of the **functions**—that is, positive consequences—of the family are that it provides an expedient way for humans to

....

Theory: A collection of related concepts.

Concepts: Ideas that sociologists have about some aspect of the social world.

Paradigms: Theoretical perspectives.

Structural functionalism (or functionalism): The sociological theory that considers how various social phenomena function, or work in a positive way, to maintain unity and order in society.

Functions: Positive consequences of social structures or social institutions.

reproduce themselves biologically; it provides emotional support to family members; and it teaches, or *socializes,* children in the rules of society. Some of the functions of religion are that it gives answers to the larger questions of existence (What existed before the Big Bang? What happens after death?); it presents us with ideas about what is right and wrong; and it brings members of a particular religious group closer together in their shared beliefs. In short, social institutions have functions for society.

Talcott Parsons (1902–1979) was the most famous theorist of structural functionalism. His theory of the functions of social systems is very complex, but here we are concerned only with what he called "the problem of order." Simply put, Parsons believed that for society as a social system to keep functioning smoothly, it needs to maintain social order. And because the social institutions already provide functions for society, social order is common. However, sometimes strains and tensions threaten to disrupt social integration and stability. Think of wars, revolutions, political polarization, racial tensions, and terrorist attacks. Parsons believed that one way societies can prevent such disruptions is by encouraging people to conform to society's expectations. This is best achieved by having them abide by the same shared **norms**, or rules, and **values**, or beliefs. Thus, for Parsons, consensus produces social order.

Sociologist Robert K. Merton (1910–2003) agreed that social institutions and social structures can have functions. But he saw that they can also have **dysfunctions**, or negative consequences. Consider how the family can be a refuge from the larger world, where family members can get nurturance, love, and acceptance in ways that are not available to them in other institutional settings. But also consider how the family can be the setting where domestic violence, contentious divorce, and the sexual and emotional abuse of children may occur.

Merton would have us examine both the functions and the dysfunctions of social phenomena, and he would also have us ask about our social structures, "Functional for whom?" In other words, we must be aware that while a social phenomenon like income inequality in the social structure of U.S. society is dysfunctional for one group (the poor), it may be quite functional for another (the wealthy). This may be one reason why the rich, as stakeholders in the economic institution, may not define income inequality as a social problem or may not want to change the social structure that creates it.

Conflict Theory

Conflict theory is the sociological theory that focuses on dissent, coercion, and antagonism in society. In this sense we may see conflict theory as the opposite of structural functionalism. It too has its roots in the 19th century, particularly in the ideas of Karl Marx.

▶ Karl Marx was a 19th-century revolutionary and critic of the economic institution known as capitalism. He believed that capitalist societies like England and the United States would eventually become communist societies. His best-known work, which he coauthored with Friedrich Engels, is *The Communist Manifesto*, first published in 1848.

Karl Marx (1818–1883) was first and foremost engaged in critiquing **capitalism**, the economic system that includes the ownership of private property, the making of financial profit, and the hiring of workers. Marx saw two main antagonistic social classes in capitalist society. The first, the **capitalists** (or bourgeoisie), make up the economically dominant class that privately owns and controls human

....

Norms: Social rules.

Values: Social beliefs.

Dysfunctions: Negative consequences of social structures or social institutions.

Conflict theory: The sociological theory that focuses on dissent, coercion, and antagonism in society.

Capitalism: An economic system that includes the ownership of private property, the making of financial profit, and the hiring of workers.

Capitalists: The economically dominant class that privately owns and controls human labor, raw materials, land, tools, machinery, technologies, and factories.

labor, raw materials, land, tools, machinery, technologies, and factories. The second social class consists of the **workers** (or proletariat), who own no property and must work for the capitalists in order to support themselves and their families financially. In their effort to maximize their profits, capitalists exploit workers by not paying them the full value of their work. Because their labor is bought and sold by the capitalists who hire and fire them, workers are treated as machines, not as human beings. Many sociologists have been influenced by Marx's conflict theory and examine the frictions that exist between the powerful social classes (the rich, the 1%, the wealthy) and the powerless social classes (the working class, the 99%, the poor), and that give rise to a variety of social problems related to the unequal distribution of wealth.

Ralf Dahrendorf departed from Marx's focus on the conflict between social classes and looked instead to the conflict between **interest groups**, organized associations of people mobilized into action because of their membership in those associations. For Dahrendorf (1959), social inequalities have their basis not only in economic differences but also in *political power*. Simply put, those with power give orders and those without power take orders.

▶ George Herbert Mead, who taught at the University of Chicago in the early 20th century, was one of the first scholars to take seriously the study of the social self. His most famous book, which was published by his students after he died, is *Mind, Self, and Society*. This book is regarded by many as the "bible" of symbolic interactionism.

Power relationships lead to the tensions between interest groups (also called advocacy groups, or lobbying groups). Thus, for Dahrendorf, social conflict in relationship to social problems occurs among interest groups—such as Americans for Prosperity, Heritage Action for America, the Southern Poverty Law Center, and People for the American Way—some of which are politically progressive while others are politically conservative.

Those groups with sufficient political power use it, usually by influencing legislation, to protect their interests. Consider the politically powerful interest groups on opposite sides of the issue of gun control, such as those that support required background checks for all gun purchases (Everytown for Gun Safety) and those that oppose such checks (National Rifle Association). Or consider interest groups that favor abortion rights (Planned Parenthood and the National Organization for Women) and those that do not (Americans United for Life and the National Right to Life Committee).

In short, conflict theory looks at how one group or social class tries to dominate another in situations it perceives as threatening to its interests and well-being. In this sense, what one group considers to be a social problem (say, the sale of assault rifles), another group may not.

Symbolic Interactionism

As mentioned above, in the discussion of the subjective element of social problems, the *social constructionist* approach says that certain social conditions, events, or patterns of behavior are social problems because people *define* them as such. The third major sociological theory, symbolic interactionism, also takes a definitional approach to understanding social problems, but rather than looking at the social structure it tends to focus on **social interaction**, or the communication that occurs between two or more people. **Symbolic interactionism** is the sociological perspective that sees society as the product of symbols (words, gestures, objects) that are given meaning by people in their interactions with each other. Symbolic interactionism has its origins in the ideas of George Herbert Mead.

....

Workers: Those who own no property and must work for the capitalists in order to support themselves and their families financially.

Interest groups: Organized associations of people mobilized into action because of their membership in those associations.

Social interaction: The communication that occurs between two or more people.

Symbolic interactionism: The sociological perspective that sees society as the product of symbols (words, gestures, objects) given meaning by people in their interactions with each other.

George Herbert Mead (1863–1931) was interested in understanding the relationship between mind, self, and society (Mead, 1934). For Mead, **mind** refers to the internal conversations we have within ourselves. In other words, we continuously think about ourselves and about what is going on around us, and all this requires the use of language. Language is nothing more than a system of **symbols** (objects that represent something else) that we interpret. For example, you are reading the words on this page because you have learned to interpret the symbols (the written words) of the English language. But unless you can read Russian, the following words are not meaningful to you: Эти слова для вас не имеют никакого значения. In the same way you learned to read words, you learned to read or "define" a clock (symbolic of time), a map (symbolic of a particular physical place), a smile (symbolic of an emotion), and so on.

Just as important as our ability to define symbols is our ability to define our *self*. The **social self** is a process by which we are able to see ourselves in relationship to others. We are not born with a social self, which is why newborns do not have a sense of who they are. They have no self-consciousness. We can acquire the social self only after we have learned to consider who we are in relationship to the attitudes and expectations of others, of *society*.

Charles Horton Cooley (1864–1929) went further and proposed the concept of the **looking-glass self,** or the idea that we see ourselves as we think others see us (Cooley, 1902a). For example, if our friends, family, and teachers continually tell us we are clever, then we are likely to see ourselves as clever. If, on the other hand, teachers, police, and judges define, or "label," us as delinquent, we are likely to take on the identity of delinquent.

In addition to defining symbols (words, gestures, objects) and our social self (who we are), we define social situations. Long ago, sociologist W. I. Thomas noted that *if people define a social situation as real, it will be real in its consequences* (Thomas & Thomas, 1928). This means, for example, that if you and other students define what is going on in the classroom as a lecture, you will then listen closely to the speaker and take lecture notes. But if you define it as a funeral or a religious revival (admittedly harder to do), then it is that situation instead, and you will act appropriately. And if you define it as a party, then the consequences are that you stop taking notes and stop raising your hand to ask questions and instead mingle, talk to your friends, and have a good time.

As an extension of these ideas we may also propose a concept originated by Merton: the **self-fulfilling prophecy,** or the social process whereby a false definition of a situation brings about behavior that makes the false definition "come true." Let's combine and apply the self-fulfilling prophecy and the looking-glass self. Imagine a 5-year-old child, Marisol, who is a recent immigrant from Mexico and speaks only Spanish. Her parents enroll her in an English-only school, and her teacher notices that Marisol does not say much in class, does not raise

her hand to ask questions like the other students, and does not interact with playmates on the playground. After a while the teacher—and other teachers and students—may label Marisol as shy, introverted, a slow learner, asocial, and so on. Now, Marisol is actually none of these things, but she eventually starts to see herself that way and then becomes timid and unsure of herself. A couple of years later, Marisol is placed in a classroom for slow learners with interpersonal issues.

ASK YOURSELF: Think of a social problem you would like to research. Which of the three theoretical perspectives discussed above do you think is best suited for your purposes? Why?

APPLYING THE THREE THEORIES TO SOCIAL PROBLEMS

1.6 Evaluate how each of the three theoretical perspectives can be applied to improve our understanding of social problems.

Let us now consider how we can apply each of the three main theoretical perspectives in sociology to gain a better understanding of social problems.

Structural Functionalism and Suicide

To illustrate how functionalism has been applied to the real world, we turn to the French sociologist Émile Durkheim (1858–1917) and his classic study on the social problem of suicide. Durkheim understood that all societies, in order to continue as they are, need two things. The first, **social integration,** describes a certain degree of unity. In order words, people need to come together and stay together. The opposite of social integration is *social disintegration,* which leads to the collapse of society. The

Mind: The internal conversations we have within ourselves.

Symbols: Words, gestures, and objects to which people give meaning.

Social self: A process by which people are able to see themselves in relationship to others.

Looking-glass self: The idea that we see ourselves as we think others see us.

Self-fulfilling prophecy: The social process whereby a false definition of a situation brings about behavior that makes the false definition "come true."

Social integration: The unity or cohesiveness of society.

second necessary condition, **social regulation**, means that to maintain social order, societies need to have a certain degree of control over the behavior of their members. This is typically achieved by having people follow social norms. The opposite of social regulation is *social disorder,* which may lead to what Durkheim called **anomie**, or a state of normlessness. Both social integration and social regulation are functional for society, but they can become dysfunctional and lead to social problems when there is too much or too little of them.

Turning to the differences in suicide rates among various groups, Durkheim (1979/1897) found, for example, that suicide rates are higher among men than among women, higher for those who are single than for those who are married, and higher among Protestants than among Catholics or Jews. He explained these and other group differences by looking at the degree of social integration and social regulation and identified four types of social suicide.

► The French sociologist Émile Durkheim is regarded as one of the early founders of sociology. Working in the late 19th and early 20th centuries, he made many contributions to the topics of social solidarity, suicide, and religion. His most famous books include *The Division of Labor in Society, Suicide,* and *The Rules of Sociological Method.*

When a group has too much social integration, when it is overly cohesive, conditions lead to **altruistic suicide**. Here, group members sacrifice their lives for the group. For example, although many complex reasons motivate suicide bombers, suicide bombing is a type of altruistic suicide because it requires that the bombers place less value on their own lives than on the group's honor, religion, or some other collective interest (Hassan, 2011). By contrast, when a society has too little social integration, when its social bonds are weak, **egoistic suicide** may result. In this case, persons in certain populations kill themselves due to extreme isolation. For example, several studies indicate that while a number of risk factors cause older adults to commit suicide, one of the leading ones is social disconnectedness, which stems from living alone, losing a spouse, experiencing loneliness, or having low social support (Van Orden & Conwell, 2011).

Too much social regulation, or excessive social control over people's behavior, can cause **fatalistic suicide**. Members of certain groups end their lives because they see no escape from their oppressive situation. For example, among women in Iranian society, fatalistic is the dominant type of suicide due to a traditional male-dominated social structure that, among other things, forces women into marriage at an early age and prohibits divorce, even in the case of domestic violence (Aliverdinia & Pridemore, 2009). On the other hand, too little social regulation, which leads to the absence of norms, causes an increase in **anomic suicide**. This means that people kill themselves because they lack rules to give them social direction for meeting their needs. For example, a long-term causal relationship exists between the unemployment rate and men's suicide rate. One study explains that when men lose their jobs, society's regulating influence on their need to work is disrupted, causing an increase in their suicides (Riley, 2010).

In sum, Durkheim demonstrates how an unbalanced degree of social integration and social regulation can be dysfunctional for society, thus resulting in high rates of suicide.

....

Social regulation: The control society has over the behavior of its members.

Anomie: A state of normlessness in society.

Altruistic suicide: Suicide that occurs as a result of too much social integration.

Egoistic suicide: Suicide that occurs as a result of too little social integration.

Fatalistic suicide: Suicide that occurs as a result of too much social regulation.

Anomic suicide: Suicide that occurs as a result of too little social regulation.

Conflict Theory and Alcohol Consumption

The use of conflict theory is demonstrated by Joseph R. Gusfield's (1986) examination of how a particular group—rural, middle-class evangelical Protestants—tried to preserve its own **culture**, or style of life, in U.S. society during the 19th and early 20th centuries. This cultural group, which Gusfield calls "the Dry forces," were reformers who wanted to correct what they saw as a major social problem: the drinking habits of ethnic immigrants. The ethnic immigrants who threatened the moral way of life of the Dry forces, and who therefore needed to be reformed and controlled, were mainly urban, lower-class Irish and Italian Catholics and German Lutherans whose cultures did not prohibit the consumption of alcohol. These ethnic groups were also generally ranked at the bottom of the U.S. social and economic ladder and thus had limited political power.

In order to retain the dominance of their way of life, the middle-class Protestants attempted to reform the ethnic drinkers. They did this, first, by trying to persuade them to stop their "immoral" drinking voluntarily and by inviting them to membership in the middle class. However, by the last quarter of the 19th century, as the United States was becoming more urban, secular, and Catholic, the Dry forces changed their tactics, substituting for persuasion a method that was more hostile and antagonistic: They tried to *coerce* reform through legislation. This coercive strategy culminated in a national policy of prohibition in 1919, when Congress ratified the 18th Amendment to the U.S. Constitution, which prohibited the manufacture, sale, and transportation of intoxicating liquors. This application of conflict theory clearly shows that the interest group with the most political power can prohibit behaviors it considers problematic.

Symbolic Interactionism and Precarious Living

Waverly Duck (2015) takes a symbolic interactionist perspective to explain how the residents of a poor African American neighborhood where drug dealing was prevalent were able to survive their precarious existence. He found that they lacked decent jobs and schools, were likely to get in trouble with the criminal justice system, had little public assistance, and so on. Duck also found that the young black male residents who sold cocaine to white suburbanites were well integrated into the community. Duck's most important finding, however, was that the community possessed an **interaction order**. This was a lifestyle that shaped residents' everyday interactions with each other in order to help them cope with their poverty and racial isolation.

Because this interaction order involved personal interactions that differed sharply with those of the American

▶ Inspired by Marx's writings, Vladimir Lenin became the chief architect of the first successful socialist revolution, the Russian Revolution of 1917. In this painting he is shown delivering a speech to workers on May Day, 1920. Now that the Soviet Union has collapsed and communism is waning, do you think that Marx's ideas are still relevant today?

mainstream, outsiders saw the neighborhood as disordered, and community routine activities appeared to them as senseless and chaotic. For the residents, however, it was the opposite. The interaction order allowed them to accurately interpret and appropriately respond to the social situations in which they daily found themselves. It helped them to define what was meant by a particular gaze, a way of walking, or a way of dressing. It made it possible for residents to move safely through their community's organized drug trade, to educate themselves and their children, and to make money. Indeed, it gave everyone—law-abiding citizens and drug dealers—a sense of order, predictability, and solidarity.

The interaction order provided residents with a shared understanding of reciprocity and respect. For example, it ensured that no one broke into the homes of elderly

Culture: A style of life.

Interaction order: A culture that shapes everyday social interactions.

people or mugged them on the street. In taking a symbolic interactionist approach, Waverly Duck shows how neighborhood residents navigated challenges by defining their everyday interactions as involving relationships of trust, mutual understanding, and cohesiveness.

ASK YOURSELF: Think of three different social problems. What are the strengths of each of the theoretical perspectives in helping you to understand each of the social problems? What are the weaknesses?

SOCIAL POLICY

1.7 Discuss the role of social policy in managing social problems.

We've noted above that one possible way to deal with pervasive social problems like poverty is to change the social structure radically. However, short of a **social revolution**—a total and complete transformation in the social structure of society (such as the French Revolution of 1789, the Russian Revolution of 1917, the Chinese Revolution of 1948)—most social change is achieved piecemeal, and frequently reforms are begun through **social policy**, a more or less clearly articulated and usually written set of strategies for addressing a social problem.

Governmental implementation of social policy takes the form of **legislation** that makes some condition or pattern of behavior legal or illegal. The Civil Rights Act of 1964, a piece of legislation passed by Congress and signed by President Lyndon B. Johnson, made racial segregation in public accommodations illegal in the United States. Another type of social policy consists of an organization's guidelines about what ought to happen or not happen between members in regard to a particular issue, such as sexual harassment, bullying, smoking, infection control, and conflicts of interest. These guidelines are usually disseminated through handbooks, manuals, and official websites.

Although social policy has many goals, our concern here is with its role in managing social problems. Each chapter includes a section proposing policy recommendations for social change that arise from the three main theoretical perspectives.

ASK YOURSELF: Think of some policies (rules and regulations) of a workplace where you have been employed. Do you think these policies may have prevented unacceptable or harmful behaviors in that workplace? How?

SPECIALIZED THEORIES

1.8 Explore the role of specialized theories in sociology.

Structural functionalism, conflict theory, and symbolic interactionism are the three most general theoretical frameworks in sociology. But given that the study of society and social behavior is a complicated business, and that there is a wide variety of social problems to consider, sociologists have constructed specialized theories to deal with this complexity and variety. Specialized concepts and theories examine narrower features of society (say, the institution of the economy) or specific social problems (the rising rates of unemployment). There are many such specialized concepts and theories within sociology—hundreds, in fact. We will not examine them all in this book, however.

All the chapter authors have expertise in particular areas of social problems research, and they employ specialized concepts and theories intended to address their concerns. You will see that some of these concepts and theories are interrelated across chapters, whereas others are more narrowly focused. In either event, the idea is to go beyond—deeper and further—what the three theoretical perspectives can offer.

ASK YOURSELF: Think of a social problem you would like to research. In what ways are the three sociological theories discussed above too broad to provide a specific understanding of that social problem? Imagine some characteristics of a specialized theory that might give you less breadth but more depth on the issue. What types of questions about your research area would it help you answer?

SERVICE SOCIOLOGY AND SOCIAL PROBLEMS

1.9 Identify ways in which service sociology can make a difference.

Social revolution: A total and complete transformation in the social structure of society.

Social policy: A more or less clearly articulated and usually written set of strategies for addressing a social problem.

Legislation: Enacted laws that make some condition or pattern of behavior legal or illegal.

This is a textbook about social *problems,* which means we will be dealing with many issues that are troubling, harmful, or just plain distressing. It is understandable that you may feel "it's all bad news," that something needs to be done, that things need to change. But how? If sociology is the discipline that studies social problems, you may want to know what solutions it has to offer. Indeed, you may be interested in finding out what *you* can do to make a difference.

Concerns about the problems of urban life and ways to alleviate them go back to the early days of U.S. sociology, at the beginning of the 20th century. As sociology became a more popular subject of study in colleges and universities around the country, it took two basic forms: the study of sociological theory and the practice of ameliorative reform and service. At that time, most people thought of sociology as a form of philanthropy (Ward, 1902), and courses with titles such as Methods of Social Amelioration, Charities and Corrections, and Preventive Philanthropy were common (Breslau, 2007). Undergraduate sociology programs were even more focused on training in charity and social service work.

After its founding in 1892, the University of Chicago established the first full-fledged department of sociology in the country. At least initially, sociologists there were diligently engaged with applied social reform and philanthropy (Calhoun, 2007). Indeed, the founder of the department, Albion W. Small (1903, p. 477), pointed out that sociology "is good for nothing unless it can enrich average life; our primary task is to work out correct statements of social problems and valid methods of solving them."

Along with the development of sociology at Chicago, between 1885 and 1930 a unique, active, and engaged sociology was being implemented in many of the **settlement houses**—neighborhood centers providing services to poor immigrants—that had been founded in major cities throughout the United States. Settlement sociologists considered the settlement an experimental effort in the solution of the social problems of the modern city. Jane Addams (1860–1935), who in 1889 cofounded the most famous of the settlement houses, Hull House, in one Chicago's poorest neighborhoods, was among them. Addams, and others like her, sought to compile empirical data on various social problems by gathering detailed descriptions of the conditions of groups living in poverty. In addition, Hull House provided a wide variety of community services, including securing support for deserted women, conducting a kindergarten and day nursery, implementing various enterprises for neighborhood improvement, and establishing a relief station.

A new type of sociology, devoted to the practical amelioration of social problems and with the early U.S. sociology of relief and reform as its heritage, has emerged. **Service sociology** is a socially responsible and mission-oriented sociology of action and alleviation (Treviño, 2011, 2012, 2013; Treviño & McCormack, 2014;

▶ In 1889, Jane Addams cofounded Hull House, a settlement house in a poor neighborhood in Chicago. Hull House provided a wide variety of community services for poor immigrants, especially women and children. Addams received the Nobel Peace Prize in recognition of her work in 1931.

Treviño, 2018). Motivated by care and compassion, service sociology is concerned with helping people meet their pressing social needs. Its practitioners believe the personal needs of one individual are not so different from the collective needs of others in similar life circumstances. This belief is the reason why service sociology treats individuals as people in community with each other. Its main goal is to help people by meeting their essential needs and concerns through service, including community counseling, coaching, mentoring, tutoring, conflict resolution, community gardening, friendly visiting, community cleanup, block activities, giving circles, crime prevention, community organizing, advocacy, voter registration, participatory action research, service learning, and mediation.

Today, more than ever, we need service sociology, and student involvement in it. Consider that, during the Barack Obama presidency, there had been a renewed interest in volunteering and social service—a so-called compassion

Settlement houses: Neighborhood centers that provide services to poor immigrants.

Service sociology: A socially responsible and mission-oriented sociology of action and alleviation.

boom—particularly among the millennial generation. Today, about one-quarter of all U.S. adults take part in some form of community service, with more than 62 million volunteers serving. In 2015, these volunteers dedicated nearly 8 billion hours to volunteer service, and the economic value of this service was about $184 billion (Corporation for National and Community Service, 2017a). Across the country, millions of volunteers are engaged in a range of critical areas, including tutoring and teaching; participating in fund-raising activities or selling items to raise money for charitable or religious organizations; collecting, preparing, distributing, or serving food; and contributing general labor (Corporation for National and Community Service, 2017a).

What is more, no less than 25.7% of college students volunteered in 2015, and about 3 million of them dedicated more than 286 million hours of service to communities across the country, primarily in activities like youth mentoring, fund-raising, and teaching and tutoring (Corporation for National and Community Service, 2017b). In addition to community service, many citizens across the country are engaged civically. Indeed, in 2013, 36% of U.S. adults participated in groups or organizations, and nearly 63% engaged in "informal volunteering" such as doing favors for neighbors (Corporation for National and Community Service, 2017a).

There are also high-profile national service initiatives, such as the annual Martin Luther King Jr. National Day of Service and the 9/11 National Day of Service and Remembrance. In addition, Americans participate in civil society programs such as AmeriCorps, which engages about 80,000 people in intensive public service work, and Senior Corps, with about 400,000 volunteers over the age of 55 who provide aid to senior citizens. This service work is being done by many ordinary people who are picking up the slack for a city, a state, a nation unwilling or unable to attend to many critical matters that directly affect thousands, even millions, of people (Coles, 1993).

On his travels through the United States during the early 19th century, the French sociologist Alexis de Tocqueville famously remarked on the American spirit of voluntary cooperation. In *Democracy in America*, Tocqueville (1899) observed that Americans, "if they do not proffer services eagerly, yet they do not refuse to render them" (p. 185). Proffering helpful services to others in the context of civil society has been a core American value since the beginning of the republic. That value is practiced today as a **culture of service**—including various forms of civic engagement, community service, and volunteerism—that allows citizens to work together to ease or mitigate the predicaments and uncertainties created by poverty, hunger, racism, sexism, epidemics, calamities, and so on. It is in this culture of service, with its numerous pressing needs and concerns, that we can consider the emergence of a sociology of social problems based on service. At the ends of the chapters to follow, the authors suggest ways in which you can get personally engaged in helping to alleviate social problems.

....

Culture of service: A style of life that includes various forms of civic engagement, community service, and volunteerism intended to help alleviate social problems.

WHAT DOES AMERICA THINK?

Questions About Sociology and Social Problems From the General Social Survey*

▶▶ Turn to the beginning of the chapter to compare your answers to those of the total population.

1. How scientific is sociology?
   SCIENTIFIC: 55.4%
   NOT SCIENTIFIC: 44.6%

2. People need not overly worry about others.
   AGREE: 31.6%
   DISAGREE: 44.4%
   NEITHER AGREE NOR DISAGREE: 24%

3. Are people helpful or looking out for themselves?
   HELPFUL: 50.6%
   LOOKING OUT FOR THEMSELVES: 49.4%

4. People are treated with respect.
   AGREE: 90.8%
   DISAGREE: 9.2%

5. Can people be trusted?
   YES: 33.4%
   NO: 66.6%

*Since 1972, the General Social Survey (GSS) has been monitoring the characteristics, behaviors, and attitudes of Americans on an annual basis. Along with data collected in the U.S. Census, GSS data play a vital role in helping researchers, journalists, policy makers, and educators understand our complex society.

CHAPTER SUMMARY

 1.1 Describe how working-class young adults are currently experiencing their lives.

When we look at young adults as a generational cohort and consider demographic factors, we get a larger picture of their life situation. Many people's personal troubles are, in fact, also collective problems. Because some groups of people experience social conditions differently than other groups, sociologists examine the intersectionality of several demographic factors.

 1.2 Define what constitutes a social problem.

The objective aspect of social problems relies on statistical data and other empirical facts to identify patterns, trends, and rates of occurrence. The subjective aspect of social problems considers how people define a certain condition, event, or pattern of behavior as a social problem. Social constructionism states that social problems are social problems for no other reason than that people say they are. The type of action needed to bring about large-scale social change is usually aimed at transforming the social structure. The type of action needed to ameliorate a problematic condition is usually aimed at helping people in need.

 1.3 Explain the sociological imagination.

The sociological imagination allows us to see personal troubles as social problems. When we take a global perspective, we compare our own society to other societies in all the world's regions. In this way we understand the social problems of U.S. society in relationship to social problems in other countries.

 1.4 Discuss how sociological research can be used to study social problems.

Quantitative research investigates social problems through statistical analysis. Qualitative research explains how people define, experience, or understand problematic situations. Three common research methods are survey, participant observation, and interviewing. Using multiple methods gives sociologists a fuller picture of the social problems they are studying.

 1.5 Explain the three main sociological perspectives of structural functionalism, conflict theory, and symbolic interactionism.

Functionalism is the sociological theory that considers how various social phenomena function, or work in a positive way, to maintain unity and order in society. Conflict theory is the sociological theory that focuses on dissent, coercion, and antagonism among groups in society. Symbolic interactionism sees society as the product of symbols (words, gestures, objects) that are given meaning by people in their interactions with each other.

 1.6 Evaluate how each of the three theoretical perspectives can be applied to improve our understanding of social problems.

Durkheim's functionalism demonstrates how the degree of social integration and social regulation can result in high rates of suicide. Conflict theory shows how the interest group that has the most political power can prohibit behaviors it considers to be problematic. The symbolic interactionist perspective can help us explain how people with clinical depression make sense of their identity and illness.

 1.7 Discuss the role of social policy in managing social problems.

Most social change happens piecemeal, and frequently the transformations are begun through social policy. Governmental implementation of social policy takes the form of legislation. Other forms are the delivery of services, the regulation of certain practices (such as drug use), and the establishment of welfare programs.

1.8 Explore the role of specialized theories in sociology.

Specialized concepts and theories examine particular aspects of society or specific social problems. They go beyond what the three theoretical perspectives can offer.

1.9 Identify ways in which service sociology can make a difference.

Service sociology is a socially responsible and mission-oriented sociology of action and alleviation. A culture of service—including various forms of civic engagement, community service, and volunteerism—allows citizens, including students, to work together to alleviate social problems.

KEY TERMS

altruistic suicide 16

anomic suicide 16

anomie 16

capitalism 13

capitalists 13

cohort 2

concepts 12

conflict theory 13

culture 17

culture of service 20

data sources 4

demographic factors 2

dysfunctions 13

egoistic suicide 16

fatalistic suicide 16

functions 12

global perspective 8

interaction order 17

interest groups 14

intersectionality 3

interviewing 10

legislation 18

looking-glass self 15

mind 15

norms 13

objective aspect of social problems 5

paradigms 12

participant observation 9

qualitative research 8

quantitative research 8

research methods 8

self-fulfilling prophecy 15

service sociology 19

settlement houses 19

social class 3

social constructionism 6

social institutions 2

social integration 15

social interaction 14

social movements 6

social policy 18

social problem 4

social regulation 16

social revolution 18

social self 15

social structure 6

sociological imagination 7

sociology 4

structural functionalism (or functionalism) 12

subjective aspect of social problems 5

survey 8

symbolic interactionism 14

symbols 15

theory 12

values 13

workers 14

⑤SAGE edge™ **Want a better grade?**

Get the tools you need to sharpen your study skills. Access practice quizzes, eFlashcards, video, and multimedia at **http://edge.sagepub.com/trevino2e**

2 POVERTY AND CLASS INEQUALITY

Leslie Hossfeld, E. Brooke Kelly, and Julia Waity

A woman and her daughter arrive at the Mitchell County food bank in Osage, Iowa, to receive donated food for their family. What do you think can be done for people living on the financial margins of society?

Investigating Poverty and Class Inequality: Our Stories

LEARNING OBJECTIVES

2.1 Explain how poverty, class, and inequality are social constructions.

2.2 Discuss patterns and trends in defining and measuring poverty.

2.3 Describe social class and mobility.

2.4 Discuss income, wealth, and other dimensions of inequality.

2.5 Apply the functionalist, conflict, and symbolic interactionist perspectives to the problems of poverty, class, and inequality.

2.6 Apply specialized theories to poverty and inequality.

2.7 Identify steps toward social change in regard to poverty.

Leslie Hossfeld

I grew up in rural Mississippi and recall vividly when schools were desegregated. My parents never really told my brothers and me that things would change at school—they chose not to draw attention to it, so I don't recall family meetings about changes that would be occurring at school. Yet I did learn later that my parents were fervently committed to us remaining in public schools, something very different from our white friends at the time who were moving to private, all-white schools. Living in rural Mississippi meant about a 30-minute drive to school each morning. But when it rained, and when the floods came, our pick-up time would be different, and we would be the first kids picked up for the ride to school—not the last ones, as was the normal, daily routine. On these days, when the bus route was reversed, I was made aware of the remarkable poverty that other kids on the bus experienced. We were middle-class, white kids who had a home, food, electricity, running water—things that as a kid I would never consider luxuries. But on these reverse bus-route days, I learned why the kids who were normally picked up before me were asleep on the bus; why their clothes were considerably different from mine; why they sometimes wore the same clothes over and over. I would marvel at the long journey we had to get to school. How long was their bus ride before I got on in the morning? What must their homes look like inside? They appeared to be shacks on the outside. Was there electricity in these homes? How long did it take them to get to a store? This simple change in a bus route had such a profound effect on me, shaping my interests and framing my worldview.

As an undergraduate I majored in history, and this provided a context for my own lived experiences, particularly growing up in the Deep South. I completed a master's degree in sociology and then moved to South Africa for many years during the 1980s and 1990s. It was during this period that I came to understand the need for social action and how academia had an important role in informing and implementing social change. I returned to the United States to study sociology, focusing on inequalities and rural economic development.

I have chosen to be a public sociologist. By that I mean taking the tools of the discipline outside the academy to inform social problems, primarily through social action. I find I am happiest and feel the greatest rewards when I am working *in* and *with* communities, addressing critical needs identified by those who live them, and using my sociological tool belt to do the heavy lifting.

E. Brooke Kelly

Being raised by a single mother for a significant portion of my childhood made me realize how tenuous one's economic prospects could be. Though we did not rely on public assistance or food stamps, I knew that without our social and economic support system, that could easily have been our story and drastically changed my life. Later, my undergraduate studies in sociology helped me better understand the way social inequalities impact life chances. In graduate school I became involved in a

University of North Carolina at Pembroke

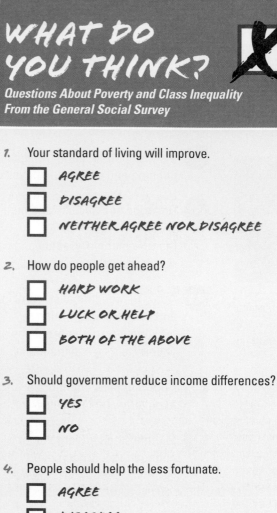

WHAT DO YOU THINK?

Questions About Poverty and Class Inequality From the General Social Survey

1. Your standard of living will improve.

☐ *AGREE*

☐ *DISAGREE*

☐ *NEITHER AGREE NOR DISAGREE*

2. How do people get ahead?

☐ *HARD WORK*

☐ *LUCK OR HELP*

☐ *BOTH OF THE ABOVE*

3. Should government reduce income differences?

☐ *YES*

☐ *NO*

4. People should help the less fortunate.

☐ *AGREE*

☐ *DISAGREE*

☐ *NEITHER AGREE NOR DISAGREE*

5. In the United States, do you think we're spending too much money on assistance to the poor, too little money, or about the right amount?

☐ *TOO MUCH*

☐ *TOO LITTLE*

☐ *ABOUT THE RIGHT AMOUNT*

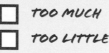 Turn to the end of the chapter to view the results for the total population.

SOURCE: National Opinion Research Center, University of Chicago.

multistate study of rural, low-income families. Through several years of interviews with Latino farmworkers, many of whom migrated with their families from their homes in Texas, Florida, or Mexico to Michigan to work the seasonal crops, I came to better understand lived experiences of poverty and the resiliency of those who struggle with such circumstances. Real-life stories, such as having to drop out of school at a young age to earn money for food, families stranded when a car broke down on the way to Michigan, or mothers who made their children labor in the fields to show them the importance of staying in school, remain with me.

Today I continue to learn about, write about, and attempt to address poverty and inequalities as a professor of sociology at the University of North Carolina at Pembroke. UNC Pembroke is located in Robeson County, the highest-poverty county in the state of North Carolina. As home of the Lumbee tribe, it is also one of the most racially and ethnically diverse rural counties in the United States. Students at UNCP reflect some of the characteristics of the county, as one of the most racially and ethnically diverse campuses in the South, with many first-generation college students, nontraditional students by age, and a majority of students relying on financial aid. Over a little more than a decade, I think I have learned as much from my students as they have from me, as many struggle with challenges of limited resources, working, and/or raising families while going to school. As a professor, I enjoy helping students learn about sociology in a way that also raises their awareness of and benefits the surrounding community and campus. My students and I have worked on projects with the nearby low-income housing authority, raised awareness on campus about the conditions of farmworkers, and surveyed students on campus about whether they are getting enough healthy foods to eat, a growing problem on college campuses.

Julia Waity

University of North Carolina Wilmington

From when I was young, I have always been involved in volunteer work in my community. My parents encouraged me in this endeavor, and I continued to pursue this involvement in college at Washington and Lee University, where I led our campus service organization. I complemented my sociology/anthropology degree with a certificate in poverty studies. After working in Baltimore for a year at a nonprofit organization that worked with low-income youth, I decided to pursue a PhD in sociology with a minor in public policy. I conducted research in the community, and consider myself to be a public sociologist. My research focuses on one specific aspect of poverty: food insecurity. In particular, I consider spatial inequalities that are present in access to food and food assistance across the rural–urban continuum. I regularly teach Sociology of Poverty to both undergraduate and graduate students, where we explore the information presented in this chapter in great detail.

WHO IS HUNGRY ON CAMPUS?

Do you ever struggle with food insecurity? Food insecurity refers to the fact that "access to adequate food is limited by a lack of money and other resources" (Coleman-Jensen et al., 2016, p. v). You may be surprised to hear that many college students struggle with food insecurity. In a 2017 study of 33,000 community college students from 24 states, two-thirds were food insecure, and one-third were hungry (Goldrick-Rab, Richardson, & Hernandez, 2017). Overall, about 12.7% of American households deal with food insecurity. While not all those who are food insecure are poor, and not all those who are poor are food insecure, low-income households have food insecurity rates substantially higher than the U.S. average. As with poverty rates, we see higher food insecurity rates among single-parent households, black and Hispanic households, and households where children are present (although not the children themselves). Food insecurity is higher in rural areas than suburban areas, with urban areas in-between. These food-insecure households can turn to government benefits like SNAP, formerly called food stamps, but that may not be enough to make ends meet. They might turn to food pantries or soup kitchens as well.

Increasingly, more colleges and universities are opening up food pantries and soup kitchens to assist these food-insecure students. In 2017, the College and University Food Bank Alliance had 492 registered members. Other strides are also being made to help food-insecure students. A pilot grant from the United States Department of Agriculture at nine California State University campuses encourages eligible students to apply for SNAP benefits and use them on campus.

With the costs of college already so high (the average yearly cost ranges from $9,586 for 2-year public colleges to $37,424 for 4-year private universities, including room and board, according to the National Center for Education Statistics), there may not be enough money left over for food, especially if students are paying their own way through college. Or the food that students can afford might not be healthy and nutritious.

ASK YOURSELF: How effective do you think that food pantries and other food assistance programs like soups kitchens and BackPack programs (which provide food to children on weekends and school breaks) are in dealing with food insecurity?

POVERTY, CLASS, AND INEQUALITY ARE SOCIAL CONSTRUCTIONS

 2.1 Explain how poverty, class, and inequality are social constructions.

Some 43 million people in the United States live below the official poverty line, and millions more live barely above it, while those in the top 1% possess 33% of the wealth of the country (Bricker et al., 2016). Class sharply divides who has access to which opportunities and resources, including a decent education and adequate health care. Inequality is growing, making it more difficult for those at the bottom to improve their lives or those of their children.

Poverty, class, and inequality are complex and intertwined concepts. They are also social constructions, yet they are more than just ideas, because they frame our everyday lives, the way we navigate through social space. Our ideas about poverty, class, and inequality are based not simply on facts but also on images and perceptions. Poverty is not just people with incomes below a certain level; it is also images of poorly dressed people begging on street corners. We know that we live in a society where some people have very little and others have immense wealth. But is that good or bad? Is inequality a useful incentive to spur people to work hard? Or is the gap between rich and poor unfair? That is what we mean by saying that concepts are socially constructed. Where do our ideas and images about poverty, class, and inequality come from?

What is social class? Are there only a few social classes, or is class in U.S. society represented by a continuum with many gradations? What is poverty? How is it related to inequality? Is poverty inevitable, or can we eradicate it? Should we define poverty exclusively in economic terms, or should we include social and political dimensions? Is inequality only an economic term, or does it too have other facets? These are the central issues on which we will focus in this chapter. As Gerhard Lenski (1966, p. 3) put it many years ago, the basic question is, "Who gets what and why?"

▶ A woman holds up her checkbook that shows "We're Broke!!" Many American families are in financial trouble. Do you think the government should help them get food, education, and full-time jobs?

PATTERNS AND TRENDS

2.2 Discuss patterns and trends in defining and measuring poverty.

Defining Poverty

More than 50 years ago, Michael Harrington published *The Other America* (1962), a book that opened the eyes of a complacent nation to deep poverty in the midst of affluence. Eradicating poverty, from Appalachia to inner cities, soon became a major focus of public policy. Critical legislation included the Economic Opportunity Act of 1964, the Civil Rights Act of 1964, and the Voting Rights Act of 1965 (Karger & Stoesz, 2006). But to eradicate or even reduce poverty, we must be able to measure it. There are two ways.

An **absolute measure of poverty** sets a threshold, usually based on annual income. A person or family with an annual income at the line or below it is identified as being in **poverty**. If income is above the line—by even one dollar—the person or family is identified as not being in poverty.

The line is arbitrary but set by policy makers to help guide them in developing programs for the poor or in evaluating the effectiveness of antipoverty programs or in deciding who is eligible for some services. In 1963, Mollie Orshansky, an economist in the Social Security Administration, developed an absolute measure of poverty built on the cost of food. On the assumption that a family spends about one-third of its disposable income on food, Orshansky proposed a poverty threshold of three times the cost of a market basket of food, adjusted for family size (see Figure 2.1). This standard has been used ever since, and the federal government adjusts the rate for inflation each year so comparisons can be made across time. The poverty line in 2017 was $24,600 for a family of four.

There are many criticisms of this measure. For example, it uses a subsistence-level basket of food rather than a basket based on a more nutritionally sound diet, and the assumption that a family spends a third of its annual income on food is likely no longer accurate. In fact, most low-income families spend about half their income on rent (Karger & Stoesz, 2006). Still, policy makers use the poverty line to guide them in developing and evaluating programs and in deciding who is eligible for certain services.

A **relative measure of poverty** looks at a person, or a group such as a family, in relationship to the rest of the community or society. Is the person or group far below or well above others in terms of income, quality of housing, educational levels or opportunities, or household possessions? One common relative measure uses the *median* household income for a nation, the point that half the households are below and half are above. We might then consider poverty to be the income at half the median, indicating how some families compare to what is typical in their society. For example, the median U.S. household income for 2015 was $56,516. Half of that is $28,258. However, unlike an absolute measure, a relative measure is not a hard-and-fast line, so it changes depending on conditions in the society as a whole. The idea of a relative measure is that we see how individuals or families compare with others in their society; that is, are they relatively similar or more disadvantaged than most?

ASK YOURSELF: What advantages do you see in continuing to use the current method of calculating the poverty rate? What disadvantages? What other ways might poverty be measured? How do you feel poverty should be defined?

Absolute measure of poverty: A threshold or line (usually based on income) at or below which individuals or groups are identified as living in poverty.

Poverty: Deficiencies in necessary material goods or desirable qualities, including economic, social, political, and cultural.

Relative measure of poverty: A measure that looks at individuals or groups relative to the rest of their community or society rather than setting an absolute line.

FIGURE 2.1 The Poverty Threshold Calculation

3 x Crisis Food Basket
Adjusted for family size
and age of
head of household

SOURCE: U.S. Census Bureau. (2010). Poverty: 2008 and 2009. American community survey briefs. Washington, DC: A. Bishaw & S. Maccartney.

Poverty Rates Over Time and Among Different Social Groups

The U.S. Census Bureau releases an annual report on household income, poverty, and health insurance coverage, usually in the early fall. In the 2015 report, the poverty rate stood at 13.5% (Proctor, Semega, & Kollar, 2016). That is, more than 43.1 million U.S. men, women, and children fell below the official poverty line.

The Census Bureau takes into account age, family size, and number of children in a household in counting the number of people below the poverty line. This creates a grid of what the Census Bureau calls the **poverty thresholds**, and a new set of thresholds is produced annually to take inflation into account. In 2016, the poverty threshold was $24,339 for a four-person household, which includes two children under age 18, and $19,337 for a three-person household including two children.

The U.S. Department of Health and Human Services uses a simplified version of the Census Bureau thresholds, called the **poverty guidelines**, which set what is known as the federal poverty level (FPL) (see Table 2.1). The main difference is the Census Bureau's focus on the number of persons, including adults and children, in the household. The FPL, as developed by Orshansky, is the number generally referred to in the media when they mention the poverty line and also the guideline used to determine eligibility for many public services.

For many years, U.S. poverty rates declined (see Figure 2.2). The historic high was 1959, the first year for which figures were estimated. Nearly 40 million people were then in poverty, or about 23% of the U.S. population. Both absolute numbers and rates declined for most of the next two decades, especially among the elderly,

since Social Security pensions were increasing not only in amount but also in extent of coverage. However, the Census Bureau uses a lower threshold for older people, so some of the decline in poverty among this group may be artificial.

By 1980, poverty rates began to grow again, peaking in the early 1990s and then dropping again until the 2000s. The poverty rate increased sharply during the Great Recession and its aftermath. The absolute number of people in poverty was higher than in 1959 and the poverty rate went from 11.7% to 15.1%, an increase of 29%. In 2015, the poverty rate finally started to decrease, although at 13.5% this was still higher than before the Great Recession. Some categories of people are more likely to be in poverty than others. The poverty rate for non-Hispanic whites was 9.1% in 2015, compared to 24.1% for African Americans, 21.4% for Hispanics (any race), and 11.4% for Asian Americans. If we look just at families, the rate for female-headed households is 28.2%, compared to 14.9% for male-headed households and 5.4% for married couples (see Table 2.2). Looking specifically at age, we see children under 18 have the highest poverty rate at 19.7%, while

TABLE 2.1 Poverty Guidelines in the United States, 2017

Persons in Family	Poverty Guideline (annual income in $)
1	12,060
2	16,240
3	20,420
4	24,600
5	28,780
6	32,960
7	37,140
8	41,320

SOURCE: Department of Health and Human Services, "HHS Poverty Guidelines For 2017."

NOTE: For families with more than eight persons, add $4,180 for each additional person.

Poverty thresholds: Measures of poverty used by the U.S. Census Bureau that take into account family size, number of children, and their ages.

Poverty guidelines: A simplified version of the U.S. Census Bureau poverty thresholds, which take into account only family size; the poverty guidelines are used to set the federal poverty level (FPL).

adults aged 65 and older have the lowest poverty rate at 8.8%. Those living in rural areas and principal cities have higher poverty rates (16.7% and 16.8%) than those living in suburban areas (10.8%).

ASK YOURSELF: Why do you think poverty rates and numbers have increased in the past decade? Why are rates so much higher among female-headed households and lower among married-couple families?

TABLE 2.2 Poverty Rates of Selected U.S. Subgroups, 2015

Category	Percentage
White, non-Hispanic	9.1
Black	24.1
Hispanic	21.4
Asian	11.4
Female heads of household, no husband present	28.2
Male heads of household, no wife present	14.9
Married couples	5.4
Children under 18	19.7
Adults age 18–64	12.4
Adults age 65 and older	8.8
Inside metropolitan statistical areas	13.0
Inside principal cities (urban)	16.8
Outside principal cities (suburban)	10.8
Outside metropolitan statistical areas (rural)	16.7

SOURCE: Proctor, Bernadette D., Jessica L. Semega, and Melissa A. Kollar. U.S. Census Bureau, Current Population Reports, P60-256(RV), *Income and Poverty in the United States: 2015*, U.S. Government Printing Office, Washington, DC, 2016.

"Extreme" Poverty and Low Income

It is not just the poverty rate or the number of people in poverty that is rising. The poor seem to be concentrated in particular neighborhoods, according to a recent report from the Brookings Institution (Kneebone, Nadeau, & Berube, 2011). **Extreme poverty neighborhoods** are areas, usually U.S. Census tracts, with poverty rates of 40% or more. The numbers of such neighborhoods declined throughout the 1990s but rose by a third between 2000 and 2009 (Kneebone, Nadeau, & Berube, 2011). According to Kneebone and colleagues (2011, p. 3): "Rather than spread evenly, the poor tend to cluster and concentrate in certain neighborhoods or groups of neighborhoods within a community. Very poor neighborhoods face a whole host of challenges that come from concentrated disadvantage—from higher crime rates and poorer health outcomes to lower-quality educational opportunities and weaker job networks."

Not only are more people falling into poverty, but their plight is also more severe now than in the past. Access to public assistance programs is declining, making the living conditions of those at the bottom of our society more difficult. Public assistance programs require individuals or families to meet eligibility requirements, such as having income below a certain level (for instance, the FPL) and

Extreme poverty neighborhoods: Areas (usually based on census tracts) that have poverty rates of 40% or more.

FIGURE 2.2 Poverty Levels in the United States, 1959–2015

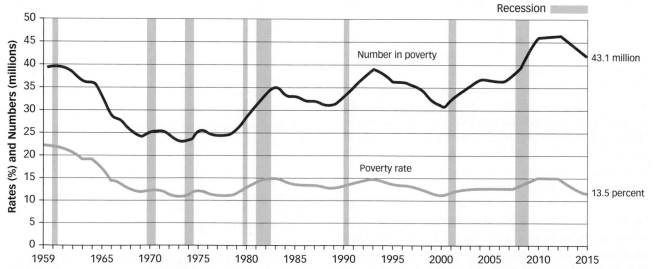

SOURCE: Proctor, Bernadette D., Jessica L. Semega, and Melissa A. Kollar. U.S. Census Bureau, Current Population Reports, P60-256(RV), *Income and Poverty in the United States: 2015*, U.S. Government Printing Office, Washington, DC, 2016.

meeting asset limits. During the past 15 years, more households have begun to live on less and less, becoming what Shaefer and Edin (2012) label the "extreme poor": households that have children present but little or no income.

The "Social Safety Net"

What we now call the **social safety net** consists of programs that emerged during the Great Depression. Until then, most charitable programs were either private, often church-based, or state and local in scope. Unfortunately, these social programs could not begin to alleviate the widespread suffering of the 1930s. The roots of the safety net are found in the Social Security Act of 1935. Most people probably think of Social Security as providing old-age pensions, but also included in this legislation were provisions for a number of additional programs: unemployment insurance; assistance to the aged, blind, and disabled; survivor benefits; and public assistance (originally for widows with children). Since its initial signing, the act has been amended, and some services have been modified or combined and others added.

A second period of expansion in federal programs occurred during the 1960s, when poverty emerged as a national concern. In addition, in response to the civil rights movement of the 1950s and 1960s, important federal legislation was enacted, including the Civil Rights Act of 1964 and the Voting Rights Act of 1965. Researchers focused not only on the problem of poverty but also on how minority status, including race and sex, was connected to poverty and being poor.

Some parts of the social safety net are social insurance programs, such as OASDI—or Old-Age, Survivors, and Disability Insurance—in which individuals pay into the system (or have spouses who pay into the system) and earn "entitlement" to services. One of the programs that has had the most impact on poverty is old-age insurance, or Social Security pensions for older people. By the 1960s, increasing numbers of workers were covered, and the level of payments helped to keep many older individuals and couples above the poverty line. Social Security pensions are now the most common form of income for older people, with more than 97% of older households receiving or about to receive such income. In fact, more than half of all elderly households receive half their income from these benefits. The average monthly benefit at the end of 2016 was $1,360.

In 1965, Medicare was added to the Social Security program. This is a public health care program for people aged 65 and older, and most older people now participate in it. Medicaid is another important part of the social safety net. This is a public health insurance program for the poor, which now includes the State Children's Health Insurance Program (SCHIP). While most doctors and hospitals accept patients insured by Medicare, fewer are willing to accept Medicaid patients, making it difficult for many individuals who qualify for Medicaid to find physicians or hospitals that will treat them.

Some other social safety net elements, in contrast to social insurance programs, are **means-tested programs** for which people usually qualify by having a poverty-level income, as described earlier. For many years, the general public has had a negative image of means-tested public assistance programs, which are often associated with racial stereotypes. Some politicians have used images of "welfare cheats" and "welfare queens" to advance their careers, though there has been little evidence of widespread cheating among welfare recipients (Segal & Kilty, 2003).

Means-tested programs include Temporary Assistance for Needy Families (TANF), a program of cash assistance to poor families; and the **Supplemental Nutrition Assistance Program (SNAP)**, from which more than 44 million people receive benefits each month. (SNAP used to be known as the food stamp program.) Another important food-related program is the Special Supplemental Nutrition Program for Women, Infants, and Children (WIC), which provides nutrition education and a small amount of supplemental income that can be used with authorized vendors. In North Carolina, for example, the average monthly WIC benefit per person is $45.14. Some means-tested programs allow recipients to have incomes somewhat higher than the official poverty line. The National School Lunch Program, for instance, provides free or reduced-cost meals for students whose family incomes are between 130% and 185% of the poverty line.

While the programs that make up the social safety net are valuable and help many people, especially the social insurance programs, fewer people are receiving benefits such as TANF, and the levels of benefits have dropped. Using North Carolina as an example, TANF benefits were $272 in 2016 for a single-parent family of three, the same as when welfare reform was enacted in 1996. This represents a 34.4% decrease in benefit levels (Stanley, Floyd, & Hill, 2014). In fact, the amount of help available for low-income individuals and families in the United States falls far short of what is accessible in many other countries, especially other industrialized nations (Waddan, 2010).

....

Social safety net: Public programs intended to help those who are most vulnerable in a society.

Means-tested programs: Programs for which people qualify by having a certain income level, usually at or up to 185% of the poverty line.

Supplemental Nutrition Assistance Program (SNAP): Federal program that provides low-income Americans with subsidies for food purchases; formerly known as the food stamp program.

The Social Safety Net

About a decade ago a friend, Melanie, was living and working abroad for an American company in Paris, France. She was 7 months pregnant with her first child when her water broke. She managed to get to a hospital, and because of the complications with her early labor was transferred to two other hospitals. Not once during all of those transfers was she asked to fill out paperwork or produce an insurance card or identification. In France, by law medical personnel are required to treat anyone coming in on an emergency basis, regardless of whether patients have insurance or income. Any unpaid expenses are picked up by the universal health care system. Even though Melanie was a U.S. citizen, the French health care system covered much of her extended stay in the hospital (over 2 weeks) and her newborn's month-long stay in neonatal intensive care. Melanie remarked that the cost of the month-long NICU stay in France was four times less expensive than that of a friend in the United States who had a similar experience with a premature birth around the same time.

Because Melanie had been living and working in France throughout her pregnancy, she had already become aware of the differences in health care and parental support that extend before and after birth. In France, not only is the cost of the delivery covered, but prenatal care before the birth and postnatal care after the birth are also covered. Preventative health care is emphasized, and expectant mothers are obligated to go to prenatal exams starting around 12 weeks. This is in contrast with the circumstances of many parents in the United States and in other countries who have trouble finding a place for prenatal care and/or cannot afford it, which can lead to health complications for both mothers and babies.

After the birth, Melanie found that a support system followed her home from the hospital. Services to help her adjust to her new role as a parent, such as figuring out how to breastfeed, assessing postpartum depression, nurse assistance or general help at home so she could rest at night, came to her home. Free medical clinics were available throughout the city to provide all the follow-up exams and routine checkups, sick visits, as well as access to mother support groups. Melanie was also provided basic supplies, such as a breast pump free of charge once she left the hospital.

Melanie continued to live and work in France for about 6 months after the birth of her child, long enough to get a glimpse at some other key differences in parental support. Day cares in France are free, and they are encouraged, especially around preschool age, to prepare children for school.

In contrast, child care is very expensive in the United States (Ireland, Switzerland, and the UK are the only countries where it is more expensive). In North Carolina, for example, the average cost for infant care is $9,255 a year, about 40% more than the average cost of in-state tuition at a public college. Low-income families can qualify for child care subsidies, but even with a subsidy, it is difficult to find high-quality child care without long waiting lists. Even if child care were available and affordable, it wouldn't solve every problem. Many

Other Dimensions of Poverty

So far, we have looked at poverty in economic terms, focusing specifically on income. Are there other components to poverty?

We noted above that with a relative measure of poverty we are trying to get a picture of how individuals or families compare to their communities or societies. That suggests we should look at the extent to which particular individuals or families can actively participate in society. Are they accepted as legitimate members? Do they see themselves as legitimate members? When a child goes to school, can his or her family provide adequate resources, such as crayons? How does the child dress? Will he or she be accepted or shunned by peers?

People are unequal not just in income or wealth but also in desirable social and political qualities. Many now argue for considering certain "economic human rights" as part of our fundamental human rights. For instance, who can vote in the United States? Recent legislative efforts to limit voting rights have included restrictions on voter registration and the requirement to show photo identification at the polls. In some states, a person loses the right to vote if convicted of a felony, including simple drug possession. If you cannot vote, are you then deficient in a specific quality, in the same way as being below a certain income level? Should lack of political rights be included in a definition of poverty?

What about the right to choose to be public or not about your sexual orientation? What about the right to be low-income jobs (like waitressing) require hours outside the times that child care centers are open, or they have schedules that change weekly or monthly (like many retail jobs), so it is especially difficult for those parents to access child care. Despite the high cost of child care, the Bureau of Labor Statistics reports that child care workers make a median annual wage of $21,170, which keeps them near or below the poverty line.

The United States has some public preschool programs, but only 28% of 4-year-olds are enrolled in them. In France, there are government-run day cares with a sliding fee scale based on income, as well as free universal preschool. Having this affordable, accessible, high-quality day care translates into more French women returning to work after having children than American women.

Also crucial to the ability of parents to return to work are family leave policies. Unlike most other industrialized nations, the United States has no federally mandated paid parental leave (Livingston, 2016). Many jobs do offer paid maternity leave, but these jobs tend to be well-paid, white-collar jobs. While the United States does have federally mandated family and medical leave for most employees, this is unpaid, so those with limited resources may not be able to take the decrease in pay associated with the leave. In contrast, paid maternity leave is universal for all mothers in France, with the amount of leave varying based on the circumstances of the birth. Fathers get 2 weeks of paid leave as well.

To further assist parents with the costs of raising children, France and other countries provide parents with family allowances and other subsidies that increase based on the number of children they have. Family allowances are cash benefits provided by the government to those with children as a right of citizenship. Note that unlike some policies in the United States that focus on income requirements, family allowances are universal.

After Melanie returned to the United States and gave birth to her other children there, the contrast in parental support between the two countries became more apparent. Not only was there a difference in coverage of services, but in France she was assisted in accessing services in a culture where everyone seemed to view her child's care as their responsibility as much as hers. In contrast, parents in the United States must seek out scarce services, such as quality child care, often at great personal costs in time, energy, and money.

The way children are thought of—as the sole responsibility of their parents, or as a responsibility of the larger society—and the way supports for children and families are structured have implications for parents and children. According to OECD data, the United States has a higher child poverty rate than most of its peer nations (except for Chile, Israel, Spain, and Turkey) using the relative poverty measure of 50% of the national median income.

▶ **THINK ABOUT IT:** Do you think that these differences in social safety nets for parents affect children? If so, how? Why do you think the social safety net is so much more limited in the United States than in France and other countries?

public about your gender identity? Should some people be so anxious about losing—or even getting—a job that they feel they must keep that part of their humanity hidden? Should we think of social conditions as a part of poverty?

ASK YOURSELF: What components do you think a definition of poverty should include? How would you define poverty?

SOCIAL CLASS

2.3 Describe social class and mobility

All societies are organized or stratified, most often into social classes, which are groups with different access to resources. In other words, inequalities in wealth, income, education, and occupation are common, and the system of social stratification we find in a particular society helps us to understand who gets what and why.

Many American citizens believe the United States is unique and that social class does not really exist here. We tend to see our nation as egalitarian and open, a place where, through hard work and self-reliance, social mobility is not only possible but common. A majority claim "middle-class" status, and about a quarter label themselves "working-class"; barely 1% identify as "upper-class," and only 7% as "lower-class" (Robinson, 2003). More of us have recently come to acknowledge a conflict

▶ During the Great Depression, hundreds of hungry, homeless men lined up at the Municipal Lodging House in New York City for a free Thanksgiving Day dinner. The unemployment rate rose to 25% in the United States during the 1930s. Do you think this could happen again?

between rich and poor (Morin, 2012), but few Americans seem to question the nature of the social class structure or whether it seriously affects opportunities. In fact, challenging whether the rich possess too much typically leads to charges of "class warfare"—especially from the rich and their conservative political allies.

Roots of the "Classless" Society

The roots of U.S. beliefs in egalitarianism and openness go back to colonial days. By the 17th century, when colonies in North America were firmly established, the English, French, and Dutch colonists found themselves in a vast expanse of open and what they perceived as unclaimed land. There was an indigenous population, but it was not as large as the one the Spanish and Portuguese found and subdued in South and Central America or the southern part of North America. For the hardy, the opportunities seemed boundless.

Yet opportunities were actually extremely limited for most European colonists. In the 13 English colonies, large landowners were generally given tracts of land by the English Crown, particularly in the southern colonies, where plantation farming and slavery were developing in the early 1600s. Most early colonists, and Africans brought to North America, were indentured servants obligated to work for landowners, merchants, or craftsmen for set periods of time, usually 7 to 10 years. Chattel

slavery developed between 1620 and 1660, when the rights and freedom of Africans were gradually taken away. However, in the early 1600s, black and white settlers were treated largely the same, and they lived lives of abject poverty. Since the average life expectancy then was only about 35 years, many indentured servants did not survive to become "free."

A class structure was developing, based on land and slave ownership in the southern colonies and on land and industry in the North. Opportunities were mainly reserved for those who arrived with advantage by birth. All the same, by the 19th century, a powerful narrative of success based on hard work, self-reliance, and perseverance had developed. This was the concept of the self-made man—the idea that anyone could rise from humble beginnings and become wealthy and successful simply by applying him- or herself (Miller & Lapham, 2012). In this view, social position is a matter of individual achievement and has little or nothing to do with a person's origins in the social hierarchy.

One of the major advocates of this **self-made myth** was the 19th-century author Horatio Alger (1832–1899), who wrote more than 100 "rags to riches" novels and stories. Although his work had its critics even then, his vision became a central part of the American image. Later, the libertarian writer Ayn Rand (1905–1982) came to have a powerful influence on the continuing acceptance of the self-made myth, especially through her novel *Atlas Shrugged*. Her writings provided the foundation for the political philosophy and ethics of capitalism that lie behind modern conservative political thought and that advocate self-reliance and limited government influence on the economy. This is a powerful ideology that we hear today expressed in the political rhetoric of such figures as Senators Rand Paul and Ted Cruz, and House Speaker Paul D. Ryan.

ASK YOURSELF: How do you feel about the self-made myth? Is a person's success based mainly on how hard that person works? Or does an individual succeed because of advantages received from family and social position? Does luck have anything to do with economic success? What about collective resources, such as schools, roads, and courts?

Class as a Social Science Concept

Two of the most important social scientists in the development of social class as a scientific concept were Karl

Self-made myth: The belief that anyone can rise from humble beginnings to become wealthy and successful simply by applying him- or herself.

Marx (1818–1883) and Max Weber (1881–1961). According to Marx, social position revolves around one important factor: ownership of the means of production. In essence, there are capitalists, who own the factories and other means of producing goods, and there are the working class, who sell their labor in order to survive. Many of Marx's critics, including Weber, have focused on this oversimplification of social stratification (Marx does identify other classes as well).

Marxist analysis of social structure has not been widely accepted in popular or academic circles in the United States because of the link between Marx and communist ideology. Much more acceptable have been the writings of Weber, who identifies three aspects of social structure: class, status, and power. **Class** refers to a person's position relative to the economic sector, such as proprietor, wage laborer, or renter. **Status** refers to social position in the context of characteristics like education, prestige, and religious affiliation. **Power** refers to political affiliations and connections.

Weber's ideas led to a conceptualization of U.S. social class as a continuum of **socioeconomic status (SES)**, rather than as a set of discrete categories that are easily distinguished from each other. Taking this perspective, we need to create an index of class based on a series of concepts, such as education, income, and occupation. That is how social science research generally treats class —by using a quantitative index or scale that measures several variables.

In many surveys and polls, in contrast, individuals are still often asked to self-identify as members of social classes using a subjective series of categories such as "upper class," "middle class," "working class," or "lower class." As we have seen, a majority of respondents identify themselves as members of the middle class.

....

ASK YOURSELF: What is your social class? Why?

....

Social Mobility

Social mobility is upward or downward movement in social position over time in a society. That movement can be specific to individuals who change social positions or to categories of people, such as racial or ethnic groups. Social mobility between generations is referred to as intergenerational mobility. As we saw earlier, the self-made myth suggests that social position in the United States is largely up to the individual, implying that mobility is quite common and easy to achieve for those who apply themselves. However, what people believe and what is fact are often not the same. A recent experimental study found that Americans substantially and consistently overestimate the amount of income mobility and educational access in society. The higher one's social class, the more

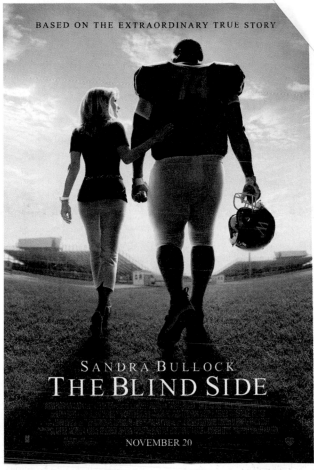

BASED ON THE EXTRAORDINARY TRUE STORY

SANDRA BULLOCK
THE BLIND SIDE

NOVEMBER 20

▶ The 2009 movie *The Blind Side* tells the rags-to-riches story of Michael "Big Mike" Oher, an offensive lineman who has played for the Baltimore Ravens, the Tennessee Titans, and the Carolina Panthers in the NFL. Can you think of other movies or books that serve to inspire people to financial success?

likely they are to overestimate social mobility. In other words, wealthy Americans tend to subscribe to the belief that pulling one's self out of poverty is easier than it actually is and that one's wealth is a result of hard work and initiative, rather than luck or birth (Kraus & Tan, 2015).

....

Class: A person's social position relative to the economic sector.

Status: Social position, revolving around characteristics such as education, prestige, and religious affiliation.

Power: The aspect of social structure related to political affiliations and connections.

Socioeconomic status (SES): A conceptualization of social class in terms of a continuum or index based on social and economic factors.

Social mobility: Upward or downward movement in social position by groups or individuals over time.

TABLE 2.3 Annual Household Income in the United States by Quintile, 2015

Quintile	Mean ($)	Share of Total (%)
Top ($117,003 or more)	202,366	51.1
Fourth ($72,002–$117,002)	92,031	23.2
Third ($43,512–$72,001)	56,832	14.3
Second ($22,801–$43,511)	32,631	8.2
Bottom ($22,800 or less)	12,457	3.1

SOURCE: "Income and Poverty in the United States: 2015," by B. D. Proctor, J. L. Semega, & M. A. Kollar, 2016. Washington, D.C.: U.S. Census Bureau.

While social mobility has always been limited in the United States, it has become even more so in the past three or four decades. Furthermore, it lags well behind mobility in most Western European nations (Miller & Lapham, 2012).

Declining social mobility is a relevant issue for current college students. Not only will many graduate with considerable debt, but they are the first generation in U.S. history likely to end up at a lower social position than that of their parents (Ermisch et al., 2012).

An Alternate Way of Understanding the U.S. Class Structure

Focusing on income as an indicator of social class is an oversimplified way of looking at class. However, it may help us get a basic picture of the structure of our society. Table 2.3 presents the U.S. household income distribution for 2015 by quintile—that is, broken into five equal parts. The table shows the mean income for each quintile, as well as the share of the total income going to that group. Keep in mind that these income numbers are for *households*, not individuals.

For 2015, the median household income was $56,516, compared to a mean of $79,263. The median is the midpoint in a distribution where half the scores are above and half are below, while the mean is computed by adding all the scores together and dividing by the number of scores. The gap between the mean and median is important because it illustrates how unequal the distribution of household income is. Income is a skewed distribution, or a distribution in which a few values are at one extreme. In this case, the skewness is due to a few very high income values, compared to many more in the lower ranges.

Even more telling indicators of the depth of inequality in the United States are the upper limits for each of the quintiles. We saw in Table 2.1 that the 2017 poverty guideline for a family of two was $16,240, and for a family of three $20,420. Virtually the entire bottom quintile falls below those thresholds. The numbers for the second quintile are also striking, with many families barely above the FPL. In fact, the bottom 40% of all U.S. households received only 11.3% of all earned income in 2014. The top quintile, in contrast, received 51.1% of household income, with a mean of $202,366. In the top 5%, the mean household income was $350,870.

While income is useful as a metric variable, another way to consider social class is to use the quintiles as rough indicators. The bottom quintile represents the poor (with those below the mean for that group representing the extreme poor), the second quintile the near poor or working poor, the third the middle class, the fourth the upper-middle class, and the top quintile the upper class. We could also divide that top quintile into the affluent (the first 15%), the rich (the next 4%), and the super-rich (the top 1%).

ASK YOURSELF: Should such extreme differences exist among U.S. economic groups? Why or why not? Is that fair? Moral?

INEQUALITY

2.4 Discuss income, wealth, and other dimensions of inequality.

When we ask who gets what and why, we are dealing with the issue of **inequality**—the fact that some in a society have more than others. Inequality is increasing throughout the world, but the gap between those at the top and those at the bottom is greater in the United States than in nearly all other industrialized societies, especially those in Europe. The same is true when we measure the proportion of the population below 50% of the median income (a measure of relative poverty, as described earlier). Only Poland and Portugal come close to the United States.

We use the term *poverty* to depict the status of those at the very bottom. A good way to think of inequality, then, is as a continuum, with extreme poverty (or the poor) at one end and wealth (or the super-rich) at the other:

Poverty ←——————————————→ Wealth

Inequality: Differences between individuals or groups in the quantities of scarce resources they possess.

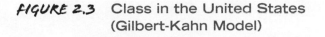

FIGURE 2.3 Class in the United States (Gilbert-Kahn Model)

TYPICAL OCCUPATIONS		TYPICAL INCOMES
Investors, heirs, and executives	capitalist class	Top 1% make about $2.0 million per year
Upper managers, professionals, and medium-sized business owners	upper middle class	14% make about $150,000 per year
Lower managers, semi-professionals, craftsmen, foremen, and non-retail sales	middle class	30% make about $70,000 per year
Low-skill manual, clerical, and retail sales	working class	30% make about $40,000 per year
Lowest-paid manual, retail, and service workers	working poor	13% make about $25,000 per year
Unemployed or part-time menial jobs, public assistance	under class	Bottom 13% make about $15,000 per year

SOURCE. Gilbert, D.L. (2011). *The American class structure in an age of growing inequality*. Thousand Oaks, CA: Sage.

While income is an important aspect of this divide between top and bottom, it is not all there is to inequality.

What about housing? Or access to health care, good jobs, and education? What about assets (which we'll discuss below)? We also need to understand that no population or country is evenly distributed on this continuum—in fact, distribution is generally far from even. The continuum will not look like a flat line, such as we saw when we broke the income distribution into five equal parts or quintiles. It will not look like a bell curve, in which most of the population falls in the middle, with equal numbers of extreme cases on both sides. The continuum of inequality is a highly skewed distribution in which many more individuals fall toward the bottom than the top, as Figure 2.3 shows.

Income and Wealth

What is the difference between income and wealth? Each year, the Census Bureau releases a report on U.S. household income that defines **income** as the money that flows into a family or household from a variety of sources, such as earnings, unemployment compensation, Social Security benefits, interest and dividends, and rental income.

FIGURE 2.4 Share of Income by Percentiles, 1989–2013

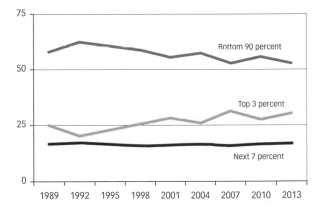

SOURCE: Bricker et al., "Changes in U.S. Family Finances from 2010 to 2013: Evidence from the Survey of Consumer Finances," *Federal Reserve Bulletin*, 2014, 100:4, pp. 10–11.

FIGURE 2.5 Share of Wealth by Percentiles, 1989–2013

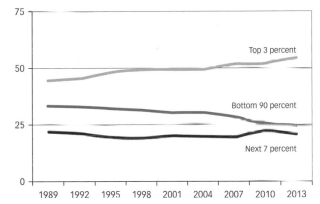

SOURCE: Bricker et al., "Changes in U.S. Family Finances from 2010 to 2013: Evidence from the Survey of Consumer Finances," *Federal Reserve Bulletin*, 2014, 100:4, pp. 10–11.

Wealth, in contrast, is often defined as a family or household's assets or possessions, or as *net worth*—the difference between the value of these assets and the amount of the family or household's debt. Many wealthy people may have high incomes as well as plentiful assets, but because income from investments often is subject to capital gains taxes rather than to income taxes, it is not included in surveys of household income. As a result, many wealthy people may not appear to have large

....

Income: Money that comes into a family or household from a variety of sources, such as earnings, unemployment compensation, workers' compensation, Social Security, pension or retirement income, interest, and dividends.

Wealth: Assets (or possessions) or net worth (the difference between the value of assets and the amount of debt for an individual, family, or household).

Researching Poverty and Class Inequality

Social Mobility for Daughters and Sons in the United States and Sweden

To understand how mobility works in a particular society, it is often helpful to look at other countries. Comparing results from a study of mobility in Sweden with similar research in the United States, Lalaina Hirvonen (2008) found that intergenerational mobility, in terms of earnings, is greater in Sweden. That is, Sweden shows higher rates of mobility from one generation to another than does the United States, contrary to popular perceptions by Americans about mobility in their country.

The impact of family background on economic status is not as strong in Sweden as in the United States. Sweden is more egalitarian in that where someone comes from is much less of a determinant of where he or she ends up. In contrast, there is more likelihood of inheriting social position in the United States, contrary to what most U.S. adults believe. This likelihood is an important indicator of equality of opportunity in a society. When family background influences an individual's future social position, that means family background puts limits on mobility, especially for those lower in the social hierarchy. In other words, in such a society, opportunity for advancement is more limited than elsewhere.

Hirvonen also found that daughters in Sweden had somewhat greater mobility than sons; however, much of the research on U.S. social mobility has focused on sons and their fathers. That may have been appropriate in the past, when men's careers and earnings were more important than women's for family well-being, but more women have now entered the paid labor force and are remaining in it for longer periods, changing the dynamics of social mobility, especially for U.S. families or households. More research remains to be done.

▶ **THINK ABOUT IT:** Are you surprised there is more social mobility in Sweden than in the United States? Why or why not? What makes Sweden more egalitarian than the United States?

---

incomes based on statistics from the Internal Revenue Service. But they still have plenty of money to spend and live very well compared to others. Currently, 10% of the population possesses about 75% of all the wealth in the United States, meaning the other 90% together share a meager 25% of everything there is to own (see Figure 2.5). Even then, there are extremes among that top 10%. And the divide between those at the top and the rest of U.S. society has been growing rapidly in the past 30 years (Bricker et al., 2014).

We need to be careful, then, to distinguish between income and wealth when we are discussing the extent of inequality in a society. Typically, distributions of income and wealth will be similar, but they will not give identical depictions of the depth of inequality because the distribution of wealth is generally more unequal than the distribution of income, as we see in Figures 2.4 and 2.5.

We know that household or family income stagnated or declined during the Great Recession. Yet we can see in Figure 2.4, which uses income data from the Federal Reserve's triannual survey of consumer finances, that not all segments of the population have been affected in the same way. Although the share of income received by the top 3% of families fell from 2007 to 2010 as business and asset income declined during the recession, their income share rebounded to 30.2% in 2013. In contrast, the income share of the bottom 90% fell to 52.7% in 2013 (Bricker et al., 2014, p. 10).

We see similar results for net worth in Figure 2.5. The wealth shared by the top 3% increased from 44.8% in 1989 to 51.8% in 2007 and 54.4% in 2013. In contrast to the rising wealth of the top 3%, the share of wealth the bottom 90% possessed declined from 33.2% in 1989 to 24.7% in 2013. During the Great Recession, those at the top of the wealth distribution were largely protected from declines felt by the remaining 90%. Changes in the share of wealth held by different segments of the wealth distribution have been less cyclical than changes in income. Yet the share of wealth held by affluent families is at modern historically high levels (Bricker et al., 2014, p. 10).

These figures are striking, and the widening gap between rich and poor should actually be even more of a public concern. According to Thomas M. Shapiro (2017, pp. 13, 14, 33):

- "The rise of wealth inequality is almost entirely due to the increase in the top 0.1 percent's wealth share." (p. 14)

- "Nearly half of the wealth accumulated over the past thirty years has gone to the top 0.1 percent of households." (p. 33)

- "The wealthiest 1 percent owned 42 percent of all wealth in 2012 and took in 18 percent of all income." (p. 13)

- "In 2015, the United States had the highest wealth inequality among industrialized nations." (p. 13)

- "Half of the U.S. population has less than $500 in savings." (p. 14)

Although these numbers are staggering, we must also remember that wealth affects people's everyday lives. In the late 1990s and early 2000s, Shapiro and his research team interviewed families from white and black middle-income and lower-income communities. His accounts of these families illustrate the way wealth or the lack it can help or hinder in profound ways. For those who possess it, wealth provides a safety net for getting through difficult times, such as unanticipated health problems, unemployment, or loss of a spouse, without incurring debt. In contrast, the absence of wealth can turn small crises into major disasters. Wealth provides transformative advantages, such as a down payment on a home in a resource-rich neighborhood, the ability to send one's children to private schools, to start a business, or to plan for retirement. Advantages such as safe neighborhoods and quality schools positively impact, or when absent, present serious obstacles for future generations. And as the wealth gap increases, the prevalence of high-poverty neighborhoods is on the rise. "A child born into a wealthy family is more than six times as likely to become a wealthy adult than a child born into a poor family" (Shapiro, 2017, p. 26).

The way people believe wealth is distributed in the United States is very different from the way it is actually distributed. The middle bar in Figure 2.6 shows the way people believe wealth is distributed, while the bottom bar shows the way they would like it to be. Contrast both these views to the top bar, which shows the actual amount of wealth held by those at the very top of U.S. society.

It is not only in economic terms—in measures of income or the value of assets and possessions—that inequality is growing in our society. We can also see rising inequality in access to education, good jobs, health care, and incarceration.

ASK YOURSELF: Some people believe inequality in income and wealth is inevitable and natural. How do you feel about that? Is inequality unfair? Or is it just to be expected?

FIGURE 2.6 Wealth of the Top 20% of U.S. Residents: Popular Views Versus Reality

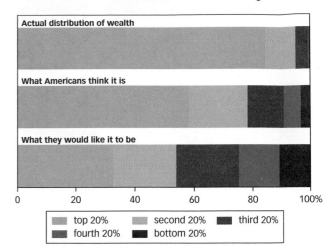

SOURCE: "Building a Better America—One Wealth Quintile at a Time," by M. I. Norton & D. Ariely, 2011, *Perspectives on Psychological Science*, 6(1), 9–12.

Other Dimensions of Inequality

Economic disparity is the central aspect of inequality, but many other social forces drive inequality in the United States and around the world. Two of the most significant of these are gender and race/ethnicity. It has been more than 50 years since the Civil Rights Act of 1964 was passed, but sexual and racial discrimination persist. While many hailed the election of Barack Obama to the U.S. presidency in 2008 as the beginning of a "postracial" era in the United States, for example, racial discrimination is still a fact of life. We also find major differences among racial and ethnic groups in income and wealth, particularly when we compare African Americans and Hispanics with whites (refer back to Table 2.2).

Shapiro (addressed above) argues that we cannot understand contemporary class inequality without considering the widening racial wealth gap, a combination he refers to as *toxic inequality*. Indeed, class and racial inequality are inextricably linked. The gap between white and black family wealth has increased nearly threefold over the past generation. The Great Recession produced the largest loss of minority wealth in U.S. history, with a wealth loss of 50% for African Americans and 66% for Hispanics (Shapiro, 2017, p. 40). In 2013, median net wealth of white families was $142,000, compared to $11,000 for African American families and $13,700 for Hispanic families (Shapiro, p. 16). Mobility is also a greater challenge for black families, who are not only more likely to be stuck at the bottom of the income and wealth ladders, but also have a harder time exceeding

Farmworkers as Forgotten Faces of Poverty

When you are at the grocery store, have you ever thought about where the food came from? Whose hands labored in the sun to pick the produce you find neatly packaged in the store? Much of the way our food is produced and distributed remains invisible to us, but the stories of farmworkers in particular often go unheard. The story of Afra and her family, who were interviewed over the course of several years in Michigan, illustrates many of the challenges that farmworkers still face today.

Afra and her husband, Reynaldo, had been working in the fields harvesting crops since they were young. Over the years, they typically migrated from a home in Texas to work harvesting the seasonal crops in Michigan. In a typical season they worked through a series of crops for about 6 months of the year, working 40–60 hours per week. Reynaldo sometimes returns to Michigan again in October to harvest Christmas trees and works at construction when back in Texas. The amount of work and pay vary based on the crop and the weather.

On a typical workday in Michigan, Afra gets up at 4:30 or 5:30 a.m. She makes lunches and cooks breakfast. She takes her children to her niece's home and usually arrives at work at 6:30 a.m. They work from 7 until sometimes as late as 7:00 or 8:00 at night.

Like Afra and Reynaldo, many farmworkers face challenging working conditions and low pay.

- More than three-fifths of farmworkers are poor.

- Farmworkers' average annual income is $11,000; for a family it is approximately $16,000. This makes farm work the second lowest-paid job in the nation (after domestic labor).

- Agriculture is consistently listed as one of the three most dangerous occupations in the

▶ Farmworkers plant, cultivate, harvest, and pack the fruits, vegetables, and nuts we consume in the United States. Migrant farmworkers, most of whom are Latino, make only about $10,000 a year. They have higher rates of death and illness than most Americans, due in part to a combination of poverty, limited access to health care, and hazardous working conditions.

United States. Among the reasons why this is so:

○ It has the highest rate of toxic chemical injuries and skin disorders of any workers in the country, as well as significant rates of eye injuries.

○ Workers often lack adequate toilet facilities and drinking water in the field.

○ There are higher incidences than other wage-earners of heat stress, dermatitis, urinary-tract infections, parasitic infections, and tuberculosis.

Over the course of 3 years, Afra and her family had some serious health problems. After having her gallbladder removed, the next year she developed

their parents' family income and wealth than whites do (Shapiro, 2017, p. 43).

Another important dimension of inequality is access to health care. During the Great Recession, the number of people without health insurance in the United States increased, partly because of the rise in unemployment and the loss of job-based health insurance for the newly unemployed. With the implementation of the Patient Protection and Affordable Care Act, often referred to as Obamacare, the number of people with health insurance increased. Yet in 2015, 9.1% of the U.S. population was without health insurance coverage for the entire calendar year. Potential future changes in health care legislation could increase the numbers of those who are uninsured. Hispanics and African Americans fell well behind whites, and lower-income groups lagged behind higher-income groups (Barnett & Vornovitsky, 2016). If we look at actual health conditions, we find that mortality, self-rated health, and specific serious illnesses are all associated with poverty. Some conditions may be due to occupations in which toxic conditions are more likely to be part of the environment. Others may occur or worsen because of inadequate or nonexistent health insurance. Lower-income workers are much more likely than higher-income workers to be underinsured or to have insurance that covers only themselves and not their spouses or dependent a hernia from working in the fields. After working through the rest of the season with the hernia, she had to have another operation to remove it when they returned to Texas. The next year she developed pancreatitis, with which she'd had trouble previously. "So, the doctor just told me that they can't do anything. . . . And I'm going to be like that, that I can die any day or they never know." She experienced sporadic pain due to the pancreatitis. Afra's husband was also diagnosed with diabetes.

- Farmworkers face many health issues, such as high blood pressure, inadequate prenatal care or health care for children, and depression.

- Nearly five out of 10 farmworker households in North Carolina cannot afford enough food for their families, which can be related to higher rates of diabetes and other health issues.

- Farmworkers are excluded from nearly all federal labor laws that protect other workers:
  - Labor organizing
  - Minimum wage
  - Overtime pay
  - Child labor laws

Not all of these health issues were directly related to the conditions of farm work; nonetheless, with their limited financial resources, Afra's illnesses placed financial strain on the family. In addition to having difficulties keeping up with bills due to lost wages from not being able to work and medical expenses from surgeries, they lost a lot and the trailer home on which they'd been making payments. Although she recently qualified for Medicaid, a health program for low-income families, it would not cover the hospital bills from before the coverage began.

- Most farmworkers are not eligible for social services. Less than 1% of all farmworkers use general assistance welfare, only 2% use Social Security, and fewer than 15% are Medicaid recipients.

Afra completed eighth grade, and Reynoldo made it through 11th grade. When asked why she did not complete high school, Afra explained that she left school when their house burned down: "We all started helping my dad to build another house." They had no other place to live, so they all stayed with a neighbor until the house was finished. Afra began field work when she was 12 years old. She has done this work ever since.

- The median highest schooling completed by farmworkers is sixth grade; 13% have completed less than 3 years of schooling, and 13% have completed high school.

Like Afra's family, dire circumstance and economic need propel many children of farmworkers out of school and into the fields. Since many farmworkers migrate, sometimes with families, the need to move to follow crops can also interrupt children's schooling and require regular changes in schools attended, presenting challenges to remaining in and doing well in school.

▶ **THINK ABOUT IT:** Is it fair that those who labor to provide our food do not earn enough to eat healthily themselves? Why or why not? If not, what can be done?

children. Chronic conditions often develop slowly, but with no or limited insurance they go untreated until they become much more serious. Preventive treatments and screenings are also often unavailable to many.

The likelihood of being imprisoned in the United States is directly related to race and ethnicity (Bonczar, 2003). Although incarceration rates for all racial groups have decreased since 2005, when we look at race and ethnicity, we find the incarceration rate per 100,000 adults is 312 for whites, 820 for Hispanics, and 1,745 for African Americans (Carson & Anderson, 2016). Black adults, then, are 5.6 times as likely as white adults to be incarcerated, and Hispanic adults are 2.6 times as likely as white adults.

In 2015, 501,300 black men were in prisons across the United States, making up 34% of the total prison population, while 21.6% of all prisoners were Hispanic and 33.8% were white. Compare these numbers to the proportions of these groups in the general U.S. population: African Americans, 12.6%; Hispanics, 17.1%; and whites, 73.6%. Who commits crimes and who goes to prison? Are certain groups of people more likely to commit crimes, or are other factors, such as racial discrimination, at work in sending people to jail?

There are many other dimensions to inequality as well. We could look at educational rates, unemployment rates, quality and location of housing, likelihood of being hungry or participating in programs like SNAP, and many other measures. Clearly, however, despite what many believe about the extent of social mobility in the United States, especially in comparison to other countries, inequality is a fact of American life. For those who believe social change is possible and something to work toward, facing that reality is just the first step.

USING THEORY TO EXPLAIN POVERTY, CLASS, AND INEQUALITY: THE VIEWS FROM THE FUNCTIONALIST, SYMBOLIC INTERACTIONIST, AND CONFLICT PERSPECTIVES

2.5 Apply the functionalist, conflict, and symbolic interactionist perspectives to the problems of poverty, class, and inequality.

Sociologists and other social scientists have grappled with the issues of poverty, class, and inequality for decades. Some theoretical explanations have focused on individual situations and characteristics, while others have looked at the structures of societies, institutions, and organizations. Still others have tried to bring the individual and the social together by describing how individuals manage within social contexts. We look at these three different perspectives in turn below.

Functionalism

Functionalism examines the nature of society and the way it is organized. **Functionalist theory** sees societies as complex systems whose various institutions and organizations work together to maintain a level of cohesion and stability. Society's norms, mores, values, traditions, and beliefs give individuals a sense of what to do and when to do it, as well as how to interact with others, particularly when they differ in social status. This shared awareness and acceptance of the structure of society is our particular culture, in which individual members accept their particular positions, whether at the top, in the middle, or at the bottom.

Drawing on the work of modern structural functionalist Talcott Parsons, the seminal work on functionalism and its application to poverty, class, and inequality is a 1945 article by Kingsley Davis and Wilbert E. Moore, "Some Principles of Stratification." Even though more than 70 years have passed since its publication, the principles outlined by Davis and Moore still largely reflect the functionalist view of poverty, class, and inequality: (a) Some positions in a society are more valuable than others and require special skills to perform; (b) only a few people have the talent for the more important positions; (c) learning those skills requires sacrifices on the part of those who have the talent to learn; (d) to induce them to make the sacrifices requires that they receive more of society's scarce resources and rewards than others in less important positions; (e) access to scarce resources and rewards becomes attached to different positions in the social hierarchy. As a result, (f) different positions in the social hierarchy have different levels of prestige and esteem, and (g) social inequality among these positions is both inevitable and functional to society's maintenance.

Herbert J. Gans (1971) presents a clear application of these principles in "The Uses of Poverty," in which he described 15 "positive functions" for poverty. These include getting the "dirty work" of society done cheaply (garbage collection and working in farm fields); ensuring the purchase of low-quality products (wilting produce and day-old bread); and guaranteeing higher social status for those who are not poor, since someone has to be at the bottom. However, Gans goes on to demonstrate that these presumably positive functions can be quite costly for society and the affluent, not just financially but also in moral terms, by requiring the toleration of exclusionary practices.

More recent theorists, including George Gilbert, Lawrence Mead, and Charles Murray, have continued to argue that social inequality is necessary and inevitable for the maintenance of any society, including the United States. To be a doctor or a banker requires much more training—which is time-consuming and arduous—than to be a janitor or a police officer. As a result, higher positions carry greater prestige and authority as well as access to scarce resources and rewards such as higher income and better housing. In *Coming Apart*, Murray (2012) argues that those in the top 5% of the population, particularly CEOs and policy makers, have extremely high IQs that lead to their success and for which they are rightly highly compensated.

ASK YOURSELF: Imagine yourself poor, and consider the functionalist provision that inequality is inevitable and functional. Would you accept your status as unavoidable and necessary?

Functionalist theory: The hypothesis that societies are complex systems whose parts work together to maintain cohesion and stability.

Policy Implications of Functionalism

According to the functionalist perspective, inequality is not only inevitable but necessary for the functioning of society. Certain positions need higher levels of rewards because of the difficulty in acquiring the skills to perform them. Therefore, while some are advantaged, others should be disadvantaged, since anyone could perform the tasks of lower positions with minimal effort. In fact, society may need to threaten those at the bottom with sanctions simply to get them to do anything.

A good example of this approach in action is welfare reform. The welfare rights movement of the 1960s was successful in expanding both coverage and benefits provided by the Aid to Families With Dependent Children (AFDC) program. However, after the election of Richard M. Nixon to the presidency in 1968, critics of the War on Poverty began a concerted attack on public assistance, arguing that many recipients were merely unwilling to work and instead were taking advantage of public benefits. These arguments escalated during the years Ronald Reagan was in office, leading to a call for welfare reform based on the propositions that many able-bodied individuals were avoiding work or job training, had become entrenched in a "culture of poverty," and needed to be pushed to learn appropriate work habits and values. Critics of welfare rejected structural explanations for poverty and believed that welfare recipients should take personal responsibility for their disadvantaged situation. By the 1990s, "welfare reform" had become policy at the federal level, leading to the **Personal Responsibility and Work Opportunity Reconciliation Act (PRWORA)** of 1996. Among this act's major provisions were time limits for receipt of benefits (no more than 60 months in a lifetime at the federal level, but less time at any state's discretion) and work requirements whereby individuals refusing to work could be sanctioned (including by losing monthly benefits).

Austerity programs—typically taking the form of cutbacks to social welfare programs that assist those at the bottom—are clearly reflections of functionalism. Many of the politicians and other commentators currently arguing for limiting the social safety net and reducing so-called entitlement programs (such as Social Security) take the functionalist approach. Other types of public assistance, such as SNAP and Medicaid, are also facing possible reductions by the U.S. Congress, even though they are vital to the health and well-being of many lower-income individuals and families. Austerity is proposed and often enacted for social safety net programs, while bailouts for banks are not seen in the same light. In fact, those programs (which some would call corporate welfare) are seen as essential to the national economy, and no one has raised the need for "personal responsibility" on the part of Wall Street bankers.

Symbolic Interactionism

Symbolic interactionism grew from George Herbert Mead's hypothesis that the meanings of social events emerge from the interactions among individuals, who are actors rather than reactors. An interaction is a negotiation, a learning process, in which the individuals involved absorb not only relevant norms and traditions but also beliefs and values—the core elements of a shared culture. In a sense, then, we learn culture or collective consciousness through the interaction process.

One of the most significant applications of interactionism to poverty, class, and inequality is the **culture of poverty thesis** proposed by Oscar Lewis (1969). Lewis believed people are poor not just because they lack resources but also because they hold a unique set of values that makes it difficult for them to escape poverty, including a sense of powerlessness that leads to feelings of helplessness and inferiority, and lack of a work ethic.

This thesis is similar to *labeling theory,* which applies interactionism to the understanding of deviance (Kilty & Meenaghan, 1977). Individuals seen as deviant or as outsiders become labeled by others who are more advantaged because of their sex, race, ethnicity, class, or age. Labeling effectively reduces the options for both labeled and labelers. The poor are among the most disadvantaged in our society, and many are at further disadvantage because in addition they are women, are people of color, and/or have limited education and occupational histories. These were the groups—poor women, poor blacks, poor Hispanics, poor Native Americans, poor Appalachians—to whom the culture of poverty thesis was applied beginning in the 1960s. Many in these groups likely did feel powerless or appear to lack a work ethic. What were their options? Rather than looking at opportunity structures, the culture of poverty thesis focuses on the presumed failings of individuals—or, in William Ryan's (1976) words, on blaming the victim.

ASK YOURSELF: Why do some people get labeled in a positive way and others in a negative way? Why do certain ideas about some groups become widely accepted, such as who is good at certain sports or who is best able to work certain jobs?

Personal Responsibility and Work Opportunity Reconciliation Act (PRWORA): U.S. federal legislation passed in 1996 that eliminated Assistance for Families With Dependent Children (AFDC) and established Temporary Assistance for Needy Families (TANF). Also known as welfare reform.

Culture of poverty thesis: The idea that living in poverty leads to the acquisition of certain values and beliefs that perpetuate remaining in poverty.

Peter Charlesworth/LightRocket / Getty Images

▶ About 16 female Nike factory workers share this single rented room near Ho Chi Minh City, Vietnam. Toilet facilities are outside and the women cook on the floor. None of the women would show their faces in this picture for fear of reprisals from their Nike bosses. If you knew that your sports footwear and equipment were manufactured in a labor camp, would you stop buying them?

Policy Implications of Symbolic Interactionism

The most striking application of symbolic interactionism to social policy is the continuing assault on public assistance—not only welfare but also other public services such as SNAP, Medicaid, and Head Start. A study of comments by members of the U.S. House of Representatives about PRWORA revealed that the legislators sounded certain themes, including personal responsibility, getting something for nothing, out-of-wedlock births, and fraud and abuse (Segal & Kilty, 2003). The notion that only the "deserving" poor should get help was common, as was the idea that welfare encourages many to remain in a "cycle of dependency." Nearly all adult welfare recipients in 1996 were women, while 89% of members of the House were men. Male representatives were more likely to speak in favor of the "need" for welfare reform and to vote for the legislation than were women—although women representatives were certainly more privileged than women welfare recipients.

Labeling theory was not intended to be a mechanism for blaming the victim. In fact, it was meant to be quite the opposite: a means for identifying how power differentials marginalize particular groups, such as women or racial and ethnic minorities. To a large extent, it drew from the principles of *critical theory*, which argues that we need to examine cultural ideas in terms of which groups benefit from them and who then advocate their points of view. In this case, we need to examine carefully who was applying particular labels to the poor as a way

of ostracizing them on the grounds that the poor are themselves responsible for their circumstances, rather than focusing on the systemic causes of poverty—who gets what and why.

Conflict Theory

At the heart of Marxist thought, from which conflict theory developed, is the division of class into two basic groups: the capitalists, or owners of the means of production, and the proletariat, or working class. Capitalists do not produce anything themselves. Rather, they extract surplus value from the work of those who make things the capitalists sell for a profit. The conflict is the struggle to control the means of production.

The point of capitalism is to make as much profit as possible, forever. In the early days of capitalism, the profit extracted from the production of material goods or commodities was invested in the making of new goods. But profit can also be accumulated for its own sake, and money can be hoarded, just like material goods. Furthermore, anything can be a commodity, including items essential for life, such as water, utilities, and food, which then are available only to those who can afford them. A modern commodity in the United States is health care. Those who can afford it (or who can afford health insurance) can have it, and those who cannot have to do without or rely on public and charitable programs. Even money can be a commodity, packaged and traded in various ways, as are home mortgages and other financial instruments that most of us need.

While anything can be a commodity, often the thing itself becomes what is of value rather than the human labor that makes it—what Marx referred to as a commodity fetish. Many of us are consumed with possessing "things," and we pay little attention to the labor that goes into them, or the conditions in which the laborers work, such as the Chinese sweatshops where iPhones are made.

Marx proposed the concept of **alienation** to describe the separation between the workers' labor to make something and the object itself, about which workers have little or no say. Workers sell their labor to capitalists and

Alienation: The separation of workers from their human nature in the capitalist production process—that is, the separation between the labor to make something and the object itself.

have little or no say in what they do as part of that production process. Alienation is not a psychological condition but rather a division between workers and their true human nature. Marx saw this as a key development in capitalist society, and it applies to all workers, whether laborers or farmworkers or professors. Marx believed in **dialectical materialism**—the idea that contradictions in an existing economic and social order, such as the conflict between owners and laborers, would create a push for change, eventually leading to new economic conditions and social relationships (Allan, 2011).

From these ideas emerged conflict theory, which proposes that we need to examine the nature of power relationships in society. Do we actually have a shared acceptance or collective consciousness, or are different groups struggling to ensure that their positions and views remain predominant?

C. Wright Mills began an important tradition in U.S. social thought by examining how those in power assert themselves. In *The Power Elite,* originally published in 1956, Mills (2000) focused on the interconnections among corporate leaders, the military, and the government—what President Dwight D. Eisenhower would later term the military-industrial complex. By the late 20th century, academic leaders were also identified as part of this matrix, participating in a process in which individuals moved readily from one position to another in the corporate world, the academic world, and the government. Economists Timothy Geithner and Lawrence Summers, for instance, have both held powerful positions in corporations, the federal government, and higher education (see below). G. William Domhoff has published a series of studies identifying these "interlocking directorates," which show that the United States, like many other countries, is dominated by a powerful elite whose members are able to maintain their control based on their own or others' wealth and social positions.

Those concerned with poverty, class, and inequality have employed conflict theory to examine the dynamics of wealth and poverty (Piven & Cloward, 1993). They have shown that poverty is systemic, rather than a function of the values or personal inclinations or attributes of the poor. As Gans (1971) has shown, poverty serves a "useful" function in society, in the sense that the threat of poverty hangs over the head of every working person. No matter how bad the situation is for a person with a job, it would be worse if he or she lost that job—a possibility that is part of everyday life for most of us. How many paychecks away from destitution are we? Are we willing to challenge our bosses and organize our coworkers, or are we afraid we will lose our jobs if we raise our voices? Those in power have the money to propagate their desired messages—that the poor are shiftless and lazy, that anyone who applies him- or herself and works hard enough

will be successful—through what Frances Fox Piven calls the propaganda machine.

> **ASK YOURSELF:** Can anything—not just material objects—be a commodity? Should we treat such necessities as food and health care as commodities? Should people have a right to necessities, whether they can afford them or not? Do you believe there is a "power elite" in the United States?

Policy Implications of Conflict Theory

From the conflict theory perspective, those at the bottom serve to keep wages for other workers low, since employers can fight efforts to raise wages by replacing outspoken workers with the unemployed. Who has the power is the critical element in the conflict theorist's view of society, and those with wealth have much more power than those at the bottom. Wealth not only buys influence through corporate leadership positions and access to the media for disseminating particular messages, but it also buys legislators and policy makers through campaign contributions and jobs outside government—as in the cases of Lawrence Summers, who became president of Harvard University after serving as secretary of the Treasury, and Timothy Geithner, who was president of the Federal Reserve Bank of New York before becoming secretary of the Treasury. Recent examples are the White House cabinet appointments of President Donald Trump, which the *New York Times* described as "more white and male than any first cabinet since Ronald Reagan" (Lee, 2017). For example, Rex Tillerson, U.S. secretary of state, was the president and chief executive of ExxonMobil. Steven Mnuchin, U.S. Treasury secretary, was a Goldman Sachs executive. James Mattis, U.S. secretary of defense, was a military general. These appointments reflect a true "interlocking directorate" of power.

Challenging the welfare "reform" of the 1990s means working with the poor as they struggle to organize. In the 1960s, it was not just federal legislation that created a War on Poverty but also the National Welfare Rights Union, which advocated for the plight of poor women and children, and the civil rights movement, which led to legislation that established voting rights and protected minorities and women from discrimination in the labor market. According to Frances Fox Piven (2006) and Mimi Abramovitz (2000), change is likely only when social movements like these are strong. Electoral politics can

Dialectical materialism: The contradictions in an existing economic and social order that create a push for change, which eventually leads to new economic conditions and social relations.

▶ University of Missouri student Davis Hurth volunteers his time with a client at the Aspire Career Academy in Hillside, Illinois. Students drove to Chicago for their alternative spring break to help adults with disabilities. Do you think it is necessary for volunteers to have a certain degree of empathy with the people they are trying to help?

stigmatized affects people's interconnections. Distributive justice is concerned with the relationship between perceptions of inequality and the principle of fairness.

Social Empathy

According to Segal (2007, p. 75), many people lack **social empathy**—"the insights one has about other people's lives that allow one to understand the circumstances and realities of other people's living conditions." If people cannot appreciate the circumstances of others, social bonds are increasingly likely to weaken, and it may become very difficult for those at the top to act in a humane way toward those at the bottom. Social empathy is thus a crucial trait for policy makers who are responsible for developing and managing programs intended to respond to the needs of those in poverty. As Segal (2006) has documented, members of Congress and recipients of TANF benefits share few characteristics such as age, gender, race, ethnicity, or degree of wealth. The two groups come from very different worlds, and those in decision-making positions have little awareness of the lives of those at the bottom—a situation very different from the one that existed for the members of Congress who helped develop the New Deal programs of the Great Depression era.

Nickols and Nielsen (2011) have demonstrated that participation in a poverty simulation exercise can lead to greater understanding of the structural conditions responsible for poverty and greater awareness of the difficult lives of the poor. Exercises like this are often used in classrooms and with volunteers and staff in social service programs and charitable organizations. Putting a human face on poverty is a necessary step in changing misconceptions about poverty.

Social Inclusion

How is it possible for someone on the margins of society to feel a sense of inclusion? Without **social inclusion**, individuals do not have a sense of interconnection with

open possibilities, but political figures will advocate for the poor only when the poor themselves challenge authority in dramatic ways.

When the economic meltdown began in 2007, many blamed those who had overreached and taken on large, high-risk (subprime) mortgages. While that certainly happened, thousands were led by unscrupulous bankers into taking out risky loans for houses with inflated values, without being informed they had other options. Once again, those in power—the bankers, the corporate leaders, the media—chose to blame the victims rather than to accept any responsibility themselves.

SPECIALIZED THEORIES APPLIED TO POVERTY AND INEQUALITY

2.6 Apply specialized theories to poverty and inequality.

Other theoretical frameworks have been used to understand the nature of poverty, class, and inequality. Theories concerned with social empathy, for example, focus on why some people seem more able than others to identify with the experiences of other people and on whether or not empathy can be learned. Frameworks that examine social inclusion look at how being marginalized and

....

Social empathy: The insights individuals have about other people's lives that allow them to understand the circumstances and realities of other people's living conditions.

Social inclusion: A sense of belonging to or membership in a group or a society.

Antonio Perez/Chicago Tribune/Getty Images

others, nor do they have incentives that may help them work toward changing their circumstances. We have seen that those at the top have not only high incomes but also considerable assets, unlike the poor. Social policies favoring these assets exclude the poor, and many public programs require the poor to have few or no assets in order to qualify for aid. Yet moving out of poverty requires not only an adequate income but also the development of assets, without which home and auto ownership, for instance, are not possible. According to Christy-McMullin and colleagues (2010, p. 252), "This Catch-22 mentality, whereby the poor do not have access to the wealth accumulation they need to move out of poverty, contributes to the economic injustice and intergenerational poverty that is prevalent in this country."

The goal of the Individual Development Account (IDA) is to help people of limited means obtain and then accumulate assets in the form of personal savings (Lombe & Sherraden, p. 2008). Usually, this takes the form of a structured social program that both matches an individual's savings and provides that person with information about the benefits of acquiring and maintaining savings or assets. IDAs have been shown to produce an increasing sense of social inclusion and economic participation.

Distributive Justice

One of the predominant principles of social welfare is **distributive justice**—relative equality in the distribution of society's social and economic resources (DiNitto, 2005). Where inequalities exist, those who believe in distributive justice propose that government efforts be applied to reduce or eliminate them. In political terms, this is the approach of liberals or progressives. On the other side, conservatives argue that inequality is not only necessary but essential for the maintenance of society—the functionalist perspective.

Appeals about fairness in public policy often focus on tax policy and whether the rich are paying their "fair share." Since the Reagan administration, the tax burden on the wealthiest Americans has been steadily reduced, on the grounds that low tax rates on the wealthy will increase the number of jobs. Jobs have not materialized, however, and at least three major recessions have occurred since Reagan left office—including the so-called Great Recession that began in 2007 (Mishel et al., 2013).

Another common argument for reducing taxes on the wealthy is that they pay the bulk of the income taxes collected by the federal government. This is true, but the reason why is they have very high incomes, and they have benefited the most from tax cuts over the past 30 years.

Another tool of tax policy is the payroll or Social Security tax. Until recently this was a flat tax of 6.2% on earned income (with a temporary reduction in 2011 and 2012). A flat tax is an example of a *regressive tax,* one whose burden is greater on lower-income people. But the payroll tax is even more regressive because it has a cap, currently $118,500 for 2016. Income above the cap is not subject to the payroll tax, no matter how much higher that income may be. Table 2.4 shows how the Social Security payroll tax works. For incomes up to the cap, individuals pay a flat rate of 7.65% of their income. However, the maximum tax anyone pays is $9,065.25 If someone makes $125,000 in a year, that person still pays only that amount, which means her or his effective tax rate is no longer 7.65% but drops to 7.25% ($9065.25/$125,000). If someone makes $250,000, her or his effective tax rate drops to 3.62% ($9065.25/$250,000). As the table shows, the effective tax rate continues to shrink as income rises. The burden of the tax falls especially on those at the low end, since they must meet their basic expenses of housing, food, clothing, and transportation from a much smaller after-tax (or discretionary) income. Ongoing legislation proposes to eliminate the cap in order to make the payroll tax more equitable (Torry & Wehrman, 2013).

Total tax burden is heavier on lower-income people who have less discretionary income, especially women

TABLE 2.4 Social Security (Payroll) Tax at Various Income Levels, With Effective Tax Rate

Income ($)	Subject to Tax ($)	Actual Tax ($)	Less Paid ($)*	Effective Tax Rate (%)
20,000	20,000	1,530.00	0	7.65
50,000	50,000	3,825.00	0	7.65
70,000	70,000	5,355.00	0	7.65
95,000	95,000	7,267.50	0	7.65
118,500	118,500	9,065.25	0	7.65
125,000	118,500	9,065.25	497.25	7.25
150,000	118,500	9,065.25	2,409.75	6.04
250,000	118,500	9,065.25	10,059.75	3.62
500,000	118,500	9,065.25	27,184.75	1.81
1,000,000	118,500	9,065.25	63,434.75	.90

SOURCE: Social Security Administration.

*"Less paid" is the difference between what an individual paid and what he or she would have paid if Social Security taxes applied to total income.

Distributive justice: Relative equality in how social and economic resources are distributed in a society.

and minorities (Abramovitz & Morgen, 2006). In addition to federal income and payroll taxes, they pay state income taxes, sales taxes, property taxes (which renters pay as part of their rent, but which owners can deduct from their taxes), and state and federal excise taxes and fees, such as on gasoline, cigarettes, and alcohol. In addition, deductions from income taxes for interest paid on mortgages benefit mostly the affluent, who realize about 60% of the $68 billion in savings this federal housing subsidy is worth. Those with incomes under $40,000 a year benefit little from such deductions (Kilty, 2009).

Tax policy, then, has great potential for distributive purposes. While the principle of distributive justice is that we should reduce inequality, the policy question we face is whether we will reduce inequality or increase it. As it now stands, U.S. tax policy benefits those at the top while hurting those at the bottom (Marr & Huang, 2012). Those who believe in distributive justice assert that that is unfair and needs to be changed. Taxing those at the top in a more equitable way would provide resources that could be used to help those at the bottom.

ASK YOURSELF: Do you feel that there is not enough social empathy? Why or why not? Why don't the poor save unless there are special programs to help them? What are your thoughts about distributive justice? What can we do to affect social policy? Should tax policy be used to reduce inequality?

SOCIAL CHANGE: WHAT CAN YOU DO?

 2.7 Identify steps toward social change in regard to poverty.

One of the most powerful moments in a person's life is when they recognize their potential to create meaningful social change. Sociologists call this "social agency." A good example of social agency and social change is evident in the number of protests that have developed in response to the 2016 U.S. presidential election results, and the many organized protest movements that have been carried out under the "Resist" or "Anti-Trump" movement (Dreier, 2017). Indeed, immediately after Trump was sworn into office, one of the largest single-day demonstrations in U.S. history was held. On January 21, 2017, it is estimated that 3–5 million people organized and marched in the United States alone; similar marches were held across the world, including major cities like Berlin, Cape Town, Johannesburg, London, Mexico City, Nairobi, Paris, and Sydney, to name a few. This movement has continued, with subsequent marches organized around immigration, climate change, science, and labor.

We all have a role in social change, yet taking action can be scary. What will our family and friends think? Will we get in trouble with school officials or the police? What can we actually achieve when the problems are so big? But we can take action; we all have the strength to change the way things are.

Melanie Stetson Freeman/The Christian Science Monitor/Getty Images

▶ Linda Amrou (right) and Aya Khalil volunteer to help build a Habitat for Humanity home near Holland, Ohio. Volunteers from many different faiths—Muslim, Buddhist, Christian—came together to help build a house that is sponsored by the local multifaith council. If poverty and homelessness have their origins in the social structure, what, if anything, can be done about them?

Many colleges and universities now offer alternative activities during spring break and other breaks in the academic year, in which student volunteers take part in service immersion projects, working at homeless shelters, food and clothing banks, or soup kitchens, or participating in neighborhood cleanups. Many college students themselves face hunger and challenges surrounding food access. Many colleges and universities have created food pantries to address student hunger. Find out if your university offers such a program. You can help by volunteering at your university food pantry—perhaps you yourself are in need of the services these programs provide.

As you have read in this chapter, hunger is a very real problem in the United States today, affecting people on many different levels. How can you address food insecurity and food access in your communities? There are many nonprofit and other organizations that focus on alleviating hunger in various ways, including access to farmers' markets for low-income consumers using Electronic Benefits Transfer of SNAP dollars, and BackPack Programs that provide children who receive free and reduced lunch at school with nutritional staple items that are sent home over the weekend so they are sure to have weekend food outside of school. These organizations thrive on volunteer hours and are great ways to get involved in your local community (Hossfeld, Kelly, & Waity, 2016).

Raising awareness is another meaningful action. Arranging screenings of relevant films, such as the documentary *A Place at the Table* about poverty and food insecurity in the United States, or *Harvest of Dignity* about the conditions that farmworkers face, can help many see what they may never have experienced on a personal level. If a student group doesn't already exist that would be open to doing this, you might try creating one. Forums and panels where local experts provide information about community problems of poverty or inequality are also useful educational opportunities.

Many students who live off campus find themselves in low-income neighborhoods. What are the housing conditions like? Are food banks or clothing banks needed in your neighborhood? Is good-quality day care a problem? Is there a local public health clinic? Are community organizing groups or settlement houses active? Such

agencies are always looking for volunteers. Other informal community groups may be trying to organize around such issues as renters' rights, quality of housing, availability of public transportation, and health care access. Unions sometimes provide legal or health services for their members and others in local communities.

Groups like Habitat for Humanity are looking for volunteers to help build new houses for low-income families. Other organizations, such as welfare rights unions and civil rights groups, may be more concerned with organizing people to challenge local, state, or federal authorities regarding the rights of the poor and near poor.

Members of state legislatures, city councils, and school boards sometimes engage in electoral politics from their commitment to public service. If you believe change can come through the electoral process, working with politicians who share your views is another option for bringing about change.

A great resource that provides concrete ways for citizens and policy makers to get involved and make change is a publication entitled *Agenda for Social Justice* (Muschert, Klocke, Perrucci, & Shafner, 2016). This volume examines social problems like the environment, health, race, poverty, gender, sexuality, housing, criminal justice, and many more. It outlines an agenda to make meaningful social change and ways we can all get involved.

Change rarely happens as the result of the efforts of a solitary person. As individuals, we are limited in what we can do and whom we can reach. But when we join organizations—whether student clubs, local or national organizations, religious groups, secular community groups, social service organizations, or professional organizations—we gain strength through numbers. Then we have the opportunity to try to change the world. What better legacy can we leave?

WHAT DOES AMERICA THINK?

Questions About Poverty and Class Inequality From the General Social Survey

Turn to the beginning of the chapter to compare your answers to those of the total population.

1. Your standard of living will improve.

   AGREE: 57.7%

   DISAGREE: 25.2%

   NEITHER AGREE NOR DISAGREE: 17.1%

2. How do people get ahead?

   HARD WORK: 70.9%

   LUCK OR HELP: 12.3%

   BOTH OF THE ABOVE: 16.8%

3. Should government reduce income differences?

YES: 60%

NO: 40%

4. People should help the less fortunate.

AGREE: 91.6%

DISAGREE: 2.3%

NEITHER AGREE NOR DISAGREE: 6.1%

5. In the United States, do you think we're spending too much money on assistance to the poor, too little money, or about the right amount?

TOO MUCH: 7.1%

TOO LITTLE: 71.4%

ABOUT THE RIGHT AMOUNT: 21.5%

SOURCE: National Opinion Research Center, University of Chicago.

CHAPTER SUMMARY

 2.1 Explain how poverty, class, and inequality are social constructions.

Poverty, class, and inequality are complex and interconnected issues, and we cannot discuss one without the others. Our ideas about poverty, class, and inequality are based not simply on facts but also on images and perceptions, meaning they are socially constructed. We often think of poverty in economic terms, but being in poverty means having deficiencies in necessary material goods or desirable qualities—not only in economic status but also in social, political, and cultural status. Class describes the positions in a society, usually based on a social, economic, and political hierarchy. We cannot have poverty or class without inequality, or differences in the quantities of scarce resources individuals or groups possess.

2.2 Discuss patterns and trends in defining and measuring poverty.

We measure poverty in the United States using an absolute measure, an income threshold at or below which households or families are considered to be in poverty. During the 1960s and 1970s the U.S. poverty rate dropped, especially during the government's War on Poverty. Throughout the 1980s and 1990s it stayed relatively constant, increased dramatically during the Great Recession, and decreased slightly to 13.5% in 2015. Poverty is also harsher now and more difficult to escape.

2.3 Describe social class and mobility.

Social mobility is much more limited in the United States than most people believe, especially in comparison with social mobility in industrialized European countries. Those in the middle continue to fall further behind those at the top.

 2.4 Discuss income, wealth, and other dimensions of inequality.

Inequality in income and in wealth has been increasing steadily for the past 30 years. While the United States is one of the wealthiest nations in the world, it is also one of the most unequal. Inequality also exists in terms of race and ethnicity, gender, opportunity, and other social and political characteristics.

2.5 Apply the functionalist, conflict, and symbolic interactionist perspectives to the problems of poverty, class, and inequality.

From the functionalist perspective, some positions in society (doctor, lawyer) are more valuable than others; the talented need to be motivated to make the sacrifices necessary to learn the skills to hold these positions; these positions deserve greater rewards than others; and there is a shared awareness and acceptance of social position. Symbolic interactionism focuses on interactions among individuals and the development of shared meaning. One approach here is labeling theory, originally applied to understanding why some groups become marginalized and learn to accept their disadvantaged position. It also led to the "culture of poverty" thesis, which argues that the poor learn a dysfunctional set of values that keeps them in poverty and thus are responsible for their own situation. Rather than arguing for a shared awareness and acceptance of social conditions, conflict theory focuses on power dynamics and the way those at the top of a social structure try to maintain their privileged position at the expense of those at the bottom. From this perspective, those at the bottom will try to change those conditions, often through social and protest movements challenging those in authority.

2.6 Apply specialized theories to poverty and inequality.

We can apply many other theoretical frameworks to understanding poverty, class, and inequality. One is social empathy, which looks at why some people seem more able than others to identify with people in positions different from their own and how those who are less able to do so can be taught how to develop social empathy. Another is social inclusion, which is concerned with how being marginalized and stigmatized affects people's social connectivity. A last example is distributive justice, which is concerned with the relationship between perceptions of inequality and the principle of fairness.

 2.7 Identify steps toward social change in regard to poverty.

A wide variety of community groups work to make change, such as settlement houses and organizations like Habitat for Humanity, which uses volunteer labor to build new homes for poor families. When we put our energy together through groups and organizations, we can change the world.

KEY TERMS

absolute measure of poverty 28

alienation 44

class 35

culture of poverty thesis 43

dialectical materialism 45

distributive justice 47

extreme poverty neighborhoods 30

functionalist theory 42

income 37

inequality 36

means-tested programs 31

Personal Responsibility and Work Opportunity Reconciliation Act (PRWORA) 43

poverty 28

poverty guidelines 29

poverty thresholds 29

power 35

relative measure of poverty 28

self-made myth 34

social empathy 46

social inclusion 46

social mobility 35

social safety net 31

socioeconomic status (SES) 35

status 35

Supplemental Nutrition Assistance Program (SNAP) 31

wealth 37

3 RACE AND ETHNICITY

Eileen O'Brien

A multicultural group of boys at a park celebration in Los Angeles, California. How tolerant would you say you are of people from racial and cultural groups different from your own?

Investigating Race and Ethnicity: My Story

Eileen O'Brien

My eye-opener as a white girl dating across the color line in the American South drove my passion for racism education. As a sociology undergraduate at the College of William & Mary in Virginia, thousands of miles from Los Angeles, I saw students marching in protest after the not-guilty verdicts in the trial of the police officers accused of beating Rodney King. I experienced the college classroom as a space of transformative power and wanted to be part of that energy as my life's work.

As a doctoral student, I helped interview the proprietors of minority-owned businesses about the racism they faced in seeking government contracts. I've interviewed whites about their color-blind racism and Latinos and Asian Americans about their experiences with prejudice and discrimination (as reported in my book *The Racial Middle,* 2008). I've led workshops on confronting racism in local schools and religious and community organizations. Recently, I've been studying hip-hop culture and race, and I'm investigating the U.S. military, both as a haven of racial open-mindedness and as the site of a persistent "brass ceiling."

A parent of two biracial children, I've been asked what I was doing with a dark-skinned baby. My son (who I'm told resembles Barack Obama) was delivered in a hospital where his own father could not be born because it did not serve black patients in the 1960s. My family is a constant reminder to me of how far we as a society have come and how far we have yet to go to achieve true racial equality.

LEARNING OBJECTIVES

 3.1 Define race and ethnicity in the new millennium.

3.2 Discuss patterns and trends linking race and ethnicity to immigration, income, criminal justice, and health.

 3.3 Apply the functionalist, symbolic interactionist, and conflict perspectives to social policy on racial inequality.

 3.4 Apply specialized theories of racism.

3.5 Identify steps toward social change in racial inequality.

 # WHAT DO YOU THINK?

Questions About Race and Ethnicity From the General Social Survey

1. Do you feel discriminated against because of your race?

   ☐ YES
   ☐ NO

2. What is the racial makeup of your workplace?

   ☐ ALL WHITE
   ☐ MOSTLY WHITE
   ☐ HALF WHITE, HALF BLACK
   ☐ MOSTLY BLACK
   ☐ ALL BLACK

3. Should a homeowner be able to decide who they sell their house to based on race?

   ☐ OWNER DECIDES
   ☐ CAN'T DISCRIMINATE
   ☐ NEITHER

4. Blacks overcome prejudice without favors.

   ☐ AGREE
   ☐ DISAGREE
   ☐ NEITHER AGREE NOR DISAGREE

5. Should the number of immigrants to America be increased, remain the same, or be decreased?

   ☐ INCREASED
   ☐ REMAIN THE SAME
   ☐ DECREASED

 Turn to the end of the chapter to view the results for the total population.

SOURCE: National Opinion Research Center, University of Chicago.

WHITE RACIAL PRIVILEGE

In the aftermath of the Great Recession, when even a college degree cannot guarantee a job, many whites do not see themselves as particularly privileged. In fact, when Tim Wise first investigated his own background for signs of privilege, he knew his upbringing was humble at best. Wise grew up in a shabby Nashville apartment complex. His father was a stand-up comedian whose work was an irregular source of income. Even with his mother's job as a market researcher, there were times the family could have qualified for food stamps. However, Wise graduated from college, became the author of several successful books, and now lives a comfortably middle-class lifestyle. From his own research into the social problem of racism, he quickly discovered that many of his successes—while certainly due in part to his own hard work—were equally the product of white racial privilege.

Although she did not own a home, for example, his mother was able to use his grandmother's house as collateral to finance Wise's education at Tulane University. Due to open and legal discrimination in the real estate market, however, Wise's African American peers would not have had a relative with that kind of housing worth—no matter how hard or how long their families worked. In his book *White Like Me,* Wise reflects that his getting into college at all—and certainly his graduating—had everything to do with racial privilege.

Wise believes that white privilege and the double racial standards he witnessed among police allowed him to indulge in "boys will be boys" deviant behavior in college and emerge unscathed. When he interviewed scholar Michelle Alexander for his documentary film *White Like Me,* she said, "Part of white privilege is, to me, the freedom to make mistakes, and go on." Wise runs out of fingers on his hands to count all the breaks he has received as a white male in a persistently unequal society. He writes: "I am where I am today, doing what I am doing today, in large part because I was born white. I say this not to detract from whatever genuine abilities I may have, nor to take away from the hard work that helped my family in previous generations afford certain homes, but simply to say that ability and

hard work alone could not have paved the way for me, just as they have not paved the way for anyone in isolation. . . . We always have help along the way, some of us a lot more than others. My help came color-coded, and that has made all the difference" (Wise, 2008, p. 16).

DEFINING RACE AND ETHNICITY IN A NEW MILLENNIUM

 3.1 Define race and ethnicity in the new millennium.

Social scientists who study race, ethnicity, and immigration as social problems often document systematic patterns of racial and ethnic inequality. They also examine the way we develop racialized identities or create narratives or **ideologies** to rationalize and justify our positions. Ideologies can make it difficult for us to accept that racial inequality continues to exist centuries after slavery, in an age when it seems a person of color can do anything, even become president of the United States. Color-blind racism (Bonilla-Silva, 2013; Frankenberg, 1993), for instance, claims that race is irrelevant and racial discrimination is a thing of the past, so the problems minorities encounter must instead be the fault of individual inadequacies such as a poor work ethic. Clearly this view can hinder public policy efforts to curtail racial inequality. Yet as we'll see, **racism**—a system of advantage based on race (Tatum, 2003)—plays a significant role in perpetuating racial inequalities in the United States and elsewhere.

Social scientists have reached near consensus that there is no biological basis for the separation of human beings into "races" (Adelman, 2003; Graves, 2004). **Race** is now largely understood to be a social construction that uses certain traits—physical, religious, cultural, socioeconomic, or some combination—to organize people into hierarchical groups.

....

Ideologies: Belief systems that serve to rationalize/justify existing social arrangements.

Racism: A system that advantages the dominant racial group in a society.

Race: A socially and politically constructed category of persons that is often created with certain physical traits (e.g., skin color, eye color, eye shape, hair texture) in mind but can also incorporate religion, culture, nationality, and social class, depending on the time, place, and political/economic structure of the society.

Despite the lack of evidence that race exists, constructions of it are entrenched in social structures and organizations, leading scholars to view it as a "well-founded fiction" (Desmond & Emirbayer, 2010, p. 21).

Asked to define race, students often begin with skin color. But suppose someone we classify as "white" (perhaps of Italian American descent) stands beside someone who identifies as Hispanic, and beside them is someone known as Asian American, a Native American, and finally a light-skinned African American. If we had them all hold out their arms, we might see that they all have exactly the same skin color. So clearly, there is something more to race.

Societies have also incorporated hair texture, nose shape, eye shape, religion, and socioeconomic status into their racial formulas. In Nazi Germany, Jews were considered a separate race, and for several decades the U.S. Census Bureau considered "Hindu" a race (Lee, 1993). In some Latin American cultures, the saying "money whitens" reflects how mixed-race persons are perceived—the wealthier they are, the more likely they are to be considered "white" (O'Brien, 2008). Under the "one-drop rule," a U.S. legacy that continued well after slavery's end, anyone identified with black ancestry (no matter how distant) was considered "Negro," even those with skin so light they could pass as white. Today, the U.S. Census Bureau considers Hispanic to be an origin, not a race, so those who identify as Hispanic must choose "some other race" on the census form. Various social and political arrangements thus shape what we know as race, but we treat it as a fixed biological reality rather than merely a human idea.

How would you answer if asked, What is your ethnicity? The terms *race* and *ethnicity* often are used interchangeably, but **ethnicity** is a distinct concept that refers to a person's cultural heritage. Mary may be racially black, but ethnically Jamaican or Dominican. Bob may be racially white, but ethnically Irish or Italian. Cheryl may be racially Native American, but ethnically she is part of the Cherokee nation. Ethnicity is often connected to particular nation-states, but not always. It can also be associated with particular languages, surnames, holidays, clothing styles—anything we think of as culture. Furthermore, ethnicity ranges on a continuum of strength from thick to thin, depending on how big a part ethnic practices play in everyday life (Vasquez, 2011). Patrick O'Malley's name identifies him as ethnically Irish, but other than celebrating Saint Patrick's Day once a year, he may not take part in anything notably Irish during his daily activities. He participates largely in **symbolic ethnicity** (Gans, 1979)—that is, ethnicity that derives more from the heritage of his distant relatives than from his own life.

Ethnicity affects the everyday lives of many, however. Social scientists who document racial segregation in housing or racialized poverty rates understand its influence, especially for Asian Americans and Hispanics. Chinese and Japanese Americans, on average, are much less likely to live in poverty than Cambodian, Hmong, Laotian, and Vietnamese Americans. Lighter-skinned Hispanics whose ethnicity is Argentinian or Peruvian are much less likely to be stuck in racially segregated housing than darker-skinned Dominican or Puerto Rican Americans (Desmond & Emirbayer, 2010).

Notice that the way someone *personally* identifies racially or ethnically is only one piece of this puzzle. The way *society* perceives or categorizes that individual is equally, and sometimes more, influential. Karen may be ethnically Korean because of her parents and ancestors, but if she is adopted by a white U.S. family and lives the typical suburban lifestyle, she may feel culturally "white." However, in her daily life she is perceived as "Asian" and often stereotyped as such—people may call her names like *chink* and assume she cannot speak English well. Therefore, we refer to her race as Asian American (given that race is a social construction, and this is the societal response to her), but her ethnicity—the cultural heritage with which she identifies—is a bit more complicated. Some U.S. families with Korean adoptees incorporate Korean culture into their everyday lives, even visiting their native land on a regular basis. Other families choose to de-emphasize the ethnicity of foreign-born adoptees. But whether or not Karen feels connected to a Korean ethnicity, she cannot escape the racialized experience of being Asian in a nation that privileges whiteness.

Imagine that Karen was adopted by a family racially marked as "white" but culturally African American; they live in a black neighborhood, worship at a black church, eat "soul food," and listen to R&B music. If Karen exhibits black cultural styles and preferences at school, her teachers and peers may draw on racial stereotypes that depict African Americans (not Asian Americans) as academically unmotivated, and her school performance may suffer.

That we are even referring to a black culture here is significant, because many African Americans cannot trace their African nationality back to any particular ethnicity; a distinct African American culture emerged instead from rigid social divisions in the U.S. context. "Black" can also be both a race and an ethnicity. Some who are racially black but identify with Haitian, Jamaican, or Nigerian

....

Ethnicity: Cultural background, often tied to nationality of origin and/or the culture practiced by the individual and his or her family of origin.

Symbolic ethnicity: An ethnicity that is not particularly salient in an individual's daily life and becomes relevant only at certain symbolic times or events.

► Future U.S. president Barack Obama, with his mother Ann Dunham, stepfather Lolo Soetoro, and younger half-sister, Maya Soetoro, during the four years they lived together in Indonesia. Many Americans identify themselves as multiracial, or as belonging to more than one race. Do you think that the racial tensions of the past will lessen as more people identify as multiracial?

culture/ethnicity rather than African American may be more culturally similar to Europeans, due to European colonization. We can expect to find many ethnic groups within a particular race, but because any race is a social construction that varies with time and place, the ethnicities within it will vary too. Still, race and ethnicity matter when we analyze social problems, in part because social scientists have consistently measured disparities in social outcomes among racial and ethnic groups.

PATTERNS AND TRENDS

3.2 Discuss patterns and trends linking race and ethnicity to immigration, income, criminal justice, and health.

Racial and Ethnic Groups

Social scientists' primary source of comprehensive data for the U.S. population by race, ethnicity, and Hispanic origin is the U.S. Bureau of the Census. Figure 3.1 shows two different questions from the census—race and Hispanic origin—and Table 3.1 shows the results. Why a separate question on Hispanic origin? As the Census Bureau says, "Hispanics can be of any race." According to 2010 figures, of the 16% of the U.S. population that is Hispanic, more than half (53%) identified as "white" and

a third identified as "other" (36.7%) (Ennis, Ríos-Vargas, & Albert, 2011). As Figure 3.1 shows, the 2010 form does not invite write-in answers about ethnicity from those who identify as white or black. Thus we have less census information on ethnicity for whites and blacks.

Whites still make up the numerical majority of the U.S. population. However, Hispanics have overtaken blacks as the largest minority group, and Asian Americans as a group grew by 43% between 2000 and 2010 (Humes, Jones, & Ramirez, 2011). Asians and Hispanics are the two fastest-growing minority groups (see Figure 3.2).

For social scientists, the term **minority group** denotes not so much a group's size as the share of societal power and resources its members hold. Women are considered a minority group despite the fact that they represent a numerical majority of the population, because they lack the income and political power of men.

TABLE 3.1 Race and Hispanic Origin as Percentage of U.S. Population, 2015

Category	Percentage
White*	77
Non-Hispanic white	62
Hispanic/Latino (any race)	18
Black/African American*	13
Some other race*	6
Asian American	6
Native American	1

SOURCE: Humes, Karen R., Nicholas A. Jones and Robert R. Ramirez. "Overview of Race and Hispanic Origin: 2010." 2010 Census Briefs, U.S. Bureau of the Census, March 2011.

*These totals include Hispanics, who are also counted in the 18% figure, which is why the individual percentages add up to more than 100%.

Minority group: A group that does not hold a sizable share of power and resources in a society; often the share of such resources is disproportionately small relative to the group's numerical presence in the overall population, and the group has a history of being systemically excluded from those resources.

People of color are the numerical majority globally, but they hold minority status within the United States due to their income, wealth, and health outcomes.

Though whites are a majority nationwide, in several U.S. states and about one-tenth of all counties, they are already a numerical minority. In 2010, Texas joined California, the District of Columbia, Hawaii, and New Mexico in having a "majority-minority" population—less than half the state's population is non-Hispanic whites. States approaching 50% minority populations in 2010 included Arizona, Florida, Georgia, Maryland, and Nevada (Humes et al., 2011, p. 19). Throughout U.S. history, anti-immigration sentiment has flared with fear and economic uncertainty, and law enforcement agencies in some states, including Arizona, have come down hard especially on Hispanic immigrants (Romero, 2011). Minority population growth will intersect with race- and immigration-related social problems as these trends continue.

ASK YOURSELF: Beginning with the 2000 U.S. Census, respondents could choose to identify themselves as members of more than one race. When certain people identify as multiracial, why does society not see them as such? Past U.S. president Obama had a white mother and a black father, but he is often called the nation's first black president, while George Zimmerman (shooter of Trayvon Martin, 2012) has a white father and a Hispanic mother and has been variously described as white, Hispanic, or multiracial in the media. How does society decide whether persons of mixed-race parentage are white, people of color, or both, and is the logic consistent? What factors seem to affect these choices?

Immigration Patterns

The United States, often called a nation of immigrants, has regarded the influx of persons from other nations differently depending on the time and the immigrants' races or places of origin. The early settlers in North America were of Northern and Western European descent, followed by Germans in the 1830s, Irish in the 1840s, Chinese in the 1850s–1880s, and Southern and Eastern Europeans and Russian Jews in the early 20th century (see Figure 3.3) (Desmond & Emirbayer, 2010). The Irish, Italians, and Jews were all subject to **racialization** in one way or another—caricatured with exaggerated features in popular media—while signs posted by businesses saying things like "Irish need not apply" revealed the prejudice and discrimination of the period. The National Origins Act of 1924, which limited the number of immigrants allowed from each region of the world, is now regarded

FIGURE 3.1   Race, Ethnicity, and Hispanic Origin Questions, U.S. Census Bureau Form, 2010

Please answer BOTH Question #5 about Hispanic origin and Question #6 about race. For this census, Hispanic origins are not races.

5. Is this person of Hispanic, Latino, or Spanish origin?
__ No, not of Hispanic, Latino, or Spanish origin
__ Yes, Mexican, Mexican American, Chicano
__ Yes, Puerto Rican
__ Yes, Cuban
__ Yes, another Hispanic, Latino, or Spanish origin *(Print origin—for example, Argentinian, Colombian, Dominican, Nicaraguan, Salvadorian, Spaniard, etc.)*
_____

6. What is this person's race? *Mark one or more boxes.*
__ White
__ Black, African American, or Negro
__ American Indian or Alaskan Native *(Print name of enrolled or principal tribe.)* _____
__ Asian Indian   __ Japanese   __ Native Hawaiian
__ Chinese   __ Korean   __ Guamanian or Chamorro
__ Filipino   __ Vietnamese   __ Samoan
__ Other Asian *(Print race—for example Hmong, Laotian, Pakistani, Thai, and so on.)* _____
__ Other Pacific Islander *(Print race—for example, Fijian, Tongan, and so on.)* _____

__ Some other race _____

SOURCE: U.S. Census Bureau.

as among the more blatantly racist laws ever passed in the United States. With Asian and African quotas of zero, it clearly favored Northern and Western Europeans, yet it remained the basis of U.S. immigration law until 1965 (Healey, 2009).

The 1965 Immigration and Nationality Act abolished racist quotas, and in 1980 the Refugee Act was passed. These reforms help explain why Hispanics and Asians are the fastest-growing U.S. groups (Desmond & Emirbayer, 2010). Between 2009 and 2011, the most common country of origin for persons obtaining naturalized citizenship was Mexico, followed by India, China, the Philippines, Colombia, Cuba, Vietnam, Jamaica, Haiti, El Salvador, and South Korea (Lee, 2012).

Whether we imagine an immigrant as a successful Cuban entrepreneur in Miami, a Korean student admitted to one of the nation's best universities, a struggling

Racialization: The process by which a society incorporates and clearly demarcates individuals who fit a certain profile into a particular racial group.

FIGURE 3.2 U.S. Population by Race and Hispanic Origin, 2012 and 2060 (projected)

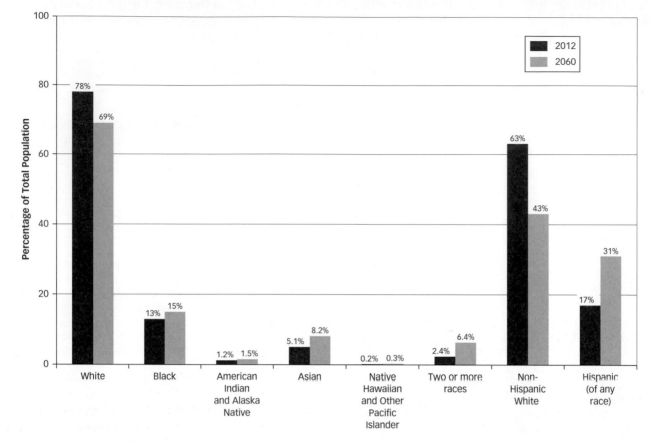

SOURCE: Based on data from the U.S. Census Bureau.

Mexican laborer, or an impoverished Vietnamese refugee with no family in this country, we cannot overlook recurrent and troubling patterns. An average of one in three children of immigrants lives in poverty (Chitose, 2005; Van Hook, Brown, & Kwenda, 2004). Motivating supporters of the Dream Act is the worry that foreign-born children of illegal immigrants could spend their entire lives in the United States, graduate from high school, and even earn college degrees, yet be at risk for deportation to countries utterly foreign to them where they may have no connections. Even if they have college degrees, their employment opportunities are limited by their immigration status, and their socioeconomic status can remain as dismal as their parents' (Preston, 2011).

From Dream Act to "Protecting the Nation"

More than 2 million immigrant children in the "1.5 generation" (foreign-born but raised from childhood in the United States) could have benefited from the passage of the Development, Relief, and Education for Alien Minors Act, popularly known as the Dream Act. This proposed legislation would have prevented their being deported, provided they meet certain requirements, and grant any who entered the United States before age 16 a 6-year period during which they could either join the military or attend college, rights they are currently denied, provided they pass extensive background checks and refrain from all criminal activity.

The bill was first introduced into the U.S. Congress in 2001 by Senators Orrin Hatch (R-UT) and Richard Durbin (D-IL), but failed to gain support when reintroduced between 2009 and 2011. So in 2012, President Obama signed an executive order freezing deportations of youth for 2 years, known as Deferred Action for Childhood Arrivals (DACA), which benefited 740,000 young people but was not guaranteed to last past the end of Obama's term in office. President Donald Trump began his term in 2017 by stating that a repeal of DACA was not an administration priority (*Miami Herald*, 2017). However, Trump did sign an executive order called "Protecting the Nation From Foreign Terrorist Entry Into the United States" in January 2017, revoking visas from anyone on a list of seven (predominantly Muslim) countries, prompting concern that campaign promises like a "Muslim ban" and a

FIGURE 3.3 Legal Migration to the United States by Region of Origin, 1820–2015

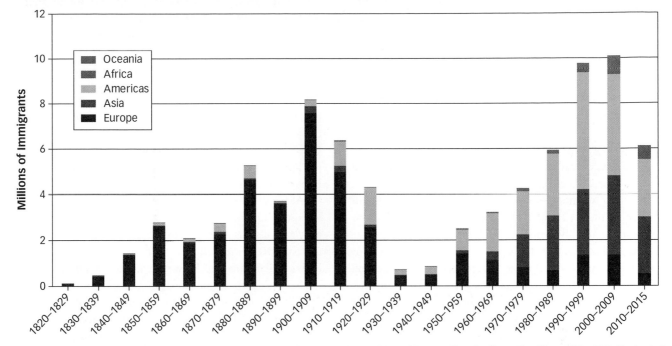

SOURCE: Data from Table 2, Persons Obtaining Legal Permanent Resident Status by Region and Selected Country of Last Residence: Fiscal Years 1820 to 2012. *Yearbook of Immigration Statistics: 2012 Legal Permanent Residents.* U.S. Department of Homeland Security.

wall on the U.S.–Mexican border were imminent. Tens of thousands gathered in many U.S. cities and airports to protest the executive order and affirm the United States as a nation of immigrants (McGurty & Frandino, 2017).

Income, Wealth, and Race

It is often difficult to disentangle class from race. When people speak of "at-risk" communities, "inner cities," and "welfare queens," without any mention of race, many imagine blacks and Hispanics (Bonilla-Silva, 2010). While nonwhites in the United States are more likely to be poor and much less likely to be wealthy than whites, it is naive to assume that by addressing poverty we can also some- how eliminate racial inequality. Even among socioeconom- ically similar individuals, the U.S. white majority enjoys racial privilege in income and wealth. As Table 3.2 shows, among male high school graduates, a white non-Hispanic earns an annual average income of $41,714, compared to $32,325 for blacks, $32,291 for Asians, and $31,668 for Hispanics. That's an advantage of nearly $10,000 per year for white males, even with the same education.

We see a similar pattern for college-educated folks. A white male with a bachelor's degree earns an annual aver- age of $66,065, compared to a similarly educated black man's $51,504, an Asian man's $60,044, and a Hispanic man's $55,867. A black man has to earn an associate degree to make the same amount as a white male high school graduate, and a bachelor's degree to reach the earn- ings level of a white male with an associate degree. Only

with postgraduate education do male Asians' earnings approach those of whites. Across every category, women earn substantially less than men, sometimes as much as $20,000 less per year, particularly women of color.

This is a cautionary tale against the **tokenistic fallacy** the assumption that, because one or a few members of a minority group have achieved equality with majority counterparts, the group no longer experiences racial disadvantage or racism no longer exists (Desmond & Emirbayer, 2010). Success stories notwithstanding, the data show a pattern of income inequality that lower levels of education cannot fully explain.

What, then, explains racial income inequality? Race dis- crimination in employment takes many forms, both overt and covert, and social scientists have used several innovative strategies to study it. Title VII of the Civil Rights Act of 1964 prohibits employment discrimination based on race, color, sex, religion, or national origin (U.S. Equal Employment Opportunity Commission, 2009), so we might expect that since 1964 most such bias has operated covertly. However, recently settled civil rights cases reveal everyday situations where employees have been made to feel uncomfortable, denied promotions, fired, or never hired because of their race.

One Hispanic worker experienced so many racial/ ethnic taunts that he finally complained to authorities.

Tokenistic fallacy: The common misunderstanding that when a small number of persons from a minority group become successful in a society there must no longer be racism in that society.

For retaliating against him, his employer, the township of Green Brook, New Jersey, had to pay him $35,000 in damages. The same year (2010), the Vanguard Group settled a suit for $300,000 by a black woman who was told she was not hired for lack of a training certificate, after it hired a white male without one (Pincus, 2011). In the first example, the bias was overt—the employee knew he was singled out because of race. In the second example, the applicant needed to be a sleuth to uncover more subtle discrimination, because nonracial reasons were given to cover up the truth of why she was not hired.

A little critical thinking reveals that the number of cases of racial discrimination that are successfully fought in court far underrepresents the real extent of employment discrimination. Consider also that civil rights violations are just that—civil—and a victim's only recourse is to sue for monetary damages; there are no criminal penalties for racial discrimination. It takes time, energy, resources, and legal representation to file a successful lawsuit. Many victims simply take their talents elsewhere rather than invest in suing employers who discriminate against them. Thus social scientists cannot merely count successful court cases to reliably estimate the extent of racial discrimination. They must adopt more innovative methods.

Because color-blind ideology makes some mistrust self-reporting about job discrimination, researchers have begun using experimental audit studies as an alternative. This methodology matches a group of testers on all relevant characteristics—résumé, qualifications, speaking patterns, and scripted answers for live interviews—except race (or gender). The researchers send the testers out to interview for jobs, find housing, or buy automobiles and then examine the results the testers report to assess whether black and white testers were treated differently. The federal government has long used this methodology to monitor housing discrimination (Feagin, 2000), but it can also be used to explore employment discrimination, most notably hiring.

Economists Marianne Bertrand and Sendhil Mullainathan (2004) conducted a study in which they sent out 5,000 résumés in the Boston and Chicago areas, four to each employer. Two of the fictional job candidates (one white, one black) had weak work histories and experiences, while the other two (one white, one black) had stronger qualifications. As the title of their article reporting on the study suggests ("Are Emily and Greg More Employable Than Lakisha and Jamal?"), they also wanted to test for the effects of names typically associated with blacks and whites. The applicants with white-sounding names got callbacks 1 in 10 times, while those with black-sounding names got callbacks only 1 in 15 times. Having a strong résumé had a bigger effect for whites (increasing callbacks by 30%) than for blacks (9%).

You might think a criminal record matters more than race, but sociologist Devah Pager (2003) found that a white male *with* a criminal record was more likely to get a callback from a prospective employer than a black male *without* such a record. By revealing employer preferences for hiring members of the majority/dominant group, these two studies help explain the racial differences in income shown in Table 3.2, as well as in unemployment rates—blacks have unemployment rates about twice as high as those of whites, especially in economic downturns. In June 2012, the white unemployment rate was 7.4%, while the black unemployment rate was 14.4% (U.S. Bureau of Labor Statistics, 2012a) (see Figure 3.4).

Although these experiences happen in the context of economic institutions, sociologists consider them cases of **individual discrimination** (Yetman, 1999) because individual employers are acting in discriminatory ways against individual applicants. However, **institutional discrimination** is also partly to blame. Institutional discrimination happens as a matter of policy. It may not be racially intended, but regardless of intent, it has disparate impacts on members of minority groups. Consider the Baltimore City Fire Department, which raised eyebrows in 2004 by recruiting an entirely white incoming trainee class in a city that is 65% black. Although individual applicants were not turned away because of black-sounding names or appearances (individual discrimination), various institutional practices combined to result in a narrower pool of black applicants than white. Many rural areas where whites lived had volunteer fire department opportunities, where applicants gained insider knowledge that helped them achieve better

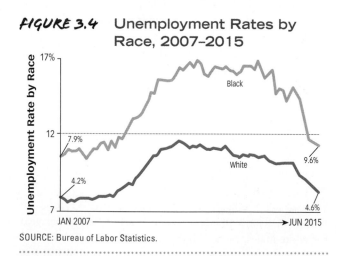

FIGURE 3.4 Unemployment Rates by Race, 2007–2015

SOURCE: Bureau of Labor Statistics.

Individual discrimination: Discrimination in which actors carry out their own intentions to exclude based on race, as opposed to being explicitly supported in doing so or directed to do so by an organization.

Institutional discrimination: Discrimination based in policies often written without overt racial language that nonetheless have disproportionately negative impacts on people of color.

entrance exam scores, and new positions were advertised internally and not predictably. Perhaps no one was thinking, "We'll do it this way so few black people will be able to apply successfully," but that was the result.

Sociologists who study racial economic inequality tend to look at either (1) dire unemployment and poverty faced by an inner-city black "underclass" whose members often do not complete high school, or (2) glass ceilings faced by middle- to upper-class college-educated blacks. In her 2003 book *Race and the Invisible Hand,* Deirdre Royster reports on her study of 50 working-class men in Baltimore, in which she examined the overlooked middle between those two extremes. Royster studied some of the stronger students at a vocational and trade school she calls "Glendale" and found striking racial differences postgraduation. Among all male students, blacks were less likely than whites to be employed in the skilled trade in which they had been trained; blacks also earned less per hour, experienced fewer promotions, held lower-status positions, and experienced longer bouts of unemployment than whites.

Royster argues that lack of education or willingness to work hard cannot explain these outcomes. Rather, blue-collar networks function to privilege white workers and disadvantage blacks. White interviewees often talked about opportunities that "fell into their laps" because of family connections or contacts made in bars and other gathering places. Even white teachers at Glendale, who spoke highly of the black students, were much more likely to recommend white students for job openings. Black interviewees called the teachers "nice" and "fair," while whites called them instrumental in job placements—clearly a much more practical outcome than simply good grades.

Royster also explains that older men in hiring positions felt more comfortable recruiting employees who reminded them of themselves. She describes this dynamic as the "invisible hand" because such networking privileges do not fit traditional definitions of racial discrimination. Nevertheless, they create white privilege and black disadvantage, however unintentional.

Institutional discrimination is often difficult to pinpoint because contemporary media and even courts of law focus our attention on discerning the "true intentions" of alleged discriminators, yet social scientists stress that the effect of discrimination remains harmful regardless of intent. We can think of racial discrimination as an iceberg, with the tip being cases such as that of the Hispanic worker in Green Brook, New Jersey—above the surface of the water, in plain view. Most racism occurs below the surface, and the untrained eye often struggles to identify it. This is due, in part, to our individualistic society's search for an individual to blame, when, in cases of institutional discrimination, such an individual does not exist.

An examination of wealth as opposed to income (see Chapter 2) further illustrates the consequences of institutional discrimination. It is difficult to save money when you are receiving less income than your counterparts; however, income differentials are only part of the story of wealth differences. As the PBS documentary *Race: The Power of an Illusion* explains, no statistic shows the extent of continuing racial inequality like the black/white wealth gap (Adelman, 2003). The wealth of the average black family is one-tenth that of the average white family (Shapiro, Meschede, & Sullivan, 2010) (see Figure 3.5). Sociologist Dalton Conley (1999, p. 26) used data from the Panel Study of Income Dynamics to show that this gap is "not a result of lower earnings among the black population.... [When income is controlled for,] at every income level, blacks have substantially fewer assets than whites." Conley also tested the hypothesis that blacks' savings rates are not as high as whites' (the "rampant consumerism" stereotype) and found no support for this explanation either.

Oliver and Shapiro (1995) coined the term *sedimentation of racial inequality* to describe how a history of institutional discrimination has reinforced the wealth gap. For example, when Social Security was established in 1935, it excluded virtually all blacks and Latinos—not by identifying specific racial groups as ineligible, but rather by excluding people in certain job categories, such as agricultural and domestic workers. As a result, this government-subsidized national savings and retirement program underserved nonwhites. Notably,

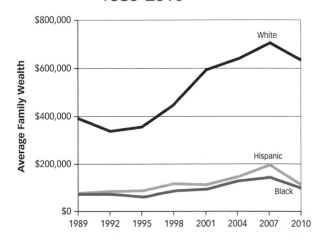

FIGURE 3.5 U.S. Average Family Wealth by Race and Ethnicity, 1989–2010

SOURCE: "The Racial Wealth Gap Is Not Improving," by S-M. McKernan, C. Ratcliff, E. Steuerie, and S. Zhang, 2013. *Less Than Equal: Racial Disparities in Wealth Accumulation,* April, p. 3. The Urban Institute. Used by permission.

however, a few exceptional non-whites could "make it"—Madame C. J. Walker's hair-care products made her an 1880s black millionaire (Desmond & Emirbayer, 2010). Institutional discrimination creates systematized patterns of racial exclusion, but it is not 100% exclusionary—it has always allowed for tokens. This is one reason why some people find it difficult to realize that racism still exists.

As Chapter 2 showed, wealth inequality is more severe than income inequality due to the intergenerational transmission of wealth. Homeownership forms the basis of most U.S. adults' net worth, but government policy on homeownership was racially biased for much of U.S. history. For example, the Federal Housing Authority played a

▶ Protesters demonstrate against President Trump's immigration ban at Portland International Airport in Portland, Oregon, in 2017 after the president signed an executive order suspending all refugee admissions, as well as blocking entry for citizens from seven Muslim-majority countries. Do you think that people of any religion, race, ethnicity, or country should be allowed to enter the United States?

TABLE 3.2 Median Annual Income of Year-Round Full-Time U.S. Workers by Race/Ethnicity, Sex, and Education, 2009

Sex/Education	Median Annual Income ($)			
	White, Non-Hispanics	Blacks	Asians	Hispanics
Males				
Some high school	32,560	26,524	23,737	25,096
High school graduate	41,714	32,325	32,291	31,668
Some college	50,360	40,138	42,129	41,274
Associate degree	51,460	41,797	46,074	42,348
Bachelor's degree	66,065	51,504	60,044	55,867
Master's degree	80,362	61,101	89,472	72,180
Females				
Some high school	21,917	22,298	–	20,038
High school graduate	30,539	26,843	27,266	25,768
Some college	35,432	31,724	35,002	31,566
Associate degree	39,784	31,936	38,089	31,794
Bachelor's degree	46,863	46,224	51,089	44,085
Master's degree	61,034	55,875	72,415	55,187

SOURCE: U.S. Census Bureau 2010.

Race and Ethnicity Beyond Our Borders

Immigration and Ethnic Diversity in Western Europe

The United States is not alone in struggling to manage resource and power imbalances in a diverse society. France, Germany, and the United Kingdom are among the top 10 nations in the world receiving international migrants (United Nations, 2009), yet their unemployment rates for foreign-born residents are significantly higher than those for their native-born (Hansen, 2012). Most of these immigrants are also European, but culturally distinct Muslims among them often draw anti-immigrant sentiment, and poor language skills and low earnings persist for two or three generations (Hansen, 2012). Some analysts draw analogies between blacks in the United States and Muslims in Western Europe in that both suffer high unemployment and school dropout rates.

These and other economic concerns, coupled with fears among the public about security, crime, and terrorism, have raised *nativist* sentiment, which combines nationalism and xenophobia (fear of difference) to view the entry of foreign-born people as a threat to stability (Mudde, 2012). Minority political parties can become viable forces in many European nations, and Austria, Denmark, the Netherlands, Sweden, and Switzerland have all seen a nativist political groundswell (Glazer, 2010; Mudde, 2012). In Switzerland, once known for cultural tolerance, the Swiss People's Party (SVP) helped win 58% of the popular vote to ban minarets (spires) atop mosques, though Muslims make up less than 6% of the population (Glazer, 2010; Papademetriou, 2012). The SVP also advocated banning burkas; Belgium, France, and the Netherlands already have such bans in place (Mudde, 2012). Moreover, the United Kingdom Independence Party (UKIP) admittedly drew upon anti-immigrant xenophobic sentiments to gain support for the UK's exit from the European Union (known as Brexit) successfully through popular vote in June 2016 (Taylor, 2016). Though movement leaders described the original motivations as largely economic, the Brexit win seemed to embolden racists, who became more vocal and active immediately following the election (Al Jazeera, 2016).

Bettmann/Getty Images

▶ A man walks past graffiti in central Athens. A major gateway for Asian and African immigrants trying to enter Europe, Greece has long struggled with illegal immigration. In the past few years, the problem exploded into a full-blown crisis as Greece sank into a deep recession, leaving one in four jobless and hardening attitudes toward migrants, who were blamed for a rise in crime. In what ways are Americans intolerant of immigrants coming into the United States?

▶ **THINK ABOUT IT**: Why is the perceived face of immigration for many Western Europeans a Muslim to be feared, when the data show the average immigrant is most likely from Europe?

major role in the sedimentation of racial inequality, particularly in the 1950s, when U.S. suburbia was created. Even now, the nest eggs that many middle- to upper-middle-class families depend on—the value of their homes—can be traced directly to parents' and grandparents' racialized experiences. Before the Fair Housing Act of 1969, banks and home insurance companies could legally charge higher mortgage and insurance rates for homes in black neighborhoods and exclude blacks from more prosperous white neighborhoods. This means, for example, that when President Obama was attending college, many black families in the United States did not own homes with enough value against which to borrow to send their children to college.

Wealth makes the difference among various "middle-class" experiences. Even when their educations and incomes are comparable to those of their white counterparts, black middle-class families are often "asset poor" by comparison (Conley, 1999), as are Asian American, Hispanic, and Native American families (Lui et al., 2006). Color-blind solutions like ensuring equal access to education and good jobs will not suffice—even with comparable income and education, racial inequality still persists.

Criminal Justice Outcomes and Race

Some researchers argue that a prison term is now a coming-of-age event for many poor nonwhite urban males, much as military service or college is for other young men. Among black males born from 1965 through 1969, 60% who did not graduate high school had been in prison by 1999 (Pettit & Western, 2004).

Some argue that deindustrialization and the loss of jobs in urban centers led this jobless cohort to crime as a means of economic survival. Others point to the War on Drugs and differential enforcement of drug laws (1960–1990). Michelle Alexander (2012) contends that mass incarceration is the "new Jim Crow." The term **Jim Crow** refers to the system of racialized segregation that existed from the time of the Emancipation Proclamation of 1865 to the landmark civil rights legislations of the late 1960s. Blacks remained unable to own their own labor, testify as witnesses, obtain education equal to that available to whites, or vote (due to the Ku Klux Klan's reign of terror). Alexander argues that the criminal justice system is the major enforcer of Jim Crow today, locking predominantly nonwhites at the bottom of a racial caste system from which they cannot escape, even after they have completed their prison sentences. Pager's (2003) work supports this legal argument, demonstrating how the stigma of a criminal record disproportionately affects the lives of black adults.

On noting that prison populations consist mainly of blacks and Hispanics, some may assume that nonwhites are more likely than whites to commit crimes; even sympathetic observers who cite unfortunate lives of poverty as a cause may draw this conclusion. Sociological perspectives such as Robert K. Merton's strain theory (discussed in Chapter 11) may reinforce this view. However, most inmates in U.S. prisons are nonviolent drug offenders incarcerated for possession, not sale, despite yearly data from the U.S. Department of Health and Human Services showing nearly identical drug use rates for blacks and whites. When rates do differ, those for whites are slightly higher, particularly for cocaine and heroin (Alexander, 2012). Thus evidence does not support the argument that more blacks and Hispanics are in jail because they commit more crimes.

We do know, however, that blacks and Hispanics are more likely than whites to be poor (Macartney, Bishaw, & Fontenot, 2013), and socioeconomic status plays a role in criminal justice outcomes. A defendant who can hire a skillful and well-connected attorney might circumvent prison or probation altogether by negotiating for community service hours or treatment in a substance abuse program (Reiman, 2001). A Seattle study found that white users of crack cocaine were more likely to be sentenced to treatment than to prison; only 25% were arrested, compared to 63% of black users (Beckett et al., 2005).

Most criminal cases are settled by plea bargain, not trial. Whether a defendant can afford bail has a major effect (Reiman, 2001); those who cannot pay must wait in jail for a court date even if innocent. Thus they cannot assist in gathering evidence for their defense or provide for their families, circumstances that can make a plea bargain more alluring. A first-time offender may plead guilty and avoid jail, which in the short term returns him or her to job and family. In the long run, however, this person now has a criminal record. This disadvantages the person on the job market (particularly if he or she is not white), prevents him or her from voting, and makes avoiding prison highly unlikely for the individual in case of another arrest (Alexander, 2012). While the intended or **manifest function** of plea bargains may be to facilitate quicker outcomes, their unintended or **latent function** is to create class and racial inequality in sentencing, even in identical cases. Sociologists find this feature of the system racist and classist because even if judges, juries, lawyers, and police officers are not prejudiced, racial inequality still results.

Institutional racism in the criminal justice system results not only from the way the court system is structured but also from the way policing works. First, it is easier for officers to patrol urban areas than it is for them to patrol in gated communities or other affluent areas, because in urban dwellings people are more densely packed and therefore criminal activities are more likely to occur

---

Jim Crow: The system of racialized segregation that existed in the United States from the Emancipation Proclamation of 1865 to the landmark civil rights legislation of the late 1960s. During this era, legal segregation was enforced by both law enforcement and white terror perpetrated by groups such as the Ku Klux Klan.

Manifest function: The intended positive outcome of social institutions or policies; the reason why they were designed or created.

Latent function: An unintentional or unanticipated positive outcome of social institutions or policies.

Institutional racism: Policies and practices embedded in social institutions that consistently and disproportionately favor members of the dominant/majority group while systematically excluding/disadvantaging people of color.

outdoors, in easily visible spaces. Illegal activity is not more likely to occur in poorer areas; it is just easier to find. Second, police are rewarded for arrests that lead to convictions ("collars"), and they safely assume that poorer individuals (lacking high-quality counsel and vulnerable to plea bargain) are more likely to be convicted than affluent ones (Chambliss, 1999). Thus, while individual officers may not be racially or class-biased, their workplace incentives make targeting poor people and minorities for law enforcement a logical choice to help them gain better pay and advancement.

Data from the 2005 Police Public Contact Survey reveal that black men were 2.5 times more likely to be arrested than white males and twice as likely to be searched during a routine traffic stop. Hispanic men were 1.5 times more likely to be stopped and three times more likely to be searched (Kansas State University, 2012). Researchers in Minnesota who collected video data on 200,000 traffic stops in 2002 found that black, Hispanic, and Native American drivers were more likely than whites to be stopped and searched. Searches of whites were more likely to uncover contraband, however, so the most serious offenders were not being targeted (Associated Press, 2003).

Sometimes the "anything but race" (Bonilla-Silva, 2010) argument emerges if a black officer targets an African American for surveillance. Is that racial profiling? **Internalized racism** happens when people of color buy into the dominant ideology and view themselves as inferior (Yamato, 2001). Whether individual internalized racism motivates racial profiling or the structure of policing does so, officers of color are affected by the social forces supporting it. The study cited above that used data from the Police Public Contact Survey noted that the officer's race was not significant in the profiling patterns, demonstrating that institutionalized racism is powerful regardless of the individuals in the institution (Kansas State University, 2012).

▶ The Memphis Sanitation Workers' Strike began on February 11, 1968, when some 1,300 black sanitation workers walked off the job to protest poor treatment, discrimination, and dangerous working conditions. Support for the black workers was divided along racial lines, and the strike became a major civil rights event, attracting the attention of the national news media and Rev. Martin Luther King Jr. Why do you suppose the striking workers wore signs declaring "I *am* a man"?

a person's life. Health indicators such as mortality rates and mental health are positive for first-generation black and Latino immigrants, but these decline significantly by the third generation (Williams & Sternthall, 2010). Asian Americans in counties that are predominantly white have markedly better life expectancy and lower death rates than all other Asian Americans (Murray et al., 2006). It is not biology that contributes to racial disparities in health. This is a profoundly *social* problem.

Some racial minorities live a "third world" existence in the United States in terms of health outcomes like mortality, life expectancy, and infant mortality. Table 3.3 shows that African American infants are more than twice as likely as white infants to die before reaching the age of 1 year, and an entire decade of life expectancy separates white females and black males. This table (compiled before the Affordable Care Act took effect) shows that nearly one-third of Hispanics lack health insurance coverage. But blacks and Native Americans are more likely than Hispanics to lag behind whites on life expectancy, death rate, and health care utilization (Murray et al., 2006; Williams & Sternthall, 2010).

Color-blind ideology might suggest that socioeconomic or cultural factors such as types of food, exercise rates, and other lifestyle behaviors explain these differences. However,

ASK YOURSELF: Analyze the complex interplay among public opinion, data on the causes of a social problem, and the creation of public policy about immigration. Why have politicians been successful at using the "immigrants cause crime" argument to garner support for recent changes in the law even when evidence suggests otherwise? Are average voters fact-checking their politicians? Is this even easy to do? What social changes might facilitate this process?

Health by Race and Ethnicity

In the United States, belonging to a racial minority increases a person's likelihood of being unemployed, of having lower income and net worth, of being subjected to racial profiling, and of spending time in prison. It also shortens

Internalized racism: Feelings that occur in people of color when they buy into racist ideology that characterizes their own group as inferior—for example, when they believe that they themselves and/or other members of their group are not deserving of prestigious positions in society, or they assume that members of their group are prone to exhibiting stereotypical behaviors.

TABLE 3.3 U.S. Life Expectancy, Infant Mortality, and Lack of Health Insurance by Race and Ethnicity

Life Expectancy (2014)	
White female	81.4
Black female	78.4
White male	76.7
Black male	72.5
Infant Mortality Rate* (2013)	
Black	10.8
Native American	7.6
White	5.1
Mexican	4.9
Asian	4.1
No Health Insurance (2014) (%)	
Hispanic	34.1
Black	17.6
White	11.5

SOURCE: National Center for Health Statistics, Center for Disease Control, 2011.

*Infant deaths per 1,000 live births; black and white totals exclude Hispanics.

sociological evidence points toward racial discrimination. In fact, some health disparities between blacks and whites manifest most strongly in the highest socioeconomic categories (Graves, 2004). Figure 3.6 shows that the difference between whites and blacks in life expectancy at age 25 actually increases with education. Health researchers refer to a "diminishing returns" hypothesis, whereby African Americans receive fewer health advantages relative to whites with each step up in education (Williams & Sternthall, 2010) because of increased stress from daily discrimination that contributes to hypertension and other health problems (Geronimus et al., 2006). Racial discrimination has as great or greater effect on blood pressure than smoking, lack of exercise, and diet combined (Krieger & Sidney, 1996).

This is not to say that diet, exercise, and education do not matter, but we cannot ignore racial discrimination and segregation. Racial segregation has been linked to a host of health-related problems, due to its correlation with social disorder, concentration of poverty, lack of safe spaces for exercise, lack of infrastructure and trust in neighbors, and poor proximity to good-quality health care (Williams & Sternthall, 2010). Native American reservations and predominantly black neighborhoods, regardless of income level, have also been routinely targeted for toxic waste dumping and strip mining (Desmond & Emirbayer, 2010; Maher, 1998), in a form of **environmental racism**. An area of Louisiana known as "Cancer Alley" holds more than a dozen toxic waste sites concentrated near poor, minority communities (Bullard, 2000). A proposed rerouting of the Dakota Access Pipeline near Standing Rock reservation that led to a standoff between police and protesters—and prompted Rev. Jesse Jackson to identify it as "the ripest case of environmental racism I've seen in a long time"—is but just one example of many environmental health hazards facing communities of color in recent years (McKibben, 2016; Thorbecke, 2016). Contaminated water in Flint, Michigan, is another (Eligon, 2016). Even the best diet, exercise, and health insurance offer little protection against the dangers posed by such toxic risks.

Native American men have the highest rates of suicide, alcoholism, and death by automobile accident among all groups (Centers for Disease Control and Prevention [CDC], 2011). Because men in general are more likely to engage in risk taking, race and gender intersect in interesting ways in health. For example, while HIV diagnoses have been declining in white males, troubling increases in HIV are occurring among Native American and black men. Both black men and black women are more than twice as likely as their white counterparts to die from stroke and coronary heart disease as their white counterparts (CDC, 2011). Thus, particularly for Native Americans, blacks, and Hispanics, racism can shave years, sometimes a decade or more, from a life. Better education and socioeconomic resources alone cannot remedy these problems.

USING THEORY TO EXPLAIN RACIAL INEQUALITY: THE VIEWS FROM THE FUNCTIONALIST, SYMBOLIC INTERACTIONIST, AND CONFLICT PERSPECTIVES

3.3 Apply the functionalist, symbolic interactionist, and conflict perspectives to social policy on racial inequality.

Environmental racism: The process by which the dominant race in society is shielded from the most toxic/harmful environmental threats, while such health risks/hazards are located closest to neighborhoods where minority groups reside.

FIGURE 3.6 Life Expectancy at Birth, by Years of Education at Age 25, by Race and Sex, 2008

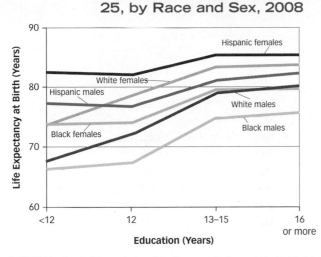

SOURCE: Reprinted with permission of the Center on Society and Health, Virginia Commonwealth University. *It Matters More to Health Than Ever Before.* Center on Society and Health Issue Brief, January 2014. Adapted from "Differences in Life Expectancy Due to Race and Educational Differences Are Widening, and Many May Not Catch Up," by S. Jay Olshansky et al., *Health Affairs*, 2012, *31*(8), pp. 1803–1813.

Many theories seek to explain the causes of racial inequality. For particular groups or geographic areas, some may be more powerful explanatory tools than others. Below we sample work in the functionalist, conflict, and symbolic interactionist perspectives and a few others.

Structural Functionalism: Assimilation

Structural functionalism assumes that the structures of society function to produce stability. Thus in a healthy society, where resources and rewards are appropriately distributed, racial and ethnic minorities that are poorly integrated throw off the equilibrium. Minorities must therefore assimilate into the dominant culture and become like the dominant group.

Robert E. Park developed the theory of the **race relations cycle** to explain the incorporation of various groups (mainly Southern and Eastern European immigrants) into U.S. society (Park & Burgess, 1924; Park, Burgess, & McKenzie, 1925). He identified four steps in this cycle: contact, competition, accommodation, and eventual assimilation (Feagin & Feagin, 2008). Park's model assumes that a society characterized by rules of law will eventually evaluate even a culturally different minority group fairly based on universal standards (Healey, 2009). During the accommodation step, the minority group essentially proves itself by adapting as required, and the dominant culture rewards its efforts until **assimilation** occurs.

Milton Gordon (1964) proposed seven stages of assimilation and described the institutions and cultural practices that a minority group is required to accommodate for full assimilation; these are listed in Table 3.4. Gordon developed his theory before the 1965 Immigration and Nationality Act, based on groups whose members encountered fewer barriers to assimilation than the darker-skinned and refugee populations who came after. His "straight-line assimilation" theory has since been challenged and refined. Portes and Rumbaut (2006) describe **segmented assimilation**, whereby a minority group embeds itself within a particular segment of the host society on one of three pathways: assimilation to the white middle class (traditional), "downward assimilation" to an impoverished class (e.g., West Indian immigrants to New York City; Waters 1999), or a hybrid path combining economic/structural assimilation with strong cultural ties to the family of origin. In an increasingly globalized world, a second-generation immigrant following this third path might have advantages in a job market that values intercultural familiarity and bilingualism. Thus straight-line assimilation may not be the most functional in the modern context.

Herbert J. Gans (1992) proposed the idea of **bumpy-line assimilation**, in which individuals can have "thick" or "thin" ties to their parents' culture of origin. And in her innovative study of three generations of Mexican American families, Jessica Vasquez (2011) identified two types that have "made it" by U.S. standards. Both were highly educated, fluent in English, and economically successful. "Thinned attachment" families had members who had intermarried and no longer spoke Spanish by the third generation, while "cultural maintenance" families were fluently bilingual, married within the group, and were visibly and culturally Hispanic. Vasquez's research shows that immigrants do not have to complete all seven of Gordon's stages to succeed in the dominant society.

Maintaining cultural heritage can even prevent some negative consequences of being a member of a minority

Race relations cycle: A pathway of incorporation into a host society that immigrants follow; includes four stages: contact, competition, accommodation, and eventual assimilation.

Assimilation: The act of literally "becoming like" the dominant group of the host society; in its purest sense, when assimilation is complete an immigrant would be indistinguishable from the dominant group in society.

Segmented assimilation: A theory acknowledging different segments of the host society into which an immigrant can assimilate (not just the white middle class).

Bumpy-line assimilation: A modification of early 20th-century assimilation theory that challenges the traditional linear one-way progression; instead, immigrants can become full participating members of the host society while still retaining certain ties to their nationalities of origin (incorporates notion of "thick" versus "thin" ties).

Experiencing Race and Ethnicity

Which Racism? Gender, Class, and Sexual Orientation Matter

It is impossible to review the data on racial inequality in income, health, criminal justice outcomes, and immigration policy without recognizing the ways gender, class, sexual orientation, and other forms of difference affect them. As Patricia Hill Collins (2008) argues, these statuses do not always interact with each other in predictable ways. While Hispanics are the racial/ethnic group most likely to be without health insurance in the United States, Hispanics do not face the same high infant mortality rates African Americans and Native Americans do (see Table 3.3). And at certain education levels, Asian American women are almost on par with or even outearn white women, but white men decisively dominate their Asian American counterparts (see Table 3.2).

Racial inequalities are conditioned not only by gender but also by social class. Particularly as measured by level of education, social class makes a tremendous difference in whether someone goes to prison (Pettit & Western, 2004). Michelle Alexander (2012) argues that policies like affirmative action, aimed at reducing racial inequality in earnings, do little to help members of the black underclass, more of whom are under some form of correctional control today than the numbers of blacks ever affected by slavery in the United States. The U.S. media identify "model minorities"

to differentiate between highly skilled educated migrants like those from India (NBC News, 2011) and unskilled laborers like those from Mexico, who conjure fear of crime even where data show it is unwarranted (Desmond & Emirbayer, 2010). Ethnic hierarchies that emerge within racial groups often have a basis in social class (O'Brien, 2008), leading some scholars to predict that certain ethnicities will soon be seen as "honorary whites" while others get left behind (Bonilla-Silva, 2010).

Immigration policy debates also cannot ignore differences like sexual orientation. While marriage to a native-born citizen can smooth the path to citizenship, those in same-sex partnerships do not have access to those same privileges if their country does not legally extend them federal marriage benefits.

Despite the complexity of intersectionality, there is great potential for social change when women, labor unions, and LGBT rights groups unite with antiracist activists around issues such as police brutality, hate crimes, and immigration law to pursue legislation

Marcos del Mazo/LightRocket/Getty Images

▶ Demonstration in Madrid, Spain, for the International Day Against Homophobia, Transphobia, and Biphobia. The banner reads, "Your hate does not fit in our streets." Do you think that in the United States, black, Hispanic, and Asian American gay, lesbian, and transgender people are doubly or triply stigmatized?

that benefits all groups. Many set aside their differences to come together for a Women's March in 2017, and made plans for future coalition work (Alter, 2017).

▶ **THINK ABOUT IT**

1. Is a woman always doubly disadvantaged if she is also a person of color? How are women affected differently from men by racism in criminal justice, income, and health?

2. Some propose that affirmative action policies in higher education should be altered to focus on social class and not race. Does your understanding of intersectionality suggest other options?

3. Social change advocacy groups fighting for racial equality are often diverse in class, gender, and sexual orientation. What strengths and challenges might such diversity present for these groups?

group in an unequal society. Children who lack nurturing kinship ties, maintained primarily through shared language, have consistently lower educational and socioeconomic outcomes than fluently bilingual children

(Fernandez-Kelly & Schauffler, 1994; Rumburger & Larson, 1998). Thus, while certain forms of assimilation are desirable, others may be detrimental, particularly in an increasingly global economy.

TABLE 3.4 Gordon's Seven Stages of Assimilation

Cultural assimilation	Adopt language, surname, style of dress, foods, holidays/celebrations, leisure activities of the dominant group.
Structural assimilation	Fully participate in economic structure—labor market, unions—educational opportunities/training, and other voluntary associations of the dominant group.
Marital assimilation	Intermarry in significant numbers with the dominant group.
Identification assimilation	See self as "American" above other ethnic or nation-state identifiers.
Attitude-receptional assimilation	Adopt the stereotyping and prejudice of the dominant group, deflecting stereotyping of own group.
Behavior-receptional assimilation	Refrain from intentional discrimination.
Civic assimilation	Vote and participate in the political structures of citizenship; embrace values of the new nation-state.

Policy Implications of Structural Functionalist Theories

Assimilation theory places the burden of avoiding racial/ethnic inequality on minority group members. Thus policy solutions that follow from it require immigrants to follow assimilation steps within a specified period. Citizenship tests that require English literacy and a basic knowledge of the U.S. political process reflect structural functionalist priorities, as do voluntary associations that teach English to immigrants and bilingual education programs. While nativist proposals to make English the official U.S. language have failed at the national level, many states have amended their constitutions to require "English only" (Costantini, 2012), despite evidence that immigrants benefit from being fluently bilingual.

Many critiques of assimilation theories rightly point out that even when minority groups play by all the rules, they face barriers erected by the dominant society (Feagin & Feagin, 2008). We must look outside structural functionalist theory for a more complete understanding of the minority group experience.

Conflict Theory

Conflict theory sees society as characterized by an imbalance of power and resources that the group in control will maintain to its advantage. It is thus not the minority group that needs to be changed but rather the dominant/majority group's exclusionary practices, intentional or not. Conflict theorists study institutional discrimination and suggest ways to restructure society and public policy to reduce it.

In *The Philadelphia Negro* (1995/1899), first published in 1899, W. E. B. Du Bois highlighted the poverty and unequal access to jobs and good health that African Americans experienced in the U.S. North. A highly educated black man (the first to receive a Ph.D. from Harvard) in the Jim Crow era, Du Bois understood firsthand that no matter how much a minority group attempted to assimilate, the majority group would resist its full inclusion. He demonstrated that unequal access to wealth and power gave blacks and whites vastly different understandings of the world and their place within it. The majority group's ideology, tied up in its sense of superiority, prevented it from seeing the disadvantaged group clearly. Du Bois (2003/1920) used the concept of the **veil** to describe this psychic distance between unequal racial groups.

Paul Marotta/Getty Images

▶ A mural in Philadelphia depicts black sociologist W. E. B. Du Bois. After graduating from Harvard, Du Bois conducted research in Philadelphia's black neighborhoods for his study *The Philadelphia Negro*. He is best known for *The Souls of Black Folk*, published in 1903, in which he famously proclaimed that "the problem of the Twentieth Century is the problem of the color-line."

Veil: A metaphor for the physical and psychic separation between the dominant/majority group and subordinate/minority groups.

His idea of **double consciousness** suggests that blacks possess a dual understanding of (1) themselves as fully capable human beings, and (2) the majority group's obscured perception of them. They use this double consciousness to negotiate their relationships with the majority group. For example, middle-class African Americans may adjust their dress and speech in commercial settings to minimize the possibility that they will be discriminated against during their transactions (Feagin & Sikes, 1994). They know they are not going to shoplift, but they anticipate the assumptions of people in power and adjust their behavior accordingly. The modern concept of **white privilege** (McIntosh, 2001)—whereby whites are unaware of the advantages their race gives them—owes an intellectual debt to Du Bois and his work. Other conflict theorists, such as Bob Blauner (1996), Charles Gallagher (2003a), and Andrew Hacker (2003), have examined how double consciousness creates "two worlds" that make it difficult to overcome majority group resistance to racial equality.

Contemporary conflict theorists also examine how rivalry between minority groups solidifies the dominant group's advantage. Edna Bonacich (1972) proposes a **split labor market theory** to describe how the (white) capitalist class divides the working class by race to keep workers from uniting to demand better pay and benefits. This analysis builds on Du Bois's concept of the **psychological wage**, whereby white capitalists simply make white workers feel superior to nonwhites to keep them from realizing they do not earn much more than the workers they look down upon (Roediger, 1991).

In an analysis of Japanese Americans, Bonacich and Modell (1980) developed the concept of the **middleman minority** to show how certain minority groups act as a buffer when they are elevated in status (though not rivaling the majority), protecting the majority from those on the bottom and serving as a scapegoat for the aggression of those below. In 1992, blacks in Los Angeles were angry about their powerlessness in the aftermath of the so-called Rodney King trial, in which officers were acquitted of police brutality in the beating of King, an African American, and they lashed out against the closest targets—Korean merchants in their own communities. From a conflict perspective, the tragedy of incidents like this is that the group on top, which makes money from both minority groups, remains unscathed. Middleman minority theory has implications for groups wanting to build alliances between minority groups in order to address their common interests.

Policy Implications of Conflict Theories

For conflict theorists, the focus is not on better training or cultural adaptation of minorities, but rather on adjusting institutional practices that have historically benefited whites so others who contribute to society can get greater access to society's benefits. Thus many related policy initiatives would benefit not only people of color but working-class and poor whites as well. Policy initiatives such as inheritance taxes and wealth creation accounts would seek to remedy the entrenched wealth inequalities that exist between whites and people of color (Conley, 1999; Oliver & Shapiro, 1995) but would also benefit asset-poor whites. Finding better solutions to drug offenses than prison would help to reduce the education and employment gap between whites and blacks. Conflict theorists since Du Bois have advocated for reduced criminalization of nonwhites, and groups like Books Not Bars and Let's Get Free, which organized a "Stop the Super-Jail" campaign in California, are multiracial coalitions that have worked toward this kind of change (Watkins, 2005). The United States is unique among nations in that individual states can bar felons from voting indefinitely, even after release from prison. Not surprisingly, this disproportionately affects African Americans, who make up 40% of ex-felons (Enten, 2012). Groups like Color of Change seek to address these and other racial power imbalances.

Symbolic Interactionist Theories

Symbolic interactionist theorists are interested in how the messages we internalize from socialization agents such as significant others and mass media affect the ways in which we, as everyday actors, maintain and perpetuate racial inequalities. Gordon Allport (1954) proposed the **contact hypothesis**, predicting that the more intergroup contact whites have with members of racial/ethnic

....

Double consciousness: African Americans' ability to see themselves both as active agents with full humanity and as they are seen through the eyes of whites who view them as inferior and problematic.

White privilege: The often unseen or unacknowledged benefits that members of the majority group receive in a society unequally structured by race.

Split labor market theory: The theory that white elites encourage divisions between working-class whites and blacks so that little unity can form between the two groups, preventing their coordinated revolt against exploitation.

Psychological wage: Feelings of racial superiority accorded to poor/working-class whites in the absence of actual monetary compensation for labor.

Middleman minority: A racial group that is not in the majority but is held up by the majority as a "positive" example of a minority and is used by those in power to pit minority groups against each other.

Contact hypothesis: The prediction that persons with greater degrees of cross-racial contact will have lower levels of racial prejudice than those with less contact.

The Myth of the "Model Minority": An Interview With Rosalind Chou

Many adults in the United States perceive Asian Americans as the "model minority" and even admire and covet this group's perceived educational and economic successes. In your book The Myth of the Model Minority *(Chou & Feagin, 2008), what types of stigma, discrimination, and prejudice did your young interviewees report facing?* My interviewees each faced racial prejudice and discrimination that ranged from racialized verbal taunts and mocking to violent physical attacks. In some cases the discrimination was subtle and respondents felt excluded or invisible. Other times, they were overtly targeted for their race or ethnicity.

How did they manage the stress these incidents caused them, and in what ways did society's ignorance about Asian Americans make it difficult for them to manage that stress more effectively? Most of the Asian Americans I spoke with were ill equipped to manage the stress. Often their families preferred to not talk about it, discuss their feelings, or "rock the boat." They did not want to come off as "problem minorities." The stigma associated with African Americans and their collective resistance against racial oppression seemed undesirable to many Asian Americans, especially if they were first-generation Americans. Strikingly, many respondents suppressed memories, chose to turn off emotions, and/or internalized the mistreatment, with alarming effects on emotional and psychological growth. On the rare occasions that my respondents did seek help, they were often misunderstood or brushed aside. Some who went to their teachers when they were bullied in school were asked to "toughen up." One student sought help from a school counselor to deal with overwhelming stress, but the counselor was more interested in the student's academic achievement, stereotyping her as a "model minority."

In your analysis, what are some of the root causes of anti-Asian racism and negative Asian American mental health outcomes as social problems? The root cause of anti-Asian racism is that racism is embedded in the foundation of our society. We are not in a "postracial" society. Anti-Asian sentiment continues because Asians are still stereotyped as "others," "foreign," and "alien." The "model minority" stereotyping has been used to create a hierarchy of people of color and Asians, and Asian Americans sometimes believe the stereotype, making it more difficult to form racial coalitions. Racial discrimination, stigma, and prejudice have solidly documented negative outcomes on mental health. Combined with a lack of services, reluctance to talk about racial discrimination within the Asian American community, and internalization of negative stereotypes, these effects produce alarming rates of depression and suicide for Asian Americans.

▶ Sociologist Rosalind S. Chou is a native of Florida, where her parents settled after emigrating from Taiwan in the 1970s. She is coauthor, with Joe R. Feagin, of *The Myth of the Model Minority: Asian Americans Facing Racism.* She is also the author of *Asian American Sexual Politics: The Construction of Race, Gender, and Sexuality* and *Asian Americans on Campus: Racialized Space and White Power.*

What concrete solutions can be put into place to deal with anti-Asian racism and its victims more effectively? Multiracial coalitions are imperative to move forward. Many Asian Americans are not aware they share experiences of racial discrimination with each other and with other groups. We have to continue to educate all our citizens about our racial past and present. Awareness and understanding of the racist foundation of the United States will help combat the inequality and disparity related to discrimination. Asian Americans must also develop counternarratives to the racialized stereotypes that exist.

▶ **THINK ABOUT IT:** How can even seemingly positive stereotypes and prejudices (whether aimed at Asian Americans or other groups) create unintended negative consequences?

minority groups, the less likely they are to be prejudiced. Empirical testing has consistently revealed that not just any contact is effective, however. Intergroup contact in which members are of equal status and contact is regular and sanctioned by an authority is more likely than other forms of contact to reduce racial prejudice (Jackman & Crane, 1986).

The positive impact of interracial contact is increasingly muted by the dominance of color blindness, however. Cross-racial friends often ignore or joke about race, not considering it a topic for serious exploration and leaving the white friend with the same beliefs as before (Korgen, 2002). The contact hypothesis was also proposed before the expansion of mass media and the Internet. To the extent these venues substitute for face-to-face contacts, they can have both positive (O'Brien & Korgen, 2007) and negative (Gallagher, 2003b) effects on users' racial outlooks.

Symbolic interactionist theories examine how racial messages affect individual performance and how people view themselves. Claude Steele (1997; Steele & Aronson, 1995) coined the term **stereotype threat** to describe how minorities' self-concepts and performance on tasks are harmed by societal stereotypes that portray them as less competent than other racial groups. Steele's test subjects were told either that their group tended to perform well on a test or that their group tended to perform poorly. Individual test scores reflected what subjects were told. Similarly, we saw above that internalized racism occurs when people of color come to believe they deserve mistreatment (Yamato, 2001) or accept stereotypes about their own group. These negative messages that permeate the culture in everyday racism known as **microaggressions** have become a focus of protests and teach-ins on many U.S. college campuses where students of color have been made to feel unwelcome (Sue, 2010). Student movements like those at the University of Missouri where the football team went on strike were aimed at drawing attention to these "slights," which can have powerful negative psychological and societal effects (Binkley & Whack, 2015; Chun & Evans, 2012).

The symbolic interactionist perspective is also useful for considering the **costs of privilege** for the majority group. For example, despite substantial material advantages, whites lose out on the interactional benefits of being bicultural/multicultural and able to get along with diverse groups—a marketable skill in the global economy. Internalized superiority can also sometimes encourage excessive risk taking; whites are more likely than other racial groups to binge drink and to die from drug-related causes (CDC, 2011). The advantages of racial privilege far outweigh the costs on the macro level, but looking at the micro level reveals the complex ways privilege and advantage interact in everyday lives. This vantage point also allows for optimism, because change can begin if we simply start the process of unlearning the detrimental aspects of our own racial/ethnic conditioning.

Policy Implications of the Symbolic Interactionist Perspective

The symbolic interactionist perspective suggests the need for more equal-status interracial contact with open and honest dialogue about race and racism. Educational settings are ideal, and the earlier the better. Advocates of antiracist education face challenges in getting schools to do more than just "celebrate multiculturalism" or promote diversity in token ways. Publishers such as Rethinking Schools are trying to make this happen (Kailin, 2002). Symbolic interactionist research also underscores the need to revamp media portrayals of people of color. Internalized racism is difficult to avoid when the news media are more likely to present African Americans in deviant criminal roles than as "Good Samaritan" figures (Feagin, 2000). The NAACP and the Anti-Defamation League try to raise awareness about media biases, but consumers must exercise their buying power and send a message to media executives that they will not tolerate racially biased programming.

ASK YOURSELF: What are some common media messages about racial/ethnic minorities, such as African Americans, Asian Americans, Hispanics, and Native Americans, and how might internalized racism based on such stereotypes play out specifically for these groups in real life?

SPECIALIZED THEORIES ABOUT RACIAL INEQUALITY

3.4 Apply specialized theories of racism.

Other theorists have approached racial inequality from more innovative vantage points, such as those discussed below.

Stereotype threat: The tendency of individuals to perform better or worse on standardized tests depending on what they have been told about their group's abilities.

Microaggressions: Everyday acts (intentional or unintentional) that serve to marginalize persons due to perceived subordinate group status.

Costs of privilege: Experiences that members of the majority group may miss out on due to racial isolation and limited worldviews.

Spatial Mismatch Theory

William Julius Wilson's (1978, 1987, 1996, 2009) research highlights the conditions faced by the worst-off African Americans. His **spatial mismatch theory** shows how deindustrialization left blacks without employment in the inner cities. With factory work, a man with barely a high school diploma could still do quite well for himself, but in the global transition from industry to a service/information-based economy, jobs moved to the suburbs, where many poor blacks could not afford to live. Such jobs also require education beyond high school, which poor blacks could also not easily afford. Furthermore, Wilson shows how federal government housing and transportation policies upended previously stable low-income black communities, changing family structure and culture. The **feminization of poverty** occurs because of black men's joblessness rather than because of any characteristic of black culture. It becomes a rational choice for poor women to avoid marriage when pregnant (Edin & Kefalas, 2005), yet children with one parent face disadvantages compounded by low socioeconomic status. And as long as work disappears, they will confront the same conditions as their parents, as the cycle continues (Wilson, 1996).

Answering those who blame black culture for racial inequality, Wilson points to structural and economic factors. While many solutions flowing from his work as an adviser to the federal government and advocate for raising the minimum wage seem to mirror those of conflict theory (they benefit the poor as well as minorities), Wilson's focus is less on an oppressive dominant group and more on impersonal structural forces. Thus he believes his public policy framing will be more palatable to those weary of race-specific policies.

Color-Blind Racism

We have seen above that **color-blind racism**—the tendency to focus on "anything but race" to explain racial inequality—has actually made it increasingly difficult to address the problem. Bonilla-Silva (2001, 2013) innovatively combines quantitative data with in-depth interviews to demonstrate how whites avoid the appearance of being racially prejudiced on standard survey instruments, while in more candid interviews they reveal troubling points of view conforming to a popular ideology increasingly resistant

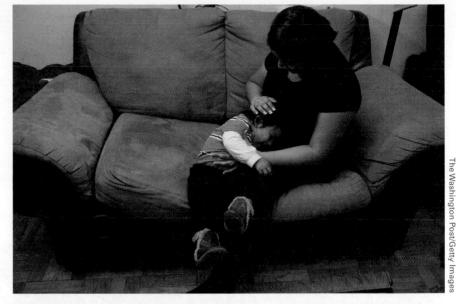

▶ Victoria Perez Cruz, 18, is an honor roll student at Northwestern High School in Prince George's County and a single mother of two-year-old Christian, who attends a nursery in the school during the day. They cuddle on their sofa in their apartment. Black and Hispanic single mothers are among those hit hardest by poverty in the United States. Do you think that the media ignore their situation?

to antiracist public policy. He identifies four means by which people resist efforts to reduce racial inequalities: (1) abstract liberalism (blindly trusting that nation-states lean toward equity without any government interference), (2) cultural racism (blaming black culture's assumed values in regard to work ethic, education, and family structure), (3) naturalization (assuming people are hardwired to avoid other races, so public policy can achieve nothing), and (4) minimization (assuming people of color are exaggerating claims of discrimination). Common personal stories ("I didn't get that job because of a black man") and rhetorical strategies ("Some of my best friends are black") underlie this powerful racial ideology.

Bonilla-Silva also hypothesizes that as Asian Americans and U.S. Hispanics become a more sizable presence, some will be incorporated as "honorary whites" to support color-blind ideology. Other empirical analyses support this prediction (O'Brien, 2008; Yancey, 2003). Bonilla-Silva (2013, p. 307) calls on white people to "begin challenging color-blind nonsense from within" and to avoid

....

Spatial mismatch theory: The theory that the movement of jobs away from central cities in the postindustrial era left many African Americans without employment.

Feminization of poverty: The trend of poverty being concentrated disproportionately in female-headed single-parent families.

Color-blind racism: A type of racism that avoids overt arguments of biological superiority/inferiority and instead uses ideologies that do not always mention race specifically.

language of "equal opportunity," demanding equality of results instead. Rather than avoiding "bad neighborhoods" and poor-quality schools, he asserts, whites should remain there and join people of color in refusing to accept substandard resources and conditions. Bonilla-Silva advocates **antiracism**, the active struggle against racism. As Tatum (2003) explains, antiracists are different from both active racists and passive racists (who allow racism to continue without confronting it). Antiracists actively walk against the flow of racism—obviously quite a challenge, yet necessary to combat the inertia of color blindness.

ASK YOURSELF: According to sociological definitions, is it "racist" for white families to move out of the city in pursuit of a better quality of education for their school-age children? What are some antiracist alternatives such families might be able to pursue instead? What would need to change to encourage more whites to do so?

Antiracism: The active struggle against racism in everyday life (micro) and/or institutionally (macro).

SOCIAL CHANGE: WHAT CAN YOU DO?

 3.5 Identify steps toward social change in racial inequality.

There are a number of ways you can get involved in working to solve the social problem of racial inequality. Using **micropolitics**—that is, simply challenging friends and coworkers in everyday conversation—you can make a difference on a larger scale than you might expect (Pincus, 2011). In addition, you might get involved with one or more of the many organizations devoted to addressing racial inequality, a few of which are described briefly below.

Color of Change

Color of Change is an Internet-based organization founded in 2005 after the race and class atrocities of Hurricane Katrina's aftermath became known. Its e-mail alerts and blogs organize petitions to pressure organizations and political leaders to act on specific issues of concern to African Americans and their allies. This group favors many of the solutions discussed in the conflict theory section of this chapter. For instance, Color of Change asked its members to contact their legislators to end "stop and frisk" procedures and low-level marijuana arrests in Manhattan that disproportionately target people of color (and poor whites). It also exposes states and organizations trying to curtail voter registration among people of color, the very old, and the very young. Since the founding of Black Lives Matter in 2013, it has also worked to alert its members of any police misconduct and helped to support

Mario Tama/Getty Images

▶ College students on the NAACP's "Vote Hard" bus tour encourage black residents of a housing project in Selma, Alabama, to vote. Why is it important to vote? How can voting in presidential elections help minority communities?

local BLM activists where incidents occur. You can sign up for e-mail alerts and participate in many petitions and citizen actions at http://www.colorofchange.org.

National Association for the Advancement of Colored People (NAACP)

Founded in 1909, the NAACP is the world's oldest civil rights organization; one of its cofounders was sociologist W. E. B. Du Bois. Anyone can become a member. This organization takes stands on practically

Micropolitics: An individual's use of his or her own personal sphere of influence to affect social change.

all the problems of racial inequality discussed in this chapter—health care, environmental racism, criminal justice, economics, and even the symbolic interactionist concern of media representation—and issues action alerts to encourage members to contact their legislative representatives. You can visit the website to join the national organization (http://www.naacp.org), but there are also more than 2,000 local chapters and an active college/youth division, so it is easy to get involved in regular meetings and actions.

▶▶ National Immigrant Solidarity Network (NISN)

Like Color of Change, National Immigrant Solidarity Network is a relatively new organization, founded in 2003, and does much of its work through e-mail action alerts to members. It is easy to get involved just by pointing and clicking (http://www.immigrantsolidarity .org). However, NISN also has four local offices in Chicago, Los Angeles, New York, and Washington, D.C., and it organizes marches and days of action in these and other areas. NISN supports the Dream Act and rejects

militarization of the border, for example. Joining is a way to stay informed on issues of concern to immigrants, to get educated on your rights during a police stop, and to take action if you choose.

▶▶ Community-Based Literacy Organizations

Most immigrants to the United States desperately want to learn English, yet there are not enough opportunities for them to do so with their grueling work schedules. Many adult literacy centers around the country are nonprofit, volunteer-based organizations looking for tutors to help immigrants with English-language skills as well as with civics education needed to pass citizenship tests. Using the Literacy Information and Communication System's literacy directory (http://www.literacydirectory.org), you can locate such a community-based center near you. Many towns and cities also have nonprofit community resource centers for refugees, where English-language and citizenship skills are taught by volunteers. If you are interested in hands-on social service and volunteer work, this would be a great place to start.

WHAT DOES AMERICA THINK?

Questions About Race and Ethnicity From the General Social Survey

▶▶ Turn to the beginning of the chapter to compare your answers to those of the total population.

1. Do you feel discriminated against because of your race?

YES: 3.8%

NO: 96.2%

2. What is the racial makeup of your workplace?

ALL WHITE: 19.3%

MOSTLY WHITE: 44.5%

HALF WHITE, HALF BLACK: 31.3%

MOSTLY BLACK: 3.9%

ALL BLACK: 1%

3. Should a homeowner be able to decide who they sell their house to based on race?

OWNER DECIDES: 19.5%

CAN'T DISCRIMINATE: 77.4%

NEITHER: 3.1%

4. Blacks overcome prejudice without favors.

AGREE: 62.5%

DISAGREE: 21.6%

NEITHER AGREE NOR DISAGREE: 15.9%

5. Should the number of immigrants to America be increased, remain the same, or be decreased?

INCREASED: 17.7%

REMAIN THE SAME: 40.2%

DECREASED: 42.1%

SOURCE: National Opinion Research Center, University of Chicago.

CHAPTER SUMMARY

 3.1 Define race and ethnicity in the new millennium.

Today, "Race" is understood to be a social construct that varies across time and place—it is a human invention tied to relationships of power and privilege and continues to have measurable consequences for minority groups worldwide. Groups that were once smaller minorities are now growing. Individual identities and experiences do not always fit neatly into socially defined racial and ethnic categories.

3.2 Discuss patterns and trends linking race and ethnicity to immigration, income, criminal justice, and health.

Racial discrimination exists at both individual and institutional levels and can be overt or covert, intentional or unintentional. Large gaps in income, rates of imprisonment, and health exist between whites (the majority group) and people of color (minority groups) that are not attributable to differences in education, socioeconomic status, or criminal activities alone. Sociological evidence points us away from color-blind explanations for these differences and toward an examination of institutional structures that produce these racial inequalities. Immigration policies, the ways in which residents of the host society treat immigrants, and global political and economic changes affect racial and ethnic relationships in any society. The United States has had periods of openness and acceptance of immigrants as well as periods of repression and suspicion of them.

 3.3 Apply the functionalist, symbolic interactionist, and conflict perspectives to social policy on racial inequality.

Structural functionalists assume smoothly functioning societies characterized by balance, equilibrium, and meritocracy, and regard the assimilation process as the key for reducing racial/ethnic tensions. Assimilation theories better explain the experiences of pre-1965 European immigrants, however, and immigrants in today's globalized world often fare better when they both assimilate and retain some cultural traditions. Rather than focusing on minorities' efforts to assimilate, conflict theorists analyze the structures created and sustained by the dominant group that forestall equality, such as keeping workers divided by their own interethnic and interracial tensions. The policy solutions conflict theorists advocate thus benefit minorities as well as poor and working-class whites. Symbolic interactionists look on a micro level, explaining how racial ideology is socialized into the dominant group and internalized by minority groups, who may begin to believe in their own supposed inferiority.

 3.4 Apply specialized theories of racism.

Wilson's spatial mismatch theory identifies impersonal structural forces, like global shifts from industry to service economies, as the major cause of contemporary racial inequalities. Bonilla-Silva's focus on color-blind racism demonstrates how we rationalize racial inequality in the social structure by convincing ourselves that a certain degree of separation is "natural," and/or that minorities bring on their own problems. These seemingly nonracial ideologies perpetuate racism and prevent voters from supporting policies that explicitly address racial inequality.

3.5 Identify steps toward social change in racial inequality.

Organizations such as Color of Change, the NAACP, NISN, and local literacy groups all offer opportunities to get involved. Simply practicing the micropolitics of change by opening up conversations about racial/ethnic inequalities and their sociological roots with friends, family, and coworkers can also have an indirect yet powerful impact.

KEY TERMS

antiracism 74

assimilation 67

bumpy-line assimilation 67

color-blind racism 73

contact hypothesis 70

costs of privilege 72

double consciousness 70

environmental racism 66

ethnicity 55

feminization of poverty 73

ideologies 54

individual discrimination 60

institutional discrimination 60

institutional racism 64

internalized racism 65

Jim Crow 64

latent function 64

manifest function 64

microaggressions 72

micropolitics 74

middleman minority 70

minority group 56

psychological wage 70

race 54

race relations cycle 67

racialization 57

racism 54

segmented assimilation 67

spatial mismatch theory 73

split labor market theory 70

stereotype threat 72

symbolic ethnicity 55

tokenistic fallacy 59

veil 69

white privilege 70

$SAGE edge™ **Want a better grade?**

Get the tools you need to sharpen your study skills. Access practice quizzes, eFlashcards, video, and multimedia at
http://edge.sagepub.com/trevino2e

4 GENDER

Katie Ann Hasson

▶▶▶ Girls at the Women's March on Washington wearing pink capes that say, "I am the Future." How will gender play a role in these girls' future lives?

Investigating Gender: My Story

Katie Ann Hasson

Living with my sister, mother, and grandmother as a teenager made me very aware of the taken-for-granted, gendered assumptions about who should do what in the home and outside it that I saw playing out in other families. In my first year of college, I discovered sociology and feminism almost simultaneously, and quickly shifted from my planned physics concentration to sociology. When gender studies was added as a new concentration, I became one of the first class of five to receive a
gender studies degree from the University of Chicago. After working for a few years as a domestic violence crisis counselor/advocate, I returned to school and earned my doctorate at UC Berkeley, again combining sociology with an emphasis in women, gender, and sexuality. For 5 years, I taught classes in sociology and gender studies at the University of Southern California.

LEARNING OBJECTIVES

4.1 Define gender.

4.2 Describe gender inequality and the study of gender as a social problem.

4.3 Identify gender problems on college campuses and beyond.

4.4 Apply the functionalist, conflict, and symbolic interactionist perspectives to the problem of gender inequality.

4.5 Apply queer theory's interdisciplinary perspective to gender inequality.

4.6 Identify steps toward social change in gender inequality.

WHAT DO YOU THINK?

Questions About Gender from the General Social Survey

1. It is better for men to work and women to tend home.
   - ☐ AGREE
   - ☐ DISAGREE

2. Most women really want a home and kids.
   - ☐ AGREE
   - ☐ DISAGREE

3. Women are not suited for politics.
   - ☐ AGREE
   - ☐ DISAGREE

4. Are you for or against the preferential hiring of women?
   - ☐ FOR
   - ☐ AGAINST

5. The mother working doesn't hurt children.
   - ☐ AGREE
   - ☐ DISAGREE

▶▶ Turn to the end of the chapter to view the results for the total population.

SOURCE: National Opinion Research Center, University of Chicago.

WAVES OF PROTEST AND PINK HATS

On January 21, 2017, an estimated 4 million women and men in cities and towns across the United States participated in Women's Marches to support women's rights, environmental issues, racial justice, and LGBTQ rights in what has been called the largest single-day protest in U.S. history (Chenoweth & Pressman, 2017; Dow et al., 2017). In doing so, they continued a tradition of feminist and other mass marches and political actions, and potentially signaled a new multi-issue, intersectional approach to mass feminist and social justice activism.

Over the past 100 years, women in the United States have achieved the right to vote (1920), were granted legal access to contraception regardless of marital status (1963) and legal abortion (1973), and gained legal protections against gender discrimination and sexual harassment after the mass entry of (middle-class) women into the labor force in the 1970s. These and other improvements represent dramatic progress toward gender equality. But many would agree that there is still much more to do. Men still earn more than women, hold the majority of political offices, and sit at the top levels of most companies. Many women still lack affordable access to health care and child care and experience high rates of sexual assault and domestic violence. Furthermore, it depends on which women you are considering. Women's economic success, health, and political participation look vastly different when race, class, sexuality, and immigration are taken into account, which highlights the importance of taking an **intersectional approach** to examining inequality.

What can we learn by considering gender inequality as a social problem? Is gender itself a social problem, or only the inequality that results from gender? Is it even possible to separate gender from gender inequality, or is inequality the inevitable result of distinguishing people as men and women? These are some of the questions we'll explore in this chapter, but first we need to understand exactly what we're talking about when we speak of gender.

DEFINING GENDER INEQUALITY

4.1   Define gender.

Do you wake up in the morning and think about your gender as a pressing social problem? Do you think about it much at all? If you live safely within the boundaries of what your particular society defines as "normal" for gender, you probably have the luxury of not thinking a lot about it in general, let alone as a pressing social problem. If you are a person who, in the words of Kate Bornstein (1994), is "let down" by the gender system, you probably *do* think of gender as a social problem that needs to be solved. In fact, all of us—*everyone* in society, regardless of where we are in or outside the gender hierarchy—can see gender as a social problem, and we can argue that at some point the gender system has let us down. What exactly does that mean?

First, what is **gender**? A common definition says gender is the social meaning layered on top of our sex categories. In this way of thinking, there are two discrete sex categories: You can be female or you can be male; you cannot be both. Once we are assigned a sex category, usually at birth, the way we are treated in the world and the way we think about ourselves are shaped by it. Look around a hospital nursery at all the babies with their pink or blue hats and blankets. There's nothing about the anatomy of a baby boy that requires him to wear a blue hat, but already gender has become important: In our culture at this time it tells us that male babies should wear blue and female babies pink. In other times and other places, male and female babies would wear completely different colors. It is precisely those social variations that make up gender—the social meanings we impose onto biological reality.

···

ASK YOURSELF: Can you think of other ways in which we begin to treat infants and young children differently based on sex category?

···

When we say the colors associated with male and female babies vary across time and culture, we are

···

Intersectional approach: A sociological approach that examines how gender as a social category intersects with other social statuses such as race, class, and sexuality.

Gender: The social meanings layered on top of sex categories.

▶ Three brothers in their bedroom with their rustic bunk bed and belongings. A girl in her bedroom with a stuffed pink unicorn. Why do you think boys say that blue is their favorite color? Why is pink considered a feminine color? How do companies market products like toys and clothes differently to boys and girls?

acknowledging that gender is socially constructed. That is, like many aspects of social life, gender is a concept created and modified over time and across cultures to produce a certain account of reality. Whether it has an underlying biological reality based on sex is less important than that we *believe* in that underlying reality. If we believe gender is real, then our beliefs make it real through our actions and assumptions. When a baby is born and placed into the male sex category and a blue hat is put on his head, everyone will treat him in a particular way based on belief in the underlying reality of gender. Because of the way we treat this blue-hatted baby, he probably will, in fact, grow up to be masculine, making our belief in his gender become reality.

Supporting the argument that gender is socially constructed are the many variations in the ways different cultures understand gender. In the United States men generally don't wear skirts, but in Scotland and India they do. In the United States, once women reach puberty, we expect that certain parts of their bodies be free of hair—usually their legs and armpits, but also their faces—and that their breasts be covered and supported by bras. But in other parts of the world, women don't shave; nor do they wear bras. These and other variations in the meanings assigned to biological sex categories convince us that gender is socially constructed.

This seems fairly straightforward, but some scholars go further and argue that not only is gender socially constructed, but biological sex is as well. From this perspective, our belief that there are two distinct types of people in the world—males and females—is just a belief, called **sexual dimorphism**, and does not represent objective reality. As evidence, scholars cite the ways in which sex has been

defined differently across times and places. Today in the United States, sex assignment happens at birth based on the infant's genitals and is largely in the hands of medical professionals. Some infants are born with genitals that cannot easily be categorized as male or female. In the past, doctors have decided where to assign those infants, often performing surgeries to make the genitals match the assigned category. This is what happens to many **intersex** individuals, those born with anatomical or genetic ambiguity about their biological sex. Their existence is important evidence for the social construction of sex, because it suggests there are not just two kinds of bodies but a continuum of different kinds (Fausto-Sterling, 2000).

In ancient Greece, sex was seen as existing along a spectrum, with men at the top and women and other lesser beings, like dwarves and slaves, at the bottom. Females were viewed not as wholly different sorts of persons from males, but rather as inferior versions of males. The ancient Greeks had knowledge of external and internal anatomy, but their beliefs about sex categories led them to understand male and female anatomy differently. While we think of a penis and a vagina as two different sexual organs, the ancient Greeks saw them as the same organ; a vagina was merely an inverted penis. Ovaries and gonads were the same organ in slightly different

Sexual dimorphism: The belief that there are two discrete types of people—male and female—who can be distinguished on the basis of real, objective, biological criteria.

Intersex: Born with some range of biological conditions that make sex category ambiguous.

versions. This is just one of the many ways cultures have made sense of our underlying biological reality. The wide biological variability that exists is too complex to be summarized in just two categories, suggesting that sex categories are socially constructed just as gender is.

People who identify as **transgender**—whose gender identity differs from the gender they were assigned at birth—reveal another aspect of gender as socially constructed. The term **cisgender** describes individuals whose gender identities match the categories they were assigned at birth. Transgender people may make a number of changes in order to live as the gender they identify with, including changing their names and pronouns (he/him, she/her, or even gender-neutral pronouns like they, zie, or hir), appearance (including clothes, hair, binding breasts), or bodies (by taking hormones or having surgery). Depending on the laws in their state, they may also be able to change their legal gender. The experiences of transgender people challenge assumptions that gender is a direct expression of biology that does not change: Not all male infants become men, not all female infants become women.

► Fa'afafine are people who identify themselves as a third gender in Samoan society. Tafi Toleafoa, who cuts a striking tall figure as a fa'afafine, is biologically male but was raised as a girl. Toleafoa often wears a plumeria blossom in her hair. What do you see as the social functions of a third gender?

FEMINISM, MEN, AND THE STUDY OF GENDER AS A SOCIAL PROBLEM

4.2 Describe gender inequality and the study of gender as a social problem.

While gender is certainly not the only social problem we can regard as socially constructed, it is unique in also being an identity to which many of us are deeply attached. What parts of your personality, behaviors, beliefs, and feelings are due to your gender, and what parts exist independent of that identity? For some theorists, as we'll discover below, every part of us and every interaction we have is touched by gender. They believe ungendering ourselves might be impossible. Would it be at all desirable?

It's easier to see gender as a social problem if we focus more specifically on gender inequality. Gender is an important source of social identity for many people, meaning it forms an important basis for how we think about ourselves as people. It is also a category that creates and sustains inequality. **Gender inequality** is the way in which the meanings assigned to sex and gender as social categories create disparities in resources such as income, power, and status. In most—if not all—societies, those categorized as female are at a disadvantage relative to those categorized as males. There are many explanations for these inequalities, some of which we explore below. But first we should consider the relationship between gender as a concept and gender inequality.

ASK YOURSELF: Do you think it is possible to ungender ourselves? Would getting rid of gender as a social category be a good thing for society? If you believe that both sex and gender are socially constructed categories, can they take very different forms? John Stoltenberg (2006) imagines a society in which sex hormones become "individuality inducers" and sex organs like the penis and clitoris are seen as different forms of the same basic anatomy. What would gender look like in such a society, or would it exist at all?

Transgender: Gender identity differs from the sex category assigned at birth.

Cisgender: Gender identity matches the sex category assigned at birth.

Gender inequality: The way in which the meanings assigned to sex and gender as social categories create disparities in resources such as income, power, and status.

For some, gender is a social category that makes distinctions between people, but these distinctions do not necessarily have to lead to inequality. Saying that women are more nurturing and men less so is a distinction, but we can keep gender as a social identity and still reduce gender inequality by valuing nurturing as much as we value qualities considered masculine, like rationality and aggressiveness. Women can go on being more nurturing and men more rational; we just have to make sure we place equal value and importance on the qualities seen as masculine and feminine.

On the other hand, some argue that every time we make a distinction, an inequality is already implied. It is not just that women are seen as more nurturing than men; nurturing, if it reflects gender categories, will always be considered inferior to whatever qualities are seen as masculine. From this perspective, the whole point of gender as a social category is to distribute power by creating and sustaining inequality. Getting rid of gender inequality then requires getting rid of gender as a social category and all the distinctions it entails.

These two perspectives lead in different directions when we examine gender as a social problem. The first suggests we can address gender inequality separately from the concept of gender as a whole. Gender is not a social problem in and of itself; rather, gender inequality is. But if gender distinctions always imply gender inequality, as in the second view, then gender itself *is* the social problem. Gender and inequality go hand in hand, and if we want to reduce inequality, we must attack the problem at its root—the existence of gender. Keep these two perspectives and their implications in mind as we further explore gender as a social problem.

One sure sign that enough people in society consider something to be a social problem is the development of a social movement to solve it. Feminism is both a body of knowledge and a social movement that addresses the problem of gender inequality, seeking to end it through a wide variety of approaches. If women are usually seen as the disadvantaged group, it makes sense they would be motivated to end gender inequality. But feminists are not only motivated to improve the status of women, they highlight the ways that our current gender hierarchy harms everyone.

....

ASK YOURSELF: Pick one of the perspectives on the relationship between gender and gender inequality described above. Imagine you are engaged in a debate to defend this perspective. What evidence might you use in support of your position? Now imagine what evidence you might use for the opposite perspective.

....

For example, men in the United States do not live as long on average as women, are more likely to die a violent death, and commit suicide at higher rates than do women. Some men who label themselves feminists point to the ways in which the demands of masculinity damage men, even as it may benefit them in other ways. Masculinity leads men to engage in risk-taking behaviors that can put their lives and health in danger. It can make meaningful and intimate relationships with other men and women difficult by inserting the constant need to demonstrate dominance and control. For these reasons, most scholars and activists who consider gender a social problem see it as a social problem for women *and* men. The gender system lets all of us down, though often in very different ways.

LOOKING AT GENDER ON CAMPUS AND BEYOND

4.3 Identify gender problems on college campuses and beyond.

Can the gender binary itself be a source of inequality? To examine this question, we can think about areas of society in which we make the division of men and women socially important. There are plenty of examples of this on any college campus. We have single-gender dorm rooms and even entire dorms, separate men's and women's bathrooms and locker rooms, separate men's and women's sports teams. On the other hand, gender-neutral or mixed-gender facilities and teams can be seen as controversial.

Many colleges used to be single-sex. At the turn of the 20th century, 29% of college students were women, and 40% of those women attended all-women colleges (Goldin & Katz, 2010). Those who opposed college education for women argued that women weren't capable of higher learning and that too much education conflicted with their roles as wives and mothers. Some even claimed that the strains of education would cause infertility! The number of coeducational colleges increased steadily over time, then increased sharply in the 1960s and '70s. In 1976, the U.S. Military Academy and Naval Academy first admitted women. Columbia University, in part because of its relationship with all-women Barnard College, was the last of the Ivy League universities to admit women as undergraduates—in 1983! Today, there are very few single-sex colleges remaining. Nationwide, 57% of bachelor's degrees are awarded to women and women have outnumbered men on college campuses for the past few decades. For comparison, in 1970, only 43% of bachelor's degrees were awarded to women (National Center for Education Statistics, 2015). While there are more women than men in college, these figures vary greatly by region, type of institution, race, and income level. In what ways do we continue to organize our college campuses according to gender, and what effects does this have? How does the gender binary itself become a social problem in these spaces, particularly for individuals who do not fit expected gender categories?

Two Teams? The Gender Binary

For much of the 20th century, women's participation in athletics was discouraged and very few sports opportunities existed for women. This changed dramatically in the 1970s when, encouraged by the feminist movement and many (white, middle-class) women's entry into the labor force, there was a surge in women's interest and participation in sports. The ability of girls and women to participate in sports at school was guaranteed in 1972 by Title IX.

Title IX states, "No person in the United States shall, on the basis of sex, be excluded from participation in, be denied the benefits of, or be subjected to discrimination under any education program or activity receiving Federal financial assistance." Issues covered by Title IX include discrimination in admissions, sexual harassment, and students who are pregnant. Title IX has had perhaps its biggest impact on schools in the area of athletics because it requires that all schools that receive federal funding provide parity for women's and men's athletic opportunities. In 1970, prior to Title IX, there were a total of 16,000 women intercollegiate athletes. For the 2015–2016 academic year, there were 214,000 women and 278,000 men participating in college sports (NCAA sponsorship and participation study). Forty years after its introduction, nearly two in five women participate in high school sports, compared to just one in 27 in 1972 (Women's Sports Foundation, 2015).

Do these increased opportunities mean there is no longer gender inequality in school sports? Not really.

Sociologists of sport have shown that there are still inequalities in access, media coverage and representation, employment, and pay. While access to athletic opportunities have increased astronomically, girls in middle-class and wealthy communities have far greater access than those in poorer communities, and girls of color participate in sports at much lower rates than whites. At the college level, even though 57% of college students are women, women receive only 43% of collegiate athletic opportunities and 45% of athletic scholarships. Men hold more coaching positions, even in women's sports, and coaches of men's teams have median salaries more than twice as much as coaches of women's teams (Women's Sports Foundation, 2015). A study of local television news and cable sports coverage from 1989–2014 found that over the past 25 years women's sports have been almost completely excluded coverage (Cooky, Messner, & Musto, 2015).

This is an example of how unequal treatment can lead to inequalities between men and women. But what about gender itself? In some cases, the very act of dividing by gender can disadvantage people whose bodies or identities don't match the male/female binary we expect. The division of sports by gender is based on our social beliefs about gender difference as much as any underlying differences in sports abilities. Our assumptions about differences between women and men shape the sports available to each group (baseball vs. softball), the rules of the game (different rules for men's and women's basketball, tennis, and lacrosse), and even the equipment used (as in men's and women's gymnastics). Training to succeed in these different events, according to different rules, has the result of emphasizing differences between men and women. We then interpret these outcomes as proof that men and women are fundamentally different (Lorber, 1993).

Although we believe that dividing sports by gender is essential because of clear biological differences between men and women, biology does not split into male and female so neatly. Although the numbers are difficult to determine, some scholars estimate that as many as 1 in

FIGURE 4.1 Participation in High School and College Sports, by Gender

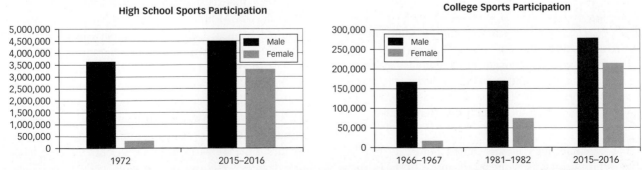

SOURCE: Data from Acosta, Vivian and Linda Jean Carpenter. 2012. *Women in Intercollegiate Sport: A Longitudinal, National Study, Thirty-five Year Update.*

2,000 infants are born with an intersex trait. Intersex refers to being born with some combination of traits, like chromosomes, genitalia, and internal sex organs, that we usually expect to be all male or all female. Thus someone might have XXY chromosomes (instead of XX or XY), ambiguous genitalia, or a vagina and internal testes (Davis, 2015). If someone naturally has some elements of female biology and some elements of male biology, what happens when our institutions require that everyone be sorted into the category of male or female?

Highly publicized cases of female athletes whose gender was challenged, such as South African runner Caster Semenya after her 2009 Junior World Championship win in the 800m or Indian sprinter Dutee Chand in the lead-up to the 2016 Summer Olympics, made public the problematic history of "gender testing" in sports. Since women's first participation in competitive sports, female athletes—especially very successful ones—have had their femininity called into question. In the Olympics, fears and accusations that some countries were fielding men disguised as women resulted in required medical inspections (dubbed "nude parades"), in which female athletes (but not male athletes) had to allow a doctor to examine their genitalia before they could be certified to compete (Karkazis et al., 2012).

More recently, gender testing of female athletes has focused on testosterone levels. Both men and women naturally produce testosterone, although on average men have higher levels of testosterone than women. In 2011, the International Olympic Committee and the International Association of Athletics Federations implemented new policies stating that female athletes with testosterone levels that were "in the normal male range" could not compete without having surgery or taking medication to reduce their testosterone levels (Karkazis et al., 2012). What kinds of assumptions are built into these policies? Focusing solely on testosterone levels assumes that (1) testosterone is the single factor that differentiates men's and women's athletic abilities, and (2) more testosterone directly produces more strength and speed. Critics of this policy point out that there is no clear evidence showing a direct link between higher testosterone and improved ability. Men are not tested for abnormally high natural levels of testosterone and would not be disqualified if their bodies produced testosterone levels that were "too high." Furthermore, elite athletes' bodies are exceptional in many ways, including

Michael Loccisano/Getty Images

▶ Mayor Bill de Blasio with soccer players Carli Lloyd, Megan Rapinoe, Chirlane McCray, and U.S. coach Jill Ellis aboard a float in a ticker tape parade on July 10, 2015, in New York City. The U.S. Women's Soccer national team were World Cup champions. How would you compare men's sports with women's sports?

having genetic variations that do provide a direct advantage. For example, several athletes are known to have genetic variations that increase muscle growth, blood flow, and endurance. Why should high testosterone levels be seen as more unfair than these other biological advantages? In fact, based on these arguments, the policies on high levels of testosterone were suspended in 2015. What do you think? Do you think that gender verification is fair?

....

ASK YOURSELF: Should men and women compete against each other in sports? Does it seem possible that men and women might have more similar skill, speed, or strength if they did?

....

Another way we can observe gender itself as a social problem would be to consider transgender individuals' experiences entering single-gender spaces and institutions, such as when a female-to-male (FTM) transgender student seeks to enroll in a women's college or a transgender woman (MTF) chooses to use the locker room that matches her gender identity. As Laurel Westbrook and Kristen Schilt show in their research, trans individuals can experience a range of reactions to their identity—and these reactions often vary by gender and context. For example, Schilt shows how individuals who openly transitioned from female to male in their workplace were accepted as men and incorporated into men's workplace culture as "one of the guys." However, by analyzing media accounts of violence against transgender individuals, Westbrook has shown that in private

John Tlumacki/Boston Globe/Getty Images

► The sign for the gender-neutral bathrooms on the 5th floor of Boston City Hall across from the reception area for the mayor's office. The answer to the question of what restroom signs should say is not clear as transgender activists fight to use the facility that matches their identity. What do you think the sign says about who can use the restroom?

men "pretending" to be trans in order to gain access to women's bathrooms and assault them. However, there is no evidence of this ever happening. In fact, research has shown that trans and gender nonconforming individuals are the ones who *experience* violence in bathrooms. The exact same arguments about bathrooms have occurred for decades in response to panics about racial integration, women's rights, and gay rights (Stone, 2012). What does this tell us about when and why we police gender? What about gender's intersections with race and sexuality?

> *ASK YOURSELF:* Why do we police gender more strictly in some situations than in others? Do you think that other identities, like race or class, might affect how someone's gender is determined?

relationships and situations defined as sexual, the shape of the genitals is often portrayed as defining the person's "true gender" (Schilt & Westbrook, 2009).

Westbrook and Schilt describe the process of **determining gender** as the variety of ways we place someone in a gender category, whether in face-to-face interactions, court cases and policy, or imagined situations (Westbrook & Schilt, 2014). They extend their previous research to show that in mixed-gender spaces and situations that are not defined as sexual, people often accept someone as the gender they say they are. However, when considering gender-segregated spaces, like bathrooms or locker rooms, "gender panics" arise. In order to resolve the panic and reaffirm that there is a natural gender binary, biology—usually genital surgery or hormones—becomes the criteria for determining gender. Gender panics reveal a double standard at work in determining gender: Gender is policed in women's spaces but not in men's, often on the basis of stereotypes of men as sexually aggressive and women as vulnerable. So-called "bathroom bills"— laws that require individuals to use the bathroom of the sex on their birth certificate, regardless of their current gender—are a good example of this. One such law, H.B. 2, was passed in North Carolina in March 2016 and in 2017, sixteen additional states had considered similar legislation (although none have been signed into law as of September 2017) (National Conference of State Legislatures, 2017). Support for these bills is spurred by panics about cisgender

The Gender Gap in STEM

Certain areas of education and work, such as STEM (science, technology, engineering, and math) fields, show significant gender imbalances. Women earn less than 20% of undergraduate degrees in physics, engineering, and computer science, but over 50% of undergraduate degrees in biosciences and social sciences. Women from underrepresented minority groups earn just over 10% of all undergraduate degrees in science and engineering fields, with psychology and social sciences making up roughly one-third of these (National Science Foundation, 2015).

Some argue that this is because men are naturally better at math and science. However, research has shown repeatedly that this is not the case. The differences in test scores or brain scans that have been found are usually quite small and not enough to explain the large gap between men and women in STEM fields. Given how much our brains grow and change throughout our lives in response to the world around us, it is just as likely that observed differences in men's and women's brains are actually a *result* of gender inequality, not a cause (Fausto-Sterling, 2005; Pitts-Taylor, 2016). Furthermore, this imbalance does not look the same in other countries. For example, in Malaysia, computer science is

Determining gender: The process of placing someone in a gender category.

seen as a female-dominated field (Mellstrom, 2009). Overall, gender gaps in science and math testing are fairly small, vary by country, and are not clearly socially significant. In international testing in math, there were 28 countries where boys scored higher; in the remaining 39 countries, girls scored the same or higher than boys. In science testing, boys scored higher in 24 countries, and girls scored the same or higher in 45 countries. In general, test scores like these have not turned out to be a good predictor of who enters or stays in STEM education and careers (National Center for Education Statistics, 2016a, b; Xie, Fang, & Shauman, 2015).

At the high school level, the proportion of boys and girls in science courses is evening out. However, the proportion of women earning undergraduate degrees in many fields has stayed the same since the 1980s and women continue to be underrepresented in physical sciences, engineering, math, and computer science. Perhaps the answer is that women choose not to take science classes or work in STEM fields because they are just less interested in science. To some extent, this is true. Studies have shown that girls express less interest in learning math and science and lower confidence and assessments of their skills, even among high achievers. But this doesn't tell the whole story. We should ask *why* women are less likely to choose these fields. Social and cultural influences, including stereotypes that math = male; lack of support or encouragement from family, friends, and teachers; and lack of role models or mentors have all been shown to contribute to girls' lower interest in math and science (Xie, Fang, & Shauman, 2015).

▶ The 2016 movie *Hidden Figures* told the true story of a team of African American women who provided NASA with important mathematical data needed to launch the program's first successful space missions. Why is so little known about these women's contributions to the space race?

ASK YOURSELF: Can you think of examples of media messages that would discourage girls from pursuing science? Have you heard friends, family, or teachers say things that might suggest to girls that science is not for them?

Gender, Work, and Family

Women in the United States still earn 19% less than men on average (Institute for Women's Policy Research, 2016). Another way of thinking about this **gender wage gap** is to say that for every dollar a man makes, his female counterpart makes about 81 cents. Why do women earn less than men on average? A great deal of research has attempted to answer this question. Some of the explanations are that women and men have different levels of education or different fields of study; that occupations are segregated by sex, meaning that men and women are actually doing different kinds of work; that the work done associated with women is valued less than that associated with men (nurses vs. doctors, or administrative assistant vs. executive); that women accept lower salaries and are less likely to negotiate for higher pay; and that women are penalized for being mothers.

No model has been fully able to explain the gap or its persistence despite women's many gains. Occupational segregation is one factor that contributes to the pay gap. Male-dominated occupations have higher pay on average than female-dominated occupations at similar skill levels. Out of the top 20 occupations for men and for women, only four overlap (Institute for Women's Policy Research, 2016). Looking at the wage gap intersectionally shows that there are significant differences when you take race and gender into account. Black women, for example, make 35% less than white men, while black men make 27% less than white men (Pew Research Center, 2016). Another example of differences within women's wages is the **"motherhood penalty."** Research has found that mothers

Gender wage gap: The gap in earnings between women and men, usually expressed as a percentage or proportion of what women are paid relative to their male equivalents.

"Motherhood penalty": Mothers earn less than both men and women without children.

Reproductive Justice

The freedom to choose when and whether to have children has been a main focus of feminist activism. Abortion was made legal throughout the United States in 1973 with the Supreme Court's decision in *Roe v. Wade*. Since 1973, the fight has been to preserve *access* to abortion. Violent attacks and legal restrictions have closed numerous clinics. Travel, waiting periods, and the legal ban on the use of federal funds to pay for abortion have made it extremely difficult for poor women, in particular, to access abortion and other reproductive health services. Because the United States is heavily involved in international development and health funding, political campaigns to restrict abortion and other reproductive services can affect women's reproductive health around the world.

While mainstream feminist activism has focused primarily on the freedom of choice, poor women and women of color have fought for their right *to have* children. The United States has a long history of forcibly sterilizing large numbers of primarily poor, nonwhite, or immigrant women and men. Sexuality, physical or mental disabilities, number of children, incarceration, and drug addiction have all been used to justify forced sterilization. Women-of-color activists have developed the framework of *reproductive justice* to address these abuses. Loretta Ross, of the activist group SisterSong, describes reproductive justice as "an intersectional theory emerging from the experiences of women of color whose multiple communities experience a complex set of reproductive oppressions." Beginning from this context, reproductive justice champions the right of every woman to decide when and if she will have a baby, to choose how she will give birth or end her pregnancy, and to parent her children in healthy communities free from violence (Ross, 2011).

The reproductive justice framework expands on the concept of reproductive rights by centering on the right to have and raise children.

Decisions about reproduction and parenting cannot be considered simply as individual choices, but need to be understood in the context of communities and the resources necessary to support women's autonomy. A reproductive justice framework can be used to understand and address a range of issues, such as the treatment of pregnant incarcerated women, access to reproductive technologies for poor women and women of color (who have high rates of infertility), and foster care reform (Luna & Luker, 2013; Ross & Solinger, 2017). It also provides insight into complex issues, such as balancing the desire of gay couples to have children by surrogacy or adoption with the needs and rights of impoverished women around the world who work as surrogates or whose children are adopted (Briggs, 2012; Rudrappa, 2015).

▶ **THINK ABOUT IT:** How does the discussion change when we think in terms of reproductive justice, rather than "choice"?

---

make less than nonmothers, while fathers are more likely to benefit from a "daddy bonus" (Correll & Paik, 2007; Hodges & Budig, 2010).

Sometimes, the value placed on career success contradicts deeply held beliefs about gender—for example, the expectation that women should take care of children and the home. Sociologists have found that women's decisions about work and family are shaped by a widely shared set of beliefs that women should be responsible for child care, which is understood to require a great deal of time, attention, and resources, while men should be responsible for supporting the family financially. In this framework, working outside the home conflicts with motherhood; domestic and childrearing activities are not considered a part of fatherhood. We can see these ideas at work behind stories of "mommy wars" between working and stay-at-home mothers, or those about women with high-power, high-paying careers who "opt out" of the workforce because they want to spend more time with their children.

In the United States, 70% of women with children under the age of 18 are in the labor force (U.S. Bureau of Labor Statistics, 2016p). Mothers can use a number of strategies to resolve the conflict between their work and cultural ideals of motherhood. Some choose to emphasize the importance of career over family, or vice versa. Some emphasize the quality of time they spend with children, rather than quantity. And some claim that work makes them better mothers (Blair-Loy, 2003; Gerson, 1985; Hays, 1996). While ideas about the conflict between work and motherhood are dominant in our culture, they do not apply equally to all mothers. Women of color have historically been culturally, economically, and legally excluded from these dominant ideals of motherhood. African American women, for example, have historically had little choice but to integrate work and motherhood out of economic necessity. The "family wage" paid to middle-class white men that allowed their wives to stay home was not extended to African American men. And African American women were explicitly excluded from government programs supporting widows and single mothers (Glenn, 2002). Based on this history of constraints, women of color have developed ideals of motherhood that do include working outside the home (Dow, 2016).

▶ Paolo Diaz at the grocery store with his kids Maile, 6, and son Elijah, 3. Maile wrote the grocery list and shops with her dad for that evening's dinner. How common do you think it is for fathers to buy groceries and cook meals for their families?

While we might think that women's decisions about whether to have children or to pursue a career are individual choices based on personal preferences, these choices are made within a social context that provides support for some and discourages others. Cultural ideals about work and motherhood, national laws and policies, company practices, and negotiations within individual families all influence what choices are available. For example, the United States is one of the only countries in the world that does not guarantee paid maternity leave. If a woman's employer does not voluntarily offer to pay her salary during maternity leave, she may not be able to afford taking time off to recover from childbirth and care for her newborn. Unlike many other wealthy countries, the United States does not offer state-subsidized child care, and the high cost of child care means that many families cannot afford the child care that would make it possible for both parents to work. How might these policies affect women's decisions about how to combine work and parenting in ways that are more complex than individual preferences?

In most families, women are responsible for the majority of domestic tasks—cleaning, cooking, shopping, etc.—and many women find that they work a **"second shift"** of domestic work after their paid workday (Hochschild, 1989). Men are doing more housework and child care than they have in the past, but they still spend far less time than women on these tasks. Women have moved

into male domains and work, but men have not made a similar move into the domestic sphere (England, 2010). Middle- and upper-income families often hire domestic workers to take over some portion of this care work. Often these workers are immigrant women, who care for children in wealthier families to make money to send back to their own children (Hondagneu-Sotelo & Avila, 1997; Parreñas, 2005).

In her interviews with 18–32-year-olds, Kathleen Gerson found that most women *and* men desire egalitarian relationships, in which both partners contribute financially and as caretakers. However, aware of the obstacles to this kind of partnership—such as demanding careers, expectations that men will be the breadwinner, and the devaluation of care work—both men and women had a "fallback position" in mind. However, men's and women's "Plan Bs" looked very different: Women wanted to be self-sufficient and able to support children themselves, while men expected they would be able to fall back on a more traditional arrangement and their partner would take care of children while they prioritized their career (Gerson, 2010). One model for more egalitarian arrangements comes from same-sex couples. Without an assumed division of tasks by gender, partners actively negotiate who will do what according to their interests and abilities, often resulting in a more equal

....

"Second shift": Unpaid housework and child care done, primarily by women, in addition to paid work outside the home.

Race and the Glass Escalator: Black Male Nurses

Although 95% of registered nurses are women, they are still paid 5% less than their male counterparts. In her study of men in predominantly female occupations like nursing, Christine Williams (1992) found that these men encounter a *glass escalator,* or invisible pressure to move up in their professions, sometimes in spite of their intentions. In her own study of black male nurses, Adia Harvey Wingfield (2009) found that the glass escalator may work better for white men than for African American men. Earlier research suggested that white male nurses receive a congenial welcome from their female colleagues and male supervisors; this was not the experience of the black male nurses Wingfield interviewed.

Both Williams's original study and Wingfield's research used in-depth interviews that allowed respondents to tell stories about their experiences in the nursing field. In Williams's study, 90% of the respondents were white,

while Wingfield interviewed 17 male nurses who all identified as black or African American. This difference in sampling led to very different research results.

▶ Nursing is a profession that has historically been dominated by white women. Black male nurses are a minority within a minority in the profession.

Gendered racism, which grounds racial stereotypes, images, and beliefs in gendered ideals, caused the mostly white colleagues of black male nurses to perceive them as dangerous and threatening in a way white male nurses did not encounter.

Black male nurses also do not benefit from the automatic assumption that they are capable of and qualified for "better" work that white male nurses are granted. Finally, while patients often mistake white male nurses for doctors, a black male nurse is more likely to find himself mistaken for a janitor. Wingfield's study demonstrates the importance of an intersectional approach to the examination of gender—that is, an approach that takes into consideration the many identities we occupy that overlap with gender and interact in complex ways. Though being a man seems to be a distinct advantage for white men, Wingfield's findings suggest that masculinity does not similarly privilege black male nurses.

▶ **THINK ABOUT IT:** How might the intersections of race and gender produce different treatment in other professions?

---

distribution (Biblarz & Savci, 2010). What are your future plans for work and family? How do you think you will negotiate a fair distribution of career and domestic tasks with your partner?

ASK YOURSELF: Think about your own family and your friends' families. Who worked outside of the home? Who did what kinds of household work? How do you think your generation will sort out these decisions?

Gender Inequality in Global Perspective

How does the United States stack up to the rest of the world when it comes to women's education,

employment, and health? In the UN Development Programme's 2015 Gender Inequality Index, the United States ranked 43rd out of 188 countries—behind Canada, the UK, and most European countries. Although women in the United States have attained high rates of educational achievement and participation in the workforce, they also experience very high maternal mortality rates and hold a low proportion of elected offices compared to similar countries (United Nations Development Programme, 2016).

Women with more education have much lower mortality rates, in part because they marry and have children later. Because of this, increasing women's education can significantly reduce both maternal and child deaths. If all women in sub-Saharan Africa completed primary education, 50,000 maternal deaths would be prevented—a 70% reduction. Worldwide, there would be 50% fewer child deaths if all women completed secondary education. And according to USAID, if 1% more girls in India enrolled in secondary school, the country's GDP would increase by 5.5% (United States Agency for International Development, n.d.). Despite such benefits, there are still significant barriers to women's education around the world. UNESCO estimated in 2013 that there are 31 million girls out of school, 4 million more than the number of boys. In Somalia, 95% of the poorest girls have never been to school, and in Pakistan that figure is 62% (United Nations Educational, Scientific, and Cultural Organization, 2013). Outbreaks of violence, ongoing conflicts, and war can prevent all children from attending school. In South Sudan in 2015, less than half of school-age boys and one-third of school-age girls were in school (United Nations Population Fund, 2016). The case of Malala Yousafzai—who gained worldwide attention after surviving an assassination attempt by the Taliban and who later won the Nobel Peace Prize—demonstrates the obstacles girls face in Pakistan when they advocate for women's education.

There are also large global gaps in women's poverty, labor, and health. Economic inequality can take many forms for women around the world. In both wealthy and low-income countries, women and girls perform much more unpaid labor, like child care and cleaning, than do men and boys (World Economic Forum, 2016). In wealthy Scandinavian countries, progressive laws and government programs, such as paid parental leave for both parents and subsidized child care, support women's participation in the workforce. However, gender inequality takes different forms in these countries, where women more often work part time or are concentrated in lower-paid, female-dominated occupations (Pettit & Hook, 2009).

Around the world, women live longer than men but are also sicker. In the United States, average life expectancy is 81.6 years for women and 76.9 years for men, and in Canada it is 84.1 years for women and 80.2 for men. In Nigeria, women's life expectancy is 55.6 years and men's is 53.4 years—almost 30 years less than in Canada! (World Health Organization, 2016b). However, there can also be large differences within groups, depending on race/ethnicity, income, or education. For example, black men in the United States with a college degree or more live 4 years less than white men with the same education, but 7 years longer than white men with less than a high school education (Olshansky et al., 2012). Maternal mortality rates contribute to the variation in women's life expectancy around the world. For example, in Nigeria, there are eight maternal deaths

for every 1,000 births, compared to seven maternal deaths for every 100,000 births in Canada. The United States has a very high maternal mortality rate compared to similar wealthy countries: 14 in 100,000 (World Health Organization, 2016a). Gender-based violence and sexual assault are problems for women in many parts of the world. WHO estimates that 35% of women worldwide have experienced sexual or intimate partner violence (World Health Organization, 2016b).

USING THEORY TO UNDERSTAND GENDER INEQUALITY: THE VIEWS FROM THE FUNCTIONALIST, SYMBOLIC INTERACTIONIST, AND CONFLICT PERSPECTIVES

4.4 Apply the functionalist, symbolic interactionist, and conflict perspectives to the problem of gender inequality.

Many of the theoretical perspectives through which we can view gender have been influenced by feminist scholarship and activism. Before the 1960s, sociologists reflected the views of their time in assuming that most of the important things about social life happen among and between men. Beginning in the 1960s and 1970s, however, more women entered the field and began a serious consideration of the role of gender across many areas of social life. The gender theories that feminists and sociologists developed line up with sociology's three dominant theoretical frameworks—structural functionalism, symbolic interactionism, and conflict theory. Each focuses attention on particular aspects and dynamics of social life, giving us different views of the same social phenomenon.

Structural Functionalism

The macro-level theory of structural functionalism dates from the birth of the discipline, when scholars proposed the metaphor of society as an organism and each of its social institutions as an organ in a body. A social institution is an established pattern of behavior, group, or organization that fulfills a specific need in society. The government is a social institution that we might see as the brain of the organism; government plays a large role in setting the rules for a given society.

Menstrual Health as a Human Right

Menstruation may not be the first thing that comes to mind when you think of a *social* problem that is a global issue. At first thought, it seems like one of the most individual and natural experiences someone could have. However, there are myriad ways that the experience of menstruation is shaped by, for example, our cultural attitudes toward gender, bodies, and sexuality; the ways we organize time and physical space in our homes, schools, and workplaces; or the technologies made available to manage menstruation and their production, advertisement, regulation, and taxation (Fingerson, 2006; Freidenfelds, 2009; Mamo & Fosket, 2009; Vostral, 2008). There are even social movements focused on menstruation! (Bobel, 2010).

Taking a global view makes this even clearer. In recent years, the international development field has begun to focus on the issue of menstrual hygiene management in low-income countries.

One researcher describes the problem this way: "Every day, schoolgirls in low-income countries around the world discover blood on their underwear for the first time, feel an uncomfortable cramping in their lower abdomen, and find themselves in a setting without toilets, water, or a supportive female teacher to explain the change happening in their body" (Sommer & Sahin, 2013, p. 1556). Menstrual hygiene management campaigns highlight how cultural taboos, poverty, inadequate knowledge, and lack of infrastructure keep girls and women from being able to manage their menstruation in effective and healthy ways. These campaigns advocate for water and sanitation infrastructure improvements that would benefit all. However, some critics of menstrual hygiene campaigns argue that they perpetuate stereotypes of ignorance and uncleanliness used to justify colonial oppression and replace traditional practices with environmentally unsustainable disposable products (Lahiri-Dutt, 2015; *Mythri Speaks*, 2016).

Stefan Heunis/AFP/Getty Images

▶ Girls from the Madibane High School in Soweto, South Africa receive an educational talk about menstruation and the female reproductive system. Sanitary pads are too expensive for many African teenagers to afford. What do you see as local solutions to this problem?

▶ **THINK ABOUT IT:** How does menstruation as a social problem affect both girls and boys?

As applied to gender, structural functionalism takes the specific form of sex role theory. The idea of a sex role begins with the more general idea of a **social role**, a set of expectations attached to a particular status or position, such as white or black, man or woman, gay or straight. Certain expectations or norms go along with different statuses. A **sex role** is a set of expectations attached to a particular sex category. An easy way to think about this is to consider what kinds of behaviors might seem strange for a man or woman in your society. For example, in the United States one expectation of straight men is that they not hold hands with or kiss other men, even on the cheek. But in Egypt and India, it is normal to see straight men holding hands with other men, and in France, men kiss other men on the cheek in greeting. Social roles vary by society, but most cultures impose some set of expectations on individuals based on their assignment into a sex category.

> *ASK YOURSELF:* Can you think of other examples of behaviors that are seen as appropriate for women or men in one culture and not in another?

Sex role theory fits within the structural functionalist view because it assumes that different sex roles for women and men are functional for society. Functionalist sociologists such as Talcott Parsons have explained these differences in terms of instrumental versus expressive roles (Parsons & Bales, 1955). Men are taught in childhood and throughout their lives to be **instrumental**, or goal- and

Social role: A set of expectations attached to a particular status or position in society.

Sex role: The set of expectations attached to a particular sex category—male or female.

Instrumental: Oriented toward goals and tasks.

TABLE 4.1 Gender Inequality Index and Related Indicators for Select Countries

Country	Gender Inequality Index Rank* (2014)	Maternal Mortality Ratio (2013)	Seats in National Parliament (% female) (2014)	Population With at Least Secondary Education (% ages 25 and older) (2014)		Labor Force Participation Rate (%) (2013)	
				Female	Male	Female	Male
Slovenia	1	7	27.7	95.8	98.0	52.3	63.2
Netherlands	2	6	28.5	95.0	96.6	61.8	74.9
Germany	3	7	36.9	96.3	97.0	53.6	66.4
Denmark	4	5	38.0	95.5	96.6	58.7	66.4
Austria	5	4	30.3	100.0	100.0	54.6	67.7
Sweden	6	4	43.6	86.5	87.3	60.3	67.9
Netherlands	7	6	36.9	87.7	90.5	58.5	70.6
Belgium	8	6	42.4	77.5	82.9	47.5	59.3
Norway	9	4	39.6	97.4	96.7	61.2	68.7
Italy	10	4	30.1	71.2	80.5	39.6	59.5
Australia	19	6	30.5	94.3	94.6	58.8	71.8
Ireland	21	9	19.9	80.5	78.6	53.1	68.1
Korea (Republic of)	23	27	16.3	77.0	89.1	50.1	72.1
Canada	25	11	28.2	100.0	100.0	61.6	71.0
Japan	26	6	11.6	87.0	85.8	48.8	70.4
Libya	27	15	16.0	55.5	41.9	30.0	76.4
United Kingdom	39	8	23.5	99.8	99.9	55.7	00.7
China	40	32	23.6	58.7	71.9	63.9	78.3
United Arab Emirates	47	8	17.5	73.1	61.2	46.5	92.0
Kazakhstan	52	26	20.1	95.3	98.8	67.7	77.9
United States	55	28	19.4	95.1	95.8	56.3	68.9
Saudi Arabia	56	16	19.9	60.5	70.3	20.2	78.3
Cuba	68	80	48.9	74.3	78.8	43.4	70.0
Mexico	74	49	37.1	55.7	60.6	45.1	79.9
Rwanda	80	320	57.5	8.0	8.8	86.4	85.3
South Africa	83	140	40.7	72.7	75.9	44.5	60.5
Pakistan	121	170	19.7	19.3	46.1	24.6	82.9
Kenya	126	400	20.8	25.3	31.4	62.2	72.4
India	130	190	12.2	27.0	56.6	27.0	79.9
Yemen	155	270	0.7	8.6	26.7	25.4	72.2

SOURCE: Gender Inequality Index and Related Indicators, United Nations Development Project, Human Development Reports.

*The Gender Inequality Index is calculated based on three dimensions (reproductive health, empowerment, and labor market) and five indicators (maternal mortality, adolescent fertility, parliamentary representation, educational attainment, and labor force participation).

FIGURE 4.2 The 10 Leading Causes of Death for Women in Low- and High-Income Countries, 2011

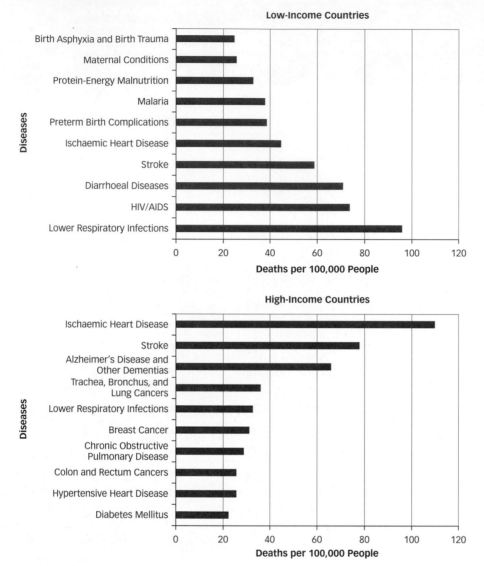

SOURCE: World Health Organization

task-oriented, while women are taught to be **expressive**, or oriented toward their interactions with other people. Theorists see this division of labor as functional for society, because women who work outside the home and men who want to stay home and take care of their children create dysfunction for society.

ASK YOURSELF: Sex role theory predicts that men will be more oriented toward the instrumental while women will be more oriented toward the expressive. Can you think of examples that support this assertion? Can you think of exceptions, or situations that contradict this assertion?

Policy Implications of Structural Functionalism

Applied to policy, sex role theory presumes that a functional family unit is one that consists of a man who fulfills an instrumental role and a woman who occupies an expressive role. Policies that support the centrality of the nuclear family—husband, wife, and children—are thus consistent with sex role theory. For example, one of the goals of the welfare reforms passed in the United States in 1996 was to encourage the formation of two-parent families, and a 2002 welfare reform bill in the House of Representatives included $300 million for policies to promote marriage (Hu, 2003). Temporary Assistance for Needy Families

Expressive: Oriented toward interactions with other people.

(TANF), which replaced Aid to Families With Dependent Children (AFDC) in 1996, requires that single women work in order to receive welfare, while married women do not have to be employed in order to receive welfare benefits. Some states have included marriage education classes as part of the training single women are required to undergo as a condition for receiving welfare benefits. Paternity establishment and child-support rules included in TANF encourage a woman receiving benefits to form some kind of relationship with the father of her children (Mink, 2001). All these policies support the assumptions of sex role theory that the most functional model of a family is a father who works outside the home to support his family and a mother who takes care of the children (and the father). Feminists have criticized TANF as a policy that violates women's rights to work, to support themselves financially, and to live independent of men. Yet, acting consistently with sex role theory, many politicians see a family unit composed of a male provider, a female caregiver, and their children as the most beneficial for society.

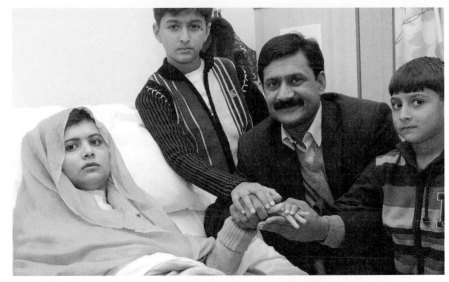

▶ Malala Yousafzai is the Pakistani girl who was shot in the head by the Taliban in 2012 for advocating girls' education. Here she is seen with her father and two younger brothers as she recuperates at the Queen Elizabeth Hospital in Birmingham, England. Malala won the Nobel Peace Prize in 2014. Why do you suppose girls' education is such a threat to the Taliban?

Symbolic Interactionism

Whereas structural functionalism and sex role theory are good examples of theories at the macro level in sociology, symbolic interactionism is generally a theory that works at the micro level. It looks at the details of social interaction and group life rather than at the big picture of how larger structures in society fit together.

In the world of symbolic interactionism, everything is a symbol, including the way you wear your hair, the way you sit, your facial expressions, the words you choose, and your inflection, as well as whether you look at me or not while you speak. Crucial to understanding social life from a symbolic interactionist perspective is understanding the meanings we give to all these things, and those meanings vary. The idea of social construction is especially important, then, from a symbolic interactionist perspective.

One specific gender theory that fits within symbolic interactionism is **doing gender theory**. Doing gender draws its legacy from a specific branch of symbolic interactionism in sociology called ethnomethodology. **Ethnomethodology** is essentially the study of folkways and the meaning and operation of what at first appear to be

very mundane and taken-for-granted aspects of social life. Harold Garfinkel became interested in what we might assume in relationship to gender. He studied a male-to-female transsexual named Agnes because he reasoned that the aspects of gender the rest of us take for granted would probably be more apparent to someone like Agnes, who was forced to try to pass as a gender different from the one in which she had been socialized (Garfinkel, 1967). Doing gender as a theory builds on Garfinkel's work to argue that gender is not a set of internalized norms for behavior, as suggested by sex role theory. Rather, gender is an interactive performance we are all constantly staging through our interactions with others. In addition, we are all accountable to our audience—the other people with whom we are interacting.

Accountability in doing gender theory refers to whether the audience for our performance understands our actions as we have intended for them to be understood. For example, if I tell a joke, you may not laugh at it, or you may think it's a particularly bad joke. But either of

....

Doing gender theory: A theory of gender that claims gender is an accountable performance created and reinforced through individuals' interactions.

Ethnomethodology: A sociological approach that seeks to uncover the taken-for-granted assumptions that lie behind the basic stuff of social life and interaction.

Accountability: The ways in which people gear their actions to specific circumstances so others will correctly recognize the actions for what they are.

those reactions still implies that the story I just told you is accountable as a joke. I meant it as a joke and you understood it as such. If I tell you a story I intended to be a joke and you stare at me blankly and wonder what the point of it was, I have failed to create an accountable joke. Doing gender as a theory assumes a deeply interactive relationship between the gender performer and the audience, because accountability is decided by both.

While sex role theory argues that gender exists internally to individuals as a set of norms and expectations, one of doing gender theory's key insights is that it is our constant performance of gender that leads us to believe that gender has some deeper underlying reality. Like a magic act, our accomplishment of gender is powerful enough to convince us there are, in fact, natural divisions of human beings into two types—male and female, masculine and feminine, man and woman. But from the doing gender perspective, sex and gender consist only of our performances.

●●

ASK YOURSELF: How does doing gender theory fit within a social constructionist perspective on gender? Based on what you know about doing gender theory, would this approach agree or disagree with sexual dimorphism?

●●

Policy Implications of Symbolic Interactionism

If gender is a performance, how does this explain the existence of gender inequality? Those using the doing gender perspective argue that gender inequality becomes part of our performances of gender, largely through allocation. **Allocation** is simply the way decisions get made about who does what, who gets what and who does not, who gets to make plans, and who gets to give orders or take them (West & Fenstermaker, 1993). The doing gender perspective assumes a widespread and deeply held belief in our society that women are both different from and inferior to men. This shapes the way in which women are held accountable for gender, especially when it comes to allocation and even in something as simple as a routine conversation.

Research has demonstrated allocation in simple conversations, each between a white middle-class man and a white middle-class woman, where the particular kind of work to be allocated is changing to a new topic when the old one runs out of steam. Two people in conversation usually change topics collaboratively, but sometimes one person does it alone. West and Garcia (1988) found that in their sample, such unilateral topic changes were always initiated by men, and from the doing gender perspective, this is an issue of allocation, controlling what two people will talk about. Men accomplish gender in conversation by changing the topic, and this seems to be especially true

when women move the conversation toward topics that are not necessarily seen as consistent with ideas of masculinity (West & Garcia, 1988). In this small way, men produce an accountable performance of masculinity.

If both gender and sex are largely performances and gender inequality is due to allocation, what are the policy implications of doing a gender perspective? A study of women in various occupations within the criminal justice system found that some did feel compelled by the organizational logic of institutions like law enforcement and prisons to do masculinity while on the job. These women emulated the styles of reasoning, speech, and demeanor thought to characterize men in their occupations (Martin & Jurik, 1996, p. 218). Even those who avoided the adaptive strategy of doing masculinity felt pressured to act like men.

As a solution to gender inequality, asking women to act like men seems inadequate. Though doing gender theory emphasizes the importance of social interaction to the construction of gender, the best solutions from this theoretical perspective still lie at the level of organizations and institutions. The reason why is if one person decides not to perform his or her gender, that decision generally does not call into question the larger institutional arrangement of gender. If as a woman I stop performing an accountable version of femininity, most people will assume something is wrong with me, not with the way gender is structured in my society. Our performances of gender certainly reinforce the larger structural status quo, but we would have to change our interactions on a massive scale to significantly change the larger social structures in regard to gender.

●●

ASK YOURSELF: Imagine situations in your own life that seem to demand different performances of gender. Are there situations in which you feel pressured to act in ways more or less consistent with your own gender? Can you identify any trends in the kinds of situations that seem to demand different types of gender performances?

●●

Because of this relationship between social structures and interaction, the locations and contexts in which we stage our performances of gender are important. We can therefore alter our gender performances best by altering those environments. Though many women in criminal justice occupations feel pressure to do masculinity, this pressure is reduced in occupations characterized by an ethic of professionalization. Where women can project themselves as professionals, they can find ways to make

---

Allocation: The way decisions get made about who does what, who gets what and who does not, who gets to make plans, and who gets to give orders or take them.

femininity and competence in their jobs more compatible. Doing gender theory suggests that organizations and institutions should restructure in ways that put less pressure on women and men to perform gender.

Conflict Theory

If structural functionalism emphasizes the relatively smooth functioning of society, conflict theory draws our attention to the importance of struggles over power and resources in society. Most theories that fall under the conflict paradigm can trace their origins to Karl Marx and his ideas about social class. **Socialist feminism**, for instance, translates Marx's theories about class oppression into a different context, arguing that the best way to understand gender relations is to see women as an oppressed social class.

Gender inequality, however, is different from social class inequality in that almost all women live intimately with their oppressors. The United States exhibits a high level of social class segregation; most people live, work, and socialize alongside people whose social class backgrounds are similar to their own. Social class segregation creates social inequality by concentrating resources geographically; poor neighborhoods have less money for schools, fewer amenities (like grocery stores), and fewer jobs available than do more affluent neighborhoods. Even if women are socially segregated within their own households, as happens in some countries, such as Egypt and Saudi Arabia, they still live with their male relatives. So though socialist feminists may argue that women are an oppressed social class, they are a unique kind of social class.

Radical feminism borrows from conflict theory the central idea of groups in conflict over power and resources. But rather than locating this conflict in class relationships as socialist feminists do, radical feminists see **patriarchy**, or male dominance, as the root of the problem. Patriarchal societies are designed in ways that quite explicitly favor men over women. Patriarchy can manifest in many ways, some subtle and some not so subtle. In many societies, parents prefer male children over female children and may abort female children or take other measures to increase their chances of having sons rather than daughters. More subtle forms of patriarchy include uses of language, such as the way the word *man* is often used to refer to all humanity, as in *mankind*. In general, patriarchal societies are characterized by **androcentrism**, the belief that masculinity and what men do are superior to femininity and what women do.

> **ASK YOURSELF:** What are some examples of androcentrism in your own society?

Liberal feminism posits that gender inequality is rooted in the ways institutions such as government treat men and women. When these institutions limit women's opportunities to compete with men in economic and political arenas, they create inequality. Why should women and men be provided with equal rights? Liberal feminists assert that all humans in modern societies are entitled to a set of basic rights. Thus they base their arguments regarding inequality on the *similarities* between men and women: Because we are all basically the same, we all deserve the same basic rights.

Policy Implications of Conflict Theory

From a liberal feminist perspective, the best way to reduce gender inequality is to reduce the barriers that stand in the way of women's advancement. Because women and men are essentially the same, once these barriers have been removed, gender inequality will gradually disappear. But as we've seen, from the radical feminist perspective gender inequality is explained by the prevalence of patriarchy as a defining characteristic of society. Thus merely changing a few laws here and there will not rid us of gender inequality. Instead, any effort to reduce gender inequality must involve a fairly radical restructuring of society—not just government but also educational institutions, religious institutions, the family, the media, work, and so on. (This explains why radical feminism is, in fact, *radical* compared to liberal feminism.)

> **ASK YOURSELF:** From a radical feminist perspective, patriarchy penetrates all areas of social life. Can you think of some examples that seem to support this assertion?

Some radical feminists argue that the first step toward ending gender inequality is for women to form their own separate institutions and organizations free of male domination. For instance, radical feminist Mary Daly famously advocated

Socialist feminism: A version of feminist thought that employs Marxist paradigms to view women as an oppressed social class.

Radical feminism: A version of feminist thought that suggests gender is a fundamental aspect of the way society functions and serves as an integral tool for distributing power and resources among people and groups.

Patriarchy: A society characterized by male dominance.

Androcentrism: The belief that masculinity and what men do are superior to femininity and what women do.

Liberal feminism: A type of feminism that suggests men and women are essentially the same and gender inequality can be eliminated through the reduction of legal barriers to women's full participation in society.

leaving Christianity behind as an institution deeply flawed by patriarchy. Other radical feminists have formed music festivals for women, women's businesses, and collectives where women could live and work apart from men.

This is not to say that radical feminists do not also support changing laws; in the 1970s, many were active in efforts to ratify the Equal Rights Amendment, which would have amended the U.S. Constitution to make any discrimination on the basis of sex illegal. But radical feminists often also engage in forms of protest and consciousness-raising activities that target institutions beyond the government. **Consciousness-raising** is a process intended to help women see the connections between their personal experiences with gender exploitation and the larger structure and politics of society—to see sexual harassment, for instance, as a fundamental and inevitable product of the patriarchal way our society is structured, part of the way men maintain control through fear and intimidation. Consciousness-raising is at the core of the popular feminist slogan "The personal is political."

Thus laws against sexual harassment and legislation aimed at protecting victims of domestic violence are part of the legacy of radical feminist organizing. It is difficult for many of us to imagine today, but as recently as the 1970s, it was not technically illegal in any U.S. state for a husband to physically assault or abuse his wife or children. This type of violence was considered strictly within the realm of the personal, and therefore not subject to public laws governing behavior. Radical feminists argued that because gender permeates all aspects of society, including the family, what happens inside the family home has very important public implications.

The laws making sexual harassment in the workplace illegal show a similar radical feminist influence because they acknowledge that merely removing legal barriers is not enough to end inequality. Many workplaces are structured in ways that make it difficult for women to occupy certain jobs; if you are the victim of constant harassment at work, just having the job does not guarantee success. Laws against sexual harassment acknowledge that sexism is part of the status quo of some work environments, or that patriarchy is built into the very fabric of our social lives.

QUEER THEORY: AN INTERDISCIPLINARY PERSPECTIVE ON GENDER

4.5 Apply queer theory's interdisciplinary perspective to gender inequality.

Our final theory draws on both the social constructionist aspect of doing gender theory and the society-wide approach of radical feminism. The use of the word *queer* in the name of this theory is partly political, a way of refusing and rechanneling the negative connotations this word often has. But the word also fits very well with the ideological agenda of the theory. The literal dictionary meanings of *queer* include "not usual," "eccentric," and "suspicious." A theory that is queer is therefore strange or unusual, different in some important way. It is just this type of rather eccentric and suspicious theory that queer theorists have set about to produce.

Queer theory is a hybrid perspective, and its beginnings can be traced to many different sources. Like many of the global social movements that flourished in the 1960s and 1970s, the gay and lesbian rights movement began to face internal problems in the 1980s and 1990s. For instance, lesbian feminists were sometimes at odds with gay men, who as men may benefit from systems of gender inequality. Women and men of color argued that the gay movement and its ideology reflected a white middle-class bias (Seidman, 1996). Questions arose about whether it was possible for one movement to represent all lesbians and gays, given the vast differences in the two groups' experiences. Thus from the gay and lesbian rights movement and feminist movements, queer theory draws its distrust of categories of identity.

From postmodernism, queer theory borrows a distrust of grand narratives, or metanarratives (Lyotard, 1984). A **metanarrative** is any attempt at a comprehensive and universal explanation of some phenomenon. Science itself is a metanarrative, as it seeks to develop theories that explain the way the universe works. The problem with metanarratives is that they inevitably leave some people at the margins or attempt to force their experiences into the grand story being told. Metanarratives as claims to knowledge have power implications for those who don't fit. If I define what it means to be a man in a certain way and you don't fit that definition, you're not as likely to receive the privileges that go along with being defined as a man.

So what does queer theory do with all these intellectual threads? It seeks to pull the metaphorical rug out from under our feet by pointing out that there was never any clear place to stand to begin with; the rug didn't really exist anyway, and this is demonstrated in three basic features of queer theory.

First, queer theory is distrustful of categories related to sexuality—gay, straight, lesbian, bisexual, transsexual,

Consciousness-raising: A radical feminist social movement technique designed to help women make connections between the personal and the political in their lives.

Metanarrative: An attempted comprehensive and universal explanation of some phenomenon.

and so on—and as a social movement it works to do away with them in their current form. The use of *queer* as a way of self-identifying among these groups represents an "aggressive impulse of generalization" and an attempt to disrupt conceptions of what is normal (Warner, 1993). Categories of identity, as discussed above, are incomplete and can never successfully encompass all the diversity contained within. For example, is a male-to-female post-operative transsexual who is romantically and sexually attracted to women straight or gay? What about some women in Native American cultures who live socially as men and marry other women? Native Americans don't consider them lesbians, and whom they have sex with is much less important than the gender they are acting out (Whitehead, 1981). How can a category labeled *lesbian* possibly hope to take account of all these differences? Queer theory answers that it can't. It doesn't stop there, though. Drawing on its feminist lineage, queer theory questions categories of gender as well, because all categories have these same fundamental flaws.

One solution queer theory proposes is to think of these identity categories as always open and fluid. You might think of this second feature of queer theory as suggesting that everyone can be, and in fact already is, queer. At some point all of us—straight, gay, feminine, masculine, intersexual, transgender—fail to live up perfectly to the demands placed on us by gender and are therefore hurt by this system. Heterosexual men in Anglo-European society are not supposed to show affection toward other men except in appropriate ways and venues (the slap on the butt during a sporting event), and many would argue that forbidding expressions of affection among any group of people goes against our basic human tendencies and is a form of oppression. The straight man who hugs his male friend a little too long is likely to be sanctioned in some way for not conforming perfectly to his particular category and in this way is "let down" by the gender

system. The ways categories of gender and sexuality are constructed affect all of us, regardless of where we fall within those categories. None of us conform to them perfectly, and this makes all of us "queer" in some way.

This assumption connects to the third feature of queer theory, its ambition to "queer" many features of academic and social life that are generally considered within the bounds of normality. Queer theory aspires to be not just a theory of sexuality, or even of gender and sexuality, but also a broad and far-reaching social theory (Seidman, 1996). Queer theorists believe sexuality is an important way in which knowledge and power are organized in society, and a theory of sexuality is therefore a theory of society in general. They argue that studying only gays and lesbians produces an incomplete picture of how sexuality works to produce identities such as "straight" and "gay." For that reason, queer theory is just as concerned with studying heterosexuality as it is with studying homosexuality, and with investigating how sexual practices permeate all aspects of society. Queer studies programs look at all types of literature, not just that which focuses on gays and lesbians or is written by them, arguing that sexuality is an integral part of all cultural productions. Rather than focusing strictly on the portrayal of gays and lesbians in the media, queer theory also examines the portrayal of heterosexuality. It studies science for the ways in which it is used to create many categories of difference, rather than solely for how it applies to issues of sexuality. For queer studies, the object of study is society itself, not just sexuality.

SOCIAL CHANGE: WHAT CAN YOU DO?

 4.4 Identify steps toward social change in gender inequality.

Much progress has been made toward reducing gender inequality on many fronts. Sociology emphasizes the structural nature of social life and draws our attention to the ways in which structural forces limit our individual choices. But emphasizing the power of structural forces in our own lives is not the same as saying those

social structures *cannot* be changed. History tells us they do change in fairly radical ways, and all of us as individuals have the choice to either contribute to the status quo or take intentional actions to change the way things are. Change may be slow and difficult, but it is always possible. Here are a few ideas for how you might contribute to social change in the area of gender inequality.

Sylvia Rivera Law Project

"Bathroom bills" have made legal battles over transgender rights newly visible, but transgender activism and advocacy cover a broad range of concerns. The Sylvia Rivera Law Project "works to guarantee that all people are free to self-determine their gender identity and expression, regardless of income or race, and without facing harassment, discrimination, or violence." Its intersectional approach joins transgender rights to immigration and incarceration. On its website (https://srlp.org) you can learn more about its legal services and advocacy, educational programs, and training for campuses and service providers, as well as find information about trans legal rights and health care, and how trans communities of color are disproportionately affected by poverty, homelessness, deportation, and incarceration.

Malala Fund

Malala Yousafzai became a global advocate for girls' education after she was attacked by the Taliban for speaking out about girls' rights to attend school in Pakistan. In 2013, 1 year after being attacked, she founded the Malala Fund with her father, a teacher and education advocate. The organization's goal is to raise awareness of the social, political, and legal issues that prevent girls from going to school; to advocate for and invest in girls' education; and to encourage girls to speak out for their right to education. Malala Fund's work includes education advocacy at local, national, and international levels. It also funds programs that provide schooling to girls in crisis situations, such as schools for Syrian refugee girls and radio learning courses during the Ebola outbreak in Sierra Leone. You can learn more about these programs and how to support girls' education worldwide at the website: www.malala.org.

The National Domestic Workers Alliance

The majority of the 2 million domestic workers—nannies, housekeepers, and home health aides—in the United States are immigrants and women of color. These workers are poorly paid and vulnerable to abuse and exploitation by their employers, even more so because they are explicitly excluded from most of the laws and regulations designed to protect workers. These women have joined together to form the National Domestic Workers Alliance (www.give2ndwa.org), fighting to

▶ Domestic workers rally for legal protections and improved working conditions.

establish and enforce legal protections for domestic work and to obtain better pay and working conditions. Since 2010, they have succeeded in getting domestic worker bill of rights laws passed in seven states.

▶▶ Techbridge

Techbridge is an organization that seeks to help parents, educators, and organizations encourage young girls to pursue interests that might eventually lead them to high-paying STEM jobs. Its website (http://www.techbridgegirls.org) provides a wealth of information about how to encourage girls to get excited about science. Girls Who Code (girlswhocode.com) and Black Girls Code (www.blackgirlscode.com) are organizations that seek to increase the number of girls and women in computer science, by matching girls with mentors and organizing clubs, workshops, and camps to teach computer programming. Visit these sites to start thinking about how you might help create the next generation of women scientists and programmers.

▶▶ SisterSong

SisterSong is a collective of women of color and indigenous activists organizing for reproductive justice. These activists aim to change the institutions and systems that impact the reproductive lives of marginalized communities by training, supporting, and organizing individuals and organizations working on reproductive justice and related issues. Their projects include training new reproductive justice activists, helping organizations integrate the reproductive justice framework into their own work, and advocating for policy changes that would reduce maternal mortality rates by increasing access to health care for low-income women and women of color. Learn more about reproductive justice on sistersong.net and www.trustblackwomen.org.

WHAT DOES AMERICA THINK?

Questions About Gender From the General Social Survey

▶▶▶ Turn to the beginning of the chapter to compare your answers to those of the total population.

1. It is better for men to work and women to tend home.

   AGREE: 27.5%

   DISAGREE: 72.5%

2. Most women really want a home and kids.

   AGREE: 47.4%

   DISAGREE: 52.6%

3. Women are not suited for politics.

   AGREE: 19.5%

   DISAGREE: 80.5%

4. Are you for or against the preferential hiring of women?

   FOR: 35.1%

   AGAINST: 64.9%

5. The mother working doesn't hurt children.

   AGREE: 75.4%

   DISAGREE: 24.6%

SOURCE: National Opinion Research Center, University of Chicago.

CHAPTER SUMMARY

 Define gender.

Gender is the belief that there are two distinct types of people in the world—males and females—and that there are social meanings attached to those categories.

 Describe gender inequality and the study of gender as a social problem.

Gender inequality is the way in which the meanings assigned to sex and gender as social categories create disparities in resources such as income, power, and status. Some argue that to make a distinction on the basis of gender is always to also assume an inequality. Others say we can keep gender as a social category without necessarily seeing women or men as better than the other. Regardless of your perspective, gender, like most social problems, is socially constructed. The particular ways in which various societies understand what gender means and how it relates to inequality vary across times and places. Some gender scholars believe sex is socially constructed as well, and that our culture affects the way we understand biological reality.

4.3 Identify gender problems on college campuses today and beyond.

Feminists and others who study gender argue that gender as a social system hurts both women and men, though often in different ways. Some boys feel pressure not to do well academically because their particular subculture defines schoolwork as feminine. However, the gender wage gap demonstrates that men still make more on average than women do around the world, even if this disparity has decreased over time. Differences between men and women in choices of college majors might be one way to explain the gender wage gap, but research suggests that women are disadvantaged in the job market by more than what they did in their college years. In some cases, the very act of dividing by gender can disadvantage people whose bodies or identities don't match the male/female binary society expects.

4.4 Apply the functionalist, conflict, and symbolic interactionist perspectives to the problem of gender inequality.

An example of structural functionalism is sex role theory, which argues that the division of men and women into gender-specific sex roles is functional for society. Doing gender theory, an example of a symbolic interactionist approach, emphasizes how we create gender through our interactional performances. Radical feminism, borrowing from conflict theory, sees patriarchy as the root of the problem of gender inequality; when a society is built on a solid foundation of male domination, the result is that men maintain power over women.

4.5 Apply queer theory's interdisciplinary perspective to gender inequality.

Queer theory incorporates feminism, concepts based in the gay and lesbian rights movement, and postmodernist mistrust of metanarratives to question the existence and usefulness of categories in our understanding of gender and larger social life.

4.6 Identify steps toward social change in gender inequality.

However we may understand the relationship between gender and inequality, as sociologists we know our actions contribute to and create the larger structural forces that make up society. We can choose to continue to contribute to the status quo of gender inequality and the gender system that, as Kate Bornstein says, lets all of us down at some point. Or we can make a conscious choice to help reduce gender inequality on college campuses and elsewhere around the world by becoming involved with organizations like the Sylvia Rivera Law Project, the Malala Fund, the National Domestic Workers Alliance, Techbridge, and SisterSong.

KEY TERMS

accountability 95

allocation 96

androcentrism 97

cisgender 82

consciousness-raising 98

determining gender 86

doing gender theory 95

ethnomethodology 95

expressive 94

gender 80

gender inequality 82

gender wage gap 87

instrumental 92

intersectional approach 80

intersex 81

liberal feminism 97

metanarrative 98

"motherhood penalty" 87

patriarchy 97

radical feminism 97

"second shift" 89

sex role 92

sexual dimorphism 81

social role 92

socialist feminism 97

transgender 82

$SAGE edge™ **Want a better grade?**

Get the tools you need to sharpen your study skills. Access practice quizzes, eFlashcards, video, and multimedia at
http://edge.sagepub.com/trevino2e

5 SEXUALITIES

Elroi J. Windsor

Men kiss in defiance of a counterprotest from street preachers at the annual LA Pride Festival in West Hollywood, California. Why do you think sexual identity is important to people?

Investigating Sexualities: My Story

Elroi J. Windsor

Sally Gupton/Sally Gupton Photography

As a teenager in Northeastern Pennsylvania, I was drawn to punk rock and feminist activism. I started a Riot Grrrl chapter in my hometown before moving to Pittsburgh for college, where I helped start another. In my first year of college, I came into my queer sexual identity, joined a queercore punk band, and hooked up with the local Lesbian Avengers group. I graduated with a degree in Women's Studies in a college that didn't have a sociology major, then moved to New York City for more activist opportunities.

While in New York, I lived in a queer collective where we hosted shows for bands, drag performances, and films in our industrial Brooklyn loft space. I got involved with a drag king troupe and worked in a feminist bookstore while organizing with other queer and transgender activist groups. Eventually, I started working as a health educator in community nonprofits funded to conduct HIV/AIDS prevention strategies. There, I learned more about sociology and decided to research in graduate school the barriers faced by trans people in health care settings.

I now teach at a small liberal arts college, and continue to study issues related to gender, the body, and sexuality. I see the relevance of sociology in everyday life, including in the ways people embody their sexual selves. As a queer and trans scholar, a same-sex married partner, and a parent to two young children, I find the sociology of sexuality to be both personally and intellectually interesting. In this chapter, I invite you to consider how the seemingly private subject of sex is, in reality, tied to so many parts of our society.

LEARNING OBJECTIVES

5.1 Explain how sexuality is a social construction.

5.2 Discuss patterns and trends of sexuality-related social problems.

5.3 Apply the functionalist, conflict, and symbolic interactionist perspectives to the study of sexuality-related social problems, specifically sexual violence.

5.4 Apply specialized theories of sexualities.

5.5 Identify steps toward social change regarding problems related to sexuality.

WHAT DO YOU THINK?

Questions About Sexuality From the General Social Survey

1. What is your belief on having sex before marriage?
   - ☐ WRONG
   - ☐ NOT WRONG

2. Do you believe that homosexuals should have the right to marry?
   - ☐ YES
   - ☐ NO
   - ☐ NEITHER

3. What is your level of happiness with your partner?
   - ☐ VERY HAPPY
   - ☐ SOMEWHAT HAPPY
   - ☐ NOT TOO HAPPY

4. Should a homosexual be allowed to teach?
   - ☐ ALLOW
   - ☐ DO NOT ALLOW

5. Should homosexual books be allowed in the library?
   - ☐ YES
   - ☐ NO

6. Married people are happier than unmarried people.
   - ☐ AGREE
   - ☐ DISAGREE
   - ☐ NEITHER AGREE NOR DISAGREE

7. What is your opinion of sex before marriage in teens between 14 and 16 years of age?
   - ☐ ALWAYS WRONG
   - ☐ SOMETIMES WRONG
   - ☐ NOT WRONG AT ALL

8. Should sex education be taught in public schools?
   - ☐ YES
   - ☐ NO

 Turn to the end of the chapter to view the results for the total population.

SOURCE: National Opinion Research Center, University of Chicago.

AND THEN, SHE WAS GONE

Audrie Pott and Daisy Coleman were typical teenage girls growing up in small towns. Audrie lived in California; Daisy lived in Missouri. Both girls were active in school. They liked hanging out with friends and uploading selfies to Instagram. Audrie and Daisy shared something else in common: They were both sexually assaulted by teenage boys whom they knew. Both girls tried to end their lives. One succeeded, the other survived.

The story of these girls plays out in the 2016 documentary film *Audrie & Daisy* (Cohen & Shenk, 2016). The film illuminates the deep personal effects of sexual assault on victims, but it also explores the way this violence impacts families, schools, and communities. The assaults on Audrie and Daisy were captured on camera. Yet documentation of the crime did not result in easy convictions for the perpetrators. Instead, the images of the assault were used to revictimize Audrie and Daisy as they spread across social media. Both girls were subjected to insults, mockery, and incredulous scrutiny from their teenage peers and from adults in the community, including law enforcement officers. They experienced what has become known as "**sexual bullying**" and "cyberbullying," a form of sexual violence often misunderstood by a legal system that lags behind technological innovation.

Using footage from the communities, the film demonstrates how justice for the girls was less important than protecting the boys accused. Audrie was just 15 years old when she took her life in 2012. Her father described her as: "[S]o large in life, she was a great athlete, great musician, good student, good kid. And then, she was gone. . . . We had to do something. We are giving a voice to our daughter, we have to so nobody else dies" (Pott, 2017). Unlike Audrie, Daisy lived on to challenge the ways sexual assault survivors are treated, as did her brother, mother, and countless other people whose lives were destroyed by sexual assault and its amplification through social media. Their efforts join a growing movement against sexual violence in the United States.

RAINN (Rape, Abuse and Incest National Network) is the largest organization in the United States that works to address sexual violence. It estimates that one out of every six women in the United States has been sexually assaulted. Young women between the ages of 13 and 34 are at the highest risk for sexual violence. And for young women in college, their risks are even higher. College women aged 18–24 face a risk of sexual violence three times higher than women overall (Rape, Abuse and Incest National Network, 2016).

The problem of sexual violence is linked to gender inequality. Among all juvenile victims of sexual assault, 82% are girls. Among adult victims, 90% are women (Rape, Abuse and Incest National Network, 2016). These statistics provide a context for understanding what happened to Daisy and Audrie. Their experiences are not uncommon. Instead, their assaults reflect a bigger social problem in the United States, and one that many people have been organizing to resist.

This chapter will focus on social problems related to sexualities. We will view sex and sexuality through the sociological lens of social construction as a way to understand the taken-for-granted meanings about sex. By viewing sex as socially constructed, we will be able to see why certain sexual practices are thought of as problems, and how these problems impact individuals and communities. By examining patterns within the United States, we will develop an understanding of sexuality as closely connected to its cultural context. In this way, sexuality-based problems that seem to be individualistic can be interpreted as reflections of that individual's society. We'll focus on hookup culture, commercial sex, and sexual health and disease as potential social problems. Then, we will review mainstream and specialized theories of sexuality to enrich our understanding. We conclude the chapter by looking at organizations that deal with sexuality and are devoted to social change.

UNDERSTANDING HOW SEXUALITIES CAN BE SOCIAL PROBLEMS

5.1 Explain how sexuality is a social construction.

"Sex is not a natural act" (Tiefer, 2004, p. 1).

This assertion contrasts with the common perception in the United States about **sex** and **sexuality**, where we think sex is a natural part of human behavior. People talk about sex as a biological urge or an instinctual survival tactic dating back to the Stone Age. We say we have a sex drive that's out of our control, and that we are "born that way" regarding our sexual identities. People treat their sexual preferences as unchosen and independent of the society in which they live. But when we examine sex across cultures and throughout history, it becomes very clear how *un*natural it really is.

Of course, it is true that sex typically involves what nature gives us—our bodies. Sexual acts can involve genitals, mouths, hands, and other body parts. But how we interpret these practices varies across disciplines. Biologists and others in the physical sciences have attributed sexual behavior to bodily functions—hormones, brain chemistry, evolutionary adaptations, and chromosomal expression. Psychologists tend to think about sexuality as more influenced by how people's psyches have developed since birth, or as determined by children's attachments to their immediate family members. Religious perspectives associate divine properties to blessed sex, and may define countless practices as sinful. Each of these perspectives has people devoted to their accuracy.

Within sociology, sexuality is thought of as dependent on culture. We interpret sexuality as **socially constructed**, or based on society's agreed-upon meanings for sexual behaviors, feelings, and identities. When we imagine sexuality as a social construct, we are able to explain why it is so different across cultures, and why the meanings of sex have changed over time. This sociological perspective enables us to critically interpret sexuality and the taken-for-granted assumptions that surround it. With this view, we can begin to understand how aspects of human sexuality can be viewed as social problems.

Consider the following scenario. A person enjoys sex, but does not experience orgasm. No matter whether they are alone or with a partner, they do not reach sexual climax. Depending on to whom they disclose this information, they would encounter different reactions. A physician might run tests to determine if this person's hormone levels were in the appropriate range. A psychologist might explore this person's past through therapy to identify a point where psychosexual development was stunted. A religious leader might question this person's faith and instruct them to pray harder. Each of these responses reflects discipline-specific interpretations. Which explanation is correct? Does this person have imbalanced hormones? Improper psychosexual development? Inadequate worship habits? Perhaps all three explanations are applicable. What if none of them are? Is it possible that the enjoyment of sex without orgasm is only a problem if the person defines it as such? Maybe this experience only

appears to be a troublesome issue because of the importance our society places on sexual climax as a definitive endpoint to a sexual experience.

The fact that sexuality can be explained differently depending on which lens is used shows us how sexuality is not really that natural. In other words, sex cannot simply be attributed to our body's natural responses. Today, people in the United States rely heavily on Western medical professionals to provide answers around sexuality. But about 150 years ago, Christianity held the most authority (Fee, 1988). In fact, the prevalence of one lens over another may be viewed as a social problem in itself. Religious leaders may eschew psychological explanations for sexuality, for example. Biologists may dismiss sociologists' reliance on cultural relativity. In each of these viewpoints, a number of significant people could define the other viewpoints as problems to be ameliorated.

But beyond these disciplinary disagreements, many issues related to sexuality can be considered social problems: sexual violence, sexually transmitted infections, and public masturbation. Most people in the United States consider these issues to be clear-cut problems. In other words, a significant number of people believe these aspects of sexuality are harmful. But other sexuality-related issues are more controversial. Some people want to keep prostitution illegal; others want to decriminalize sex work. Some people fret about teens "sexting" on smart phones; others see this as a way for teens to express their sexualities without the risks associated with pregnancy and disease. Surely, a significant number of people consider these sexual behaviors harmful. But a significant number of people disagree with that assertion. These gray areas complicate what counts as a sexuality-related social problem and reinforce sex and sexuality as socially constructed.

When we examine sexuality as socially constructed, it becomes clear that sexuality-related social problems are also socially constructed. What counts as a social problem in one society is quite normal in another. In Saudi Arabia and parts of Zimbabwe, for example, consensual same-sex activity is punishable by death. But Mozambique and Mexico offer legal protections for people who engage in same-sex sexual activity (United Nations, 2015). In

....

Sexual bullying: A pattern of sexual harassment that can include spreading rumors about a person's sexual behavior or identity, forcing someone to do something sexual, and writing sexual messages about a person online or as graffiti.

Sex: The behaviors of two or more people who consent to the pursuit of pleasure and define these behaviors as such.

Sexuality: A combination of sexual behaviors, attractions, identities, and communities.

Social construction: Society's agreed-upon meanings that vary across culture and throughout history.

the United States, the criminalization of same-sex sex through sodomy laws ended in 2003. Then in 2015, same-sex marriage was legalized (Smith, 2016). Rights for the lesbian, gay, bisexual, transgender, and queer/questioning (LGBTQ) community have come a long way in the United States. Back in 1777, founding father Thomas Jefferson advocated that men who committed sodomy be castrated. For women sodomites, he suggested boring holes through their noses. Jefferson viewed these punishments as more humane alternatives to Virginia's death penalty sentences (Gay and Lesbian Archives of the Pacific Northwest, 2007). And although public support for LGBTQ rights has been increasing, no national law currently exists to protect workers from being fired for being gay or lesbian (Human Rights Campaign, 2016). So whether sexual relations between people of the same sex are a social problem depends on time and place.

In this chapter, we will consider some of the key patterns and trends related to sexuality. Then we will address some current issues related to sexuality that many people consider to be sexual problems: hookup culture and the sexual double standard, sexual labor, and sexually transmitted diseases and sexual health.

ASK YOURSELF: What factors are most influential in classifying certain kinds of sexual behaviors as problems? What social problems related to sexuality exist now, but might not in 50 years? Can you think of any sexuality issue that is unique to the individual and not influenced by their social context?

PATTERNS AND TRENDS

5.2 Discuss patterns and trends of sexuality-related social problems.

If we are going to discuss the patterns and trends related to sex and sexuality, it would be helpful to start with a working definition of sex. In your opinion, what counts as sex? For heterosexual pairings, most people agree that sex includes penile-vaginal intercourse (PVI). Most would also include penile-anal intercourse as sex, and still, a majority view oral-genital contact as sex. The research on what counts as sex shows that other types of sexual contact are less likely to be described as "sex," but some people still consider hand-genital contact and mutual masturbation to be sex (see Table 5.1; Sanders et al., 2010). These statistics are useful in identifying patterns in what counts as sex, but notice that no behavior achieves consensus on the issue. Even in the most commonly agreed-upon behavior—PVI—the numbers fail to reach 100%. Some people still hesitate to classify PVI as "sex." What could be happening here?

There are many factors that go into determining what counts as sex. For some people, a simple list of behaviors leaves out key factors that are useful in deciding whether an act counts as sex or not. For example, many people would classify PVI as sex only if it was consensual. Nonconsensual PVI could be considered rape, and survivors of sexual assault may hesitate to call those experiences sex. Other factors in defining sex may relate to the quantity and quality of the act. If PVI lasts only a few seconds, is it sex? What if no one has an orgasm? If one person thinks they just had sex, but their partner does not, did sex occur? Beyond heterosexual contexts, what acts qualify as "going all the way"? Research on gay and lesbian definitions of sex also shows a lack of agreement. One study found that 90% of men who have sex with men define penile-anal intercourse as sex, and just over 60% count oral-genital contact as sex. The same research study found less consensus among women who partner with women. Among them, close to 80% considered oral-genital contact sex, and about 70% of the sample also included penetration with toys, genital-genital contact, and hand-genital contact to be sex (Sewell, McGarrity, & Strassberg, 2016). An author of several books on lesbian sexuality asserts,

FIGURE 5.1 American Support for Same-Sex Relations, 1978–2017

Do you think gay or lesbian relations between consenting adults should or should not be legal?

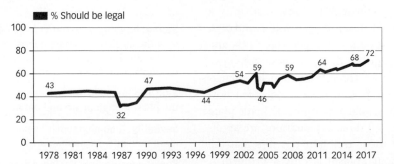

SOURCE: From "US Support for Gay Marriage Edges to New High," by Justin McCarthy. Gallup News, May 15, 2017. Reprinted with permission from Gallup Inc.

FIGURE 5.2   Employment Protections by State, 2017

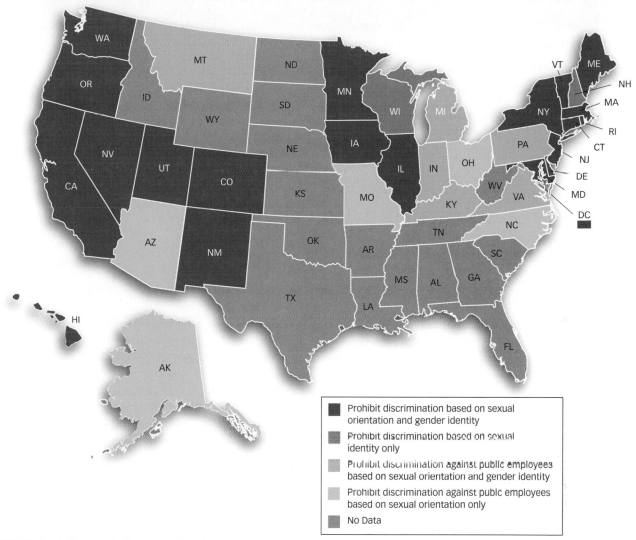

Legend:
- Prohibit discrimination based on sexual orientation and gender identity
- Prohibit discrimination based on sexual identity only
- Prohibit discrimination against public employees based on sexual orientation and gender identity
- Prohibit discrimination against public employees based on sexual orientation only
- No Data

SOURCE: Reprinted with permission from Human Rights Campaign.

"There's no ultimate act of lesbian sex" (Cage, 2014, p. 16). What does sex really mean if there are different definitions of "sex" based on the genders of the people involved? The definition offered in the previous section defined sex as "the behaviors of two or more people who consent to the pursuit of pleasure and define these behaviors as such." But as we can see in the research, offering a definition that is applicable to everyone in every situation is elusive. How can we tell the difference, if any, between sex and hooking up? Does it matter? In the next section, we consider the relevance of "hookup culture" as a social problem.

ASK YOURSELF: What counts as sex to you? Has your definition of sex changed over time based on your own experiences? How does consent matter in your definition? Does the quality of the sex or the length of the act matter in how you define whether you've had sex?

Hookup Culture and the Sexual Double Standard

Imagine receiving a text message from a good friend: "I hooked up with my study group partner last night." What exactly is your friend describing? The term **hooking up** is rather vague, perhaps purposefully so. Based on research studying it, hooking up can refer to kissing, but it can also refer to sex. It can include all of the other sexual behaviors that fall between these two ends of the sexual continuum, as well. The ambiguous nature of the term allows young people to feel like they can satisfy their friends' expectations while maintaining their own privacy and independence (Bogle, 2008).

Hooking up: A casual sexual encounter without emotional or romantic expectations, often occurring within an intoxicating party atmosphere.

TABLE 5.1 Attitudes Regarding Which Behaviors Count as Sex

Would you say you "had sex" with someone if the most intimate behavior you engaged in was . . .	% said "yes"
You touched, fondled, or manually stimulated a partner's genitals?	44.9
A partner touched, fondled, or manually stimulated your genitals?	48.1
You had oral (mouth) contact with a partner's genitals?	71.0
A partner had oral (mouth) contact with your genitals?	72.9
Penile-anal intercourse?	80.8
Penile-vaginal intercourse?	94.8
Penile-vaginal intercourse with no ejaculation (the man did not "come")?	89.1
Penile-vaginal intercourse with no female orgasm (the woman did not "come")?	92.7
Penile-vaginal intercourse, but very brief?	94.4
Penile-vaginal intercourse with a condom?	93.3

SOURCE: Sanders, Stephanie A., Brandon J. Hill, William L. Yarber, Cynthia A. Graham, Richard A. Crosby, and Robin R. Milhausen. 2010. "Misclassification Bias: Diversity in Conceptualisations about Having 'Had Sex'." *Sexual Health* 7(1):31–4.

Without doubt, hooking up has become a defining feature of young adult sexuality, and its roots are in higher education. On college campuses across the United States, students can expect to encounter what is known as "hookup culture." Characterized by sexually charged party atmospheres, copious alcohol consumption, and casual sex, hookup culture has become a defining feature of present-day life for young adults (Wade, 2017). Some people find the existence of hookup culture to be a problem in and of itself, objecting on moral or religious grounds. They may long for a fantastical version of the good ol' days, modeled in 1950s-era portrayals of dating in popular culture. But from a sociological standpoint, hookup culture is marked by other kinds of social problems.

Although not all college students buy into hookup culture, its pervasiveness influences the ways young people think about their sexualities. Students who opt out of hooking up often experience social marginalization. If a college student does not drink alcohol, dislikes the party scene, or just chooses to prioritize their studies, how do they fit into college life? What social life options are available to them? Some of these students manage long-term, monogamous relationships, but others who are unattached can find it difficult to find stable partners within the hookup culture context (Bogle, 2008; Wade, 2017). Other young adults participate in hookup culture and hope to find a more serious relationship within it. In a sense, the old dating rituals have become reversed. Instead of meeting someone, getting to know them, calling them your boyfriend or girlfriend, and eventually having sex, hookup culture often starts with the sexual encounter before the people involved really know much about each other (Bogle, 2008). This can cause confusion and

hurt feelings for people who envision settling down in a marriage one day, but are unsure of the steps they need to take to get there (Bogle, 2008; Kelly, 2012). Students who participate in hookup culture sometimes regret it, especially if their encounters caused embarrassment (Thomas, 2010). Beyond the emotional well-being that comes with a satisfying social life, some researchers express concern over the effects of hookup culture on other aspects of health. The ubiquitous presence of alcohol in hookup culture means that young adults may engage in risky sexual behaviors. The overconsumption of alcohol may also raise important questions about whether intoxicated actors are freely consenting to sexual activity (LaBrie et al., 2014). Overall, there is a lot of public fear around the costs of hookup culture.

Despite these concerns, however, college students seem to accept hookup culture. Research shows that students who support hookup culture agree that "hooking up is fun, harmless, status-enhancing, a way to assert control and power, and a way to express sexual freedom" (Aubrey & Smith, 2013, p. 446). In contrast to other studies, some research shows that hooking up poses no negative long-term effects on students' well-being when they are motivated to participate more autonomously instead of due to pressure from other peers (Vrangalova, 2015). This contrasts with widespread concern about the effects of casual sex on young women, in particular. Although research has found that men are more comfortable with hooking up (Lambert, Kahn, & Apple, 2003), other studies have found no significant gender differences among those who participate in hookup culture (Aubrey & Smith, 2013; Vrangalova, 2015). Given the evidence, does hooking up present equal opportunities for engaging in casual sex with equal benefits for everyone involved?

The cultural phenomenon of hooking up may mirror other inequalities. Most of the studies noted above relied on quantitative measures, which give us a little bit of information about large groups of people. A closer look at hookup culture in qualitative research, however, reveals some important gender differences. The kind of sex that happens in a hookup culture tends to benefit men more than women. Research has found that women are more likely to experience orgasm when they have sex within relationships. In hookup culture, women are less likely to participate in the kinds of sex acts most associated with their own orgasms. In more committed relationships, they can communicate their desires more easily with a person they know and trust. They also describe receiving oral sex more in relationship contexts, which is more likely to result in orgasm for many women. Women reported that hookup partners typically disregarded women's pleasure, and men confirmed this selfishness (Armstrong, England, & Fogarty, 2012a). One man told researchers he was committed to his partner's pleasure, saying, "'I'm all about just making her orgasm,' but when asked if he meant 'the general her or like the specific her?' he replied, 'Girlfriend her. In a hookup her, I don't give a shit'" (Armstrong et al., 2012a, p. 456). These gender differences in hookup culture have been referred to as contributing to an "orgasm gap" between heterosexual women and men (Armstrong et al., 2012a, p. 454). According to research on orgasm frequency, the group most likely to say they "usually" or "always" climaxed during sex was heterosexual men (95% of them). Eighty-nine percent of gay men and 88% of bisexual men reported orgasming usually or always. These numbers among men were higher than all women, though lesbians (86%) had higher orgasm frequency than bisexual (66%) and heterosexual (65%) women (Frederick, St. John, Garcia, & Lloyd, 2017).

Men's entitlement to pleasure in a hookup, and disregard for women's, reflects a type of gender inequality informed by the **sexual double standard** (Armstrong et al., 2012a; Wade, 2017). The sexual double standard is a term used to describe the ways men are rewarded for their sexually permissive attitudes and behaviors, while women are negatively labeled for doing the same things (Zaikman et al., 2016). This double standard can affect women's sexual autonomy. Although heterosexual women put effort

Andrew Lichtenstein/Sygma/Getty Images

▶ Having fun is an integral part of the college experience for many students. On college campuses across the country, young people party in sexually charged environments where alcohol consumption is paramount. Hookup culture thrives within these alcohol-soaked parties. Do you think that these events make it more likely that students will engage in risky sexual behaviors?

into looking sexually attractive and pleasing men, they compromise their own sexual agency in return. Although hookup culture may not necessarily be bad for women overall, its focus on men's pleasure may normalize men's sexual aggression and be a contributing factor to rape culture (Wade, 2017).

Ultimately, many people do consider hookup culture a social problem. Some critics reject the casualness of the sex acts outright. Others do not object to the casual sex that defines hookup culture, but to the ways the social dynamics can marginalize some groups of people. What do you think?

....

ASK YOURSELF: How does the research on hookup culture compare to your own college experiences? Do you think hooking up advantages men and disadvantages women? Would you classify hookup culture as a social problem?

....

Sex Work and Human Trafficking

As a society, we generally agree that sex is special. Social institutions like religion, family, and the media convey messages about sex as an intimate act that is done

....

Sexual double standard: A term describing the ways that men are rewarded—and women are negatively labeled—for sexually permissive attitudes and behaviors.

Penises, Reconsidered

Imagine the scene:

A woman lies sleeping in her room. She is a widow. She sleeps in bed with her youngest child, while her other children slumber nearby on a mattress. Suddenly, she awakes in the night to find a man climbing into her bed. He tells her to hush, and takes hold of her shoulder.

What happens next?

Chances are, you assume the woman is about to get raped. And if you grew up in the United States, this may be the ultimate outcome. Without doubt, the scenario above is terrifying for most women in the United States.

But this home invasion took place in Indonesia, where sexual norms are different. The woman suppressed her initial fright and responded with defiance. She sat up, pushed the man off her, and shouted at him as he stumbled away, out of a window, and into the village streets. Later the next morning, she joked about the event with others in the neighborhood. Amid uproarious laughter, a neighbor mocked the man's stupidity. The woman was also angry—she wanted the man to pay a fee for his mistake.

This story was recounted by anthropologist Christine Helliwell (2000) as part of her research with the Indonesian community. When Helliwell first heard about the attack, she was alarmed. She considered it an attempted rape, worthy of punishment. When she tried to discuss the incident with the woman, she struggled to convey her anger. Unable to find a word for *rape* within the people's native language, she asked the woman if she had thought to hurt the man while she was shooing him out of her room. The woman was confused and shocked, replying, "It's only a penis. How can a penis hurt anyone?"

For this community, penises were not imposing weapons, waiting to inflict harm onto women's more vulnerable organs. In fact, genitals were not tied to sex and gender. Instead, a person's work tasks were greater signifiers of gender. Genitals weren't even crucial for determining sexual desire (Helliwell, 2001).

The ways this community gives meaning to genitalia illustrate how meanings of the sexual body are not universal. Meanings of sexual bodies vary around the world. One interesting example is found among

the Dani people of West New Guinea. From about the age of 6, Dani boys wear a long gourd over their penises nearly all the time. This culture is known for its low interest in sex. In his research with the Dani, Heider (1976) found that new parents viewed sex as procreative. They abstained from sex for 5 years after the birth of a child. This practice was customary and caused little concern for its practitioners. Another example closer to home is the reverence for bigger penises in the United States. As much as U.S. culture takes lessons from the ancient Greeks, it is noteworthy that the Greeks valued small penises as the more admirable male body type (Dover, 2016/1989). Contrast the evidence you see on ancient Greek statues with the current reverence for larger phalluses. If size matters, it matters differently across cultures and throughout history.

1. How do views and meanings of genitals affect the ways people define their sexualities?

2. What do you think about living in a society where attempted rape is a laughable infraction? Could your own country ever hold that same idea?

between two people who care about each other. Due to these socially constructed meanings, the selling of sex for money violates commonly held ideas about sex. Many people view **sexual labor** as immoral and indicative of a social problem. Sociologist Ronald Weitzer (2015) argues, "Prostitution is universally seen as a problem rather than an opportunity. There is a strong and widespread antipathy toward it on the part of most individuals, most NGOs, and most governments. Prostitution is viewed as dangerous for the sellers, as attracting perverse customers (deviants and abusers), as disruptive for communities where prostitution is visibly present, and as unmanageable by state authorities" (p. 81). But like most social issues, the public does not always agree. Research suggests that

people who have conservative political ideologies are more likely to oppose prostitution, while people who are more liberal, less religious, and of a higher social status are more accepting of it (Chon, 2015).

Sexual labor can take on different forms. The commercial sex industry includes street prostitution, brothels, high-status escorting services, exotic dancing and strip clubs, Internet video camming, and pornography. People who labor in this industry are often referred to as "sex workers," though they do not always have sex with the people paying for their services. Some sex work

Sexual labor: The selling of sexual services for money.

includes labor provided for legal sexual entertainment, such as peepshows, stripping, and pornography featuring adult actors. Although it is legal to pay for sex in some countries, such as Australia and Germany, prostitution is mostly illegal in the United States. Only a few counties in Nevada have decriminalized prostitution (Weitzer, 2012).

The number of people affected by a problem typically informs public policies targeting its prevention or elimination. But getting accurate statistics about the commercial sex industry is extremely difficult. One problem lies in how one defines commercial sex. Providers of erotic massage, online exhibitions of sex, and street prostitution are all types of sex work. Some people may choose to participate in these occupations, while others may be coerced into it. In addition, police arrest records often reflect local economies where prostitution is clustered, and not national trends. Prostitution is also known to have a high turnover of workers who are highly mobile (Wagenaar, Amesberger, & Altink, 2017). And although the buyers of sex greatly outnumber the sellers, it is the workers themselves who are most often subjected to arrest (Weitzer, 2012). These factors make tracking the sex industry nearly impossible (Wagenaar, Amesberger, & Altink, 2017). Commercial sex scholars have voiced critiques of attempts to present figures on the industry. They caution people to carefully assess sources for any statistics used to characterize this stigmatized population (Wagenaar et al., 2017; Weitzer, 2012). Still, many articles are published with dubious statistics about sex work.

One example of inaccurate reporting within the commercial sex industry relates to the trafficking of sex workers, which is included in information about human trafficking. The United Nations defines **human trafficking**, or "trafficking in persons," as

> the recruitment, transportation, transfer, harbouring or receipt of persons, by means of the threat or use of force or other forms of coercion, of abduction, of fraud, of deception, of the abuse of power or of a position of vulnerability or of the giving or receiving of payments or benefits to achieve the consent of a person having control over another person, for the purpose of exploitation. Exploitation shall include, at a minimum, the exploitation of the prostitution of others or other forms of sexual exploitation, forced labour or services, slavery or practices similar to slavery, servitude or the removal of organs. (United Nations, 2004, p. 42)

According to the most recent report issued by the U.S. Department of State, human trafficking is a $150 billion industry that enslaves millions of children, women, and men (U.S. Department of State, 2016). Yet this same report also acknowledges the unreliable nature of research on trafficking.

A central focus within the problem of trafficking people is what many organizations call "sex trafficking." These organizations condemn the practice of transporting and selling people for sexual services. Polaris, an organization focused on ending modern slavery and restoring freedom to trafficked victims, reports that it has received over 22,000 reports of cases where people have been trafficked for sex. It characterizes traffickers as deceptive and violent, who victimize youth who run away and are homeless (Polaris, 2017). The Half the Sky Movement has tried to raise awareness of the problem, claiming "far more women and girls are shipped into brothels annually now, in the early 21st century, than African slaves were shipped into slave plantations each year in the 18th century" (Half the Sky Movement, n.d.).

But sex work activists challenge the bold claims made about what these groups call "sex trafficking." They critique the way the term "prioritizes moralistic, limited, and objectifying notions of the product ('sex') rather than on the people producing that labor (sex workers)" (Lerum, 2015). They also object to the dominant narrative around sexual labor that portrays young women and girls as stolen and exploited by their captors. Popular movies like *Taken* and *Abduction of Eden* feature dramatic storylines where girls are kidnapped, drugged, and forced into sex with older men. Critics argue that stories like these mislead the public about human trafficking and bolster the need for heroic interventions from Western men. They also object to the way antitrafficking activists distort real life, heart-wrenching stories of abuse as a way to promote their efforts to rescue people from dangerous conditions. Although these stories are alarming and indeed warrant attention, they tend to justify the criminalization of all sex workers (Lerum, 2015). Most people find the abduction of children for sexual exploitation indefensible. But questions remain about the scope of the problem.

What do you think about commercial sex? Is the selling of sex a social problem? Most people would likely agree that coercing or forcing people into the commercial sex trade is a social problem. But what about people who freely choose to engage in sex work? Is the selling of their sexual services a problem? And why do we focus more on the sellers of sex than the buyers? What drives men (and some women) to purchase sex? What conditions in society drive women (and some men) to sell sex? Issues of gender and economic inequality inform this issue. Women are sexually objectified in our society. And poverty can be a factor that pushes poor people to sell their bodies. But even though people may barter for sex in their committed relationships (e.g., doing the laundry in exchange for oral

....

Human trafficking: Recruiting, transporting, and harboring vulnerable people through threats or force to exploit their labor, including sexual labor.

Guy Corbishley/Alamy Stock Photo

▶ Sex workers march in London, England to claim their right to practice their profession without fear of being arrested and assaulted. Some prostitutes say that the more their work must be clandestine, the more it becomes a danger to public health and an invitation to crime. Do you agree with them?

sex), we still seem to treat the exchange of sex for money with disdain. Ultimately, social taboos around sexuality have allowed our society to stigmatize people who sell their sexual labor for cash.

··

ASK YOURSELF: How is sexual labor like other kinds of jobs that involve the exploitation or even abuse of the body? Are some kinds of commercial sex more acceptable than others? Which social forces construct commercial sex as a social problem, and how have you been influenced by these ideologies?

··

Sexually Transmitted Diseases and Sexual Health

"All Americans should have the opportunity to make choices that lead to health and wellness" (Centers for Disease Control and Prevention [CDC], 2016b, p. 1). This statement asserts a basic human right—the right to choose a healthy life. The assertion is the first line on the first page of the most recent statistical publication on **sexually transmitted diseases (STDs)** in the United States. It is published by the Centers for Disease Control and Prevention (CDC), a national governmental organization tasked with the surveillance of risks to human health, including STDs. Therefore, the statement that people are entitled to choose health relates to our sexual health as well.

The existence of STDs is considered a social problem by many people who care about human sexuality.

According to the CDC (2016b), there were 1,526,658 cases of chlamydia, 395,216 cases of gonorrhea, and 23,872 cases of syphilis reported in 2015. Based on messages you have heard about STDs, do you think the rates of infection are on the rise, on the decline, or staying the same? The answer depends on the STD and the time period that is being examined. Although chlamydia had the highest incidence rates reported among these three STDs in 2015, it experienced the lowest increase. From 2014 to 2015, chlamydia increased by 5.9%, while gonorrhea saw a 12.8% increase and syphilis saw a 19% increased during the same year (CDC, 2016b). Although 2015 brought the highest number of reported cases ever for these three STDs combined, STD rates had been on the decline up until the early 2000s (CDC, 2016b). For HIV, an incurable STD that can cause death, 40,000 new HIV infections are diagnosed each year. But HIV rates experienced a 19% decline between 2005 and 2014 (CDC, 2016c). The most common STD, Human Papilloma Virus (HPV), affects nearly 80 million people in the United States (Satterwhite et al., 2013). In fact, HPV is so commonplace that most people who are sexually active will get it, though it may never result in any symptoms (CDC, 2016a). Figure 5.3 provides an overview of the rates of common STDs. Most sexually active people will be affected by an STD at some point in their lives (Satterwhite et al., 2013).

Although anyone can get an STD, some groups are more at risk than others. Young people between the ages of 15 and 24 years are most at risk for acquiring an STD (CDC, 2016b; Satterwhite et al., 2013). Compared to men, women face serious long-term health complications, such as infertility. Men who have sex with men are at greater risk of acquiring STDs compared to men who are exclusively heterosexual and women (CDC, 2016b). STD rates also vary based on race and ethnicity. For example, reports of chlamydia cases increased for Asians (7.8%), whites (14.6%), and multiracial people (43.1%); decreased among black people (11.2%); and stayed stable for Native Americans and Hispanics between 2011 and 2015. But for syphilis, rates increased for all race and ethnicity groups during that same time period (CDC, 2016b).

··

Sexually transmitted diseases (STDs): Bacterial and viral infections of the human body that are passed through sexual behaviors.

Despite these alarming statistics, they must be taken with a grain of salt. Private and public STD reporting systems are imperfect. For example, consider what happens when a person goes to a public health clinic and tests positive for syphilis, but wants a second opinion. They then go to their family doctor and get another syphilis test, with positive results again. If both the clinic and the private doctor report the syphilis case to the CDC, the same person's STD case is reported twice as two separate cases. In reality, there is only one case of syphilis to be reported. The same is true for a person who gets a positive result and never gets treatment, but retests as positive again in the future. In addition, people from lower socioeconomic statuses are more likely seek health care at free clinics, which may have more systematic STD reporting mechanisms in place compared to small family practices where those with private insurance get care. These situations contribute to overreporting of some STD cases.

On the other hand, some STDs are underreported. Some people are less likely to seek health care. Men, especially those who hold traditional beliefs about masculinity, go to the doctor less frequently (Himmelstein & Sanchez, 2016). And due to the high prevalence of racial discrimination, people of color may be less inclined to seek health care services and to get treatment (Burgess et al., 2008). Thus, men and racial minorities may be less likely to know they have an STD. STDs among these groups would be less likely to wind up in official statistics. Finally, many STDs are asymptomatic, which means people can have an STD without ever showing any signs. Without recognizable symptoms, they may never get tested, and may be omitted from national data on STDs.

With the amount of attention placed on tracking STDs, it becomes clear that the U.S. government defines STDs as a social problem. But are STDs truly a *social* problem? Indeed, a sexually transmitted infection, or STI, requires medical invention. But why is the sexual transmission of a virus or bacterial strain more problematic than other infections? The common cold can be transmitted during a sexual encounter, yet it is not classified as an STD or STI. And with many STIs being curable or becoming undetectable with treatments, is it really appropriate to classify them as diseases? The existence of social stigma affects the ways we view STDs. Is it plausible that herpes can be thought of as a temporary skin rash, like poison ivy? Or do societal taboos around sexuality inevitably influence how we think about genital infections?

Stigma regarding sexual health extends beyond physical infections to psychological problems. The American Psychiatric Association (APA) designates a range of sexual practices as indicative of mental disorder in its diagnostic manual. The APA classifies some aspects of sexuality as "dysfunctional." People who lack desire for sex, experience limited or delayed sexual arousal, or feel pelvic pain during sex may be diagnosed by psychotherapists as having a sexual dysfunction (American Psychiatric Association, 2013a). However, self-identified asexuals may find no problems with their disinterest in sex or lack of erotic arousal (Carrigan, 2011). And pelvic pain may be a symptom of a physical problem.

Why are these aspects of sexuality considered mental disorders? The APA does not simply label atypical sexual interest as mental disorder. Instead, it requires that people who exhibit those interests "feel personal distress about their interest, not merely distress resulting from society's disapproval; or have a sexual desire or behavior that involves another person's psychological distress, injury, or death, or a desire for sexual behaviors involving unwilling persons or persons unable to give legal consent" (American Psychiatric Association, 2013b, p. 1). However, it is unclear how a person can express distress that is independent of social stigma. For example, sexual arousal while cross-dressing can be diagnosed as "transvestic disorder." But if a person feels ashamed about this interest primarily because society has rigid gender expectations, then is the interest truly a disorder? In addition, the paraphilias of sexual sadism and sexual masochism can involve distress and even injury as part of the consensually negotiated scenes. These issues raise questions about the ways some atypical practices become classified as psychological disturbances. Psychomedical institutions have tremendous power in defining some sexual practices as unhealthy. At the same time, the APA's diagnostic manual lacks any definition for what counts as healthy or functional sexuality. These issues have caused sexualities scholars to challenge the ways mental health professionals pathologize some sexualities (e.g., Moser & Kleinplatz, 2005; Windsor, 2014).

Like the CDC stated in the quotation that started this section, people should be able to choose paths to sexual health. It is possible for a person to have an STD or a diagnosable sexual dysfunction (or both!) while feeling good and healthy about one's sexuality. Much of how we pathologize sexuality in the United States is related to social stigma. Perhaps the social problems related to sexual health, then, are more about societal health than physical or psychological conditions.

****

ASK YOURSELF: Why do you think STDs are classified according to the method of transmission rather than the symptoms or affected body parts? Can you think of any other disease classification that relies on the method of transmission? How does stigma affect the way people view STDs compared to other communicable diseases? How does stigma affect the way we treat some sexual practices as disordered?

****

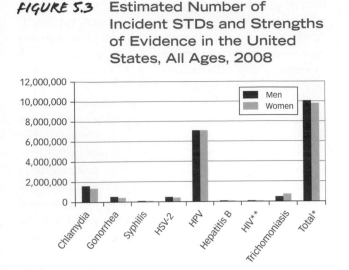

FIGURE 5.3 Estimated Number of Incident STDs and Strengths of Evidence in the United States, All Ages, 2008

SOURCE: Satterwhite, Catherine Lindsey, Elizabeth Torrone, Elissa Meites, Eileen F. Dunne, Reena Mahajan, Cheryl Bañez Ocfemia, John Su, Fujie Xu, and Hillard Weinstock. 2013. "Sexually Transmitted Infections among Us Women and Men: Prevalence and Incidence Estimates, 2008." *Sexually Transmitted Diseases* 40(3):187–93. Reprinted with permission from Wolters Kluwer Health, Inc.

*Totals may not add exactly due to missing data on sex and rounding.

**HIV estimates for men and women only include data for blacks/African Americans, Hispanics/Latinos, and whites; these three racial/ethnic groups accounted for 96% of all incident HIV infections. The total estimate includes all races.

USING THEORY TO UNDERSTAND SEXUAL VIOLENCE: THE VIEWS FROM THE FUNCTIONALIST, CONFLICT, AND SYMBOLIC INTERACTIONIST PERSPECTIVES

5.3 Apply the functionalist, conflict, and symbolic interactionist perspectives to the study of sexuality-related social problems, specifically sexual violence.

Making someone feel obligated, pressured or forced into doing something of a sexual nature that they don't want to is sexual coercion. This includes persistent attempts at sexual contact when the person has already refused you. Nobody owes you sex, ever; and no means no, always.

—Miya Yamanouchi, author of *Embrace Your Sexual Self: A Practical Guide for Women* (2015)

The quotation above belies certain realities at work in our society. Namely, there is an air of entitlement around our sexual exchanges. Why do we need to be told that no

always means no when it comes to sex? Isn't that assertion common sense? Unfortunately, the commonplace nature of sexual violence means that statements like Yamanouchi's are needed. But society is moving toward understanding consent as a key part of sexual experiences. In this way, people have started talking about the need for establishing consent during sexual encounters, and avoiding situations where consent is compromised, such as when a person is intoxicated, impaired, or subjected to an exploitative power dynamic (e.g., a prisoner and a prison guard). Part of understanding consent is in detailing what counts as nonconsensual sex, which is often thought of as sexual violence.

The three primary sociological theories provide a basic framework for understanding sexual violence in the United States. How can we understand the commonplace nature of rape and sexual assault? What roles do institutions, individuals, and inequalities play in the ways sexual violence exists in the United States? What are the policy implications associated with the main theoretical approaches? The next section applies the functionalist, conflict, and symbolic interactionist theories to sexual violence.

Structural Functionalism

Theories within structural functionalism focus on how a society works, or functions, to maintain itself. It examines the ways different social institutions work together to maintain order within society. Within this framework, we would consider what function sexual violence serves in society. A structural functionalist explanation for sexual violence relates to gender inequality. As the previous chapter discussed, men have substantial advantages over women. In a patriarchal, or male-dominated, society like the United States, sexual violence can be understood as serving to maintain the status quo of gender differences. A structural functionalist explanation for sexual violence might argue that because many women live in fear of being raped, their ability to live freely in the world is stifled, thus perpetuating their continued subordination as women. The threat of sexual violence, then, serves to inhibit women's independence and sexual autonomy (Jones, 2012). Conversely, it sustains men's roles as the dominant actors in sexual exchanges and in social life more broadly.

Another structural functionalist approach would consider the **latent functions** of sexual violence, or its unintended positive consequences. Sociologist Robert K. Merton (1968) argued that the latent functions of a social action may be more interesting sociologically.

Sexual violence may have important latent functions. Widespread sexual violence may serve to mobilize

Latent function: An unintended, or indirect, consequence of a social action; results that occur but were not the primary purpose of the action.

women to act with collective resistance. By sharing their experiences with sexual violence, women may engage in consciousness-raising and develop a commitment to feminism (Donovan, 2012). The 2017 Women's March on Washington, for example, demonstrated women's collective outrage over the continuing normalization of men's sexual violence against women (Sauder, 2017). Although sexual violence is a chief way women experience oppression, women's resistance to it is fierce. In addition to political actions like marches and Take Back the Night rallies to end sexual violence, sexuality scholars have theorized rape as part of broader cultural dynamics. Thus, an unintended consequence to sexual violence from a structural functionalist perspective may be the new ways we understand sexual violence as occurring in a **rape culture**. Here, rape is not something committed by "bad" or pathological men, but is something that fits within masculinity constructs that encourage men's dominance over women and promotes relationships based on sexual coercion (Pascoe & Hollander, 2016).

Policy Implications of Structural Functionalism

If we acknowledge that sexual assault occurs because of cultural norms, then strategies to end sexual violence should address the institutional factors that contribute to rape culture. In recent years, the Internet has been a site for challenging rape culture. Through social media hashtags like #BeenRapedNeverReported, anti–street harassment apps like HollaBack!, and countless feminist blogs, digital activism is raising awareness about the problem of sexual violence. These forums foster community and dialogue among young women and girls (Keller, Mendes, & Ringrose, 2016; Rentschler, 2014). And these initiatives pervade social media, a powerful structure in socializing youth. Other strategies focus on preventative efforts that engage communities with educational programming. These advocates work to identify the social supports necessary to prevent sexual violence from occurring in the first place (Dunn, 2015).

GABRIELLE LURIE/AFP/Getty Images

▶ A student carries a sign in solidarity for a rape victim during graduation at Stanford University. Stanford students were protesting the university's handling of rape cases, alleging that the campus keeps secret the names of students found to be responsible for sexual assault and misconduct. How does society blame women for sexual assault?

Evelyn Hockstein/For The Washington Post via Getty Images

▶ Savannah Badalich, the founder of the Bruin Consent Coalition, a campaign against sexual assault, sits in front of signs bearing 7,000 ribbons at UCLA. The student club held an event to pay respect to the 7,000 UCLA students who have experienced or will experience sexual violence over the course of their lifetime.

ASK YOURSELF: When should we start teaching youth about sex? If we need to change the climate around sex to eliminate rape culture, then how young is too young? What social institutions should teach youth about sex? Is this education best delivered at home among family, in schools among peers, or in religious spaces? How should we talk about the need for consent in sexual relations?

Rape culture: The societal conditions that encourage men's dominance over women where men feel entitled to sexually coerce women in order to fit conventional standards of masculinity.

Trans Sexuality, With Differences Across Gender, Race, and Class

LGBTQ—which one of these letters does not belong? The acronym stands for Lesbian, Gay, Bisexual, Transgender, and Queer/Questioning. Sometimes the letters extend to I (Intersex), A (Asexual), and more. As our understanding of sexuality and gender evolves, so too does the language used to describe our diverse experiences. But in the commonly used LGBTQ descriptor, all of the letters represent a sexual identity, except for T—transgender—which represents a gender term. In reality, transgender people can be any sexual identity. They can be L, G, B, Q, or any other sexuality. The inclusion of "transgender" in this acronym reflects the ways trans people are part of queer communities and organizations. The acronym seems to account for the ways that gender and sexuality intersect. Beyond its sexual diversity, the transgender community contains people from all walks of life. And when we examine the most common problems faced by trans people, it becomes immediately clear that intersectionality provides an important lens to understand the issues.

The National Center for Transgender Equality published the largest study of trans people in the United States in 2015. It found that trans people encounter hardships in everyday life: family, housing, work, health care, and violence. But some trans people are more affected than others. For example, trans people live with HIV (1.4%) at almost five times the overall U.S. rate (0.3%), but 19% of black trans women were HIV positive. And although nearly half of trans people reported being sexually assaulted in their lifetime, the rates varied across gender and race. Female-to-male trans men (51%) and nonbinary people with female on their original birth certificate (58%) reported higher rates of sexual assault compared to trans women (37%). The highest rates for sexual assault by race were among Native Americans (65%), multiracial people (59%), and Middle Easterners (58%), compared to the lowest rates among Latino/as (48%), whites (45%), and Asians (41%) (James et al., 2016).

Compared to the general population, these figures are startling. They are likely related to higher rates of poverty endured by trans people. While 14% of the general U.S. population lives in poverty, the number doubles for trans people, who also have an unemployment rate three times higher than the national average (James et al., 2016).

▶ *Orange Is the New Black* actress Laverne Cox speaks during a news conference at the U.S. Capitol to call for federal surveys to include data on sexual orientation and gender identity. Why is the "T" part of the LGBTQ community? What do trans people have in common with sexual minorities?

Bill Clark/CQ Roll Call/Getty Images

These numbers are important, but they can take away from the human experience of trans people. As one respondent in the above survey stated: "When people have tried to grope me in the street or have verbally harassed me, it's usually either because they see me as a sexual target or because they can't figure out whether I am a 'man' or a 'woman' and they think they have the right to demand an explanation" (James et al., 2016, p. 201). For trans people, this experience is all too common. But beyond the links between gender and sexuality, the effects of race and class cannot be overlooked.

▶ **THINK ABOUT IT**

How have trans celebrities like Laverne Cox and Caitlyn Jenner affected public opinion on transgender people?

Conflict Theory

As we have seen in previous chapters, conflict theory represents a struggle between the "haves" and the "have nots." In Marx's (1978/1844) classic theory, this conflict was between the owners of production (the bourgeoisie) and the workers (the proletariat). Other Marxist theorists expanded the scope of conflict, including Nancy Hartsock (2013/1983), who identified parallels between the bourgeoisie–proletariat conflict and the relationship between men and women. In comparison to women of the same race, men in the United States retain control over most resources. They hold the majority of power in most social institutions: government, religion, and the economy. This dominance throughout society is known as patriarchy, and is a primary reason for gender inequality. The problem of sexual violence is one that reflects gender inequality at its core, where women report much higher rates of sexual victimization than men. A conflict theory approach to sexual violence considers the ways men control resources and are therefore positioned to set the sexual agenda in heterosexual contexts.

In reviewing sexual assault prevalence, young women between the ages of 18 and 24 report the highest rates of rape compared to all other age groups among women (Sinozich & Langton, 2014). What is unique about this age group? A conflict theory approach would explore the social worlds of this age group compared to others. This age group reflects a time period of independence, when many young adults leave home for work or college. On college campuses, for example, social resources are distributed along gender lines. In a study on college life, researchers described how college party culture laid the grounds for sexual coercion. They showed how fraternities dominated the social scene and controlled nearly everything related to social life. From choosing raunchy party themes with accompanying dress codes to supplying alcohol and transportation, fraternity brothers held the power in these interactions. They controlled the resources and limited women's resources in this context (Armstrong, Hamilton, & Sweeney, 2006). A conflict theorist would conclude that in this patriarchal context, men are the beneficiaries who have more power to sexually exploit women.

Policy Implications of the Conflict Perspective

It can be hard for women to report being raped. The United States Bureau of Justice revealed that only 32.5% of rape and sexual assaults were reported to police in 2015 (Truman & Morgan, 2016). Compared to other original felony charges that accused defendants face, rape and assault have a lower chance of resulting in convictions (Reaves, 2013). Even though sexual violence includes criminal offences, it appears that legal protections are not working for women. To foster justice for women who have been sexually assaulted, it is important to understand the reasons why they are unlikely to report these incidents to the police. Young women may fear that law enforcement officers may judge them negatively, especially if they were involved with older men or were drinking alcohol while underage. Disclosing these highly sensitive stories is more likely with officers who exhibit care and compassion in hearing them (Greeson, Campbell, & Fehler-Cabral, 2014). And when people are convicted of rape, 84% of them receive a prison sentence (Reaves, 2013).

Symbolic Interactionism

The symbolic interactionist theoretical framework focuses on the interpersonal relationships between the people involved and the meanings of their interactions. One symbolic interactionist concept is the looking-glass self, theorized by Charles Horton Cooley (1902b). This concept explains that individuals imagine how others view them and respond according to how they think others are judging them. We experience emotional reactions to our sense of how others perceive us, which makes the idea of the "self" a very social experience. For example, in getting ready to go out to a nightclub, a woman may want to wear a short, tight skirt. In the looking-glass self framework, she may imagine others' reactions to her outfit. In thinking about the reactions of people she wants to attract, she may anticipate that they will judge her as attractive and want to flirt with her. While considering the reactions of the friends she will see at the club, she imagines they will compliment her as looking cute and ready to have fun. Consequently, she may feel excited about going to the club, happy to interact in a party atmosphere.

If we apply a symbolic interactionist theory to sexual violence, we would consider the problem on the individual, or micro, level. This theory can help us understand why people involved in the same interaction may ascribe different meanings to it. In the scenario described above, a different person at the club may interpret the woman's attire as an invitation to touch her. Due to buying into the myth that women ask to be raped (Edwards et al., 2011), this club-goer may attribute her clothing as a sign that she is interested in sexual activity. To this person, the clothing symbolizes a possibility for a physical encounter, but for the woman, she may have just wanted to flirt and have a good time dancing.

The symbolic interactionist theory helps us to understand how people interpret the same symbols with different meanings. It can demonstrate how people normalize sexual violence in everyday interactions, such as seeing men's unwelcome groping and sexual dominance as just a regular part of heterosexual life (Hlavka, 2014). At the same time, symbolic interactionism is a useful tool in thinking about how we understand sexual victimization. The labeling of "victims" and "victimization" may not be experienced as such by everyone, even when the behaviors involved are similar (Gavey, 1999). These conundrums raise important issues to consider in theorizing about sexual violence and sexuality more generally.

Policy Implications of Symbolic Interactionism

How can change be felt in one-on-one interactions? Like the previous two theories have addressed, policy changes can happen in structures like media and education, and through reforming legal avenues. Perhaps by changing these institutional factors, people will learn to treat each other differently. One study of college students found that sexual stereotypes affect how people expect to negotiate consent in their interpersonal relationships (Hust, Rodgers, & Bayly, 2017). This research drives home the need for sexuality education programs that combat harmful sexual stereotypes while teaching young people how to talk about their wants, needs, and boundaries. Openly discussing desires and limits with prospective partners lays the foundation for consensual encounters to occur.

Pride in Pakistan? An Interview With Moon Charania

LGBTQ Pride parades are often thought of as celebrations where sexual minorities are free to be who they are. But the freedom experienced by participants can be affected by the way the parades are organized.

What did you notice when researching Pakistan's one and only LGBT Pride parade?

The 2011 Pride event in Pakistan was sponsored by the U.S. embassy. Attendees included U.S. military representatives, foreign diplomats, and elite leaders of Pakistani LGBT advocacy groups. There was no widely distributed press release, so other queer activists, artists, and individuals were not invited. Further, the event was held on the embassy premises, and appeared limited to the goal of U.S. patronage for select Pakistani gay and lesbian individuals and groups. As the first promotion of gay rights by U.S. diplomats in an Islamic nation, the event provoked right-wing protests, but also condemnation from local gay rights activists, who either were not among the invitees or deliberately chose not to participate in the event.

Despite more radical roots, Pride events have been reduced to visibility politics, mainstream assimilation, and sexual transgression celebrations. Pride tends to be a depoliticized party for queers and their straight allies. I don't think these objectives are necessarily interesting or important to queers in the Pakistani context where (1) visibility, identity politics, and marching in, say, pink underwear, carry less political import, and (2) queer politics is inextricably linked to decoloniality

Andrew Lichtenstein/Sygma/Getty Images

▶ Moon Charania is an assistant professor of International Studies at Spelman College. She authored *Will the Real Pakistani Woman Please Stand Up: Empire, Visual Culture, and the Brown Body* (McFarland Press, 2015). Her scholarship examines visual culture, trauma narratives, and decolonial politics. The research discussed here, "Outing the Pakistani Queer: Pride, Paranoia and Politics in U.S. Visual Culture," was published in *Sexualities* (2016, p. 20).

and class justice. Isolating LGBTQ identity from neocolonial violence is not a viable political strategy for queers who live at the intersection of multiple identities.

SPECIFIC THEORIES IN SEXUALITIES AND SOCIAL PROBLEMS SCHOLARSHIP

5.4 Apply specialized theories of sexualities.

Erotic Habitus: Understanding Both Marginalized and Normalized Sexualities

A more recent theoretical framework for understanding sexuality includes the concept of "erotic habitus" (Green, 2008), which expands Pierre Bourdieu's (1980) idea of *habitus*. Bourdieu (1980) described *habitus* as "embodied history" that "is the active presence of the whole past of which it is the product" (p. 56). He argued that people develop a habitus over time through the process of socialization and life experiences. We internalize ways of being and acting in our social worlds, and learn to behave in expected ways. The *habitus* we acquire structures how we act in different social contexts and influences our ability to change social life. To Bourdieu (1980), the habitus represents a realm of action that is both a prerequisite and an obstacle to social change. He believed that people's habitus could change slowly over time as people constructed new ways of interacting. In short, the habitus unpacks what we think of as "common sense."

....

Habitus: How people learn and develop ways to embody actions in a given social context.

Basically, notions of sexual justice and citizenship cannot be simply celebrated (e.g., Pride) when Pakistanis experience daily violence under empire, which then turns around and offers an exclusive Pride event, claiming that the U.S. stands for human rights in Pakistan.

How did the 2011 Pride parade in Islamabad relate to U.S. politics?

Gay Pride, an event imagined as the paradigmatic site of "free expression" of sexuality, and the U.S. embassy, make strange bedfellows. While the U.S. disregards queer people of color (QPOC) in the U.S., it shows a hyper-intrigue for QPOC outside the United States, particularly in Muslim nations. If the state that exacts violence on Muslims is also the same state that grants visibility to queer Muslims, we must question that visibility. People invested in sexual justice must remain vigilant toward seemingly positive practices deployed by those in power.

In your view, what does Pakistani queer resistance look like?

I am often reminded when I think of both queerness and queer resistance in the Pakistani context of José Muñoz, who so beautifully said: "We may never touch queerness, but we can feel it as the warm illumination of a horizon imbued with potentiality" (2009, p. 1). In Pakistan, and other parts of the Global South, there is this deep poetic queer resistance that comes in many forms, where queerness is informed by sexual irregularities, where queerness is bodily and challenges the limits of what can be understood as a body, where queerness assumes the presence of queer desire despite the silence, and where queerness carves out spaces for its survival, flourishment, and pleasure.

Of course, there are also more straightforward judicial triumphs. In September 2012, the Pakistani Supreme Court ruled that members of the transgender community are entitled to every right enjoyed by other citizens. In early 2011, the Court also ruled to allow a third gender category on national identity cards. Both these rulings came out of grassroots activism around the relationship between the body and human rights. There are also organizations like the Pakistan Queer Movement and Tehrik-e-Niswan (Women's Movement), which depart from Western modalities of visibility and invest in deliberate sites of art and music, like street theatre, to construct and affirm queerness, decoloniality, and critical social justice. Local Pakistani queer groups and individuals demonstrate the ambiguity and anxiety of being seen as global citizens and the complex realities of living out queer desire in the backyard of empire and state power.

▶ **THINK ABOUT IT**

1. How do LGBTQ Pride parades reflect the politics of the area in which they are organized?

2. What is the difference between LGBTQ rights and queer justice?

Building off of Bourdieu's theory of habitus, Adam Isaiah Green (2008) suggested that people also have an **erotic habitus** that guides their sexual interactions and inclinations. Green's (2008) theory of erotic habitus explains that the ways we embody our sexualities are informed by our social worlds. The theory explores how individual psychological processes like sexual desire connect to the ways institutions influence the formation of sexual ideas and manifest through our bodies in sexual practices. It "is the *sociological* component of sexual desire that straddles social structure and unconscious processes" (Green, 2008, p. 622). Having an erotic habitus means that individuals have developed certain dispositions, or inclinations. What we find sexually arousing is based on the interplay between our psychic processing of social factors (Green, 2008).

The theory of erotic habitus is a useful way to understand a variety of sexual practices. This framework has been applied to research on urban gay and bisexual men's sexual interactions (Green, 2011). It has been expanded upon to explain transgender men's evolving *sexual* habitus, which helps account for the ways trans men's changes in gendered embodiment accommodate the sexual practices they experience (Schilt & Windsor, 2014). Another study found that the framework helped explore the ways heterosexual and bisexual cisgender men reconciled their sexual attraction to transgender women who had penises (Weinberg & Williams, 2014). These studies examined the effects of habitus for people navigating more marginalized sexualities.

Erotic habitus: The interplay between psychological processes and structural influences at work when people negotiate sexual desires and behaviors.

But the theory of erotic habitus can also help us to understand more normative sexual desires. For example, erotic habitus can explain why women's breasts are sexualized in U.S. society. Why do heterosexual men identify women's breasts as sexually arousing compared to other body parts, like women's elbows or armpits? For some straight guys, paying attention to women's breasts may feel natural. They may experience sexual arousal upon seeing breasts and attribute their embodied reactions as totally normal. But the erotic habitus theory would explain that their sexual desires stem from a combination of their life experiences, structural factors in society, and their psychological processing of this information. The sexualization of breasts is a social construction, which means the meanings people ascribe to breasts vary across cultures and throughout history. Despite evolutionary biologists' and psychologists' efforts to pinpoint the effects of nuanced breast features on sexual mate selection, anthropological research reveals that not all cultures treat female breasts as objects of sexual attention (Yalom, 1997). This means that in some societies, women's breasts are not sexualized. The sexualization of breasts, then, is dependent on one's culture. So, in the United States, where breasts are featured as a prominent attribute of women's sexuality, people learn to treat them as such. Consider all the ways breasts are sexualized in U.S. media, or how religious leaders and school officials encourage girls and women to modestly cover up their breasts. When you really think about it, social institutions play a major role in teaching us how to be sexual. The erotic habitus theory argues that these structural forces imprint on our psyches and affect the ways we experience desire. In this way, heterosexual men's sexual desire for women's breasts has become normalized.

ASK YOURSELF: Think about your thoughts during a sexual experience—how are they informed by family, religion, and media? How does your thinking affect your psychological state before, during, and after the act? How might this way of being in the world, your habitus, change over time?

Black Feminist Theory: Representing Sexuality in the Media

As a pop music superstar and a multimillion-dollar business executive, Beyoncé is the embodiment of what it means to be a media mogul. So when she released the 2016 visual album *Lemonade*, it was not surprising that people paid attention and reacted with enthusiasm. Much of the excitement around Beyoncé's latest work centered on its political messages. Her work addressed issues from police brutality to Second Amendment gun rights, and included a resounding celebration of blackness and women's empowerment. She wove her political messages of liberation through a personal story of infidelity and reconciliation, and in so doing, contributed to a familiar feminist idea: The personal is political (Harris-Perry, 2017). Consequently, black women collectively assembled a syllabus of resources to engage with Beyoncé's art and its connections to feminism (Benbow, 2016).

Not all black feminists were celebrating, however. Esteemed black feminist theorist bell hooks blogged about her disappointment with Beyoncé's album. Although she appreciated Beyoncé's "positive exploitation" of black women's diverse bodies and her ability to challenge mainstream perceptions, hooks dismissed the work as a money-making venture that glamorized female violence and perpetuated dominance in intimate relationships (hooks, 2016). She rejected Beyoncé's vision of feminism as a simple formula of equality between women and men (hooks, 2016). In this way, hooks expanded on a core black feminist theory tenet—that feminism must work against all injustices and include in its analyses other axes of oppression, such as those based on race, class, and sexuality (Collins, 2000).

Black feminist theory, also known as intersectional feminist theory, has a rich history in the United States. The concept of analyzing gender and race was introduced by black women long ago. At a women's rights convention in 1851, Sojourner Truth gave an impromptu speech, "Ain't I a Woman," that questioned the ways women's rights were characterized based only on white women's struggles (Brezina, 2005). Later, in 1892, Anna Julia Cooper echoed Truth's point in "The Colored Woman's Office," which argued that the black woman was "confronted by both a woman question and a race problem, and [was] as yet an unknown or an acknowledged factor in both" (Cooper, 2010/1892, p. 182). But it was not until the 1980s that critical race theorist Kimberlé Crenshaw coined the term *intersectionality* in response to second-wave mainstream feminism's inattention to race and racism as well as the sexism within antiracist activist campaigns (Adewunmi, 2014). Now, intersectionality enjoys renewed interest, as scholars, activists, and Internet commentators deploy the term to analyze many aspects of social life.

In her 2005 book, *Black Sexual Politics*, sociologist Patricia Hill Collins applied black feminist theory to mass media representations of women and men. She argued that mass media is an important site to analyze how ideas about black sexuality are represented. As an influential institution in society, media can shape how people perceive reality. Controlling, stereotyped images of black women and men in movies, on television, and in music videos may be interpreted as authoritative (Collins, 2005), especially to youth who lack the media literacy required to analyze them.

Even when these representations are fictional, they can have harmful consequences. For example, Collins (2005) argued that media that depict black people as hypersexual and wild can help justify racial inequality to white people: "Representations that reduce Black men to the physicality of their bodies, that depict an inherent promiscuity as part of authentic Black masculinity, that highlight the predatory skills of the hustler, and that repeatedly associate young Black men in particular with violence converge in the controlling image of Black men as booty call–seeking rapists" (Collins, 2005, p. 166). Commercial hip hop videos that portray black men as sex-obsessed and black women as perpetually sexually available can lead viewers to internalize these stereotypes. But Collins (2005) also rejected attempts to sanitize these representations, arguing that such impulses reflect a "politics of respectability" that cater to middle-class white versions of masculinity and femininity (p. 71). Instead, she saw media images as ever-changing sites of struggle that reflect black people's heterogeneous experiences. In mass media, images and language can both replicate and resist intersecting oppressions based on gender, race, class, and sexuality (Collins, 2005). Collins (2005) proposed redefining black gender ideology to include an empowered erotic of sexual autonomy. She called for an ideology that "uncoupled strength from notions of sexual dominance and exploitation" (Collins, 2005, p. 209), which brings us back to Beyoncé.

Although bell hooks (2016) accused Beyoncé of trotting out tired stereotypes that served to keep women sexually exploited and subdued under patriarchal and capitalist oppression, other black feminist theorists challenged her interpretations. Jamilah Lemieux (2016) argued that Beyoncé's *Lemonade* was a symbol of sex positivity, and appreciated the way it showcased the pleasure a black woman can find in her own body, in sex, and in the masculine point of view. Joy-Ann Reid (2016) lauded Beyoncé for depicting black women as deserving of "the kind of adoration and admiration of the feminine that white women have always taken for granted." She challenged hooks's (2016) dismissal of the work as capitalist exploitation, contending, "If Beyoncé is commodifying our sexual beings, she is doing so by seizing the receipts from the dominant culture's hands."

Jason LaVeris/FilmMagic/Getty Images

▶ Beyoncé, performing at the 2014 MTV Video Music Awards, puts a different twist on the word *feminist*. Her latest music, film, and art have caused her to be celebrated as an icon of black feminism. How do Beyoncé's feminist messages differ from popular stereotypes about feminism?

These divergent reactions to a celebrity's creative work illustrate the ways that black feminist theory can encompass multiple perspectives. Just like mainstream feminist theory can include varying theoretical orientations, so too can black feminist theory. At its core, however, black feminist theory will always examine the intersections between gender, race, class, sexuality, and other aspects of identity that shape human experiences in complex ways.

ASK YOURSELF: Do you think sexually explicit media representations cause harm? Can sexual imagery be positive? How do media portray people of varying races and genders differently? How can intersectionality help us to understand media portrayals and their effects on society? What other social problems are connected to the issue of media representations?

SOCIAL CHANGE: WHAT CAN YOU DO?

5.5 Identify steps toward social change regarding problems related to sexuality.

The problems related to sexuality will not be solved with an easy, quick-fix solution. Social problems rarely are. Instead, these issues benefit from increased awareness, collective action, and social movements. Important lessons can be taken from history. If we look to the past, we can see that many things in our society have changed. The meanings of sex and what is considered acceptable behavior have changed over time. Practices that were once outlawed as criminal—using contraception, masturbating to pornography, having sex with a person of the same sex—are now completely legal and treated as pretty normal. Realizing these historical changes should give us hope. Things can and do change.

Many groups and organizations around the world are working to address problems related to sexuality. Some are more focused on addressing specific issues, like prison rape, sex workers' rights, and sex education. Others have a broader scope and deal with diverse sexuality issues. If you are interested in making a change,

▶ LGBTQ rights organizations hold a rally to oppose the Trump administration's attack on trans students at the Stonewall National Monument in New York City. Participating trans speakers and city officials made it clear they would fight to keep protections for trans and gender nonconforming people and students.

it is very likely that you can find an initiative out there to plug into. This final section of the chapter provides a sample of organizations doing great work around sexuality. But there are many more organizations out there.

▶▶ Sexuality Advocacy, Southern Style: SONG and SPARK

Two regional organizations focusing on sexuality issues are SONG and SPARK. Southerners on New Ground (SONG) has been fighting for queer liberation since 1993. It prioritizes community organizing and works collectively with diverse groups of marginalized people, such as immigrants, people with disabilities, and working class and rural residents of the South. SONG creates educational media and conducts trainings that recognize the interconnectedness of all oppressions. Check out its website for news and events (http://southernersonnewground.org/). SPARK is a pro-sex organization that focuses on reproductive health and justice issues. Based in Atlanta, Georgia, SPARK

prioritizes southern communities as sites of resistance. This anti-oppression organization uses an intersectional framework to empower LGBTQ youth of color leadership. SPARK's work includes community and political organizing, media training, sexual health advocacy, and activism. Its website contains great resources for reproductive justice work (http://www.sparkrj.org/).

▶▶ Sexual Assault: What Men Can Do

To end rape, men must be part of the solution. Two organizations that take this call to action seriously are White Ribbon and Men's Resources International (MRI). Both organizations promote positive masculinity and work to end gendered violence around the world. White Ribbon is a Canada-based organization that began in 1991 with a call for men to wear white ribbons to declare their stance against violence toward women and girls. This organization conducts workshops and presentations aimed at engaging men and boys and challenging their ideas around manhood and its connection to violence. Its website posts information about conferences to facilitate change and partner with other organizations to help men and boys form healthy relationships with each other and with women and girls (http://www.whiteribbon.ca/). MRI offers support to people by using community-based leadership. It works with women to encourage unity and peace in families and in local communities. The global partnership of MRI connects people from parts of the United States with communities in Bolivia, Brussels, Liberia, Nigeria, Pakistan, Rwanda, and Zambia. On its website, you can find links to the trainings and educational services it offers, including documents with strategies for effectively reaching out to men on these important issues (http://mensresourcesinternational.org/).

Trans Sexualities: INCITE! and NCTE

INCITE! began in 2000 as a small group of women of color concerned about violence and has grown to a national collective of grassroots chapters around the United States. It centers the experiences of women, gender-nonconforming, and trans people of color in its work. As a radical feminist political project, it tackles violence in all its forms—within the community and against the community. INCITE! addresses sexuality issues such as street harassment, sterilization abuse against disenfranchised communities, and sexual and intimate partner violence. Learn more about what it does and how you can get involved on its website (http://www.incite-national.org/home). The National Center for Transgender Equality (NCTE) is a social justice organization run by and for transgender people. Founded in 2003, NCTE mobilizes around diverse issues that affect trans communities, including violence, discrimination, sexual health, sex work, and identity documentation. It is also responsible for compiling data from the largest survey on trans people's experiences. Visit its website for information on its advocacy efforts and to read the research on trans lives (http://www.transequality.org/).

WHAT DOES AMERICA THINK?

Questions About Sexuality From the General Social Survey

Turn to the beginning of the chapter to compare your answers to those of the total population.

1. What is your belief on having sex before marriage?

   WRONG: 40.6%

   NOT WRONG: 59.4%

2. Do you believe that homosexuals should have the right to marry?

   YES: 59.3%

   NO: 28.7%

   NEITHER: 12%

3. What is your level of happiness with your partner?

   VERY HAPPY: 56.9%

   SOMEWHAT HAPPY: 38.9%

   NOT TOO HAPPY: 4.2%

4. Should a homosexual be allowed to teach?

   ALLOW: 88.1%

   DO NOT ALLOW: 11.9%

5. Should homosexual books be allowed in the library?

   YES: 82.7%

   NO: 17.3%

6. Married people are happier than unmarried people.

   AGREE: 36.8%

   DISAGREE: 31.7%

   NEITHER AGREE NOR DISAGREE: 31.5%

7. What is your opinion of sex before marriage in teens between 14 and 16 years of age?

   ALWAYS WRONG: 61.3%

   SOMETIMES WRONG: 29%

   NOT WRONG AT ALL: 9.7%

8. Should sex education be taught in public schools?

   YES: 92.2%

   NO: 7.8%

SOURCE: National Opinion Research Center, University of Chicago.

CHAPTER SUMMARY

5.1 Explain how sexuality is a social construction.

The assertion that sex and sexuality are social constructions contrasts with the way we often talk about sex and sexuality in the United States. People frequently treat their sex and sexuality as independent of the society in which they live. But when we examine sex across cultures and throughout history, it becomes clear that sex and sexuality truly are social constructions.

5.2 Discuss patterns and trends of sexuality-related social problems.

Hookup culture is pervasive on college campuses. College students tend to accept the realities of hookup culture, but these practices may reaffirm gender inequalities, specifically those related to the sexual double standard. The commercial sex industry, especially trafficking of people for sexual labor, is depicted as a problem, but sex worker rights groups challenge popular portrayals. Sexually transmitted diseases affect millions of people, but the pathologization of sexual practices is often influenced by societal stigmas around sexuality.

5.3 Apply the functionalist, conflict, and symbolic interactionist perspectives to the study of sexuality-related social problems, specifically sexual violence.

Functionalist perspectives argue that sexual violence serves a social function, such as maintaining gendered divisions in society. *Critical* functionalist analysis would suggest that sexual violence sustains gender inequality, where men remain the dominant actors in heterosexual exchanges. Conflict theorists contextualize sexual violence within historical inequalities that grant men more control over resources that bolster their power to sexually exploit women. Symbolic interactionists prioritize the ways individuals make sense of their sexual encounters and may arrive at different conclusions based on how they think others perceive them. The policy implications of all three perspectives include changes on the institutional, individual, and interpersonal levels.

5.4 Apply specialized theories of sexualities.

The theory of erotic habitus considers the ways social structures and psychological processes interact to shape our sexual desires and practices, and can be used to understand both normative and marginalized sexualities. Black feminist theory, also known as intersectional feminist theory examines the complex ways identities—race, gender, class, sexual identity, and more—interact to shape our experiences.

5.5 Identify steps toward social change regarding problems related to sexuality.

Many organizations have mobilized to address different problems related to sexuality. Some take intersectional and whole-person approaches to issues like reproductive justice, while others focus on men's roles in ending sexual violence. Other organizations focus on issues that affect specific populations, like trans people and women of color. All of these efforts reflect the broad strategies used to address complex problems about a seemingly private issue.

KEY TERMS

erotic habitus 121

habitus 120

hooking up 109

human trafficking 113

latent function 116

LGBTQ 118

rape culture 117

sex 107

sexual bullying 106

sexual double standard 111

sexual labor 112

sexuality 107

sexually transmitted diseases (STDs) 114

social construction 107

AGING

Duane A. Matcha

BSIP/Getty Images

Gisele, who is 87 years old and suffering from Alzheimer's disease, moved in with her eldest daughter, who helps her with all her daily actions. As the U.S. population continues to age, which social problems do you think will be exacerbated, and which ones do you think will be reduced?

Investigating Aging: My Story

Duane A. Matcha

When I graduated from college with an undergraduate degree in social science, I had no idea what I was going to do. An ad in the local newspaper for a position as an outreach worker with the local Commission on Aging sounded interesting, so I applied, not knowing what to expect. The position was temporary, since funding was provided through a 2-year state/federal grant. In those 2 years, however, I discovered a great deal about myself and the lives of older people.

While my job was to advocate for lower- and middle-income older persons and help them get tangible assistance, many needed only someone to talk to. Others experienced a variety of problems, ranging from illegal eviction to navigating the paperwork of a public bureaucracy. My experiences, while individually significant, also highlighted the role of the sociological imagination in addressing aging in the United States. It was not one older person but many who lacked food or meaningful human interaction. Realizing that when I provided one person with the help he or she needed others would ask for the same assistance helped me understand the difference between an individual problem and a social problem that could be addressed by public policy.

As a result of my accidental job experience, aging became the foundation of my graduate training in sociology and remains the core of my research. I've examined end-of-life decision making among older populations; the relationship between aging and health care costs; and, most recently, the way the print media portray the aging population in the United States and other countries.

LEARNING OBJECTIVES

6.1 Discuss aging as a social construct.

6.2 Discuss patterns and trends in the demographics of aging.

6.3 Apply the functionalist, symbolic interactionist, and conflict perspectives to social policy for the aging.

6.4 Apply specialized theories to the social construction of aging.

6.5 Identify steps toward social change for the aging.

WHAT DO YOU THINK?
Questions About Aging From the General Social Survey

1. Adult children are important to help elderly parents.
   - [ ] AGREE
   - [ ] DISAGREE

2. Who should provide help for the elderly?
   - [ ] FAMILY MEMBERS
   - [ ] GOVERNMENT AGENCIES
   - [ ] NONPROFIT ORGANIZATIONS
   - [ ] PRIVATE PROVIDERS

3. Should the aged live with their children?
   - [ ] YES
   - [ ] NO
   - [ ] DEPENDS

4. Who should pay for help for the elderly?
   - [ ] ELDERLY PEOPLE THEMSELVES OR THEIR FAMILY
   - [ ] THE GOVERNMENT/ PUBLIC FUNDS

5. In the United States, do you think we're spending too much money on Social Security, too little money, or about the right amount?
   - [ ] TOO MUCH
   - [ ] TOO LITTLE
   - [ ] ABOUT THE RIGHT AMOUNT

 Turn to the end of the chapter to view the results for the total population.

SOURCE: National Opinion Research Center, University of Chicago.

HOMESHARING: MILLENNIALS AND OLDER INDIVIDUALS

A recent article on BBC News.com discussed a solution to two social problems: young millennials unable to afford housing and older individuals often living alone in homes they were unable to maintain and in need of companionship. The program, Ensemble2Generations, matches young students with older individuals living alone. The article, focusing on arrangements in France, noted that face-to-face interviews are necessary to determine compatibility between the generations. In addition, student applicants must write an essay explaining why they want to be placed with an older person. Such homeshare arrangements currently exist in some 16 countries.

There are two different arrangements that can be made. In one, the student is allowed to live rent free in the home but is required to provide aid to the older person. Such aid would be in the form of cooking, cleaning, or helping with grocery shopping. In the second arrangements, the student pays into the household budget in exchange for greater freedom from providing assistance.

While some homeshare placements are not successful, research indicates most are. According to the article, homeshare projects in Spain and the United States found that 93.2% of older people and 98.7% of students felt that they benefited from the program. Interviews with students and older persons involved in these programs illustrate the enjoyment and learning opportunities both generations experienced by having a housemate. Such programs are positive efforts to bridge the generational divide (Bright, 2017).

We begin with a brief look at the historical background of aging in the United States and then turn to a wide variety of issues and theoretical perspectives associated with the aging process. Most important, this chapter explains why aging is a socially constructed social problem and develops an alternate understanding of the older population as an integral component of the larger society, not the "problem" that has been constructed. For example, the aging population is often blamed for the rising cost of health care in the United States. In reality, older patients are responsible for a relatively small proportion of this increase.

IS AGING A SOCIAL PROBLEM?

6.1 Discuss aging as a social construct.

Ted is a 75-year-old white male living in Sun City, Arizona. He's enjoying his life of leisure, playing golf on a daily basis and spending time with his grandchildren, who visit regularly. Ted retired 10 years ago from a management position with a multinational company. During the 40 years he worked for the company, he saved for retirement, and his company now provides him with a pension. He lives a comfortable life and has no financial concerns because he is in relatively good health and has a sufficient retirement income. His home is paid for, and he enjoys going out to eat on a regular basis. He volunteers 3 days a week at a local school, where he mentors at-risk children.

Diane is a 75-year-old minority female living in a working-class section of a major city. She worked at low-wage jobs most of her life and had not been able to save more than $1,000 by the time she retired 10 years ago. She receives Social Security benefits but no pension. Because of her low income, she was unable to afford a home and has lived in an apartment all her life. Her neighborhood is now in transition and becoming less safe, but she cannot move because she cannot afford the higher rent she would have to pay elsewhere. Her health is fine, but she does take a number of medications for a variety of medical conditions she developed over her lifetime.

▶ An 88-year-old and an 89-year-old celebrate after winning the Super Grandmother and Super Grandfather annual contest in Tbilisi, Republic of Georgia. Did you know that in the United States, May has been designated as Older Americans Month since 1963?

VANO SHLAMOV/AFP/Getty Images

Ted and Diane are both considered "old" because of their chronological age, but are they a social problem? Neither was considered a social problem before retirement, so why is their aging a social problem?

What do we know about aging and its consequences? The process of aging is complex and results in any number of outcomes. In other words, older people are not homogeneous. They are as diverse as any other age group. Beyond sharing a common chronological age (65 and over), older persons fit into all the social class positions members of other age groups do. They also exhibit as wide a diversity of political and religious thought as we find in the larger society. They engage in a variety of familial relationships and experience intimate discord, as do others. Thus, to understand the aging of Ted and Diane and millions of others who are 65 and older, we begin by examining how aging is socially constructed as a social problem.

The Social Construction of Aging as a Social Problem

When we think about aging, we generally think in terms of chronology. In other words, how old am I, and how does my age compare to the ages of others? While chronological age is important, it is limited as a description because it locates an individual in a single point in time. In this chapter we will use chronological age to identify segments of the larger population that fall into a category society generally classifies as "old." However, rather than focusing only on a specific chronological age, we will utilize the concept of **aging**, "a social process that is constructed from the expectations and belief systems of the structural characteristics of society" (Matcha, 1997, p. 20).

··
ASK YOURSELF: How did age become, and how does it persist as, a socially constructed social *problem?*
··

Today, baby boomers in the United States are entering retirement age in growing numbers. By 2050, the number of people age 65 and over in the United States will more than double from approximately 35 million today to some 88 million (see Figure 6.1; Federal Interagency Forum on Aging-Related Statistics, 2016). This growth has fostered concern among politicians and policy makers as they try to understand the implications of such rapid demographic change. Some politicians have said the country cannot afford to care for so many older people. Others have argued that government programs supporting the older population, such as Social Security and Medicare, will go broke and be unable to meet the financial and health needs of older citizens. Given the range of potential responses to these demographic changes, what is society to do?

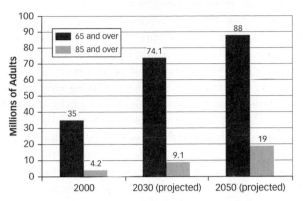

FIGURE 6.1 Increase in Numbers of U.S. Adults 65 and Over and 85 and Over, 2000–2050

SOURCE: Federal Interagency Forum on Ageing-Related Statistics. Older Americans 2016: Key Indicators of Well-Being. Federal Interagency on Aging-Related Statistics. Washington, DC: U.S. Government printing Office. August 2016.

··
ASK YOURSELF: If we could ensure that Social Security will remain solvent throughout this century by reducing the benefits it pays out, would you be in favor of doing so? Why or why not? Some options for protecting Social Security place the economic burden of doing so on the individual, while others place it on the larger society. Why does the choice matter?
··

This is not the first time older people have been thought of as a social problem. In the late 18th and early 19th centuries, earlier traditions of responsibility to older members of society gave way to norms of increased individual responsibility, and wealth inequality—believed to be relatively low during the colonial period—began increasing and creating greater generational differences at the same time (Fischer, 1978). Public attitudes toward older citizens thus became increasingly negative, particularly if the elderly were not wealthy, white, and male.

The result of these changing societal attitudes was a rising level of poverty in old age and the transformation of older age into a socially constructed social problem throughout the 19th and 20th centuries. Individuals remained in the workplace because pensions, private or public, did not exist. With the emergence of **welfare state**

···

Aging: A social process constructed from the expectations and belief systems of the structural characteristics of society.

Welfare state: Government provision of services essential to the well-being of large or significant segments of the population that are not possible or profitable within the private sector.

policies such as Social Security in 1935 and Medicare in 1965, however, as well as society's recognition that assistance in old age was necessary, the overall well-being of older adults improved significantly.

By the late 1980s, however, the socially constructed impression of older people changed again. This time, they were perceived as too wealthy! Terms such as "greedy geezers" conveyed an image of older people living the good life in Florida or elsewhere, playing shuffleboard while younger generations struggled to get by (Street & Cossman, 2006). Currently, older adults in the United States are caught in a political vortex in which programs upon which they rely are being attacked as too expensive and no longer viable for younger generations. They are being asked to "sacrifice" for the well-being of their children and grandchildren. Efforts to frame the recent economic recession as a generational divide blame the older-age population rather than the larger structural framework of institutionalized inequality. To understand more fully how aging has been, and continues to be, socially constructed as a social problem, we next examine the role of ageism.

Ageism

Ageism is the use of a person's perceived or real chronological age as the basis for discriminatory actions. Connecting ageism to the demographic shift discussed above, Longino (2005, p. 81) notes that "this apocalyptic picture of the future is indeed ageist, because it objectifies people who are aging and treats them as though they are all alike. They are not people anymore; they are 'the burden.'" In the context of this commonly held view, we will explore why ageism remains a potent negative force in U.S. culture, whether among younger adults who hold stereotypical beliefs about their elders, employers who do not believe older workers can be as productive as their younger counterparts, or media outlets that promote outdated portrayals of older persons.

For example, in U.S. print advertisements, older people are generally nonexistent and are negatively stereotyped when they do appear. In newspaper articles, they are generally depicted as poor, in poor health, and needing assistance (Miller et al., 1999). The portrayal of the health and illness of Canadian seniors has been associated with the following themes: "aging as disease, individual responsibility for healthy aging, and apocalyptic demography/costs of [un]healthy aging" (Rozanova, 2006, p. 131). A comparison of U.S. and European newspaper articles about aging found differences in the ways older persons were portrayed. For example, European newspaper articles were more likely to suggest age-related connections with rising health care costs (Matcha & Sessing-Matcha, 2007). In Ireland, Fealy et al. (2012,

p. 99) found that "the proposition that older people might be healthy, self-reliant and capable of autonomy in the way they live their lives was largely absent" from the newspaper articles the researchers examined. In American television programs and commercials, older citizens are again nonexistent or, if visible, are portrayed in stereotypical fashion, such as being forgetful, slow, and useless (Blakeborough, 2008). One study found that older people made up only 3% of characters, while children accounted for 7% and young and middle-age adults were disproportionately represented. As a result, the more hours survey respondents spent watching television, the less they understood the older-age population (Signorielli, 2001). Similarly, Donlon, Ashman, and Levy (2005, p. 314) found that "exposure to television is a significant predictor of more negative stereotypes of aging."

We see that perhaps the most pervasive ageist attitudes are the result of an anti-aging culture in the United States. This culture is framed as a way of "helping" people address the myriad problems of an aging body. Hair coloring, wrinkle creams, plastic surgery, and other aids are intended to remake the image of older individuals—again, particularly women (Hurd Clarke, 2011). Ageism thus fosters the socially constructed reality that being old is a social problem.

As a result of these socially constructed images, we are less likely to have a realistic impression of older persons. Here, for example, are some common myths about aging (Kart, 1994), along with the reasons each is false:

- *Myth: Senility inevitably accompanies old age.* Achieving a particular chronological age does not make a person senile, as evidenced by the many older individuals who have accomplished a great deal in later life. For instance, singers such as Bob Dylan, Mick Jagger, and Paul McCartney, and actors Robert Redford, Samuel L. Jackson, and Betty White range in age from late 60s to early 90s, and all of them continue to perform. Older political figures include Hillary Rodham Clinton and U.S. senator John McCain.

- *Myth: Most old people are lonely and isolated from their families.* Research has demonstrated that most older individuals have at least one child living within an hour's drive, and that the amount of interaction they have with children and other family members is less important than the quality of that interaction (Fingerman, 2001).

....

Ageism: The use of real or perceived chronological age as a basis for discrimination.

TABLE 6.1 Overview of Social Security, Medicare, and Medicaid

Social Security	• Signed into law in 1935. • Initially eligibility for Social Security was at age 65. Eligibility age increased to 66 in 2005 and will begin increasing to 67 in 2017. • Retired workers and dependents account for 71% of total benefits paid, with an average monthly benefit of $1,348 in 2016. • Disabled workers and their dependents account for 16% of total benefits paid. • Survivors of deceased workers account for about 13% of total benefits paid. • Nine out of 10 individuals age 65 and older receive Social Security benefits. • There are currently 2.8 workers for each Social Security beneficiary. By 2035, there will be 2.2 workers for each beneficiary.

Medicare	• Signed into law in 1965.
	• Medicare is a health insurance program for the following people: those ages 65 and older; those under 65 with certain disabilities; those of any age with end-stage renal disease (permanent kidney failure requiring dialysis or a kidney transplant).
	
	• **Medicare Part A (hospital insurance):**
	  ○ Helps cover inpatient care in hospitals.
	  ○ Helps cover skilled nursing facility, hospice, and home health care.
	
	• **Medicare Part B (medical insurance):**
	  ○ Helps cover doctors' and other health care providers' services, outpatient care, durable medical equipment, and home health care.
	  ○ Helps cover some preventive services to help maintain health and to keep certain illnesses from getting worse.
	
	• **Medicare Part C (also known as Medicare Advantage):**
	  ○ Offers health plan options run by Medicare-approved private insurance companies.
	  ○ Provides benefits and services covered under Part A and Part B.
	  ○ Covers Medicare prescription drug coverage (Part D).
	  ○ Includes extra benefits for extra costs in some plans.
	
	• **Medicare Part D (Medicare prescription drug coverage):**
	  ○ Helps cover the cost of prescription drugs.
	  ○ May help lower prescription drug costs and help protect against higher costs in the future.
	  ○ Is run by Medicare approved private insurance companies.

Medicaid	• Signed into law in 1965.
	• Medicaid is a state and federal partnership that provides coverage for people with lower incomes, older people, people with disabilities, and some families and children.
	• Each state operates a Medicaid program that provides health coverage for lower-income people, families and children, the elderly, and people with disabilities.
	• Eligibility rules differ from state to state.
	• Medicaid expansion exists in some states but not others. States with Medicaid expansion will cover all people if income is below 133% of the federal poverty level.
	• Benefits covered for adults differ from state to state, but certain benefits are covered in every Medicaid program.
	• Doctors' services that are covered by Medicaid that are applicable to older citizens include the following:
	  ○ Laboratory and X-ray services
	  ○ Inpatient hospital services
	  ○ Outpatient hospital services
	  ○ Long-term care services and supports
	  ○ Medical and surgical dental services for adults
	  ○ Services provided in health clinics
	  ○ Nursing facility services for adults
	  ○ Home health care services for certain people
	  ○ Prescription drugs
	• The Affordable Care Act has expanded options for community-based care, increasing opportunities for people of all ages who have disabilities to get help with daily activities while remaining in their homes. The Medicaid program continues to move toward providing more community-based care options as alternatives to nursing homes.

SOURCES: Social Security Administration, Fact Sheet (www.ssa.gov/pressoffice/factssheet/basicfact-alt.pdf), accessed January 4, 2017; Medicare Benefits, _Medicare and You 2017_, U.S. Department of Health and Human Services, Centers for Medicare and Medicaid Services, Baltimore, MD; Medicaid (https://www.healthcare.gov/medicaid-chip/medicaid-expansion-and-you/), accessed February 19, 2017.

- *Myth: Most old people are in poor health.* While a small percentage of older individuals have difficulty engaging in at least one activity of daily living (ADL), the rest are capable of independent living and remaining active within their communities (Ferraro, 2011).

- *Myth: Old people are more likely than younger people to be victimized by crime.* While crime rates have decreased overall in the recent past, they have dropped significantly among older people, and nationally those ages 65 and over have the lowest rate of victimization (Truman & Morgan, 2016). When victimized, however, older people do have a more difficult time recovering, physically, emotionally, and financially (Peguero & Lauck, 2008).

- *Myth: The majority of old people live in poverty.* The majority of older adults in the United States have modest incomes that allow them to enjoy their later years. However, poverty is greater among older women, the widowed, and minority elderly. The triple threat of poverty is being female, widowed, and a member of a minority group (U.S. Department of Health and Human Services, 2015).

- *Myth: Old people tend to become more religious as they age.* In reality, older individuals who are religious were so in middle age and earlier (Moody & Sasser, 2012). Older individuals are more likely to attend religious services than are people in other age groups, but that does not make them more religious (Hill, Burdette, & Idler, 2011).

- *Myth: Older workers are less productive than younger workers.* Older workers do not experience significant declines in mental and physical abilities. They are less likely than younger persons to be in the labor market, but not because they cannot do the work. In fact, they are generally as productive as younger workers (Schulz & Binstock, 2006).

- *Myth: Old people who retire usually suffer a decline in health.* In reality, if an older person suffers a decline in health after retirement, it is generally the result of a medical condition that existed before retirement (Ekerdt, 2007).

- *Myth: Most old people have no interest in, or capacity for, sexual relations.* The greater the frequency of sexual activity among middle-aged adults, the greater the chance they will remain sexually active in older age. Unless there are physical problems, older men and women can remain sexually active well into their seventh and eighth decades of life (Masters & Johnson, 2010).

- *Myth: Most old people end up in nursing homes and other long-term care institutions.* On any given day, only about 4% of Americans ages 65 and over are in nursing homes, although the percentage among the oldest-old (age 85+) is much higher. In reality, most older U.S. adults remain in their own homes and have no need for any type of institutionalized care (Kahana, Lovegreen, & Kahana, 2011).

With this more realistic view of older people in mind, we turn next to a number of patterns and trends that define current and future realities for older adults—and that perpetuate the social construction of aging as a social problem.

PATTERNS AND TRENDS

 Discuss patterns and trends in the demographics of aging.

Demographics

One hundred years ago, the 4 million U.S. adults age 65 and over made up about 4% of the population. Today, some 40 million people in that age category represent approximately 13% of the population. By 2050, some 88 million over the age of 65 will be representing 20% of the total population. This is actually a relatively minor shift in the population pyramid compared with that in other industrialized countries. For example, in Japan and Italy those over age 65 are expected soon to make up the largest percentage of the population (35% and 36%, respectively; United Nations, 2015). Figure 6.2 shows the differences between the United States and other industrialized countries in terms of population aging.

REUTERS/Harrison McClary

▶ Dr. Byron Harbolt treats a patient at his clinic in Altamont, Tennessee. Harbolt, 89, who charges as little as $15 for an office visit, sees patients 6 days a week in the rural clinic he opened in 1960. Would you feel comfortable having a doctor who is 89 years old?

Behind the increasing number of older people in the population are a variety of other sociodemographic factors, including decreased fertility and increased life expectancy rates. **Fertility rate** is a count of the number of children born to women during their prime fertility period. Fertility rates have decreased significantly in the United States and throughout the developed world. At the same time, people are living longer. **Life expectancy** is the average number of years a person born in a given year can expect to live. When we combine decreasing fertility rates and increasing life expectancy, we find that fewer children are being born and those who are born are living longer, resulting in a demographic shift from a younger population to one that is rapidly aging. In fact, the fastest-growing segment of the population consists of those ages 85 and over.

Digging deeper into the numbers, we find there are more older-age women than older-age men because women, on average, have longer life expectancy. The **sex ratio** identifies the number of men per 100 women (see Figure 6.3). These numbers are important because they measure the availability of potential mates for those who are widowed or divorced in older age. In other words, an older male has a much larger pool of eligible older women from which to select, if he is interested in a relationship, whereas an older woman finds a much smaller pool of eligible men.

Finally, the demographic shift is also changing the dependency ratio. This ratio consists of three different numbers. First is the **child dependency ratio,** which counts the number of children under age 16 for every 100 people ages 16 to 64. The **old-age dependency ratio** counts the number of older persons age 65 and over for every 100 people ages 16 to 64. Finally, the **total dependency ratio** is the number of children under 16 and the number of older persons 65 and over for every 100 persons ages 16 to 64.

The higher the total dependency ratio, the more services are necessary to provide for those identified as dependent on the larger society. The projected changes in the child and old-age dependency ratios in the United States shown in Table 6.2 are consistent with those in other developed countries. However, the overall U.S. dependency ratio is generally lower than that in most other developed countries. Demographic changes like these do not themselves make aging a social problem, but framing them as a "disaster for society" or a "tsunami of historical proportions" constructs aging as a social problem by implying that older adults are responsible for their consequences.

Next we turn to the family and the changes it is experiencing as a result of the changing demographic structure of the population.

Family

The family represents the foundation of social institutions and as such is experiencing fundamental changes (see Chapter 9). Declining fertility rates, for instance, mean families are having fewer children, making it more difficult for those children to care for older parents. On the economic front, women's increased participation in the workforce has fundamentally reshaped economic relationships in families, as well as caregiving and domestic responsibilities, although these still rest mostly with women.

Meanwhile, the growing life expectancy rates at birth and at age 65, along with declining fertility rates, mean that the numbers of older adults, and particularly the oldest-old (85 and over), are increasing. These demographic changes within the family are putting greater pressure on adult children as they care for multiple generations of family members. These increased demands are not the fault of older people, but rather structural conditions that force family members to address competing demands without the necessary formal support systems.

The role of grandparent, a primary family role, is often viewed as a welcome opportunity to provide social-emotional support to a younger generation. Increasingly, grandparents are also becoming the primary caregivers for their grandchildren, helped by the fact that, as noted above, many live relatively close to at least one of their children.

Family relationships are also evolving in terms of sexual expectations between aging couples. The phrase "use it or lose it" has been applied to the extent to which couples engage in sexual activity in middle age (Moody & Sasser, 2012). Generally speaking, men and women are capable of remaining sexually active well into their later years (Masters & Johnson, 2010). While the frequency of sexual activity may decline over time, the need for intimacy remains regardless of age. Another change in family relationships is occurring as same-sex marriage becomes more widely accepted and recognized by law. As gay couples adopt children or have their own via surrogacy, their opportunities to eventually enjoy the role of grandparent increase.

....

Fertility rate: The number of children born per 1,000 women during their prime fertility period.

Life expectancy: The average number of years a baby born in any given year can expect to live.

Sex ratio: The number of males for every 100 females in the general population or within some designated segment, such as among those ages 65 and over.

Child dependency ratio: The number of children under the age of 16 per 100 adults ages 16 to 64.

Old-age dependency ratio: The number of older persons ages 65 and over for every 100 adults between the ages of 16 and 64.

Total dependency ratio: The number of children under the age of 16 and the number of older persons age 65 and over for every 100 adults ages 16 to 64.

Elder Abuse

Elder abuse is an unfortunate reality that can take various forms—sexual, financial, physical, and emotional. Elder neglect is also common. The National Center on Elder Abuse (1999, p. 1) identifies the following types of abuse and neglect:

- *Physical abuse:* Use of physical force that may result in bodily injury, physical pain, or impairment

- *Sexual abuse:* Nonconsensual sexual contact of any kind with an elderly person

FIGURE 6.2 Percentage of the Population Age 65 and Over, 2015–2050

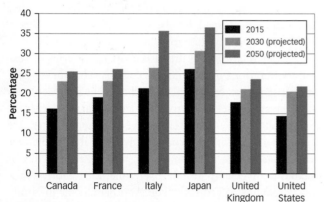

SOURCE: United Nations, Department of Economic and Social Affairs, Population Division (2015). *World Population Prospects: The 2015 Revision, Key Findings and Advance Tables.* Working Paper No. ESA/P/WP.241.

FIGURE 6.3 Males per 100 Females in the United States by Age, 2015, 2030, and 2050

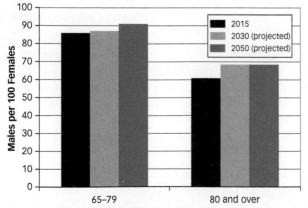

SOURCE: He, Wan, Daniel Goodkind, and Paul Kowai. U.S. Census Bureau, International Population Reports, P95/16-1, An Aging World: 2015, U.S. Government Publishing Office, Washington, DC, 2016.

TABLE 6.2 Child and Old-Age Dependency Ratios in the United States, 2000 and 2050

Year	Total dependency ratio	Child dependency ratio	Old-age dependency ratio
2000	50.5	32	18.5
2050	65.8	28.9	36.9

SOURCE: United Nations 2015. Population Division of the Department of Economic and Social Affairs of the United Nations Secretariat, *World Population Prospects: the 2015 Revision.*

- *Emotional abuse:* Infliction of anguish, pain, or distress through verbal or nonverbal acts

- *Financial/material exploitation:* Illegal or improper use of an elder's funds, property, or assets

- *Neglect:* A person's refusal, or failure, to fulfill any part of his or her obligations or duties to an elderly person

Statistics reported in 2016 showed that more than half (58.5%) of the non-self-neglect substantiated reports of elder abuse in the United States—in other words, reports of abuse that were made by someone else and were investigated and found to be true—involved neglect, followed by physical abuse (15.7%), financial/material exploitation (12.3%), emotional abuse (7.3%), all other types (5.1%), and sexual abuse (0.04%) (Statistic Brain, 2017). Whether they have been swindled out of their life savings by con artists, beaten by family members, or simply ignored because they are too much trouble for their overworked spouses, a growing number of older citizens suffer serious harm from these forms of abuse and neglect.

How common are crimes of elder abuse? In 2016, the National Center on Elder Abuse reported that over 2 million cases of elder abuse are reported each year and that 9.5% of older Americans will experience some form of elder abuse. Victims of elder abuse are primarily female, white, with an average age of 77.9 years (Statistic Brain, 2017). Given the increased level of dependency that can occur with age, elder abuse will persist as the baby boom generation moves into old age.

Economics

For more than two centuries, older adults were identified as a social problem in the United States because they did not have the economic means to care for themselves. Recently, however, critics accused them of demanding a lifestyle beyond their ability to afford. What is the economic reality? We can sum it up as "diverse." (Much of the information provided in this section comes from the Federal Interagency Forum on Aging-Related Statistics, 2016.)

The **poverty rate** is a measure of the number of people whose incomes fall below the level set by official poverty guidelines. It is calculated for the entire population and for subsections, such as by age and family size. The U.S. government established poverty guidelines in the early 1960s based on the belief that a family spends one-third of its income on food. Each year the government calculates the cost of food for different household sizes, ranging from one person to eight, and multiplies the resulting figures by three to determine the poverty guidelines for the various household sizes. In 2016, the federal poverty line for a one-person family/household was $11,880, and for a two-person family/household it was $16,020 (U.S. Department of Health and Human Services, 2016).

Compared to other age groups in the United States, those ages 65 and over have the lowest poverty rate. That being said, as age increases, so does the likelihood of poverty (see Figure 6.4). The picture grows more complex when we also look at the profoundly influential characteristics of sex, race, ethnicity, and marital status. For example, older women who live alone, regardless of race or ethnicity, are more likely than older men to live in poverty. Elderly minority women living alone experience a significantly higher poverty rate than do elderly white women living alone. In 2014, the poverty rate for older African American women living alone was 31.1%, for Hispanic older women living alone, it was 41.5%. By contrast, the poverty rate for elderly white women who were married was 3.1% (Federal Interagency on Aging-Related Statistics, Older Americans, 2016).

Table 6.3 examines the distribution of income among those 65 and over. It is evident that over the 40 year period covered in the table, the distribution of older adults across income brackets has skewed upward. We also know that median household income among those 65 and over increased between 1974 and 2014 from $22,921 to $36,895 (all in 2014 dollars). While seemingly impressive, this is not a significant growth rate. The data also point to the economic diversity that exists among older U.S. adults (Federal Interagency on Aging-Related Statistics, Older Americans, 2016).

We can also see changes since the 1960s in the sources of income for married and nonmarried persons 65 and older. Figure 6.5 indicates how Social Security, pensions, and earnings have grown increasingly important to them over time. Some 60% of older citizens rely on Social Security as their primary source of income, which explains why any reference to reducing government funding to this program is met with concern. The data in Figure 6.6 are divided into quintiles, or fifths of the population, so we can examine differences between segments of the older-age

REUTERS/Lucy Nicholson

▶ A 98-year-old man kisses his wife at the end of a dance in Sun City, Arizona. Many older adults maintain sexual interest and activity well into their 80s and 90s. Why do you suppose media images of romance and sexual attractiveness ignore older people?

FIGURE 6.4 Poverty Rate Among U.S. Elderly by Age and Marital Status, 2015

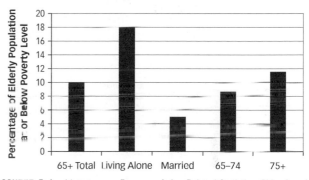

SOURCE: Federal Interagency Forum on Aging-Related Statistics. Older Americans 2016: Key Indicators of Well-Being. Federal Interagency Forum on Aging-Related Statistics. Washington, DC: U.S. Government Printing Office, August, 2016.

TABLE 6.3 Income Distribution of the U.S. Population Age 65 and Over, 1974, 2000, and 2014

	Poverty	Low income	Middle income	High income
1974	14.6%	34.6%	32.6%	18.2%
2000	9.9%	27.5%	35.5%	27.1%
2014	10.0%	22.5%	31.1%	36.4%

SOURCE: Federal Interagency Forum on Aging-Related Statistics. Older Americans 2016: Key Indicators of Well-Being. Federal Interagency Forum on Aging-Related Statistics. Washington, DC: U.S. Government Printing Office, August, 2016.

population. While we can say that older adults are truly economically diverse, that diversity is limited.

Poverty rate: A measure of the number of individuals or groups in poverty, expressed in absolute or relative terms.

FIGURE 6.5 Sources of Income for Older U.S. Adults, 1962 and 2014

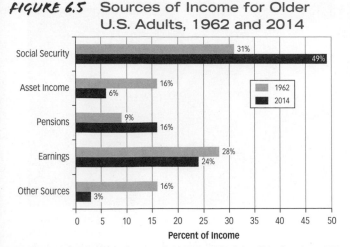

Percent of Income

	1962	2014
Social Security	31%	49%
Asset Income	16%	6%
Pensions	9%	16%
Earnings	28%	24%
Other Sources	16%	3%

SOURCE: Federal Interagency Forum on Aging-Related Statistics. Older Americans 2016: Key Indicators of Well-Being. Federal Interagency Forum on Aging-Related Statistics. Washington, DC: U.S. Government Printing Office, August, 2016.

NOTE: The definition of "other" includes, but is not limited to, unemployment compensation, workers' compensation, veterans' payments, and personal contributions. Estimates may not sum to the totals because of rounding. These data refer to the civilian noninstitutionalized population.

FIGURE 6.6 Economic Well-Being and Source of Income in Old Age by U.S. Population Quintiles, 2016

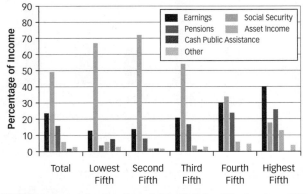

SOURCE: Interagency Forum on Aging-Related Statistics. Older Americans 2016: Key Indicators of Well-Being. Federal Interagency Forum on Aging-Related Statistics. Washington, DC: U.S. Government Printing Office. June 2016.

Social Security is central to the needs of most older citizens. What can we do to ensure the long-term viability of the Social Security program? In a brief published by the National Academy of Social Insurance, Reno and Lavery (2005) reported on the economic benefits of various proposals to reduce the anticipated shortfall in Social Security benefits. According to these authors, if the earnings cap (currently about $110,000) were removed so that *all* earned income were taxed, the additional revenue generated would reduce the shortfall by 93%. Increasing the Social Security tax by 1% on individuals and employers would generate additional revenue that would cover 104% of the shortfall, effectively ensuring the well-being of Social Security through the end of the 21st century. Another

▶ A homeless, older black man is a resident at this shelter in Jacksonville, Florida. Such a person may experience discrimination when looking for a job not only because of his race but also because of his age.

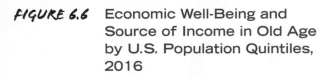

option is to reduce the cost-of-living benefit that keeps Social Security in line with the inflation rate; this change would cover 111% of the expected shortfall. It would also reduce future Social Security income for middle-class recipients by as much as 46%, however. Other suggested changes would have much smaller impacts on the shortfall. They include increasing the age for full retirement from 67 to 68, lowering the yearly cost-of-living adjustments by 1%, and extending coverage to new state and local government workers. The resulting outcomes would cover 28%, 79%, and 10% of the gap, respectively.

Health

Despite efforts by some to connect rising health care costs in the United States to the increasing number of older citizens, the relationship between the two is in fact minimal. For example, "neither the percentage of GDP that a nation spends on health care on all of its people, nor the percentage of its GDP devoted to health care strictly for the elderly, seem to be driven by the percentage of the population that is aged" (Reinhardt, 2000, p. 73). More recently, Quesnel-Vallee, Farrah, and Jenkins (2011, p. 564) have noted that "population age per se is not the main driver of health care costs." The deeper question, then, is how to improve the overall health of older citizens and not blame them for higher health care costs.

Today's older adults are significantly healthier than those of 100 or even 50 years ago. One way to measure the health of a population is to examine life expectancy at birth and at age 65. In the United States, life expectancy at birth has increased from approximately 47 years at the beginning of the 20th century to about 79 years today.

Social Security: A federal program that provides monthly benefit payments to older workers who have participated in the workforce and paid into the system.

Experiencing Aging

Food Insecurity Among Baby Boomers

When we think of Americans experiencing hunger, we generally do not think of older-age Americans. According to a recent report by Feeding America, some 8 million baby boomers (those born between 1946 and 1964) experience food insecurity. While that number may appear to be small compared to the total number of older Americans, the number is expected to increase as baby boomers continue to age.

Why are older Americans experiencing food insecurity? Quite literally, many do not have enough money to buy food. They may have worked at low-wage jobs all their life and upon retirement, simply do not have enough money to purchase an adequate supply of food. Others may have lost everything during the economic crisis of 2008–2009. Many older-age workers lost their jobs during the economic crisis but were too young to begin collecting Social Security. Many were simply unprepared for an early retirement.

What can be done to address this problem? Feeding America suggests a plan that incorporates multiple organizations such as service providers, advocates for older Americans, and policy makers to create programs that will alleviate or at least lessen the problem in the future. It would also be helpful if workers of all ages were paid more for the work they perform, thus allowing them to have more money available to buy the food necessary to sustain themselves and their families (McGarvey, 2015).

▶ **THINK ABOUT IT**

1. Although it is not identified in the article, who do you think is more at risk for food insecurity—men or women? What about by race and ethnic identity? Why?

2. What is the impact on society of an increasing number of older Americans going hungry every day?

That increase has occurred for a number of reasons, such as improved public health, increased income, better living and working conditions, and improved medical services. At age 65, an American adult today can expect to live an additional 19.3 years on average. This is an increase of roughly 2.5 years since 1981 (Federal Interagency Forum on Aging-Related Statistics, 2016).

Improved health is allowing more people to live longer lives, thus fueling the increase in the numbers of older persons. In particular, those surviving into oldest-old age (85 and over) are now the fastest-growing segment of the population. As people age, their utilization of health services also increases. Therefore, the growth in the oldest-old population should predict increased health care costs among this segment of the population. What we also know, however, is that only a small percentage of older individuals accounts for the majority of Medicare spending (Budrys, 2012). More specifically, Medicare costs are approximately six times greater for those recipients who die than for those who do not (Hogan et al., 2001). In other words, aging is not the cause of rising health care costs—the cost of dying is.

In the United States, health care for older citizens is provided through **Medicare**, a universal health care system for those 65 and over. The Medicare insurance program, which became part of the Social Security Act in 1965 under President Lyndon B. Johnson, along with **Medicaid**, ensures access to health care services for older citizens and those living in poverty. The program has been credited with improving the overall health of older persons. However, its costs have grown significantly, and it now faces an uncertain economic and political future.

Projections currently indicate that Medicare Part A (hospital insurance) will be able to pay only 87% of hospital costs by 2024 if no changes are made to its financing mechanisms. Parts B (medical insurance) and D (prescription drug coverage), however, are not in danger (Van de Water, 2013). While the economic crisis facing Medicare has been building for some time, the program and its beneficiaries have recently become political pawns in the ongoing debate regarding the role of government in everyday life. While the system could be strengthened by

Medicare: A federal health care program for those ages 65 and over. The program is divided into four parts that address health coverage for services provided by physicians and hospitals as well as prescription drug coverage.

Medicaid: A federal/state program that provides a variety of social services to those identified as eligible based on state-specific criteria.

an increase in the Medicare tax rate, some have proposed turning it into a voucher program instead. Under such a program, an older person would receive a yearly voucher to be used to purchase health coverage. If the person were to use up the total value of the voucher before the end of the year, he or she would have to pay for additional medical services or do without until the next year.

It is not surprising that health care has become an area of significant political debate in this country. With health care costs rising at levels well beyond the rate of inflation, efforts to control costs will continue, and in the process, the health of older citizens may be affected.

ASK YOURSELF: Should Medicare be converted to a voucher system, or should the program remain as it is? Which of these choices is in the best interests of older citizens and of the general public? How can Medicare be made more efficient and less expensive?

Political Power

Will the United States become a **gerontocracy**, a country in which the political system is run by and for older citizens at the expense of younger generations? Chances are that this will not occur. So what is the political reality for older U.S. adults?

Although older voters now enjoy a larger public presence than voters in other age groups because of their numbers, the extent to which they influence public policy is unclear. All Americans who vote can have input into their political destiny, and historically, older U.S. citizens have been more likely to vote than those in any other age group (see Table 6.4). However, older Americans are just as diverse in their political beliefs, and in their voting patterns, as Americans in other age groups.

The emergence of welfare state programs has, without a doubt, played a crucial role in improving the overall health, well-being, and financial security of older citizens in the United States and throughout the developed world. It has also, by definition, increased dependence on government programs. In recent years, some politicians have undertaken efforts to dismantle such programs, though they have proven beneficial to older persons in the United States and elsewhere, and return the services the programs offer to the private sector. Older U.S. adults have begun to make their concerns about these efforts known through membership groups such as AARP (formerly the American Association of Retired Persons) and the more activist advocacy organization the Gray Panthers.

One of the more sensitive political issues for older voters is **generational inequity,** or the idea that they are unfairly receiving more benefits than other groups in

TABLE 6.4 Voting Patterns in the United States by Age, 2008–2014

	2008	2010	2012	2014
Total population 18 years and over	58.2%	41.8%	56.5%	38.5%
18–24 years old	44.3	19.6	38.0	15.9
25–34 years old	48.5	26.9	46.1	24.2
35–44 years old	55.1	37.7	52.9	32.8
45–54 years old	62.6	46.9	60.0	41.0
55–64 years old	68.1	56.3	67.1	51.4
65–74 years old	70.1	59.9	71.1	59.1
75 years and over	65.8	57.7	67.9	53.3

SOURCE: U.S. Census Bureau, Current Population Survey, November 2014, and earlier reports.

society thanks to age-specific legislation that favors them. Programs such as Social Security and Medicare, for instance, can raise the question of fairness to other age groups. Do children receive less from the government because they do not have an advocacy group like AARP?

Social Security and Medicare do provide age-specific benefits to individuals above a certain chronological age (Kapp, 1996, 2006). The problem, however, is not that older people are better at advocating for government to meet their needs, but that Congress has been unwilling to create universal support programs that provide services to *all* age groups, other than a few examples like the Americans With Disabilities Act.

Crime

As noted above, and as Figure 6.7 shows, older persons are less likely to be victims of crime in the United States

Gerontocracy: A system in which older-age citizens have the power to run the government and dictate policies that primarily support people in their age category.

Generational inequity: A situation in which older-age members of a society receive a disproportionate share of the society's resources relative to younger members; perceptions that such inequity exists lead to calls for adjustments to ensure greater economic and social parity between generations.

than are members of other age groups (Bachman & Meloy, 2008). However, research shows that older Americans believe they are *more* likely to be victimized (a finding first noted by Harris, 1976). What accounts for this difference between perception and reality?

There are several possible explanations. As noted above, when older persons are victimized, they have more difficulty recovering from injuries than do younger persons, and hospitalization can be a bigger financial strain for them. Older persons are also less likely to be in the labor force; thus, they may have limited ability to replenish their financial reserves after an assault. For older persons, being a victim of crime appears to be related to socioeconomic status; that is, wealthier older people have the economic means to live in areas in which they are less likely to experience victimization (Peguero & Lauck, 2008). Many urban areas undergo physical and demographic transformation over a number of decades, resulting in environments that are newly daunting and sometimes difficult to navigate for older persons who have lived there for many years. Finally, the deaths of friends and family leave many older persons alone, without adequate bases of emotional support and assistance.

In addition to being victims, older people also commit crimes. They currently make up the fastest-growing segment of the American prison population, not because they are committing more crimes, but because of the lengthy sentences now imposed, particularly on drug offenders. When older-age persons commit crimes

REUTERS/Lucy Nicholson

▶ Sometimes people assume that the elderly are too out of shape, sick, tired, or just plain old to exercise. But many adults ages 65 and older take part in physical activities such as walking, dancing, gardening, swimming, and cycling. Some people in their 70s and 80s even run marathons.

they tend to commit many of the same types of crimes as members of other age groups, but in far lower proportions. They are most likely to be charged with gambling, sex offenses, vagrancy, and public drunkenness (Feldmeyer & Steffensmeier, 2007). Because it costs more to care for older prisoners than younger ones, researchers have begun to look closely at sentencing guidelines and at how states can imprison older inmates without increasing the overall cost of care (Matcha, 2011). Again, some frame the rising costs associated with an increasingly older prison population as a social problem of aging when, in reality, the problem lies with the criminal justice system and sentencing policies.

ASK YOURSELF: Should older perpetrators of crimes be treated differently from others because of their age? Is it important to incarcerate an 80-year-old who has committed a serious crime, or should he or she experience a different type of punishment? If we treat an 80-year-old differently, what about a 75-year-old? Or a 65-year-old? Where should the chronological cutoff be for a different prison experience?

Global Perspective

The demographic shift toward an older population is not confined to the United States. In fact, the United States has, and will continue to have, one of the lowest percentages of people age 65 and over in the industrialized world. By the middle of the 21st century, the percentage of older-age people in the developing world will be increasing faster than the

FIGURE 6.7 **Violent Victimization Rates in the United States by Age, 2005–2015**

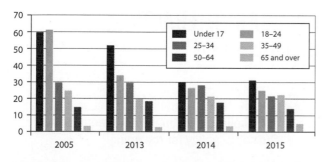

Legend:
- Under 17
- 25–34
- 50–64
- 18–24
- 35–49
- 65 and over

SOURCE: Truman, Jennifer I. and Lynn Langton. *Criminal Victimization, 2014.* Office of Justice Programs, Bureau of Justice Statistics. U.S. Department of Justice. (Revised September 29, 2015). NCJ 248973. Truman, Jennifer I. and Rachel E. Morgan. *Criminal Victimization, 2015.* Office of Justice Programs, Bureau of Justice Statistics, U.S. Department of Justice. NCJ 250180.

percentage in the developed world. Tables 6.5, 6.6, and 6.7 show the changes that are expected to continue well into the middle of this century in various regions of the world.

Notice the extent to which all regions of the world will experience significant growth of their aging populations between now and 2050. In the countries of Africa, the percentage of those 65 and over will almost double by 2050, while in Asia and Latin America it will triple. In all regions of the world except Africa and Oceania, the old-age dependency ratio will be greater than the child dependency ratio. Similarly, the median age will be at least 40 in all regions except Africa and Oceania. These demographic changes will alter economic and social landscapes throughout the world.

Let's look more closely at Japan and Italy. Japan is the country most representative of the future of aging. Over 17% of its population in 2000 was age 65 or over, and by 2050, that figure will be just over 36%. The government's ability to provide services in the future is in doubt because the old-age dependency ratio is expected to increase from 27.6 in 2000 to 77.4 in 2050. One reason is that life expectancy in Japan has increased steadily since the middle of the 20th century. In 2000–2005, it was 78.3 and 85.2 years for males and females, respectively. By 2050–2055, it will reach 85.5 and 91.9 years, and by the end of the 21st century it could be as high as 90.5 and an impressive 96.99 years (United Nations, 2015).

Italy's demographics are similar to Japan's. In 2000, about 18% of the population was 65 or over; by 2050, just over 35% will be. The old-age dependency ratio is expected to increase from 29.1 in 2000 to 73.9 in 2050. Finally, life expectancy rates in Italy have also increased from 83 for females and 77.2 for males in 2000 to 91 and 86.4, respectively, in 2050 and 96.5 and 91.9 in 2100 (United Nations, 2015). These changes go beyond mere numbers, of course. For instance, how many aging workers are remaining in the workforce? In Japan, more than 20% of older workers are still employed, while Italy may have a problem because less than 6% of older Italians are in the workforce. Why is this low percentage a problem? Perhaps the clearest answer is the ratio of retirees who collect government benefits to workers whose taxes help pay for them. By 2050, Japan is expected to have 96 pensioners for every 100 workers. In Italy, however, there will be 155 pensioners for every 100 workers (Bongaarts, 2004). Such ratios, particularly Italy's, are not sustainable because funding the pension system would take much of the workers' salary. The impact this situation will have on retiring Italians is expected to be dramatic. Both Japan and Italy will need to reevaluate their public policies and encourage greater numbers of older citizens to continue working.

Older-age populations around the world are under increasing pressure to reduce their impact on the societies in which they live. At the same time, they are being viewed

TABLE 6.5 Percentage of Population Age 65 and Over by Region, 2010 and 2050

Region	2010	2050
Africa	3.5	5.9
Asia	6.8	18.2
Europe	16.4	27.6
Latin America	6.8	19.5
Northern America	13.1	22.7
Oceania	10.7	18.2

SOURCE: United Nations, 2015. Population Division of the Department of Economic and Social Affairs of the United Nations Secretariat, *World Population Prospects: The 2015 Revision.*

as the vanguard of a new era in which changing political and economic conditions can offer them a renewed sense of purpose. It is this dichotomy that frames the lives of older persons throughout the developed world.

Before we go on to the discussion of theoretical perspectives in the next section, let's return for a moment to an earlier point and reinforce that aging is not in itself a social problem. Rather, older-age populations are diverse and are growing because of societal changes in family, work, and health. It is the way aging is socially constructed, in the patterns and trends reviewed above, that creates an image of aging as a social problem, of older people as the driving force of change, and therefore of the aging population as the culprit in any disruption these changes bring to the broader society.

USING THEORY TO UNDERSTAND AGING: THE VIEWS FROM THE FUNCTIONALIST, CONFLICT, AND SYMBOLIC INTERACTIONIST PERSPECTIVES

6.3 Apply the functionalist, conflict, and symbolic interactionist perspectives to social policy for the aging.

The sociological study of aging has historically focused on finding ways to improve the lives of older persons

TABLE 6.6 Child and Old-Age Dependency Ratios by Region, 2010 and 2050

	Africa	Asia	Europe	Latin America	Northern America	Oceania
Total dependency ratio, 2010	81.2	47.6	46.6	52.7	48.3	53.3
Child	74.9	37.6	22.6	42.4	28.8	36.8
Old-age	6.3	10.0	24.0	10.3	19.5	16.4
Total dependency ratio, 2050	61.5	56.6	74.6	57.8	66.3	61.9
Child	52.0	28.2	26.4	27.0	28.6	32.4
Old-age	9.5	28.4	48.1	30.8	37.7	29.5

SOURCE: United Nations, 2015. Population Division of the Department of Economic and Social Affairs of the United Nations Secretariat, *World Population Prospects: The 2015 Revision.*

TABLE 6.7 Median Age by Region, 2010 and 2050

Region	2010	2050
Africa	19.1	24.8
Asia	28.8	39.9
Europe	40.4	46.2
Latin America	27.5	41.2
Northern America	37.4	42.1
Oceania	32.2	37.4

SOURCE: United Nations, 2015. Population Division of the Department of Economic and Social Affairs of the United Nations Secretariat, *World Population Prospects. The 2015 Revision.*

rather than on building theories. Nevertheless, theoretical frameworks have evolved and offer a range of explanations that address the aging process and its outcomes. We begin with an assessment of the primary theoretical perspectives within sociology as they apply to aging.

Structural Functionalism

Recall that structural functionalism provides a view of society in which balance and social order are central, and every action has consequences and thus a function. Manifest functions are intended, while latent functions are unintended. For example, a retirement system is a manifest function of work because it allows for the smooth transition of older workers out of the system and provides employment opportunities for younger workers. A latent function of retirement is the creation of a population with the time to engage in volunteer efforts that reduce the need for full-time paid workers.

Structural functionalism is also built around the concept of structure and the need for social institutions such as the family, education, and religion to regulate the norms and values of society. A change in one part of the system will result in reactions from other parts. For example, the ongoing demographic shift toward a larger older population is resulting in an expanded effort to provide necessary health and social services to those in need.

Policy Implications of Structural Functionalism

While functionalism has its critics, some of the policy implications of this perspective are valuable. For instance, is the retirement of older workers functional for the individual and for society? It provides a ready supply of job openings for younger workers, ensuring that they become wage earners who provide for their own economic stability and that of society rather than disengaging from society's economic well-being. The establishment of a retirement "age" also provides society with a framework of work activity to which workers are expected to adhere; not retiring "on time" is viewed as dysfunctional. Although age-defined mandatory retirement no longer exists for most U.S. workers, most in fact still leave the workforce as soon as they find it economically feasible to do so.

Conflict Theory

While functionalism is based on balance and social order, conflict theory offers a distinctively different view of society in which inherent inequality allows the dominant group to impose its norms and values on the less powerful, maintaining an economic and social advantage and igniting power struggles over the use of society's resources. While initially focused on social class differences, conflict theory has evolved and today examines any

The Challenges of Aging in the Developing World

A recent article by Panruti, Liebig, and Duvvuru (2015) offers insight into the societal consequences of a rapid expansion of the aging population in India. The article includes an overview of the demographics of India's population; shows developments in research, education, and training; and concludes by addressing three emerging issues associated with aging in India.

As a country, India has the second-largest population in the world. Currently 1.2 billion, it is expected to increase to 1.4 billion by 2030. Although India's elderly population, as a percentage of the total population, is relatively small, it will continue to grow because of a continuing decrease in the overall fertility rate. As a result, the current 90 million elderly will increase to some 130 million by 2030.

While India has established research and education programs that examine the aging process, more work remains. The authors point to medical/geriatric research, biological gerontology, and social and behavioral gerontology as efforts to expand the knowledge base as well as provide increased levels of care for the aging population.

According to the authors, the emerging aging issues in India address fundamental needs of the growing elderly population. The first emerging aging issue is who is responsible for their support—the government or the family? This has become increasingly important with the trend toward a nuclear family structure rather than the traditional multigenerational family in which older members are provided care by their children.

The second emerging issue is that of health care—specifically, health care that meets the needs of an expanding aging population. As in other countries, older citizens are in need of care for chronic health conditions that are more expensive and result in greater dependency on others. In response, the government has begun implementing the development of regional geriatric centers and local health clinics.

The third emerging aging issue is that of income inequality for the aging population. Because most the elderly

NARINDER NANU/AFP/Getty Images

▶ An Indian street dentist installs dentures on an elderly patient at his roadside dentistry stall. Do you expect that street dentistry in India will be a booming business as the country's population ages?

live in rural areas, the need for adequate income in old age is significant, as most do not have any form of a pension plan.

▶ **THINK ABOUT IT**

1. Which emerging aging issue should be the primary issue of the Indian government? Why?

2. As birth rates continue to decline and life expectancy increases, the older-age population will continue to increase. What other aging-related issues will become important in the near future?

3. Given that the majority of older-age Indians live in rural areas and are poor, how could they help in the development of social policies for the aging population?

---

number of power issues involving race, class, sex, age, and other factors.

Conflict theory thus reflects the ongoing struggles within the aging population. Because older U.S. adults are diverse economically, politically, racially, ethnically, and religiously, they do not all reach the same outcome in life. For instance, the earliest baby boomers, known as front-enders, were born in the period 1946 through 1954. When they were eligible for the draft during the Vietnam War, the latest boomers, born from 1955 through 1964, were in preschool. Today, those early boomers can retire, while the youngest are vulnerable to layoffs and a bleak financial future.

Thus, conflicts have arisen between the segments of this population, and baby boomers as a whole are less able to unite behind their common needs. Exploiting this conflict, government and the private sector can win concessions on the policies and services they provide. For example, cries of the financial ruin of Social Security and the bankruptcy of Medicare drown out the economic realities, fragmenting the millions of baby boomers as they jockey for position within the public policy arena.

Policy Implications of the Conflict Perspective

If we limit conflict theory to a Marxist interpretation, then its only application is in how work affects older

Researching Aging

"Successful Aging" in Iran

What does the word *successful* mean to you, and how do you apply the word? Does passing this course make you successful? Is successful ever applied to your age group—such as "successful" young adults? If so, what criteria can be identified to determine whether you, as a young adult, are successful?

An article by Zanjari, Sani, Chavoshi, Rariey, and Shahboulaghi (2016) examines the perceptions of successful aging among Iranian elderly. The concept of successful aging was originally developed by Rowe and Kahn (1998). They believed that successful aging involved several factors that included the avoidance of disease and a continued engagement in everyday life via mental and physical stimulation. As one ages, the chance that they can meet these criteria suggests that successful aging is difficult to attain and maintain.

Zanjari and colleagues interviewed 60 residents of Tehran City. The sample was stratified by the social class of the participants and the socioeconomics of the neighborhood.

Participants were at least 60 years old, with a mean age of 72 and not experiencing cognitive impairment. The researchers found that the subjects mentioned several categories and subcategories associated with successful aging. The six main categories, in order of importance by the respondents, were: social well-being, psychological well-being, physical health, spirituality and transcendence, financial security, and elder-friendly environmental and social context. In other words, successful aging can be understood as a multidimensional concept. The researchers also found that social class position and gender influenced older Iranian views of what constitutes successful aging. For example, lower-class Iranians described financial security, while those from higher social classes were more likely to identify recreational activities that signify successful aging. Similarly,

► An elderly husband and wife in Abyaneh, Iran. What do you think a married couple in the United States that has aged successfully would look like?

Eric Lafforgue/Art in All of Us/Corbis/Getty Images

Iranian males considered retirement and disengaging from their work as indications of successful aging, while older women connected successful aging to raising successful children.

► **THINK ABOUT IT**

1. Some Iranian respondents did not like the word *successful* because it implied that some older individuals were "winners" and others "losers." Do you agree with this view of the concept of successful when applied to an age group? Why?

2. Are there other categories that could be identified with aging successfully?

3. How does culture influence our interpretation of successful aging?

BSIP/UIG/Getty Images

► A retiree volunteers at a kindergarten in Switzerland. What other contributions can older citizens make to their communities?

citizens. In other words, if what we do (work) defines who we are and what we have (or do not have) in a capitalist society, then older individuals are disadvantaged because access to work is controlled by those in the upper class, who create work to maintain their privileged position. Older citizens are thus viewed as nonproductive members of society, devalued and at the mercy of the more productive. Thus, "a Marxist view of the situation of people considered too old to be effective in the workplace places the blame for their circumstances on the general problems of capitalist society" (Cockerham, 1997, p. 70).

But the policy implications of conflict theory also apply to the distribution of power and resources. For example, the current debate in the United States over the proper role of government in providing services to the less fortunate is fundamentally grounded in the availability of resources: Should older citizens receive health care services through a government agency (Medicare) or through the private sector? Should workers of all ages be allowed to deposit some or all of their current Social Security funds into the stock market in an effort to grow their retirement funds at their own risk, or should the federal government control the funds and offer a safe but lower rate of return? These competing ideas and the belief systems behind them characterize the way power and resources affect the future of a growing segment of older people.

Symbolic Interactionism

Symbolic interactionism assumes that individuals in a society communicate via cultural symbols and shared meanings, and it looks at the ways we create our identities, the representations of who we believe we are in relationship to those around us. For older adults in the United States, identity is grounded in the past as well as in the present. What is an older person? Cultural symbols like white hair, wrinkles, reading glasses, and nursing homes are all components that endure as identity features. Other features are shared experiences of historical significance—such as the Great Depression, World War II, the Vietnam War, and 9/11—that connect individuals to an identity.

Policy Implications of Symbolic Interactionism

The policy implications of symbolic interactionism are significant. For years, the mass media in the United States have labeled aging adults as slow, politically conservative, overweight, hard of hearing, intellectually challenged, and overbearing toward the young. The problem with these labels is their consequences. For example, if an older person applies for a job, will the potential employer view him or her as someone who can perform the job, or as someone too slow to keep up with its demands?

Symbolic interactionism also has policy implications for efforts to address the problems older individuals experience as they attempt to adapt to changes, either social changes such as advancements in technology or changes that affect their personal lives, such as moving from environments they have known for decades into nursing homes or relinquishing car keys because they can no longer drive without endangering themselves and others. Society compensates older individuals for changes like these by creating public policies that increase their dependence on others, such as senior transportation for those who can no longer drive. While commendable, these programs miss the larger problems of where older persons live and the lack of local services that could enable them to maintain their independence.

SPECIALIZED THEORIES ABOUT AGING

6.4 Apply specialized theories to the social construction of aging.

Theoretical frameworks specific to the sociological study of aging have been few because of the interdisciplinary nature of aging research, its problem-solving focus, and its emphasis on the individual rather than society (Bengtson, Putney, & Johnson, 2005). Beginning in the 1950s, however, several distinct theories have been developed, each of which offers a variety of explanations of the aging process. We look at them in roughly chronological order.

Disengagement Theory

Disengagement theory was developed from the Kansas City Study of Adult Life in the 1950s and became one of the first theories of aging. Originally designed to reflect the functionalist relationship between the individual and society, it suggests that the aging individual and society engage in a mutual withdrawal in the sixth decade of life, allowing the individual to begin the socialization into old age. We see the application of functionalism in disengagement theory, because this theory conceptualizes the relationship between the individual and society as one of balance and, when applied to the world of work, as one of maintaining social order between generations.

The three basic tenets of disengagement theory are that disengagement is a mutual process, that it is universal, and that it is inevitable (Cumming & Henry, 1961). Further research efforts in the United States and other countries have not found support for the theory; nevertheless, it offered a beginning point from which further theoretical development has emerged.

When disengagement theory was first developed, most American workers faced mandatory retirement based on age. According to the theory, people understood that after working for an organization for a number of years and growing older, they would be replaced by younger workers, and the process was generally mutually agreeable. This is only a limited example of the mutual benefit shared by the worker and society, and other problems with the theory arose.

The assumption that disengagement occurs universally in all societies is problematic because work, the work role, and the role of older workers vary not only between but also within cultures. Finally, disengagement is not inevitable. In the current economic environment, many baby boomers will be forced to remain engaged in the workforce and in other middle-age-related roles; and, with the elimination of mandatory retirement for most occupations, others will not disengage from the workforce because they do not want to.

Activity Theory

Activity theory originated in the late 1940s and early 1950s (Cavan et al., 1949; Havighurst & Albrecht, 1953), but it was not officially established until the early 1970s (Lemon, Bengtson, & Peterson, 1972). Theoretically, activity theory is built on the work of symbolic interactionism.

Essentially, activity theory argues the opposite of disengagement theory by positing that as people age, they assume new roles more consistent with their current identities. Thus, they remain actively engaged in the social world and maintain their self-concepts and life satisfaction, but at levels different from before. Thus, identified as aging successfully, they enjoy new sets of activities they find as satisfying as their previous ones from middle age.

On a basic level, activity theory reflects modern U.S. society and its cultural values of individualism and independence. It represents a middle-class orientation to aging and identifies it as successful. At the same time, "activity theory neglects issues of power, inequality, and conflict between age groups" (Powell, 2006, p. 49). And, as with disengagement theory, efforts to replicate the initial work of activity theory have yielded only partial support (Longino & Kart, 1982).

Political Economy of Aging

Political economy of aging is less a unified theory than a broad perspective in which factors like inequality and structural forces help us understand aging in an economic and political context. For example, this perspective's focus on the way the provisions of the welfare state are distributed within a society shows us how social and economic inequalities are perpetuated that are then manifested in old age (Quadagno & Reid, 1999).

The basic tenets of the political economy of aging are as follows:

- An older person's sense of worth and power is shaped by the broader social structure.

- Labels attached to the elderly affect not only their beliefs about themselves, but also the way society creates public policies for them.

- Inequalities within society are reflected in the social policies and politics of aging. As a result, these policies enforce group-based advantages and disadvantages consistent with those in the larger society.

Joe Raedle/Getty Images

▶ Anita Dante searches for a job in a local newspaper's classified section at her home in Margate, Florida. After working for most of her life, Dante had planned on retiring, but her plans have changed. Dante lost most of her retirement nest egg and must now get a job to continue to support herself.

- Dominant political and economic ideological beliefs that reinforce advantages and disadvantages in the larger society are the basis for social policy (Estes, 1991).

- This perspective thus frames the relationship between the aging population and the larger society as one in which broader social and economic inequalities dominate the creation of social policy. In addition, older-age populations experience the generally negative impact that labeling can have on their lives and opportunities.

Continuity Theory

Building on activity theory, **continuity theory** utilizes the concept of normal aging as a basis for explaining how older individuals adjust. Here, "normal aging" describes the circumstances of those who are able to live independently, provide for their economic well-being, purchase nutritious foods, and meet their clothing and transportation needs. These are individuals who enjoy stability in this transitory life period as well as active involvement in the process itself. According to Atchley (1989, p. 183), "A central premise of continuity theory is that, in making adaptive choices, middle-aged and older adults attempt to preserve and maintain existing internal and external structures and that they prefer to accomplish this objective by using continuity (i.e., applying familiar strategies in familiar arenas of life)."

The crux of continuity theory is the existence of internal and external continuity. Inner continuity is our definition of who we are. It refers to inner qualities such as our preferences, temperament, and skills we have acquired. Atchley uses the Alzheimer's patient as an example of

Continuity theory: A theory that utilizes the concept of normal aging as a basis for explaining how older individuals adjust.

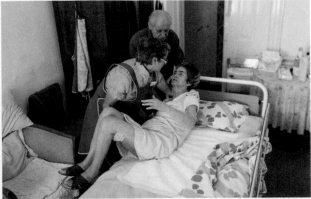

REUTERS/Nacho Doce

► Alzheimer's disease patient Isidora Tomaz is carried to bed by an aid worker from the Portuguese Alzheimer Association, a charity in Lisbon, Portugal. Isidora's husband looks on. Many patients receiving care from the association live at home.

External continuity relates to our physical and social environments, roles we perform, and activities in which we engage. Thus, for an older person the familiarity of his or her own home or other places where he or she spends time is important. The persistence of a particular role that a person has performed for years also provides a connection to the past as well as to the future. When external continuity is lost, the person experiences distress because surroundings are not familiar or must be experienced without access to all senses. External continuity allows an individual to cope with physical and mental changes that challenge the ability to function. If a person experiences difficulty walking or has short memory lapses, knowing the layout of his or her home enables the person to navigate hallways or stairs with less difficulty.

someone without inner continuity, because the person does not remember his or her identity, behavior patterns, or abilities. The loss of inner continuity is also problematic for others who attempt to interact with the person; they will experience lack of predictability in their interactions with the individual.

Finally, continuity can be too little, optimal, or too much. Too little continuity results in a lack of patterned activity, leading to unpredictability. Optimal continuity results when life adjustments are occurring at a rate consistent with the person's coping mechanisms. Too much continuity results in a lack of change, and the person feels stuck in a nonchanging environment (Atchley, 1989).

SOCIAL CHANGE: WHAT CAN YOU DO?

6.5 Identify steps toward social change for the aging.

Aging continues to be socially constructed as a social problem. What can you do? In a word: everything. Utilizing the material in this chapter as a guide, become involved in changing the way aging is socially constructed from a problem to an asset. The first step is to become aware of your own ageist attitudes and behaviors. Recognizing them allows you to think about what you say and how you behave toward older individuals. You can also engage in broader activities such as those described below.

older person receive what he or she is due. If you know of older individuals who are experiencing difficulties because they are poor, or who have a particular medical condition, you can advocate for them as a group. For example, in New York State, Tuesday is lobby day at the state capitol in Albany. Individuals meet with state legislators and attempt to convince them to write legislation that will advance the needs of the groups for which they are advocating. Finally, if you are concerned about issues affecting older persons, such as potential changes to Social Security or Medicare, you could join an advocacy organization that fights for the rights of all older persons.

Advocacy

Advocacy can take many forms. If you have a grandparent or know of another older person who needs help with housing or financial support, you can become that person's advocate, going to the appropriate agencies with him or her and helping the

Internships

Does your educational institution provide internships for students? If so, an internship with a local office on aging, senior center, or any other aging-related agency offers hands-on experience that can translate into exciting opportunities. You will also meet a number of

▶ Nurses feed elderly patients in a nursing home in Moscow, Russia. The home houses nearly 20 patients who were left without other forms of care. Russia's population continues to age rapidly, with over 13% of the population now 65 years or older.

great people who will be thrilled you are taking the time to provide them with the assistance they need. Often, it's the small things that make a difference. I've had students do internships in a senior center if they were interested in direct service with older adults. I have also placed students in the state office on aging if they are more interested in public policy related to aging. You might also look for internships in other organizations that advocate for older individuals, such as the Gray Panthers.

▶▶ Volunteering

Volunteer your time at a nursing home or wherever groups of older persons congregate. However, you should not assume that all older people want or need assistance. Generally, if they do, they will ask. Simply assuming they need help and doing things for them can create a feeling of dependence.

Become involved with organizations that promote active and engaged aging. For example, the National Council on Aging provides information about how advocates can help the organization and, by extension, older citizens. Area Agencies on Aging, which are part of a national organization, are located in all states; the organization's local and national offices offer a wealth of information about advocacy for older persons.

▶▶ Service Learning

If your college or university offers a service learning component, become involved. Different from internships or volunteering, service learning provides benefits to both the student and the recipient of the services. Beyond the service provided is the learning that occurs. In other words, take what you have learned in the classroom and apply it in the broader world of aging.

Turn to the beginning of the chapter to compare your answers to those of the total population.

1. Adult children are important to help elderly parents.

   AGREE: 94%

   DISAGREE: 6%

2. Who should provide help for the elderly?

   FAMILY MEMBERS: 66%

   GOVERNMENT AGENCIES: 16.5%

   NONPROFIT ORGANIZATIONS: 8.2%

   PRIVATE PROVIDERS: 9.3%

3. Should the aged live with their children?

   YES: 57.7%

   NO: 27.6%

   DEPENDS: 14.7%

SOURCE: National Opinion Research Center, University of Chicago.

4. Who should pay for help for the elderly?

   ELDERLY PEOPLE THEMSELVES OR THEIR FAMILY: 54.1%

   THE GOVERNMENT/PUBLIC FUNDS: 45.9%

5. In the United States, do you think we're spending too much money on Social Security, too little money, or about the right amount?

   TOO MUCH: 5.2%

   TOO LITTLE: 61.3%

   ABOUT THE RIGHT AMOUNT: 33.5%

CHAPTER SUMMARY

6.1 Discuss aging as a social construct.

Because aging is constructed from the expectations and beliefs of society, it has been identified as a social problem throughout U.S. history. Initially, older adults were considered a social problem because they were unable to provide for their own well-being. More recently, they have been identified as a social problem because of the cost of providing for their financial well-being and health care through taxpayer-supported government programs such as Social Security and Medicare. The construction of aging as a social problem is reinforced through the use of ageism, or the use of a person's chronological age as a basis for discrimination. We see the labeling of older citizens as a social problem on television, in newspapers and magazines, and around the Internet. As a result, societal expectations and beliefs about aging are rooted in a number of myths.

6.2 Discuss patterns and trends in the demographics of aging.

The percentage of the population age 65 and over is increasing and will continue to increase from 13% to 20% in virtually all countries. In the United States this demographic shift may harden the socially constructed belief that aging itself is a social problem. Smaller families place increased pressure on those caring for older members even as more people are living longer. In addition to elder abuse, older U.S. adults are also victims of crime, though at much lower rates than other age groups.

6.3 Apply the functionalist, symbolic interactionist, and conflict perspectives to social policy for the aging.

Functionalism offers insight into issues such as work and retirement. Is the retirement role functional for society and the individual, or does it create a power imbalance whereby individuals are expected to remove themselves from the workplace even though they want to remain employed? Conflict theory offers insight into power relations and the availability of resources, both within the aging community and between older persons and the larger society. Symbolic interactionism cuts through the media-created images and offers a realistic interpretation of aging in a changing world.

 6.4 Apply specialized theories to the social construction of aging.

Several specialized theories, from disengagement to the political economy of aging, offer a variety of interpretations that allow us to understand the complexity of the aging process and the ways in which perspectives have changed from the early 1950s to the present day. These theories are interconnected with social policies of aging through the expectations placed on older citizens. For example, disengagement theory supports the idea of mandatory retirement of older workers, while the political economy of aging perspective questions how social policies control older citizens.

 6.5 Identify steps toward social change for the aging.

Finally, what can you do? Become involved; become aware. Reject stereotypes of aging and volunteer, seek out an internship or service learning opportunity, or become an advocate for older persons.

KEY TERMS

ageism 132	fertility rate 135	Medicaid 139	sex ratio 135
aging 131	generational inequity 140	Medicare 139	Social Security 138
child dependency ratio 135	gerontocracy 140	old-age dependency ratio 135	total dependency ratio 135
continuity theory 147	life expectancy 135	poverty rate 137	welfare state 131

EDUCATION

Jenny Stuber

Students work on their math in their fourth-grade classroom at Carman-Buckner Elementary School in Waukegan, Illinois. In what ways does education get people to conform to society's expectations?

Investigating Education: Our Stories

Jenny Stuber

My story as a sociologist of education begins at Northwestern University. As a first-generation student, I was mystified by the class privilege I observed around me, but from which I often felt excluded. I could "pass" as any other white, middle-class student, but lacked some of the cultural know-how and financial resources to which many of my peers had access. Their access to these resources facilitated participation in Greek life, unpaid internships, and cultural events in Chicago and on campus. The disjuncture between my own social class background—having spent time on welfare growing up, attending college only by virtue of a full financial aid package—and the backgrounds of my peers raised profound questions about the paths that students take through the educational system and the ways in which schools both promote social mobility and reproduce inequality.

As a scholar, I continue to ask these questions, paying special attention to social class inequalities in higher education. As an educator, I inspire students to see the power and potential within the education system, along with its enduring social injustices.

LEARNING OBJECTIVES

7.1 Describe the role of education in the United States.

7.2 Discuss patterns of inequality in education.

7.3 Describe the history of the U.S. educational system and how it has affected different demographic groups.

7.4 Apply the functionalist, interactionist, and conflict perspectives to social policy for education.

7.5 Apply specialized theories to the social institution of education.

7.6 Evaluate explanations for educational inequality.

7.7 Describe recent reforms in education.

7.8 Identify steps toward social change in education.

WHAT DO YOU THINK?

Questions About Education From the General Social Survey

1. What is your interest level in local school issues?
   - [ ] VERY INTERESTED
   - [ ] MODERATELY INTERESTED
   - [ ] NOT AT ALL INTERESTED

2. What is your confidence level in education?
   - [ ] A GREAT DEAL
   - [ ] ONLY SOME
   - [ ] HARDLY ANY

3. In the United States, do you think we're spending too much money on improving the nation's education system, too little money, or about the right amount?
   - [ ] TOO MUCH
   - [ ] TOO LITTLE
   - [ ] ABOUT THE RIGHT AMOUNT

4. Do you think that sex education should be taught in public schools?
   - [ ] YES
   - [ ] NO

5. On the average, African Americans have worse jobs, income, and housing than white people. Do you think these differences are because most African Americans don't have the chance for the education that it takes to rise out of poverty?
   - [ ] YES
   - [ ] NO

Turn to the end of the chapter to view the results for the total population.

SOURCE: National Opinion Research Center, University of Chicago.

IDRIS AND SEUN

 7.1 Describe the role of education in the United States.

American Promise, a documentary film released in 2013, chronicles the educational experiences of two black children, from two families within the same neighborhood, following them from kindergarten into college. The film reveals a number of complex issues related to race, social class, and educational achievement (Dargis, 2013). Both Idris and Seun begin their formal education at age 5 in an elite private school in one of Manhattan's wealthiest neighborhoods. According to the filmmakers, the boys are attending the school in response to the school administration's efforts to increase diversity among the student body, alongside their parents' desire to provide their sons with the best possible education—one they do not view as available in their neighborhood public school. As the film progresses, and the boys get older, Seun leaves the private school and enters a public high school, while Idris persists at the private school, despite numerous obstacles.

Throughout the film, the documentarians press the children, their parents, their teachers, and school administrators to consider the ways in which race and class affect the day-to-day lives of Idris and Seun and their life chances. From an early age, Seun and Idris are aware of differences between themselves and their predominantly white, upper-class peers at school. Simultaneously, they are aware of the differences between themselves and their predominantly black, lower- and middle-class friends in their Brooklyn neighborhood. Seun struggles to make friends at school and is unable to get classmates to visit his home in Brooklyn. While playing basketball near his house, Idris is made fun of and accused of "talking like a white boy." Both appear caught between the high-achieving world of their largely white and affluent school and their Brooklyn neighborhood.

As the boys get older and begin to struggle academically, the filmmakers begin to explore the factors that contribute to the boys' relatively poor academic achievement. While the film does not offer

any clear answers, it does shed light on a few factors that contribute to some children doing better than others in school. First, both Seun and Idris have a difficult time establishing a sense of identity. They face conflicting pressures about who they should be from parents, neighborhood friends, classmates, and school staff. Many times these values and expectations clash, making it difficult for the boys to meet everyone's expectations.

A second factor shaping these boys' academic experiences is that as Idris and Seun grow older, it becomes clear that they have learning disabilities. While they both get much-needed help to manage their disabilities, they continue to face academic challenges.

A third factor that the film makes evident is that social class matters. Idris's father is a doctor and his mother is a lawyer. They live comfortably and have the resources and knowledge to support him; they are more similar than Seun's family to the families at the private school, although they are not nearly as wealthy. Seun's mom, in contrast, is a nurse who works long hours and cannot take the time to offer Seun the level of academic support found in Idris's home. Seun's family also faces the tragic death of one of his siblings. Given Seun's family's limited financial circumstances, managing this death is particularly challenging, and negatively impacts Seun's academic experiences.

All of these racial, circumstantial, social, and economic factors contribute to the challenges the boys encounter at school and affect their life chances. For Seun, the conditions surrounding his life lead to his parents' decision to remove him from the private school and enroll him in the local public school instead. For Idris, intensive parental involvement aids him in persisting at the private school, but he ultimately fails to be accepted at his first-choice college.

Filmed over 13 years, *American Promise* tells a poignant story—one that raises questions about the differences between public and private schools and the ways in which students' backgrounds are related to what occurs in and outside schools. This chapter explores many of the issues illustrated by the story of Idris and Seun, and focuses on how sociological theories can explain the role of schools in providing social mobility or reproducing inequality. These theories focus on the family, the peer group, the school context, and the educational system itself, to explain the problems and possibilities that emerge from the educational system. By examining the sociological perspective on education, you will be able to analyze the roles that schools play in their societies and explain why a sociological perspective on educational problems is essential to developing solutions to those problems.

▶ The 19th-century education reformer Horace Mann once said, "A teacher who is attempting to teach without inspiring the pupil with a desire to learn is hammering on a cold iron." How does a teacher forge an educated mind in a young student?

As a nation, the United States has long placed a great deal of faith in education. Americans tend to view schools as providing opportunities for social mobility, places that nurture and develop the hearts and minds of children, an antidote for ignorance and prejudice, and the solution to myriad social problems. Throughout the United States' history, countless citizens have regarded schools as the setting in which the American Dream is realized; as meritocratic institutions where members of each successive generation, through hard work and initiative, can achieve their full potential.

This is not to say that Americans have not been critical of our educational system—quite the contrary! Debates concerning teaching methods, politics, curricula, racial desegregation, equality of opportunity, and other issues have always defined the educational arena. It is precisely because Americans believe so passionately in education and expect so much from their schools that the U.S. educational system has been subject to such disagreements.

Today, many observers believe that education in the United States is in crisis. In the early 1970s, the American education system experienced crises related to inequalities of educational opportunity and the allegedly authoritarian and oppressive nature of schools. In the 1980s and 1990s, concerns about education shifted to the decline of standards and authority, which were blamed for the erosion of U.S. economic superiority. Today, an emphasis on standards has resulted in a preoccupation with accountability, with related concerns about achievement gaps along race, class, and gender lines. With the appointment of President Donald Trump's secretary of education, Betsy DeVos, renewed attention has been granted to questions of school choice, and whether public schools are able to deliver the kind of education that parents demand and taxpayers deserve.

PATTERNS AND TRENDS

7.2 Discuss patterns of inequality in education.

To begin our discussion of social problems in education, we start with some statistical snapshots on the state of education in the United States. These snapshots highlight key aspects of educational achievement—how much students know and how they score on various assessments—and educational attainment—how much education they have received. These data reveal that Americans have lower levels of achievement than many peer nations, and that significant inequalities exist among Americans.

Educational Achievement and the Decline of Basic Skills

Critics of public education in the United States have pointed to the failure of schools to teach basic skills in reading, writing, science, and mathematics. Although there is debate over which skills and knowledge should be measured, and whether a decline in skills is responsible for the United States' economic decline, it appears that schools in the United States have become less effective in transmitting skills and knowledge. Comparisons of American adults to adults living in other economically advanced countries show, for example, that American adults score about average on international tests of literacy and below average on tests of numeracy (Rampey et al., 2016).

Indeed, the problem of illiteracy in the United States is concerning. Rather than being "literate" or "illiterate," literacy is measured as a scale that reflects an individual's ability to understand, evaluate, and engage with written texts to participate in society, achieve one's goals, and develop one's knowledge and potential. Currently, about 17% of adult Americans possess only the most basic or functional levels of literacy (Rampey et al., 2016). Scores on numeracy are even lower. This means that tens of millions of Americans are limited in their own potential because they cannot use texts to learn, develop, or seek opportunities. Moreover, the nation itself may be hindered because these individuals lack the higher-order reading and comprehension skills that are necessary in today's labor market. According to the College Board (2015), only about 43% of recent high school students are "college or career ready" upon high school graduation.

Gaps in Educational Achievement

Since the 1960s, educational policy has focused on differences in student achievement across social classes, races, ethnicities, and genders. The **achievement gap** is often measured using standardized tests. Federal educational policy has attempted to reduce the achievement gap, beginning with the **Elementary and Secondary Education Act (ESEA)** of 1965; continuing through the **No Child Left Behind Act (NCLB)** of 2001; and with the most recent initiative, **Race to the Top (RTT)**, introduced in 2010 under President Barack Obama.

Figure 7.1 highlights trends in the achievement gap in reading, showing the test scores of white, Asian and Pacific Islander, black, and Hispanic eighth graders since 1980 (NCES, 2013, 2017). Scores are drawn from the **National Assessment of Educational Progress (NAEP)**, sometimes called "The Nation's Report Card." These data show significant and persistent gaps in achievement over time, with white and Asian American students posting the highest average scores. Inequalities in achievement are also found along social class lines. Figure 7.2 compares the eighth grade reading scores of students who are eligible for free or reduced lunch—a proxy for students who meet federal definitions of poor or low income—to those who are not (NCES, 2013, 2017). These data show a clear advantage for students who grow up in economically advantaged homes. While the size of the test score gap is typically smaller, scores of math performance exhibit similar patterns of inequality across groups.

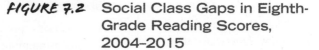

FIGURE 7.1 Racial Gaps in Eighth-Grade Reading Scores, 1971–2015

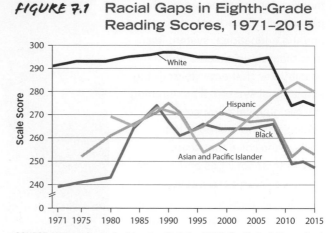

SOURCE: National Center for Education Statistics (2013). The Nation's Report Card: Trends in Academic Progress 2012 (NCES 2013 456). Institute of Education Sciences, U.S. Department of Education, Washington, D.C.

FIGURE 7.2 Social Class Gaps in Eighth-Grade Reading Scores, 2004–2015

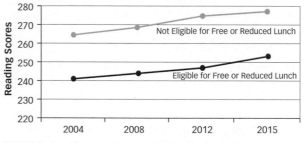

SOURCE: National Center for Education Statistics. 2017. https://www.nationsreportcard.gov/reading_math_2015/#reading/gaps?grade=8 Retrieved on May 5th, 2016.

Achievement gap: The consistent difference in scores on tests of student achievement across different demographic groups, including groups based on race, gender, and socioeconomic status.

Elementary and Secondary Education Act (ESEA): The primary piece of federal legislation concerning K–12 education in the United States; this act, first passed in 1965, was most dramatically revised through its reauthorization in 2001 as the No Child Left Behind Act.

No Child Left Behind Act (NCLB): U.S. federal legislation passed in 2001 as the reauthorization of the Elementary and Secondary Education Act; established a range of reforms mandating uniform standards for all students with the aim of reducing and eventually eliminating the social class and race achievement gap by 2014. It was reauthorized by President Obama in 2015 as the Every Student Succeeds Act (ESSA).

Race to the Top (RTT): Federal program established by President Obama in 2010 with the goal of aiding states in meeting various components of NCLB by offering grants to states to improve student outcomes and close achievement gaps.

National Assessment of Educational Progress (NAEP): A congressionally mandated set of standardized tests intended to assess the progress of a sample of U.S. students at various grade levels from all demographic groups and parts of the country.

Gaps in Educational Attainment

Many jobs in the United States have minimum education requirements; therefore, educational attainment is an indicator of who is eligible for which jobs, as well as who may be qualify for higher education. Figure 7.3 shows the gap in high school graduation rates across racial lines (Snyder, de Bray, & Dillow, 2016). These patterns parallel those of racial gaps in educational achievement, and set the stage for inequalities in college enrollment and eventual completion. As shown in Figure 7.4, significant racial and social class gaps exist in the percentage of high school students who enroll in 2- or 4-year degree programs following graduation. Finally, Figure 7.5 shows that these gaps persist among adults who eventually complete a 4-year degree (Ryan & Bauman, 2016). Because educational attainment is so highly correlated with income, as well as health and political/civic engagement, it is clear that inequalities in education set the stage for inequalities in other areas of social life.

ASK YOURSELF: Which of these patterns of inequality in U.S. education do you find most alarming or most problematic? Why? What do you think are the causes of these patterns? What does our society need to do to reverse these trends?

U.S. EDUCATION SYSTEM: A BRIEF HISTORY

7.3 Describe the history of the U.S. educational system and how it has affected different demographic groups.

So how did we get to the current state of inequalities in education? A brief history of education in the United States shows that despite the ideal of schools serving as the "great equalizers," and continual efforts to level the playing field, this history is marked by enduring inequalities in access, funding, and more.

Prior to the 1830s, education in the United States was loosely organized and noncompulsory. While elites were privately educated in subjects like math, philosophy, and religion, everyone else was taught basic literacy in the home, if at all. The birth of the "common school movement" in the 1830s changed that. With the growth of urbanization and industrialization, education advocates like Horace Mann lobbied for a system that would be universal, free, and nonsectarian (not rooted in specific religious beliefs). Accordingly, formal education expanded and became democratized at this time—at least with respect to social class. Through the second half of the 1800s, primary and secondary schools spread from

FIGURE 7.3 Racial Gaps in High School Graduation, 2013–2014

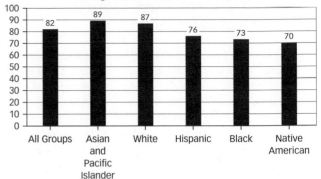

SOURCE: Snyder, T.D., de Brey, C., and Dillow, S.A. (2016). Digest of Education Statistics 2015 (NCES 2016-014). National Center for Education Statistics, Institute of Education Sciences, U.S. Department of Education. Washington, DC.

FIGURE 7.4 Racial and Social Class Gaps in College Enrollment, 2014

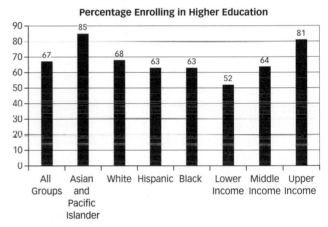

SOURCE: Snyder, T.D., de Brey, C., and Dillow, S.A. (2016). Digest of Education Statistics 2015 (NCES 2016-014). National Center for Education Statistics, Institute of Education Sciences, U.S. Department of Education. Washington, DC.

FIGURE 7.5 Percentage of Adult Population (25 and Older) With Bachelor's Degree or Higher, by Race

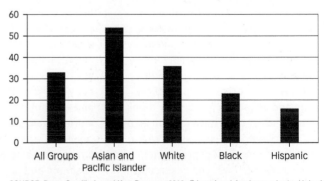

SOURCE: Ryan, Camille L. and Kurt Bauman. 2016. *Educational Attainment in the United States: 2015 Population Characteristics.* Washington, D.C.: The U.S. Census Bureau.

Race, Class, and the Gender Gap in Achievement

Whereas researchers once asked whether schools were "failing at fairness" when it came to educating girls (Sadker & Sadker, 1994), today concerns focus on the lower levels of achievement and college completion among boys and young men (DiPrete & Buchmann, 2013). When it comes to many standardized tests, GPA, high school completion, and college enrollment, girls and young women outperform their male counterparts. For example, about 85% of girls finish high school on time, while only 78% of boys do so (Stetser & Stillwell, 2014); 71% of those female high school graduates enroll in some form of postsecondary education, while only 61% of male graduates do so (Lopez & Gonzalez-Barrera, 2014). In fact, the gender gap in scores on the National Assessment of Educational Progress *widens* between fourth and 12th grade—something that has prompted researchers to look to social processes to explain.

Many sociologists see the gender gap in education as an issue of socialization and messages about masculinity. Yet notions of how masculinity and school success are related require an intersectional perspective: It is not a simple story about how young men understand education, but a complex story of how notions of masculinity intersect with race and social class. In his book *Learning the Hard Way*, Edward Morris (2012) suggests that some boys disengage from school because they see school success as a girl thing, one that requires students to follow rules and develop a mastery of "book smarts." Over time, boys take on an air of "contrived carelessness"—where they flaunt their lack of preparation, mock studious boys, and assert that

common sense and street smarts trump book smarts. According to Morris, this response emerges among white, working-class boys growing up in lower-income communities, as they begin to recognize that traditional avenues for adult male success no longer exist. Within their rural and de-industrialized communities, jobs have disappeared, and a sense of masculine identity and achievement along with them. In response, some boys reject academic success as a legitimate basis for identity and instead gain status by asserting an alternative standard of masculinity—one that emphasizes toughness, fighting, and an interest in traditionally masculine pursuits like sports, hunting, and fishing.

Similar processes are evident among black and Latino males—where the gender gap is even larger. According to both Edward Morris and Prudence Carter (2006), when black males succeed in school, they risk being labeled gay or effeminate. Because these are stigmatized identities, young black men must choose between academic success and masculinity. In inner-city environments where young men of color have limited opportunities to achieve economic success, they seek alternative yardsticks for measuring their worth. They may emphasize "hardness" and a streetwise demeanor as a more certain path toward attaining respect (Carter, 2006). Instead of striving for success by achieving in school and one day earning a

▶ Members of the Bloods street gang sitting in front of their homeboy's gravesite in 1995. How did these young men assert their masculinity? Where do you suppose they are now?

decent income, they gain immediate respect by being *ballers* and *gangstas*, or by demonstrating cleverness and verbal skills through *clownin'* and *riffin'* (Morris, 2012). Although the responses of white and nonwhite boys parallel each other, Morris finds that black and Latino boys have additional personas available to them to reassert their masculinity.

Finally, it is important to note that the gender gap in achievement is negligible or nonexistent among middle- and upper-class boys (DiPrete & Buchmann, 2013); among the more affluent, boys and girls go on to college at similar rates. DiPrete and Buchmann assert that boys' "educational attainment appears to be more sensitive to the level of educational resources in the family" (p. 153), with vulnerabilities for boys with less-educated or absent fathers. Where young men perceive legitimate opportunities for adult occupational success, and where they have examples of such success within their families, they are less inclined to disengage from school. This finding has important implications for the need for mentoring and role modeling within lower-income schools and communities.

PYMCA/UIG/Getty Images

New England to the South and then West. From the start, boys and girls were largely educated together, yet legalized racial segregation was the norm. Because schooling was compulsory only through age 14, many adolescents left school to work at home, in factories, or on farms. At the start of the 20th century, between 50% and 60% of school-aged children (ages 5–19) were enrolled in school (Snyder, 1993).

Schools in the United States have long struggled with efforts to incorporate and educate students from diverse backgrounds. Indeed, the earliest education reformers considered the promotion of civic education and social integration to be the highest goal of schooling. During the mid-1800s Catholic immigrants from Ireland and Lutherans from Germany pressed for their own public schools; ones where their religious traditions were permitted alongside academic instruction. Starting in 1875, however, 38 states passed a Blaine Amendment, barring the use of taxpayer funds for religious schools or instruction. With increased immigration from Southern and Eastern Europe in the late-18th and early-19th centuries came increased efforts aimed to limit private, religious schools and encourage secular, public education that would help integrate an increasingly diverse nation. Perhaps no group experienced these efforts at "Americanization" more than Native Americans, who throughout the 20th century were taken from their families and forced to attend boarding schools, where they were stripped of their language and customs with the goal of complete assimilation into Anglo society.

While assimilation and social cohesion have been persistent story lines in the educational history of the United States, so has segregation. During slavery, literacy among blacks was explicitly forbidden, the assumption being that education would threaten the slave system, making slaves less dependent on their masters and more able to exert autonomy or organize a rebellion. Yet a desire for knowledge—whether for self-empowerment, personal expression, or religious guidance—existed among slaves, as did underground systems of education. (*Note:* Communities of free blacks existed in the North at this time.) After the Civil War, free public education was extended to black Americans. From the very beginning, schools attended by black students have been overcrowded and underfunded. Up until the 1950s, black schools in the Deep South received an average of 30 cents for every dollar of funding received by white schools; in the Mid-Atlantic states, black schools received an average of 60 cents for every dollar received by white schools (Margo, 1990).

Although the U.S. Supreme Court ruled racial segregation to be legal in the 1896 case *Plessy v. Ferguson* (as long as facilities were "separate but equal"), it reversed this decision with *Brown v. Board of Education* in 1954. Here, the justices unanimously agreed that even if segregated schools have equivalent resources, they would still be guilty of inflicting unconstitutional social and psychological harm on minority students—with segregation inherently marking them as different, and therefore lesser. Yet because the Court's decision lacked a legal enforcement mechanism, few school districts moved to desegregate. It was not until the Civil Rights Act of 1964 that the government began requiring districts to develop desegregation plans, and used the threat of funding cuts to enforce them. In the 1970s and 1980s, busing across school boundaries was used to racially integrate schools. By the late 1990s, opposition to such plans brought this policy to an end. Today, *de facto* segregation (segregation by choice or preference) has replaced *de jure* segregation, with many white families choosing to live in majority-white communities or exit the public school system altogether. Whites constitute more than 60% of all school-aged children in the United States, but they make up only about 50% of public school students (Snyder, de Brey, & Dillow, 2016). These patterns of segregation contribute to persistent problems with funding and resources in schools attended by black and other minority students. This disparity in resources is embedded in the fact that nearly 50% of a school's budget comes from local property taxes, with higher tax bases in majority-white neighborhoods.

The recent history of education in the United States has focused on questions of equity for immigrant students—which will likely remain a focus in the near future. As Figure 7.6 shows, it is predicted that by 2025 Hispanic

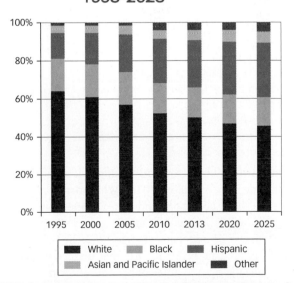

FIGURE 7.6 U.S. Public School Enrollments by Race, 1995–2025

Legend: White | Black | Hispanic | Asian and Pacific Islander | Other

SOURCE: Snyder, T.D., de Brey, C., and Dillow, S.A. (2016). Digest of Education Statistics 2015 (NCES 2016-014). National Center for Education Statistics, Institute of Education Sciences, U.S. Department of Education. Washington, DC.

Education Beyond Our Borders

International Tests of Student Achievement

Because many in the United States are concerned about educational achievement within our borders, it is useful to explore how the United States "stacks up" to other nations. Policy makers and scholars have increasingly used international tests of student achievement to rank the education systems of different countries. Whenever a new round of testing data is released, there is renewed attrition to the relatively poor performance of students in the

TABLE 7.1 PISA Math Scores for 15-Year-Olds, OECD Countries, 2015

Rank	Country	Average Score	Rank	Country	Average Score
1	Singapore	564	17	Poland	504
2	Hong Kong	548	17	Ireland	504
3	Macao	544	19	Norway	502
4	Taiwan	542	20	Austria	497
5	Japan	532	21	New Zealand	495
6	China	531	21	Vietnam	495
7	Korea	524	23	Russia	494
8	Switzerland	521	23	Sweden	494
9	Estonia	520	23	Australia	494
10	Canada	516	26	France	493
11	Netherlands	512	27	United Kingdom	492
12	Denmark	511	28	Czech Republic	492
12	Finland	511	28	Portugal	492
14	Slovenia	510		OECD average	490
15	Belgium	507		. . .	
16	Germany	506	~37	United States	470

SOURCE: Kastberg, D., Chan, J.Y., and Murray, G. (2016). Performance of U.S. 15-Year-Old Students in Science, Reading, and Mathematics Literacy in an International Context: First Look at PISA 2015 (NCES 2017-048). U.S. Department of Education. Washington, DC: National Center for Education Statistics. Retrieved May 7th, 2017, from http://nces.ed.gov/ pubsearch.

students will make up close to 30% of public school students (Snyder, de Brey, & Dillow, 2016). While many of these students will have been born and raised in the United States, a significant portion will be immigrants. Some portion of these will also be undocumented. In 1982, the U.S. Supreme Court declared in *Plyler v. Doe* that undocumented students have the right to a free public education in the United States (through the 12th grade). For immigrant students, questions have been raised about language instruction. In conjunction with the Bilingual Education Act of 1968, the 1974 U.S. Supreme Court decision *Lau v. Nichols* mandated that schools provide appropriate instruction to English language learners (ELLs). The law is vague, however, on how long and in which subjects students should be educated in English versus their native language. In recent years, critics have emerged, promoting English-only laws and banning multicultural education. These efforts reflect persistent anxieties about immigrant groups and conflicts over whether education should accommodate cultural differences or promote social cohesion.

FIGURE 7.7   Child Poverty Rates in Select OECD Nations, 2013

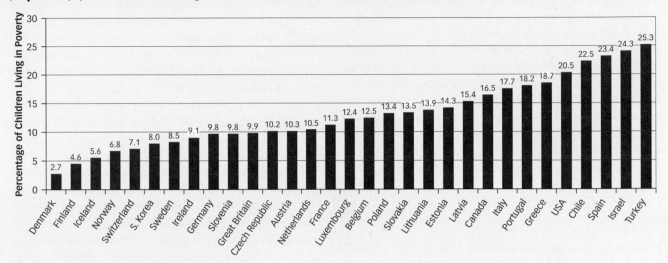

SOURCE: Data from Organization for Economic Cooperation and Development. (2012) OECD Income distribution questionnaire. OECD (2017), Poverty rate (indicator).

United States. As Table 7.1 shows, the United States scores below average on international tests of math achievement, as measured by the Program for International Student Assessment (PISA), where it ranks approximately 37th. Scores on science and reading literacy are higher, with the United States ranking about 19th and 15th, respectively (Kastberg, Chan, & Murray, 2016).

Many view these results as a sign of the U.S. education system's decline. However, scholars such as Diane Ravitch (2013) and David Berliner and Bruce Biddle (1995) point out that the United States has always done relatively poorly on international student assessments.

Ravitch contends that standardized test scores mask other important educational goals, such as critical thinking and creativity. Ravitch notes that some top-scoring nations that have historically emphasized memorization are now trying to emulate aspects of the U.S. education system that encourage independent thought and creativity. Unfortunately, the U.S. system seems to be moving away from these practices, while it increasingly focuses on memorization and test-taking skills.

Another important element in this international comparison is the degree to which poverty affects student outcomes. As Figure 7.7 shows, the United States

has one of the highest child poverty rates among OECD (Organization of Economic Cooperation and Development) nations. Berliner (2006) argues that there is a relationship between high child poverty rates and low student test scores. Berliner shows that individual U.S. states with low poverty rates, such as Massachusetts, have scores that are similar to the highest-achieving nations. Like all data, international achievement numbers must be viewed with a careful and critical eye.

▶ **THINK ABOUT IT:** How would you explain the relationship between high child poverty rates and low math scores?

ASK YOURSELF: How have your educational experiences compared to those of your parents and grandparents (or other guardians)? How do you think your educational experiences may have been different if you were from a different race/ethnicity or social class group?

International Comparisons: Situating Education in the United States

As noted above, students in the United States tend to perform more poorly than students in other developed countries. But how does the U.S. *system* of education compare to systems in other countries? Countries vary considerably in how they organize their school systems: what subjects are required, how many years are required, and the degree to which students are tracked. Few systems are as complex as the United States'. For instance, most countries have a national ministry of education that exerts control from the top down, as opposed to the localized system of education that exists across the United States, where decisions about funding and curriculum are made at the state or district level. In addition, education in the United States tends to be inclusive and undifferentiated, where all students basically receive the same secondary school credential (although variations exist in the quality of education). Students in other systems are often placed in different streams or tracks, separating students as gifted and less gifted, or vocationally versus academically inclined. This may result in different types of secondary school diplomas being granted. Ultimately, each country's system of education reflects its unique history and culture. Let's take a look!

Germany

Imagine having your occupational fate decided around age 11. Such a proposition would strike many Americans as odd, given our cultural emphasis on personal autonomy, growth, and discovery. Yet this kind of tracking is at the heart of Germany's education system. While most students attend the same type of school until age 11 (*Grundschule*), the following year students are sorted into one of five tracks, with the main distinction between them that students can enter higher education only if they were sorted into the *Gymnasium* track and passed the *Abitur* exam (some students in the *Gesamtschule* track also qualify); the other tracks prepare students for professional or vocational roles, with separate schools for engineering, skilled manual labor, and business (basic accounting, human resources, clerical fields). Elementary school teachers play a powerful a role in determining a student's path, making judgments about students' academic ability and comportment during early elementary grades; parents play a more limited role.

In the United States, being assigned to a vocational track may be considered a disappointment, given our emphasis on college as the route to economic stability and respect. Yet in Germany, a cultural tradition of respect for craftspeople, along with strong union organization, means that students who complete the vocational track often end up in jobs that are well respected and well paid. A system of apprenticeships is built into the education of students attending *Realschules* and *Hauptschules*, with students landing positions in skilled engineering and manufacturing with companies like Mercedes-Benz and Siemens.

What about students' experiences *at* school? The German system places less emphasis on exams than does the United States, and exams are typically essay based. Moreover, don't expect homecoming games or prom activities—German schools tend to be academic in

orientation, with little emphasis on sports or extracurricular activities.

Finland

So far in the 21st century, Finland has posted some of the highest scores on international assessments of math, science, and reading exams. Even more impressive is the low variation in scores across racial, ethnic, and socioeconomic groups. So how has Finland achieved such impressive and consistent results?

During the past 40 years, a major overhaul of Finland's education system has focused on high-quality teacher education, equality across the curriculum, and the provision of wraparound services. Finland eliminated all forms of tracking and standardized testing and instead ensures that students attain a high level of success through formative evaluation and oral and narrative dialogues between teachers and students. The one standardized exam that Finland administers is a college entrance exam consisting of items designed to evaluate students' problem-solving, analytic, and writing skills (Darling-Hammond, 2010).

Perhaps the most remarkable characteristic of the Finnish system is the way it recruits, educates, and retains teachers. With only 15% of college graduates who apply for teacher education programs being admitted, teaching is a very selective career. Students receive stipends and free tuition as they complete a 3-year graduate program preparing them to be classroom teachers. Finnish teachers earn good wages, are treated as professionals, and maintain a large degree of autonomy over their teaching practices. They oversee small classes of students and are given time to collaborate with coworkers, develop curricula, and review student work. As a result, they can develop innovative practices that meet students' individualized needs. Finnish teachers also have a high degree of work satisfaction, which has eliminated job turnover and shortages.

Education reform in Finland has taken a different path from education reform in the United States and has achieved markedly better results. To what extent can the United States learn from Finland as it works to improve its education system? One potential barrier is that there are currently too few students enrolling in teacher preparation programs in the United States, perhaps reflecting concerns about the teaching profession having too little respect and autonomy, and insufficient salaries.

Ghana

While literacy rates reach upwards of 95–100% in Western industrialized countries, educational attainment and achievement lag behind in many nations of the Global South (a term for the poor, less-developed countries of Africa, Asia, and Central and South America). In these nations, poverty, hunger, and corruption are barriers to educational progress. After winning independence in 1957, Ghana proceeded to build a universal system of education. As in many countries colonized by European powers, the educational system mirrors that of their colonizers, with preschool (ages 3–5), basic primary school (6–11), junior high school (12–14), senior high school (15–17), and college (18–21). With courses taught in both native languages and English, much of the curriculum mirrors what is taught in the Global North. Some critics suggest that the educational system place greater emphasis on local knowledge, history, and culture, and ensure that education is useful and culturally relevant. Organizations like the World Bank, however, mandate that certain provisions be met by their education systems, if countries are to receive economic assistance for development. Corruption also plagues such systems, as bribery and waste mean insufficient funds for high-quality teachers or materials.

Currently, about 85–90% of primary age children are enrolled in Ghana's schools. Literacy rates exceed 70%, but a 10 point gap exists between male and female students. As in many countries of the Global South, the education of females lags behind males in Ghana, where the average level of attainment is 8 years for boys but less than 6 for girls (UNESCO, 2015). Gender role expectations and structural conditions heighten educational expectations for males, who are more likely to be the economic leaders. Female education is considered a luxury, as girls are pulled out of school, often to assist with domestic tasks (Ballantine, Hammack, & Stuber, 2017). Increasingly, activists are concerned that negative attitudes toward menstruation, and the lack of effective menstrual products (and limited access to bathrooms with running water), hinder the education of women in such countries, as many girls miss up to 1 month of school each year due to their periods. Harassment of female students and feelings of safety are also a major concern (Lambert, Perino, & Barreras, 2012). Accordingly, a "Girls Education Unit" has been established to take on such issues.

Ulrich Baumgarten/Getty Images

▶ Fourth-grade children attend class at an elementary school in Bonn, Germany. The German education system is different in many ways from that in the United States. In Germany, children in Grades 1–4 attend elementary school (*Grundschule*), where the subjects taught are the same for all. Then after the fourth grade, they are separated according to their academic abilities and the wishes of their families.

USING SOCIOLOGICAL THEORIES IN EDUCATION

7.4 Apply the functionalist, interactionist, and conflict perspectives to social policy for education.

So how can we understand inequalities in education, and how can we apply sociological theories to address social policies in the educational domain? The **sociology of education** mirrors larger theoretical debates within sociology. This section provides an overview of the major theoretical perspectives used by sociologists—functionalism, conflict theory, and symbolic interactionism—and then applies them to educational policy questions.

Functionalist Theory

Functionalist sociologists view society as a kind of machine—one in which each component performs a unique job and contributes to the functioning of the whole. For functionalists, the family, religion, school, and

Sociology of education: The study of how individuals and institutions throughout society affect the education system and how the system produces educational outcomes.

ASK YOURSELF: To what extent is an international perspective on education necessary? What kinds of insights can be gained by looking at other systems of education?

other social institutions each play important roles in how society as a whole functions.

Functionalist theories of school and society trace their origins to French sociologist Émile Durkheim (1858–1917). Durkheim (1977) believed that in virtually all societies, education is critical in creating the moral unity necessary for social cohesion and harmony. Functionalists assume that consensus and cooperation are the normal state in society and that conflict represents a temporary breakdown of shared values. In a well-functioning society, schools socialize students with appropriate values, unify them into a collective whole, and sort them into necessary adult roles.

Al Seib/Los Angeles Times/Getty Images

▶ Sandy Torres is quick to answer questions from Gabriel Robles (left), a site director who is reading to first, second, and third grade students at the Stevenson YMCA Community School in Long Beach, California, which provided reading instruction to 1,000 low-income kids. Education has historically been seen as offering the opportunity for economic mobility. Do you think a child of poor or poorly educated parents is as likely to get a good education as someone born to middle-class parents with college degrees?

Talcott Parsons (1959) believed that education is a vital part of a modern society. He argued that education sets modern society apart from earlier time periods because it establishes a system of **meritocracy**—a system in which people achieve their social positions based on talent and hard work (i.e., merit), rather than the circumstances of their birth. In modern societies education plays a key role in meritocratic selection processes, at least assuming that schools provide equal opportunity for all citizens.

Policy Implications of Functionalist Theory

Functionalists typically see schools as providing equality of opportunity. The just society is one in which each member has an equal shot at social and economic success, where merit and talent replace family background as the essential determinants of one's adult status. From this perspective, inequality in pay or status is normal and can be tolerated, as long as these inequalities reflect differences in talent and effort. Education provides the setting in which society can achieve this meritocratic ideal.

Functionalism leads to support for educational policies that promote a uniform curriculum and one that emphasizes a common history and shared cultural values. Such policies also promote equality of educational opportunity and strive to provide all children with access to high-quality teachers and equitable funding. However, functionalists do not believe that schools within a meritocracy should guarantee equal *outcomes*; rather, schooling should provide equal *opportunity* for students to compete for unequal results.

ASK YOURSELF: What is the role of schools in society from a functionalist perspective? How would you critique this theory—how does functionalism fail to capture the role of schools in society?

Conflict Theory

Conflict theorists argue that society is held together not by shared values and collective identity alone, but by the ability of dominant groups to impose their will on subordinate groups. This will is not imposed through overt force; instead, ideologies promoted by the powerful are designed to convince everyone that inequalities are fair.

Whereas functionalists emphasize cohesion in explaining social order, conflict sociologists emphasize struggle. Karl Marx (1818–1883) is considered the founder of conflict theory. From this perspective, schools are

Meritocracy: A system in which personal advancement and social position result from merit, based on knowledge and skill.

social battlefields. Marx argued that society's competing groups—the bourgeoisie, or the "haves," and the proletariat, or the "have-nots"—were in a constant state of tension. The bourgeoisie control power, wealth, privilege, and social opportunities (including access to education), while the proletariat seek a larger share of the good stuff. Yet because the bourgeoisie maintain control over society's institutions, they are able to use coercive power and manipulation to mold society to their benefit.

Drawing on Karl Marx's theories, Samuel Bowles and Herbert Gintis (1976) examined the role of schooling in the United States. They argued that there is a direct correspondence between the organization of schools and the economic organization of capitalist society. The main function of schools, they asserted, is to produce workers. Not creative, productive, autonomous workers, but workers who are obedient, follow rules, and do not ask too many questions or make too many waves. From this perspective, until society itself fundamentally changes, there is little hope for genuine school reform.

Randall Collins offered another take on social conflict in education. Whereas functionalists view the expansion of education as a necessary response to the expansion of democracy and technology, Collins (1979) argued that the rise in the level of credentials required by specific jobs is not a natural response to the needs of the labor market. Instead, it emerges from status competition among groups battling over scarce cultural, political, and economic rewards. Collins demonstrated that demand for educational credentials has increased more than the skill requirements needed for those jobs. For example, while the actual knowledge and skills of their profession have not increased dramatically, pharmacists must now complete a 6-year college program leading to a doctorate, rather than the apprenticeship program of the 1930s or the baccalaureate degree that was required a decade ago. The upgrading of credentials is seen in other occupations as well, despite a lack of evidence showing that workers with higher credentials outperform those without. The rise in credential requirements is a result of middle-class professionals' attempts to raise their status. As historically marginalized groups have made gains in their own educational attainment, advantaged groups have pushed for the need for more credentials, once again asserting their advantage. Through this competition, basic degree requirements for different jobs spiral ever upwards. Thus, conflict theorists see educational institutions as an instrument for perpetuating class differences, rather than a tool for promoting a democratic and meritocratic society.

Policy Implications of Conflict Theory

Conflict theorists stress the role of education in reproducing social and educational inequalities and the need to eliminate them. Like functionalists, they support policies to ensure equality of opportunity, but they go further by also supporting policies meant to reduce inequality of results in and beyond the school. Many conflict theorists contend that the roots of unequal educational outcomes lie within deeper, more basic social inequalities. Therefore, rather than focusing on schools as the site for social change, conflict theorists believe that the basic dynamics of capitalism—especially the poverty and inequality associated with it—need to be altered in order to produce true educational equity.

ASK YOURSELF: How do functionalists and conflict theorists differ in their assessment of the role of schools in helping to change societies? What should be the goal of education—training individuals for employment or for critical thinking and creativity? Or are these two goals compatible?

Interactionist Theory

Interactionist theories of education shift the focus from the structure of education at the macro-level to the experience of education at the micro-level. What do students and teachers actually do, they ask? How do people within schools understand the meaning of education and their roles within that setting? Interactionist theories attempt to "make the commonplace strange" by exploring the deeper meanings of people's everyday, taken-for-granted behaviors and interactions.

Interactionist theory has its origins in the social psychology of early-20th-century sociologists George Herbert Mead (1863–1931) and Charles Horton Cooley (1864–1929). This school of thought, known as symbolic interactionism, views the self as socially constructed in relation to social forces and structures; self and society are the product of ongoing interactions and the negotiation of meaning.

Researchers often combine interactionist theory with functionalism and/or conflict theory to produce a more comprehensive theory of society. One of the most influential interactionist theorists was Raymond Rist, whose research demonstrates how teacher expectations of students, based on categories like race, class, ethnicity, and gender, affect students' perceptions of themselves and their achievement. Rist (1977) showed how labeling students based on social class resulted in the placement of low-income students in lower-ability reading groups and middle-class students in higher-ability groups, regardless of students' actual abilities. These labels became "life sentences" with profoundly negative effects on the achievement of the low-income students, who remained in low-ability groups throughout their careers. Rist concluded that the interactional processes of the school resulted in educational inequality mirroring the larger structures of society. Combined with the findings of conflict theory, Rist's interactionist approach provides empirical documentation of one way that schools reproduce inequality.

Policy Implications of Interactionist Theory

Interactionist theory stresses the need to base education policies on a keen examination of what goes on inside schools and classrooms. For example, interactionists argue that to develop policies that will ensure equality of opportunity or reduce gaps in education, sociologists must get inside the "black box" of schooling to understand precisely how schools reproduce inequalities (conflict theory) or increase opportunities (functionalist theory). Policy interventions will not work if they do not take account of how teachers and students actually interact and understand their roles in school.

> **ASK YOURSELF:** How does interactionist theory differ in its focus from functionalist and conflict theories? Can it complement one or both of the other theories?

SPECIALIZED THEORIES IN THE SOCIOLOGY OF EDUCATION

7.5 Apply specialized theories to the social institution of education.

Specialized theories of education are best suited to explain what really happens in schools, and how educational gaps and social problems in education get produced. Many of these theories are inspired by one of the main theoretical paradigms, but are more refined based on research conducted within educational settings.

Code Theory

British sociologist Basil Bernstein (1924–2000) drew on functionalist, conflict, and interactionist perspectives to develop **code theory** (Bernstein 1977a, 1977b, 1990, 1996). Code theory explains some of the subtle cultural and interactional mechanisms that perpetuate inequalities in education and society. Codes are systems that people use to communicate. Bernstein (1973a, 1973b) observed differences in the communication codes of working-class and middle-class children, reflecting class and power relationships in schools and society. For example, when asked to tell a story based on a set of

photographs, working-class boys used primarily pronouns (*he, she, it*) while middle-class boys used specific nouns (*the boys, a woman, a man*). Bernstein noted that in order to understand the working-class boys' stories, one would need the photographs; one would not need the photographs to understand the middle-class boys' stories. He described the language codes of the working-class boys as "restricted"—that is, useful for communicating in situations where context is shared. He described middle-class language codes as "elaborated"—containing enough detail and context to be understood more broadly. Working-class speech codes are not worse than middle-class speech codes, Bernstein argued; rather, they simply reflect the functional context of working-class jobs and family life. Likewise, the codes of the middle classes reflect the fact that their jobs require them to communicate across groups and settings. But because schools rely on middle-class codes for instruction and for organizing interactions between students and teachers, working-class children are disadvantaged.

Bernstein's study of language interactions within the educational system showed how schools (especially in the United Kingdom and United States) inadvertently reproduce what they are meant to eradicate—social class advantages in schooling and society. Based on his work, sociologists argue that policies to reduce educational inequalities need to provide low-income students access to the dominant modes of communication and advise teachers to become more aware of their own biases in how language functions.

Theories of Economic, Social, and Cultural Capital

French sociologist Pierre Bourdieu (1930–2002) provides a conflict approach to understanding how education reproduces inequality (Bourdieu, 1977, 1984; Bourdieu & Passeron, 1977). Like Bernstein, Bourdieu asserts that educational gaps are not so much a reflection of differences in ability as differences in cultural styles. Bourdieu distinguishes three forms of capital—economic (wealth), social (networks and connections), and cultural (personal appearance and forms of knowledge, including music, art, and literature)—to which different groups have unequal access. Bourdieu's **cultural capital theory** asserts that

Code theory: Basil Bernstein's concept that society reproduces social classes by favoring the communication codes, or manners of speaking and representing thoughts and ideas, of more powerful socioeconomic groups.

Cultural capital theory: Pierre Bourdieu's concept that a range of nonfinancial assets, such as education, physical appearance, and familiarity with various kinds of music, art, and literature, empower individuals to advance in a social group that values these cultural assets.

although schools appear to operate neutrally, they actually advantage the cultural styles of the upper and middle classes. These classes possess more economic, social, and cultural capital, which have exchange value in the educational marketplace. For example, economic capital can purchase better schools and services such as tutoring, social capital allows groups to use connections to their advantage, and cultural capital is rewarded at school. Furthermore, teachers may "naturally" reward students who are responsive during story time or who share interesting travel stories about what they did over summer vacation, lacking an awareness that such students are not necessarily brighter than others, but that such students exhibit the cultural styles of the dominant classes. Thus, schooling corresponds to society's dominant interests, and upper- and middle-class forms of capital become codified in the curriculum. Unlike functionalists, Bourdieu saw these patterns as leading to class domination rather than social cohesion.

From the conflict perspective, educational policies can reduce inequalities by providing low-income students with access to the dominant forms of social and cultural capital, and by changing curriculum and pedagogy in ways that acknowledge and counteract these cultural biases.

Institutional Theory

John W. Meyer's (1977) **institutional theory** argues that schools are global institutions and have developed similarly across the world since the 19th century, whereby mass systems have democratized access to public education. At the institutional level, schools develop policies, processes, and rituals that legitimate their existence and functions in society. Like Randall Collins, Meyer does not believe that educational expansion is driven primarily by the needs of the labor market; instead, he views mass schooling as springing from society's support for an expanded democratic civil society and a desire to be recognized as a modern nation.

Based on Meyer's theory, David Baker and Gerald LeTendre (2005) argue that a fundamental set of beliefs has influenced the development of mass schooling, including the idea that all children should be educated, that nations should invest in schooling, that education serves the collective good, that children should receive early and ongoing schooling, that the cognitive skills learned in schools are good for individuals and society, and that access to schooling should not be limited by social, economic, or racial status.

Although Meyer and colleagues believe national differences in systems of education are important, they stress the remarkable commonalities that exist among educational institutions, regardless of local cultures. Furthermore, this perspective highlights the benefits associated with mass education, namely, those associated with democratic and economic uplift.

Feminist Theory

Feminist educators and sociologists of education have examined the ways that schools perpetuate sexist attitudes and behaviors, as well as unequal educational outcomes based on gender. Such theorists draw attention to how gender representations in the formal curriculum, expectations and role modeling in schools and society, and interactions between students and teachers contribute to different and unequal educational experiences and outcomes.

Feminist theories lend support for policies aimed at providing equality of opportunity for women and reducing gender-based inequalities of educational achievement. At least in Western industrialized countries, these policies have helped reduce or eliminate the gender gap in education. Some feminist scholars are now grappling with the lower levels of achievement among boys to ensure gender equity in education. Despite the fact that female students have higher grades and levels of educational attainment compared to male students, they still lag behind in STEM fields. Policy experts have focused on efforts to make the culture of science more appealing to girls and identifying mentors that tap into the skills and interests of female students.

ASK YOURSELF: Which of the specialized theories in the sociology of education are most useful for evaluating problems with the education system in the United States, and why? Moreover, what recommendations would Bernstein, Bourdieu, and Collins make to reform the U.S. education system?

EXPLANATIONS FOR EDUCATIONAL INEQUALITY

7.6 Evaluate explanations for educational inequality.

Significant differences in educational achievement and attainment in the United States call into question the

Institutional theory: The concept that schools are global institutions and have developed similarly throughout the world since the 19th century as a result of processes of globalization and democratization.

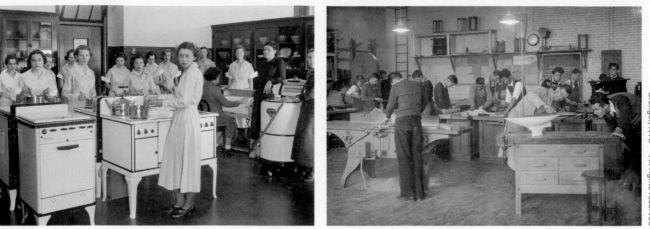

▶ Girls attend a cooking and cleaning class at Chevy Chase High School in Bethesda, Maryland, in 1935. Boys work in a carpentry shop class at Anacostia High School in Washington, D.C., in 1939. Does such gender segregation exist in American high schools today?

country's ideology of equality of educational opportunity. Although the data suggest that higher levels of schooling do pay off in the labor market, the data do not support the democratic-liberal faith that schooling provides the mechanism for reducing inequalities between social groups. In fact, family background remains a powerful predictor of educational achievement and attainment and economic outcomes.

How do sociologists explain these unequal outcomes? Moving beyond the theoretical frames of functionalism and conflict theory, we find the unique contribution of sociology: a perspective that combines understandings of both the person (micro-level) and the system (macro-level). At the micro-level, **student-centered explanations** look at factors outside the school as the source of educational inequalities, including the family, the community, the peer group, and the individual student. In contrast, **school-centered explanations** focus on factors within the school as the source of educational inequalities, including policies and procedures like ability grouping, as well as the school climate.

Student-Centered Explanations

In the 1960s, sociologists suggested that economically disadvantaged students lagged behind because they attended inferior schools—schools that spent less money on each student, spent less on materials and extracurricular activities, and had worse teachers. A number of research studies in the 1960s and 1970s demonstrated, however, that this conventional liberal wisdom was too simplistic and that solutions were far more complex than simply spending more money on education.

In the landmark publication *Equality of Educational Opportunity* (1966), James S. Coleman and colleagues argued that differences among students have a greater impact on educational performance than do differences among schools. Based on this work, known as the Coleman Report, educational researchers and policy makers concluded that students from lower socioeconomic backgrounds did less well in school because of characteristics of the students themselves, their families, their neighborhoods and communities, their cultures, and perhaps even their genetic makeup. These student-centered explanations became dominant in the 1960s and 1970s, and persist today, even though they are politically charged.

Genetic Difference Theory

Some researchers have argued that race and social class gaps in educational performance are the result of genetic differences in intelligence (Herrnstein & Murray, 1994; Jensen, 1969). Empirical research, however, has challenged this assertion, indicating that lower educational performance among some groups is due in part to the cultural bias of IQ test questions, the conditions under which educational tests are administered (Steele, 1997), and cultural and family differences (Hurn, 1993). Ultimately, there is little or no empirical evidence to support **genetic difference theory**.

Student-centered explanations: Explanations for educational inequalities that focus on factors outside the school, such as the family, the community, the culture of the group, the peer group, and the individual student.

School-centered explanations: Explanations for educational inequalities that focus on factors within the school, such as teachers and teaching methods, curriculum, ability grouping and curriculum tracking, school climate, and teacher expectations.

Genetic difference theory: The discredited concept that differences in educational performance between working-class and nonwhite students and their middle- and upper-class and white counterparts are due to genetic differences in intelligence.

Cultural Deprivation Theory

Cultural deprivation theory suggests that working-class, poor, and nonwhite families often lack cultural resources, such as books and other educational stimuli, and thus arrive at school at a significant disadvantage (Lewis, 1966). Indeed, research on *summer learning loss* suggests that less-advantaged students lose upwards of 2 months of learning during the summer, in large part because they do not have age-appropriate reading materials at home (Alexander, Entwisle, & Olson, 2001). Other researchers speculate that language socialization, and how parents talk to children—whether they talk a lot or a little, use questions or directives—is another aspect of students' home culture that advantages some students and disadvantages others at school (Hart & Risley, 2003).

Cultural Difference Theories

Cultural difference theories agree that cultural and family differences distinguish white middle-class students from working-class and nonwhite students, who may arrive at school without the skills and attitudes required for success. They do not see this as a deficiency, however, but as a reflection of their being part of minority groups with different ways of life, and who may be subject to racism, discrimination, and unequal life chances. The cultural styles that students have been raised with clash with the cultural expectations that govern the educational system, resulting in educational struggles. Echoing Basil Bernstein's research on language codes: It is not that working-class students speak in ways that are worse than middle-class students; it is that they speak in ways that are *different* from the cultural expectations of the educational system.

Scholars have connected the "underachievement" of some Hispanic students to cultural clashes between home and school. In her study of Mexican American and Mexican immigrant families living in Texas, Guadalupe Valdes (1996) found that in a culture where family comes first (*familism*), parents may pull children out of school to spend time with a sick or dying family member, causing school personnel to question parents' commitment to education. Parents, meanwhile, mistrust the schools for sending the message that success in life is dependent on higher education. With the emphasis on *respeto*, some Hispanic immigrants may view kids who go off to college as abandoning their families. Although these kids may obtain stable jobs with good pay, family members may see them as morally deficient for leaving them behind. Students from many minority groups must balance similar pressures when navigating the competing expectations of school and family.

ASK YOURSELF: Which student-centered explanation for educational inequalities do you find most compelling, and why? How do such explanations relate to your own educational experiences and observations?

School-Centered Explanations

While the Coleman Report argued that between-school differences are not the key factor in explaining different student outcomes between groups, it did not say that schools have *no* effect. In fact, Coleman's later work suggested that schools do vary and may indeed differentially impact student outcomes (Coleman & Hoffer, 1987; Coleman, Hoffer, & Kilgore, 1982). In the 1980s, sociologists of education began to examine policies at the macro-level and processes within school that may contribute to educational inequalities.

Effective Schools Research

School cultures or environments can have a decisive impact on educational outcomes, as indicated by research on effective schools. Students in effective schools outperform expectations through a combination of high expectations, strong and effective leadership, accountability for students and teachers, monitoring of student learning, extensive time spent on teaching and learning, and flexibility for teachers and administrators to experiment and adapt to new situations and problems (Stedman, 1987). These findings suggest that schools in lower socioeconomic communities can take steps to improve student achievement by addressing school climate.

One element of the **effective schools movement** is the small-schools movement, which strives to change school climate and improve educational outcomes from inside. Research points to benefits associated with small schools, including greater interest in school activities, higher achievement levels, and more social equality (Griffith, 1995; Lee, 1995). In smaller schools, students can have greater influence, hold more leadership positions, and interact more informally with teachers and administrators. As more schools have adopted the small-school or school-within-a-school model, researchers have found it difficult to re-create the benefits that appear to exist in naturally

....

Cultural deprivation theory: The theory based in the concept that children from working-class and nonwhite families lack certain cultural resources, such as books and other educational stimuli, and thus arrive at school at a significant disadvantage.

Cultural difference theories: Theories based in the concept that there are cultural and family differences between working-class and nonwhite students and white middle-class students attributable to social forces such as poverty, racism, and discrimination.

Effective schools movement: A movement for school improvement based on the concept that effective schools have certain characteristics (such as effective leadership, accountability, and high expectations of teachers and administrators) that help explain why their students achieve academically despite disadvantaged backgrounds.

occurring small schools (Lee & Ready, 2007). A Chicago-based study found that while small schools had more supportive environments, with higher graduation rates, they did not have higher rates of achievement (Kahne et al., 2008). National-level studies echo these findings (Levine, 2010). Yet one study of New York's 150 small schools did show improved learning (Abdulkadiroğlu, Weiwei, & Pathak, 2013). There is good research also suggesting that smaller schools can produce higher levels of engagement and feelings of connectedness and safety (Carolan, 2012; Weiss, Carolan, & Baker-Smith, 2010).

Between-School Differences: Curriculum and Pedagogic Practices

Conflict theorists argue that significant differences exist in terms of culture and climate between schools in lower socioeconomic communities and those in higher socioeconomic communities (MacLeod, 2009). Of course, different life chances begin with different family backgrounds, but different school environments teach children to dream different sets of dreams. For conflict theorists, variations in funding, teacher quality, curriculum, pedagogy, and teacher expectations are all important factors shaping educational outcomes. In her classic research, Jean Anyon (1980, 1981) found that schools serving working-class students feature curriculum and instruction that emphasize rule-following and respect for authority. Lessons focus on memorization of facts and completion of worksheets, rather than activities involving analysis or interpretation. By contrast, schools serving economically privileged children emphasize independence, creativity, and critical thinking. Students in those schools are taught to see themselves as creators of knowledge, whereas their less-privileged peers are socialized to see themselves as passive recipients of facts, whose opinions matter little.

Within-School Differences: Curriculum and Ability Grouping

When groups of students perform very differently in the same school, school policies may be in effect. The practice of ability grouping (often referred to as **tracking**) is likely responsible to some degree. Functionalists believe tracking is a valuable technique to separate students based on ability and to ensure all students learn at an appropriate level and pace. Supporters of tracking insist, however, that track placements should be fair and meritocratic, based on ability and hard work, rather than race, ethnicity, social class, or gender.

Conflict theorists, conversely, suggest that tracking is a mechanism for separating groups and for reproducing inequalities. Research shows that track placement is associated with student race and social characteristics, with working-class and nonwhite students more likely to be

assigned to lower tracks. Tracking, then, results in unequal education, as students are exposed to different and unequal expectations, curricula, and pedagogies (Kalogrides, Loeb, & Béteille, 2013; Oakes, 1985; Watanabe, 2008). Differences in the curriculum and pedagogic practices implemented across tracks is one school-based policy that at least partially contributes to unequal academic outcomes (Oakes, Gamoran, & Page, 1992).

> **ASK YOURSELF:** Which school-centered explanations for educational inequalities do you think are most important, and why? How do these explanations relate to your own educational experiences?

Do Schools Reproduce Inequality? Evaluating Theory and Evidence

Some researchers believe that schools unfairly perpetuate social inequalities and thus confirm conflict theorists' belief that schools advantage the dominant groups in society. Other researchers believe there is insufficient evidence to support much of conflict theory in regard to school processes, with some evidence supporting the functionalist view that school selection processes are meritocratic and produce genuine learning and opportunities for mobility.

We think there is evidence for some of the functionalists' hypotheses, but on the whole, more evidence supports conflict theorists' claim that schools help to reproduce inequality and help dominant groups maintain their advantages. Schools are only part of this process, however; we must see them within the context of a larger set of institutional forces operating within a highly unequal society. Schools do not reproduce inequality by themselves, but are part of a process in which social inequalities are transmitted across generations.

> **ASK YOURSELF:** What do you think are the most important factors contributing to inequalities in education? What can society do to eliminate these inequalities? Do you think schools reproduce social inequalities?

Researching Education

Ever since the publication of The Coleman Report in 1966, researchers have been trying to determine just

Tracking: An educational practice in which students are divided into groups, purportedly based on their academic ability.

how much schools matter in educating children and closing the achievement gap (Downey & Condron, 2016). That's because the Coleman Report arrived at the surprising conclusion that variations among schools have little impact on student achievement, while variations among students—having to do with their race, class, and family backgrounds—seem to have the greatest impact. Practically, this finding suggested that schools play only a small role in shaping students' achievement, and that even spending more money and improving the quality of schools may not help close the gap.

As it turns out, determining how much schools themselves—versus students' backgrounds and experiences outside of schools—impact learning and educational outcomes is an incredibly difficult task. One reason for this difficulty is that answering this question requires that researchers gather lots of information and control for the right variables. After all, there are many reasons why some students may have higher achievements than others. Over the years, sociologists and other researchers have developed innovative techniques to determine that schools do, indeed, play a powerful role in closing the education gap. We now know this due to the discovery of what has been called "summer setback," "summer slide," and "summer learning loss."

To understand how schooling impacts students and closes the achievement gap, researchers like Barbara Heyns (1978); Doris Entwisle and Karl Alexander (1992); Alexander, Entwisle, and Olson (2007); and others have developed a unique approach: Measure students' achievement at the beginning of the school year and then again at the end of the school year. While researchers know that students enter school already unequal in terms of their achievement, documenting changes at various points in the school year can provide insight into the independent role that schools play in closing the achievement gap. What these researchers have found is that the achievement gap does, indeed, narrow over the course of the school year. That is, students of all races and social classes experience learning gains during the school year, possibly even learning at similar rates. The fact that the achievement gap widens again over the summer shows that persistent disadvantages at home continue to hinder the schooling outcomes of poor and minority students.

By the time students reach the fifth grade, less-advantaged students have lost nearly a year and a half's worth of learning due to the existence of an academic calendar that includes an extended summer break (Allington & McGill-Franzen, 2003; Cooper, Borman, & Fairchild, 2010). It is likely that the pattern of learning gains and losses persists into high school, with less-advantaged students continuing to fall behind. Over the years, researchers have become increasingly confident in these findings, with new data sets and new research techniques providing substantial support for the positive impact of schooling and the devastating impact of "summer learning loss." Despite this evidence, there appears to be little desire to make fundamental changes to the school calendar to thwart the summer slide. Instead, schools and community groups have invested their time and energy in developing programs that encourage less-advantaged students to read and remain academically engaged over the summer. While helpful, this is not the type of systemwide reform that would seriously address the achievement gap.

EDUCATIONAL REFORM FROM THE 1980S TO 2017

7.7 Describe recent reforms in education.

As long as there has been a system of education in the United States (and elsewhere, presumably), there have been efforts at educational reform. In recent decades, the federal government has taken on a more dominant role in educational policy. This became especially evident in 2001, when President George W. Bush's No Child Left Behind policy led to increased emphasis on testing, accountability, and the insistence on steady improvements in outcomes. This emphasis continued under President Obama's Race to the Top initiative; time will tell as to how President Trump responds to the trends toward accountability and federal influence in education.

Two general approaches characterize educational reform. The first, school-based reform, stresses the independent power of schools to eliminate the achievement gap for low-income students. The second, the societal-level approach, stresses that school-level reform is necessary but insufficient to close the achievement gap, and that societal and community-level reforms are an essential part of this process.

School-Based Reforms

Assessment and Accountability

Since the adoption of No Child Left Behind (NCLB) in 2001, the federal government has directed state and local governments to adopt a neoliberal approach to school reform. A logical progression of the standards movement initiated in 1983 by the *A Nation at Risk* report and in federal legislation under Presidents George W. Bush (America 2000) and Bill Clinton (Goals 2000), NCLB is the most comprehensive federal education policy in U.S. history. Based on the critique that education in the United States has historically underserved low-income

► President Barack Obama fist-bumps a young middle-school student. Obama had tasked the Federal Communications Commission to help build high-speed digital connections to America's schools and libraries, with the goal of getting 99% of students access to next-generation broadband and wireless technology.

and minority children, NCLB mandated uniform standards for all students in order to reduce and eventually eliminate achievement gaps by 2014. Testing was conducted annually to determine whether schools were making "adequate yearly progress." Unfortunately, the law did not reach its goal of eliminating achievement gaps in 2014, and this aspect of this law has since been changed.

Advocates of NCLB argued that it would force states to ensure that low-income students are held to the same standards as more affluent students. Schools that did not reach these goals were threatened with cuts to funding or administrative intervention. Yet critics argued that however noble the goal of eliminating the achievement gap, NCLB did not provide sufficient funds to improve failing schools and relied on punishment, instead of building school capacity (Sadovnik, 2008).

Shortly after taking office in 2009, President Barack Obama established the Race to the Top, a program designed to spur innovation and continue the emphasis on standards and accountability that were at the core of NCLB. This legislation provided $4.35 billion in competitive grants, awarded to states pledging to increase opportunities for charter schools, adopt common educational standards (including Common Core), and gather fine-grained data on student and teacher performance.

In December 2015, No Child Left Behind was reauthorized by President Obama as the **Every Student Succeeds Act (ESSA)**. While some elements of the earlier act remained, others changed. The new act, for example, retains the emphasis on uniform standards, testing, and accountability. Yet states now have more authority over the content of those standards and exams, with the federal government barred from imposing specific curriculum or achievement benchmarks. In addition, federal

penalties are no longer imposed on states and districts that perform poorly. Instead, low-performing schools are required to adopt specific plans for improvement. States and schools have more autonomy over this process, however—which some education advocates see as essential to ensuring teacher autonomy. Others worry that these new provisions will allow states to do less than what is needed to close the achievement gaps (Davis, 2015).

Together, these federal reform initiatives have led to increases in school choice, charter schools, and voucher systems; efforts to improve teacher education and teacher quality; and attempts to develop effective school models. The goals and outcomes associated with these school-based reforms are discussed below.

School Choice

During the 1980s, some researchers reasoned that **magnet schools** (public schools open to students from different neighborhoods) and private schools were superior to neighborhood public schools because, as schools of choice, they reflect the desires and needs of their constituents and were thus responsive to change (Coleman et al., 1982). By the late 1980s, **school choice** was at the forefront of the educational reform movement. Today, it stands as one of the chief goals of President Trump's secretary of education, Betsy DeVos. School choice emphasizes market forces rather than educational bureaucracy as key to reforming the schools. The two most popular varieties of school choice are charter schools and school vouchers.

Charter Schools. Dating back to the early 1990s, **charter schools** are public schools that are free of many of the regulations applied to traditional public schools; in return, they are held accountable for student performance. As public schools, charter schools are funded with tax dollars (unlike private schools, they do not charge tuition) and must be open to all students in the school districts where they are located. Admissions processes for charter schools are dictated by the laws of the individual states, but in low-income areas

Every Student Succeeds Act (ESSA): The reauthorized version of No Child Left Behind, which returned some power back to the states concerning educational standards and testing.

Magnet schools: Publicly funded schools designed to recruit students from across entire districts by offering particular disciplinary focuses such as arts, technology, science, or mathematics.

School choice: A school reform approach that introduces market forces to shape school policies by offering parents a range of school options, including magnet schools, voucher schools, charter schools, and regular public schools.

Charter schools: Publicly funded schools that operate independent of school districts and are free of many of the regulations that apply to traditional public schools.

admission is usually based on a lottery. If a charter school fails to meet the provisions of its charter, based on student outcomes and fiscal soundness, it can be forced to close.

Davis Guggenheim's popular documentary film *Waiting for "Superman"* (2010) drew attention to charter schools by contrasting high-quality charter schools with failing traditional public schools. The film presents heart-wrenching scenes of families who do not win the lottery for charter school admission. It argues that zip code should not be destiny and champions school choice as the solution to low-performing urban schools. Guggenheim notes that there are excellent public schools and teachers, but his film provides no examples of these, nor of ineffective charter schools. Critics argue that the film is simplistic, biased, and does not adequately reflect existing research. In fact, research shows a wide range of performance among charter schools. In math achievement, 29% of charter schools have scores where students learn more than those in traditional public schools; the scores of 40% of charter schools are no different; and 31% of charter schools perform more poorly than traditional public schools (Center for Research on Education Outcomes, 2013).

Vouchers. **School voucher** programs operate in 17 states. Advocates argue that school voucher programs that provide families with funds to send children to private schools (including parochial schools) have three important educational impacts. First, vouchers provide low-income parents with the same educational choices that middle-class parents have, and thus lead to increased parental satisfaction with their children's schools. Second, given that private schools, like charter schools, do not have to contend with a large educational bureaucracy, they provide a more innovative, responsive learning environment, which results in higher achievement for low-income students. Third, with increased competition from charter and voucher schools, urban public schools will eventually be forced to improve or close their doors. This will produce higher achievement in the public schools that remain.

These claims about voucher programs have stirred considerable debate. For one thing, voucher programs blur the line between church and state, with taxpayer dollars going to fund private school education. Furthermore, critics argue that voucher proponents make unfounded assumptions based on faulty research; in fact, evidence is mixed on whether students do better in voucher schools than in traditional public schools. Finally, critics worry that voucher systems drain resources from public schools and further exacerbate educational inequalities.

Teacher and School Quality

What does an effective school look like? There is general agreement that it sets high standards and high expectations

► U.S. Secretary of Education Betsy DeVos is a supporter of the school voucher program.

for students, holds teachers and administrators accountable for student performance and goals, creates a safe and orderly environment, employs experienced and qualified teachers who have access to high-quality professional development, hires committed administrators, and encourages parental and community engagement.

At the classroom level, course content, pedagogy, technology, and class size have impacts on student achievement. However, without effective teachers, these factors mean little. Sound instructional practices, implemented by effective teachers, are a prerequisite of school improvement (Darling-Hammond, 2010).

Research reveals that the most qualified teachers possess strong academic skills, the equivalent of a major in the field in which they are teaching, at least 3 years' teaching experience, and participation in high-quality professional development programs (Ingersoll, 2003). Yet many teachers do not have these characteristics. Therefore, recruiting and retaining high-quality teachers are among the most important challenges for U.S. education. At the secondary school level, especially in low-income urban schools, a disproportionate share of classes in core academic subjects (math, science, English, social studies) are taught by teachers who do not hold teaching certificates in those subjects. Urban schools with high levels of minority students also typically have larger percentages of novice teachers than do other schools (National Center for Education Statistics, 2008) and more difficulty filling vacancies (Malkus, Hoyer, & Sparks, 2015).

Since the 1990s, a number of alternatives to traditional university-based teacher education have emerged, such as

School voucher: An approach to school choice in which parents of school-age children receive government-issued vouchers that they can apply toward tuition at private schools.

Teach for America (TFA) and the New Teacher Project (NTP), as ways to attract talented teachers to lower-income schools. Through these alternative certification programs, rather than enrolling in traditional multiyear university teacher education programs, high-performing college graduates complete a summer training program and are immediately placed in teaching positions in underserved schools. Critics argue that because many alternative programs require only 2 years of service, the attrition rate is very high (Ingersoll, 2004). High levels of attrition and the lack of experience within lower-income schools are significant barriers to those students' academic success.

Recently, school reformers have examined the role of teacher tenure as one roadblock to improving teacher quality. In 2014, the California State Supreme Court ruled that teacher tenure policies violate students' rights to an adequate education because they retain ineffective teachers. Accordingly, the federal government and some states have taken steps toward gathering detailed data on teacher performance and implementing policies that make it easier to fire teachers deemed ineffective. President Obama's secretary of education, Arne Duncan, expressed support for the decision in *Vergara v. California,* describing it as "an opportunity for a progressive state with a tradition of innovation to build a new framework for the teaching profession that protects students' rights to equal educational opportunities while providing teachers the support, respect and rewarding careers they deserve." Many teachers' organizations, like the **National Education Association (NEA)** and the **American Federation of Teachers (AFT)**, have expressed opposition to these developments, with the AFT's Randi Weingarten accusing then-secretary Duncan of adding "to the polarization" in education debate and undermining teachers' due process rights.

Evidence suggests that reforms aimed at improving teacher quality and the overall effectiveness of schools have the potential to improve low-income, high-minority schools. The Education Trust (2010a) provides examples and argues that some districts (like Aldine and El Paso, Texas) and some states (Delaware, Illinois, Massachusetts, North Carolina, and Texas) have significantly reduced achievement gaps related to race, ethnicity, and social class by enhancing professional development among their teaching staff. However, such reforms often fail to improve consistently failing schools, and more drastic action is needed.

> **ASK YOURSELF:** Which school-based reforms do you think have the greatest potential to improve student achievement and reduce educational inequalities? Why? How might some of these school-based education reforms worsen problems in the U.S. education system?

Societal, Community, Economic, and Political Reforms

Although school-level reforms have demonstrated the potential to improve the educational experiences of low-income and minority children, by themselves they are limited unless they also address factors outside of schools that lay the foundation for educational inequalities. In addition to school-based approaches, such as early childhood programs, summer programs, and after-school programs, many scholars call for fundamental social change, including economic initiatives to reduce income inequality and to create stable and affordable housing, and for the expansion of school-community clinics to provide health care and counseling (Rothstein, 2010). Ultimately, school reform can accomplish only so much without attention to broader social and economic policies aimed at addressing poverty.

School Finance Reforms

Financing for schools has been a contentious issue since the establishment of public education. In 1973, the U.S. Supreme Court declared in *Rodriguez v. San Antonio* that there is no constitutional right to an *equal* education under the 14th Amendment. Since then, advocates for school finance equity have litigated at the state level. They argue that the current method of funding schools through local property taxes means that affluent communities can spend significantly more on education than can low-income areas, and that these spending differences violate students' constitutional right to an *adequate* education (per the wording of their state's constitution) in lower-income schools.

As a result of these legal efforts, 27 states now have financing plans where low-income districts receive an average of 8% *more* funding than high-income districts (LaFortune, Rothstein, & Schanzenbach, 2015). Research suggests that these funding reforms have been successful. Julien LaFortune and his coauthors show that these reforms have reduced the social class gap on the NAEP (National Assessment of Educational Progress) exam by 20%. By contrast, in the states that have not adopted such school finance reforms, the social class gap in test scores has *increased*. Looking at the long-term impact of school

....

Teach for America (TFA): A nonprofit organization that recruits students and professionals from high-profile institutions, trains these individuals to enter the teaching profession, and places them in disadvantaged schools for a period of at least 2 years.

National Education Association (NEA): The largest union representing teachers in the United States.

American Federation of Teachers (AFT): One of the two largest unions representing teachers in the United States.

funding increases, Jackson, Johnson, and Persico (2015) found that when poorly funded schools receive a budget boost, students attending those schools went on to have higher graduation rates, as well as greater educational attainment and earnings.

Full-Service and Community Schools

Another way to attack education inequity is to educate both the *whole child* and the *whole community*. Full-service and **community schools** provide "wrap-around services" that address the educational, physical, psychological, and social needs of students and their families in a coordinated and collaborative fashion (Dryfoos, Quinn, & Barkin, 2005). They serve as community centers, health clinics, and recreation facilities, and provide services such as adult education, job training and placement, tutoring, after-school programs, mental health services, and drug and alcohol programs. Specifically designed to improve at-risk neighborhoods, community schools place an emphasis on building collective efficacy and developing a communal political voice that works toward justice for everyone in the neighborhood. Notable examples of community schools that are also full-service schools are Geoffrey Canada's Harlem Children's Zone schools in New York City. As the president and CEO of Harlem Children's Zone, Canada has sought to create the conditions through which children can positively "contaminate" Harlem and spread the "virus" of educational excellence. Canada has stated:

> When you've got most of the kids in a neighborhood involved in high-quality programs, you begin to change the cultural context of that neighborhood. If you are surrounded by people who are always talking about going to college, you're going to end up thinking, "Hey, maybe this is something I could do, too." You can't help but get contaminated by the idea. It just seeps into your pores, and you don't even know that you've caught the virus. (quoted in Tough, 2008, p. 125)

Geoffrey Canada's programs use a "cradle to college" approach to improve students' academic outcomes. Even before their children are born, parents in "Baby College" learn how to have academic conversations with children, and how to provide children with a healthy home environment and acceptable forms of discipline. Baby College even distributes household items that promote health and well-being to families who cannot afford them. This intensive approach has been emulated in communities across the country.

Canada's formula of starting education as early as possible, extending the school day, and offering tutoring for at-risk students seems to produce results. Studies that compare students who participated in Canada's program to similar students who were not selected for the program show higher test scores and lower rates of teen pregnancy and juvenile delinquency among Harlem Children's Zone students (Dobbie & Fryer, 2011, 2015).

Although supporters laud the achievements of reformers like Canada, the costs associated with his program make it hard to replicate. Other critics worry that the program uses a cultural deficit model based on changing one's home culture and instilling high levels of discipline. Indeed, one study suggests that while the program increases academic outcomes, "no-excuses" schools like Canada's and KIPP (Knowledge Is Power Program) may turn students into passive learners, good at following direction but lacking educational autonomy and self-direction (Golann, 2015).

> *ASK YOURSELF:* Which school-centered reforms do you think are most important to reducing educational inequalities? What challenges might a district face if it attempts to create full-service and community schools?

Education Reform: Concluding Thoughts

To summarize, education reform in the United States from the 1980s through today has sought both excellence and equity; reforms have increasingly stressed accountability through testing and the implementation of consequences—as key to reducing the achievement gap. Although federal, state, and local reforms have produced some improvement in achievement, critics point out that the U.S. educational system was never as problematic as its critics have suggested (Berliner & Biddle, 1995). They suggest the real problem is that U.S. education works exceptionally well for children from higher socioeconomic backgrounds and exceptionally poorly for those from lower socioeconomic backgrounds. Despite efforts to address these inequalities—using vouchers and charter schools—the existing evidence does not overwhelmingly support advocates' claims that school choice initiatives reduce educational inequality. As the nation moves further into the new millennium, with higher levels of economic inequality, broad-based social reforms need to be paired with educational reform to achieve educational equity.

In her 2010 book *The Flat World and Education: How America's Commitment to Equity Will Determine*

Community schools: Schools that strive to meet all the basic academic, physical, and emotional needs of students and their families while building strong, cohesive bonds among teachers, students, and students' families.

Our Future, Linda Darling-Hammond reviews education reforms around the world and outlines five key elements that should inform efforts to reform U.S. education:

1. Meaningful learning goals
2. Intelligent, reciprocal accountability systems
3. Equitable and adequate resources
4. Strong professional standards and supports
5. Organization of schools for student and teacher learning

Darling-Hammond notes that the United States must meet the basic needs of all children so they can focus their attention on academic work instead of on survival. She agrees with many that the U.S. education system will continue to fail its students, at great cost to society, if it does not equalize access to educational opportunity and support meaningful learning. An examination of the sociological evidence suggests that successful school improvement will require systemic reform aimed at the school, student, community, economic, and societal levels.

SOCIAL CHANGE: WHAT CAN YOU DO?

 7.8 Identify steps toward social change in education.

A tremendous amount of work needs to be done at the school, community, and societal levels to improve our schools and reduce achievement gaps. Individuals like you can take a number of steps to help bring about positive change, including volunteering to be mentors or tutors in programs for disadvantaged or at-risk students, or pursuing a career as an educator. Because a substantial portion of the achievement gap results from "summer learning loss," becoming active and committed during the summer may be an especially effective way to get involved.

Whether you choose to become an educator or not, you can contribute to the improvement of the education system as a citizen. As philosopher of education John Dewey argued a century ago, education is key to the development of the informed citizenry that is essential for defending democracy. As an educated citizen, you can support policies aimed at reducing the achievement gaps. When others argue for policies that may exacerbate educational inequalities, you can support political leaders who promote policies that advocate for the strengthening of public education, including equitable school funding policies and policies aimed at aiding schools, families, and neighborhoods. You may even choose to serve on an educational committee or organization, or run for a position on the local school board. By voicing your opinions and sharing your knowledge of the education system with others, you can positively shape the public discussion about education and influence the future direction of schooling in this country.

▶ Danielle Cavanaugh goes over a writing exercise with a young student at a learning and tutoring center in Aurora, Colorado. What are some benefits of volunteering to tutor school-aged children?

▶▶ Opportunities for Volunteering

- Volunteer through a program on your college campus.
- Become a Big Brother or Big Sister (http://www.bbbs.org).
- Tutor at a local school or community organization, such as the Boys and Girls Club (http://www.bgca.org).

▶▶ Become an Educator

- Become a licensed teacher through your university if such a program is available.
- Seek out an alternative certification program such as Teach for America (http://www.tfa.org) or the New York City Teaching Fellows Program (http://www.nyctf.org).

- Participate in a "gap year" program like City Year, to provide organized, intensive mentoring to students in an at-risk school (cityyear.org).

Stay Informed and Engaged

- Read about changes in education policy in sources such as the Education section of the *New York Times* (http://www.nytimes.com/pages/education/index.html).

- Learn about your political leaders' views on education, thank them for upholding policies you support, and contact them when you disagree with their views and votes (http://www.usa.gov/Contact/Elected.shtml).

- Become aware that much is implemented and achieved at the local level. You can attend meetings of your local school boards and district superintendents, and vote in elections, if eligible.

WHAT DOES AMERICA THINK?

Questions About Education From the General Social Survey

Turn to the beginning of the chapter to compare your answers to those of the total population.

1. What is your interest level in local school issues?

    VERY INTERESTED: 43.7%

    MODERATELY INTERESTED: 42.7%

    NOT AT ALL INTERESTED: 13.6%

2. What is your confidence level in education?

    A GREAT DEAL: 25.3%

    ONLY SOME: 56.4%

    HARDLY ANY: 18.3%

3. In the United States, do you think we're spending too much money on improving the nation's education system, too little money, or about the right amount?

SOURCE: National Opinion Research Center, University of Chicago.

TOO MUCH: 6.1%

TOO LITTLE: 72.1%

ABOUT THE RIGHT AMOUNT: 21.8%

4. Do you think that sex education should be taught in public schools?

    YES: 92.2%

    NO: 7.8%

5. On the average, African Americans have worse jobs, income, and housing than white people. Do you think these differences are because most African Americans don't have the chance for the education that it takes to rise out of poverty?

    YES: 52.3%

    NO: 47.7%

CHAPTER SUMMARY

7.1 Describe the role of education in the United States.

Americans tend to view schools as providing opportunities for social mobility, personal development, and skill building. Education is often seen as a solution to a variety of social problems. In reality, the U.S. education system also plays a role in reproducing social inequalities and

other problems. Many critics of public education in the U.S. point to the failure of schools to effectively teach basic skills, including reading, writing, science, and math.

7.2 Discuss patterns of inequality in education.

Education in the United States is also characterized by significant gaps in educational achievement and educational attainment. Persistent achievement gaps exist among different groups, with white, Asian American, and affluent students performing at higher levels on standardized tests than black, Hispanic, and low-income students. U.S. students also score only about average on tests of academic achievement among students in industrialized nations.

 7.3 Describe the history of the U.S. educational system and how it has affected different demographic groups.

The educational inequalities that exist today are deeply rooted in the history of American education. While public school education was integrated by gender from its inception in the 1820s, racial segregation has existed throughout, with persistent underfunding for schools serving minority students. Schools in the United States have also balanced the impetus to segregate with the goal of using education as the site for assimilating citizens into a diverse nation. Today, this battle continues, with questions about how to educate English language learners and immigrants.

7.4 Apply the functionalist, interactionist, and conflict perspectives to social policy for education.

Functionalist ideals of a meritocratic education system shaped the development of the public education system in the United States and continue to mold democratic visions of education as the source of equal opportunity. Conflict theory, by contrast, highlights the ways in which social and economic privilege define education in the United States and create marked gaps in achievement between people of different races and social classes. Interactionist theory guides researchers in evaluating how students, teachers, administrators, and other community members actively make meaning of schooling, and their interactions within educational environments.

7.5 Apply specialized theories to the social institution of education.

Many specialized theories focus on the cultural clashes between students' home environments and the cultural expectations of the educational system. Code and social reproduction theorists argue that educational institutions reproduce social inequalities by rewarding class-specific forms of language and social, cultural, and economic capital. Institutional theorists argue that the development of mass education systems around the world has been a result of the commitment to democratic civil societies. Finally, feminist theorists argue that schools reproduce gender inequalities for both girls and boys.

 7.6 Evaluate explanations for educational inequality.

School-centered explanations for educational inequality look at the roles of educational organization and processes, such as funding, teacher quality, and school quality, in producing unequal educational achievement by different groups. Student-centered explanations examine how factors outside schools, such as biology, families, communities, and poverty, produce unequal achievement. Research indicates that student achievement is affected by a combination of school- and student-centered factors.

7.7 Describe recent reforms in education.

Recent school reforms have increased the role of the federal government and emphasized the use of standardized testing to identify and reduce educational gaps. While administrators and teachers can take many steps to improve student achievement, schools are embedded in communities that have their own sets of complex social, economic, and political issues. Education reformers must account for the role of factors outside the schools that affect student achievement, focusing especially on poverty and inequality in society at large.

7.8 Identify steps toward social change in education.

Everyone can take steps to improve the U.S. education system. By volunteering in underserved areas or becoming a teacher, you can directly influence students and schools. By remaining informed and pressing elected leaders to support sound education policies, you can help improve schooling through the democratic process.

KEY TERMS

achievement gap 156

American Federation of Teachers (AFT) 174

charter schools 172

code theory 166

community schools 175

cultural capital theory 166

cultural deprivation theory 169

cultural difference theories 169

effective schools movement 169

Elementary and Secondary Education Act (ESEA) 156

Every Student Succeeds Act (ESSA) 172

genetic difference theory 168

institutional theory 167

magnet schools 172

meritocracy 164

National Assessment of Educational Progress (NAEP) 156

National Education Association (NEA) 174

No Child Left Behind Act (NCLB) 156

Race to the Top (RTT) 156

school-centered explanations 168

school choice 172

school voucher 173

sociology of education 163

student-centered explanations 168

Teach for America (TFA) 174

tracking 170

 **Want a better grade?**

Get the tools you need to sharpen your study skills. Access practice quizzes, eFlashcards, video, and multimedia at
http://edge.sagepub.com/trevino2e

MEDIA

William Hoynes

Members of the press look on as U.S. Senator Angus King addresses clients at a drug rehabilitation center in Portland, where he talked about new legislation that would confront the opioid epidemic facing Maine and much of the country.

Investigating Media: My Story

William Hoynes

Watching, reading, and listening to news has been my daily routine since my teenage years. In college, I learned to read the news with a critical eye, questioning journalistic quality, depth, and perspective. In graduate school at Boston College, I was an active member of the Media Research and Action Project (MRAP), codirected by William Gamson and Charlotte Ryan, working with community activists to challenge barriers to media access and promoting greater media diversity.

Working with MRAP opened a window for me onto broader questions about the ways news contributes to public understanding of political issues and current events. In the 1980s and 1990s, I began working with my colleague David Croteau, with whom I still write today, on a series of studies of the range of perspectives featured on prestigious television news programs. Our studies examining ABC's *Nightline*, PBS's *NewsHour*, and the public affairs lineup on PBS stations were published by the media watch group FAIR (Fairness & Accuracy In Reporting) and helped generate public debate about the consequences of limited political diversity on U.S. television news.

Over the past 25 years, I have worked on monitoring of the local news media in Boston and Philadelphia, activist efforts to prevent the increasing commercialization of public schools, and nationwide campaigns to maintain federal regulations limiting the size of major media conglomerates and to reform the funding and structure of public broadcasting. I continue to work with media education and media activist organizations, including the Spark Media Project in Poughkeepsie, New York, and FAIR.

LEARNING OBJECTIVES

8.1 Describe the relationship between media and social problems.

8.2 Discuss patterns and trends in media portrayals of social problems.

8.3 Describe the debate about the role of media as a potential cause of social problems.

8.4 Discuss emergent social problems associated with new media technologies.

8.5 Explain how the functionalist, conflict, and symbolic interactionist perspectives conceptualize the media–social problems relationship.

8.6 Explain how contemporary theories conceptualize the media–social problems relationship.

8.7 Identify steps toward media-related social change.

 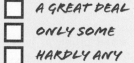 **WHAT DO YOU THINK?**

Questions About Media From the General Social Survey

1. What is your main source of information about events in the news?
- [ ] NEWSPAPERS
- [ ] THE INTERNET
- [ ] TV
- [ ] OTHER

2. What is your confidence level in the press?
- [ ] A GREAT DEAL
- [ ] ONLY SOME
- [ ] HARDLY ANY

3. How many hours do you watch TV each day?
- [ ] 0
- [ ] 1–2
- [ ] 3–4
- [ ] 5 OR MORE

4. What is your confidence level in television?
- [ ] A GREAT DEAL
- [ ] ONLY SOME
- [ ] HARDLY ANY

5. How often do you read the newspaper?
- [ ] DAILY
- [ ] A FEW TIMES A WEEK
- [ ] ONCE A WEEK
- [ ] LESS THAN ONCE A WEEK
- [ ] NEVER

 Turn to the end of the chapter to view the results for the total population.

SOURCE: National Opinion Research Center, University of Chicago.

THE DRAMA OF "ROAD RAGE"

8.1 Describe the relationship between media and social problems.

A minor traffic dispute in Carteret County, North Carolina, escalated into a dramatic confrontation in March 2013 when 40-year-old Bradley Turner jumped out of his car and threw a punch at 20-year-old William Berry, who Turner believed had cut him off. Berry and Nathan Brotzman, the 21-year-old passenger in his pickup truck, responded by punching and kicking Turner, beating him to the ground. Turner's wife stepped out of their car and handed him a pistol, which Turner pointed at Berry and Brotzman, who quickly ran away and called 911. Turner fired several shots in Berry's direction but no one was hurt.

Much of the incident was captured on cell phone video by one of Berry's neighbors, and the clip circulated widely on the Internet. Local and national news outlets—from the Greenville, North Carolina, television station WNCT and the local *Gaston Gazette* to the *New York Daily News* and Gawker—posted it. While Bradley and Christy Turner were actually charged with gun-related crimes, media reports instead highlighted the drama of "road rage."

Media play a prominent role in shaping what we define as a social problem. By calling attention to some issues, such as "road rage," they help to identify the social issues that attract our concern and action. By downplaying or neglecting other issues, they signal that, for example, the abundance of guns on the streets is not a serious social problem. Exploring the relationship between social problems and the media will help us to understand how and why some issues emerge as widely discussed social problems—and why others remain on the margins of public discussion, relegated to the category of personal trouble rather than social problem.

Sociologists have long explored the complex relationship between media and social problems. Recently, however, changes in the media environment and developments in social problems scholarship have produced three distinct sets of questions about media and social problems.

One set focuses on media *content* and the role of media in defining issues as social problems. How, for example, do news and entertainment media portray emerging and long-standing social problems? How, if at all, do such portrayals change over time, and how do advocates shape media portrayals of specific social problems? Are new forms of digital media, including user-generated and social media, changing the way the media construct social problems?

A second set of questions looks at the potential *role* of media as a cause of, or contributor to, social problems. Does exposure to violent media imagery produce violent behavior? Do media contribute to health problems such as obesity or anorexia? And how do media influence our understanding of, and responses to, social problems?

The final set of questions about media and social problems focuses on the emergence of *new social problems* related to the development of new media technologies. For example, what are the consequences of the digital divide—that is, persistent inequality in people's access to and knowledge about new digital media? How can we understand media-related social problems such as cyberbullying and distracted driving? What new challenges do these pose for policy makers?

This chapter traces these three areas of social problems scholarship, exploring the intersection of media and social problems in the context of classic as well as more specialized theories.

PATTERNS AND TRENDS

8.2 Discuss patterns and trends in media portrayals of social problems.

The media regularly portray social problems. Crime, for example, is a staple of local television news coverage, and print, broadcast, and online journalists routinely cover a range of issues associated with health, education, and the environment. A steady stream of Hollywood films and prime-time television programs include implicit references to school violence, homelessness, and drug abuse. Both news and entertainment media also often offer in-depth and dramatic portrayals of the causes and consequences of social problems. But what counts as a social problem?

Media and the Construction of Social Problems

The conditions that become social problems have both objective and subjective dimensions that interact. The objective dimension includes evidence of the existence, prevalence, and severity of potentially troubling issues, such as illegal drug use, gun violence, or child abuse. The subjective dimension includes collective interpretations of and public attitudes about these issues. Media are a primary arena within which the two dimensions interact, offering a prominent space where we debate and interpret the meaning and significance of incidents and trends associated with potential social problems. For example, citizens seeking to raise awareness about gun violence may offer journalists evidence of the problem—from official statistics to details of dramatic gun incidents—hoping the media will report it. Such news reports typically generate commentary, in which media become an arena for interpreting the significance of the statistics and incidents and for discussion of the appropriate ways to respond, leading to additional reporting on the debate over gun violence. Thus media help define the context within which both public policy and public opinion develop.

Only some troubling social conditions emerge as social problems earmarked for public discussion about potential solutions. **Moral entrepreneurs** are advocates who organize to focus public attention on these issues. They do so through the process of **claims making**, whereby groups compete to have authorities acknowledge, accept, and respond to their claims about difficult social issues. Claims making, then, is at the center of the process by which some social issues are defined as social problems (Kitsuse & Spector, 1973).

Media are a central and increasingly influential venue for defining troubling issues as social problems. Claims makers often use the news and online media for circulating their interpretations of social problems to policy makers and the public, jockeying for position to do so. Thus media attention is not distributed equally across issues, nor is it a simple reflection of the prevalence or severity of a given issue. Looking at examples of news coverage of crime and drugs will help us see *how* media construct social problems.

....

ASK YOURSELF: Consider news coverage of a current social problem. Can you identify the claims makers? Do reports feature various claims makers and multiple definitions of the problem or potential solutions? If so, how do you assess their competing interpretations?

....

Crime, Drugs, and Media Routines

Consider the contents of front-page headlines, lead stories on the evening news, the cable TV news crawl, and top-of-the-screen stories on news websites. Publicity—often the result of sustained media attention—is a major factor in shaping what citizens and public officials recognize as social problems requiring policy responses. However, this

GREG DALE/National Geographic Creative

▶ Do we live in a "network society" in which media networks such as Twitter, texting, and e-mail influence the social, political, economic, and cultural lives of people across the country and around the world? Some say that online media like Facebook and YouTube helped protesters launch the Tunisian revolution of 2010 and the Egyptian revolution of 2011. How many friends do you have who live in different countries with whom you can communicate instantly?

increased attention does not usually follow the worsening of a troubling issue. In fact, researchers have found it can occur when a social issue is stable or even improving. In recent years, for example, even as violent crime rates in the United States declined, a growing proportion of the public believed crime was getting worse (Bridges, 2017). News coverage of crime is a classic example.

For more than half a century, the volume of news coverage of crime—that is, the number of crime stories in the major news media—has been independent of the crime rate. In other words, we should not assume that an increase in crime *news* is the result of an increase in *crime,* or that a drop in crime news reflects a decline in the crime rate. F. James Davis's (1952, p. 330) pioneering study of crime reporting in Colorado newspapers found "there is no consistent relationship between the amount of crime news in newspapers and the local crime rates," and this finding has been replicated in later studies (see Katz, 1987).

Yet crime news remains a staple of U.S. journalism. Local television news programs and newspapers consistently report on crime and the courts, and national and online news outlets spend considerable time covering high-profile criminal cases. If the actual occurrence of crime is not the foundation of news coverage, what explains this intensity of coverage?

....

Moral entrepreneurs: Advocates who organize to focus broad public attention on troubling issues.

Claims making: The process whereby groups compete to have their claims about difficult social issues acknowledged, accepted, and responded to by authorities.

FIGURE 8.1 Cocaine and LSD Use Among U.S. High School Seniors, 1975–1990

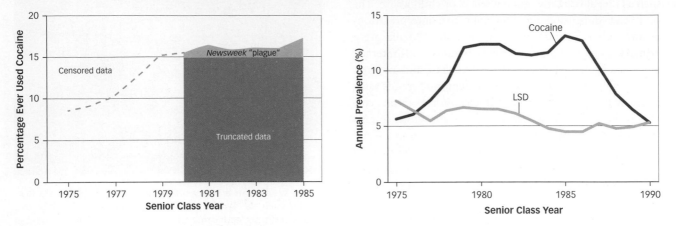

SOURCE: Johnston, Lloyd D., Patrick M. O'Malley, and Jerald G. Bachman. 1991. *Drug Use Among American High School Seniors, College Students and Young Adults, 1975-1990. Volume I: High School Seniors.* Rockville, MD: National Institute on Drug Abuse.

Research indicates that **journalists' professional routines**, the daily activities around which news reporters organize their work, are the key to understanding the consistently high level of crime coverage in the U.S. news media. Journalists know they can expect a steady stream of information from police and the courts, so they can count on crime stories to make the day-to-day work of producing news more manageable and less uncertain, just as weather and sports reports do. Crime—including stories about wayward celebrities, unusual offenses, and unfolding dramas—is a tried-and-true theme that draws the audiences that commercial and online news organizations need to earn advertising revenue.

In one classic study, sociologist Mark Fishman (1978, p. 533) sought to understand the roots of crime news by examining "how and why news organizations construct crime waves." Reports of a crime wave, Fishman found, result in large part from three key journalistic practices. First, in evaluating the newsworthiness of potential stories, journalists implicitly classify events by theme—"crimes against the elderly" was the theme in Fishman's study. Events are more likely to become news—and to be featured prominently—when they fit a continuing news theme.

Second, most crime reporting relies overwhelmingly on information from authorities, especially local police, whose publicity specialists know how news organizations operate. Fishman (1978, p. 540) reports that "police who transmit crime dispatches to the media select incidents that they think will interest journalists," mainly the kinds of stories they have reported before, and they provide reporters with continuing examples of a currently popular theme as long as such stories exist.

Third, news organizations track their competitors, making sure they do not miss important or interesting stories their rivals are covering. The news media outlets in one city or region thus often end up reporting the same stories, reinforcing the significance of a specific theme—such as a crime wave—and further encouraging police sources to supply similar leads.

For example, understanding journalistic routines gives us insight into the way news media circulate what sociologists Orcutt and Turner (1993) call "distorted images of drug problems." The U.S. news media's focus on cocaine in 1986—highlighted by a March 17 *Newsweek* cover story, "Kids and Cocaine: An Epidemic Strikes Middle America," that identified "A Coke Plague"—relied on alarming numbers and powerful graphic representations of cocaine use to describe the crisis. These numbers and graphics, however, required significant interpretive and creative work to be consistent with a story of a cocaine crisis. Orcutt and Turner show how *Newsweek* graphically illustrated a very small, 1-year increase that masked a longer-term trend of relative stability in cocaine use, selectively citing survey findings in ways that were not consistent with the overall research results (see Figure 8.1a).

Reports of a growing LSD problem in the early 1990s similarly pointed to a survey showing a small increase in LSD use among high school seniors from 1989 to 1990. The reports failed to note, however, that the increase from 4.9% to 5.4% of high school seniors was not statistically significant, and that LSD use among this group had been higher in the late 1970s and early 1980s (see Figure 8.1b).

Most recently, the use of methamphetamine emerged in the first decade of the 2000s as a new national drug problem. Again, news media played a prominent role in the construction of the meth crisis (Shafer, 2007), with *Newsweek* using familiar language in its August 2005 cover story, "The

....

Journalists' professional routines: The daily activities around which news reporters organize their work.

Meth Epidemic: Inside America's New Drug Crisis."

Drug abuse is a complex social issue, and reporting can help the public understand it. But the examples noted above show that claims makers do not necessarily need to offer research data to legitimate their definitions of social problems. In fact, Deseran and Orcutt (2009, p. 883) argue, "if anything, there appears to be an inverse relationship between media legitimation of drug crises and empirical documentation based on drug surveys."

Sometimes news organizations are themselves the primary claims makers, and editors and reporters play a crucial role in constructing social problems. Sometimes, however, journalists are skeptical of other claims makers' efforts. During the 1996 U.S. presidential campaign, rather than running headlines about a documented marijuana crisis, news media raised critical questions about survey results and identified the primary claims makers regarding an increasing teen drug problem—President Bill Clinton and presidential candidate Bob Dole—as political actors seeking to gain media attention and sway voters (Deseran & Orcutt, 2009). The debate about drugs became part of the political campaign, with reporters paying more attention to the candidates' performances than to the "problem" of increasing marijuana use. News media, in this case, effectively deterred politicians from defining a new marijuana problem.

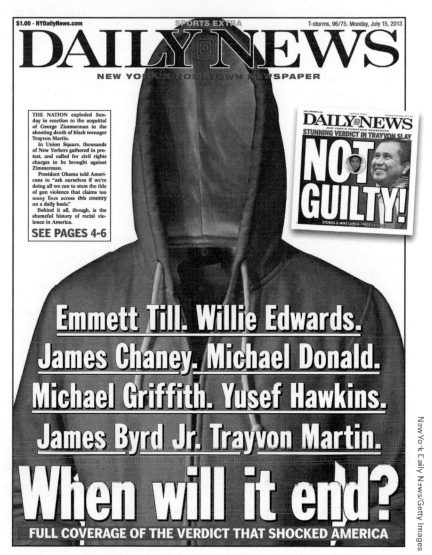

▶ Is there an element of sensationalism in many news stories in which the messages are overdrawn? Has tabloid journalism become a major part of how serious crime is reported? Are newspapers like the *Daily News,* "New York's most momentous newspaper," responsible for stoking the feelings of their readers?

Media Frames and Sponsors

The ways that news media define social problems—that is, the common **media frames,** conventions of journalistic storytelling that situate a social problem within a broader context (Gamson, 1992)—are dynamic, changing over time in response to newsworthy events and broader cultural changes. One of the most powerful factors shaping the way media frame social problems is what Gamson and Modigliani (1987) call **sponsor activities,** the advocacy and promotional work of publicizing and advancing a specific interpretation of an issue. As these researchers note, prominent media frames that define social issues "frequently have

sponsors interested in promoting their careers. Sponsorship is more than merely advocacy, involving such tangible activities as speech-making, advertising, article and pamphlet writing, and the filing of legal briefs to promote a preferred package" (p. 165).

For example, in the years after the civil rights movement, with sponsorship from civil rights organizations and several presidential administrations in the 1960s and 1970s, news media typically framed racial discrimination toward blacks as a serious problem and affirmative

Media frames: Conventions of journalistic storytelling that situate a social problem within a broader context.

Sponsor activities: The work of promoting and publicizing specific media frames.

action as an appropriate remedial action. In later years, particularly the late 1970s and early 1980s, a network of neoconservative journals, think tanks, and organizations emerged as powerful sponsors of a very different interpretation, defining the problem as reverse discrimination, and this frame became increasingly prominent in the news media in the 1980s (Gamson & Modigliani, 1987).

News Coverage Builds on Culturally Resonant Themes

We've seen that routine media practices, the need for audiences that drive advertising revenue, and the public's desire for dramatic and unusual stories shape media reporting on social problems. In addition, news coverage often invokes **culturally resonant themes**, widely held beliefs, values, and preferences familiar to potential audiences.

Media characterizations of food-related social problems—overweight/obesity and anorexia/bulimia—are a prime example of portrayals rooted in deep-seated assumptions about our bodies and our eating habits, individual responsibility, and health. In the 2000s, the news media described obesity as a growing U.S. health crisis, an "epidemic." Much reporting drew on scientific research, but journalists selected, simplified, and dramatized the findings (Saguy & Almeling, 2008). News coverage constructed obesity in ways that identified individuals as both the problem and the likely solution.

Media accounts typically blamed individuals' eating habits and inactivity and suggested that making better food and exercise choices would be the most productive response. They typically underplayed the social structural and genetic roots of obesity and potential policy-based responses. This individual-oriented approach to a social problem is consistent with cultural themes that value individual responsibility, as well as with long-standing stereotypes that define body weight in moral terms and overweight people as lazy and weak.

Media portrayals of anorexia and bulimia frame these eating disorders in very different terms, identifying them as legitimate eating disorders with both individual and social structural causes as well as biological, medical, psychological, and cultural foundations. Medical intervention is portrayed as a common and effective way to treat them. The volume of coverage of anorexia and bulimia remained relatively stable during the 1990s and 2000s, while news coverage of obesity, in contrast, grew dramatically as the crisis frame emerged (see Figure 8.2).

Saguy and Gruys (2010, p. 247) note: "In the contemporary U.S. society, where thinness is highly prized, news articles are less likely to blame individuals for being (or trying to be) *too thin* than they are to blame them for being *too fat*. This suggests that, more generally,

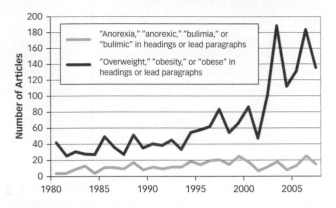

FIGURE 8.2 Number of U.S. News Articles About Anorexia/Bulimia and Overweight/Obesity, 1980–2007

SOURCE: Morality and Health: News Media Constructions of Overweight and Eating Disorders, by A. C. Saguy and K. Gruys, 2010, *Social Problems*, 57(2), 231–250. Reprinted with permission from the University of California Press.

cultural values shape how the news media assign blame and responsibility." In short, news media portrayals of social problems often invoke popular assumptions and stereotypes about their causes and consequences, and about appropriate responses.

Entertainment Media

Entertainment media play a significant role in publicizing social problems, helping identify emerging issues, and focusing attention on persistent problems. For example, according to sociologist Stephen Pfohl (1977, p. 320), both news media and television medical dramas helped establish child abuse as a legitimate social problem: "The proliferation of the idea of abuse by the media cannot be underestimated. Though its stories were sensational, its credibility went unchallenged." Two decades later, popular music helped revive concern about child abuse as a social problem. Hit songs from artists such as 10,000 Maniacs ("What's the Matter Here," 1987), Suzanne Vega ("Luka," 1987), and Pearl Jam ("Daughter," 1993) refocused national attention on the continuing problem.

The Media and Moral Panics

News media sometimes shine a dramatic spotlight on a social issue in a way that can help constitute, and inflame, a moral panic. Sociologist Stanley Cohen coined the term

Culturally resonant themes: Themes that invoke widely held beliefs, values, and preferences that are familiar to potential audiences; such themes are common in news stories of social problems.

Experiencing Media

Defining the Problem: Race, Gender, and Sport

The Rutgers University women's basketball team had just completed the best season in program history, and its regional semifinal upset victory over top-seeded Duke helped propel a Cinderella story line in the sports pages. Then the team lost the NCAA National Championship game to Tennessee, and talk-radio host Don Imus referred to the women on the Rutgers team as "nappy-headed hos" on his nationally syndicated program. Over the next 8 days, Imus apologized, lost his televised simulcast partner (MSNBC), and ultimately had his radio show cancelled by CBS.

News coverage of Imus's derogatory remarks was far more extensive than reporting on the game. Most news media framed the incident as a story about race and racism. Undoubtedly, race was at the center. A white "shock jock" made racist remarks about a team consisting mostly of black players. However, sociologist Cheryl Cooky and her colleagues (2010) suggest that an understanding of intersectionality—in this case, the way race, gender, class, and sexuality are woven together—offers a deeper insight into the events.

In framing the incident as a "race story," major news media quoted prominent black men such as Jesse Jackson and Al Sharpton, but recognized leaders of women's organizations—and the Rutgers athletes—were far less visible; news reports mentioned black leaders or organizations more than six times as often as they mentioned female leaders or women's groups (Cooky et al., 2010, p. 149). And the coverage generally ignored the on-campus protests at the Rutgers Women's Center, which sought to emphasize the intersection of racism and sexism in Imus's remarks.

Cooky and her colleagues suggest that "the media's uncritical positioning of Sharpton and Jackson as the primary spokespeople racialized the controversy. Moreover, this frame silenced intersectional ways of knowing given that the quotations from Black leaders featured in the articles focused only on the racial/racist aspects of the controversy, while neglecting themes on race, gender, and sexuality in sport" (p. 150). Journalists covered the incident as a high-profile controversy, missing the opportunity to examine its deeper meaning within the continuing problems of racism and sexism in U.S. society.

▶ Members of the Rutgers University women's basketball team appear at a news conference in 2007. The team and school officials held the news conference after radio personality Don Imus made racist and sexist remarks about the team on his radio and television shows.

REUTERS/Mike Segar

▶ **THINK ABOUT IT**

1. Why do you think news reports emphasized race rather than gender as the key issue in this story?

2. How do you think an intersectional approach would change the media's framing of this incident?

---

moral panic in his influential 1972 book *Folk Devils and Moral Panics.* Since then, a large research literature has explored this concept.

In **moral panics**, public fear and anxiety about particular social problems are disproportionate to the actual danger posed by those problems. In some cases, such as news coverage of the cocaine "crisis," media play an active role in promoting moral panics. In other cases, such as news reporting about child abuse, media serve more as channels for stories that fuel the panics. As Erich Goode and Nachman Ben-Yehuda (2009, p. 106) note, "The media are usually the vehicle that conveys the stories and claims on which moral panics are based; they are the most effective means by which indignation over a given threat is propagated because, unlike word of mouth, they reach large audiences over a brief time, often even simultaneously."

Goode and Ben-Yehuda observe that news organizations contribute to moral panics most commonly through **media exaggeration**, strategies that dramatize

....

Moral panics: Situations in which broad public fears and anxieties about particular social problems are disproportionate to the dangers of those problems.

Media exaggeration: Strategies of dramatizing and embellishing media stories involving social issues to attract and hold the attention of an audience.

and embellish social issues to attract an audience. Media exaggeration takes two primary forms. First, journalists pay inordinate attention to events that are uncommon or statistically unusual. Second, they overstate the extent or size of a social problem, using the language of epidemic, crisis, or plague. This kind of reporting produces dramatic headlines and news stories that go viral, and it is one of the principal ways media can contribute to a moral panic.

Media Activism and Social Problems

Much of the media reporting on social problems emerges from official government sources, but activists can intervene to try to highlight social problems in the news. Reporting of domestic violence is one example.

Beginning in the late 1990s, sociologist Charlotte Ryan began working with the Rhode Island Coalition Against Domestic Violence to improve the way local news outlets covered domestic violence issues. Leaders of the coalition knew that even sympathetic reporters often wrote stories that helped perpetuate what the leaders saw as destructive myths about domestic violence, including that it is a private family problem rather than a social problem worthy of sustained public attention. The members of the coalition sought a better understanding of how reporters gathered their information, so they could work with local journalists to improve their coverage.

Ryan examined local newspaper coverage of 12 domestic violence murders in Rhode Island from 1996 through 1999, consisting of 88 articles, most of which appeared in the first week following each murder. Her findings were striking. News stories focused primarily on the perpetrators; the victims were nearly invisible. The murders were generally portrayed as unpredictable family tragedies, and the sources quoted in news reports played key roles in defining the stories. Some, including neighbors and witnesses, emphasized the individual tragedy, and police sources focused on the details of the crime. Only when reporters turned to domestic violence experts—shelter providers, public health workers, and victims' advocates—did their stories link the murders to the problem of domestic violence. Ryan concluded: "With a few notable exceptions, the media reinforced the perception that domestic violence murders are isolated family tragedies and did not challenge common myths about domestic violence. In doing so, reporters missed opportunities to broaden the public's understanding of domestic violence, its warning signs and possibilities for prevention and community intervention" (Rhode Island Coalition Against Domestic Violence, 2000, pp. 5–4).

Ryan and the Rhode Island Coalition (2000) went on to produce a reporters' handbook about domestic violence and the law, with recommendations from survivors, that was distributed throughout the state, and a training program for survivors and advocates about how reporters work so they could become more effective news sources. The Rhode Island Coalition is now one of the principal sources in newspaper coverage of domestic violence in the state, and the coverage has changed in ways that reflect the coalition's emphasis on understanding domestic violence as a social problem, not just a private tragedy.

Claims Making in the Era of YouTube and Facebook

Just about anyone with a computer and an Internet connection can be an amateur media producer. Now, if mainstream journalists overlook an issue, advocates and claims makers can bypass traditional news outlets and create their own advocacy media to gain publicity, mobilize support, and pressure policy makers to take action. In this new media environment, claims making is more accessible to a wider range of advocates, but it is also more diffuse, with many voices competing for public attention.

ASK YOURSELF: What kind of social problems commentary do you see on Facebook? Do the claims draw from, and link to, traditional media? Do they point to the Facebook pages or websites of advocacy organizations? Do you think social networking sites are effective at focusing public attention on new social problems? Why or why not?

Digital media can democratize the process of social problem construction, opening new communication channels, additional opportunities for information sharing, and a new infrastructure for public discussion. Most **user-generated media content** reaches only very small networks of friends and family of the generators, and many people remain spectators, consuming content distributed largely by the major media companies that have long dominated our information environment. Still, as more people get their news and information through social media, there is growing evidence that popular social media such as Facebook and Twitter are becoming increasingly

User-generated media content: Publicly shared media content produced by users (often amateurs) rather than media companies.

Researching Media

Comparing Media Constructions of Obesity in the United States and France

If you've ever travelled outside the United States, you may have observed that news broadcasts in other countries can look quite different from U.S. news. Do American news media depictions of social problems reflect a specific national cultural context? To explore this question, sociologists Abigail C. Saguy, Kjerstin Gruys, and Shanna Gong (2010) compared American and French newspaper coverage of overweight and obesity over a 10-year period. Newspapers in both countries portrayed obesity as a social problem, but the coverage in the two framed the sources and solutions to the problem very differently.

The obesity rate in France is far lower than that in the United States, but newspapers in France were twice as likely as U.S. papers to frame obesity as a health "crisis." About half the French news stories also included discussion of other countries, while the American press focused exclusively on the United States in 95% of articles. While coverage in both countries was equally likely to highlight individual blame for increased body weight, French news was far more likely to point to social structural causes of overweight/

obesity. Saguy and her colleagues note that "an emphasis on individual blame dominates U.S. news framing, while being more equally balanced by other frames in French news reporting" (p. 599). This difference likely reflects broader cultural differences, such as that Europeans are more likely to frame social problems in structural terms.

When it came to solving the problem of obesity, U.S. media emphasized individual solutions such as diet and exercise (56% of stories) and paid comparatively little attention to policy solutions (21%) such as the nutritional quality of school lunches. In contrast, the French press offered equal emphasis on individual and policy solutions (44% for both). In discussing dietary solutions, the American press focused primarily on low-fat, low-carbohydrate, and low-calorie diets, while the French emphasized healthy foods.

Saguy and her colleagues conclude that the distinctive national news

▶ An overweight woman sits on a chair in Times Square in New York City. In 2013, New York City mayor Michael Bloomberg launched an initiative to ban supersize sodas and limit the sizes of other sugary drinks that could be sold by restaurants, delis, movie theaters, sports stadiums, and food carts. Approximately 60% of New Yorkers opposed the measure, saying that purchasing such drinks should be a matter of individual choice. Most Americans see obesity as an individual problem.

REUTERS/Lucas Jackson

coverage "probably echoes general patterns in how social problems are addressed differently in each nation, with a U.S. press focusing more on individual autonomy and the French press envisaging a larger role for the state" (p. 605).

▶ **THINK ABOUT IT**

1. Why do you think French and American news media report differently on obesity?

2. Do you think a journalistic emphasis on social structural causes of, and policy solutions to, obesity would help newspaper readers develop a deeper understanding of weight-related social problems? Why or why not?

---

significant claims-making arenas. For example, "fake news" sites, many of which originated in Russia, used Facebook to generate millions of views during the 2016 U.S. presidential election (Allcott & Gentzkow, 2017). Such fake news sites, which were not operated by professional journalists, posted false stories designed to attract committed ideologically conservative audience

segments and give voice to hyperpartisan claims makers. In addition, during the 2016 presidential campaign and since taking office, President Donald Trump has used Twitter—and his more than 25 million followers—to advance often-dubious claims about various social problems, including crime, voter fraud, and government surveillance.

DEBATING MEDIA AS A CAUSE OF SOCIAL PROBLEMS

 8.3 Describe the debate about the role of media as a potential cause of social problems.

For decades, critics have identified media as one of the fundamental *sources* of social problems, and social science researchers have debated whether, and how, media exposure might encourage behaviors and attitudes associated with social problems, including crime and delinquency, violence, unhealthy eating, and smoking. You may be familiar with some of the claims—such as that violent video games help cause school violence or that advertising is a cause of eating disorders—but you may not know how long these debates have raged or how complex the causes of social problems are.

In her thorough exploration of contemporary arguments that blame media for social problems, sociologist Karen Sternheimer (2013) identifies nine **media phobias**, or broad public fears about the negative impact of media, as listed in Table 8.1. Sternheimer does not discount the significance of these social problems; in fact, she argues that they warrant significant public attention. However, she finds little evidence that media are the cause of any of them: "Despite the commonsense view that media must be at least partly to blame for these issues, the evidence suggests that there are many more important factors that create serious social problems in the United States today. Popular culture gets a lot of attention, but it is rarely a central causal factor" (p. 2). Media are, for Sternheimer, little more than "sheep in wolf's clothing" (p. 285) that appear to be far more powerful drivers of social problems than they really are.

> **ASK YOURSELF:** Why do you think media are so often blamed for social problems? What do we neglect when we focus on media as the cause of social problems? How would you respond to Sternheimer's characterization of media as "sheep in wolf's clothing"?

Next we review both the claims and the counterclaims about media causing, facilitating, or worsening various social problems, to help you draw your own conclusions.

Youth and Crime: The Payne Fund Studies and Comic Books

We can conclude that exposure to media has significant influence on what we think and how we behave only if

TABLE 8.1 Nine Media Phobias

	Media Phobias
1	Media are ruining childhood
2	Media are putting people at greater risk for suicide, depression, kidnapping, and sexual abuse
3	Media are making people dumber
4	Media are causing violence
5	Media are endorsing teenage sex
6	Media are encouraging teen pregnancy and single parenthood
7	Media are causing health problems, such as obesity and anorexia
8	Media are promoting substance abuse
9	Media are making children increasingly materialistic

SOURCE: Sternheimer, Karen. 2013. *Connecting Social Problems and Popular Culture*. 2nd Edition. Boulder, CO: Westview Press.

we assume that media are powerful. Public concern about media power has persisted since the early 20th century, and it often seems to intensify when new media technologies emerge. The introduction of the telephone, for example, aroused fears that the new device would threaten privacy. The development of video games and the Internet produced a new wave of concern that violent media content would produce violent children.

One of the earliest social science research efforts to study the relationship between media and social problems was the Payne Fund Studies in the 1930s. Several prominent sociologists—including social theorist Herbert Blumer and youth gang researcher Frederic Thrasher—participated in the multibook research project aimed at offering "a comprehensive study of the influence of motion pictures upon children" (Charters, 1933, p. v).

The conclusions of the Payne Fund Studies emphasized the complexity of the relationship between movies and children. The authors noted that children learn from movies, and that the emotional responses movies evoke constitute a key component of their power. At the same time, they recognized movies' differing influence on individual children, suggesting that social context and children's experiences were a key part of the picture.

Media phobias: Fears about the negative impacts of media that lead to identifying media as the causes of persistent social problems.

The Payne Fund authors paid particular attention to whether heavy movie attendance led children to engage in crime or other troublesome behavior. The results were decidedly mixed. In his historical review of 20th-century media effects research, McDonald (2004, p. 186) notes that the Payne Fund data point to a "reciprocal relationship—movies do have an effect on children, but those children who are most attracted to the worst movies tend to be those with the most problems to begin with."

Sociologist Herbert Blumer (1933) conducted the most in-depth investigation of the movies-delinquency relationship. He found movies to be a factor in the delinquent activities of only a minority of boys and girls, with an indirect effect on crime and delinquency. Still, he found, movies can exert "indirect influences disposing or leading persons to delinquency or crime," including "through the display of crime techniques and criminal patterns of behavior; by arousing desires for easy money and luxury, and by suggesting questionable methods for their achievement; by inducing a spirit of bravado, toughness, and adventurousness; by arousing intense sexual desires; and by invoking daydreaming of criminal roles" (p. 198). Despite scholars' efforts to highlight the complex two-way relationship, the Payne Fund Studies generally affirmed public anxiety about the negative influence of movies on young people and helped pave the way for future research on media as a cause of social problems.

Comic books, too, became a focus of concern. In the 1940s and 1950s, critics led by psychiatrist Fredric Wertham (1954) identified the reading of comic books as a cause of juvenile delinquency. Wertham argued that comic books' frequent depictions of violence, crime, and horror glamorize crime and teach criminal techniques, effectively promoting crime, delinquency, and generally antisocial behavior among youth. A U.S. Senate subcommittee on juvenile delinquency held hearings on comic books in 1954, with Wertham as a prominent witness. Other social scientists weighed in to support Wertham's critique, including C. Wright Mills (1954), who offered a glowing review of Wertham's book *Seduction of the Innocent,* which was published just a few days after the hearings.

Yet social science research findings demonstrating a relationship between comic book reading and juvenile delinquency were scant. As sociologist Frederic Thrasher (1949, p. 205), who had previously been involved in the Payne Fund Studies, argued, "It may be said that no acceptable evidence has been produced by Wertham or anyone else for the conclusion that the reading of comic magazines has, or has not, a significant relation to delinquent behavior." Later research found little evidence of a comic book–delinquency connection, and a 1980 study concluded, "This study does not support the hypothesis that reading violent comic books leads to greater aggression among children" (Tan & Scruggs, 1980, p. 583).

▶ In the 1940s, despite limited evidence, there was significant public concern that comic book reading promoted juvenile delinquency.

In response to the hearings and to widespread publicity, the comic book industry adopted a proactive plan of **self-regulation,** proposing to police itself to stave off government regulation. Some of the principles of the code the industry initiated appear in Table 8.2.

The Payne Fund Studies of motion pictures and Wertham's critique of comic books helped sustain the idea that media can be more than simple entertainment, that they offer genuine educational opportunities, and that government has an interest in promoting policies that support public-spirited educational forms of media (see McChesney, 1996). With television rapidly emerging as the dominant form of U.S. media in the 1950s, the earlier debates about movies and comics served as backdrop to an ongoing battle over television's role, if any, in causing or worsening social problems.

Media and Violence

Violence is a foundation of contemporary television, so common that many viewers find it unremarkable. Television executives believe violence sells, that viewers—especially

Self-regulation: A process whereby media industries propose to police themselves to stave off the imposition of government regulation.

Morris Engel/Premium Archive/Getty Images

TABLE 8.2 Select Stipulations of the 1954 Comics Code Adopted by the Comic Magazine Association of America

- "Policemen, judges, government officials and respected institutions shall never be presented in such a way as to create disrespect for established authority."

- "No comics shall explicitly present the unique details and methods of a crime."

- "All scenes of horror, excessive bloodshed, gory or gruesome crimes, depravity, lust, sadism, masochism shall not be permitted."

- "Profanity, obscenity, smut, vulgarity or words or symbols that have acquired undesirable meanings are forbidden."

SOURCE: Quoted in Hajdu, David. 2008. *The Ten-Cent Plague: The Great Comic Book Scare and How it Changed America*. New York: Farrar, Straus and Giroux.

highly coveted young adults—are attracted to violent programming. Why do some viewers find media violence compelling? What are the limits of its allure?

The underlying question of much research in this area is whether watching violent television promotes violent behavior, and if so, how much? By analyzing the relationship between consuming violent entertainment and enacting real-world violence, researchers may increase understanding of, and perhaps help to alleviate, social problems associated with violence.

On the surface, questions about the influence of television violence are straightforward and intuitive. Television violence (and, more generally, media violence) is pervasive. Young people ages 8 to 12 ("tweens") spend, on average, about 4.5 hours with screen media each day; teens ages 13 to 18 average more than 6.5 hours of screen media per day (Common Sense Media, 2015) (see Table 8.3). Much popular television programming and other video content include violent images, themes, and events. In this context, it is reasonable to ask whether regular exposure to images of violence has any significant influence on viewers' behavior, attitudes, or understanding of their world.

Let's begin with the most direct question: Does television violence cause real-world violence? The answer appears to be simple common sense. How could watching heavy doses of violence on television *not* encourage people to commit acts of violence by glorifying violent behavior, suggesting that violence is rewarding, depicting violence as an acceptable way to resolve conflict, encouraging imitation, and linking violence and aggression with pleasure?

It is difficult, however, to establish a clear causal link between television violence and violent behavior. In laboratory experiments, psychologists have found that exposure to violent television images produces a short-term increase in aggressive feelings. Some lab experiments have shown that watching violent television increases postviewing aggressive behavior, such as playing aggressively with toys, and in some surveys viewers have reported an increase in aggressive behavior after watching violent television (Comstock, 2008).

While many researchers accept that there is a relationship between violent television and aggression, the specific dynamics of that relationship remain contested. Perhaps most important, the evidence linking media violence to violent behavior—the core of the claim that violent television is a key cause of violence-related social problems—is weak. This should come as no surprise. Aggression, even aggressive play, in a laboratory setting is clearly different from real-world violent behavior. If we want to understand the potential relationship between consuming violent media and acting aggressively or violently, we need to recognize all the other factors that intervene. Children attracted to media violence, and compulsive viewers of media violence, are likely different in important respects from viewers less interested in media violence. Similarly, some children may find that televised violence—and other forms of entertainment violence—provides an arena for working through their emotions, including feelings of aggression, in the world of fantasy. And differently situated viewers may respond differently to distinct forms of television violence.

This is notoriously tricky terrain to navigate. There is good reason to be wary of television violence. It crowds out other kinds of television, and to many viewers (and parents), it ranges from distasteful to downright scary. But this does not mean it causes violent behavior or juvenile crime. There is no simple consensus about which specific forms of television violence are most worrisome. For example, if you worry that media violence causes violent behavior, which of these kinds of violent television programs do you find most troubling?

1. A prime-time drama focused on the grisly activities of a serial killer

2. A broadcast of the *Lord of the Rings* film trilogy

3. A news program with images of graphic violence from the war in Afghanistan

4. A dramatic reality program about local law enforcement

5. An animated comedy full of ostensibly humorous family violence

Is it the sheer magnitude of the violence on display? Its goriness or casualness? The degree to which it appears to be real? The viewer's emotional connection to the perpetrators or the victims? The perpetrators' identities as authorities or criminals? Let's face it. Daily news viewers and *Lord of the Rings* fans are likely to object to different forms of television violence.

Let's return to the core question: Does watching television cause violent behavior? There is little empirical basis for an answer of yes. When one criminologist weighed in on the effects of media violence, she concluded: "The evidence suggests that there is no urgency in addressing the media violence problem under the auspices of preventing violent crime. Even a generous reading of the literature suggests that these effects are very small by comparison with the effects of other factors" (Savage, 2008, p. 1134).

Even if watching violent television does not cause violent crime, other potential links between televised violence and social problems merit attention. For instance, scholars have found that violent television—and other forms of media violence—can affect the way people understand and respond to violence in their communities.

Consuming a regular diet of television violence may also desensitize viewers to violence in the real world by making it ordinary, taken for granted. Communication scholar Erica Scharrer (2008, p. 301) summarizes how desensitization occurs "through the long-term development of emotional tolerance, in which individuals become inured through repeated exposure to violence, ultimately registering a diminished physiological response as well as a higher threshold at which to label something as violent and a greater tendency to think of violence as simply part of the everyday fabric of society."

Watching television violence may also enhance viewers' fear of violence. For example, television programs show crime and violence far more frequently than they occur in real life, and these portrayals seem to influence heavy viewers, who are more likely than others to worry about crime and violence in their own lives (Gerbner et al., 1994). During the 1990s, the volume of crime stories on television news increased dramatically, though real violent crime declined throughout the decade. In creating entertaining and emotionally engaging stories, news outlets can promote fear and anxiety and contribute to the widespread expectation that we are all in danger, contradicting the actual data on crime rates (Altheide, 2002, 2009). George Gerbner and his colleagues (1986, p. 10) labeled this the "mean world" syndrome, whereby "for most viewers, television's mean and dangerous world tends to cultivate a sense of relative danger, mistrust, dependence, and—despite its supposedly 'entertaining' nature—alienation and gloom."

Of course, the relationship between media and public attitudes is complex; both media content and audience experiences matter. Local news seems especially influential in promoting fear of crime, regardless of actual local

▶ The popular television series *Game of Thrones* has been criticized for the amount of sexual violence it depicts. Graphic scenes of rape and torture have been featured in several episodes. Do you think that this level of violence is necessary for the story?

crime rates (Escholz, Chiricos, & Gertz, 2003; Romer, Jamieson, & Aday, 2003). Reality television programs about law enforcement also seem to promote fear of crime. Audience experiences are influential, too; one study found that local news viewing enhanced fear of crime among all kinds of viewers, but especially viewers in high-crime neighborhoods, those with recent experiences as crime victims, and those who perceived crime stories as realistic (Chiricos, Padgett, & Gertz, 2000).

Scholars have asked many of the same questions about violence in video games, which sometimes occurs in highly realistic settings. The popular game *Grand Theft Auto* is a case in point. While many perceive it as a satiric commentary on violence in U.S. society, the game has attracted considerable attention because players are permitted to kill police officers and engage in other violent and criminal behaviors. Some studies have found that playing violent video games desensitizes players to real-world violence and can increase aggressive behavior (Bartholow, Sestir, & Davis, 2005; Carnagey, Anderson, & Bushman, 2007). However, there is no simple consensus on the effects, and other researchers argue that concerns are overstated (Ferguson, 2007; Kutner & Olson, 2008).

Ads, Films, and Youth Smoking

Media have also been implicated in social problems related to health, especially among youth. Tobacco advertising has long portrayed cigarette smoking as sexy, cool, mature, and independent, and most research suggests such ads are effective in promoting smoking among adolescents. One comprehensive review evaluated studies in a variety of countries, including Australia, England, India, Japan, Norway, Spain, and the United States, and the researchers conclude that tobacco ad campaigns

TABLE 8.3 Time Spent on Screen Media Among Tweens (8- to 12-Year-Olds) and Teens (13- to 18-Year-Olds) in the United States, 2015

	Tweens	Teens
Total Screen Media	4:36	6:40
Watching TV/DVDs/videos	2:26	2:38
Playing video, computer, or mobile games	1:19	1:21
Using social media	0:16	1:11
Browsing websites	0:12	0:36
Other screen activities	0:23	0:54

Proportion Who Spend Time With Screen Media Each Day

	Tweens	Teens
No time	6%	6%
2 hours or less	28%	17%
2–4 hours	27%	20%
4–8 hours	27%	31%
More than 8 hours	11%	26%

SOURCE: Common Sense Media. 2015. *The Common Sense Census: Media Use by Tweens and Teens.*

work: "Exposure to promotion causes children to initiate tobacco use" (DiFranza et al., 2006, p. 1244).

Hollywood films also appear to have a significant impact on attitudes and behaviors regarding tobacco. The National Cancer Institute's in-depth review *The Role of the Media in Promoting and Reducing Tobacco Use* (2008) shows that studies using various research methods have all yielded similar findings about the influence of smoking in the movies. High levels of exposure to on-screen smoking are associated with more positive beliefs about tobacco and higher rates of smoking. The authors conclude: "Along with the results of cross-sectional and longitudinal population-based studies, experimental research indicates that images of smoking in film can influence people's beliefs about social norms for smoking, beliefs about the function and consequences of smoking, and ultimately their personal propensity to smoke" (p. 392).

Media are certainly not the sole, or even the primary, cause of youth tobacco use. Family members who smoke, connections to peer smokers, and various psychological traits also influence youth smoking habits. But tobacco advertisements and a steady dose of smoking images in popular culture—including those resulting from **product placement,** in which manufacturers pay for their products to be used or mentioned by film or television characters— can effectively promote smoking. By associating cigarettes with adventure, sexuality, and adult lifestyles, media help to sustain a set of cultural meanings that define smoking in terms that are attractive to some youth.

Media and Obesity

We've seen that the definition of obesity as an "epidemic" in recent years highlights the role of media in constructing social problems. At the same time, scholars and public health officials have identified media as a *contributor*

James Leynse/Corbis/Getty Images

▶ Joe Camel was a character used to advertise Camel cigarettes from 1987 to 1997; he appeared in magazines, on billboards, and, as shown in this photo, on the side of a building in New York City. Highly recognizable, Joe Camel was presented in various entertaining situations and in bold and bright colors. The R. J. Reynolds Tobacco Company denied the character was directed at the under-18 market. What do you think?

Product placement: A form of advertising in which products are used or mentioned by film or television characters.

to the growth in childhood obesity (Brown & Bobkowski, 2011; Zhang et al., 2016): "Most large national cross-sectional studies and several longitudinal studies indicate that children who spend more time with media are more likely to be overweight than children who don't" (Kaiser Family Foundation, 2004, p. 10). What dynamic produces the connection between media use and obesity? It is possible, for example, that children who are heavy media users are less active, and their lower levels of physical activity help cause weight gain. And the vast amount of advertising aimed at children for high-calorie, nonnutritious fast food, sugary snacks, and soda appears to have an impact on their dietary habits that leads to an increase in obesity.

Children in the early 21st century are deluged by more advertisements than were the children of any previous generation. In the 1970s, children watched an estimated 20,000 television commercials per year; by the 1990s this figure had doubled, to 40,000 a year (Kunkel, 2001), and it has continued to increase in the 2000s. Today's children are also exposed to heavy advertising in other media platforms, including online, in video games, and on billboards.

Many children have a keen awareness of themselves as consumers and are often the first in their households to try new media technologies. In her study of children's consumption, *Born to Buy*, sociologist Juliet Schor (2004, p. 11) points out, "Children have become conduits from the consumer marketplace into the household, the link between advertisers and the family purse." As a result, children drive many forms of family consumption, often pressuring parents until they relent or using their own allowances to purchase products. Advertisers understand this process and have learned to target children accordingly.

In response to concerns about media as a factor in childhood obesity, the Walt Disney Company in 2012 instituted a requirement that foods appearing in its children's television, radio, and website programming meet strict nutritional guidelines. According to the *New York Times*, the new guidelines would lead to a change in the food items advertised to children: "Products like Capri Sun drinks and Kraft Lunchables meals—both current Disney advertisers—along with a wide range of candy, sugared cereal and fast food, will no longer be acceptable advertising material" (Barnes 2012, p. B1).

▶ Two women look at a billboard showing an emaciated naked woman in Milan, Italy. The picture, used to promote the Italian women's clothing brand Nolita, appeared in double-page spreads in Italian newspapers and on city billboards to coincide with fashion week in Milan. Do you think that images like this have any effect on viewers beyond the immediate one of shock?

Disney executives were quick to point out that promoting nutrition among children is good business for a kid-oriented brand, and then–first lady Michelle Obama praised Disney's commitment, encouraging other media companies to develop similar nutritional standards. And recent research has shown broad public support for policies that limit ads for high-sugar, high-fat foods during children's television programs (Tripicchio et al., 2016). With continuing research showing a link between food ads and obesity—a 2012 study found youth who recognize fast-food advertisements are more likely to be obese (American Academy of Pediatrics, 2012)—pressure on media to develop new advertising guidelines will likely continue to grow.

Media and Eating Disorders

Sociologists and feminist scholars have long recognized that eating disorders such as anorexia and bulimia are more than just individual troubles. Defining eating disorders as a social problem leads us to consider the cultural norms that contribute to them (Hesse-Biber et al., 2006).

Many young people, disproportionately girls, desire thinner bodies. One recent study of a nationally representative sample of 11- to 16-year-olds in the United States found that 26% of girls were currently on a diet and another 28% were not dieting but thought they should lose weight. Among adolescent boys, 18% were dieting and another 17% thought they should lose weight (Iannotti & Wang, 2013). Many young people take extreme measures to lose weight. A 10-year study that followed more than 1,700 adolescents into young adulthood found that 43.7%

of young women and 18.7% of young men reported persistent use of "unhealthy weight control behaviors" such as fasting, skipping meals, smoking cigarettes, taking diet pills, vomiting, or taking laxatives (Neumark-Sztainer et al., 2012). Those who struggle with eating disorders such as anorexia nervosa (an unwillingness to eat, accompanied by a distorted sense of being overweight) or bulimia (binge eating, often accompanied by attempts to rid the body of its effects through purging) are conforming to cultural norms that encourage thinness but following extreme—and dangerous—methods to achieve an exaggeration of the culturally preferred body type.

Media play a prominent role in promoting and circulating what sociologist Sharlene Hesse-Biber (2006) calls the **cult of thinness**, which idealizes a decidedly slim body type unachievable for the vast majority of the population. While little evidence suggests that exposure to media *causes* eating disorders, media are among the central communicators of this cultural ideal (Stice & Shaw, 1994), equating a slender body with beauty, intelligence, morality, and success.

Entertainment media—from prime-time television programs and Hollywood films to fashion magazines and music videos—routinely emphasize the virtues of the thin body, not always subtly. One review of research on images of the female body in contemporary visual media notes that the findings "can be easily summarized in two phrases: 'thin is normative and attractive' and 'fat is aberrant and repulsive'" (Levine & Harrison, 2009, p. 494).

Advertising, however, may be the most consistent promoter of the ideal of the thin body. Ads for products from clothing and automobiles to beer and vacation packages typically feature slender bodies as part of the sales pitch. Advertisements about products and services associated with dieting and weight loss, exercise and fitness, and even cosmetic surgery highlight thin bodies and promote body dissatisfaction among potential consumers. In his pioneering study of the development of the emergence of consumer culture in the early 20th century, *Captains of Consciousness,* Stuart Ewen (1977) reminds us that mass advertising encourages potential customers to be dissatisfied with their bodies as a way to build demand for new consumer products. It can be difficult to escape an ad culture that consistently bombards us with reminders that we are not as thin as the bodies on billboards, in magazines, and on television—and that we can (and should!) do something to change our bodies. This idealization is so deeply embedded in our cultural fabric that we may not even recognize the ways media images celebrate the cult of thinness.

Some user-generated media content can idealize the thin body quite aggressively. A number of so-called pro-ana or pro-mia websites support women seeking to maintain an anorexic or bulimic lifestyle (Boero &

Pasco, 2012). Blogs, social networks, and websites offer an online community where persons with anorexia and bulimia share dieting tips, fasting strategies, purging techniques, and advice on how to hide these practices from family and friends. These sites display "thinspiration" photos showing remarkably thin women as models to inspire those who deny that their eating habits are unhealthy or in need of treatment.

Media do not simply or directly cause social problems, but the relationship between media and social problems is complex and contested. Now we turn to several examples of evolving social problems associated with new forms of media.

EMERGENT SOCIAL PROBLEMS AND NEW MEDIA TECHNOLOGIES

8.4 Discuss emergent social problems associated with new media technologies.

Digital media offer many ways to interact with friends, community, and work colleagues as well as to take courses and engage in politics. Some of the ways we use new media are also producing new kinds of social problems.

Distracted Driving

Although the combination of alcohol consumption and driving has been a cause of accidents since the development of automobiles, and U.S. states started passing laws against drunk driving in 1910, drunk driving did not emerge as a widely recognized social problem until the early 1980s, thanks to advocacy by Mothers Against Drunk Driving (MADD) and others. Just as dangerous as drunk driving is **distracted driving**, operating a motor vehicle while engaged in other attention-requiring activities (Strayer, Drews, & Crouch, 2006), and the proliferation of smart phones offers increased possibilities for distracted driving. Do you send text or e-mail messages while you drive? The National Highway Traffic Safety Administration (NHTSA) says that more than 70% of drivers between the ages of 18 and 24 report sometimes doing so. You probably know this is a hazardous

....

Cult of thinness: Idealization of a decidedly slim body type that is unachievable for the vast majority of the population.

Distracted driving: The operation of a motor vehicle while engaged in other attention-requiring activities, such as texting or talking on the phone.

activity. In fact, the NHTSA (2016) reported more than 3,000 fatalities and 430,000 injuries in 2014 from distraction-affected crashes "when drivers divert their attention from the driving task to focus on some other activity," and texting is among the most common ways drivers are distracted.

Individuals recognize the dangers of distracted driving. The Pew Research Center found that 44% of adults and 40% of teens report having been in a car when a driver used a cell phone in a dangerous way (Madden & Rainie, 2010). With mounting evidence of its toll, the U.S. Department of Transportation has been among the primary advocates seeking to frame distracted driving as a social problem. Former U.S. secretary of transportation Ray LaHood has called distracted driving "an epidemic of America's roadways," and the Department

of Transportation has launched an information website devoted to the problem (http://www.distraction.gov).

Thanks, in part, to government efforts to define it as a serious social problem, distracted driving is becoming an issue of public concern. Many high school health classes and driver education programs now emphasize its dangers; 46 states and Washington, D.C., have passed laws specifically outlawing texting while driving (see Figure 8.3); and the news media are full of stories about distracted driving.

ASK YOURSELF: Is distracted driving recognized as a serious problem among your network of friends? Why or why not? How do attitudes about distracted driving compare with attitudes about drunk driving?

FIGURE 8.3 State Texting-While-Driving Laws, 2017

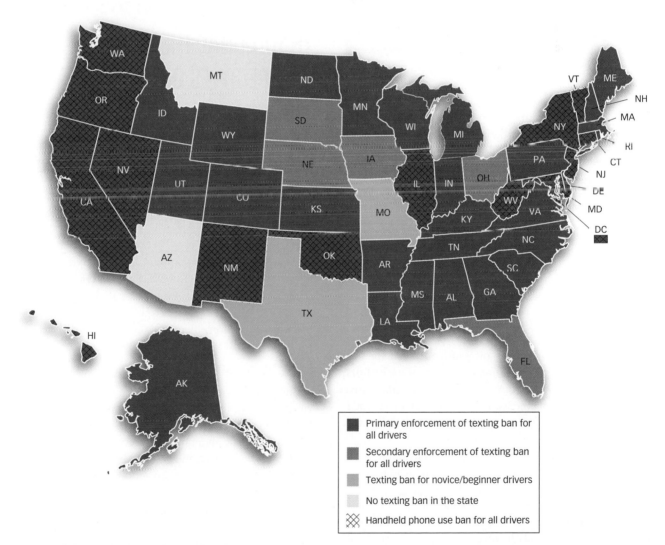

- ■ Primary enforcement of texting ban for all drivers
- Secondary enforcement of texting ban for all drivers
- Texting ban for novice/beginner drivers
- No texting ban in the state
- ⊠ Handheld phone use ban for all drivers

SOURCE: Governor's Highway Safety Association, 2017, Distracted Driving Laws by State. January.

NOTE: Under secondary laws, an officer must have some other reason to stop a vehicle before citing a driver for using a cell phone. Laws without this restriction are called primary.

Cyberbullying

Several high-profile cases of repeated harassment through text messages and on social networking sites, including incidents in Missouri and Massachusetts that involved teenage suicides, helped make **cyberbullying**, or electronic forms of bullying, an issue of national concern. Definitions of what constitutes cyberbullying are still evolving, as are the legal issues associated with mediated and sometimes anonymous harassment and appropriate sanctions, if any. Cyberbullying usually follows a pattern of repetitive actions, such as sending hostile or insulting text messages, posting inappropriate photos to embarrass someone, and rumormongering and harassment on social networks. Two leading scholars of cyberbullying offer the following definition: "willful and repeated harm inflicted through the use of computers, cell phones, and other electronic devices" (Hinduja & Patchin, 2009, p. 5).

The primary victims and perpetrators are teenagers. Research suggests cyberbullying "is a prevalent problem, similar to school bullying," experienced by up to one-quarter of students (Wade & Beran, 2011, p. 45). Educators, parents, and others who work with young people have succeeded in identifying cyberbullying as an issue of public concern, and the media have helped focus public attention on the problem. The federal government includes information about reporting and preventing cyberbullying on its StopBullying. gov website, and the U.S. Centers for Disease Control and Prevention distributes information about how to protect youth from electronic aggression. Any sustained public discussion of cyberbullying will need to recognize how it is similar to traditional forms of bullying, as well as how new media technologies amplify the visibility of bullying. As social media scholar danah boyd notes, "Social media has not radically altered the dynamics of bullying, but it has made these dynamics more visible to more people" (2014, p. 152).

The Digital Divide

Evolving media technologies offer the potential for new forms of civic engagement, more flexible work schedules, new patterns of global communication, even innovative solutions to social problems. High hopes for these possibilities, however, are tempered by the fact that all forms of media are not equally accessible to all individuals, nationally or globally. The consumption of media requires money, and the richer nations that own and produce most global media also disproportionately consume media.

In the United States, educational attainment is a major determinant of the **digital divide**. In 2015, about 94% of U.S. households headed by a person with a college degree had high-speed Internet access at home (see Table 8.4). In contrast, a much smaller proportion, only 64%, of households headed by a person who had not completed high school had the same access (U.S. Census Bureau, American Community Survey, 2016). Inequality in Internet access intersects with other social issues. For example, the Internet offers new possibilities for communication between health care providers and their patients. However, one study of community health center patients in a low-income urban neighborhood found that a large percentage did not regularly access the Internet from home. The researchers note that these "findings overall support the ongoing concerns about a 'digital divide' and should make clinicians in this clinic cautious about referring patients to the internet for health information" (Denizard-Thompson et al., 2011, p. 458).

As more people gain access to electronic media, the influence of these media will continue to grow, playing an increasingly powerful role in social life. However, persistent economic inequality will continue to create socially significant inequities in media access and use.

TRADITIONAL THEORETICAL PERSPECTIVES ON MEDIA AND SOCIAL PROBLEMS

8.5 Explain how the functionalist, conflict, and symbolic interactionist perspectives conceptualize the media–social problems relationship.

The three traditional sociological perspectives—functionalism, conflict theory, and symbolic interactionism—are significant for the kinds of questions they direct us to consider. Let's look at how each applies to the intersection of media and social problems.

Functionalism

A functionalist approach suggests that media play the vital role of calling attention to pressing social problems, functioning as a kind of alarm system that can warn and inform the public about new and persistent social problems. From this perspective, media are a vital cultural resource, an arena for both official distribution of information about

....

Cyberbullying: Electronic forms of bullying.

Digital divide: The gap in access to information and communication technologies between more advantaged and less advantaged groups, such as between the wealthy and poor regions of the world (the global digital divide) and between social classes within a country.

TABLE 8.4 Home Internet Connections for U.S. Households, 2016 (in percentages)

	Computer in Household	Home Internet Connection	Home Broadband Subscription
Total U.S. Population in Households	93.1	92.5	85.2
Householder Education			
Less than high school graduate	77.5	87.0	64.0
High school graduate, some college	90.8	91.9	82.2
Bachelor's degree or higher	97.8	96.4	93.9
Householder Race and Ethnicity			
White	93.3	93.3	86.3
African American	89.3	88.3	77.4
Hispanic/Latino	92.5	88.8	81.1
Asian American	97.1	95.7	92.6
Employment Status			
Employed	96.3	93.5	89.5
Unemployed	93.3	90.2	83.2
Not in labor force	85.1	91.3	75.8
Householder Age			
Under 18	96.6	92.3	88.6
18–64 years	95.0	92.6	87.4
65 years and older	79.8	92.3	71.1

SOURCE: U.S. Census Bureau. 2015. 2015 American Community Survey.

problems and public deliberation about potential solutions. For example, media have played a vital role in calling attention to problems associated with smoking, and public health officials define a robust antismoking advertising campaign as a powerful form of public education (Centers for Disease Control and Prevention, 2013a). At the same time, the functionalist approach asks whether the media industry's dynamics make the alarm system dysfunctional, calling selective attention to social problems in a way that undermines a working public information system. We might consider, for example, how the media system operates when companies that are heavy polluters are also major sources of advertising dollars for national news outlets.

ASK YOURSELF: With so much media content circulating in the digital age, do you think televised ad campaigns can effectively sound the alarm about troubling issues? Do you think graphic antismoking commercials are effective at curbing youth smoking, for example? Why or why not?

Policy Implications of Functionalism

From a functionalist perspective, public policy should promote a media system that broadly distributes information and ideas about a wide range of social issues and promotes free expression and vigorous public debate. Public policy that protects press freedom, including in digital media and often referencing the First Amendment, is consistent with this approach. Efforts to restrict online speech—such as the Communications Decency Act of 1996 and the Child Online Protection Act of 1998, two failed efforts to restrict expression on the Internet—are likely to weaken the media system's ability to operate effectively in the collective process of defining social problems.

Conflict Theory

A conflict theory approach identifies media as a contested arena, where powerful actors seek to promote their definitions of social problems. In thinking about media and power, conflict theorists ask us to consider who owns and

The Global Digital Divide

According to the International Telecommunications Union (ITU, 2016), approximately 47% of the world's population was online in 2016. However, citizens of the developed world (81%) are twice as likely as people in the developing world (40%) to be online. In Europe, 79% of the population has Internet access, while 65% of people in the Americas are online. In contrast, the Internet is available to just 42% in Asia and the Pacific and only 25% in Africa.

While many Northern Americans and Europeans can access news and information from around the globe, network with like-minded people near and far, and explore online virtual worlds, most people in the so-called global South have little or no access to basic Internet service. Instead, they live in a world where even regularly delivered electricity can be a scarce commodity. Recognizing the significance of the global digital divide, two agencies of the United Nations, the ITU and UNESCO (United Nations Educational, Scientific and Cultural Organization), established the Broadband Commission for Digital Development to try to expand global Internet access. In 2014, the ITU adopted a resolution establishing a series of global telecommunication and information technology goals and targets aimed at the year 2020 (International Telecommunications Union, 2017). The *Connect 2020* agenda highlights four key goals:

1. "Growth—Enable and foster access to and increased use of telecommunications/ ICTs." Targets include increasing worldwide Internet access to 55 percent of households and making telecommunications 40 percent more affordable by 2020.

2. "Inclusiveness— Bridge the digital divide and provide broadband for all." Targets include 50 percent of households in the developing world and 15 percent of households in least developed countries with Internet access, 90 percent of the worldwide rural population covered by broadband service, and gender equity among Internet users reached by 2020.

3. "Sustainability—Manage challenges resulting from telecommunication/ ICT development." Targets include reducing e-waste by 50 percent and decrease telecommunications industry-generated greenhouse gases by 30 percent by 2020.

4. "Innovation and partnership— Lead, improve and adapt to the changing telecommunication/ ICT environment." Targets include building effective partnerships among global stakeholders and continuing to enhance innovation in the telecommunications sector.

REUTERS/Paulo Whitaker

▶ Brazilian indigenous people use computers inside a tent in Cuiaba, Brazil. Who does and does not have access to computers is an important question for media sociologists. In countries such as China and Myanmar (formerly Burma) in the Far East and Iran and Saudi Arabia in the Middle East, censorship of the Internet is pervasive. Should governments limit their citizens' access to the Internet? Should there be any censorship at all?

The rapid development of various mobile communications technologies may offer new ways of challenging digital inequality. Even so, achieving results will require a consistent commitment from national governments, international organizations, and the telecommunications industry, beginning with defining the global digital divide as a social problem.

▶ **THINK ABOUT IT**

1. What do you think are the social and economic consequences of the global digital divide?

2. How, if at all, do you think new forms of mobile communications technology will help reduce the global digital divide?

---

controls media, and how ownership patterns shape media portrayals of social problems. We should also consider how powerful actors seek to influence media representations of social issues, promoting coverage of some and downplaying others. In addition, conflict theory highlights the relationships among media, social problems, and inequality, asking how media can either reinforce or challenge social problems rooted in social and economic inequality.

For example, news and entertainment media offer a steady diet of dramatic stories about crime and the police, but a conflict perspective suggests that media's general inattention to the causes, consequences, and racial dynamics of mass incarceration in the United States actually reinforces social inequality. In short, from a conflict theory perspective, media are significant precisely because they are a valuable resource for dominant groups that seek to exercise power over both what we recognize as social problems and what solutions are considered legitimate for subordinate groups that oppose or resist such definitions.

Policy Implications of Conflict Theory

With its emphasis on questions of ownership and control, a conflict theory approach suggests that media policy can effectively limit powerful actors' capacity to influence media representations of social issues. Federal regulations that prevent companies from owning both television stations and daily newspapers in the same markets, for example, are part of a larger policy agenda to promote diverse ownership and stop the trend toward media consolidation. Policies governing the operation of the Internet—including "net neutrality," the principle that Internet service providers cannot discriminate among or charge users differently for different kinds of online applications and content—spark substantial debate about media power.

Symbolic Interactionism

A symbolic interactionist approach to media and social problems says social problems emerge from "a process of collective definition" (Blumer, 1971) in the news and entertainment media. Symbolic interactionist theories are generally associated with the micro-level dimensions of social life. Through interaction, in other words, individuals create a shared understanding of reality, including definitions of what constitute legitimate social problems as well as reasonable potential responses. Interactionist approaches can offer insight into how media workers—including journalists, editors, bloggers, filmmakers, and television producers—define social problems within their professional communities.

Symbolic interactionists consider, for example, how reporters learn about, discuss, and ultimately identify concussions among young athletes as a serious problem worthy of ongoing, in-depth news coverage. They also look at the way people interact with and interpret media representations of social problems, as well as how media inform public discussion about the meaning of, significance of, and potential responses to long-standing and new social problems.

Policy Implications of Symbolic Interactionism

A symbolic interactionist approach has little to say about the content of specific media; instead, it looks at the policy-making process and the way policy makers collectively define media goals and possibilities. How, for example, do federal regulators interact with members of the public, with representatives of the media industry, and with media

An employee walks past signage inside Comcast Corp. headquarters in Philadelphia, Pennsylvania. Comcast is the largest broadcasting and cable television company in the world. It operates NBC, Telemundo, MSNBC, CNBC, USA Network, NBCSN, E!, The Weather Channel, and Universal Pictures. Do you see such consolidation in the media industry as good or bad?

Charles Mostoller/Bloomberg/Getty Images

policy experts as they develop, implement, and evaluate media policies? This perspective also suggests that we should pay attention to the ways policy advocates identify media-related social problems and frame social problems to mobilize constituents and pressure policy makers.

THEORIES IN CONTEMPORARY MEDIA AND SOCIAL PROBLEMS SCHOLARSHIP

8.6 Explain how contemporary theories conceptualize the media–social problems relationship.

While traditional theoretical perspectives offer a broad foundation for the study of social problems, the more specialized constructionist, public arenas, and agenda-setting theories help us understand the role of media in the processes of defining, disseminating, and responding to social problems.

Constructionist Approach

The most fully developed theory of social problems is the **constructionist approach** (Kitsuse & Spector, 2000;

....

Constructionist approach: An approach to social problems theory that highlights the process whereby troubling social issues become recognized as social problems.

Chapter 8: Media **201**

Loseke & Best, 2003; Schneider, 1985), which highlights the process by which troubling social issues become recognized as social problems. Constructionists acknowledge a vast pool of candidate issues, only some of which gain the status of legitimate social problem. Objective measures of the prevalence, severity, or danger of a social issue are not the principal determinants of a social problem's status in the constructionist view, although advocates may invoke them. Instead, constructionists ask *how* issues become problems, and they see media as a central part of the process.

Public Arenas Model

One theoretical approach to explaining how public attention is turned toward some social problems and away from others is Hilgartner and Bosk's (1988) **public arenas model**, which offers a framework for analyzing the rise and fall in public attention to different social problems. This model assumes that public attention is limited—not all potential social problems can be the focus of public attention—and highlights media as a primary arena in which "social problems are framed and grow" (p. 58). It identifies several key factors that influence the extent of media attention to social problems, including the "carrying capacity" of media outlets (space in newspapers, time on television, budgets for reporters); the "principles of selection" that guide decisions about media attention to social problems (including drama, novelty, powerful sponsors, and shared understandings of importance); and the patterns of feedback among media and other public arenas, such as Congress and the presidency, the courts, activist groups, religious organizations, research communities, and foundations. The public arenas model helps us to think about how, for example, the emergence of a new social problem such as an increase in the numbers of home foreclosures can squeeze other troubling issues, such as the employment and health challenges facing soldiers returning from combat deployments, out of the media spotlight and off the public agenda.

Sociologist Ray Maratea (2008) has extended the public arenas model to include the blogosphere as a venue for directing public attention to social problems, explaining how blogs, with their near-constant updating and unlimited space, run at a faster pace than traditional media and offer a larger carrying capacity than newspapers or television. Maratea recognizes that bloggers have not supplanted the traditional news media, noting, "While the Internet may indeed provide an expanded capacity to carry problem claims, bloggers must still rely on mainstream news outlets to distribute their claims to larger audiences" (p. 156). The public arenas model offers a helpful framework for making sense of the ways various forms of online media, especially user-generated media and social media, help to focus public attention on social problems.

Agenda-Setting Theory

Media may not tell people what to think, but they can significantly influence what people think *about*. This ability to direct people's attention toward certain issues is the foundation of **agenda-setting theory**, which emphasizes the role media play in influencing public understanding of social issues and social problems (McCombs, 2004). Agenda setting results from patterns of news coverage of (or silence about) social issues and from the relative prominence news gives to various social problems. Early agenda-setting research demonstrated that media coverage of social issues influences public opinion more than does the issues' objective prominence (Funkhouser, 1973). Experimental research later confirmed that media coverage influences audience assessments of an issue's importance (Iyengar & Kinder, 2010).

Still, theorists suggest caution in making generalizations about agenda setting. One study of television news and public opinion in Germany found strong agenda-setting effects for some issues but not for others (Brosius & Kepplinger, 1990). The agenda-setting role of media may be most powerful when people have no direct experience with an issue and are therefore dependent on media for basic information. Agenda-setting theory asks us to consider the process through which some social problems—for example, increasing student debt or government surveillance—become matters of broad public concern, highlighting the role of media in that process.

> *ASK YOURSELF:* How, if at all, do you think media influence your understanding of which social problems are worthy of public attention?

Public arenas model: A model that offers a framework for analyzing the rise and fall in the amount of attention the public pays to different social problems.

Agenda-setting theory: A theory that emphasizes the important role media play in influencing public understanding of social issues and social problems.

SOCIAL CHANGE: WHAT CAN YOU DO?

 8.7 Identify steps toward media-related social change.

Activist organizations often develop media strategies aimed at influencing, and sometimes presenting alternatives to, the narratives that circulate in the major media. Such "media activism" takes a wide variety of forms, with different organizations focused on different media-related problems, offering concerned citizens a range of different ways to get involved.

▶▶ Media Reform

In the early 2010s, media reform activists began seeking to restructure the U.S. media system, advocating for policies that highlight the public interest stakes in media policy, promote openness and accessibility, and emphasize the democratic role of media. Among the leading media reform organizations is Free Press (http://www.freepress.net), a national organization that "fight[s] to save the free and open internet, curb runaway media consolidation, protect press freedom, and ensure diverse voices are represented in our media." Free Press seeks to democratize the media policy-making process; engage the public in federal media policy decisions through public education campaigns; mobilize citizens to communicate directly with elected officials; and participate in policy debates in Washington, including ongoing policy research and advocacy. Students can become members of Free Press, sign up for the organization's regular e-mail updates, attend the National Conference for Media Reform, and take action by participating in one of Free Press's timely campaigns.

▶▶ Media Literacy

In our media-saturated society, citizens face a daily barrage of images and messages. Advocates of media literacy argue that citizens need to be equipped with the skills and experiences that will enable them to engage critically with the media they consume and to learn the fundamentals of producing their own media. Some advocates work inside schools, others with community organizations in community centers, libraries, and local media arts organizations. Many efforts are locally focused, such as Healthy Youth Peer Education in Allentown, Pennsylvania, and the Spark Media Project in Poughkeepsie, New York. Several national media literacy organizations try to connect media literacy activists, forging links among them so they can build strategy and share resources, and develop curricula for school and community use. Among the most prominent of these organizations are the Center for Media Literacy (http://www.medialit.org), which works to help citizens "develop critical thinking and media production skills needed to live fully in the 21st century media culture," and the National Association for Media Literacy Education (http://namle.net), which seeks to "help individuals of all ages develop the habits of inquiry and skills of expression that they need to be critical thinkers, effective communicators and active citizens in today's world."

Media literacy groups around the United States are sponsored by schools and universities or run by community-based nonprofit organizations. You can become a media literacy activist by joining a group in your community, or by partnering with a local high school or elementary school to develop new media literacy activities. Either way, you will find valuable resources for media literacy education on the Center for Media Literacy's website, including the CML MediaLit Kit.

▶▶ Efforts to Limit Commercialism

With ads appearing almost anywhere we can imagine—from our computer screens and smart phones to inside school buses and even pieces of fruit—it is increasingly difficult to identify any commercial-free zones in contemporary society. Some media activists define the omnipresence of advertising as a growing social problem in need of a sustained response. They try to protect and promote public spaces free of constant sales pitches. Commercial Alert (http://www.commercialalert.org), for example, is a national organization dedicated to limiting the reach of commercial culture, seeking "to prevent it from exploiting children and subverting the higher values of family, community, environmental integrity and democracy." Similarly, the Campaign for Commercial

► WikiTribune is a news website that posts articles on local and global events that can be easily verified and improved. It is intended to counter the fake news and "alternative facts" that arose after the presidential election of 2016.

AP Photo/Jeff Blackler

Free Childhood (http://commercialfreechildhood .org) works to build a movement "to end the exploitive practice of marketing to children and promote a modern childhood shaped by what's best for kids, not corporate profits." Both organizations, which offer students various ways to get involved, are part of a growing movement to limit the presence of advertising in media and in public places.

WHAT DOES AMERICA THINK?

Questions About Media From the General Social Survey

► Turn to the beginning of the chapter to compare your answers to those of the total population.

1. What is your main source of information about events in the news?

   NEWSPAPERS: 7.9%

   THE INTERNET: 43.4%

   TV: 38.4%

   OTHER: 10.3%

2. What is your confidence level in the press?

   A GREAT DEAL: 8.2%

   ONLY SOME: 42.1%

   HARDLY ANY: 49.7%

3. How many hours do you watch TV each day?

0: 8.6%

1–2: 45.4%

3–4: 27.5%

5 OR MORE: 18.5%

4. What is your confidence level in television?

A GREAT DEAL: 10.2%

ONLY SOME: 47.2%

HARDLY ANY: 42.7%

SOURCE: National Opinion Research Center, University of Chicago.

5. How often do you read the newspaper?

DAILY: 21.1%

A FEW TIMES A WEEK: 14.3%

ONCE A WEEK: 12.1%

LESS THAN ONCE A WEEK: 15.9%

NEVER: 36.6%

CHAPTER SUMMARY

 8.1 Describe the relationship between media and social problems.

Media have a complex and multifaceted connection to social problems. They are embedded in the process of social problem construction, become a focus of concern as a source of social problems, and are associated with emerging social problems.

8.2 Discuss patterns and trends in media portrayals of social problems.

Media offer a prominent space where we debate and interpret the meaning and significance of incidents and trends associated with potential social problems. Journalists' professional routines and the sponsor activities of issue advocates help explain the amount of social problems coverage in the news as well as media approaches to social problems. Media sometimes contribute to moral panics by dramatizing and embellishing social issues to attract an audience.

8.3 Describe the debate about the role of media as a potential cause of social problems.

Researchers have long debated how media exposure might encourage behaviors and attitudes associated with social problems. The 1930s Payne Fund Studies found that movies were a factor in the delinquent activities of only a minority of boys and girls, with an indirect effect on crime and delinquency. While many researchers accept that there is a relationship between violent media and aggression, the specific dynamics of that relationship remain contested—and the evidence linking media violence to violent behavior is weak. Media are not the primary cause of youth tobacco use, but by associating cigarettes with adventure, sexuality, and adult lifestyles, media help to sustain a set of cultural meanings that define smoking in terms that are attractive to some youth. Media play a prominent role in idealizing a slim body type that is unachievable for the vast majority of the population. Little evidence suggests that exposure to media causes eating disorders, but media help to communicate this powerful cultural ideal. Media do not simply or directly cause social problems; the relationship between media and social problems is complex and contested.

 8.4 Discuss emergent social problems associated with new media technologies.

Digital media offer us many ways to interact, and some of the ways we use new media are producing new kinds of social problems. Distracted driving, cyberbullying, and the digital divide are emerging as widely recognized social problems, generating both broad public discussion and new government policies.

8.5 Explain how the functionalist, conflict, and symbolic interactionist perspectives conceptualize the media–social problems relationship.

The three traditional sociological perspectives direct us to consider different kinds of questions about media and social problems. A functionalist approach defines media as a kind of alarm system that can warn the public about new and persistent social problems. A conflict theory approach identifies media as a contested arena, where powerful actors seek to promote their definitions of social problems. A symbolic interactionist approach to media and social problems points to the ways people create a shared understanding of reality, including definitions of what constitute legitimate social problems as well as reasonable responses.

8.6 Explain how contemporary theories conceptualize the media–social problems relationship.

Contemporary theories help us understand the role of media in the processes of defining, disseminating, and responding to social problems. The constructionist approach asks how some troubling issues become defined as social problems and sees media as a central part of the process. The public arenas model helps explain the rise and fall in public attention paid to different social problems, highlighting several key factors that influence the extent of media attention to social problems. Agenda-setting theory emphasizes how media influence public understanding of social problems, highlighting patterns of news coverage of social issues and the relative prominence news gives to various social problems.

8.7 Identify steps toward media-related social change.

Media activism takes a variety of forms, with different organizations focused on different media-related problems, offering concerned citizens a range of different ways to get involved. Media reform activists seek to restructure the U.S. media system, advocating for policies that highlight the public interest stakes in media policy, promote openness and accessibility, and emphasize the democratic role of media. Media literacy advocates work to equip citizens with the skills and experiences they need to engage critically with the media they consume and to learn the fundamentals of producing their own media. Media activists concerned about the omnipresence of advertising try to protect and promote public spaces that are free of advertisements.

KEY TERMS

agenda-setting theory 202

claims making 183

constructionist approach 201

cult of thinness 196

culturally resonant themes 186

cyberbullying 198

digital divide 198

distracted driving 196

journalists' professional routines 184

media exaggeration 187

media frames 185

media phobias 190

moral entrepreneurs 183

moral panics 187

product placement 194

public arenas model 202

self-regulation 191

sponsor activities 185

user-generated media content 188

9 FAMILY

Meg Wilkes Karraker

Vyacheslav Prokofyev/TASS/Getty Images

Mikhail Alyoshin, a single father, and his daughters Anastasia and Darya in their apartment near Moscow, Russia. What do you envision as the typical family?

Investigating Family: My Story

Meg Wilkes Karraker

I often tell students about my father, Herbert Wilkes, born in a rural area in the South still known for staggering poverty and associated social problems. Abandoned by his father, Herbert dropped out of high school. Although he was one of the smartest and hardest-working people I have ever known, I hate to think how different his life, and likely my own, would have been had history not been in his favor. A decorated veteran of three wars (World War II, the Korean War, the Vietnam War), he drew the attention of a commanding officer who shepherded him on to Officer Candidate School.

My father also had the good fortune to fall in love with Mary, a home economics teacher whose family had also struggled to make a living for six children on a south Georgia farm. My mother helped my father "polish" his presentation of self to fit him for further opportunities. In exchange, she saw the world, making loving homes for my sister and me as we moved around the United States and Europe every 3 years.

When my father retired from the army as a lieutenant colonel, he had completed his graduate equivalency degree. Within a year he had a B.A. in sociology from the University of Nebraska at Omaha and then worked with the South Carolina Department of Corrections until his second retirement. My mother returned to teaching and completed her own master's degree.

During their half century of marriage, Herbert and Mary exemplified the role not only of biography but also of social structure in shaping individual opportunity. They have long inspired me in my own sociological quest to understand families and society.

LEARNING OBJECTIVES

9.1 Define the concept of family.

9.2 Discuss patterns and trends in marriage, cohabitation, and divorce.

9.3 Describe family problems related to economics, religion, and government.

9.4 Apply the functionalist, conflict, and symbolic interactionist perspectives to the concept of family.

9.5 Apply specialized theories to the family.

9.6 Identify steps toward social change to address family problems.

WHAT DO YOU THINK?
Questions About Family From the General Social Survey

1. Children are a financial burden on parents.
   - ☐ AGREE
   - ☐ DISAGREE
   - ☐ NEITHER AGREE NOR DISAGREE

2. A same-sex female couple can raise a child as well as a male-female couple.
   - ☐ AGREE
   - ☐ DISAGREE
   - ☐ NEITHER AGREE NOR DISAGREE

3. Having children increases social standing in society.
   - ☐ AGREE
   - ☐ DISAGREE
   - ☐ NEITHER AGREE NOR DISAGREE

4. A same-sex male couple can raise a child as well as a male-female couple.
   - ☐ AGREE
   - ☐ DISAGREE
   - ☐ NEITHER AGREE NOR DISAGREE

5. Single parents can raise kids as well as parents.
   - ☐ AGREE
   - ☐ DISAGREE
   - ☐ NEITHER AGREE NOR DISAGREE

6. Divorce is the best solution to marital problems.
   - ☐ AGREE
   - ☐ DISAGREE
   - ☐ NEITHER AGREE NOR DISAGREE

 Turn to the end of the chapter to view the results for the total population.

SOURCE: National Opinion Research Center, University of Chicago.

A RETREAT FROM MARRIAGE AND FAMILY

9.1 Define the concept of family.

Like so many women in her deteriorating South Philadelphia neighborhood, Deena met her son's father when she was only 15 and he was 20. Three years later, Deena was living with Kevin, they were engaged to be married, and she was happily pregnant. But soon Kevin began staying out late, drinking, and cheating on her. After giving birth prematurely, Deena left Kevin and moved in with her grandmother, disenchanted about what a family should be. Today, she has a new boyfriend, Patrick, with whom she is expecting her second child. Deena and Patrick have been together 2 years and both are recently drug-free, but they still live in the old neighborhood, where the temptation to return to their old way of life hangs like a shadow over their present (Edin & Kefalas, 2005).

What led Deena and Kevin to have a baby without marrying? Why has Deena been in relationships with men who say they want to have a baby with her but who do not appear to be good potential husbands? Could Deena and Patrick set up their own household instead of living with relatives? What keeps couples such as Deena and Patrick from remaining faithful to one another? Why do their lives appear to be in such disarray? Do Deena, Kevin, Patrick, and their families serve as evidence that "American society is coming apart at the seams" (Edin & Kefalas, 2005, p. 6), especially when it comes to families?

At first glance, Deena, who is struggling to make "promises [she] can keep" around childbearing (if not marriage), exemplifies many of the social problems facing families across U.S. society today. She has not married her children's fathers. Some would say she is too young to be having children. She became a mother before she could acquire the education and employment that would increase her chances of attaining socioeconomic stability. Some may question how parents like Deena can rear the next generation. How will they and their children contribute to the economy and other basic institutions in U.S. society? As we shall see in this chapter, it is not only the economically disadvantaged who are in what some call a retreat from marriage and family.

Based on their research with 162 low-income single mothers in economically strapped neighborhoods in central Philadelphia and Camden, New Jersey, Kathryn Edin and Maria Kefalas (2005) conclude that we are not witnessing a rejection of the *ideal* of marriage and the American dream of family. On the contrary, the women Edin and Kefalas studied (and Edin lived among) hold extremely high expectations for marriage. In fact, they would rather forgo a risky marriage that might fail and instead hold out for a "good marriage," one characterized by sexual fidelity, happiness, and a "long list of middle-class accoutrements, like a house, a lawn, a car, a couch, a TV, and a 'nice' wedding" (pp. 108–109). When Edin and Kefalas asked Deena and Patrick (the couple in the story at the beginning of this chapter) about marriage, Patrick said, "I like to do things right though, instead of cutting corners, and doing everything half-assed. I'd rather get engaged for two years, save money, get a house, make sure . . . the baby's got a bedroom, [than get married now]" (p. 106). Deena added, "And I get a yard with grass. [And] I want a nice wedding" (p. 107).

We have ample evidence that economic hardship makes family formation and marital stability difficult. Katherine S. Newman and Victor Tan Chen (2007) have studied the "near poor" in the United States, the 50 million who earn between $20,000 and $40,000 per year and live just above poverty yet well below the middle class. Newman and Chen's research on this relatively invisible "missing class" confirms that it is not just the abjectly poor who have difficulty forming stable relationships. Among the missing class, grueling hours at low-wage jobs take a severe toll on the formation and maintenance of long-term bonds like marriage. Women cannot afford to look upon potential partners only in terms of romance, because they have bills to pay and children to feed. In other words, "money is the constant calculus underlying decisions to join and separate incomes, merge and split households" (p. 151).

What about those who are not among the poor or the near poor? Do middle-class and better-off U.S. adults retain faith in marriage and the kind of traditional family marriage creates? Or, as some have suggested, is the family in decline across all segments of U.S. society? As we will see, people across social classes are marrying less and living in arrangements that are anything but traditional.

The Decline of the Family?

Just how extensive are these shifts in the demography of families? And do they indicate a growing disenchantment with the social institution of family? The debate over what some call the decline of the family has been raging for decades, part of the broader **culture wars** over the future direction of U.S. society as a whole. Initially, the debate focused on certain types of families, especially those living in poverty and those of particular races or ethnicities. But the second half of the 20th century also brought some striking changes in the picture of all U.S. families. The number of divorces shot up, as did the number of children born to unmarried partners. Consequently, the number of families headed by divorced or never-married women rose dramatically. Likewise, the 1960s saw the arrival of a generation that sometimes favored **cohabitation**—that is, living in an intimate relationship outside marriage.

▶ Magazines and tabloids keep track of celebrities' on-again, off-again romantic relationships. Why do you suppose readers are interested in such scandalous gossip?

Taking one position in the culture wars are advocates of the **marriage movement**, who warn against the sexual revolution, teenage pregnancy, and same-sex marriage while advocating traditional marriage. Alarmed at what he saw as the collapse of the traditional family, in 1977 child psychologist James Dobson founded Focus on the Family, a Christian ministry whose mission is "nurturing and defending the God-ordained institution of the family and promoting biblical truths worldwide" (Focus on the Family, 2016). Some other social scientists followed suit. In a series of provocative books and articles, sociologist David Popenoe (1988, 1993, 1996, 2004, 2009), founder and codirector of the National Marriage Project, has argued that the modern family is failing in its primary social functions: sexual regulation, procreation, and socialization of children in a stable, economically productive, and emotionally supportive unit formed by the lifelong union of a man and a woman.

Family battles in the culture wars are accompanied by heated arguments around what some call "family values," often framed in terms of hot-button issues such as abortion. Yet, as we shall see later in the discussion of government policy in support of families, for all the rhetoric

around family values, when it comes to a comprehensive family policy, the United States does not appear to *value families* as much as do many other developed countries (Karraker & Grochowski, 2012).

Other writers, such as sociologist Judith Stacey (2011), professor emerita of gender and sexuality studies and social and cultural analysis at New York University, see a much more complicated story than the culture wars would suggest. Stacey argues that "adaptation" describes the changing family better than "decline." Part of the debate centers on exactly how we define family, and how we understand the processes that help change family structures.

Defining the Family

Part of the answer to the question "Is the family in trouble?" depends on how we define family. The U.S. Census Bureau defines **family** as two or more people who are related

Culture wars: Disputes over the state of American society, including the presumed decline of the family as well as "family values."

Cohabitation: Unrelated, unmarried adults in an intimate relationship sharing living quarters.

Marriage movement: Social movement that advocates traditional marriage and warns against the sexual revolution, teenage pregnancy, and same-sex marriage.

Family: (1) Two or more people related by birth, marriage, or adoption who share living quarters (U.S. Census Bureau definition), or (2) members of a social group who are in an intimate, long-term, committed relationship and who share mutual expectations of rights and responsibilities.

Experiencing Family

Feminism and Intersectionality

Feminist sociologists are among action-oriented social scientists seeking a more just world, not only around gender equity issues but also around intersections of gender with race and ethnicity, social class, sexual orientation, immigration status, (dis)ability, age, veteran status, and other social locations.

In her pioneering work *Black Feminist Thought: Knowledge, Consciousness, and the Politics of Empowerment,* Patricia Hill Collins (1990) argues that systems of oppression are bound up with the linkages among race, social class, and gender. In this chapter, we see how race and ethnicity affect the likelihood that a woman will marry or that children will grow up in a two-parent family. We also see how, although cohabitation is more common among those with lower levels of education, those with college educations (a correlate of social class) fare better economically when they do cohabit. Still other research finds that social class

and gender determine the ability to control one's time at home and at work, aggravating inequalities between people with more or less economic privilege and between men and women (Clawson & Gerstel, 2014).Other studies examine the challenges gay men face in being fathers in a heterosexist society (Berkowitz, 2011).

An intersectional approach, particularly one from a **feminist perspective**, is vital to understanding how patriarchy and sexism privilege or oppress certain social categories of women and men, relationships, and families.

▶ **THINK ABOUT IT:** Identify a pressing social problem for families and ask yourself: Can we address this problem without taking into account intersections between gender and at least one other social status? How does intersectionality inform efforts to make a more just society for families?

▶ Patricia Hill Collins is Distinguished University Professor of Sociology at the University of Maryland, College Park, and Charles Phelps Taft Distinguished Emeritus Professor of Sociology at the University of Cincinnati. She has served as president of the American Sociological Association. In her book *Black Feminist Thought* she uses the concept of intersectionality to examine how race, class, gender, and sexuality are interconnected in experiences of oppression. For example, black women have the double burden of both racial and gender discrimination.

---

to each other by birth, marriage, or adoption and who share living quarters. The Census Bureau (2012a) differentiates family from **household**, which is defined as people, related or not, who share living quarters. In everyday life, the definition of family is not only highly contested but also socially constructed (Karraker & Grochowski, 2012, p. 5). In research in which unmarried mothers were asked to draw pictures of their families, they first drew mothers and fathers, parents and children, and other extended kin. However, when asked to add individuals who were important to their family life but who might not fit the usual definition of family, those women added close friends and neighbors on whom they depended, individuals who might be considered **fictive kin** (Stack, 1974). Finally, when asked to subtract individuals who did not fit their personal definitions of family, those women quickly

excluded some persons to whom they or their children were related by blood, marriage, or adoption but who were not important to their family life. Several women excluded the mothers of their children's fathers. Even if their children's fathers were important parts of their children's lives, these mothers reported that the older women often hindered the mothers' efforts to forge good relationships with their children's fathers (Karraker & Grochowski, 1998).

Feminist perspective: A theoretical approach that emphasizes the extent to which patriarchy and sexism undermine women (and men), relationships, and families.

Household: All the related and unrelated people who share living quarters.

Fictive kin: People to whom one is not related by blood, marriage, or adoption but on whom one nonetheless depends.

ASK YOURSELF: Does the U.S. Census Bureau definition of family speak to the meaning of family in the 21st century? Why or why not? (If not, offer an alternative definition.) Why is the definition of family so important?

▶ A promotional photo for *Modern Family*. The comedy series has been described as being about "one big (straight, gay, multi-cultural, traditional) happy family." The sitcom portrays our evolving ideas of family. What is your idea of family?

Bob DAmico/ABC/Getty Images

Clearly, our definition of precisely what is *family* is shifting. On September 26, 2012, about 14.5 million television viewers tuned in to watch the season premiere of the ABC situation comedy *Modern Family*, making it the ninth-most-watched show that week (Nielsen, 2012). The sitcom, which debuted in 2009, received the Emmy Award for Outstanding Comedy Series for a third year in a row in 2012. The show portrays three parts of a complex, extended family: Phil Dunphy, his wife Claire, and their three children; Claire's brother Mitchell, his partner Cameron, and their adopted daughter Lily; Claire and Mitchell's father Jay Pritchett, his much younger wife Gloria, her son Manny from a previous marriage, and a baby born to Jay and Gloria.

The classic definition of family devised by cultural anthropologist George Peter Murdock (1949) more than half a century ago—characterized by common residence and the social functions of economic cooperation, sexual regulation, and child socialization—goes only so far. Another way to envision families in the 21st century is to recognize that each of us lives not just in one family but in a series of families over a lifetime. Thus, we derive a definition of family not just from biology and law but also from experience with kin, friends, and others, as well as from lived experience through institutions including educational settings, faith communities, health care institutions, the media, and the workplace. Grochowski (1998) avoids the term *family* altogether, instead favoring "strategic living community," which she defines as all members of a social group who are in an intimate, long-term, committed relationship. We should add to that definition the idea that family members share expectations of rights and responsibilities to one another and to the family as a whole.

PATTERNS AND TRENDS

9.2 Discuss patterns and trends in marriage, cohabitation, and divorce.

Part of the debate around the social problems of families has to do with changes in the very structures the family assumes. In this section, we explore the ways patterns and trends in marriage, cohabitation, and divorce change family structures, and the effects of these changes on the well-being of children.

Marriage

However we define it, the family is undergoing substantial demographic change, and the women described by Edin and Kefalas (2005), such as Deena in this chapter's opening vignette, are not too far from the norm. U.S. society in the 21st century is facing what we can call a growing **marriage dearth**, meaning people are dramatically less likely to be living in the state of matrimony than were comparable people a half-century ago. As shown in Figure 9.1, the U.S. Census Bureau (2012a) uses four major categories for marital status: never married, married, widowed, and divorced. The Census Bureau reserves the term *married couple* for a husband and wife who share the same household but allows that, rather than being "married, spouse present," a married person might be "separated" or "married, spouse absent." Keep in mind that a person who is described as single can therefore be never married, widowed, or divorced.

Marriage dearth: The decline in the proportion of adult Americans who are married.

FIGURE 9.1 U.S. Marital Status, 1960–2014

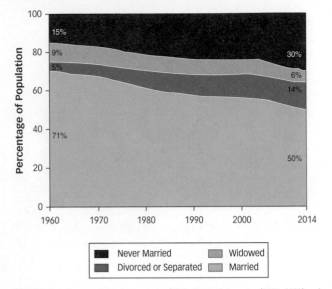

SOURCE: Pew Research Center analysis of U.S. decennial census (1960–2000) and American Community Survey data (2008, 2010–2014), IPUMS.

Just what it means to be married varies widely across societies. For data collection purposes, the United Nations (2016a) defines marriage as "the act, ceremony, or process by which the legal relationship of husband or wife is constituted." We find the highest marriage rates in the Cook Islands (34.0) and Mongolia (19.0), two of the least developed countries in the world (United Nations, 2016a). In contrast, the percentage of U.S. adults ages 25 and older who have never married doubled between 1960 and 2012, from one in 10 to one in five (Wang & Parker, 2014). Does societal development in some way "doom" marriage as we know it?

When we discuss the "retreat from marriage" (Edin & Kefalas, 2005, p. 5) in the United States, we must recognize that the choice—some would say the privilege—to marry intersects with a wide range of other social factors. For instance, as shown in Figure 9.2, younger people are dramatically less likely to be married today than were their counterparts 50 years ago, partly because the median age at marriage has never been higher. Likewise, while whites are still more likely than either blacks or Hispanics to be married, only among whites do we see a majority who are currently married, and a slim one at that. The decline in marriage for those with less than a college education is even more striking. Only among the college educated do we find a majority currently married (Wang & Parker, 2014).

Just how much of the marriage dearth is caused by extraneous "supply" factors? The **pool of eligibles**, or the supply of potential marriageable partners, is shaped by a number of factors. For example, given the **marriage gradient**,

Pool of eligibles: The quantity and quality of potential partners for marriage.

Marriage gradient: The tendency for women to "marry up"— that is, to marry older men.

FIGURE 9.2 Percentage of U.S. Adults Married in 1960 and 2010

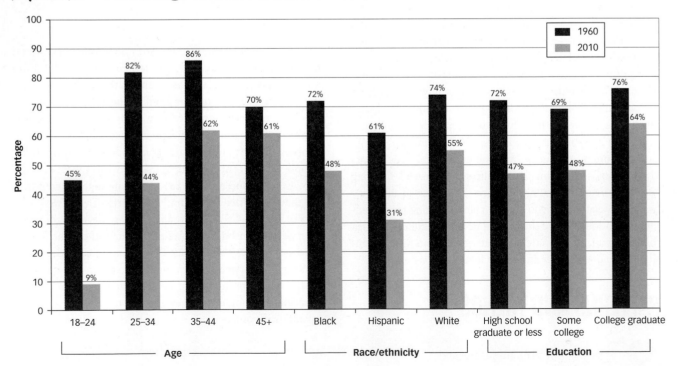

SOURCE: Cohn, D'Vera, Jeffrey S. Passell, Wendy Wang, and Gretchen Livingston. Barely Half of U.S. *Adults Are Married – A Record Low*. December 4, 2011. Washington, DC: Pew Research Center. Reprinted with permission.

or the tendency for women to marry men who are slightly older, the older a woman is, the less likely she is to find a potential husband. Black women in particular face a severely imbalanced sex ratio (Lichter et al., 1992; South & Lloyd, 1992). First, this **marriage squeeze** for black women is affected by the number of potential marriage partners. Death—including unarmed men shot by police (and who have mobilized the Black Lives Matter movement), imprisonment, and military enlistment rates effectively reduce the number of black men available as potential husbands. Second, higher rates of unemployment among black men reduce their perceived suitability as mates, as almost eight out of 10 unmarried American women want a spouse with a steady job (Wang & Parker, 2014). Furthermore, black men are more likely than black women to marry someone of another race (Crowder & Tolnay, 2000). As a result, at 90 men to every 100 women, the gender ratio is more imbalanced for blacks than for any other racial or ethnic group in the United States (Spraggins, 2005).

When we take all these factors into account, the race of the householder makes a great difference in the household type. As shown in Table 9.1, whites are much more likely to live in husband-wife households than are blacks. However, and in spite of their having lower median family income, Hispanic households have essentially the same percentage of husband-wife households as do whites (U.S. Census Bureau, 2012c). William Julius Wilson (1987)

found that, when faced with a pregnancy, white, black, and Hispanic women living in poverty on the South Side of Chicago were unlikely to marry the fathers of their babies unless the men were employed. Today, some social policy makers would like to see marriage higher on the list of priorities for single mothers (and the fathers of their children).

ASK YOURSELF: What reasons can you think of that a single mother living in poverty should marry the father of her child if he does not have a job?

Marriage dearth aside, many in the United States are clearly not ready to give up on marriages or on families. Among those who have never been married, 53% say they wish to do so. Only 32% say they do not wish to marry, while another 13% are not sure. While a majority (68%) of Americans believe it is important for a couple to marry if they plan to spend the rest of their lives together, only 48% agree that society is better off if people make marriage and having children a priority (Wang & Parker, 2014). Yet, as shown in Figure 9.3, a Pew Research Center study found that "public attitudes about the institution

Marriage squeeze: The severely imbalanced sex ratio experienced by black women in regard to potential marriage partners.

FIGURE 9.3 Attitudes Toward Marriage in the United States, 2010

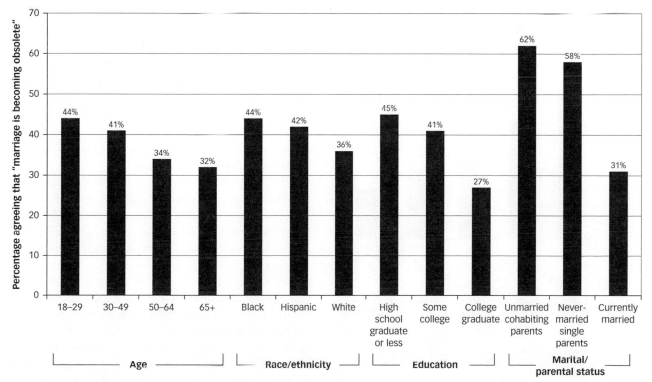

SOURCE: Cohn, D'Vera, Jeffrey S. Passell, Wendy Wang, and Gretchen Livingston. Barely Half of U.S. *Adults Are Married – A Record Low.* December 4, 2011. Washington, DC: Pew Research Center. Reprinted with permission.

of marriage are mixed" (Cohn et al., 2011, p. 2). When asked, "Is marriage becoming obsolete?" in 2011, almost four of 10 U.S. adults answered yes, compared to almost three of 10 in 1978 (a year when the divorce rate was at an all-time high). The percentages of affirmative responses to that statement are lowest among older white adults, those with a college degree, and the currently married.

The economic benefits of marriage are considerable. The continuously married are better off financially than those who are cohabiting, divorced and not remarried, or never married. The reasons for these differences include economies of scale (two can live more cheaply than one), but, as the National Marriage Project (2011) notes, married couples may also save and invest more in the future and act as insurance for one another in the case of illness and job loss. Married couples also receive more employment-based benefits (such as prorated health insurance) and often more help from two sets of extended families and friends. Married people, especially husbands, enjoy better health and live longer than the unmarried (Drefahl, 2012).

Finally, in terms of median income, married-couple households are far better off than either female-headed households or even male-headed households. And the families that fare best of all in economic terms? As shown in Figure 9.4, married-couple households in which the wife is employed.

However, the positive effects of marriage may not be as great as they might seem, at least when compared to the effects of stable cohabiting relationships. Researchers have found that marriage and cohabitation have similar effects

TABLE 9.1 Husband-Wife Households by Race and Ethnicity, 2010

Race/Ethnicity of Household	Percentage
White	51.2
Non-Hispanic white	51.1
Black	28.5
Native American and Alaskan Native	40.1
Asian	59.7
Native Hawaiian and Pacific Islander	51.3
Some other race	49.6
Two or more races	41.0
Hispanic or Latino of any race	50.1
All racial and ethnic groups combined	48.4

SOURCE: U.S. Census Bureau, 2012b. "Households and Families: 2010." *2010 Census Briefs.* Issued April 2012.

on psychological well-being, health, and social ties. Any differences tend to be small and to grow smaller the longer couples are together, whether they are married or not. What matters may not be the form of a partnership—whether the couple are married or not—but rather the duration and stability of the relationship (Musick & Bumpass, 2012). This leads us to consider the dramatic rise in unmarried partnerships.

Cohabitation

As the proportion of adults who are married falls toward less than half (perhaps as soon as when this book goes to print), the prevalence of single-person households (those formed by never-married as well as divorced and widowed individuals) will very likely increase. Already, just as the number of people choosing not to marry has risen, the rate of cohabitation has increased.

The U.S. Census Bureau has been collecting data on unmarried-couple households for several decades. Today, a census survey respondent can identify her- or himself as an unmarried partner in one of three ways: (1) as an unmarried partner of the householder and of the opposite sex, (2) as an unmarried partner of the householder and of the same sex, or (3) as a spouse of the householder and of the same sex (U.S. Census Bureau, 2010). The number of unmarried-partner households has increased dramatically over the past half-century, more than doubling in the past 20 years alone (U.S. Census Bureau, 2010). Today, a majority of adults report having cohabited at some point in their lives (Frey & Cohn, 2011).

FIGURE 9.4 U.S. Median Income by Family Type, 2009

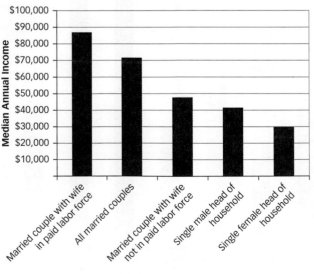

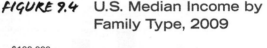

SOURCE: U.S. Census Bureau, 2012f. Statistical Abstract of the United States: 2012. Table 699. "Median Income of Families by Type of Family in Current and Constant (2009) Dollars, 1990 to 2009."

NOTE: Calculations exclude California, Georgia, Hawaii, Indiana, Louisiana, and Minnesota, which did not report data for some of the periods.

Unmarried partners are more likely to be young, have lower levels of education and income, and be less religious than those who do not cohabit. They are also more likely to have been divorced or to have parents who were divorced, to have lived without a father in the home, or to have lived in families with high levels of marital conflict when growing up (National Marriage Project, 2011).

Today, more than six of 10 first marriages begin with the couple living together; 50 years ago, almost none did (Kennedy & Bumpass, 2008). Does living together give a couple a chance to check out their compatibility, and thus perhaps avoid a future divorce? Any such effects related to cohabitation—and they are inconclusive—are less likely the result of the cohabitation and more likely the result of a **selection effect**. In other words, individuals who choose to cohabit may have some attitudes and characteristics that predispose them to marital instability. Research indicates that when couples enter into cohabitation after they have become engaged or have definite plans to marry, premarital cohabitation does not appear to be associated with the probability of later divorce. In fact, women (but not men) who cohabit after they have become engaged or have definite plans to marry may even have a lower probability of divorce than those who do not cohabit (Manning & Cohen, 2012). On the other hand, couples who cohabit prior to becoming engaged may be more likely to have marital problems and to be less happy in their marriages (Rhoades, Stanley, & Markman, 2009). Indeed, research points to age at marriage, not premarital cohabitation, as the better predictor of divorce (Kupperbert, 2014).

What about the socioeconomics of cohabitation? Although cohabitation is more common among those with lower levels of education, among cohabitors with college degrees, median household income in 2009 was $106,400, slightly higher than the $101,160 among college-educated married adults. The mean household income of cohabitors without college degrees ($46,540) was significantly below that of married couples without degrees ($56,800) (Frey & Cohn, 2011, p. 1).

ASK YOURSELF: When asked whether cohabitation is a reasonable predictor of marital success, many college students say, "Of course! Living together is a good way to test whether a more serious commitment will last." However, as the research indicates, this is hardly the case. Why do you think these attitudes persist in the face of empirical evidence to the contrary?

Divorce

In the mid-20th century, the clamor over the state of the family centered on rising rates of divorce. Since then, the percentage of U.S. adults who have been married at least once has dropped, from 85% in 1960 to 72% in 2010. Moreover, those who do marry are less likely to stay married. In the past 50 years, the proportion of American adults who are divorced or separated has almost tripled, increasing from just 5% to 14% (Cohn et al., 2011). Worldwide, as the marriage rate has been dropping, the crude divorce rate has been rising, almost doubling between 1970 and 2012, from 1.1 to 1.9 (Organisation for Economic Co-operation and Development, 2015). Compared to most other developed countries, the United States has higher rates of marriage, but it also has higher rates of divorce and remarriage and more short-term cohabiting relationships (Cherlin, 2009). In fact, the United States has the fifth-highest crude divorce rate, just behind Russia, Gibraltar, Ukraine, and Moldova.

U.S. divorce statistics were first recorded in 1867. Data collection methods were not always reliable and have varied over the years, but the best information indicates that the **crude divorce rate**, the number of divorces per 1,000 population, increased very slowly but steadily from 1867, when very few marriages ended in divorce. By 1967, 100 years later, around one-quarter of marriages ended in divorce. Figure 9.5 shows the **refined divorce rate**, the number of divorces per 1,000 married women, and a more stable indicator, as it includes only members of the population who are actually at risk of divorce (married women).

Divorce rates in those years were shaped by several factors, including the stigma attached to divorce; restrictive laws that granted divorce only when the plaintiff could prove adultery, abuse, or abandonment; and, especially, limited economic opportunities for women. The Great Depression of the 1930s dampened divorce rates somewhat, because many who might have wished to could not afford the costs of obtaining divorces and living apart. Then the divorce rate resumed its slow but steady increase until World War II, spiking as the war and its effects strained family life and increased labor force participation by women, giving women the means to leave unsatisfactory marriages. That rise was followed by a decline in divorce rates during the baby boom years of the 1950s and 1960s (Elder, 1974; Plateris, 1973).

The incidence of divorce again increased in the early 1960s to a high in the 1980s, before falling in the first decade of the 21st century. The more recent effects of

Selection effect: In contrast to the experience effect, attitudes and characteristics that predispose an individual to a relationship outcome, such as divorce.

Crude divorce rate: The number of divorces per 1,000 population.

Refined divorce rate: The number of divorces per 1,000 married women.

the Great Recession on divorce are discussed later in this chapter. Research has found some cautionary evidence for a link with this economic downturn, with divorce rates higher in areas where home foreclosure rates were high. However, given the already downward trend in divorces, we should interpret such data with caution (Cohen, 2012).

The dramatic rise in divorce rates from the 1960s to the 1980s occurred at a time of remarkable social and cultural change. Women were achieving higher levels of education and greater labor force participation, making it more economically feasible for those who wanted to leave their marriages to do so. California's Family Law Act of 1969 ushered in "no-fault" divorce, now an option for terminating a marriage in all 50 states (American Bar Association, Section on Family Law, 2012). The effect of allowing divorce based on "irreconcilable differences" or "irretrievable breakdown," rather than on the former adversarial criterion of wrongdoing by one party, is not easy to decipher. Early research suggested that divorce rates increased as states instituted no-fault divorce laws (see, for example, Nakonezny, Shull, & Rogers, 1995), but the question remains whether the increases were caused by changes in the law or simply occurred at the same time as other significant social and cultural changes.

Approximately 20% of divorces occur in the first 5 years of marriage (Centers for Disease Control and Prevention, 2012c). The National Marriage Project (2011) estimates the chance of any U.S. adult getting divorced at between 40% and 50% and identifies several risk factors in the first 10 years of marriage, as shown in Table 9.2. Note how many risk factors are related to socioeconomic factors, either directly (annual income, education) or indirectly (age at marriage, birth of a child before marriage).

Ironically, divorce rates are highest in some Bible Belt states (Arkansas, Oklahoma, and West Virginia), as well as in some western states (Idaho, Nevada, and Wyoming). States with the lowest rates are scattered across the Midwest (Illinois, Iowa) and the Northeast (Connecticut, Maryland, Massachusetts, New York, and Pennsylvania) (U.S. Census Bureau, 2012b). Clearly, sociocultural factors such as more conservative religious traditions must be intersecting with other factors, such as early age at first marriage (a significant predictor of divorce), as well as socioeconomic and other factors.

In 2017, twice-divorced and thrice-married Donald J. Trump became the 45th president of the United States. Described as "a devoted and loving husband, father, and grandfather" by some of his supporters (Citizens for Trump, 2016), perhaps this signals a shift in attitudes—including the stigma—of divorce, at least for some Americans.

> **ASK YOURSELF:** In 2014, the U.S. Census Bureau proposed dropping some of the questions on marriage and divorce from the American Community Survey, but reversed those plans under opposition from researchers. What value, if any, do you see in national data collection on marriage and divorce?

FIGURE 9.5 Number of Divorces per 1,000 Married Women, 1960–2009

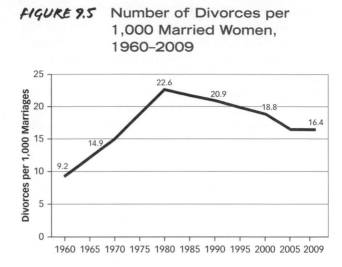

SOURCE: Centers for Disease Control and Prevention 2000, 2009; U.S. Census Bureau 2000, 2001.

What About the Children?

In 1960, almost nine of 10 children under age 18 in the United States were living with two married parents. By 2010, only two-thirds were doing so (U.S. Census Bureau, 2010). In 2010, four in 10 births were to unmarried

FIGURE 9.6 Relationship of Unmarried Couples at Child's Birth, 2012

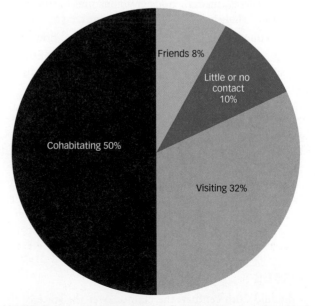

SOURCE: From the Fragile Families and Child Wellbeing Study Fact Sheet, accessed at: http://www.fragilefamilies.princeton.edu/documents/FragileFamiliesandChildWellbeingStudyFactSheet.pdf

parents, and four in 10 cohabiting households included at least one child. (When we are referring to a mother or father not married to the other parent, the term *unmarried parent* is more precise than *single parent*.) As revealed in the Fragile Families and Child Wellbeing Study, many unmarried parents are either living together or in a **visiting union**, meaning they live apart but are romantically involved at the time of their child's birth (McLanahan, 2011). Only one in 10 had little or no contact when their child was born. However, most of those relationships formed during early parenthood do not last. Less than one-third of unmarried-parent couples are still together 5 years after their child's birth. Almost four in 10 unmarried mothers form at least one new partnership, and one in seven have a child with a new partner. Fathers in these unmarried couples tend to become less engaged with their offspring over time. By the time the child is 5 years old, only half of nonresident fathers had seen the child in the last month.

The Fragile Families Study confirms that unmarried parents are much more disadvantaged than married parents (McLanahan, 2011). Unmarried parents are themselves less likely to have grown up with both biological parents and are more likely to be poor and black or Hispanic. They have often begun parenting in their teens and have had children with more than one partner. They are also more likely to suffer from depression, report substance abuse, and spend time in jail. Their families are much more likely to be welfare dependent. For example, at the time the child was 5 years old, only 2% of married-parent families were receiving food stamps,

compared to 33% of families in which the parents were single and not living together.

What about the children in these unions? Again, the Fragile Families Study (2012) has found that children born to unmarried parents are less advantaged than children whose parents are married. Their mothers are more likely to use harsher parenting techniques and less likely to participate in literacy activities like reading aloud. These children, especially the boys, have lower cognitive test scores than do children of married parents and exhibit more aggression.

FAMILY PROBLEMS AND THREE INSTITUTIONAL STAKEHOLDERS

9.3 Describe family problems related to economics, religion, and government.

Every institution in society has a stake in the family. In this section, we examine concerns and interests around the family of three major institutions: economics, religion, and government. First, we focus on how the economic downturn of the Great Recession played out in families of the middle class. Second, we contemplate the roles of religion and spirituality (which are not necessarily the same thing) in family life. Third, we consider the place of government policy in regard to violence against women.

Struggles of the Middle Class: Effects of the Great Recession on Families

Socioeconomic status remains a powerful indicator of the structure and also the quality of family life. Economic hardship can reduce the chance that a couple will marry or stay married, and that a child will grow up in a two-parent family (Child Trends, 2012). Social class can also shape the quality of conjugal and parent-child relationships (Hill, 2012). The changes in the structure of family life described above are reshaping the economic resources available to many families. The economic downturn that began in 2008 changed the portrait of even middle-class families, determining which will retain their middle-class existence and which will fall behind.

TABLE 9.2 Background Characteristics and Risk of Divorce During First 10 Years of Marriage

Factor	Decrease in Divorce Risk (%)
Annual income over $50,000 (vs. under $25,000)	30
College (vs. high school dropout)	25
Marriage at over 25 years of age (vs. under 18)	24
Birth of a baby 7 months or more after marriage (vs. before marriage)	24
Intact family of origin (vs. divorced parents)	14
Religious affiliation (vs. none)	14

SOURCE: National Marriage Project and the Institute for American Values. 2012. Social Indicators of Marital Health & Well-Being, Trends of the Past Five Decades in *The State of Our Unions: Marriage in America 2012*. Reprinted with permission.

Visiting union: Unmarried parents who are romantically involved but living apart.

Researching Family

The Fragile Families and Child Wellbeing Study

Sociologists and other social scientists at Columbia University, Pennsylvania State University, and Princeton University are following almost 5,000 children born in large U.S. cities from 1998 through 2000. Approximately three-quarters of the children were born to unmarried parents. Because these families are more likely to break up and to live in poverty than are other families, the investigators refer to them as "fragile families."

The Fragile Families Study addresses four important questions:

1. What are the conditions and capabilities of unmarried parents, especially fathers?

2. What is the nature of the relationship between unmarried parents?

3. How do children born into these families fare?

4. How do public policies and environmental conditions affect families and children?

Researchers interviewed both mothers and fathers when the children were born and when they were 1, 3, and 5 years old to collect data on attitudes, relationships, parenting behavior, demographic characteristics, mental and physical health, economic and employment status, neighborhood characteristics, and program participation. They also conducted in-home assessments of the children and their home environments.

More information about the study, including a list of publications, is available online at http://www .fragilefamilies.princeton.edu.

▶ **THINK ABOUT IT:** The findings of the Fragile Families Study provide powerful evidence of the connections among social structure, family organization, and child well-being. But what kinds of "grades" do parents give themselves? A study found that two-thirds or more of black and white parents give themselves high marks for parenting, yet only a bit more than half of Hispanic parents do so (Parker & Wang, 2013). What do you think accounts for this difference?

The full verdict is not yet in on the effects of the Great Recession. How has it affected families you know? In what the Pew Research Center (2012) calls "the lost decade of the middle class," the Great Recession reverberates through families in the form of unemployment and underemployment, stagnant and reduced pay, and foreclosures on homes (Greenstone & Looney, 2011). Today, 86% of U.S. adults consider a secure job an important part of what it takes to be middle class, compared to 33% in 1991 who considered a white-collar job necessary to achieving middle-class status (Wang, 2012). But achieving employment stability has become increasingly difficult with the rise in long-term unemployment that accompanied the Great Recession, especially among males ages 35–54 and white-collar workers (Kallberg, 2012). The average monthly unemployment rate almost doubled in the years immediately before and then again after the Great Recession, to just under 10%. During the same period, median family income fell from $49,600 to $45,800.

But it was median family net worth that took the greatest hit, falling from $126,400 to $77,300 in 2010. That level had not been seen since the early 1990s, and the drop effectively did away with the accumulated prosperity of the preceding 20 years. Moreover, middle-income families lost more wealth than either the wealthiest or the poorest families (Bricker et al., 2012). Even in that presumed bastion of the middle class, the U.S. suburb, "hardship has built a stronghold" as the percentage of people living below the poverty line grew by 66% (*New York Times*, 2012).

In the last few years, the unemployment rate has fallen, but much of the jobs gained have been lower-paying service jobs, rather than higher-paying positions (Morath, 2014), leaving families still to worry about employment and earnings (Belz, 2015). A recent survey by the Federal Reserve Board revealed that 47% of respondents would have difficulty securing $400 to cover an emergency (National Public Radio, 2016). By 2016, most Americans said that their household was faring well, but they were "strikingly pessimistic . . . about risks beyond their control" (Boak & Swanson, 2016).

Even without the Great Recession, maintaining a middle-class family life is not easy. Dual-earner spouses strain for work–life balance (Gootman & Saint Louis, 2012; Jang, Zippay, & Park, 2012; Karraker & Grochowski, 2012). Parents wrestle with how to manage

Family Beyond Our Borders

Children and the Changing Family

What about the effects of changes in family structure on children worldwide? First, children appear to fare better in societies where strong bonds exist between parents. However, they do not necessarily fare better in societies in which their parents marry, or worse in societies in which their parents do not. The gap in the quality of life between children living in two-parent families and those in single-parent families is much greater in some countries (the United States, the United Kingdom, Austria) than in others (Belgium, Denmark, France, Germany, Italy, Sweden).

The difference? Germany, Italy, and Sweden all provide a universal child benefit structure that guarantees a minimum income to every child, regardless of parental situation; the United States does not (Kamerman, 1996). Among economically advanced nations, the United States is at the bottom in terms of child poverty (only Romania ranks lower). In the United States, nearly a quarter of children live in households with incomes lower than 50% of the national median (Adamson, 2012). So, is the problem that parents fail to marry, or that society fails to provide a safety net for struggling families, regardless of how they are structured?

The United States is not alone in experiencing dramatically shifting trends in the demography that makes up family. Are we seeing a worldwide decline in interest in family as we know it? Families composed of parents, children, and extended kin have been at the core of societies around the world, with members often living and working as a unit. This is no longer true, as more and more people around the world are choosing to forgo marriage and childbearing (Kotkin, 2012).

Reasons for this global shift, while complex and variable across societies and cultures, include competitive capitalism, widespread movement away from traditional values, urbanization, and global economics. In pursuit of economic advantage, individuals are often forced to choose between family formation and career advancement. Movement away from traditional religious values (Judeo-Christian, but also Muslim, Hindu, Confucian, and Buddhist) prioritizes more secular values, including individualism and the pursuit of personal happiness and socioeconomic achievement. Urbanization suppresses both marriage and fertility rates, not only in the large urban centers of North America, Europe, and especially East Asia, but also in the fast-growing cities in developing areas of Asia, North Africa, and parts of the Middle East. Finally, a weak global economy and global fiscal crises, accompanied by a drop in the number of well-paying jobs, could dampen hope for future generations and, consequently, the desire to form families and bear children.

▶ **THINK ABOUT IT:** Do you think we will see fewer children being raised in families around the world in your lifetime? What factors worldwide do you expect to shape the answer to that question?

---

the advantages that come with affluence, such as unlimited Internet access (Kreutzer, 2012; Seltzer et al., 2012), and fret over how much is too much to give their children. They agonize over caregiving for children, elders, and grandchildren (Karraker, 2015; Rogers & Welter, 2012). All the while, family scholars warn that families may not be providing their members with sufficient developmental assets (Search Institute, 2012).

As noted above, the divorce rate dropped during the Great Depression of the 1930s, but how has the Great Recession of 2008 affected family structure? Apparently, marriage, cohabitation, and divorce rates have changed very little during the period since the economic downturn began. While divorce rates did not rise in states with high unemployment, they did so in states with high rates of home foreclosures, but only among individuals with education beyond high school (which may be an artifact of the correlation between higher education and homeownership; Cohen, 2012). However, since 2008 the percentage of young adults (especially women! [Fry, 2015]) living with their parents has increased and fertility rates have fallen, with the steepest declines in states most affected by the recession (Morgan, Cumberworth, & Wimer, 2012).

Economic distress taxes any family's **resilience**, the ability not just to bounce back from change or troubles (McCubbin, Thompson, & McCubbin, 1996) but to spring forward into the future (Grochowski, 2000). Have families experienced changes in their quality of life since the onset of the Great Recession? Overall negative effects on physical or mental health, as well as on access to health care, have been few, with some exceptions. Among adults

....

Resilience: The ability not just to bounce back from change or troubles but to spring forward into the future.

► A woman and her husband prepare supper for their two children at the Breezeway Motel in Fairfax, Virginia. They are temporarily staying at the hotel while waiting for a shelter and looking for work. The couple had previously fallen behind on their rent and were laid off from their jobs.

ages 25 to 44, more have reported experiencing serious psychological distress. Among black children, asthma rates have risen. Among adults, more have gone without medical care. Preliminary research does not reveal how many of these effects have been experienced by individuals whose lives have actually been touched by the Great Recession, but housing instability in particular may be related to such mental health consequences as anxiety attacks, depression, and self-ratings of health as fair to poor (Burgard, 2012).

"The Family That Prays Together . . . ": Religion, Spirituality, and Family Resilience in Tough Times

Religion has often been cited as a source of strength during times of economic and other hardships. I recall my mother (and grandmother) saying, "God never asks you to bear a burden greater than you can carry." In light of today's declining religious identification, how often do you now hear someone call so explicitly on a deity or religious teaching as a way to address family problems? Do such beliefs help or hinder families as they respond to economic difficulties or other troubled times?

Individuals who identify with a religion tend to form traditional marriages (Mahoney, 2010). But religious identification is not what it used to be. Approximately 51% of all U.S. adults do not adhere to a particular faith tradition (Association of Religion Data Archives, 2010). However, not belonging to a religious body or attending religious services does not preclude a person from having a sense of **spirituality**, or an underlying moral or value system. Families with religious or, more broadly, spiritual foundations express a sense of meaning and purpose on which they can draw during hard times. They also exhibit

greater resilience than do families without such foundations (Karraker & Grochowski, 2012). Research has found a positive relation between religiosity and marital satisfaction and well-being. For example, marital satisfaction has been found to be associated with a couple's shared religion, prayer for one's spouse, and forgiveness (Olson et al., 2015). Moreover, as Émile Durkheim (1915) argued in the early 20th century, religion can serve as a kind of "social glue," binding society together. Solidarity with others with whom a family shares faith or beliefs may generate powerful social networks. I found that to be the case in the small city in the midwestern United States I call Bluffton, where two-thirds of the population is Catholic. There Catholic nuns have partnered with educational, government, philanthropic, and religious institutions to ensure that the city's disadvantaged families receive the social and cultural support they need. The sisters' efforts to create a "good society" in Bluffton have included founding and funding shelters for homeless women and their children, regardless of their religious identification (Karraker, 2011, 2013a, 2013b).

Government efforts on behalf of families took a new "faith-based" turn in the 21st century. In 2001, the administration of President George W. Bush introduced the $300 million Faith-Based and Community Initiative to promote heterosexual marriage as a way to address poverty and reduce the dependence of unmarried mothers and their children on welfare (Berkowitz, 2002). Today, the Center for Faith-Based and Neighborhood Partnerships, an office of the U.S. Department of Health and Human Services (2012), sponsors several initiatives around social problems that deeply touch families, including responsible fatherhood. (Information about these government initiatives is available online at http://www.fatherhood.gov/for-dads.)

ASK YOURSELF: Visit the website of the U.S. Department of Health and Human Services' Center for Faith-Based and Neighborhood Partnerships (http://www.hhs.gov/partnerships). If you were to apply for a grant through this office, what would you propose? What might be the pros and cons of such a faith-based initiative?

Like the culture wars around family values, discussions about what government can do about family problems are often highly contentious, and (by their very title and tradition) faith-based initiatives may take on moral, especially religious, overtones (Karraker & Grochowski, 2012). Especially given current debates about abortion

Spirituality: An underlying moral or value system, which may be in the absence of membership in a religious body or attendance at religious events.

rights, same-sex marriage, and other charged issues, we might well be concerned about maintaining the separation of church and state.

Some faith-based programs also come up short on effectiveness. For example, Frank Furstenberg (2002, 2004), who has studied families—including teen mothers and their children—for more than five decades, offers criticisms of initiatives to promote marriage among unmarried mothers. Furstenberg found that although more than half of unmarried mothers eventually marry the fathers of their children, four in five of those marriages end within 15 years. Marriages between women and men who are not the fathers of their children have even higher rates of dissolution. Still, for all their controversy (and potential promise), partnerships between faith-based groups and government that aim to address family social problems appear to be here to stay.

▶ The Lima family prays before dinner at their home in Rockville, Maryland. Do you think daily rituals can help families develop resilience in times of trouble?

Government on Behalf of Families: The Violence Against Women Act

Families appear to have fewer problems and fare best in societies that value them and make them a priority for forging civil society. Unlike most other developed nations around the world, the United States lacks a comprehensive family policy. The United States also invests less in government programs for families than does any other developed nation. Denmark, Ireland, and the United Kingdom spend 4% or more of their gross domestic product on family benefits. The United States spends less than 1.5% (Organization for Economic Development and Cooperation, 2014). Societies that invest the most in family policy tend toward a commitment to equity across genders and all family forms: "inclusive, enabling, developmental, and nonmoralistic" (Ozawa, 2004, p. 302). In contrast, U.S. family policy is a product of the high value American society has traditionally placed on individual responsibility, limited government, and the marketplace as a way to solve social problems (Danziger, Danziger, & Stern, 1997).

However, public spending on families has increased in the United States since the beginning of the 21st century (Bogenschneider & Corbett, 2010), reaching the highest level in the nation's history (Moffitt, 2008). Congress has enacted legislation that directly affects families in a multitude of arenas. Some of this legislation, such as the Patient Protection and Affordable Care Act (widely known as Obamacare), has been quite contentious. Other legislation, such as the Violence Against Women Act (VAWA), has a history of bipartisan support.

Domestic violence is difficult for any victim, but Native American women living on reservations have found escaping and prosecuting such violence especially difficult because of a lack of access to medical and other resources as well as the scarcity of law enforcement officers and judges on the reservations (and their lack of jurisdiction over non–Native Americans; Childress, 2013). Research has found that 46% of these women suffer rape, physical violence, and/or stalking by intimate partners, a rate much higher than that experienced by women of other races (Black et al., 2011). A recent change to VAWA allows tribal courts to try non–Native Americans who are alleged to have committed violence against Native American women on reservations.

USING THEORY TO EXPLAIN FAMILY PROBLEMS: THE VIEW FROM THE FUNCTIONALIST, CONFLICT, AND SYMBOLIC INTERACTIONIST PERSPECTIVES

9.4 Apply the functionalist, conflict, and symbolic interactionist perspectives to the concept of family.

▶ Diverse groups join a rally in support of the Violence Against Women Act on Capitol Hill in Washington, D.C. In early 2014, three Native American tribes—the Yaqui of Arizona, the Tulalip of Washington, and the Umatilla of Oregon—were the first in the nation to exercise their inherent right to protect Native American women from domestic violence and rape, regardless of the offenders' Native or non-Native status.

As of May 2016, same-sex marriage is legal in 20 countries and legal in jurisdictions in two other countries (Human Rights Campaign, 2016). In 1996, both houses of the U.S. Congress passed the **Defense of Marriage Act (DOMA)** by very large margins. DOMA defined marriage as the legal union of one man and one woman for federal and interstate purposes. On June 26, 2015, the U.S. Supreme Court (*Obergefell v. Hodges, 2015*) ruled, "The Court now holds that same-sex couples may exercise the fundamental right to marry." But the battle over same-sex marriage has been and remains a contentious one, as illustrated by the case of Minnesota (Joughlin, 2014).

On November 6, 2012, Minnesota voters failed to approve an amendment to the state's constitution that would have instituted a ban on same-sex marriage. The question posed in the ballot read, "Shall the Minnesota Constitution be amended to provide that only a union of one man and one woman shall be valid or recognized as a marriage in Minnesota?" The voters rejected the amendment (Helgeson, 2012). To the surprise of many, just 6 months later, on May 14, 2013, Governor Mark Dayton signed a bill passed by the Minnesota legislature that legalized same-sex marriages in Minnesota (Minnesota Department of Human Rights, 2014).

Few issues have engendered as much public debate, personal angst, and campaign expenditures as same-sex marriage. More than $10 million was spent by both sides combined in the case of the proposed Minnesota constitutional amendment in 2012 (Mitchell, 2012). Campaigns were also launched to pass legislation that recognizes same-sex marriages. The Human Rights Campaign (HRC) is a large nonprofit organization that works "for lesbian, gay, bisexual, and transgender equal rights." HRC's Marriage Center (http://www .hrc.org/marriage-center) tracks the rapidly changing status of same-sex marriage and **civil unions**—legal arrangements that grant some or all of the provisions of marriage to same-sex couples—across the United States, state by state.

The Human Rights Campaign maintained that President Trump "has been a consistent opponent of marriage equality," favoring instead domestic partnerships benefits, but later opposing civil unions, and pledging to appoint judges to the U.S. Supreme Court who would overturn marriage equality (Human Rights Campaign, 2017). All this in the face of public opinion polls finding increasing support for same-sex marriage (Masci, Brown, and Kiley, 2017).

Sociological theories offer several ways to address the policy implications of banning or recognizing same-sex marriage, such as the following:

- What would be the social consequences of legalizing same-sex marriage?

- Who stands to gain and who stands to lose if same-sex marriage is legalized?

- What does the debate over same-sex marriage say about the meaning of marriage?

We next consider questions like these from the viewpoint of the functionalist, conflict, and symbolic interactionist perspectives.

Functionalism

Structural functionalism shines a macrosociological light on the family as the primary institution for economic support, emotional security, and especially childhood

---

Defense of Marriage Act (DOMA): U.S. federal law, enacted in 1996, that defines marriage as the legal union of one man and one woman for federal and interstate purposes.

Civil unions: Legal provisions that grant some or all of the legal rights of marriage to unmarried couples.

socialization. In this view, the family serves to maintain equilibrium in society. Writing in the mid-20th century, structural functionalists like Talcott Parsons argued that families are best organized around the instrumental and expressive needs of their members (Parsons & Bales, 1955), with men traditionally serving as breadwinners for their families and women traditionally serving as what we might call C.Em.O.s (chief emotional officers). It might be tempting to think of structural functionalism only as a theory that supports the status quo. However, we can also use concepts such as manifest and latent functions and dysfunctions to understand the intended and unintended consequences of social changes facing families.

▶ James Obergefell, the named plaintiff in the *Obergefell v. Hodges* case, speaks to the media after the same-sex marriage ruling outside the U.S. Supreme Court on June 26, 2015. The court said that same-sex couples have a constitutional right to marry anywhere in the United States. Do you think that countries in Africa, Asia, and the Middle East will follow suit?

Policy Implications of Structural Functionalism

Minnesota for Marriage was a coalition of people who supported the Minnesota marriage amendment described above. The organization's website (which is no longer live) described the traditional functions of marriage as including controlling sexuality and caring for children: "Marriage is society's mechanism for increasing the likelihood that children will be born and raised by the two people responsible for bringing them into the world—their mother and father" (Minnesota for Marriage, 2012). Those who supported the Minnesota marriage amendment warned that any marital union other than that between a man and a woman would compromise the functions of that union, particularly the well-being of children (Heaney, 2012).

Others, like attorney Michael Rodning Bash (2012), challenged the premise that marriage between a man and a woman is "natural." They made the argument that passage of the amendment would compromise the common good of society, children, and their parents. As Bash wrote: "It is difficult to imagine a good-faith argument that society is better off when certain children grow up with parents who are denied access to the social and legal resources and benefits that other parents and their children enjoy." Instead, opponents of the amendment asserted, social policy should be in the business of supporting parents, regardless of their sexual orientation.

What would a structural functionalist theorist say? First, although in postmodern societies like ours the family increasingly shares responsibility for the socialization of

▶ Mercedes Santos (second from right) shares a laugh with her partner, Theresa Volpe (second from left), while playing cards with their son and daughter at their home in Chicago. Santos and Volpe are a same-sex couple raising their two biological children.

children with other institutions (day-care facilities, schools, extracurricular clubs and teams), the family remains the primary institution through which children are socialized. What appears to be in dispute is the definition of the family and, in particular, the ability of different parental configurations to socialize the next generation effectively.

Research on parenting outcomes affirms that socioeconomic conditions are a primary factor in socialization, as are quality of parenting, family climate and stability, and social networks. However, for children growing up with lesbian or gay parents, research has failed to find any negative developmental outcomes (Stacey & Biblarz, 2001); any effects on academic achievement, behavior, emotional development, or self-esteem (Patterson & Hastings, 2007; Potter 2012); or any self-concept, peer relations, conduct, or gender development differences. The only differences in parenting that have been reported in research may actually favor the children of lesbian mothers. Compared with other mothers, lesbian mothers are more likely to engage in imaginative play with their children and less likely to report using corporal punishment (Goldberg & Allen, 2013).

In other words, research does not support the contention that same-sex marriage is dysfunctional in terms of the socialization of children. Research conducted by the Urban Institute has estimated that same-sex couples are raising children in virtually every county (96%) in the United States (Bennett & Gates, 2004). However, the same research found that same-sex couples with children are in fact disadvantaged in that they are less likely than other couples to have access to family health insurance through their employers.

Conflict Theory

Structural functionalist theory sees society as structured to ensure a stable, effective social order. Conflict theory, on the other hand, sees society as organized around competing vested interests. In the late 19th century, Karl Marx and Friedrich Engels linked the existence of social class and private property to the oppression of women in the family (see Engels, 1972/1884). A century later, Randall Collins and Scott Coltrane (1991) made a sociological argument for conflict theory as a way to examine the conflicts inevitable in day-to-day family life. Today, conflict theorists see social relationships in society, including injustices related to the intersections of social class, race and ethnicity, gender, and sexual orientation, as being replicated in the family.

Policy Implications of the Conflict Perspective

Sociologist Melissa Sheridan Embser-Herbert (2012) has described the position of same-sex families in North American society and the tax and other financial, logistical, and time burdens borne by couples who cannot marry. A lesbian and an attorney, she has also outlined the heroic challenges of establishing legal custody of her son should her partner die before adoption proceedings could be completed. The organization Minnesotans United for All Families (2012) offered citizens the following rationale for opposing the marriage amendment: "This amendment violates the core Minnesotan value of treating others as we would want to be treated. It is not our place to limit the freedoms of others." From a conflict perspective, Minnesotans United made the argument that enacting a constitutional ban on same-sex marriage would oppress people like Embser-Herbert and her family while maintaining a status quo that benefits others.

Conflict theorists often see social institutions such as workplaces, schools, and religion as shoring up the claims of that status quo. Early on, the Minnesota amendment had the backing of the powerful Catholic Archdiocese of Minneapolis and Saint Paul (2010), which, 2 years before the amendment was to appear on the ballot, distributed to all parishioners an 8-minute DVD opposing same-sex marriage. (Those urging Minnesotans to "vote no" on the amendment had a coalition of faith-based organizations and religious leaders on their side as well.) However, a visible number of Catholics in some neighborhoods displayed lawn signs and bumper stickers that read "Another Catholic Voting *No*."

Had some of the social solidarity the Catholic Church has enjoyed, not only with the faithful but across society on important moral issues, been challenged by the social capital expended on the Minnesota marriage amendment? Since 2001, a majority of people who are unaffiliated have supported same-sex marriage. By 2016, a majority of white mainline Protestants (64%) and Catholics (54%) did as well. Even support among black Protestants and white evangelicals has also increased (Pew Social Research, 2016).

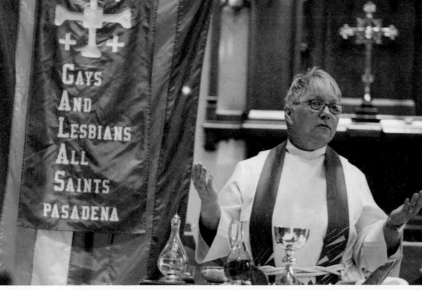

▶ The Rev. Susan Russell, an openly gay priest, leads a service at All Saints Episcopal Church in Pasadena, California. Can we expect to see more openly gay clergy in the future?

ROBYN BECK/AFP/Getty Images

Symbolic Interactionism

Laws and constitutional amendments around same-sex marriage are about more than the structure and function of society, or even the oppression and freedom of disadvantaged groups. For an understanding of how social policy might play out in the daily lives of families and their members, we turn to microsociological theories like symbolic interactionism. Rather than focusing on macrosocial forces such as institutions and social classes, symbolic interactionism focuses on patterns of interaction among individuals. Symbolic interactionists are particularly interested in the meanings that interaction creates and the ways language and other symbolic systems maintain social relationships and society. For example, some advocates of same-sex marriage rights oppose the use of the term *civil union*, arguing that it connotes more limited rights and responsibilities than the more widely accepted *same-sex marriage*.

Policy Implications of Symbolic Interactionism

Words have mattered mightily in the debates over same-sex marriage. Should we "limit" the opportunity to wed? Would matrimony be somehow "redefined" if gays were eligible to marry? Most important, what does "marriage" mean? The policy debate around who may marry provides powerful testimony about the importance of language and symbolic meanings.

Both sides in the Minnesota marriage amendment fight strongly recommended that their followers use interactional techniques to persuade others to vote their way. For example, the Minnesota for Marriage website (http://www.minnesotaformarriage.com) provided downloads aimed at helping supporters of the amendment organize house parties and print business cards and small flyers that could be personalized with supporters' contact information. The Minnesotans United for All Families website (http://mnunited.org) provided a download for a "conversation toolkit" and a way for opponents of the amendment to create their own fund-raising pages. Minnesotans United's "Family Stories" and "Gallery" were intended to create a sense that all Minnesotans, regardless of sexual orientation, share the same meaning of "family": "They believe family is about love and commitment, working together, bettering their communities, raising children, and growing old together. They believe marriage matters."

In this social media age, both sides also made heavy use of Internet communication technologies like Facebook, Twitter, Flickr, and YouTube to get their messages across to the public. Perhaps even more important, these technologies enabled supporters to connect easily with one another and with the campaign. Both Minnesota for Marriage and Minnesotans United for All Families also offered merchandise for sale on their websites, providing supporters yet another way to self-identify symbolically with their cause. Public policy campaigns will never be the same.

FOUR SPECIALIZED THEORIES BEYOND FUNCTIONALISM, CONFLICT, AND SYMBOLIC INTERACTIONISM

 9.5 Apply specialized theories to the family.

Like the other social problems addressed in this book, the study of families has its own set of specialized theories, in addition to structural functionalist, conflict, and symbolic interactionist theories. This section briefly describes four such theories and applies them to family social problems: social exchange theory and sexual engagement, life course development theory and boomerang kids, family systems theory and (dis)connected families, and family ecology theory and raising families in dangerous neighborhoods.

Social Exchange Theory: Transactional Sexual Exchanges

Social exchange theory is a microsociological theory based on the idea that individuals will draw on their personal resources to maximize their rewards and minimize their costs. Furthermore, the theory suggests that we form, maintain, and dissolve social relationships based in large part on our perceptions of equity and balance in the calculus of exchange (Karraker & Grochowski, 2012). In other words, we commit to and continue in long-term intimate relationships to the extent that we trust we will be treated fairly in the long run (Marsiglio & Scanzoni, 1995; Scanzoni, 1978, 1982).

Among the family social problems that interest sociologists is why young men and women often become sexually active before they are developmentally or socially ready to do so. Have you ever considered that sexual engagement might be driven by patterns of exchange? Nancy Luke and her colleagues (2011) in the United States and Kenya have studied premarital relationships among women in sub-Saharan Africa. They found that unmarried women who are poor are more likely to engage

....

Social exchange theory: A theory that posits individuals will draw on personal resources to maximize rewards and minimize costs when forming, maintaining, or dissolving relationships.

in **transactional sex**, the receipt of money and gifts from a male partner in exchange for sexual activities, and that engaging in transactional sex decreases a young woman's power to negotiate a relationship to her advantage (such as requiring the man to use a condom). As a young woman's income increases, so does the likelihood that she will delay sex and engage in safer sexual practices

Family Life Course Development Theory: Boomerang Kids

Are you a "boomerang kid" (or do you expect you might become one in the future)? Thinking of young adults you know who have moved back in with their parents (or never left the family home), what social factors do you believe shaped their decisions? In what ways might this "new normal" of deferred adulthood affect the life course development of young adults and their parents?

Family life course development theory seeks to understand developmental processes and outcomes as families move through a series of stages across the life course. These stages are set in part by historical and social conditions and often come to be socially acceptable, as in the case of age norms for marriage and childbearing (Karraker & Grochowski, 2012). For example, much recent research has examined the social problem of adult children moving back in with their parents, described as "accordion families and boomerang kids" (Newman, 2012) or "helicopter parents and landing pad kids" (Fingerman et al., 2012). In 2014, one-third (32.1%) of 18-to-34-year-olds lived with their parents (Fry, 2016). Furthermore, among those living with their parents, eight in 10 were satisfied with the arrangement (Parker, 2012).

So, what is the social problem here? Overly dependent adult children who just will not grow up? Smothering parents who enable their children's dependency? Or social forces that are changing the very nature of the transition from child to adult? Katherine S. Newman (2012) interviewed and observed families in six developed countries: Denmark, Italy, Japan, Spain, Sweden, and the United States. Her conclusion: Global economic forces have changed cultures around the world, causing the cost of living to rise along with unemployment rates. As globalization has challenged normative markers for adulthood, families have welcomed back young adults, allowing them to draw on "the bank of mom and dad" (p. xi) and creating a "slippery state of adulthood" (p. 10). This may be creating a deferred crisis, as members of the younger generation are unable to establish financial and other independence, leaving them even more vulnerable as their parents age and die. In the meantime, what it means to be an adult is clearly undergoing a substantial shift worldwide.

Family Systems Theory: (Dis)connected Families

Family systems theory has received wide play among counselors, nurses, social workers, sociologists, and others who work with troubled families. This theory views the family as a series of subsystems, such as parent-child, siblings, and spouses, and proposes that a change in any part of the family system will have consequences for the other parts. Families therefore strive to maintain a sense of equilibrium (Karraker & Grochowski, 2012). Scholars have examined a range of family social problems from a family systems approach, including marital conflict, parent-child conflict, and child sexual abuse. One of the most immediate problems facing family systems today is the association between media use and increasing disconnection among family members (Padilla-Walker, Coyne, & Fraser, 2012).

In *Alone Together: Why We Expect More From Technology and Less From Each Other* (2011), Sherry Turkle (who is both a sociologist and a clinical psychologist) uses 15 years of research to describe how blogs, cell phones, Facebook, and other information and communication technologies have ramped up our professional productivity and enabled us to remain connected with family members when we are physically separated from them. The effects on family subsystems of these new ways of communicating, and the dissatisfaction and even anger they sometimes create, are exemplified by the case of Trey, whose brother shared the news that his wife was pregnant not with a visit or a personal call, but with a blog posted to the world. For people like Trey, Turkle notes, the new technologies have created (dis)connected families, compromising the quality of authentic interaction and relationships among partners, parents, children, and other family members, threatening connections and intimacy with the "erosion of boundaries between the real and the virtual" (p. xi).

Family Ecology Theory: Raising Children in Dangerous Neighborhoods

Families are embedded in broader natural and human-built environments (Karraker & Grochowski, 2012).

....

Transactional sex: The exchange of money and gifts for sexual activities.

Family life course development theory: A theory that examines the developmental processes and outcomes as families move through a series of normative stages across the life course.

Family systems theory: A theory that views the family as a set of subsystems defined by boundaries and striving toward social equilibrium.

Family ecology theory helps us understand how they function and adapt within these physical, social, and other ecosystems (Bubolz & Sontag, 1993). Could you construct a diagram that illustrates the social ecology of an immigrant family in the United States? How does this ecology differ from that of a family that does not have immigrant status? How do key social institutions like education, economics, government, religion, and extended and other kin create potential assets (or deficits) for immigrant families? (For in-depth information about immigrant families, see the award-winning research of Joanna Dreby, 2010, 2012.)

Some of the most compelling applications of family ecology theory help us understand the importance of safe neighborhoods for families raising children. For example, research has found that mothers who perceive the neighborhoods in which they live to be dangerous spend significantly less time in outdoor activities with their children than do mothers who perceive their neighborhoods to be safe (Frech & Kimbro, 2011). Organizations like MAD DADS (Men Against Destruction—Defending Against Drugs and Social Disorder) understand the role of the family ecosystem in raising healthy children. Founded in 1989 by a group of black fathers in Omaha, Nebraska, and now with chapters worldwide, MAD DADS (http://maddads.com)

REUTERS/Jim Young

▶ A Neighborhood Watch sign posted in a neighborhood in Detroit, Michigan. How does living in a high-crime neighborhood challenge family life?

works at the local level to provide positive male role models as leaders in neighborhoods, communities, and cities, hoping to counter the effects of crime, drugs, and violence and make urban neighborhoods safer for youth and families.

Family ecology theory: A theory that views family systems as embedded in natural or human-made physical, social, and other environments.

SOCIAL CHANGE: WHAT CAN YOU DO?

9.6 Identify steps toward social change to address family problems.

Social Problems, the journal of the Society for the Study of Social Problems, includes reports of cutting-edge research on family social problems, such as families in the child welfare system (Hook, Romich, Lee, Marcenko, & Kang, 2016), the effects of incarceration on relationship dissolution (Turney, 2015), and family socioeconomic status and the path to college (Crosenoe & Muller, 2014). But let us not neglect the power of sociology to spur change for the common good. One 20-year veteran of studying families offers a pragmatic approach to research on families and their problems: "I do what I do because I'm hoping that the knowledge we gain will make the world a better place for kids, [and] for families" (quoted in Friese & Bogenschneider, 2009, p. 234).

Below, three undergraduate students reflect on the ways peers on their campuses have engaged in social action around three pressing family problems: affordable housing,

Scott Cunningham/NBAE/Getty Images

▶ Members of the Atlanta Dream assist with Habitat for Humanity to help build homes in Lovejoy, Georgia. Have you ever been involved in a service project like this?

food insecurity, and intimate partner violence. In addition, you can assess how your school or workplace stacks up against *Working Mother* magazine's "100 Best Places to Work" in terms of a culture of work–family balance.

Affordable Housing: Habitat for Humanity With the University of Minnesota

Brandon Haugrud

Like so many others in the United States, Minnesota families were devastated by the subprime mortgage crisis of 2008 that forced thousands to default on their mortgages and seek substandard housing. According to a recent study by the National Association of Realtors (2015), home foreclosures in Minnesota had fallen to nearly 0.4% by May 2015, the lowest level since December 2007 and an indication that the housing market in Minnesota has essentially recovered. In the greater Twin Cities, however, about a third of households spend more than 30% of their income on housing. When families spend more than they can afford on their housing, they are less about to afford food, clothing, transportation, medical care, and other necessities (Metropolitan Council, 2016). When nearly 50% of families in the Twin Cities with annual incomes under $35,000 pay more than they can afford on their housing, they are less able to afford health care, nutritious food, high-quality education, and long-term savings.

Students at the University of Minnesota, many from families that experienced home foreclosures, have partnered with Twin Cities Habitat for Humanity to eliminate poverty housing and make the dream of homeownership a reality for hardworking families. In addition to constructing safe, decent, affordable homes, students have become politically engaged with the Minnesota state legislature in their efforts to persuade lawmakers to support affordable-housing legislation. They also assist communities outside Minnesota, taking winter and spring break trips to build homes with other Habitat affiliates across the United States, as well as raising thousands of dollars each year for new home construction. To learn more about the work of Habitat for Humanity and its efforts to eliminate poverty housing, or to become involved with a Habitat affiliate in your community, visit http://www.habitat.org.

Food Insecurity: Lewis & Clark College's Hunger Banquet

Miriam Wilkes Karraker

What social problem could be more pressing for parents than the inability to feed their children? Almost one-third of Oregon's children experience **food insecurity**, or uncertain access to nutritious food. This is one of the highest rates in the United States. In Portland, home of Lewis & Clark College, 14% of households do not have access to nutritious food on a regular basis (Yeager, 2012).

In what Barry Glassner (2012), sociologist and former president of Lewis & Clark College, describes as "an impressive flip side to the absurd *Portlandia* sketch and the excess and privilege it skewers," students at Lewis & Clark organize "hunger banquets" to raise awareness of food insecurity. Upon arriving at the dining hall, each Lewis & Clark student receives a lunch ticket. Each is then served a meal typical for a public school student based on the social class and neighborhood of a particular school. Afterward, a Feeding America Child Hunger Corps member of the Oregon Food Bank and other community partners discuss food insecurity and the social, developmental, and academic significance of food deprivation for children in the public schools. Students leave the "hunger banquet" with information about how they can better serve children and families by keeping food banks well stocked and by advocating against hunger.

Intimate Partner Violence: The Clothesline Project at the University of St. Thomas

Emilee Sirek and Victoria Speake

Intimate partner violence (IPV) is "a serious, preventable public health problem that affects millions of Americans" (Centers for Disease Control and Prevention, 2012b). It includes physical, sexual, and psychological/emotional harm, or the threat of such harm, by a current or former partner or spouse, and it occurs among both heterosexual and same-sex couples. IPV varies in frequency and severity and ranges from one blow to chronic, severe battering. Men and women are violent at nearly equal rates, but men make up the majority (87%) of offenders who come to the attention of the police (Melton & Sillito, 2012).

The Clothesline Project (CLP) was started in 1990 to bear "witness to violence against women." Women affected by violence decorate a shirt and then hang it on a clothesline to spread community awareness of violence against women and generate support for those affected

---

Food insecurity: A household's lack of access to nutritious food on a regular basis.

Intimate partner violence (IPV): Physical, sexual, or psychological/emotional harm or the threat of harm by a current or former intimate partner or spouse.

by family violence and other traumatic experiences. The colors of the shirts represent different forms of violence, from sexual abuse to political attack. Since it began on Cape Cod, Massachusetts, the CLP has crossed state and international borders, appearing in Germany, Lebanon, Namibia, and Taiwan. Friends and family members of victims and survivors of IPV can now also decorate shirts with or on behalf of their loved ones.

Students at the University of St. Thomas in St. Paul, Minnesota, have elaborated on the CLP model to engage students, faculty, and staff who may not have experienced IPV directly. All campus community members are invited to decorate or write the name of a survivor or victim on a shirt to be hung on a clothesline strung in the campus quad. This inclusive event serves as a visual reminder that everyone is connected to interpersonal violence in some way. For more information about the CLP and instructions on how to start a project on your own campus, visit http://www.clotheslineproject.org.

▶▶ The Work–Family Climate at Your School or Workplace

For more than 30 years, *Working Mother* magazine has invited companies to be recognized for their support of working mothers and their families; it "encourage[s] policies and programs to help all employees balance work and family." The application for recognition asks more than 500 detailed questions about issues such as child care, flexible scheduling, and advancement programs. *Working Mother* then recognizes the "100 Best" companies for women, hourly workers, executive women, and multicultural women, as well as the best law firms and nonprofit companies. The Top 10 for 2015 included such well-known corporations as General Mills and IBM, but the full list includes lesser-known companies as well.

▶ University of Kansas students make their way along an installation of the Clothesline Project, which publicly displays T-shirts decorated by survivors of rape, domestic violence, or both.

How does your school or workplace measure up on indicators of quality of work–family life? Read some of the profiles of *Working Mother*'s "100 Best" at http://www.workingmother.com/2015-working-mother-100-best-companies-hub?filter[3]=11203. Contact your human resources department for information on workplace policies, but also collect data on child care and other work–family issues from your organization's website for current or potential employees. Use social media to gather unofficial information about employee satisfaction and your organization's reputation in the community around work–family issues. You may find additional information and support if your organization has a women's center or related affinity group. When you complete your research, prepare a white paper in which you assess the status of work–family support at your organization and offer recommendations. Share it with the offices and individuals who assisted you, as well as with other leaders in the organization.

WHAT DOES AMERICA THINK?
Questions About Family From the General Social Survey

▶ Turn to the beginning of the chapter to compare your answers to those of the total population.

1. Children are a financial burden on parents.

   AGREE: 26.8%

   DISAGREE: 57.6%

   NEITHER AGREE NOR DISAGREE: 15.6%

2. A same-sex female couple can raise a child as well as a male-female couple.

   AGREE: 46.7%

   DISAGREE: 40.9%

   NEITHER AGREE NOR DISAGREE: 12.4%

3. Having children increases social standing in society.

AGREE: 33.2%

DISAGREE: 36.3%

NEITHER AGREE NOR DISAGREE: 30.5%

4. A same-sex male couple can raise a child as well as a male-female couple.

AGREE: 42.9%

DISAGREE: 44.2%

NEITHER AGREE NOR DISAGREE: 12.9%

5. Single parents can raise kids as well as two parents.

AGREE: 48.8%

DISAGREE: 41.7%

NEITHER AGREE NOR DISAGREE: 9.5%

6. Divorce is the best solution to marital problems.

AGREE: 51.5%

DISAGREE: 33.7%

NEITHER AGREE NOR DISAGREE: 14.8%

SOURCE: National Opinion Research Center, University of Chicago.

CHAPTER SUMMARY

 Define the concept of family.

Falling marriage rates, rising divorce rates, and increases in cohabitation fuel the culture wars around the family. The marriage movement asserts that the lifelong union of a man and a woman is best suited to fulfilling the traditional social functions of the family. Yet other scholars see changes in family as representing not decline, but adaptation. The U.S. Census Bureau defines family as two or more people who are related to one another by birth, marriage, or adoption and who share living quarters. A household is defined as people, related or not, who share living quarters. Beyond those definitions, the meaning of family is both contested and changing, sometimes including, for example, fictive kin. A more contemporary definition recognizes that each of us lives in a series of families over a lifetime and that family is defined not only by biology and law but also by experience with kin, friends, and others.

 Discuss patterns and trends in marriage, cohabitation, and divorce.

The United States is facing a marriage dearth. The proportion of adults who are currently married has dropped steadily over the past 50 years, to around 50%. At the same time, the percentage of adults who are divorced has almost tripled, and the percentage of those who have never married has almost doubled. The choice to marry intersects with a wide range of other social factors, including age (age at first marriage has never been higher), race and ethnicity (whites are more likely than either blacks or Hispanics to be married), and college education (a majority who are currently married hold college degrees). These patterns also reflect the available pool of eligibles and the marriage gradient, as well as the possibility of heterogamous unions. Still, a clear majority of those who have never been married say they wish to be married, although many believe marriage is becoming obsolete in spite of its advantages.

9.3 Describe family problems related to economics, religion, and government.

The onset of the Great Recession saw family income and especially family wealth drop, the latter to the lowest level since 1990, adding to the challenges middle-class families already face. Overall, marriage, cohabitation, and divorce rates have changed very little since the economic downturn began in 2008, but circumstances like housing instability put a special strain on family resilience. Religious beliefs and practices have been linked to family resilience, but declining numbers of U.S. adults profess identification with a religious faith tradition. Although the United States lacks a comprehensive family policy, one example of government intervention on behalf of families is the Violence Against Women Act. A provision of the act is specifically targeted at aiding Native American women living on reservations, who experience higher rates of violence than do women of other races.

9.4 Apply the functionalist, conflict, and symbolic interactionist perspectives to the concept of family.

The case of same-sex marriage effectively illustrates the three theories applied throughout this book to illuminate social policy alternatives. Structural functionalist theory calls to mind the efforts of those who wish to retain traditional marriage through passage of legislation such as the Defense of Marriage Act. Conflict theory reminds us that maintaining the status quo in the form of traditional family structures disadvantages families led by gays and lesbians in profound ways. Symbolic interactionism demonstrates the power of language in social policies affecting families, as well as the role of social media and new communication technologies in shaping public opinion around social policy.

9.5 Apply specialized theories to the family.

Social exchange theory offers an opportunity to understand why young women might engage in transactional sex. Life course development theory examines the rise of the "boomerang kids" phenomenon and the likely consequences of delayed adulthood. Family systems theory sees families as a set of systems and subsystems and explains why these systems are becoming increasingly disconnected by technology. Finally, family ecology theory reveals how parenting styles are affected by parents' perceptions of the safety of their neighborhoods.

 9.6 Identify steps toward social change to address family problems.

Habitat for Humanity volunteers help provide affordable housing for families. Taking part in a "hunger banquet" can help students or members of any organization understand family food insecurity and encourage them to take action to alleviate the problem in their communities. The Clothesline Project raises awareness about intimate partner violence and promotes healing. You can conduct your own survey to assess the balance between work and family supported at your own school or workplace.

KEY TERMS

civil unions 224

cohabitation 211

crude divorce rate 217

culture wars 211

Defense of Marriage Act (DOMA) 224

family 211

family ecology theory 229

family life course development theory 228

family systems theory 228

feminist perspective 212

fictive kin 212

food insecurity 230

household 212

intimate partner violence (IPV) 230

marriage dearth 213

marriage gradient 214

marriage movement 211

marriage squeeze 214

pool of eligibles 214

refined divorce rate 217

resilience 221

selection effect 217

social exchange theory 227

spirituality 222

transactional sex 228

visiting union 219

10 WORK AND THE ECONOMY

Rudi Volti

▶▶▶ A worker installs parts in a vehicle frame as they move down the production line at the Mercedes-Benz factory in Vance, Alabama. Do you think these types of manufacturing jobs will still be around in 20 years in the United States?

Investigating Work and the Economy: My Story

Rudi Volti

When I was a boy I was fascinated with airplanes, trains, cars, and motorcycles. But my family was anything but affluent, so several years passed before I could get a car, a very tired 1955 Chevrolet that did not take well to my efforts to improve its performance. In college and graduate school my interest in mechanical devices led me to a more general consideration of technology and its interaction with the economy, culture, and society, and especially its effects on jobs and employment. I took this interest into my career as a college professor, where I taught a course on technology and society almost every year. These classes were the motivation for my textbook *Society and Technological Change,* now in its eighth edition. Of course, many forces besides technology shape the way work is structured and performed, and I have tried to account for them in *An Introduction to the Sociology of Work and Occupations,* now in its second edition. Observing the effects of technological and other changes on work and occupations will continue to be a source of fascination for me.

LEARNING OBJECTIVES

10.1 Explain the general shape of the U.S. workforce today.

10.2 Identify patterns and trends in employment and unemployment.

10.3 Discuss the role of unions and the issues of wage inequities, discrimination, and stress in the workplace.

10.4 Apply the functionalist, conflict, and symbolic interactionist perspectives to workplace issues.

10.5 Apply specialized theories to workplace issues.

10.6 Identify steps toward social change for work-related problems.

 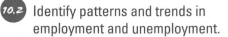

WHAT DO YOU THINK?
Questions About Work and the Economy From the General Social Survey

1. If you were to become rich, would you continue to work or stop working?

   ☐ CONTINUE TO WORK

   ☐ STOP WORKING

2. With regard to your income tax, do you think it is too high, about right, or too low?

   ☐ TOO HIGH

   ☐ ABOUT THE RIGHT AMOUNT

   ☐ TOO LOW

3. Do you think that work is most important to feel accomplished?

   ☐ MOST IMPORTANT

   ☐ NOT THE MOST IMPORTANT

4. What is your interest level in economic issues?

   ☐ VERY INTERESTED

   ☐ MODERATELY INTERESTED

   ☐ NOT INTERESTED AT ALL

5. What is your confidence level in banks and financial institutions?

   ☐ A GREAT DEAL

   ☐ ONLY SOME

   ☐ HARDLY ANY

 Turn to the end of the chapter to view the results for the total population.

SOURCE: National Opinion Research Center, University of Chicago.

FROM 500 TO 750 ENVELOPES

Lisa Weber isn't exactly a newbie at the National Envelope Company; she has been there for 28 years, having started when she was 19 years old. For many years the company paid decent wages and offered occasional perks like company picnics and holiday turkeys. These are now gone, and at the same time the pace of work has increased substantially. Today, says Weber, "It's harder for me to want to get up and go to work than it used to be. It's not something I would wish on anybody. I'm worn out. I get home and I can barely stand up" (quoted in Semuels, 2013, p. A1).

Lisa Weber's job is the flip side of one seemingly bright spot in the Great Recession that according to the government's reckoning stretched from late 2007 to early 2010: Although the period was marred by widespread unemployment, it also was the scene of a strong advance in worker productivity. For Weber, improved productivity meant having gone from producing 500 envelopes per hour to 750. When she started with the firm, it was owned by a Holocaust survivor who believed benevolent treatment of employees was not only a good thing in itself but also good for business. Then e-mail came along, and with it a reduced demand for paper envelopes. The firm filed for bankruptcy in 2010 and was acquired by a private equity firm. As the new owners saw it, changes had to be made in order to return the company to solvency. Some workers were laid off permanently, while those who hung on to their jobs had to work harder. As one executive summed up the situation, "It became clear that as the market began to soften, what was in place was not a sustainable business model. . . . Sometimes you have to make dramatic changes to save the jobs that you can."

The basic elements of the National Envelope story have been repeated at thousands of other firms. Technological change has undermined the foundations of many jobs, especially those in the manufacturing sector. The profitability and even the survival of many firms has hinged on their ability to pare production costs to a minimum, often by reducing numbers of workers and requiring higher output from those who remain. For National Envelope, cost-reduction efforts were not enough. Shortly after

Lisa Weber's story appeared in print, the firm once again filed for bankruptcy and was subsequently liquidated. For National Envelope and its workers, it all ended badly.

At the same time, however, technological change, globalization, and social and cultural changes are also creating new opportunities for those able to take advantage of them. The dynamic world of the early 21st century is constantly creating winners and losers; the challenge is to encourage potential winners while at the same time creating a more humane society for all. In this chapter we will examine work and unemployment against the backdrop of major technological, social, and economic changes. Along the way we will consider immigration, the trajectory of wages and salaries, labor unions, race- and gender-based discrimination, human capital, affirmative action, workplace stresses and dangers, and job satisfaction. By examining these topics we can better understand the forces that had made Lisa Weber's working life so difficult, and what, if anything, might be done to improve the working lives of men and women like her.

WORK AND THE LABOR FORCE

10.1 Explain the general shape of the U.S. workforce today.

We begin with some basic terms. Unless they are self-employed or unpaid volunteers, workers receive wages or salaries in return for their efforts. A **wage** is a sum of money paid on an hourly basis. In general, a wage earner is not as well paid as an employee who receives a **salary**, which generally is paid on a monthly or bimonthly basis. A salary provides more stable earnings, but it also may require working beyond the customary 40-hour workweek for no additional pay.

Many workers also receive a variety of **benefits** in addition to their wages or salaries. In the past, many salaried workers were entitled to pensions after they

....

Wage: Payment for work done on an hourly basis.

Salary: Remuneration paid on a monthly or bimonthly basis and not directly tied to the number of hours worked.

Benefits: Noncash compensation paid to employees, such as health insurance and pension plans. Also known as fringe benefits.

TABLE 10.1 The U.S. Labor Force in Late 2016

Total Labor Force Over the Age of 20	Men	Women	Employed Men	Employed Women	Unemployed Men	Unemployed Women
159,451	81,751,000	72,109,000	78,405,000	69,203,000	3,347,000	2,906,000

SOURCE: United States Department of Labor, Bureau of Labor Statistics. Table A-1. "Employment Status of the Civilian Population by Sex and Age."

retired. "Defined benefit" plans that paid a stipulated sum of money on a regular basis have become rare in the private sector, and in their place many employers now offer "defined contribution" plans in which both the employers and the employees contribute to employees' retirement funds. Both employers and employees also put funds into the latter's Social Security account. Another important benefit, when it is available, is employer-provided health insurance. The United States has relied much more heavily on employers to provide health insurance than other countries do, creating a number of social and economic problems, especially for workers whose insurance is terminated when they lose their jobs. Other employer-supplied benefits may include contributions to disability insurance and perhaps financial support for employees' further education and training. Together, a wage or salary along with benefits add up to an employee's **total compensation**.

The **labor force** is conventionally defined as all persons in the civilian noninstitutional population who are either employed or unemployed but actively seeking work. In turn, the "noninstitutional population" is defined by the U.S. Department of Labor as "persons 16 years of age and older residing in the 50 states and the District of Columbia, who are not inmates of institutions (e.g., penal and mental facilities, homes for the aged), and who are not on active duty in the Armed Forces" (U.S. Bureau of Labor Statistics, 2013). The size of the labor force can change over time, substantially affecting employment and unemployment statistics.

A statistical tabulation of the U.S. labor force in late 2016 is presented in Table 10.1. The jobs of employed men and women fall into one of three broad sectors of the economy, which have been labeled as the primary, secondary, and tertiary (or service) sectors. In 2014, about 2,982,100 workers were employed in the **primary sector**, consisting mostly of farming and mining, while 18,326,700 worked in the **secondary sector**, which includes construction and manufacturing. This leaves no fewer than 120,641,100—or more than 80% of employed workers—in the tertiary or **service sector**, a varied mix that includes health care, education, financial services, utilities, retail and wholesale trade, leisure and hospitality, transportation, and all levels of government (U.S. Bureau of Labor Statistics, 2015a).

▶ People walk past clocks at Reuters Plaza in London on their way to work. Many see their jobs as the "daily grind" in which their lives are dictated by time and making money. The popular phrases "working for the weekend" and "thank God it's Friday" connote how some people feel about their workaday worlds.

PATTERNS AND TRENDS

10.2   Identify patterns and trends in employment and unemployment.

The shift of the majority of the labor force into the service sector has been one of the most important long-term changes in human history. Very few of us now produce tangible goods as farmers or factory workers. Our livelihoods are based on the work we do as nurses, teachers,

Total compensation: Remuneration that includes a wage or salary plus benefits.

Labor force: The segment of the population either employed or actively seeking employment.

Primary sector: The sector of the economy centered on farming, fishing, and the extraction of raw materials.

Secondary sector: The sector of the economy that includes manufacturing and other activities that produce material goods.

Service sector: The sector of the economy that provides services such as education, health care, and government. Also known as the tertiary sector.

musicians, government employees, food-service workers, and employees in all the other varied occupations in the service sector.

Employment and Unemployment

Many workers lost their jobs during the course of the Great Recession (2007–2009), and although employment has rebounded since then, for many people joblessness remains a problem, as does underemployment—that is, working part-time when a full-time job is preferred. We calculate the percentage of unemployed men and women by dividing the number of jobless people by the number of individuals in the labor force (see Figure 10.1).

We need to treat these numbers with caution, however. Far from being a stable number, the size of the labor force may vary widely. In recent years it has shrunk to a substantial degree; in late 2016, 88.6% of men between the ages of 25 to 54 were in the labor force, leaving about 7 million men neither employed nor "available for work" (Puzzanghera, 2016). Some of them could be found in the ranks of **discouraged workers** who had quit looking for jobs and were therefore no longer counted as unemployed. Others had significant medical problems that prevented them from working. A fair number of these had been caught up in an opioid epidemic that may have begun as a search for pain relief, but became a debilitating addiction. Another group not counted as part of the labor force were those in jail or prison, whose numbers had grown substantially in recent years. At the end of 2015, 2,173,800 men and women were incarcerated in federal, state, and local jails and prisons, most of whom were of working age (Kaeble & Gaze, 2016). (For a discussion of the effects of increased levels of incarceration on official employment rates for African Americans, see Western, 2006, pp. 86–107.)

Whatever the reasons for the reduced size of the labor force, the shrinking pool of potential workers obscures the true extent of joblessness. Since unemployment statistics are determined by dividing the number of unemployed by the total workforce, a smaller official workforce will lower the unemployment rate. The converse also applies: With the same extent of employment, a larger workforce results in a higher rate of unemployment. This leads to the paradoxical situation whereby official tabulations of unemployment may actually go up in the early months of an economic recovery as more job seekers cease being discouraged workers when they return to the labor force. Finally, government statistics make no distinction between workers who were employed for the whole year and workers who happened to have jobs at the time they were surveyed. The unemployment rate is a snapshot, and as such, it does not adequately capture the situations of many workers who have experienced periods of joblessness during a given year. In 2015, 16.9 million men and women were unemployed at some point during the year, more than 10% of the total labor force (U.S. Bureau of Labor Statistics, 2016). The unemployment rate also does not take into account individuals who have jobs but work only part-time, even though they would prefer a full-time job. In late 2015, there were 5.8 million involuntary part-time workers (U.S. Bureau of Labor Statistics, 2015f).

For these reasons, some believe the official unemployment rate may give an overly optimistic picture of employment and unemployment. On the other hand, a substantial number of workers elude the statistical net by working in the **underground economy** (also known as the shadow economy). Some work done in this sector is clearly illegal in all or most parts of the country—drug manufacture and dealing, prostitution, bookmaking, and bootlegging, for example. A considerable amount of work also occurs in legitimate areas but is done "off the books," including repair work, gardening, and personal services performed on a cash basis to avoid sales and income taxes. Some workers are hired clandestinely so their employers can avoid making contributions to Social Security, Medicare, and other mandated programs, or because their businesses are violating health and safety codes.

By its very nature, employment in the underground economy is difficult to measure, but according to one careful study, it accounts for an average of 12% of gross national income in industrially developed economies and much more in underdeveloped ones (Schneider & Enste, 2002). Including these workers in official statistics would decrease the unemployment rate by a significant margin.

The Consequences of Unemployment

Periods of high unemployment do not affect all members of the labor force in the same way. As you might expect, unemployment is negatively correlated with educational levels. Race and ethnicity also have clear associations with employment and unemployment (see Figures 10.3 and 10.4). The worst unemployment situation is that of black teenagers, who had an unemployment rate of 28% toward the end of 2016. During that period the overall unemployment rate for white, black, Hispanic, and Asian American members of the labor force were 4.3, 8.9, 5.2, and 3.6%, respectively.

....

Discouraged workers: Unemployed workers who have given up looking for jobs and hence are no longer counted as members of the labor force.

Underground economy: Work that is illegal or is designed to avoid the reporting of payments to government authorities such as tax collectors. Also known as the shadow economy.

Researching Work and the Economy

Finding a Job

How do you get a job? How effective are formal means of finding a job such as website listings, social media, newspaper advertisements, employment agencies, university placement services, and cold calls to prospective employers?

A classic study by Mark Granovetter (1995) began with the assumption that crucial to any job search is access to information about job openings and various aspects of potential jobs. Granovetter found that "formal means" of learning about jobs often were useful but accounted for fewer than half of job leads. What was really crucial for the majority of successful job searches was membership in a social network that included people connected in some way to employers with openings to fill. For prospective employers, an applicant's network provided important clues. Instead of using elaborate procedures for determining a candidate's suitability, employers could simply assume that a social connection to one of their employees (or even a friend or relative of an employee) at least qualified the person for further consideration. When that employee or employee's friend was known to be competent and trustworthy, an employer would be more inclined to hire an applicant who had a connection, however tenuous, to one or the other.

Granovetter also discovered something that seems counterintuitive. We might assume that strong interpersonal ties, the sort found among kinfolk, friends, and neighbors living in close proximity, would form the core of the social networks that led to successful job placements. In fact, the opposite prevailed: *Weak* ties were much more important than strong ones. Weak ties connected acquaintances rather than close friends, customers, merchants, and second-order relationships such as "a friend of my aunt Beatrice." This follows from the likelihood that our close personal relationships link people who travel in economic and social circles similar to ours. As a result, their information regarding available job opportunities is not much better than our own. In contrast, connecting with a less intimate social network considerably expands the sources of information about where work can be found. These kinds of connections can be particularly important for low-status job seekers; as subsequent research indicated, weak ties are more likely than strong ones to connect them with higher-status individuals.

▶ Today, social media sites are of limited use in finding a job, but they likely will be more important in the years to come.

To be sure, a lot has changed since Granovetter conducted his research. In particular, social networking sites and other digital media have become important sources of information about employment opportunities, and most prospective employers use social media to announce job openings. Job seekers have made abundant use of them, but have these media reduced the importance of personal connections? At this point there is no firm evidence that social media have become the dominant means of connecting job seekers with prospective employers. But that doesn't mean that sites like Twitter and Facebook are of little importance. Rather, the unwise use of social media can be a hindrance to being hired. According to one survey, three of four recruiters and hiring managers consult social media entries when making hiring decisions, and one of three candidates is rejected because something objectionable appears in a social media account (J. Smith, 2013). In sum, despite the massive growth of social media in recent years, personal rather than digital connections are essential for the majority of successful job hires. Perhaps we should not make too much of the limited utility of social media for finding jobs. Social media sites are relatively new, and employers and job seekers are still learning how to use them effectively. In the long run, users of social media may benefit from the fact that, as Granovetter discovered, more distant network relationships are particularly helpful when it comes to finding jobs. After all, how many of your Facebook friends are acquaintances rather than friends in the fullest sense of the word?

▶ **THINK ABOUT IT**

1. What sorts of social networks do you belong to? Which of them might be especially useful in helping you find a job?

2. Many people, especially members of minority groups, lack connections with social networks that can be useful for finding jobs. What might be done to help such job seekers expand and develop their social networks?

FIGURE 10.1 Unemployment in the United States, 2002–2016

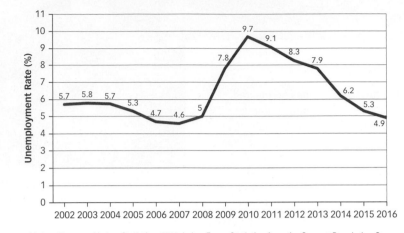

SOURCE: United States Department of Labor, Bureau of Labor Statistics, 2012. Labor Force Statistics from the Current Population Survey.

The median time without a job also varies. In 2016, 27.4% of the unemployed were jobless for 27 weeks, while 31.6% were in this situation for 5 weeks or less. In the middle were 27.5% with 5–14 weeks of joblessness and 16.2% who were out of work for 15–26 weeks (U.S. Bureau of Labor Statistics, 2017b). The economic costs of unemployment can be severe for individuals. They lose not only wages and salaries but also employer-provided health care benefits. Under these circumstances, medical problems have pushed many Americans into bankruptcy. Some can maintain their coverage by paying their former employers' shares of their insurance premiums, but this high cost adds considerably to the financial stress of unemployment.

In addition to making it more difficult to afford health care, joblessness itself can be hazardous to physical and psychological health. According to one study, workers between the ages of 51 and 61 who lost their jobs were twice as likely as employed workers to suffer a heart attack over the next 6 to 10 years (Bassett, 2010). Another study of workers who lost their jobs during the severe recession of the early 1980s found that in the year following a job loss, the death rates of high-seniority workers increased by 50% to 100%. The consequences of unemployment also persisted for a long time; this cohort still exhibited a 10–15% higher death rate 20 years after the initial job loss (Luo, 2010).

The manner in which unemployment produces these negative health consequences is not entirely clear, but unemployment does seem to be associated with poor health habits that increase the risk of diabetes and heart disease (Bassett, 2010). It also seems highly likely that unemployment is accompanied by increased levels of stress, which can be the source of a multitude of physical ailments.

High unemployment levels affect the personal finances not only of the unemployed but also of those still working. According to one study, each percentage point increase in the unemployment rate lowers the incomes of families in the bottom **quintile** by 1.8%, by 1.4% in the middle quintile, and by 1% in the top quintile (Mishel, Bernstein, & Shierholz, 2009, p. 48). Many employees become willing to accept lower wages, or longer hours for the same wages, in order to get or keep their jobs. As we saw in the story that opened this chapter, firms may try to boost productivity and profits by increasing the workloads of diminished numbers of employees. Finally, in addition to financial and health consequences, simply having been unemployed may have negative consequences that last long afterward. A study of workers who lost their jobs during the severe recession of 1981–1982 found that two decades later their earnings were 30% less than those of workers who had remained employed during this period (*The Economist*, 2010). Another study found that white men who graduated from college during the 1981–1982 recession earned 6% to 8% less for each percentage point increase in the unemployment rate when compared with employees who graduated during more prosperous times. Their situation improved by about one-quarter of a percentage point in each following year, but 15 years after graduation their earnings were still 2.5% less than those of workers who graduated in better economic circumstances (Kahn, 2009).

Quintile: One-fifth of anything that can be divided.

Jobs, Secure and Insecure

Given the many unfortunate consequences of unemployment, job security is one of the most important features a job can offer. Some occupations, notably teaching, offer the prospect of tenure in order to protect academic freedom. Tenure, however, is not ironclad; teachers and professors can lose their jobs for serious rule breaches or because their institutions have to cut staff for financial reasons. Other professions offer de facto tenure, as occurs when an attorney is made a partner in a law firm. Government workers and employees in some unionized industries and firms can be fired only after their employers have gone through formal procedures, some of them quite extensive. Employers also are prevented from firing workers for trying to organize a union or for **whistle-blowing**—that is, drawing public attention to malfeasance within the firm. Civil rights laws forbid dismissals based on race, color, gender, creed, age, or national origin. But in general, the relationship between employers and employees in the United States is governed by the doctrine of **employment at will**. This means that in most states, unless there is a specific agreement or discrimination of some sort has occurred, an employee can be summarily fired for any reason or for no reason at all (Muhl, 2001).

Some of the most precariously employed are contingent workers, many of whom are "temps" placed by specialized agencies to do short-term work in offices and other work sites. Because they do not have to give contingent workers benefits such as health insurance, some businesses make frequent use of them, while others retain them for periods of time that stretch "temporary" beyond recognition. Industries vary considerably in the extent to which they employ temporary workers. Almost 70% of

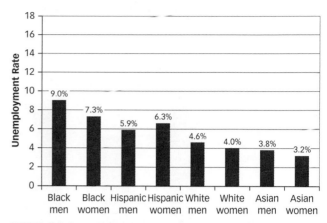

FIGURE 10.3 U.S. Unemployment by Race/Ethnicity, 2017

SOURCE: U.S. Dept. of Labor, Bureau of Labor Statistics, 2017C "Labor Force Characteristics by Race and Ethnicity."

FIGURE 10.4 Unemployment Rate by Educational Attainment for Blacks and Whites Age 25 and Older in the United States, 2011 Annual Average

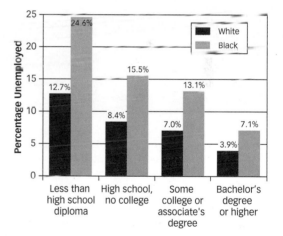

SOURCE: United States Department of Labor, Bureau of Labor Statistics, 2011. "The African-American Labor Force in the Recovery," Chart 3.

temporary workers are employed in only three industries: transportation and materials handling, production, and office and administrative support. The remainder are scattered in a wide variety of industries (Nicholson, 2015).

....

Whistle-blowing: The act of calling attention to malfeasance in one's organization.

Employment at will: The legal practice that allows an employer to terminate a worker's employment even if no specific reason for the termination is given.

FIGURE 10.2 U.S. Unemployment Rates by Educational Level, 2017

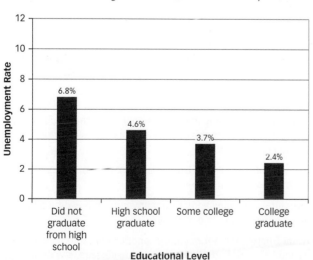

SOURCE: United States Department of Labor, Bureau of Labor Statistics, 2017B.

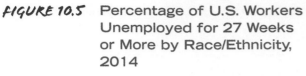

FIGURE 10.5 Percentage of U.S. Workers Unemployed for 27 Weeks or More by Race/Ethnicity, 2014

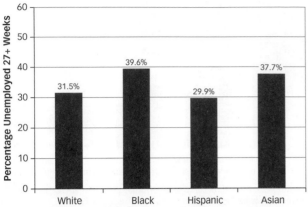
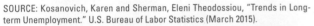

SOURCE: Kosanovich, Karen and Sherman, Eleni Theodossiou, "Trends in Long-term Unemployment." U.S. Bureau of Labor Statistics (March 2015).

▶ A man rubs his eyes as he waits in a line of job seekers to attend a career fair in New York City. Long-term unemployment may lead not only to eviction and foreclosure on people's houses but also to mental stress and loss of self-esteem.

Compared with members of the permanent workforce, temporary workers tend to be younger; less likely to be high school or college graduates; and more likely to be female, black, or Hispanic. About 40% are part-timers. The main advantage of working as a temp is flexibility, but temporary workers earn less per hour than regular employees, and most lack health insurance and pension plans. They are often given the most routine tasks and sometimes experience social isolation and poor self-image from being "just a temp" (Henson, 1996).

Employment and Technological Change

What the statistics about employment and unemployment don't tell us is why jobs are abundant during certain times and scarce during others. While the business cycle, demographic trends, government policies, and even fluctuations in the weather affect the numbers, some degree of unemployment is inevitable. People may be jobless because they have moved or voluntarily left their jobs. In good economic times this **"frictional unemployment"** is not problematic because workers readily find new jobs. Even recessions may not be too painful if they are short and followed by economic expansions. This has unfortunately not been the case for the aftermath of the Great Recession; as often happens when a recession is triggered by a crisis in the financial sector, economic and employment growth tend to proceed at a very slow pace.

In considering the causes of present-day unemployment, it is useful to distinguish between two types of unemployment. **Cyclical unemployment** occurs during the periods of weak economic growth that seem to be inevitable features of a modern economy. Although these episodes are painful, they tend to be fairly short-lived and can be somewhat lessened by government actions to stimulate the economy. Economic growth follows to help make up for the losses incurred. **Structural unemployment**, as its name implies, is joblessness resulting from major changes in the basic structure of the economy, such as the rise and fall of entire industries and a reordering of the occupational structure. A major cause of structural change is the introduction of new technologies, accompanied by the obsolescence of established ones. Computerization, the Internet, and smart phones have been transforming the ways we make things, communicate with one another, and send, receive, and store information. But with these benefits, has technological transformation also brought us widespread and persistent unemployment?

The pluses and minuses of new technologies have been endlessly debated. Back in the 16th century, the government of Tudor England banned "engines for working of tape, lace, ribbon, and such wherein one man doth more amongst them than seven English men can do" (quoted in Thomis, 1972, pp. 14–15). Concerns about employment being destroyed by technological advances were common during the **Great Depression** of

....

"Frictional unemployment": Unemployment that results from workers being temporarily jobless while transitioning from one job to another.

Cyclical unemployment: Unemployment caused by cyclical downturns in the economy.

Structural unemployment: Unemployment that is caused by basic changes in the economy.

Great Depression: Worldwide economic downturn in the period 1929–1941, marked by failing businesses, low or at times negative economic growth, and widespread unemployment.

the 1930s, when a "technotax" was seriously considered for employers who replaced their workers with new equipment (Bix, 2000).

The high levels of employment that followed the Great Depression should have eased these fears, but today's rapid advances in computers, robotics, expert systems, and automated processes have reignited them. At the same time, however, it should be recognized that technological advances have created new work opportunities; who was employed as a designer of Web pages before the Internet? Besides creating new jobs, technological change can create employment opportunities indirectly. A machine that reduces the cost of production puts more money in the pockets of the firm's owners or remaining workers, who then purchase more goods and services, creating more employment opportunities for the workers who produce them. Cheaper production also lowers prices, resulting in higher sales and yet more production and employment opportunities. In all these cases, increased productivity need not diminish employment prospects.

The false connection between technological change and unemployment is based on what economists call the **lump of labor fallacy**. This is the assumption that there is only so much work to be done and hence only a fixed number of jobs, so when labor-saving technologies take over some of the work, some workers necessarily lose their jobs. Some governments that subscribe to this idea have mandated a shorter workweek in the hope of creating more jobs. There are several good reasons for shortening the workweek, but creating new employment opportunities isn't one of them. There is no shortage of essential tasks to be done, now or in the future. For example, workers are needed to rectify environmental damage, rebuild crumbling infrastructure, and bring medical services to underserved populations. The paradox of unemployment coexisting with unmet needs for workers suggests, first, that workers' skills are not matched to the kinds of jobs they require, and second, that governments and their citizens are unable or unwilling to pay for these jobs.

Should we not worry about technological advances having unfortunate consequences for work and employment? In fact, we should worry. Although technological change need not destroy *work* as a whole, it can certainly annihilate particular *jobs*. And as technological change alters the mix of jobs, it can substantially affect the distribution of income. Before we look at these issues, let us consider another force deeply affecting work and employment.

Globalization

Innovations from containerized freight traffic to e-mail to trade pacts between nations have allowed firms today

▶ Today, the automotive industry is highly automated, relying on robots—series of mechanical arms—in assembly lines and factories like this one in India. Robots are cost-effective, efficient, and safe. What do you see as the drawbacks of having robots in the factory for human workers?

to treat the whole world as a market for their products and services. Like technological advances, increasing **globalization** can lower production costs and result in some combination of lower prices, higher wages and salaries, and greater profits. Consequently, spendable income will increase, at least for some segments of the society. This in turn expands the demand for goods and services, at least some of which will be supplied by workers in the country that lost some jobs to offshore production. This is the good news, but it is not the whole story. Globalization, as well as technological change, has contributed to widening disparities in wealth and income around the world.

Chronic unemployment and underemployment are major problems in many poor countries, but jobs created by foreign firms are often dangerous, exhausting, and poorly paid. China has experienced astonishing rates of economic growth in recent years by using its huge labor supply for the production of exported goods bearing the labels of foreign firms. Many Chinese have achieved middle-class status or better as a result, but tens of millions of workers in apparel, electronics, and other labor-intensive enterprises continue to face serious workplace problems. According to one study of nine factories conducted by

Lump of labor fallacy: The notion that there is a fixed number of jobs and that unemployed individuals can find jobs only when others lose their jobs or reduce the number of hours they work.

Globalization: The process through which business firms, political authority, and cultural patterns spread throughout the world.

Work and the Economy Beyond Our Borders

The North American Free Trade Agreement

In 1965, Mexico enacted its Border Industrialization Plan, which for the most part removed tariffs for enterprises near the U.S.–Mexican border. This policy encouraged the construction of maquiladoras, foreign-owned factories producing a wide range of industrial products along the Mexican side of the border. The number of factories expanded following the signing of the **North American Free Trade Agreement (NAFTA)** in 1994, which gradually eliminated tariff barriers between the United States, Canada, and Mexico.

Thousands of maquiladoras operate in Mexico today, many manufacturing products once made in the United States. Beyond question, U.S. workers have lost jobs due to factories relocating to Mexico and elsewhere, a form of globalization that has devastated entire communities unable to compete with workers earning roughly $2 per hour. At the same time, however, NAFTA has had some positive results. Trade between the United States and Mexico amounted to $583.6 in 2015. In that year the value of goods and services U.S. firms sold in Mexico came to $267.2 billion (Office of the U.S. Trade Representative, 2016). Only Canada and China buy more U.S.-made goods. Although U.S.–Mexico trade has cost some U.S. jobs, it has also stimulated the expansion of others.

Assessing the impact of NAFTA on employment in the United States poses a number of methodological problems, but the consensus among economists is that the overall effects have been modest. Some studies show no net effect, while others indicate a net gain of a bit under a million U.S. jobs (O'Neil, 2013, p. 96).

For Mexico and its workers, the picture is mixed. Some Mexican manufacturers closed their doors because they could not compete with foreign firms. The Mexican economy's tighter connection with the North American market has left it more vulnerable to economic slowdowns in the United States and Canada. Work in export-oriented maquiladoras, much of it done by women, is poorly compensated in comparison to work in the United States and other developed countries, but for many Mexicans it is an improvement over the widespread poverty of many parts of the country.

Despite expectations when it was enacted, NAFTA by itself has neither transformed the Mexican economy nor done much to stem the flow of undocumented immigration to the United States. Like any significant alteration in the economic status quo, it has brought significant gains to some and losses to others. Although the overall balance has been positive, those who have been adversely affected have had to make some painful adjustments.

► People work in a maquiladora, or garment assembly plant, in Mexico. Factories producing blue jeans have given jobs to thousands of workers, but they are pumping chemicals into rivers used to irrigate corn fields downstream. Locals say they do not know if the wastewater presents a long-term risk to their health, but some complain of chemical fumes that smell bad and irritate their throats.

REUTERS/Jennifer Szymaszek

► **THINK ABOUT IT**

1. Although globalized production has benefited consumers by lowering the prices of many items, it has also led to job losses in some industries. Should those who have lost their jobs due to globalization receive some sort of compensation? If so, from whom?

2. Some employees in poor countries work for miserable wages in appalling workplace conditions. How might these inequities be eliminated? What can you as a consumer do about this situation?

the nonprofit China Labor Center in 2015, workers' pay was inadequate to meet ordinary expenses, and overtime work of more than 100 hours a month was necessary just to get by. Work proceeded at a very fast pace, and rest breaks were few and far between. Workplace deaths through accident and suicide were not uncommon; some have been well publicized because they occurred at factories supplying products for Apple, Samsung, and other makers of high-tech consumer products (China Labor Watch, 2015).

North American Free Trade Agreement (NAFTA): A pact initiated in 1994 to stimulate trade among the United States, Canada, and Mexico by lowering or eliminating tariff barriers.

An employee looks up from her work on a production line in the Suzhou Etron Electronics Factory in Suzhou, China. China may be "the workshop of the world," but young rural migrant workers are less accepting than their parents were of life in the factories—low pay, grueling hours, and very strict workplace rules. Do you think that as its economy continues to grow, China will turn toward a service economy, with more teachers, nurses, and hairdressers than factory workers?

STAKEHOLDERS

10.3 Discuss the role of unions and the issues of wage inequities, discrimination, and stress in the workplace.

All of us have a direct interest in work and its correlates. As individual workers and as members of society as a whole, we are affected by the composition of the workforce, levels of employment and unemployment, the rise and fall of particular occupations, and the manner in which work organizations are structured. Although the money earned as a wage or salary is not the only reward for holding a job, it is hard to live a fulfilling life when unemployed or working at a minimum-wage job. Many things affect a worker's level of remuneration. Having a skill that is in high demand is one, but not the only one. As we shall see, a person's wage or salary is likely to reflect when he or she entered the labor force, prior access to education, the extent of unionization, and the extent of discriminatory behavior by employers and potential employers.

Wages and Salaries: Winners and Losers

One inescapable aspect of economic and social change in recent decades has been persistently weak growth in wages and salaries for most workers. According to the liberal-leaning Progressive Policy Institute, from 1979 to 2013 the wages of the middle segment of the workforce have gone up by only 6% in real (i.e., corrected for inflation) dollars, while low-wage workers have suffered an actual decline of 5% (Mishel, Gould, & Blivins, 2015). Not all economists accept these figures, but there is a general consensus that recent decades have been characterized by a widening income and wealth gap separating a relatively few individuals and families from the bulk of the population (see Chapter 2).

Not only is today's income and wealth gap greater than it has been for many decades, but there appear to be fewer opportunities to move up economically. In the past, people were willing to accept a fair amount of economic inequality because they or their children would be able to improve their financial circumstances. This was true in the past; in 1970, 90% of 30-year-olds were earning more money than their parents when they were the same age. In 2014, only half did so (*The Economist*, 2017, p. 21).

Unions and Their Decline

Income inequality in the United States has been increasing for many reasons, one of which is the steady erosion of union membership. In 1955, when the two largest union organizations merged, 37% of U.S. workers were members of labor unions (Freeman 2007, p. 77). By 2015, union membership had skidded to a mere 11.1% of workers (see Figure 10.6). The decline has been especially notable in the private sector, where only 6.7% of employees belonged to unions. In contrast, the unionization rates for federal, state, and local government workers are 27.3%, 30.2%, and 41.3%, respectively (U.S. Bureau of Labor Statistics, 2016g).

Unionization confers a number of benefits. On average, union workers earn wages 14.1% higher than those of their nonunionized counterparts, even after education and experience, type of industry, region, and occupation are controlled for (Blanchflower & Bryson, 2007; Mishel et al., 2009, p. 200). They also receive 15–25% more benefits, such as health insurance (Budd, 2007, pp. 165–166; Mishel et al., 2009, pp. 123, 202–203), as well as more workplace training and employee development.

In recent years, black and Hispanic workers have benefited from unionization more than white workers, and men more than women (Mishel et al., 2009, p. 200). The benefits are particularly evident among low-skilled workers (Pencavel, 2007, p. 434). Even nonunion workers benefit when good wages are paid to dampen the appeal of unionization, such as at nonunion auto factories in the South.

Although the general trend of unionization has been downward, the private-sector Service Employees International Union won a recent victory in organizing workers in low-paid occupations in the health care, private security, food and beverage, and hospitality industries. At the other end of the income scale, unionized pilots, upper-echelon public officials, and professional athletes have done very well as a result of union actions (Gladwell, 2010). Ironically, the success of their unions has contributed to the wide income gap separating some very well-paid employees from the rest of the working population.

Is Increasing Human Capital the Answer to Wage Disparities?

The combination of technological advances and outsourcing to foreign lands has eliminated many manufacturing jobs in the United States, along with the decent wages they once paid. What is needed now is an accelerated development of **human capital**—that is, improvements in workers' skills and attitudes that will allow them to develop and effectively utilize modern workplace technologies. However, for many workers the key to earning a good income is not simply having the ability to use computers and other sophisticated equipment; what matters is being able to contribute to the development of organizational systems and processes that make the best use of these technologies (Brynjolffson & McAfee, 2011, p. 42). Yet in recent years educational budgets have been cut and college tuition has steadily increased. It is also difficult for the United States to develop a well-educated workforce when one-fifth of the children in the nation are living in poverty.

Over a working life, college graduates, on average, earn considerably more than high school graduates (see Figure 10.7). The extent to which a college degree increases earning power depends on a number of factors, such as an individual's major (Taylor et al., 2011, pp. 83–114), but on the whole, college is a good investment. Why is this so? Is the greater earning power of college graduates a reflection of the superior skills that college graduates bring to their jobs? Or have these workers simply passed through an educational "filter" to gain credentials attesting to their superior qualities? Does it matter what they actually learned? It is the rare prospective employer who asks for an applicant's academic transcript or even inquires about his or her grade-point average.

The content of most graduates' formal education is of less importance than what they are able to learn while on the job. Many firms still do a fair amount of worker training, but the benefits are not distributed equally. One study found that 35% of young college graduates received on-the-job training, but only 19% of high school graduates did (Levine, 1998, p. 109). (The extent of employee training is notoriously difficult to determine, however; see Levine, 1998, pp. 136–137.) Race and ethnicity also affect access to these programs; one study based on the 2001–2002 California Workforce Survey found that Hispanic workers are less likely to have opportunities for training even after variables like prior education and the industries in which they work are controlled for (Yang, 2007). Gender can be a factor, too. Mentorship, the process in which more experienced workers guide less experienced employees to develop their skills and abilities, is usually confined to members of the same sex; unfortunately, a connection of a sexual nature may be inferred when an older man mentors a younger woman. Since it's still the case that fewer women than men have achieved leadership positions, young women have correspondingly fewer opportunities to find mentors than do their male counterparts.

It hardly requires great insight to observe that work today is being substantially altered, if not transformed, by globalization and technological change. Under these circumstances, worker skills can quickly become obsolete and irrelevant. Yet despite an obvious need for retraining, the proportion of workers receiving either company-sponsored or on-the-job retraining has actually fallen in recent years. Making matters worse, training programs have been disproportionately aimed at well-educated, highly skilled workers, largely forsaking those with the greatest need to upgrade their job skills (*The Economist*, 2017).

Discrimination in the Workplace

Unequal access to on-the-job training programs is only one aspect of a much larger issue: lingering employment discrimination on the basis of race, ethnicity, gender, and age. Maintaining an equitable workplace is not just a matter of treating individuals fairly; to be successful, it is imperative that employers effectively leverage the abilities of their increasingly diverse workforces. A few decades ago the statistically typical worker in the United States was a white male. Today, white men are a minority in a diverse

FIGURE 10.6 **U.S. Union Membership by Sector, 1973–2015**

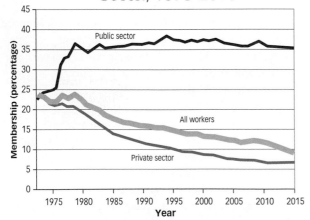

SOURCE: Adapted from Barry T. Hirsch and David A. Macpherson, "Union Membership and Coverage Database from the Current Population Survey: Note," *Industrial and Labor Relations Review*, Vol. 56, No. 2, January 2003, pp. 349–54.

Human capital: The package of cognitive, physical, and social skills of individual workers.

FIGURE 10.7   Earnings and Employment by Educational Attainment in the United States, 2016

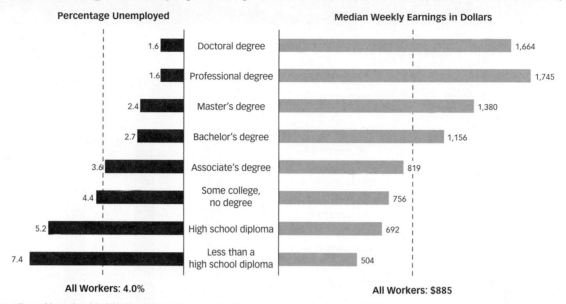

Percentage Unemployed		Median Weekly Earnings in Dollars
1.6	Doctoral degree	1,664
1.6	Professional degree	1,745
2.4	Master's degree	1,380
2.7	Bachelor's degree	1,156
3.6	Associate's degree	819
4.4	Some college, no degree	756
5.2	High school diploma	692
7.4	Less than a high school diploma	504
All Workers: 4.0%		**All Workers: $885**

SOURCE: https://www.bls.gov/opub/ted/2016/weekly-earnings-by-educational-attainment-in-first-quarter-2016.htm
https://www.bls.gov/emp/ep_table_001.htm.

workforce in which women comprise 46.8%, blacks are 12.6%, Hispanics are 16%, and Asian Americans are 6% (U.S. Bureau of Labor Statistics, 2015c).

Overt discrimination is illegal. Title VII, Section 703, of the Civil Rights Act of 1964 made it a federal crime "to fail or refuse to hire or to discharge any individual" based on "such individual's race, color, religion, sex, or national origin." Similar provisions apply to employment agencies and labor unions. The passage of the Civil Rights Act and other legislation has not eliminated disparities based on race, ethnicity, and gender, however. We have seen above that unemployment rates differ substantially for racial and ethnic groups. So do incomes (see Figure 10.9). Toward the end of 2016, for men and women at or over the age of 25 median weekly earnings for white workers came to $909. The figures for black and Hispanic families were $724 and $675, respectively. Asian American workers fared best of all, at $1,077 (U.S. Bureau of Labor Statistics, 2017g). How much discrimination contributes to unequal outcomes in pay and employment is difficult to say. One clue comes from a study conducted in New York City that asked closely matched groups of black, Latino, and white applicants to answer 169 newspaper want ads for low-level positions such as restaurant worker, stock clerk, mover, and telemarketer. Of these, 31.0% of white applicants were offered a job or called back for a second interview, while only 25.1% of Latinos and 15.2% of blacks received positive responses (Pager, Western, & Bonikowski, 2009). White applicants had a higher rate of positive responses even when their application forms indicated they had criminal records, although the difference was not statistically significant.

> **ASK YOURSELF:** Many believe that past and current discrimination against women and minorities require the enactment and implementation of **affirmative action** policies and programs. Critics of affirmative action, however, note that many women and minority members come from more privileged circumstances than do many white males. Would it be better, then, to use social class as a basis for affirmative action programs? If this were to be done, how would social class be defined? Is it simply a matter of income and wealth?

Women in the Workforce

Female employees face problems similar to those encountered by racial and ethnic minorities, but some are unique to them regardless of race and ethnicity. Women have always worked, but until the past few decades most were not paid members of the working population. In 1947, only about one-third of adult women in the United States were employed or actively looking for work (Moen & Roehling, 2005, pp. 13–14). Today, women's labor participation rate is only slightly below that for men (see Figure 10.10), although men on average put in more hours on the job.

Much of the increase in women's labor force participation comes from white women joining the workforce; black women were already there. In 1920, for example,

Affirmative action: Policies enacted by governments and private organizations to increase work and educational opportunities for women and members of certain minority groups.

Education, Race, and Income

A major dividing line in U.S. society separates the incomes of college graduates from the incomes of those who lack college degrees. The dollar amount of the difference is a matter of some dispute, but it certainly comes to several hundred thousand dollars over a lifetime (Day & Newburger, 2002). (For a more modest estimate, see Pilon, 2010.) To be sure, attaining a college education has become massively expensive, and many graduates struggle for years to pay off the loans they incurred as students. Nor does possessing a college diploma guarantee economic success. Even so, it's clear that having a college degree considerably improves a person's odds of finding steady employment with a decent wage or salary.

Although African American and Hispanic students have made substantial strides in educational attainment in recent years, they still lag behind whites (as Figure 10.8 shows). But educational attainment is not the sole cause of income differences, as we can see by comparing the incomes of college-educated whites and minority group members (Aud, Fox, & KewalRamani, 2010). In 2014, white men over the age of 25 with college degrees had a median weekly income of $1,249, a significantly higher income than those of blacks ($895) and Hispanics ($937) with college degrees. Asian Americans did better, but at a weekly income of

$1,149 still trailed the white median by $100 per week (U.S. Bureau of Labor Statistics, 2015e). The income gap was less pronounced among women; the annual income of black women with college degrees was only $5,000 less than that of white women with college degrees. For college-educated Hispanic women the gap was larger, at $7,000, while Asian American women actually out-earned their white counterparts by $4,000.

Are these differences solely the results of prejudice and discrimination? Not all college degrees are equal, and it is possible that most white graduates went to institutions that prepared them for work better than those attended by minority graduates. Age also has to be taken into account, especially for Hispanics, who on average are younger than the workforce as a whole. Still, the income gap that separates white women and black women is smaller than the one that

divides white men and black men. It does seem possible, then, that black men face more discrimination in the labor market than do black women.

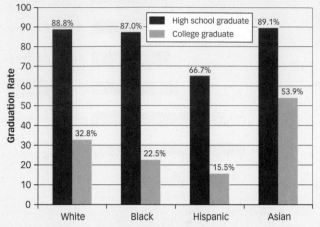

FIGURE 10.8 Educational Attainment in the United States, 2015

Legend: High school graduate / College graduate

White: 88.8%, 32.8%
Black: 87.0%, 22.5%
Hispanic: 66.7%, 15.5%
Asian: 89.1%, 53.9%

(Y-axis: Graduation Rate, 0–100)

SOURCE: http://www.census.gov/content/dam/Census/library/publications/2016/demo/p20-578.pdfExperiencing Work and the Economy

▶ **THINK ABOUT IT**

1. Why does possession of a college degree enhance someone's ability to find a job? What are the most important job-related skills, attitudes, and habits learned in college?

2. Although having a college degree is correlated with having higher life-time earnings, correlation does not necessarily imply causality. Is there a causal relationship in this case?

33% of married and 59% of unmarried black women were in the U.S. labor force, while for white women, the figures were 7% and 45%, respectively (Reskin & Padavic, 1994, pp. 22–23). It was not until the 1990s that white women's labor force participation catch up to that of black women.

Though women now participate in the labor force in numbers nearly equal to those of men, they are massively overrepresented within the ranks of secretaries, nurses, child-care workers, and receptionists. Of the hundreds

of occupations tallied by the U.S. Census Bureau, just 10 account for one-third of U.S. women workers (Institute for Women's Policy Research, 2011). Some observers would argue that such gender-based **occupational segregation** simply reflects the different interests and abilities of men and

Occupational segregation: The tendency of certain jobs to be predominantly filled on the basis of gender or according to race and ethnicity.

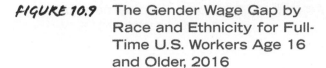

FIGURE 10.9 The Gender Wage Gap by Race and Ethnicity for Full-Time U.S. Workers Age 16 and Older, 2016

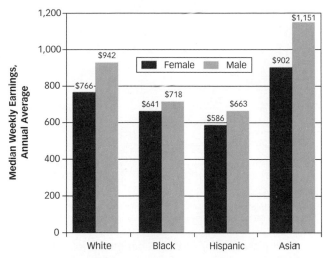

SOURCE: United States Department of Labor, Bureau of Labor Statistics 2012. "Median usual weekly earnings of full-time wage and salary workers by selected characteristics, annual averages."

women. Whether these are due to inherent differences, prior socialization, or the interaction of the two has long been a matter of scholarly and popular debate. In any event, segregation by gender is problematic when it contributes to long-standing disparities in the wages and salaries of men and women. In 2014, full-time women workers received an average of 83 cents for every dollar earned by male workers (U.S. Bureau of Labor Statistics, 2016). This represents an improvement over the recent past; in 1979, the ratio was 62 cents to the dollar (U.S. Bureau of Labor Statistics, 2012b). Note, however, that these statistics refer to weekly earnings. Women are more likely to work on a part-time basis than men (26–12%). But in contrast to the overall male-female income gap, women working part-time out-earn male part-timers by $242 to $236 (U.S. Bureau of Labor Statistics, 2015b, p. 7).

Occupations in which there are high proportions of women workers almost always have lower wages and salaries than do male-dominated occupations. The division between "men's jobs" and "women's jobs" contributes substantially to the lower average earnings of women workers; according to one calculation, it accounts for about 20% of the male-female wage gap (see Figure 10.11; Cotter, Hermson, & Vanneman, 2006, p. 201).

Gender-based occupational segregation diminishes women's wages and salaries in several ways. One is a consequence of supply-and-demand economics. When large numbers of women are confined to a few occupations, the supply of workers there will be large relative to the demand, keeping wages and salaries low. Another is that some

employers, most of whom are men, believe that by its very nature the kind of work women perform is of less value than the work done by men. Few tasks are more important than the care and education of young children, for example, but categorizing these tasks as "women's work" results in low pay for day-care workers. At the other end of the occupational spectrum, pediatric medicine, which has a relatively high number of female practitioners, is also one of the lowest-paid medical specialties (J. Smith, 2012b).

Women have begun to move into male-dominated occupations in significant numbers. Some of this activity can be attributed to the fact that women are now more likely than men to get a college degree. They also have made substantial advancements in earning postgraduate degrees. For the period 2011–2012, 47.6% of medical school graduates were women (Jolliff et al., 2012). During that same period, the percentage of law school graduates who were women was almost identical, at 47.3% (American Bar Association, 2013, p. 4). More educational preparation for women addresses only one aspect of occupational segregation, of course, but soon we may no longer automatically associate medicine and law with male practitioners.

The income of female workers has also been undermined by another difference between women and men: the continuity of their occupational careers. The moment when employees typically arrive at the make-or-break phase of their careers is precisely the time when many women take on the massive responsibilities of bearing and raising children. Very few men leave their jobs to be stay-at-home fathers or even cut back on their workloads to spend more time with their children. This may be an economically rational decision, given that fathers are likely to earn more than mothers. Whatever the reason, far more women than men have interrupted careers, or careers with serious role conflicts, making advancement more difficult and dampening their long-term earnings.

Women on average earn less than men for many reasons, though the gap has been narrowing in recent years. But here we must make an important qualification: Between 1979 and 2010, the gap narrowed for workers lacking college degrees because men's earnings declined, not because women's earnings increased (Autor & Wasserman, 2013, pp. 11–12, 21). For college-educated women workers, the news has been mixed. Contrary to the general stagnation in wages in recent decades, these workers have enjoyed increases in pay. Even so, the male-female earnings gap has *widened* for college-educated workers because women's wages and salaries have not risen as rapidly as men's. (Keep in mind that these statements apply to the national labor force; there can be considerable deviation from general trends within regional labor markets. See McCall, 2001, pp. 123, 126.) College-educated women workers have enjoyed rising incomes, but their male counterparts have done even better (Autor & Wasserman, 2013, p. 25).

Working May Be Hazardous to Your Health

Work is a dangerous activity for many employees. According to the U.S. Department of Labor, 4,836 workers died in 2015 as a result of work-related injuries (U.S. Bureau of Labor Statistics, 2016b). Highway accidents involving truckers and other drivers were the leading cause of job-related deaths, followed by falls, slips, and trips; contact with objects or equipment; injuries caused by persons or animals; and exposure to harmful substances or environments (U.S. Bureau of Labor Statistics, 2016b). In 2015, the category encompassing agriculture, forestry, fishing, and hunting earned the dubious distinction of having the highest fatality rate, at 25.3 deaths per 100,000 full-time equivalent workers. Next came transportation and material moving at 14.7, followed by construction at 12.5 per 100,000. In contrast, the category of office and administrative support had only 0.5 fatalities per 100,000 full-time equivalent workers (U.S. Bureau of Labor Statistics, 2016f).

FIGURE 10.10 Global Employment by Gender, 1962–2015

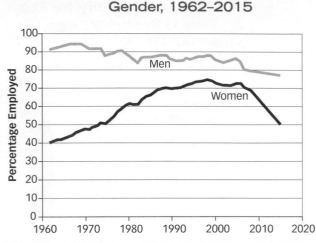

SOURCE: Based on "End of the Gender Revolution," Reeve Vanneman, Department of Sociology, University of Maryland. Authors' calculations from Current Population Survey (CPS) data provided by the Integrated Public Use Microdata (IPUMS) files.

Workplace fatalities are rare, but on-the-job injuries are fairly common. In total, 2.9 million U.S. workers suffered nonfatal injuries on the job in 2015, or 3 injuries for every

FIGURE 10.11 Educational Attainment and Lifetime Earnings in the United States by Gender

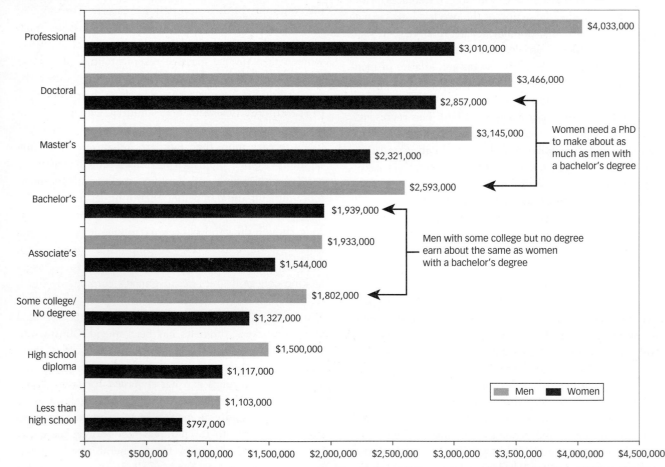

SOURCE: From *The College Payoff: Education, Occupations, and Lifetime Earnings*, Anthony P. Carnevale, Stephen J. Rose, and Ban Cheah. The Georgetown University Center on Education and Workplace. August 5, 2011. Reprinted with permission.

100 full-time equivalent workers (U.S. Bureau of Labor Statistics, 2016d). Manufacturing jobs are more dangerous than those in the service sector, with 3.8 injuries per 100 full-time equivalent workers in the former and 2.9 in the latter. There is, however, a considerable spread within the service sector. Some services, such as finance and insurance, have only 0.5 injuries per 100 workers, a sharp contrast with the 12.0 ratio for workers employed in nursing and residential care facilities, a ratio considerably higher than the one for truck driving, which comes out to 4.3 per 100 (U.S. Bureau of Labor Statistics, 2016d).

Workplace Stress

In addition to causing physical injuries and even death, a job that poses physical hazards can also induce the psychological condition known as **stress**. Some degree of job-related stress is not necessarily a bad thing. The stress of facing a challenging set of tasks can promote a high level of performance and feelings of accomplishment. But beyond a certain point, stress becomes an overwhelmingly negative aspect of working life that has been implicated in a number of physical and psychological ailments, such as depression, high blood pressure, and lower back pain, along with alcoholism and drug abuse.

Although it seems a bit counterintuitive, a monotonous job can also be quite stressful, particularly one that requires steady concentration, such as data entry or assembly-line work. Having inadequate resources is another source of stress. Anyone who has faced a deadline can attest that time is one of the most crucial resources. Power and authority also are important. A worker who is charged with implementing decisions but lacks the authority to do so will feel stress. Perhaps most important, workers have lives that extend beyond the workplace, and trying to accommodate the competing demands of work and family can be profoundly stressful.

Stressful work situations are not always offset by higher wages or salaries, nor does a well-paid position high in the organizational hierarchy necessarily result in elevated stress levels. In fact, the opposite seems to be the case. Low-wage occupations that afford little control over the work environment are associated with elevated risks of hypertension, cardiovascular disease, and mental illness (Schulman, 2003, pp. 98–100). In a study of British government officials, one key indication of stress—elevated blood pressure during working hours—was found to be more pronounced among low-status workers than among high-status workers. The lower-level workers also had higher death rates, even when variables such as age were taken into account (Job Stress Network, 2005).

Although we usually characterize stress as an individual psychological problem, it also has a clear organizational dimension. The way work is structured, especially the

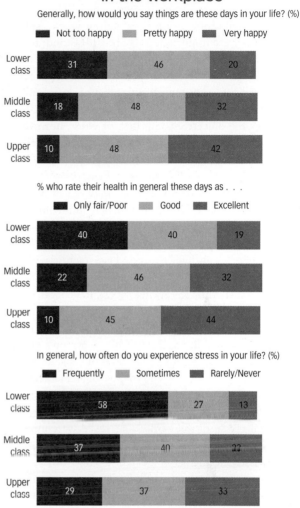

FIGURE 10.12 Physical and Mental Health in the Workplace

Generally, how would you say things are these days in your life? (%)

- Not too happy
- Pretty happy
- Very happy

Lower class: 31 / 46 / 20
Middle class: 18 / 48 / 32
Upper class: 10 / 48 / 42

% who rate their health in general these days as . . .

- Only fair/Poor
- Good
- Excellent

Lower class: 40 / 40 / 19
Middle class: 22 / 46 / 32
Upper class: 10 / 45 / 44

In general, how often do you experience stress in your life? (%)

- Frequently
- Sometimes
- Rarely/Never

Lower class: 58 / 27 / 13
Middle class: 37 / 40 / 22
Upper class: 29 / 37 / 33

SOURCE: "A Third of Americans Now Say They Are in the Lower Classes" by Rich Morin and Seth Motel. September 10, 2012. Pew Research: Pew Social and Demographic Trends. Reprinted with permission.

NOTE: "Does not apply" and "Don't know/Refused" responses not shown.

balance between responsibilities and access to adequate resources, greatly affects stress levels. In general, workers who are able to control the demands of their working environments are less likely to experience stress than are those with little of this ability (O'Toole & Lawler, 2006, p. 105).

Job Satisfaction and Dissatisfaction

Stress is a major contributor to dissatisfaction with a job, but it is hardly the only one. Sociologists, psychologists, and enlightened managers have long been concerned about working conditions that harm workers and reduce their productivity. On the whole, the majority of workers are at least reasonably satisfied with their jobs. A survey conducted in 2015 by the Society for Human Resource

Stress: The negative psychological and physiological effects of difficulties at work and elsewhere.

Management (2016) found that 88% of the workers surveyed were satisfied with their jobs, although only half that number reported being "very satisfied." The most significant contributors to job satisfaction, wages, salaries, and benefits were important, but came in second; topping the list was "respectful treatment of all employees at all levels." Job security came in next, followed by interactions with supervisors and opportunities to use skills and abilities (Society for Human Resource Management, 2016).

Besides the objective conditions of work, however, we must also consider the values, attitudes, and especially the expectations that workers bring to their jobs. Academics and other well-educated members of the upper-middle class who research and write about work may reflect their own responses to particular jobs, but the men and women actually doing the work may bring different sets of values and expectations. Even workers in some of the most unpleasant and low-paying jobs have expressed satisfaction with their work because, if nothing else, it is the basis of their friendship network (Bryant & Perkins, 1982). In general, on-the-job friendships are often important sources of both worker satisfaction and organizational success (West, 2017).

As with most other aspects of life, a person's expectations about a job affect his or her level of satisfaction with that job. Younger workers tend to have higher expectations than older workers, who have become more realistic and more resigned. This can be seen in the results of a recent Harris poll: 78% of the workers surveyed were interested in changing their careers, but only 54% of workers in their 40s expressed an interest in a career change (Boyle, 2013). Differing expectations also help explain why women generally exhibit the same levels of job satisfaction as male workers, even though their jobs on the whole pay less, are less intrinsically interesting, and offer fewer opportunities for advancement. Rather than having lower aspirations than men, women may be comparing their job situations with those of other women (Hodson, 1989).

> **ASK YOURSELF:** What sorts of trade-offs would you make in order to have a satisfying job? Specifically, would you rather have a high-paying but not very satisfying job, or one that paid less but offered more job satisfaction? What characteristics of work and the workplace contribute to job satisfaction for you, and what characteristics detract from it?

Work in the 21st Century

In the 1950s, futurists were making bold predictions about the way automated processes would take over most of the work then being done by humans. The "age of leisure" they envisioned never came to pass, of course, although advances in production technologies went far beyond

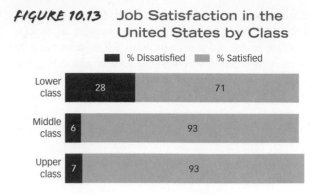

FIGURE 10.13 Job Satisfaction in the United States by Class

Legend: ■ % Dissatisfied ■ % Satisfied

Lower class: 28 / 71
Middle class: 6 / 93
Upper class: 7 / 93

SOURCE: "A Third of Americans Now Say They Are in the Lower Classes" by Rich Morin and Seth Motel. September 10, 2012. Pew Research: Pew Social and Demographic Trends. Reprinted with permission.

NOTE: "Don't know/Refused" responses not shown. Shares combine proportions who say they are "completely" or "mostly" satisfied.

what they prophesied. Today's problem is not how to fill up vast amounts of leisure time, but how to deal with involuntary unemployment. Technological advances and globalization have profoundly influenced work, but, as noted above, a key distinction has to be made between the loss of particular *jobs* and *employment* as a whole.

Technological change is only one of the forces shaping work today and in the future. Climate change, government policies, and cultural shifts will change the mix of jobs we do, who does them, and the extent to which they are rewarded. Additionally, shifts in the size and composition of the workforce will profoundly affect jobs and the economy. The most important trend is, and likely will continue to be, a slowdown in population growth, and its complement, an aging society. These trends have been particularly evident in Japan and many European countries, but they also affect the United States. According to the U.S. Department of Labor Statistics, from 2014 to 2024, the labor force will grow at an annual rate of 0.5% (U.S. Bureau of Labor Statistics, 2015d). Such a slow rate of growth will result in a labor force of about 164 million men and women in 2024, composed of fewer younger workers, more older ones, and more retirees. Demographic trends will also change the composition of the labor force, which, due to immigration, somewhat higher fertility rates, and higher rates of labor force participation, will have relatively more Latinos and Asian Americans, and relatively fewer whites.

The aging of a slowly growing labor force will pose a number of challenges, but not nearly as severe as the ones confronting Japan and some other countries, which are facing both aging populations and smaller labor forces. Taking care of elderly people and maintaining the financial integrity of private and government pensions will be difficult tasks. The United States is fortunate that it has large numbers of immigrants, most of whom are in their prime working age, to pick up the slack.

Members of the labor force, both immigrant and native-born, will hold down jobs in industries and workplaces that are likely to differ markedly from what we now think to be the normal state of affairs. Some of the changes will be beneficial for workers and the populations as a whole; others may not. As has always been the case, the jobs we hold are shaped by the societies we live in, but in the final analysis, we shape society through the work we do.

USING THEORY TO EXAMINE WORK AND THE ECONOMY: THE FUNCTIONALIST, CONFLICT, AND SYMBOLIC INTERACTIONIST PERSPECTIVES

10.4 Apply the functionalist, conflict, and symbolic interactionist perspectives to workplace issues.

Many theories are relevant to understanding work and its social context. Some have been created by sociologists, some by others. All provide useful insights, but none covers all aspects of work. Three major theoretical approaches are discussed in this section: functionalism, conflict theory, and symbolic interactionism.

Functionalism

Functionalism views society as a system of interconnected parts that support and depend on one another. The dominant theoretical approach in sociology and anthropology during the first half of the 20th century, it met with heavy criticism beginning in the late 1960s, but its influence continues today.

Functionalism has obvious relevance to the study of work. One of the fundamental characteristics of work in modern society is the **division of labor**, through which work is divided into many specialized occupational roles and tasks. To illustrate, the *Dictionary of Occupational Titles* compiled by the U.S. Bureau of the Census lists 842 separate occupational categories, encompassing 30,000 distinct job titles such as "emulsification operator," "welt trimmer," and "pickling grader" (U.S. Department of Labor, 2011).

One of the first discussions of the benefits of the division of labor appears in Adam Smith's classic 1776 work *The Wealth of Nations*. In a section containing his

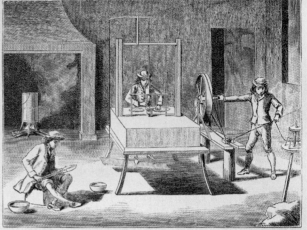

Old Images/Alamy Stock Photo

▶ A depiction of 17th-century pin makers. The division of labor proceeds something like this: One worker stretches the wire, another straightens it, a third cuts it, a fourth points it, a fifth grinds it at the top, and another affixes the head on the top.

famous presentation of pin manufacture, Smith showed that dividing pin making into several specialized tasks resulted in great improvements in productivity; where one pin maker working alone might make 20 pins a day, 10 workers performing specialized tasks could produce 48,000 pins, an average of 4,800 pins per worker (A. Smith, 2012/1776).

In a single pin factory a manager can organize and coordinate the operations of a few workers, but how can this be done when a vast number of tasks are being performed in thousands of separate enterprises? Smith's answer focused on the role of market exchanges in tying together all these diverse activities. In an effective market, the providers of specialized goods and services enter into explicit and implicit contracts when engaging in mutually beneficial exchanges with the providers of other goods and services (A. Smith, 2012/1776).

In Smith's vision, individuals and businesses enter into these contracts out of self-interest. This is at best a partial answer, however, because it misses the crucial social dimension of marketplace exchanges. In his *Division of Labor in Society*, originally published in 1893, Émile Durkheim (1984) emphasized the role of the extralegal elements of contracts—the values and norms that make up the cultural core of society—in maintaining a durable economic and social order (Goodwin & Scimecca, 2006, p. 121). In short, culture provides the rules governing market exchanges, without which these exchanges would not be possible.

Labor markets are populated not by socially isolated individuals but by men and women strongly influenced

Division of labor: The division of work into a multiplicity of specialized occupational roles and tasks.

by preexisting social and cultural rules. Wages and salaries are not solely determined by negotiations between an employer and an employee; in many instances, they often reflect norms and values regarding the value of the work being done. In the United States, some professional baseball and football players make enormous salaries, but this is not the case in countries where baseball and football are minor sports at best. More ominously, the allocation of jobs and rates of remuneration may reflect biases and prejudices that may be part of the values and norms of some segments of the society.

Policy Implications of Functionalism

The norms and values that support discrimination on the basis of race, ethnicity, and gender were once more prevalent than they are today, but they are by no means extinct. A functionalist theorist would likely argue that lingering prejudices and discriminatory behavior hinder the effective interconnectedness of the various elements that contribute to a well-functioning society. In particular, the jobs that people hold and the work they do should be a reflection of their abilities, and not of their race, ethnicity, and gender. A society is not functioning well, for example, when a woman takes a job as a salesclerk because she is barred from studying to be a physician.

Most of today's sociologists who take a functionalist approach would not argue that a society will align itself in such a way that existing cultural values and norms will naturally result in the functionally optimal allocation of jobs and work. Rather, they would agree that it may be necessary to pass and enforce employment laws that prevent discrimination on the basis of race, ethnicity, and gender. It is to be hoped that these laws also will act as transformative forces that contribute to a shift to a set of values and norms that do not support biased behavior.

The Conflict Theory of C. Wright Mills

A number of approaches—Marxist theory, critical theory, feminist theory, world systems theory, poststructural theory, and queer theory—can be included in the ranks of conflict theories. Here, we will briefly focus on the sociological analysis of C. Wright Mills (1916–1962). Although he wrote prior to the designation of "conflict theory" as a theoretical approach, Mills's approach to sociology and the study of work resides firmly within it.

One of Mills's earliest works, *The New Men of Power,* originally published in 1948, looked at the way union officials shape the relationship between employers and employees (Mills, 2001/1948). In his later book *The Power Elite* (1956), Mills portrayed U.S. society in the 1950s as dominated by three interlinked elites: the managers of large corporations, upper-level government officials, and top

military brass. In Mills's analysis, the rise of these forces threatened U.S. democracy itself. Unlike Marxists, however, he did not expect class-conscious workers to challenge this triumvirate. Absorbed in their efforts to acquire the consumer goods churned out by a booming postwar economy, members of the working class were not much inclined to dispute the prevailing distribution of power.

Nor did Mills put much hope in the political consciousness of middle-class workers, a group he analyzed in another book, *White Collar* (1951). Although their ranks had grown spectacularly during the 20th century, white-collar workers did not lean toward concentrated political action. As with the working class, this group's "usual demands are for a larger slice of a growing yield, and its conscious expectations are short-run expectations of immediate material improvements, not in any change in the system of work and life" (Mills, 1951, p. 331). In Mills's glum summation, "the jump from numerical growth and importance of function to increased political power requires, at a minimum, political awareness and political organization. The white-collar workers do not have either to any appreciable extent" (Mills, 1951, pp. 352–353).

Mills also sought to connect what he called "private problems" and "public issues." As individuals we tend to think our problems are unique to ourselves, failing to note that they are often produced by social forces beyond our control (Mills, 1959). For instance, we might view unemployment as a result of personal failings such as a lack of requisite skills or motivation. In fact, the widespread unemployment that followed the financial collapse of 2007–2008 was brought on by reckless and even criminal activities perpetrated by a financial sector liberated from prior government oversight.

Policy Implications of Mills's Conflict Theory

Mills wrote primarily in the 1950s, and much of his work was an attack on the complacency of that postwar decade. The policy implications of his ideas are not evident when it comes to governmental actions, but they have some applicability to present-day labor unions. If unions took Mills seriously, they would remain concerned with the wages and salaries of their members, but they also would organize in support of their interests and press employers more aggressively for actions to benefit the working class and the middle class as a whole. Unions would promote specific government policies that benefit members, but they would also educate union members so they better understand how today's society is structured, and who benefits the most from that structure.

Symbolic Interactionism

Symbolic interactionism is the theoretical approach that looks into the significance of symbols in structuring society and affecting individual behavior. Anyone familiar with working environments will be at least subconsciously aware of the many symbols that distinguish workers and workplaces. Organizations as diverse as the Ford Motor Company, Goodwill, the Central Intelligence Agency, and Facebook all have their distinctive logos. The design and selection of these logos has grown into an entire industry, and organizations try to embed themselves in the consciousness of potential customers and the public at large by displaying their logos whenever and wherever possible. Logos as old as Coca-Cola's and as new as Twitter's are burned vividly into our consciousness.

The places where people work also can be rich in symbolism. Buildings are places to get work done, but they may also denote something important about organizations and the people who work for them. As architectural critics have noted, skyscrapers that loom over a city are often not justifiable in economic terms; instead, they are designed and built for their symbolic value. The skyscraper used to be a distinctively U.S. construction, but today the world's tallest buildings are located in China, Dubai, and Malaysia, countries enjoying rapid increases in wealth. As the saying goes, "If you've got it, flaunt it."

The way a building is divided and furnished also may say a lot about what goes on inside it. An office with a single occupant says one thing about that person's value to the organization, while a large, undivided work space housing many workers says something quite different. An office on the topmost floor may symbolize being at the summit of the organization's hierarchy. A corner office with a sweeping view may also denote high organizational status. The type and quality of office furnishings are often tied to employees' positions in an organization. For example, the phrase "to be called on the carpet," meaning to be called to account or castigated by a higher-up, comes from the fact that in the past low-ranking employees would be summoned to the carpeted offices of workplace superiors to be reprimanded.

Uniforms are another symbol, an obvious occupational marker. Some uniforms, such as those of police officers, denote authority. Others, like the jumpsuits worn by prisoners, convey just the opposite. At one time, many manual workers wore blue work shirts or blue coveralls, hence the term *blue collar,* still shorthand for manual work and generally low status. In contrast, in some organizations, middle- or upper-level managers are derisively known as "suits."

▶ Construction crews work on a project in New York City where glass skyscrapers are being built. They wear hard hats and yellow safety vests as part of their "uniform." Manual laborers like construction workers are often referred to as blue-collar workers.

Andrew Lichtenstein/Corbis/Getty Images

Policy Implications of Symbolic Interactionism

The world contains much that we can usefully analyze from the perspective of symbolic interactionism. One symbol with obvious policy implications is the police uniform. On the one hand, the policeman-as-soldier uniform strongly connotes power and authority with dark colors, a badge, and a prominently displayed sidearm and baton. Garb like this conveys the image of a powerful individual capable of bringing order and security to a harsh environment populated by dangerous people. In contrast, in community policing, an officer acts as a member of the community, working closely with residents to preserve the peace. Under these circumstances, uniforms with a less military air may better convey the intended image.

SPECIALIZED THEORIES: WEBER AND SCIENTIFIC MANAGEMENT

 Apply specialized theories to workplace issues.

Max Weber's Theoretical Approach to Bureaucracy

In the description and analysis of the organizational structures of workplaces, one term is inescapable: *bureaucracy.* Although the word has strong connotations of inefficiency, waste, coldness, and petty rules, under the right circumstances bureaucracy can be the most effective way of getting things done.

The foundation of sociological thinking about bureaucracy was built by Max Weber (1864–1920) (Weber, 1958). Weber delineated the key elements of bureaucratic organization: (1) specialized personnel, (2) division of labor, (3) hierarchical authority, (4) impersonality, (5) clearly articulated rules and regulations, and (6) written records. In addition to presenting the major components of bureaucratic organization, Weber devoted considerable attention to the cultural values and modes of thought that gave rise to modern bureaucracies. Bureaucratic structures and processes reflected what Weber took to be the dominant cognitive orientation of modern societies: rationality. For Weber, rational thought patterns were prime elements of a historical process he called "the disenchantment of the world." By this, he meant the ability and willingness to explain the causes of worldly events without invoking supernatural agents such as devils, ghosts, and genies. Instead, logic and empiricism are the basis for understanding why things happen as they do.

Weber saw rationality as crucial to the design and operation of modern organizations because this mode of thought provides the most effective and efficient way of attaining particular goals. However, the goals a person or organization pursues may not themselves be the result of rational thought. Rationally designed structures and processes can be used to achieve goals that defy rational comprehension; as Captain Ahab in *Moby-Dick* notes of his pursuit of the great white whale, "All my means are sane, my motive and my object mad." Equally important, rationality can serve goals that are not just irrational but unethical, immoral, and criminal as well. History has provided us with plenty of examples of rationality being used for barbaric ends, Nazi Germany being a particularly repellant case.

Bureaucracy is an inescapable element of modern life. Most of us are born in bureaucratic settings, receive our education in them, and live out our working lives in them. Many of us rely on bureaucratically organized religious bodies to assist us in our final days. For employees who work in bureaucratic settings this mode of organization has both advantages and disadvantages. Work in a bureaucratically structured organization can entail being snarled in red tape, constricted by a multiplicity of rules and regulations, and thwarted when one attempts to act in an innovative and creative manner. On the other hand, a bureaucratic structure can protect an employee from unreasonable demands made by both clients and superiors. It prevents endless rumination over what to do in a particular situation, and it adds a dose of predictability in an unpredictable world.

Whether bureaucratic organization is good or bad, effective or ineffective, depends to a great extent on the nature of the work to be done. What works in one setting may be counterproductive in another. In similar fashion, what helps workers to do their jobs effectively in one set of circumstances may block them in another. For individual workers, bureaucratic organizational structures can offer protection from capricious, unreasonable, and oppressive bosses, but it can also leave workers as little more than flesh-and-blood robots performing monotonous, routinized tasks. Which path is taken depends heavily on workers' ability to shape the rules and organizational structures that govern the way they do their work.

Scientific Management

The decades that bracketed the turn of the 20th century were marked by widespread and at times violent labor unrest. Conflicts between labor and management, capitalists and proletarians, were endemic, and some countries seemed on the brink of revolution. But to Frederick W. Taylor (1856–1915) these conflicts were not inevitable; he believed that what was needed was a scientific approach to the management of workers.

The scion of a well-established Philadelphia family, Taylor had distinguished himself by developing improved techniques for the machining of steel and other metals. If obdurate metals could be more effectively managed through the development and use of scientific principles, thought Taylor, then surely these principles could be used for the more effective management of workers. During the latter part of the 19th century and the early 20th, he and his followers created what they called "scientific management." The fundamental assumption of scientific management was that both workers and traditional managers had failed to develop and use the most efficient production methods. Much better results would follow through the development and application of precise time-and-motion studies. When work was studied in this "scientific" manner, superfluous motions would be eliminated, and "the one best way" of doing things would prevail (Kanigel, 1997).

Workers were to be completely excluded from the formulation of maximally efficient procedures, because it was assumed they lacked the ability to generate efficient working procedures on their own. To compensate for their complete loss of on-the-job power, workers would be rewarded through a piece-rate wage system that would ensure they received their fair share of the financial gains that came with improved production methods. As Taylor saw it, labor strife had been fueled by endless squabbles between workers and managers over how to divide a small pie. In contrast, under scientific management production would be maximized, and workers and enterprise owners would share a much larger pie.

Scientific management thinking was very influential in its heyday. Taylor was an effective publicist who claimed that the principles of scientific management were equally valid outside factory settings; they could be used to good effect for the management of schools, hospitals, and even churches. Scientific management had a wide following outside the United States; even Vladimir Lenin encouraged the application of scientific management in the newly founded Soviet Union. But as with many great ideas, its implementation failed to meet its promise. As might be expected, workers naturally objected to the rigid control of their actions, and some employers manipulated piece rates so that workers saw no improvement in their wages. Of equal or greater importance, established managers were decidedly unenthusiastic about scientific management, and many resisted the efforts of Taylor's followers to tell them how to manage their businesses. Jealously guarding their authority, they were unwilling to cede it to teams of college-educated men with stopwatches and clipboards.

Subsequent research in industrial sociology and psychology called into question one of the key assumptions of scientific management, that the main source of worker motivation is the hope of making more money. Beginning with the famous Hawthorne studies of the 1920s and 1930s, researchers came to the realization that workplaces are social systems in their own right, often with strong cultural norms. As these research projects discovered, the norms of working groups affect the speed with which workers go about their tasks and prevent the most efficient workers from outpacing fellow workers. The opportunity to earn more money is an important source of motivation, but it is not the only one.

SOCIAL CHANGE: WHAT CAN YOU DO?

 10.6 Identify steps toward social change for work-related problems.

Some social problems are not solved by massive, sweeping changes. Sometimes improvement comes through relatively small-scale actions at the local level. The first example below describes a cluster of actions that have had global consequences. The second also deals with an aspect of globalization, but one tied directly to local concerns.

▶▶ United Students Against Sweatshops

Bangladesh is one of the world's poorest countries. Its largest industry is garment manufacture, accounting for 80% of its export earnings and heavily dependent on extremely cheap labor, most of it done by women. Five garment factories were housed in the Rana Plaza building in Dhaka, the nation's capital. In April 2013, the building's owner and the factory managers dismissed engineers' concerns about safety even though the building had developed cracks and had begun to shake. Workers were ordered back to their jobs, and the next day the building collapsed, killing 1,127 people (Manik & Yardley, 2013).

The tragedy in Bangladesh is a reminder of the sad history of the garment industry. After a fire swept through the Triangle Shirtwaist Factory in New York City in 1911, killing 146 young women from Eastern European Jewish and Italian immigrant families, stronger safety laws were passed and the movement to unionize garment workers gained strength in the United States. Higher wages and safer working conditions increased production costs in a price-sensitive industry, and in the decades that followed, much of the work in the industry moved to parts of the world where wages were still low and safety was not always a prime consideration.

The ultimate responsibility for enacting and administering effective laws that protect workers necessarily rests with the countries where the factories are located. Even so, outsiders can exert a significant amount of pressure to improve the working lives of garment workers. Apparel is produced to be sold at a profit, and if a significant number of consumers decide to boycott goods produced in sweatshops, manufacturers will be strongly motivated to improve working conditions. Colleges and universities often earn sizable revenues from the sale of apparel bearing the names and logos of their institutions, making a boycott of the manufacturers of that apparel financially painful for them.

One group committed to pressuring sweatshop employers is United Students Against Sweatshops. Activists in this organization have taken advantage of the fact that colleges and universities are major retailers of T-shirts, hoodies, caps, and other items of apparel (United Students Against Sweatshops, 2017). Because students are concentrated in a particular geographic locality, they are

▶ Fast-food workers, cashiers, cooks, delivery people, and their supporters hold a rally outside New York City Hall. They expected the city council to vote on legislation that would provide a fair workweek for fast-food and retail workers as well as a bill that would enable them to have a united voice on the job.

in a good position to organize themselves and pressure their institutions to require independent inspections of firms that supply merchandise carrying their schools' brands. Such efforts have produced some notable successes. In the 1990s, student activism was directed at Nike's suppliers in Indonesia, who eventually raised their workers' wages by 50%. In another case, Pennsylvania State University terminated its relationship with Adidas after one of the firm's contractors abruptly shut down a factory and refused to give employees severance pay.

United Students Against Sweatshops has shown that an organized group can affect the purchasing decisions of retailers. Still, extensive changes will come about only through the combined efforts of consumers, retailers, and larger organizations such as churches and municipalities. Your campus is a place to begin.

▶▶ Pitzer College and the Day Labor Center

Day laborers are workers who station themselves in public places, often the parking lots of big-box hardware stores, in the hope of being recruited for short-term work. Their employers are typically small businesses and homeowners who need temporary workers to do semiskilled jobs such as painting, tree trimming, and moving. Day laborers are usually immigrants, and many lack documentation for legal residence in the United States. Their existence is difficult; their working conditions may be unsafe, and they have little recourse if they are taken advantage of or not paid.

Many communities have banned the solicitation of work in public places. Pomona, California, for instance, passed an ordinance that prohibited "the solicitation of or for work on any street or highway, public area or non-residential parking area." Fortunately for the men needing work in the Pomona area, in 1998 students and faculty at Pitzer College, in the adjacent town of Claremont, founded the Pomona Economic Opportunity Center (PEOC) to serve their interests. As a result of the efforts of Pitzer students and faculty, the Pomona ordinance was amended to allow day laborers a single place within the city at which to seek temporary work from prospective employers. The PEOC was then designated as this sole lawful place.

In addition to connecting workers with prospective employers, the center is a gathering site for laborers that also promotes safe and fair working conditions for them. It aids workers and their families in a multitude of ways. According to its statement of purpose, "The Center's primary goals include increasing the financial security, safety, health, civic participation and human rights of day laborers in the Pomona Valley region, along with addressing and working to change the systemic obstacles that stand in the way of achieving those goals" (Pitzer College, 2017). The activities of the center include the following:

- Identifying well-paid and safe employment opportunities for day laborers

- Improving access to existing resources in the local community and building coalitions to create new resources

- Providing educational opportunities on worker and immigrant rights

- Identifying training opportunities in work and language skills

- Developing strong day laborer leaders through organizing and training

Many of the problems day laborers encounter can be traced to their lack of fluency in written and spoken English, so since 1999 the PEOC has sponsored classes in English as a second language taught by student volunteers from Pitzer and other Claremont colleges. The instruction is not all one-way; workers affiliated with the PEOC participate in weekly lunchtime meetings with Pitzer students seeking to enhance their command of Spanish and gain a better understanding of cultures different from their own as well as the family issues and working lives of day laborers. Many communities have significant immigrant populations, and organizing informal language classes is a good way for students to strengthen ties between themselves and recent immigrants, and to benefit their communities.

WHAT DOES AMERICA THINK?

Questions About Work and the Economy From the General Social Survey

Turn to the beginning of the chapter to compare your answers to those of the total population.

1. If you were to become rich, would you continue to work or stop working?

   CONTINUE TO WORK: 71.4%

   STOP WORKING: 28.6%

2. With regard to your income tax, do you think it is too high, about right, or too low?

   TOO HIGH: 55.2%

   ABOUT THE RIGHT AMOUNT: 42.2%

   TOO LOW: 2.6%

3. Do you think that work is most important to feel accomplished?

   MOST IMPORTANT: 45.7%

   NOT THE MOST IMPORTANT: 54.3%

4. What is your interest level in economic issues?

   VERY INTERESTED: 39.4%

   MODERATELY INTERESTED: 46.1%

   NOT INTERESTED AT ALL: 14.5%

5. What is your confidence level in banks and financial institutions?

   A GREAT DEAL: 14.1%

   ONLY SOME: 54.3%

   HARDLY ANY: 31.6%

SOURCE: National Opinion Research Center, University of Chicago.

CHAPTER SUMMARY

 10.1 Explain the general shape of the U.S. workforce today.

The labor force is conventionally defined as all persons in the civilian noninstitutional population who are either employed or unemployed but actively seeking work. More than 80% of American workers are employed by the service sector, while the remaining work in the primary sector (farming and mining) and the secondary sector (construction and manufacturing).

 10.2 Identify patterns and trends in employment and unemployment.

Work is an essential activity that, like most human endeavors, has its problematic aspects. Today, the most problematic is the absence of work, often for large periods of time, for a significant portion of the labor force. Unemployment has not been spread evenly over all segments of the labor force, and some who are unemployed have become so discouraged about the prospects of finding a job that they have given up and are no longer counted as members of the labor force (discouraged workers). As in many other arenas, race, ethnicity, and gender are important, influencing a person's likelihood of being unemployed and the duration of joblessness.

10.3 Discuss the role of unions and the issues of wage inequities, discrimination, and stress in the workplace.

Globalization and technological change have greatly affected employment and unemployment. They have also been implicated in the widening income gap that has been a prominent feature of the U.S. economy for several decades; other causes are the decline of unionization, educational disparities, and the persistent difficulties faced by women and members of racial and ethnic minority groups. Unemployment creates many present and future difficulties for the jobless. Some jobs are inherently dangerous, and all modes of work have their stressful elements. Yet work has the potential to bring personal satisfaction, even if the sources of job satisfaction are not always obvious.

10.4 Apply the functionalist, conflict, and symbolic interactionist perspectives to workplace issues.

Functionalism makes evident the interconnected nature of the great variety of occupations found in a modern society and offers some ideas about what holds everything together. Conflict theorist C. Wright Mills pointed to unemployment as a public issue often mistaken for a private problem. Symbolic interactionism notes the ways in which work and occupations are suffused with symbols that give important clues about the nature of particular jobs and the workers doing them.

 10.5 Apply specialized theories to workplace issues.

Max Weber delineated the key elements of the bureaucratic organization: specialized personnel, division of labor, hierarchical authority, impersonality, clearly articulated rules and regulations, and written records. Bureaucracy is an inescapable element in modern life. Work in a bureaucratically structured organization can entail dealing with red tape and rules and regulations that may stifle creativity. On the other hand, a bureaucratic structure can protect an employee from unreasonable demands made by both clients and superiors. It prevents endless rumination over what to do in a particular situation, and it adds a dose of predictability in an unpredictable world. Scientific management, promoted by Frederick W. Taylor, had its heyday around the turn of the 20th century. Its thesis that "one best way" exists to do a particular job was an attempt to find maximum efficiency in production methods and reward workers by piece-rate wage systems. Subsequent research in industrial sociology and psychology called into question one of the key assumptions of scientific management, that the main source of worker motivation is the hope of making more money.

10.6 Identify steps toward social change for work-related problems.

Some problematic aspects of work and unemployment seem intractable, but immobilizing despair is not a proper response. To take two examples of effective activism, United Students Against Sweatshops has challenged the use of sweatshop labor on an international scale, and at the local level, Pitzer College and the Pomona Economic Opportunity Center has helped immigrant workers improve their working situations as well as their lives in general.

KEY TERMS

affirmative action 247

benefits 236

cyclical unemployment 242

discouraged workers 238

division of labor 253

employment at will 241

"frictional unemployment" 242

globalization 243

Great Depression 242

human capital 246

labor force 237

lump of labor fallacy 243

North American Free Trade Agreement (NAFTA) 244

occupational segregation 248

primary sector 237

quintile 240

salary 236

secondary sector 237

service sector 237

stress 251

structural unemployment 242

total compensation 237

underground economy 238

wage 236

whistle-blowing 241

$SAGE edge™   Want a better grade?

Get the tools you need to sharpen your study skills. Access practice quizzes, eFlashcards, video, and multimedia at
http://edge.sagepub.com/trevino2e

11 CRIME

Kyle J. Thomas and Benjamin C. Hamilton

Bilgin S. Sasmaz/Anadolu Agency/Getty Images

▶▶▶ People light candles at a makeshift memorial for the mass shooting victims who lost their lives after a gunman fired on thousands attending a concert in Las Vegas on October 1, 2017, killing 59 people and injuring more than 500.

Investigating Crime: Our Stories

LEARNING OBJECTIVES

11.1 Discuss crime as a social problem.

11.2 Explain how crime is socially defined.

11.3 Discuss the sources of crime data.

11.4 Discuss patterns and trends in crime and crime measurement.

11.5 Describe the U.S. criminal justice system and its stakeholders.

11.6 Apply the functionalist, conflict, and symbolic interactionist perspectives to the problem of crime.

11.7 Apply specialized theories of crime.

11.8 Identify steps toward social change concerning crime.

Kyle J. Thomas

As with many scholars, my interest in crime and deviance spawned largely from my own experiences. In my undergraduate studies at Washington State University I became fascinated with the question of why I engaged in deviant behavior in groups that I would otherwise not engage in alone. This ultimately bloomed into a broader interest in why people break rules and the social causes that factor into this decision. Once I finished my undergraduate degree, I moved across the country to the University of Maryland to pursue a Ph.D. in criminology. There I was exposed to an in-depth education on criminological theories and research that has had a profound impact on my career.

In 2015, I completed my Ph.D. and accepted a position at the University of Missouri–St. Louis (UMSL). My research focuses on how subjective expectations influence the decision to offend. More specifically, much of my work examines peer and attitudinal influences on offending. I have also worked to incorporate behavioral economics into the study of crime and deviance. At UMSL I teach criminological theory and research methods at the undergraduate level, and advanced statistics at the graduate level.

Benjamin C. Hamilton

My desire to pursue a career in crime and social research was first sparked in Philadelphia at a conference at the Academy of Criminal Justice Sciences during my senior year as an undergraduate. Before then, my exposure to research had primarily been limited to reading assignments and individual papers I had written for classes. Many of the papers had been several decades old, with results already revisited and challenged by contemporary scholars and practitioners. The conference, by contrast, was my first opportunity to get a first-hand glimpse of cutting-edge, contemporary research, as well as hear from scholars directly as to how they conducted their studies, what methods they employed to gather their data, and how they dealt with any issues that arose throughout the process.

I knew shortly afterward that I wanted to focus my professional development toward conducting research in the social sciences. A few weeks later, I sent an application for a master's program in criminology and criminal justice at the University of Missouri–St. Louis, and now am currently enrolled in their Ph.D. program. Most of the projects I have been involved in up to now have primarily focused on offender decision making—namely, on how offending populations respond to "rational" incentives—and measurement issues in crime research. I also teach an undergraduate-level class on statistical applications in criminology and criminal justice.

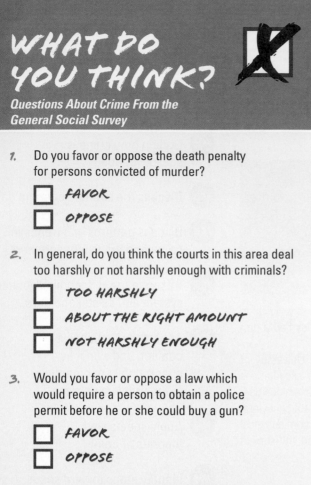
1. Do you favor or oppose the death penalty for persons convicted of murder?

   ☐ FAVOR

   ☐ OPPOSE

2. In general, do you think the courts in this area deal too harshly or not harshly enough with criminals?

   ☐ TOO HARSHLY

   ☐ ABOUT THE RIGHT AMOUNT

   ☐ NOT HARSHLY ENOUGH

3. Would you favor or oppose a law which would require a person to obtain a police permit before he or she could buy a gun?

   ☐ FAVOR

   ☐ OPPOSE

4. In the United States, do you think we're spending too much money on law enforcement, too little money, or about the right amount?

   ☐ TOO MUCH

   ☐ TOO LITTLE

   ☐ ABOUT THE RIGHT AMOUNT

5. Are there any situations you can imagine in which you would approve of a policeman striking an adult male citizen?

   ☐ YES

   ☐ NO

6. Are you ever afraid to walk at night in your neighborhood?

   ☐ YES

   ☐ NO

  Turn to the end of the chapter to view the results for the total population.

SOURCE: National Opinion Research Center, University of Chicago.

IN A HOODED SWEATSHIRT

Suppose an African American friend of yours, a high school senior, is staying at a friend's house in a gated community. It's a chilly, rainy day and he's home taking care of his younger stepbrother. Bored, he decides to walk to a nearby convenience store. On his way back from the store, he notices a man following him, and, nervous, he calls his girlfriend on his cell phone. She tells him to run away, but a violent struggle between the men ensues.

This describes the case of Trayvon Martin and George Zimmerman. According to police, residents of Zimmerman's Florida neighborhood had reason to worry about crime. Home foreclosures had left many houses empty and made the neighborhood a target for thefts, so Zimmerman had formed a Neighborhood Watch group. On February 26, 2012, when he spotted Martin, a black youth in a hooded sweatshirt, he called 911. Even though the police dispatcher instructed him not to pursue Martin, he did so anyway (Blow, 2012). In the confrontation that then took place, Martin was killed. Zimmerman was subsequently tried on charges of second-degree murder and manslaughter. The prosecutor in the case suggested that Martin had been racially profiled by Zimmerman, a civilian. Racial profiling occurs when police use race or ethnicity as a

REUTERS/Lucas Jackson

▶ LeTasha Brown stands with her arms around Anthony Dixon Jr. during a rally in front of the Sanford Police Department following the killing of Trayvon Martin in Sanford, Florida, in 2012. Martin was shot dead in a confrontation with George Zimmerman, a Neighborhood Watch captain who believed the young black man looked suspicious as he walked through the gated community in a hooded sweatshirt.

factor in determining whether a particular individual is suspected of committing a crime.

Zimmerman's attorneys claimed he was defending himself against Martin and looked to Florida's controversial "stand your ground" law, which justifies an individual's using force if he or she reasonably believes it is necessary to prevent imminent death or great bodily harm. Since Martin's death, many have argued that this law needs to be repealed. However, staunch defenders of the law, including small retail businesses and the powerful National Rifle Association, will challenge any efforts to repeal. On July 13, 2013, after deliberating 16.5 hours, a jury of six women, five of them white, found Zimmerman not guilty of the charges against him.

INTRODUCTION: CRIME AS A SOCIAL PROBLEM

 11.1 Discuss crime as a social problem.

Most people attest to having some basic understanding of what crime is, as well as what causes crime. This is likely due to the popularity of crime as a topic in news reports, politics, and television shows, and because crime is a concept that seems easy to understand. If an individual robs a bank, one could imagine that the motivation stems simply from obtaining large sums of cash. If someone murders a spouse, then one might assume that he did it to cash in on a life insurance policy. While the various monetary rewards to offending aid in explaining why individuals find some crimes appealing, it fails to account for the fact that the overwhelming majority of criminal acts yield few material gains, and often come with substantial risk of arrest. Even if crime does yield material rewards for relatively little effort, the majority of people—even those seemingly in "need"—lead lives of conformity. If criminal and delinquent behavior is easy, fun, and rewarding, why do individuals refrain from giving in to its temptations? Is it because they have been socialized to hold moral beliefs against harming others? Do they fear the prospect of punishment if caught by authorities? Or are they concerned with what their parents, friends, or employers might think if they were to commit a crime? The question of why individuals commit crime is fundamental in sociology, as it has clear implications for how societies function.

Crime can also have direct and long-term impacts on offenders and victims of crime. Victims of robbery, burglary, or petty theft not only experience the loss of capital, but also the frustration and fear associated with being held at gunpoint, or knowing a stranger broke into their home. Victims of aggravated and sexual assaults frequently live with the serious physical, mental, and emotional consequences of their offenders' actions. The offenders themselves may experience substantial costs. Individuals in jails and prisons lose out on valuable time that could be used to improve themselves and parent their children. A felony record can be highly detrimental to future employment prospects, often forcing prior offenders to accept low-wage jobs. Although it is easy and tempting to think of offenders as "bad people," many law violators commit crimes because of momentary lapses in judgment or due to adverse life circumstances. A single criminal event can have complex and long-term social, economic, and physical consequences for both victims and offenders.

Crime also negatively impacts local communities. Residents of high-crime neighborhoods may be afraid to leave their homes, and are less able to forge and maintain relationships with neighbors in ways that can improve community conditions. This results in a breakdown in "collective efficacy," in which residents are unable to come together and address problems such as criminal activity (Sampson et al., 1997). Additionally, schools, public libraries, and recreation centers in high-crime areas tend to be underfunded or nonexistent, in part because community members are unable to lobby politicians for valuable resources (Bursik & Grasmick, 1993).

There is also substantial financial cost to the public associated with crime. Property crimes incur hundreds of millions of dollars in losses each year (Chalfin, 2013). The average medical expenses and productivity losses associated with aggravated assault is over $100,000 *per offense* (McCollister et al., 2010). In 2007, the criminal actions of big banks played a direct role in the collapse of the housing market, leaving thousands of people with no savings or financial support. Even further, the costs of running and maintaining jails and prisons can reach billions of dollars annually (Henrichson & Delaney, 2012), and these funds often come from the same pool of money that funds public education.

The creation and enforcement of laws also have consequences for the perceived legitimacy of the government. Some laws adversely affect certain social groups. We can see examples of this with the "War on Drugs," which prioritized the policing and punishment of possessing crack cocaine (mostly used within poor, largely African American communities) over that of other types, such as powder cocaine (mostly used by middle/upper-class whites). Even though both drug types are similar chemically, one has been policed more heavily than the other due to the social groups that are associated with its use. We can also see this discrimination with stop-and-frisk laws, which were predominantly employed in minority communities. These policies have had devastating effects on certain social groups. While drug convictions for whites doubled from 1986 through 1996, for blacks they quintupled. Today, roughly 60% of prison inmates are black or Latino. As sociologist Loïc Wacquant has observed, the racial composition of prisons today is the reverse of what it was in the 1950s, when only 30% of inmates were persons of color. The fact that these had such drastic adverse impacts on minority communities led many to question the true motivations beyond their enactments.

The impact that criminal justice stakeholders have on the perceived legitimacy of the government is perhaps most visible in the actions of law enforcement. Police officers are uniquely granted the power to take away freedoms of those suspected of breaking the law and to use deadly force against individuals perceived as an imminent threat. These powers, when abused, can have profound effects on society. In August 2014 in Ferguson, Missouri, the police shooting of Michael Brown, an unarmed, 18-year-old black male, prompted massive civil unrest throughout the country. Even though the officer was exonerated of misconduct by a grand jury, the event sparked widespread media coverage and a highly vocal response by civil rights communities.

Although the shooting itself was no doubt tragic, the implications of how actions of law enforcement can adversely impact police–community relations was on full display. This, in turn, can affect law enforcement's ability to deter and solve crimes. Research on police legitimacy has found that when members of the public harbor unfavorable attitudes toward law enforcement, people are more likely to refuse to aid police officers in investigations, or even seek the help of the police when they are victimized. This can lead to increased rates of crime, as the police are less able to perform their necessary tasks toward controlling crime, and members of the local community may seek to "get even" with those who victimize them. Put simply, law enforcement may, ironically, encourage crime incidences to occur, given how specific actions of police officers (such as the Ferguson shooting) are handled.

Crime is a complex social problem that can affect day-to-day lives directly and indirectly. As such, understanding its causes and consequences is important. This chapter will revisit some of the issues discussed above in more detail, with the goal of highlighting the complexity of crime as a social problem, and the extent and nature of crime in the United States and around the world. It will introduce how sociological theories have been used to explain crime, and finally, discuss some ways that society can work to prevent crime in the future.

CRIMES ARE SOCIALLY DEFINED

11.2 Explain how crime is socially defined.

The seemingly simple question "What is crime?" is more complex than many people realize. Criminologists are in the predicament of being unable to define their subject of interest. Crime is behavior defined as illegal by legislatures and other governing agencies. But even the idea that crime is behavior that is illegal is not so straightforward. Some behaviors, such as the recreational use of marijuana, are illegal in some states but not others. Other behaviors are illegal in some circumstances but not others (e.g., killing someone in self-defense), and this too can vary across states. Even further, the legal status of many behaviors can drastically change over time. For decades in parts of the United States, African Americans were prohibited from using drinking fountains designated for whites. Concerns over terrorist attacks after 9/11 led to the criminalization of many previously permissible behaviors at airports, such as boarding the plane with small knives and box cutters. Accordingly, while it exists in all societies, there is no *single* understanding of crime as a social problem.

It is helpful to consider *why* some behaviors are deemed illegal and others are not. The **normative consensus** perspective holds that behaviors are illegal because there is agreement among members of society that the behaviors are morally wrong. Most people believe that murder, rape, and theft are repugnant, and that even if they were not formally defined as illegal, it is likely society would regulate and punish them informally. The **normative conflict** perspective, on the other hand, views the creation of laws as a way for those in power to maintain their position in society. Consider the example of the "War on Drugs" described above. That crack cocaine carried a sentence 100 times harsher than that of powdered cocaine is an example of lawmakers choosing to more harshly punish minority groups. In the most basic sense, crimes are behaviors that *violate society's norms at a given time, defined by those in power*. In the United States, state legislatures are responsible for writing criminal laws that formally define what is "criminal" and the possible punishments for violating those laws.

Normative consensus: Perspective that holds that behaviors get codified illegal because there is general agreement among members of society that the behavior is morally wrong.

Normative conflict: Perspective that views the creation of laws as a means for those in power to maintain their position in society.

"Crimes" can be also grouped into two categories: *mala in se* and *mala prohibita*. **Mala in se crimes** are those that violate the moral conscience and are thought of as wrong in and of themselves. They include acts such as murder, theft, and assault. **Mala prohibita crimes** are acts that may not be inherently evil but are viewed as wrong because they are defined as illegal by those in power. Recreational use of marijuana is prohibited in many states, but many individuals who are otherwise law-abiding have no problem using marijuana and may highlight that the adverse consequences of marijuana use are not as injurious as excessive alcohol consumption. In this way, the recreational use of marijuana is not in and of itself evil, but its use invokes a stigma and may result in formal sanctions. Other *mala prohibita* crimes include gambling and prostitution. The way the law treats mala prohibita behaviors depends on many factors, including social and political climate, socioeconomic factors, and geographic location. While most college students probably hold strong attitudes against driving while drunk, this was not necessarily the case before the 1980s, when Mothers Against Drunk Driving (MADD) began to organize and influence lawmakers and social norms.

▶ Three demonstrators at a lunch counter in Jackson, Mississippi, are smeared with ketchup, mustard, and sugar by integration opponents in 1963. Jim Crow laws mandated racial segregation in all public facilities in southern U.S. states. Until 1965 these laws prohibited blacks from using restrooms, restaurants, and drinking fountains that were intended for whites only.

ASK YOURSELF: College students and office workers often set up pools in which they fill out brackets for the NCAA Basketball Championship tournament, a socially accepted form of gambling. Can you think of other *mala prohibita* crimes in which your peers commonly engage? Do you think they are acceptable behaviors? Why or why not?

DATA SOURCES AND CORRELATES OF CRIME

11.3   Discuss the sources of crime data.

Official Crime Measurement

Each year the Federal Bureau of Investigation (FBI) provides a national overview of crimes reported to the police through the Uniform Crime Reports (UCR). The FBI categorizes crimes as either Part 1 "index crimes" or Part 2 crimes. The index crimes consist of eight offenses that the FBI uses to produce the annual crime index. The UCR categorizes these offenses as either violent or property crimes, with the former including homicide, rape, aggravated assault, and robbery, and the latter including motor vehicle theft, burglary, larceny, and arson. The UCR is useful for understanding trends in crime over time, since it has been collected in essentially the same way for many years. There are two exceptions. Arson was not one of the original index crimes but was added in 1979. In addition, a new definition of rape took effect in 2013 that removed the requirement of "forcible" assault and the restriction that the attack must be on a woman. Table 11.1 provides the FBI's definitions of index crimes as of 2013.

There are several strengths of the UCR. First, there is a standardized reporting process that allows for comparisons of crime rates both over time and across regions. Second, roughly 70% of all police agencies report information to the

Mala in se **crimes:** Acts that may not be inherently evil but are viewed as wrong because they are defined as illegal by those in power.

Mala prohibita **crimes:** Crimes that violate the moral conscience and are thought of as wrong in and of themselves.

TABLE 11.1 Serious Violent Crimes

Crime	Description
Murder and manslaughter	*Murder and nonnegligent manslaughter:* The willful killing of one person by another. *Manslaughter by negligence:* The killing of another person through gross negligence.
Forcible rape	Penetration, no matter how slight, of the vagina or anus of any body part or object, or oral penetration by a sex organ of another person without the consent of the victim.
Robbery	The taking or attempted taking of anything of value from the care, custody, and control of a person or persons by force or threat of force or violence and/or by putting the victim in fear.
Aggravated assault	An unlawful attack by one person upon another for the purpose of inflicting severe or aggravated bodily injury. This type of assault usually is accompanied by the use of a weapon or by means likely to produce death or great bodily harm.
Burglary (breaking and entering)	The unlawful entry of a structure to commit a felony or a theft.
Larceny-theft (except motor vehicle theft)	The unlawful taking, carrying, leading, or riding away of property from the possession or constructive possession of another.
Motor vehicle theft	The theft or attempted theft of a motor vehicle.
Arson	Any willful or malicious burning or attempt to burn, with or without intent to defraud, a dwelling house, public building, motor vehicle or aircraft, personal property of another, etc.

SOURCE: FBI Uniform Crime Report, 2012 and Criminal Justice Information Services (CJIS) Decision, Uniform Crime Reporting (UCR) Program, *Reporting Rape* in 2013.

FBI, covering about 95% of the U.S. population. Thus, the UCR data are nationally representative. Third, the FBI also reports whether each criminal event resulted in an arrest, which can allow for an estimation of **clearance rates**—the number of arrests divided by the total number of reported crimes. Despite these strengths, there are disadvantages to the UCR data. Crimes that are unreported are not captured in the data. Research indicates that only about half of all crimes are formally reported to the police (Langton et al.,

2012), meaning that the UCR substantially underestimates crime in the United States. The amount of unreported crime is known as the **dark figure of crime**. Another limitation of the UCR comes from the **hierarchy rule**, where in any single crime event law enforcement agencies report only the most serious crime committed. If an individual robs a convenience store and in the process shoots the clerk, only the shooting will be reported to the FBI. This can underestimate the prevalence of certain crime types. A final limitation of the UCR is the lack of specific information provided concerning the criminal events. For example, there is no mention of the type of relationship between victim and offender or of the number of offenders involved. The FBI has attempted to address the problems stemming from the hierarchy rule by phasing out the UCR and replacing it with the National Incident-Based Reporting System (NIBRS). This process has been gradual and will not capture the dark figure of crime.

Self-Report Surveys

Another way to study the causes of criminal behavior is through self-report surveys among potential offenders. This involves researchers administering a survey in a school or prison and asking respondents, "How many times in the last year have you stolen something worth less than $50?" The self-report method is used extensively because of and its ability to capture crimes that go unreported to the police, as well as its ability to ask about victimless crimes such as drug use. Researchers must trust respondents to accurately and honestly report their own offending behavior, which may be biased due to memory and social desirability. Another concern with the self-report method is that much of this research is conducted in middle schools and high schools, and is therefore likely to miss students who are absent the day of the survey, or who have already dropped out of schools—which may include those who are most likely to be delinquent.

Victimization Surveys

A final method to measure the nature and extent of crime is using victimization surveys. These ask about respondents' experiences being victims of crime. The National Crime Victimization Survey (NCVS) is collected by interviewing individuals within randomly selected households across the United States. The NCVS is capable of overcoming the "dark figure of crime" by estimating the annual rate of victimization in the United States

Clearance rates: The number of arrests divided by the total number of reported crimes.

Dark figure of crime: The amount of unreported crime.

Hierarchy rule: A reporting, where in any single crime event police agencies are asked only to report the most serious crime committed.

Researching Crime

Subculture Norms on Philadelphia's Streets

Criminologist Elijah Anderson (1999) set out to explain the high rates of violence in mostly black, poor, and violent neighborhoods in Pennsylvania. He discovered that a code governed interactions between neighborhood residents and sanctioned the use of violence to resolve conflict and show "nerve." While most of the people he spoke to were more "decent" than "street," everyone had to know the rules of the code for self-preservation.

The primary rule was to look and act tough, rejecting mainstream customs associated with white society. Young men wore untied sneakers, pants with waistbands hanging well below the waist, and hats turned backward. While these styles were later adopted by middle-class adolescents, at first they signified antagonism toward conventional styles. The appearance of the young men gave the community a bad reputation, which also contributed to the stereotyping and demonizing of young black males. As Anderson observes:

> Many ghetto males are caught in a bind because they are espousing their particular ways

of dressing and acting simply to be self-respecting among their neighborhood peers. A boy may be completely decent, but to the extent that he takes on the *presentation* of "badness" to enhance his local public image, even as a form of self-defense, he further alienates himself in the eyes of the wider society, which has denounced people like him as inclined to violate its norms, values, rules, and conventions to threaten it. (pp. 112–113)

▶ Display of thousands of pairs of shoes representing victims killed by gang violence in Philadelphia. A west Philly neighborhood is home turf of the 60th Street Posse, also known as Six-O, which controls organized criminal activity in the area. Today's gangs tend to be smaller and less regimented than gangs of the past.

Harry Hamburg/NY Daily News Archive/Getty Images

▶ **THINK ABOUT IT:** Anderson describes the way a subculture's norms encouraged young people to become alienated from society, often leading to violence and crime. How do you think community leaders could reverse these patterns and encourage positive behaviors among youth in such communities?

(rather than only that which is reported to the police). Like self-report surveys, the NCVS derives its estimations from individual citizens directly, which can then be compared to official crime trends captured by the UCR. Crime trends reported by both sources tend to reflect one another in overall direction but not in magnitude. This suggests that both the NCVS and UCR are capable of accurately assessing the extent to which crime is increasing or decreasing over time. Like other measures of crime, the NCVS has its limitations. First, as with self-report surveys, respondents may lie about, or not fully understand, their victimization experiences. Second, the

NCVS records multiple instances of victimizations as a "series incident." This limits the number of victimizations individuals are allowed to report at a single time period to a maximum of 10 occurrences. Nonetheless, the NCVS is a useful tool for estimating the overall level of crime.

PATTERNS AND TRENDS

 Discuss patterns and trends in crime and crime measurement.

TABLE 11.2 Violent and Property Crimes Reported to the Police, 2014

Violent Crime	
Murder and nonnegligent manslaughter	14,249
Forcible rape	84,041 (116,645)*
Robbery	325,802
Aggravated assault	741,291
Total	1,165,383
Property Crime	
Burglary	1,729,806
Larceny-theft	5,858,496
Motor vehicle theft	689,527
Total	8,277,829

SOURCE: Compiled from FBI Uniform Crime Reports 1995–2014.

*Total rape reported according to the revised definition underneath the UCR.

TABLE 11.3 Violent and Property Crime Arrests by Gender, 2014

Offense Charged	Percentage Male	Percentage Female
Violent crime	79.8	20.2
Murder and nonnegligent manslaughter	88.5	11.5
Forcible rape	97.2	2.8
Robbery	86.1	13.9
Aggravated assault	77.0	23.0
Property crime	61.8	38.2
Burglary	82.2	17.8
Larceny-theft	56.8	43.2
Motor vehicle theft	79.7	20.3
Arson	80.5	19.5
Total	73.3	26.7

SOURCE: Compiled from FBI Uniform Crime Reports 1995–2014.

Profiles of Offenders: Gender and Race

The UCR's arrest data provide demographic profiles of persons arrested, including gender and race. As Table 11.3 shows, men are overwhelmingly more likely than women to be arrested for crime, with certain exceptions, such as larceny-theft.

The male predisposition toward crime, among both offenders and victims, is well illustrated by the crime of homicide. Two-thirds of homicides involve male offenders and male victims. Men are twice as likely to murder women as women are to murder men. And women murdering other women makes up only 2% of all homicides.

ASK YOURSELF: Does it surprise you that criminal behavior is dominated by men? What might be some reasons for this?

The UCR also looks at race. With a couple of important exceptions (murder and robbery), whites make up the modal arrest group for each of the index crimes (see Table 11.4). We would expect this because whites make up 78% of the U.S. population, while African Americans make up just 13%. But given their numbers in the population, blacks are overrepresented in arrest data for many crimes, both as offenders and as victims. Most crime is intraracial, meaning that the victim and offender are from the same racial background. For example, from 1980 through 2008, 84% of white victims were killed by whites, while 93% of black victims were killed by blacks (Cooper & Smith, 2011).

Self-report surveys, such as the National Youth Survey (NYS), tell a similar story concerning the demographic profiles of offenders. Not only are males also more likely to report committing crimes than females, but ethnic minorities (such as African Americans and Hispanics) report committing more crimes than whites.

ASK YOURSELF: What reasons might account for the overrepresentation of black persons found in arrest data, particularly for the crimes of murder and robbery?

Profiles of Victims: Gender and Race

Yearly reports by the NCVS show that there is considerable overlap between the characteristics of offenders and the characteristics of victims. African Americans, for instance, are more likely to be victims of both violent and property crimes than are whites (in spite of black individuals making up a substantially smaller portion of the total population), and older individuals tend to experience fewer violent victimizations than are adolescents.

Unlike offending trends (where males are much more likely to commit violence than females), the data indicate that differences between male and female violent victimization are smaller. Between 1993 and the late 2000s, the NCVS showed that males were shown to be more likely to be violently victimized than were females. However, since 2010 males and females have reported similar rates of serious violent victimization, with the gap in robbery victimization and aggravated assaults slowly decreasing until 2015, when women reported a slightly higher rate of

TABLE 11.4 Arrests by Race, 2014

Offense Charged	Percentage White	Percentage Black
Violent crime	59.4	37.7
Murder and nonnegligent manslaughter	46.3	51.3
Forcible rape	67.2	29.9
Robbery	42.3	55.9
Aggravated assault	63.7	33.1
Other assaults	65.4	31.9
Offenses against the family and children	64.4	32.9
Property crime	68.8	28.4
Burglary	67.6	30.2
Larceny-theft	69.2	28.0
Motor vehicle theft	66.5	30.7
Arson	73.1	23.4
Forgery and counterfeiting	63.8	34.0
Fraud	66.1	31.8
Embezzlement	61.9	35.6
Stolen property; buying, receiving, possessing	65.5	32.2
Vandalism	70.1	27.0
Weapons: carrying, possessing, etc.	57.3	40.7
Prostitution and commercialized vice	53.7	41.8
Sex offenses (except forcible rape and prostitution)	72.5	24.3
Drug abuse violations	68.9	29.1
Gambling	35.8	58.9
Driving under the influence	83.7	13.0
Liquor laws	80.2	14.5
Drunkenness	80.9	15.7
Disorderly conduct	63.0	33.9
Vagrancy	68.7	28.3
All other offenses (except traffic)	67.1	30.5
Suspicion	53.5	46.2
Curfew and loitering law violations	51.4	46.2
Total crimes	69.4	27.8

SOURCE: Compiled from FBI Uniform Crime Reports 1991–2010.

aggravated assault and serious violent victimization than did men. Sexual assaults and rapes, however, are consistently reported at a much higher rate for women. Thus, while men report higher rates of violent victimization than women, women have always reported being victims of rape or sexual assault more often than men.

Current Crime Trends

Since the early 2000s, Gallup polls have indicated that the majority of Americans believe crime is on the rise. Crime is also consistently mentioned as one of the most important social problems facing the country. If public perception can be taken to be an accurate measure of crime, then one might suspect we are living in a hyperviolent and crime-ridden time. On the contrary, reported violent and property crime substantially decreased between 1995 and 2015 (see Figures 11.1 and 11.2). Among violent crimes, murder declined by 45.1%, rape (old definition) by 29.8%, and robbery by 53.7%. Aggravated assault went down by 44.4%. Of the property crimes, burglary declined by 45%, larceny-theft by 39.6%, and motor vehicle theft by 61.4%. Put simply, crime is substantially lower today than it was when it reached its peak a little over two decades ago.

FIGURE 11.1 Reported Violent Crime, 1990–2015

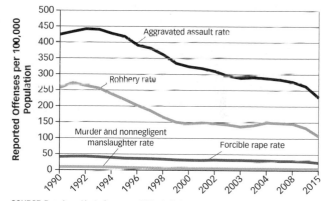

SOURCE: Data from Alexia Cooper and Erica L. Smith, *Homicide Trends in the United States, 1980–2008.* U.S. Department of Justice, Bureau of Justice Statistics, November, 2011.

FIGURE 11.2 Reported Property Crime, 1990–2015

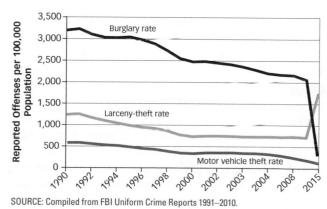

SOURCE: Compiled from FBI Uniform Crime Reports 1991–2010.

Criminologists have had considerable difficulty accounting for this substantial decline in the crime rate. Multiple explanations have been proposed, including the aging population in the United States, the decline of the crack cocaine market, increases in the incarceration of offenders, as well as improvements in the economy (see Blumstein & Wallman, 2000).

ASK YOURSELF: Why might people perceive that crime is increasing when the official data show otherwise?

Crime From a Global Perspective

Making cross-national comparisons of violent crime rates can be like comparing apples to oranges, as it is difficult to compare crime rates of Western industrialized countries to nonindustrialized countries. Nations also differ substantially in the legal definitions of crimes. As just one example, Haiti, Morocco, and Syria have "honor crimes" laws that legally justify a man killing his wife or daughter because she offended his honor (MacKinnon, 2008). The lack of worldwide consensus regarding definitions of criminal behavior extends to a host of different crimes. Further complicating cross-national comparisons are disparities in national data sources and the fact that data are not collected reliably in many developing countries.

One approach to conducting a comparative international study is to compare two countries that are similar. For example, the United States is often depicted (both internationally and domestically) as exceptionally violent and crime prone when compared to other Western democracies such as England and France. In fact, data from the World Health Organization indicate that nonlethal violent crime rates in the United States are similar to other economically developed countries. The notable exception, however, is for gun-related homicide, in which the U.S. rate is seven times higher than other countries (Grinshteyn & Hemenway, 2016). In other words, violence may not be much more common in the United States, but when it occurs it is more likely to be deadly. One possible explanation is the relatively easy access to firearms in the United States, which can greatly influence whether an aggravated assault turns fatal.

ASK YOURSELF: What might explain the comparatively high rates of lethal violence in the United States?

Understanding crime through a global perspective is also important because globalization itself is changing the nature of crime. Crime is becoming increasingly transnational, meaning that each criminal event is not limited within a single border. **Transnational crimes** include drug trafficking, cybercrime, and human trafficking, a lucrative

REUTERS/Larry Downing

▶ A Department of Homeland Security (DHS) worker at the National Cybersecurity and Communications Integration Center in Arlington, Virginia. The United States Intelligence Community, including the DHS, concluded that the Russian government interfered in the 2016 U.S. presidential election. Do you see this as a type of cybercrime?

form of modern-day slavery. The U.S. State Department estimates that 27 million people are victims of human trafficking worldwide. A common scheme victimizes young women who are lured by false job prospects to the United States, Japan, and many countries in Western Europe, but on arrival are told they owe large debts for their transportation. They are then enslaved in brothels or forced into street prostitution. In other cases, such as cybercrimes, the offender and the victim(s) can be in different countries at the time of the crime. In 2014, millions of Target customers had their credit and debit card information stolen in a cyberattack, and it is believed the perpetrators were living in Eastern Europe. Such crimes can be difficult to regulate and investigate because of the limited jurisdictions of individual policing agencies, and because they can be inhibited by international relations.

The effect of globalization on crime is evident in the United States by growing interest in understanding the causes and consequences of **terrorism**, which is defined as the unlawful use of violence in the pursuit of political aims. Terrorism is, by definition, a criminal act, and it is increasingly receiving the attention and resources of policing agencies in the United States. After 9/11 the FBI changed its mission statement from focusing only on domestic crimes and law enforcement to national security and preventing terrorism.

Transnational crimes: Crimes that have effects across national borders.

Terrorism: Violence perpetrated for political reasons by subnational groups or secret state agents, often directed at noncombatant targets, and usually intended to influence an audience.

Transnational Crime: An Interview With Criminologist Jay S. Albanese

In your book Transnational Crime and the 21st Century *(2011), you discuss the problem of human trafficking. What is human trafficking?* Human trafficking takes different forms, but its essence is coerced servitude. The basic elements of human trafficking are three:

- Exploitative labor (sex, manual labor, servitude)

- The harboring of victims (through recruitment, transport, or receipt)

- Coercion (accomplished through deception, force, or threats)

Is human trafficking similar to other transnational crimes? The defining feature of transnational crime is violations of law that involve more than one country in their planning, execution, or impact. These offenses are distinguished from other crimes in their multinational nature and cross-border impact, which pose unique problems in understanding causation, developing prevention strategies, and mounting effective adjudication procedures.

What different elements contribute to human trafficking as a social problem? We should not underestimate the seriousness of human trafficking as crime. Unlike most transnational crimes, which involve the buying and selling of consumable products, human trafficking entails the buying and selling of human beings who are exploited over and over again in an ongoing form of enslavement.

What is needed to combat the problem more effectively? A great deal remains to be done to better protect victims, understand the true nature and scope of trafficking enterprises, and increase the number of successful prosecutions in order to fulfill the promise of coordinated international action made by the United Nations' binding Protocol to Prevent, Suppress and Punish Trafficking in Persons, Especially Women and Children (enacted in 2003). Some progress has

REUTERS/Brian Snyder

▶ Flight attendant Mary Furlong-Ferguson carries educational materials to help airline personnel spot sex-trafficking through the Dallas–Fort Worth International Airport. Pimps traffic thousands of underage prostitutes.

clearly been made, as suggested by the fact that 63% of 155 countries have passed laws against human trafficking pursuant to the U.N. Protocol. More than half of countries have developed a national action plan and an anti–human trafficking police unit. Nevertheless, progress has been slow, and we need to more effectively identify and uncover trafficking networks, protect victims, and prosecute traffickers.

▶ **THINK ABOUT IT:** What are the advantages to human traffickers of carrying out their crimes transnationally? What can be done to combat human trafficking?

THE U.S. CRIMINAL JUSTICE SYSTEM AND ITS STAKEHOLDERS

11.5 Describe the U.S. criminal justice system and its stakeholders.

The U.S. criminal justice system attempts to address the social problem of crime. It employs **stakeholders**—including police, prosecutors, defense attorneys, and judges—who make decisions about arrests, prosecutions, and sentencing. The operation of the criminal justice system is a discretionary process that can yield different versions of justice from one defendant to the next. Issues of intersectionality are present at every stage. Who is accused? What does he or she look like? What legal representation can the accused afford? What does the victim look like? The variables that affect potential outcomes are vast and complex.

Police

The police are the most visible stakeholders of the criminal justice system. This leads to high levels of scrutiny by the general

Stakeholders: All individuals who have an interest in and are affected by the workings of a given system; in the criminal justice system, stakeholders include those accused of crimes as well as those who process cases, including police, attorneys, and court and correctional staff.

REUTERS/Lucy Nicholson

▶ Among the major responsibilities of the police are to identify criminal offenders and criminal activity and, when appropriate, to apprehend offenders and participate in later court proceedings. Police officers in Britain typically do not carry firearms, while those in the United States, such as these officers in Los Angeles, California, are usually heavily armed. Which do you think is most effective in maintaining order and controlling crime?

public. This scrutiny is valuable, as police are afforded considerable powers that common citizens are not. For instance, police have the power to arrest, or to use deadly force in a greater range of situations than are often allowed to other citizens. But the responsibilities of police are much broader than are often depicted in television shows, and include activities such as responding to public order complaints, directing traffic, and offering first aid to those in need. They also have the challenging tasks of entering dangerous situations, investigating the circumstances around a criminal event, and preventing criminal acts.

The structure of police departments in the United States is grounded in English tradition (Walker & Katz, 2008) and is characterized by local control and **decentralization of power**. This means that unless the circumstances are extreme, police hold limited power and respond to calls only within their own geographic boundaries. Decentralization of power has social implications in that enforcement varies from place to place according to the traditions and norms of local communities. Police in high-crime neighborhoods, for example, might prioritize crimes differently than police in suburban communities and overlook relatively low-level offenses, such as disorderly conduct.

While the English influence is still prevalent today (Manning, 2005), some aspects of policing have changed over time in the United States. During the "political era" of law enforcement history, 1840–1920, politicians and police officers worked together closely, a practice that sometimes led to payoffs and other corruption of the force (Cole & Smith, 2008a). The "professional era," 1920–1970, brought more training and education for police officers, more equal enforcement of laws, reduced political interference, merit-based employment procedures, and a focus on fighting crime. The current era, which began around 1970, has

been called the "community policing era" because police work has expanded to include more proactive and community-oriented strategies. At first, police departments accomplished this goal by taking officers out of patrol cars and putting them on the streets, in schools, and in communities to increase cooperation and trust between private citizens and the police force (Walker & Katz, 2008).

Increasing the size of police forces is often an appealing topic for political candidates. Despite this fact, research indicates that *how* police departments allocate resources is more effective than the sheer size of the force. Beginning in the 1970s, many urban police departments began incorporating data-mapping tools that plot the locations of crimes across different parts of a city. These techniques have shown that crime is not spread evenly across city neighborhoods. Instead, about 6% of clusters, or hot spots, account for half of all criminal events (Braga & Weisburd, 2010; Pierce, 1989). Police officers can more effectively reduce crime when resources are directed at these hot spots, a policing strategy known as **hot-spot policing**. Figure 11.3 is an example of a hot-spot map showing that, in the period from January 2008 through February 2009, firearms incidents in Brockton, Massachusetts, occurred near bar locations between midnight and 4:00 a.m. By focusing police resources on such hot spots, cities can prevent further crime.

Courts

After the police make a formal arrest, the case proceeds to the courts. The three major actors of the courts are the prosecutors, defense attorneys, and judges. Prosecutors are attorneys who prosecute offenders on behalf of the state. They begin by reviewing the evidence gathered through the police investigation and determine whether the evidence is convincing enough to proceed through the court process. If the prosecutor decides to file charges, there is a **presumption of innocence**, and the prosecution is charged with proving every element of the case beyond a reasonable doubt, a legal standard established in the 1850 case of *Commonwealth v. Webster*. This standard requires a high amount of certainty that the accused committed the acts; when there is doubt the verdict must be "not guilty." In a small number of cases defendants will assert **affirmative defenses**, which can include insanity, self-defense,

Decentralization of power: The distribution of functions and responsibilities of police officers to different local authorities.

Hot-spot policing: A method employed by police departments to track the ordered spatial patterns of crime by monitoring when crimes occur disproportionately in particular geographic areas and responding to those areas.

Presumption of innocence: The principle that a criminal defendant is innocent until proven guilty, placing the burden on the government to establish proof of guilt beyond a reasonable doubt.

Affirmative defenses: Legal defenses in which new facts or sets of facts operate to defeat claims even if the facts supporting the claims are true.

FIGURE 11.3 Firearms-Related Incidents, City of Brockton, Midnight to 4:00 a.m., January 1, 2008–February 28, 2009

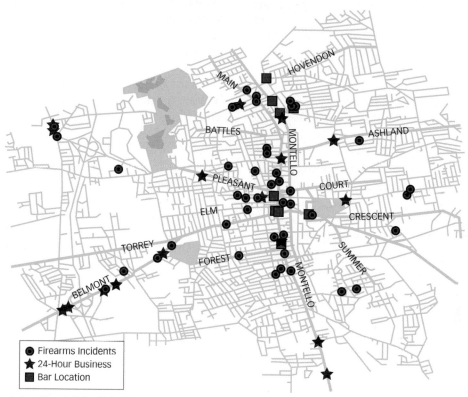

SOURCE: Reprinted by permission of Pamela Kelley, Kelley Research Associates.

and mistake. An affirmative defense is different from mere reliance on the government to meet its burden of proof and often requires an additional showing by the defendant.

In the United States, any defendant whose crime could result in a jail or prison sentence is entitled to representation by a defense attorney, whose main purpose is to protect the defendant's rights and guide him or her through the criminal justice process. A defense attorney may be retained and compensated by the accused. Defendants who lack the financial resources to secure their own private attorney must rely on publicly appointed lawyers—also known as **public defenders**—to defend them during the **adjudication** process. Oftentimes public defenders are dealing with very large caseloads, which raises questions about the quality of the representation these defendants received (Feeney & Jackson, 1990–1991).

ASK YOURSELF: In 2009, Amanda Knox, an American college student who had been living in Perugia, Italy, was convicted by an Italian court of murdering her roommate, a conviction later overturned when the DNA evidence presented was found to be inconclusive and unreliable. In Italy's criminal justice system the judge is not an unbiased finder of law but rather an active participant in the investigation. Do you think Knox would have had a different experience in the U.S. adversarial system, in which two parties argue a case before a judge? Why or why not?

Ideally, the court process would be adversarial, whereby the prosecution attempts to receive the best outcome for the state and the defense attorney the best outcome for the defendant. In reality, the court process can better be characterized as involving a **courtroom workgroup**, where the prosecutors and defense attorneys work closely together and the shared goal of the two sides is efficiency. This often involves closing cases through *plea bargaining*. The benefit of this process is that the U.S. courts are bogged down by a heavy backlog of cases, and plea bargains are more efficient than trials. While every citizen has a constitutional right to a jury trial, if all persons accused of crimes were actually to claim that right, the court system would be overwhelmed. About 95% of all felony convictions in state courts were the results of plea bargains (U.S. Bureau of Justice Statistics, 2005). If the defendant opts for a jury trial, however, jurors (individuals selected from the general community to serve as

Public defenders: Publicly appointed lawyers.

Adjudication: The process in which a final judicial decision or sentence is made in a criminal case.

Courtroom workgroup: The informal and working relationships between the prosecutor, defense attorney, and judicial officer.

the "finder of fact") will be brought in to identify the evidence they believe to be true beyond a reasonable doubt and render a verdict.

The role of judges in the court process is to rule on all **matters of law**. Judges are also afforded the right to make sentencing decisions within the confines of the law. However, judicial discretion in sentencing has changed over time. For many years the goal of the criminal justice system was rehabilitation, and judges had considerable discretion to sentence each offender to a very broad length under the idea that he or she would be released when rehabilitated—a principle known as **indeterminate sentencing**. Interestingly, both liberal and conservative politicians came together to get rid of the indeterminate sentencing strategy, albeit for different reasons. Liberal policy makers were concerned over the racial disparities in sentence length, while conservatives were primarily concerned with whether rehabilitation is effective or simply "soft on crime." With this, judicial discretion was replaced by a system of **determinate sentencing**, in which legislatures determined a narrower length of sentences through **sentencing guidelines**. There is some evidence that the use of sentencing guidelines has curbed some racial disparities in the criminal sentencing process, but there is still evidence of some disparities (Tonry, 2008). Moreover, there is growing concern that the curbing of judicial discretion has simply displaced discretion to the prosecutor—a courtroom actor with less public oversight.

Traditional courts in the United States operate under an adjudicative model of justice. Typical steps in the process are arraignment (in which charges against the defendant are formally announced), pretrial hearings (in which discovery of evidence is held to determine the strength of the prosecutor's case), motion hearings, and disposition (trial, plea bargain, or dismissal). Cases are dealt with individually, efficiency is the goal, and outcomes can depend on a number of factors, both legal and extralegal. Legal factors include characteristics of the case, such as seriousness of the crime, length of the defendant's criminal record if any, and sufficiency of evidence. Extralegal factors include characteristics of the defendant, such as gender, race, and socioeconomic status.

Traditional courts make no attempt to deal with the larger social problems affecting the community. Efforts to overcome this limitation have recently given rise to courts of limited jurisdiction, or **specialized courts**. Rather than using a case efficiency model of justice, specialized courts make problem solving their primary goal and orient their proceedings toward social justice. Many of these courts try to bring about social change for defendants (e.g., to end their drug abuse), for the community (e.g., to take guns off the street), and for victims (e.g., to end the cycle of violence in which they have been trapped). Collaboration,

nontraditional roles, and the participation of private agencies are also distinguishing features of specialized courts (Hemmens et al., 2010). Drug courts, for example, typically work with defendants before their cases are resolved, with the aim of helping them end their drug abuse and assisting them in finding better lives for themselves. Drug offenders who do not have histories of violence can choose to enter substance abuse treatment programs for counseling, therapy, and education; such programs might last 12 to 18 months. Drug courts have been found to be effective at reducing substance abuse and crime (Rossman et al., 2011).

ASK YOURSELF: What are some advantages of specialized courts? Can you think of any disadvantages from the defendant's point of view? Can you think of any other kinds of specialized courts that could be beneficial?

Corrections

If a defendant is found guilty, he or she is sentenced by the presiding judge and goes under the supervision of corrections officials who are in charge of overseeing the offender's punishment. The most prominent purposes of punishment are incapacitation, rehabilitation, retribution, and deterrence. **Incapacitation** involves the loss of individual freedom and liberty. Here, the offender, sentenced to jail or prison time, cannot victimize another person in the community due to the simple fact that he or she is incarcerated. **Rehabilitation** involves helping the offender with the root cause of the criminal behavior in the hope that this will prevent it from happening again. This can include educational programs, mental health counseling, treatment for drug and alcohol abuse, anger

Matters of law: The legal process issues that arise during court proceedings and that are in the exclusive jurisdiction of a judge to resolve.

Indeterminate sentencing: Sentencing for convicted offenders in which the length of incarceration is undetermined.

Determinate sentencing: A sentence for a fixed period that is determined by statute.

Sentencing guidelines: A set of standards that are created to establish consistent sentencing practices within a jurisdiction.

Specialized courts: Problem-solving courts set up within local district courts to deal with social problems affecting the surrounding communities.

Incapacitation: Loss of liberty due to incarceration.

Rehabilitation: A goal of punishment that seeks to restore the offender to a more law-abiding life, free of the encumbrances that may have caused him or her to commit a crime.

▶ In this courtroom artist's sketch, former congressman Anthony Weiner, accompanied by his attorney, reads a statement during a hearing in New York federal court. Weiner pleaded guilty to transmitting sexual material to a minor and was sentenced to 21 months in prison.

management, and other behavioral therapies. **Retribution** involves punishment for the sake of punishment. It has no purpose other than to communicate to the wrongdoer that the criminal behavior is not tolerated. Finally, **deterrence** aims either to stop crime in the first place (**general deterrence**) or to stop an offender from offending again (**specific deterrence**). For example, strict laws against drunk driving have a general deterrent effect on the public at large, while the experience of losing his or her driver's license might specifically deter an individual from driving drunk again.

• •

ASK YOURSELF: Studies have shown that courts in Florida deemed African American youths to be less amenable to rehabilitation than their white counterparts who had committed the same types of crimes and had similar records. Thus, African American teenagers were transferred to adult courts for processing while white teenagers were kept in the rehabilitative juvenile justice model. Why do you think this occurred?

• •

Corrections in the United States have a violent past. Before 1800, U.S. and European criminal justice systems employed harsh physical punishments (Cole & Smith, 2008). Early in the 19th century, massive penitentiaries were created in Pennsylvania and New York to make punishment less vengeful. The primary theory behind these institutions was that the religious reformation of offenders, in combination with the instillation of a good work ethic, could help them become law-abiding and moral citizens. By the end of the 1800s, this idea of a religiously motivated reformation was replaced with a "medical model" of rehabilitation. Crime was seen as similar to a disease, in

that the root causes for each individual needed to be identified and addressed in order for crime to be reduced. Thus, through the 1970s, there was focus on rehabilitation, and correctional facilities offered numerous programs to rehabilitate offenders. Then, in 1974, criminologist Robert Martinson evaluated the effectiveness of "treatment" programs offered by prisons and found that the programs being implemented at the time were mostly ineffective. Martinson's conclusions were more of a testimony to the fidelity of prison programming, but his report was interpreted as concluding that "nothing works." As a result, the "get tough" model of crime control took hold. It calls for longer and increased use of prison sentences, and has continued to dominate criminal justice policy in the United States. Nevertheless, **recidivism** (or reoffending) remains high (Cole & Smith, 2008).

Probation and parole keep offenders in the community and out of prison. **Probation** is an alternative to incarceration (e.g., prison or jails) and allows a convicted individual to stay in the community under certain conditions such as supervision, counseling, drug-free status, and a clean record. If an offender fails to comply, probation can be revoked, resulting in incarceration. **Parole** allows an inmate to leave prison early and finish his or her sentence within the community, also under supervision and other conditions. The transition from prison back into the community can be difficult for many, and support is not always available, a situation that often leads to new offenses.

• •

ASK YOURSELF: Why is the transition from prison back to the community a vulnerable time for ex-inmates?

• •

• •

Retribution: Punishment that serves no purpose except to punish and communicate to the wrongdoer that his or her behavior is not tolerated.

Deterrence: A purpose of punishment that sets out to prevent rational people from committing crimes.

General deterrence: A law or policy written to stop a person from committing a crime in the first place.

Specific deterrence: A law or policy written to stop those who break laws from offending again.

Recidivism: The habit of reoffending.

Probation: An alternative to incarceration that offers an individual freedom if he or she can abide by the law and comply with the terms and conditions mandated by the court.

Parole: The release, under supervision, of a convicted criminal defendant after he or she has completed part of his or her sentence, based on the concept that the defendant will follow the law and become a part of society.

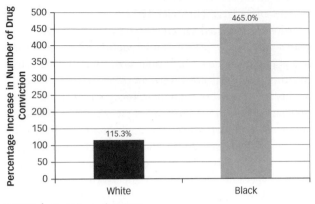

FIGURE 11.4 Increase in Drug Convictions for U.S. Whites and Blacks, 1986–1996

SOURCE: Justice Policy Institute, 2000.

CRIME FROM THE STRUCTURAL FUNCTIONIST, SYMBOLIC INTERACTIONIST, AND CONFLICT PERSPECTIVES

11.6 Apply the functionalist, conflict, and symbolic interactionist perspectives to the problem of crime.

Theoretical criminologists attempt to discover why people do (or do not) commit crimes, but often approach these explanations from different theoretical orientations. Some argue that individuals violate social norms because they desire a certain level of economic success but lack the opportunities to achieve it legitimately. Or perhaps individuals offend because they learn to define criminal conduct as right, warranted, or justified in certain situations. Even further still, crime may be a product of the conflict that exists within society between the powerful and the working class. Regardless of orientation, a number of criminological theories attempt to explain the causes of crime and question the sociolegal orientation of laws, and the ways they affect society.

Structural Functionalism

The functionalist perspective begins with a normative consensus assumption that there is general agreement across all aspects of society regarding goals and moral standards. Ideally, the complex institutions making up society should stress adherence to norms and values

and thus regulate behaviors. Nevertheless, at times these institutions break down, and this can cause individuals to engage in crime. In other words, the organization of society itself may cause or contribute to crime and its patterns. The functionalist perspective traces back to the work of Émile Durkheim (1984). As noted in Chapter 1, Durkheim demonstrated that suicide—typically thought of as a selfish behavior resulting from individual pathologies—could be explained by sociological conditions, specifically anomie. Anomie, or normlessness, is an episodic or permanent condition caused by broad social changes in society that render institutions designed to regulate goals and behavior ineffective. The result is ambiguity in behavioral norms. Durkheim's ideas in *Suicide* were influential in the development of two perspectives in criminology—strain theories and control theories.

Robert K. Merton (1938) drew heavily on Durkheim in his "Social Structure and Anomie," arguing that high crime rates in the United States were the result of a permanent anomic state. Whereas in a well-functioning society institutions adequately define both the goals one should seek to attain and the appropriate means to achieve those goals, in the United States there is an overemphasis on the desired goals (e.g., economic success) and an underemphasis on the means (legitimate vs. illegitimate). This is further exacerbated by the fact that the legitimate means to attain economic success are not equally distributed across society. Merton offers a **strain theory** of crime and deviance that seeks to explain why crime rates are differentially distributed across different class structures in society. It is assumed that in American society financial success is a universal goal, but society is structured such that not every individual has a fair shot at achieving that goal through legitimate avenues. This goal–means disconnect "pushes" people—particularly those in lower classes—to look for ways to improve the likelihood of achieving economic success, and individuals are thought to respond to strain in one of five ways, or *adaptations*.

The first response to strain discussed by Merton is *conformity,* in which individuals accept both the means and goals of society. Conformists continue to work hard to achieve financial success legitimately, but even when it is not attained they refrain from crime because they value moral behavior and doing things "the right way." A second adaptation is *innovation,* in which individuals embrace the goal of economic success but reject the idea that this success must be attained through legal means. Individuals who feel they are not earning as much as they desire may turn to drug dealing or white-collar crime,

Strain theory: A theory of crime that posits individuals commit crimes because of the strains caused by the imbalance between socially accepted goals and the individuals' inadequate means to achieve those goals.

thus retaining the goal of economic success but using "innovative" yet illicit means to do so. *Ritualists* reject the ends but accept the means of society. They do not commit crime because they are not necessarily seeking economic success. *Retreatists* such as drug users and alcoholics reject society's goals and means and remove themselves from conventional society altogether. *Rebels*, such as terrorists, reject conventional goals and replace them with new ones, advocating for a new system and the destruction of the current one.

Merton's (1938) theory of anomie embraces the functionalist view that the cause of crime is rooted in social structure. Humans are assumed to be inherently social beings not naturally inclined to deviate, but the emphasis on the universal goal of monetary success in combination with the unequal distribution in legitimate opportunities to achieve success can "pressure" people into crime, particularly those in the lower classes. Merton's theory laid the foundation for numerous other functionalist-rooted strain theories, including Cohen (1955), Cloward and Ohlin (1960), and Messner and Rosenfeld (2013).

Another set of criminological theories is rooted in the functionalist perspective. Travis Hirschi (1969) believed that Durkheim's discussion of anomie was consistent with the Hobbesian notion that individuals are inherently *self-interested*. For Hobbes, man's natural state of life is "nasty, brutish, and short" because individuals are naturally inclined to go after their own self-interests. Drawing on this idea, Hirschi argued that the motivation to engage in crime is innate, and that the question that criminologists should be asking is not "why do people commit crime?" but rather "why *don't* people commit crime?" Hirschi offers a **social control theory** that argues that when institutions effectively socialize members of society, behavior is regulated; but when these institutions break down and are ineffective at socializing, individuals are "free to deviate." According to Hirschi (1969), the bond to society has four elements. *Attachment* is the emotional element of the social bond that starts with the warmth felt toward parents and extends to other family members, teachers, and friends. When a criminal opportunity appears, an individual who is strongly attached to others will refrain from engaging in crime out of fear of disappointing others—in other words, the attached institutions are psychologically present. Those with weak attachments have less at stake and are more likely to deviate. *Commitment* is the rational component of the social bond, and describes how long-term, pro-social goals regulate behavior. Fear of getting kicked out of school and thus not graduating can effectively prevent individuals from engaging in behavior that may result in expulsion. *Involvement* is the temporal element of the social bond, as spending time in conventional activities (e.g., sports teams) leaves less free time to deviate; those with little structured time are more likely to

commit crime. Finally, *beliefs* represent the moral element of the bond: When young people believe in the validity of the rules of society, they are less likely to violate them (Hirschi, 1969, p. 26).

Thus, like strain theories, control theories adopt the functionalist view of normative consensus and that crime is affected by structural factors. Control theories differ, however, by arguing that individuals naturally possess the motivation to engage in force and fraud, and structural conditions are related to crime when they fail to restrain people from engaging in their natural desires. This control theory notion is also exemplified in **social disorganization theory**, which was developed by University of Chicago sociologists Clifford Shaw and Henry McKay (1942). They argue that in socially disorganized communities—characterized by poverty, residential mobility, and racial/ethnic heterogeneity—institutions such as schools, religious organizations, and family are unable to effectively socialize youth to hold values that restrain criminal and delinquent behaviors.

Policy Implications of Structural Functionalism

Although strain and control theories are based on different assumptions of human nature, they both offer similar and practical ideas on crime prevention. Although Merton's strain theory identifies the motivational source of crime in the unequal distribution of opportunities for success, he is clear that effectively socializing individuals in the appropriate means of achieving success can reduce the likelihood that individuals turn to crime. Control theories similarly emphasize the importance of effective socialization in reducing crime. Accordingly, schools, parents, and other institutions that bear the responsibility of socializing youth need the resources and skills to take on this role. Increased funds for schools and parenting classes are effective strategies for crime prevention. Importantly, and unique to functionalist theories, crime can be a good thing in society when it is committed at a proper amount. Individuals violating social norms allow the institutions designed to regulate behavior to punish the deviance, thus reinforcing the shared values that promote conformity.

....

ASK YOURSELF: If you got into trouble on campus, who would you be afraid of disappointing? Does the potential for disappointing someone make you think twice about doing something prohibited?

....

....

Social control theory: A theory of crime that assumes all people are capable of committing crimes and that some are stopped by their strong bonds to society.

Social disorganization theory: A theory that links crime rates to neighborhood ecological characteristics: poverty, residential mobility, and racial heterogeneity.

▶ Dylann Roof is charged with murder in the shooting deaths of nine people, all African American, at the Emanuel African Methodist Episcopal Church in Charleston, South Carolina, in 2015. Motivated by white supremacist beliefs, Roof said he engaged in mass murder with the intention of starting a race war. Do you see Roof as a "rebel" wanting to change Americans' ideas about race relations?

Symbolic Interactionism

Symbolic interactionism is a microsociological theory that views all human behavior as resulting from a complex interaction between persons and situations. The theory begins with the assumption that our identities, and the situational contexts in which behavior occurs, have relatively little meaning until we interact with others who communicate and define them for us. For example, without communicating with others we may not know the significance of someone staring us down. By being exposed to patterns of behavior conducive to delinquent conduct we may "learn" that this is a sign of a challenge and that the appropriate way to respond to such disrespect is violence. Furthermore, when others see us or treat us as criminals, we may be more likely to see ourselves in a similar light and act in a manner that is consistent with this identity. Two theoretical perspectives of criminology are rooted in the symbolic interactionist framework: differential association and labeling theories.

Edwin H. Sutherland developed **differential association theory** and drew heavily on his social psychological and symbolic interactionist training from the University of Chicago. Sutherland (1947) specifically drew on the work of W. I. Thomas—who defined social psychology as the scientific study of attitudes—and argued that the proximal cause of criminal behavior was one's evaluation of that behavior (the rationalization). He also drew on the work of George Herbert Mead and Charles Horton Cooley and argued that one's ability to fit a deviant rationalization into a concrete circumstance is dependent on his or her definition of that situation. According to Sutherland, we learn these definitions through structured interactions with others, who communicate that crime is either (1) wrong in all circumstances, (2) appropriate but only under some circumstances, or (3) appropriate in virtually all

circumstances (Matsueda, 1988). However, our associates often give us mixed messages, and we are exposed to definitions that are both favorable and unfavorable to crime. When one's definitions favorable to crime exceed one's definitions unfavorable to crime, he or she is predicted to deviate. The differential association process is hypothesized to explain not just if or how often one is deviant, but also the types of criminal acts he or she commits (Thomas, 2015). Sutherland's (1947) differential association theory is considered a quintessential sociological explanation, as it identifies the causes of crime through interactions with social groups, one's learned attitudes toward crime, and in the meaning individuals place on immediate circumstances. Differential association theory has impressive empirical support. Associating with delinquent friends and possessing delinquent attitudes are two of the strongest predictors of deviant conduct (Pratt et al., 2010).

Other criminological theories incorporate the identity aspect of symbolic interactionism. The central premise of these theories is that individuals can embrace a deviant conception of themselves, and that the solidification of this identity can affect subsequent behavior through a self-fulfilling prophecy. For example, **labeling theories** emphasize how the application of sanctions can lead to a deviant stigma applied by others, which in turn affects one's identity and subsequent delinquency. Lemert (1951) believes that most adolescents experiment with **primary deviance**, or low-level, nonserious offending. In fact, he argued that the causes of primary deviance are multifaceted, and that it is so normative that it is of little sociological significance. What is important is how society responds to this minor deviance. In some instances, society overreacts—what Tannenbaum (1938) calls a "dramatization of evil." When this occurs, individuals can embrace the idea that they are a "bad person" and begin to act in accordance with this identity. These adolescents who are labeled deviant and embrace a delinquent identity are more likely to reoffend in the future, and escalate their offending into more serious forms of deviance, known as **secondary deviance**.

....

Differential association theory: A theory of crime that asserts that all behavior is learned, both criminal and noncriminal.

Labeling theories: Theories that emphasize how the application of sanctions can lead to a deviant stigma applied by others, which in turn affects one's identity and subsequent delinquency.

Primary deviance: In societal reaction theory, this refers to individuals' engagement in low-level offending, like speeding or experimenting with alcohol.

Secondary deviance: In societal reaction theory, this refers to individuals' engagement in more serious forms of crime after they have been labeled and treated as criminals.

Identity and labeling theories can be difficult to test empirically, but there is some support for the notion that they may contribute to the explanation for crime. For example, there is research indicating that the application of formal sanctions tends to increase future criminal behavior rather than decrease it (Paternoster & Ioavanni, 1989).

Policy Implications of the Symbolic Interactionist Perspective

While the symbolic interactionist perspective lends itself well to explaining deviant behavior, trying to prevent said behavior through public policy, underneath this perspective, can often be challenging. After all, one cannot "force" adolescent teens to form friendships solely with nondelinquent peers. Nonetheless, efforts have been made toward targeting certain types of interactions, such as "gang activity," by penalizing the congregation of youths in specific public spaces (street corners, for instance) while donning certain symbols/gang-related attire, etc. Whether these sorts of policies actually prevent associations with deviant peers, however, is another matter entirely. Some programs, such as "Big Brothers Big Sisters," attempt to provide younger individuals with pro-social definitions and goals by pairing them directly to pro-social "mentors" who act as surrogate friends/parental figures. Research has supported the program's capability in reducing "anti-social behavior" among adolescents (Grossman & Garry, 1997). Finally, arresting and incarcerating juveniles may have detrimental consequences, as incarcerated youth are more likely to be exposed to deviant norms and attitudes held by other inmates. Additionally, youth who are formally sanctioned maintain a permanent criminal record, and thus should, underneath the labeling perspective, be more likely to offend in the future. Thus, alternatives to sanctioning, such as diversion programs, should be employed (when suitable) to reduce further instances of criminal behavior.

Conflict Theory

Conflict theory stresses that the social inequities that exist among classes, races, and genders are all sources of conflict that may potentially lead to crime. In general, the weak are made to suffer at the hands of the powerful: the poor held down by the rich, ethnic minorities by the white majority, and women exploited and demeaned by men. Conflict theorists also examine how the powerful write and use the laws to their own advantage and to the detriment of weaker groups. We have seen in this chapter that punishments for possession of crack cocaine, weak enforcement of wage laws, and stop-and-frisk policies all contribute to the disproportionate incarceration of people of color—and all could be explored through a conflict lens. We next explore the injustices that exist between classes and genders through the same lens.

Karl Marx was a German philosopher who lived in the 1800s. While he said very little about crime directly, many conflict criminologists have used his general view of society to explain crime in a model known as **Marxist criminology**. Marx described two dominant classes: the **bourgeoisie**, or the wealthy class, who own the means of production; and the **proletariat**, or the working class, who contribute their labor.

Marxist criminologists believe the struggles between classes affect crime in many ways. For instance, **bourgeoisie legality** allows the members of the wealthy class—through their connections to officials and lawmakers—to write and use the law as a tool of oppression. The "deviant" behaviors of the poor are viewed as "street crimes," while similar behaviors by the ruling class are largely ignored. Furthermore, members of the working class are excluded from higher-paying jobs, from receiving better employee benefits, and from achieving a more comfortable lifestyle; this exclusion causes them to behave in a criminal manner.

> **ASK YOURSELF:** Do you think it is a crime for corporations to impose unfavorable working conditions on employees? Why or why not?

An example of this is the U.S. economic crisis that began in 2007. As housing prices declined following reckless lending by banks, many financial institutions suffered huge losses and faced bankruptcy. The government bailed out the largest of these even as many U.S. workers faced job loss, home foreclosure, and rising food and fuel prices. Seeing how the bourgeoisie lawmakers stepped in to serve their own class members, the Occupy Wall Street movement took flight nationwide.

> **ASK YOURSELF:** Do you think Occupy Wall Street is a modern example of the proletariat rising up against the bourgeoisie? Has it been an effective approach to gaining more equality and power for "the 99%"? Explain your reasoning. Would you ever join such a movement? Why or why not?

Marxist criminology: A view based on the writings of Karl Marx that sees the law as the mechanism by which the ruling class keeps the members of the surplus population in their disadvantaged position.

Bourgeoisie: In Marxist theory, the wealthy class that owns and controls the means of production and is at odds with the lower class.

Proletariat: In Marxist theory, the working class, which is at odds with the bourgeoisie.

Bourgeoisie legality: The theory that members of the upper class make the laws to serve and protect their own interests to the detriment of the lower class.

Employees take part in a protest for better wages outside a Walmart store in Los Angeles. Can these employees use current laws to obtain higher wages? Do laws always advantage the rich?

Feminist criminology is often viewed as a part of the conflict perspective because it questions the inequities between the genders that permeate the criminal justice system in myriad ways. Some feminist criminologists believe that **paternalism**—that is, the practice of treating or governing women in a fatherly manner, especially by providing for their needs without giving them rights or responsibilities—explains why women are more likely than men to be victims of crimes at the hands of men they know and with whom they have relationships (Belknap, 2007). Others criticize the way the criminal justice system treats male and female offenders differentially. Kathleen Daly and Meda Chesney-Lind (1988) found that female juvenile delinquents are punished more harshly than boys for minor offenses because their behaviors are contrary to beliefs about how girls should behave.

The feminist/conflict perspective finds that other aspects of the criminal justice system have had disproportionately negative impacts on women. For example, under marital privilege, an individual cannot be compelled to testify against his or her spouse; abusive husbands sometimes use a poor understanding of the privilege to threaten their wives with harm if they plan to testify voluntarily against them. Feminist criminologists have also studied chivalry, or a tendency to overprotect women and girls. Some researchers have found that a chivalrous attitude toward women leads to leniency for female defendants in criminal cases (Mallicoat, 2007), while others have found that women who violate gendered expectations are treated more harshly (MacDonald & Chesney-Lind, 2001). Regardless of case outcomes, feminist criminologists find that gender is an important variable that causes difference due to an imbalance of power between men and women.

Policy Implications of the Conflict Perspective

The policy implications of the conflict perspective are macro in nature and call for radical social changes that can resolve economic and social inequalities. This can be done by creating better work conditions, eliminating race and gender discrimination in the workplace, providing universal health care, and offering equal opportunity in housing and education. Conflict theorists who have looked into the impacts of race and gender on charging and sentencing decisions have suggested that possible solutions to current inequities include an increase in the numbers of minorities and women in positions in the criminal justice system and changes in laws to eliminate criminalization of the behavior of the disenfranchised (Amster, 2004; Ferrell, 2013). Feminist criminologists also question the androcentric nature of the laws and continue to challenge laws that place women in a disadvantaged position relative to men (Chesney-Lind & Morash, 2013).

SPECIALIZED THEORIES ABOUT CRIME

11.7 Apply specialized theories of crime.

Many prominent criminological theories directly descend from the sociological theories of functionalism, symbolic interactionism, and conflict. But other theories exist that do not derive directly from sociology and can be thought of as specialized theories of criminal behavior.

Rational Choice Theories of Criminal Behavior

One subset of theories is based on the standard economic assumption that humans are rational beings and break the law when the benefits of crime outweigh the costs. This idea traces back to Enlightenment thinkers Cesare Beccaria and Jeremy Bentham. Beccaria (1764) was not directly interested in specifying a criminological theory, but in writing a treatise critical of the punishment practices of the time. Most formal punishments handed down by governments were arbitrary and excessive, and were driven primarily by the goal of retribution. Beccaria believed that the purpose of punishments should not be limited to retribution, and that effective punishments could prevent crime from happening in the first

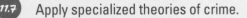

Feminist criminology: A theory of crime that includes gender in its analysis.

Paternalism: The system, principle, or practice of managing or governing individuals in the manner of a father dealing with his children.

REUTERS/Lucy Nicholson

Experiencing Crime

Fighting Stereotypes With Hate Crime Legislation

Matthew Shepard was a student at the University of Wyoming in 1998. One night he met two individuals at a bar who agreed to give him a ride home, but instead they drove him to a remote area, beat and tortured him, and finally tied him to a fence to die. Alive but in a coma, Shepard was discovered 18 hours later by a bicyclist who initially mistook him for a scarecrow. He had suffered fractures to his skull and severe brain damage, and he died without regaining consciousness.

On June 7, 1998, in Jasper, Texas, three white men (known white supremacists) tied a black man named James Byrd Jr. to the back of their pickup truck and dragged him along an asphalt road. Byrd did not die until he smashed into a pipe at the side of the road that severed his head and arm. The defendants then dumped his remains in a cemetery.

Social statuses like race, gender, and social class all factor into the development of hate crime legislation. The attack on Matthew Shepard was motivated by the defendants' perceptions of his sexual orientation, but Wyoming did not include this category in its hate crime law at the time. Texas did not have any hate crime law in place at the time of James Byrd's murder, but after his death it was finally passed.

Today, 45 U.S. states have adopted some form of hate crime legislation, making it a crime to victimize a person simply because of his or her identity or beliefs. These laws allow courts to impose stiff punishments and send a message of intolerance of hate crime. Originally, only acts committed on

► Stella and James Byrd Sr. arrange flowers around the headstone of their son, James Byrd Jr., in Jasper, Texas.

the basis of a person's race, religion, ethnicity, or nationality were prosecuted under federal law, but in 2009 President Barack Obama signed the Matthew Shepard and James Byrd Jr. Hate Crimes Prevention Act, expanding the law to include crimes motivated by victims' gender, sexual orientation, gender identity, or disability.

► **THINK ABOUT IT:** Do you think that James Byrd Jr.'s murder was especially heinous not only because he was black but also because he was male?

SOURCES: Matthew Shepard Foundation (2014) and Wong (2009).

---

place. Effective punishments, according to Beccaria, are *certain, swift,* and *severe.* Certainty refers to the likelihood of apprehension (i.e., arrest) if the crime is committed. If there is a 100% chance of arrest it is unlikely an individual will offend. Swiftness refers to how quickly a punishment is applied, with the idea being that when punishments are employed closer in time to the act itself, individuals are more likely to associate a negative consequence with the behavior. Severity concerns the harshness of the punishment, but Beccaria does not mean that punishments should be excessively cruel; rather, the punishments of crime should be proportional to the crime that is committed. Beccaria was calling for criminal justice reform, but in doing so outlined deterrence theory, a perspective arguing that individuals rationally decide to

commit crime and weigh formal sanction threats heavily in this rational calculus. Deterrence theory accords institutions formally designed to regulate crime—the police, courts, and corrections—a seminal role in crime prevention, and it serves as the theoretical foundation for the criminal justice system in the United States.

Deterrence theory falls under a more general **rational choice theory.** Rational choice is broader in that it more formally specifies the benefits of crime, and extends potential costs beyond the threat of formal sanctions. Benefits to crime can include potential monetary gains,

....

Rational choice theory: A theory of crime that says humans are reasoning actors who weigh costs and benefits and make rational choices to commit crimes.

accruement of peer status, and psychological thrills, while costs can include time spent incarcerated, anticipated disapproval of parents, and the potential loss of a job. The theory simply states that before taking a course of action, individuals consider and weigh the possible consequences (both positive and negative), and choose the behavioral response that will yield them the most pleasure and the least pain. Initial presentations of rational choice treated individuals—at least implicitly—as being purely rational agents. This could not explain why individuals made "bad" offending decisions that resulted in arrest. Most criminologists now believe in a concept known as **bounded rationality**, which means we make choices but our choices are limited by the time we have to make a decision, the information that is available to us, and our own cognitive capacity. The future of the rational choice perspective likely lies in the decision-making advancements identified in behavioral economics. This work has shown that many decisions that seem irrational may not be irrational at all. For example, individuals consistently report that they would rather have $100 today than $110 one year from now, which is difficult to account for in a traditional subjective utility model since $110 is greater than $100. Research has indicated, however, that individuals weigh immediate stimuli greater than stimuli that will be experienced at a later point in time. This may explain why individuals engage in criminal behaviors that are immediately rewarding but seemingly go against long-term interests.

••

ASK YOURSELF: When is rational choice "bounded," and how might these bounds affect someone's decision to commit crimes?

••

Environmental Theories of Crime

Most sociological theories of crime use structural characteristics to explain differences in the propensity to commit crime. Merton as well as Shaw and McKay, for example, suggest that poverty is a condition that can affect the rate of offending. Some criminological perspectives point out that the individual offender is just one element of a criminal event. That is, crime also involves a victim and a situational element, and these too are important. Consider that crime was on the rise in the 1960s despite the fact that poverty was declining and other social conditions were improving. This fact was difficult to reconcile for most sociological explanations. Cohen and Felson (1979) argued that the rise in crime was the result of the increase in the number of criminal opportunities. Specifically, items that were worth stealing became smaller and easier to carry and conceal. The increased presence of women in the workforce also meant that fewer individuals were home during the day

David Grossman/Alamy Stock Photo

▶ Many poor neighborhoods have conditions of urban decay, with abandoned and severely neglected buildings, streets, and lots. Do you think these physical conditions of disrepair and decrepitude ("broken windows") lead to crime? Or is it poverty and lack of money that lead to crime?

to prevent burglaries from occurring. Even further, more people were living in single-person units, meaning that individuals were often walking home alone at night. Crime increased in the 1960s not because the number of potential criminals changed, but because our daily activities changed. Cohen and Felson's (1979) **routine activity theory** suggests that crime occurs when three things converge in space and time: (1) a motivated offender, (2) a suitable target, and (3) the absence of a capable guardian.

The routine activity perspective has important implications for policy. Most theoretically rooted policy implications are based on the notion that crime can only be prevented by addressing individual or macrosociological risk factors. Routine activity theory suggests that we can prevent crime by reducing the suitableness of targets or by increasing the presence of capable guardians. Theft from department stores can be reduced by attaching ink tags on items that explode when forcibly removed (target suitability). Importantly, a "capable guardian" does not necessarily refer to a human being but can include security systems, cameras, or even improved lighting.

Another example of an environmental theory is George L. Kelling and James Q. Wilson's (1982) **broken windows theory**. The central premise of this theory is that minor

•••

Bounded rationality: The idea that an individual's thought processes are deemed to be rational even when they are constrained by low intelligence, chemical dependence, or mental illness.

Routine activity theory: The theory that proposes that crime occurs when three things converge in space and time: a motivated offender, a suitable target, and the absence of a capable guardian.

Broken windows theory: The theory that maintaining an urban environment in an orderly manner will deter both low-level and serious offending.

signs of disorder (such as graffiti, loitering, and broken windows), if not properly addressed, can ultimately lead to more serious forms of criminal activity. This can occur for several reasons. First, disorder can act as a signal to offenders that individuals do not care about an area and that crime could be committed there without concern of reporting. Put simply, disordered communities attract criminals. Second, signs of disorder can stoke fear among law-abiding citizens and cause them to refrain from leaving their homes. These are individuals who would likely intervene on the commission of criminal acts if witnessed, but their fear of crime prompts them to retreat from the community altogether. Third, signs of disorder drive down housing prices, which, in turn, increases residential mobility in the neighborhood. The policy implications of broken windows theory are clear: Police may effectively prevent serious forms of criminal behavior by addressing the minor forms of criminal behavior.

SOCIAL CHANGE: WHAT CAN YOU DO?

 11.8 Identify steps toward social change concerning crime.

Action to address the problem of crime must include all interested stakeholders— offenders, victims, vulnerable populations, the criminal justice system—and society at large. Fortunately, there are many ways for students to participate in social change, often by helping one person at a time and learning valuable skills along the way. Here are some opportunities for effecting social change.

▶▶ Take Back the Night

In October 1975, Susan Speeth was stabbed to death by a stranger just a block from her home. At the time, the 911 emergency system had only recently been implemented, and other crime prevention measures we now take for granted—lighting, cameras, building design features—were nonexistent. Moreover, violence against women was not considered a social problem; rather, it was often dismissed as the "fault" of the victims for being out at night. Speeth's murder inspired women and men to rally on campuses to raise awareness about crimes against women, and to call upon those in control to make public areas safe. Thus, Take Back the Night, a national foundation, was born, and public events during April and October became established features on many campuses.

Is Take Back the Night relevant today? In 2010, fraternity pledges for the Delta Kappa Epsilon fraternity at Yale University surrounded the campus Women's Center, chanting, "No means yes" and "Yes means anal," and "My name is Jack, I am a necrophiliac, I f**k dead women." Although measures were taken to suspend the fraternity, its message fed the old myth that crimes against women are somehow the victims' fault. Take Back the Night

Tribune Content Agency LLC/Alamy Stock Photo

▶ Programs like Big Brothers Big Sisters match adult volunteers to children in need of mentorship.

continues to be an important organization that welcomes participation from both women and men and drives home the message that women have the right to walk safely in their communities. Are crimes against women a problem on your campus or in your community? Take Back the Night provides planning support to help you promote your own Shine Your Light Walk (http://www.takebackthenight.org/TBTNfoundation.html).

▶▶ Big Brothers Big Sisters

Taking social action often means partnering with established community organizations. Big Brothers Big Sisters (BBBS; http://www.bbbs.org) is a 100-year-old international organization that matches adult mentors to children of single parents in every U.S. state and a dozen other countries. Mentoring is one of the most effective strategies for delinquency prevention. In the largest evaluation of BBBS to date, researchers found that even though the organization provides neither tutoring nor antidrug counseling, participating young people achieve substantial improvements in school performance and reductions in antisocial behavior (Grossman & Garry, 1997).

Many chapters of BBBS are in dire need of mentors, especially males. College students can be excellent mentors. Training is provided, and the commitment period is 1 year. Most BBBS chapters accept volunteers as young as 18.

Here's a story of one of our students who made a difference through mentoring. He had been mentored as a teenager after the death of his father, and then later, as a college student, he served as a mentor at the local BBBS. After graduation, he was hired by our college as an assistant football coach. In that capacity, he and the coaching staff and most of the players partnered with BBBS to start a program called SportsMENship, which mentored middle school boys. The program later expanded to include the college's baseball team, ensuring a yearlong experience for the "littles," who tend to be drawn to sports rather than academics and are excited to be around college athletes. Moreover, they learn to recognize the importance of being a student-athlete, rather than just an athlete. Through their relationships with the mentors, they see that they need academic success in order to pursue their interests in athletics, and that their role models are serious about getting their college degrees and plan to pursue careers outside sports.

►► Operation Swordphish

Students at the University of Alabama–Birmingham are assisting police in fighting computer-based fraud and theft in a program called Operation Swordphish, which began in 2010. Nearly 7,000 cybercrimes in Alabama went uninvestigated each year, because individually they were too small for federal agencies to intervene. Students now help to build a database of reported cybercrimes, such as "phishing" e-mails. As savvy users of Facebook and other social media are probably aware, phishing is a computer-based method for acquiring confidential information, including user names, passwords, and credit card details, by masquerading as a trustworthy source.

Operation Swordphish is essentially an information center for accumulating data in such a way as to build cases against scam artists. The program is designed to encourage victims to volunteer details about how they were fooled. Through collaboration with the law enforcement community, the program can measure the incidence of specific scams and the damage caused in order to calculate the statewide impact of each. This

information in turn can support a federal investigation. Public education campaigns make residents aware of what to do if they believe they have been victims of a financial-based cybercrime. Students help to gather and analyze the information received from victims. The program's directors hope it will be a model for other jurisdictions.

►► College-Led Initiatives

A college course called Arts Outreach is part of a nationally recognized program that partners Stonehill College (near Brockton, Massachusetts) with the local district attorney's office and local arts programs. The course provides positive role models for fourth, fifth, and sixth grade children by matching them with college students and high school student leaders for weekly painting, dance, and photography classes taught by faculty. The children are drawn from a Brockton census tract with high rates of juvenile court arraignment, weapons in school, poverty, school dropout, teen pregnancy, foster care, domestic and child abuse, and drug and alcohol abuse. Since 1998, Arts Outreach has provided a safe learning environment where children are taught new artistic skills, build healthy friendships, and develop individual and group problem-solving skills. In the classes, elementary school children are paired with college mentors, and high school students act as co-mentors. All student mentors attend 3 to 4 days of training in conflict resolution techniques, responsibilities, and expectations; take a guided tour of the school and neighborhood; and are briefed about the selected children. The program culminates in a collaborative project at a local museum. For more information, visit http://www.afhboston.org.

At Mercer University in Macon, Georgia, what began as a first-year seminar called Engaging the World grew into a coalition of students, faculty, and local human rights experts who formed the campus-wide Sex Trafficking Opposition Project (STOP; http://www.mercer.edu/stop). Following reports of police raids on local massage parlors, student STOP members spoke out in conventional and alternative news media to express concern that potentially trafficked women were being arrested and then released to their traffickers. They helped bring antitrafficking training to the Macon police force and members of the Macon Crisis Line and Safe House. The Macon police chief credited STOP's community activism with helping to transform traditional police raids into potential rescues, to free one child-sex-trafficking victim, and to shut down five massage parlors. More than 900 people from around the region heard from national experts on human trafficking at a campus conference organized by STOP.

Turn to the beginning of the chapter to compare your answers to those of the total population.

1. Do you favor or oppose the death penalty for persons convicted of murder?

FAVOR: 60.4%

OPPOSE: 39.6%

2. In general, do you think the courts in this area deal too harshly or not harshly enough with criminals?

TOO HARSHLY: 20.1%

ABOUT THE RIGHT AMOUNT: 18%

NOT HARSHLY ENOUGH: 61.9%

3. Would you favor or oppose a law which would require a person to obtain a police permit before he or she could buy a gun?

FAVOR: 71.6%

OPPOSE: 28.4%

4. In the United States, do you think we're spending too much money on law enforcement, too little money, or about the right amount?

TOO MUCH: 10.7%

TOO LITTLE: 54.4%

ABOUT THE RIGHT AMOUNT: 34.9%

5. Are there any situations you can imagine in which you would approve of a policeman striking an adult male citizen?

YES: 68.9%

NO: 31.1%

6. Are you ever afraid to walk at night in your neighborhood?

YES: 32.2%

NO: 67.8%

SOURCE: National Opinion Research Center, University of Chicago.

CHAPTER SUMMARY

 11.1 Discuss crime as a social problem.

Because crime is risky and often results in few material gains, the question of why individuals commit crimes is fundamental to sociology. Crime affects both individuals and communities and the creation and enforcement of laws can even determine the perceived legitimacy of a government.

 11.2 Explain how crime is socially defined.

Our reactions to many crimes are shaped not by an absolute consensus of which are the most important or serious, but by socially constructed definitions that change over time and place.

 11.3 Discuss the sources of crime data.

The FBI's Uniform Crime Reports (UFR) are useful for understanding trends in crime over time and include data from police departments across the U.S. Importantly, however, research has found that roughly half of crime is reported to the police. Other data sources include self-reporting and victimization surveys, which come with their own unique set of limitations.

 11.4 Discuss patterns and trends in crime and crime measurement.

In the United States, street crimes such as burglary and robbery have generally been on the decline, as law enforcement resources have become more strategic. However, enforcement of laws against **white-collar crimes**—illegal acts, punishable by criminal sanctions, committed in the course of legitimate occupations or by corporations—lags, despite the fact that such crimes have far-reaching impacts. As a society, we are more concerned with crimes committed by low-income minority individuals than with crimes committed by mid- to high-income white people. Our stereotypes regarding what is "criminal" affect the way we perceive and fear crime and possibly how we allocate precious resources. Having a global view of crime allows us to learn from our differences and similarities about topics such as definitions of crime, styles of enforcement, methods of punishment, and the influence of globalization on crime itself.

 11.5 Describe the U.S. criminal justice system and its stakeholders.

The criminal justice system is made up of stakeholders (police, attorneys, and court and correctional staff) whose job is to work within the law and, ideally, achieve justice. A reliance on plea bargains and an emphasis on case efficiency lead to high incarceration rates, along with high recidivism. Specialized courts have been created to target crimes that pose extreme hardships on communities; they aim for collaboration and problem solving, not merely case processing.

11.6 Apply the functionalist, conflict, and symbolic interactionist perspectives to the problem of crime.

Theories from a structural functionalist view include strain and control theories. These theories question individuals' experiences with society and seek explanations for why they commit crimes, such as failure to achieve financial success or weak bonds to society. They call for policies that can alleviate strain or strengthen individuals' bonds to society. The conflict perspective is a macro view of crime that blames criminal behavior on the imbalance of power among members of society. According to this model, economic, racial, and gender injustices can lead individuals to commit crime. Thus, feminist criminology falls under the conflict perspective. Policy implications are macro in nature and call for radical social change. Symbolic interactionist theories include differential association theory and societal reaction theories. The policy implications of these theories are micro in nature and look to influence young people's social choices and the way we respond as a society when they commit crime.

 11.7 Apply specialized theories of crime.

Specialized theories seek to understand offenders' choices and the socioecological conditions that support crime. They include rational choice theory, routine activities theory, broken windows theory, and social disorganization theory.

11.8 Identify steps toward social change concerning crime.

Crime affects not only those who engage in it and those who are victimized by it but also members of society at large who want to create peaceful and safe communities. By taking part in crime awareness programs, you can raise the public's consciousness about crime. By agreeing to mentor children at risk for crime, you can serve as a positive role model and help prevent future criminalization or victimization. By being active in your community and seeking out opportunities to help, you can become an agent of social justice and be part of the solution.

KEY TERMS

adjudication 275

affirmative defenses 274

bounded rationality 284

bourgeoisie 281

bourgeoisie legality 281

broken windows theory 284

clearance rates 268

courtroom workgroup 275

dark figure of crime 268

decentralization of power 274

determinate sentencing 276

deterrence 277

differential association theory 280

feminist criminology 282

general deterrence 277

hierarchy rule 268

hot-spot policing 274

incapacitation 276

indeterminate sentencing 276

labeling theories 280

mala in se crimes 267

⑤SAGE edge™ **Want a better grade?**

Get the tools you need to sharpen your study skills. Access practice quizzes, eFlashcards, video, and multimedia at
http://edge.sagepub.com/trevino2e

12 DRUGS

Carrie B. Oser

▶▶▶ A door is painted with the message to stop selling heroin in a neighborhood with a high rate of illegal drug use in New York City. What can poor communities like this one do to stem the tide of drug use?

Investigating Drugs: My Story

Carrie B. Oser

My research interests in alcohol and drug use were solidified in graduate school, when I traveled around the United States interviewing substance abuse treatment directors for the National Institute on Drug Abuse (NIDA)–supported National Treatment Center Study. This experience provided practical research skills and real-world insights into the daily challenges faced by people with substance use disorders, as I was able to hear their stories. It also shed light on the various treatment approaches commonly used and the various organizational-level differences in treatment centers. After reading Adrian Nicole LeBlanc's *Random Family: Love, Drugs, Trouble, and Coming of Age in the Bronx* (2003), I began to appreciate intersectionality and decided to focus my career on the health of people with substance use disorders involved in the criminal justice system. After receiving my M.A. and Ph.D. in sociology at the University of Georgia, I joined the faculty at the University of Kentucky. I am currently professor and associate chair of the Department of Sociology, with joint appointments in the College of Medicine's Department of Behavioral Science and the Center on Drug and Alcohol Research (CDAR).

My research focuses on special populations of drug users (e.g., criminal offenders, rural residents, and minorities) in a variety of topical areas including implementation science, health services utilization, social networks, and infectious disease prevention. I have over a decade of experience in leading projects supported by NIDA and have published over 100 papers on these topics. I also promote social change by regularly teaching a course on drugs and crime using the Inside-Out Prison Exchange Program model, which brings together persons who are incarcerated with undergraduate students to study as peers in a college class behind prison walls.

LEARNING OBJECTIVES

12.1 Discuss drug use as a social problem.

12.2 Describe the problems of drug dependence.

12.3 Relate patterns of drug use to the life course, gender, race/ethnicity, and sexual orientation.

12.4 Apply the functionalist, symbolic interactionist, and conflict perspectives to social policy on drug use.

12.5 Apply specialized theories to the social problems of drug use.

12.6 Identify steps toward social change on drugs.

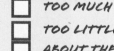 

WHAT DO YOU THINK?
Questions About Alcohol and Other Drugs From the General Social Survey

 1. How often do you spend the evening at a bar?
- ☐ AT LEAST ONCE A WEEK
- ☐ AT LEAST ONCE A MONTH
- ☐ AT LEAST ONCE A YEAR
- ☐ NEVER

2. Should marijuana be made legal?
- ☐ YES
- ☐ NO

3. In the United States, do you think we're spending too much money on dealing with drug addiction, too little money, or about the right amount?
- ☐ TOO MUCH
- ☐ TOO LITTLE
- ☐ ABOUT THE RIGHT AMOUNT

4. In the United States, do you think we're spending too much money on dealing with drug

rehabilitation, too little money, or about the right amount?
- ☐ TOO MUCH
- ☐ TOO LITTLE
- ☐ ABOUT THE RIGHT AMOUNT

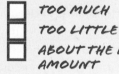

Turn to the end of the chapter to view the results for the total population.

SOURCE: National Opinion Research Center, University of Chicago.

A CANARY IN A COAL MINE?

Imagine working as a health care practitioner in the infectious disease clinic at the local public health department in a small rural town where a lot of the residents know each other. Your clinic offers free, confidential walk-in testing for syphilis, gonorrhea, chlamydia, and the human immunodeficiency virus (HIV), as well as safer sex counseling, free condoms, treatment for sexually transmitted diseases (STDs), and referrals for HIV-infected clients. It is a cold December morning, and your first client comes into the clinic looking tired and stressed. He softly requests an HIV and STD test. You proceed with pretest counseling according to the Centers for Disease Control and Prevention (CDC) guidelines. During the pretest counseling and screening processes, your client discloses he thought it was a good idea to get tested for STDs because his girlfriend has been cheating on him and then later reveals he has been injecting drugs. After explaining the testing processes, you first collect a saliva sample for the rapid HIV antibody testing. Within 20 minutes, he screens positive for HIV. This is a bit unexpected, as your clinic usually doesn't see that many people who screen positive for HIV. It is a shock for the client, too, as he doesn't know anyone with HIV, and you proceed with additional counseling and referrals. Later that day, you have two more clients come in requesting HIV testing, both of whom also screen positive. You begin to wonder if this is a "canary in the coal mine" scenario and immediately notify the director of the public health department about a potential HIV outbreak.

The scenario described above actually occurred in Scott County, Indiana, in December 2014. By March 2015, Governor Mike Pence (now Vice President Pence) declared a public health emergency, as 72 confirmed cases and eight additional preliminary HIV cases had been reported during that 3-month time frame. Usually, the Scott County public health department sees less than five HIV cases per year. Clearly, the proverbial canary in the coal mine stopped singing, signifying the need for public health intervention and the involvement of the CDC to address the HIV epidemic. Indiana and CDC health officials have primarily attributed this outbreak to the

sharing of drug injection equipment and the drug Opana, a powerful opioid pain reliever, although a few cases were identified as sexually transmitted. While the HIV outbreak was tragic, it has been the impetus for social change. For example, needle exchange programs, which were previously illegal in Indiana, have been implemented in public health departments across the region, including Kentucky and Ohio. This outbreak may have been prevented with increased access to medication-assisted treatments for drug-dependent individuals and increased promotion of condom use during oral, anal, and vaginal sex. Finally, encouraging people to get tested for HIV is another key piece of the prevention puzzle. The CDC recommends HIV testing should be part of preventative routine care, and occur at least annually for high-risk groups such as persons who inject drugs. The CDC is currently tracking the potential for future HIV and the Hepatitis C Virus (HCV) outbreaks in rural counties similar to Scott, which are characterized by insular networks of injection drug users.

► Many U.S. states allow the legal use of marijuana for medical purposes. The sale of marijuana for recreational use became legal in Colorado on January 1, 2014. In addition to marijuana buds, pot shops in Colorado sell marijuana-infused foods ranging from brownies and hard candies to cookies, olive oil, granola bars, chocolate truffles, and even spaghetti sauce.

LLOYD K. TOWNSEND JR./National Geographic Creative

DRUGS IN SOCIETIES

 12.1 Discuss drug use as a social problem.

As a child, do you remember spinning in a circle as fast as you could until you got too dizzy and fell down? This is an example of the innate desire to alter our consciousness. In addition to these childhood play experiences, humans have long desired to eat or drink substances that also alter their consciousness and make them feel stimulated, relaxed, or euphoric. A **drug** is any substance whose properties produce psychophysiological changes when ingested. By this definition, we can consider a whole host of substances to be drugs regardless of their legality, medicinal nature, or social value including alcohol, over-the-counter cold medicines, and illegal drugs such as cocaine. The earliest drugs, such as psychedelic mushrooms, were found naturally occurring, and humans could use their psychoactive properties with little effort. Over time, humans began to manipulate substances for psychoactive purposes—for spiritual, recreational, and medical reasons—eventually becoming increasingly scientific and ultimately giving birth to the modern pharmaceutical industry.

Why do people use drugs? All drugs produce psychophysiological changes that fundamentally alter the way an individual experiences the world. Some people use drugs to induce transcendent states or enhance consciousness; they seek to feel more closely connected to the spiritual realm. Others use drugs to alter their moods—to enter into a state of relaxation, induce excitement, or loosen up at a party. Drugs are a common means of enhancing social interaction and are used as a way to connect to others. The desires to "fit in" and reduce social anxieties are commonly touted reasons for initial drug use during adolescence. Also, sharing drugs can serve as a ritual for developing social intimacy. Drugs, whether legal or illegal, have also long had medicinal uses precisely because of their ability to make people feel different. Whether it is to cope with childhood trauma, depression, or chronic back pain, altering one's state with drugs serves as a psychic palliative. People are able to manage the symptoms of illness, and drugs play this vital role in many societies.

Drug encounters are inherently social phenomena. The experience of altered states through the use of a psychoactive substance is due not simply to the substance itself but also to the user's psychological state and the social environment in which he or she consumes the drug. Mood, expectations, and personal history influence the drug experience in conscious and subconscious ways. In other words, we learn about how to experience drugs and how to conceive of them through our social contexts and social encounters.

The social and physical contexts can also shape whether a drug encounter is positive or negative. For example, the experience of an individual using ecstasy at a rave or club will be different from the experience of a trauma victim using ecstasy during a therapeutic session. In one context, the focus is on the pleasure and exuberance the drug can produce, and in the other the drug serves as a palliative, facilitating emotional closure with difficult experiences. Indeed, the experience of a "bad trip" on LSD is often attributed more to the user's state of mind and environment than to the substance's pharmacological properties.

All societies have normative patterns of drug use. While we are most familiar with drug laws, not all societies rely only on the threat of legal sanction to enforce standards of behavior in the course of psychoactive drug use. Often, members of a community "police" each other with regard to the acceptable standards of behavior within that community. In fact, all societies, even those with laws against the use of certain drugs, have social norms and values governing the use of psychoactive drugs, who may use them, and how those users should behave. The social context of drug use matters. For example, in the United States, drinking a beer at a professional sporting event such as a baseball game is perfectly acceptable behavior for an adult. However, if the same adult were to drink a beer while attending a play performed by 8-year-olds at the local elementary school, he or she would likely face disapproval and social sanctions from others. One location is deemed socially acceptable for alcohol use by the community, the other is not.

Community norms also shape what is considered acceptable behavior for persons under the influence of a drug, which is often different from acceptable behavior for those in a sober state. For instance, while the expectation that they will be disinhibited enables drug users to act in ways typically out of bounds for sober citizens, communities generally set boundaries for permitted and expected behaviors on the part of those under the influence of drugs. The social context is important for determining the applicability of these rules. Yelling and chanting with drunken enthusiasm at a tailgate party before the big game may be socially acceptable or even encouraged, but at a holiday dinner party where wine is casually sipped, such behavior may cause a person's ejection, with no return invitation.

Drugs as a Social Problem

While drugs are often considered a social problem in U.S. society, as inanimate substances they are neither inherently good nor inherently bad. Their effects depend on

....

Drug: A substance that has properties that produce psychophysiological changes in the individual who ingests it.

▶ Young men enjoy a night of drinking in Glasgow, Scotland. The Glasgow City Council banned "happy hours" when cut price drinks can be bought at specific times. In what ways do you think people might act differently when drinking with friends than when drinking alone?

the social contexts and the ways, good or bad, in which humans put them to use. Opiate drugs, for instance, can relieve excruciating pain and play an important role in reducing human suffering after a medical surgery. However, recreational users of these substances can fall into a problematic cycle of dependence, leading to other forms of deviant behavior, comorbid health conditions, and even the possibility of death from overdose. Thus, the ways in which we integrate drugs into our lives shape the impacts they have on individuals and societies.

In the United States, federal efforts to control psychoactive substances began in the early 20th century, but a heightened focus on policing the use of drugs emerged in the 1970s. President Richard M. Nixon first declared the **War on Drugs**, calling drugs "public enemy number one," channeling unprecedented resources toward drug abuse treatment programs, and addressing drug use as a public health problem. For example, the National Institute on Drug Abuse (NIDA)—the leading government agency on the health impacts of drug use, abuse, and dependence—was founded during the Nixon administration in 1974, as was the Office of Drug Abuse Law Enforcement (ODALE), created specifically to police narcotics. ODALE became the Drug Enforcement Agency (DEA) in 1973. Public policy on drugs has since built upon the foundation of these 1970s efforts, and the issue of drugs as a social problem has become fixed in the American popular consciousness. However, the War on Drugs is popularly associated with President Ronald Reagan because of his administration's massive increase in spending on both federal law enforcement and the drug enforcement agency, while drastically reducing the drug education, prevention, and treatment budgets. When the Reagan administration began its own War on Drugs in 1982, less than 2% of Americans considered drugs the most important issue facing the nation. The

media were used to reinforce the rhetoric and link drugs to crime, especially in impoverished inner-city minority neighborhoods. Then, crack came onto the scene in 1985. Due to these efforts and the emergence of the crack epidemic, by 1989, 63% of Americans viewed drugs as the most important issue facing the country, according to a *New York Times* poll.

Today, the U.S. government allocates about 52% of its drug-related funding to **supply reduction** programs, such as federal, state, local, and international law enforcement, while the remainder goes toward **demand reduction**, such as prevention and treatment (Office of National Drug Control Policy, 2016). Supply and demand reduction are intertwined, and additional investments are needed in the domestic demand reduction strategies to promote sustained reductions. In contrast, other countries around the world have reduced or even eliminated their criminal justice focus on drugs. For example, in 2001, Portugal decriminalized the possession of personal-use amounts of all drugs (including marijuana, crystal methamphetamine, and cocaine). If you are a Portuguese citizen walking down the street in Lisbon and a police search uncovers an amount of heroin small enough for personal use in your pocket, you will not be arrested. While you may think such a policy would increase drug use, a recent study found that both injection drug use and teen drug use have actually declined in Portugal (Hughes & Stevens, 2010).

ASK YOURSELF: What might be some of the effects if the United States were to decriminalize simple possession of all drugs? How would such a policy shift affect the way law enforcement occurs on a day-to-day basis?

Differences Among Drug Use, Drug Abuse, and Drug Dependence

How do we distinguish among drug use, drug abuse, and drug dependence? **Drug use** is simply the ingestion of

War on Drugs: The comprehensive policy first formulated by President Richard M. Nixon to address the drug problem in the 1970s and significantly promoted by President Ronald Reagan in the 1980s.

Supply reduction: An approach to drug policy aimed at disrupting the manufacturing and distribution supply chains of drugs.

Demand reduction: An approach to drug policy aimed at providing education, prevention, and treatment.

Drug use: The ingestion of substances so as to produce changes in the body that alter the way the user experiences the world.

substances in order to produce changes in the body or mind that alter the way the world is experienced. Any consumption of psychoactive substances (including legal drugs such as alcohol) for any purpose is considered drug use.

Drug abuse, on the other hand, is the use of psychoactive substances in a way that creates social, psychological, or physical problems for the user. All drugs can be abused, including legal ones such as alcohol, tobacco, diet pills, decongestants, and even caffeine. The fundamental distinction between drug use and drug abuse is that abuse creates harm in the life of the user. Thus, all drug abuse includes drug use; however, all drug use is not necessarily drug abuse.

Drug dependence is characterized by compulsive drug use behaviors despite negative consequences and produces psychophysiological changes in the user. This dependence can be physiological or psychological in nature, or both, and its effects can vary considerably. For example, compared with more socioeconomically disadvantaged persons, those with sufficient resources or wealth may experience fewer problems associated with drug dependence and be less likely to be arrested, fired from their jobs, or lose custody of their children. Table 12.1 recaps the distinctions among these terms.

> *ASK YOURSELF*: How might wealth and fame affect a person's experiences with drugs, the criminal justice system, and family court?

To illuminate the differences among use, abuse, and dependence, let us consider the consumption of alcohol, for which there is no legal prohibition among adults over the age of 21. Enjoying a glass of wine or two with dinner is not considered deviant behavior in U.S. society and is a socially sanctioned means of celebrating. This kind of alcohol consumption can be categorized as drug use.

However, consider the person who goes to happy hour on Wednesday, consumes enough beer to make herself sick, and is unable to show up for work the following day. In this instance, the user has not only brought on physical illness as a result of her drinking but has also failed to meet her responsibilities in the workplace. This is an instance of alcohol consumption leading to social and physical problems; we may consider this pattern of drinking to be alcohol abuse.

Finally, consider an individual who drinks daily, often beginning early, because he feels he needs to drink. He may be anxious about the prospect of not being able to drink, so he hides alcohol in his jacket, office, or car and takes sips while at work to be comfortable and avoid hand tremors. He may go home after work to prepare another drink for himself or stop at a bar for some additional drinks on the way. This person would be considered alcohol dependent.

TABLE 12.1 **Differences Among Drug Use, Drug Abuse, and Drug Dependence**

Term	Definition
Drug use	The ingestion of substances to produce changes in the body or mind that alter how the world is experienced
Drug abuse	The use of psychoactive substances in a way that creates social, psychological, or physical problems for the user
Drug dependence	A state that produces psychophysiological changes in the user and is characterized by compulsive drug use and drug-seeking behaviors despite harmful consequences

DRUG DEPENDENCE AND ASSOCIATED HARMS

12.2 Describe the problems of drug dependence.

In *Righteous Dopefiend* (2009), Philippe Bourgois and Jeff Schonberg highlight the suffering often associated with drug dependence and the complex social, political, and institutional forces that shape drug users' lives. As illustrated by their research, the experience of managing drug dependence can be a grueling one. They describe one person's experience of "dopesickness"—withdrawal from opiate drugs—and quote his own description:

> Felix tried to urinate into the plastic water bottle that he kept next to his blankets, but his body was shaking too hard. He stood up, but his leg muscles spasmed and he fell down the highway embankment. He had to drag himself on his hands and knees to get back up to his mattress, pausing twice to retch. . . .
>
> "First I'm cold; then poof! Heat flashes, and I'm ripping the covers off. But it's cold out here,

Drug abuse: The use of psychoactive substances in a way that creates problematic outcomes for the user.

Drug dependence: A state that produces psychophysiological changes in the user and is characterized by compulsive drug use and drug-seeking behaviors despite harmful consequences.

Researching Drugs

Misuse of Prescription Drugs

Prescription drug misuse—defined by Compton and Volkow (2006, p. S4) as "any intentional use of a medication with intoxicating properties outside of a physician's prescription for a bona fide medical condition"—has risen significantly during the past decade, particularly among adolescents and young adults. Commonly misused prescription drugs include those used to treat pain (e.g., drugs containing the active ingredients codeine, hydrocodone, and oxycodone), anxiety (e.g., benzodiazepines including Valium or Xanax), or attention deficit hyperactivity disorder (e.g., stimulants including Ritalin or Adderall). During 2000, an estimated 8.7 million people aged 12 and older in the United States had used prescription drugs nonmedically within the previous year. By 2014, this figure had increased to 15 million (Substance Abuse and Mental Health Services Administration, 2015). After marijuana and alcohol use, the nonmedical use of prescription drugs is the most widespread drug issue in the United States.

Young adults ages 18–25 are the segment of the U.S. population with the highest rates of prescription drug misuse. Many are introduced to prescription drugs by means of legitimate prescriptions or through their social networks. Recent research has shown that young adults in various nightlife scenes are especially likely to misuse prescription drugs (Kelly et al., 2013b), such as those in the indie rock scene or those who frequent electronic dance music clubs (Kelly et al., 2013a). Networks are also salient in the lives of young adults who inject prescription drugs in rural areas, as those more central to the drug-using network are more likely have the Hepatitis C Virus (Havens, Lofwall, Frost, Oser, Leukefeld, & Crosby,

2013; Zibbell, Hart-Mallory, Barry, Fan, & Flanigan, 2014).

A key problem with prescription drug misuse is that some users may perceive the drugs to be safe because physicians prescribe them for medical problems. Yet a host of dangers arise with misuse, including the possibility of overdose, high blood pressure, drug interactions, and seizures. Because prescription drugs are still needed for legitimate treatment of severe or chronic conditions including cancer, the policies surrounding them are complex. Government and industry cannot simply make them illegal to inhibit access to those who misuse them (even though criminalization does not necessarily reduce their use). The need to ensure care for patients thus makes it difficult to police the abuse of these medications, but efforts are in progress. For example, in 2010, OxyContin was reformulated by Purdue Pharma to a noncrushable, noninjectable formula. The abuse-deterrent formulation has reduced the misuse of this pain medication, but much of reduction in OxyContin is associated with a transition to other opiate drugs such as heroin (Cicerco & Ellis, 2015; Cicero, Ellis, & Surratt, 2012). Also, 40 states have implemented prescription drug monitoring programs (PDMPs), which collect data on dispensed prescription

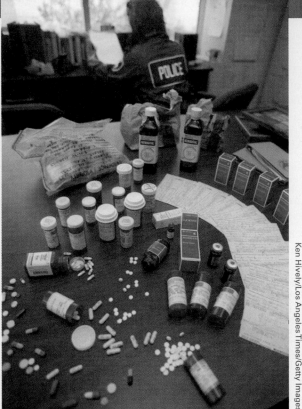

Ken Hively/Los Angeles Times/Getty Images

▶ Prescription drug misuse can have serious medical and legal consequences. "Doctor shoppers" are people who go from doctor-to-doctor seeking prescriptions for drugs for a number of reasons, including getting high, self medication of pain, anxiety, and depression.

controlled substances and store them in a central database where they can be accessed by authorized users (e.g., health care professionals, law enforcement agents). PDMPs aim to reduce drug abuse by discouraging "doctor shopping" and inappropriate prescribing practices.

▶ THINK ABOUT IT

1. Why do you think prescription drug misuse has increased so dramatically among young adults in recent years?

2. What are some problems associated with PDMPs?

3. Can you think of any other strategies that might help to prevent the misuse of prescription drugs?

so I get like freezing, 'cause I'm covered with wet sweat. I try to spit, and all this green stuff comes out. Then I'm just squirtin' out my guts. My heart feels like it's going to stop. I can't pick up my bones. My knees hurt; my legs are locked; I can't breathe; I can't even think; I feel every nerve in my fingertips, every single one. I can't stand still. I can't lie down." (p. 80)

Bourgois and Schonberg's graphic field notes describe the physical and psychological agony of withdrawal from opiate drugs. This suffering can be alleviated by another dose of opiates, a powerful physiological imperative that makes dependence on the drugs difficult to overcome.

The Problem of Drug Dependence

We have seen that drug dependence can be both physiological and psychological. Physiological dependence leads the user to experience physical withdrawal symptoms in the absence of the drug, as Felix did in the description above. Not all aspects of dependence are physiological, however. Psychological dependence leads to distress or anxiety when the user is without the drug. These symptoms are not simply expressions of moral or constitutional weakness. Rather, they are very real experiences including intense cravings that can prevent the individual from carrying out a normal routine.

Opiate dependence provides an illustration. The physiological properties of opiates increase the likelihood of dependence. Heroin, for instance, binds with opioid receptors in the brain to enhance endorphins and enkephalins. The body becomes physically dependent on this chemical response, such that withdrawal symptoms occur if the user reduces or stops using the drug. Withdrawal from an opiate drug can be an extremely unpleasant experience. In heavy users, symptoms may begin only hours after the previous use and typically peak within 2 days. As Felix's experience shows, they include cold sweats, insomnia, bone and muscle pain, cramping, diarrhea, vomiting, nausea, and intense drug cravings. For very heavy users, sudden withdrawal may even lead to death because the symptoms are so severe.

Not everyone who uses opiates becomes addicted, and not everyone who uses them experiences withdrawal symptoms upon stopping their use. You may have used opiate pills to alleviate pain after having a wisdom tooth extracted, but when you stopped taking the pills you likely did not experience the severe symptoms that accompanied Felix's withdrawal because your body had not become physically habituated. Yet those who use opiate painkillers medically beyond a few days may in fact experience mild physical symptoms of withdrawal, such

▶ A pregnant woman smokes crack in the neighborhood known as Cracolandia (Crackland) in São Paulo, Brazil. In the United States, crack is designated a Class A (or Schedule I) drug by the Drug Enforcement Agency because it is thought to cause great harm. Ed Sheeran's popular song "The A Team" is about a crack-addicted prostitute. Do you think there are as many songs that glamorize street drugs as there are that focus on their addictive effects?

as aches or diarrhea, when they stop. Acclimation to such drugs builds over time. This is called tolerance. For those who are drug dependent, this results in increased dosages or more potent forms of drug administration such as snorting or injecting drugs.

During 2014, an estimated 21.5 million people in the United States had a substance dependence problem in the preceding year (Substance Abuse and Mental Health Services Administration, 2015). This is almost double the 2010 estimate of 11.3 million people with a substance use disorder (Substance Abuse and Mental Health Services Administration, 2011)! Of the 21.5 million individuals, 17.0 million were dependent on alcohol, 7.1 million were dependent on illegal drugs, and 2.6 million were dependent on both alcohol and illegal drugs (see Figure 12.1). Individuals with comorbid issues can make dependence even more difficult to treat.

Drug Treatment

Recovery from drug dependence can be a difficult and complicated process; relapse rates are high. In addition to the physiological dependence some drugs induce, individuals with substance use disorders must contend with the powerful social and psychological forces that shape drug cravings. The people, locations, and events associated with the drug-dependent person's use provide powerful stimuli that provoke desires to use again. The strength of these social and environmental factors in drug dependence is a key reason why the most effective treatment programs do not seek merely to cease use of the drug. Rather,

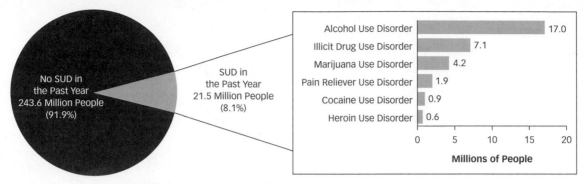

SOURCE: *Behavioral Health Trends in the United States: Results from the 2014 National Survey on Drug Use and Health.* Center for Behavioral Health Statistics and Quality, Substance Abuse and Mental Health Services Administration, U.S. Department of Health and Human Services.

they also strive to stimulate behavioral changes in the individual's wider life, attending to his or her emotional, material, and social needs and not just to the immediate physical circumstances of his or her drug addiction.

Social contexts can also encourage people to seek treatment for drug dependence. If social relationships, career, status, or self-esteem seem threatened, users may feel driven to seek out help. Other personal motivators include anxiety about the need to support a drug habit, negative health consequences, a fear of bodily injury or death, and the user's need to improve the quality of his or her life or better care for any children. Others may be involved in the criminal justice system and required to attend drug treatment. Individuals mandated to treatment as part of sentencing have shown improved treatment outcomes (National Institute on Drug Abuse, 2014).

While many drug-dependent individuals need assistance with recovery, high-quality treatment can be difficult to obtain. In fact, only 10.9% of those who need treatment actually received it at a drug treatment center (Substance Abuse and Mental Health Services Administration, 2014). Uninsured or underinsured individuals have limited access to some of the most basic treatments. Private drug treatment programs are quite expensive, and public treatment programs—particularly for individuals with special circumstances, such as women with children—often have long waiting lists. Thus, a grave paradox exists: Compared to those who are not drug dependent, people with substance use disorders are both more likely to need help and less likely to have health insurance. The 2010 passage of the Patient Protection and Affordable Care Act (also known as ACA, or Obamacare) was the first piece of legislation mandating that individuals have insurance coverage and that insurance companies cover substance abuse treatment as essential health benefits by 2014 (see Chapter 13 for additional details on the ACA). The ACA will likely increase substance abuse treatment access, but there is current discussion of repealing the ACA.

In addition, many treatment approaches and typologies are available, including 28-day residential programs, outpatient treatment, medication assisted treatments (MAT), and mutual self-help groups such as Alcoholics Anonymous (AA) or Narcotics Anonymous (NA). Residential and outpatient treatment are more costly but are more likely to employ evidence-based treatment approaches and have access to formally trained or licensed clinical professionals. Medication assisted treatment (such as methadone, buprenorphine, or naltrexone) is helpful for certain substance use disorders such as alcohol or opiate dependence. However, these medications are often costly and controversial, as some MATs have the potential for drug diversion and many individuals and clinicians are proponents of an "abstinence only" lifestyle. The primary benefits of AA/NA are that meetings are readily available in most urban/suburban areas, it is free, and it can be used in combination with outpatient and medication assisted treatments.

While many drug abusers depend on drug treatment, others recover in different ways. Some experience a kind of spontaneous remission, giving up drug habits without treatment in a fashion typically referred to as **natural recovery**. Natural recovery often occurs as a response to changing social conditions—the user changes residential location or finds a new job or romantic partner—and usually when the user has access to resources and support for assistance.

Drugs and Health

A significant reason why societies concern themselves with drug control is the health impact of drug consumption.

....

Natural recovery: A person's cessation of a drug habit without the assistance of a drug treatment program.

We cannot fully describe here all the harms associated with the use of a wide variety of drugs. Nonetheless, although the definition of *excess* may vary from drug to drug and from individual to individual, excessive consumption is what leads to harm. For example, marijuana has been shown to have many medical benefits, including as a treatment for glaucoma and for the side effects of chemotherapy; Figure 12.2 shows the U.S. states that allow its use for medical purposes, although federal law still prohibits it. However, some studies have shown that long-term, excessive marijuana use can lead to cognitive impairments. Whether a result of heavy use on one occasion or substantial use over an extended period of time, excessive consumption of any drug, regardless of legality, can create a range of problems for some individual users that include overdose, mental health problems, cognitive impairment, organ damage, infectious disease transmission, violence, and accidents.

Beyond the suffering of individual users, the health impact of drug use on society as a whole is also significant. For example, the financial cost imposed by alcohol and drug problems (not including tobacco) in the United States is approximately $417 billion per year (National Institute on Drug Abuse, 2015). Thus, the societal costs of drug use are substantial, at $417 billion, especially when compared to the $15 million spent on drug prevention and treatment in the United States (Office of National Drug Control Policy, 2016).

Most of these costs are productivity losses, particularly those related to abuse-related illness, crime/incarceration, black market activities, and premature death. Economists have estimated that substance-using employees claim more sick days, are late to work more often, have more job-related accidents, and file more workers' compensation insurance claims than do nonusing employees. Clearly, drug and alcohol use can create

FIGURE 12.2   Medical Marijuana Laws, 2016

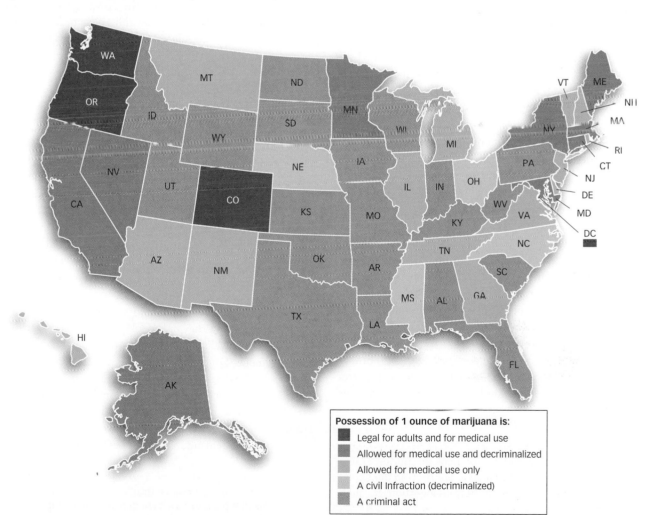

Possession of 1 ounce of marijuana is:

- Legal for adults and for medical use
- Allowed for medical use and decriminalized
- Allowed for medical use only
- A civil infraction (decriminalized)
- A criminal act

costs for employers as well as for the economy more generally.

There are also societal costs specifically related to the health of drug users and the potential for disease transmission. Injection drug use can facilitate the transmission of infectious diseases such as HIV and HCV, affecting not only drug users but also those within their social networks; needle-borne epidemics travel faster than sexually transmitted ones. Even trace amounts of blood infected with HIV can rest within a used syringe, making its reuse highly risky. HIV and HCV can also remain in blood on other injection paraphernalia, such as cookers and cottons used for injection. In addition, drug use can reduce inhibitions and increase the potential to engage in sex without a condom, which increases one's potential for contracting HIV or other STDs.

Many European governments have implemented innovative approaches to address the employment, health, and legal costs associated with heroin injection. Germany, Spain, and Switzerland have implemented heroin-assisted therapy programs and/or drug consumption rooms that provide a safe venue for drug use. Individuals are required to register, complete an assessment intake, and adhere to strict rules (e.g., no drug sharing). These programs aim to reduce disease transmission, have professional staff on-site to address health issues (e.g., wound care, overdoses, other health issues), and promote referrals to treatment programs and other needed social services. In heroin-assisted treatment programs, HIV transmissions have declined, criminal offending has declined, and many participants have stopped heroin use because the programs provide points of entry for drug treatment and other health care services. Participants have also been able to obtain stable employment and housing (Fischer et al., 2007).

In the United States, in contrast, since the onset of the HIV epidemic, injection drug users have accounted for almost one of every three HIV infections. Though major public health efforts have reduced infections within this population, new infections continue to emerge along the same fault lines as many other health disparities. African Americans and Hispanics are disproportionately affected by drug-related HIV exposures, for example. Policies shown to be effective elsewhere (such as **needle exchange programs**) continue to lack support among federal officials in the United States but have been gaining recent traction in light of the HIV outbreak in rural southeastern Indiana.

ASK YOURSELF: Why do you think the United States has not followed Europe's lead in addressing the social problems associated with heroin injection through harm reduction programs?

PATTERNS OF DRUG USE ACROSS SOCIAL GROUPS

12.3 Relate patterns of drug use to the life course, gender, race/ethnicity, and sexual orientation.

Patterns of drug use differ across various groups within any society. This occurs not necessarily because of any innate characteristics of the people themselves, but because of the ways in which statuses, social norms, and societal treatment organize and define people's behaviors and interactions. Various aspects of people's lives, and the expectations people have of others, shape a wide range of behaviors, including how drugs are consumed as well as who consumes them and what drugs are defined as legal. Let's consider data from the National Survey on Drug Use and Health (NSDUH) to see how age, gender, race, and sexual orientation influence drug use. NSDUH is a main governmental source on the prevalence, trends, and consequences of substance use and abuse in the noninstitutionalized U.S. population aged 12 and older and collects data through face-to-face interviews. Unfortunately, NSDUH does not present aggregate statistics on income categories. (To investigate other drug trends yourself, visit https://www.samhsa.gov/data/population-data-nsduh.)

Drugs and the Life Course

In many societies, the use of drugs is most prevalent among youth. As Figure 12.3 shows, drug use in the United States peaks during the early adulthood ages of 18 to 25. A variety of socially structured factors shape this pattern. In some instances, drug consumption may occur during the intense period of identity development expected during adolescence and early adulthood. In attempting to more clearly define their identities, young people may see risks as a challenge and sensation seeking as a part of personal growth. Young people also often attempt to forge independent decisions, including about drug and alcohol use, because self-sufficiency and self-reliance are bound up with their conceptions of adulthood. Drug use may be one way for them to engage in risky behaviors in an effort to distance themselves from their parents and parental values. Finally, early adulthood is distinguished by relative independence from social roles and normative expectations, a freedom that allows young people to be tremendously self-oriented and to engage in

Needle exchange programs: Drug abuse harm reduction programs that provide new syringes to intravenous drug users who exchange used syringes.

Drugs Beyond Our Borders

Methamphetamine in China

Illicit drug use has spread quickly in China since the late 1980s, after many years of political suppression. While emerging social and economic freedoms have opened up many positive opportunities for Chinese citizens, they have also provided openings for growth in drug markets. The number of drug abusers officially documented by Chinese public security departments has increased from 70,000 in 1990 to well over 1 million today. Illicit drug use continues to escalate across the country as China modernizes. In addition to a continuing heroin problem, China has seen a surge in the consumption of other drugs, including methamphetamine, ecstasy, and ketamine during the past decade.

Methamphetamine, often in the form known as ice, is domestically produced within China. According to the United Nations Office on Drugs and Crime, among countries surveyed China had the highest number of methamphetamine seizures and has recently become one of the world's largest methamphetamine markets. Most

of the recently detected drug laboratories in China produced methamphetamine, representing a significant increase over earlier years. Of registered drug users in 2004, only 1.7% used methamphetamine, but that number grew to 11.1% by 2007 and has continued to increase since that time.

Chinese society has experienced rapid changes in the past generation that have benefited many people, including a newly forming urban middle class, but these changes have also introduced new social problems, such as the rise in drug use. The growth in methamphetamine use in Chinese society reflects the way changes within societies can bring negative consequences along with positive ones. Many of these results are unintended, though perhaps they are an inevitable outgrowth of rapid social change; they also highlight the

▶ Blocks of methamphetamine confiscated by Chinese police during a crackdown on drugs are displayed. In China, crystal meth is generally called "ice" and doing meth is called "ice skating." Methamphetamine is China's second most popular drug after heroin.

AP Photo/Huang qiqing

extent to which the expansion of social freedoms within a society sometimes leads individuals to act in ways that are not the healthiest or most beneficial.

▶ THINK ABOUT IT

1. Why do you think that methamphetamine use might be growing so extensively in China?

2. How do you think rapid social change may shape drug use in China and elsewhere?

---

behaviors such as drug use. Some indicate they are doing drugs because youth is "the time to get it out of my system."

Drug use, including drinking alcohol, typically declines beginning in the mid-20s as young adults assume the social roles and responsibilities of full adulthood. Note that it is changes in the social features of their lives—not physiological or cognitive changes—that enable this shift. The significant decline in drug use across young adulthood, often referred to as **maturing out**, occurs naturally, without treatment or other forms of intervention. Not only weekend pot smokers but even those engaged in more frequent or "hard" drug use can experience maturing out. This is not to say that aging is a substitute for drug treatment, but users of many substances tend to follow this pattern.

Gender and Drug Use

Age is not the only influence on drug use. We take on different roles within the family, the workplace, social

circles, and other areas depending on how we understand gender within our society. Much as with any other cultural practice, the meanings and significance of drug use are viewed through the lens of our gender identities. As Figure 12.4 shows, while just over 54% of young women in the United States have ever used an illegal drug, more than 60% of young men have done so. Some of this difference has to do with the fact that young men are often offered greater opportunities to begin drug use within their peer networks and experience less supervision as adolescents. When we look at use in the past year, these trends hold. Thus, we can see the ways in which our gender identities affect our peers, interactions, experiences, and decisions about whether to use drugs.

Maturing out: The decline and cessation of psychoactive drug use among younger people as they age into different social roles and responsibilities.

Throughout human history, both men and women have used drugs—though at times in different ways influenced by gender. For example, ideals of masculinity influence not only the drugs men choose to consume but also the ways they consume them. Binge drinking can be a means for men to make claims of masculinity through stamina, willingness to take risks, power, strength, and outperforming peers or winning a social competition. This is part of the reason why U.S. society experiences many more deaths from alcohol poisoning among men than among women. The gender disparity in alcohol-induced fatalities is a direct result of our cultural framing of alcohol consumption as an act with gendered meanings.

Research also indicates that the pathways leading into and out of drug-using careers differ for men and women and can be partially explained by gender socialization. The beginnings of many women's drug-using careers are related significantly to their relationships with men. Women exit drug-using careers for family reasons and because their using interferes with work responsibilities more often than do men. Women's stopping drug use tends to center on the personal and emotional aspects of drug experiences, while men's cessation is more directly related to external and financial factors.

Race/Ethnicity and Drug Use

Race and ethnicity are also significant influences on drug use among young adults in the United States. Throughout the nation's history of drug control, race has played a significant role in the ways drugs are used, the ways they are perceived, and the ways their use is policed. As Figure 12.5 shows, data from the 2015 NSDUH indicate that white young adults are mostly likely to have used illegal drugs. By contrast, Asian American youth have some of the lowest rates of drug use. These trends tend to hold for the use of individual types of drugs. For marijuana, cocaine, hallucinogens, and illegal prescription drugs, white young adults report the highest prevalence of use, while Asian young adults report the lowest. Black and Hispanic youth tend to fall between these groups. We also find these patterns in the use of legal substances such as alcohol and cigarettes.

These figures may surprise you, since you may have been led to believe that racial and ethnic minorities report more experiences with drug use than do whites. Popular conceptions of drug use and drug users are shaped covertly through the news and social media as well as through the entertainment industry including films, music, and television. Many media depictions highlight drug use by members of racial and ethnic minority groups, and exposure to these depictions can create unconscious social stereotypes and influence the ways we think about the lives of drug users.

FIGURE 12.3 **Illegal Drug Use in the United States by Age, 2015**

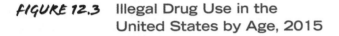
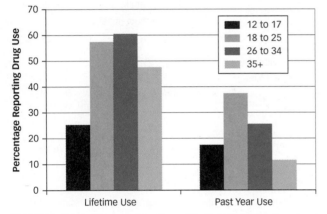

SOURCE: The National Survey on Drug Use and Health. United States Department of Health and Human Services.

FIGURE 12.4 **Illegal Drug Use Among U.S. 18- to 25-Year-Olds by Gender, 2015**

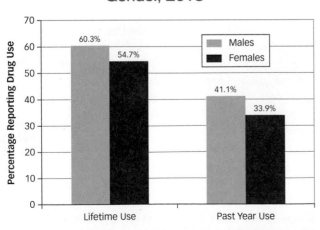

SOURCE: The National Survey on Drug Use and Health. United States Department of Health and Human Services.

FIGURE 12.5 **Prevalence of Illegal Drug Use Among U.S. 18- to 25-Year-Olds by Race/Ethnicity, 2015**

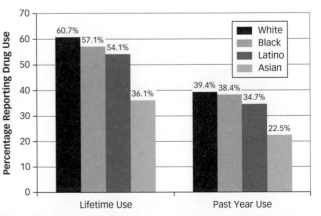

SOURCE: The National Survey on Drug Use and Health. United States Department of Health and Human Services.

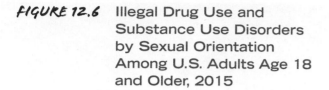

FIGURE 12.6   Illegal Drug Use and Substance Use Disorders by Sexual Orientation Among U.S. Adults Age 18 and Older, 2015

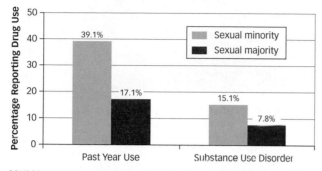

SOURCE: https://www.samhsa.gov/data/sites/default/files/NSDUH-SexualOrien tation-2015/NSDUH-SexualOrientation-2015/NSDUH-SexualOrientation-2015.pdf.

ASK YOURSELF: How have drug users and drug dealers been portrayed in the media? What messages do these representations send to viewers? To see how representations have changed over the past 75 years, you may want to spend one evening watching *Reefer Madness* and another watching *Pineapple Express* and consider how these films differ in their depictions of marijuana smokers.

Sexual Orientation and Drug Use

Our sexual orientation, including both sexual identity and sexual attraction, significantly shapes our social interactions and is delicately intertwined with our gender identity. Sexual minorities are individuals who identify as lesbian, gay, or bisexual, while the sexual majority population self-identifies as heterosexual. Existing research suggests that sexual minorities are more likely to use and abuse drugs, as compared to their sexual majority counterparts. For the first time, the NHSDU included two measures of sexual orientation in 2015, which make these data the first nationally representative data set on sexual minority drug use in the United States. About 4.3% of those aged 18 or older identify as a sexual minority. As Figure 12.6 shows, sexual minority adults aged 18 and older were more likely to both report past-year illegal drug use and meet criteria for a substance use disorder, as compared to sexual majority adults. In contrast to the sexual majority population, in which males are more likely to report past-year drug use (20.4% for males, as compared to 13.9% for females), sexual minority females are more likely to use drugs than sexual minority males (41.1% for women, as compared to 36.3%).

Intersections of Social Difference

While race, socioeconomic status, age, sexual orientation, and gender identity may each influence drug use behaviors, it is the intersection of all these social differences that shapes individuals' experiences in society. In particular, this intersection affects experiences of privilege and oppression; governs access to and experiences with the education system, housing, and peers; and influences the ways people engage with and respond to the world. Your race, ethnicity, gender, sexual orientation, and socioeconomic status also affect your likes and dislikes, your friends, your high school, your neighborhood, your choice of college or university, and your employment opportunities. They influence the music to which you listen, the food you eat, the movies you like, and even the drugs with which you come into contact. It is likely that some of your classmates had access to marijuana and crack cocaine in the neighborhoods where they grew up, for instance, while others could easily find only marijuana.

Our individual characteristics and the meanings these characteristics have in society thus shape our lives in numerous ways. From influencing our access to drugs to setting normative expectations about drug use to creating stress through oppressive life conditions, features of our lives function separately and together to influence the ways we experience the world around us and the ways we behave, including our substance use.

USING THEORY TO UNDERSTAND DRUG USE: THE VIEWS FROM THE FUNCTIONALIST, CONFLICT, AND SYMBOLIC INTERACTIONIST PERSPECTIVES

12.4 Apply the functionalist, symbolic interactionist, and conflict perspectives to social policy on drug use.

In this section we consider sociology's three classic theories to explore how they explain the initiation, continuation, and cessation of drug use.

Functionalism

Functionalism primarily considers how societies maintain themselves by creating a certain order for those living within them. Overall, the theory argues, the functioning of

Experiencing Drugs

How Drug Enforcement Is Shaped by Race, Class, Age, Sexual Orientation, and Gender Identity

REUTERS/Jim Young

▶ Cook County Sheriff police officers search a vehicle and a woman in a known drug-selling area of Chicago. Young people of color are likely to be stopped by police, especially if they are thought to be acting "suspiciously." Do you think that their race and the way they are dressed have anything to do with the police being suspicious of them?

Can you count the number of times you have witnessed police officers canvassing the dorms and knocking down doors in search of drugs? How often have you been at a fraternity party that was raided by the police and resulted in drug convictions? How many of your university friends have been very drunk or high on marijuana in public but were never stopped and frisked by police? How many friends have illegally purchased prescription drugs like Adderall but have never been arrested?

Young black men living in the inner city are much more likely than students at your university to have contacts with the police in search of drugs—on their streets, at their homes, and in their cars. Even though drugs are used illegally across the socioeconomic spectrum and among all racial groups, drug-using and drug-dealing offenders are much more accessible and visible in inner-city neighborhoods than in university dorms, fraternity houses, middle-class homes, and white communities. In addition, policing street-level drug dealing is less complex than investigating large drug operations. As a result, arrests of young, poor black men for drug offenses have risen at a much faster rate than have the arrests of others for similar offenses—even though drug use is not higher among black men than among white men.

One police practice in particular, known as stop and frisk, disproportionately affects people of color. In June 2012, the *New York Times* reported that in 2011 the New York Police Department (NYPD) documented 685,724 instances of stop and frisk, 87% of which involved blacks or Hispanics (on average only 6% of stops lead to actual arrests). In Brownsville, Brooklyn, population 14,000, the NYPD made about 52,000 stops from January 2006 to March 2010. One young black male, Tyquan Brehon, told the *New York Times* he was stopped by police more than 60 times before he was 18 years old (Dressner & Martinez, 2012). While race matters, females in these communities are less likely to be stopped than males, and males wearing suits are less likely to be stopped than males wearing hoodies (clothing often serves as an indicator of class position). Thus, race, gender, and social class intersect to leave poor black men highly vulnerable to stop-and-frisk procedures. Use of stop-and-frisk tactics have been decreasing, largely due to accusations of racial profiling; however, the benefits of stop-and-frisk tactics have been promoted under the Trump administration.

Clearly, the intersection of race, class, age, sexual orientation, and gender identity influences the ways people use drugs, their access to resources, and their experience of harms (physical, criminal justice) associated with drug use and sales. It explains why all white people do not experience the same issues with drugs and why all women do not face the same risks. Recognizing the intersectionality of multiple characteristics is critical to understanding the experience of substance use and substance-related harms.

▶ **THINK ABOUT IT**

1. Inner-city communities are disproportionately under the gaze of policing agencies. Should the police alter the way they approach drug problems? Should they focus more frequently on drug sales and use on college campuses?

2. If the harms associated with drug use are determined not by the drugs used but rather by the intersectionality of race, class, age, sexual orientation, and gender identity, how should society address the social problem of drugs?

society is managed through the collective behavior of the society's members.

A living organism makes a useful analogy for society as functionalists see it. The circulatory system allows oxygen and nutrients to flow throughout the body, while internal organs perform various functions such as digestion and absorption of nutrients, minerals, and oxygen, and sensory organs such as the eyes take in the information necessary for the body to act in certain ways. If any of these functions is disrupted, it becomes more difficult for the organism to maintain its existence. According to functionalists, the collective group shares norms, institutions, and rituals that allow expectations of behavior to be passed down from one member to another, society's form and organization to be maintained, and society itself to remain stable. When individuals break social norms, for instance, they disrupt the social fabric and damage society's ability to maintain itself.

When rapid social changes are occurring, society's expectations and regulation of behavior become less clear, and anomie emerges. (Recall that anomie is a condition in which individuals feel disconnected from society and its social standards.) Individuals are more likely to break social norms when they experience anomie.

Functionalists may consider the use of certain drugs—those on which society has placed social and legal sanctions—to be an act of deviance and rejection of social norms that emerge from feelings of anomie. For example, a young man beginning heroin use is likely to know this act breaks social norms against the drug's use. His act of deviance, according to a functionalist perspective, disrupts the established social standard and contributes to the society's instability.

On the other hand, when a drug is socially sanctioned, functionalists would argue that, rather than disrupting the social fabric, its ritualized use may contribute to community cohesion and solidarity. For example, the use of ayahuasca—a hallucinogenic brew—in ritual fashion among indigenous peoples of the Amazon provides the community with the opportunity to come together during a time of crisis, such as when a member is ill. From a functionalist perspective, they promote community solidarity and cohesion by bringing members together for a shared purpose.

In many Western societies, alcohol is a permitted drug that serves to enhance social bonds and community cohesion

REUTERS/Fred Thornill

▶ Fans cheer at a football game and raise their cups of beer. Fans frequently have tailgate parties during which they drink beer and grill food. Tailgating usually occurs in the parking lots of stadiums and arenas, before and sometimes after games and concerts. Is there a tailgating culture on your campus?

in rituals from wedding toasts to tailgating to happy hour. During happy hour, coworkers are able to forge social bonds outside the workplace, collectively blow off steam related to job stress, and relax at the end of the workday. From a functionalist perspective, happy hour serves to maintain the social fabric by facilitating solidarity in a socially sanctioned forum. This behavior is seen as normative in society and, as such, contributes to its maintenance.

Policy Implications of Functionalism

According to the functionalist perspective, it remains imperative for society to create supportive communities in order to prevent the use and abuse of illegal drugs. Fostering community cohesion and solidarity is critical in this regard, because individuals will be less likely to abuse drugs—legal and illegal—if they feel a deeper connection to the community. By reducing anomie and feelings of social dislocation, communities will be in a better position to prevent the abuse of drugs as well as the harms associated with drug use.

Local policies that encourage communities to come together are important pieces of the puzzle from the functionalist perspective. For example, the creation of public spaces, such as parks, malls, and public venues, in which members of the community feel invested facilitates social bonds, inhibiting behaviors like illegal drug use that break social norms. Policies that stimulate community participation can reduce individuals' needs to use drugs in response to social dislocation.

Efforts to build social capital—the social, material, and symbolic resources inherent within social ties—in

Peter Stackpole/The LIFE Picture Collection/Getty Images

▶ Members of the Women's Christian Temperance Union invade a bar while customers continue drinking. In 1919, Congress ratified the 18th Amendment to the U.S. Constitution, which prohibited the manufacture, sale, and transportation of alcoholic beverages. This ushered in the era known as Prohibition (1920–1933). Prohibition ended with the repeal of the 18th Amendment; it has been called "the experiment that failed."

communities also fall within functionalist policies on reducing drug abuse. For example, consider how your neighbors may act as resources to enhance your neighborhood quality of life, whether through beautifying the neighborhood, watching out for neighborhood kids, keeping an eye on your house while you're on vacation, or lending you tools. Harnessing the strength and potential of these resources allows communities to further their drug education, prevention, and intervention efforts. They can more effectively communicate information that may either inhibit the use of drugs among young people or reduce the level of harm among active drug users. By enhancing social capital, communities also more effectively position themselves to facilitate drug treatment.

For example, the Office of National Drug Control Policy's Drug Free Communities Support Program provides funding for community-based efforts to reduce drug use among youth. These initiatives bring youth and adults together in community programs that inhibit drug use. Creating youth athletic leagues in resource-poor communities can provide structured activities for young people, for instance, thus reducing the likelihood they will engage in delinquent activities. Since its inception in 1997, the Drug Free Communities Support Program has provided grants to over 2,000 local communities in the United States, with 698 grant awards totaling $85.9 million in FY 2016.

Conflict Theory

In contrast to functionalism, conflict theory considers how conflicts between groups in society come about, often finding evidence of collective behavior that leads to the creation of social disparities and social exclusion. Rather than examining the ways in which society maintains itself, conflict theorists consider how collective behavior creates ruptures in the social fabric. At the core of conflict theory is the issue of power, grounded in political and economic structures. Those in positions of power—that is, those with high status and abundant resources—act to facilitate inequality by ensuring the uneven distribution of power and resources across society. Conflicts then emerge over these inequitable allocations.

With regard to drugs, conflict theorists would argue that decisions and policies about which drugs are legal and who can access them are products of the social structure. Those in positions of power have greater ability to shape policies on drugs, often in ways that permit them to legitimate their own social position and exert social control over those less powerful. For example, sociologist Joseph R. Gusfield (1986) describes the temperance movement in the United States as an upper-class social movement and the abstinence from alcohol that accompanied it as a signifier of status. This movement occurred in the wake of immigration from Ireland and southern European nations in which the use of alcohol was a routine and normative behavior. The temperance movement was a means of articulating social distinctions between the upper class and the poor and newer immigrants within society.

Some have also suggested that the outlawing of drugs such as heroin and cocaine during the early 20th century was tied to the emergence of the modern pharmaceutical industry, which profited from the control of these substances. The same argument has been made more recently in the debate over medical marijuana. From a conflict theory perspective, the prohibition of medical marijuana protects the revenue streams of corporate firms. (For an excellent sociological examination of medical marijuana, see *Dying to Get High: Marijuana as Medicine* [2008], by Wendy Chapkis and Richard J. Webb.)

For conflict theorists, the creation of laws governing drugs provides a means of exerting social control and policing over those who are less powerful. And as we saw earlier in this chapter, young whites use illegal drugs at higher rates than black youth, yet black youth are arrested for drug crimes at rates 3.5 to 5.5 times higher than the white arrest rate (Human Rights Watch, 2009). This is a stark difference. Legal scholar Michelle Alexander makes a compelling argument in her prominent book, *The New Jim Crow: Mass Incarceration in the Age of Colorblindness* (2012), that the War on Drugs is a strategy to continue the racial caste structure and push back the progress from the civil rights movement. The War on Drugs has largely contributed to the fact that one in three black men will spend time in prison in their lifetime (Lyons & Pettit, 2011), and prisons have become the new slave plantations for black men. As another example, drug-using pregnant black women, who are already socially marginalized on the basis of race, class, and gender, are more likely to be reported to the authorities by health care providers than are their white counterparts. In this respect, the social control exerted through drug laws extends beyond the simple act of public policing to reach the private sphere of the clinical medical encounter, resulting in drug-using black women delaying prenatal care or drug treatment to avoid criminal sanctions. A conflict theory perspective considers that these disparities occur as a means of strengthening the position of racial privilege that whites occupy.

Conflict theory also describes how the social structure influences human behavior more broadly. Because everyone acts in response to the conditions of society, drug use becomes reasonable to individuals as a means of coping with marginalization and societal inequalities. Conflict theorists would argue that this explains why whites have higher rates of drug *use*, while blacks and Hispanics are more likely to experience drug *dependence*. Similar patterns emerge along social class lines. The poor are especially vulnerable to experiencing drug problems and drug harms because they also lack the resources to recover from drug dependence.

Policy Implications of Conflict Theory

Policies derived from a conflict theory perspective focus on bringing about change in the inequalities in society, and subsequently reducing the adverse impacts of drug abuse. Individuals may be less likely to abuse drugs if they are not experiencing the impacts of inequality and its accompanying marginalization. Moreover, ensuring equality promotes greater access to resources that reduce the drug-related harms. For example, opening economic opportunities like jobs and developing programs that reduce poverty are important bases for policy making according to conflict theory. Currently, the distance between classes is growing, with the poor getting poorer while at the same time the rich are getting richer. Legal reform is another policy implication of conflict theory,

which would allow individuals with felony drug convictions to be eligible for federal student aid, to obtain public housing, and to vote. By enabling all members of society to have resources beyond those that merely enable survival, societies can inhibit the abuse and harms of drugs.

As another example, early childhood intervention programs, such as the Infant Health and Development Program, the Perry Preschool Project, the Carolina Abecedarian Project, and the Chicago Child-Parent Center Program, have been shown to be very effective in reducing inequality and substance use (Pungello, Campbell, & Barnett, 2006). Children who completed these programs were less likely to use substances or to be arrested and more likely to graduate from high school and earn college degrees. These are demonstrated efforts to reduce disorganization associated with political and economic decay in inner-city communities.

Conflict theorists examine policies based not only on their intent but also on their consequences. Policies generated during the War on Drugs may appear on their face to be "race-neutral," but they have had considerable effects on racial disparities in sentencing for drug-related crimes. Mandatory minimum sentences and laws concerning school-zone enhancements, which increase the penalties for selling or using drugs near schools, tend to have their most significant influence on sentencing for crimes in inner-city neighborhoods, where racial/ethnic minorities are more likely to live.

ASK YOURSELF: In the United States, federal law requires controlled substances to be classified as Schedule I, II, III, IV, or V drugs based on their medical utility, safety profile, and abuse potential. Why do you think the federal law in the United States still has marijuana classified as a Schedule I drug, meaning it has a no medical utility and high abuse potential, when over half of the states in the United States have passed laws permitting medical marijuana?

Symbolic Interactionism

Symbolic interactionism focuses on how individuals understand themselves in relationship to society. We constantly manage our concept of self through our interactions with others in society, and we behave on the basis of the meanings we interpret from these interactions, internalizing our perceptions of the way others see us. This internalization is what George Herbert Mead (1934) referred to as the "self"; it depends on the attitudes, values, and norms we perceive during interactions.

These attitudes, values, and norms are subject to change over time on the basis of our interactions. For example, heroin users have been considered normal, sick,

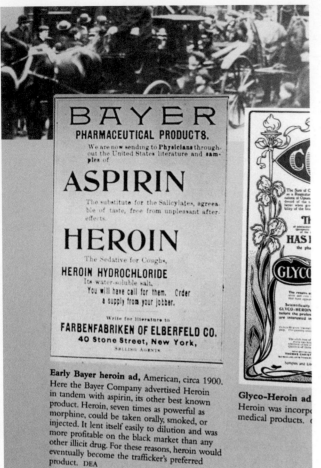

Early Bayer heroin ad, American, circa 1900. Here the Bayer Company advertised Heroin in tandem with aspirin, its other best known product. Heroin, seven times as powerful as morphine, could be taken orally, smoked, or injected. It lent itself easily to dilution and was more profitable on the black market than any other illicit drug. For these reasons, heroin would eventually become the trafficker's preferred product. DEA

Glyco-Heroin ad Heroin was incorp medical products.

▶ An early advertisement for Bayer Aspirin shows heroin presented in the same ad. In the late 19th century, cocaine was commonly used as a general tonic for sinusitis and hay fever. Sigmund Freud experimented with cocaine and Arthur Conan Doyle's fictional detective Sherlock Holmes frequently injected himself with a 7% solution of the drug.

and criminal at different times in history. In the mid-1800s, heroin was legally purchased and commonly used recreationally by middle- and upper-class women. Their use of the drug was acceptable; hence, they were normal. In the late 1890s, heroin was believed to be a miracle cure for coughs, and Bayer sold heroin-based cough syrups with directions for use by both adults and children. The users of heroin then were considered ill. When heroin was criminalized in 1914 under the Harrison Act, users became criminals. With the shifting social and legal labels for the drug, users have reinterpreted their identities.

ASK YOURSELF: Can you think of any substances other than heroin for which the labels placed on users have shifted over time? What might be the social impacts of such label changes?

Consider Howard S. Becker's classic study "Becoming a Marihuana User" (1963a). Becker describes the process of jazz men becoming socialized into using marijuana and learning to experience its effects in particular ways. The experiences individuals have under the influence of drugs must be interpreted, and the process of learning how to interpret the sensations and experiences of a drug high is a critical component of becoming a drug user. The subtleties and nuances of the drug's effects must be learned and understood within a particular context, and these processes unfold only in the course of interactions before, during, and after the drug is used. Certain sensations may be interpreted differently over time, and feelings that may have been uncomfortable are redefined as key components of the drug experience.

Just as becoming a drug user is a process that occurs in the course of social interaction, so is becoming a recovering drug user. Through interactions with peers or counselors in recovery, the person learns the language, norms, and manners of being in recovery and reconstructs his or her identity. Through interactions with and support from others in recovery, the newly sober person redefines his or her past drug-using behaviors as faults of the addiction disease. The identity of the individual transforms from "addict" to "sober."

Thus, when we change the people with whom we interact, we may shift our interpretations and transform our identities. When we spend more time with peers who use drugs and drink, we may have a more positive interpretation of those behaviors than when we spend time with family or with Narcotics Anonymous members. Symbolic interactionism stresses the importance of social context and the groups with whom we associate, since the way we interpret society and its symbols is dependent on our interactions with these contexts and groups. This is particularly important in adolescence, when the individual's primary interaction group shifts from the family to peers. Symbolic interactionism suggests that this transition facilitates the initiation into drug use among adolescents, because their primary interactions, attitudes, and perspectives about normative behaviors are changing.

Policy Implications of Symbolic Interactionism

From the perspective of symbolic interactionism, our understanding of drug use within a social context and the creation of programs that help facilitate positive identity change are key points of intervention for drug policies. Policy makers can either change the ways individuals and groups interpret behavior or change the types of people with whom at-risk individuals interact.

The symbolic interactionist perspective offers several policy options. One is to try to prevent drug use from achieving enhanced status within social networks, groups of people connected through their social ties to others. Policies affecting the meanings of drug use within these social circles may inhibit the way groups of people interact around drugs. Social marketing campaigns are often directed at shaping the ways people perceive particular drugs. For example, in response to a significant rise in methamphetamine use among gay men, a public service campaign targeted these men with the message, "Buy meth, get HIV free." By linking the use of methamphetamine to HIV, the campaign highlighted the risks of drug use and associated the drug with an infectious disease.

Another approach is to shape people's interpretations of drug use in order to reduce the harms associated with particular patterns of consumption. For example, college students typically perceive that their peers drink more alcohol and more often than is actually the case. The perception of such heavy drinking as a "normal" part of college life can lead some students to overindulge. By highlighting the reality that the average college student actually drinks less, and less often, health promotion campaigns may influence students to have fewer drinks and to drink less regularly. This approach is illustrated by the Social Norms Program, which was implemented in New Jersey high schools (Connell et al., 2009). There, a survey of high school students showed that many thought their friends were engaging in frequent drug use, alcohol use, and sex. However, the survey also revealed that the peers were not using drugs, drinking, or having sex as often as was perceived. Thus, the schools, with the help of researchers, implemented a social marketing campaign to educate the students about the true amount of deviance occurring among their peers. This program shifted the high schoolers' perceptions of the prevalence and acceptance of drug and alcohol use and sex.

Mentoring programs may also reduce drug use among young people by offering them the opportunity for routine interactions with good role models. Such interactions can provide positive ways for young people to interpret their lives, since the mentors display positive norms. From the symbolic interactionist perspective, through exposure to these positive norms and the development of positive interpretations of young people's lives, these programs may reduce the potential for engaging in drug use. In fact, many studies have shown that youth who participate in Big Brothers Big Sisters programs are less likely than their peers who do not to start using drugs and alcohol (see, e.g., Grossman & Tierney, 1998).

Symbolic interactionists further recommend policies that remove the stigma of drug use and thus create positive drug-using or drug-recovering identities. For example, decriminalization efforts, such as the laws implemented in 18 U.S. states where possession of small amounts of marijuana is not a criminal offense, remove the criminal label from users and free them of the stigma of being

criminal offenders. The Netherlands also has decriminalized marijuana. There, adults have been able to buy small quantities of marijuana in coffee shops since 1976. Yet a higher percentage of adults use marijuana in the United States, where it cannot be legally purchased, than in the Netherlands (Reinarman, Cohen, & Kaal, 2004).

SPECIALIZED THEORIES ON DRUG USE

 12.5 Apply specialized theories to the social problems of drug use.

We now turn briefly to some of the more specialized sociological theories on drinking and drug use: general strain theory, social disorganization theory, and social learning theory.

General Strain Theory

Robert Agnew (1992) developed general strain theory from the Durkheim tradition of functionalism. The theory suggests individuals may feel strain as a result of their experiences in society, and that strain shapes the way they behave. Strain can result from losses in individuals' social lives—whether relationship or status losses. People may also experience strain when their aspirations for status do not meet their achieved status, or when they encounter negative stimuli in their social environments, such as being bullied or physically abused. The cumulative experience of strain can lead some individuals to engage in deviant behaviors as a coping mechanism.

Drug use has been widely documented as a coping mechanism that may be induced by the cumulative experience of various forms of strain. For example, among adolescents, strain may emerge from conflicts with parents over the discrepancy between the adolescents' status claims and the parents' perception of the adolescents' status. From the perspective of strain theory, such strain may be related to initiation into drug use among teenagers. In other instances, strain stemming from personal failures to meet expected goals in school, work, or social life can lead to drug use.

Social Disorganization Theory

Social disorganization theory, which emerged from the Chicago School of Sociology in the early 20th century as a means of explaining social problems in urban environments, is a classic theory of the influence of social ecology. According

▶ "Squatters," people who live in an abandoned building, sit in their squat and get high. Crack houses are usually old, abandoned, or burned-out buildings, frequently located in run-down neighborhoods. It is in places like these that drug dealers and drug users buy, sell, produce, and use illegal drugs.

to social disorganization theory, the social environment—particularly the neighborhood environment—is a key influence on behavior. When a community is socially disorganized, primarily through concentrated poverty and residential instability, the community loses its inherent social controls, and deviant behaviors rise. Thus, the ecological characteristics of a neighborhood influence behaviors, above and beyond the individual characteristics of those living within the neighborhood.

In particular, social disorganization theorists like Sampson and Wilson (1995) describe how macro-level factors—such as deindustrialization, wage polarization, outsourcing, racism, poor housing, and discrimination—can create structurally disorganized and culturally isolated communities. Cut off from mainstream society, residents in those communities lack or have only minimal access to conventional institutions, including resources, conventional role models, and social networks that facilitate social and economic advancement. A crime-inducing landscape results, and crime, violence, and drug use become acceptable, expected, and valuable. The community then is unable to exert informal control over its members.

Social disorganization theorists warn that the policies of the War on Drugs have actually facilitated the development and maintenance of socially disorganized communities. The drug war has channeled money into the criminal justice system rather than into improving communities. Thus, police officers tend to focus efforts on particular communities (mostly those that are disorganized) where drug use and sales are visible. In these communities,

arrest, conviction, and incarceration for drug offenses are more likely, and these have harmed the families, economic strength, and informal social controls of those areas. In particular, when most drug offenders return to their communities after arrest and incarceration, they do not have access to drug treatment, have fewer marketable skills, have limited experiences in the conventional work world, and are less likely to marry. Concentrated poverty, family instability, and hence the lack of informal social control will remain part of that community, and it will continue to be disorganized.

Social Learning Theory

Social learning theory is related to the symbolic interactionist tradition, and primarily associated with the theorist Ronald Akers (1998). It assumes individuals are conditioned by their social environment to behave in particular ways and to model the behaviors of those around them. When an individual is in a social environment in which normative behaviors are routinely enacted and rewarded, that individual becomes conditioned (i.e., they learn) to engage in normative behaviors. Similarly, in a social environment in which deviant behaviors are routinely enacted, the individual becomes conditioned to engage in acts of deviance. The kinds of behavior that are reinforced depend on who is in the social environment.

Aker's (1998) social learning theory assumes individuals are not born drug users, but rather learn to become drug users by being in a drug-using social environment in which drug-using behavior is positively reinforced. The individual's drug use is thus a response to his or her having been conditioned toward it and is shaped directly by the social context. This is one reason why scholars of adolescent deviance have been concerned with deviant peer groups. If their peers use drugs, adolescents will be more likely to use drugs. In fact, most drug users learn about drugs from friends and have friends who are drug users.

For social learning theorists, then, the process of rehabilitation from drug abuse is rooted in reconditioning the individual in an environment in which abstinence is valued and encouraged by others. This explains why the mutual self-help groups such as AA/NA programs have been successful in promoting abstinence for many. Through these programs, substance abusers begin to associate with others who encourage sobriety, which helps recondition their behavior.

SOCIAL CHANGE: WHAT CAN YOU DO?

 12.6 Identify steps toward social change on drugs.

Drug use and responses to drug use can become social problems that affect the users and users' families, friends, and communities. It is important, then, that we all make an effort to ensure that effective, humane, and fair drug policies are implemented; that drug users and their families, friends, and communities are treated with respect and dignity; and that improving the health of drug users and their communities is paramount. You are an important asset in addressing drug use as a social problem, and in addressing the multitude of social problems that arise from both drug use and drug policy. You can educate yourself and your friends, participate in harm reduction activities, and engage in social activism to promote responsible drug policies. Here's how.

Educate Yourself and Your Friends

Many misconceptions and myths persist about who uses drugs, the harms of drug use, the effectiveness of drug policies, and the benefits of incarcerating drug users. Educating yourself and others, however, is actually quite easy. Excellent resources are available online, and books and documentary films can also provide reliable information (see Table 12.2 for some suggestions). Sharing information about the effects and harms of substance use and safer ways to use substances can help support and implement drug policies that are effective, humane, and fair; that treat drug users with respect; and that improve the health of drug users and their communities.

Erowid is a nonprofit organization whose trusted website (http://www.erowid.org) provides up-to-date information about emerging drugs, harms of use, and legal sanctions for use. Erowid also provides a forum where users can describe their own experiences. The website organized by Students for Safe Drinking (http://www.collegedrinking .org) will help you educate yourself about how to drink alcohol while reducing harm to yourself and your friends (e.g., eat first, travel in pairs, carry condoms, and don't do shots for each year of your age).

There are also ways to get involved and formally educate yourself through college coursework. Many colleges have undergraduate drug use/abuse research opportunities to work with graduate students and faculty on research projects, but the responsibility is on the student to seek out these research opportunities with faculty. Internships or service learning courses provide applied experiences in real-world settings such as health care, substance abuse treatment centers, nonprofit community-based organizations, law enforcement agencies, and the department of corrections. Internships and service learning courses are useful tools when on the job and provide networking opportunities with potential employers. Over 300 universities in the United States offer courses based on the Inside-Out Prison Exchange Program (http://www.insideoutcenter.org/), which provides social change opportunities through transformative education experiences. Classes based on the Inside-Out model are taught in a variety of disciplines inside a prison, and are based on the premise that both people who are incarcerated (i.e., inside students) and college undergraduates (i.e., outside students) can learn a great deal from each other when operating as peers in a classroom. Regardless of the class topic, drug use and abuse will come up, as most people who are incarcerated have drug use histories.

Participate in Harm Reduction Activities

Participating in harm reduction activities that promote safer drug-using practices and that educate others about the benefits of **harm reduction** is another way to help. You probably do not realize it, but you already participate in many harm reduction activities. You may wear a seatbelt when you get in a car, look both ways before you cross the street, and refrain from eating certain foods to avoid heartburn. So incorporating others into your life or volunteering to help them reduce harm associated with their choices could be a natural next step.

Many organized harm reduction activities related to drug and alcohol use were actually started by young people. For example, DanceSafe, a nonprofit organization operating throughout the United States, educates and

Harm reduction: An approach to drug policy aimed at minimizing or eliminating the harms associated with drug use behaviors.

TABLE 12.2 Some Helpful Resources

Websites	Books	Documentaries
DanceSafe http://www.dancesafe.org	Alexander, M. 2012. *The New Jim Crow: Mass Incarceration in the Age of Colorblindness*. New York: New Press.	*American Drug War: The Last White Hope* (2007)
DRCNet Online Library of Drug Policy http://www.druglibrary.org	Bourgois, P. 1995. *In Search of Respect: Selling Crack in El Barrio*. Cambridge, UK: Cambridge University Press.	*Chasing Heroin* (2016)
Drug Policy Alliance http://www.drugpolicy.org	Becker, H. S. 1963. *Outsiders: Studies in the Sociology of Deviance*. New York: Free Press.	*Drugs Inc.* (2010)
Erowid http://www.erowid.org	Chapkis, W., and R. J. Webb. 2008. *Dying to Get High: Marijuana as Medicine*. New York: New York University Press.	*From Heroin to Methadonia* (2006)
Harm Reduction Coalition http://www.harmreduction.org	Gusfield, J. R. 1986. *Symbolic Crusade: Status Politics and the American Temperance Movement*, 2nd ed. Urbana: University of Illinois Press.	*Project Lazarus* (2009)
Students for Safe Drinking http://www.collegedrinking.org	Musto, D. F. 1999. *The American Disease: Origins of Narcotic Control*, 3rd ed. New York: Oxford University Press.	*The House I Live In* (2012)
Students for Sensible Drug Policy http://www.ssdp.org	Weil, A., and W. Rosen. 2004. *From Chocolate to Morphine: Everything You Need to Know About Mind-Altering Drugs*, rev. ed. Boston: Houghton Mifflin.	*13th* (2016)

provides tools for harm reduction at raves and other dance music venues. DanceSafe also sells testing kits for ecstasy and cocaine so users can be aware of the substances that are actually contained in the drugs they plan to take. Find your local DanceSafe chapter and volunteer (https://dancesafe.org/).

If loud music is not your style, you can always focus your volunteer efforts on a program devoted to syringe exchange, safe crack use, or overdose prevention. Here, you may be trained in street outreach, in which you provide harm reduction kits to those who enter the program and those in the surrounding streets. You may also be trained in the proper use and disposal of syringes, safe crack pipe use, and the prevention of overdose from opiates.

The resources these programs provide are invaluable in reducing the spread of Hepatitis B and C, HIV, and other infectious diseases. Access to clean syringes also reduces the likelihood of abscesses, which can result in emergency room visits, and endocarditis, a potentially fatal inflammation of the lining inside the heart. Most important, overdose prevention reduces deaths and other adverse effects associated with substance abuse. By volunteering with such harm reduction programs, you can help to humanize drug users, improve their health and the

health of their communities, and promote the adoption of effective and fair drug policies.

You can learn more from the Harm Reduction Coalition (http://www.harmreduction.org), which also offers training in harm reduction techniques. This organization is an excellent resource that promotes effective, humane, and fair drug policies. One of its most critical efforts is to address the issues of inequality related to race, gender, sexual orientation, gender identity, and socioeconomic status that make some individuals particularly vulnerable to drug use and drug harms. Through its work, the coalition aims to enhance the dignity and health of drug users and their communities.

▶▶ Engage in Social Activism to Promote Responsible Drug Policies

On a macro-level, you can engage in social activism to promote the adoption of responsible drug policies both domestically and internationally. You can join your campus's chapter of Students for Sensible Drug Policy (SSDP), or, if your college does not have a chapter, you can start one. SSDP (http://www.ssdp.org) lobbies college administrators, local government officials, and representatives in Washington, D.C., to

▶ Protesters in the Black Lives Matter social movement have held marches all over the United States as a call to action to address systemic racism, including the calling for the end of the War on Drugs and its resulting mass incarceration. The Black Lives Matter movement stemmed from the acquittal of George Zimmerman after the shooting of Trayvon Martin and gained traction after a series of killings of unarmed black men and boys (Tamir Rice, Eric Garner, and Michael Brown) by police. Do you think that social activism is the answer to ending the War on Drugs?

NICHOLAS KAMM/AFP/Getty Images

advocate for drug policies that do not violate individual rights and are effective in reducing drug-related harms. For example, SSDP is currently campaigning against zero-tolerance policies on campuses, student drug testing, and financial aid and higher education restrictions on drug offenders. SSDP is also working with the Amethyst Initiative to lower the legal drinking age in the United States, as the U.S. is one of only nine countries where the legal drinking age is above 18 or 19 years old.

You can also engage in drug policy activism by working with SAFER (Safer Alternative for Enjoyable Recreation; https://www.facebook.com/SAFERchoice/). SAFER is an educational campaign on college campuses that aims to teach people about the harms of alcohol use versus the harms of marijuana use in order to get people to

think critically about the differences in the ways these substances are treated legally. SAFER has been at the forefront of changing zero-tolerance policies on college campuses where many students have been kicked out of dorms for marijuana use.

Both SAFER and SSDP work closely with the Drug Policy Alliance (DPA; http://www.drugpolicy.org), an international nonprofit organization that advocates for alternatives to the drug war and for harm reduction policies rooted in equality and compassion. DPA's executive director, Ethan Nadelmann, has been a guest on the *Colbert Report,* the *O'Reilly Factor,* and *Fox and Friends* to discuss the harms of the drug war and promote effective and humane drug policies. You could volunteer your time to this organization, assist in its letter-writing campaigns, or donate some money to its many causes.

WHAT DOES AMERICA THINK?

Questions About Alcohol and Other Drugs From the General Social Survey

Turn to the beginning of the chapter to compare your answers to those of the total population.

1. How often do you spend the evening at a bar?

   AT LEAST ONCE A WEEK: 7.1%

   AT LEAST ONCE A MONTH: 19.9%

   AT LEAST ONCE A YEAR: 27.9%

   NEVER: 45.1%

2. Should marijuana be made legal?

   YES: 61.1%

   NO: 38.9%

3. In the United States, do you think we're spending too much money on dealing with drug addiction, too little money, or about the right amount?

   TOO MUCH: 7.9%

   TOO LITTLE: 65.8%

   ABOUT THE RIGHT AMOUNT: 26.3%

4. In the United States, do you think we're spending too much money on dealing with drug rehabilitation, too little money, or about the right amount?

   TOO MUCH: 11.1%

   TOO LITTLE: 62.6%

   ABOUT THE RIGHT AMOUNT: 26.3%

SOURCE: National Opinion Research Center, University of Chicago.

CHAPTER SUMMARY

 12.1 Discuss drug use as a social problem.

The use of drugs has occurred in societies over a long period of human history and for a wide range of reasons. As inanimate substances, drugs are neither inherently good nor inherently bad. Their effects depend on the social context and the ways, good or bad, in which humans put them to use. The use of drugs can create a range of physical, psychological, and social problems, especially when social norms about such use are broken.

 12.2 Describe the problems of drug dependence.

Drug use can create physiological or psychological dependence on a substance. Being deprived of the drug can be a painful experience for a user, which contributes significantly toward continued use. Patterns of drug use and abuse are not evenly distributed through society but are influenced by social aspects of individuals' lives.

12.3 Relate patterns of drug use to the life course, gender, race/ethnicity, and sexual orientation.

Use, abuse, and misuse of and dependence on drugs and alcohol occur and/or become social problems in ways that vary both within and across societies and social contexts by individual, group, culture, social norms, socioeconomic status, gender, race, age, sexual orientation, mind-set, and setting. In the United States, whites are more likely to use illegal drugs than are blacks, and males are more likely to use drugs than are females. Young adults are the age group most likely to use drugs, as are sexual minorities. Those in a lower socioeconomic stratum are more likely than those in a higher one to experience drug problems and the harms associated with drug use.

Apply the functionalist, symbolic interactionist, and conflict perspectives to social policy on drug use.

The functionalist and conflict theories focus on social structure, inequalities, and/or lack of social control as causes of drug use, while symbolic interaction theories center their explanations of drug use on people's interactions and relationships with others.

Apply specialized theories to the social problems of drug use.

General strain theory assumes that individuals use drugs to cope with negative relationships. Social disorganization theory explains the influence of the local environment on patterns of drug use. Social learning theory explains how individuals become socialized into drug use.

Identify steps toward social change on drugs.

You can take part in programs that can help to reduce the social problem of drugs by participating in harm reduction activities and engaging in social activism to promote responsible drug policies.

KEY TERMS

demand reduction 294	drug dependence 295	maturing out 301	supply reduction 294
drug 293	drug use 294	natural recovery 298	War on Drugs 294
drug abuse 295	harm reduction 311	needle exchange programs 300	

 $SAGE edge **Want a better grade?**

Get the tools you need to sharpen your study skills. Access practice quizzes, eFlashcards, video, and multimedia at
http://edge.sagepub.com/trevino2e

13 HEALTH

Valerie Leiter

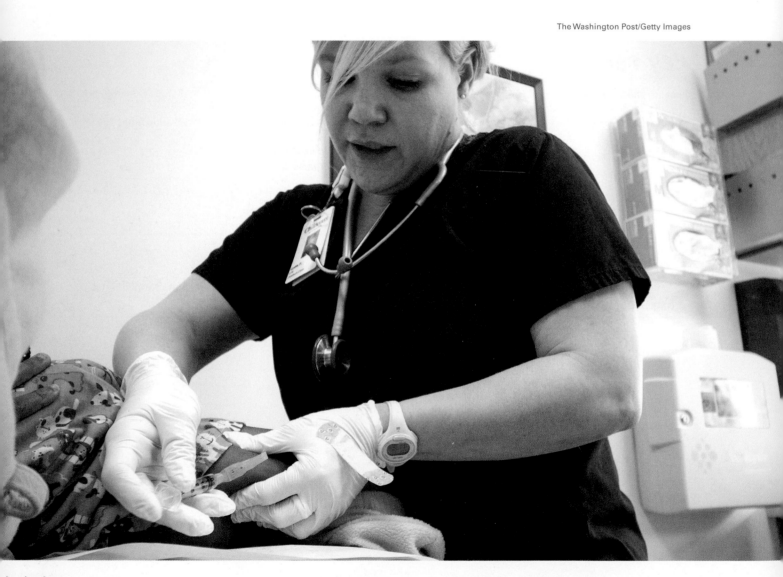

A nurse administers the measles, mumps, and rubella (MMR) vaccine to a child at Children's Primary Care Clinic in Minneapolis, Minnesota. Do you think states should allow exemptions to the MMR vaccine on religious and philosophical grounds?

Investigating Health: My Story

Valerie Leiter

I was born in Albany, New York, into a working-class family that struggled financially. When I was less than 3 years old, I almost died from a bacterial meningitis infection. I was in a coma for 3 days and was extremely fortunate to survive and heal completely. My family did not have health insurance. Only my mother's determined advocacy, with the help of a friend who was a nurse who recognized the dangerous symptoms, got me admitted to the hospital in time to save my life.

As a poor kid growing up in middle-class neighborhoods, I understood social inequality first-hand. When I was in high school, I had the opportunity to take introduction to sociology as a senior, paying for the AP credit with money that I earned through my job at a local donut shop. That allowed me to take a class on social problems my very first semester of college, which hooked me on sociology, with its focus on real-world issues. Since then, I have earned a masters in sociology and a joint Ph.D. in sociology and social policy. I worked for a while doing policy research for state and federal agencies, and am now a sociology professor. I love working with my students and especially try to mentor those who, like me, are first-generation college students.

My research has one foot in sociology and the other in the world of policy. I have looked at how disability policy affects the transition to adulthood among youth with disabilities, and am currently examining how the U.S. government regulates medical devices for women's health. My understanding of health as a social problem is rooted in both personal and professional experiences.

LEARNING OBJECTIVES

13.1 Describe health, disease, and illness as socially defined.

13.2 Discuss patterns and trends in health, illness, and treatment.

13.3 Describe the health care system and its stakeholders.

13.4 Apply the functionalist, conflict, and symbolic interactionist perspectives to the concept of health.

13.5 Apply specialized theories of health.

13.6 Identify steps toward social change to promote health.

WHAT DO YOU THINK?

Questions About Health From the General Social Survey

1. Do you think that the government should help pay for medical care?
   - ☐ YES
   - ☐ NO

2. In the United States, do you think we're spending too much money on improving and protecting the nation's health, too little money, or about the right amount?
   - ☐ TOO MUCH
   - ☐ TOO LITTLE
   - ☐ ABOUT THE RIGHT AMOUNT

3. What is your confidence level in medicine?
   - ☐ A GREAT DEAL
   - ☐ ONLY SOME
   - ☐ HARDLY ANY

4. What is your interest level in medical discoveries?
   - ☐ VERY INTERESTED
   - ☐ MODERATELY INTERESTED
   - ☐ NOT AT ALL INTERESTED

5. Do you think that incurable patients should be allowed to die?
   - ☐ YES
   - ☐ NO

6. Do you think a person has the right to end his or her own life if this person has an incurable disease?
   - ☐ YES
   - ☐ NO

 Turn to the end of the chapter to view the results for the total population.

SOURCE: National Opinion Research Center, University of Chicago.

SUFFERING FROM DRAPETOMANIA

It is 1845 in the American South. The cotton trade is in full swing and so is slavery. Kendrick, a slave on the largest cotton plantation in Maryland, has been working in the fields in the sun all summer long with little water and no rest or shade. His back aches, his feet are swollen, his hands are raw, and he has a constant dry cough.

While those around him have been beaten into submissive obedience, Kendrick is different. No matter how severely he is oppressed or how exhausting his days are, he cannot accept his position in life. He comes to a decision. Early the next morning he will make a run for it.

It is 3:00 a.m. and the only light falls from the stars. The moon has long since gone to rest. The cool night air bathes Kendrick's skin. He feels alive and alert, as if he has been floating through a nightmare his entire life only to finally wake and feel the fresh wind of freedom just one tree line away. . . .

Do you hope he makes it?

According to some 19th-century literature, Kendrick is not displaying strong resilience and an admirable will to live and be free. Rather, he is suffering from a disease. The disease, called drapetomania, was defined as the tendency for a slave to run away from their master (Cartwright, 1851). This was a real diagnosis made by medical professionals and believed to require treatment, including the surgical removal of both big toes, so running away became a physical impossibility. What do you think about doctors' involvement in "treating" slaves for this condition?

In the course of this chapter we will look at patterns and trends in health and health care, and at theories of health and health care, and ask how the spread of sickness and disease and the social construction of sickness and disease today are still embedded in systems of social inequality.

The *Oxford English Dictionary* defines *illness* as a disease or period of sickness affecting the body or mind and *health* as the state of being free of illness or injury. So

▶ The front page of the French newspaper *Le Petit Journal Illustré* from October 30, 1921, shows a poor family suffering from tuberculosis as a result of living in a squalid flat in Paris. In the United States, Jacob Riis, a social reformer and photographer, documented the squalid living conditions in New York City slums in his 1890 book *How the Other Half Lives*. Riis brought attention to the spread of diseases like smallpox, typhus, and measles in the unhygienic and overpopulated tenements.

what does sociology have to do with a physical problem occurring within an individual?

We will examine how social location determines your quality of life, how long you will live, and how you will die. This chapter challenges common definitions of illness and disease as personal experiences and shows that these are not static or objective states but rather socially constructed notions. The disadvantaged, the oppressed, and the segregated in societies suffer illness at far greater rates than do the wealthy. They do so because they are exposed to health problems more often than are wealthier people who have money and privilege, and are less able to purchase health care to address their problems.

WHAT ARE DISEASE AND ILLNESS?

13.1 Describe health, disease, and illness as socially defined.

It is common logic that illness is a physical event caused by physical factors. For example, bacterial meningitis is an infectious, acute inflammation of the lining of the brain and spinal column. In this disease, bacteria interfere with bodily functions. To cure diseases, we consult with doctors, use medications, and adopt physical strategies such as resting.

Sociologists call this taken-for-granted way of thinking about sickness and disease in our society the medical model (Engel, 1981). Medicine reaches beyond disease, however, and permeates our lives. The prominence of medical television shows, healthy-eating magazines, exercise magazines, and self-help books demonstrates that medicine and health care are not merely constructs that exist to help us prevent and overcome illness.

This taken-for-granted way of thinking also does not take into account the social aspects of disease. It is helpful to think of disease as the biophysiological phenomena that affect the body, and as illness as the social phenomena that accompany the disease (Conrad & Leiter, 2012). This view helps us understand the interaction between the sick individual and society. In the meningitis example, the disease involved a high fever, stiff and painful neck, vomiting, and confusion. Those symptoms were treated through the use of IV antibiotics, hospital care, and rest. But there are also powerful social factors involved, shaping an individual's chances of contracting the disease, and also how the individual is treated after becoming sick. The risk factors associated with getting meningitis include: overcrowded living conditions, not getting childhood immunizations, and being exposed to insects and rodents—these social and environmental factors place people at greater risk for the disease. And after the disease is contracted, other people may stigmatize and shun the individual, for fear that they will somehow also become ill. It is the experience of disease, with its uncomfortable and sometimes life-threatening symptoms, that often catches our attention. Yet the experience of illness is just as important.

In contemporary societies, we need to ask ourselves some key questions about illnesses: Why are some illnesses seen as the fault of the individuals who contract them? To what extent do individuals actually have control over the conditions that place them at risk? Why is medical treatment often seen as the solution to these problems, rather than looking upstream at causes and focusing on preventing the illness from occurring? What other functions does medicine serve apart from the repair of our physical bodies? And how is the power of medicine entangled in our lives?

Some sociological theorists argue that medicine has gone beyond its functional role of fixing physical bodies and is used in our everyday lives as a form of **social control**. Sociologists consider how diseases or sicknesses, and those who are sick or diseased, are labeled and treated. In many instances, what we call a "disease" may have very weak links to what is actually going on within the diseased person's body (Zola, 1972; for discussion of Zola's foundational theory, see Hyde et al., 2006). Treatment is not simply a utilitarian method of curing illness. It incorporates wider social expectations about appropriate social behavior of both the sick person and others who interact with them.

Consider depression. At its most basic, depression is characterized by prolonged periods of sadness and feelings of worthlessness and has been linked strongly to lower levels of the neurotransmitter serotonin within the brain. However, a taboo still surrounds the experience of depression. Those suffering it may be labeled lazy or weak and be too embarrassed to seek help. If the medical profession links this illness directly to serotonin level and other bodily symptoms, why do we treat it differently from other physical illnesses, such as the flu or AIDS or cancer?

Social behavior itself may be labeled as a disease. When we diverge from society's norms, society reins us back in to label us sick and diseased and "treat" us so we again conform. For example, recent additions and amendments to the *Diagnostic and Statistical Manual of Mental Disorders* (DSM) medicalize behaviors that traditionally were never thought to be illnesses or medical problems. The DSM is published by the American Psychiatric Association and provides standard criteria for the classification of mental disorders. Clinicians, insurance companies, and legal systems around the world use it extensively in diagnosis and treatment. The fifth edition of the manual, known as *DSM-5*, was published in 2013. Some of its newest entries include excoriation disorder (obsessive-compulsive skin picking) and hoarding disorder. The medicalization of skin picking and hoarding raises the question whether such labeling of social behaviors exceeds the realm of medical issues. The British Psychological Society (2011, p. 6) has recognized concerns about the increasing scope of medicalization in the *DSM* that it stated were "clearly based on social norms, with 'symptoms' that all rely on subjective judgments." The diagnoses "reflect current normative social expectations."

Furthermore, gender-specific sexual dysfunctions have been added. For females, sexual desire and arousal disorders have been combined into one disorder: female sexual interest/arousal disorder (American Psychiatric Association, 2013). The idea that a behavior in females may constitute an illness while the same or similar behavior in males does not raises serious concerns about whether the manual promotes social ideals of gender. Since this diagnosis was added to the *DSM*, the U.S. Food and Drug Administration (FDA) has approved a drug called Addyi

....

Social control: The ability of a strong group in society to control the actions of subordinate groups.

for low sexual desire among premenopausal women. The medicalization cycle is complete here: There is a diagnosis and a medical treatment to address it. Pharmaceutical companies have become increasingly important agents in the medicalization of life (Conrad & Leiter, 2008).

This chapter does not argue that all illnesses, whether physical or mental, are social constructs. The diagnosis and subsequent treatment of many behaviors that interfere with a person's life are extremely worthwhile and important. What the chapter proposes is that the labeling of certain behaviors as illnesses may exceed the traditional functions of medicine and may reflect prevailing norms and prejudices.

> *ASK YOURSELF:* How do depression and other mental illnesses demonstrate the setting of social standards through the medicalization of behavior? Who decides when a person is overweight? Obese? Do you think the range of medical disorders has exceeded its function in diagnosing and treating medical problems? Why are certain behaviors labeled diseases, whereas others (for example, being a workaholic) are not?

Characteristics of a Medicalized Society

We live in a medicalized society, one in which we explain social problems in medical terms. For example, responding to social encounters with heavy drinking is deemed a disease. Being exceedingly shy may be labeled as "social anxiety disorder." Research regarding the prevalence and incidence of ADHD reveals how, as societies develop over time, certain behaviors may become medicalized (see Figure 13.1).

Four general points can be made about many possible examples of medicalized behavior:

1. Medicine sets the limits of normal behavior and defines people as sick who fall outside these limits. It sorts, labels, and treats the deviant, the nonconformist, the malingerer, and the sick. Thus the way in which medical problems are produced, conceptualized, and treated is the outcome of specific social and historical factors.

2. The way we conceptualize some social issues as medical problems has immense significance. It makes health and illness the outcome of the individual's behavioral or biological malfunctioning and independent of their existence in a wider social environment. For example, obesity is often conceptualized as a problem with that person's will or morality, regardless of the fact that the environment in which they live may not provide healthy food or safe places to exercise.

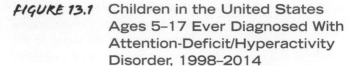

FIGURE 13.1 Children in the United States Ages 5–17 Ever Diagnosed With Attention-Deficit/Hyperactivity Disorder, 1998–2014

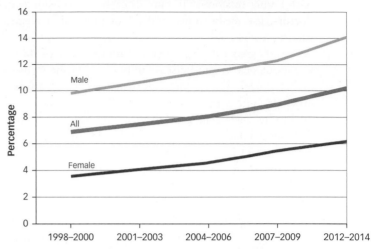

SOURCE: Center for Disease Control and Prevention, 2013. "ADHD Throughout the Years."

3. Medicalization makes these problems appear to be products of nature—of genetics, of biological dysfunction, or of innate characteristics of individuals. Thus it puts the problems safely beyond political and social interventions and solutions.

4. Medical solutions to social problems give additional power to health care providers and systems, and individuals who refuse treatment may face being labeled as "bad patients" who are at fault for continuing to experience their conditions.

Although using medicine to categorize diseases and exert some level of social control, such as by promoting exercise, is undeniably a benefit to society, sociologists recognize that the medicalization of society also has a dark side. The argument against it does not denounce medicine as a whole. Rather, it argues against the labeling, value-laden norms, and stigmatization associated with excess medicalization. The medicalization of society exceeds the diagnosis and treatment of physical conditions and extends into the labeling and control of social and behavioral deviance. It deems medical issues to be largely the consequences of personal choice, rather than recognizing that disease and illness occur within a framework of hierarchical social structures and broader governmental policies.

Two False Assumptions About Health

To distinguish the necessary functions of medicine from the overzealous, medicalizing ones, we must think of disease as being as much a social process as a biological product

The Medicalization of Attention-Deficit/Hyperactivity Disorder

The term *attention-deficit/hyperactivity disorder* (ADHD) did not emerge in the United States until the 1950s, when Smith (2010, p. 939) asserts, "a lot was expected of the baby boom generation" and there was concern about "perceived American deficiencies in science and technology [and] education critics demanded more of students." He states that "action was taken by school guidance counsellors . . . to identify and help such underachieving children," and this "coincided with the emergence of many psychoactive drugs to treat . . . hyperactivity."

ADHD is characterized by inattention and hyperactivity and impulsivity. These symptoms must be present before the person reaches 12 years of age; occur in two or more settings; interfere with or reduce the quality of social, school, or work functioning; and not occur during the course of some other psychotic disorder. They must occur for at least 6 months and include behavior inappropriate for the person's developmental level (American Psychiatric Association, 2013; Centers for Disease Control and Prevention, 2013b).

Data from the 2011 National Survey of Children's Health (NSCH), analyzed by the Centers for Disease Control and Prevention (2017), are instructive because they are derived from almost 100,000 respondents. The survey asked parents about their children's health, and the CDC analysis found that the diagnosis of ADHD had increased markedly from 2003 to 2011. In 2003, 7.8% of children's parents reported that they had been diagnosed with ADHD. In 2007, it increased to 9.5%, and in 2011, to 11% of all children. This represents an increase of 5% in each year.

Among children in the United States in 2011, 6% took medication for the disorder, including drugs sold under a range of names such as Aderall, Dexedrine, and Ritalin. These drugs act by increasing certain neurotransmitters in the frontal region of the brain—the area associated with executive functioning (Weiss, 2011). The percentage of children being medicated for ADHD increased 7% each year.

There are marked differences in children's chances of being diagnosed with ADHD:

- Boys are 2.3 times more likely than girls;

- Black children are 20% less likely and Latino children are 54% less likely than white children;

- Children in households where the primary language is not English are 86% less likely than households where the primary language is English; and

- Children with Medicaid insurance coverage are 1.5 times more likely than those with private insurance to be diagnosed.

There has been an explosion in the diagnosis and treatment of ADHD. There are no biological markers for ADHD. Rather, physicians diagnose the disorder based on subjective terms, partially on evidence provided by teachers and parents. From a social problems perspective, the increase in ADHD diagnoses represents the medicalization of unacceptable behavior, particularly among boys and white middle-class children who underperform at school. Starting in the 1990s, ADHD adults also began to be diagnosed with it (Conrad & Potter, 2000). ADHD diagnosis and treatment have increasingly been globalized, facilitated by pharmaceutical companies, Western psychiatry, use of *DSM* criteria, use of the Internet, and activism by advocacy groups (Conrad & Bergey, 2014).

▶ **THINK ABOUT IT:** Why do you think there has been a steady increase in the numbers of children diagnosed with ADHD? Why do you think boys are more than twice as likely as girls to be diagnosed with ADHD? Do you think that behavioral illnesses such as ADHD are being overdiagnosed and overmedicated? If so, why?

of nature. Illness and disease are the products of biology, genetic risk factors, and personal behaviors. However, all these factors operate within social arrangements that, when we consider health issues epidemiologically, heavily influence both who gets ill and what makes them ill.

Two flawed assumptions about disease recur constantly in our daily lives and in the media:

1. Genetics explains illness and disease to the exclusion of social factors.

2. People have control over the factors that make them ill.

Let us examine each of these to understand why they are misleading.

Genetics Alone Explains Disease

Genetic explanations are offered regularly for a range of conditions and illnesses, including obesity, drug addiction, and alcoholism. There is, however, no evidence for a genetic contribution to what are actually cultural practices such as drug use, nor any scientific justification for making negative moral evaluations couched in the language of medical science. The categorization of such behaviors as illnesses thus lies not in science but in a social evaluation of them.

Sociologists consider health from a perspective that is different from modern conceptions of science and medicine. Rather than view illness as an individual problem, they analyze illness by social factors such as ethnicity, socioeconomic status, age, and gender to better understand how broader patterns of social inequality result in health inequalities—both illness (morbidity) and death (mortality). Single biological risk factors do not account for the social patterning of disease—genetics combined with social and physical environmental factors cause disease.

So what does a genetic explanation achieve? Information about your own genes, now available through genetic testing, may allow you to plan for the future, to undertake preventive measures to halt or delay the development of a disease or illness. However, this limited utility may not justify the weight that we place on genetics. By reducing the explanation of disease to biology alone, the genetic explanation systematically excludes sociological explanations and deflects our attention from the ways in which social life shapes our experience of disease. Between the genetic predisposition for a specific disease and its occurrence actually lie the intervening variables of politics, economics, gender roles, and social marginalization on the basis of race and ethnicity. Ironically, it is exactly these considerations that may determine whether a person has access to genetic testing to predict vulnerability to some conditions, and it is these variables we must take into account in explaining who gets sick—that is, how a genetic risk is transformed into a social reality.

People Who Are Ill Have Made Poor Lifestyle Choices

The second flawed assumption is that people adopt lifestyles that make them sick—freely making bad choices about diet, smoking, and exercise, for example—and are therefore individually responsible for their conditions. However, from a social problems perspective, remember that individual lifestyles are themselves socially patterned, and that those lower down in the stratification system can

► Sandy Wright looks over her bag of medications in her home in Peoria, Illinois. Americans are taking record numbers of prescription drugs, over-the-counter medications, and supplements. The overprescribing of antibiotics has led to the emergence of "superbugs," antibiotic-resistant bacteria.

make fewer choices about the foods they consume, the exercise they take, and even their smoking and drinking habits (Subramanyam et al., 2012). Research on programs targeted at individual behavior, such as the Stanford Five-City Project and the Pawtucket Heart Health Program, two large-scale studies examining the effects of lifestyle on heart disease, demonstrates that changes in lifestyle have little effect on the reduction of cardiovascular disease (Everage et al., 2013).

Common Features

For sociologists of health, these flawed assumptions have two common features. First, they claim that when an individual becomes diseased, it is a problem of the individual's own body and unique biology. Sociologists, however, argue that the distinct patterns of health and illness that we can observe along the intersections of class, gender, race, and ethnicity demonstrate that we should not consider health and illness merely as an individual problem; rather, health and illness are heavily determined by patterns of social inequality. By arguing that illness and disease are matters for societal consideration, sociologists show that we can understand, treat, and experience disease differently than we do. There is no pure, value-free scientific knowledge about disease. Our knowledge of health and illness, the organizations and professions that deal with health care, and our own responses to our bodily states are shaped and formed by the history of our society and our place in it.

Second, even if lifestyle behaviors were the sole cause of disease, extensive studies have shown that it is almost impossible for people to change their lifestyles on their own and in isolation from their social circumstances (Everage et al., 2013). The social factors that predispose people to adopt unhealthy lifestyles—work stress, for example—are often ignored in treatment plans that focus on individual-level causes like diet, cholesterol, or drinking. Instead, we need to see these risk factors in context, to understand how individuals are exposed to them and why they have limited access to resources for responding to them (Clougherty, Souza, & Cullen, 2010). If we want to change the patterns of disease, we must change the patterns of social inequality that produce them, and not focus solely on their downstream impact on the individual.

PATTERNS AND TRENDS

 13.2 Discuss patterns and trends in health, illness, and treatment.

Now that we have examined the notion of illness as socially constructed and a means to set norms of social behavior, let us consider who suffers illness, and why. What patterns and trends in illness do we find?

Who Gets Sick?

In modern Western societies, it is usually assumed that health differences are biologically caused or that individual lifestyles result in people becoming sicker and dying earlier. People from disadvantaged backgrounds choose to smoke more, drink more, and exercise less, choices leading to biological changes that cause disease, damage health, and lead to shorter lives. The argument of this chapter, however, and of sociological thought in general, is that disease is not caused by purely biological factors and individual choices. On the contrary, individual lifestyle choices are shaped socially.

Sociologists traditionally argue that disease is shaped by broad social determinants rather than by personal choices individuals make. People from lower socioeconomic backgrounds drink more, smoke more, eat less healthy diets, and exercise less than do their counterparts in higher socioeconomic groups. But these decisions are not made in a vacuum and should not be considered pure choices. Rather, a wide range of mediating social factors intervenes between the biology of disease, individual lifestyle, and the social experience to shape and produce disease. These factors range from standards of housing and workplace conditions to emotional and psychological experiences at work and at home, to men's and women's social and gender roles, to membership in **status groups** based on ethnicity.

Thus we need to consider these factors against the background of overall patterns of inequality that exist

▶ A father holds his child, who has asthma, with a smokestack in the background. What other kinds of air pollution have you seen in your community or elsewhere?

Simon Marcus Taplin/Corbis/Getty Images

within society. For example, is there a political commitment to reducing inequality and providing a social environment that prevents illness and disease? Are there guaranteed housing standards, access to and affordability of fresh and healthy food, and safe working conditions, as well as safe and available resources and places where people can get physical exercise, both intentionally and incidentally?

Whether they seek to promote equality by sharing wealth or adopt strictly capitalist ideals, governments directly affect the health of people living under middle-class and poorer circumstances. Other social institutions also shape the experience of health within a population. For example, landlords who neglect apartments place children at risk for asthma because of their exposure to molds and cockroaches, known asthma triggers. Employers who allow substandard working

....
Status groups: Social groups that are either negatively or positively privileged.

conditions can make workers more likely to get sick (including textile factory workers) or injured on the job (such as meatpacking factory workers). Professional sports leagues that fail to prevent damage to players' health through injury can leave the athletes and their families with heavy burdens. Industries that promote unhealthy habits like smoking and eating junk food can harm health, as do companies and industries that pollute air, soil, and water. Even given improved living conditions and medical practices, if inequalities based on class, gender, race, and ethnicity are not tackled, the differences between the rich and the poor persist and widen. Disease and social inequality are linked intimately. If you want to know who is disadvantaged socially in any society, look at who gets sick and lives shorter lives. It is not merely who is poor and who is rich that is at work—there is a **social gradient of health** (Lynch et al., 2006), a kind of sliding scale where your socioeconomic status shapes your exposure to health problems. Those at the top of the social system are healthier and live longer, while those at the bottom are sicker, do not live as long, and die more from preventable diseases and accidents, with middle-class people somewhere in between those two extremes.

> *ASK YOURSELF:* Do you think it is more difficult for a person from a low socioeconomic background to take care of their health than it is for a person from a high socioeconomic background? Why or why not?

Growing Inequality and Its Impact on Health

While our health appears to us as a personal issue, from a social problems perspective it is socially patterned: Who gets sick, when we die, and what we die of are closely linked to wider patterns of inequality in society. British studies have found marked differences in health levels between occupational classes, for men and women, and for all ages (Rowlingson, 2011). Poor people have a much higher mortality rate than do those at the top. They suffer from more chronic illness, and their children weigh less at birth and have shorter bodies (White, 2012).

There are also marked inequalities in access to health services, particularly preventive care. For example, in Southern California, researchers found that 97% of otolaryngologists (doctors specializing in treating the ear, nose, and throat) would offer an appointment to a child with commercial insurance, but only 27% would do so for a child on Medi-Cal (publicly funded health care). Of that 27%, only 19% would offer to perform a tonsillectomy; the remaining 8% would refer the child to another physician. The surgeons said they did not want to operate on those without commercial insurance due to the excessive administrative burdens (96%), low reimbursement rates (92%), and high administrative fees (87%) associated with treating Medi-Cal patients (Wang et al., 2004).

The growing inequalities of wealth and income observed within and between nations in recent years mean that inequalities of health are also widening. Income inequality in the United States—the gap between the richest and the poorest—is now greater than at any period since the 1920s. The Congressional Budget Office (2016) found that among the top 1% of households in the United States, income grew by 188% between 1979 and 2013, compared with just 18% growth among the bottom 80% of households and 63% growth in the 81st to 99th percentiles.

It is not just the extent of poverty within a society but also the extent of income inequality that determines the distribution of health and illness. Countries with relatively minor differences between richest and poorest are the healthiest. Zheng and George (2012, p. 2179) speculate that income inequality may result in "underinvestment in human resources and social goods, while intensifying social comparisons and subsequent psychological stress and frustration . . . [and] as increasing income inequality exacerbates these disadvantageous social conditions, personal resources, especially socioeconomic status, increase in importance as tools for accessing social and health resources." Health, like every other service, relies on profitability.

The Gini coefficient is an index measuring the level of inequality in a society: A coefficient of zero indicates total equality and a coefficient of one indicates total inequality. Karlsson et al. (2012) used the Gini coefficient to assess the impact of income inequality on health across 21 countries; their findings are represented in Figure 13.2. The degree of inequality of income within a high-income country also influences the citizen's experience of health (Hallerod & Gustafsson, 2011). Inequality matters two ways: where an individual is placed in the social class hierarchy, and also how unequal the society is.

Age at death and cause of death are all linked to social class. In 1978, Michael G. Marmot and his colleagues published the first major study of class differences in health in Britain. Skilled white-collar workers at the bottom of the British civil service hierarchy had disease rates four times those of workers at the top. Those one step below the top had disease rates twice those at the top. This finding was confirmed over a wide range of diseases.

Social gradient of health: The consistent finding that inequality and health are related, with those at the top of the social system being healthier and living longer than those at the bottom.

FIGURE 13.2 Relationship Between Health and Income Inequality for Selected Countries, 2010

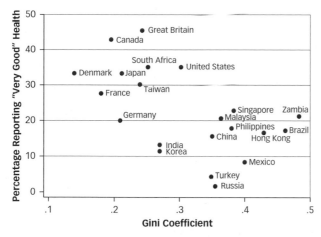

SOURCE: Karlsson et. al. (2012) 'Income inequality and health: Importance of a cross-country perspective' *Social Science & Medicine* 70(6): 875–885.

Even when they took into account lifestyle factors such as smoking, high-fat diets, obesity, and high blood pressure, those at the bottom of the hierarchy were three times as vulnerable as those at the top (Marmot et al., 1978).

Some commentators have used Marmot's studies to argue that everyone experiences the impact of social position on health, not just the poor (Marmot, 2006). More recently, Shishehbor et al. (2006) found that the lower someone's socioeconomic status, the higher the risk of death. The poorest people had higher mortality in every year of the study, and the differences between socioeconomic groups grew over time. After adjusting for other variables that could account for the differences, they found that socioeconomic status was still strongly related to mortality rates.

Gender Differences

Although gender discrimination has been reduced in modernized Western societies, gender stereotypes and gender roles remain prominent. Consider the roles females usually play in advertising, television shows, and films. What characteristics and qualities do they embody? How do these compare with the ways males are presented and the roles men play?

The saturation of gender stereotypes in mass media may appear harmless, yet we all internalize such stereotypes, perceiving ourselves and our health and behavior in comparison with what we see around us. How do you think this exposure affects men's and women's experiences of health and illness? We examine these experiences next, beginning with women's.

ASK YOURSELF: Over the next few days, note the advertisements for painkillers that you see online and in other media. Are there differences in the ways men and women are portrayed in these ads? Are different kinds of pain relievers targeted at men and women? (See Greene & Herzberg, 2010; Kempner, 2006.)

Women's Experience of Health

Research reveals two consistent findings relating to the health of women in Western societies. They are diagnosed as suffering from more ill health than men. Yet, paradoxically, they live longer than men (see Figure 13.3). In the United States in 2013, women's life expectancy was 81.2 years and men's 76.4 (Centers for Disease Control, 2015). This gives rise to a gendered health paradox. Are women more likely than men to experience illness, or are gender differences due largely to men underreporting health problems?

The concept of medicalization is particularly useful for explaining women's experiences in Western medicine. Medical textbooks and journals have been criticized for their sexist attitudes (Niland & Lyons, 2011), and gender-specific information is scarce or absent for various conditions such as cardiovascular disease, alcohol abuse, and pharmacology. Furthermore, there is an underlying theme in the literature that women's health problems are aberrations from male norms (Dijkstra, Verdonk, & Largo-Janssen, 2008). For example, medical textbooks portray menopause as a deficiency disease (Hvas & Gannik, 2008). Menopause is simply the cessation of menses in women (White, 2006). In Western cultures, where aging is negatively perceived and womanhood is strongly associated with fertility, menopause is overwhelmingly understood as a problem requiring medical treatment (Colombo et al., 2010).

Several factors explain women's higher rate of medical diagnosis. For instance, between the ages of 15 and 44, women are hospitalized at a higher rate than men, largely

FIGURE 13.3 U.S. Life Expectancy, 1950–2050 (projected)

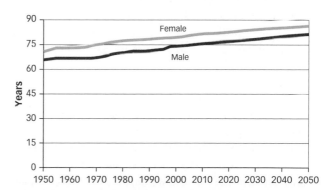

SOURCE: Reprinted with permission from Data360, http://www.data360.org/dsg.aspx ?Data_Set_Group_Id=195

due to childbirth. Women go to doctors more than men do, especially during their childbearing years, when many have family planning needs and receive prenatal care (Drapeau, Boyer, & Lesage, 2009). Women are encouraged to have Pap smears for cervical cancer and mammograms for breast cancer detection.

Women are also overrepresented in health statistics as a consequence of their caretaker roles for children, for other adults in the household, and for their extended families. Such carework can have social and health consequences like lower social status, longer work hours, persistently lower wages, unpaid work, greater social and emotional commitments, and fewer hours of sleep and leisure (Drapeau et al., 2009).

The final factor explaining the apparent high numbers of sick women is that women and men are socialized to experience and report their bodily sensations differently. Women are more likely to consult doctors based on how they feel, whereas men are more likely to avoid consultation with doctors. Men are less likely than women to be diagnosed as suffering from stress or depression and more likely to be diagnosed as having physical ailments (Galdas, Cheater, & Marshall, 2005).

ASK YOURSELF: How do you think age and gender interact in the context of the medical encounter? Think about the types of health problems women of different ages experience. How does their health link to their gender? Do men experience the same shifts in disease over their lifetimes? What do we learn from this comparison?

Men's Experience of Health

Although practices and attitudes are constantly changing, it is still not the norm for women to engage in contact sports, reckless driving, and other displays traditionally associated with masculinity. To conform to their social role and establish their social standing, however, men engage in these and other activities that can put them in danger of serious injury and death.

Construction and other jobs, such as mining, that require significant manual labor continue to be dominated by men. Dangerous and sometimes unhealthy workplaces have serious consequences for men's health, including exposure to far greater levels of chemicals. Asbestos, a fiber commonly used in building products and insulation until the early 1990s, is now known as a carcinogen to which many men in the construction trades were exposed. And the mere fact of performing demanding physical labor for 8 hours a day over many years creates stress and injuries.

Gender also has significant impacts on the way men understand and experience sickness and disease. Men's health, and ill health, is often framed in the context of masculinity. Traits that are dominantly linked to masculinity, such as stoicism and an emphasis on physical health rather than on emotional or mental distress, encourage men to delay visiting doctors and to underreport pain or other symptoms in medical encounters (Galdas et al., 2005).

Men delay seeking medical advice for even the most overt physical symptoms. In a review of the international literature, Kiss and Meryn (2001) found that men often fail to appear for scheduled medical checkups and examinations. We can also infer that men are actively trying to negotiate their gender identity in the face of chronic illnesses that challenge key attributes of their masculinity—their ability to stay in control, act rationally, not complain, and "be a man." Thus men's reactions to ill health may well be to protect their socially determined sense of gender identity from threats.

ASK YOURSELF: Make a list of five character traits you think are seen as typically "masculine." How might each of these traits affect the way in which men experience health and illness?

Socioeconomic and Occupational Differences

Sociologists have consistently demonstrated a strong correlation between socioeconomic status and health (Zheng & George, 2012). The likely causes of this relationship are practical: A person in a lower socioeconomic demographic has greater exposure to stress and hardship and more limited access to valuable resources such as food, housing, health care, and medical knowledge (George, 2005).

Members of lower socioeconomic groups are also more vulnerable to the worst effects of urbanism: slum dwellings, poor ventilation, garbage, and overcrowding (Craddock, 2000). They are exposed to the unregulated labor market of sweatshops and home work. The poor pay higher cash costs; have less access to informal sources of financial assistance, such as friends and family; and depend on insecure incomes. Ironically, the poorer you are, the more it costs you to live. Poorer people have lower life expectancies, higher overall mortality rates, and higher infant mortality rates. Low socioeconomic status is associated with higher rates of death from the 14 major causes of death in the International Classification of Diseases (Chandola, 2000). Men in unskilled manual labor are five times more likely to die prematurely than are men working in professions (Chandola, 2000).

Work experiences account for at least part of the difference in the experience of health between different socioeconomic classes. Those in the lower or "blue-collar"

How Race and Ethnicity Influence Health

Race has direct effects on health, and combines with class in significant ways. Racism affects nondominant racial populations directly in three ways: institutional racism (policies and procedures that reduce access to housing, education, employment, and other life opportunities), cultural racism (policy environments that involve stereotypes and are hostile to egalitarian policies), and interpersonal racial discrimination (which causes psychosocial stress and may alter behavioral patterns, increasing health risks) (Williams & Mohammed, 2013).

The differences in sickness and death rates between African Americans and whites are not biological, not natural, and not genetic. A study of the management of appendicitis revealed that, compared to Caucasian children in the United States, African American children have a much lower rate of hospitalization, higher rates of perforation of the appendix, higher rates of invasive surgery, and longer delays in surgical management of the condition (Kokoska et al., 2007).

Disparities in treatment between members of indigenous groups and nonindigenous persons may be a result of clinical services not being set up to serve indigenous communities. Such services may be located far away from where indigenous populations live, and they may function to remove people from their environment and isolate them in hospitals. For example, Australian Aboriginals have a mortality rate up to five times that of their non-Aboriginal counterparts, related to heart disease, diabetes, and tuberculosis. Indigenous Australian women are 10 times more likely to die from cervical cancer than are nonindigenous women, and it is the number one cause of cancer deaths among indigenous women despite the fact that it is one of the most easily preventable forms of cancer. Low participation of indigenous women in cervical screening (Pap smear) programs because of lack of access to services is a particular problem (Coory et al., 2002).

Native American populations in the United States are disadvantaged in terms of both mental and physical health, even when factors such as location in rural areas are accounted for (Baldwin et al., 2002; Gone, 2007). Maternal and infant health is a key area in which Native American populations fall behind. Power relationships between dominant and subordinate groups based on class, gender, and race and ethnicity determine the health and sickness of people, rather than facts of nature or biology. Group differences in health reflect inequalities in societies.

Jupiterimages/Getty Images

▶ A young black woman is rejected by teenage girls sitting in a limo. Do you see this kind of informal segregation of people anywhere in your everyday life?

▶ **THINK ABOUT IT**

1. Can you see ways in which your own ethnicity has impacts on your health?

2. Is the ethnic patterning of disease the outcome of a racist society?

3. If you were asked to advise your congressional representative about strategies to improve the health of ethnic minorities, what would you suggest?

working classes are often exposed to harmful chemicals or dangerous machinery or practices. Every 10th lung cancer death is related to workplace risks (World Health Organization, 2011). Moreover, cancer is one of the leading causes of work-related deaths in the United States, contributing to a much higher proportion of fatalities than workplace accidents or injuries (Hämäläinen, Takala, & Saarela, 2007). The stress of working conditions that combine low autonomy and high workloads in unsupportive environments causes up to 35% of cardiovascular mortality in the United States (Kuper et al., 2002).

In 2015, there were 4,836 fatal occupational injuries in the United States. Of these, most occurred in working-class industries and working-class occupations (see Table 13.1). In contrast, there are very few dangers in a typical office environment. It is increasingly recognized that the health of the individual worker does not necessarily have to be physically at risk for the impact of

Valentin Sprinchak/TASS/Getty Images

▶ A miner works inside a coal mine in eastern Ukraine. Coal mining is one of the most dangerous jobs in the world. Not only is there a constant risk of cave-ins, but there is also the danger of coal workers' pneumoconiosis, or black lung disease, which is caused by long-term exposure to coal dust. What other occupations are hazardous to workers' health?

TABLE 13.1 Fatal Occupational Injuries in the United States by Occupation and Industry, 2015

Occupation	
Management	379
Protective service	213
Sales and related	228
Farming, fishing, and forestry	284
Construction and extraction	924
Installation, maintenance, and repair	392
Transportation and material moving	1,301
Military	73
Industry	
Goods producing	2,035
Natural resources and mining	697
Agriculture, forestry, fishing, and hunting	577
Construction	985
Manufacturing	353
Service providing	2,801
Wholesale trade	175
Retail trade	269
Transportation and warehousing	799
Professional and business services	491
Leisure and hospitality	233
Government	270

SOURCE: Table modified from Bureau of Labor Statistics, 2016.

capitalist employment practices to make themselves felt. Lack of autonomy at work, lack of control over the production process, and separation from fellow workers—the key components to Marx's account of alienation—are all causes of disease (Benach & Muntaner, 2007).

THE U.S. HEALTH CARE SYSTEM AND ITS STAKEHOLDERS

13.3 Describe the health care system and its stakeholders.

The ways in which people seek health care, its provision, and its funding are all factors that heavily influence access to services and therefore quality and standards of health. While government policy may be the most important mediating factor in the U.S. health care system, many stakeholders influence the way the general population experiences health and illness. Next we look at government policy in the form of the Patient Protection and Affordable Care Act, widely known as Obamacare, and then at stakeholders, including private health insurers, pharmaceutical companies, members of the medical profession, and alternative practitioners.

The Government: Obamacare

The U.S. health care system stands in contrast to many others in the Western world. Health care in welfare states such as Australia, New Zealand, and the United Kingdom has traditionally been provided by the government. From a sociological perspective, these systems have been extremely beneficial. The government is responsible for the provision of health care, and taxpayers' money (with the wealthiest paying the greater portion) goes directly to benefit those in lower socioeconomic groups in the most necessary and fundamental of ways. This model is directly in line with the traditional conception of the state as the means of providing minimum standards of living for all its citizens (White, 2009, Chapter 4).

The United States, on the other hand, has operated under a neoliberal system of governance since its inception, with a health care sector that is a mix of private

Health Beyond Our Borders

Health in Russia and Greece After Political and Financial Crises

Life expectancy in Russia declined significantly after the collapse of the Soviet Union in the early 1990s and the major economic collapse in 1998. Between 1987 and 1994, life expectancy of Russian adult males fell by 7.4 years, to 57.5. Female life expectancy followed a similar path, falling by 2.6 years between 1989 and 1994. These significant declines were mainly due to mortality from preventable factors such as cardiovascular disease, alcohol abuse, and traffic accidents (Levintova & Novotny, 2004).

Greece provides a startling example of what may happen when a government severs health care funding. Following the global financial crisis that began in 2007, the government of Greece attempted to restore the country's faltering economy by adopting austerity measures that have proven extremely controversial. These cost-cutting efforts have had serious social and health effects on the country's population. The Ministry of Health was

downsized by 24%, so health services were cut and many once-free services are no longer available. Unemployment more than tripled, from 7.2% in 2008 to 23% in 2016.

Cuts in publicly funded health services coupled with the huge loss of employment had drastic consequences for the people's health (Kondilis et al., 2013). Between 2007 and 2009 suicide rates rose by 16%, and the murder rate climbed almost 26%, with men overrepresented as victims in both cases. Deaths from infectious diseases increased by 13%, outbreaks of malaria and West Nile virus occurred, and rates of HIV infection grew. In response to these problems, Greece in 2016 began a large-scale health sector reform to

REUTERS/Yannis Behrakis

▶ Prosthetics placed by people with disabilities are seen in front of the Greek parliament during a protest against new austerity measures in Athens. In 2013, Greek doctors and nurses saw their paychecks reduced by nearly a third, and the country experienced serious shortages of drugs and medical supplies. Some effects of austerity included increases in heart disease, suicide, and HIV infection. Cuts in health care have major and long-lasting effects.

improve health, with support from the World Health Organization (WHO, 2016).

▶ **THINK ABOUT IT:** Have you lived in a community that was affected by sudden economic change (such as the closing of a major industry)? Can you think of any impact that change may have had on the health and well-being of community members?

and government interests. As of 2013, 47% of people had employment-based private insurance, 7% had individual private insurance, 33% had government-financed insurance (such as Medicare for elderly people or Medicaid for low-income people), and 13% remained uninsured (Bodenheimer & Grumbach, 2016).

Whereas many countries that traditionally have operated under welfare state capitalism are now shifting toward privatization of their health care industries (a change many scholars find extremely concerning), in 2010, the U.S. government took a broad step in the other direction. The Patient Protection and Affordable Care Act (ACA) of 2010, upheld by the U.S. Supreme Court in 2012, supplements to increase U.S. citizens' access to health insurance and thus appropriate health care. Before the passage of this law, 44 million people in the United States did not have any form of health insurance (ObamaCare Facts, 2013). The new law stipulates that all U.S. citizens are to have health insurance by 2014 or pay a penalty.

Under Obamacare, all of these means of obtaining health insurance have expanded to encompass more people. Companies with 50 or more employees are required to provide health insurance to their employees, for instance. Tax breaks and other incentives encourage smaller businesses to provide insurance to their employees. Medicare has not changed, but Medicaid's low-income threshold has been lowered in some states, to cover more people. Those who do not have coverage can shop for insurance through so-called health insurance marketplaces that make private plans comparable and accessible. Many people buying insurance through these marketplaces qualify for tax credits to subsidize their monthly insurance premiums. Furthermore, young people are now able to stay on their parents' insurance plans until they are 26 years old.

This legislation changed the regulation of insurance companies, which now must insure everyone, including those who have preexisting conditions. These sweeping reforms have met with enormous and highly organized

▶ The U.S. House Rules Committee meets to shape the final version of the Republican health care bill before it goes to the floor for debate and a vote, at the U.S. Capitol in Washington, D.C. This was the Republicans' effort to repeal and replace the Patient Protection and Affordable Care Act (Obamacare).

complex are corporate ownership of hospitals and the interlocking ownership and production of health care. Many governments have pursued privatization policies, believing that private enterprise is more efficient and effective and enables greater choice. Essentially, community family doctors have been replaced by larger clinics, and more hospitals have been privatized.

This worldwide trend toward privatization troubles sociologists and other academics. Company directors and managers have a duty to exercise their powers in the best interests of their companies on behalf of their shareholders' financial interests. In contrast, governments' interest in health care is to promote the public good. Thus the goals of public and private enterprise are at odds in the context of health care.

opposition from big business, the health insurance industry, and political parties representing wealthy citizens. All these groups are to be taxed more to fund the new insurance system.

Congress and the president of the United States in 2017 have pledged to revise Obamacare substantially. Proposals include a total repeal of the law, giving individuals with Medicare vouchers to buy private insurance, eliminating the expansion of Medicaid that covered 11 million new people, and turning the Medicaid program into a block grant (which allows the federal government to give states blocks of money to use as they determine).

The Medical-Industrial Complex

In the 1970s and 1980s, the private sector purchased many independent hospitals and health services, and chains of related services were forged together under large corporate structures (Relman, 1980). Relman called this a transition from "cottage industry" health care to a vertically and horizontally integrated "medical-industrial complex." Horizontal integration yielded broad market share, while vertical integration enabled providers to funnel consumers through health networks, referring patients to affiliated specialists, radiologists, pathologists, and hospitals.

The medical-industrial complex is a large and growing network of private corporations engaged in the business of supplying health care services to patients for profit—services that used to be provided by government, nonprofit institutions, or individual practitioners. At the base of this

Pharmaceutical Companies

Pharmaceutical companies are among the largest companies in the world. One commentator has described the U.S. pharmaceutical industry, sometimes referred to as "Big Pharma," as the "$200 billion colossus" (Angell, 2005), estimating that expenditures on prescription medicines account for approximately 15% of the U.S. gross national product. Pharmaceutical companies are not only major players in the health care system; they also make up a significant proportion of many Western economies.

Ironically, because they are private companies seeking to further their profits, pharmaceutical companies actually benefit from a sicker society. The more sick people in the community, the more demand for pharmaceuticals, driving up their market price and profitability. Sometimes, demand increases competition as new companies enter the market and drive down prices. However, the research, development, and clinical trial phases required to bring a new pharmaceutical to market incur massive costs, estimated to range between $92 million and $884 million, with an estimated clinical success rate of under 11% (Morgan et al., 2011). The cost of producing a new drug effectively discourages new market entrants and thus reduces competition in the sector.

Have you ever watched a television commercial for a fast-food chain and suddenly felt hungry? Drug advertising does exactly the same thing, which explains why U.S. pharmaceutical companies are now such heavy advertisers. Pharmaceutical

▶ Generic drugs have exactly the same pharmacological effect as their brand-name counterparts. The U.S. Food and Drug Administration requires that generic drugs be as safe and effective as brand-name drugs. Many people still prefer brand-name drugs even though generic drugs cost 80–85% less. How much of this do you think is due to pharmaceutical advertising?

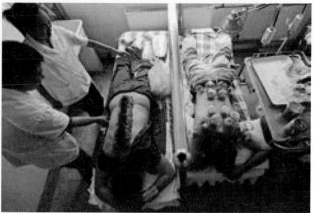

▶ A patient (table on left) receives acupuncture treatment with mashed garlic, herbs, and ignited dry moxa leaves placed on the back to treat rheumatism as another patient receives cupping treatment at a hospital in Hefei, China. In the United States, alternative forms of medicine are not typically covered by health insurance, yet many Americans spend billions of dollars every year on treatments such as yoga, acupuncture, aromatherapy, herbalism, hypnotherapy, osteopathy, and reflexology. Why do you think that is the case?

companies spent over $3 billion on advertising to consumers in 2012 (Pew Charitable Trusts, 2013). Advertising prescription drugs directly to consumers has many implications for the sociology of health. It increases the market base by raising awareness of health issues and encouraging people to consult their doctors if they are experiencing the symptoms noted in the ads. However, critics argue that such advertising misinforms patients, overemphasizes drug benefits, manufactures disease, and encourages the overutilization of drugs, leading to inappropriate prescribing and wasting appointment time (Ventola, 2011). Most countries have recognized the problems associated with direct-to-consumer pharmaceutical advertising. New Zealand and the United States are the only two member countries of the Organisation for Economic Co-operation and Development that allow pharmaceutical companies to advertise directly to consumers (Ventola, 2011).

Pharmaceutical advertising to consumers is another form of *medicalization*, the definition and treatment of social issues as medical problems. Two major "illnesses" have been identified as heavily medicalized by the pharmaceutical industry: erectile dysfunction (Conrad, 2007) and menopause (Hunter, 2007). As discussed above, menopause is a natural phase in a woman's life; it is not a medical condition requiring treatment. With respect to erectile dysfunction, 10% of U.S. men are unable to achieve an erection (Feldman et al., 2000), and pharmaceutical advertising is said to target men experiencing what are merely normal variations in sexual performance (Shaw, 2008). Pharmaceutical advertising can change our social perceptions of what it is to be healthy and what is normal behavior or bodily function. Medical

professionals are people and are not immune to such societal shifts in norms. They are therefore also more likely to diagnose and prescribe pharmaceuticals in circumstances that may not warrant such action.

ASK YOURSELF: Have you ever diagnosed yourself after watching a pharmaceutical advertisement? Do you think pharmaceutical advertising is shifting social conceptions of what it is to be healthy and what behaviors or bodily functions are normal or deemed illnesses? Do you think direct-to-consumer pharmaceutical advertising should be banned?

Alternative Practitioners

The most widely known therapies not supported by orthodox medicine are homeopathy, chiropractic, osteopathy, acupuncture, and herbalism. Paradoxically, "alternative" medicine shares many of the characteristics of orthodox medicine: focusing on the individual rather than on social factors as the source of disease and increasingly depending on a wide range of preparations marketed by multinational drug companies (Barnes, Bloom, & Nahin, 2008). Alternative practitioners treat conditions that orthodox medicine finds hard to deal with, such as chronic back pain. They also provide treatments for contested conditions—that is, those the medical profession does not consider diseases, such as chronic fatigue syndrome. Most people who use alternative practitioners do so in combination with orthodox practices (Barnes et al., 2008).

Patients and Patient Groups

Although they are the least powerful members of the health care system, patients do most of the health care work. Experiencing biological symptoms does not automatically trigger a visit to the doctor, and up to one-third of the population will ignore symptoms, self-medicate, or consult friends and family about the meaning of the experience. Folk health knowledge still plays a powerful role in modern societies. We could say that medicine deals with disease, whereas individuals construct the meanings their symptoms have for them. It is this lay culture that organizes the ways in which individuals perceive their symptoms, and whether or not they will consult medical professionals.

Most patient groups take the form of self-help groups, in which people with similar conditions come together voluntarily to share knowledge and support one another. Support groups have been found particularly valuable at the psychosocial level for those suffering from chronic illnesses, but participation in such groups may also lead to *illness identity dependency*, in which individuals identify themselves as their disease even after successful treatment—for example, "I am a cancer patient" (Corbin, 2003).

USING THEORY TO UNDERSTAND HEALTH: THE VIEWS FROM THE FUNCTIONALIST, CONFLICT, AND SYMBOLIC INTERACTIONIST PERSPECTIVES

 13.4 Apply the functionalist, conflict, and symbolic interactionist perspectives to the concept of health.

We've seen that health is not merely an individual and biological function. It is affected significantly by social factors such as race, gender, socioeconomic status, and the various influences of stakeholders. In this section we consider three of the major theoretical frameworks through which sociologists perceive issues of health and illness. We will also examine the policy implications we can derive from considering health and illness through each of these theoretical lenses.

Functionalism

The structural functionalist perspective sees society as a harmonious, balanced set of interacting institutions, like a living organism with interrelated parts. Each institution (structure) serves a particular set of social needs (functions) to ensure a stable society. For example, the religious, educational, and medical institutions of our society all interact to socialize, train, and repair individuals to ensure their smooth integration into society.

Talcott Parsons (1951), the major theorist of this position, identified a shared set of expectations between the patient and the doctor. The doctor is a highly skilled professional who applies scientific knowledge to the patient's trouble. The patient seeks out the doctor and complies with the doctor's directives so as to get better. For Parsons, illness is not just a physiological issue; it is a deviant behavior. People adopt "the sick role" as a way of avoiding social responsibilities (Parsons, 1951, p. 43). At the crux of Parsons's argument are the four dimensions of the sick role:

1. A sick person is excused from undertaking normal social obligations.

2. Deviant behavior through illness is viewed as being caused by nature, and thus the sick person's neglect of social obligations is not considered a personal fault or an intentional act of deviance.

3. The sick role is legitimated by the person's being socially required to seek treatment for the illness.

4. The sick person must comply with practitioners' instructions and follow general social norms, like resting or taking medication, to get better as soon as possible, thereby exiting the sick role.

Thus Parsons argued that the sick role is a means for a person to escape arduous social responsibilities by adopting a role with different and less demanding social obligations. However, as discussed above, society often attributes illness to individuals' actions and behaviors. Alan is held accountable for suffering emphysema because he chose to smoke. Julie is responsible for her diabetes because she failed to eat well or exercise regularly. This shift in social conceptions of illness raises questions about whether Parsons's sick role is a valid social framework from which to consider questions of health and illness today.

Furthermore, Parsons's conception of society as a cohesive, effectively functioning set of structures is also questionable. After attaining dominance in the 20th and 21st centuries, the medical profession has recently undergone significant challenges to its authority, including technological developments, the growth of an increasingly educated public, direct-to-consumer advertising of drugs, use of the Internet, and the rise of corporate medicine (see Table 13.2). These challenges demonstrate the transformation of medicine from what some considered an altruistic profession into a business model that pursues profit.

Whereas medicine once undertook the responsibility for health alone, now it must share it with a wide range of other practitioners, financially and institutionally. This forced sharing has decreased the status of the medical profession and the public's trust in it. For example, the medical information available on the Internet allows patients to challenge medical diagnoses (Dent, 2006), hand in hand with the rise of the knowledgeable patient (Broom, 2005). These developments have had profound effects on the doctor-patient relationship. The ability to access information (and misinformation) online can provide patients with a sense of knowledge and empowerment (Korp, 2006), which they bring to the medical encounter. Some studies have found that medical professionals see better-informed patients as challenges to their power, leading them to develop strategies to reinforce traditional patient roles (Broom, 2005). Patients are affected by the increasing fragmentation of the medical profession: Patients now seek medical advice from a number of different specialists, rather than relying on a single practitioner for all their health care needs (Martin, Currie, & Finn, 2009). "Doctor shopping" is a more common practice, as patients seek medical practitioners who will diagnose them with the conditions they think they have.

Policy Implications of Structural Functionalism

At the heart of Parsons's structural functionalism is interpersonal trust, particularly patients' trust in their health care providers. Parsons argued that *value congruence*, or shared norms and values, is a key component of trust (Kehoe & Ponting, 2003, p. 1066). Trust in the reliability, effectiveness, and legitimacy of "symbolic structures"—such as white coats and stethoscopes— is essential (Parsons, 1968, p. 155). With respect to health this means that for hospitals, primary care physicians, specialists, and nurses to function effectively, patients must trust in the ability of these structures to improve their health.

Kehoe and Ponting (2003) investigated the trust Canadians place in their health care providers, government departments, and legislative reform in the area of health. They found that Canadians are very proud of their public health care system and trust their medical and allied health workers. However, their trust in the bureaucracy is breached when hospitals are closed or there are changes to the public health system—Medicare—which "is a source of pride and part of Canadians' national identity" (p. 1074). When trust in the health care system is lost, the system also loses the legitimacy that, according to structural functionalists, is critical to its operation and effectiveness.

This analysis raises interesting questions for recent health care reforms in the United States. We might interpret the debate over Obamacare as critically affecting

Ian McVea/Fort Worth Star-Telegram/ Getty Images

▶ According to Talcott Parsons, medical practice involves reciprocity in the doctor-patient relationship. What kind of relationship do you have with your doctor? Do you have complete confidence and trust in his or her abilities?

TABLE 13.2 Six Current Challenges to the Medical Profession

Trend	Result
Bureaucratization of medical practice	Doctors have become employees of large health care firms and have lost some of their autonomy.
Competitive threat from other health care workers	There has been a large increase in the number of allied and alternative health professionals, who compete with the medical profession.
Globalization and the information revolution	Consumers are better informed, and via "medical tourism" patients travel to other countries for cheaper treatments.
Changing patterns of disease	Many conditions are now chronic, such as type 2 diabetes. The lack of effective medical treatment has taken the shine off the "magic bullet" medicine of the mid-20th century.
Erosion of trust in the doctor-patient relationship	Patients are now much more likely to seek legal redress against their doctors.
Fragmentation of medical specialties	The once-unified medical profession is now divided into specialists and generalists with their own representative bodies.

SOURCE: Developed from McKinlay and Marceau (2002) 'The End of the Golden Age of Doctoring' *International Journal of Health Services* 32(2): 379–416.

U.S. citizens' trust that the government can manage health care. The legislation may also reestablish those same people's trust in the legitimacy of the government as an institution that ensures minimum standards of health for all, or may be interpreted as government imposing its own values on individuals.

The policy implications from a structural functionalist perspective are paradoxical. On the one hand, it would seem that to solve the social problems of the health care system we need more doctors, hospitals, technology, and drugs. In short, structural functionalism says there is nothing wrong with the health care system that more of what we already have won't fix. On the other hand, noneconomic relationships based on trust are central to the smooth working of market economies—and these are undermined by the for-profit, high-tech, corporate form U.S. medicine has developed.

Conflict Theory

From a conflict perspective, medicine in advanced capitalist societies is oriented toward curing disease through the application of sophisticated drugs and the use of high-cost technology. There are two major conflicts:

1. Those who suffer the most illness in modern Western societies are those who can least afford high-cost treatments and sophisticated drugs.

2. The development of costly treatments and pharmaceuticals is not the most effective way to improve health outcomes for the general population.

In the developed world today, the leading causes of mortality and of **morbidity** are heart disease, stroke, various cancers, mental and nervous disorders, and chronic respiratory diseases, which conflict theorists see as the result not of internally caused bodily processes but of social conditions. These illnesses are not open to cure by intensive care or the use of drugs (Miniño et al., 2010).

REUTERS/Jim Bourg

▶ A cancer patient lies inside the tube of a magnetic resonance imaging scanner during an MRI examination of her breasts at Georgetown University Hospital in Washington, D.C. Many cancer patients spend a great deal of time undergoing medical examinations and treatments.

ASK YOURSELF: Do you think the billions of dollars spent on developing pharmaceuticals and diagnostic treatments would be better spent on reducing environmental hazards, not only in developing countries but also in developed ones like the United States?

If medical and scientific advances are relatively ineffective at improving health compared to social reforms, why then do societies and the medical profession push forward with expensive new medical treatments, sustaining life at any cost and neglecting the social problems that cause disease and illness in the first place?

Conflict theorists explain that the U.S. health care system is a central part of the capitalist economy that functions to produce profit (Waitzkin, 2000). Some theorists take this further, arguing that scientific medicine equates healing with consumption. Illness and disease create a market for medicine and treatment, and therefore health care is a business. The demand for health care legitimates and facilitates capitalist economic growth, despite its negative health consequences. From this perspective, the health care industry has four interrelated economic functions in capitalist society (see Figure 13.4): accumulation of capital, provision of investment opportunities, absorption of surplus labor, and maintenance of the labor force (Waitzkin, 2000).

In addition, the organization of health care provides three important ideological functions (Waitzkin, 2000):

1. By delivering health care, however inadequately, it legitimates the status quo, acting as an agent of social control by reducing what are basically social problems to an individual level.

2. When "health care" means the consumption of health care and drugs, it reproduces the capitalist mode of production.

3. It reproduces the capitalist class structure both in the organization of health workers and by rationing care on the ability to pay for it.

According to the conflict perspective, U.S. society sees health as an individual problem, to be met with individual solutions such as medication, behavioral change, and technology-based therapies. This way of looking at health and illness serves the interests of powerful groups within society, such as pharmaceutical corporations (which sell medication) and employers (who may place workers' health

Morbidity: The number of diagnoses of disease or other conditions in a given population at a designated time, usually expressed as a rate per 100,000.

FIGURE 13.4 Economic Functions of the
U.S. Health Care System

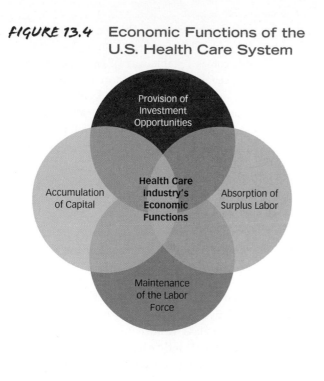

in jeopardy through hazardous conditions). The conflict perspective highlights the role of wider social structure in causing illness; it is not the individual who is ill but the structure of society that causes illness and frames healing.

Policy Implications of the Conflict Perspective

From a conflict theory perspective, the contemporary capitalist organization of health care systematically neglects the environmental, occupational, and social production of health and disease. Hence the source of sickness and disease is the capitalist economic system itself, and only with its transformation will health be transformed. Change will not occur while for-profit health care and pharmaceutical companies dominate the health care system. The United States will continue to have the world's most expensive health care system, unequal access to health care, and some of the poorest health outcomes in the developed world.

For more moderate conflict theorists, it is clear that capitalism will not be displaced any time in the near future. While Marx argued that capitalism would eventually self-destruct as worsening working conditions and wages left the working class unable to buy the products and services the ruling class was selling, he did not foresee that workers would unite to demand better treatment through unions. Although unions have been in decline for some years, Western capitalists have seen that it is far cheaper to provide safe working environments than to lose productivity and pay compensation when employees are injured and cannot work.

Symbolic Interactionism

The key to the symbolic interactionist perspective is that people construct meaning from situations and objects. Situations that we define as real have real consequences (Thomas & Thomas, 1928). Thus human beings are not stimulus-response mechanisms: The way we define a situation defines the way we will act in it. What bearing does this perspective have on the way we understand health?

The Western model of health predicts that drugs should have a straightforward biochemical effect and cure the conditions at which they are targeted. Theoretically, they should work the same way for everyone. However, sociologists have shown that this is not the case (Moerman & Jonas, 2002). When a new drug is tested, the experimental group is given the drug, a control group is given a placebo (a sugar pill that is chemically inert), and a third group is given nothing. A double-blind trial is conducted in which neither the patients nor the doctors know who is getting which substance. In a study of the placebo effect in Parkinson's disease patients, the placebo was found to have a very powerful positive effect on patients' symptoms (de la Fuente-Fernández et al., 2001). This placebo effect cannot be explained by Western medicine, which separates the mind from the body (Moerman & Jonas, 2002). For sociologists, however, such findings provide evidence that the way we define a situation affects what happens. In other words, if you think you've received a drug, your body may respond as if you had received it.

Policy Implications of Symbolic Interactionism

Symbolic interactionism can help us look at how policy issues are framed. For instance, the placebo effect seems particularly profound for people being treated with antidepressants. Most commentators now agree that the difference between an antidepressant drug and a placebo is insignificant, and 57% of trials funded by pharmaceutical companies have failed to demonstrate that antidepressant drugs had an impact, a finding that came to light only when Kirsch, Scoboria, and Moore (2002) gained access to U.S. Food and Drug Administration documents. They refer to these data as a "dirty little secret"— well known within the pharmaceutical industry but not to the general public, doctors, or their patients.

Kirsch (2009) went on to analyze 38 published clinical trials that enrolled more than 3,000 depressed patients. He found that 75% of the antidepressant effect of drugs was also produced by placebos. "Placebos instill hope in patients by promising them relief from their distress," Kirsch wrote in his book *The Emperor's New Drugs*. "Genuine medical treatments also instill hope, and this is the placebo component of their effectiveness" (p. 3). The clear policy implication is that a very large number of prescriptions for costly antidepressants are not needed and that costs to consumers could be reduced significantly.

SPECIALIZED THEORIES

13.5 Apply specialized theories of health.

Bourdieu and Physical, Social, and Cultural Capital

Pierre Bourdieu (1984) developed an innovative theory of the relationship of the body to class position in society. He saw health as socially patterned and reflected in the individual's body. Health is a source of capital we can use to gain valued social goods—jobs, education, and social status. Bourdieu's position thus complements Marx's belief that social class as determined by the economy is central to modern societies, but he also argued that other forms of capital exist, which he labeled *cultural, social,* and *symbolic.* Possessing these forms of capital allows individuals to position themselves in society.

The healthy body, Bourdieu argued, represents a form of physical as well as symbolic capital. The well-maintained, the fit, and the not-overweight body represents claims to being a member of society in good social standing. Bourdieu argued that the body is inscribed with social and cultural relationships—that is, it is socially produced and not just a fact of nature. We internalize our positions in the social hierarchy of society, learning the appropriate ways of dressing our bodies and presenting them, ways of standing

and sitting and even of walking. This set of learned practices, which Bourdieu (1990) called "habitus," is culturally provided and becomes a stable way of enacting ourselves in the social world. Our bodies then form our physical capital, alongside our economic, social, and cultural capital, and "the way people treat their bodies reveals the deepest dispositions of their habitus" (Bourdieu, 1984, p. 190).

One way of illustrating Bourdieu's argument is to look at patterns of eating in different classes in our society. Affluent individuals are likely to enjoy higher-quality diets, whereas individuals of lower socioeconomic status consume diets that are nutrient-poor (Darmon & Drewnowski, 2008). This leads to a downward social distribution of obesity, with higher obesity rates among poorer people. Using a Bourdieuian approach, seeing the body as socially produced and a cultural marker of social standing, Calnan and Cant (1990) have shown that food consumption is an underlying factor in this distribution of obesity. Middle-class women in their study emphasized a "balanced diet" and "everything in moderation," whereas working-class women stressed that a meal should be "substantial" and "filling," though not necessarily nutrient-rich. While we may think of obesity as linked to individual diets, Calnan and Cant's work demonstrates that there are class-specific ways of relating to food. Let us look at this insight a bit further.

The interplay of physical, social, cultural, and economic capital is relevant to childhood obesity. Among lower-class children, the tendency to obesity is facilitated by environments that reinforce unhealthy eating and low physical activity and that are served by fast-food outlets and poorly maintained recreational facilities (Cohen, Doyle, & Baum, 2006). Consequences include respiratory disorders, type 2 diabetes, depression, and social exclusion (Storch et al., 2007). In adulthood these individuals are then at greater risk of obesity (Freedman et al., 2005), diabetes, and cancer (Ogden et al., 2010). Thus the working-class habitus and its resulting body create a circular effect of increasing disease in childhood leading into adulthood, thus producing reduction in life expectancies.

▶ Many poorer communities have been described as "food deserts," where affordable healthy food is not available. They may have corner stores and fast-food restaurants, but no supermarkets. Constant consumption of nutrient-poor foods can lead to heart disease, obesity, and diabetes.

Social Capital Theory

Émile Durkheim argued in his book *The Division of Labor in Society,* originally published in 1893, that social harmony would come about in industrial society through the formation of communities based on shared occupational interests, producing a new moral individual whose actions would be guided by a concern for the common good. Contemporary social capital theorists argue that increased population concentration and improved communication will revitalize the idea of the common good and alleviate social conflict. In communities where there is strong social capital—neighborhood organizations, social clubs, strong sports groups, and a sense of belonging—there are also better health rates (Poortinga, 2006). When communities do not generate social capital, theorists see this failure as the fault of community dysfunction.

What their approach overlooks is that economic resources and political rights are also necessary parts of a strong sense of community. Arguing that those at lower socioeconomic levels suffer poor health because they do not generate social capital suggests they are responsible for their own shortcomings and should solve them on their own. The social capital approach thus appeals to conservative, post–welfare state governments, which see it as a way of shifting responsibility for what used to be state-provided services to the local level.

Fundamental Cause Theory

Bruce Link and Jo Phelan have proposed a theory that emphasizes basic social conditions as a source of health inequalities, rather than individually based risk factors. This theory focuses on social factors such as socioeconomic status and social support that are "fundamental causes of disease," affecting multiple diseases through multiple mechanisms (Link & Phelan, 1995). Socioeconomic status is associated with resources including money, knowledge, power, and social connections that can protect individuals' health, regardless of the specific disease. In more recent work, they note that medical advances may not benefit all groups, and emphasize using policies to weaken the link between having socioeconomic resources and gaining access to health care treatments (Phelan, Link, & Tehranifar, 2010).

SOCIAL CHANGE: WHAT CAN YOU DO?

 Identify steps toward social change to promote health.

If most of what affects our health is a product of our social environment, it follows that changing our health means changing our social environment. Most proposals for improving health focus on individual-level solutions, such as eating better and exercising more. Yet individuals often do not have complete control over their environments. Here are some ways in which you can create social changes, starting right now:

- *Change the menu.* Lobby for a better diet at your workplace or campus. Ask for and eat unprocessed foods—such as fresh fruits and vegetables, brown rice, and whole-grain breads—and low-sugar, low-sodium options.

- *Improve access to water.* Get your workplace or campus to install a water fountain that allows users to refill their own bottles with filtered water.

- *Reduce the number of smokers.* Start a self-help group to support people who want to quit smoking. You don't have to be a smoker to help others kick the habit. Help ensure that no-smoking rules on campus are honored. Find resources at the National Cancer Institute's Smokefree website (http://www.smokefree.gov).

- *Promote occupational health and safety.* Young workers represent about 13% of the U.S. workforce and have relatively high rates of occupational injury. Visit the National Institute for Occupational Safety and Health's website (http://www.cdc.gov/niosh). Know the hazards and dangers present in your workplace, educate your peers, and ensure that your workplace is operating in a health- and safety-conscious manner.

- *Contribute to a culture of health.* The Robert Wood Johnson Foundation is promoting community-level ideas for creating cultures of health. Check out its blog for more ideas about how you could improve the health opportunities for your entire community (http://www.rwjf.org/en/culture-of-health.html).

Jaap Arriens/NurPhoto/Getty Images

▶ Over 100 mostly female participants showed up at a park in Poland for physical training exercises. For an hour participants did aerobic and body weight exercises under the guidance of personal trainers with music provided by a DJ. Are there places in your community where people can exercise and enjoy the outdoors?

WHAT DOES AMERICA THINK?

Questions About Health From the General Social Survey

▶▶ Turn to the beginning of the chapter to compare your answers to those of the total population.

1. Do you think that the government should help pay for medical care?

   YES: 72%
   NO: 28%

2. In the United States, do you think we're spending too much money on improving and protecting the nation's health, too little money, or about the right amount?

   TOO MUCH: 9.8%
   TOO LITTLE: 65.1%
   ABOUT THE RIGHT AMOUNT: 25.1%

3. What is your confidence level in medicine?

   A GREAT DEAL: 35.7%
   ONLY SOME: 49.9%
   HARDLY ANY: 14.4%

SOURCE: National Opinion Research Center, University of Chicago.

4. What is your interest level in medical discoveries?

   VERY INTERESTED: 59.5%
   MODERATELY INTERESTED: 35.6%
   NOT AT ALL INTERESTED: 4.9%

5. Do you think that incurable patients should be allowed to die?

   YES: 73.7%
   NO: 26.3%

6. Do you think a person has the right to end his or her own life if this person has an incurable disease?

   YES: 65.5%
   NO: 34.5%

CHAPTER SUMMARY

 13.1 Describe health, disease, and illness as socially defined.

Illness and disease are socially constructed notions. Medicine is pervasive in society and acts as a form of social control in our lives. Much social behavior has been medicalized. Sociologists look to social factors to explain illness and disease.

 13.2 Discuss patterns and trends in health, illness, and treatment.

Demographic and economic factors shape lifestyle choices that cause disease. Social inequality determines the distribution of health and illness. Who gets sick, when we die, and what we die of are linked closely to wider patterns of inequalities of power and other resources. Men's health is threatened by engagement in risky activities and unsafe work conditions, while women's health is managed heavily by the medical system, not always to their benefit.

 13.3 Describe the health care system and its stakeholders.

Unlike many wealthy countries where government has traditionally provided health care, the United States' health care system is a mix of public and private sector efforts. The medical-industrial complex is a large and growing network of private corporations that provide health care services to patients for profit. Pharmaceutical companies are for-profit enterprises that advertise prescription drugs directly to consumers. Practitioners of alternative medicine and patient groups provide health care outside traditional medicine.

 13.4 Apply the functionalist, conflict, and symbolic interactionist perspectives to the concept of health.

Functionalists believe that in order for healthcare professionals to deliver health care effectively, patients must have trust in their ability and must adopt a "sick role," which excuses them from normal social obligations. Conflict theorists see the U.S. health care system, particularly the pharmaceutical industry, as having as its main goal not the delivery of health care but the generation of profit. According to the symbolic interactionist perspective, the meanings that patients give to particular drugs will largely determine their effectiveness.

 13.5 Apply specialized theories of health.

According to Bourdieu's notion of physical capital, maintaining a healthy body is symbolic of good social standing. Communities high in social capital have higher rates of health among their populations. Social capital theorists argue that concentration and communication alleviate social conflict. In communities with strong social capital, members generally experience better health. Fundamental cause theory focuses on the idea that socioeconomic status and levels of social support are essential to understanding disease.

13.6 Identify steps toward social change to promote health.

Take action to ensure a healthy diet in your workplace and community. Be informed about the hazards and dangers present in your workplace. Promote community-level improvements in health opportunities.

KEY TERMS

morbidity 334

social control 319

social gradient of health 324

status groups 323

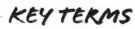

THE ENVIRONMENT

Katharine A. Legun and Michael M. Bell

A Los Angeles County Fire Department helicopter flies over a wildfire in Castaic, California. How is an environmental problem like a wildfire also a social problem?

Investigating the Environment: Our Stories

LEARNING OBJECTIVES

14.1 Explain how environmental problems are social problems.

14.2 Discuss patterns and trends in environmental issues.

14.3 Apply the functionalist, conflict, and symbolic interactionist perspectives to environmental problems and policy.

14.4 Apply specialized theories to the environment.

14.5 Identify steps toward social change concerning the environment.

Katharine A. Legun

I was born in a resource town in Northern Canada, where my family lived in a house in the woods beside a large lake. I remember running through the woods with my brother, emerging hours later in some neighbor's backyard. We would walk out onto the frozen lake in the winter while my mother and her friends would fly kites. At dinnertime, I would overhear conversations about too many trees being cleared on the neighbor's land, oil discovered nearby, or too many sheep being attacked by bears on our friend's farm.

We moved to the city. We still shared green spaces with neighbors, talked about the removal or placement of trees, and watched the salmon runs at the provincial park. Years later, when I took a course on the sociology of natural resources as an undergraduate, conversations about access to environmental goods and community development resonated heavily. Who would I be had my access been different?

As I learned more about changes to the environment and the governance of these resources, my interests only expanded. Whenever I move, the landscape changes, but the question in my mind stays the same: How do we make sure that access to resources is fair and fosters good relationships, while also making sure that those resources are healthy for future generations? I don't think I will ever have a definitive answer, but I'm amazed at the vibrant, heartfelt conversations that follow when I ask the question.

Michael M. Bell

When I was 19 years old, I found myself looking over a lake high in the Talamanca Mountains of Costa Rica, accompanied by two men who had impressed me deeply: Emanuel, a sugarcane worker, and Frederico, a Cabécar Indian.

I was taking a semester off my undergraduate geology studies to work for a copper company looking to open a mine in these remote mountains, now a UN Biosphere Reserve and reserve for native peoples like the Cabécar. The company had hired Emanuel and Frederico to help me collect samples for lab analysis. I didn't realize it then, but I was a tool of economic, social, and ecological imperialism. And the company had conscripted my two companions in their own exploitation.

Frederico, who knew the lake well, quietly said, "There is a song for this place." He began to sing a slow, hymnlike melody in Cabécar. I didn't understand the words, and Frederico didn't try to translate them. He didn't have to. I understood its more fundamental meaning: There is a song for this whole place, this whole Earth and its inhabitants.

When I got back to school, I realized I had to try to learn that big song. I switched to environmental studies and then got a joint Ph.D. in sociology and environmental studies. I also took up an active second life as a composer and musician of grassroots and classical music. I know a bit of the big song now, I think. But I've got so, so much more to learn.

1. What is your interest level in environmental issues?

☐ *VERY INTERESTED*

☐ *MODERATELY INTERESTED*

☐ *NOT AT ALL INTERESTED*

2. In the United States, do you think we're spending too much money on the environment, too little money, or about the right amount?

☐ *TOO MUCH*

☐ *TOO LITTLE*

☐ *ABOUT THE RIGHT AMOUNT*

3. In the United States, do you think we're spending too much money on improving and protecting the environment, too little money, or about the right amount?

☐ *TOO MUCH*

☐ *TOO LITTLE*

☐ *ABOUT THE RIGHT AMOUNT*

4. What is your interest level in farm issues?

☐ *VERY INTERESTED*

☐ *MODERATELY INTERESTED*

☐ *NOT AT ALL INTERESTED*

Turn to the end of the chapter to view the results for the total population.

SOURCE: National Opinion Research Center, University of Chicago.

EXPERIENCING THE HEAT WAVE

Gerald lived in South Chicago. He had retired from his job 5 years ago and spent much of his day in his apartment. He often went for a walk to the corner store in the morning to pick up groceries or cat food, or just to chat with Frank, who had operated the store for almost 20 years. Gerald rarely spoke to his children, except for his daughter, Janelle, who occasionally took him to the pharmacy to pick up his medication.

It had been an unusually hot July that summer of 1995. Gerald couldn't make it to the store—he could barely muster the energy to get to the fridge or pour himself a glass of water. His air conditioner had broken years ago, and he couldn't justify purchasing a new one. After falling into a deep sleep, Gerald woke up in a hospital bed, surrounded by other people who had collapsed from heat exhaustion as he had. Luckily, Frank had sent his son to check on Gerald, who found him unconscious in his favorite blue armchair.

What factors caused Gerald to experience life-threatening heat exhaustion? Is a heat wave like the one in Chicago in 1995 an environmental problem? Or is it a social problem? What social arrangements and activities precipitated the high heat-related death toll in Chicago that year? Is Gerald's experience an example of environmental inequality?

Gerald's story exemplifies the social complexity of environmental problems. We could argue that an increase in heat waves is an example of human-induced climate change and identify a broad range of possible culprits, from excessive traveling to overproduction and overconsumption. Yet Gerald also experienced the heat wave differently from others. The elderly, particularly those who take medications and live alone, are the most likely to die from heat exhaustion. Those who don't have air conditioners or access to cool spaces like movie theaters and shopping malls are also at increased risk. For some, heat waves are not such a big deal, while for others they are monumental. So how do we identify and define environmental problems when their earthly manifestations are so diverse? As we will discuss in this chapter, while many environmental problems have clearly observable effects, the perceptions of those effects and the solutions they inspire vary across populations. At times, they vary so significantly that they create conflicts between groups and spark social movements. In this sense, environmental problems are always, in part, social problems.

ENVIRONMENTAL PROBLEMS AS SOCIAL PROBLEMS

14.1 Explain how environmental problems are social problems.

We often think of environmental phenomena as objectively observable within the realm of hard sciences. For example, we can identify a heat wave as the presence of unusually high temperatures several days in a row. In Chicago in 1995, for 3 consecutive days the heat index was around 120 degrees. Similarly, we measure pollution by sampling the air or water and determining the quantities of toxic particles it contains. We quantify biodiversity by counting the number of species in a given area. We can measure deforestation and resource depletion. The point is, these are ways to identify environmental problems and translate them into real, hard data that can clearly define the ecological dimensions of the problem (for example, see Figure 14.1). Yet how do we know these data represent environmental problems rather than just normal patterns in the natural world?

After all, the average high temperature in Las Vegas in July is around 106 degrees, but we wouldn't say that Las Vegas experiences a monthlong heat wave. Similarly, not all logging is considered an environmental problem, and many of the toxins in a test tube of tap water are naturally occurring. There is nothing necessarily bad about heat, fewer trees, or foreign substances in new landscapes or natural materials, but of course we don't talk about the environment with such neutrality. Instead, we talk about heat waves, deforestation, and pollution. We also talk about climate change, desertification, and environmental collapse. These concepts encompass not simply events happening in the natural world but also the relationships people have with the environment and its characteristics. These relationships are all informed by our social lives.

In fact, our view of what constitutes an environmental problem has as much to do with effects on people as with events and processes in nature. Those effects are always experienced socially. They depend on how we have organized our lives and the types of information we have received from various social sources. For example, the Chicago heat wave led to high levels of illness and death. Without that human experience, those hot days would be less troubling. We commonly think of an environmental issue that is a threat to humans as an environmental problem. The *unsustainability* of a situation or process is another marker of problems in

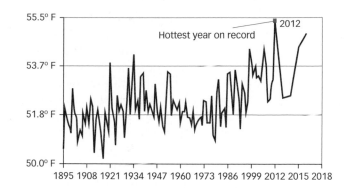

FIGURE 14.1 Average Annual Temperature in Contiguous United States, 1895–2016

SOURCE: Climate Central, compiled from NOAA's National Climate Data Center and Applied Climate Information System.

resource use and pollution. That is, if human activities are depleting or degrading resources faster than they can be renewed, the long-term effects are economic, social, and cultural stresses tied to the scarcity of those resources. While it seems the environment is nonsocial because it exists and functions without people, in practice, the only environment we know is one we can see and experience, and when those sights and experiences are unpleasant, the state of the environment becomes a problem.

We could say that an environmental problem is an ecological phenomenon that has an effect people do not want. That seems pretty straightforward, so what does a sociological perspective add? Throughout this chapter, we will discuss the ways in which the creation, identification, and experience of environmental problems are all social. They relate to our beliefs about the environment and how it influences the practices of everyday life. Even health impacts are sometimes social phenomena. For example, during the Chicago heat wave, children became ill as their school buses got mired in traffic. Two children died as a result of being stuck in a car after a trip to the movies. Using buses to get to school and driving to the movies on a hot day are social practices that influence the experience of a heat wave (Klinenberg, 2002).

In short, environmental problems are *social* problems. Your experience of them is tied to where you are, who you are, and what you do. As a university student on campus, you will experience a heat wave as moderated by a cooling system. If you are a gardener, the climate index and the number of growing degree-days in a year determine what you can plant. If you are a fruit farmer, a heat wave in February can mean premature blooming and vulnerability to frost for your crop. If you are an elder whose life can be threatened by summer's extreme heat, an early heat wave may be cause for alarm.

The way you *interpret* the heat wave also has a lot to do with the social world around you. If you are engaged in conversations about climate change, you may link your daily experiences to what you know about global climate patterns. If you are majoring in plant biology, perhaps you look immediately for signs of an early spring: The grass is becoming greener sooner; daffodils are emerging from the soil too early. (One of the authors went to a grade school where the students counted the crocus and snowdrop flowers every spring. How jarring would it be to count the spring flowers in January or February instead of April?)

Experience and interpretation are not independent of each other. What you experience and the way you experience it influence the way you interpret it. Likewise, what you know can affect the way you feel. When the environment poses a threat, it can also threaten people's identities, making the experience and management of environmental problems more difficult. What some people experience as a problem may be unnoticeable or unimportant for others because their lives are organized differently. Environmental problems, for this reason, can be highly contested and difficult to resolve. We'll take up the relationship between experiences and ideas later in the chapter, but for now, the important point is that *environmental problems are also social problems,* and members of a population experience environmental phenomena differently.

The causes of environmental problems are also social. We extract too many resources, produce too much stuff, and throw too much stuff away. We use hazardous extraction and production methods and generate toxic materials that we release into the environment. Why do we do these things? Environmental sociologists would suggest that our society encourages us to. We economically reward industrial activities that are environmentally harmful, like cheaply producing oil or cutting down trees. Our society says it's normal to live far away from work and commute long distances in personal vehicles. We gain social status by purchasing the latest computer models and throwing the old ones away. In short, we benefit from behaving badly. We do not all benefit, however, and some of us suffer from the environmental ills of our modern lives. Some groups of people, often those already marginalized by society, are disproportionately affected by environmental problems. Much of this chapter will focus on how environmental problems are invariably related to social inequality.

It is no wonder that social organization is a focal point for social scientists interested in environmental problems. Social organization, or social structure, is the way people are divided into groups and categories and placed in a social hierarchy. This hierarchy influences people's access

▶ A worker loads coal into a furnace as smoke and steam rise from an unauthorized steel factory in Inner Mongolia, China. To meet China's targets to slash emissions of carbon dioxide, authorities have shut down privately owned steel, coal, and other high-polluting factories scattered across rural areas.

to economic, cultural, social, and political resources. Some scholars talk about the outcome of this hierarchy as *social inequality,* and some discuss *social stratification,* but these mean basically the same thing: These forces sometimes differentiate people based on race, ethnicity, gender, or social class. When we think about the environment specifically, these characteristics are also influential and have environment-specific implications. In particular, social organization influences *environmental rights.* These could be rights to clean air, water, and food; the right to practice a livelihood like farming or fishing; or the right to maintain traditional landscapes that play a role in people's cultural practices. In the section below we discuss environmental rights, paying attention to inequalities based on class and race. We also show why a global perspective increasingly matters in any conversation about environmental problems and environmental inequalities.

PATTERNS AND TRENDS

 Discuss patterns and trends in environmental issues.

Environmental Justice and Globalization

Ensuring the health of our environment isn't just about easing ecological disruption or threats to human health. It also requires us to consider social inequality and social equity. While we often think of social inequality as just the space between the rich and the poor, this description doesn't get at the unfairness or inequity of that difference.

Social equity, on the other hand, refers to equality and takes into account the different contexts that shape opportunities, needs, and resources.

Equality can actually be quite unfair, because by applying the same rules to different people, or giving everyone the same resources, we ignore the differences that already exist in their lives. In his book *The Red Lily* (1894), the French poet Anatole France writes about the efforts the lower classes must exert to keep a prosperous country prosperous, while the benefits of living in a prosperous country are unfair:

> The poor must work for [the comfort of the wealthy], in presence of the majestic quality of the law which prohibits the wealthy as well as the poor from sleeping under the bridges, from begging in the streets, and from stealing bread.

This passage follows a long description of the oppression of peasants, who were being removed from their farmlands to go to war and defend France, returning landless and in the service of the wealthy population who had remained in the protected state. In the text quoted above, France is emphasizing the irony of applying the same law to the rich and the poor when clearly the poor—and not the wealthy—are compelled to seek shelter under bridges, beg in the streets, and steal their food. Moreover, the impoverishment of the poor generated the wealth and security of the rich, and the **environmental dispossession** they experienced perpetuates their vulnerability.

Environmental dispossession is the reduction or removal of access to environmental resources previously accessible by powerful people who generally benefit from the process. Issues of equity and dispossession are commonly used in the context of colonialism to refer to processes where indigenous peoples are denied access to land and resources they had inhabited, sometimes for millennia. Environmental dispossession can make it difficult for people to access food and traditional medicine, causing health challenges (Richmond & Ross, 2009; Tobias & Richmond, 2014). Dispossession can also have a double effect, as ecological knowledge that has been crafted over many years is no longer able to be used in the management of the space and its resources, but also, when spaces are taken from one group and given to another, it's often

► Protesters march against the Dakota Access Pipeline (DAPL) in Portland, Oregon. The DAPL is a 1,172-mile-long underground oil pipeline that extends through four U.S. states: North Dakota, South Dakota, Iowa, and Illinois. Several North American tribal nations oppose the pipeline because it threatens sacred burial grounds and the quality of water. What do you see as the pros and cons of the pipeline?

because those resources are valuable and can be used for economic production. Using those resources intensively, but excluding people who may have significant knowledge about those resources, can quickly create environmental problems (see Latorre, Farrell, & Martínez-Alier, 2015; Letnic, 2000).

In their work in South Africa, Stull, Bell, and Ncwadi (2016) have suggested that a particularly extreme form of environmental dispossession occurred through the apartheid system, where black South Africans were excluded from a range of rights, including access to fertile and economically productive land. The authors call this extreme and particular form of environmental dispossession "environmental apartheid." Like with the peasants of France's poem, environmental apartheid has meant that those who were politically disenfranchised and officially excluded from economic opportunities also had to graze cattle on marginal land, produce food on depleted soil, and retrieve water from poor sources, with the social and economic effects lasting long after racial segregation was officially abandoned as a national policy. In such a context, environmental degradation is clearly entangled with questions of justice.

Social equity: Closely related to the concept of social equality, social equity stresses fairness and justice.

Environmental dispossession: The reduction or removal of access to environmental resources previously accessible, largely by a dominant group of beneficiaries.

A critical question to ask when we consider climate change, waste management, deforestation, and nuclear radiation is who benefits from the processes that create environmental problems like these, and who suffers? Often, when we are concerned about social equity, we talk about justice, because it implies a broader commitment to equity and an effort to produce that equity. Justice is equity being enacted. In the context of the environment, we often talk explicitly about environmental justice. This means making sure people aren't being exploited for the benefit of others and that access to environmental resources is fair. John Rawls, in *A Theory of Justice* (1971), suggested we try to imagine what sorts of principles we would come up with for a just society if we were ignorant of where we would end up on the resulting social spectrum. Rawls believed we would arrive at two principles:

1. Each person is to have an equal right to the most extensive basic liberty compatible with a similar liberty for others.

2. Social and economic liberties are to be arranged so they are both (a) reasonably expected to be to everyone's advantage, and (b) attached to positions and offices open to all.

In other words, if we were committed to a just society, we would want the best for *everyone,* not just the majority of people or the people who seem most worthy. It will always be unjust to sacrifice the well-being of some for the benefit of others, or to limit the rights of some to expand the rights of others. Access to fish or timber or fertile farmland, and the right to sell the produce, is an economically important, environmentally based right. Equally vital is the right to clean air and water and the space to engage in local economic activities without a risk to health. We can also apply the standard of environmental justice to cultural rights, and to the significance of places and landscapes in the lives of community members.

Inequality can be fair only when it benefits everyone—for example, the inequality of allowing only people who are trained and certified to serve as doctors. But how do we know whether something benefits everyone? Who gets to decide? Environmental justice requires that everyone be able to participate fairly in decisions about the environment regardless of race, class, gender, or nationality; that no one coerce or force another to make an agreement; and that all stakeholders—the people who are affected by the decisions—are able to participate in the negotiation process.

The loss of environmental rights is not always unjust. If members of a minority group disproportionately lose access to a resource or are the only ones barred from disposing of waste at a waterway, the result is unjust. But some people may lose the right to use a resource because it is being overused, or because they are polluting it. This, under Rawls's definition, can arguably be quite just.

Environmental justice is increasingly complicated in the age of globalization. For example, some countries choose to have few or no environmental regulations as a strategy for attracting the subsidiary operations of wealthy transnational corporations. Because these subsidiaries are unregulated and foreign-owned, local populations suffering the environmental hazards and degradation they may create have little recourse. One outcome of this relocation of environmentally damaging production to poorer countries is the new international division of labor (Cohen, 1981; Marin, 2006): Manufacturing jobs move to underdeveloped countries, while white-collar jobs stay in the industrialized countries. In some cases, the management of highly toxic waste moves to poorer countries and regions while the products that generate the waste are enjoyed by the wealthy in richer regions. Under conditions of considerable political inequality, this process is referred to as **toxic colonialism.**

In the following sections, we discuss climate change, natural disasters, waste disposal, and radiation to illustrate some of the issues around inequality and globalization. They are only a few among many environmental problems, and we hope you will consider the approaches discussed in this chapter when you expand your critical scope to other issues.

• •

ASK YOURSELF: What might prevent a society from becoming just? What are some examples of environmental injustice that you have witnessed in your community? What injustices do you find particularly problematic? What do you think shapes local experiences of globalization? How do you think globalization shapes local environments?

• •

Climate Change

Claims about the existence of climate change often rely on data provided by the U.S. Environmental Protection Agency, the Intergovernmental Panel on Climate Change, and the Goddard Institute for Space Studies. These data indicate that the warmest years around the globe have all occurred since 1998, and each decade has been a little balmier than the one before. Yet there are still cold winters and regions that seem to have gotten *colder* over the

• •

Toxic colonialism: When toxic waste is moved from wealthy countries to economically and politically marginalized regions.

► These two photos present a contrast between a Central American woman carrying a bucket of green tomatoes that she picked in a field and a wealthy couple enjoying their meal at a fancy restaurant. How can you interpret these two photos in terms of environmental justice?

past century, indicating that the effects of the warming of Earth's atmosphere on climate are uneven and difficult to predict. However, overall trends point to a warming climate, with higher sea level and less snowpack.

The way we define climate change has a big influence on what we see when we look at the data. Parts of Alabama, Georgia, and Mississippi have experienced little warming, and some areas have even cooled over the past century (data extracted from U.S. Environmental Protection Agency, 2012a). Areas that are warm year-round and experience less seasonal variation in climate, such as around the equator and near water, will also experience less change in surface temperature as the atmosphere warms. However, recent research has found that many of those climates that have historically experienced the least climate variability will be the most sensitive to change (Mora et al., 2013). Given that they also contain the most biodiverse regions on the planet, as well as some of the poorest populations, these regions will see much greater effects of climate change, and much sooner than other regions.

The same could be said for climate change over time. If we compare this year to last year, perhaps there is not much of a story to tell. Even over centuries there are patterns, but they do not give a full picture of the changes. Often, scientists who look at global climate change will look at *anomalies* in temperature and other aspects of weather. They take a period of time, often 1951 to 1980, and measure the degree to which current conditions diverge from the averages over those decades. For example, the graph in Figure 14.3 displays deviations from a normal temperature range, so we can see there are many more occurrences of temperatures above a normal range after 1980. While it may be generally a bit warmer than before and the winters a bit milder, it is also occasionally *much* hotter—and occasionally much wetter, drier, windier, or even colder than usual. This increase in extremes is as significant as the warming of some locations, such as the Earth's poles.

This is why scientists often object to defining the issue as "global warming" and favor the more accurate

► Environmental activists in Chicago protest President Donald Trump's decision to exit the Paris climate accord. In 2017, Trump withdrew the United States from the agreement, stating it imposed unfair standards on American businesses and workers. Countries that abide by the Paris agreement—including China, the European Union, India, Japan, and Russia—agree to reduce carbon dioxide emissions to mitigate global warming.

FIGURE 14.2 Temperature Anomalies, December 2016 to February 2017

Dec–Jan–Feb 2016–2017   **L-OTI (°C) Anomaly vs. 1951–1980**

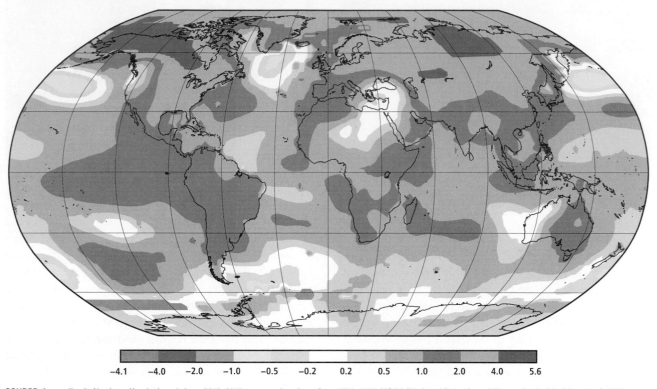

| −4.1 | −4.0 | −2.0 | −1.0 | −0.5 | −0.2 | 0.2 | 0.5 | 1.0 | 2.0 | 4.0 | 5.6 |

SOURCE: Anomalies in Northern Hemisphere/winter 2016–2017 compared to those from 1951–1980, NOAA (National Oceanic and Atmospheric Administration). 2016.

FIGURE 14.3 Deviations From Normal Temperatures, 1850–2016

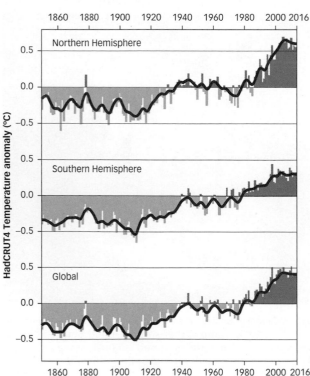

SOURCE: Hemispheric and global averages graph. Climate Research Unit, University of East Anglia.

term *climate change*. Placing the emphasis on warming suggests that we should focus on heat alone, and the point, welcome to some, that winters are getting warmer too—in fact, they are warming faster than summers. In early 2017, northern parts of the United States were experiencing unusually warm weather for February, precipitating both delight at the return of barbecue-appropriate warmth and dread at the implications for climate change. But if our definition of this environmental problem reminds us that greater heat in winter is likely to be accompanied by other effects—like stronger winter winds, bigger snowfalls, and faster evaporation of snowpack—we will consider the problem differently and act on it differently. Definitions matter enormously in social life.

One of the most profound visible aspects of climate change is the melting of polar ice. Ice melts have a number of different consequences for different people. Research has shown that Inuit living in Northern Canada already face respiratory health problems associated with warmer summers (Furgal & Seguin, 2006). Moving across the ice has also become less predictable and more dangerous. For a traditionally nomadic population with strong cultural and economic roots in hunting, an increase in the risks associated with travel is highly problematic (Furgal & Seguin, 2006; Laidler, 2007). Climate change threatens the Inuit physically but also culturally, because many of their traditional activities now place them in danger.

As the ice melts, the sea level also rises because of thermal expansion, and as water gets warmer, it takes up more space. The Intergovernmental Panel on Climate Change's Third Assessment Report, completed in 2001, projected that sea level will rise between 0.5 and 1.4 meters by 2100. In low-lying coastal regions, even small increases in sea level can flood wetlands and leave people who live in these areas at greater risk of flooding and vulnerability to storm surges; more than a billion people could be displaced (Small & Nicholls, 2003). Developing countries are likely to be the hardest hit, with sea-level rise potentially crippling the Bahamas, Egypt, and Vietnam (Dasgupta et al., 2009). Refugees fleeing endangered areas may face new or worsened conflicts with neighbors (Buhaug, Gleditsch, & Theisen, 2010). Moving populations paired with shifting access and increasing scarcity of natural resources has the potential to increase violent conflict (Barnett & Adger, 2007). Policy that anticipates these social dimensions of climate change may help to alleviate some of this potential distress.

ASK YOURSELF: We've discussed northern communities and climate change. What social and political problems may influence their resilience to the effects of a changing climate? Who is to blame for the changes? Does it matter? Who should take responsibility for alleviating the impacts of climate change on coastal communities? Why?

Natural Disasters

With global climate change, extreme weather events are also expected to increase (Meehl et al., 2000). Natural disasters have uneven effects on people, as we discussed in the case of the Chicago heat wave at the beginning of the chapter. More generally, the places where people live are associated with different levels of risk. Some locations are more prone than others to tornados, heat waves, or hurricanes. Often, these higher-risk areas are also associated with lower property values and may be occupied by people with lower incomes. These populations may also be less resilient to the effects of natural disasters, and there is evidence to suggest that their vulnerability is only increasing (Van Aalst, 2006). Research has also suggested that minorities, women, and low-income populations suffer more emotional stress from natural disasters (Fothergill, Maestas, & Darlington, 1999; Tierney, 2007).

Hurricane Katrina is a good example of a natural disaster that was experienced differently by different people. Katrina formed over the Bahamas in 2005 and ran along the Gulf Coast from Florida to Texas. The greatest destruction occurred in New Orleans, Louisiana, where the levee system failed. Katrina was one of the five deadliest hurricanes in U.S. history, with a death toll of more than 1,800. Just over half those deaths occurred in Louisiana, and many of those were in New Orleans. Black people in New Orleans were much more likely to die than whites, and more generally the elderly were also at higher risk (Brunkard, Namulanda, & Ratard, 2008; Sharkey, 2007). Income also influenced the death rate: Low economic resources made it difficult for people to evacuate and relocate while the city flooded with water (Lavelle & Feagin, 2006). Thus, income, race, and age all influenced the magnitude of the disaster for groups of people.

Waste

The disposal of human waste is a social problem and a problem of social justice (see Figure 14.6). While everyone produces waste, nobody wants to have to deal with it. In much of the world, intricate systems have been built to whisk away refuse, quickly and effortlessly, never to be seen again. For the most part, we wash our hands, literally and figuratively, of our everyday pollution.

Clearly, waste does not simply evaporate but instead gets deposited in particular locations. While technologies for containing and treating landfills have improved, such facilities often remain unwelcome additions to local neighborhoods. Many adopt the NIMBY (not-in-my-backyard) approach, whereby people who may not be opposed to the establishment of landfills object to having them located near their own homes and businesses (Camacho, 1998; Cole & Foster, 2001; Saha & Mohai, 2005). The health effects of living near a landfill or incinerator are unclear, but there is evidence that low birth weight, birth defects, and some types of cancer are more common among populations that live near such facilities (Elliott et al., 2009; Goldberg et al., 1999; Porta et al., 2009). Health effects aside, the presence of a landfill does seem to consistently decrease the value of nearby residential property (Ready, 2005).

Research has also shown that waste sites are more likely to emerge in less wealthy communities. Often, these are minority communities. Mohai and Saha (2007) found that, in the United States in 1990, more than 40% of people living within a mile of a disposal site were persons of color. The minority population in 1990 was only a quarter of the U.S. total, meaning that disposal sites were disproportionately placed in those neighborhoods. Mohai and Saha contend that the disproportionately high numbers of waste sites in Hispanic and African American communities may result from a number of economic, sociopolitical, and racial factors. Firms may locate waste management plants in areas where the cost of land is low, and these areas tend to be occupied by the economically disadvantaged, who are disproportionately people of

FIGURE 14.4 Climate Change Vulnerability Index, 2016

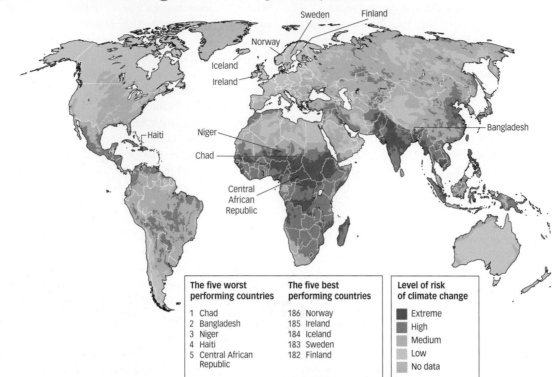

The five worst performing countries	The five best performing countries	Level of risk of climate change
1 Chad	186 Norway	■ Extreme
2 Bangladesh	185 Ireland	■ High
3 Niger	184 Iceland	■ Medium
4 Haiti	183 Sweden	■ Low
5 Central African Republic	182 Finland	■ No data

SOURCE: © Maplecroft 2014. Reprinted with permission from the global risk analytics company, Maplecroft.

FIGURE 14.5 Natural Catastrophes Worldwide, 2015

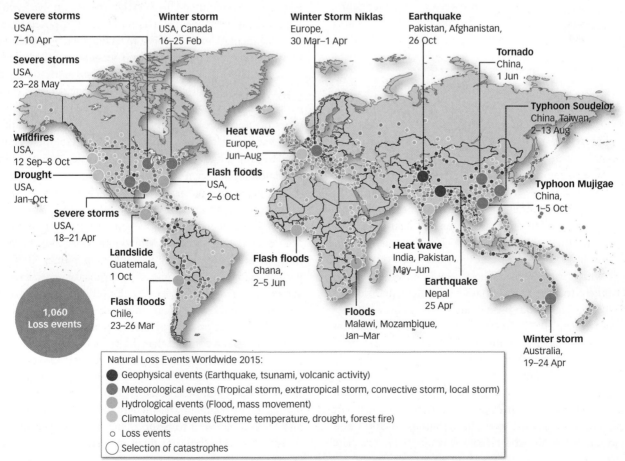

Severe storms
USA,
7–10 Apr

Severe storms
USA,
23–28 May

Wildfires
USA,
12 Sep–8 Oct

Drought
USA,
Jan–Oct

Severe storms
USA,
18–21 Apr

Winter storm
USA, Canada
16–25 Feb

Heat wave
Europe,
Jun–Aug

Flash floods
USA,
2–6 Oct

Winter Storm Niklas
Europe,
30 Mar–1 Apr

Earthquake
Pakistan, Afghanistan,
26 Oct

Tornado
China,
1 Jun

Typhoon Soudelor
China, Taiwan,
2–13 Aug

Typhoon Mujigae
China,
1–5 Oct

Landslide
Guatemala,
1 Oct

Flash floods
Chile,
23–26 Mar

Flash floods
Ghana,
2–5 Jun

Heat wave
India, Pakistan,
May–Jun

Earthquake
Nepal
25 Apr

Floods
Malawi, Mozambique,
Jan–Mar

Winter storm
Australia,
19–24 Apr

1,060 Loss events

Natural Loss Events Worldwide 2015:
- ● Geophysical events (Earthquake, tsunami, volcanic activity)
- ● Meteorological events (Tropical storm, extratropical storm, convective storm, local storm)
- ● Hydrological events (Flood, mass movement)
- ○ Climatological events (Extreme temperature, drought, forest fire)
- ○ Loss events
- ○ Selection of catastrophes

SOURCE: Natural Catastrophes, 2012 World Map. © 2013 Münchener Rückversicherungs-Gesellschaft, Geo Risks Research, NatCatSERVICE.

FIGURE 14.6 Municipal Solid Waste (MSW) Generation Rates, 1960–2014

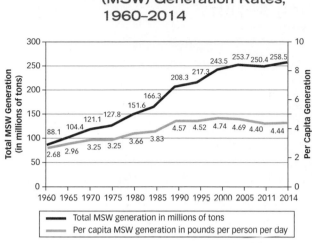

Total MSW generation in millions of tons

Per capita MSW generation in pounds per person per day

SOURCE: Municipal Solid Waste, United States Environmental Protection Agency.

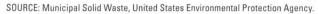

color. Once a plant has been built, the more affluent may move away from the area. From a sociopolitical perspective, wealthy communities may have more political clout to influence the placement of waste management sites. Lastly, Mohai and Saha suggest, racial factors may influence the placement of sites. Waste management firms may see minority neighborhoods as the least likely to resist the development of such sites and therefore as easy targets. We might therefore conclude that the placement of waste management systems exemplifies environmental racism, in which environmental degradation is more pronounced in places occupied or utilized by minority communities.

Radiation

We've seen above that globalization makes it difficult to identify the stakeholders in environmental decisions, particularly given the scope and longevity of the outcomes. What happens in one part of the globe often has far-reaching consequences. The effects of the disaster that took place at the nuclear power plant in Chernobyl, Ukraine, in 1986, for example, were not contained to the city, region, or state that surrounded it. All over Europe, people experienced the consequences of radioactive fallout. Some have estimated the total premature deaths globally resulting from the Chernobyl disaster to be as high as 985,000 (Yablokov et al., 2009). But still, some groups have suffered the effects more than others.

The population that experienced the highest radioactivity from Chernobyl in Norway were the Saami, a minority group of reindeer herders (Mehli et al., 2000). Most of their exposure was through the consumption of reindeer meat contaminated when the animals grazed in areas that received fallout. This exposure created a threat to the Saamis' health and to their economic well-being. The Norwegian government introduced a range of measures

to try to reduce their health risk, including restricting the slaughter of reindeer for food to particular times of the year and moving the reindeer to less contaminated areas. The Saami were also prevented from selling any contaminated meat and encouraged to reduce their own consumption.

These measures of protection were highly disruptive to the Saami and came with significant social and economic consequences. Not only were their traditional grazing and slaughtering practices disrupted, but their cultural identities as herders with traditional knowledge and a unique relationship to nature were challenged. An environmental justice framework would suggest that they should have been protected from the unequal burden of contamination that they faced, but also that they should have been able to maintain access to the resources that are economically and culturally so important for them.

Hardly a specter of the past, people in Japan have recently faced similar challenges to the Saami after the Daiichi nuclear plant disaster in Fukushima. In 2011, following the Tōhoku earthquake and subsequent tsunami, the cooling system for the reactors at the coastal Daiichi plant failed, causing a meltdown and release of radioactive material into the surrounding area (see Figure 14.7). The effects of the disaster are multifaceted and continue to unfold. As a basic level, radioactive waste has been released into the environment and poses a threat to human ecosystems. Appropriately responding to those threats is a complicated task. People within 20 kilometers of the nuclear power plant were immediately evacuated to reduce exposure, but evacuation had its own consequences, as an estimated 600 people died as a result of being displaced from their homes (Ten Hoeve & Jacobsen, 2012). Imagine suddenly having to abandon your community and livelihood temporarily, but being unsure of when you could return?

In addition to the direct effects of radiation exposure and evacuation, there are lasting psychological effects, and governance challenges, associated with the ongoing management of the radiation. The appropriate level of exposure, particularly for the consumption of food, remains debated and generates anxiety among citizens (Burch, 2012, 2016). Fukushima is a farming region, and the government has encouraged a return to farming in areas deemed to be safe. Food is tested and sold if it registers below a government-approved threshold. However, these values remain under debate to this day, as some people in Japan think the levels are too high and shouldn't be deemed safe for consumption (Burch et al., forthcoming). The psychological stress of eating food that people feel may be unsafe is significant, and poses a significant challenge to well-being even if the negative physical health effects are thought to be low (Von Hippel, 2011). The intersection of food and radiation also has unique gendered effects, as women are more likely to be responsible for the preparation of food and ensuring the safety of their family. In her work on radiation and citizen science, Kimura (2016)

FIGURE 14.7   Radiation From the Daiichi Nuclear Power Plant Disaster

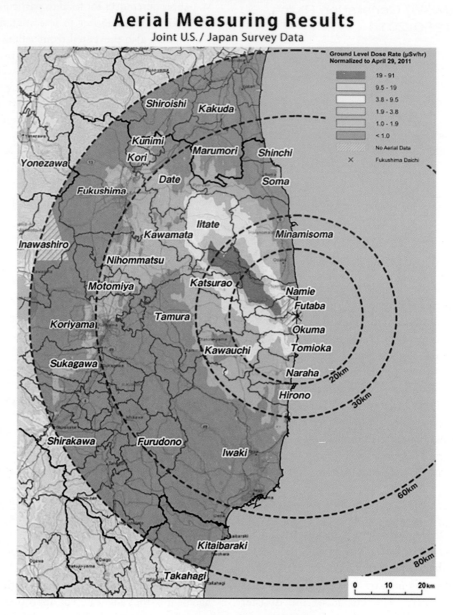

Aerial Measuring Results
Joint U.S. / Japan Survey Data

SOURCE: UNEP.

finds that mothers who sought out their own information about the safety of radiation, and developed practices that went against government policy, would often be labeled as "irrational" and face social condemnation. The invisibility and uncertainty surrounding radiation has led to unique governance issues and remains a challenge for regions dealing with exposure.

ASK YOURSELF: What are the benefits of nuclear power production? Who benefits from nuclear power? Who should be responsible for testing and compensating people for health problems resulting from nuclear radiation?

THEORETICAL APPROACHES IN ENVIRONMENTAL SOCIOLOGY

14.3 Apply the functionalist, conflict, and symbolic interactionist perspectives to environmental problems and policy.

Environmental problems, like climate change, natural disasters, waste disposal, and nuclear radiation, are actually abstract, social concepts, and the experiences associated with them are rarely immediate and direct. Consider

Experiencing the Environment

Marginalization and Hurricane Katrina

Natural disasters like Hurricane Katrina do not have the same effects on everyone who experiences them. James R. Elliott and Jeremy Pais (2006) suggest that the history of race and class in New Orleans, where there are strong divisions that have not been significantly altered by migration, had a strong influence on how different residents were affected by the hurricane. They also suggest that the reasons for the differences were intersectional. That is, differences among residents in their experiences of the hurricane could not be explained purely by class, nor could they be explained entirely by race. Instead, race and class intersected to create unique experiences.

Elliott and Pais measured residents' evacuation timing, short-term recovery, stress and emotional support, and likelihood of return. They found that low-income African Americans were the most likely to

have never left the city. Black workers were 3.8 times more likely to have lost their jobs, and particularly workers earning $10,000 to $20,000 a year. Low-income African Americans were also the least likely to return to their pre-Katrina communities.

Depending on their experiences, livelihoods, and resources, people experience environmental problems differently. Those who have historically been socially marginalized based on race, class, religion, or gender may feel these events more profoundly, in part because they receive the least social protection and meet more barriers to recovery resources. Understanding how those experiences of marginalization intersect, as in the case of Hurricane Katrina, helps us understand the

Scott Olson/Getty Images

▶ Residents hang out in front of their homes, which are surrounded by floodwater after Hurricane Harvey caused widespread destruction during the summer of 2017. Harvey dumped nearly 50 inches of rain in and around the Houston area.

social dimensions of environmental problems so that we can generate sound and just solutions.

▶ **THINK ABOUT IT**

1. How does intersectionality relate to justice?

2. What policy recommendations might you make to encourage a fair and just recovery for New Orleans?

3. What does an intersectional approach say about other environmental problems, such as climate change?

---

climate change: We cannot see carbon dioxide rising to the sky and getting trapped in the atmosphere and then immediately feel the temperature rise. In a sense, there are no direct effects—only **indicators** that we place within a larger context of meaning. This is true not only of climate change but also of anything we seek to understand. Scientists may have the most precise, detailed, sophisticated, and extensive technologies with which to make observations, but what are these observations of?

The numbers on a digital thermometer go up, but does that indicate higher temperatures? Or is it changing electrical pulses passing through a series of tiny diodes that result in different patterns of light? Perhaps it's both (or, if the thermometer is broken, maybe neither). All perceptions require conceptions. The tools we use may

be technical and oriented toward developing an objective assessment, but they are also cultural and social, in the sense that they are developed by and used by specific groups of people in the pursuit of their interests. This does not make scientific claims any less valid. On the contrary, the culture of scientific production overall is highly specialized, laborious, and laudable. We are merely suggesting that everything gets filtered through some social and cultural lens, whether the lens of climate science or the lens of local knowledge practices.

....

Indicators: Observable changes in social and ecological behaviors that are used to indirectly measure other changes that are less visible.

Waste in a Global Context

As electronics become cheaper and more available to consumers, the waste generated in their production and disposal also becomes an increasing problem.

Electronic waste is highly toxic and difficult to recycle (Schmidt, 2002). As a result, nations like the United States often ship their electronic waste to China, India, or Pakistan to be recycled or dumped (Robinson, 2009; Silicon Valley Toxics Coalition, 2002). Alastair Iles (2004) has discussed the ways that technology flows—in which electronics are designed in one location, produced in another, and dumped in another—raise questions of environmental justice.

Thousands are employed in the disposal of electronics, and while there may be financial benefits, the health and environmental costs are huge. Not only are there risks associated with handling the e-waste, but spills and pollution from disposal and recycling can contaminate the groundwater and air, causing a bevy of illnesses for those who occupy nearby areas (Grant et al., 2013). These areas, Iles suggests, suffer disproportionate ills from the electronics industry, while the benefits are enjoyed to a much greater extent in other parts of the globe.

Computer manufacturers have an obligation to develop greener technologies to alleviate the problems associated with disposal. On the other hand, we should also reconsider any trade agreements and development programs that make it difficult for underdeveloped countries and regions to negotiate healthier and more environmentally friendly working conditions.

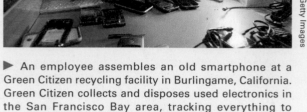

David Paul Morris/Bloomberg/Getty Images

▶ An employee assembles an old smartphone at a Green Citizen recycling facility in Burlingame, California. Green Citizen collects and disposes used electronics in the San Francisco Bay area, tracking everything to ensure the electronic waste is recycled back into raw material, or refurbished and resold.

▶ **THINK ABOUT IT**

1. Who benefits from the global trade of hazardous waste?

2. How might electronic waste disposal differ if it couldn't be conducted across national borders?

Social scientists use different theoretical lenses to try to make sense of the world too. A phenomenon like climate change has a particular meaning among climatologists and perhaps a slightly different meaning to Inuit living in Northern Canada. Sociologists may be more concerned with the process of meaning making and what those different meanings say about social structures and the distribution of power among the different stakeholders. We will deal with a few popular sociological lenses next and discuss how environmental sociologists have honed them in ways that work particularly well for environmental problems.

Functionalism

Structural functionalism focuses on the macro-level structures and processes that shape society. In environmental sociology, a structural functionalist perspective directs our attention to the organization of society and how it might create environmental problems. We might also consider how environmental problems themselves reproduce types of social organization.

Our society is organized in ways that encourage some behaviors while making others more difficult. For instance, it is easy to engage in the types of activities that have higher environmental costs, and in some cases avoiding those activities will put you at a disadvantage. The paving of roads and expansion of highways enable speedy movement between suburbs and cities by way of motor vehicles. Unless you live in a fairly dense city with excellent public transportation, driving your own car may best enable you to accept a better job, arrive at that job on time, and significantly reduce your daily commute. In such circumstances, even people with environmentally friendly attitudes may find it hard to put their beliefs into practice (Kollmuss & Agyeman, 2002).

We have become too dependent on environmentally bad behaviors in our everyday lives, building a world in which those behaviors are easier and more rewarding than environmentally considerate behaviors (Stern, 1992; Stern, Dietz, & Guagnano, 1995; Stern, Dietz, & Kalof). It is simply too much work to avoid driving, or too expensive to buy local fresh produce, or too harmful for our careers to forgo the latest gadgets, even if we are perfectly aware of the problems those actions create. We do too well at being environmental villains.

Policy Implications of Structural Functionalism

If we adopt a structural functionalist perspective, we need to focus on reorganizing society to make bad environmental behaviors less appealing and more inconvenient, perhaps by raising the economic costs associated with them, or we could make good practices cheaper and more convenient. A third strategy is simply to make bad practices much less harmful.

We've basically described the ecological modernization (EM) perspective. **Ecological modernization theory** suggests that we can find solutions to our environmental problems by altering our current economic system to encourage good environmental behaviors. Competition, management, and taxes can reduce our inclinations to use the environment for free. The production of green technology will follow, as efficiency and better use of resources become driving forces in research and development. Rather than rejecting modernization, as some environmental sociologists do, we should solve problems by modernizing further (Mol & Spaargaren, 2000). We can keep our basic standard of living and engage in the same types of activities with a much smaller environmental impact.

Perhaps the greatest benefit of the EM approach is that it does not ask for massive changes to people's lifestyles or challenge the cultural practices they enjoy. It does not require any radical economic restructuring. The changes are subtle and organic and can occur without significant discomfort. The government can offer incentives for green changes too. The "cash for clunkers" program, or Car Allowance Rebate System (CARS), was an EM-style program introduced in 2009 in the United States to subsidize the purchase of high-efficiency vehicles when the buyers traded in old low-efficiency vehicles. Fuel is expensive, and people are willing to pay more for a clean environmental conscience, so high-efficiency technology is being developed and refined, and cars that utilize it are increasingly accessible and affordable.

Ecological modernization theory has its critics, however. Some challenges invoke the idea of social inequality. Many countries now switching to green technology have undergone industrialization processes that were far from environmentally friendly, such as Australia, the United States, and the United Kingdom. If other countries undertake similar economic development, the environmental impacts

► The PS10 solar power plant near Seville, Spain, was designed to produce 11 megawatts of electricity from the sun's rays, collected by more than 600 giant movable mirrors. The mirrors concentrate the sun's rays onto the top of a 300-foot tower, where the resulting heat produces steam to drive a turbine.

will be significant and potentially disastrous. Yet the economic disadvantages in these countries, and their need for economic growth and infrastructure development, make it difficult for them to gain access to expensive new green technologies. Critics question whether EM theory is appropriate outside industrialized nations, where the need for environmentally sound economic development is greatest.

Some argue that current levels of consumption are unsustainable, even if we switch to green technologies. Electric cars still require considerable energy and resources in their manufacture and may be using nonrenewable energy depending on the electricity available to their owner (Arar, 2010). Perhaps if we all switched to electric cars *and* renewable electricity sources, the environmental benefits would be considerable, but the general observation remains: An increase in green consumerism does not necessarily reduce environmental impacts or have positive environmental effects. For example, rather than forgoing disposable food containers, we may use them more if they were compostable, recyclable, or made from organic materials. Producing and consuming less is always the better option. Critics are particularly skeptical of green technologies given capitalist societies' need to continue growing, and the ways that green consumption may participate in **conspicuous consumption**, or consumption for the sake of showing social status. If you're

Ecological modernization theory: The theory that society can become environmentally sustainable through the development of greener technologies and government regulations.

Conspicuous consumption: Using the consumption of goods to display social status, like prominently carrying a designer handbag.

proud of your electric car, you may be tempted to drive it everywhere, even if it's charging with electricity generated through nonrenewables like gas, oil, or coal.

Many of these critiques are aimed at the technological and market-based aspects of EM and the faith it places in green consumers. Skeptics are even more critical of corporate greenwashing, the practice in which organizations advertise themselves as green when their actions are not. For example, "clean" coal technology and oil-drilling innovations might reduce the environmental impacts of the coal and oil industries, but these will never be green industries, given that they are highly polluting in their production and consumption. Ecological modernization cannot guarantee that companies' ecological politics are anything but a thin veneer.

But EM also sees a big role for government. While globalization has long been seen as unfriendly to environmental conservation, Sonnenfeld and Mol (2002) suggest that the right types of global governance could make globalization positive for the environment (see also Mol, 2003). Governments could set a baseline gas mileage for all new cars, for example, so that auto companies would be forced to produce high-efficiency vehicles.

> *ASK YOURSELF:* What are some examples of ecological modernization in your community? Where might you see resistance to ecological modernization? Do you feel the ecological modernization approach is too optimistic? Why or why not?

Conflict Theory

Conflict theory is often associated with Karl Marx and his understanding of society's structure as being tied to the distribution of materials and resources. For the conflict theorist in environmental sociology, materials are pulled from the environment and used to generate profit, essentially without being paid for. Our economic system rewards companies for producing more and reducing costs, which encourages them to exploit the environment.

From the conflict perspective, we could think of the environment as engaged in a type of labor: It generates goods, such as wood and steel, and services, such as waste disposal. We could also consider how the desire to accumulate capital and wealth leads to an attempt to reduce both human and environmental labor costs while expanding production and increasing inequality and environmental degradation. The free labor of the environment then simply participates in the class conflict inherent in capitalist production. Why is environmental labor free?

First, the environment produces goods but has no ability to negotiate prices for those goods. There may even be ecological value in not selling: An apple left unpicked can feed insects, attract wildlife, and fertilize the ground when it falls. But without price negotiation, most environmental products are treated as free because they cannot be withheld. In this sense, the environment may be seen as our most voiceless laborer, with power only exercised at times of resource collapse or crisis.

Second, many environmental consequences of human activities are shared and do not fall specifically on the individuals who caused the problems. Once carbon dioxide (CO_2) is in the air, there is no way to contain it and attach it to the exact producer who put it there. To make matters worse, CO_2 may interact with other pollutants to produce further negative consequences—for example, climate change that combines with habitat loss to undermine the reproductive abilities of wildlife. How do we tie these compounded costs back to an individual?

A third reason why environmental labor is free is that many actions don't show their environmental consequences for many years, sometimes centuries. Even if we know exactly what those consequences are, and even if they would directly affect the person responsible for them, it is easy to put off future suffering for immediate gains. Some say it is impossible to fully predict the future outcomes of our present actions. The world is too complicated, and we haven't been studying the environment long enough to know.

The absence of environmental costs in the economy feeds what environmental sociologists call a **treadmill of production** (ToP) (Pellow, Schnaiberg, & Weinberg, 2000; Schnaiberg & Gould, 1994; Schnaiberg, Pellow, & Weinberg, 2002). The ToP describes the production cycle, where, in its simplest form, resources and work generate goods that are sold for a profit, the profit is reinvested into the system, and waste from the production process is deposited back into the environment. Competition between producers causes companies to search out ways to cut production costs through more technology, or cheaper employees, cheaper resources, or cheaper ways to dispose of waste. As the profit-investment cycle spins, it spins at an increasing speed to produce more goods for less.

Rather than solving environmental problems, ToP theorists say, ecological modernization is more likely to perpetuate them by supporting a fundamentally unsustainable economic system. Under capitalism there will always be pressure for economic growth and the increased use of environmental resources. Even greener consumption will encourage production to expand and propel environmental degradation at an increasing rate as competition forces firms to cut their costs of labor and other inputs. What we

Treadmill of production: A theory that describes the ways that production is constantly accelerating without moving forward.

need is a different economic system. We need to get off the treadmill of production.

Sometimes reducing the costs of inputs can be good for the environment. Technology that makes resource extraction more efficient, for example, means less waste in the extraction process. We can reduce the costs of getting rid of waste by producing less waste in the first place, and the less energy used to produce energy, the better. These are all possible positive aspects of pushing firms to reduce costs through ecological modernization.

Unfortunately, there is still a problem, as the ToP perspective illuminates. First, even if we reduce costs through technology and efficiency, we still cannot reduce the environmental impact to zero. Second, competition in capitalism is so fierce that even if technology improves the efficient use of resources, firms will still be compelled to find the cheapest supply sources, which often means locating factories where energy is cheap, getting resources from places where the land and labor for extraction are cheap, and finding waste sites that are cheap. Third, the treadmill is always accelerating: If firms get more from their resources, they won't necessarily use less but instead might expand production. If a firm can use half the amount of energy to make the same number of cars, for example, why not double the number made and sell them for less, expanding market share and putting pressure on competitors before they can catch up? The ToP perspective suggests that the capitalist economy is organized to promote cost cutting and expansion, so the environmental benefits of new technology will always be limited.

Policy Implications of the Conflict Perspective

Conflict theory suggests that we must deal with the problems of consumption, competition, labor, and environmental degradation simultaneously, by addressing the capitalist economic system. One solution is to legislate labor and environmental protections. After all, if the treadmill of production is propelled by competition, legislation that has similar effects on all firms will curb inequality and the overuse of resources while still allowing firms to compete in other areas. Yet because firms exist in particular locations, and because local governments want to protect their tax bases and constituents' jobs by keeping them there, legislation that might harm or curtail particular firms is a tough sell. Globalization has also significantly curbed governments' ability to resolve environmental abuses and labor exploitation through governance because, as we've seen, companies can now operate in many places where they are not closely regulated.

For conflict theorists, the plight of the environment is closely tied to the plight of labor. One of the only ways to resolve environmental problems from a conflict theory perspective is to drastically reduce inequality among

► Climate change is causing the Arctic to warm more quickly than the rest of the world, causing a dramatic loss of Arctic sea ice. The primary role that sea ice plays in the global climate is its ability to reflect the sun's radiation efficiently. As sea ice is lost, more sunlight is absorbed into the newly open ocean, shifting the ocean surface from highly reflective to one that absorbs most of the sun's energy. What meaning do you suppose the average person would give to all of this?

people, both within and between nations, while developing a strong, environmentally protective state. Reducing inequality would change the nature of competition by reducing producers' ability to find cheaper labor and laxer environmental regulations. For example, if the people working in e-waste plants in China had a higher standard of living and stronger local government, they could demand a higher wage for such dangerous work, and environmental protections could drive the cost of disposal up. The result may be a higher price for electronics or a stronger incentive to make their disposal greener.

ASK YOURSELF: From a conflict theory perspective, fostering equality will help resolve environmental problems, but this might take a while to achieve. What should we do in the meantime? What would happen if we just factored environmental labor into production costs? What problems could arise from decreasing inequality and increasing production costs?

Symbolic Interactionism

We've seen that people often attach different meanings to environmental problems depending on who they are and what they want to accomplish. Symbolic interactionist theorists might say that every environmental problem is really a conflict over the meanings different groups attach to a phenomenon, and these meanings are important, because they shape what is deemed an appropriate response to the phenomenon. For example, consider the bulk movement of undesirable materials from one site to another. When is this called waste management and when is it constructed as an environmental problem? Some might say it is a very efficient way of dealing with the by-products of a healthy economic life. What if the material is organic and moved to a farm for fertilizer? Or plastic and moved to a recycling facility? The disposal of waste becomes an environmental problem when it is seen as a threat to our health, our sense of justice, or our visions of a beautiful landscape and functioning ecosystem.

Environmental sociologists often rely on the social constructionist perspective rather than on symbolic interactionism, but the two are closely related. Social constructionism highlights the ways we give environmental materials meanings through social interactions, even though we often think those meanings are inherent in the things themselves. That is, socialization gives us conceptual tools with which to see the world, and the way we see it therefore depends on the shape and character of those tools. We have no means to grasp what is happening in a pure, unmediated way, because we make sense of the world through knowledge we generate and share socially.

Climate change is the perfect example. The concept of climate change is not something anyone comes up with in a vacuum. Even scientists who can observe CO_2 levels in the atmosphere use technologies developed for that purpose by others and shared by others. They talk to other people about their findings and publish in journals where dialogues between scientists occur. The average person confronted with some hotter days, higher sea level, or odd species behavior probably wouldn't think, "Ah, it's carbon dioxide trapped in the atmosphere. It must be global warming." The concept of global warming is necessary for us to know what we are seeing and interpret it and give it meaning. Hotter days become much more ominous when the concept of global warming is available to us.

In fact, we do not just absorb all the concepts around us that help make sense of the environment. Instead, we focus on those that resonate with us and that are shared by our friends, family members, and society. Knowledge is not something we pick up as we encounter it; rather, what we take to be knowledge gains credence through our identification with those who extend it to us. In short, gaining knowledge is an active process of culture, closely bound up in our sense of identity, which we can call the *cultivation of knowledge* (Bell, 2004).

For example, we use a common language when trying to describe an idea like global warming, and that language develops more depth and becomes more meaningful the more we use it. Even if you don't believe global warming is taking place, you know people like you find the idea important and compelling, so you pay attention to it. If you are a student at a university, those conversations may be shaped by campus culture and discussions of research and science.

If you are a city planner, the concept of global warming might be ripe with future scenarios and adaptations that relate to things like sea level and water supplies. If you are a manufacturer, public discussion about global warming may seem accusatory and uninformed about business practices, or it may make people feel on edge. The way people build environmental knowledge depends on the social foundations from which they are building. The result can be a clash of visions in which people are not simply debating global warming but defending their identities.

In her work on logging on the northwest coast of Canada, for example, anthropologist Terre Satterfield (2002) suggests that debates about logging are about much more than trees and environmental preservation; they are about the identities of local groups and their claims to legitimacy in the area. Whose forest is it? Who should decide what the forest means and does? Is it a sacred place? A cultural, recreational space? Or is the forest a productive space that can feed families? These contested values were so hotly debated in the community Satterfield studied that elementary school children were divided into those who perceived logging as a part of their own positive cultural heritage and those who demonized it.

The theory of **frame analysis** is associated with social interactionism and social constructionism because it focuses on the meanings people give to elements in the environment. Frame analysis suggests that people present issues in ways that elicit particular types of responses. For example, fishermen frame a river with deformed fish as contaminated and threatened by economic interests, while the oil company upriver frames the river as healthy and an economic resource for oil production. If the public accepts the fishermen's frame, it not only produces a tangible outcome—such as new legislation about acceptable levels of contaminants—but also signals that the fishermen's knowledge is valid and that the fishermen have more right to fish than the oil company has to pump oil. If the oil company's frame becomes more widely accepted instead, its legitimacy on the river is validated and its rights are confirmed.

At its crudest, framing is about the framer's ability to convince people to see things the same way as the framer so they will form the same opinions. That skill is determined by the communicator's use of what Snow and Benford (1988) call **frame alignment,** or the presentation of information in a way that is congruent with or complementary to the knowledge the frame recipient already has.

···

Frame analysis: A sociological approach that focuses on the presentation of information and ideas in ways that are intended to elicit particular understanding and responses.

Frame alignment: A situation in which multiple frames work together to enhance the efficacy of each.

Framing that serves political interests isn't always bad. If people are concerned about an environmental problem because it threatens their well-being, they will use frames for their own benefit. Some argue that it is in fact impossible to avoid framing, because we are always presenting information from our own standpoints and seeking agreement. Without framing, it would be difficult for scientists to communicate ideas like global warming to the public or to get the public to support efforts to resolve environmental issues. People generally like information that fits with what they already know, and they don't like information that challenges their perceptions of the world. Psychologists call the clashing of incongruent information **cognitive dissonance**. Rather than hold on to contradictory information, people will often reject it. To some degree, environmental activists need to frame ideas in particular ways so that others can hear and consider those ideas. No environmental battle is won without some rhetoric.

▶ Police and emergency personnel stand near damaged cars following a multivehicle accident north of Athens, Greece. Fog was blamed for the 28-car pileup. We live in a "risk society." Do you ever think about how many risks you take on a daily basis, from crossing the street to eating food that could be contaminated?

Policy Implications of Symbolic Interactionism

If the meanings we attribute to the environment are products of social interaction, does that make them less real? If social constructions and frames are political and integral to the process of environmental claims making, should we then remain critical and skeptical of all environmental problems? Even if we accept that the meanings people give to environmental problems are generally self-interested, we do not necessarily have to become cynics. Instead, we could consider the types of representations particular constructions and frames enable, and to what extent they include a variety of voices and encourage conversation as opposed to silence. For example, one way to evaluate and accept frames with a critical eye is to consider the processes through which they are made and the flexibility and inclusiveness of their boundaries. Frame analysis is useful for directing attention to the interests embedded in a frame and the interests the frame advances. These interests are not necessarily bad. Indeed, social justice is all about responding to interests—the interests of those whose legitimate concerns have been neglected or actively suppressed.

We could make this observation about symbolic interactionism more general. If environmental problems are at least partly about conflicts between social groups and threats to the identities of their members, we can reach resolution only when we recognize and legitimate different perspectives. For example, suppose people downstream from an industrial production facility begin feeling sick. They notice fewer birds migrating to the shore, and the grasses that normally grow in the water in the spring aren't there anymore. The managers at the production facility have had the water tested recently, and they suggest the residents are merely upset because their company had to let some people go in response to the recession. To resolve the problem, we need to make sure all parties, both the community members and the managers of the facility, have the resources to perform the necessary research and to test and vocalize their concerns. The solutions to environmental problems lie as much in the processes taken to address them as in the outcomes.

> **ASK YOURSELF:** Do some motivations make a frame seem more legitimate? Do some motivations invalidate a frame? From a symbolic interactionist perspective, what factors may prevent environmental problems from being resolved? Who do you think has the right to participate in discussions about climate change, natural disasters, waste management, or radiation? What about other environmental problems?

Cognitive dissonance: The discomfort of holding conflicting beliefs or values.

SPECIALIZED THEORIES IN ENVIRONMENTAL SOCIOLOGY

14.4 Apply specialized theories to the environment.

We look next at two specialized theories within environmental sociology that tie some of the other perspectives together: risk society and ecological dialogue. Risk society emphasizes the ways in which conflicts between groups of people are increasingly tied to the groups' different perceptions of risk. Ecological dialogue considers how the meanings people give to environmental problems are constantly being renegotiated by the types of direct material experiences more commonly associated with ecological modernization or the treadmill of production. In these two theories, our social experiences and environmental experiences are very explicitly intertwined.

Risk Society

Leaving the house in the morning is risky. Driving to work is certainly risky, and even heading to work on foot requires navigating some dangerous situations. Then again, staying home can be risky, too, depriving you of exercise and reducing your exposure to fresh air and sunlight. Some basic risks are unavoidable. Our choices of which risks to take are influenced by our culture, the benefits associated with the risks, and the costs of avoiding them.

For example, many people live far from where they work. They could live closer, but the housing near work is too expensive. They could work at home, but they don't have the money or time to set up their own businesses. It's easier to take the job in the city and live in the suburbs. But that means driving, and risking becoming one of the 2 million people injured and 35,000 killed every year in traffic accidents in the United States (U.S. Census Bureau, 2012g). Driving to work may be a known risk, but it's one we perceive as normal and acceptable. As public transportation networks grow, bicycle lanes spread, and housing prices near business areas decline, the risk of driving may begin to seem too great and the rewards too low. Some may decide it is now unacceptable and leave the car at home or get rid of it altogether. Others may decide they enjoy their space and the drive to work so much that they will continue to take the chance.

Many of the risks to which we are exposed are more complicated and less predictable, and much less visible, than that of driving to work. Take, for example, the use of DDT. DDT (dichlorodiphenyltrichloroethane) is an insecticide best known for its use in agriculture. During the middle of the 20th century, however, when it was thought that humans were not affected by it, DDT was also sprayed over towns to kill mosquitoes and used to exterminate mammals, like bats, and invertebrates, like sea crustaceans. Adults and children were doused with DDT to get rid of lice.

In the 1950s and 1960s, concern about the effects of DDT began to mount. It reached a pinnacle in 1962 with the publication of Rachel Carson's book *Silent Spring*. Carson was a marine biologist and conservationist who had seen the effects of DDT in birds (the title of her book is meant to conjure up the idea of a spring without birdsong). As it happens, when DDT builds up in a female bird's system, the shells of the eggs she lays become paper thin, and successful reproduction is unlikely. Carson suggested that pesticides like DDT hurt not only mammals and birds but humans as well. She was right. If people ingest enough DDT, they develop nausea and tremors and can even die, but there are also more subtle effects, like low birth weight in children born to women with high DDT levels. Evidence also links DDT to diabetes and cancer.

DDT is still sometimes used overseas to fight malaria because it is so effective at killing mosquitoes—although even where malaria rates are extremely high, there is much concern that the benefits aren't high enough to justify its use (Paull, 2007). Yet an assessment of the risk of using DDT is not a simple, straightforward calculation. It is contested and socially situated. The U.S. Department of Agriculture deems DDT to be moderately toxic, and most people have some DDT stored in their bodies. Even when Carson published her book and evidence against DDT was mounting, some scientists were extremely critical of her blanket condemnation and the public frenzy that resulted. Dr. Robert White-Stevens, a former biochemist and spokesman for the chemical industry, suggested at the time, "If man were to follow the teachings of Miss Carson, we would return to the Dark Ages, and the insects and diseases and vermin would once again inherit the earth" (quoted in McLaughlin, 1998). DDT is not all bad, some would say. It's bad only when it's used thoughtlessly and excessively. If we know more about the risks, we can use it better and without major impacts on the ecosystem. After all, even *nutmeg* is toxic at some level.

Of course, nutmeg and DDT are not the same thing. The trick is to make more educated decisions about what we are using and to what effect. To modernize and develop, some risk is necessary, because otherwise we would be constrained to the knowledge we already have and the practices already in place. At least some technology we have now is better than what we had in the 1950s, and we can produce some things with much less environmental impact than before. Certainly, we have undergone some level of ecological modernization. Those changes would have been impossible, however, if we had insisted that there be no possibility of unforeseen effects. So we blunder ahead, but in the best case we do so only after considering what the consequences might be and with our eyes open for what we may have missed. Increasingly, modernization is accompanied by anxiety and caution, and the sense that projects should be undertaken only after scientific testing and due consideration. While still committed to the advancement of living standards and the refinement of human practices, societies are increasingly driven by what Ulrich Beck (1992; Beck, Giddens, & Lash, 1994) calls **reflexive modernization**—that is, modernization that is increasingly *reflective* about what it is doing. No longer confident that all technological changes will necessarily be for the best, we debate and investigate and insist on those open eyes.

Beck (1992) suggests this form of modernization is part of what he calls the **risk society**. His overarching thesis is that risks are everywhere and play an increasing role in shaping society. The ability to avoid risk exposure creates a new way in which people are divided into social groups, replacing old systems that differentiated them by their access to money and other economic resources. Whereas conflict used to arise over the distribution of goods, with everyone wanting more, it now arises over dodging bads and wanting less of the undesirables. According to Beck, "The driving force in the class society can be summarized in the phrase: *I am hungry!* The movement set in motion by the risk society, on the other hand, is expressed in the statement: *I am afraid!*" (p. 49). Our fear is spurred by our inability to predict the future and our lack of assurance that the government can and will protect society. If risk is about a subjective evaluation of whether the benefits of some activity are worth the potential future costs, leaving it up to the government seems foolhardy. We have lost faith in what Beck calls the **risk contract**, or the implicit understanding that government will enact rules to make sure people will be protected as society bounds progressively forward.

Governments still have rules about acceptable levels of risk, but people in the risk society are less likely to place their faith in these figures. New scientific studies often find that what we knew before was wrong, and different people can draw different conclusions and even significantly different facts from the same phenomena. The industry scientists say one thing, while those employed by the environmentalists say another. Sometimes it seems there's science to back up any claim, and all you need to be right are some really deep pockets.

Even if our science were flawless, there is still the problem of averages. What we consider to be an acceptable level of risk is based on average exposure, but some people are much more exposed or susceptible than others. For example, young children drink large volumes of apple juice, and apples have relatively high levels of trace pesticides due to the difficulty of producing the crop. Environmental sociologist John Wargo (2009) points out that because of their faster rate of development and new-cell formation, children are more likely than adults to form flawed cells that will become cancerous. Assuming that the government has factored in social and physical differences like these when setting acceptable levels of pesticides could be dangerous, especially as cultural practices change. On the other hand, rejecting the role of government is also wrong. Information about risk levels may not be easily available, and the burden of negotiating those risks shouldn't fall entirely on the shoulders of the individual.

> **ASK YOURSELF:** If a group's cultural practices expose group members to unsafe levels of risk, is anyone at fault? What can or should be done to protect people in these circumstances?

Beck has said that risk is the great class equalizer in this age of global environmental problems. Critics argue that he takes this point too far, however. To some degree, risks do confront everyone, but air pollution, for instance, tends to settle in lower elevations, commonly poorer neighborhoods. Waterborne illnesses disproportionately afflict those with lower socioeconomic status. The farmworkers who apply pesticides are typically poor and can't afford expensive organic food. Radiation from nuclear weapons testing conducted many years ago in sparsely populated Nevada has shown up all along the East Coast of the United States (Beck & Bennett, 2002), yet various forms of cancer disproportionately affect people in Nevada and Utah. Environmental risks do have impacts on everyone, to some degree, but they certainly seem to come down more heavily on some—and some, generally the wealthy, are better positioned to avoid the worst consequences. Perhaps this is one reason why surveys usually show that the socially advantaged are the least concerned about environmental problems.

Reflexive modernization: A form of economic development focused on revising current systems of production and making careful assessments of future outcomes of projects and decisions.

Risk society: A society stratified by the ability to avoid risk.

Risk contract: The implicit understanding that government will enact rules to make sure people are protected as society bounds progressively forward.

▶ A homesteader sprays potatoes with pesticide in the Tygart Valley of West Virginia. In the 1940s and 1950s, many American neighborhoods were sprayed with DDT to suppress gypsy moths, mosquitoes, beetles, and other insects. Children would sometimes run into the spray as the DDT trucks went by. Today, thousands of migrant farmworkers (many of whom are undocumented) are injured by pesticide poisoning.

Ecological Dialogue

In the structural functionalist and conflict theory approaches, we largely assume that environmental problems have an objective, scientific grounding. This is called **realism** in environmental sociology, and it is often contrasted with social constructionism. In practice, however, the distinction between realism and constructionism can be a little fuzzy. Many theories that claim to be realist creep into social constructionism, and much social constructionism depends on the existence of material realities. But realists argue that we can separate ecological problems from human relationships and social organization, whereas constructionists claim that environmental problems are human problems and are impossible for us to parse out from human relations and experience in

any sort of objective way. Theoretically, it sounds fairly straightforward. Practically, it becomes much more difficult to be clearly planted on one side or the other. Instead, sociologists often travel between the two when trying to think through environmental problems.

Perhaps we should look at environmental problems using an **ecological dialogue** approach (Bell, 2012; Bell & Lowe, 2000), in which the material and the ideal interact and inform each other, together creating the world in which we live. That interplay between things and thoughts never generates a static product. It is constantly in flux with conflict, collaboration, and creativity.

The ecological dialogue approach assumes that the world we experience is not a complete or stable thing that we can pin down and know definitely and conclusively. There has not been, and will not be, a historical moment when we fully know the world. But there are moments when we can know it *better*—and not better merely in the positivist sense of more accurately, but with greater depth and richness. We can know the world better by seeing it in multiple ways and engaging with it experientially and intellectually. How poorly would we know the world if we didn't think about what we saw and felt? How poorly would we know the world if we only read about it and talked about it with others? We can see redwood trees and know them. We can read about redwood trees and know them. How much better do we know them when we've read about the ancient forests and marveled about these arboreal giants with friends, having also stood amid them, touched their bark, and looked up, trying to imagine how they taper off, 300 feet up in the air? How much better do we know them after a lifetime of reading, seeing, touching, smelling, thinking, and talking, all these things playing together in our bodies and minds? Practically, the line between the material tree and our ideal tree is unclear, although sometimes it makes sense for analytic purposes to make a momentary distinction.

When we think about environmental problems as an ecological dialogue, we also open ourselves to learning from others and their experiences—whether those others are human or nonhuman, alive today, or rocks with 4.5 billion years of history. When we bring them together into dialogue, they push us to create new information that may be more complicated and uncomfortable, but also more nuanced and better able to help us consider such varied and dynamic global environmental issues as climate change.

Realism: The point of view that the world is directly knowable.

Ecological dialogue: An approach to the environment and society that focuses on the interactions between aspects of human environmental relationships.

Researching the Environment

The Work of Riley E. Dunlap and Aaron M. McCright

What people notice and how they think about what they've experienced depends on how it fits with what they already know and the frameworks they've developed to process information. We all have sociocultural lenses through which we peer to see the world. Along these lines, Riley E. Dunlap and Aaron M. McCright have worked at analyzing those social and demographic characteristics that correlate to attitudes about climate change, and how these demographic-attitude couplings become reinforced when they confront each other (McCright & Dunlap, 2011).

Self-identified liberals are more likely than self-identified conservatives to be concerned about climate change (Dunlap & McCright, 2008). While we could not say that all liberals are green activists and all conservatives are nonbelievers, the pattern is significantly strong. Nor does the research mean that being a Democrat makes a person believe the climate is changing, or that being a Republican makes a person disagree. On the other hand, Dunlap and McCright (2010) have found increasing polarization between Democrats and Republicans on the issue of climate change (see also McCright & Dunlap, 2003, 2010).

In recent work, McCright (2011) found that some systems of thought or general orientations predispose people to be more or less likely to believe that climate change is taking place. Those more critical of industrial capitalism are more likely to believe, whereas defenders of industrial capitalism are more likely to challenge the existence of climate change. Those who practice reflexive modernization, who look for ways to critique and refine industry, differ from those who advocate for industrial expansion. It makes sense: If your interests lie in changing industry, you're looking for problems and see them readily. If you are more oriented to expansion, you may be more hesitant to rework the past and present. These predispositions also translate into the types of knowledge that is produced and where it circulates, evident in the relationship between conservative think tanks and climate denial books (Dunlap & Jacques, 2013).

One of the problems faced by climate science is that when the news media report on it, they want to appear to be evenhanded and unbiased, and the resulting coverage doesn't accurately reflect the relative weight of the arguments. Instead, the news media treat both perspectives as equally valid. Moreover, they often focus on disagreement and controversy to make stories more compelling, making it seem that there is much more dissent about the existence of climate change than there actually is. McCright (2011) suggests this presentation of divisive information can polarize people into different climate change camps. It doesn't help that media outlets

► Effigy of Donald Trump during a massive march against climate change as part of the North American Day of Action in downtown Toronto, Canada.

themselves are often polarized into two camps: those that are more conservative and critical of climate change claims (such as Fox News) and those that are more liberal and concerned about climate change (such as MSNBC). Increasingly, the worlds that political groups occupy are isolated from one another. As a result, the disagreement in public opinion exceeds the disagreement in the scientific community, increasing both the challenge to and need for ecological dialogue.

► **THINK ABOUT IT:** Why do you suppose that liberals tend to be concerned about global warming while conservatives tend to deny it exists?

SOCIAL CHANGE: WHAT CAN YOU DO?

 14.5 Identify steps toward social change concerning the environment.

If we are on an ever-accelerating treadmill of production that makes ecological modernization ever harder to attain, it seems that small environmentalist actions might keep the treadmill going longer. For example, driving a hybrid car only modestly contributes to curbing global warming. After all, such a car is still using gasoline. Maybe buying a hybrid even supports the present car-based transportation system. The environmentalist who just bought a hybrid will now be less inclined to put up with the inconvenience of a poor bus system, thus denying the bus system the additional ridership it needs to fund better service. Does buying a hybrid then make larger, society-level changes less likely to happen?

We don't think so—one of us owns a hybrid and we both frequently use the bus! We like to think of the problem as the social equivalent of how landscapes change. We rarely see the hills and valleys of the land change much in our own lifetimes, but geology tells us that, over time, they change enormously. Geology also tells us that the really noticeable and important changes take place in short, dramatic moments: through floods, earthquakes, and eruptions that cause the bonds of rock and soil to slip and slide in great masses of movement, until the land is almost unrecognizable. So it is with social change. We may desire a landslide in the order of things, but without the preparation provided by countless cultural and political raindrops on the soil and rock of social life, nothing would move. *For things to change, we need both the rain and the landslide.* Few of us will experience the landslide, but we can all be part of the rain.

So what can you do to get fired up about an environmental problem as large as climate change? Ask questions, and think through them thoughtfully, acknowledging that the questions you choose predispose you to a particular type of answer. That's okay. Sometimes we need to limit our vision to focus and gain some depth and detail. But keep in mind that your answer is probably not *the* answer. There will never be an end to the conversation, unless we withdraw from participation, and that doesn't help anyone. While it may be valuable to see one aspect of a problem clearly, we also need to engage in conversations, be they heated disagreements

▶ Recycling cans and bottles on Community Service Day in Wellsville, New York. Recycling is the third component of the "reduce, reuse, and recycle" approach to waste management.

or wholehearted camaraderie, or perhaps some of both. Sometimes the rain is stormy.

Environmental problems may seem to have relatively straightforward technical solutions. Stop CO_2 emissions, stop climate change. Stop using paper, plastics, electronics, and manufacturing chemical compounds like pesticides, and the problem of waste disposal virtually disappears. Make the globe a nuclear-free zone, stop the problem of radiation. What we've tried to illustrate is that environmental problems are social, and even solutions that seem technically straightforward are socially very messy. While different perspectives may have slightly different policy implications, they all suggest that some attention to social justice is important. Along these lines, we have tried to emphasize that we are engaging in an ecological dialogue, and encouraging that dialogue to be more representative and vibrant is a fundamental part of any solution.

So whether people in your community are discussing oil drilling, logging, toxic waste, bicycle lanes, or just access to resources for marginalized groups, learn about the issue and get involved, however you can. It doesn't matter whether you agree with everyone who's voicing their opinions. It's great if you don't agree, so you can add something new to the conversation. Be sure you respect the different contexts people come from and think about what they might know that you don't, and vice versa. You'll leave those conversations better equipped to take a critical look

Education Images/UIG/Getty Images

at how you've organized your life and consider whether there is anything you might be able to revise to be more environmentally friendly and more environmentally just. Try to find an ethical way to dispose of that old computer. Ride a bike to work, and if your city isn't bike-friendly, participate in the growing movement to lobby local governments for better bike lanes. Attend a political rally for rights to clean water. These efforts might seem small, but aggregated among those of other people engaging in similar actions, they can be raindrops in a landslide.

WHAT DOES AMERICA THINK?

Questions About Environment From the General Social Survey

Turn to the beginning of the chapter to compare your answers to those of the total population.

1. **What is your interest level in environmental issues?**

   VERY INTERESTED: 42.2%

   MODERATELY INTERESTED: 47%

   NOT AT ALL INTERESTED: 10.8%

2. **In the United States, do you think we're spending too much money on the environment, too little money, or about the right amount?**

   TOO MUCH: 9.8%

   TOO LITTLE: 65.3%

   ABOUT THE RIGHT AMOUNT: 24.9%

3. **In the United States, do you think we're spending too much money on improving and protecting the environment, too little money, or about the right amount?**

   TOO MUCH: 8.1%

   TOO LITTLE: 62.7%

   ABOUT THE RIGHT AMOUNT: 29.2%

4. **What is your interest level in farm issues?**

   VERY INTERESTED: 21.8%

   MODERATELY INTERESTED: 47.5%

   NOT AT ALL INTERESTED: 30.7%

SOURCE: National Opinion Research Center, University of Chicago.

CHAPTER SUMMARY

 Explain how environmental problems are social problems.

Environmental problems occur in the natural world, but they are experienced and interpreted by people who exist in the social world. What we see as problems depends on who we are, where we live, and how we interact with the environment in our daily lives. The solutions we dream up depend on the way we envision ourselves in the environment in the future.

 Discuss patterns and trends in environmental issues.

Environmental justice and globalization are major trends influencing the way we think of patterns in environmental problems. Environmental justice entices us to look at fairness in the distribution of environmental hazards and bounties, while globalization draws our attention to the scope of modern environmental problems and their geographic and political complexity. Climate change, waste management, natural disasters, and radiation are all issues that bring attention to questions of fairness and the global qualities of environmental problems.

14.3 Apply the functionalist, conflict, and symbolic interactionist perspectives to environmental problems and policy.

A functionalist perspective shows us how society has organized everyday life in ways that create environmental problems, so we can recognize how reorganizing life and building more efficient technologies can alleviate the negative effects of human action. Conflict theory suggests that our economy is going to continue to exploit the environment as competition puts pressure on industry to produce more while reducing environmental costs, so a fundamental economic reorganization of society is the only way to truly resolve our environmental problems. Symbolic interactionists consider how people identify environmental problems and give them meanings in ways that relate to identity, access to resources, and what people hold to be culturally valuable.

14.4 Apply specialized theories to the environment.

According to risk theory, people are increasingly concerned with avoiding environmental risks. Moreover, society is organized hierarchically according to levels of safety or hazard, so wealth is less determinant of class position than the ability to avoid harm. The ecological dialogue suggests that the environmental world is never fully knowable, but that we can gain more knowledge about the environment through interaction. We will never be able to see perfectly what happens in an ecosystem, so that we can predict with perfect accuracy how it will behave under certain conditions, but we can gain a better understanding by experiencing nature and sharing those experiences through dialogue.

14.5 Identify steps toward social change concerning the environment.

One of the biggest challenges to solving environmental problems is that we all have personal relationships with the environment and ways of seeing the environment that are culturally, socially, and economically important to us. In order to think critically about our own practices, we need to engage in open conversations with others about their environmental experiences and beliefs. Environmental problems can also seem global and insurmountable. Yet we can make small changes to our everyday practices that add up over time, and across our communities, so the effects can be significant. For example, using environmentally friendly transportation, reducing waste, and sourcing more environmentally just products seem like good places to start, as long as the conversations about the bigger issues continue.

KEY TERMS

cognitive dissonance 359

conspicuous consumption 355

ecological dialogue 362

ecological modernization theory 355

environmental dispossession 345

frame alignment 358

frame analysis 358

indicators 353

realism 362

reflexive modernization 361

risk contract 361

risk society 361

social equity 345

toxic colonialism 346

treadmill of production 356

75 SCIENCE AND TECHNOLOGY

Michael Mascarenhas

A participant in the Science March on Washington holds a sign that says, "Science Has No Borders." Why is it that science and politics are sometimes in tension with each other?

Investigating Science and Technology: My Story

Michael Mascarenhas

In the spring of 2010 I joined an eight-person interdisciplinary team to help a nongovernmental organization based in the United States conduct a baseline assessment of water, sanitation, and hygiene education programs in Rwanda. My participation as a social scientist, I was told, would be crucial in helping this and similar organizations improve future humanitarian efforts both in the field and in policy discussions with donors and other supporters.

Toward the end of our fieldwork I began to reflect on how our research efforts would contribute to the lives of rural Rwandans. In the field, decisions have to be made about whose voices to include *as data*, and, as I found out, these decisions have more to do with *who* was counting than *what* was counted. From this and other fieldwork experiences, I have become increasingly interested in how knowledge travels from one place to another, and the different ways in which expertise is weaved, separated, and assembled in debates about modern society and our contemporary social and environmental problems.

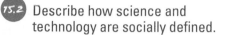

LEARNING OBJECTIVES

15.1 Identify social problems related to science and technology.

15.2 Describe how science and technology are socially defined.

15.3 Discuss patterns and trends in science and technology.

15.4 Identify the stakeholders in science and technology.

15.5 Apply the functionalist, conflict, and symbolic interactionist perspectives to science and technology issues.

15.6 Apply specialized theories to science and technology issues.

15.7 Identify steps toward social change regarding science and technology.

 WHAT DO YOU THINK?
Questions About Science and Technology From the General Social Survey

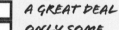

1. What is your interest level in scientific discoveries?
- ☐ VERY INTERESTED
- ☐ MODERATELY INTERESTED
- ☐ NOT AT ALL INTERESTED

2. What is your confidence level in the scientific community?
- ☐ A GREAT DEAL
- ☐ ONLY SOME
- ☐ HARDLY ANY

3. Does science make our way of life change too fast?
- ☐ YES
- ☐ NO

4. Do the benefits of scientific research outweigh harmful results?
- ☐ YES
- ☐ NO

5. Scientific research is necessary and should be supported by the federal government.
- ☐ AGREE
- ☐ DISAGREE

6. What is your interest level in technologies?
- ☐ VERY INTERESTED
- ☐ MODERATELY INTERESTED
- ☐ NOT AT ALL INTERESTED

7. Do you use the home Internet through a mobile device?
- ☐ YES
- ☐ NO

▶▶ Turn to the end of the chapter to view the results for the total population.

SOURCE: National Opinion Research Center, University of Chicago.

SCIENCE AND THE PUBLIC TRUST

It appears that science has never been further from the truth. For example, climate scientists aver that climate change is occurring and is the result of human activity. The climate change science webpage of the U.S. Environmental Protection Agency, for example, states the "earth's climate is changing" and "human activities are contributing to climate change," resulting in adverse effects to "our health, environment, and economy" (United States Environmental Protection Agency, 2017, p. 1). Yet this scientific knowledge exists amid the election of a U.S. president who believes global warming was a concept created by and for the Chinese in order to make U.S. manufacturing noncompetitive. Climate change is a hoax, according to President Donald Trump. In effect, politics and not science is the central factor in shaping people's belief in the effects of climate change (Pew Research Center, 2016).

Sociologist Ulrich Beck (1992, 1999) has argued that science has become so central to modern society that it can neither predict nor control its effects. Science, Beck (1992, 1999) argues, generates risks too vast to calculate, too complex to solve. In the era of nuclear fission, genetic engineering, and a changing climate, society itself has become a scientific laboratory, and science a social problem. Physicist J. Robert Oppenheimer recognized this paradox in 1945, as he and other scientists unlocked the secrets of the atom, and in so doing, gave humanity the knowledge and technology to destroy itself.

Today, we use cell phones, computers, and other technological devices to communicate, shop, bank, and do business online. These technologies, we are told, make our lives easier, and free us to spend more time doing what we want. And, unlike the atom bomb, they expose us to minor risks or dangers. We get our news 24/7 from Google, Facebook, and Twitter, and design new online communities, forging new connections between once-distant and disparate groups. Consider what happened in the months that followed the South Asian tsunami of 2004. Bombarded with media reporting and seduced by YouTube videos, viewers watched live as millions of people lost their homes, livelihoods, and in many cases their lives. These horrific images provoked an outpouring of empathy and generosity of global proportions. Governments, corporations, and individuals from around the world scrambled to offer aid, medicine, other vital supplies, and technical support to the helpless victims. Within 6 months, official aid and private donations raised over $13 billion for the victims of this *natural* disaster (Mascarenhas, 2017).

New communication technologies such as Skype, FaceTime, Google Hangout, and Houseparty offer more convenience and intimacy, and supposedly more privacy, than landlines that could be wiretapped. But do they? Consider the experience of Edward J. Snowden, a former contractor for the National Security Agency (NSA). During his employment Snowden discovered that the NSA and the British government were conducting a top-secret mass surveillance of civilians' phones and e-mails. He leaked the classified information to the British newspaper *The Guardian.* Some consider Snowden a hero, a patriot, and a whistle-blower; others consider him a dissident and a traitor. How would you label Snowden's actions? Is using a portable digital device to store sensitive documents a safe or a dangerous practice? Do we need stricter policies and new technologies to ensure that top-secret information stays top-secret? Are U.S.-based hosting and other Web service companies losing business to overseas competitors? If so, does that pose a danger to U.S. security? Has Snowden's leak damaged the U.S. government's espionage capabilities and left the nation at higher risk to terrorism? Or are governments in fact going too far and endangering the privacy of their citizens? In tandem with these questions, sociologists are asking how the incorporation of surveillance technologies into everyday life is redefining social inequality, social relations, and the concepts of public versus private space. Technology is at the center of a new social problem: the shifting balance between privacy and security.

Google, Facebook, and Amazon freely engage in sophisticated consumer surveillance and data mining to boost their profits. Their collection and analysis of data is part of the **big data** revolution. The benefits to society of this revolution will be myriad "as big data becomes part of the solution to pressing global problems like addressing climate change, eradicating disease, and fostering good governance and economic development" (Mayer-Schönberger & Cukier, 2013, p. 17). This revolution is often referred to as the **fourth paradigm**, a new scientific methodology based on data-intensive computing, where knowledge and understanding are gained with sophisticated algorithms and statistical techniques. Supporters argue that the rise of big data is nothing short of a historical turning point in humanity's quest to solve its most pressing social problems. Using technological advances, corporations are able to aggregate large quantities of digital data to tailor services, advertising, and products to particular consumers. Medical institutions are using big data too. They use it to sift hospital statistics on infections, mortality rates, durations of patient stays, and health care providers, hoping to make hospitals safer and improve medical outcomes.

However, the production of big data is never a simple undertaking. Numbers can't speak for themselves, and data sets—no matter their scale—are still objects of human design. Identity thieves, insurance companies, prospective employers, and opponents of individuals or nations may also be using big data, compiling consumers' personal information, passwords, bank account information, or medical histories intending to cause harm. For example, identity fraud is on the rise, with the number of global victims topping 1 million a day, causing the loss of more than $110 billion annually worldwide (Javelin Strategy & Research, 2013). In 2014, there were 12.7 million U.S. victims of identity fraud, with a new identity fraud victim every 2 seconds (Javelin Strategy & Research, 2015). Have you or has someone you know been a victim of identity fraud? Do you know where your data are?

ASK YOURSELF: Can governments use surveillance to increase security while still respecting civil liberties such as the right to privacy? What trade-offs between privacy and safety shape public and private security and surveillance activities? How does our usual assumption that the Internet is secure shape our social relationships there?

Science and technology play a prominent role in shaping what we define as a social problem. By exploring the relationship between social problems and science and technology, this chapter will help you understand how and why some technology issues emerge as widely discussed social problems while others remain in the category of purely technological or scientific problems.

HACKING AND CYBERCRIME AROUND THE WORLD

 15.1 Identify social problems related to science and technology.

"I'm a computer hacker. I haven't hurt anyone," says a young male being questioned by a detective in a TV show. In fact, more than 75% of hacking worldwide is done by men between the ages of 18 and 30, most likely living in California, Florida, New York, or Texas (Internet Crime Complaint Center, 2011; United Nations Office on Drugs and Crime, 2013; see Figure 15.1). The original hackers were members of the MIT Tech Model Railroad Club who tinkered with the circuitry of model railroads in the 1950s. Some of them discovered that the toy whistles of the train engines could fool the telephone system and allow them to make long-distance calls for free. Here we see the origin of the term *hacking* as we know it—tinkering with a technology to gain an advantage, still the core practice of hacking today.

A *white hat hacker* hacks to protect companies and help identify individuals engaged in cybercrime. A *black-hat hacker*, in contrast, aims to break into company computers to steal data or vandalize computer networks or websites. A hacker can also be a "hacktivist"—someone who steals or manipulates data to make a political or social statement. Aaron Swartz believed that information on the Internet should be available to all for free, so he downloaded 4.8 million academic articles from a subscription-only service in the United States. Though he acted for political reasons rather than for financial gain, he was charged with wire and computer fraud. Whether it is done for political, financial, or personal gain, hacking is on the increase worldwide. Approximately 3% of the hackers worldwide are based in China, where the government places major restrictions on citizens' Internet access and online communication. In China, hacking offers some individuals a chance to tinker with the Internet in order

Big data: The large quantities of digital data produced by digital societies, including data from cell phones, keystrokes, and GPS units.

Fourth paradigm: A new scientific methodology based on data-intensive computing, where knowledge and understanding are gained with sophisticated algorithms and statistical techniques of extensive or mega-scale databases.

to gain freedom of expression, autonomy, and empowerment, while other Chinese hackers have attacked government and corporate websites and networks around the world, hitting organizations such as the U.S. Federal Election Commission, Google, and Microsoft. The 2016 election of U.S. president Donald Trump was mired by the fact that Russian civilian and military intelligence services hacked the databases of Democratic Party organizations in order to sway the U.S. election in favor of Trump.

About six in 10 global Internet users have been touched by cybercrimes such as identity theft, computer viruses, or online fraud. Are you one of them? Globally, there are 14 cybervictims every second (Norton, 2012). Your chance of being a victim of cybercrime depends on your geographic location, your Internet habits, and your Internet technologies. The theft of real property is a long-familiar social problem, whereas the theft or manipulation of electronic data has become one of the top four economic crimes of the early 21st century (PricewaterhouseCoopers, 2011). New forms of cyberespionage and cyberwarfare are also proliferating. A nonprofit organization called Spamhaus in London identified Cyberbunker in the Netherlands as a host for spammers and requested that it be blacklisted. In response, Spamhaus e-mails and webservers were flooded with traffic at 300 gigabits per second for over a week in March 2013. The attack affected millions of Internet users by slowing down global Internet traffic. Another form of espionage that is becoming a problem worldwide is the stealing of human resource files as a means of terrorism. The human resource records of the Nigerian secret service were hacked in August 2012 by Boko Haram, an anti-Western group known for attacking Christians, schools, and police stations in Nigeria. This attack illustrates the growing capabilities of the cyber-arsenal available to groups or nations wanting to employ new forms of warfare or espionage.

As we have seen throughout this book, to understand social problems sociologists ask questions about who, why, how, and what. In cybercrime or hacking, the "who" can be anyone from a local employee to a customer to a stranger halfway around the world, acting alone or in a group. The "why" may be motivated by economic gain, espionage, activism, terrorism, or warfare. The "how" is the use of knowledge and skills to manipulate software and to take advantage of Internet behaviors. The "what" is as dynamic as the Internet, ranging from an individual being scammed out of money to sensitive data being stolen and sold. Hacking thus attempts to modify an existing socio-technical system like the Internet by introducing new social practices and technologies. A **sociotechnical system** is a system that includes material artifacts, human skills, and social practices defined by social norms within an organizational pattern to obtain or address a goal or objective.

Social problems like cybercrime and hacking are unique because of the role technology plays in them. That is, without the Internet and electronic hardware and software, there would be no cybercrime. However, not all cyberthreats come from criminals or black-hat hackers. They can also originate from the unintended consequences of software upgrades or defective equipment. Regardless of their origins, cyberthreats are defined by the skill levels, motivations, and abilities of the actors.

ASK YOURSELF: Consider the information displayed in Figure 15.1. Why might Russia, China, and the United States be hot-spots for hackers? What do the other seven top locations for hacking have in common with these three countries that might explain why they all support hackers in large numbers? Is there a correlation with tinkering to gain advantage? What social factors support or suppress Internet hacking?

SCIENCE AND TECHNOLOGY AS SOCIALLY DEFINED

15.2 Describe how science and technology are socially defined.

Barton Gellman / Getty Images

▶ Former intelligence contractor Edward J. Snowden poses for a photo during an interview in an undisclosed location in Moscow, Russia. Snowden, who exposed extensive details of global electronic surveillance by the National Security Agency, was given temporary asylum by Russia, allowing him to evade prosecution by authorities in the United States. Do you consider him a patriot or a traitor? An idealist or an opportunist?

Sociotechnical system: A system that includes material artifacts, human skills, and social practices defined by social norms within an organizational pattern to obtain or address a goal or objective.

What Is Science?

To understand the role of science in a social problem like hacking, we begin by defining it. The term *science* can refer to particular fields of study, such as biology, physics, or geology. Science is a method of systematically collecting and verifying observed facts. It is the entire societal institution of gathering, reproducing, and maintaining knowledge, and it includes actors, material culture, and resources. Robert K. Merton (1942), the first sociologist of science, called it a "deceptively inclusive word" because it is all of these. For our purposes, **science** is the accumulation of knowledge by specific methods within a particular culture that certifies, applies, and governs what is named science.

Science as a form of knowledge plays an active role in what becomes a social problem. Take, for example, the case of Flint, Michigan, when in the spring of 2014 officials switched the water supply to the Flint River to save money. Community members immediately reported that their water changed color and had a strange odor. Some residents suffered from skin rashes and hair loss, others complained about back and muscle aches, and still others experienced gut bacteria problems. The county health department refused to act, downplaying any danger, and a spokesperson for the Michigan Department of Environmental Quality declared that anyone concerned about lead in their drinking water should "relax." However, it was only after citizens collaborated with scientists to confirm that the drinking water contained

Samuel Corum/Anadolu Agency/Getty Images

▶ What influence did Russia's hacking of the 2016 U.S. presidential election have? What should governments do to ensure their democratic processes are safe from the influence of hackers?

Science: The accumulation of knowledge by specific methods within a particular culture that certifies, applies, and governs what is named science.

FIGURE 15.1 Origins of Hacks and Global Cost, 2012

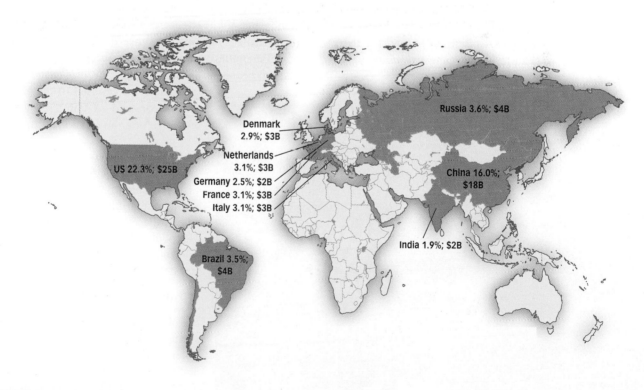

Denmark 2.9%; $3B
Netherlands 3.1%; $3B
Germany 2.5%; $2B
France 3.1%; $3B
Italy 3.1%; $3B
US 22.3%; $25B
Brazil 3.5%; $4B
Russia 3.6%; $4B
China 16.0%; $18B
India 1.9%; $2B

SOURCE: Businessworks 2012.

NOTE: Percentages indicated by country of origin, and dollar amounts are the estimated costs to the global economy.

E. coli, cancer-causing trihalomethanes, and lead, did government agencies declare a state of emergency. Over a period of 18 months over 100,000 people were poisoned from water that government scientists told them was safe to drink. In reflecting on the Flint water crisis, Mark Edwards, a professor of civil engineering at Virginia Tech, declared that "the idea of science as a public good is being lost." This is because in Flint the scientific agencies charged with protecting citizens weren't solving the problem of a contaminated drinking water supply; "they *were* the problem" (Kolowich, 2016, p. 1).

What we consider knowledge and who knows it often defines social problems. Science is a social problem gatekeeper because it designates what knowledge has authority and when. In the case of Flint, Michigan, only scientists were believed when they labeled the community unsafe, while the concerns of community residents were brushed aside. Eventually both science and local knowledge came into alignment when in October 2015 the county declared a health emergency and switched back to Detroit water. Science has the power to determine what knowledge is relevant and when, and how other knowledge is interpreted within and outside social problems.

However, the case of Flint was not the first in which scientific studies did not support community members' health concerns. The Love Canal neighborhood in Niagara Falls, New York, was the home of Hooker Chemical before that company's property was sold for suburban development in the 1950s. The area was known to have puddles of oil and other chemicals in which children often played. In 1976, journalists reported that the community was suffering an unusual number of miscarriages, birth defects, and other health problems, and that toxic chemicals were present in the soil and water. Local authorities denied there was a problem, ignoring local activists' complaints of strange odors and documentation of residents' birth defects. Scientists were divided, and studies were inconclusive about whether chemicals caused the reported illnesses. Studies by the U.S. Environmental Protection Agency (EPA) found harm to residents' chromosomes, while another study found that Love Canal residents had no more chromosome damage than did people who lived nearby but had not been exposed to the leaking chemicals. Only after 2 years of concerted public pressure by activists did President Jimmy Carter name Love Canal a federal health emergency and relocate the remaining 550 families (Tesh, 2001). In both cases, we see how science has the power to determine what knowledge is relevant and what is not when interpreting social problems.

In December 1984 a gas leak in Bhopal, India, became one of the world's worst industrial disasters, killing more than 2,200 people outright and exposing 500,000 others to a toxic cloud. Today, the Indian government argues that there is no contamination at the site, and that documented birth defects are unrelated to the disaster. In this case, scientific studies of local groundwater and the breast milk of residents show the continued presence of toxic chemicals above typical levels in the community. As a result, environmental scientists, the environmental advocacy group Greenpeace, and local community members are asking for renewed efforts to clean up the site and its contaminated groundwater. While science as a form of knowledge plays an active role in defining how governments, corporations, and communities respond to and accept responsibility for social problems, in the absence of a long-term health study of those exposed to the gas at Bhopal, or lead in Flint, science is unable to offer an opinion.

SAUL LOEB/AFP/Getty Images

▶ People wait in line to attend a House Oversight and Government Reform Committee hearing on Capitol Hill in Washington, D.C., about the tainted water in Flint, Michigan.

ASK YOURSELF: In the case of Flint, Michigan, the truth won out. Does the truth always win out? Does the moment before science identifies the "truth" augment or diminish social problems?

What Is Technology?

We often think of technology as consisting of material objects like computers, handheld electronic devices, and other machines. But a broader and more useful definition identifies technology as the means to serve a need, work efficiently, make a profit, or offer a service. Thus technology, like science, has multiple meanings. It can be a computer, but it can also be a complex whole consisting of the knowledge, methods, and materials needed to make and use a computer. More formally, **technology** is an artifact that is defined by social practices, and a product of the way in which social institutions and social relationships are organized.

Consider a slaughterhouse at the beginning of the 20th century in the midwestern United States, and think about how, as a technology, it was defined and constrained by wider social practices. Male butchers gained income and status in the slaughterhouse and in their community because of their skill with the knife. After World War I, black men entered knife work and gained stature as well. Women were a small minority in the meatpacking industry and were paid less than men through the 1960s. Within this minority a hierarchy based on race defined the activity, technology, and location of "women's work." After men cut up the meat, certain parts were sent down a chute to the women's work areas for processing. Black women were given the least desirable women's jobs in the offal part of the slaughterhouse, though they could still earn more doing the lowest-paid work there than they could working as maids elsewhere. Native-born white women were considered temporary workers who earned the same as black women. However, they did clean work in the packing department, where visitors were shown the modern business of meatpacking. Eastern European women did the work that required the most training and skill because they were long-term dependable workers. Societal notions about race and gender structured what men and women did in the slaughterhouse, what technologies they used, and where they used them (Horowitz, 1997).

> *ASK YOURSELF:* Make a list of technologies in your home. Does everyone in the household use the same technologies, and in the same manner? How do people of different genders and races use technologies differently or similarly?

What Is Technoscience?

Where is the boundary between science and technology? To answer this question, we return to the topic of hacking. Early hackers were a few individuals with high-level computer skills and techniques. An early hacker action made a political statement with the WANK worm, which declared "Worms Against Nuclear Killers" when it infected computers at NASA and the U.S. Department of Energy. Such malware, or software intended to disrupt computer operations, was a type of "science" because the knowledge to wield it was maintained and produced by a small group of people. Today, malware tool kits are readily available and make participation in cybercrimes and hacking easier. They have become a technology.

In its history, hacking has sometimes behaved as a "science" and sometimes as a "technology." **Technoscience** includes all supporters, detractors, and social relationships that define the categories of science and technology. A technoscientific analysis can help capture the "messiness" around the boundaries of each term by exploring how hacking is both a science and a technology simultaneously. For example, technoscience would address how a computer infected with a virus could turn an unwitting computer user into a hacker, or how the skills and knowledge of computer science become a means for espionage between nations.

Science as a Social Problem

Traditional images of science portrayed it as a truth-seeking activity that used quantitative assessments and expert knowledge to arrive at facts, until we began to question the facts of science. For example, society recognized that the atom bomb was a military marvel as well as a device of horrific destruction. Industrialization brought labor-saving devices into the factory and the home while also polluting environments with chemical by-products. These complications prompt us to ask the question: Is science a social problem?

Mary Shelley's early-19th-century novel *Frankenstein* provided a similar warning of how unbridled scientific experimentation can have destructive consequences for its creator. The issues it raised have not gone away: How much should we experiment with gene modification? What might its consequences be for biodiversity and species survival? What are the ethical implications and limits of scientific research? To frame science as a social problem, we must understand it as a human endeavor rather than as a method that creates rationality, objectivity, and purity. As long as science offers us certainty, authority, and answers, we see it as a solution. When it creates uncertainty, risk, and danger, we identify and study science as a social problem.

One of the clearest examples of science as a social problem is the Tuskegee Syphilis Study. In 1932, the U.S. Public Health Service intentionally infected 400 black men with syphilis, a sexually transmitted disease. Government scientists allowed these men to go untreated for 40 years.

Technology: An artifact that is composed of social practices, social institutions, and systems that create and constrain it.

Technoscience: A concept that encompasses the boundary between science and technology and includes all supporters, detractors, and social relations that work to eventually close the division between the categories of science and technology.

The purpose of this study was to examine the effects of "untreated syphilis in the male negro." Untreated syphilis causes damage to the brain, nerves, eyes, heart, blood vessels, liver, bones, and joints. In extreme cases it can cause blindness, paralysis, mental retardation, and death, and this is how many of the untreated suffered. Moreover, in the 1950s, penicillin was discovered as an effective treatment for syphilis. However, scientists withheld treatment on the grounds that it would interfere with their study. Only after sustained public pressure did the U.S. government end the study in the mid-1970s. By that time over 100 black men had died, and many others were forced to live with major mental and physical damage.

Technology as a Social Problem

Modern Times, a film written and directed by Charlie Chaplin in 1936, examines the idea of technology as a social problem. The film asks whether technology has gotten too big and made humans its servants, merely parts of the machine. With the entrance of industrialization, workers' skills and knowledge become obsolete next to the machine. This deskilling of workers shifts control from them to a centralized authority.

AP Photo / National Archives

▶ In this 1950s photo, a black man included in the Tuskegee Syphilis Study has blood drawn by a doctor. For 40 years medical workers withheld treatment from unsuspecting men infected with a sexually transmitted disease simply so that doctors could track the ravages of the illness and dissect their bodies afterward. What ethical obligations do scientists have when conducting experiments on human subjects?

Lewis Mumford, one of the founders of technology studies, wrote about the changes the increased mechanization of human labor brought to society and suggested that the way we use technology may threaten what it means to be human. Mumford argued that technology is an integral part of civilization that reflects the entire society. A society where everyone visits the well daily to obtain water develops social interactions that are different from those of a society where members use water in isolation, inside rooms devoted to water usage. Mumford criticized the machine-dominated culture for altering community engagement, individual autonomy, and quality of life. In other words, he foresaw the possibility of technology being a social problem that dehumanizes humanity. The introduction of household water sources decreased community solidarity in communities that formerly depended on limited numbers of common wells, even as it decreased physical labor and improved water quality.

In his later work, Mumford (1967) wrote of the **megamachine**, a new social order composed of humans and technology that is dominated by technological rather than human needs. Megamachines alter human **social organization**, the pattern of relationships among individuals and groups. Could they become reality?

In South Korea, 90% of households have broadband, and 66% of the population have smart phones. More than 2.55 million South Koreans are using their Internet devices longer than 8 hours a day. More than half the nation plays online games regularly. Teachers report that children ages 5 to 9 are animated when using smart phones and distracted and nervous without them. One young girl said she gets nervous when she has less than 20% power on her device. This intense engagement with the Internet is a megamachine, in which humans and technology are creating a new social organization and people may be spending more time with machines than with other people. Government officials, health care practitioners, and teachers have called this social problem "Internet addiction," and ask whether it might become an illness (Lee, 2012). Educators are responding by introducing curricula to teach elementary school children about safe and healthy uses of connectivity.

Megamachine: A new social order composed of humans and technology that is dominated by technological rather than human needs.

Social organization: The pattern of relationships between individuals and groups.

Researching Science and Technology

Vaccines and Autism

Do vaccines cause autism? Medical experts say no, yet many parents of children diagnosed with autism continue to doubt the science. Actress-turned-activist Jenny McCarthy, for example, has attributed her son's autistic behavior to a series of vaccinations he received as a child. The author of three books on autism, McCarthy helped organize a growing movement of parents concerned about a vaccine-autism link.

The vaccine-autism debate began in 1998 with the research findings of gastroenterologist Andrew Wakefield published in *The Lancet*, Britain's oldest medical journal. Wakefield's paper described 12 children showing autistic behaviors and severe intestinal inflammation. Wakefield also reported that he found traces of the measles virus in his participants' intestinal tracts, and speculated that a three part combination—gut issues, autism, and measles virus—comprised the basis for a single syndrome. His hypothesis of a causal link was strengthened by the fact that eight out of the 12 children in his study had been

developing normally, and within days of getting the measles, mumps, and rubella (MMR) injection began to display classic symptoms of autism, including loss of speech (Donvan & Zucker, 2016).

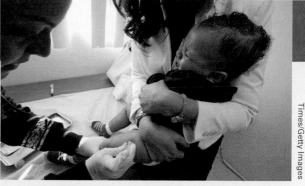

▶ A medical assistant administers an MMR vaccine to a 1-year-old boy in Los Angeles.

Mel Melcon/Los Angeles Times/Getty Images

Nearly every virologist, pediatrician, and public health official regarded the MMR vaccine as a notable example of applied science and public health policy. It had effectively eliminated all three of the targeted diseases. Still, for many parents the lack of data to support Wakefield's claims was beside the point. Rates of autism have skyrocketed from an estimated one child in 3,000 to one in 150 kids. For parents with autistic children, Wakefield was the first scientist who had ever really listened to them. His hypothesis vindicated their concerns, and showed the world they were neither crazy nor ignorant. Many of them came to his defense even after his research was exposed as

fraudulent, his conflicts of interest revealed, his publications withdrawn, and his medical license revoked.

For all the controversy surrounding the science, those leading the autism movement found a new voice and platform to speak about this condition. For many, it was no longer seen as a sickness in need of a cure but a medical condition that needed to be further researched, understood, and cared about.

▶ **THINK ABOUT IT:** Most believe that the scientific controversy surrounding vaccinations in children and the rise of autism has been resolved. Or has it? Do you believe vaccinations are safe? How do you know?

PATTERNS AND TRENDS

 15.3 Discuss patterns and trends in science and technology.

If we view science and technology as a social problem, the trends and patterns that emerge illustrate a connection between modern science, "personal troubles," and "public issues" that is often overlooked when we view science, technology, and society separately. C. Wright Mills (1961, p. 16) described this connection between science and society as a

science machine that is built by a community of individuals who share a common culture. He suggested that once we see the science machine driving science, we can begin to understand its connections and relationships to society and its problems. Moreover, the practice of science is embedded in the social, economic, political, and cultural institutions that support it; in the priorities of research centers (universities, corporations, nonprofits, and national laboratories) where scientists work; in the cultural biases and prejudices

....

Science machine: A connection between science and society that is built by a community of individuals who share a common culture.

▶ In the movie *I, Robot*, a technophobic cop (played by Will Smith) investigates a supercomputer that programs robots to kill humans. The film *2001: A Space Odyssey* is about the HAL 9000 computer that takes over a spacecraft with two astronauts in it. In the television series *Westworld*, android hosts terrorize guests at a futuristic Western-themed amusement park. Can you think of other films and novels with similar themes?

of the scientists themselves; and in the economic and academic pressures of doing modern science.

Values and Doing Science

For decades, modern science has been sampling our blood and studying our genes to evaluate our health, identify our predispositions for certain illnesses, and prescribe treatments. We assign to science the power to discover the truth about our health. This power is reinforced by the success of science in developing new vaccines, insecticides, and drugs to solve social problems. However, what happens when an illness moves through a population faster than science can find an answer? The science's protocol is to do research in the laboratory. When a solution is suspected, it is tested carefully in a controlled environment until guidelines are established to protect people from unintended consequences. Once the efficacy of the science has been established, the solution is introduced to the general public.

What happens when there isn't sufficient time to go through the established protocols? In response to social scientific problems such as HIV/AIDS, activists have suggested the need to implement **crisis science**, or triage science, when there is no time to follow time-consuming research protocols. The goal of crisis science is to respond quickly and produce results quickly, allowing individuals to participate in studies that may be risky and soliciting community participation in the research (Hood, 2003). Crisis science works in tandem with the normal protocols of science while simultaneously engaging activists and patients in the coproduction of knowledge through experimental procedures of drug testing. This occurred in

the case of AIDS research (Epstein, 1995).

Another growing response to doing science that supports citizens' claims about exposure to pollution and their health problems are **health social movements** (HSMs), the practice of linking health research with community activism to influence health policy. HSMs embrace the principles of science—the systematic use of theory, methods, and evidence—and use them to challenge the authority of scientific institutions in public debates about health (Brown et al., 2012). What sets HSMs apart from other social movements is less the fact that they challenge science than how they go about doing science. HSMs often engage in citizen science alliances (CSAs) in which activists, community members, scientists, and health professionals collaborate in pursuing research, treatment, and funding of particular health problems (Brown et al., 2012). Studies of Gulf War–related illnesses such as chronic multisymptom illness (CMI), and the environmental breast cancer movement (EBCM), are two of a growing body of HSMs.

A practice of knowledge production that embraces a broad set of participatory research methods in the investigation of social scientific problems is **street science**. When local knowledge is combined with insights, tools, and techniques from disciplinary science, local knowledge forms the basis of street science, seeking to improve the democratic character of science-based policy making (Corburn, 2005).

Another response of the scientific community to social problems is the development of **science shops**, facilities hosted by universities where citizens can participate in science, ask scientific questions, and become part of the

---

Crisis science: Medical science that works in tandem with Mode 1 science and has the freedom to respond to crises and the needs of patients faster than traditional science.

Health social movements: The practice of linking health research with community activism to influence health policy. HSMs embrace the principles of science.

Street science: A practice of knowledge production that embraces a broad set of participatory research methods in the investigation of social scientific problems.

Science shops: Facilities hosted by universities where citizens can participate in science, ask scientific questions, and become part of the scientific process.

scientific process. Science shops began in the Netherlands in the 1980s as a bottom-up strategy for bringing the social needs of communities into universities' scientific research agendas. They can now be found at universities around the globe from Europe to South Korea, demonstrating how science is being redefined by the organizations that create it.

Reform movements that typically address health or social problems, such as advocacy for nutritional cancer therapies and environmental change, have also generated their own research (by the Gerson Research Organization and the World Wide Fund for Nature, for instance). They have conducted peer-reviewed research and in some cases provided alternative theories to engage with mainstream science (Hess, 1999, 2009). Thus science is being redefined by social problems to include more active roles for actors typically excluded from the production of knowledge.

When we analyze social problems and science simultaneously, our view of science changes from certainty, facts, and objectivity to uncertainty, conflicting values, high stakes, and urgent decisions (Ravetz, 2005). By broadening the products of science from ones that offer certainty, objectivity, and established knowledge to ones that recognize the risks of the unknown, we redefine our understanding of science to acknowledge the complexities rather than to eliminate them. By recognizing human values, risks, and uncertainties, science engages with social problems to find new solutions.

Today, corporations, citizens, governments, and nonprofit organizations are interested in the knowledge, technologies, and patents of a newly interdisciplinary science. The shift in what science is, whom it serves, and how it does what it does is summarized in Table 15.1, which distinguishes the traits of classic scientific discovery as **Mode 1** and socially responsible and application-oriented science as **Mode 2**.

> *ASK YOURSELF:* What are the advantages and disadvantages of applying Mode 1, Mode 2, and crisis science to the solution of social problems?

Technology and Values

One of the responses to threats of terrorism in the United States was the development of an all-body scanner to be used in airports as a quick and efficient means of searching for concealed weapons. Two types of three-dimensional millimeter wave machines were developed: "naked" machines and "blob" machines. The naked machines showed graphic naked images of the human body and anything concealed under the clothing. The blob machines displayed sexless avatars with baseball caps that indicated where on the body something was

TABLE 15.1 Traits of Mode 1 and Mode 2 Forms of Knowledge Production

Traits	Mode 1	Mode 2
Audience	Academic	Wider society
Context	Disciplinary	Transdisciplinary
Organization	Hierarchical	Egalitarian
Priority	Academic freedom	Social responsibility
Evaluation	Peer review	Social relevance
Validation	Scientific certainty	Acknowledges uncertainty
Planning	Long-term and linear	Exploratory

SOURCE: Gross, Matthias. 2010. *Ignorance and Surprise: Science, Society, and Ecological Design.* Cambridge, Mass: MIT Press

hidden. Public response to the naked machines was negative enough for the Obama administration to order that they be retrofitted as blob machines. This is a case in which a technological solution to one social problem—security—spurred a new social problem by invading privacy. The technological solution that solved the social problem of body scanning embraced the value of protecting privacy as well as security (Rosen & Wittes, 2011).

The example of the naked and blob machines demonstrates that there may be several technological solutions to a social problem. The technological solution that meets the most needs of all the actors will be the ideal solution. Unfortunately, this ideal technological solution doesn't always get designed or implemented. However, by identifying different actors in social problems and their needs, we can begin to design technology that is more inclusive of multiple needs.

A popular do-it-yourself (DIY) movement dedicated to actively experimenting, designing, and sharing technological solutions to social problems is the **makerspace**. While often associated with the subversive acts and political interventions of hackerspaces and hacklabs, individuals

Mode 1: A type of scientific discovery or knowledge production done by scientists in universities through the application of experimental science within distinct disciplines.

Mode 2: A type of scientific discovery or knowledge production that is done by experts and nonexperts working together in transdisciplinary environments to create applications that are socially responsible.

Makerspace: A popular do-it-yourself (DIY) movement dedicated to actively experimenting, designing, and sharing technological solutions to social problems.

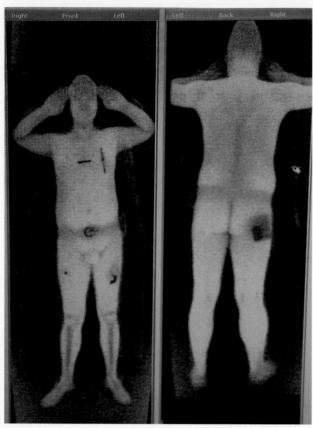

▶ A computer screen shows a scan of an airport security officer in a RapiScan full-body scanner. Found in many airports, the scanner, used for security screening purposes, produces an image of a person's naked body. Do you see this technology as a good way to protect travelers from terrorist attacks or as an infringement on people's privacy?

participating in makerspaces are interested in manipulating, innovating, and designing new technology directed toward social entrepreneurship; consumerist material production; and, increasingly, social justice and community needs (Lyles et al., 2016).

Science Constructs and Solves a Social Problem

Chagas disease affects roughly 18 million people in Latin America. The *Trypanosoma cruzi* parasite is transmitted to humans by an insect called the vinchuca that nests in walls and roofs made of adobe. Once infected, a person may not show external signs of the disease, but his or her nervous, digestive, and circulatory systems are being attacked by the parasite. If a patient is treated early, the parasite can be controlled or killed; however, if left untreated the disease is fatal—it is the fourth-leading cause of death in Latin America. The World Health Organization (WHO) considers Chagas disease a neglected killer that others have called a disease of poverty.

In 1909, Carlos Chagas, a physician, discovered the disease in Brazil while working on urban epidemics for the Manguinhos Serum Therapy Institute, an internationally recognized center of experimental science. However, the disease that was named for him was not immediately recognized as a social problem in Latin America and did not draw the attention of scientists and public health administrators. In the 1930s, Salvador Mazza, an Argentinean epidemiologist working on Chagas disease, carefully researched acute cases to document the symptoms and identified traces of parasites in the blood of infected patients. Mazza's commitment to documenting evidence of infection of the parasite contributed to the recognition of Chagas disease by national public health departments and the Pan American Health Organization.

In the 1940s and 1950s, Chagas disease gained recognition as a chronic ailment and a social problem. Scientists shifted from studying individual patients to studying the disease in the general population. These larger-scale studies led to statistical analyses that estimated the number of people afflicted. Public health officials could then mobilize to fight the problem through hygiene education and improved access to health care. In addition, a new insecticide, gammexane, was found to eliminate vinchucas, and massive fumigation of housing was implemented by the El Salvadoran Ministry of Health.

By the 1970s, the *T. cruzi* parasite had become the focus of study, instead of the person infected with Chagas disease. Researchers studied the physiology of the parasite and its insect host in order to find a means to attack the parasite and create a vaccine against it. A vaccine would solve the social problem and replace fumigation and education as a first defense. Though no vaccine was discovered, the study of *T. cruzi* became an important biological model that legitimated Latin American scientists in the eyes of the international scientific community. Today, the primary strategy for addressing Chagas disease is to control and attack the parasite (Kreimer & Zabala, 2007).

Different social actors choose different facts and frameworks from which to approach and understand the social problem of Chagas disease. For the infected patient, Chagas is the cause of illness. For the scientific community and public health officials, knowledge of Chagas and its environment, host, and parasite helped identify a potential social problem, construct the social problem, and offer solutions. Science's role as authority remained constant even as solutions and constructions of the social problem changed.

Technological Fixes

In the United States and other Western cultures, people generally associate technological improvements with progress. In the late 18th century, science and technology were seen as instruments of societal transformation and began to symbolize progress. Today, the ideal of **technocracy**, a system in which science and technology provide rationality, expertise, and logic and create a better world, is still widely considered desirable. This technocratic view of progress sees technology as a means to fix social problems.

For example, we use radar to deter speeding on the highways by monitoring automobiles and identifying those in violation of the speed limit. Drivers still speed, of course, and some buy radar detectors and occasionally get tickets. Their **technological fix** uses technology to solve a problem that is nontechnical and ignores the social components of the problem. In other words, when we use technology to solve a social problem like speeding, we may create another like the use of radar detectors. Or our solution may isolate the problem from the social context, such as ignoring the fact that the average speed of cars traveling on a particular highway is always 10 miles per hour over the speed limit.

Industrialized Science Creates Social Problems

Science was once done by educated European male elites such as Galileo, Newton, and Kepler. Today, it is the primary activity of a broad range of experts in academia, industry, and government. We have moved from an era of little science to big science, with the number of researchers growing steadily throughout the 20th century (see Figure 15.2). Science itself is now an industry. With the rise of **industrialized science**, in which science is done on a large scale for profit, new social problems are emerging (Ravetz, 1971). With industry pursuing genomics, robotics, and nanotechnology for profit, for instance, the possibilities for intervention in and manipulation of human life and our environment are raising new questions.

In rich countries around the world, backbreaking labor and repetitive physical work have already been taken over by machines in an example of technology making life easier for many. With the help of robotics, more types of human labor could become unnecessary and alter what humans do. What types of work will everyone do in a robotic world? We depend on our livelihoods to define who we are in society and where we fit. What will define the social order in a robotic world?

We now can create genetically modified organisms (GMOs) for food production, though some safety issues about manipulating genes in the food we eat remain unresolved. Nanotechnology offers similar engineering possibilities, such as genomics to modify our bodies and our world. Will we bioengineer ourselves to eliminate genetic propensities or vulnerabilities to disease? Who will be eligible, and who will decide what engineered traits will be desirable? Industrialized science may be offering us a "brave new world," or it may recreate our current world with social problems even more complex than those we already face. The problem is that we don't know what the outcomes will be. One solution is to redirect science to focus on safety, health, environment, and ethics rather than on industrialized goals (Ravetz, 2005). This focus would ensure that science's agenda stays in tune with and responsive to contemporary social problems.

Social Problems Within Science

Worldwide, there are more than 7 million scientists and engineers, approximately 62% of them in industrialized nations. We know from Chapter 4 that women are a minority within science. But science is also demarcated by the absence of people of color, both in developed countries like the United States and in developing countries in general. Thus a social problem within science is the dearth of diversity in the science, technology, engineering, and math (STEM) workforce. We can examine the diversity of STEM education and science and technology studies schools to get a better sense of this inequity.

Science and technology studies scholars have developed a critical understanding of "science" as something that is inherently social. Today, STEM and science and technology programs and departments can be found in universities throughout the United States. These programs train future researchers, academics, and scientists. Some departments have made gains in terms of gender balance. For example, at Brown University, the University of California, Berkeley, and the University of Michigan, women researchers outnumber men researchers. Yet this situation remains the

---

Technocracy: A means of governing that is guided by rationality, expertise, and logic.

Technological fix: The use of technology to solve a social problem that is nontechnical. In fixing the problem it creates another, because the underlying social issue is still present and has been isolated from the social context.

Industrialized science: Science that is done on the large scale for profit.

FIGURE 15.2 Total Numbers of Researchers Employed Around the Globe, 2002–2014

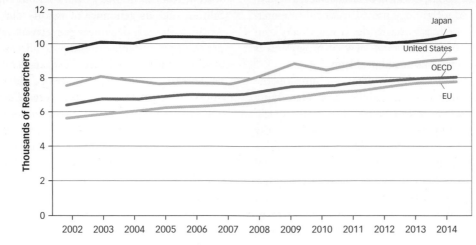

SOURCE: Organization for Economic Cooperation and Development, Main Science and Technology Indicators. Reprinted with permission.

FIGURE 15.3 Gender and Race of Some STS Departments and Programs in the United States

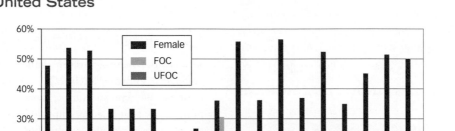

exception, as most schools are still male dominant, particularly Drexel University, Rensselaer Polytechnic Institute, and Stanford University. We also see real disparities in faculty of color (FOC) and major gaps in underrepresented faculty of color (UFOC), Latinos and African Americans. In fact, many institutions have no underrepresented faculty of color. Moreover, while some, like Worcester Polytechnic Institute, seem diverse, most faculty of color at WPI do not hold permanent positions. (See Figure 15.3.)

Today, colleges in the United States remain as racially segregated as they were in the mid-1950s, and this is particularly true in the STEM disciplines. In 2014, 9,568 doctorates were awarded to students in engineering, many of whom were to be faculty and leaders of industry and government—the same government that funds science research. Only 1.7% of these doctorates were awarded to blacks and 2.5% to Hispanics. Similarly, for every 100 students matriculated in medical schools, only 15 are students of color (American Educational Research Association, 2015). In 2012, a total of 1,690 doctorates were awarded in computer science, 2% were awarded to blacks, 1.5% to Hispanics, and 0.1% to Native Americans. This segregation in higher education is occurring at a time when nonwhite students outnumber whites in America's K–12 schools. Looking at science from a global perspective, we see a similar trend among scientists working in the Global South. Thus a social problem within science is the dearth of diversity in the science, technology, engineering, and math (STEM) workforce. There is also strong evidence for the benefits of diversity in STEM, which is consistent with the research showing that analytical problem-solving skills are positively related to informal interactions with diverse peers (American Educational Research Association, 2015).

Some of the same obstacles that have prevented women from entering science fields in the United States have also prevented citizens of developing countries from becoming scientists. Scarcity of role models and lack of access to education and resources are all potential obstacles to developing scientific capacity. Removing these can enrich the culture of science and expand its abilities to respond to social problems.

The National Science Foundation (NSF), an independent U.S. government agency authorized to initiate and support scientific research, requires that all research proposals consider the social impacts of science and engineering research. The NSF had emphasized the need to broaden participation and enhance diversity in its programs by increasing the participation of groups based on gender, ethnicity, disability, and geographic differences; enhancing the infrastructure for research and education; disseminating scientific results broadly; and outlining the benefits of the research to society (National Science Foundation, 2003).

***

ASK YOURSELF: Consider the data displayed in Figure 15.3. What types of social problems would science be addressing if more scientists were women or people of color?

***

SCIENCE, TECHNOLOGY, AND THEIR STAKEHOLDERS

15.4 Identify the stakeholders in science and technology.

One of the roles of science in modern society is to be the authority or voice of truth about the natural world. Science and technology validate programs and policies that tell us what we should eat, how we should treat illness, and what is best for our safety. They do this by providing knowledge and techniques that let us describe problems with certainty and prescribe solutions with accuracy. For example, when we are ill and visit a doctor, we expect that he or she will diagnose our illness with certainty and prescribe the correct treatment.

In this section we will look at how different social actors or stakeholders use science and technology in specific and deliberate ways to frame, respond to, and solve social problems. Typical stakeholders of science and technology include the experts (scientists, engineers, and technicians), the funders (government, nonprofit organizations, and corporations), the producers (universities, corporations, and professional societies), and the consumers (average citizens, groups, and entire communities).

Social problems involving science and technology often take the form of complex controversies among scientific, medical, or technical experts. The social, political, and economic implications of these disagreements affect stakeholder groups unequally. Let us look at one example of corn production in the United States and Mexico, where the stakeholders are government agencies, farmers, and consumers in both countries.

In 2003, approximately 5% of total arable land worldwide was planted with transgenic crops. *Transgenic crops* are grown from seed that has had genes artificially inserted (rather than acquired through pollination) in order to increase yields, raise pest or disease resistance, or improve tolerance of heat, cold, or drought. The majority of transgenic crops grown today are herbicide-tolerant soybeans, insect-resistant cotton, and maize that is either herbicide-tolerant or insect-resistant. Of these crops, 90% are grown in the United States and Argentina, with Canada and China producing most of the remaining 10%. Concerns about the widespread adoption of transgenic crops include the potential for damage to human health, destruction of the environment, and disruptions to farming practices and food production.

Different governments have taken different stances on transgenic crops that reflect cultural, economic, and political factors. In the United States three federal agencies—the Department of Agriculture, the Environmental Protection Agency, and the Food and Drug Administration—ensure the safety of transgenic crops. There are no sexually compatible wild relatives for transgenic maize to pollinate in the United States; thus the primary concern of the U.S. government is the biosafety of humans and the environment, not the spread of transgenic maize into the local maize germplasm.

Mexico welcomes the importation of U.S. transgenic maize for food consumption. However, it has banned the planting of transgenic maize in its own soil since 1998 in order to keep the locally bred maize free of GMOs. Maize was first domesticated in Mexico several thousand years ago, and its wild ancestor still grows there. Thus the primary concern of the Mexican government is to maintain the genetic diversity of the landraces of maize in Mexico that are open-pollinated and bred by local farmers. **Landraces** are local varieties of seeds that have been domesticated by communities over time and have adapted to local cultural and environmental needs.

***

Landraces: Local varieties of seeds that have been domesticated by communities over time and have adapted to local cultural and environmental needs.

The Mexican government's interest in controlling transgenic maize is to preserve genetic diversity, while the U.S. government's concern centers on ensuring food and environmental safety. Thus similar types of stakeholders may have different interpretations or approaches to the same social problem. If transgenic crops become a social problem in the United States, it will likely focus on the safety of the crop for humans or the potential destruction of habitats for insects like the monarch butterfly. In Mexico, the social problem will be preventing the flow of genes from transgenic crops to wild ancestors of maize and farmer-bred landraces of maize. Or it might be maintaining the traditional breeding practices of Mexican farmers if transgenic crops are introduced.

U.S. farmers prefer high-yielding maize and buy the first-generation hybrids yearly. Typically they do not save seeds for replanting from year to year, and their primary goal is the production of crops. Transgenic crops and large-scale farmers are both part of an industrial agricultural system.

In contrast, Mexican farmers produce maize and conserve landraces that have often been handed down through their families for generations. These traditional farmers develop new plant varieties, process their crops, and consume what they grow. They select and grow different varieties of maize based on cropping systems, local environmental conditions, and consumer preferences for color, texture, cookability, and shelf life. Mexican farmers trade seeds with relatives and neighbors in exchanges that reflect and reinforce their social relationships (Snow, 2005).

One common concern among most of the stakeholders involved with transgenic crops is the safety of the crops for human consumption. Risks associated with these crops include allergic reactions to food and antibiotic resistance. Only two transgenic crops, of all that have been studied, have been found to cause allergies. One was never developed further, and the safety of the other, StarLink corn, is still being debated by scientists. Research continues, but it is commonly believed that GMOs cause no greater risk of allergy than conventional foods. In the laboratory stage, transgenic crops are given antibiotic resistance markers that become part of the final product. Another concern is thus about the risk that a horizontal transfer of these drugs could lead to antibiotic resistance in humans. This too is believed to be highly unlikely, though the potential risk is there.

Little scientific evidence to date indicates that transgenic crops are riskier than conventionally bred crops. However, Zimbabwe refused to import GMO corn in 2010 because of concerns about its safety for the population and the purity of future crops.

The creation of transgenic crops is an expensive but powerful technology the industry has been quick to patent for profit. In the United States, the ability to secure intellectual property rights on living organisms and biological processes has helped the seed industry—once a regional business that supported a broad range of genetic diversity—to consolidate and become big business. Today, the industry is dominated by only a few companies. In traditional agriculture, seed stock was a public good that individuals traded for the community's benefit. The entrance of transgenic crops into traditional agricultural communities threatens contamination of the seed stock, reduction of genetic diversity, and the pursuit of legal action by patent holders against smallholder farmers (Gepts, 2005).

Transgenic crops that are insect-resistant are designed to address particular pests in particular regions. However, these pests and nontarget pests are different in other locations, so the introduction of a transgenic crop to a new area may cause unintended harm in the new ecosystem. For example, the monarch butterfly is susceptible to the *Bacillus thuringiensis* (Bt) toxin used in transgenic crops. Studies indicate there is minimal effect on the monarch in the short term, but further investigation is needed to measure any long-term effects. Other insects may be affected by the introduction of transgenic crops in ways we have yet to identify. Thus insects are additional potential stakeholders in the debate surrounding transgenic crops.

Science is an active stakeholder in this debate. However, within science there are different sorts of stakeholders among agribusiness and individual scientists, critics, and scientific publishers. In 2001, two biologists, David Quist and Ignacio Chapela, documented the presence of transgenic genes in maize landraces in Mexico. Their paper, published in the science journal *Nature,* created a controversy in science and highlighted a social problem in agricultural biotechnology. Critics asked how the transgenes came to be there. It is a normal part of science for new theories to be challenged, but in this case the critique was used to obscure the primary finding that transgenes were present in Mexican landraces of maize. The challengers' research was funded in part by an agriculture biotech firm involved in transgenic crop production. Their financial and political ties to industry raised questions about their motives for critiquing the findings of Quist and Chapela, who themselves were critics of the university-industry alliance.

Uncharacteristically, the editors of *Nature* disowned the original report by Quist and Chapela in a response that reflected the interests of the publication's sponsors. The controversy highlighted "the intensity of the marriage of science to corporations" in the field of agricultural biotechnology (Worthy et al., 2005, p. 143). In 2005, the area in Mexico where Quist and Chapela had discovered transgenic genes was retested. Such genes were no longer present in the landraces of maize.

Pallava Bagla/Corbis/Getty Images

▶ People in New Delhi, India, demand a ban on the introduction of genetically modified mustard in Indian fields. Would you eat foods—plants or animals—that you knew were genetically engineered?

USING THEORY TO EXAMINE SCIENCE AND TECHNOLOGY: THE VIEWS FROM THE FUNCTIONALIST, CONFLICT, AND SYMBOLIC INTERACTIONIST PERSPECTIVES

 15.5 Apply the functionalist, conflict, and symbolic interactionist perspectives to science and technology issues.

Social scientists have long used the traditional three sociological perspectives—functionalism, conflict theory, and symbolic interactionism—to suggest alternative points of view from which to assess social problems. Contemporary scholarship on science, technology, and social problems uses these theories in conjunction with feminist theory, science and technology studies, and cultural studies to extend the analysis, definition, and content of social problems research.

Functionalism

A structural functionalist approach to science and social problems illustrates the positive and negative functions of social structures. One social problem within science is that top scientists receive the lion's share of scientific credit. A structural functionalist explanation for this would cite **cumulative advantage**, which multiplies the advantage for those who have resources and limits the capacity of those

without. Cumulative advantage explains why graduate students who attend top-tier American research universities such as Harvard, MIT, and Stanford are more likely to become prominent scientists than those who attend nonresearch universities. At a top-tier research university students have access to active scientists and their scientific networks. These resources provide students with a cumulative advantage over their peers who lack such access.

Another example of cumulative advantage is the accumulation of cultural capital—that is, social assets that promote social mobility, such as a parent's educational background. Doctoral students are more likely to have a parent with an advanced degree (43%) than a parent with only some college (12%) (National Science Foundation, 2013). Cumulative advantage helps explain the absence from science of individuals from a wide variety of backgrounds, socioeconomic levels, and educational institutions. Lack of diversity reinforces the preexisting scientific social networks, which means most scientists train at the same institutions with comparable cultural capital from the same recognized scientific leaders. This sameness, in turn, stabilizes the scientific culture by ensuring that similar questions are asked and studied by similar people. This form of **academic capital** enables scientists at elite

Cumulative advantage: A position that multiplies advantages for those who have them and limits the capacity for those without resources.

Academic capital: An example of cumulative advantage where scientists in elite institutions build enduring networks, resources, and schools of thought.

Experiencing Science and Technology

What Does It Mean to Be a Black Woman in Science?

Minority groups in the United States are underrepresented within the science and engineering professions compared to their proportions in the general population. Of all scientists and engineers in the United States, 2% are black women, compared to 51% who are white men (see Figure 15.4).

While all students need to be encouraged in scientific pursuits by parents, teachers, and mentors, minority students may receive less parental and school support to study science than are their nonminority peers. High schools that serve minority populations often have limited offerings in math and science, lacking classes in subjects like analytical geometry, precalculus, and calculus that provide the foundation for majoring in science in college. A white male can always find a peer who shares his interests because he is in the majority, while minority students may have fewer peers with whom to discuss and explore science or engineering. Students who form study groups and complete their homework together are generally more successful than isolated students.

One black scientist described her shock at being overlooked by her

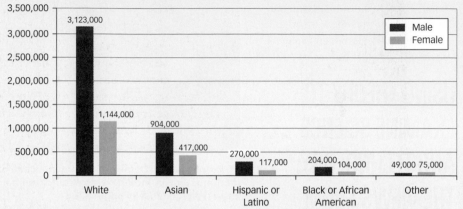

FIGURE 15.4 Scientists and Engineers Working in the United States by Race and Gender, 2015

SOURCE: National Science Foundation.

peers and teachers, not because she was black but because she was a woman. Black women in science encounter not only racism but also sexism in the scientific culture. As students they may fail to be elected to student science organizations, may find their male lab partners (whether black or white) dismantling the labs they set up and redoing them, or may be advised to take freshman physics when male peers are taking junior-level quantum mechanics.

The culture of science is aware that minority women are rare in science and that many potential scientists

are exiting the pathway before achieving their goal. Supplementary educational programs, efforts to change cultural norms, and mentoring are strategies that can change scientific culture and create a more welcoming community for minorities and women.

▶ **THINK ABOUT IT:** What stereotypes might the following individuals encounter: A Hispanic man working in a laboratory? An Asian woman directing a laboratory? A black woman giving a scientific presentation? A white homosexual man running for president of a scientific association?

---

institutions to build enduring networks, resources, and schools of thought.

A structural functionalist position may also help researchers pose questions about what role science or technology is playing in the creation of a social problem. That is, researchers might trace what knowledge is defining a social problem and how it is being applied in order to describe the relationship between science and the social problem. Or they might focus on a technology (such as

the automobile) and ask how individuals and communities are using it in order to understand the role of the technology in social problems (such as traffic accidents or poor air quality).

Policy Implications of Structural Functionalism

Public policy can use a structural functionalist perspective to recognize what role science or technology plays in a social problem. When science is the authority that names a social problem, policy makers can ask for opposing scientific views or views outside the realm of scientific expertise. Historically, the absent voice in social problems has been the lay perspective. Remember the story of Love Canal, in which local residents were not believed about the high levels of illness in their community? A structural functionalist perspective applied to policy can ensure that lay perspectives and other previously unheard voices are heard and considered along with scientific ones.

We can ask a similar question about technologies associated with social problems. People use automobiles to travel for work, play, and everyday needs. The use of this technology contributes to poor air quality for all, but not everyone uses cars. If we identify who uses cars for what, as well as when and where cars are not used and why, we can begin to identify economic, cultural, and historical factors that may not have been visible before. These invisible aspects—such as nondrivers depending on friends who drive or people choosing to live close to shops and work—offer clues to solving social problems related to air quality. By including technology's role in a social problem, structural functional analysis helps to broaden the potential solution sets by revealing interests and factors that may have been invisible.

Conflict Theory

A conflict theory approach studies aspects of social problems that are contested within the scientific culture. For example, the use of male subjects in the majority of clinical trials in the United States was identified as a social problem in the late 1980s. The social problem was addressed by the 1993 National Institutes of Health Revitalization Act, which mandated the inclusion of previously underrepresented groups in clinical trials. As a result, BiDil was licensed as an antihypertension drug specifically for African Americans. BiDil symbolizes a shift in biomedicine from a universal model of medicine to one that focuses on niches or specific social groups. Some within the scientific community see this as a potential new social problem, while others believe it has solved one. A conflict perspective can help identify scientific controversies and show how they shape the framing or solving of social problems by science (Epstein, 2007).

Conflict theory can also expose the social relationships defined by material and social conditions within social problems. For example, the unpaid labor of housewives emerged as a social problem in the 1960s, at the same time that industrialized nations were adopting household technologies. The sales of domestic laundry appliances increased dramatically in the 1960s, with the increase continuing to the present. In 2003 alone, nearly 15 million laundry appliances were sold in the United States. Washing machines made washing clothes less physically demanding and raised household expectations about cleanliness and the number of clothes needed. In other words, the new domestic technologies of the home industrial revolution altered the way laundry was done. Before machines, women helped each other (or hired help) on wash day and washed fewer clothes. With washing machines in their homes, women were washing more clothes and doing it alone (Cowan, 1983).

Cash or credit is required to buy a washing machine today, rather than labor to trade, as women had previously traded with others on wash day. If households were to participate in the formal economy, they needed more cash or access to credit to buy items such as washing machines. The need for money highlighted that women's household labor was unpaid and that their domestic responsibilities prevented them from joining the labor market to bring income into the household. By using conflict theory to look at the material and social conditions of women's activities in the home, we can describe the social and technological changes that contribute to the social problem.

Policy Implications of the Conflict Perspective

When we merge conflict theory with science and technology studies, issues of inequality, power, and control are highlighted. By considering how material power is played out through technology, or how science can reinforce inequality, we can reframe social problem definitions and solutions and perhaps develop policies more responsive to changes in society. For example, nearly every major car manufacturer, not to mention Google and Amazon, is planning to sell autonomous (self-driving) cars by the year 2020, predicting that traffic accidents and fatalities will decrease or be eliminated. Driving rules may stay the same with autonomous cars, or new policies may be adopted. Conflict theory would suggest that we consider access and control—who sets boundaries for the autonomous car, and how? Will anyone be able to operate an autonomous car? Who will be responsible if there is an accident? Conflict theorists might also consider the ethical issues, like the effect on jobs and tax revenue that will accompany this new technology. These are just a few of the questions conflict theory might ask about technological changes that require new policies.

Symbolic Interactionism

Instead of thinking of society in terms of the institutions of science and technology, symbolic interactionists consider immediate social interaction and the meanings people develop and rely on in addressing social problems. By studying the meanings and practices attached to a technology by different actors, for instance, scholars have documented how that technology becomes the right tool for the task.

Cervical cancer was identified as a women's health problem in the United States in the early 1940s. One solution to this social problem was the development of a technology to screen for cervical cancer. The Pap smear became the "right tool" for cancer screening because it was shaped by various practices, from cost juggling and hiring low-wage lab workers to negotiating local disagreements between clinicians and laboratories about test results. For all the women whose cancer was successfully detected and treated, the Pap smear *was* the right tool. However, it was the wrong tool for the underpaid female cytotechnologists and the women whose screenings resulted in false negatives or false positives. With symbolic interactionism, we can illustrate the diverse ways technologies are used and applied, as well as the involvement of social organizations, actors, and diverse agendas in social problems (Casper & Clarke, 1998; Wajcman, 2000).

Policy Implications of Symbolic Interactionism

A symbolic interactionist approach can help identify the interaction and negotiation of the actors engaged in defining or solving social problems, as well as the symbolic meanings that people develop in shaping the problem. If policy makers assume science is normal and providing them with facts, truth, and objectivity, they will use it very differently than if they recognize its postnormal attributes of being risky, uncertain, and shaped by different interests. Mode 1 science and Mode 2 science will inform very different types of policies to solve the same social problem. If we assume nanotechnology is safe because of Mode 1 science, we will readily buy and use sunscreen that relies on nanotechnology or approve it for general use in the population. A Mode 2 science perspective would encourage us to ask: What are the risks? Who is most at risk or least at risk? What is unknown about this technology, and how might we address it?

> *ASK YOURSELF:* Pick a technology currently being used to solve a social problem. Identify the different actors and interests that would argue the technology is the right one or the wrong one for this social problem.

SPECIALIZED THEORIES

15.6 Apply specialized theories to science and technology issues.

Traditional theoretical perspectives offer a broad foundation for the study of social problems. Contemporary scholarship on the relationships among science, technology, and

social problems builds upon traditional views to develop more specialized theoretical approaches. These, in turn, help us identify the sociocultural contexts in which science and technology interact and affect social problems.

Social Construction of Science

When scholars focus on science as a social institution they study the biographies, methods, and experiments of scientists. Biographies of scientists tell us about their social networks, education, and experiences; we can use this information to explain and describe the development of scientific knowledge. Knowing what scientists do and how they do it also contributes to our understanding of the emergence of ideas, facts, and questions in science. This information helps sociologists to identify the social facts of science. Émile Durkheim (1982/1895) describes **social facts**, the ways of thinking, acting, and feeling that are external to and exert pressure on the individual. Social facts like methods and findings allow us to understand science as a social institution and describe its beliefs, tendencies, and practices. The social facts of science highlight how science is socially constructed. In other words, science is produced by people within social networks and a scientific culture.

Sociologist Robert K. Merton saw science as a social institution governed by a set of distinct norms and values shared among the scientific community. Merton identified an elaborate reward system in American science, including honorific rewards, memberships in learned societies, positions in prestigious departments, citations, and journal editorships that motivated scientists to strive in the name of science (Morris, 2015). "When the institution of science works efficiently," Merton suggested, "recognition and esteem accrue to those who have best fulfilled their roles" as scientists (Merton, 1957, p. 639).

In his book *The Structure of Scientific Revolutions,* Thomas Kuhn (1962) argued that science was characterized by phases of very conservative practices followed by periods of revolutionary upheaval. Scientists, according to Kuhn, are socialized into the academic culture of scientific communities, which appeal to a particular theoretical or methodological orientation. Scientists, far from being dispassionate, are strongly committed to their theories, and engage in "normal science" in an effort to solve scientific problems that fit within their existing paradigm. Kuhn (1962) suggested that social factors do not only affect the conditions under which scientific knowledge is produced but also affect the theoretical judgments of

Social facts: The ways of thinking, acting, and feeling that are external to the individual and exert pressure on the individual.

scientists. Such scientists become conservative researchers providing data and analysis in support of the dominant paradigm.

The early 1970s saw the emergence of the sociology of scientific knowledge (SSK) approach to thinking about science. This approach examined how social factors influence "technical" questions such as design choices, scientists' relationship with funding agencies, the methodologies and theories utilized, the interpretation of data, and the publication and dissemination of research results. The SSK perspective focused on the production of knowledge and insisted that because science was social, scientific knowledge had to be understood as a social product. The existence of social facts in science helps social scientists to uncover the role of science within social problems. When we analyze science as a human endeavor, we can begin to understand the multiple roles science plays in social problems.

ASK YOURSELF: In labeling samples according to race, is it better to use the label the individual employs or the generic label used by the society at that particular time? (Remember that race is a socially constructed label.) What is the impact on science of using labels based on social norms?

Social Construction of Technology

New technologies often create new social problems. In 1898, a woman bicyclist was refused service in an English pub because she was wearing knickerbockers (baggy trousers) when the norm was for women to wear long skirts. That norm made it difficult for women to ride bicycles until both bicycle designs and clothing styles began to change.

The social construction of technology is a theory that analyzes social problems associated with technology. It begins with the perspective of users as agents of technological change in order to understand how human actions and values shape technology. For example, when a new technology such as the bicycle is introduced, different groups assign different meanings to the technology. Male users of high-wheeler bicycles used them for sport, and the bicycles came to symbolize "machismo." Female users and elderly men wanted bikes for transport and labeled the high-wheeler "unsafe." These identities of macho and unsafe influenced the bicycle's development paths. Ultimately, the safety bicycle was developed, which featured a steerable front wheel, equally sized wheels, and a chain drive to the rear wheel. It dominated other designs due to its **interpretive flexibility,** or ability of the development path to respond to different users' needs. By studying the ways different user groups define and label an

Granger NYC

▶ A female telegraph messenger in Berlin, Germany, circa 1910. Despite their long skirts, women could easily maneuver the "safety" bicycles without risking the headlong falls common among the more "masculine" high-wheeler bicycles.

emerging social problem connected to a new technology, the social construction of technology highlights the way technological change responds to cultural influences and the way a technology develops into a working artifact.

Actor-Network Theory

In the 1970s, science and technology scholars began studying the laboratory spaces in which scientists work using social science research methods that included participant observation, discourse analysis, and interviews (Knorr-Cetina, 1981; Latour & Woolgar, 1979; Lynch, 1985). These early ethnographies were germane to the actor-network approach of Michel Callon and Bruno Latour (see, for example, Callon, 1999; Latour, 1987; Law, 1999) and the laboratory studies of Karin Knorr-Cetina (1992, 1995, 1999). This new line of research represented a shift away from studying the products of science to studying how science and technology are socially shaped or constructed.

Interpretive flexibility: The ability of the development path to respond to different users' needs.

Nuclear Power

France is the world's largest net exporter of electricity, because electricity from nuclear power, which provides 75% of France's own electricity needs, has low production costs. Areva, the third-largest uranium producer in the world, is a French public multinational conglomerate based in Paris, and the strategic partner in uranium for Niger, the fourth-ranking producer of the metal.

Areva has been operating in Niger for more than 40 years and will soon be opening the Imouraren mine there, which is expected to produce 5,000 tons of uranium per year for 35 years. In addition to its investment in the mine of 1.2 billion euros (about $1.6 billion), Areva will spend 6 million euros (about $8 million) per year on health care, education, training, transport, and access to water and energy for the local people (World Nuclear Association, 2013). Niger is one of the poorest countries in the world; most of its people live on less than a dollar a day. Is this a human success story about how France has solved a major social problem by providing electricity to its citizens while also improving the lives of citizens in another country?

In the past decade, allegations have arisen of contaminated scrap metals finding their way into Niger's local housing construction, kitchen utensils, and tools. It is suspected that radioactive waste has been used in road construction. Increased respiratory problems from blown radioactive dust are afflicting people living in the region near the mine. Radioactivity has been reported at more than 100 times the level recommended by international standards. Wells have been contaminated and depleted. Areva denies culpability and maintains that it has ensured the highest levels of safety in its operations. Is this a story of failure caused by corporate greed, government corruption, and poor implementation?

The way we see this situation will play a major role in determining what type of social problem it is, and for whom. France and Areva have the science

▶ The Salem Nuclear Power plant is located at the Hope Creek Generating Station in New Jersey. In 2017 there were 61 nuclear power plants operating in the United States.

Mark Reinstein/Corbis via Getty Images

and technology to build and the ability to define this as a success story. Their expertise and access to resources facilitate their ability to negotiate with another country that lacks the means to mine and use its uranium for its own people. It is the citizens of that country who may define the mine as a failure because they do not have the ability to make informed decisions about their health, livelihoods, and energy choices in light of corporate and nation-state actions.

▶ **THINK ABOUT IT:** What are the roles and responsibilities of citizen groups, corporations, and nation-states in resolving a social problem like nuclear power?

Their analyses using actor-network theory revealed how scientific facts are constructed in laboratories through social networks, communication technologies, and shared interests. This approach to studying the laboratory illustrated the mundane processes, social ordering, and social organization required to produce a scientific fact. Scientific knowledge is negotiated between scientists in laboratories and funders, suppliers, governments, investors, and clients outside the laboratories. Actor-network theory also places nonhuman actors, such as microscopes and laboratory benches, into studies of science, acknowledging that these nonhuman actors define and regulate the context or place of science. Actor-network theory studies the heterogeneous networks of human and nonhuman actors in order to identify the material and social actions and forces of science and technology (Callon, Law, & Rip, 1986; Latour, 1987; Law, 1991).

Feminist Epistemologies

Feminist epistemologies have generally been critical of the actor-network approach because of general disregard of race, gender, and to a lesser degree class inequalities inherent in the practices of modern science. Building on the work of Carolyn Merchant's *The Death of Nature* (1980, 1996) feminist scholars have developed distinct theories of knowledge and critiques of Western modern science. Many science studies scholars, Donna Haraway

(1997) argues, have forgotten how gender, race, and class are also constructed in the mundane processes of science. Haraway (1997, p. 35) insists, "Either critical scholars in antiracist, feminist cultural studies of science and technology have not been clear enough about racial formation, gender-in-the-making, the forging of class, and the discursive production of sexuality *through the constitutive practices of technoscience production themselves*, or the science studies scholars aren't listening—or both."

Similarly, Sandra Harding (1993, 1998) calls for a different approach to the practice of science, one that systematically examines all the social values that shape a particular process. To what extent is science multicultural, Harding (1998) asks. Privileged ways of knowing, Harding (2009) concludes, do not recognize their own location in either the history of human knowledge production or in natural and social relations. *Standpoint theories* (Hartsock, 1983; Longino, 1994), *strong objectivity* (Harding, 1991, 1998, 2009), and *situated knowledges* (Haraway, 1991, 1997) argue for feminism as the precondition for knowledge making.

SOCIAL CHANGE: WHAT CAN YOU DO?

15.7 Identify steps toward social change regarding science and technology.

In order to ensure that science and technology contribute to beneficial solutions and do not create or reinforce social problems, all interested stakeholders—including you—must perform certain roles. By engaging in community service opportunities, you can have a direct impact on the ways in which science and technology are developed, applied, and integrated into society. A few opportunities for you to get involved are described below.

▶▶ Engineers Without Borders

Join or start a chapter of Engineers Without Borders (EWB) on your campus (http://www.ewb-usa.org). The goal of EWB is to provide clean water, power, and sanitation to communities in need. Students and professionals from all disciplines, including public health, anthropology, geology, business, communications, and engineering, apply a holistic approach to community development and community projects requiring an element of engineering design. Individuals gain leadership experiences, apply technical and management skills, and help communities create solutions they can sustain for the long term.

▶▶ EPA Office of Water

The U.S. Environmental Protection Agency's Office of Water encourages all citizens to learn about their water resources and supports volunteer monitoring because of its many benefits. Participants in the EPA Volunteer Monitoring Program build awareness of pollution problems, become

Fairfax Media/Fairfax Media/Getty Images

▶ Nicole Teo and Susan Conyers, who work for Engineers Without Borders, use a simple water purification system. Engineers Without Borders uses volunteer engineers and engineering students to design and undertake water, sanitation, and energy projects in developing countries worldwide.

trained in pollution prevention, help clean up problem sites, provide data on waters that may otherwise be unassessed, and increase the amount of information on water quality available to decision makers at all levels of government. The data resulting from volunteer monitoring are used for delineating and characterizing watersheds, screening for water quality problems, and measuring baseline conditions and trends. For more information, see the EPA's website at http://water.epa.gov/type/watersheds/monitoring/vol.cfm.

▶▶ Campus Sustainability Initiatives

Become active in your school's sustainable campus initiative program, or if one doesn't exist, create one. Such a program identifies a social problem on campus that has or could have a scientific or technological component. At the University of Utah, for example, every student pays a small fee into the Sustainable Campus Initiative Fund, which pays for sustainable projects or businesses on campus. All students are eligible to submit project proposals. To be funded, a project must have a positive environmental impact; encourage Earth-conscious habits; and incorporate economic, social, and scientific factors. For more on the University of Utah initiative, see http://sustainability.utah.edu/get-involved/students/sustainable-campus-fund.php.

Join or start an interdisciplinary student organization on your campus to tackle a social problem. At Cornell University, students are composting, turning lights out, eliminating carbon emissions, and identifying and discussing social problems. One interdisciplinary campus group is called Design, Engineering, Education, and Development; its members work with developing communities to improve equity and sustainability. Another group designs and builds

resilient structures for ecological, social, and economical sustainability. Some Cornell undergraduates have collaborated to establish an accessible, sustainable, and free bike-share program on campus. For more information, visit http://www.sustainablecampus.cornell.edu/getinvolved/studentorgs.cfm.

▶▶ No-Impact Living

Conduct a "no-impact project" alone, as a class, or as a family for 1 week to see what a difference no-impact living can have on your quality of life. Keep a journal of the impact of modern technology and "conveniences" on your life, emotions, relationships, time, and money. At the end of the week identify one change you will retain in your life to minimize your impact on the environment. Two students at Drake University turned their no-impact project into a campus-wide effort that banned bottled-water sales on campus. For more information, see the No Impact Project website at http://noimpactproject.org.

WHAT DOES AMERICA THINK?

Questions About Science and Technology From the General Social Survey

Turn to the beginning of the chapter to compare your answers to those of the total population.

1. What is your interest level in scientific discoveries?

    VERY INTERESTED: 42.2%

    MODERATELY INTERESTED: 42.1%

    NOT AT ALL INTERESTED: 15.7%

2. What is your confidence level in the scientific community?

    A GREAT DEAL: 42%

    ONLY SOME: 51.8%

    HARDLY ANY: 6.2%

3. Does science make our way of life change too fast?

    YES: 52.4%

    NO: 47.6%

4. Do the benefits of scientific research outweigh harmful results?

    YES: 78.5%

    NO: 8.7%

5. Scientific research is necessary and should be supported by the federal government.

    AGREE: 85.4%

    DISAGREE: 14.6%

6. What is your interest level in technologies?

    VERY INTERESTED: 41.1%

    MODERATELY INTERESTED: 46%

    NOT AT ALL INTERESTED: 12.9%

7. Do you use the home Internet through a mobile device?

    YES: 39.7%

    NO: 60.3%

SOURCE: National Opinion Research Center, University of Chicago.

CHAPTER SUMMARY

 Identify social problems related to science and technology.

Science and technology scholars ask questions about the incorporation of science and technology into society; how science and technology are redefining social inequality, social relationships, and public/private space; and how and why some issues emerge as widely discussed social problems while others are relegated to the category of technological or scientific problems.

 Describe how science and technology are socially defined.

Science as a form of knowledge plays an active role in defining how governments, corporations, and communities respond to and accept responsibility for social problems. Technology is embedded as an artifact in social practices, social institutions, and systems that are part of emerging social problems and their solutions. By analyzing science and technology as technoscience, we can broaden our analysis of them to raise new questions about social problems, science, and technology. Science plays an active role in social problems, sometimes as part of the authority that solves them and sometimes as a factor creating the culture and the social problem. Science can be a social problem or it can have its own social problems. Our cultural beliefs about technology and progress can define what is and is not a social problem. Technology too can be a social problem or part of the solution.

15.3 Discuss patterns and trends in science and technology.

By viewing science and technology as social problems, we can identify trends and patterns illustrating that the way we do science, and the values that shape science, change over time; that technologies we use are shaped by values; and that we use technologies to fix social problems. In addition, the way we use science to solve social problems is dynamic; science as a social institution can have social problems.

15.4 Identify the stakeholders in science and technology.

Stakeholders use science and technology in specific and deliberate ways to frame, respond to, and solve social problems. They shape the way science is done, what science is done, and where it is applied. Stakeholders of science and technology include experts, funders, producers, and consumers.

 Apply the functionalist, conflict, and symbolic interactionist perspectives to science and technology issues.

Structural functionalism, symbolic interactionism, and conflict theory are important theories in the analysis of science, technology, and social problems. Structural functionalism explains that one reason why eminent scientists receive most of the credit in their fields is that, because they have access to resources like elite education and cultural capital, their advantages are compounded. Conversely, those without these resources are not as likely to get credit. Conflict theory shows how scientific controversies can help to frame or solve social problems. By studying the meanings and practices that different people give to a particular technology, symbolic interactionists can demonstrate how that technology can benefit them.

15.6 Apply specialized theories to science and technology issues.

Specialized theories such as social construction of science, social construction of technology, and actor-network theory are used to describe, interpret, and troubleshoot science, technology, and social problems.

 Identify steps toward social change regarding science and technology.

You can take several actions to ensure that science and technology contribute to beneficial solutions and do not create problematic situations. Some of these actions include joining or starting a chapter of Engineers Without Borders on your campus; becoming active in your university's sustainable campus initiative program, or, if one doesn't exist, creating one; and conducting a "no-impact project" to see what difference no-impact living has on your quality of life.

KEY TERMS

academic capital 385

big data 370

crisis science 378

cumulative advantage 385

fourth paradigm 371

health social movements 378

industrialized science 381

interpretive flexibility 389

landraces 383

makerspace 379

megamachine 376

Mode 1 379

Mode 2 379

science 373

science machine 377

science shops 378

social facts 388

social organization 376

sociotechnical system 372

street science 378

technocracy 381

technological fix 381

technology 375

technoscience 375

---

16 WAR AND TERRORISM

Ori Swed

Iraqi forces during the advance to retake the last district in Mosul, Iraq still held by the Islamic State (ISIS) group fighters. What do you see as the relationship between war and terrorism?

Investigating War and Terrorism: My Story

Ori Swed

My interest in studying war and terrorism stems from personal experience. I grew up in Israel, a country that regularly experiences security threats and seasonal armed conflicts, so I was exposed to terrorism and the reality of armed conflict from a young age. I lived through my first war at the age of 11, and at 18 I joined the Israeli armed forces. In Israel, military service is mandatory, and the armed forces are one of the major socialization institutions in the nation. From the Israeli point of view, military service is an important civil duty. Because of the omnipresence of security threats, and their related impact over the culture as a whole, Israelis associate service with protection of family and friends as well as with serving their country. In many surveys, popular support for the Israeli military ranks higher than for any other institution.

After my military service, I began my academic career at the Hebrew University in Jerusalem, later completing my Ph.D. in sociology at the University of Texas at Austin. Sociological research helped me to better understand my society and culture, seeing how security issues define Israeli culture and examining the role of security forces and institutions in Israeli society, politics, and economy. My research focuses on those issues as well as others outside of the Israeli case. In my work, I examine the interaction between armed forces and nonstate actors, such as aid organizations, peace activists, and private security workers. My current work examines the increasing role of private military and security companies in contemporary warfare and counterterrorism efforts.

LEARNING OBJECTIVES

16.1 Describe war as a social concept.

16.2 Discuss patterns and trends in the incidence and costs of war.

16.3 Describe the future of war.

16.4 Apply the functionalist, symbolic interactionist, and conflict perspectives to war.

16.5 Apply the two-society thesis to the relationship between the U.S. military and U.S. society.

16.6 Discuss the Global War on Terror.

16.7 Identify steps toward social change to foster peace.

 WHAT DO YOU THINK?

Questions About War and Terrorism From the General Social Survey

1. Do you expect the United States to be in a world war in the next 10 years?

   ☐ YES
   ☐ NO

2. What is your confidence level in Congress?

   ☐ A GREAT DEAL
   ☐ ONLY SOME
   ☐ HARDLY ANY

3. What is your interest level in international issues?

   ☐ VERY INTERESTED
   ☐ MODERATELY INTERESTED
   ☐ NOT AT ALL INTERESTED

4. What is your interest level in military policy?

   ☐ VERY INTERESTED
   ☐ MODERATELY INTERESTED
   ☐ NOT AT ALL INTERESTED

5. In the United States, do you think we're spending too much money on military, armaments, and defense, too little money, or about the right amount?

   ☐ TOO MUCH
   ☐ TOO LITTLE
   ☐ ABOUT THE RIGHT AMOUNT

   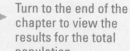 Turn to the end of the chapter to view the results for the total population.

SOURCE: National Opinion Research Center, University of Chicago.

THE ISLAMIC STATE AND THE BLURRING LINES BETWEEN WAR AND COUNTERTERRORISM

On September 2, 2014, the Islamic State in Iraq and Syria (ISIS), an organization almost unknown except in circles of security experts, released a videotape showing the beheading of U.S. journalist James Foley. Foley was shown kneeling in the middle of the desert, wearing an orange prisoner suit, while above him a masked figure in black waved a knife. This horrible video, which quickly went viral, was merely the opening chord of ISIS's terror campaign.

ISIS developed in Eastern Syria and Western Iraq, territories suffering from a power vacuum due to weak governance and internal conflict. In a short period of time ISIS gained control of a territory the size of France, taking over rural areas and important cities like Mosul, Palmyra, and Al-Raqqah. In the territories under its control, ISIS instituted religious laws and economies, the latter based mostly on plunder. It also initiated health services and a justice system, and collected taxes, thus assuming the characteristics of a nation-state. ISIS's expansion ended with the military intervention of international and regional powers, among them a coalition led by Russia and another by the United States. In mid-2017, the two coalitions and other regional actors, such as Turkey and Iran, engaged with ISIS on several fronts, attempting to curb the organization's influence in rural Syria and to drive it out of Mosul, Iraq.

The rise of ISIS has drawn attention to the blurry line between combatant and terrorist, and between war and counterterrorism. Designated a terrorist organization, ISIS has been engaging in "classic" terrorist activity across the Middle East and Europe, such as the 2015 attacks in Tunisia and Paris, and the 2017 attack in Manchester, England, and Barcelona, Spain. However, ISIS is also a state-like entity in control of vast strips of land, with significant resources behind it, and sustaining a military force with capabilities greater than those of most countries. This odd situation poses a challenge to security forces and scholars.

WAR AS A SOCIAL CONCEPT

16.1 Describe war as a social concept.

We can define **war** as organized, collective fighting between at least one political unit that seeks political or economic control over a territory or other important resource and another political unit or social group. This definition expands the traditional focus on state-to-state war (the military of one government against the military of another fought over a specific territory) by including war waged by substate units, as well as the possibility that a distinct political, religious, ethnic, or racial group might become the target. War is "organized and collective," which sets it off from more individual, sporadic, and spontaneous acts of violence. It is "political" because the fighting units use violence deliberately in the search for a particular outcome, such as control over a governing structure, natural resources, or suppression of a population that is regarded as oppositional.

In the past, war was conventionally seen as organized violence carried out between national states and across national borders. Other forms of organized violence also existed, such as the wars conducted against the native populations of the Americas, but the decolonization process that began following the end of World War II in 1945 brought new recognition that parties in conflict do not have to be states, war is usually not formally declared, and fighting may be carried out solely within rather than across the borders. For example, colonial powers such as the French in Vietnam and Algerians and Portuguese in Africa fought against substate groups seeking national liberation to retain parts of their empires. They often enlisted local elites, who in turn recruited soldiers from the local population, creating elements of civil war as well.

Wars also take the form of *campaigns of ethnic cleansing*, such as in the former Yugoslavia in the early 1990s; *genocide*, such as in Rwanda in 1994; and *violent political repression*, such as the so-called Dirty War carried out against those opposed to military rule in Argentina, or against Buddhist monks in Myanmar (the former Burma). The scale of this sometimes catastrophic killing is one important reason to include these actions in our definition of war. In Cambodia, over the last half of the 1970s, as much as 25% of the population was decimated, as Cambodians were either executed by the Khmer

....

War: Organized, collective fighting involving at least one political unit that seeks political or economic control over a territory or other important resource against another political unit or social group.

Rouge, an ultraleft political group that had seized power, or died in a famine aggravated by the destruction of agricultural production during the Indochina War. In all these cases, states waged wars against their own populations.

In globalized intrastate wars, organized violence is less political and more economic because the motive is to control valuable resources. These resources include diamonds (Sierra Leone); the production and distribution of drugs (Colombia and Mexico); timber (East Timor); oil (the Niger Delta); and valuable minerals and ore such as coltan, used in the manufacture of electronic products (Democratic Republic of the Congo). Sometimes called "resource wars," these conflicts differ from classic war in several ways: (1) They include multiple types of fighting units, such as paramilitary forces, mercenaries, self-defense units, militaries from other countries, and even peacekeeping forces; (2) they frequently target civilians, often by employing sexual violence; (3) they often conscript child soldiers; and (4) they establish connections between in-country actors, such as local warlords and traders in the valuable commodity, and international players such as corporations, banking interests, and global agencies such as the United Nations. In many respects, resource wars are similar to organized crime, but on a larger scale.

ASK YOURSELF: What wars are being fought as you read this chapter? Who are the fighting parties? Are they armies controlled by states, or other types of combatants?

War is a social concept because it involves culture, politics, and economics, the features of human society examined throughout this textbook. While no doubt some elements of human nature are expressed in war, sociologists try to understand this form of activity not by examining genes or biology but instead by describing the social relationships contained within it. Situating war in social life does not imply approval, any more than our social understandings of crime and racism imply support for those behaviors. War can also be said to be "social" because it has important impacts on society: There are physical casualties, of course, but also effects on nationalism, psychology, patterns of inequality, issues concerning race and ethnicity, economic performance, technology, and the environment. In these respects, war can be said to have a "long tail," or a social legacy that continues to influence social life long after the fighting itself has subsided.

PATTERNS AND TRENDS

 16.2 Discuss patterns and trends in the incidence and costs of war.

▶ Iraqi soldiers of the Ninth and 16th companies take part in an operation to liberate the city of Mosul in northern Iraq from the terrorist group ISIS.

As a "social activity," war contains several patterns and new trends that are important to understand, especially if we want to reduce if not eliminate its occurrence. Among the most important questions is whether fewer wars are being fought now than a generation ago. Another is whether wars are becoming less deadly, as measured by the number of battlefield deaths. Are we, as some commentators have suggested, winning the "war against war" (Gat, 2008; Goldstein, 2011; Pinker, 2011)?

Incidence of Interstate War

When we watch in the news the vocal exchanges of threats between President Donald Trump and Kim Jong Un, the supreme leader of North Korea, we may think that war between states is an inevitable human condition. However, data on wars tell us a different story. It does appear that wars waged between states are declining in number (Human Security Report Project, 2012, 2013). This decline is ascribed to political and economic changes on a global level. Since the end of World War II the international community has developed mechanisms and institutions that facilitate conflict mediation and resolution among nations. Furthermore, the steady movement from autocracies to democracies throughout the globe has provided an additional stability to the world system. The **democratic theory of peace** proposes that political democracies are less likely to wage war, at least with each other, so as more nations become democratic, the chances of interstate armed conflict decrease. Europe has become a zone of peace, the probability of war between Latin American

Democratic theory of peace: The theory that political democracies are less likely than nondemocracies to wage war with each other.

countries is remote, and it appears that many East and South Asian nations, at least those advancing toward democracy, will also not go to war with each other.

What other features of democracy might make us optimistic about the future of interstate war? Among democracies, leaders are more likely to believe that negotiation and diplomacy will work because the leaders of other countries think so as well. Citizens see war as a measure of last resort; they are less likely to cherish martial values or welcome combat as an opportunity to test their bravery and heroism. War is expensive, financially and in human terms, and is to be avoided, especially when countries are facing others whose populations feel much the same way. If these features of democratic systems are real, and as many countries lurch, however unevenly, in the direction of democracy, then over time the incidence of interstate war will continue to decline.

Economic factors play a significant role in this trend as well. The fast pace of globalization has made war less effective in achieving economic goals than it was in the past. Today, it is almost always cheaper to buy resources on the global market than to acquire them by force. Participation in advanced consumer societies does seem to reduce significantly, if not quite eliminate, the likelihood of countries going to war with other prosperous countries. The "McDonald's theory of conflict resolution" suggests that countries where McDonald's fast-food restaurants have been established do not go to war with each other (Friedman, 2005). There have been exceptions to this rule. In 1999, during the war with Serbia over Kosovo, the United States and other countries in the North Atlantic Treaty Organization (NATO), all possessing McDonald's, bombed Belgrade, which also had several McDonald's outlets. The dark blue section in Figure 16.1 represents interstate war; note that it has declined, especially since the end of the Cold War in 1989.

Similar predictions apply to politically motivated civil wars. The European colonial systems of the 19th century have been almost entirely dismantled; the green section in Figure 16.1 reveals that colonial wars ended after 1973. Former colonies now enjoy at least formal political sovereignty. They may suffer different forms of subordination, including high levels of poverty, poor governance, and inadequate education and health care—conditions often called "structural violence" and "neocolonialism"—but they no longer need to engage in direct violence to achieve independence.

We find a similar pattern in Figure 16.2, which captures the rate of battle deaths in state-based conflicts between 1946 and 2009. There are three peaks of casualties, one around 1950 and the Korean War; another in the late 1960s and early 1970s, marking the most intense fighting in Vietnam; and finally a third, an extremely

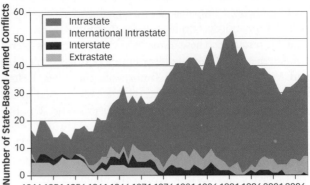

FIGURE 16.1 Trends in State-Based Conflicts by Type, 1946–2009

"State-based conflicts" are those in which the warring parties include a state and one of more nonstate armed groups. Extrastate—or anticolonial—conflicts ended by 1975, while interstate conflicts became rare in the 2000s. As a result of this shift, all conflicts in 2009 were intrastate, though nearly a quarter were internationalized.

SOURCE: Human Security Report Project. *Human Security Report 2012: Sexual Violence, Education, and War: Beyond the Mainstream Narrative.* Vancouver: Human Security Press, 2012. Reprinted with permission.

NOTE: This figure is a "stacked graph," meaning the number of conflicts in each category is indicated by the depth of the band of color. The top line shows the total number of conflicts of all types in each year.

bloody war between Iran and Iraq in the early 1980s. Since then the rate of deaths from state-based conflicts has declined significantly.

With the end of the Cold War, neither the United States nor the former Soviet Union needs to wage "proxy wars" through allies. For example, one important feature of the Vietnam War was Moscow's support for North Vietnam and U.S. support for South Vietnam. Several African conflicts were fought with the two superpowers lurking in the background. The United States and (now) Russia may continue their shadow dance on many fronts, as they did during the Soviet–Afghan War of the 1980s and the Syrian Civil War of the 2010s, but the pattern of fighting via subordinate partners appears to have decreased. The United Nations, now free of the constraints of the Cold War, has been able to play a more active peacekeeping role. That too has reduced violence, even if the record is imperfect.

Unfortunately, wars between states and battlefield deaths are not the only measures of the future of war. We look at civilian casualties next.

Civilian Casualties

During World War I, the combatants often deployed their forces in trenches relatively close to each other. The defenses were usually much stronger than any offensive, and the consequences were usually tragic. At the Battle of

FIGURE 16.2 Reported Battle Deaths
From State-Based Conflicts,
1946–2009

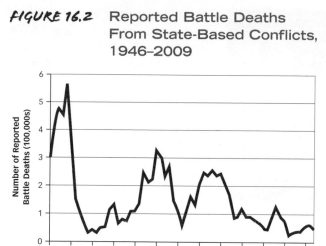

SOURCE: Human Security Report Project. *Human Security Report 2012: Sexual Violence, Education, and War: Beyond the Mainstream Narrative.* Vancouver: Human Security Press, 2012. Reprinted with permission.

the Somme, the British took nearly 60,000 casualties on the first day. Despite appalling losses on all sides, civilians were relatively protected. Noncombatants made up less than 10% of the war's total losses.

About two decades later, on April 26, 1937, the German air force, supporting General Francisco Franco during the Spanish Civil War, deliberately targeted the market areas of the Basque village of Guernica to make a point about the costs it was willing to impose on civilians. Bombing civilians was not entirely new, but Guernica was a turning point (Tanaka & Young, 2009). World War II was devastating to the militaries on all sides, but even more for civilians. The Soviet Union lost 25 million people, 75% of them civilians. German bombers attacked London and other cities in England, and British and U.S. bombers struck German cities. Kurt Vonnegut's famous novel *Slaughterhouse-Five* grapples with the firebombing of the German city of Dresden, where 40,000 inhabitants were killed. Japanese occupation in the Pacific was responsible for the deaths of millions. Toward the end of the war, U.S. incendiary bombing set many Japanese cities on fire, including Tokyo, where 100,000 people died in one night. The technology employed in the atomic bombs used on Hiroshima and Nagasaki was new, but the targeting of civilians on a mass scale was not.

The United States lost approximately 58,000 soldiers during the Vietnam War. About 1 million Vietnamese, counting government forces from both North and South and revolutionary forces, also died. Yet another million Vietnamese civilians were killed (some sources put the figure closer to 2 million). In the post-Vietnam era, the ratio of military to civilian deaths has often been entirely reversed. In many globalized intrastate wars, noncombatant deaths have reached 9:1, so for every combatant nine civilians died—the exact inverse ratio of World War I. In Bosnia,

the militaries on both sides even colluded to target civilians and thereby intensify the pace of ethnic cleansing (Andreas, 2008). Civilians have suffered by far the largest losses in armed conflicts in East Timor, Sierra Leone, and Colombia, with catastrophic results. Conflict in south-central Somalia was made more devastating by extremist militants' decision to ban the delivery of humanitarian assistance. An estimated 258,000 people died between October 2010 and April 2012, including 133,000 children under the age of 5 (Food Security and Nutrition Analysis Unit–Somalia, 2013). Due to the intersection of fighting and disruption of normal social life, civil war in Syria had by 2016 cost the lives of over 400,000 people and displaced another 12.3 million (International Rescue Committee, 2016).

These figures temper our optimism about the future of interstate war. National armies, particularly from democracies, may be less likely to engage each other, but other forms of war continue, and a true accounting recognizes the loss of noncombatants as well as those in uniform. As of the beginning of 2017, the United States had lost 2,386 soldiers in Afghanistan, in addition to the 4,486 casualties in Iraq (Coalition Casualty Count, 2016). These are significant, painful losses to their families and friends, and to the country as a whole. At least 170,000 civilians have also died in Iraq; the actual number is probably considerably higher (Iraq Body Count, 2016). In Afghanistan, the United Nations Mission for the Protection of Civilians in Armed Conflict places the number of noncombatant dead at over 26,000 from 2007 through 2016.

Globalized Intrastate Wars

The number of state-based wars per year has declined. However, this comparatively bright note is balanced by the emergence of another type of conflict: globalized intrastate war. The most important goal of such a war is control of the flow of valuable natural resources. **Globalized intrastate wars** are fought largely for economic gain rather than for political reasons (Kaldor, 2012).

Globalized intrastate wars engage many types of fighting units. Paramilitary forces play a major role, with warlords operating largely in their own self-interest and sometimes abducting and enlisting children to fight. Foreign mercenaries, private military contractors, and international forces, sometimes backed by the United Nations, may also be involved. Deliberate expulsion of civilians in ethnic cleansing campaigns allows the warlords to tighten control over territory. Civilians bear the

....

Globalized intrastate wars: Organized violence used to control territory containing valuable resources, often fought by paramilitary forces, targeting civilians, containing high levels of sexual violence, and using child soldiers.

▶ Pablo Picasso's *Guernica*, 1937. Picasso created this painting to bring the world's attention to the atrocities committed against the defenseless civilian population of the little Basque village of Guernica in northern Spain. *Guernica* has become a powerful antiwar symbol. The gratuitous horrors of modern war and the suffering it inflicts on individuals, particularly innocent civilians, are depicted in the painting through tortured images of people, animals, and buildings wrenched by violence and chaos.

total of the military budgets of all of Washington's allies, including NATO, Japan, and South Korea, *plus* the combined total of the military budgets of all potential enemies, including China, Russia, North Korea, and Iran (Stockholm International Peace Research Institute, 2017).

In fiscal year 2015, the official U.S. defense budget came to $596 billion. The true figure is significantly larger. This does not include additional allocation for the U.S. military operations in Iraq and Afghanistan, which are not part of the official budget. Additional military expenditures by the Department of Homeland Security, State Department, Veterans Administration, NASA, and Department of Energy (for the production of nuclear warheads) bring annual U.S. military spending to nearly a trillion dollars, significantly more than the annual federal deficit.

During World War II, U.S. military spending accounted for an astonishing 40% of the gross domestic product (GDP). The country finally escaped the Great Depression, not through President Franklin D. Roosevelt's New Deal but through the huge stimulus provided to the automobile industry by orders for tanks, trucks, and jeeps; to the steel industry for naval ships; to clothing manufactures for uniforms, boots, and the like; and to the new aircraft industry for fighter planes and bombers. Military spending later fell from that unique high point but remained significant as the Cold War set in, reaching 8% to 10% of GDP as the government maintained a sizable army, navy, and air force; garrisoned troops in Germany; established military bases in the Pacific; and developed and deployed nuclear weapons. Expenditures on the Vietnam War became so large that many argued they were actually undermining U.S. strength. National debt increased, as did inflation, and the U.S. dollar declined in value. Research and development for civilian manufacturing dropped in priority, and innovation fell relative to Europe and Japan. Many were reminded of President Dwight D. Eisenhower's warning, made in an April 16, 1953, speech, that "every gun that is made, every warship launched, every rocket fired signifies, in the final sense, a theft from those who hunger and are not fed, those who are cold and not clothed."

Not until the end of the Cold War and the transformation of the Soviet Union did the United States reap a "peace dividend." During President Bill Clinton's administration military spending declined, especially relative to

brunt of these conflicts, with tens and even hundreds of thousands of deaths and high levels of sexual violence.

International agencies, nations, nongovernmental organizations, and private donors may provide humanitarian assistance to vulnerable populations, instead of undertaking riskier efforts to reduce fighting. Unfortunately, humanitarian aid can become an additional lootable resource that, despite donors' good intentions, fuels the conflict and makes the war self-financing. During the war in Bosnia in 1992 and 1995, both Serbian militia and Bosnian criminal gangs kept violence high so as to maintain a flow of humanitarian assistance to besieged Sarajevo. Some of this aid was diverted into black markets. But the violence was not high enough to invite direct intervention by Europe and the United States (Andreas, 2008). In this case, enemies engaged in a peculiar type of cooperation because each had an interest in keeping assistance coming in. Civilian aid officials and nongovernmental organizations had to allow some aid to enter the black market in return for ensuring that some of it be used for its intended purposes (Polman, 2010). In another case, the U.S. military paid contractors to transport supplies across Afghanistan, but the social networks included criminal groups, Afghan power brokers, and subcontractors with links to insurgents. This form of corruption, called "threat financing," involved U.S.-funded development efforts in Afghanistan but inadvertently supported the Taliban.

Economic Costs of War and War Preparation

The United States spends almost as much on its military as the rest of the world combined. In other words, the budget of the U.S. Department of Defense equals the combined

Experiencing War and Terrorism

Who Serves in the U.S. Armed Forces?

The Vietnam War was called the "working-class war" because U.S. college students who were drafted were able to defer their military service. Since they were more likely to come from middle- and upper-income brackets, deferment created a bias in which those located in the lower brackets were more likely to be drafted, fight, and die. After Vietnam, the Pentagon moved to an all-volunteer force. How has this decision affected the composition of the current U.S. military?

The clearest change is in the sex distribution of the armed forces. Since 1973, the proportion of female soldiers has moved from only 2% to approximately 15%. This shift carries profound implications, which we explore later in this chapter.

Yet there continues to be substantial class patterning in the armed forces. As before, the middle- and top-income brackets are significantly underrepresented. For example, in 2007, during the height of the war in Iraq, census districts with mean incomes between $30,000 and $60,000 contributed significantly more than their share of active-duty army recruits. Districts with higher incomes contributed significantly fewer than we would expect if soldiers were drawn evenly from the whole population. Districts with average incomes over $120,000 contributed only one-third their "fair share" (National Priorities Project, 2008).

However, contrary to many impressions, the military does not draw from the lowest levels of society, either. Discipline, teamwork, and basic education skills are highly valued in the modern force. The Pentagon's goal is for 80% of recruits to have high school diplomas. Except during the worst years in Iraq, it has met that goal. (During that time, to meet pressing needs, the way was eased for the recruitment of individuals with felony records, histories of drug use, problematic character backgrounds, and lack of the educational requirement.)

Historically, African Americans have been overrepresented in the post–World War II military. There they have been able to achieve success and social mobility—often more so than in civilian society. On the other hand, the wars in Iraq and Afghanistan have not been very popular in the black community, and the proportion of the military that is African American, while still higher than average, has declined somewhat. Meanwhile, Latinos have steadily increased their representation.

▶ Cadets at the United States Military Academy (West Point) march during formation. Cadets who graduate from West Point are commissioned as second lieutenants in the U.S. Army. In 2016, the demographic profile of cadets attending West Point was as follows: male, 84%; female, 16%; white, 72%; Hispanic, 10%; and black, 9.13%.

Geographically, the military is disproportionately drawn from rural areas, the South, and the Mountain states. The Midwest, major cities, and the two coasts are underrepresented. In 1968, ROTC training programs had 123 units in the East and 147 in the South. Six years later, there were 180 branches in the South and only 93 in the East (Nelson, 2010). Due to base consolidations and closings, only 10 states serve as home to 70% of those in uniform.

▶ **THINK ABOUT IT**

1. Do you think each income class in the United States should contribute its "fair share" to the military? Why or why not?

2. Since World War II, blacks have been overrepresented in the U.S. military. Why has their proportion declined during the past decade while the proportion of Latinos has increased?

the size of the overall economy, reaching a low point of 3.5% of GDP in 1999.

After the terrorist attacks on New York City and Washington, D.C., on September 11, 2001, however, budget increases over the next decade for the Global War on Terror and the new wars in Afghanistan and Iraq doubled U.S. defense spending. Yet the uncertain outcomes of both wars, and debate over federal spending in general, have renewed the question of whether military spending should be reduced.

REUTERS/Tim Shaffer

Psychological Costs of War

As early as Homer's *Iliad*, humans have recognized that no one returns from war unchanged. Political authorities and military leaders have generally underplayed the psychological damage of war to avoid negative impacts on recruitment and public opinion. Early in World War II, political and military leaders expected that "real men" would be relatively immune from the effects of war and that conventional heterosexual masculinity would protect against combat's psychological effects. Unfortunately, the intensity of fighting soon demonstrated the consequences of exposure to violence.

Post-traumatic stress disorder (PTSD) is a specific set of symptoms associated with the aftermath of exposure to traumatic experiences. These include flashbacks, sleep disturbances, extreme sensitivity to noise, disturbing dreams, and poor concentration. Those with PTSD are also more likely to suffer alcohol and drug abuse, family problems, and suicide. The term did not become official until after the end of the Vietnam War, when a determined group of veterans, advocates, and medical professionals lobbied to include it in the *Diagnostic and Statistical Manual of Mental Disorders* (Scott, 1990) so soldiers could become eligible to receive treatment from the Veterans Administration.

Measuring the incidence of PTSD and other psychological consequences of war is very difficult, in part because symptoms may not appear for months or even years. A RAND Corporation study conducted during the early part of the Iraq War found between one-sixth and one-third of veterans experiencing PTSD, depression, or other significant psychological trauma (Tanielian & Jaycox, 2008). The consequences are significant. Approximately 2.5 million have served in Iraq and Afghanistan, of whom 400,000 to 800,000 have or will have significant psychological wounds. Less than half will seek professional help for their conditions, however. Many fear being stigmatized, while others are immersed in a culture that emphasizes self-reliance and individual response to adversity. If treatment were extended to all in need, the cost would be approximately $1 trillion over 40 years, about equal to the direct cost of the Iraq and Afghanistan wars themselves (Stiglitz & Bilmes, 2008).

THE FUTURE OF WAR

16.3 Describe the future of war.

Drones

Unmanned vehicles, or drones, are among the more innovative—and controversial—instruments of war.

TABLE 16.1 Trade-offs for Costs of War

Military Expenditures	Comparable Domestic Priorities
Taxpayers in Fort Lauderdale, Florida, payed $13.74 million as their share of the F-35 Joint Strike Fighter Jet.	Those funds are sufficient to pay the salaries of 206 elementary school teachers for 1 year.
Taxpayers in Denver, Colorado, payed $54.98 million for nuclear weapons and associated costs.	Those funds are sufficient to pay for 1,745 scholarships for university students for 4 years.
Taxpayers in Burlington, Vermont, payed $53.79 million for their share of overall Department of Defense expenditures.	Those funds are sufficient to enable 14,929 children receiving low-income health care for 1 year.

SOURCE: www.costofwar.com; www.nationalpriorities.org.

NOTE: All data are projected for FY 2017.

Drones constitute a key component of the so-called Revolution in Military Affairs (RMA) that applies new digital technologies to enhance the accuracy and effectiveness of weapons. Drones have become key counterterrorism instruments; their enhanced surveillance capacity makes it possible for users to track and destroy targets in real time.

The military use of drones increased dramatically during the first years of President Barack Obama's administration, especially in northwest Pakistan but also in Afghanistan, Yemen, and Africa, most notably Somalia. Drones appear to offer an effective and less expensive substitute for ground forces. Also, the drone program over Pakistan is run by the Central Intelligence Agency and is not officially acknowledged by the government. It is therefore possible for the CIA to use lethal force covertly, while the government of Pakistan can deny it is allowing a foreign power to wage war on its territory.

But there are also social problems associated with drone use. Using official numbers, the ratio of militant to civilian deaths has improved over the relatively short life of the program (see Table 16.2). For example, civilians accounted for roughly 70% of deaths from drone strikes between 2004 and 2007, but 0% in 2013 (New America Foundation, 2013). Yet the rules for defining "militant" and "civilian" remain contentious; some reports indicate that all armed men under age 40 in the vicinity are counted as "militant." Since virtually all

Post-traumatic stress disorder (PTSD): A mental health condition triggered by a terrifying event. Symptoms include flashbacks, nightmares, and severe anxiety, as well as thoughts about the event that cannot be controlled.

men in northwest Pakistan are armed, lower reported deaths may not actually prove noncombatants are being protected. Drone operations sometimes employ a "double-tap" strategy, in which a target is hit with a missile and then struck again when others come to help or investigate. Regardless of the actual number of fatalities, the widespread impression that drones do kill many innocent people undermines U.S. credibility among Pakistan's population.

Nor are the rules of engagement that govern the drone program transparent. At least four U.S. citizens have been assassinated by drones, and some point out that these individuals were not granted the legal "due process" the Constitution guarantees. The Obama administration said that it conducted extensive reviews before selecting any target, and the president himself signed off on any attack on an American citizen (Becker & Shane, 2012). Drones also have considerable "second-order effects," or indirect impacts, on local populations. Even where killings are largely limited to militants, the constant buzzing of hovering drones and the unpredictable threat of attack have limited normal social functions like weddings and funerals, religious gatherings, schools, and bazaars. Agriculture may also be disrupted, with significant economic impact. Surviving militants may blame locals for providing intelligence to guide the strikes and may take revenge (Stanford Law School/NYU Law School, 2012). When people leave targeted areas, they contribute to the flow of refugees to already overcrowded urban areas. The use of drones can also become a grievance point that enables opposition fighters to recruit new members (Sluka, 2011).

Finally, drone operators are not immune to psychological fallout from being agents of violence. Though physically safe on military bases in the United States, these pilots can suffer the effects of PTSD. All the pieces—civilian casualties, the hidden chain of command, second-order effects, and psychological toll on all sides—speak to the need for a more sociologically grounded interpretation of the use of drones rather than one limited to conventional military measures.

Women in Combat Roles

In January 2013, Defense Secretary Leon Panetta and the Joint Chiefs of Staff announced the end of the ban on women serving in combat roles in the U.S. Army. Nearly 15% of the 1.4 million active-duty military are female, and more than 255,000 women had deployed to Iraq or Afghanistan. Before 1973, women in the U.S. military served mostly as nurses or clerks; now they serve on surface ships, pilot helicopters, and fighter jets, and are deployed overseas as cooks, mechanics, drivers, military police, and intelligence officers. In 2015, Secretary of Defense Ashton Carter approved implementation plans for the integration of women into direct ground combat roles.

▶ U.S. Army General Laura Richardson sits behind U.S. Army Chief of Staff Mark Milley while he testifies about opening combat units to women in the military during a Senate Armed Services Committee hearing on Capitol Hill, in 2016 in Washington, D.C.

TABLE 16.2   **Annual Drone Casualties in Pakistan by Category, 2004–2013**

Year	Militant	Civilian	Unknown
2004–2007	43–76	95–107	16–18
2008	157–265	23–28	49–54
2009	241–508	66–80	44–136
2010	555–960	16–21	38–50
2011	304–488	56–64	31–36
2012	197–317	5	19–31
2013	44–76	0	3–5
Total	1,588–2,700	261–305	200–330

SOURCE: New American Foundation.

Many of these changes have placed more women in harm's way. In fact, the new policies only formalize what was already happening in Iraq and Afghanistan. Women have demonstrated bravery under fire, been captured, won medals, and served in many difficult circumstances. Although their casualty rate remains lower than that of men, more than 800 women have been wounded or killed in Iraq and Afghanistan.

The movement of women into combat roles, phasing in over several years, will continue a controversy that has been brewing for more than a decade. For example, a commander can still make a case for an exception, preserving the traditional all-male fighting unit.

The social construction of gender is one of the key sociological questions in the end of the ban on women in combat. Historically, masculine traits have been considered crucial for the proper training and performance of soldiers, especially those directly engaged in fighting. Will the presence of women constitute a "social problem" in the front lines? Must warriors always be male?

Some suggest the warrior role requires a hypermasculine culture (Leatherman, 2011; Titunik, 2008; Wood, 2006). **Hypermasculinity** is an intensification of traits typically associated with stereotypical male behavior: physical strength, aggressiveness, assertiveness, risk taking, virility, and an appreciation for danger and adventure. Military training, and the goal of strengthening bonding within small units, may also rest on shared male identity. Songs ("This is my rifle, this is my gun; this one is for fighting, this one is for fun"), shaved heads, a steady stream of references to intimate body parts, and a major role for sexual innuendo consolidate this identity. Masculinity may be as crucial for group performance as competence in handling weapons. Women may still face opposition in taking combat roles, but not because they are physically weaker. The "problem" is that their presence may rupture male solidarity.

Another sociological perspective concentrates on professionalism rather than masculinity. In this view, the military is a complex institution in which male warrior traits are not as important for success as are the skills and attitudes that create group cohesion. With bare chest and bulging muscles, hefting a huge heavy machine gun and exuding anger with every step, Sylvester Stallone's Rambo character may have done well at the box office, but he does not embody the teamwork, discipline, obedience, and service considered more important to fulfilling most military missions. In the not-so-distant past, women were excluded from serving on police patrols, performing complex surgery, long-distance running, and arguing legal cases in court. Many believed that women were physically incapable of performing these activities properly. But women have gained widespread acceptance in these and other activities because they are able to carry out their functional roles. Biological sex has not disappeared, but it has become much less important than task or functional training. While some style differences may remain between the sexes, women have shown their ability to achieve and contribute on par with men.

Those who favor continuing the ban on women in combat often invoke more traditional perspectives on gender relations. For example, women have limited upper-body strength and would be unable to carry heavy loads or drag wounded comrades to safety. Moreover, their presence encourages distractions that compromise morale and interfere with the bonding necessary for an effective fighting force. During the 2012 presidential campaign, Republican candidate Rick Santorum argued,

"When you have men and women together in combat, I think men have emotions when you see a woman in harm's way. I think it is something that's natural. It's very much in our culture to be protective." While still chief of staff of the U.S. Air Force, General Merrill McPeak testified to the Senate Armed Services Committee, then considering allowing women to fly combat aircraft, that he would choose a less qualified male pilot over a more qualified female because "even though logic tells us that women can [conduct combat operations] as well as men, I have a very traditional attitude about wives and mothers and daughters being ordered to kill people" (quoted in McSally, 2011). The Center for Military Readiness, based in Washington, D.C., is one organization that is particularly vociferous in defending the exclusion of women from combat.

Those favoring an end to the combat ban focus on more fluid construction of gender roles, with new possibilities for women. For example, technology may be more important to the contemporary soldier than strength. Many standard-issue weapons are relatively light, making it possible even for children to use them. All recruits could be required to meet standards of strength, speed, and endurance that apply evenly to women and men. Men might have an easier time meeting the marks, but some women would qualify while some men would fail. Furthermore, the distinction between combat and noncombat positions has already been blurred. Early in Operation Iraqi Freedom, Private First Class Jessica Lynch and two other female soldiers, Lori Piestewa and Shoshana Johnson, were captured and suffered injuries. All three were members of the 507th Maintenance Company. Lynch and Piestewa were unit supply specialists; Johnson prepared meals. All were clearly in harm's way.

Ending the combat ban enabled the rules to catch up with reality. Female soldiers were "colocated" with combat teams and participated in patrols for many years, primarily because they are better able than male soldiers to avoid offending cultural sensitivities when local women need to be searched. In the Marine Corps, Female Engagement Teams serve on the front lines in Afghanistan. Cultural Support Teams have deployed with the Special Forces. Public opinion polls show most U.S. adults generally agree with lifting the ban (*New York Times*, 2009).

Finally, eligibility for full combat will be necessary for women if they are to achieve full equality in the armed forces. Without that opportunity they will always be considered second-class citizens and held back unfairly. A final, crucial argument is that ending the combat ban may

....

Hypermasculinity: An intensification of traits normally associated with stereotypical male behavior: physical strength, aggressiveness, assertiveness, risk taking, and appreciation for danger and adventure.

be necessary to reduce sexual violence and harassment in the armed forces and service academies.

USING THEORY TO EXAMINE WAR AND TERRORISM: THE VIEWS FROM THE FUNCTIONALIST, CONFLICT, AND SYMBOLIC INTERACTIONIST PERSPECTIVES

16.4 Apply the functionalist, symbolic interactionist, and conflict perspectives to war.

Political scientists and international relations theorists have long studied war. Nonetheless, sociology has much to contribute. All the major theories—functionalism, symbolic interactionism, and conflict theory—address the sociological relationships found in war, each through distinct approaches.

Functionalism

The structural functionalist approach takes a macro view and looks at the relationships between particular phenomena, such as crime or health, and the overall organization of society. Its tendency is to focus on social order. "Structures" can be said to be "functional" when they strengthen the capacity of society to hold itself together.

Given its devastation, war may seem an odd contributor to the stability and functioning of society. And its dysfunctions usually do outweigh the benefits. Even in trying to understand the functions of war, we must not forget the multiple tragedies that always accompany human beings' use of violence against other human beings.

The United States' experience during World War II illustrates the structural functionalist perspective.

The entire country was mobilized behind the war effort. Every medically eligible male served in the armed forces, intelligence, administration, or government. The economy was largely driven by the war, women flowed into the workforce to replace men fighting overseas, and the participation of minorities improved on the past record of discrimination. Though blacks fought in segregated units led by white officers, their service made it more difficult for them to accept the racial status quo after the war. Japanese Americans were herded into detention centers, a shameful practice that violated their rights as U.S. citizens. But many young men from these camps ended up in Europe fighting for their country. This experience helped lay the groundwork for the expansion of citizenship rights after the war. Finally, women demonstrated that they could build tanks, construct aircraft, and forge steel. Though the effects were not immediate—men came home to reclaim these jobs—the experience helped women prepare for new postwar opportunities to work outside the home.

World War II also helped the United States finally emerge from the Great Depression. Some technical innovations of the war, such as radar and improvements in aircraft engines, were applied in the postwar civilian sector. And lower spending on consumption during the war and the resulting savings helped create the groundwork for a postwar period of prosperity, including the expansion of homeownership and the purchase of automobiles. Still, we can be excused for hoping there might be a better way to achieve such benefits.

Scott Olson/Getty Images

▶ Female marine recruit Kylieanne Fortin goes through close combat training at the U.S. Marine Corps training depot in Parris Island, South Carolina. Marine Corps boot camp, with its combination of strict discipline and exhaustive physical training, is considered the most rigorous of all U.S. armed forces recruit training. The first three women ever to graduate from the infantry training course completed the program in November 2013.

Sexual Violence in the Military

Under pressure from different constituencies and after years of complaints about avoiding the problem, the U.S. Department of Defense now issues an annual report on sexual assault in the military. The department estimated that about 14,900 service members experienced some kind of sexual assault in 2016. This figure was down from an estimated 20,300 active-duty members experiencing a sexual assault in 2014 (U.S. Department of Defense, 2016). These reports certainly undercount the actual number of assaults.

Equally controversial are the actions being taken to respond to this epidemic. The military has introduced hotlines, mandatory online training, zero-tolerance policies, workshops, and specialized units charged with reducing sexual violence. These steps may have an effect, but advocacy groups outside the military and many soldiers themselves claim the problem has actually worsened over the past decade.

Because some commanders have set aside convictions on sexual assault charges and even forced victims to continue working alongside perpetrators, Senator Kirsten Gillibrand (D-NY) unsuccessfully championed legislation that would remove military commanders from the process of deciding whether sexual misconduct cases should go to military trial. In 2013, a Pentagon report found that 5,061 troops reported cases of assault. Of these only 484 cases went to trial, and only 376 resulted in convictions (*New York Times*, 2014).

Chip Somodevilla/Getty Images

▶ Military Academy Cadet Stephanie Gross (r), a survivor of sexual assault, testifies before the House Armed Services Committee's Subcommittee on Military Personnel with Naval Academy Midshipman Second Class Shiela Craine (l) and Ariana Bullard on Capitol Hill. Gross was raped twice while at West Point.

▶ **THINK ABOUT IT**

1. Why do you think sexual assault occurs at a higher rate in the military than in civilian life?

2. What can be done about the problem of underreporting of such assaults?

3. What would you do to reduce the level of sexual assault within the military?

Policy Implications of Structural Functionalism

The most important policy implication of the structural functionalist perspective is that war, or at least preparation for war, might be necessary to defend a society against outside threats. Supporters of nuclear deterrence would argue that during the Cold War, the mutual threat of the United States and the Soviet Union to destroy each other with atomic weapons did maintain a certain kind of peace between them. In this view, the capacity to wage war—even extreme war—contributed to each side's national security. Many would argue instead, however, that peace can be achieved without the threat of nuclear annihilation.

The production and control of atomic weapons imply a strong concentration of power, calling attention to Max Weber's (1958) definition of the state as the organization that holds the only legitimate means of violence. For Weber, the emergence of the nation-state was useful because force could now be centralized in a single organization governed by norms or rules that most people found acceptable. Moreover, the use of that force was increasingly professionalized, meaning it was more carefully regulated and subject to political authority. In this way of thinking, a country can live with nuclear weapons when the public believes the weapons are carefully controlled and an elaborate decision-making structure ensures they will be used only as a last resort. When properly managed, the possession of the weapons' deadly force might lead to carefully regulated threats that are never carried out instead of actual violence.

Structural functionalists take a similar stance toward the armed forces as a whole: Lethal force can be used, but only under clearly defined circumstances and with the approval of civilian leaders. Ultimately, the *raison d'être* of the military is to keep the country safe. Maintaining the security of society by means of its military certainly falls short of a nonviolent ideal, but it is preferable to the existence of numerous armed substate actors, all using or threatening violence to achieve private interests.

Time Life Pictures/National Archives/The LIFE Picture Collection/Getty Images

It's Our Fight Too!

▶ American World War II–era recruitment poster for women workers. "Rosie the Riveter" was the iconic image representing American women working in factories during the war. The equivalent image of women working for the war effort in Canada was "Ronnie the Bren Gun Girl," and in Britain it was the painting *Ruby Loftus Screwing a Breech Ring*.

Conflict Theory

Conflict theory focuses on power structures and the domestic and international inequalities that drive the war system. One of the most important concepts conflict theorists employ is the idea of the **military-industrial complex**, or the relationships among government forces, the Pentagon, and defense contractors that promote the acquisition of weapons systems and a militarized foreign policy.

In his January 17, 1961, farewell address to the nation, President Dwight D. Eisenhower warned of

> an immense military establishment and a large arms industry [that] is new in the American experience. The total influence—economic, political, even spiritual—is felt in every city, every statehouse, every office of the federal government. . . . In the councils of government, we must guard against the acquisition of unwarranted influence, whether sought or unsought, by the military-industrial complex. The potential for the disastrous rise of misplaced power exists, and will persist.

This remarkable statement came from an individual who was not only president of the United States but also the former commanding general of Allied forces in Europe and the head of the D-Day invasion of Normandy. With Eisenhower's speech, the term *military-industrial complex* entered the national vocabulary.

Sociologically, the military-industrial complex contains a series of distinct features. These include a strong compatibility of interest among top Pentagon officials, defense contractors, and members of Congress (Adams, 1981). This common interest results in the purchase of expensive weapons systems that are often unneeded or that underperform (Hartung, 2011). The military-industrial complex is guided by self-interest rather than policy. For example, the military continues to invest in the acquisition of large tanks, weapons of a method of conducting war that is largely obsolete. Members of Congress often support weapons procurement programs that benefit their districts, regardless of whether the programs contribute to national security. Even liberals, generally doves with respect to war policy, vote to retain military bases that are no longer useful, or armaments the military itself may oppose, in order to benefit their local constituencies. Counterinsurgency capabilities such as language skills, intelligence gathering, and social science–based cultural knowledge do appear in the Department of Defense budget, but they receive less support than expensive heavy-weapons hardware.

Ideology plays an important role in the military-industrial complex, especially a view of the world that C. Wright Mills (1956) called the "military definition of reality." According to Mills, most civilian and military leaders in the United States see the world as an unsettled, competitive, often hostile arena in which military prowess is the best option for securing national interests and maintaining U.S. status as the most powerful nation in the world. According to the Constitution and formal regulations, the U.S. military is under civilian control. Civilians, however, share the military mind-set regarding the importance of projecting power, ensuring that nonmilitary options such as diplomacy receive less attention and lower policy priorities. Military leaders and their values thus play a significant role in Washington's policies, not conspiring against civilians, but working alongside and often supported by them.

Mills is unusual among conflict theorists because he regarded the military as a source of power in its own right. He was certainly aware of corporate power, but unlike conventional Marxists, who call attention to

. . . .

Military-industrial complex: The relationships among government, the Pentagon, and defense contractors that promote the acquisition of weapons systems and a militarized foreign policy.

▶ An American soldier, wounded by an exploding land mine, is carried to a helicopter by his comrades during the Vietnam War in 1969. Military and civilian casualties and losses on both sides of the conflict were massive.

property rights and market forces, Mills identified power as rooted in the control of large-scale, bureaucratically structured organizations, be they big business, the executive branch of government, or the military itself. Mills thought the Cold War had degraded the capacity of the United States to engage in productive diplomacy with other nations. Though he wrote more than 50 years ago, his ideas remain influential.

Policy Implications of the Conflict Perspective

One policy implication of the thesis that the military-industrial complex holds considerable influence is that the United States is more war-prone than most Americans believe. The chance that it will fight other democracies is fairly remote, yet Washington has certainly established a belligerent record, especially since the end of World War II. During the Cold War, the Pentagon fought major wars in Korea and Vietnam as well as numerous smaller conflicts. Defense spending averaged 8% to 10% of GDP. And the country provided military aid and training to many repressive regimes, such as those of Mobutu in Zaire, Pinochet in Chile, and Sukarno in Indonesia. According to conflict theorists, the war system proved expensive at home and shrank the possibilities for democratic reform abroad.

Ideology has operated in the post–Cold War era as well. In 2002, President George W. Bush endorsed an internal government report titled *National Security Strategy of the United States of America,* which outlined a strategy of preventive war in which the United States would have to "act against emerging threats before they are fully formed." The document declared the nation's right to "dissuade potential adversaries from pursuing a military buildup in the hopes of surpassing, or equaling, the power of the United States." Simple deterrence, or preventing war by threatening retaliation, was thought less likely to work. The conclusion called for "anticipatory action to defend ourselves—even if uncertainty remains as to the time and place of the enemy's attack. To forestall or prevent such hostile acts by our adversaries, the United States will, if necessary, act preemptively." In this controversial statement—the authors of which were civilians—diplomacy, negotiation, and multilateral cooperation with allies take a backseat.

Conflict theorists also note profiteering in the recent wars in Iraq and Afghanistan, especially because new policies relied more heavily on private military contractors such as Halliburton and Blackwater. While humanitarian aid and development projects existed, both wars saw strategies that relied more on "hard power" military options. The Global War on Terror (discussed below) also favors a militarized approach to security rather than a combination of policing, building a broader range of allies, and conflict resolution. Meanwhile, the illegal "rendition" of terror suspects to foreign prisons, abuse and torture conducted by the United States itself, negative images of the detention center at Guantánamo Bay, and the use of drones have provided robust recruitment incentives for the very insurgents the United States is trying to defeat. Conflict theorists say these policies are counterproductive for most U.S. citizens but reflect the priorities of the country's power elite.

Symbolic Interactionism

Symbolic interaction theorists try to understand how individuals acquire the meanings and understandings that govern their interactions with other individuals and social groups. Human beings do not automatically act out directives from authorities or dominant structures. They interpret the surrounding circumstances and then play out these interpretations. They may even change the script depending on time, place, and key engagements with other people. Social interaction is a bottom-up rather than a top-down approach to social life.

Symbolic interactionism is a very human perspective because it examines the constant exchange, dialogue, and communication that guide social life. We could not get through the day without utilizing a huge tool box of social skills that enable us to peacefully coordinate our actions with our families, neighbors, and coworkers. Even when we disagree with them or consider them different, strange, or possibly threatening, we usually do not want to kill them. Many people believe we are condemned to competition, even conflict and violence, by our genetic makeup. It would be far more accurate to say our biology "condemns" us to cooperation (Fry, 2006; United Nations Educational, Scientific and Cultural Organization, 1986).

But if we are predominantly cooperative, how can we also engage in torture, rape, killing, and other destructive acts, at times on a stupefying scale? The Rwanda genocide, the bombing of civilians by both sides in World War II, rape camps in Bosnia, and the use of child soldiers all serve as social alarm bells. Humans do carry the potential to do great harm. What does symbolic interactionism tell us about this more tragic side of social behavior?

Several factors must come together for humans to exercise violence on a horrific scale. Three in particular mark the passage from acceptance of others to violent killing: authorization, routinization, and dehumanization (Fellman, 1998; Gamson, 1995; Kelman & Hamilton, 1989). Fortunately, the combination of these three is rare.

Under **authorization**, leaders define a situation so that individuals are absolved of responsibility for making personal moral choices. People act badly because an authority has given them approval to do so. Hutu militia butchered Tutsi during the Rwanda genocide believing their leaders had been given approval for these actions. Those who dropped the atomic bombs on civilians in Hiroshima and Nagasaki did not have to think about the consequences because they were following orders from the president and the military chain of command. Japanese soldiers killed hundreds of thousands of civilians in Nanjing because they believed they were authorized by the highest military officers (Chang, 1997).

Under **routinization**, actions become organized by well-established procedures so there is no opportunity for raising moral questions. Individuals act badly because they believe in a routine that determines how they are to behave; they no longer have to make deliberate decisions. For example, those who ran the Nazi death camps followed closely prescribed procedures governing how many people they were to kill on each shift, how they were to administer the gas, how hot they were to make each oven, and how they were to dispose of the bodies.

Under **dehumanization**, attitudes reflect perceptions that the targets are less than human. People act badly because they see only objects, animals, or vicious enemies, not

▶ An old woman and children on their way to the gas chambers at the Auschwitz concentration camp in Poland, 1944. The "Final Solution" was the systematic effort by the Nazi bureaucracy to exterminate the Jews of Europe during World War II by gassing, shooting, and other means. Can you think of other examples of systematic killing that are rational, efficient, and devoid of emotion?

human beings. For example, the terrible medical experiments the Japanese conducted on prisoners of war during World War II were carried out on what they called *maruta*, or wooden logs. The Nazi regime portrayed Jews as rats or other vermin. During the 1994 genocide in Rwanda, Hutu hate propaganda referred to Tutsis as *inyenzi*, or cockroaches.

In all these cases, the scale of enemy making intensified. Leaders gave their approval, perpetrators were given instructions and mechanisms to follow, and those killed no longer counted as human beings. All moral decision making was suspended. The symbolic interactionist perspective helps us understand how these meanings, no matter how heinous, can be acquired—and, fortunately, how unusual they are.

Policy Implications of Symbolic Interactionism

One striking sociological finding is that it is actually very difficult to get human beings to kill each other, even in the midst of war. It can be done, obviously—we have

---

Authorization: Enemy-making behavior facilitated by leaders that absolves individuals of the responsibility to make personal moral choices.

Routinization: The organizing and structuring of enemy-making behavior so thoroughly that there is no opportunity for raising moral questions.

Dehumanization: Enemy-making behavior that makes the other side appear to be less than human; eliminates the need to raise moral questions.

just reviewed several dismaying examples. But we cannot assume soldiers will kill just because they have been given orders to do so. Killing is, sociologically speaking, extremely problematic.

One of the earliest applications of sociological studies to the battlefield found that complexity and contradiction were the rule rather than devotion to duty as defined by superior officers. During World War II, less than 25% of combat soldiers could be counted on to fire their weapons at the enemy. Everyone else fired in the air, refused to shoot, or huddled near the ground. Lieutenant Colonel Robert Cole described the behavior of his soldiers under attack in 1944: "Not one man in twenty-five voluntarily used his weapon . . . they fired only while I watched them or while some other soldier stood over them" (quoted in Malesevic, 2010, p. 221). Almost all the actual fighting was carried out by a relatively small number of combatants.

Firing ratios improved during the Vietnam War and among front-line soldiers in Iraq and Afghanistan. This rise in efficiency rested on findings of other studies that in the heat of battle, soldiers fight not for abstractions such as "democracy" or "freedom," or even to protect the homeland from attack. Instead, they fight because they are loyal to the people in their immediate unit. Training therefore now focuses on deepening the micro-level solidarity of small fighting units; comradeship, mutual respect, and not letting others down are the key motivations. Left to themselves, individuals generally do not kill efficiently; only through close attention to social organization and the creation of new norms forged in the intensity of small-group interaction do soldiers perform as their leaders desire.

SPECIALIZED THEORY: THE TWO-SOCIETY THESIS

16.5 Apply the two-society thesis to the relationship between the U.S. military and U.S. society.

The political and social turmoil surrounding the Vietnam conflict in the 1960s, especially opposition to the draft, fundamentally altered the U.S. military's enlistment policy. In 1973, the Pentagon ended the draft and established an all-volunteer force (AVF). Conscription still exists in theory; young men must register with the Selective Service System, but few expect they will be forced to serve. Entering the military is an option to choose—or not.

One important result of an AVF is that the military may become a society within a society. This relationship between the civilian and military sectors might become a social problem if the two sectors exhibit differences in members' social backgrounds, cultural values, and political beliefs. A significant gap between military and civilian experiences and attitudes threatens a cornerstone of democratic society—that the fighting force is drawn from and is representative of everyone. The two-society thesis recognizes that most U.S. adults support the military in many ways. But beneath that important social fact, disparities between classes, cultures, and belief systems structure a divide between military and civilian life. An AVF may actually be easier to commit to fighting, whereas a military in which soldiers are drafted, despite problems, is subject to more constraints before those soldiers are sent into battle.

The two-society thesis assumes that soldiers, both enlisted and officers, will make military service a career lasting significantly longer than the 18 to 24 months draftees served. Pay scales and benefits have improved dramatically in the AVF. The military has become more family-oriented; more than half its members have children, and more than 100,000 are married to other service members. Military bases resemble towns and often provide schools, recreational and medical facilities, and subsidized shopping. During times of considerable economic uncertainty in the civilian sector, these features attract volunteers to become absorbed into the military's thinking, perspective, and attitudes. One study of marines returning home after boot camp found them repulsed by "the physical unfitness of civilians, by the uncouth behavior they witnessed, and by what they saw as pervasive selfishness and consumerism" (Ricks, quoted in Rahbek-Clemmensen et al., 2012, p. 672).

Yet a very small proportion of U.S. citizens serve in the armed forces. During the long-running wars in Iraq and Afghanistan, more than 2.5 million soldiers deployed to combat theaters. That is a large number—but significantly less than 1% of the population. During the Cold War, the percentage of veterans in Congress was higher than the percentage in the country as a whole. Now, less than a quarter of Americans have served in the military. At the beginning of the 2003 war with Iraq, among 535 members of Congress, only one had a child deployed to Iraq. Among the general public, the proportion who know someone who has served in the military has also declined (Parker, 2011). These concentrations seem to have influenced political and social views on different topics.

Members of the military are significantly more conservative than the rest of the population. One large-scale survey found 63.9% of leaders in the armed forces identifying as Republicans, compared with only 30.3%

The Network of U.S. Foreign Military Bases

The United States has established an enormous number of military bases throughout the world, reaching a total of over 1,000 (see Figure 16.3). Some are large: In 2015, approximately 37,000 military personnel were stationed in Germany; almost 12,000 in Italy; and nearly 49,000 in Japan. Others are relatively small and contain only small contingents of advisers. One growing subcategory is that of bases connected to the use of drones, especially in Africa and the Middle East. The Pentagon places the annual cost of maintaining these bases at $22.1 billion, but others offer estimates as high as $170 billion (Vine, 2012).

At times, U.S. military personnel on foreign bases have become embroiled in sex scandals with locals and have committed violence against women and girls living nearby. Okinawa, islands south of Japan and the site of several important U.S. military bases, was the scene of the 1995 rape and murder of a young girl by several U.S. servicemen. The local population's reaction led to the election of political leaders hostile to the continued presence of American military personnel and forced dramatic restructuring of the bases themselves.

Other kinds of incidents can turn local opinion against U.S. military bases as well.

In Italy, the severing of a gondola cable by the tail of a U.S. jet flying below its permitted altitude led to a dozen deaths. Other criminal acts have included murder in Afghanistan, more incidents of rape in Japan, and environmental spoilage in the Philippines. The United States has also tortured prisoners at bases in Iraq, Afghanistan, and Guantánamo Bay, and in CIA secret prisons (Shane, 2013b). In almost all these cases adjudication, where it has occurred at all, has taken place in the United States. Structural functionalists might argue that the bases are a vital component of U.S. defense; conflict theorists might suggest they are better understood as agents of influence and control.

▶ **THINK ABOUT IT**

1. How would you regard the presence of a foreign military base on the outskirts of your town? Would the fact that your government has approved this base affect your views?

2. Do you think U.S. staff on foreign bases should be governed by the local legal process, or by U.S. procedures? Why?

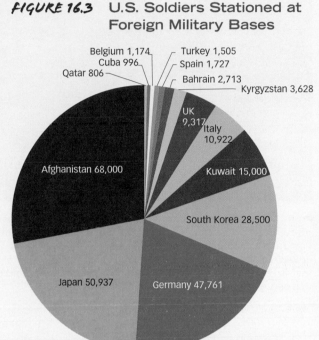

FIGURE 16.3 U.S. Soldiers Stationed at Foreign Military Bases

Belgium 1,174
Cuba 996
Qatar 806
Turkey 1,505
Spain 1,727
Bahrain 2,713
Kyrgyzstan 3,628
UK 9,317
Italy 10,922
Afghanistan 68,000
Kuwait 15,000
South Korea 28,500
Japan 50,937
Germany 47,761

SOURCE: Department of Defense, September 30, 2012.

---

of civilian nonveteran leaders. About two-thirds of military leaders called themselves "somewhat conservative" or "very conservative," compared with less than a third of civilian nonveteran leaders (Feaver & Kohn, 2001). Meanwhile, less than 5% of the military elite identified as "very liberal" or "somewhat liberal," compared with 37.5% of civilian leaders.

Serving in the military is also a distinct experience. While flying a fighter jet for the air force is very different from fixing a tank in the army, important commonalities make military culture in all branches substantially different from civilian life. These include the following (Burk, 2008):

- *Cohesion:* The emotional bond of shared identity and camaraderie among soldiers in their local unit.

- *Esprit de corps:* The pride soldiers take in the effectiveness and importance of their organization.

- *Discipline:* The commitment soldiers make to conform to rules, command, instruction, and drill.

Scott Olson/Getty Images

▶ A recruit responds to a motivational speech being made by his commanding officer before graduation from boot camp at the U.S. Marine Corps recruit depot in Parris Island, South Carolina. The French sociologist Émile Durkheim used the term *collective effervescence* to describe the shared emotional excitement or "electricity" that is created in a group when people come together and participate in an activity that serves to unify them.

- *Etiquette:* The elaborate prescriptions that guide interpersonal interactions, especially between individuals of different ranks.

- *Ceremonies:* The rituals that mark events and convey the distinct experiences and expectations of soldiers as different from civilians.

Beyond these cultural elements, it is not difficult to imagine how the combination of overseas deployment, exposure to hazard, the possibility of killing, and the possibility of being killed all can create a sense of personal commitment and national service quite different from what we find in civilian occupations. Not everyone in the military is a warrior; the so-called tooth-to-tail ratio, which compares those trained to fight on the ground with those who provide support, is only 10%. Even among those deployed to Iraq and Afghanistan, significantly less than half have engaged in actual fighting. Nonetheless, the warrior mentality continues to play a major role in the self-conception of the military. As Burk (2008) notes, "Warfighting still determines the central beliefs, values, and complex symbolic formations that define military culture." And army veteran Matt Gallagher, who served in Iraq, has observed, "A lot of guys feel that they're part of a warrior caste, separate and distinct from society" (quoted in Thompson, 2011).

The end of the draft, longer time in service, a distinct set of political and social views, and unique features of the military experience support the two-society thesis. Is there any counterevidence?

In 1993, President Clinton modified the standing policy of excluding gays and lesbians from the military by adopting a policy of "don't ask, don't tell" (DADT). This may have eased some homophobic practices, but many gays and lesbians continued to be expelled from the armed forces once their identities became known. DADT also put the military at odds with civilian society, which had been moving, however unevenly, toward greater inclusion and the extension of more civil rights to gays and lesbians. In response to the establishment of DADT, some universities and colleges barred ROTC programs from their campuses, in part because any policy that required homosexuals to "stay in the closet" violated their nondiscrimination charters. However, over the past decade a remarkable sea change has occurred within the military, driven largely by generational changes in the larger society. Younger soldiers, marines, and junior officers moving up the ranks are not nearly so fixed in their views as their elders. Many in the military recognized that dismissing gays and lesbians, particularly when skilled, capable people were in demand, was self-destructive. A seminal article describing the negative impact of DADT on military efficacy was published in *Joint Forces Quarterly,* the main journal of the Joint Chiefs of Staff (Prakash, 2009). In 2012, following a congressional debate and extensive preparation within the armed forces, President Obama ended DADT. As in many other militaries around the world, gays and lesbians can now serve openly in the U.S. armed forces. Discrimination has not ended, and backlash still occurs, but in their general movement toward greater equality, the military and civilian worlds now appear more alike than different.

> *ASK YOURSELF:* Should a democratic society rely on an all-volunteer force, or should military service be evenly distributed across the population through a draft? If the draft were reintroduced in the United States, should women be eligible as well as men? Has the adoption of the AVF made it easier for the United States to engage in war? Why or why not?

TERRORISM

 16.6 Discuss the Global War on Terror.

Definition Issues

The U.S. State Department defines **terrorism** as "violence perpetrated for political reasons by subnational groups or secret state agents, often directed at noncombatant targets, and usually intended to influence an audience." Kidnapping, bombing, seizure of public buildings, and assassinations are intended to induce fear, often because witnesses feel the targets of these acts do not deserve the violence they suffer. There is a random element as well: Anyone could become a victim. In sociological terms, terrorism is a dramatic taboo.

The hijacking of passenger airliners on September 11, 2001, and the subsequent attacks on the World Trade Center in New York City and the Pentagon in Washington, D.C., fit this definition of terrorism and dominate public perceptions and political debate. Responses to terrorist acts often include moral outrage at the loss of civilian lives, anger at the violation of normal rules regarding public safety, desire for revenge, and, at times, gloating by perpetrators. These emotions heighten the already significant tension surrounding such acts.

Terrorism can be *international* in the sense that the attacking party is based in one part of the world and organizes violence so that perpetrators and weapons cross borders. Terrorism can also be *domestic* when attackers and targets are within a single country, even if inspiration may come from outside sources. The 9/11 al-Qaeda attacks in the United States were certainly international. The 2017 Manchester Arena bombing in Manchester, England, is considered domestic because it was carried out by a British citizen. Examples of domestic terrorism in the United States include a nail bombing during the 1996 Summer Olympic Games in Atlanta, Georgia; the destruction of a federal building in Oklahoma City in 1995; and attacks on and killings of medical professionals who provide abortions.

In addition, we must consider *repressive state terrorism,* which is the employment of systematic violence against political opposition within national borders, and *state-sponsored terrorism,* in which a government provides material support, weapons, and training to subnational units in another country so they can attack the government or civilians in that country. In both cases, the violence undermines democratic processes and holds the wrong people responsible for presumed grievances.

There are many examples of repressive state terrorism. The Communist Party in China and the Soviet Union under Josef Stalin killed millions of political opponents, both real and presumed. Other examples include the "disappearances" carried out by Argentina's military *junta* in the early 1970s and the mass execution of Cambodians by the Khmer Rouge in the late 1970s. Labeling the actions of a state or organization "terrorist" can be controversial. The U.S. State Department considers Hezbollah, a complex political organization that includes both fighting units and welfare providers, operates in Lebanon, and has fought Israel, a terrorist organization. The United States also criticizes Iran for providing military and monetary support to Hezbollah. During the 1980s, the South African government labeled the African National Congress (ANC) a "terrorist" group when it sabotaged power lines and carried out other acts of violence against property. Yet, from their own standpoint, the members of the ANC were "freedom fighters" engaged in a just struggle to overthrow the authoritarian apartheid system. As the Truth and Reconciliation Commission later documented, it was the government's brutal repression of antiapartheid activists that was fully "terrorist." Other examples are the Irish Republican Army and its struggle against British occupation, and Jewish resistance movements in British Palestine who kidnapped soldiers and bombed civilian and military facilities.

The U.S. government has participated in terrorism. In the past, the Pentagon trained military officers from Central and South America in repressive techniques aimed at suppressing local social movements. Washington has also supplied military equipment and other support to governments that have systematically violated human rights—the Saigon regime during the Vietnam War, Saddam Hussein's government in Iraq in the 1980s, and the regime of Augusto Pinochet in Chile, which overthrew the democratically elected government of Salvador Allende. Any government that possesses nuclear weapons might be considered guilty of state "terrorism" because it seeks a political outcome—deterrence of war—by threatening extreme violence against civilian noncombatants in another country.

Weighing the Risks of Terrorism

No matter the definition, terrorism is a political act that threatens the lives of innocent people. Protection against this risk is necessary, yet security measures can themselves create problems. In 2016, the United States spent over $65 billion annually on programs administered by the Department of Homeland Security. Funds are allocated to

....

Terrorism: Violence perpetrated for political reasons by subnational groups or secret state agents, often directed at noncombatant targets, and usually intended to influence an audience.

LYNN JOHNSON/National Geographic Creative

▶ Only part of the outer shell of the South Tower was left standing as a result of the 9/11 terrorist attacks on the World Trade Center in New York City. Terrorists crashed two passenger airliners into the Twin Towers, killing 2,752 people, including all 157 passengers (including the hijackers) and crew aboard the two planes.

in public mental health programs would lower the suicide rate, as would legislation making it harder for mentally unstable individuals to acquire handguns. Requiring ignition devices in automobiles that make it impossible for people to start their cars when drunk would reduce the number of fatal motor vehicle accidents, about half of which involve alcohol.

Such measures are controversial. Initiating them would cost money, although far less than is currently spent on combating the terrorist threat. But the government's monitoring of private telephone conversations and other forms of communication in the name of counterterrorism is, from a civil liberties view, also controversial. The sociological perspective makes two points when it comes to policy alternatives: First, the way we prioritize social problems has important consequences for society, and second, the way we respond to social problems—how much money we spend, which remedies we follow, and which we ignore—creates an agenda. Does a militarized approach receive greater support? Or is social reform favored?

U.S. citizens are made physically more secure by counterterrorist expenditures. The clear physical threat posed by terrorism presents itself differently than the more abstract dangers of a possible automobile accident, generalized social stress, and victimization by a storm or other natural disaster. The risks of terrorism cannot be ignored. But it is also clear that concentrating more effort on programs that address other social problems would save more lives.

The Global War on Terror

After the September 11, 2001, attacks, the Bush administration established a distinct framework for response. President Bush called for a Global War on Terror (GWOT) that would integrate a series of military, political, legal, intelligence, and policy measures, with a focus largely on militant Islamic groups such as al-Qaeda and other jihadist organizations. Under the new doctrine, countries that harbor or sponsor terrorists would be considered enemies, and the United States pledged to conduct preemptive strikes against those that even seemed like they might begin to organize attacks. Internationally, the two most visible features of the GWOT were military interventions in Afghanistan and Iraq, both undertaken in the name of pursuing terrorists in their home territory—even if the evidence did not always support this claim.

The GWOT also included several important pieces of legislation and executive findings. After 9/11 the definition of "enemy combatant" was broadened to include any person who engages in hostile acts against the United States as designated by the commander in chief. Hundreds of individuals—some dangerous, some not;

security systems at airports and other transportation systems, to many levels of police and federal agencies, to new surveillance technologies, to cooperation with foreign governments, and to counterterrorist intelligence operations. From the social problems perspective, are these commitments the best way to allocate scarce resources? The goal is to save lives. Is this the most efficient way to spend money to accomplish that goal?

The risk of a U.S. citizen becoming a victim of a terrorist attack at home is relatively low; victims number fewer than 10 a year since September 11, 2001. In comparison, about 50 people in the United States are murdered, 85 take their own lives, and 120 die in traffic accidents *every day* (Schneier, 2010). We can reduce the deaths, injuries, and other costs of many of those problems and others considered in this volume more effectively than we can reduce those from terrorism. Gun control would significantly cut the number of homicides; about 70% of murders are committed with guns. A relatively modest increase some captured on battlefields in Iraq and Afghanistan; others from various sites in Europe, the Middle East, and South Asia—were incarcerated at Guantánamo Bay, a navy base and detention center on the island of Cuba. These prisoners entered a legal limbo in which they were neither tried for specific acts nor provided a process through which they could eventually be released. All were interrogated in the search for further information by means that violated the Geneva Convention regarding the treatment of prisoners. Detainees were isolated from each other, sometimes deprived of sleep, and subjected to pain and different humiliations in an effort to break their will.

BEN STANSALL/AFP/Getty Images

▶ A man adds a rose to a mound of messages and floral tribute in Manchester, England. Twenty-two people were killed and dozens injured in the 2017 terror attack at the Ariana Grande concert at the Manchester Arena. What do you think can deter similar incidents from happening?

At home, the Bush administration and Congress passed the Patriot Act of 2001, which significantly increased the capacities of law enforcement and intelligence-gathering agencies. Phone records could now be more easily accessed. The Internet, including private e-mail exchanges, could be monitored more aggressively. And many medical, employment, and financial records could be reviewed with less judicial oversight. For example, the National Security Agency (NSA) now uses a keyword search to screen all international phone calls.

Other important domestic measures created under the Department of Homeland Security include the closer tracking of noncitizens within the United States and new requirements that they register and report to immigration authorities. Authorities can more easily detain and deport individuals suspected of engaging in terrorism-related activities. And the secretary of the Treasury has expanded authority to regulate financial transactions, particularly those of foreign individuals and other economic units.

Limitations of the Global War on Terror

The Global War on Terror has been credited with helping to prevent several attacks on U.S. soil. After the Boston Marathon bombings in April 2013, the *New York Times* argued that during the previous decade, the "United States was strikingly free of terrorist attacks, in part because of far more aggressive law enforcement tactics" (Shane, 2013a). Examples include a 2001 shoe-bomb plot that would have brought down a civilian airliner; a planned 2007 attack against Fort Dix, New Jersey; and a 2010 plot to bomb Times Square in New York City. (In the case of the 2009 Northwest Airlines bomb incident, it could also be claimed that vigilant fellow passengers

prevented a Nigerian man from setting off explosives hidden in his underwear.) Perhaps the GWOT's best claim to success lies in deterrence: Despite these incidents and the Boston Marathon bombings, the number of international terrorist acts carried out on U.S. home territory remains relatively small. At the same time, the GWOT has raised many questions, including the possibility that some of its measures violate U.S. laws and norms, and that some are actually self-defeating.

The American Civil Liberties Union has challenged many sections of the Patriot Act as infringing on civil liberties in general and on the First Amendment in particular. The government's right to search an individual's library records, book purchases, and business and private finances without disclosing that the person is being investigated is also a breach of the right to due process. Some city police departments, especially New York's, have carried out widespread surveillance on Muslim Americans, paying informants to photograph prayer sessions in mosques, recording the names of those signing protest petitions, and reporting Muslims who volunteer to feed poor families. The NYPD has used plainclothes detectives to eavesdrop on ordinary conversations and, under an organizational entity called the Demographics Unit, has cataloged Muslim businesses engaged in normal commerce. Using a strategy called "create and capture," New York and other municipalities have used undercover agents to coax young men into discussions about terrorism and then into the margins of terrorist activities. In the decade after 9/11, the FBI and Department of Justice convicted approximately 150 men in these sting operations. Most had little to no connection with international terrorist networks. Indeed, most of the questionable behavior appears to have been generated by contact with the law enforcement agencies themselves (Goldman & Apuzzo, 2013).

Many other GWOT programs have shortcomings and even negative feedback loops that undermine their original purpose of helping control terrorism. U.S. military interventions in Iraq and Afghanistan have heightened unfavorable views of the United States in the Middle East, precisely where Washington is trying to increase its influence, as have reports of conditions at Guantánamo Bay. Prisoners have been subjected to aggressive interrogation practices, including physical assaults, insults such as desecration of the Koran, and questionable practices such as sexual touching by female interrogators and smearing of faux menstrual blood on prisoners' bodies to create embarrassment and humiliation. Despite former president Obama's original vow to close Guantánamo, current president Trump has stated that he wants to keep it open. In 2013, a number of prisoners there went on a hunger strike. In some countries, the detention center at Guantánamo Bay has become a symbolic martyr site that encourages still more opposition to the United States.

Suspects have also been captured by foreign intelligence operators abroad with the assistance of U.S. agents and then "rendered" to facilities in other countries for waterboarding and other forms of torture. At Abu Ghraib in Iraq and Bagram in Afghanistan, prisoners have died from abusive treatment while under custody. These incidents have received some attention in the U.S. media but have secured a much higher profile abroad, especially in the countries considered most likely to harbor terrorist networks.

Counterterrorist drone attacks also contain self-defeating features. They are extremely unpopular in Pakistan, and President Obama's ambassador to Pakistan, Cameron Munter, had "wondered whether the pace of the drone war might be undercutting relations with an important ally for the quick fix of killing midlevel terrorists" (Coll, 2013).

In April 2007, the British government announced that it would no longer employ the term *war on terror*. Lady Eliza Manningham-Buller, the former director of MI5, the British intelligence service, stated her preference for the change, calling the 9/11 attacks "a crime, not an act of war" (Norton-Taylor, 2011). In May 2013, President Obama also called for a new, more precise focus on terrorist networks rather than a broad-based "war." The United States must redefine its efforts, Obama argued, "as a series of persistent, targeted efforts to dismantle specific networks of violent extremists that threaten America" (quoted in Baker, 2013).

Like any effort to grapple with a specific social problem, the shift from "war" to a more focused "targeting of networks" will shift resources, produce new agendas for some organizations, end missions for others, and call for a different language to discuss the problem. One of the most challenging issues, especially for public perceptions, is that whatever it is called, we cannot, in all probability, reduce terrorism to zero.

SOCIAL CHANGE: WHAT CAN YOU DO?

16.7 Identify steps toward social change to foster peace.

 Join a Peace Movement

In his famous military-industrial complex speech, President Eisenhower argued, "Only an alert and knowledgeable citizenry can compel the proper meshing of the huge industrial and military machinery of defense with our peaceful methods of goals, so that security and liberty may prosper together." Eisenhower was not an antiwar activist, but many citizens have felt that not only informed public opinion but also popular mobilization is necessary in order for peace to win out over war. Identify a student or community antiwar organization, determine what its strategy is, what kinds of public events it holds, and how it attempts to exert influence. (Examples include United for Peace and Justice, Peace Now, and the Women's International League for Peace and Freedom, although not all may be active in your particular area.) Where has it been successful, and where might it need to follow a different strategy? Do you feel motivated to help?

▶ Members of the Syrian American community of New York and New Jersey demand the ouster of Syrian president Bashar Al-Assad. How effective do you think such rallies are in influencing the politics of another country?

⏩ Help Provide Direct Assistance to War Victims

Many organizations provide assistance to the victims of war, like the International Red Cross and the United Nations Children's Emergency Fund (UNICEF). Others focus on particular aspects of war; examples include Save Our Children for child soldiers and Survivors Corps for those injured by antipersonnel land mines. Still other organizations offer aid along particular themes, such as helping refugees who have fled war-torn areas, women who have become widows, or persons suffering the aftermath of sexual violence. The Duvet Project (http://www.zcommunications.org/in-kabul-widows-and-orphans-move-up-by-kathy-kelly), organized by Afghan Peace Volunteers, pays women a living wage to sew wool-filled duvets and delivers them to families. Many of these organizations could do more with more money. With some friends, do some research and identify a program that carries out effective work on a particular

issue. Is it possible for your group to raise some money for this organization?

⏩ Promote Civilian–Military Dialogue

In general, the U.S. public respects the nation's armed forces. Yet most Americans do not have much contact with the military, and many students are poorly informed about its internal structure. Intersections is a nongovernmental organization that promotes peace, justice, and reconciliation. One of its most important activities is facilitating a series of veteran-civilian dialogues. Some campuses also have local clubs that attempt to create bridges between the military and civilian communities. An example is ALLIES (the Alliance Linking Leaders in Education and the Services) at Tufts University, dedicated to improving civilian-military relations through joint education, research, and training. Can you help create a similar dialogue group on your campus?

Turn to the beginning of the chapter to compare your answers to those of the total population.

1. Do you expect the United States to be in a world war in the next 10 years?

YES: 59.3%

NO: 40.7%

2. What is your confidence level in Congress?

A GREAT DEAL: 5.8%

ONLY SOME: 40.4%

HARDLY ANY: 53.8%

3. What is your interest level in international issues?

VERY INTERESTED: 21.4%

MODERATELY INTERESTED: 49.2%

NOT AT ALL INTERESTED: 29.4%

SOURCE: National Opinion Research Center, University of Chicago.

4. What is your interest level in military policy?

VERY INTERESTED: 35.3%

MODERATELY INTERESTED: 47.8%

NOT AT ALL INTERESTED: 16.9%

5. In the United States, do you think we're spending too much money on military, armaments, and defense, too little money, or about the right amount?

TOO MUCH: 26.8%

TOO LITTLE: 38.1%

ABOUT THE RIGHT AMOUNT: 35.1%

CHAPTER SUMMARY

 16.1 Describe war as a social concept.

Sociologically, war is an organized, collective activity of political units against other political units. It may or may not be carried out by states. War often has costs even greater than the numbers killed or wounded on the battlefield.

16.2 Discuss patterns and trends in the incidence and costs of war.

War between nations seems to be declining. At the same time, new types of globalized intrastate conflict are increasing. These wars carry high costs for civilians, who are often targeted in campaigns of ethnic cleansing. The economic and psychological burdens of war—and even preparing for war—are significant.

16.3 Describe the future of war.

The future of war is paradoxical. Wars are likely to be fought with high-tech weapons such as drones that promise to make conflict more precise and discriminating. These promises are not always met. At the same time, many contemporary wars are extremely bloody and include the targeting of civilians. In the U.S. armed forces, more women may move into direct combat roles.

Apply the functionalist, symbolic interactionist, and conflict perspectives to war.

Structural functionalists might focus on the small social benefits that have emerged from war, despite massive human cost. During WWII, for instance, the country was mobilized behind the war effort. Women flowed into the workforce and inclusion of minorities throughout society increased. Conflict theorists employ the idea of the military-industrial complex, or the relationships among government forces, the Pentagon, and defense contractors that promote the acquisition of weapons systems and a militarized foreign policy. One policy implication of this idea is that the United States is more war-prone than most Americans believe. Symbolic interactionists, who seek to understand how meaning is assigned, identify three factors that must come together for violence to be exercised on a horrific scale: authorization, routinization, and dehumanization. Because studies have found that soldiers fight not for abstractions such as "democracy" and "freedom" but rather out of loyalty to the people in their immediate units, training now focuses on deepening comradeship, mutual respect, and not letting others down.

 Apply the two-society thesis to the relationship between the U.S. military and U.S. society.

The two-society thesis proposes that the all-volunteer force has reduced the proportion of U.S. citizens with military experience and has widened the social gap between those who have served and those who remain in civilian occupations.

 Discuss the Global War on Terror.

While the Global War on Terror has been largely successful in terms of deterrence, it has also raised questions about the extent of government surveillance, and some programs have shortcomings; the use of drones, for instance, has become extremely unpopular. Former president Obama sought to reframe the war on terror as "a series of persistent, targeted efforts to dismantle specific networks of violent extremists that threaten America."

Identify steps toward social change to foster peace.

You might consider engaging in antiwar activities, trying to reduce the impact of war on its victims, or stimulating military-civilian dialogue on your campus.

KEY TERMS

authorization 411

dehumanization 411

democratic theory of peace 399

globalized intrastate wars 401

hypermasculinity 406

military-industrial complex 409

post-traumatic stress disorder (PTSD) 404

routinization 411

terrorism 415

war 398

 SAGE edge™ Want a better grade?

Get the tools you need to sharpen your study skills. Access practice quizzes, eFlashcards, video, and multimedia at **http://edge.sagepub.com/trevino2e**

URBANIZATION

Michael Ian Borer and Tyler S. Schafer

▶▶▶ An aerial view of New York City at dusk. Do you think that most social problems are urban problems?

Investigating Urbanization: Our Stories

LEARNING OBJECTIVES

17.1 Explain social problems that uniquely arise from urbanization and city growth.

17.2 Discuss patterns and trends in urbanization and city growth.

17.3 Apply the functionalist, conflict, and symbolic interactionist perspectives to problems that arise from urbanization and city growth.

17.4 Apply specialized theories to urbanization and city growth.

17.5 Identify steps toward social change regarding urbanization and city growth.

Michael Ian Borer

My relationship with cities began before I was even born. My grandparents fled the Nazis and arrived almost miraculously in New York City. "The City"—as we in the suburbs referred to it—was consistently a part of my life. I visited museums and green spaces. I went to baseball games with my grandfather, who adopted the Dodgers and then the Mets. I ate food from various ethnic enclaves and rode trains above- and belowground. I shuffled through busy streets avoiding eye contact with passersby. I was offered drugs and sex for sale of all varieties. Even as a kid from the 'burbs, I grew up urban. In many ways, today we've all become urban in some way.

I have always grappled with questions about social order. How could so many people from so many different places moving so quickly from one place to the next be so physically close yet so culturally far from one another? How do they get along under such conditions? The existential burden of these questions stayed with me through college, then graduate school, and remains a key motivator for my research as a professional sociologist traveling to cities across the United States and the world. Now, as a sociologist living in and studying Las Vegas, I find my early questions have led to other questions. Sometimes I have to remind myself that often the best answers are questions.

Tyler S. Schafer

Given my roots, you might assume I should have become a rural sociologist. I grew up in a small mid-Missouri town ringed with farmland in every direction. A few times a year my dad and I would hit the road to catch a St. Louis Cardinals game, and I would ask questions about the city and he would tell stories the whole way. The Arch, the massive animated Anheuser-Busch neon sign, and the bustling baseball stadium were such a contrast to the stimuli I encountered in my daily life. What I found more intriguing, however, were the people zipping along the interstate and highways. Where were they coming from? Where were they going? What were the stories of the old men playing saxophones on the street corners? What kinds of lives were the boys and girls my age in the city living?

Moving to Las Vegas for graduate school was quite a shift. It has been fascinating for me to watch Las Vegans establish institutions many older cities take for granted. Las Vegas and the Southwest have also encouraged me to think more about the relationship between cities and the natural environment. What happens here may serve as a bellwether for other cities. No doubt, my explorations as an urban sociologist in Las Vegas have provided me with research questions I will pursue for the rest of my career.

WHAT DO YOU THINK?

Questions About Urbanization From the General Social Survey

1. In the United States, do you think we're spending too much money on highways and bridges, too little money, or about the right amount?

   - ☐ TOO MUCH
   - ☐ TOO LITTLE
   - ☐ ABOUT THE RIGHT AMOUNT

2. In the United States, do you think we're spending too much money on mass transportation, too little money, or about the right amount?

   - ☐ TOO MUCH
   - ☐ TOO LITTLE
   - ☐ ABOUT THE RIGHT AMOUNT

3. In the United States, do you think we're spending too much money on assistance to big cities, too little money, or about the right amount?

   - ☐ TOO MUCH
   - ☐ TOO LITTLE
   - ☐ ABOUT THE RIGHT AMOUNT

4. In the United States, do you think we're spending too much money on solving problems of big cities, too little money, or about the right amount?

   - ☐ TOO MUCH
   - ☐ TOO LITTLE
   - ☐ ABOUT THE RIGHT AMOUNT

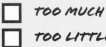 Turn to the end of the chapter to view the results for the total population.

SOURCE: National Opinion Research Center, University of Chicago.

URBANIZATION AND CITY GROWTH IN GLITTER GULCH

The urban sociologist Robert E. Park famously described cities as social laboratories. For sociologists interested in a range of issues from the environmental to the cultural, Las Vegas—with its extreme climate and its extreme adult amusements and copycat architecture—is an ideal subject. This city provides us with a fascinating, and at times unsettling, laboratory for exploring issues of urbanization. At once lauded as a testament to the ability of humans to dominate and control nature through technology, decried as the modern-day Gomorrah, celebrated as one of the nation's leading tourist destinations, and more recently site of the largest mass shooting in recent U.S. history, it is rife with complexity, contradiction, and calculated awe.

Las Vegas grabbed headlines across the globe in the 1990s as it experienced unprecedented growth, its population jumping from about 800,000 in 1980 to approximately 2 million in 2007. At the peak of its boom, in 2006, U.S. Census Bureau demographers estimated the city was adding more than 8,000 new residents per month. When the housing bubble burst and the recession began in 2008, Las Vegas earned the not-so-coveted title of "Foreclosure Capital of the World." This brief hiccup in the city's population surge provides an opportunity for the city to assess the quality of the growth, diagnose growing pains, and try to prepare for another projected boom in population.

The growing pains, it turns out, have been numerous. The flood of new residents coincided with an ongoing drought, now 14 years long, that has drastically strained the city's water supply. The increased population of children put stress on an already low-performing public school system, while health care, public transit, community centers, public parks, bike lanes, and state universities took major hits in funding due to a weak state budget and a governor who put private interests ahead of public ones. Were these developments inevitable?

URBANIZATION, GROWTH, AND SOCIAL PROBLEMS

17.1 Explain social problems that uniquely arise from urbanization and city growth.

While we may take cities for granted as simply the backdrop against which modern life unfolds, they are by no means new. Humans have been building cities for thousands of years. What is relatively new, however, is the centrality of cities to human life.

Urbanization is the process by which cities, suburbs, and metropolitan areas develop and grow over time. Migrations from rural communities to dense urban ones call for new forms of **social order** and social control; because these both solve and create social problems, growth is *not* value-neutral. What happens to working-class and poor underclass residents of neighborhoods that are demolished and replaced with highways, malls, and luxury condominiums? What happens to families who rely on social services that have been eliminated due to changes in tax structures that help some city dwellers but not all? What happens to the air that city dwellers breathe when factories move in or cars are the only means of transportation? In a city with a heterogeneous population, there will be winners and losers. The political, economic, and cultural structures of a **city** often dictate who ends up on which side. Those structures, and the processes that put them in motion, are at the heart of the social problems that result from urbanization and population growth.

In 1800, a mere 3% of the world's population lived in cities. In 2007, that figure was 50%. By 2050, it is estimated that more than 75% of the world's population will be living in metropolitan areas. This boom in urbanization will not be evenly distributed across the globe. As Table 17.1 indicates, over the past few decades the percentage of people living in cities in less developed regions of the world—for example, parts of Africa, Asia, the Caribbean, and Latin America—has approached that of more developed countries in North America and Europe and is growing at a faster pace, a trend expected to continue indefinitely into the future.

At the same time, however, the rural populations in less developed regions will remain much larger (see Figure 17.1). This boom in both metro and rural populations will have a major impact on how cities grow in developing regions, and on their ability to accommodate the needs of city dwellers. If these regions follow the path of urbanization that developed areas have, their increasing populations will require them to solve growth-related problems much more quickly and broadly.

TABLE 17.1 Percentage of Urban and Rural Population in More and Less Developed Regions of the World, 1950–2050

Area	1950	2011	2050
More Developed Regions			
Total population in billions	0.81	1.24	1.31
Percentage urban	54.5	77.7	85.9
Less Developed Regions			
Total population in billions	1.72	5.73	7.99
Percentage urban	17.6	46.5	64.1

SOURCE: Data derived from *World Population Prospects: The 2011 Revision*. Population Division of Economic and Social Affairs of the United Nations Secretariat.

The United States has also witnessed a shift to cities. In 1860, 20% of the U.S. population resided in urban areas. Forty years later, that number had doubled to 40%. Today, more than 250 million people in the United States—more than 75% of the population—live in cities. Figure 17.2 illustrates the drop in U.S. rural populations and accompanying urbanization, which occurred under conditions of slower population growth than in less developed regions. As you can see, even if cities are an old phenomenon, their role in human life has changed dramatically in recent history.

While many social problems, such as poverty, unemployment, and inequality, occur *in* cities, in this chapter we address those that arise *because of* urbanization and city growth. In a rapidly urbanizing world it is critical that we learn from past successes and failures in city building and management in order to better understand the massive urbanization occurring now in places like China, India, and throughout the African continent.

Although cities today look markedly different from those of the late 19th and early 20th centuries, the time at which sociology firmly took root as a discipline, many of the social dynamics in cities at that time have persisted. The early urban sociologists were primarily concerned with the ways city life would differ from the rural traditions many of them held dear. Much like the current shift from national economies to increasingly global ones, the shift from rural, traditional human settlements to increasingly urban, industrial ones

....

Urbanization: The movement of populations from rural to urban areas; the growth and development, and redevelopment, of cities.

Social order: The conformity of individuals to explicit and implicit social rules of behavior.

City: A relatively large, dense, and heterogeneously populated place or settlement.

FIGURE 17.1 Urban and Rural Populations by Development Group, 1950–2050 (estimated)

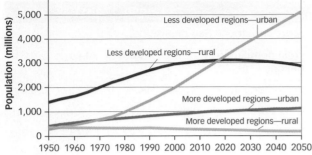

SOURCE: *World Urbanization Prospects: The 2011 Revision. Highlights.* Population Division of Economic and Social Affairs of the United Nations Secretariat. Reprinted with the permission of the United Nations.

FIGURE 17.2 Proportion of Urban and Rural Residents in the United States, 1950–2050 (projected)

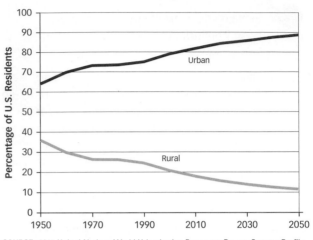

SOURCE: *2011 United Nations World Urbanization Prospects Report,* Country Profile – United States. Population Division of Economic and Social Affairs of the United Nations Secretariat. Reprinted with the permission of the United Nations.

generated a great deal of fear and anxiety in urban analysts. One of their primary concerns was the manner and extent to which social relations and communal forms that dominated traditional societies would be reproduced in urban settings.

German sociologist Ferdinand Tönnies (1855–1936) was interested in identifying the consequences of mass urbanization and the relational forms emerging in the new urban social order. In his famous text *Gemeinschaft und Gesellschaft,* originally published in 1887, Tönnies (1957) outlines two basic organizing principles of social relationships and institutions. He associates these "ideal types" loosely with towns and cities and understands them as stages in the evolution of human society. The first stage is **gemeinschaft**, or "communal association." This is the traditional, rural settlement with a homogeneous population in which everyone knows all the other residents and their biographies. Relationships are intimate and enduring, and interactions are guided by a mutual interest in the common good of the village. Because kinship, community, and religion unite individuals, the shared traditions and culture of the village, in addition to religious beliefs, function as the main instruments of social control.

At the other end of the continuum, or the next stage in human social development, is **gesellschaft**, or "societal association." This is the modern city in which "rational self-interest" or individualism eclipses community interests. Relationships are no longer steeped in sentiment but instead are primarily associational and based on calculating, economic exchanges. Given the heterogeneous populations of emerging cities, residents no longer share language, religion, and traditions, and behavior and interaction are governed by external forces like the evolving criminal justice system. For Tönnies, the process of urbanization was inseparable from the parallel process of **industrialization**. Together these forces erode social bonds and weaken the family unit, which he saw as a vital component of a healthy society.

Although Tönnies understood this evolutionary process as a necessary development in human organization, he was largely pessimistic about the likelihood of communal associations materializing in cities. His view of city life has persisted in some form for more than a century in urban studies. Though communities do exist in cities, sometimes those bonds can be very fragile. When cities undergo large development or redevelopment, neighborhoods and social networks can be torn apart as residents are dispersed throughout or driven from the city.

Georg Simmel (1858–1918) was interested more in social psychological adaptations to the heterogeneity of urban life than he was in social cohesion. His starting point was that people in cities must interact with strangers, living physically close to one another yet emotionally and culturally distant. Simmel (1971, p. 325) argued that the large size and dense concentration of strangers in cities leads urbanites to develop a new kind of defense mechanism against the potential sensory overload, the "swift and continuous shift of external and internal stimuli," of cities. City dwellers develop relational forms that are reserved and

....

Gemeinschaft: Communal association, or a sense of close-knit community relations based on shared traditions and values.

Gesellschaft: Societal association, or a sense of relationships typified by impersonal bureaucracies and contractual arrangements rather than informal ones based on kinship and family ties.

Industrialization: A process that leads to a significant increase in the proportion of a population engaged in specialized factory work and nonagricultural occupations; increases the number of people living near factories and relying on mechanically produced goods and services.

▶ Seoul, South Korea, as seen from a distance in 1905 illustrates what Ferdinand Tönnies called the *gemeinschaft* type of community. Here, rural peasants had personal interactions that gave them a feeling of togetherness, and their behavior was regulated by common social traditions. Seoul today is a *gesellschaft* society characterized by formal organization and impersonal relationships.

"intellectualistic," as opposed to sentimental and tradition based, as in small towns or villages. Simmel noted:

> Thus the metropolitan type—which naturally takes on a thousand individual modifications—creates a protective organ for itself against the profound disruption with which the fluctuations and discontinuities of the external milieu threaten it. Instead of reacting emotionally, the metropolitan type reacts primarily in a rational manner, thus creating a mental predominance through the intensification of consciousness, which in turn is caused by it. (p. 326)

This "protective organ" and intellectualistic mental state of urban dwellers is manifested most clearly in a "blasé attitude," a general indifference to the bombardment of stimuli. Simmel argued that urbanites would experience a sort of paralysis if they addressed all the stimuli they encounter. Nothing would get done.

For those who can adapt to diminished traditional social bonds and indifferent, rational interactional styles, the city provides spaces and opportunities for heightened individuality and creativity. Others, however, do not handle the shift as well and are overcome with feelings of alienation. As Simmel (1971, p. 334) stated, "Under certain circumstances, one never feels as lonely and as deserted as in this metropolitan crush of persons." For Simmel, then, cities do not guarantee but rather provide the *potential for* increases in individuality and creativity.

Not all our current social problems produced by cities were identified in classic sociology, however. Advancements in transportation have made it possible not only for more people to access or own vehicles but also for cities to spread farther into their hinterlands, taking up increasingly large amounts of space. Early urbanists could not imagine the massive surge in energy consumption that would be required to power innumerable lightbulbs and

air conditioners—two things very familiar to us from living in Las Vegas. As Chapter 14 points out, environmental problems produce social effects.

ASK YOURSELF: Why would a shift from rural, small-town settlements to urban, big-city settlements cause fear in both observers of social life and those living through those changes? What problems might emerge from rapid population growth in cities? Are the concerns of early urban observers similar to or different from those of observers, commentators, politicians, reformers, and others today?

PATTERNS AND TRENDS

 17.2 Discuss patterns and trends in urbanization and city growth.

Heterogeneity, Strangers, and Community

If we are to focus on social problems that arise uniquely from urbanization, we must address the effects of increased *heterogeneity* that come with the growth of the city and its rising centrality in the human experience. Unlike the moral homogeneity of village life, where everyone shares similar values, beliefs, rituals, traditions, symbols, and languages, cities are cultural crucibles, and their social control and social institutions have to incorporate the complex constellations of city residents' interests.

Urban heterogeneity also means a population of **biographical strangers**. People in cities regularly spend most of

Biographical strangers: Individuals who do not know each other on a personal basis or who have never met.

their time near, around, or with people they do not know who come from somewhere else, and interactions with strangers become the dominant form of social relations. How is any semblance of social order possible? Much has been written about the *perceived* threat of "strange" black men by both male and female whites (Anderson, 1990). The power differential that allows some to define others as "strange," along with the legal ramifications of such labeling, is a social problem.

Conflict can emerge from the diversity of cultures present in cities (Zukin, 1995). City dwellers—especially newcomers and outsiders—also are **cultural strangers**. That is, they do not know or share each other's values, customs, and views about what passes for acceptable behavior, especially about what is allowed when they are in public and cannot avoid each other.

Historically, cities have served as immigrant "gateways" into the United States. Of the 24 million people who arrived during the classic era of U.S. immigration (1880–1930), 19 million came between 1900 and 1930; of these, 80% were from Europe (Massey, 1995; Waters & Jiménez, 2005). They came from Czechoslovakia, Hungary, Ireland, Italy, Lithuania, Poland, and Russia and faced irresistible pressure to downplay their ethnicity, to "acculturate" or "assimilate." Ethnic identities were feared as threats to national unity.

Quotas in the 1920s, World War I, the Great Depression, and World War II limited the numbers of arrivals, but a "new regime" in immigration began in the 1970s and has persisted through today (Massey, 1995). The postwar boom brought a growing need for labor, and many immigrants from Latin American countries filled these positions. A steady flow of new immigrants is projected, blurring the boundaries between cohorts of arrivals (Massey, 1995; Waters & Jiménez, 2005). This continuous flow from Asia, the Caribbean, and Latin America is unlike the episodic bursts of the classic era and will change the nature of assimilation, and thus cities, in the United States (Massey, 1995).

Immigrant ethnicity is affected not only by differences in the sequencing and duration of the immigrant flow but also by the locations from which immigrants come. Asians and Latinos are now the largest racial and ethnic minority populations in the United States, displacing blacks in the lead (Alba & Nee, 2003). Immigrants who arrive in these flows come from similar cultures and speak similar languages. They experience less pressure to assimilate, since more people speak their native languages and adhere to their native traditions, and there are more native cultural ties onto which newer immigrants may latch (Massey, 1995).

Compared with earlier immigrants, members of this continuous and more homogeneous flow of immigrants

will have vastly different assimilation experiences, including the proliferation of foreign-language or cultural communities (Massey, 1995), or "immigrant enclaves" (Portes & Manning, 1986). Such communities used to be part of a temporary stage in an immigrant group's assimilation process. Now they are taking on more permanent and enduring forms in cities, though they are often the first to be bulldozed if they are not deemed profitable as "tourist spectacles" or "ethnic theme parks" (Krase, 2012). Think about this the next time you enter one of these neighborhoods. Is the ethnic identity of the residents being presented authentically, or is it more like what you might find at Disney's Epcot Center?

Another shift is an emphasis on multiculturalism, which encompasses a trend toward enacting policy that embraces and protects culturally diverse practices and behaviors in public schools, workplaces, and public spaces. Although cultural diversity may be increasingly protected by law, racial and ethnic prejudice and discrimination persist in cities. Since current immigrant groups are able to hold on to cultural elements of their native countries, however, it may be more accurate to describe the United States as a "salad bowl," in which different racial and ethnic groups mix together but hold their original "flavors," than as a "melting pot" in which they combine to forge new patterns of behavior. Diverse groups can exist separately while still participating in political and economic life. Moreover, there is growing consensus that preserving cultural differences is not only possible but also important.

Migration within the country's borders has also produced anxiety in U.S. cities throughout history. In the decades following the emancipation of black slaves, factories began to proliferate in northeastern and midwestern cities as industrialization took hold, creating massive labor demands in cities like Chicago, Cleveland, Detroit, New York, and Pittsburgh. When World War I broke out and men were drafted to fight, many factories recruited black laborers from the South. At around the same time, the boll weevil—an insect native to Central America that feeds on cotton buds and flowers—migrated into the U.S. South and decimated the crops of many growers. This combination of push-and-pull factors led to a massive relocation of black individuals and families from southern towns and cities to growing cities of the Northeast and Midwest. Conflict arose between newly arrived blacks and some white ethnic groups with whom they competed for jobs.

Cultural strangers: Individuals who are from different symbolic worlds or cultures.

On the heels of the Great Depression, President Franklin D. Roosevelt developed a plan for helping people rebound economically by promoting homeownership as a means for attaining and growing wealth through assets. To encourage people to buy homes, he implemented a program to back loans for home buyers through the Federal Housing Administration (FHA). These federally backed loans had fixed interest rates and could be paid off in lower payments over a longer period of time than previously available. Roosevelt was hesitant to approve all loans, however, so he told banks to approve loans for homes only in certain parts of U.S. cities. In a practice later known as redlining, he literally took a red pen and drew lines around neighborhoods he arbitrarily deemed "too risky" for loans. These were neighborhoods that had primarily black residents or were integrated. Over the next 40 years, 90% of the loans approved through the FHA program went to white home buyers. Not only did this contribute to massive accumulations of white wealth while denying such growth to black residents, it started a process of intense **segregation** in U.S. cities that persists to this day (see Figure 17.3).

Although *de jure*, or legal, racial segregation has been outlawed in the United States since the 1960s, *de facto*, or in practice, segregation persists. Social justice organizations routinely conduct experiments to see whether landlords, real estate agents, and banks discriminate against prospective homeowners or renters on the basis of race and consistently find that they do (Massey & Denton, 1993; Massey & Lundy, 2001; Oliver and Shapiro 1995; Roscigno, Karafin, & Tester, 2009; Turner et al., 2002; Yinger, 1995). In large part, these practices stem from a deep anxiety about heterogeneity in cities.

Segregation does not simply result from anxiety about heterogeneity, however; it also worsens anxiety. Researchers who have studied black ghettos argue that residents must adapt to conditions of joblessness, drug use, welfare dependency, teenage childbearing, police unresponsiveness and hostility, and hopelessness. This often results in the evolution of attitudes and behaviors that are at odds with or opposed to dominant, mainstream ones (Anderson, 1999; Massey & Denton, 1993). Severe racial and class isolation have produced language patterns among black ghetto residents so distinct from Standard American English they function as barriers to occupational and educational success (Massey & Denton, 1993).

Racial and ethnic diversity thus contribute to the heterogeneity in cities, but so too can ideological and moral differences, as well as the mere *possibility* of difference. Heterogeneity in cities is about more than the color of someone's skin or the country of his or her birth. Lyn H. Lofland (1998, p. 3) describes the connection between strangers and city life: "The city, because of its size, is the

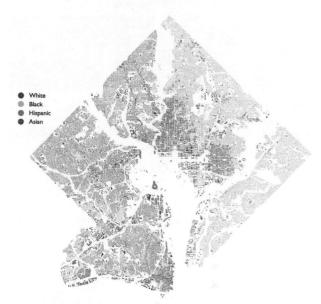

SOURCE: Ngo, Kenton. Washington, DC Racial Figure Ground. January 29, 2015. http://www.kentonngo.com/2015/01/29/figure-ground-of-race/.

locus of a peculiar social situation: the people to be found within its boundaries at any given moment know nothing personally about the vast *majority* of others with whom they share this space."

Interacting with the "Other" on a daily basis is a social problem reserved almost exclusively for cities. Urban scholars and reformers continue to be deeply troubled by the question of how to generate consensus among diverse strangers around a shared meaningful way of life that could bring continuity and predictability to a chaotic and overstimulating environment. Today, as more of the world moves to cities, migration patterns bring increasingly diverse populations together, and we become a more global society, we still grapple with questions about how to form meaningful or at least effective ties with others.

The term *globalization* refers to the often uneven development of social, political, and economic relationships that stretch worldwide. The accelerated flow of capital across international borders is the defining attribute of globalization. In our increasingly global economy, some cities fare better than others, and the most successful

Segregation: The practice of physically separating the occupants of some social statuses from the occupants of others.

So close and yet so far. These commuters on a Kiev, Ukraine, subway car sit only inches from each other but are also strangers to each other. Have you ever felt lonely in a crowded city?

Italian neighborhood with street market, Mulberry Street, New York City, circa 1900. Urban sociologists have long been interested in the ethnic enclaves of cities. In *The Ghetto* (1928), Louis Wirth examined Jewish immigrant colonies in big cities like Chicago. In *The Urban Villagers* (1962), Herbert J. Gans wrote about the Italian American working-class community in Boston's West End. Have you ever visited Chinatown in San Francisco, Little Italy in Boston, or Little Havana in Miami?

are those with financial institutions critical for the functioning of the global economy, advanced telecommunication infrastructure, and a good business climate (low real estate, payroll, revenue, and other taxes; Friedmann, 1986). These become central organizing nodes of the global economy and are known as *global cities* (Sassen, 2001). As central locations within the global economy, global cities attract people from the cities' poorer outskirts as well as from developing countries. Thus multiculturalism is as much a part of globalization as is the flow of

capital (Sassen, 2001), and the social problems of heterogeneity are now a global phenomenon. People will need to adapt swiftly in order to relate to and interact with one another in cities in more and less developed regions.

ASK YOURSELF: Although the specific contexts have changed over time, the same general issue of heterogeneity in cities continues to puzzle urban scholars. How do we create order among such a diversity of biographies, moral orders, and interests? If diversity is generally accepted as a positive attribute, why does it create social problems in cities as populations increase? Who benefits from worldwide urbanization, and who doesn't?

Urbanization and the Natural Environment

One basic component of cities is that they contain immense numbers of people. These people, in turn, consume large amounts of resources like water and energy, so as cities grow, the provision of resources and, by extension, resource scarcity become serious concerns for city planners and governments. The ways in which these concerns are addressed have impacts on the environment. In this section we will describe some of the social problems that arise as cities grow in both physical size and population, including resource scarcity, carbon dioxide emissions and climate change, and suburban sprawl and the destruction of natural ecosystems.

The intersection of urban and environmental sociology has only recently garnered the attention it deserves. Some of these issues cannot be addressed by traditional theories from urban sociology like structural functionalism, conflict theory, and symbolic interactionism, so we address them more comprehensively in the section on specialized theories below.

Water Scarcity

Humans cannot survive without water. Water also irrigates the farmlands where their growing food demands

Urbanization Beyond Our Borders

Heterogeneity in Global Cities

Some migrants who move to global cities are highly educated and highly paid corporate professionals, but many are low-skilled workers who end up in service jobs or the "informal" economies of these booming cities (Friedmann, 1986; Sassen, 2001). The wealth gap between transnational elites and low-skilled workers in global cities is widening rapidly. Accordingly, the populations of global cities are becoming more culturally diverse and income distributions more inequitable, producing more heterogeneity and interest groups with vastly different priorities. People are therefore learning new ways to interact with others in new urbanized areas.

For example, rapid urbanization in China has compelled people to change the ways they think about and treat each other. In the presence of so many new people they do not know personally and whose origins and social classes are unknown, formerly polite interactions with neighbors have been replaced by "indifference." "Neighborhood obligations," Jankowiak (2010, p. 267) observes, "have been discarded in favor of other forms of connectivity," including ties based on school affiliation, "work contacts, association with places of origin, friendship bonds, and close family relationships." Secret societies, guilds, and "common ethnic and/or religious affiliation" have also become more important.

According to Jankowiak, "Taken together, ethnicity, religion, and native place associations serve as essential bases for the formation of social connection or kinship ties" in contemporary China (pp. 260–261). Urban "kinship" ties have become more elaborate. "Individuals who are outside the formal (e.g., bilateral or patrilineal) genealogical systems are frequently transformed from casual friends into close quasi-kin," Jankowiak notes (p. 262). Bilateral grandparent ties also became more important as China's one-child policy took hold and more working parents needed help with child-rearing duties. However, the emerging "bilateral multigenerational family is a fragile institution" (pp. 265–266).

▶ **THINK ABOUT IT**

1. In what ways do people act alike or differently in cities across the world?

2. Have you seen any changes in your city or town similar to those happening in China?

---

are met. Cultural practices like green lawns—which were brought across the Atlantic from England and then into desert climates like the U.S. Southwest—require water to maintain. Water cleans urbanites' bodies, clothes, dishes, and cars; fills their swimming pools and hot tubs; and animates their decorative fountains. Water is a renewable resource, but it is also finite. As cities grow, they put increasing strains on their water supplies. At some point they must confront the possibility of exhausting their supply or locate alternate sources.

Water shortages, real or perceived, produce social relationships characterized by anxiety, resentment, hostility, and competition. Such a situation is unfolding in our home state of Nevada. Southern Nevada is proposing a pipeline to move groundwater (water naturally accumulated over many years in underground aquifers) from central and eastern Nevada to augment its existing water resources. The proposal has sparked a heated debate, with southern Nevadans arguing for the need to diversify the sources from which they draw their water and to ensure the region can support projected population growth. The project is strongly opposed by many other Nevadans, including rural residents, ranchers, Native American tribes, the Mormon Church, conservationists, and outdoor enthusiasts.

The water war between central and southern Nevada is but one side effect of a much larger resource shortage in the U.S. Southwest today, the result of a combination of massive population growth, urbanization, and climate change. The Colorado River quenches the thirst of 40 million people in seven states, and that number is rapidly rising. The river serves 22 Native American tribes, 7 national wildlife refuges, and 11 national parks (Deneen, 2013), in addition to irrigating more than 4 million acres of farmland (Kenworthy, 2013). As it flows, it passes through an area experiencing its worst drought on record. The drought has brought a steady decline in water levels at Lake Mead—the lake from which Las Vegas draws 90% of its water supply and that also serves cities and agriculture in California and Arizona. A white "bathtub ring" of mineral deposits is visible on the rocks around the lake, a reminder of where the lake's water level used to be.

Despite aggressive conservation efforts that have reduced per capita water demands by more than 29% (Southern Nevada Water Authority, 2009), hydrologists predict there is a 50% chance Lake Mead will go dry if

▶ Lake Mead near Boulder City, Nevada. The "bathtub ring" of light minerals shows the high water mark around the lake. As metropolitan areas and their populations grow, they require more and more resources such as land and water. Droughts, the appropriation of land, and the diversion of water frequently cause major social conflicts.

▶ A man wears a face mask with buildings shrouded in toxic haze in Beijing, China. As long ago as the 14th century, the Arab sociologist Ibn Khaldun (1332–1406) noted that air pollution was caused by overcrowding and recommended that urban areas preserve open, empty spaces so that the wind could carry away the fetid air.

drought conditions persist, the climate changes as predicted, and future demand is not further curtailed (Scripps Institution of Oceanography, 2008). Unfortunately for Las Vegas, the amount of water the city is allowed to draw from Lake Mead was set in 1922 when the population of Clark County, which today includes the Las Vegas Metropolitan Area, was a mere 5,000. Las Vegas thus gets 4% of the total water allotted to the Lower Basin states; California gets 58.7% and Arizona 37.3%. No one could have predicted the hyperbolic growth the area experienced at the beginning of the 21st century.

Other Sunbelt cities, like Phoenix and Los Angeles, experienced massive population growth during the same period. As the Colorado River's flow dwindles under drought conditions and climate change, the region faces serious social conflicts over how to deal with shortages. If the water levels get so low that guaranteed allotments can no longer be met, how will reductions be divided up among the states that draw from the river?

In 1968, after much debate, the Central Arizona Project (CAP), an aqueduct more than 300 miles long from Lake Havasu to Phoenix and eventually Tucson, was approved for construction. The project was a massive one, since it had to pump water over and through mountain ranges to deliver it to Arizonans. A major stipulation of the deal, called the California Guarantee, was that California would be guaranteed its full allotment for the year before Arizona got a drop. Congress accepted California's demands, altering the playing field for any future water debates in the event of severe shortage. If drought conditions persist and climate changes as predicted, states will have to cut their use of Colorado River water. But because of the California Guarantee, the cuts will not be shared across the board (Reisner,

1986). Arizona will have to sacrifice before California. This is but one example of the social struggles associated with resource shortages that stem from the processes of urbanization and city growth. These scenarios play out in urbanizing and growing regions across the globe.

The breakneck pace of urbanization in many parts of the world has created unprecedented challenges for providing clean water to booming populations. According to the United Nations (2010), 141 million urban residents worldwide lack access to clean drinking water. Cities in Ghana, Africa, have experienced rapid urbanization and slum development that has not been matched by development of water distribution infrastructure, resulting in lack of access to water in many parts of the cities, disease related to unsanitary sewer systems, and massive water waste due to faulty pipes and illegal connections. Cities in Egypt, Nicaragua, and Peru also face water shortages due to increased demands from urbanization, worsened by weak infrastructure (United Nations, 2010). Among city dwellers globally, from 2000 to 2008 there was a 20% decrease in access to clean tap water (United Nations Human Settlements Programme, 2011).

Greenhouse Gas Emissions

In 2011, the United Nations Human Settlement Programme reported that while cities occupy only 2% of land globally, they are responsible for emitting up to 70% of all harmful greenhouse gases (GHG). This relationship is complicated, however. Most of the urbanization occurring across the globe is now taking place in low- to middle-income nations, and this trend is predicted to continue well into the future. In these regions many households have incomes so low they hardly contribute to GHG levels (Satterthwaite,

2009). However, in more developed countries with some of the slowest urban population growth, GHG emission levels are much higher per person and have been growing at a much faster pace (Satterthwaite, 2009). The reason is that consumption patterns are more influential on greenhouse gas emissions than raw numbers of people.

Increasingly, researchers are suggesting that cities are not actually as bad as may have been thought in terms of GHG emissions. For instance, per capita GHG emission rates are often *lower* in cities than the average rates for the countries in which they are located (Dodman, 2009). Some also argue that the share of global GHG emissions commonly attributed to cities has been grossly overstated (Satterthwaite, 2009). This view tries to separate per capita GHG emissions from those produced in cities' outskirts in activities like agriculture, deforestation, and energy production. However, these activities occur only to meet the demands of residents in nearby cities. Recall that in the United States, more than 75% of the population resides in cities. Nonurban activities are overwhelmingly serving urban populations and should not be considered rural.

Urbanization in the Shadow of Global Climate Change

Cities are particularly vulnerable to the effects of climate change. Cities can also be key sites for climate change adaptation and mitigation. The density of many cities presents opportunities for increasing the efficiency of energy consumption and transportation. Urban density also heightens the risks associated with increasingly severe storms and "natural" disasters. Moreover, many of the world's largest cities are coastal, leaving their populations and infrastructure vulnerable to sea level rise. Cities in many developed countries have begun to implement climate change adaptation and mitigation strategies. Climate change poses an additional set of puzzles for growing cities in developing countries and rapidly urbanizing ones like China and India.

As countries compete to integrate into the global economy, they often adopt growth mantras that prioritize economic growth through industry. Manufacturing tends to be located in or near cities, which attracts more rural residents to cities for work. Other rural residents migrate to the city for employment opportunities created by the expanding population. As the population grows, more space is needed for workers to live and proponents of the growth mantra demand that more space be dedicated to industry. Historically, as countries industrialize, they also urbanize. Indeed, urbanization and industrialization propelled the United States to its powerful position in the global economy.

There is growing consensus that climate mitigation requires coordinated actions at the global level. Proposals about how to distribute responsibility for creating the problem, coupled with the challenge of identifying countries' willingness to effect change, have hindered past efforts at constructing a global climate action plan (Ehrhardt-Martinez et al., 2015). The Kyoto Protocol, adopted in 1997, was one of the first global agreements, and laid out emission reduction targets for developed countries. The United States never signed on to the agreement, which left many around the world concerned and skeptical about collective mitigation efficacy (Ehrhardt-Martinez et al., 2015).

The Kyoto Protocol was largely toothless. In the years between its ratification and implementation, free trade deals were struck that ensured the growth of global production systems guaranteed to increase emissions. Most of these involved waste-producing extraction processes to be exported to poor countries, creating the illusion that developed countries were reducing their emissions (Roberts & Parks, 2006). Often these trade relationships have the effect of inhibiting economic and industrial development and urbanization in poor countries.

Global frustration with the United States' abstention from the Kyoto Protocol highlights a central concern for many countries regarding global climate agreements. Specifically, developing countries and recently developed ones want agreements that factor in which countries have historically contributed most to the problem, and hold them responsible for paying off their "**climate debt**" to all the others who have not contributed to the problem (many of which are most vulnerable to the effects of climate change; Roberts & Parks, 2006).

The United States' refusal to ratify emissions reduction goals is rooted in fears of losing yet more jobs to China and India, a topic that continues to fuel anti-environmental sentiment and climate change denial in the United States. Rapidly urbanizing and industrializing countries like China and India have resisted compliance with emission reduction goals out of fear that regulations could destroy their global market competitiveness (Roberts, 2011).

There is a need to develop climate change agreements that make it possible for newly urbanizing and industrializing countries—and where responsibility for climate change is thus far negligible—to develop their economies and qualities of life (Klein, 2014). There have been proposals to establish global average per capita emission targets that would allow developing and urbanizing countries to grow (Ehrhardt-Martinez et al., 2015).

....

Climate debt: The idea that wealthy nations that have contributed most to the problem of climate change—through their overconsumption of resources, damage to the environment, and consumption of atmospheric space—are responsible for contributing most to efforts to mitigate it. Practically, countries with the highest climate debt would be expected to help the countries most harmed adapt to their changing ecological realities, and agree to reduce future GHG emissions to allow developing countries to be able to produce more of the global share as they grow.

The Paris agreements are the newest set of global emission reductions, adopted in 2015 by a consensus of representatives from 195 countries. By October 2016, countries with histories of high emissions like China and the United States had ratified the agreements. Some had begun heralding the agreements as the death of fossil fuels and a turning point in climate change mitigation. Others worry that the real successes of the agreements, like significant progress in global diplomacy, obscure their significant shortcomings. The global goals are laudable; however, there is no plan for how to meet them (Klein, 2016). Furthermore, U.S. president Donald Trump, who tweeted in 2012 that he believed "global warming was created by and for the Chinese in order to make U.S. manufacturing non-competitive," announced in 2017 he would be pulling the United States out of the Paris agreements. Both his comments about climate change being a hoax and his rationale for exiting the agreements are rooted in his belief that global policy that seeks to acknowledge and address historic climate change constitutes a "bad deal" for the United States and is thus economically "unfair."

The goals of the agreements are to keep global temperature rise under 2 degrees Celsius, but the plans that have been ratified are projected to result in an increase of up to 4 degrees, which would guarantee some of the worst-case scenarios predicted by climate scientists. Recent research on sea level rise (Hansen et al., 2016) paints a grim picture of the possibilities of even a 2 degree increase. Climate scientist and activist James Hansen has stated (Vaidyanathan, 2016):

> Consequences [of climate change] include sea level rise of several meters, which we estimate would occur this century or at latest next century, if fossil fuel emissions continue at a high level. That would mean loss of all coastal cities, most of the world's large cities and all their history.

President Trump has maintained that he is open to renegotiating global climate agreements that are "fairer" to the United States, but countries like France, Germany, and Italy have suggested the agreements cannot be renegotiated. Even if they could, terms to an agreement President Trump would find fair would no doubt do little in the way of keeping global temperature rise below 2 degrees.

Approximately 400 U.S. mayors have agreed their cities would do their part to uphold the commitments to which President Obama agreed. Some states, universities, and other organizations have also pledged their continued dedication to meeting the goals established in Paris. These localized initiatives are significant, but at the national level, Scott Pruitt, head of the Environmental Protection Agency, recently announced the Trump administration would be initiating the repeal of President Obama's Clean Power Plan, which pushed states away from coal and toward lower carbon-emitting sources of energy. President Trump's rejecting a national commitment to the agreements greatly undermines their initial potential to address global climate change. Without more aggressive efforts to enforce emission reductions it seems unlikely that cities—newly emerging or long-standing—will function as mitigators of climate change. Cities' acute vulnerability to the effects of climate change means urban planners will neglect developing adaptation plans at their peril.

ASK YOURSELF: How do urbanization and population growth create environmental problems? Who is responsible for the environmental problems produced by cities: City officials? Businesses located in cities? The people who live, work, and play in cities? Are cities and the problems connected to them inevitable, so that the only solution is to get rid of cities? If so, then where will the millions of displaced people live?

THEORETICAL PERSPECTIVES IN URBAN SOCIOLOGY

17.3 Apply the functionalist, conflict, and symbolic interactionist perspectives to problems that arise from urbanization and city growth.

Structural Functionalism

Herbert Spencer coined the phrase "survival of the fittest" in an attempt to incorporate Charles Darwin's ideas about natural selection into his theory of functionalism. Spencer put forth an "evolutionary" theory of societal change that suggested development is automatically and intrinsically positive. That is, social life is automatically better in the future than it was in the past due to natural processes of growth and adaptation.

Building on Spencer's basic ideas, the urban ecologists of the Chicago School of Sociology wanted to understand the natural forces behind the city's growth and diverse population. They used the term *natural* to draw an analogy between people and plants. They believed the city was a "superorganism" where competition for space was won by the "fittest." Though they dismissed other factors, like wealth and feelings, they felt understanding the natural laws of urbanization would allow them to better account for and fix persistent social problems associated with dense and heterogeneous populations.

Beginning with Roderick D. McKenzie and then Ernest W. Burgess and Amos H. Hawley, urban ecologists promoted the view that life in a human **community** functions like life in other biological communities. Like other organisms, human beings must adapt to their surroundings and fend off potential dangers. The most successful communities and people will take over the "best" areas of the city and have a higher survival rate. Chicago ecologists also noted the ways urban dwellers cooperate for the sake of mutual survival and defense against successive "invasions" of newcomers and migrants. The researchers' focus on natural competition and cooperation suggested that the city's spatial structure is a result of natural processes beyond the reach of human participation and engineering.

One of the most enduring legacies of the Chicago School ecologists is the model they constructed to depict the biological processes that created the city of Chicago and the divisions within it. Ernest W. Burgess's (1925) *concentric-zone model* showed how patterns of land use reflected successive phases of invasion and occupation. The outcome was a series of concentric circles or zones, with the **central business district (CBD)** placed firmly in the center (see Figure 17.4). This was the hub of the city's economic activity and had the highest land values. Moving outward, the CBD was surrounded by a "zone of transition" perpetually under threat of invasion by businesses and industries with growing commercial interests. Those who could leave this vulnerable area did, but those who could not afford to move were forced to stay, forming a marginal population of immigrants, criminals, and the mentally ill in an area known for poverty and vice. This is where the Jewish ghetto, Little Sicily, Chinatown, and parts of the Black Belt were located.

The next zone was for the assimilated and upwardly mobile, such as the children of immigrants. Burgess called this the "zone of working-men's homes." The second-generation immigrants and factory laborers who lived there weren't poor, but neither were they wealthy enough to own land or their own apartments. The "residential zone," instead, was populated by the middle class, mostly white-collar employees and small-business owners and managers. They lived in newer, or at least renovated, apartments and single-family homes. Crime rates were significantly lower in this zone than in the working class's natural area, which in turn was less crime-ridden than the "zone of transition" just outside the CBD. The zone farthest away was the suburbs, the "commuters' zone," filled with residents who depended on the city for their jobs but were successful enough to live in the safer periphery of the city.

With artistic license to deal with Lake Michigan (which cut the zones in half down a north–south line), Burgess's model was a pretty accurate description of the residential segregation of Chicago. But it was intended to do more than describe Chicago; the goal was to show the

FIGURE 17.4 Concentric-Zone Model of the City

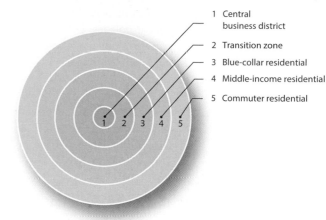

1 Central business district
2 Transition zone
3 Blue-collar residential
4 Middle-income residential
5 Commuter residential

social patterns one could expect to find in all industrial cities. Because Burgess painted in broad strokes, his model was open to criticisms that led others—including his own colleagues—to offer modified layouts of the city.

Homer Hoyt's (1939) *sector model* is based on the idea that cities' growth patterns depend on the cities' main lines of transportation. Transport corridors produce patterns of intense competition for land and real estate around them. Instead of concentric zones, in Hoyt's model "the city was pictured more like a starfish or a spoked wheel" (Karp, Stone, & Yoels, 1991, p. 55). Chauncy Harris and Edward Ullman disagreed with both Burgess and Hoyt. Their *multiple-nuclei model* deemphasizes the CBD in favor of a decentralized vision of the city, with several nuclei in areas with specific concentrations of specialized activities and facilities like manufacturing, shopping, and education.

One of the major problems with the Chicago School's ethnographic and ecological studies is their lack of attention to culture as a productive force. The researchers often assumed culture to be only reactionary, while larger natural forces in the competition for land shaped human relations. But if human agency isn't part of a model of urban life, then how can social reform be possible? The conflict-oriented urban political economists try to answer this question by focusing on the political and economic interests of powerful players, as we see next.

Community: A usually positive (though not necessarily so) form of sustained social cohesion, interaction, and organization that exists between the larger society and individuals who have similar characteristics or attributes (e.g., ethnicity, geography, beliefs).

Central business district (CBD): The commercial, office, transportation, and cultural center of a city; land values in the CBD are usually among the highest in the city.

Conflict Theory

In the late 1960s and early 1970s, social and political unrest in urban areas grew, in part, from increased racial polarization and restrictive government policies. Urban scholars were prompted to find new ways to understand these emerging realities of city life (Kleniewski, 1997, p. 35; Walton, 1993, p. 302). They drew upon Max Weber's writings and the rediscovered ideas of Karl Marx (and to a lesser extent Friedrich Engels) to explain what the Chicago School's theories could not. Developed under a few different names, this newly emerging perspective was tied together by a few basic assumptions that directly challenged the Chicago School's approach (Kleniewski, 1997, p. 37).

Of particular importance is the idea that a city's form and growth are not the result of "natural processes" but come from decisions made by people and organizations that control wealth and other key resources. Powerful decision makers, rather than some abstract evolutionary principles, are thus responsible for the conditions of cities. Due to its emphasis on powerful actors, this perspective—called the *urban political economy* approach—quickly became, and perhaps still remains, the dominant theory of urban sociology for addressing the social problems of urbanization that promote income inequality, crime, and racism.

Wealthy and politically active people are more powerful than the Chicago School allowed, and the power some people yield can be used to help some while hurting others. Weber's ideas about the ways key actors influence the distribution of social goods led sociologists to explore how individuals and organizations control urban assets and land markets. Such actors include real estate investors and agents, urban planners, housing managers, police, policy makers, mortgage lenders, and financiers. Theorists argue that these actors can determine which social groups and populations gain access to particular property markets.

In one of the first books to adopt this new perspective and address these issues, *Whose City? And Other Essays on Sociology and Planning*, R. E. Pahl (1970, p. 221) states:

> A truly urban sociology should be concerned with the social and spatial constraints on access to scarce urban resources and facilities as dependent variables and managers or controllers of the urban system, which I take as the independent variable.

Human agency is intricately connected to conflicts over the distribution of resources that, in turn, influence urban forms and social arrangements. Solidarity and cooperation are impossible because the city forces people to view others only as cogs within the urban "growth machine" (Gottdiener & Feagin, 1988; Logan & Molotch, 1987), in which cities depend on capitalism for growth and sustenance.

The "new" urban sociology, then, sought to explain cities as part of a larger story about class conflict, capital accumulation, and ideological control. Urban theorists directly inspired by Marxian theories—like Manuel Castells, David Harvey, and Henri Lefebvre—transformed general theories about the "evil and avaricious capitalist system" (Harvey, 1973, p. 133) into explanations about the struggle for urban space.

Harvey (1973) argues that the continual **redevelopment** of certain areas of cities—not the areas with the most need—is driven by profit-motivated capitalists without interference from, and sometimes with the help of, local and federal governments. According to Harvey, this tends to benefit affluent whites and hurts poor African Americans and other minorities who have trouble obtaining loans to buy houses. From this vantage point, Harvey stresses the role of the **built environment** as commodity and as a source of profit and loss:

> Under capitalism there is a perpetual struggle in which capital builds a physical landscape appropriate to its own condition at a particular moment in time, only to have to destroy it, usually in the course of a crisis, at a subsequent point in time. The temporal and geographical ebb and flow of investment in the built environment can be understood only in the terms of such a process. The effects of the internal contradictions of capitalism, when projected into the specific context of fixed and immobile investment in the built environment, are thus writ large in the historical geography of the landscape that results. (p. 124)

Investment and disinvestment by the power elite divide upper-class and working-class residential areas to avoid confrontation between them. This residential segregation, in turn, creates an unevenly developed environment with high and low land values that benefit the capitalist class at the expense of the underclass.

From the urban political economy perspective, the city is a profit-making machine fed by the reconstruction and redevelopment of the built environment wherever revenue can be generated. Manuel Castells (1977) connects Marxist theories to the city by interpreting the dual roles of the city as a unit of production (similar to Harvey's ideas) and a locus of social reproduction. Uneven and unequal social relations are reproduced by individuals' consumption of

---

Redevelopment: The rebuilding of parts of a city; sometimes large areas are completely demolished before being rebuilt, sometimes older buildings are preserved or updated.

Built environment: The human-constructed physical and material objects that make up the city, like buildings, streets, and sidewalks.

goods like food and clothing and their collective consumption of services like housing and other social services (health care, education, recreation). Castells argues that the state is a tool for the wealthy. Therefore, cities are organized so the state provides the minimal social services and facilities needed to reproduce and maintain a flexible, somewhat educated, and mostly healthy workforce at the lowest cost possible. This includes providing government-subsidized housing, often cheaply and poorly built.

Castells (2000, p. 293) stresses that the spatial form of the city reproduces the contradictions of capitalism Marx outlined long ago for cities that exhibit great disparities in wealth: "Spatial transformation must be understood in the broader context of social transformation: space does not reflect society, it expresses it, it is a fundamental dimension of society." He criticizes the Chicago School as well as other scholars who have unrealistically approached the city as a distinct ecology independent of the larger capitalist system.

Castells's structural take on cities is intended to correct the idea that urban spaces are shaped by the knowledge and actions of those who live, work, and play in them. Along with other Marxist-oriented theorists, however, Castells put himself at the other extreme, where the spatial forms of the city are determined by forces outside the control of everyday people. A new generation of urban scholars he influenced set out to study the processes and effects of the most dominant institutions that shape cities: economics and politics. Their operating assumption is that cities are products of the forces of capitalism and are therefore influenced by and a part of the global political economy. This claim has led to much research on world-systems theory (Smith & Timberlake, 1995; Wallerstein, 1979), globalization (Short, 2004), and global cities (Sassen, 2001, 2002, 2010).

Symbolic Interactionism

Influenced by symbolic interactionist writings on everyday life in cities (Karp et al., 1991; Lofland, 1998) and by cultural sociology's imperative to analyze "meaning making," the urban culturalist perspective focuses on the practices and processes of culture and community building in cities. Urban culturalists explicitly investigate the symbolic relationships between people and places and the ways that places are given meaning and value. They view the development and redevelopment of the urban built environment as a means for understanding cultural values, ideas, and practices (Borer, 2008; Bridger, 1996; Lofland, 1998; Monti, 1990). Their overarching goal is to understand the ways in which people contribute, in varying degrees and with varying reasons, to the social life of the city. They view the city, therefore, as a collective accomplishment regardless of the social problems that exist within it.

The urban culturalist perspective is place based, but it is not city based. That is, it does not view one city as the

► The low-income neighborhood known as Boca la Caja in Panama City, Panama, is adjacent to an area of expensive real estate that includes the Trump World Tower (left). Boca la Caja faces many social problems as a result of Panama City's rapid growth and urbanization: crime, poor waste management, social and economic isolation, poor infrastructure, and organizational disorder.

absolute example of 21st-century **urbanism** in the way that Los Angeles, as well as Miami (Nijman, 2000) and New York (Halle & Beveridge, 2011), have been presented by contemporary scholars. City-based theories are problematic because they don't allow comparisons between cities (or between cities, suburbs, and towns). Also, as Robert A. Beauregard (2011, p. 199) argues, they favor particular cities and schools where scholars reside, tend to be exclusionary, and reduce the utility of urban studies:

> In addition, by fueling radical uniqueness, a proliferation of city-based theories diminishes what cities have in common and often denies that an "ordinary" city can add value to urban theory. Instead the claim is that some cities have theoretical value and other cities do not. The latter receive theory; the former create it. Thus, what is needed is not an acceptance of city-based urban theories but a critical spirit that fosters skepticism.

Most urban sociologists begin with a social problem or phenomenon, then seek out places in the city or cities they're investigating where it happens. The urban culturalist perspective prompts scholars to begin with a place and ask an open and inductive question: What happens or happened here? This method provides opportunities for researchers to build new ideas and theories from the ground up, instead of making and then testing assumptions. This does not mean researchers shouldn't be aware of past theories or research on the areas and populations they are studying.

Even while allowing "local knowledge" to play a central role, urban culturalists still bring certain theories and

Urbanism: The ways of life or cultures of people in cities; the myths, symbols, and rituals of urbanites.

"sensitizing concepts" with them into the field. They have contributed to and continue to cultivate six key areas of inquiry: (1) images and representations of the city; (2) urban community and civic culture; (3) place-based myths, narratives, and collective memories; (4) sentiment and meaning of and for places; (5) urban identities and lifestyles; and (6) interaction places and practices. These can form a comparative framework for studying the similarities and distinctions between types of places and the people who use and inhabit them.

Urban culturalists have been particularly adept at investigating issues that arise from cities' heterogeneous populations. Norton E. Long (1958), a political scientist interested in the ways cultural practices influence the social lives of cities, characterized the city as an "ecology of games." He contended that while each social grouping or "game" has different rules and roles for its "players," no game within the city is so isolated that it does not come into contact with another or, for that matter, does not need to come into contact with another. In contrast with Robert E. Park's understanding of the city as a mosaic whose social worlds do not interpenetrate, Long argued that often proximity is enough to foster at least weak civic bonds between presumably incompatible interest groups. As he described it: "Sharing a common territorial field and collaborating for different and particular ends in the achievement of overall social functions, the players in one game make use of the players in another and are, in turn, made use of by them" (p. 255). Interdependence is necessary between specialized occupations and lifestyles.

While the games have their own places to be played, they also occur in places people commonly share, often referred to as **third places**. Ray Oldenburg (1999, p. 16) defines third places as "public places that host the regular, voluntary, informal, and happily anticipated gatherings of individuals beyond the realms of home and work." Coffee shops, pubs, and other small businesses (Borer & Monti, 2006; Macgregor, 2010; Milligan, 1998; Oldenburg, 1999) provide settings for the "games" played by businessmen and -women (the owners, managers, and employees); patrons (playing leisure "games"); and other groups who use the sites for gatherings and for displaying information for various causes, retail opportunities, and local events.

Because individuals utilize many different places within their city, they learn and are capable of playing by the rules for multiple "games." The rules are usually a hodgepodge of liberal and conservative values. As Monti's (1999) historical analysis of civic culture in U.S. cities shows, liberal and conservative thinkers see the world very differently, in theory. But people reconcile these different and seemingly irreconcilable points of view in their everyday routines. The civic culture of U.S. cities, and of cities around the world, is a hybrid culture made up of individuals and groups that think and act in a variety of liberal and conservative ways.

Even though communities are collective accomplishments, not everyone plays an equal role in making the decisions or follows the rules exactly the same way all the time. Urban dwellers can change their ways of thinking and acting, but only within tolerable limits. This hybrid mixing is at the heart of what Monti calls the "paradoxical community." Because the cultural influence of cities stretches beyond their physical borders, the same kinds of "paradoxical community" practices can be found in suburbs and small towns (see Macgregor, 2010).

Paradoxical or not, communities in cities are packed with meaning and emotional attachments. In 1945, Walter Firey published a study on the sentimental value attached to certain areas in Boston and the way land had been used throughout the city. His "Sentiment and Symbolism as Ecological Variables" showed that large areas of land were not only reserved for noneconomic uses but also left undeveloped because they had been collectively endowed with symbolic meaning. These areas could not be fitted into a model based on concentric circles, zones, or nuclei. Boston's "sacred sites"—the parks, cemeteries, and 48-acre area in the center of the city that formed the original "commons"—had never been developed (p. 140). Furthermore, Beacon Hill, an upper-class residential neighborhood near the center of the city, was not taken over by the CBD and maintains its privileged position inside the city.

Beacon Hill survives not merely because the people who live there share a common ecological space with rational economic functions. Rather, its existence derives from cultural values, the sentiment residents attach to their territory. According to Firey (1945, p. 144), people could have lived in less expensive districts with an "equally accessible location and even superior housing conditions. There is thus a noneconomic aspect to land use on Beacon Hill, one which is in some respects actually diseconomic in its consequences." "Sentiment" and "symbolism," which mean everything from social prestige to ethnic or racial prejudice, are ecological factors that influence spatial distribution and patterns of development and redevelopment. Firey's study has had lasting impact by showing how cultural factors affect political agendas related to land-use decisions (Borer, 2008, 2010; Maines & Bridger, 1992).

....

ASK YOURSELF: Which of the schools of thought discussed here align with your way of thinking about cities? Which are best suited for addressing the social problems that arise from urbanization and population growth? Theorists have described the city as an organism, a growth machine, an ecology of games. What term or metaphor would you use to describe the city?

....

....

Third places: Locations that serve social needs beyond work and home life (e.g., local coffee shops).

Experiencing Urbanization

Perceptions of Disorder

After we recognize that heterogeneity is a social problem caused by urbanization and population growth, we then also need to recognize that the individuals in cities, and elsewhere, are themselves heterogeneous. That is, all people's identities are made up of different attributes, such as gender, race, social class, occupation, religion, age, and marital status. It is imperative that we be aware, however, that people experience urban social problems differently depending on the configurations of attributes that make up their identities. Because urbanization is a worldwide phenomenon, all people are affected by it, though not *equally* affected.

Concerned about the role of heterogeneity on perceptions of social order and disorder in urban neighborhoods, Robert J. Sampson and Stephen W. Raudenbush (2004)

studied the cues and clues that trigger such perceptions. Do people react only to observable signs like broken windows or graffiti on walls, or do they "see" disorder based on factors such as race, ethnicity, and social class? Sampson and Raudenbush found that the latter—the racial, ethnic, and class-based composition of the neighborhood—was much more influential on perceptions of disorder among blacks, whites, and Latinos than supposedly objective measures. The sight of poor black males was the key trigger for *all* populations.

Sampson and Raudenbush argue that disorder is not just about race, but about the socially constructed and historically biased associations among race, gender, and disorder across populations. Thus policies to fix social problems through urban redevelopment that rely solely on "beautifying" neighborhoods or

increasing police presence are insufficient. A better, yet much more difficult, approach is to undo the stigma attached to poor minorities that is "due to social psychological processes of implicit bias and statistical discrimination as played out in the current (and historically durable) racialized context of cities in the United States" (p. 337). Changing the way people think has proven to be much harder, though it can be more effective, than removing graffiti or abandoned cars.

▶ **THINK ABOUT IT**

1. How does an intersectional approach help us make sense of the ways people understand social problems in their neighborhoods?

2. What are the most important social attributes to consider when you are attempting to understand others' respective identities, and your own?

SPECIALIZED THEORIES IN URBAN SOCIOLOGY

 Apply specialized theories to urbanization and city growth.

Historically, sociology has been hesitant to embrace the natural environment as a topic of study, partly because early researchers wanted to differentiate their discipline from the other social sciences. Specialized modern theories redress that oversight.

Urban Sustainability

The concept of sustainability has taken a central place in most recent discussions of development, industry, and urban planning. It has its roots in a 1987 report by the United Nations World Commission on Environment and Development titled *Our Common Future*. This document, commonly known as the Brundtland Report (for Gro Harlem Brundtland, who chaired the commission), defined sustainable development as "development that meets the needs of the present without compromising the ability of future generations to meet their own needs." One major goal of the commission was to position environmental concerns as a central factor in global development planning.

In 1992, the United Nations convened the Earth Summit, which produced Agenda 21, an action plan for implementing sustainable development at the local, national, and international levels. While the Brundtland Report emphasized the need to protect the natural environment for the sake of ecological systems and resources critical for economic and social life, Agenda 21 emphasized the importance of social issues in the sustainability puzzle (Colantonio, 2007). This triad of environmental protection, economic growth, and social justice—also known as the "triple bottom line" (Elkington, 1994,

Federal-style row houses line Beacon Street in Boston's Beacon Hill neighborhood. Through the years, Beacon Hill has been home to many wealthy and influential people, such as Oliver Wendell Holmes Sr., who, in 1860, coined the term *Boston Brahmins* to refer to the city's upper-class citizens.

environmental stewardship and avoid practices and policies that could jeopardize the health of natural resources like water, soil, and air. What about social sustainability, though?

The social dimension is focused on creating and maintaining healthy, sustainable communities. A diversity of issues gets folded into the notion of healthy communities, including trust, cohesion, community identification, cultural and community diversity, pride, sense of place, security, and high quality of life, which also tend to translate into feelings of personal and collective responsibility for future generations (Colantonio, 2007; Colantonio & Dixon, 2011). An interest in social sustainability and in healthy communities centers on urban dwellers' basic needs and social well-being, social capital, equity, and social and cultural dynamism (Colantonio, 2007). These are critical elements for fulfilling individuals' needs for belonging and attachment in cities characterized by immense heterogeneity and mutual strangeness.

1997), or the "three pillars" model of sustainability—has also been adopted by many cities as the guiding principle for achieving urban sustainability (see Figure 17.5).

The increased concern for urban sustainability represents an effort to address the social and environmental problems produced by urban growth guided simply by a desire to grow the economy. This theoretical foundation for urban growth not only addresses environmental problems in a way traditional sociological theories have not but also bridges environmental problems and social problems, understanding that they are intricately related.

Sustainability asks that we consider the long-term viability of our current actions. How long before we run up against economic, environmental, and/or social limits? How can and should we manage healthy nature–society relationships now and in the future? How can we foster and maintain healthy social and economic well-being, cultural diversity, and equity across diverse populations? This is a perspective in which we consider how the decisions we make within each of these three domains affect the others.

Economic and environmental sustainability are relatively straightforward notions if we refer back to the idea of meeting "the needs of the present without compromising the ability of future generations to meet their own needs." Economic sustainability, then, suggests that we not engage in risky financial practices that could destabilize the economy and that we ensure the existence of decent-paying jobs for future generations. Common goals are low unemployment rates, diversified economies, and labor force stability. Similarly, environmental sustainability asks that we practice

"Just" Sustainability

Critics have argued, however, that the three major dimensions of the triple bottom line are prioritized unequally (Agyeman, Bullard, & Evans, 2002; Campbell, 1996; Colantonio & Dixon, 2011; Drakakis-Smith, 1995; Littig & Grießler, 2005) because the priorities of the interest groups behind the various pillars diverge (Campbell, 1996). Left

FIGURE 17.5 The Three Components of Urban Sustainability

Researching Urbanization

The Effects of Sustained Population Growth on Community Relations: The Las Vegas Metropolitan Area Social Survey

The population growth rates in Las Vegas were among the highest in the United States at the end of the 20th century. The Las Vegas metropolitan area grew about 83% between 1990 and 2000 and continued at this rapid pace until about 2010. In 2009, a team of sociologists administered surveys and conducted focus group interviews in neighborhoods throughout the Las Vegas Valley to assess residents' knowledge and attitudes about economic, social, and environmental issues in the city (Futrell et al., 2010). The questions probed residents' knowledge about the environment and trust in environmental information as well as their perceptions about their responsibility for environmental issues and their willingness to pay to address these issues. The researchers also asked questions about migration and residential mobility, neighborhood and social bonds, and quality of life. Finally, they probed residents' economic problems, job satisfaction, and employment history.

Of the study's respondents, only 8% were born in Las Vegas, while 75% were born in other U.S. states and 16% in other countries. On average, they had lived in their homes for 12.1 years; 64% had moved from other Las Vegas Valley homes, while 34% came from outside the state. The high rate of recent arrivals was accompanied by a weak sense of belonging to both the city and the neighborhood. Those born in Las Vegas or other parts of Nevada were much more likely to feel attached to the city than those from other states or countries, and the longer they had lived in their homes the more likely they were to report attachment. More respondents felt a sense of belonging to Nevada and Las Vegas than felt a sense of belonging to their neighborhoods.

These patterns suggest potentially low levels of social capital among those who were part of the city's population boom. The data support this. Among respondents 41% reported visiting their neighbors "almost never" and 63% reported "almost never doing or receiving favors for neighbors." Focus group respondents overwhelmingly reported weak bonds among neighbors and feeling as though most people in their neighborhoods were strangers. At the same time, most reported yearning for more community bonds.

These findings imply that unmanaged rapid urbanization or population growth poses problems for creating community. The slow development of social capital and bonds to city and neighborhood suggests that as cities grow, they must take quality-of-life issues seriously and facilitate the creation and maintenance of institutions and amenities that can support community development.

▶ The Las Vegas metropolitan area experienced rapid population growth between 1990 and 2000.

▶ **THINK ABOUT IT:** What can residents of cities in flux do to create a strong sense of belonging in their neighborhoods?

---

unmediated, these priorities must vie for attention among planners, politicians, activists, and the public. For example, the ideal of sustainability emerged partly in response to the broad conflict of "human versus nature." That is, urban planning has tended to promote city building at the cost of the natural environment (Campbell, 1996), which ultimately threatens cities' persistence into the future. Similarly, efforts to grow a local economy in a capitalist city urge corporations and large businesses to keep wages low. While in the short term this increases profits, it also threatens to destabilize the labor force by pushing workers into poverty. Just like natural resources, human resources (labor) must not be exploited or they will not continue to deliver into the future (Campbell, 1996). Finally, the most complicated conflict in balancing the three pillars of sustainability is created by the need to ensure both social equity *and* environmental protection. If environmental protection entails more tempered economic growth, how do we create greater economic opportunities, and by extension social capital and high quality of life, for those at the bottom of the socioeconomic ladder? This conflict expresses the difficulty of addressing social sustainability in a way that also treats environmental and economic sustainability.

In theory, social sustainability is understood as vital to be preserved and stabilized for future generations in order to protect the achievements of human civilization (Littig & Grießler, 2005). In practice, however, the social dimension, especially the emphasis on equity, has been largely marginalized. Accordingly, Agyeman et al. (2002, p. 78) have developed the concept of "just" sustainability, which they define as "the need to ensure a better quality of life for all, now and into the future, in a just and equitable manner, whilst living within the limits of supporting ecosystems." This reworking of the economic, environmental, and social triad of sustainability emphasizes the need to extend the quality of life and social capital elements of social sustainability to communities of color and low-income populations (Alkon & Agyeman, 2011). It takes seriously the imperative to build sustainable communities for *all* people (Agyeman & Evans, 2003). Moreover, research suggests that those living in low-income and racially segregated communities face serious barriers to social

capital, social mobility (the ability to climb the social class ladder), and quality-of-life resources like access to good schools, high-quality health care, reliable transportation, and political representation (Massey & Denton, 1993).

> **ASK YOURSELF:** In what ways do or could the different types of sustainability complement each other? In what ways do or could they contradict each other? What do you think are the most important practices and principles for building sustainable cities?

Creating sustainable communities in cities helps establish a collective will to preserve the communities and the cities. This attachment to place and foundation for the establishment of shared goals and visions can serve as the social and cultural buttress for growth plans that meaningfully incorporate environmental stewardship. When communities are invested in one another and in the environment, policies and practices like New Urbanism, "smart" growth, and civic engagement in general become much more potent.

SOCIAL CHANGE: WHAT CAN YOU DO?

 17.5 Identify steps toward social change regarding urbanization and city growth.

Urban and town planners today are much more likely to talk about the ways in which given projects affect not just the economic vibrancy of particular areas but also the environment and social justice or equity. How much "social engineering" can be accomplished through better or more socially responsive kinds of planning is another issue that has gained a lot of attention among professionals. Contemporary experts have begun to cool, perhaps prematurely, to the idea that spreading "middle-class culture" will succeed in unifying a diverse urban population (Monti, 2013). At the same time, ironically, they still believe bringing more low-income and minority people to live and work in the suburbs is a good thing to do according to the "contact hypothesis," which suggests that less desirable people or places can be improved by being exposed to more desirable people or places.

More modest and scaled-down visions of what might be accomplished with better designed urban and suburban places appear in planned New Urbanist developments like Celebration and Seaside, both in Florida. These places

were supposed to manufacture a sense of community by bringing residents together a lot more often through the integration of private residential space with carefully designed public space (Talen, 2000, p. 173). We can think of **New Urbanism** as a response to urban and suburban sprawl, both of which cater to people moving in cars rather than on foot. Walking or riding a train with others instead is supposed to help foster better physical and social health.

This approach has been successful, up to a point. It turns out that people will hang out more in attractive, well-designed spaces and are more likely to "bump into each other" when they can walk to a shopping area or workplace that's within a couple blocks of where they live. At the same time, building a town or neighborhood with such principles in mind doesn't guarantee that everyone living there is going to get along or pledge undying loyalty to the place (Frantz & Collins, 1999).

New Urbanism: An approach to designing cities, towns, and neighborhoods aimed at reducing traffic and sprawl and increasing social interactions.

► Neighbors in Detroit, Michigan dance in a blocked-off street during a neighborhood block party. Events like this can foster a sense of community between neighbors.

The connection between creating a new place or improving an older one and fixing the people who live, work, or play there simply isn't as straightforward as reformers, policy makers, and planners would have us think. That shouldn't stop them from trying to make better places. It also shouldn't stop you from helping make your city, suburb, or town better. But where do you start?

There are a few things that you can do, provided you have the means, desire, and gusto. Remember, however, that since urbanization and population growth are *social* problems, individual actions are only a small first step to larger changes and reforms.

First, try to break up the everyday monotony of traveling from home to school or work and back by shaking up your daily routine. If you're in a car, take some streets you haven't been on before. Maybe park the car, get out, and walk around to see who's there and what they're doing. Second, if you're making one of these stops, try to do it in an ethnic enclave. Stop at a restaurant or food truck and take in the local delicacies. Eating foods from other ethnicities is a first step toward breaking the barrier between populations and making the "Other" less strange. Third, in your own neighborhood, get to

know those around you by spending more time in the front of your house or apartment rather than inside or in the backyard. Creating a "front porch" culture is one of the primary tools New Urbanist planners use to help foster connections between neighbor and neighbor *and* between neighbor and passerby. Fourth, be mindful of the ways city life and its built environment infringe on the natural environment. If water is an issue, use less. If air pollution is an issue, reduce the amount you drive. Take public transportation when you can. You'll be helping the environment and you might even rub elbows and chat with some fellow responsible citizens you wouldn't have met otherwise.

ASK YOURSELF: Urban planners and policy makers often assume that fixing the physical "face" of a city—the way it looks—will make the city "better." Do you think there are connections between the way a city looks and the actions and activities of the people who live and work there? Besides making changes to your own behavior, what things can you do to fix the social problems that affect people you know and people you don't in your city or town?

WHAT DOES AMERICA THINK?

Questions About Urbanization From the General Social Survey

 Turn to the beginning of the chapter to compare your answers to those of the total population.

1. In the United States, do you think we're spending too much money on highways and bridges, too little money, or about the right amount?

   TOO MUCH: 10.1%

   TOO LITTLE: 50.5%

   ABOUT THE RIGHT AMOUNT: 39.4%

2. In the United States, do you think we're spending too much money on mass transportation, too little money, or about the right amount?

   TOO MUCH: 9.2%

   TOO LITTLE: 37.6%

   ABOUT THE RIGHT AMOUNT: 53.2%

3. In the United States, do you think we're spending too much money on assistance to big cities, too little money, or about the right amount?

   TOO MUCH: 34.4%

   TOO LITTLE: 24.2%

   ABOUT THE RIGHT AMOUNT: 41.4%

4. In the United States, do you think we're spending too much money on solving problems of big cities, too little money, or about the right amount?

   TOO MUCH: 13.5%

   TOO LITTLE: 51.9%

   ABOUT THE RIGHT AMOUNT: 34.6%

CHAPTER SUMMARY

 17.1 Explain social problems that uniquely arise from urbanization and city growth.

Cities are the biggest things that humans have ever built together, but that doesn't mean that people who live in cities are all the same. In fact, people who live in cities are often quite different from their neighbors. While diversity is generally a favorable quality for healthy communities, it takes a lot of work for people of diverse backgrounds to find common ground and work together. Without some degree of trust and tolerance, social order is threatened, as is the ability of city dwellers to address important social issues like environmental degradation, education reform, and residential segregation.

17.2 Discuss patterns and trends in urbanization and city growth.

As the world becomes increasingly urban, many people fear that individuals will become further alienated from their neighbors, and consequently, the general social fabric of societies will forever be frayed and unraveled. This fear is reinforced by rising income inequalities and health disparities within and between cities as well as the impacts that cities are having on the lands they are built upon and near.

17.3 Apply the functionalist, conflict, and symbolic interactionist perspectives to problems that arise from urbanization and city growth.

A functionalist perspective or urban ecological approach shows us how cities and their respective populations develop out of natural processes of adaptation, competition, and succession. Recognizing how these processes work can help alleviate the negative effects of urbanization and population growth. A conflict theory or urban political economy approach would suggest that people in cities are always competing for scarce resources and that those who can accumulate more and more of those

Part V: Problems of Global Impact

resources will continue to exploit those who don't have many or any resources. A fundamental restructuring of the economy is therefore the only way to truly fix urban problems. A symbolic interactionist or urban culturalist perspective uncovers how people make sense of the cities they live, work, and play in and how that influences the way they interact with others and the city's built environment. By identifying the things and practices that people hold to be culturally valuable, we can gain a better understanding of what they see as the most important problems.

17.4 Apply specialized theories to urbanization and city growth.

The increased concerns for urban sustainability in recent years represent an effort to address the social and environmental problems produced by urban growth guided simply by a desire to grow the economy. Such a theoretical foundation for urban growth not only addresses environmental problems in a way traditional sociological theories have not but also bridges environmental problems and social problems, understanding that they are intricately related. Thinking about urban sustainability as a combination of environmental, economic, and social factors is a necessary way to address cities' most pressing problems. "Just" sustainability attempts to meet "the need to ensure a better quality of life for all, now and into the future, in a just and equitable manner, whilst living within the limits of supporting ecosystems" (Agyeman et al., 2002, p. 78).

17.5 Identify steps toward social change regarding urbanization and city growth.

No redevelopment scheme, no matter how successful it may be in terms of making nicer buildings and more public space for people to share, can guarantee that everyone who ends up living in the rebuilt area will behave wonderfully all the time and get along. As an approach to rebuilding inner cities, however, comparatively modest size and modestly scaled social expectations for the people living and working in these places holds more promise than massive urban clearance and bulldozing projects have ever delivered. And it is in the hands of those who are civically engaged and work hard to know others across the city's symbolic boundaries to moderate and negotiate the extent of expectations.

KEY TERMS

biographical strangers 427

built environment 436

central business district (CBD) 435

city 425

climate debt 433

community 435

cultural strangers 427

gemeinschaft 426

gesellschaft 426

industrialization 426

New Urbanism 442

redevelopment 436

segregation 429

social order 425

third places 438

urbanism 437

urbanization 425

GLOSSARY

Absolute measure of poverty: A threshold or line (usually based on income) at or below which individuals or groups are identified as living in poverty.

Academic capital: An example of cumulative advantage where scientists in elite institutions build enduring networks, resources, and schools of thought.

Accountability: The ways in which people gear their actions to specific circumstances so others will correctly recognize the actions for what they are.

Achievement gap: The consistent difference in scores on student achievement tests between students of different demographic groups, including groups based on race, gender, and socioeconomic status.

Adjudication: The process in which a final judicial decision or sentence is made in a criminal case.

Affirmative action: Policies enacted by governments and private organizations to increase work and educational opportunities for women and members of certain minority groups

Affirmative defenses: Legal defenses in which new facts or sets of facts operate to defeat claims even if the facts supporting the claims are true.

Ageism: The use of real or perceived chronological age as a basis for discrimination.

Agenda-setting theory: A theory that emphasizes the important role media play in influencing public understanding of social issues and social problems.

Aging: A social process constructed from the expectations and belief systems of the structural characteristics of society.

Alienation: The separation of workers from their human nature in the capitalist production process—that is, the separation between the labor to make something and the object itself.

Allocation: The way decisions get made about who does what, who gets what and who does not, who gets to make plans, and who gets to give orders or take them.

Altruistic suicide: Suicide that occurs as a result of too much social integration.

American Federation of Teachers (AFT): One of the two largest unions representing teachers in the United States.

Androcentrism: The belief that masculinity and what men do are superior to femininity and what women do.

Anomic suicide: Suicide that occurs as a result of too little social regulation.

Anomie: A state of normlessness in society.

Antiracism: The active struggle against racism in everyday life (micro) and/or institutionally (macro).

Assimilation: The act of literally "becoming like" the dominant group of the host society; in its purest sense, when assimilation is complete an immigrant would be indistinguishable from the dominant group in society.

Authorization: Enemy-making behavior facilitated by leaders that absolves individuals of the responsibility to make personal moral choices.

Benefits: Noncash compensation paid to employees, such as health insurance and pension plans. Also known as fringe benefits.

Big data: The large quantities of digital data produced by digital societies, including data from cell phones, keystrokes, and GPS units.

Biographical strangers: Individuals who do not know each other on a personal basis or who have never met.

Bounded rationality: The idea that an individual's thought processes are deemed to be rational even when they are constrained by low intelligence, chemical dependence, or mental illness.

Bourgeoisie: In Marxist theory, the wealthy class that owns and controls the means of production and is at odds with the lower class.

Bourgeoisie legality: The theory that members of the upper class make the laws to serve and protect their own interests to the detriment of the lower class.

Broken windows theory: The theory that maintaining an urban environment in an orderly manner will deter both low-level and serious offending.

Built environment: The human-constructed physical and material objects that make up the city, like buildings, streets, and sidewalks.

Bumpy-line assimilation: A modification of early-20th-century assimilation theory that challenges the traditional linear one-way progression; instead, immigrants can become full participating members of the host society while still retaining certain ties to their nationalities of origin (incorporates notion of "thick" versus "thin" ties).

Capitalism: An economic system that includes the ownership of private property, the making of financial profit, and the hiring of workers.

Capitalists: The economically dominant class that privately owns and controls human labor, raw materials, land, tools, machinery, technologies, and factories.

Central business district (CBD): The commercial, office, transportation, and cultural center of a city; land values in the CBD are usually among the highest in the city.

Charter schools: Publicly funded schools that operate independent of school districts and are free of many of the regulations that apply to school districts.

Child dependency ratio: The number of children under the age of 16 per 100 adults ages 16 to 64.

Cisgender: Gender identity matches the sex category assigned at birth.

City: A relatively large, dense, and heterogeneously populated place or settlement.

Civil unions: Legal provisions that grant some or all of the legal rights of marriage to unmarried couples.

Claims making: The process whereby groups compete to have their claims about difficult social issues acknowledged, accepted, and responded to by authorities.

Class: A person's social position relative to the economic sector.

Clearance rates: The ratio of reported cases of crime to cleared cases, calculated by dividing the number of crimes that result in arrests by the total number of crimes recorded.

Climate debt: The idea that wealthy nations that have contributed most to the problem of climate change—through their overconsumption of resources, damage to the environment, and consumption of atmospheric space—are responsible for contributing most to efforts to mitigate it. Practically, countries with the highest climate debt would be expected to help the countries most harmed adapt to their changing ecological realities, and agree to reduce future GHG emissions to allow developing countries to be able to produce more of the global share as they grow.

Code theory: Basil Bernstein's concept that society reproduces social classes through favoring the communication codes, or manners of speaking and representing thoughts and ideas, of more powerful socioeconomic groups.

Cognitive dissonance: The discomfort of holding conflicting beliefs or values.

Cohabitation: Unrelated (unmarried) adults in an intimate relationship sharing living quarters.

Cohort: Within a population, a group of individuals of similar age who share a particular experience.

Color-blind racism: A type of racism that avoids overt arguments of biological superiority/inferiority and instead uses ideologies that do not always mention race specifically.

Community: A usually positive (though not necessarily so) form of sustained social cohesion, interaction, and organization that exists between the larger society and individuals who have similar characteristics or attributes (e.g., ethnicity, geography, beliefs).

Community schools: Schools that strive to meet all the basic academic, physical, and emotional needs of students and their families while building strong, cohesive bonds among teachers, students, and students' families.

Concepts: Ideas that sociologists have about some aspect of the social world.

Conflict theory: The sociological theory that focuses on dissent, coercion, and antagonism in society.

Consciousness-raising: A radical feminist social movement technique designed to help women make connections between the personal and the political in their lives.

Conspicuous consumption: Using the consumption of goods to display social status, like prominently carrying a designer handbag.

Constructionist approach: An approach to social problems theory that highlights the process whereby troubling social issues become recognized as social problems.

Contact hypothesis: The prediction that persons with greater degrees of cross-racial contact will have lower levels of racial prejudice than those with less contact.

Continuity theory: A theory that utilizes the concept of normal aging as a basis for explaining how older individuals adjust.

Costs of privilege: Experiences that members of the majority group may miss out on due to racial isolation and limited worldviews.

Courtroom workgroup: The informal and working relationships between the prosecutor, defense attorney, and judicial officer.

Crisis science: Medical science that works in tandem with Mode 1 science and has the freedom to respond to crises and the needs of patients faster than traditional science.

Crude divorce rate: The number of divorces per 1,000 population.

Cult of thinness: Idealization of a decidedly slim body type that

is unachievable for the vast majority of the population.

Cultural capital theory: Pierre Bourdieu's concept that a range of nonfinancial assets, such as education, physical appearance, and familiarity with various kinds of music, art, and dance, empower individuals to advance in a social group that values a particular set of these cultural assets.

Cultural deprivation theory: A theory based in the concept that children from working-class and nonwhite families often lack certain cultural resources, such as books and other educational stimuli, and thus arrive at school at a significant disadvantage.

Cultural difference theories: Theories based in the concept that there are cultural and family differences between working-class and nonwhite students and white middle-class students attributable to social forces such as poverty, racism, discrimination, and unequal life chances.

Cultural strangers: Individuals who are from different symbolic worlds or cultures.

Culturally resonant themes: Themes that invoke widely held beliefs, values, and preferences that are familiar to potential audiences; such themes are common in news stories of social problems.

Culture: A style of life.

Culture of poverty thesis: The idea that living in poverty leads to the acquisition of certain values and beliefs that perpetuate remaining in poverty.

Culture of service: A style of life that includes various forms of civic engagement, community service, and volunteerism intended to help alleviate social problems.

Culture wars: Disputes over the state of American society, including the presumed decline of the family as well as "family values."

Cumulative advantage: A position that multiplies advantages for those who have them and limits the capacity for those without resources.

Cyberbullying: Electronic forms of bullying.

Cyclical unemployment: Unemployment caused by cyclical downturns in the economy.

Dark figure of crime: The amount of unreported or undiscovered crime, which calls into question the reliability of official crime statistics.

Data sources: Collections of information.

Decentralization of power: The distribution of functions and responsibilities of police officers to different local authorities.

Defense of Marriage Act (DOMA): U.S. federal law, enacted in 1996, that defines marriage as the legal union of one man and one woman for federal and interstate purposes.

Dehumanization: Enemy-making behavior that makes the other side appear to be less than human; eliminates the need to raise moral questions.

Demand reduction: An approach to drug policy aimed at providing education, prevention, and treatment.

Democratic theory of peace: The theory that political democracies are less likely than nondemocracies to wage war with each other

Demographic factors: Social characteristics of a population, in particular those of race, age, and gender.

Determinate sentencing: A sentence for a fixed period that is determined by statute.

Determining gender: The process of placing someone in a gender category.

Deterrence: A purpose of punishment that sets out to prevent rational people from committing crimes.

Dialectical materialism: The contradictions in an existing economic and social order that create a push for change, which eventually lead to new economic conditions and social relations.

Differential association theory: A theory of crime that asserts that all behavior is learned, both criminal and noncriminal.

Digital divide: The gap in access to information and communication technologies between more advantaged and less advantaged groups, such as between the wealthy and poor regions of the world (the global digital divide) and between social classes within a country.

Discouraged workers: Unemployed workers who have given up looking for jobs and hence are no longer counted as members of the labor force.

Distracted driving: The operation of a motor vehicle while engaged in other attention-requiring activities, such as texting or talking on the phone.

Distributive justice: Relative equality in how social and economic resources are distributed in a society.

Division of labor: The division of work into a multiplicity of specialized occupational roles and tasks.

Doing gender theory: A theory of gender that claims gender is an accountable performance created and reinforced through individuals' interactions.

Double consciousness: African Americans' ability to see themselves both as active agents with full humanity and as they are seen through the eyes of whites who view them as inferior and problematic.

Drug: A substance that has properties that produce psychophysiological changes in the individual who ingests it.

Drug abuse: The use of psychoactive substances in a way that creates problematic outcomes for the user.

Drug dependence: A state that produces psychophysiological changes in the user and is characterized by compulsive drug use and drug-seeking behaviors despite harmful consequences.

Drug use: The ingestion of substances so as to produce changes in the body that alter the way the user experiences the world.

Dysfunctions: Negative consequences of social structures or social institutions.

Ecological dialogue: An approach to the environment and society that focuses on the interactions between aspects of human environmental relationships.

Ecological modernization theory: The theory that society can become environmentally sustainable through the development of greener technologies and government regulations.

Effective schools movement: A movement for school improvement based on the concept that unusually effective schools have certain characteristics (such as effective leadership, accountability, and high expectations of teachers and administrators) that help explain why their students achieve academically despite disadvantaged backgrounds.

Egoistic suicide: Suicide that occurs as a result of too little social integration.

Elementary and Secondary Education Act (ESEA): The primary piece of federal legislation concerning K–12 education in the United States; this act, first passed in 1965, was most dramatically revised through its reauthorization in 2001 as the No Child Left Behind Act.

Employment at will: The legal practice that allows an employer to terminate a worker's employment even if no specific reason for the termination is given.

Environmental dispossession: The reduction or removal of access to environmental resources previously accessible, largely by a dominant group of beneficiaries.

Environmental racism: The process by which the dominant race in society is shielded from the most toxic/harmful environmental threats, while such health risks/hazards are located closest to neighborhoods where minority groups reside.

Erotic habitus: The interplay between psychological processes and structural influences at work when people negotiate sexual desires and behaviors.

Ethnicity: Cultural background, often tied to nationality of origin and/or the culture practiced by the individual and his or her family of origin.

Ethnomethodology: A sociological approach that seeks to uncover the taken-for-granted assumptions that lie behind the basic stuff of social life and interaction.

Every Student Succeeds Act (ESSA): The reauthorized version of No Child Left Behind, which returned some power back to the states concerning educational standards and testing.

Expressive: Oriented toward interactions with other people.

Extreme poverty neighborhoods: Areas (usually based on census tracts) that have poverty rates of 40% or more.

Family: (1) Two or more people related by birth, marriage, or adoption who share living quarters (U.S. Census Bureau definition), or (2) members of a social group who are in an intimate, long-term, committed relationship and who share mutual expectations of rights and responsibilities.

Family ecology theory: A theory that views family systems as embedded in natural or human-made physical, social, and other environments.

Family life course development theory: A theory that examines the developmental processes and outcomes as families move through a series of normative stages across the life course.

Family systems theory: A theory that views the family as a set of subsystems defined by boundaries and striving toward social equilibrium.

Fatalistic suicide: Suicide that occurs as a result of too much social regulation.

Feminist criminology: A theory of crime that includes gender in its analysis.

Feminist perspective: A theoretical approach that emphasizes the extent to which patriarchy and sexism undermine women (and men), relationships, and families.

Feminization of poverty: The trend of poverty being concentrated disproportionately in female-headed single-parent families.

Fertility rate: The number of children born per 1,000 women during their prime fertility period.

Fictive kin: People to whom one is not related by blood, marriage, or adoption but on whom one nonetheless depends.

Food insecurity: A household's lack of access to nutritious food on a regular basis.

Fourth paradigm: A new scientific methodology based on data-intensive computing, where knowledge and understanding are gained with sophisticated algorithms and statistical techniques of extensive or mega-scale databases.

Frame alignment: A situation in which multiple frames work together to enhance the efficacy of each.

Frame analysis: A sociological approach that focuses on the presentation of information and ideas in ways that are intended to elicit particular understanding and responses.

"Frictional unemployment": Unemployment that results from workers being temporarily jobless while transitioning from one job to another.

Functionalist theory: The hypothesis that societies are complex systems whose parts work together to maintain cohesion and stability.

Functions: Positive consequences of social structures or social institutions.

Gemeinschaft: Communal association, or a sense of close-knit community relations based on shared traditions and values.

Gender: The social meanings layered on top of sex categories.

Gender inequality: The way in which the meanings assigned to sex and gender as social categories create disparities in resources such as income, power, and status.

Gender wage gap: The gap in earnings between women and men, usually expressed as a percentage or proportion of what women are paid relative to their male equivalents.

General deterrence: A law or policy written to stop a person from committing a crime in the first place.

Generational inequity: A situation in which older-age members of a society receive a disproportionate share of the society's resources relative to younger members; perceptions that such inequity exists lead to calls for adjustments to ensure greater economic and social parity between generations.

Genetic difference theory: The discredited concept that differences in educational performance between working-class and nonwhite students and their middle- and upper-class and white counterparts are due to genetic differences in intelligence.

Gerontocracy: A system in which older-age citizens have the power to run the government and dictate policies that primarily support people in their age category.

Gesellschaft: Societal association, or a sense of relationships typified by impersonal bureaucracies and contractual arrangements rather than informal ones based on kinship and family ties.

Global perspective: A viewpoint from which we compare our own society to other societies around the world.

Globalization: The process through which business firms, political authority, and cultural patterns spread throughout the world.

Globalized intrastate wars: Organized violence used to control territory containing valuable resources, often fought by paramilitary forces, often targeting civilians, often containing high levels of sexual violence, and often using child soldiers.

Great Depression: Worldwide economic downturn in the period 1929–1941, marked by failing businesses, low or at times negative economic growth, and widespread unemployment.

Habitus: How people learn and develop ways to embody actions in a given social context.

Harm reduction: An approach to drug policy aimed at minimizing or eliminating the harms associated with drug use behaviors.

Health social movements: The practice of linking health research with community activism to influence health policy. HSMs embrace the principles of science.

Hierarchy rule: A reporting, where in any single crime event police agencies are asked only to report the most serious crime committed.

Hooking up: A casual sexual encounter without emotional or romantic expectations, often occurring within an intoxicating party atmosphere.

Hot-spot policing: A method employed by police departments to track the ordered spatial patterns of crime by monitoring when crimes occur disproportionately in particular geographic areas and responding to those areas.

Household: All the related and unrelated people who share living quarters.

Human capital: The package of cognitive, physical, and social skills of individual workers.

Human trafficking: Recruiting, transporting, and harboring vulnerable people through threats or force to exploit their labor, including sexual labor.

Hypermasculinity: An intensification of traits normally associated with stereotypical male behavior: physical strength, aggressiveness, assertiveness, risk taking, and appreciation for danger and adventure.

Ideologies: Belief systems that serve to rationalize/justify existing social arrangements.

Incapacitation: Loss of liberty due to incarceration.

Income: Money that comes into a family or household from a variety of sources, such as earnings, unemployment compensation, workers' compensation, Social Security, pension or retirement income, interest, and dividends.

Indeterminate sentencing: Sentencing for convicted offenders in which the length of incarceration is undetermined.

Indicators: Observable changes in social and ecological behaviors that are used to indirectly measure other changes that are less visible.

Individual discrimination: Discrimination in which actors carry out their own intentions to exclude based on race, as opposed to being explicitly supported in doing so or directed to do so by an organization.

Industrialization: A process that leads to a significant increase in the proportion of a population engaged in specialized factory work and nonagricultural occupations; increases the number of people living near factories and relying on mechanically produced goods and services.

Industrialized science: Science that is done on the large scale for profit.

Inequality: Differences between individuals or groups in the quantities of scarce resources they possess.

Institutional discrimination: Discrimination based in policies often written without overt racial language that nonetheless have disproportionately negative impacts on people of color.

Institutional racism: Policies and practices embedded in social institutions that consistently and disproportionately favor members of the dominant/majority group while systematically excluding/disadvantaging people of color.

Institutional theory: The concept that schools are global institutions and have developed similarly throughout the world since the 19th century as a result of processes of globalization and democratization.

Instrumental: Oriented toward goals and tasks.

Interaction order: A culture that shapes everyday social interactions.

Interest groups: Organized associations of people mobilized into action because of their membership in those associations.

Internalized racism: Feelings that occur in people of color when they buy into racist ideology that characterizes their own group as inferior—for example, when they believe that they themselves and/or other members of their group are not deserving of prestigious positions in society, or they assume that members of their group are prone to exhibiting stereotypical behaviors.

Interpretive flexibility: The ability of the development path to respond to different users' needs.

Intersectional approach: A sociological approach that examines how gender as a social category intersects with other social statuses such as race, class, and sexuality.

Intersectionality: The ways in which several demographic factors—especially social class, race, ethnicity, and gender—combine to affect people's experiences.

Intersex: Born with some range of biological conditions that make sex category ambiguous.

Interviewing: A method of data collection in which the researcher asks respondents a series of questions.

Intimate partner violence (IPV): Physical, sexual, or psychological/emotional harm or the threat of harm by a current or former intimate partner or spouse.

Jim Crow: The system of racialized segregation that existed in the United States from the Emancipation Proclamation of 1865 to the landmark civil rights legislation of the late 1960s. During this era, legal segregation was enforced by both law enforcement and white terror perpetrated by groups such as the Ku Klux Klan.

Journalists' professional routines: The daily activities around which news reporters organize their work.

Labeling theories: Emphasize how the application of sanctions can lead to a deviant stigma applied by others, which in turn affects one's identity and subsequent delinquency.

Labor force: The segment of the population either employed or actively seeking employment.

Landraces: Local varieties of seeds that have been domesticated by communities over time and have adapted to local cultural and environmental needs.

Latent function: An unintentional or unanticipated positive outcome of social institutions or policies.

Legislation: Enacted laws that make some condition or pattern of behavior legal or illegal.

LGBTQ: The acronym for Lesbian, Gay, Bisexual, Transgender, and Queer/Questioning.

Liberal feminism: A type of feminism that suggests men and women are essentially the same and gender inequality can be eliminated through the reduction of legal barriers to women's full participation in society.

Life expectancy: The average number of years a baby born in any given year can expect to live.

Looking-glass self: The idea that we see ourselves as we think others see us.

Lump of labor fallacy: The notion that there is a fixed number of jobs and that unemployed individuals can find jobs only when others lose their jobs or reduce the number of hours they work.

Magnet schools: Publicly funded schools designed to recruit students from across entire districts by offering particular disciplinary focuses, such as arts, technology, science, or mathematics.

Makerspace: A popular do-it-yourself (DIY) movement dedicated to actively experimenting, designing, and sharing technological solutions to social problems.

Mala in se **crimes:** Crimes that are illegal because they are bad in themselves or inherently wrong by nature.

Mala prohibita **crimes:** Crimes that are illegal because they are prohibited by law.

Manifest function: An intended, overt, planned, and/or agreed-upon (by consensus) effect or outcome of social phenomena or individual behaviors.

Marriage dearth: The decline in the proportion of adult Americans who are married.

Marriage gradient: The tendency for women to "marry up"—that is, to marry older men.

Marriage movement: Social movement that advocates traditional marriage and warns against the sexual revolution, teenage pregnancy, and same-sex marriage.

Marriage squeeze: The severely imbalanced sex ratio experienced by black women in regard to potential marriage partners.

Marxist criminology: A view based on the writings of Karl Marx that sees the law as the mechanism by which the ruling class keeps the members of the surplus population in their disadvantaged position.

Matters of law: The legal process issues that arise during court proceedings and that are in the exclusive jurisdiction of a judge to resolve.

Maturing out: The decline and cessation of psychoactive drug use among younger people as they age into different social roles and responsibilities.

Means-tested programs: Programs for which people qualify by having a certain income level, usually at or up to 185% of the poverty line.

Media exaggeration: Strategies of dramatizing and embellishing media stories involving social issues to attract and hold the attention of an audience.

Media frames: Conventions of journalistic storytelling that situate a social problem within a broader context.

Media phobias: Fears about the negative impacts of media that lead to identifying media as the causes of persistent social problems.

Medicaid: A federal/state program that provides a variety of social services to those identified as eligible based on state-specific criteria.

Medicare: A federal health care program for those age 65 and over. The program is divided into four parts that address health coverage for services provided by physicians and hospitals as well as prescription drug coverage.

Megamachine: A new social order composed of humans and technology that is dominated by technological rather than human needs.

Meritocracy: A system in which personal advancement results from merit, based on knowledge and skill.

Metanarrative: An attempted comprehensive and universal explanation of some phenomenon.

Microaggressions: Everyday acts (intentional or unintentional) that serve to marginalize persons due to perceived subordinate group status.

Micropolitics: An individual's use of his or her own personal sphere of influence to affect social change.

Middleman minority: A racial group that is not in the majority but is held up by the majority as a "positive"

example of a minority and is used by those in power to pit minority groups against each other.

Military-industrial complex: The relationships among government, the Pentagon, and defense contractors that promote the acquisition of weapons systems and a militarized foreign policy.

Mind: The internal conversations we have within ourselves.

Minority group: A group that does not hold a sizable share of power and resources in a society; often the share of such resources is disproportionately small relative to the group's numerical presence in the overall population, and the group has a history of being systemically excluded from those resources.

Mode 1: A type of scientific discovery or knowledge production done by scientists in universities through the application of experimental science within distinct disciplines.

Mode 2: A type of scientific discovery or knowledge production that is done by experts and nonexperts working together in transdisciplinary environments to create applications that are socially responsible.

Moral entrepreneurs: Advocates who organize to focus broad public attention on troubling issues.

Moral panics: Situations in which broad public fears and anxieties about particular social problems are disproportionate to the dangers of those problems.

Morbidity: The number of diagnoses of disease or other condition in a given population at a designated time, usually expressed as a rate per 100,000.

"Motherhood penalty": Mothers earn less than both men and women without children.

National Assessment of Educational Progress (NAEP): A congressionally mandated set of standardized tests intended to assess the progress of a sample of U.S. students at various grade levels from all demographic groups and all parts of the country.

National Education Association (NEA): The largest union representing teachers in the United States.

Natural recovery: A person's cessation of a drug habit without the assistance of a drug treatment program.

Needle exchange programs: Drug abuse harm reduction programs that provide new syringes to intravenous drug users who exchange used syringes.

New Urbanism: An approach to designing cities, towns, and neighborhoods aimed at reducing traffic and sprawl and increasing social interactions.

No Child Left Behind Act (NCLB): U.S. federal legislation passed in 2001 as the reauthorization of the Elementary and Secondary Education Act; established a range of reforms mandating uniform standards for all students with the aim of reducing and eventually eliminating the social class and race achievement gap by 2014.

Normative conflict: Perspective that views the creation of laws as a means for those in power to maintain their position in society.

Normative consensus: Perspective that holds that behaviors get codified illegal because there is general agreement among members of society that the behavior is morally wrong.

Norms: Social rules.

North American Free Trade Agreement (NAFTA): A pact initiated in 1994 to stimulate trade among the United States, Canada, and Mexico by lowering or eliminating tariff barriers.

Objective aspect of social problems: Those empirical conditions or facts that point to the concreteness of social problems "out there."

Occupational segregation: The tendency of certain jobs to be predominantly filled on the basis of gender or according to race and ethnicity.

Old-age dependency ratio: The number of older persons ages 65 and over for every 100 adults between the ages of 16 and 64.

Paradigms: Theoretical perspectives.

Parole: The release, under supervision, of a convicted criminal defendant after he or she has completed part of his or her sentence, based on the concept that the defendant will follow the law and become a part of society.

Participant observation: A research method that includes observing and studying people in their everyday settings.

Paternalism: The system, principle, or practice of managing or governing individuals in the manner of a father dealing with his children.

Patriarchy: A society characterized by male dominance.

Personal Responsibility and Work Opportunity Reconciliation Act (PRWORA): U.S. federal legislation passed in 1996 that eliminated Assistance for Families with Dependent Children (AFDC) and established Temporary Assistance for Needy Families (TANF). Also known as welfare reform.

Pool of eligibles: The quantity and quality of potential partners for marriage.

Post-traumatic stress disorder (PTSD): A mental health condition triggered by a terrifying event. Symptoms include flashbacks, nightmares, and severe anxiety, as well as thoughts about the event that cannot be controlled.

Poverty: Deficiencies in necessary material goods or desirable qualities, including economic, social, political, and cultural.

Poverty guidelines: A simplified version of the U.S. Census Bureau poverty thresholds, which take into account only family size; the poverty guidelines are used to set the federal poverty level (FPL).

Poverty rate: A measure of the number of individuals or groups in poverty, expressed in absolute or relative terms.

Poverty thresholds: Measures of poverty used by the U.S. Census Bureau that take into account family size, number of children, and their ages.

Power: The aspect of social structure related to political affiliations and connections.

Presumption of innocence: The principle that a criminal defendant is innocent until proven guilty, placing the burden on the government to establish proof of guilt beyond a reasonable doubt.

Primary deviance: In societal reaction theory, this refers to individuals' engagement in low-level offending, like speeding or experimenting with alcohol.

Primary sector: The sector of the economy centered on farming, fishing, and the extraction of raw materials.

Probation: An alternative to incarceration that offers an individual freedom if he or she can abide by the law and comply with the terms and conditions mandated by the court.

Product placement: A form of advertising in which products are used or mentioned by film or television characters.

Proletariat: In Marxist theory, the working class, which is at odds with the bourgeoisie.

Psychological wage: Feelings of racial superiority accorded to poor/working-class whites in the absence of actual monetary compensation for labor.

Public arenas model: A model that offers a framework for analyzing the rise and fall in the amount of attention the public pays to different social problems.

Public defenders: Publicly appointed lawyers.

Qualitative research: Research that studies how people define, experience, or understand problematic situations.

Quantitative research: Research that studies social problems through statistical analysis.

Quintile: One-fifth of anything that can be divided.

Race: A socially and politically constructed category of persons that is often created with certain physical traits (e.g., skin color, eye color, eye shape, hair texture) in mind but can also incorporate religion, culture, nationality, and social class, depending on the time, place, and political/economic structure of the society.

Race relations cycle: A pathway of incorporation into a host society that immigrants follow; includes four stages: contact, competition, accommodation, and eventual assimilation.

Race to the Top (RTT): Federal program established by President Obama with the goal of aiding states in meeting the various components of NCLB by offering grants to states to improve student outcomes and close achievement gaps.

Racialization: The process by which a society incorporates and clearly demarcates individuals who fit a certain profile into a particular racial group.

Racism: A system that advantages the dominant racial group in a society.

Radical feminism: A version of feminist thought that suggests gender is a fundamental aspect of the way society functions and serves as an integral tool for distributing power and resources among people and groups.

Rape culture: The societal conditions that encourage men's dominance over women where men feel entitled to sexually coerce women in order to fit conventional standards of masculinity.

Rational choice theory: A theory of crime that says humans are reasoning actors who weigh costs and benefits and make rational choices to commit crimes.

Realism: The point of view that the world is directly knowable.

Recidivism: The habit of reoffending.

Redevelopment: The rebuilding of parts of a city; sometimes large areas are completely demolished before being rebuilt, sometimes older buildings are preserved or updated.

Refined divorce rate: The number of divorces per 1,000 married women.

Reflexive modernization: A form of economic development focused on revising current systems of production and making careful assessment of future outcomes of projects and decisions.

Rehabilitation: A goal of punishment that seeks to restore the offender to a more law-abiding life, free of the encumbrances that may have caused him or her to commit a crime.

Relative measure of poverty: A measure that looks at individuals or groups relative to the rest of their community or society rather than setting an absolute line.

Research methods: Techniques for obtaining information.

Resilience: The ability not just to bounce back from change or troubles but to spring forward into the future.

Retribution: Punishment that serves no purpose except to punish and communicate to the wrongdoer that his or her behavior is not tolerated.

Risk contract: The implicit understanding that government will enact rules to make sure people are protected as society bounds progressively forward.

Risk society: A society stratified by the ability to avoid risk.

Routine activity theory: The theory that crimes occur when motivated offenders come across suitable targets and a lack of capable guardians.

Routinization: The organizing and structuring of enemy-making behavior so thoroughly that there is no opportunity for raising moral questions.

Salary: Remuneration paid on a monthly or bimonthly basis and not directly tied to the number of hours worked.

School-centered explanations: Explanations of educational inequalities that focus on factors within the school, such as teachers and teaching methods, curriculum, ability grouping and curriculum tracking, school climate, and teacher expectations.

School choice: A school reform approach that theoretically allows market forces to shape school policies by offering parents a range of school options, including magnet schools, voucher schools, charter schools, traditional local public schools, and regular public schools.

School voucher: An approach to school choice in which parents of school-age children receive government-issued vouchers of a certain monetary value that they can apply to tuition expenses at private schools.

Science: The accumulation of knowledge by specific methods within a particular culture that certifies, applies, and governs what is named science.

Science machine: A connection between science and society that is built by a community of individuals who share a common culture.

Science shops: Facilities hosted by universities where citizens can participate in science, ask scientific questions, and become part of the scientific process.

"Second shift": Unpaid housework and child care done, primarily by women, in addition to paid work outside the home.

Secondary deviance: In societal reaction theory, this refers to individuals' engagement in more serious forms of crime after they have been labeled and treated as criminals.

Secondary sector: The sector of the economy that includes manufacturing and other activities that produce material goods.

Segmented assimilation: A theory acknowledging different segments of the host society into which an immigrant can assimilate (not just the white middle class).

Segregation: The practice of physically separating the occupants of some social statuses from the occupants of others.

Selection effect: In contrast to the experience effect, attitudes and characteristics that predispose an individual to a relationship outcome, such as divorce.

Self-fulfilling prophecy: The social process whereby a false definition of a situation brings about behavior that makes the false definition "come true."

Self-made myth: The belief that anyone can rise from humble beginnings to become wealthy and successful simply by applying him- or herself.

Self-regulation: A process whereby media industries propose to police themselves to stave off the imposition of government regulation.

Sentencing guidelines: A set of standards that are created to establish consistent sentencing practices within a jurisdiction.

Service sector: The sector of the economy that provides services such as education, health care, and government. Also known as the tertiary sector.

Service sociology: A socially responsible and mission-oriented sociology of action and alleviation.

Settlement houses: Neighborhood centers that provide services to poor immigrants.

Sex: The behaviors of two or more people who consent to the pursuit of pleasure and define these behaviors as such.

Sex ratio: The number of males for every 100 females in the general population or within some designated segment, such as among those age 65 and over.

Sex role: The set of expectations attached to a particular sex category—male or female.

Sex tourism: Travel to destinations, typically in developing countries, specifically for the purpose of buying sex from men and women there.

Sex trafficking: A commercial, criminal activity that includes force, fraud, or coercion to exploit a person sexually for profit.

Sexual bullying: A pattern of sexual harassment that can include spreading rumors about a person's sexual behavior or identity, forcing someone to do something sexual, and writing sexual messages about a person online or as graffiti.

Sexual dimorphism: The belief that there are two discrete types of people—male and female—who can be distinguished on the basis of real, objective, biological criteria.

Sexual double standard: A term describing the ways that men are rewarded—and women are negatively labeled—for sexually permissive attitudes and behaviors.

Sexual labor: The selling of sexual services for money.

Sexuality: A combination of sexual behaviors, attractions, identities, and communities.

Sexually transmitted diseases (STDs): Bacterial and viral infections of the human body that are passed through sexual behaviors.

Social class: A category of people whose experiences in life are determined by the amount of income and wealth they own and control.

Social construction: Society's agreed-upon meanings that vary across culture and throughout history.

Social constructionism: The social process by which people define a social problem into existence.

Social control: The ability of a strong group in society to control the actions of subordinate groups.

Social control theory: A theory of crime that assumes all people are capable of committing crimes and that some are stopped by their strong bonds to society.

Social disorganization theory: A theory that links crime rates to neighborhood ecological characteristics: poverty, residential mobility, and racial heterogeneity.

Social empathy: The insights individuals have about other people's lives that allow them to understand the circumstances and realities of other people's living conditions.

Social equity: Closely related to the concept of social equality, social equity stresses fairness and justice.

Social exchange theory: A theory that posits individuals will draw on personal resources to maximize rewards and minimize costs when forming, maintaining, or dissolving relationships.

Social facts: The ways of thinking, acting, and feeling that are external to the individual and exert pressure on the individual.

Social gradient of health: The consistent finding that inequality and health are related, with those at the top of the social system being healthier and living longer than those at the bottom.

Social inclusion: A sense of belonging to or membership in a group or a society.

Social institutions: Any set of persons, such as a family, economy, government, or religion, cooperating for the purpose of organizing stable patterns of human activity.

Social integration: The unity or cohesiveness of society.

Social interaction: The communication that occurs between two or more people.

Social mobility: Upward or downward movement in social position by groups or individuals over time.

Social movements: The collective efforts of people to realize social change in order to solve social problems.

Social order: The conformity of individuals to explicit and implicit social rules of behavior.

Social organization: The pattern of relationships between individuals and groups.

Social policy: A more or less clearly articulated and usually written set of strategies for addressing a social problem.

Social problem: A social condition, event, or pattern of behavior that negatively affects the well-being of a significant number of people (or a number of significant people) who believe that the condition, event, or pattern needs to be changed or ameliorated.

Social regulation: The control society has over the behavior of its members.

Social revolution: A total and complete transformation in the social structure of society.

Social role: A set of expectations attached to a particular status or position in society.

Social safety net: Public programs intended to help those who are most vulnerable in a society.

Social Security: A federal program that provides monthly benefit payments to older workers who have participated in the workforce and paid into the system.

Social self: A process by which people are able to see themselves in relationship to others.

Social structure: The pattern of interrelated social institutions.

Socialist feminism: A version of feminist thought that employs Marxist paradigms to view women as an oppressed social class.

Societal reaction theory: A theory of crime that argues that people become criminals based on how others respond to their actions.

Socioeconomic status (SES): A conceptualization of social class in terms of a continuum or index based on social and economic factors.

Sociological imagination: A form of self-consciousness that allows us to go beyond our immediate environments of family, neighborhood, and work and understand the major structural transformations that have occurred and are occurring.

Sociology: The study of social behavior and human society.

Sociology of education: The study of how various individuals and institutions throughout society affect the education system and educational outcomes.

Sociotechnical system: A system that includes material artifacts, human skills, and social practices defined by social norms within an organizational pattern to obtain or address a goal or objective.

Spatial mismatch theory: The theory that the movement of jobs away from central cities in the postindustrial era left many African Americans without employment.

Specialized courts: Problem-solving courts set up within local district courts to deal with social problems affecting the surrounding communities.

Specific deterrence: A law or policy written to stop those who break laws from offending again.

Spirituality: An underlying moral or value system, which may be in the absence of membership in a religious body or attendance at religious events.

Split labor market theory: The theory that white elites encourage divisions between working-class whites and blacks so that little unity can form between the two groups, preventing their coordinated revolt against exploitation.

Sponsor activities: The work of promoting and publicizing specific media frames.

Stakeholders: All individuals who have an interest in and are affected by the workings of a given system; in the criminal justice system, stakeholders include those accused of crimes as well as those who process cases, including police, attorneys, and court and correctional staff.

Status: Social position, revolving around characteristics such as education, prestige, and religious affiliation.

Status groups: Social groups that are either negatively or positively privileged.

Stereotype threat: The tendency of individuals to perform better or worse on standardized tests depending on what they have been told about their group's abilities.

Strain theory: A theory of crime that posits individuals commit crimes because of the strains caused by the imbalance between societally accepted goals and the individuals' inadequate means to achieve those goals.

Street science: A practice of knowledge production that embraces a broad set of participatory research methods in the investigation of social scientific problems.

Stress: The negative psychological and physiological effects of difficulties at work and elsewhere.

Structural functionalism (or functionalism): The sociological theory that considers how various

social phenomena function, or work in a positive way, to maintain unity and order in society.

Structural unemployment: Unemployment that is caused by basic changes in the economy.

Student-centered explanations: Explanations of educational inequalities that focus on factors outside the school, such as the family, the community, the culture of the group, the peer group, and the individual student.

Subjective aspect of social problems: The process by which people define social problems.

Supplemental Nutrition Assistance Program (SNAP): Federal program that provides low-income Americans with subsidies for food purchases; formerly known as the food stamp program.

Supply reduction: An approach to drug policy aimed at disrupting the manufacturing and distribution supply chains of drugs.

Survey: A research method that asks respondents to answer questions on a written questionnaire.

Symbolic ethnicity: An ethnicity that is not particularly salient in an individual's daily life and becomes relevant only at certain symbolic times or events.

Symbolic interactionism: The sociological perspective that sees society as the product of symbols (words, gestures, objects) given meaning by people in their interactions with each other.

Symbols: Words, gestures, and objects to which people give meaning.

Teach for America (TFA): A nonprofit organization that recruits students and professionals from high-profile institutions, trains these individuals to enter the teaching profession, and places them in disadvantaged schools for a period of at least two years.

Technocracy: A means of governing that is guided by rationality, expertise, and logic.

Technological fix: The use of technology to solve a social problem that is nontechnical. In fixing the problem it creates another, because the underlying social issue is still present and has been isolated from the social context.

Technology: An artifact that is composed of social practices, social institutions, and systems that create and constrain it.

Technoscience: A concept that encompasses the boundary between science and technology and includes all supporters, detractors, and social relations that work to eventually close the division between the categories of science and technology.

Terrorism: Violence perpetrated for political reasons by subnational groups or secret state agents, often directed at noncombatant targets, and usually intended to influence an audience.

Theory: A collection of related concepts.

Third places: Locations that serve social needs beyond work and home life (e.g., local coffee shops).

Tokenistic fallacy: The common misunderstanding that when a small number of persons from a minority group become successful in a society there must no longer be racism in that society.

Total compensation: Remuneration that includes a wage or salary plus benefits.

Total dependency ratio: The number of children under the age of 16 and the number of older persons age 65 and over for every 100 adults ages 16 to 64.

Toxic colonialism: When toxic waste is moved from wealthy countries to economically and politically marginalized regions.

Tracking: An educational practice in which students are divided into groups, purportedly based on their academic ability.

Transactional sex: The exchange of money and gifts for sexual activities.

Transgender: Gender identity differs from the sex category assigned at birth.

Transnational crimes: Crimes that have effects across national borders.

Treadmill of production: A theory that describes the ways that production is constantly accelerating without moving forward.

Underground economy: Work that is illegal or is designed to avoid the reporting of payments to government authorities such as tax collectors. Also known as the shadow economy.

Urbanism: The ways of life or cultures of people in cities; the myths, symbols, and rituals of urbanites.

Urbanization: The movement of populations from rural to urban areas; the growth and development, and redevelopment, of cities.

User-generated media content: Publicly shared media content produced by users (often amateurs) rather than media companies.

Values: Social beliefs.

Veil: A metaphor for the physical and psychic separation between the dominant/majority group and subordinate/minority groups.

Visiting union: Unmarried parents who are romantically involved but living apart.

Wage: Payment for work done on an hourly basis.

War: Organized, collective fighting involving at least one political unit that seeks political or economic control over a territory or other important resource against another political unit or social group.

War on Drugs: The comprehensive policy first formulated by President Richard M. Nixon to address the drug problem in the 1970s.

Wealth: Assets (or possessions) or net worth (the difference between the value of assets and the amount of debt for an individual, family, or household).

Welfare state: Government provision of services essential to the well-being of large or significant segments of the population that are not possible or profitable within the private sector.

Whistle-blowing: The act of calling attention to malfeasance in one's organization.

White privilege: The often unseen or unacknowledged benefits that members of the majority group receive in a society unequally structured by race.

Workers: Those who own no property and must work for the capitalists in order to support themselves and their families financially.

REFERENCES

Abdulkadiroğlu, Atila, Weiwei Hu, and Parag A. Pathak. 2013. *Small High Schools and Student Achievement: Lottery-Based Evidence From New York City.* No. w19576. Cambridge, MA: National Bureau of Economic Research.

Abramovitz, Mimi. 2000. *Under Attack, Fighting Back: Women and Welfare in the United States.* New York: Monthly Review Press.

Abramovitz, Mimi, and Sandra Morgen. 2006. *Taxes Are a Woman's Issue: Reframing the Debate.* New York: Feminist Press at the City University of New York.

Acosta, Vivian, and Linda Jean Carpenter. 2012. *Women in Intercollegiate Sport: A Longitudinal, National Study, Thirty-five Year Update.* Accessed March 1, 2017. www.acostacarpenter.org.

Adams, Gordon. 1981. *The Politics of Defense Contracting: The Iron Triangle.* New York: Council on Economic Priorities.

Adamson, Peter. 2012. *Measuring Child Poverty: New League Tables of Child Poverty in the World's Richest Countries.* Innocenti Research Centre, Report Card 10. Florence, Italy: UNICEF. http://www.unicef-irc.org/publications/pdf/rc10_eng.pdf.

Adelman, Larry. 2003. *Race: The Power of an Illusion.* DVD. San Francisco: California Newsreel.

Adewunmi, Bim. 2014. "Kimberlé Crenshaw on Intersectionality: 'I Wanted to Come Up With an Everyday Metaphor That Anyone Could Use.'" *New Statesman.* Accessed May 23, 2017. http://www.newstatesman.com/lifestyle/2014/04/kimberl-crenshaw-intersectionality-i-wanted-come-everyday-metaphor-anyone-could.

Agnew, Robert. 1992. "Foundation for a General Strain Theory of Crime and Delinquency." *Criminology* 30 (1): 47–88.

Agustín, Laura María. 2007. *Sex at the Margins: Migration, Labour Markets and the Rescue Industry.* London: Zed Books.

Agyeman, Julian, Robert D. Bullard, and Bob Evans. 2002. "Exploring the Nexus: Bringing Together Sustainability, Environmental Justice, and Equity." *Space and Polity* 6 (1): 77–90.

Agyeman, Julian, and Tom Evans. 2003. "Toward Just Sustainability in Urban Communities: Building Equity Rights With Sustainable Solutions." *Annals of the American Academy of Political and Social Science* 590: 35–53.

Akers, Ronald. L. 1998. *Social Learning and Social Structure: A General Theory of Crime and Deviance.* Boston, MA: Northeastern University Press.

Al Jazeera. 2016. "UN Urges UK to End Xenophobic Attacks After Brexit Vote." June 28. Accessed February 27, 2017. http://www.aljazeera.com/news/2016/06/uk-xenophobic-attacks-brexit-vote-160628171147062.html.

Alan Guttmacher Institute. 2013. "Facts on American Teens' Sexual and Reproductive Health." http://www.guttmacher.org/pubs/FB-ATSRH.html.

Alba, Richard, and Victor Nee. 2003. *Remaking the American Mainstream: Assimilation and Contemporary Immigration.* Cambridge, MA: Harvard University Press.

Albanese, Jay S. 2011. *Transnational Crime and the 21st Century: Criminal Enterprise, Corruption, and Opportunity.* New York: Oxford University Press.

Alexander, Karl L., Doris R. Entwisle, and Linda S. Olson. 2001. "Schools, Achievement, and Inequality: A Seasonal Perspective." *Educational Evaluation and Policy Analysis* 23 (2): 171–91.

———. 2007. "Lasting Consequences of the Summer Learning Gap." *American Sociological Review* 72 (2): 167–80.

Alexander, Michelle. 2012. *The New Jim Crow: Mass Incarceration in the Age of Colorblindness.* New York: New Press.

Aliverdinia, Akbar, and William Alex Pridemore. 2009. "Women's Fatalistic Suicide in Iran: A Partial Test of Durkheim in an Islamic Republic." *Violence Against Women* 15 (3): 307–20.

Alkon, Alison Hope, and Julian Agyeman, eds. 2011. *Cultivating Food Justice: Race, Class, and Sustainability.* Cambridge, MA: MIT Press.

Allan, Kenneth. 2011. *The Social Lens: An Invitation to Social and Sociological Theory,* 2nd ed. Thousand Oaks, CA: Pine Forge Press.

Allcott, Hunt, and Matthew Gentzkow. 2017. "Social Media and Fake News in the 2016 Election." Working Paper. January. http://web.stanford.edu/~gentzkow/research/fakenews.pdf.

Allen, Charlotte. 2010. "The Quiet Preference for Men in Admissions." Minding the Campus, Manhattan Institute, June 7. http://www.mindingthecampus.com/originals/2010/06/the_quiet_preference_for_men_i.html.

Allen, Louisa. 2012. "Pleasure's Perils? Critically Reflecting on Pleasure's Inclusion in Sexuality Education." *Sexualities* 15 (3–4): 455–71.

Allington, Richard L., and Anne McGill-Franzen. 2003. "The Impact of Summer Reading Setback on the Reading Achievement Gap." *Phi Delta Kappan* 85 (1): 68–75.

Allison, Rachel, and Barbara J. Risman. 2013. "A Double Standard for 'Hooking Up': How Far Have We Come Toward Gender Equality?" *Social Science Research* 42 (5): 1191–1206.

———. 2014. "'It Goes Hand in Hand With the Parties': Race, Class, and Residence in College Student Negotiations of Hooking Up." *Sociological Perspectives* 57 (1): 102–23.

Allport, Gordon. 1954. *The Nature of Prejudice.* Cambridge, MA: Addison-Wesley.

Almodovar, Norma Jean. 2010. "The Consequences of Arbitrary and Selective Enforcement of Prostitution Laws." *Wagadu. A Journal of Transnational Women's and Gender Studies* 8: 241–57.

Alter, Charlotte. 2017. "How the Women's March Has United Progressives of All Stripes." *Time,* January 20. Accessed March 1, 2017. http://time.com/4641575/womens-march-washington-coalition.

Altheide, David L. 2002. *Creating Fear: News and the Construction of Crisis.* Piscataway, NJ: Aldine Transaction.

———. 2009. "Moral Panic: From Sociological Concept to Public Discourse." *Crime, Media, Culture* 5 (1): 79–99.

Alvaredo, Facundo, Anthony B. Atkinson, Thomas Piketty, and Emmanuel Saez. 2013. "The Top 1 Percent in International and Historical Perspective." *Journal of Economic Perspectives* 27 (3): 3–20.

Alvarez, Maria João, and Leonel Garcia-Marques. 2008. "Condom Inclusion in Cognitive Representations of Sexual Encounters." *Journal of Sex Research* 45 (4): 358–70.

American Academy of Pediatrics. 2012. "Familiarity With Television Fast-Food Ads Linked to Obesity." April 29. http://www.aap.org/en-us/about-the-aap/aap-press-room/pages/Familiarity-With-Television-Fast-Food-Ads-Linked-to-Obesity.aspx.

American Bar Association. 2013a. *A Current Glance at Women in the Law, February 2013.* Chicago: ABA, Commission on Women in the Profession. http://www.americanbar.org/content/dam/aba/marketing/women/current_glance_statistics_feb2013.authcheckdam.pdf.

———. 2013b. "Statistics From the ABA Commission on Women. February. Accessed December 16, 2013. http://www.americanbar.org/content/dam/aba/marketing/women/current_glance_statistics_feb2013.authcheckdam.pdf

American Bar Association, Section of Family Law. 2012. "Family Law in the Fifty States: Case Digests." *Family Law Quarterly* 45. http://www.americanbar.org/content/dam/aba/publications/family_law_quarterly/v0145/4win12_chart4_divorce.authcheckdam.pdf.

American Educational Research Association. 2015. (December 7, 2015). *How the Science on Diversity and Affirmative Action Matters to Fisher v. University of Texas, Austin.* Paper presented at the Bringing Science to Bear on Fisher vs. UT-Austin, Washington, D.C.

American Psychiatric Association. 2013a. *Highlights of Changes From DSM-IV-TR to DSM-5.* Arlington, VA: American Psychiatric Association. http://www.dsm5.org/Documents/changes%20from%20dsm-iv-tr%20to%20dsm-5.pdf.

———. 2013b. *Diagnostic and Statistical Manual of Mental Disorders,* 5th ed. Washington, DC: American Psychiatric Association.

———. 2013c. "Paraphilic Disorders." Accessed May 25, 2017. (file:///C:/Users/elroi.windsor/Downloads/APA_DSM-5–Paraphilic-Disorders.pdf).

Amster, Randall. 2004. *Street People and the Contested Realms of Public Space.* El Paso, TX: LFB Scholarly Publishing.

Anderson, Elijah. 1990. *Streetwise: Race, Class, and Change in an Urban Community.* Chicago: University of Chicago Press.

———. 1999. *Code of the Street: Decency, Violence, and the Moral Life of the Inner City.* New York: W. W. Norton.

Andolfatto, David, and Andrew Spewack. 2017. "Why Do Unemployment Rates Vary by Race and Ethnicity?" Federal Reserve Bank of St. Louis. February 6. Accessed May 29, 2017. https://www.stlouisfed.org/on-the-economy/2017/february/why-unemployment-rates-vary-races-ethnicity.

Andreas, Peter. 2008. *Blue Helmets and Black Markets: The Business of Survival in the Siege of Sarajevo.* Ithaca, NY: Cornell University Press.

Angell, Marcia. 2005. *The Truth About Drug Companies: How They Deceive Us and What to Do About It.* New York: Random House.

Angelon-Gaetz, Kim A., David B. Richardson, and Steve Wing. 2010. "Inequalities in the Nuclear Age: Impact of Race and Gender on Radiation Exposure at the Savannah River Site (1951–1999)." *New Solutions* 20 (2): 195–210.

Anyon, Jean. 1980. "Social Class and the Hidden Curriculum of Work." *Journal of Education* 162 (1): 67–92.

———. 1981. "Social Class and School Knowledge." *Curriculum Inquiry* 11 (1): 3–42.

———. 1997. *Ghetto Schooling: A Political Economy of Urban Educational Reform.* New York: Teachers College Press.

———. 2005. *Radical Possibilities: Public Policy, Urban Education, and a New Social Movement.* New York: Routledge.

Arar, J. I. 2010. "New Directions: The Electric Car and Carbon Emissions in the US." *Atmospheric Environment* 44 (5): 733–34.

Archdiocese of Minneapolis and Saint Paul. 2010. *Preserving Marriage in Minnesota.* DVD. Minneapolis and Saint Paul, Office of the Archbishop (John C. Nienstedt).

Armstrong, Elizabeth A., Paula England, and Alison C. K. Fogarty. 2012a. "Accounting for Women's Orgasm and Sexual Enjoyment in College Hookups and Relationships." *American Sociological Review* 77 (3): 435–62.

———. 2012b. "Orgasm in College Hookups and Relationships." In *Families as They Really Are,* edited by Barbara Risman, 362–77. New York: W. W. Norton.

Armstrong, Elizabeth A., and Laura T. Hamilton. 2013. *Paying for the Party: How College Maintains Inequality.* Cambridge, MA: Harvard University Press.

Armstrong, Elizabeth A., Laura Hamilton, and Brian Sweeney. 2006. "Sexual Assault on Campus: A Multilevel, Integrative Approach to Party Rape." *Social Problems* 53 (4): 483–99.

Arnold, Ryan. 2013. "Persistent Rape Culture at Amherst College." *AC Voice,* April 24. http://acvoice.com/2013/04/24/persistent-rape-culture-at-amherst-college.

Arnot, Madeleine. 2002. *Reproducing Gender: Selected Critical Essays on Educational Theory and Feminist Politics.* London: Falmer.

Associated Press. 2003. "Racial Profiling Study: Police Stop Minorities More Often Than Whites." *Brainerd Dispatch,* September 24.

Association of American Medical Colleges. 2017. "Women in U.S. Academic Medicine and Science: Statistics and Benchmarking Report 2011–2012. Table 1: Medical Students Selected Years 2013, 1965–2012." https://www.aamc.org/members/gwims/statistics/.

Association of Religion Data Archives. 2010. "U.S. Membership Report." http://thearda.com/rcms2010/r/u/rcms2010_99_US_name_2010.asp.

Atchley, Robert C. 1989. "A Continuity Theory of Normal Aging." *Gerontologist* 29 (2): 183–90.

Aubrey, Jennifer Stevens, and Siobhan E. Smith. 2013. "Development and Validation of the Endorsement of the Hookup Culture Index." *Journal of Sex Research* 50 (5): 435–48.

Aud, Susan, Mary Ellen Fox, and Angelina KewalRamani. 2010. *Status and Trends in the Education of Racial and Ethnic Groups.* U.S. Department of Education, National Center for Education Statistics, NCES 2010–015. Washington, DC: Government Printing Office. http://nces.ed.gov/pubs2010/2010015.pdf.

Aud, Susan, William Hussar, Frank Johnson, Grace Kena, Erin Roth, Eileen Manning, Xiaolei Wang, and Jijun Zhang. 2012. *The Condition of Education 2012.* U.S. Department of Education, National Center for Education Statistics, NCES 2012–045. Washington, DC: Government Printing Office. http://nces.ed.gov/pubs2012/2012045.pdf.

AugsJoost, Brett, Petra Jerman, Julianna Deardorff, Kim Harley, and Norman A. Constantine. 2014. "Factors Associated

With Parent Support for Condom Education and Availability." *Health Education and Behavior* 41 (2): 207–15.

Australian Institute of Health and Welfare. 2006. *Australia's Health 2006: The Tenth Biennial Health Report of the Australian Institute of Health and Welfare.* AIHW Cat. No. AUS 73. Canberra: Australian Institute of Health and Welfare.

Australian Safety and Compensation Council. 2006. Estimating the Number of Work Related Traumatic Injury Fatalities in Australia 2003–04. Canberra: Commonwealth of Australia.

Autor, David, and Melanie Wasserman. 2013. *Wayward Sons: The Emerging Gender Gap in Labor Markets and Education.* Washington, DC: Third Way. http://economics.mit.edu/files/8754.

Avis, Nancy E., and Sybil Crawford. 2008. "Cultural Differences in Symptoms and Attitudes Toward Menopause." *Menopause Management* 17 (3): 8–13.

Bachman, Ronet, and Michelle Meloy. 2008. "The Epidemiology of Violence Against the Elderly: Implications for Primary and Secondary Prevention." *Journal of Contemporary Criminal Justice* 24 (2): 186–97.

Baker, David, and Gerald K. LeTendre. 2005. *National Differences, Global Similarities: World Culture and the Future of Schooling.* Stanford, CA: Stanford Social Sciences.

Baker, Peter. 2013. "Pivoting From a War Footing, Obama Acts to Curtail Drones." *New York Times,* May 23, 1.

Balderrama, Anthony. 2010. "Is Getting a Job Really About Who You Know?" CNN. September 16. Accessed January 12, 2017. http://economics.mit.edu/files/8754.

Baldwin, Laura-Mae, David C. Grossman, Susan Casey, Walter Hollow, Jonathan R. Sugarman, William L. Freeman, and L. Gary Hart. 2002. "Perinatal and Infant Health Among Rural and Urban American Indians/Alaska Natives." *American Journal of Public Health* 92 (9): 1491–97.

Ballantine, Jeanne H., Floyd M. Hammack, and Jenny Stuber. 2017. *The Sociology of Education: A Systematic Analysis,* 8th ed. New York: Routledge.

Banks, Duren, and Denise C. Gottfredson. 2004. "Participation in Drug Treatment Court and Time to Rearrest." *Justice Quarterly* 21 (3): 637–58.

Barnes, Brooks. 2012. "Promoting Nutrition: Disney to Restrict Junk-Food Ads." *New York Times,* June 5, B1.

Barnes, Patricia M., Barbara Bloom, and Richard L. Nahin. 2008. *Complementary and Alternative Medicine Use Among Adults and Children: United States, 2007.* National Health Statistics Reports 12 (December 10). Hyattsville, MD: National Center for Health Statistics. http://www.cdc.gov/nchs/data/nhsr/nhsr012.pdf.

Barnett, J., and W. N. Adger. 2007. "Climate Change, Human Security and Violent Conflict." *Political Geography* 26 (6): 639–55.

Barnett, Jessica C., and Marina S. Vornovitsky. 2016. "Health Insurance Coverage in the United States: 2015." U.S. Census Bureau, Current Population Reports, Report (P60–257). Accessed June 1, 2017. http://www.khi.org/assets/uploads/news/14561/p60–257.pdf.

Bartholow, Bruce D., Marc A. Sestir, and Edward B. Davis. 2005. "Correlates and Consequences of Exposure to Video Game Violence: Hostile Personality, Empathy, and Aggressive Behavior." *Personality and Social Psychology Bulletin* 31 (11): 1573–86.

Bash, Michael Rodning. 2012. "Avoid This Concept in Defining Marriage: 'Natural.'" *Star Tribune,* November 2. http://www.startribune.com/opinion/commentaries/177031211.html.

Bassett, Laura. 2010. "Study: Longterm Unemployment Has Disastrous Effects on Health and Longevity." *Huffington Post,* November 5. http://www.huffingtonpost.com/2010/11/05/study-longterm-unemployme_n_779743.html.

BBC News. 2013a. "Same-Sex Marriage Becomes Law in England and Wales." July 17. http://www.bbc.com/news/uk-politics-23338279.

———. 2013b. "Same-Sex Marriage: French Parliament Approves New Law." April 23. http://www.bbc.com/news/world-europe-22261494.

Beauregard, Robert A. 2011. "Radical Uniqueness and the Flight of Urban Theory." In *The City, Revisited: Urban Theory From Chicago, Los Angeles, and New York,* edited by Dennis R. Judd and Dick Simpson, 186–202. Minneapolis: University of Minnesota Press.

Beccaria, C. 1764. *On Crimes and Punishments.* Translated by H. Paolucci. New York: Macmillan. 1963.

Beck, Harold L., and Burton G. Bennett. 2002. "Historical Overview of Atmospheric Nuclear Weapons Testing and Estimates of Fallout in the Continental United States." *Health Physics* 82 (5): 591–608.

Beck, Ulrich. 1992. *Risk Society: Towards a New Modernity.* London: Sage.

Beck, Ulrich, Anthony Giddens, and Scott Lash. 1994. *Reflexive Modernization: Politics, Tradition and Aesthetics in the Modern Social Order.* Cambridge: Polity Press.

Becker, Howard S. 1963a. "Becoming a Marihuana User." In *Outsiders: Studies in the Sociology of Deviance,* 41–58. New York: Macmillan.

———. 1963b. *Outsiders: Studies in the Sociology of Deviance.* New York: Macmillan.

Becker, Jo, and Scott Shane. 2012. "Secret 'Kill List' Proves a Test of Obama's Principles and Will." *New York Times,* May 29.

Beckett, Katherine, Kris Nyrop, Lori Pfingst, and Melissa Bowen. 2005. "Drug Use, Drug Possession Arrests, and the Question of Race: Lessons From Seattle." *Social Problems* 52 (3): 419–41.

Belknap, Joanne. 2007. "Culturally Focused Batterer Counseling." *Criminology & Public Policy* 6 (2): 337–40.

Belknap, R. A., and N. Cruz. 2007. "When I Was in My Home I Suffered a Lot: Mexican Women's Descriptions of Abuse in Family of Origin." *Health Care for Women International* 28 (5): 506–22.

Bell, Michael Mayerfeld. 2004. *Farming for Us All: Practical Agriculture and the Cultivation of Sustainability.* University Park: Pennsylvania State University Press.

———. 2012. *An Invitation to Environmental Sociology,* 4th ed. Thousand Oaks, CA: Pine Forge Press.

Bell, Michael Mayerfeld, and Philip Lowe. 2000. "Regulated Freedoms: The Market and the State, Agriculture and the Environment." *Journal of Rural Studies* 16 (3): 285–94.

Belz, A. 2015. "On the Road Again." *Star Tribune,* May 23, A1, A6.

Benach, Joan, and Carles Muntaner. 2007. "Precarious Employment and Health: Developing a Research Agenda." *Journal of Epidemiology and Community Health* 61: 276–77.

Benbow, Candice Marie. 2016. "Lemonade Syllabus: A Collection of Works Celebrating Black Womanhood." Accessed April 15, 2017. https://gisellepr.files.wordpress.com/2016/05/lemonade-syllabus.pdf.

Bengtson, Vern L., Norella M. Putney, and Malcolm L. Johnson. 2005. "The Problem of Theory in Gerontology Today." In *The Cambridge Handbook of Age and Ageing,* edited by Malcolm L. Johnson, 3–20. Cambridge: Cambridge University Press.

Bennett, James T., and Bruce E., Kaufman, eds. 2007. *What Do Unions Do? A Twenty-Year Perspective.* New Brunswick, NJ: Transaction Books.

Bennett, Lisa, and Gary J. Gates. 2004. *The Cost of Marriage Inequality to Children and Their Same-Sex Parents.* Washington, DC: Human Rights Campaign.

Berkowitz, Bill. 2002. "The Mullahs of Marriage." *The Nation,* May 14. Accessed July 9, 2010. www.thenation.com/article/mullahs-marriage.

Berkowitz, Dan, and William Marsiglio. 2007. "Gay Men: Negotiating Procreative, Father, and Family Identities." *Journal of Marriage and Family* 69: 366–81.

Berkowitz, Dana. 2011. "Maternal Instincts, Biological Clocks, and Soccer Moms: Gay Men's Parenting and Family Narratives." *Symbolic Interaction* 34 (4): 514–35.

Berkowitz, Eric. 2012. *Sex and Punishment: Four Thousand Years of Judging Desire.* Berkeley, CA: Counterpoint Press.

Berliner, David C. 2006. "Our Impoverished View of Educational Research." *Teachers College Record* 108 (6): 949–95.

Berliner, David C., and Bruce J. Biddle. 1995. *The Manufactured Crisis: Myths, Fraud, and the Attack on America's Public Schools.* Reading, MA: Addison-Wesley.

Bernstein, Basil. 1973a. *Class, Codes and Control.* Vol. 1, *Theoretical Studies Towards a Sociology of Language.* London: Routledge & Kegan Paul. First published 1971.

———. 1973b. *Class, Codes and Control.* Vol. 2, *Applied Studies Towards a Sociology of Language.* London: Routledge & Kegan Paul. First published 1971.

———. 1977a. "Class and Pedagogies: Visible and Invisible" (rev. ed.). In *Class, Codes and Control.* Vol. 3, *Towards a Theory of Educational Transmissions,* 116–56. London: Routledge & Kegan Paul.

———. 1977b. *Class, Codes and Control.* Vol. 3, *Towards a Theory of Educational Transmissions.* London: Routledge & Kegan Paul. First published 1975.

———. 1990. "Social Class and Pedagogic Practice." In *Class, Codes and Control.* Vol. 4, *The Structuring of Pedagogic Discourse,* 63–93. London: Routledge.

———. 1996. *Pedagogy, Symbolic Control and Identity: Theory, Research, Critique.* London: Taylor & Francis.

Bersamin, Melina M., Mallie J. Paschall, Robert F. Saltz, and Byron L. Zamboanga. 2012. "Young Adults and Casual Sex: The Relevance of College Drinking Settings." *Journal of Sex Research* 49 (2–3): 274–81.

Bertrand, Marianne, and Sendhil Mullainathan. 2004. "Are Emily and Greg More Employable Than Lakisha and Jamal? A Field Experiment on Labor Market Discrimination." *American Economic Review* 94 (4): 991–1013.

Best, Joel. 1999. *Random Violence: How We Talk About New Crimes and New Victims.* Berkeley: University of California Press.

Bettie, Julie. 2003. *Women Without Class: Girls, Race, and Identity.* Berkeley: University of California Press.

Bewley-Taylor, Dave, Chris Hallam, and Rob Allen. 2009. *The Incarceration of Drug Offenders: An Overview.* London: Beckley Foundation Drug Policy Programme.

Biblarz, Timothy, and Evren Savci. 2010. "Lesbian, Gay, Bisexual, and Transgender Families." *Journal of Marriage and Family* 72 (3): 480–97.

Binh, Vu Ngoc. 2006. "Trafficking of Women and Children in Vietnam: Current Issues and Problems." In *Trafficking and the Global Sex Industry,* edited by Karen Beeks and Delila Amir, 33–43. Lanham, MD: Lexington Books.

Binkley, Collin, and Errin Haines Whack. 2015. "In the Wake of Missouri Uproar, Black Students Around U.S. Complain of Casual, Everyday Racism." *U.S. News and World Report,* November 12. Accessed March 1, 2017. https://www.usnews.com/news/us/articles/2015/11/12/missouri-protests-embolden-student-leaders-on-other-campuses.

Bix, Amy Sue. 2000. *Inventing Ourselves Out of Jobs? America's Debate Over Technological Unemployment, 1929–1981.* Baltimore: Johns Hopkins University Press.

Black, Michele C., Kathleen C. Basile, Matthew J. Breiding, Sharon G. Smith, Mikel L. Walters, Melissa T. Merrick, Jieru Chen, and Mark R. Stevens. 2011. *The National Intimate Partner and Sexual Violence Survey (NISVS): 2010 Summary Report.* Atlanta, GA: National Center for Injury Prevention and Control, Centers for Disease Control and Prevention. http://www.cdc.gov/ViolencePrevention/pdf/NISVS_Report2010–a.pdf.

Blair-Loy, Mary. 2003. *Competing Devotions: Career and Family Among Women Executives.* Cambridge, MA: Harvard University Press.

Blakeborough, Darren. 2008. "'Old People Are Useless': Representations of Aging on *The Simpsons.*" *Canadian Journal on Aging* 27 (1): 57–67.

Blanchflower, David G., and Alex Bryson. 2007 "What Effect Do Unions Have on Wages Now and Would Freeman and Medoff Be Surprised?" In *What Do Unions Do? A Twenty-Year Perspective,* edited by James T. Bennett and Bruce E. Kaufman, 79–113. New Brunswick, NJ: Transaction.

Blascovich, Jim, Steven J. Spencer, Diane Quinn, and Claude Steele. 2001. "African Americans and High Blood Pressure: The Role of Stereotype Threat." *Psychological Science* 12 (3): 225–29.

Blauner, Bob. 1996. "Talking Past Each Other: Black and White Languages of Race." In *The Meaning of Difference: American Constructions of Race, Sex and Gender, Social Class, and Sexual Orientation,* edited by Karen E. Rosenblum and Toni-Michelle C. Travis, 167–76. New York: McGraw-Hill.

Blow, Charles M. 2012. "The Curious Case of Trayvon Martin." *New York Times,* March 16. http://www.nytimes.com/2012/03/17/opinion/blow-the-curious-case-of-trayvon-martin.html.

Blumer, Herbert. 1933. *Movies, Delinquency, and Crime.* New York: Macmillan.

———. 1971. "Social Problems as Collective Behavior." *Social Problems* 18: 298–306.

Blumstein, Alfred, and Joel Wallman. 2000. "The Recent Rise and Fall of American Violence." In *The Crime Drop in America,* edited by Alfred Blumstein and Joel Wallman, 1–12. New York: Cambridge University Press.

Boak, J., and E. Swanson. 2016. "Survey Shows Economic Concerns Continue." *Star Tribune,* May 19, D6.

Bobel, Chris. 2010. *New Blood: Third-Wave Feminism and the Politics of Menstruation*. Brunswick, NJ: Rutgers University Press.

Bobo, Kim. 2009. *Wage Theft in America: Why Millions of Working Americans Are Not Getting Paid—and What We Can Do About It*. New York: New Press.

Bodenheimer, Thomas, and Kevin Grumbach. 2016. *Understanding Health Policy: A Clinical Approach*. 7th ed. New York: McGraw Hill Education.

Boero, Natalie, and C. J. Pascoe. 2012. "Pro-anorexia Communities and Online Interaction: Bringing the Pro-ana Body Online." *Body & Society* 18 (2): 27–57.

Bogenschneider, Karen, and Thomas J. Corbett. 2010. "Becoming a Field of Inquiry and a Subfield of Social Policy." *Journal of Marriage and Family* 72: 783–803.

Bogle, Kathleen A. 2008. *Hooking Up: Sex, Dating, and Relationships on Campus*. New York: New York University Press.

Bonacich, Edna. 1972. "A Theory of Ethnic Antagonism: The Split Labor Market." *American Sociological Review* 37: 547–59.

Bonacich, Edna, and John Modell. 1980. *The Economic Basis of Ethnic Solidarity: Small Business in the Japanese American Community*. Berkeley: University of California Press.

Bonczar, Thomas P. 2003. *Prevalence of Imprisonment in the U.S. Population, 1974–2001*. U.S. Bureau of Justice Statistics, NCJ 1979-76. Washington, DC: U.S. Department of Justice. http://www.bjs.gov/content/pub/pdf/piusp01.pdf.

Bongaarts, John. 2004. "Population Aging and the Rising Cost of Public Pensions." *Population and Development Review* 30 (1): 1–23.

Bonilla-Silva, Eduardo. 2001. *White Supremacy and Racism in the Post–Civil Rights Era*. Boulder, CO: Lynne Rienner.

———. 2013. *Racism Without Racists: Color-Blind Racism and the Persistence of Racial Inequality in America*. Lanham, MD: Rowman and Littlefield.

Borer, Michael Ian. 2008. *Faithful to Fenway: Believing in Boston, Baseball, and America's Most Beloved Ballpark*. New York: New York University Press.

———. 2010. "From Collective Memory to Collective Imagination: Time, Place, and Urban Redevelopment." *Symbolic Interaction* 33 (1): 96–114.

Borer, Michael Ian, and Daniel J. Monti Jr. 2006. "Community, Commerce, and Consumption: Businesses as Civic Associations." In *Varieties of Urban Experience: The American City and the Practice of Culture*, edited by Michael Ian Borer. Lanham, MD: University Press of America.

Borman, Geoffrey, and Maritza Dowling. 2010. "Schools and Inequality: A Multilevel Analysis of Coleman's Equality of Educational Opportunity Data." *Teachers College Record* 112 (5): 1201–46.

Bornstein, Kate. 1994. *Gender Outlaw: On Men, Women, and the Rest of Us*. New York: Vintage Books.

Bourdieu, Pierre. 1977. *Outline of a Theory of Practice*. Cambridge: Cambridge University Press.

———. 1980. *The Logic of Practice*. Stanford, CA: Stanford University Press.

———. 1984. *Distinction: A Social Critique of the Judgment of Taste*. Cambridge, MA: Harvard University Press.

Bourdieu, Pierre, and Jean-Claude Passeron. 1977. *Reproduction in Education, Society and Culture*. London: Sage.

Bourgois, Philippe. 1995. *In Search of Respect: Selling Crack in El Barrio*. Cambridge: Cambridge University Press.

Bourgois, Philippe, and Jeff Schonberg. 2009. *Righteous Dopefiend*. Berkeley: University of California Press.

Bowleg, Lisa, Kenya J. Lucas, and Jeanne M. Tschann. 2004. "'The Ball Was Always in His Court': An Exploratory Analysis of Relationship Scripts, Sexual Scripts, and Condom Use Among African American Women." *Psychology of Women Quarterly* 28 (1): 70–82.

Bowles, Samuel, and Herbert Gintis. 1976. *Schooling in Capitalist America: Educational Reform and the Contradictions of Economic Life*. New York: Basic Books.

boyd, danah. 2014. *It's Complicated: The Social Lives of Networked Teens*. New Haven, CT: Yale University Press.

Boyle, Justin. 2013. "Millions of Americans Looking to Change Careers, Study Shows." Degree360, July 15. http://www.onlinedegrees.com/degree360/workplace/millions-of-americans-looking-to-change-careers.html.

Braga, Anthony A., and David L. Weisburd. 2010. *Policing Problem Places: Crime Hot Spots and Effective Prevention*. New York: Oxford University Press.

Brents, Barbara G., and Kathryn Hausbeck. 2005. "Violence and Legalized Brothel Prostitution in Nevada: Examining Safety, Risk, and Prostitution Policy." *Journal of Interpersonal Violence* 20 (3): 270–95.

Breslau, Daniel. 2007. "The American Spencerians: Theorizing a New Science." In *Sociology in America: A History*, edited by Craig Calhoun, 39–62. Chicago: University of Chicago Press.

Brewis, Joanna, and Stephen Linstead. 2000. "'The Worst Thing Is the Screwing': Consumption and the Management of Identity in Sex Work." *Gender, Work & Organization* 7 (2): 84–97.

Brezina, Corona. 2005. *Sojourner Truth's "Ain't I a Woman?" Speech: A Primary Source Investigation*. New York: The Rosen Publishing Group.

Bricker, Jesse, Lisa J. Dettling, Alice Henriques, Joanne W. Hsu, Kevin B. Moore, John Sabelhaus, Jeffrey Thompson, and Richard A. Windle. 2014. "Changes in U.S. Family Finances From 2010 to 2013: Evidence From the Survey of Consumer Finances." *Federal Reserve Bulletin* 100 (4): 1–41.

Bricker, Jesse, Alice Henriques, Jacob Krimmel, and John Sabelhaus. 2016. "Measuring Income and Wealth at the Top Using Administrative and Survey Data." *Brookings Papers on Economic Activity* 2016 (1): 261–331.

Bricker, Jesse, Arthur B. Kennickell, Kevin B. Moore, and John Sabelhaus. 2012. "Changes in U.S. Family Finances From 2007 to 2010: Evidence From the Survey of Consumer Finances." *Federal Reserve Bulletin* 98 (2): 1–80. http://www.federalreserve.gov/pubs/bulletin/2012/pdf/scf12.pdf.

Bridger, Jeffrey C. 1996. "Community Imagery and the Built Environment." *Sociological Quarterly* 37 (3): 353–74.

Bridges, Ana J., Robert Wosnitzer, Erica Scharrer, Chyng Sun, and Rachael Liberman. 2010. "Aggression and Sexual Behavior in Best-Selling Pornography Videos: A Content Analysis Update." *Violence Against Women* 16 (10): 1065–85.

Bridges, Tristan. 2017. "Why People Are So Averse to Facts." *Sociological Images*. February 27. https://thesocietypages.org/socimages/2017/02/27/why-the-american-public-seems-allergic-to-facts/.

Briggs, Laura. 2012. *Somebody's Children: The Politics of Transnational and Transracial Adoption.* Durham, NC: Duke University Press.

Bright, Sam. 2017. "One Solution to Two Big Social Problems." *BBC News Magazine.* January 20. http://www.bbc.com/news/magazine-38399246.

Brint, Steven G. 2006. *Schools and Societies,* 2nd ed. Stanford, CA: Stanford University Press.

British Psychological Society. 2011. "Response to the American Psychiatric Association: DSM-5 Development." http://apps.bps .org.uk/_publicationfiles/consultation -responses/DSM-5%202011%20−%20 BPS%20response.pdf.

Britz, Jennifer Delahunty. 2006. "To All the Girls I've Rejected." *New York Times,* March 23. http://www.nytimes.com/2006/03/23/opinion/23britz.html?_r=1.

Broaddus, Michelle R., Heather Morris, and Angela D. Bryan. 2010. "'It's Not What You Said, It's How You Said It': Perceptions of Condom Proposers by Gender and Strategy." *Sex Roles* 62 (9–10): 603–14.

Brooks, Siobhan. 2010. "Hypersexualization and the Dark Body: Race and Inequality Among Black and Latina Women in the Exotic Dance Industry." *Sexuality Research and Social Policy* 7 (2): 70–80.

Broom, Alex. 2005. "Medical Specialists' Accounts of the Impact of the Internet on the Doctor/Patient Relationship." *Health* 9 (3): 319–38.

Brosius, Hans-Bernd, and Hans Mathias Kepplinger. 1990. "The Agenda Setting Function of Television News: Static and Dynamic Views." *Communication Research* 17 (2): 183–211.

Brown, Jane D., and Piotr S. Bobkowski. 2011. "Older and Newer Media: Patterns of Use and Effects on Adolescents' Health and Well-Being." *Journal of Research on Adolescence* 21 (1): 95–113.

Brunkard, Joan, Gonza Namulanda, and Raoult Ratard. 2008. "Hurricane Katrina Deaths, Louisiana, 2005." *Disaster Medicine and Public Health Preparedness* 2 (4): 215–23.

Bryant, Clifton D., and Kenneth B. Perkins. 1982. "Containing Work Disaffection: The Poultry Processing Worker." In *Varieties of Work,* edited by Phyllis L. Stewart and Muriel G. Cantor, 199–212. Beverly Hills, CA: Sage.

Brynjolffson, Erik, and Andrew McAfee. 2011. *Race Against the Machine.* Lexington, MA: Digital Frontier Press.

Bubolz, Margaret M., and M. Suzanne Sontag. 1993. "Human Ecology Theory." In *Sourcebook of Family Theories and Methods: A Contextual Approach,* edited by Pauline G. Boss, William J. Doherty, Ralph LaRossa, Walter R. Schumm, and Suzanne K. Steinmetz, 419–48. New York: Plenum.

Budd, John W. 2007. "The Effect of Unions on Non-wage Compensation: Monopoly Power, Collective Voice, and Facilitation." In *What Do Unions Do? A Twenty-Year Perspective,* edited by James T. Bennett and Bruce E. Kaufman. New Brunswick, NJ: Transaction.

Budrys, Grace. 2012. *Our Unsystematic Health Care System,* 3rd ed. Lanham, MD: Rowman & Littlefield.

Buhaug, Halvard, Nils Petter Gleditsch, and Ole Magnus Theisen. 2010. "Implications of Climate Change for Armed Conflict." In *Social Dimensions of Climate Change: Equity and Vulnerability in a Warming World,* edited by Robin Mearns and Andrew Norton, 75–102. Washington, DC: World Bank.

Bullard, Robert. 2000. *Dumping in Dixie: Race, Class, and Environmental Quality.* Boulder, CO: Westview Press.

Burch, K. 2012. "Consumer Perceptions and Behaviors Related to Radionuclide Contaminated Food: An Exploratory Study From Kansai, Japan." Master's thesis, Norwegian University of Life Sciences.

———. 2016. "Fighting for Food Safety in Post-Fukushima Japan: How Consumers Are Challenging the Governance and Regulation of Radionuclides in the Food System." In *Third ISA Forum of Sociology* July 10–14.

Burch, K., K. Legun, and H. Campbell. 2017. "Not Defined by the Numbers: Authenticity and Democracy in Debating the Data." In *Agri-environmental Governance as an Assemblage: Multiplicity, Power, and Transformation,* edited by Forney, Rosin, and Campbell. London: Routledge.

Burgard, Sarah. 2012. "Is the Recession Making Us Sick?" *Pathways* (Fall): 19–23.

Burgess, Diana J., Yingmei Ding, Margaret Hargreaves, Michelle van Ryn, and Sean Phelan. 2008. "The Association Between Perceived Discrimination and Underutilization of Needed Medical and Mental Health Care in a Multi-Ethnic Community Sample." *Journal of Health Care for the Poor and Underserved* 19 (3): 894–911.

Burgess, Ernest W. 1925. "The Growth of the City: An Introduction to a Research Project." In *The City,* by Robert E. Park, Ernest W. Burgess, and Roderick D. McKenzie, 47–62. Chicago: University of Chicago Press.

Burk, James. 2008. "Military Culture." In *Encyclopedia of Violence, Peace, and Conflict,* edited by Lester Kurtz. Oxford: Elsevier Science and Technology.

Bursik, Robert J., andHarold G. Grasmick. 1993. *Neighborhoods and Crime: The Dimensions of Effective Social Control.* Lanham, MD: Lexington Books.

Cage, Diana. 2014. *Lesbian Sex Bible: The New Guide to Sexual Love for Same-Sex Couples.* Beverly, MA: Quiver.

Calhoun, Craig. 2007. "Sociology in America: An Introduction." In *Sociology in America: A History,* edited by Craig Calhoun, 1–38. Chicago: University of Chicago Press.

Callon, Michel. 1999. "Actor-Network Theory: The Market Test." In John Law and John Hassard. (Eds.), *Actor Network Theory and After* (pp. 181–195): Oxford Blackwell Publishers.

Callon, Michel, John Law, and Arie Rip. 1986. *Mapping the Dynamics of Science and Technology: Sociology of Science in the Real World.* Basingstoke, England: Macmillan.

Calnan, Michael, and Sarah Cant. 1990. "The Social Organisation of Food Consumption: A Comparison of Middle Class and Working Class Households." *International Journal of Sociology and Social Policy* 10 (2): 53–79.

Camacho, David E., ed. 1998. *Environmental Injustices, Political Struggles: Race, Class, and the Environment.* Durham, NC: Duke University Press.

Campbell, Scott. 1996. "Green Cities, Growing Cities, Just Cities? Urban Planning and the Contradictions of Sustainable Development." *Journal of the American Planning Association* 62 (3): 296–312.

CareerBuilder. 2013. "More Employers Finding Reasons Not to Hire Candidates on Social Media, Finds CareerBuilder Survey." June 27. http://www.career builder

.com/share/aboutus/pressreleasesdetail
.aspx?sd=6%2F26%2F2013&
id=pr766&ed=12%2F31%2F2013.

Carnagey, Nicholas L., Craig A. Anderson, and Brad J. Bushman. 2007. "The Effect of Video Game Violence on Physiological Desensitization to Real-Life Violence." *Journal of Experimental Social Psychology* 43 (3): 489–96.

Carnevale, Anthony P., Stephen J. Rose, and Ban Cheah. 2011. *The College Payoff: Education, Occupations, Lifetime Earnings*. Washington, DC: Georgetown University Center on Education and the Workforce.

Carolan, Brian V. 2012. "An Examination of the Relationship Among High School Size, Social Capital, and Adolescents' Mathematics Achievement." *Journal of Research on Adolescence* 22 (3): 583–95.

Carrigan, Mark. 2011. "There's More to Life Than Sex? Difference and Commonality Within the Asexual Community." *Sexualities* 14 (4): 462–78.

Carson, E. Ann, and Elizabeth Anderson. 2016. "Prisoners in 2015." *U.S. Bureau of Justice Statistics*. Accessed June 1, 2017. https://www.bjs.gov/index .cfm?ty=pbdetail&iid=5869.

Carson, E. Ann, and William J. Sabol. 2012. *Prisoners in 2011* Bureau of Justice Statistics Bulletin NCJ 239808, December. Washington, DC: U.S. Department of Justice. http://www.bjs.gov/content/pub/ pdf/p11.pdf.

Carson, Rachel. 1962. *Silent Spring*. Boston: Houghton Mifflin.

Carter, Prudence L. 2005. *Keepin' It Real: School Success Beyond Black and White*. New York: Oxford University Press.

———. 2006. "Intersecting Identities: 'Acting White,' Gender, and Academic Achievement." In *Beyond Acting White: Reframing the Debate on Black Student Achievement*, edited by Horvat, Erin McNamara, and Carla O'Connor, 111–132. Lanham, MD: Rowman & Littlefield.

Carter, Vednita, and Evelyn Giobbe. 2006. "Duet: Prostitution, Racism, and Feminist Discourse." In *Prostitution and Pornography. Philosophical Debate About the Sex Industry*, edited by Jessica Spector, 17–39. Stanford, CA: Stanford University Press.

Cartwright, Samuel. 1851. "Report on the Diseases and Physical Peculiarities of the Negro Race." *New Orleans Medical and Surgical Journal* (May): 691–715.

Casper, Monica J., and Adele E. Clarke. 1998. "Making the Pap Smear Into the 'Right Tool' for the Job: Cervical Cancer Screening in the USA, circa 1940–95." *Social Studies of Science* 28 (2): 255–90.

Castells, Manuel. 1977. *The Urban Question: A Marxist Approach*. Cambridge, MA: MIT Press.

———. 2000. *The Information Age: Economy, Society, and Culture*. Oxford: Blackwell.

Cavan, Ruth S., E. W. Burgess, Robert J. Havighurst, and Herbert Goldhamer. 1949. *Personal Adjustment in Old Age*. Chicago. Science Research Associates.

Center for Research on Education Outcomes. CREDO. 2013. "National Charter School Study." Palo Alto, CA: CREDO (Center for Research on Education Outcomes) at Stanford University.

Centers for Disease Control and Prevention. 2000. "Births, Marriages, Divorces, and Deaths: Provisional Data." National Vital Statistics Report 49.

———. 2001. *Births, Marriages, Divorces, and Deaths: Provisional Data for January– December 2000*. National Vital Statistics Reports 49, no. 6. Hyattsville, MD: National Center for Health Statistics. http://www.cdc. gov/nchs/data/nvsr/nvsr49/nvsr49_06.pdf.

———. 2010a. *Births, Marriages, Divorces, and Deaths: Provisional Data for 2009*. National Vital Statistics Reports 58, no. 25. Hyattsville, MD: National Center for Health Statistics. http://www.cdc.gov/nchs/data/ nvsr/nvsr58/nvsr58_25.pdf.

———. 2010b. "Increasing Prevalence of Parent-Reported Attention-Deficit/ Hyperactivity Disorder Among Children— United States, 2003 and 2007." *Morbidity and Mortality Weekly Report*, November 12, 1439–43. http://www.cdc.gov/mmwr/ preview/mmwrhtml/mm5944a3.htm.

———. 2011. "CDC Health Disparities and Inequalities Report—United States, 2011." *Morbidity and Mortality Weekly Report* (Suppl), January 11.

———. 2012a. "Binge Drinking: Nationwide Problem, Local Solutions." *Vital Signs*, January. http://www.cdc.gov/vitalsigns/ pdf/2012–01–vitalsigns.pdf.

———. 2012b. "Intimate Partner Violence: Definitions." Accessed December 31. http://www.cdc.gov/ViolencePrevention/ intimatepartnerviolence/definitions.html.

———. 2012c. "Marriage and Divorce." Accessed November 25. http://www.cdc .gov/nchs/fastats/divorce.htm.

———. 2012d. "STD Trends in the United States: 2011 National Data for Chlamydia, Gonorrhea, and Syphilis." Fact sheet. http://www.cdc.gov/STD/stats11/ trends-2011.pdf.

———. 2013a. "Antismoking Messages and Intention to Quit—17 Countries, 2008– 2011." *Morbidity and Mortality Weekly Report*, May 31, 417–22. http://www.cdc .gov/mmwr/pdf/wk/mm6221.pdf.

———. 2013b. "Attention-Deficit/Hyperactivity Disorder: Symptoms and Diagnosis." Accessed October 10. http://www.cdc.gov/ ncbddd/adhd/diagnosis.html.

———. 2013c. "HIV in the United States: At a Glance." http://www.cdc.gov/hiv/ statistics/basics/ataglance.html.

———. 2016a. "Genital HPV Infection - Fact Sheet." Accessed May 25, 2017. https:// www.cdc.gov/std/hpv/hpv-factsheet -march-2017.pdf.

———. 2016b. *Sexually Transmitted Disease Surveillance 2015*. Atlanta: U.S. Department of Health and Human Services.

———. 2016c. "Trends in U.S. HIV Diagnoses, 2005–2014." Accessed May 25, 2017. https://www.cdc.gov/nchhstp/newsroom/ docs/factsheets/hiv-data-trends-fact -sheet-508.pdf.

———. 2017. Key Findings: Trends in the Parent-Report of Health Care Provider- Diagnosis and Medication Treatment for ADHD: United States, 2003–2011. https:// www.cdc.gov/ncbddd/adhd/features/key -findings-adhd72013.html.

Cervantes, Mario. 2014. "Scientists and Engineers: Crisis, What Crisis?" *OECD Observer*. Accessed April 24. http://www .oecdobserver.org/news/archivestory.php/ aid/1160/Scientists_and_engineers.html.

Chalfin, A. 2013. "Economic Costs of Crime." *The Encyclopedia of Crime & Punishment*. edited by Jennings, W.G., 543–558. New York: Wiley.

Chambliss, William J. 1999. *Power, Politics, and Crime*. Boulder, CO: Westview Press.

Chandola, Tarani. 2000. "Social Class Differences in Mortality Using the New UK National Statistics Socio-economic

Classification." *Social Science & Medicine* 50 (5): 641–49.

Chang, Iris. 1997. *The Rape of Nanking: The Forgotten Holocaust of World War II*. New York. Basic Books.

Chapkis, Wendy. 1997. *Live Sex Acts: Women Performing Erotic Labor*. New York: Routledge.

———. 2011. "Sex Workers" (interview). In *Introducing the New Sexuality Studies*, 2nd ed., edited by Steven Seidman, Nancy Fischer, and Chet Meeks, 327–33. New York: Routledge.

Chapkis, Wendy, and Richard J. Webb. 2008. *Dying to Get High: Marijuana as Medicine*. New York: New York University Press.

Charters, W. W. 1933. *Motion Pictures and Youth: A Summary*. New York: Macmillan.

ChartsBin. 2014. "Current Worldwide Homicide/Murder Rate." Accessed April 17. http://chartsbin.com/view/1454#.UA650iTrKAA.mailto.

Chasteen, Amy L. 2001. "Constructing Rape: Feminism, Change, and Women's Everyday Understanding of Sexual Assault." *Sociological Spectrum* 21 (2): 101–40.

Chenoweth, Erica, and Jeremy Pressman. 2017. "This Is What We Learned by Counting the Women's Marches." *Washington Post*, Monkey Cage. February. Accessed March 4, 2017. https://www.washingtonpost.com/news/monkey-cage/wp/2017/02/07/this-is-what-we-learned-by-counting-the-womens-marches/?utm_term=.72dc8da3c830.

Cherlin, Andrew J. 2004. "The Deinstitutionalization of American Marriage." *Journal of Marriage and Family* 66: 848–61.

———. 2009. *The Marriage-Go-Round: The State of Marriage and the Family in America Today*. New York: Alfred A. Knopf.

Chesney-Lind, Meda, and Merry Morash. 2013. "Transformative Feminist Criminology: A Critical Re-thinking of a Discipline." *Critical Criminology* 21 (3): 287–304.

Cheston, Duke. 2013. "The Cruelty of the Hook-Up Culture." John William Pope Center for Higher Education Policy, March 7. http://www.popecenter.org/commentaries/article.html?id=2816.

Childress, Sarah. 2013. "Will the Violence Against Women Act Close a Tribal Justice 'Loophole'?" *Frontline,* PBS, February 4.

Child Trends. 2012. "Percent of Non-marital Births to All Women, 1940–2009." http://www.childtrends.org/index.cfm.

Chin, Ko-Lin, and James O. Finckenauer. 2012. *Selling Sex Overseas: Chinese Women and the Realities of Prostitution and Global Sex Trafficking*. New York: New York University Press.

China Labor Watch. 2013. Home page. Accessed October 17. http://www.chinalaborwatch.org.

Chiricos, Ted, Kathy Padgett, and Marc Gertz. 2000. "Fear, TV News, and the Reality of Crime." *Criminology* 38 (3): 755–85.

Chitose, Yoshimi. 2005. "Transitions Into and Out of Poverty: A Comparison Between Immigrant and Native Children." *Journal of Poverty* 9 (2): 63–88.

Chon, Don Soo. 2015. "Gender Equality, Liberalism and Attitude Toward Prostitution: Variation in Cross-National Study." *Journal of Family Violence* 30 (7): 827–38.

Chou, Rosalind S., and Joe R. Feagin. 2008. *The Myth of the Model Minority: Asian Americans Facing Racism*. Boulder, CO: Paradigm.

Chow-White, Peter. 2006. "Race, Gender and Sex on the Net: Semantic Networks of Selling and Storytelling Sex Tourism." *Media, Culture and Society* 28 (6): 883–905.

Christy-McMullin, Kameri, Yvette Murphy, Marcia Shobe, Shikkiah Jordan, Lauren Barefield, and Erika Gergerich. 2010. "Second-Generation Individual Development Account Research: Preliminary Findings." *Journal of Evidence-Based Social Work* 7 (3): 251–66.

Chun, Edna, and Alvin Evans. 2012. *Diverse Administrators in Peril: The New Indentured Class in Higher Education*. Boulder, CO: Paradigm Publishers.

Cicero, Theodore J., and Matthew Ellis. 2015. "Abuse-Deterrent Formulation and the Prescription Opioid Abuse Epidemic in the United States: Lessons Learned From Oxycontin." *JAMA Psychiatry* 72 (5): 424–30.

Cicero, Theodore J., Matthew S. Ellis, and Hilary L. Surratt. 2012. "Effect of Abuse-Deterrent Formulation of OxyContin." *New England Journal of Medicine.* 367: 187–189.

Clawson, Dan, and Naomi Gerstel. 2014. *Unequal Time: Gender, Class, and Family in Employment Schedules*. New York: Russell Sage Foundation.

Citizens for Trump. 2016. Meet Our First Family–The Trump Family. https://citizensfortrump.com/2015/12/13/meet-future-first-family-trump-family/

Clift, Stephen, and Simon Carter, eds. 2000. *Tourism and Sex: Culture, Commerce, and Coercion*. New York: Pinter.

Clougherty, Jane E., Kerry Souza, and Mark R. Cullen. 2010. "Work and Its Role in Shaping the Social Gradient of Disease." *Annals of the New York Academy of Sciences* 1186: 102–24.

Cloward, Richard A., and Lloyd E. Ohlin. 1960. *Delinquency and Opportunity: A Theory of Delinquent Gangs*. Glencoe, IL: Free Press.

Clune, William H., John F. Witte, and Robert M. LaFollette Institute of Public Affairs. 1990. *Choice and Control in American Education*. London: Falmer.

Coalition Casualty Count. 2014. Accessed April 24. http://icasualties.org.

Cockerham, William C. 1997. *This Aging Society*, 2nd ed. Upper Saddle River, NJ: Prentice Hall.

Cohen, A. K. 1955. *Delinquent Boys: The Culture of the Gang*. Glencoe, IL: Free Press.

Cohen, Bonni, and Jon Shenk. 2016. *Audrie and Daisy*. http://www.audrieanddaisy.com/about/.

Cohen, L. E., and M. Felson. 1979. "Social Change and Crime Rate Trends: A Routine Activity Approach." *American Sociological Review*, 44(4): 588–608.

Cohen, Philip N. 2012. "Recession and Divorce in the United States: Economic Conditions and the Odds of Divorce, 2008–2010." Maryland Population Research Center Working Paper. http://papers.ccpr.ucla.edu/papers/PWP-MPRC-2012–008/PWP-MPRC-2012–008.pdf.

Cohen, R. B. 1981. "The New International Division of Labor, Multinational Corporations, and Urban Hierarchy." In *Urbanization and Urban Planning in Capitalist Society,* edited by Michael Dear and Allen J. Scott, 287–315. London: Methuen.

Cohen, Sheldon, William J. Doyle, and Andrew Baum. 2006. "Socioeconomic Status Is Associated With Stress Hormones." *Psychosomatic Medicine* 68 (3): 414–20.

Cohen, Stanley. 2002. *Folk Devils and: The Moral Panics Creation of the Mods and Rockers*, 3rd ed. London: Routledge.

Cohn, D'Vera, Jeffrey S. Passell, Wendy Wang, and Gretchen Livingston. 2011. "Barely Half of U.S. Adults Are Married—A Record Low." Pew Research Center, Social and Demographic Trends, December 14. http://www.pewsocialtrends.org/files/2011/12/Marriage-Decline.pdf.

Colantonio, Andrea. 2007. "Social Sustainability: An Exploratory Analysis of Its Definition, Assessment Methods, Metrics and Tools." 2007/01: EIBURS Working Paper Series, Oxford Institute for Sustainable Development—International Land Markets Group, Oxford Brookes University.

Colantonio, Andrea, and Tim Dixon. 2011. *Urban Regeneration and Social Sustainability: Best Practice From European Cities.* Hoboken, NJ: Wiley-Blackwell.

Cole, George F., and Christopher E. Smith. 2008a. *The American System of Criminal Justice.* Belmont, CA: Wadsworth.

———. 2008b. *Criminal Justice in America,* 5th ed. Belmont, CA: Thomson Higher Education.

Cole, Luke W., and Sheila R. Foster. 2001. *From the Ground Up: Environmental Racism and the Rise of the Environmental Justice Movement.* New York: New York University Press.

Coleman, James S., et al., for the U.S. Office of Education, National Center for Education Statistics. 1966. *Equality of Educational Opportunity.* Washington, DC: Government Printing Office.

Coleman, James S., and Thomas Hoffer. 1987. *Public and Private High Schools: The Impact of Communities.* New York: Basic Books.

Coleman, James S., Thomas Hoffer, and Sally Kilgore. 1982. *High School Achievement: Public, Catholic, and Private Schools Compared.* New York: Basic Books.

Coleman-Jensen, Alisha, Matthew P. Rabbit, Christian A. Gregory, and Anita Singh. 2016. *Household Food Security in the United States in 2015.* United States Department of Agriculture.

Coles, Robert. 1993. *The Call of Service: A Witness to Idealism.* Boston: Houghton Mifflin.

Coll, Steve. 2013. "Remote Control." *New Yorker,* May 6, 77.

College Board. 2015. "2014 College Board Program Results: SAT." Accessed May 7, 2017. https://www.collegeboard.org/program-results/2014/sat.

Collier, Roger. 2009. "Rapidly Rising Clinical Trial Costs Worry Researchers." *Canadian Medical Association Journal* 180 (3): 277–78.

Collins, Chuck. 2012. *99 to 1: How Wealth Inequality Is Wrecking the World and What We Can Do About It.* San Francisco: Berrett-Koehler.

Collins, Patricia Hill. 1990. *Black Feminist Thought: Knowledge, Consciousness, and the Politics of Empowerment.* Boston: Unwin Hyman.

———. 2000. *Black Feminist Thought: Knowledge, Consciousness, and the Politics of Empowerment,* 2nd ed. New York and London: Routledge.

———. 2005. *Black Sexual Politics: African Americans, Gender, and the New Racism.* New York and London: Routledge.

———. 2008. *Black Feminist Thought: Knowledge, Consciousness, and the Politics of Empowerment,* 2nd ed. New York: Routledge.

Collins, Randall. 1979. *The Credential Society: An Historical Sociology of Education and Stratification.* New York: Academic Press.

Collins, Randall, and Scott Coltrane. 1991. *Sociology of Marriage and the Family: Gender, Love, and Property.* Chicago: Nelson-Hall.

Colombo, Cinzia, Paola Mosconi, Maria Grazia Buratti, Alessandro Liberati, Serena Donati, Alfonso Mele, and Roberto Satolli. 2010. "Press Coverage of Hormone Replacement Therapy and Menopause." *European Journal of Obstetrics & Gynecology and Reproductive Biology* 153 (1): 56–61.

Common Sense Media. 2015. *The Common Sense Census: Media Use by Tweens and Teens.* https://www.commonsensemedia.org/research/the-common-sense-census-media-use-by-tweens-and-teens.

Compton, Wilson M., and Nora D. Volkow. 2006. "Abuse of Prescription Drugs and the Risk of Addiction." *Drug & Alcohol Dependence* 83 (1) Suppl. 1: S4–7.

Comstock, George. 2008. "A Sociological Perspective on Television Violence and Aggression." *American Behavioral Scientist* 51 (8): 1184–1211.

Congressional Budget Office. 2016. *The Distribution of Household Income and Federal Taxes, 2013.* June. https://www.cbo.gov/sites/default/files/114th-congress-2015–2016/reports/51361–HouseholdIncomeFedTaxes_OneCol.pdf.

Conklin, Kurt. 2012. "Attacks on Sex Education Continue Nationwide." Reproductive Health Reality Check, October 9. http://rhrealitycheck.org/article/2012/10/09/school-controversies-in-sex-education.

Conley, Dalton. 1999. *Being Black, Living in the Red: Race, Wealth, and Social Policy in America.* Berkeley: University of California Press.

Connell, Nadine M., Pamela M. Negro, Allison N. Pearce, Dawn M. Reilly, and B. A. Fera. 2009. *New Jersey Department of Education and Rowan University Social Norms Project: Report for the 2008–2009 School Year.* Report to the New Jersey Department of Education. Trenton: State of New Jersey.

Connell, R. W. 2005. *Masculinities,* 2nd ed. Berkeley: University of California Press.

Conrad, Peter. 2007. *The Medicalization of Society: On the Transformation of Human Conditions Into Treatable Disorders.* Baltimore: Johns Hopkins University Press.

Conrad, Peter, and Meredith Bergey. 2015. "The Impending Globalization of ADHD: Notes on the Expansion and Growth of a Medicalized Disorder." *Journal of Health & Social Behavior* 122 (3): 31–43.

Conrad, Peter, and Valerie Leiter. 2004. "Medicalization, Markets and Consumers." *Journal of Health & Social Behavior* 45 (Suppl): 158–76.

Conrad, Peter, and Deborah Potter. 2000. "From Hyperactive Children to ADHD Adults: Observations on the Expansion of Medical Categories." *Social Problems* 47: 559–82.

Cookson, Peter W., Jr., Alan R. Sadovnik, and Susan F. Semel, eds. 1992. *International Handbook of Educational Reform.* New York: Greenwood Press.

Cooky, Cheryl, Mike Messner, and Michela Musto. 2015. "'It's Dude Time!': A Quarter Century of Excluding Women's Sports in Televised News and Highlight Shows." *Communication & Sport* 3 (3): 261–87.

Cooky, Cheryl, Faye L. Wachs, Michael Messner, and Shari Dworkin. 2010. "It's Not About the Game: Don Imus, Race, Class, Gender and Sexuality in Contemporary Media." *Sociology of Sport Journal* 27: 139–59.

Cooley, Charles Horton. 1902a. *Human Nature and the Social Order.* New York: Charles Scribner's Sons.

———. 1902b. "The Looking-Glass Self." In *Social Theory: The Multicultural and Classic Readings,* 4th ed., edited by Charles Lemert, 189. Philadelphia, PA: Westview Press.

Cooper, A., and E. L. Smith. 2012. *Homicide Trends in the United States, 1980–2008.* U.S. Department of Justice, Bureau of Justice Statistics.

Cooper, Al, Irene P. McLoughlin, and Kevin M. Campbell. 2000. "Sexuality in Cyberspace: Update for the 21st Century." *CyberPsychology and Behavior* 3 (4): 521–36.

Cooper, Alexia, and Erica L. Smith. 2011. *Homicide Trends in the United States, 1980–2008: Annual Rates for 2009 and 2010.* Patterns and Trends, November, NCJ 236018. Washington, DC: U.S. Department of Justice. http://www.bjs.gov/content/pub/pdf/htus8008.pdf.

Cooper, Julia Anna. 1892 (2010). "The Colored Woman's Office." In *Social Theory: The Multicultural and Classic Readings,* 4th ed., edited by Charles Lemert, 179–84. Philadelphia, PA: Westview Press.

Cooper, Harris, Geoffrey Borman, and Ron Fairchild. 2010. "School Calendars and Academic Achievement." In *Handbook of Research on Schools, Schooling, and Human Development*, edited by Judith L. Eecles and Jacquelynne S. Meece, 342–55. New York: Routledge.

Coory, Michael D., Jennifer M. Muller, Nathan A. M. Dunn, and Patricia S. Fagan. 2002. "Participation in Cervical Cancer Screening by Women in Rural and Remote Aboriginal and Torres Strait Islander Communities in Queensland." *Medical Journal of Australia* 177 (10): 544–47.

Corbin, Juliet M. 2003. "The Body in Health and Illness." *Qualitative Health Research* 13 (2): 256–67.

Corey, Ethan. 2013. "Students Protest Lenient Sexual Misconduct Sanctions." *Amherst Student,* May 1. http://amherststudent.amherst.edu/?q=article/2013/05/01/students-protest-lenient-sexual-misconduct-sanctions.

Corporation for National and Community Service. 2011. "Volunteering in America." Accessed September 8. http://www.volunteeringinamerica.gov/national.

———. 2017a. "National: Trends and Highlights Overview." Accessed April 1. https://www.nationalservice.gov/vcla/national

———. 2017b. "College Students." Accessed April 1. https://www.nationalservice.gov/vcla/demographic/college-students.

Correll, S., Benard, S., & Paik, I. 2007. "Getting a Job: Is There a Motherhood Penalty?" *American Journal of Sociology* 112 (5): 1297–1338.

———. 2013. "Volunteering and Civic Life in America." Accessed November 13. http://www.volunteer inginamerica.gov/national.

Costantini, Cristina. 2012. "Bilingual Border Cities Challenge Movement to Make English the Official Language." *Huffington Post*, February 2. http://www.huffingtonpost.com/2012/02/02/english-official-language-border-bilingual_n_1249307.html.

Cotter, David, Joan Hermson, and Reeve Vanneman. 2006. "Gender and Inequality at Work." In *Working in America: Continuity, Conflict, and Change,* 3rd ed., edited by Amy Wharton. New York: McGraw-Hill.

Cowan, Ruth Schwartz. 1983. *More Work for Mother: The Ironies of Household Technology From the Open Hearth to the Microwave.* New York: Basic Books.

Craddock, Susan. 2000. *City of Plagues: Disease, Poverty, and Deviance in San Francisco.* Minneapolis: University of Minnesota Press.

Crosnoe, Robert, and Chandra Muller. 2014. "Family Socioeconomic Status, Peers, and the Path to College." *Social Problems* 61 (4): 602–24.

Cross, Christopher. 2004. *Political Education: National Policy Comes of Age.* New York: Teachers College Press.

Crowder, Kyle D., and Stewart E. Tolnay. 2000. "A New Marriage Squeeze for Black Women: The Role of Racial Intermarriage by Black Men." *Journal of Marriage and the Family* 62: 792–807.

Cumming, Elaine, and William E. Henry. 1961. *Growing Old.* New York: Basic Books.

Currul-Dykeman, Kathleen Erin. 2014. *Domestic Violence Case Processing: A Serious Crime or a Waste of Precious Time?* El Paso, TX: LFB Scholarly Publishing.

Dabhoiwala, Faramerz. 2012. *The Origins of Sex: A History of the First Sexual Revolution.* Oxford: Oxford University Press.

Dahrendorf, Ralf. 1959. *Class and Class Conflict in Industrial Society.* Stanford, CA: Stanford University Press.

Daly, Kathleen, and Meda Chesney-Lind. 1988. "Feminism and Criminology." *Justice Quarterly* 5 (4): 497–538.

Danziger, Sheldon, Sandra Danziger, and Jonathan Stern. 1997. "The American Paradox: High Income and High Child Poverty." In *Child Poverty and Deprivation in the Industrialized Countries, 1945–1995,* edited by Giovanni Andrea Cornia and Sheldon Danziger, 181–209. Oxford: Clarendon Press.

Dargis, Manohla. 2013. "Two Boys' Schooling, for 13 Years of It: 'American Promise,' a Documentary on Dalton Students." *New York Times,* October 17.

Darling-Hammond, Linda. 2010. *The Flat World and Education: How America's Commitment to Equity Will Determine Our Future.* New York: Teachers College Press.

Darmon, Nicole, and Adam Drewnowski. 2008. "Does Social Class Predict Diet Quality?" *American Journal of Clinical Nutrition* 87 (5): 1107–17.

Dasgupta, Susmita, Benoit Laplante, Craig Meisner, David Wheeler, and Jianping Yan. 2009. "The Impact of Sea Level Rise on Developing Countries: A Comparative Analysis." *Climatic Change* 93 (3–4): 379–88.

Davis, F. James. 1952. "Crime News in Colorado Newspapers." *American Journal of Sociology* 57 (4): 325–30.

Davis, Georgiann. 2015. *Contesting Intersex: The Dubious Diagnosis.* New York: New York University Press.

Davis, Kingsley. 1937. "The Sociology of Prostitution." *American Sociological Review* 2: 744–55.

Davis, Kingsley, and Wilbert E. Moore. 1945. "Some Principles of Stratification." *American Sociological Review* 10: 242–49.

Davis, Mike. 2003. *Dead Cities, and Other Tales.* New York: New Press.

Day, Jennifer Cheeseman, and Eric C. Newburger. 2002. *The Big Payoff: Educational Attainment and Synthetic Estimates of Work-Life Earnings.* U.S. Census Bureau, Current Population Reports

P23–210. Washington, DC: Government Printing Office. http://www.census.gov/prod/2002pubs/p23–210.pdf.

de la Fuente-Fernández, R., T. J. Ruth, V. Sossi, M. Schulzer, D. B. Calne, and A. J. Stoessl. 2001. "Expectation and Dopamine Release: Mechanism of the Placebo Effect in Parkinson's Disease." *Science* 293 (5532): 1164–66.

de Zwart, Onno, Marty P. N. van Kerkhof, and Theo G. M. Sandfort. 1998. "Anal Sex and Gay Men." *Journal of Psychology and Human Sexuality* 10 (3–4): 89–102.

DeNavas-Walt, Carmen, Bernadette D. Proctor, and Jessica C. Smith. 2011. *Income, Poverty, and Health Insurance Coverage in the United States: 2010*. U.S. Census Bureau, Current Population Reports P60–239. Washington, DC: Government Printing Office. https://www.census.gov/prod/2011pubs/p60–239.pdf.

———. 2012. *Income, Poverty, and Health Insurance Coverage in the United States: 2011*. U.S. Census Bureau, Current Population Reports P60–243. Washington, DC: Government Printing Office. https://www.census.gov/prod/2012pubs/p60–243.pdf.

———. 2013. *Income, Poverty, and Health Insurance Coverage in the United States: 2012*. U.S. Census Bureau, Current Population Reports P60–245. Washington, DC: Government Printing Office. https://www.census.gov/prod/2013pubs/p60–245.pdf

———. 2015. *Income and Poverty in the United States: 2014*. U.S. Census Bureau, September 2015. https://www.census.gov/content/dam/Census/library/publications/2015/demo/p60–252.pdf.

Deneen, Sally. 2013. "Feds Slash Colorado River Release to Historic Lows." *National Geographic Daily News*, August 16. http://news.nationalgeographic.com/news/2013/08/130816–colorado-river-drought-lake-powell-mead-water-scarcity.

Denizard-Thompson, Nancy M., Kirsten B. Feiereisel, Sheila F. Stevens, David P. Miller, and James L. Wofford. 2011. "The Digital Divide at an Urban Community Health Center: Implications for Quality Improvement and Health Care Access." *Journal of Community Health* 36: 456–60.

Dent, Mike. 2006. "Disciplining the Medical Profession? Implications of Patient Choice for Medical Dominance." *Health Sociology Review* 15: 458–68.

Deseran, Travis A., and James D. Orcutt. 2009. "The Deconstruction of a Drug Crisis: Media Coverage of Drug Issues During the 1996 Presidential Campaign." *Journal of Drug Issues* 39: 871–91.

Desmond, Matthew, and Mustafa Emirbayer. 2010. *Racial Domination, Racial Progress: The Sociology of Race in America*. New York: McGraw-Hill.

DiFranza, Joseph R., Robert J. Wellman, James D. Sargent, Michael Weitzman, Bethany J. Hipple, and Jonathan P. Winickoff. 2006. "Tobacco Promotion and the Initiation of Tobacco Use: Assessing the Evidence for Causality." *Pediatrics* 117 (6): 1237–48.

Dijkstra, A. F., P. Verdonk, and A. L. Lagro-Janssen. 2008. "Gender Bias in Medical Textbooks: Examples From Coronary Heart Disease, Depression, Alcohol Abuse and Pharmacology." *Medical Education* 42 (10): 1021–28.

Diken, Bulent, and Carsten Bagge Laustsen. 2005. "Becoming Abject: Rape as a Weapon of War." *Body & Society* 11 (1): 111–28.

Dines, Gail, and Robert Jensen. 2004. "Pornography and Media: Toward a More Critical Analysis." In *Sexualities: Identities, Behaviors, and Society*, edited by Michael S. Kimmel and Rebecca F. Plante, 369–79. New York: Oxford University Press.

DiNitto, Diana M., with Linda K. Cummins. 2005. *Social Welfare: Politics and Public Policy*, 6th ed. Boston: Allyn & Bacon.

DiPrete, Thomas A., and Claudia Buchmann. 2013. *The Rise of Women: The Growing Gender Gap in Education and What It Means for American Schools*. New York: Russell Sage Foundation.

Dobbie, Will, and Roland G. Fryer Jr. 2011. "Are High-Quality Schools Enough to Increase Achievement Among the Poor? Evidence From the Harlem Children's Zone." *American Economic Journal: Applied Economics* 3 (3): 158–87.

———. 2015. "The Medium-Term Impacts of High-Achieving Charter Schools." *Journal of Political Economy* 123 (5): 985–1037.

Dodman, David. 2009. "Blaming Cities for Climate Change? An Analysis of Urban Greenhouse Gas Emissions Inventories." *Environment & Urbanization* 21 (1): 185–210.

Donlon, Margie M., Ori Ashman, and Becca R. Levy. 2005. "Re-vision of Older Television Characters: A Stereotype-Awareness Intervention." *Journal of Social Issues* 61 (2): 307–19.

Donovan, Josephine. 2012. *Feminist Theory: The Intellectual Traditions*, 4th ed. New York and London: Continuum International Publishing Group.

Dougherty, Kevin J., and Floyd M. Hammack, eds. 1990. *Education and Society: A Reader*. San Diego, CA: Harcourt Brace Jovanovich.

Dover, Kenneth J. 2016 [1989]. *Greek Homosexuality*. London and New York: Bloomsbury Academic.

Dow, Dawn M. 2016. "The Deadly Challenges of Raising African American Boys: Navigating the Controlling Image of the 'Thug.'" *Gender & Society* 30 (2): 161–88.

Dow, Dawn M., Dana R. Fisher, and Rashawn Ray. 2017. "This Is What Democracy Looks Like!" The Society Pages, Sociological Images blog. February 16. Accessed March 1, 2017. https://thesocietypages.org/socimages/2017/02/06/this-is-what-democracy-looks-like/.

Downey, Douglas B., and Dennis J. Condron. 2016. "Fifty Years Since the Coleman Report: Rethinking the Relationship Between Schools and Inequality." *Sociology of Education* 89 (3): 207–20.

Downing-Matibag, Teresa M., and Brandi Geisinger. 2009. "Hooking Up and Sexual Risk Taking Among College Students: A Health Belief Model Perspective." *Qualitative Health Research* 19 (9): 1196–1209.

Drakakis-Smith, David. 1995. "Third World Cities: Sustainable Urban Development, 1." *Urban Studies* 32 (4–5): 659–77.

Drapeau, Aline, Richard Boyer, and Alain Lesage. 2009. "The Influence of Social Anchorage on the Gender Difference in the Use of Mental Health Services." *Journal of Behavioral Health Services & Research* 36 (3): 372–84.

Dreby, Joanna. 2010. *Divided by Borders: Mexican Migrants and Their Children*. Berkeley: University of California Press.

———. 2012. "The Burden of Deportation on Children in Mexican Immigrant Families." *Journal of Marriage and Family* 74: 829–45.

Drefahl, Steven. 2012. "Do the Married Really Live Longer? The Role of Cohabitation and Socioeconomic Status." *Journal of Marriage and Family* 74: 462–75.

Dreier, Peter. 2017. "The Anti-Trump Movement: Recover, Resist, Reform." *The American Prospect*. April 4.

Dressner, Julie, and Edwin Martinez. 2012. "The Scars of Stop-and-Frisk." *New York Times,* June 12. http://www.nytimes .com/2012/06/12/opinion/the-scars-of -stop-and-frisk.html.

Dryfoos, Joy G., Jane Quinn, and Carol Barkin. 2005. *Community Schools in Action: Lessons From a Decade of Practice*. Oxford: Oxford University Press.

Du Bois, W. E. B. 1995. *The Philadelphia Negro: A Social Study*. Philadelphia: University of Pennsylvania Press. First published 1899.

———. 2003. *Darkwater: Voices From Within the Veil*. Amherst, NY: Humanity Books. First published 1920.

Duck, Waverly. 2015. *No Way Out: Precarious Living in the Shadow of Poverty and Drug-Dealing*. Chicago: University of Chicago Press.

Dunlap, R. E., and P. J. Jacques. 2013. "Climate Change Denial Books and Conservative Think Tanks Exploring the Connection." *American Behavioral Scientist* 57 (6): 699–731.

Dunlap, Riley E., and Aaron M. McCright. 2008. "A Widening Gap: Republican and Democratic Views on Climate Change." *Environment* 50 (5): 26–35.

———. 2010. "Climate Change Denial: Sources, Actors and Strategies." In *The Routledge Handbook of Climate Change and Society*, edited by Constance Lever-Tracy, 240–59. New York: Routledge.

Dunn, Donna. 2015. "Prevention Is Possible: Aligning Priorities to End Sexual Violence." *William Mitchell Law Review* 41 (3). Accessed April 19, 2017. http://open .mitchellhamline.edu/cgi/viewcontent .cgi?article=2893&context=wmlr.

Durkheim, Émile. 1915. *The Elementary Forms of Religious Life*. London: Allen & Unwin.

———. 1977. *The Evolution of Educational Thought: Lectures on the Formation and Development of Secondary Education in France*. London: Routledge & Kegan Paul.

———. 1979. *Suicide: A Study in Sociology*. New York: Free Press. First published 1897.

———. 1982. *The Rules of Sociological Method*. Edited by Steven Lukes; translated by W. D. Halls. New York: Free Press. First published 1895.

———. 1984. *The Division of Labor in Society*. Translated by W. D. Halls. New York: Free Press. First published 1893.

The Economist. 2010. "Something's Not Working." April 29. http://www.economist .com/node/16010303.

———. 2017a. "Fat Tails." January 27, 21.

———. 2017b. "Special Report: Lifelong Education." January 14.

Edgemon, Erin. 2013. "College Students Fight Human Trafficking." United Methodist Church, January 11. http://www.umc.org/ news-and-media/college-students-fight -human-trafficking.

Edin, Kathryn, and Maria Kefalas. 2005. *Promises I Can Keep: Why Poor Women Put Motherhood Before Marriage*. Berkeley: University of California Press.

Education Trust. 2010a. "Achievement in America: How Are We Doing? What Comes Next?" http://www.edtrust.org/dc/ resources.

———. 2010b. *Education Watch: Achievement Gap Summary Tables*. Washington DC: Education Trust.

Edwards, Katie M., Jessica A. Turchik, Christina M. Dardis, Nicole Reynolds, and Christine A. Gidycz. 2011. "Rape Myths: History, Individual and Institutional-Level Presence, and Implications for Change." *Sex Roles* 65 (11–12): 761–73.

Ehrhardt-Martinez, Karen, Thomas K. Rudel, Kari M. Norgaard, and Jeffrey Broadbent. 2015. "Mitigating Climate Change." In *Climate Change and Society: Sociological Perspectives*, edited by R. E. Dunlap and R. J. Brulle, 199–234. New York: Oxford University Press.

Eisenberg, Marla E., Dianne M. Ackard, Michael D. Resnick, and Dianne Neumark-Sztainer. 2009. "Casual Sex and Psychological Health Among Young Adults: Is Having 'Friends-with-Benefits' Emotionally Damaging?" *Perspectives on Sexual and Reproductive Health* 41: 231–37.

Eisenhower, Dwight D. 1961. "Farewell Address." Dwight D. Eisenhower Presidential Library. http://www .eisenhower.archives.gov/research/online_ documents/farewell_address.html.

Ekerdt, David J. 2007. "Work, Health, and Retirement." In *Encyclopedia of Health and Aging*, edited by Kyriakos S. Markides. Thousand Oaks, CA: Sage.

Elder, Glen H. 1974. *Children of the Great Depression: Social Change in Life Experience*. Chicago: University of Chicago Press.

Eligon, John. 2016. "A Question of Environmental Racism in Flint." *New York Times,* January 21. Accessed March 1, 2017. https:// www.nytimes.com/2016/01/22/us/a -question-of-environmental-racism-in-flint .html.

Elkington, John. 1994. "Towards the Sustainable Corporation: Win-Win-Win Business Strategies for Sustainable Development." *California Management Review* 36 (2): 90–100.

———. 1997. *Cannibals With Forks: The Triple Bottom Line of 21st Century Business*. Oxford: Capstone.

Elliott, James R., and Jeremy Pais. 2006. "Race, Class, and Hurricane Katrina: Social Differences in Human Responses to Disaster." *Social Science Research* 35 (2): 295–321.

Elliott, P., S. Richardson, J. J. Abellan, A. Thomson, C. de Hoog, L. Jarup, and D. J. Briggs. 2009. "Geographic Density of Landfill Sites and Risk of Congenital Anomalies in England." *Occupational and Environmental Medicine* 66 (2): 81–89.

Embser-Herbert, Melissa Sheridan. 2012. "On Being a (Lesbian) Family in North American Society." In *Families With Futures: Family Studies Into the Twenty-First Century*, edited by Meg Wilkes Karraker and Janet R. Grochowski, 33–34. London: Routledge.

Engel, George L. 1981. "The Need for a New Medical Model: A Challenge for Biomedicine." In *Concepts of Health and Disease: Interdisciplinary Perspectives*, edited by Arthur L. Caplan, H. Tristram Englehardt Jr., and James J. McCartney, 589–607 Reading, MA: Addison-Wesley.

Engels, Friedrich. 1972. *The Origin of the Family, Private Property, and the State*. Atlanta, GA: Pathfinder. First published 1884.

England, Paula. 2010. "The Gender Revolution: Uneven and Stalled." *Gender & Society* 24 (2): 149–66.

Enloe, Cynthia. 1989. *Bananas, Beaches and Bases: Making Feminist Sense of International Politics*. London: Pandora Press.

Ennis, Sharon R., Merarys Ríos-Vargas, and Nora G. Albert. 2011. *The Hispanic Population: 2010*. U.S. Census Bureau, Census Brief C2010BR-04. Washington, DC: Government Printing Office. http://www.census.gov/prod/cen2010/briefs/c2010br-04.pdf.

Enten, Harry J. 2012. "How US Rules on Former Felons Voting Can Swing Presidential Elections." *Guardian,* July 3.

Entwisle, Doris R., and Karl L. Alexander. 1992. "Summer Setback: Race, Poverty, School Composition, and Mathematics Achievement in the First Two Years of School." *American Sociological Review* 57 (1): 72–84.

Epstein, Steven. 1995. "The Construction of Lay Expertise: AIDS Activism and the Forging of Credibility in the Reform of Clinical Trials." *Science, Technology, & Human Values* 20: 408–37.

———. 2007. *Inclusion: The Politics of Difference in Medical Research*. Chicago: University of Chicago Press.

Ermisch, John, Markus Jantti, and Timothy M. Smeeding, eds. 2012. *From Parents to Children: The Intergenerational Transmission of Advantage*. New York: Russell Sage.

Escholz, Sarah, Ted Chiricos, and Marc Gertz. 2003. "Television and Fear of Crime: Program Types, Audience Traits, and the Mediating Effect of Perceived Neighborhood Racial Composition." *Social Problems* 50 (3): 395–415.

Eshbaugh, Elaine M., and Gary Gute. 2008. "Hookups and Sexual Regret Among College Women." *Journal of Social Psychology* 148 (1): 77–89.

Estes, Carroll L. 1991. "The New Political Economy of Aging: Introduction and Critique." In *Critical Perspectives on Aging: The Political and Moral Economy of Growing Old,* edited by Meredith Minkler and Carroll L. Estes, 19–36. Amityville, NY: Baywood.

Everage, Nicholas J., Crystal D. Linkletter, Annie Gjelsvik, Stephen T. McGarvey, and Eric B. Loucks. 2013. "Implementation of Permutation Testing to Determine Clustering of Social and Behavioral Risk Factors for Coronary Heart Disease, National Health and Nutrition Examination Survey 2001–2004." *Annals of Epidemiology* 23 (7): 381–87.

Ewen, Stuart. 1977. *Captains of Consciousness: Advertising and the Social Roots of Consumer Culture*. New York: McGraw-Hill.

Farrer, James. 2006. "Sexual Citizenship and the Politics of Sexual Story-Telling Among Chinese Youth." In *Sex and Sexuality in China,* edited by Elaine Jeffreys, 102–23. London: Routledge.

Farrer, James, Gefei Suo, Haruka Tsuchiya, and Zhongxin Su. 2012. "Re-embedding Sexual Meanings: A Qualitative Comparison of the Premarital Sexual Scripts of Chinese and Japanese Young Adults." *Sexuality & Culture* 16 (3): 263–86.

Fausto-Sterling, Anne. 2000. *Sexing the Body: Gender Politics and the Construction of Sexuality*. New York: Basic Books.

———. 2005. "The Bare Bones of Sex: Part 1—Sex and Gender." *Signs: Journal of Women in Culture and Society* 30 (2): 1491–27.

Feagin, Joe H. 2000. *Racist America: Roots, Current Realities, Future Reparations*. New York: Routledge.

Feagin, Joe R., and Clairece Booher Feagin. 2008. *Racial and Ethnic Relations,* 8th ed. Upper Saddle River, NJ: Prentice Hall.

Feagin, Joe R., and Melvin P. Sikes. 1994. *Living With Racism: The Black Middle-Class Experience*. Boston: Beacon Press.

Fealy, Gerard, Martin McNamara, Margaret Pearl Treacy, and Imogen Lyons. 2012. "Constructing Ageing and Age Identities: A Case Study of Newspaper Discourses." *Ageing & Society* 32: 85–102.

Feaver, Peter D., and Richard H. Kohn, eds. 2001. *Soldiers and Civilians: The Civil-Military Gap and American National Security*. Cambridge, MA: MIT Press.

Federal Bureau of Investigation. 2013a. "Crime in the United States: Offense and Population Percent Distribution by Region, 2012." Uniform Crime Reports. http://www.fbi.gov/about-us/cjis/ucr/crime-in-the-u.s/2012/crime-in-theu.s.2012/tables/3tabledatadecover viewpdf/

table_3_crime_in_the_united_states_offense_and_population_distribution_by_region_2012.

———. 2013b. "Crime in the United States: Offenses Known to Law Enforcement by State by City, 2012." Uniform Crime Reports. http://www.fbi.gov/about-us/cjis/ucr/crime-in-the-u.s/2012/crime-in-the-u.s.-2012/tables/8tabledatadecpdf/table_8_offenses_known_to_law_enforcement_by_state_by_city_2012.xls/view.

———. 2015a. "Crime in the United States: Offense and Population Percent Distribution by Region, 2015." Uniform Crime Reports. https://ucr.fbi.gov/crime-in-the-u.s/2015/crime-in-the-u.s.-2015/tables/table-3.

———. 2015b. "Crime in the United States: Offenses Known to law Enforcement by State and City, 2015." Uniform Crime Reports. https://ucr.fbi.gov/crime-in-the-u.s/2015/crime-in-the-u.s.-2015/tables/table-8/table_8_offenses_known_to_law_enforcement_by_state_by_city_2015.xls/view.

Federal Interagency Forum on Aging-Related Statistics. 2016. *Older Americans 2016: Key Indicators of Well-Being*. August. Washington, DC: Government Printing Office.

Fee, Elizabeth. 1988. "Sin Versus Science: Venereal Disease in Baltimore in the Twentieth Century." *Journal of the History of Medicine and Allied Sciences* 43 (2): 141–64.

Feeney, Floyd, and Patrick G. Jackson. 1990–1991. "Public Defenders, Assigned Counsel, Retained Counsel: Does the Type of Criminal Defense Counsel Matter?" *Rutgers Law Journal* 22: 361–456.

Feldman, H. A., C. B. Johannes, C. A. Derby, K. P. Kleinman, B. A. Mohr, A. B. Araujo, and J. B. McKinlay. 2000. "Erectile Dysfunction and Coronary Risk Factors: Prospective Results From the Massachusetts Male Aging Study." *Preventive Medicine* 30 (4): 328–38.

Feldmeyer, Ben, and Darrell Steffensmeier. 2007. "Elder Crime: Patterns and Current Trends, 1980–2004." *Research on Aging* 29 (4): 297–322.

Fellman, Gordon. 1998. *Rambo and the Dalai Lama: The Compulsion to Win and Its*

Threat to Human Survival. Albany: State University of New York Press.

Ferguson, Ann Arnett. 2000. *Bad Boys: Public Schools in the Making of Black Masculinity.* Ann Arbor: University of Michigan Press.

Ferguson, Christopher John. 2007. "The Good, the Bad and the Ugly: A Meta-analytic Review of Positive and Negative Effects of Violent Video Games." *Psychiatric Quarterly* 78: 309–16.

Fernandez-Kelly, M. Patricia, and Richard Schauffler. 1994. "Divided Fates: Immigrant Children in a Restructured Economy." *International Migration Review* 28: 662–89.

Ferraro, Kenneth F. 2011. "Health and Aging: Early Origins, Persistent Inequalities?" In *Handbook of Sociology of Aging,* edited by Richard A. Settersten Jr. and Jacqueline L. Angel, 465–75. New York: Springer.

Ferrell, Jeff. 2013. "Cultural Criminology and the Politics of Meaning." *Critical Criminology* 21 (3): 257–71.

Fields, Jessica. 2007. "Knowing Girls: Gender and Learning in School-Based Sexuality Education." In *Sexual Inequalities and Social Justice,* edited by Niels Teunis and Gilbert H. Herdt, 66–85. Berkeley: University of California Press.

Finer, Lawrence B. 2007. "Trends in Premarital Sex in the United States, 1954–2003." *Public Health Reports* 122 (1): 73–78.

Finer, Lawrence B., and Adam Sonfield. 2012. "The Evidence Mounts on the Benefits of Preventing Unintended Pregnancy." *Contraception* 87 (2): 126–27.

Fingerman, Karen L. 2001. "A Distant Closeness: Intimacy Between Parents and Their Children in Later life." *Generations* 25 (2): 26–33.

Fingerman, Karen L., Yen-Pi Cheng, Eric D. Wesselmann, Steven Zarit, Frank Furstenberg, and Kira S. Birditt. 2012. "Helicopter Parents and Landing Pad Kids: Intense Parental Support of Grown Children." *Journal of Marriage and Family* 74: 880–96.

Fingerson, Laura. 2006. *Girls in Power: Gender, Body, and Menstruation in Adolescence.* Albany, NY: SUNY Press.

Firey, Walter. 1945. "Sentiment and Symbolism as Ecological Variables." *American Sociological Review* 10: 140–48.

Fischer, Benedikt, Eugenia Oviedo-Joekes, Peter Blanken, Christian Haasan, Jürgen Rehm, Martin T. Schecter, John Strang, and Wim van den Brink. 2007. "Heroin-Assisted Treatment (HAT) a Decade Later: A Brief Update on Science and Politics." *Journal of Urban Health* 84 (4): 552–62.

Fischer, D. H. 1978. *Growing Old in America.* New York: Oxford University Press.

Fishman, Mark. 1978. "Crime Waves as Ideology." *Social Problems* 25 (5): 531–43.

Flack, William F., Jr., Kimberly A. Daubman, Marcia L. Caron, Jenica A. Asadorian, Nicole R. D'Aureli, Shannon N. Gigliotti, et al. 2007. "Risk Factors and Consequences of Unwanted Sex Among University Students: Hooking Up, Alcohol, and Stress Response." *Journal of Interpersonal Violence* 22 (2): 139–57.

Flaxman, Greg, with John Kucsera, Gary Orfield, Jennifer Ayscue, and Genevieve Siegel-Hawley. 2013. *A Status Quo of Segregation: Racial and Economic Imbalance in New Jersey Schools, 1989–2010.* Los Angeles: Civil Rights Project, UCLA. http://civilrightsproject.ucla .edu/research/k-12–education/integration -and-diver sity/a-status-quo-of-segregation -racial-and-economic-imbalance-in-new -jersey-schools-1989–2010/Norflet_NJ_ Final_101013_POSTb.pdf.

Focus on the Family. 2016. "Foundational Values." Accessed August 11, 2016. http://www.focusonthefamily.com/about/ foundational-values#vision.

Food Security and Nutrition Analysis Unit— Somalia. 2013. "Study Suggests 258,000 Somalis Died Due to Severe Food Insecurity and Famine." Press release, May 2. http://www.fsnau.org/in-focus/ technical-release-study-suggests-258000– somalis-died-due-severe-food-insecurity -and-famine-.

Fothergill, Alice, Enrique G. Maestas, and JoAnne D. Darlington. 1999. "Race, Ethnicity and Disasters in the United States: A Review of the Literature." *Disasters* 23 (2): 156–73.

Fragile Families and Child Wellbeing Study. 2012. "Fact Sheet." http://www .fragilefamilies.princeton.edu/documents/ FragileFamiliesandChild WellbeingStudyFactSheet.pdf.

Frankel, Arthur, and Debra A. Curtis. 2008. "What's in a Purse? Maybe a Woman's Reputation." *Sex Roles* 59: 615–22.

Frankenberg, Ruth. 1993. *White Women, Race Matters: The Social Construction of Whiteness.* Minneapolis: University of Minnesota Press.

Frantz, Douglas, and Catherine Collins. 1999. *Celebration, U.S.A.: Living in Disney's Brave New Town.* New York: Henry Holt.

Frech, Adrianne, and Rachel Tolbert Kimbro. 2011. "Maternal Mental Health, Neighborhood Characteristics, and Time Investments in Children." *Journal of Marriage and Family* 73: 605–20.

Frederick, David A., H. Kate St. John, Justin R. Garcia, and Elisabeth A. Lloyd. 2017. "Differences in Orgasm Frequency Among Gay, Lesbian, Bisexual, and Heterosexual Men and Women in a U.S. National Sample." *Archives of Sexual Behavior.* DOI:10.1007/s10508–017–0939–z.

Freedman, D. S., L. K. Khan, M. K. Serdula, W. H. Dietz, S. R. Srinivasan, and G. S. Berenson. 2005. "The Relation of Childhood BMI to Adult Adiposity: The Bogalusa Heart Study." *Pediatrics* 115 (1): 22–27.

Freeman, Richard B. 2007. *America Works: Critical Thoughts on the Exceptional U.S. Labor Market.* New York: Russell Sage Foundation.

Freidenfelds, Lara. 2009. *The Modern Period: Menstruation in Twentieth-Century America.* Baltimore, MD: Johns Hopkins University Press.

Frey, Richard, and D'Vera Cohn. 2011. "Living Together: The Economics of Cohabitation." Pew Research Center, Social and Demographic Trends, June 27. http://www .pewsocialtrends.org/files/2011/06/pew -social-trends-cohabitation-06–2011.pdf.

Friedman, Thomas. 2005. *The World Is Flat: A Brief History of the Twenty-First Century.* New York: Picador.

Friedmann, John. 1986. "The World City Hypothesis." *Development and Change* 17 (1): 69–83.

Friese, Bettina, and Karen Bogenschneider. 2009. "The Voice of Experience: How Social Scientists Communicate Family Research to Policymakers." *Family Relations* 58 (2): 229–43.

Fritschi, L., and T. Driscoll. 2006. "Cancer Due to Occupation in Australia." *Australian and*

New Zealand Journal of Public Health 30 (3): 213–19.

Fry, Douglas. 2006. *The Human Potential for Peace*. New York: Oxford University Press.

Fry, Richard. 2013. "A Rising Share of Young Adults Live in Their Parents' Home." Pew Research Center, Social and Demographic Trends, August 1. http://www .pewsocialtrends.org/2013/08/01/ a-rising- share-of-young-adults-live-in -their-parents-home.

————. 2015. "Record Share of Young Women are Living With their Parents, Relatives." Pew Social Research, November 11. Accessed August 11, 2016. http://www .pewresearch.org/fact-tank/2015/11/11/ record-share-of-young-women-are-living -with-their-parents-relatives/.

————. 2016a. "For First Time in Modern Era, Living With Parents Edges Out Other Living Arrangements for 18- to 34-Year-Olds." Pew Research Center, Social and Demographic Trends, May 24. http://www .pewsocialtrends.org/2016/05/24/for-first -time-in-modern-era-living-with-parents -edges out-other-living-arrangements-for -18-to-34-year-olds/.

————. 2016b. "The Evolving Landscape of Young Adult Living Arrangements." May 24. Accessed August 11. http://www .pewsocialtrends.org/2016/05/24/1-the -evolving-landscape-of-young-adult-living -arrangements/.

Funkhouser, G. Ray. 1973. "The Issues of the Sixties: An Exploratory Study in the Dynamics of Public Opinion." *Public Opinion Quarterly* 66: 942–48, 959.

Furgal, Christopher, and Jacinthe Seguin. 2006. "Climate Change, Health, and Vulnerability in Canadian Northern Aboriginal Communities." *Environmental Health Perspectives* 114 (12): 1964–70.

Furstenberg, Frank R. 2002. "What a Good Marriage Can't Do." *New York Times,* August 13. http://www.nytimes .com/2002/08/13/opinion/what-a-good -marriage-can-t-do.html.

————. 2004. "Values, Policy, and the Family." In *The Future of the Family,* edited by Daniel P. Moynihan, Timothy M. Smeeding, and Lee Rainwater, 267–75. New York: Russell Sage Foundation.

Futrell, Robert, Christie Batson, Barbara G. Brents, Andrea Dassopoulos, Chrissy

Nicholas, Mark J. Salvaggio, and Candace Griffith. 2010. *City of Las Vegas Your City Your Way Initiative: Final Report.* Las Vegas, NV: Las Vegas Metropolitan Area Research Team. http://www.lasveg asnevada.gov/files/Your_City_Your_Way_ Final_Report.pdf.

Gagnon, John H., and William Simon. 1973. *Sexual Conduct: The Social Sources of Human Sexuality.* Chicago: Aldine.

Galdas, Paul M., Francine Cheater, and Paul Marshall. 2005. "Men and Health Help-Seeking Behaviour: Literature Review." *Journal of Advanced Nursing* 49 (6): 616–23.

Gallagher, Charles A. 2003a. "Miscounting Race: Explaining Whites' Misperceptions of Racial Group Size." *Sociological Perspectives* 46 (3): 381–96.

————. 2003b. "Playing the White Ethnic Card: Using Ethnic Identity to Deny Contemporary Racism." In *White Out: The Continuing Significance of Racism,* edited by Ashley W. Doane and Eduardo Bonilla-Silva, 145–58. New York: Routledge.

Galligan, Roslyn F., and Deborah J. Terry. 1993. "Romantic Ideals, Fear of Negative Implications, and the Practice of Safe Sex." *Journal of Applied Social Psychology* 23 (20): 1685–1711.

Gamson, William A. 1992. *Talking Politics.* New York: Cambridge University Press.

————. 1995. "Hiroshima, the Holocaust, and the Politics of Exclusion: 1994 Presidential Address." *American Sociological Review* 60 (1): 1–20.

Gamson, William A., and Andre Modigliani. 1987. "The Changing Culture of Affirmative Action." *Research in Political Sociology* 3: 137–77.

Gans, Herbert J. 1971. "The Uses of Poverty: The Poor Pay All." *Social Policy* (July/August): 20–24.

————. 1979. "Symbolic Ethnicity: The Future of Ethnic Groups and Cultures in America." *Ethnic and Racial Studies* 2 (1): 1–20.

————. 1992. "Comment: Ethnic Invention and Acculturation: A Bumpy Line Approach." *Journal of American Ethnic History* 12 (1): 42–52.

Garcia, Lorena. 2009. "'Now Why Do You Want to Know About That?' Heteronormativity, Sexism, and Racism in the Sexual (Mis) education of Latina Youth." *Gender & Society* 23 (4): 520–41.

Garfinkel, Harold. 1967. *Studies in Ethnomethodology.* Englewood Cliffs, NJ: Prentice-Hall.

Gat, Azar. 2008. *War in Human Civilization.* New York: Oxford University Press.

Gavey, Nicola. 1999. "'I Wasn't Raped, but . . .': Revisiting Definitional Problems in Sexual Victimization." In *New Versions of Victims: Feminists Struggle With the Concept,* edited by Sharon Lamb, 57–81. New York: New York University Press.

————. 2005. *Just Sex? The Cultural Scaffolding of Rape.* New York: Routledge.

Gay and Lesbian Archives of the Pacific Northwest. 2007. "Sodomy Laws: Virginia." Accessed March 24, 2017. http://www.glapn.org/sodomylaws/usa/ virginia/virginia.htm.

Geisinger, Brandi N. 2011. "Critical Feminist Theory, Rape, and Hooking Up." Master's thesis, Iowa State University.

Gengler, Amanda M. 2012. "Defying (Dis) Empowerment in a Battered Women's Shelter: Moral Rhetorics, Intersectionality, and Processes of Control and Resistance." *Social Problems* 59: 501–21.

George, Linda K. 2005. "Socioeconomic Status and Health Across the Life Course: Progress and Prospects." *Journal of Gerontology: Social Sciences* 60B: 135–39.

Gepts, Paul. 2005. "Introduction of Transgenic Crops In Centers of Origin and Domestication." In *Controversies in Science and Technology: From Maize to Menopause,* edited by Daniel Lee Kleinman, Abby J. Kinchy, and Jo Handelsman, 119–134. Madison: University of Wisconsin Press.

Gerbner, George, Larry Gross, Michael Morgan, and Nancy Signorielli. 1994. "Growing Up With Television: The Cultivation Perspective." In *Media Effects: Advances in Theory and Research,* edited by Jennings Bryant and Dolf Zillmann, 17–41. Hillsdale, NJ: Lawrence Erlbaum.

Gerbner, George, Larry Gross, Nancy Signorielli, and Michael Morgan. 1986. "Television's Mean World: Violence Profile No. 14–15." Unpublished paper, Annenberg School of Communications, University of Pennsylvania.

Geronimus, Arline T., Margaret Hicken, Danya Keene, and John Bound. 2006. "'Weathering' and Age Patterns of

Allostatic Load Scores Among Blacks and Whites in the United States." *American Journal of Public Health* 96: 826–33.

Gerson, Kathleen. 1985. *Hard Choices: How Women Decide About Work, Career, and Motherhood.* Berkeley, CA: University of California Press.

———. 2010. *The Unfinished Revolution: How a New Generation Is Reshaping Family, Work, and Gender in America.* New York: Oxford University Press.

Gilbert, Dennis. 2015. *The American Class Structure in an Age of Growing Inequality.* Thousand Oaks, CA: Sage.

Gladwell, Malcolm. 2010. "Talent Grab: Why Do We Pay Our Stars So Much Money?" *New Yorker,* October 11, 85–93.

Glassner, Barry. 2012. "Organic Food for Thought on Campuses." *Chronicle of Higher Education,* March 11. http://chronicle .com/article/Organic-Food-for-Thought -on/131119.

Glaze, Lauren E., and Laura M. Maruschak. 2008. "Parents in Prison and Their Minor Children." U.S. Department of Justice, Bureau of Justice Statistics, Special Report, NCJ 222984, August. http://www .bjs.gov/content/pub/pdf/pptmc.pdf.

Glazer, Sarah. 2010. "Europe's Immigration Turmoil: Is Europe Becoming Intolerant of Foreigners?" *CQ Global Researcher* 4 (12): 289–320.

Glenn, Evelyn Nakano. 2002. *Unequal Freedom: How Race and Gender Shaped American Citizenship and Labor.* Cambridge, MA: Harvard University Press.

Glenn, Norval, and Elizabeth Marquardt. 2001. *Hooking Up, Hanging Out, and Hoping for Mr. Right: College Women on Dating and Mating Today.* New York: Institute for American Values.

Golann, Joann W. 2015. "The Paradox of Success at a No-Excuses Charter School." *Sociology of Education* 88 (2): 103–19.

Goldberg, Abbie E., and Katherine R. Allen, eds. 2013. *LGBT-Parent Families.* Heidelberg, Germany: Springer.

Goldberg, Mark S., Jack Siemiatyck, Ron DeWar, Marie Désy, and Hélène Riberdy. 1999. "Risk of Developing Cancer Relative to Living Near a Municipal Solid Waste Landfill Site in Montreal, Quebec, Canada." *Archives of Environmental Health* 54 (4): 291–96.

Goldin, Claudia, and Lawrence F. Katz. 2010. "Putting the "Co" in Education: Timing, Reasons, and Consequences of College Coeducation From 1835 to the Present." NBER Working Paper 16281. National Bureau of Economic Research.

Goldman, Adam, and Matt Apuzzo. 2013. "NYPD Linked Mosques to Terror." *New York Times,* August 29.

Goldrick-Rab, Sara, Jed Richardson, and Anthony Hernandez. 2017. *Hungry and Homeless in College: Results From a National Study of Basic Needs Insecurity in Higher Education.* Wisconsin Hope Lab.

Goldstein, Joshua. 2011. *Winning the War on War.* New York: Penguin Books.

Gone, Joseph P. 2007. "'We Never Was Happy Living Like a Whiteman': Mental Health Disparities and the Postcolonial Predicament in American Indian Communities." *American Journal of Community Psychology* 40 (3/4): 290–300.

Goode, Erich, and Nachman Ben-Yehuda. 2009. *Moral Panics: The Social Construction of Deviance,* 2nd ed. Malden, MA: Wiley-Blackwell.

Goodwin, Glenn A., and Joseph Scimecca. 2006. *Classical Sociological Theory: Rediscovering the Promise of Sociology.* Belmont, CA: Thomson Higher Education.

Gootman, Elissa, and Catherine Saint Louis. 2012. "Maternity Leave? It's More Like a Pause." *New York Times,* July 20. http:// www.nytimes.com/2012/07/22/fashion/ for-executive-women-is-maternity-leave -necessary.html?_r=1&agewanted=all.

Gordon, Milton. 1964. *Assimilation in American Life: The Role of Race, Religion, and National Origins.* New York: Oxford University Press.

Gottdiener, Mark, and Joe R. Feagin. 1988. "The Paradigm Shift in Urban Sociology." *Urban Affairs Review* 24 (2): 163–87.

Gottfredson, Michael R., and Travis Hirschi. 1990. *A General Theory of Crime.* Stanford, CA: Stanford University Press.

Goudreau, Jenna. 2010. "Most Popular College Majors for Women." *Forbes,* August 10. http://www.forbes.com/2010/08/10/most -popular-college-degrees-for-women -forbes-woman-leadership-education -business.html?boxes=Homepagechannels.

Granovetter, Mark, 1995. *Getting a Job: A Study of Contacts and Careers,* 2nd ed. Chicago: University of Chicago Press.

Grant, K., F. C. Goldizen, P. D. Sly, M. N. Brune, M. Neira, M. van den Berg, and R. E. Norman. 2013. "Health Consequences of Exposure to E-Waste: A Systematic Review." *The Lancet Global Health* 1 (6): e350–e361.

Grant, Melissa Gira. 2013. "Unpacking the Sex Trafficking Panic." *Contemporary Sexuality* 47 (2): 2–6.

Graves, Joseph L., Jr. 2004. *The Race Myth: Why We Pretend Race Exists in America.* New York: Dutton.

Green, Adam Isaiah. 2008. "Erotic Habitus: Toward a Sociology of Desire." *Theory and Society* 37 (6): 597–626.

———. 2011. "Playing the (Sexual) Field: The Interactional Basis of Systems of Sexual Stratification." *Social Psychology Quarterly* 74 (3): 244–66.

Greene, Jeremy A., and David Herzberg. 2010. "Hidden in Plain Sight: Marketing Prescription Drugs to Consumers in the Twentieth Century." *American Journal of Public Health* 100 (5): 793–803.

Greenstone, Michael. 2012. "The Uncomfortable Truth About American Wages." *New York Times,* Economix blog, October 22. http:// economix.blogs.nytimes.com/2012/10/22/ the-uncomfortable-truth-about-american -wages.

Greenstone, Michael, and Adam Looney. 2011. "The Great Recession May Be Over, but American Families Are Working Harder Than Ever." Brookings Institution, Hamilton Project blog, July 8. http://www.brookings .edu/blogs/jobs/posts/2011/07/08–jobs -greenstone-looney.

Greeson, Megan R., Rebecca Campbell, and Giannina Fehler-Cabral 2014. "Cold or Caring? Adolescent Sexual Assault Victims' Perceptions of Their Interactions With the Police." *Violence and Victims* 29 (4): 636–51.

Griffith, James. 1995. "An Empirical Examination of a Model of Social Climate in Elementary Schools." *Basic and Applied Psychology* 17 (1–2): 97–117.

Griffiths, Mark D. 2012. "Sex Addiction: A Review of Empirical Research." *Addiction Research and Theory* 20 (2): 111–24.

Grinshteyn, Erin, and David Hemenway. 2016. "Violent Death Rates: The US Compared with Other High-income OECD Countries, 2010. *The American Journal of Medicine* 129(3): 266–73.

Grochowski, Janet R. 1998. "Strategic Living Communities: Families for the Future." *Futurics: Quarterly Journal of Futures Research* 21: 24–29.

———. 2000. "Families as Strategic Living Communities." Paper presented at the annual meetings of the American Academy of Health Behavior, Santa Fe, New Mexico, September.

Gross, Matthias. 2010. *Ignorance and Surprise: Science, Society, and Ecological Design.* Cambridge, MA: MIT Press.

Grossman, Jean Baldwin, and Eileen M. Garry. 1997. *Mentoring: A Proven Delinquency Prevention Strategy.* OJJDP Juvenile Justice Bulletin, April. Washington, DC: U.S. Department of Justice. https://www.ncjrs.gov/pdffiles/164834.pdf.

Grossman, Jean Baldwin, and Joseph P. Tierney. 1998. "Does Mentoring Work? An Impact Study of the Big Brothers Big Sisters Program." *Evaluation Review* 22 (3): 403–26.

Grubb, Amy, and Emily Turner. 2012. "Attribution of Blame in Rape Cases: A Review of the Impact of Rape Myth Acceptance, Gender Role Conformity, and Substance Use on Victim Blaming." *Aggression & Violent Behavior* 17 (5): 443–52.

Guarino-Ghezzi, Susan. 1994. "Reintegrative Police Surveillance of Juvenile Offenders: Forging an Urban Model." *Crime & Delinquency* 40 (2): 131–53.

Guerino, Paul, Paige M. Harrison, and William J. Sabol. 2011. *Prisoners in 2010.* U.S. Bureau of Justice Statistics, NCJ 236096. Washington, DC: U.S. Department of Justice. http://www.bjs.gov/content/pub/pdf/p10.pdf.

Gusfield, Joseph R. 1986. *Symbolic Crusade: Status Politics and the American Temperance Movement,* 2nd ed. Urbana: University of Illinois Press.

Hacker, Andrew. 2003. *Two Nations: Black and White, Separate, Hostile, Unequal.* New York: Scribner.

Hackman, J. Richard, and Greg R. Oldham. 1976. "Motivation Through the Design of Work: Test of a Theory." *Organizational Behavior and Human Performance* 16: 250–79.

Hajdu, David. 2008. *The Ten-Cent Plague: The Great Comic Book Scare and How It Changed America.* New York: Farrar, Straus and Giroux.

Hajjar, Ihab, Jane Morley Kotchen, and Theodore A. Kotchen. 2006. "Hypertension: Trends in Prevalence, Incidence, and Control." *Annual Review of Public Health* 27: 465–90.

Hald, Gert M., Neil Malamuth, and Carlin Yuen. 2010. "Pornography and Attitudes Supporting Violence Against Women: Revisiting the Relationship in Nonexperimental Studies." *Aggressive Behavior* 36 (1): 14–20.

Half the Sky Movement. n.d. "Sex Trafficking and Forced Prostitution." Accessed March 25. http://www.halftheskymovement.org/campaigns/sex-trafficking.

Halle, David, and Andrew A. Beveridge. 2011. "The Rise and Decline of the L.A. and New York Schools." In *The City, Revisited: Urban Theory From Chicago, Los Angeles, and New York,* edited by Dennis R. Judd and Dick Simpson, 137–68. Minneapolis: University of Minnesota Press.

Hallerod, Björn, and Jan-Eric Gustafsson. 2011. "A Longitudinal Analysis of the Relationship Between Changes in Socio-economic Status and Changes in Health." *Social Science & Medicine* 72 (1): 116–23.

Hämäläinen, P., J. Takala, and K. L. Saarela. 2007. "Global Estimates of Fatal Work-Related Diseases." *American Journal of Industrial Medicine* 50 (1): 28–41.

Hamilton, Laura, and Elizabeth A. Armstrong. 2009. "Gendered Sexuality in Young Adulthood: Double Binds and Flawed Options." *Gender & Society* 23 (5): 589–616.

Hansen, James, Makiko Sato, Paul Hearty, Reto Ruedy, Maxwell Kelley, Valerie Masson-Delmotte, Gary Russell. 2016. "Ice melt, sea level rise and superstorms: evidence from paleoclimate data, climate modeling, and modern observations that 2 C global warming could be dangerous." *Atmospheric Chemistry and Physics* 16 (6): 3761–3812.

Hansen, Randall. 2012. *The Centrality of Employment in Immigrant Integration in Europe.* Washington, DC: Migration Policy Institute.

Harawa, Nina, John Williams, Hema Ramamurthi, and Trista Bingham. 2006. "Perceptions Towards Condom Use, Sexual Activity, and HIV Disclosure Among HIV-Positive African American Men Who Have Sex With Men: Implications for Heterosexual Transmission." *Journal of Urban Health* 83 (4): 682–94.

Haraway, Donna. 1991. "Situated Knowledges: The Science in Feminism and the Privilege of Partial Perspective." Pp. 183–201 in *Simians, Cyborgs and Women,* edited by Donna Haraway. London: Routledge.

Haraway, Donna. 1997. *Modest_Witness@ Second_Millennium. Femaleman_Meets_ Oncomouse.* New York: Routledge.

Harding, Sandra. 2009. "Postcolonial and Feminist Philosophies of Science and Technology: Convergences and Dissonances." *Postcolonial Studies* 12(4): 401–21.

Harding, Sandra. 1991. *Whose Science, Whose Knowledge?* Ithaca: Cornell University Press.

Harding, Sandra. 1993. *The "Radical" Economy of Science: Toward a Democratic Future.* Bloomington: Indiana University Press.

Harding, Sandra. 1998. Is *Science Multicultural?: Postcolonialisms, Feminisms, and Epistemologies.* Bloomington, IN: Indiana University Press.

Harrell, Erika. 2011. "Workplace Violence, 1993–2009: National Crime Victimization Survey and the Census of Fatal Occupational Injuries." U.S. Department of Justice, Bureau of Justice Statistics, Special Report, NCJ 233231, March. http://bjs.gov/content/pub/pdf/wv09.pdf.

Harrington, Carol. 2012. "Prostitution Policy Models and Feminist Knowledge Politics in New Zealand and Sweden." *Sexuality Research and Social Policy* 9 (4): 337–49.

Harrington, Michael. 1962. *The Other America.* New York: Macmillan.

Harris, Louis. 1976. *The Myth and Reality of Aging in America.* Washington, DC: National Council on the Aging.

Harris-Perry, Melissa. 2017. "Person of the Year 2016 Runner-Up: Beyoncé." *Time* magazine. Accessed April 15, 2017. http://time.com/time-person-of-the-year-2016–beyonce-runner-up/.

Hart, Betty, and Todd R. Risley. 2003. "The Early Catastrophe: The 30 Million Word Gap by Age 3." *American Educator* 27 (1): 4–9.

Hartsock, Nancy C. M. 1983 (2013). "The Feminist Standpoint: Toward a Specifically Feminist Historical Materialism." In *Feminist Theory Reader: Local and Global Perspectives, Third Edition,* edited by Carole R. McCann and Seung-Kyung Kim, 354–69. New York: Routledge.

Hartung, William. 2011. *Prophets of War: Lockheed Martin and the Making of the Military-Industrial Complex.* New York. Nation Books.

Harvey, David. 1973. *Social Justice and the City.* Athens: University of Georgia Press.

Hassan, Riaz. 2011. *Suicide Bombings.* New York: Routledge.

Havens, J., M. Lofwall, S. Frost, C. Oser, R. Crosby, and C. Leukefeld. 2013. "Factors Associated With Prevalent Hepatitis C Infection Among Rural Appalachian Injection Drug Users." *American Journal of Public Health*, 103 (1): 44–52.

Havighurst, Robert James, and Ruth Albrecht. 1953. *Old People.* New York: Longmans Green.

Hays, Sharon. 1996. *The Cultural Contradictions of Motherhood.* New Haven, CT: Yale University Press.

Head, Jonathan. 2004. "Japan's AIDS Time Bomb." BBC News, July 13. http://news .bbc.co.uk/2/hi/asia-pacific/3890689.stm.

Healey, Joseph F. 2009. *Race, Ethnicity, Gender, and Class: The Sociology of Group Conflict and Change,* 5th ed. Thousand Oaks, CA: Pine Forge Press.

Heaney, Stephen J. 2012. "Marriage Vote: For the Children." *Star Tribune,* October 16. http://www.startribune.com/opinion/ commentaries/174479341.html.

Heider, Karl G. 1976. "Dani Sexuality: A Low Energy System." *Man* 11 (2): 188–201.

Helgeson, Baird. 2012. "Same-Sex Marriage Ban Defeated." *Star Tribune,* November 6. http://www.startribune.com/politics/ statelocal/177544631.html?refer=y.

Helliwell, Christine. 2000. "'It's Only a Penis': Rape, Feminism, and Difference." *Signs: Journal of Women in Culture and Society* 25 (3): 789–826.

———. 2001. "Engendering Sameness." *Intersections: Gender, History and Culture in the Asian Context* 6. Accessed March 22, 2017. http://intersections.anu.edu.au/ issue6/helliwell.html.

Hemmens, Craig, David C. Brody, and Cassia C. Spohn. 2010. *Criminal Courts: A Contemporary Perspective.* Thousand Oaks, CA: Sage.

Henrichson, Christian, and Ruth Delaney. 2012. "The Price of Prisons: What Incarceration Costs Taxpayers." *Federal Sentencing Reporter,* 25: 68–74.

Henson, Kevin. 1996. *Just a Temp.* Philadelphia: Temple University Press.

Herrnstein, Richard J., and Charles Murray. 1994. *The Bell Curve: Intelligence and Class Structure in American Life.* New York: Free Press.

Hess, David J. 1999. *Evaluating Alternative Cancer Therapies.* New Brunswick, NJ: Rutgers University Press.

———. 2009. "The Potentials and Limitations of Civil Society Research: Getting Undone Science Done." *Sociological Inquiry* 79 (3): 306–27.

Hesse-Biber, Sharlene N. 2006. *The Cult of Thinness.* New York: Oxford University Press.

Hesse-Biber, Sharlene N., Patricia Leavy, Courtney E. Quinn, and Julia Zoino. 2006. "The Mass Marketing of Disordered Eating and Eating Disorders: The Social Psychology of Women, Thinness and Culture." *Women's Studies International Forum* 29 (2): 208–24.

Heyns, Barbara 1978. *Summer Learning and the Effects of Schooling.* New York: Academic Press.

Higher Education Research Institute. 2013. "CIRP Freshman Survey Results for 2013." http:// heri.ucla.edu.

Hilgartner, Stephen, and Charles L. Bosk. 1988. "The Rise and Fall of Social Problems: A Public Arenas Model." *American Journal of Sociology* 94 (1): 53–78.

Hill, Shirley A. 2012. *Families: A Social Class Perspective.* Thousand Oaks, CA: Sage.

Hill, Terrence D., Amy M. Burdette, and Ellen L. Idler. 2011. "Religious Involvement, Health Status, and Mortality Risk." In *Handbook of Aging,* edited by Richard A. Settersten Jr. and Jacqueline L. Angel, 533–46. New York: Springer.

Himmelstein, Mary S., and Diana T. Sanchez. 2016. "Masculinity in the Doctor's Office: Masculinity, Gendered Doctor Preference and Doctor-Patient Communication." *Preventive Medicine* 84: 34–40.

Hinduja, Sameer, and Justin W. Patchin. 2009. *Bullying Beyond the Schoolyard: Preventing and Responding to Cyberbullying.* Thousand Oaks, CA: Sage.

Hirschi, Travis. 1969. *Causes of Delinquency.* Berkeley, CA: University of California Press.

Hirvonen, Lalaina H. 2008. "Intergenerational Earnings Mobility Among Daughters and Sons: Evidence From Sweden and a Comparison With the United States." *Journal of Economics and Sociology* 67: 777–826.

Hlavka, Heather R. 2014. "Normalizing Sexual Violence: Young Women Account for Harassment and Abuse." *Gender & Society* 28 (3): 337–58.

Hochschild, Arlie Russel. 1989. *The Second Shift: Working Parents and the Revolution at Home.* New York: Viking.

Hodges, Melissa, and Michelle Budig. 2010. "Who Gets the Daddy Bonus? Organizational Hegemonic Masculinity and the Impact of Fatherhood on Earnings." *Gender & Society* 24 (6): 717–45.

Hodson, Randy. 1989. "Gender Differences in Job Satisfaction: Why Aren't Women More Dissatisfied?" *Sociological Quarterly* 30 (3): 385–99.

Hogan, Christopher, June Lunney, Jon Gabel, and Joanne Lynn. 2001. "Medicare Beneficiaries' Costs of Care in the Last Year of Life." *Health Affairs* 20 (4): 188–95.

Hondagneu-Sotelo, Pierrette, and Ernestine Avila. 1997. "'I'm Here, but I'm There': The Meanings of Latina Transnational Motherhood." *Gender & Society* 11(5): 548–71.

Hood, Robert. 2003. "AIDS, Crisis, and Activist Science." In *Science and Other Cultures: Issues in Philosophies of Science and Technology,* edited by Robert Figueroa and Sandra Harding, 15–25. New York: Routledge.

Hook, Jennifer L., Jennifer L. Romich, JoAnn S. Lee, Maureen O. Marcenko, and Ji Young Kang. 2016. "Trajectories of Economic Disconnection Among Families in the Child Welfare System." *Social Problems* 63 (2): 161–79.

hooks, bell. 2016. "Moving Beyond Pain." Accessed April 15, 2017. http://www .bellhooksinstitute.com/blog/2016/5/9/ moving-beyond-pain.

Horowitz, Roger. 1997. "'Where Men Will Not Work': Gender, Power, Space, and the Sexual Division of Labor in America's Meatpacking Industry, 1890–1990." *Technology and Culture* 38 (1): 187–213.

Horsfall, Jan. 2001. "Gender and Mental Illness: An Australian Overview." *Mental Health Nursing* 22 (4): 421–38.

Hossfeld, Leslie, Brooke Kelly, and Julia Waity. 2016. "Solutions to the Social Problem of

Food Insecurity in the United States." In *Agenda for Social Justice: Solutions for 2016,* edited by G. Muschert, G., Klocke, R. Perrucci, and J. Shefner. Bristol: Policy Press, 39–48.

Hoyt, Homer. 1939. *The Structure and Growth of Residential Neighborhoods in American Cities.* Atlanta, GA: Federal Highway Administration.

Hu, Wei-Yin. 2003. "Marriage and Economic Incentives: Evidence From a Welfare Experiment." *Journal of Human Resources* 38 (4): 942–63.

Hua, Cynthia. 2013. "2012–'13 Sexual Climate Assessment Released." *Yale Daily News,* May 15. http://yaledaily news.com/crosscampus/2013/05/15/2012–13–sexual-climate-assessment-released.

Hughes, Caitlin Elizabeth, and Alex Stevens. 2010. "What Can We Learn From the Portuguese Decriminalization of Illicit Drugs?" *British Journal of Criminology* 50 (6): 999–1022.

Human Rights Campaign. 2016. *Marriage Equality Around the World.* Accessed August 19, 2016. http://hrc-assets.s3 website-us-east-1.amazonaws.com//files/assets/resources/WorldMarriageMap.pdf.

Human Rights Watch. 2009. *Decades of Disparity: Drug Arrests and Race in the United States.* New York: Human Rights Watch.

Human Security Report Project. 2011. *Human Security Report 2009/2010: The Causes of Peace and the Shrinking Costs of War.* New York: Oxford University Press.

———. 2012. *Human Security Report 2012: Sexual Violence, Education, and War: Beyond the Mainstream Narrative.* Vancouver: Human Security Press.

Humes, Karen R., Nicholas A. Jones, and Roberto R. Ramirez. 2011. *Overview of Race and Hispanic Origin: 2010.* U.S. Census Bureau, Census Brief C2010BR-02. Washington, DC: Government Printing Office. http://www.census.gov/prod/cen2010/briefs/c2010br-02.pdf.

Hunter, Myra. 2007. "Bio-psycho-socio-cultural Perspectives on Menopause." *Best Practice & Research: Clinical Obstetrics & Gynaecology* 21 (2): 261–74.

Hurd Clarke, Laura. 2011. *Facing Age: Women Growing Older in Anti-Aging Culture.* Lanham, MD: Rowman & Littlefield.

Hurn, Christopher J. 1993. *The Limits and Possibilities of Schooling: An Introduction to the Sociology of Education,* 3rd ed. Boston: Allyn & Bacon.

Hust, Stacey J. T., Kathleen Boyce Rodgers, and Benjamin Bayly. 2017. "Scripting Sexual Consent: Internalized Traditional Sexual Scripts and Sexual Consent Expectancies Among College Students." *Family Relations* 66 (1): 197–210.

Hvas, Lotte, and Dorte Effersøe Gannik. 2008. "Discourses on Menopause—Part 1: Menopause Described in Texts Addressed to Danish Women 1996–2004." *Health* 12 (2): 157–75.

Hyams, Melissa. 2006. "*La Escuela:* Young Latina Women Negotiating Identities in School." In *Latina Girls: Voices of Adolescent Strength in the United States,* edited by Jill Denner and Bianca L. Guzmán, 93–108. New York: New York University Press.

Hyde, Abbey, Margaret P. Treacy, Anne P. Scott, Padraig MacNeela, Michelle Butler, Jonathan Drennan, Kate Irving, and Anne Byrne. 2006. "Social Regulation, Medicalisation, and the Nurse's Role: Insights From an Analysis of Nursing Documentation." *International Journal of Nursing Studies* 43 (6): 735–44.

Hynie, Michaela, John E. Lydon, Sylvana Cote, and Seth Wiener. 1998. "Relational Sexual Scripts and Women's Condom Use: The Importance of Internalized Norms." *Journal of Sex Research* 35 (4): 370–80.

Iannotti, Ronald J., and Jing Wang. 2013. "Patterns of Physical Activity, Sedentary Behavior, and Diet in U.S. Adolescents." *Journal of Adolescent Health* 53 (2): 280–86.

ICT Facts and Figures. 2016. International Telecommunications Union. Geneva, Switzerland, June 2016.

Iles, Alastair. 2004. "Mapping Environmental Justice In Technology Flows: Computer Waste Impacts in Asia." *Global Environmental Politics* 4 (4): 76–106.

Ingersoll, Richard. 2003. *Who Controls Teachers' Work? Power and Accountability in America's Schools.* Cambridge, MA: Harvard University Press.

———. 2004. "Why Some Schools Have More Underqualified Teachers Than Others." In *Brookings Papers on Education Policy,* edited by Diane Ravitch. Washington, DC: Brookings Institution Press.

Institute for Women's Policy Research, 2010. "The Gender Wage Gap by Occupation." April, p. 2. Accessed December 21, 2010. http://www.iwpr.org/pdf/c350a.pdf.

———. 2011. "The Gender Wage Gap: 2010." Fact Sheet, IWPR C350, September. http://www.iwpr.org.

———. 2016. "The Gender Wage Gap by Occupation 2015." Accessed March 1, 2017. https://iwpr.org/publications/the-gender-wage-gap-by-occupation-2015–and-by-race-and-ethnicity/.

International Rescue Committee. 2012. "DRC Study Shows Congo's Neglected Crisis Leaves 5.4 Million Dead." http://www.rescue.org/news/irc-study-shows-congos-neglected-crisis-leaves-54–million-dead-peace-deal-n-kivu-increased-aid—4331.

International Telecommunications Union. 2013. *The World in 2013: ICT Facts and Figures.* Geneva: International Telecommunications Union. http://www.itu.int/en/ITU-D/Statistics/Documents/facts/ICTFactsFigures2013–e.pdf.

Internet Crime Complaint Center. 2011. *2010 Internet Crime Report.* Washington, DC: National White Collar Crime Center. http://www.ic3.gov/media/annualreport/2010_ic3report.pdf.

Iraq Body Count. 2017. Accessed March 25. http://www.iraqbodycount.org.

Ivanov, Ivan D., and Kurt Straif. 2006. "Prevention of Occupational Cancer." *World Health Organization GOHNET Newsletter* 11: 1–4.

Iyengar, Shanto, and Donald R. Kinder. 2010. *News That Matters: Television and American Opinion,* updated ed. Chicago: University of Chicago Press.

Jackman, Mary, and Marie Crane. 1986. "Some of My Best Friends Are Black: Interracial Friendships and Whites' Racial Attitudes." *Public Opinion Quarterly* 50: 459–86.

Jackson, C. Kirabo, Rucker C. Johnson, and Claudia Persico. 2015. *The Effects of School Spending on Educational and Economic Outcomes: Evidence From School Finance Reforms.* No. w20847. Cambridge, MA: National Bureau of Economic Research.

Jacobs, Jessica. 2010. *Sex, Tourism and the Postcolonial Encounter: Landscapes of Longing in Egypt.* Farnham, England: Ashgate.

James, Sandy E., Jody L. Herman, Susan Rankin, Mara Keisling, Lisa Mottet, and Ma'ayan Anafi. 2016. *The Report of the 2015 U.S. Transgender Survey.* Washington, DC: National Center for Transgender Equality. Accessed March 22, 2017. http://www .transequality.org/sites/default/files/docs/ usts/USTS%20Full%20Report%20–%20 FINAL%201.6.17.pdf.

Jang, Soo Jung, Allison Zippay, and Rhokeum Park. 2012. "Family Roles as Moderators of the Relationship Between Schedule Flexibility and Stress." *Journal of Marriage and Family* 74: 897–912.

Jankowiak, William. 2010. "Neighbors and Kin in Chinese Cities." In *Urban Life: Readings in the Anthropology of the City,* 5th ed., edited by George Gmelch, Robert V. Kemper, and Walter P. Zenner, 256–68. Long Grove, IL: Waveland Press.

Jaschik, Scott. 2006. "Affirmative Action for Men." *Inside Higher Ed*, March 27. http://www.insidehighered.com/ news/2006/03/27/admit.

———. 2009. "Probe of Extra Help for Men." Inside Higher Ed, November 2. http://www .insidehighered.com/news/2009/11/02/ admit.

———. 2010. "Gender Gap Stops Growing." *Inside Higher Ed*, January 26. http://www .insidehighered.com/news/2010/01/26/ gender.

Javelin Strategy & Research. 2015. *2013 Identity Fraud Report: Data Breaches Becoming a Treasure Trove for Fraudsters.* Pleasanton, CA: Javelin Strategy & Research. https:// www.javelinstrategy.com.

Jensen, Arthur R. 1969. "How Much Can We Boost IQ and Scholastic Achievement?" *Harvard Educational Review* 39 (1): 1–123.

Job Stress Network. 2005. "The Whitehall Study." Accessed November 1. http:// www.workhealth.org/projects/pwhitew .html.

Jolliff, Lauren, Jennifer Leadley, Elizabeth Coakley, and Rae Anne Sloan. 2012. "Table 1. Medical Students, Selected Years, 1965–2012." In *Women in U.S. Academic Medicine and Science: Statistics and Benchmarking Report 2011–2012.* Washington, DC: Association of American Medical Colleges. https://www.aamc.org/ members/gwims/statistics.

Jones, Helen. 2012. "On Sociological Perspectives." In *Handbook on Sexual Violence*, edited by Jennifer M. Brown and Sandra L. Walklate, 181–202. London and New York: Routledge.

Jones, Jo, William Mosher, and Kimberly Daniels. 2012. *Current Contraceptive Use in the United States, 2006–2010, and Changes in Patterns of Use Since 1995.* National Health Statistics Reports 60 (October 18). Hyattsville, MD: National Center for Health Statistics. http://www .cdc.gov/nchs/data/nhsr/nhsr060.pdf.

Jones, Robert P., and Daniel Cox. 2011. *Catholic Attitudes on Gay and Lesbian Issues.* Washington, DC: Public Religion Research Institute. http://publicreligion.org/site/wp -content/uploads/2011/06/Catholics-and -LGBT-Issues-Survey-Report.pdf.

Joughlin, Charlie. 2014. "Today: Tenth Circuit to Hear Argument in Utah Marriage Case." Human Rights Campaign, HRC Blog, April 10. http://www.hrc.org/blog/entry/today -tenth-circuit-to-hear-argument-in-utah -marriage-case.

Joy, Lois. 2003. "Salaries of Recent Male and Female College Graduates: Educational and Labor Market Effects." *Industrial and Labor Relations Review* 56 (4): 606–21.

Kaeble, Danielle, Lauren E. Glaze, 2015. "Correctional Populations in the United States, Bureau of Justice Statistics (December 29, 2016)." Accessed January 4, 2017. https://www.bjs.gov/index .cfm?ty=pbdetail&iid=5870.

Kahana, Eva, Loren Lovegreen, and Boaz Kahana. 2011. "Long-Term Care: Tradition and Innovation." In *Handbook of Sociology of Aging*, edited by Richard A. Settersten Jr. and Jacqueline L. Angel, 583–602. New York: Springer.

Kahn, Lisa. 2009. "The Curse of the Class of 2009." *Wall Street Journal*, May 9. http://online.wsj.com/article/ SB124181970915002009.html.

Kahne, Joseph E., Susan E. Sporte, Marisa De La Torre, and John Q. Easton. 2008. "Small High Schools on a Larger Scale: The Impact of School Conversions in Chicago." *Educational Evaluation and Policy Analysis.* 30 (3): 281–515.

Kailin, Julie. 2002. *Antiracist Education: From Theory to Practice.* Boulder, CO: Rowman & Littlefield.

Kaiser Family Foundation. 2004. *The Role of Media in Childhood Obesity.* Issue Brief, February. Menlo Park, CA: Henry J. Kaiser Family Foundation.

Kaldor, Mary. 2012. *New and Old Wars: Organized Violence in a Global Era*, 3rd ed. Stanford, CA: Stanford University Press.

Kallberg, Arne L. 2012. "The Social Contract in an Era of Precarious Work." *Pathways* (Fall): 3–6.

Kalogrides, Demetra, Susanna Loeb, and Tara Béteille. 2013. "Systematic Sorting: Teacher Characteristics and Class Assignments." *Sociology of Education* 86 (2): 103–23.

Kamerman, Sheila B. 1996. "Child and Family Policies: An International Overview." In *Children, Families, and Government: Preparing for the Twenty-First Century,* edited by Edward F. Zigler, Sharon Lynn Kagan, and Nancy W. Hall, 31–48. New York: Cambridge University Press.

Kanigel, Robert. 1997. *The One Best Way: Frederick Winslow Taylor and the Enigma of Efficiency.* New York: Viking Press.

Kansas State University. 2012. "Racial and Gender Profiling Can Affect Outcome of Traffic Stops." ScienceDaily, June 12. http://www.sciencedaily.com/ releases/2012/06/120621130716.htm.

Kapp, Marshall B. 1996. "Aging and the Law." In *Handbook of Aging and the Social Sciences,* 4th ed., edited by Robert H. Binstock and Linda K. George, 467–79. San Diego, CA: Academic Press.

———. 2006. "Aging and the Law." In *Handbook of Aging and the Social Sciences,* 6th ed., edited by Robert H. Binstock and Linda K. George, 419–35. San Diego, CA: Academic Press.

Karger, Howard Jacob, and David Stoesz. 2006. *American Social Welfare Policy: A Pluralist Approach*, 5th ed. Boston: Pearson/Allyn & Bacon.

Karjane, Heather M., Bonnie S. Fisher, and Francis T. Cullen. 2005. *Sexual Assault on Campus: What Colleges and Universities Are Doing About It.* Washington, DC: National Institute of Justice. https://www .ncjrs.gov/pdffiles1/nij/205521.pdf.

Karkazis, Anastasia, Rebecca Jordan-Young, Georgiann Davis, and Silvia Camporesi. 2012. "Out of Bounds? A Critique of the New Policies on Hyperandrogenism in Elite Female Athletes." *The American Journal of Bioethics* 12 (7): 3–16.

Karlsson, Martin, Therese Nilsson, Carl Hampus Lyttkens, and George Leeson. 2012. "Income Inequality and Health: Importance of a Cross-Country Perspective." *Social Science & Medicine* 70 (6): 875–85.

Karp, David A. 1996. *Speaking of Sadness: Depression, Disconnection, and the Meanings of Illness.* New York: Oxford University Press.

Karp, David A., Gregory P. Stone, and William C. Yoels. 1991. *Being Urban: A Sociology of City Life,* 2nd ed. Westport, CT: Praeger.

Karp, David R. 2001. "Harm and Repair: Observing Restorative Justice in Vermont." *Justice Quarterly* 18 (4): 727–57.

Karraker, Meg Wilkes. 2011. "Religious, Civic, and Interpersonal Capital: Catholic Sisters in One Community's Response to Migrant Families." *Forum on Public Policy* 2011 (2). http://forumonpublicpolicy.com/vol2011 .no2/archivevol2011.no2/karraker.pdf.

———. 2013a. *Diversity and the Common Good: Civil Society, Religion, and Catholic Sisters in a Small City.* Lanham, MD: Lexington Books.

———. 2013b. *Global Families,* 2nd ed. Thousand Oaks, CA: Sage.

———. 2015. "Carework for Children and the New Austerity: Findings From the 'Middle Class in Middle America' Study." Paper presented at the Austerity, Gender and Household Finances Conference, June, University of Kent, Canterbury, UK.

Karraker, Meg Wilkes, and Janet R. Grochowski. 1998. "Dual Vision Research for a Postmodern Perspective on Single Mothers' Families." Paper presented at the annual meeting of Sociologists of Minnesota, Minneapolis, October.

———. 2012. Families With Futures: Family Studies Into the Twenty-First Century, 2nd ed. London: Routledge.

Karras, Ruth Mazo. 2000. "Active/Passion, Acts/ Passions: Greek and Roman Sexualities." *American Historical Review* 105 (4): 1250–66.

Kart, Cary S. 1994. *The Realities of Aging: An Introduction to Gerontology,* 4th ed. Boston: Allyn & Bacon.

Kastberg, D., J. Y. Chan, G. and Murray. 2016. Performance of U.S. 15-Year-Old Students in Science, Reading, and Mathematics Literacy in an International Context: First Look at PISA 2015 (NCES 2017-048). U.S. Department of Education. Washington, DC: National Center for Education Statistics. Accessed May 7, 2017. http://nces.ed.gov/ pubsearch.

Katz, Jack. 1987. "What Makes Crime 'News'?" *Media, Culture and Society* 9: 47–75.

Kehoe, Susan M., and J. Rick Ponting. 2003. "Value Importance and Value Congruence as Determinants of Trust in Health Policy Actors." *Social Science & Medicine* 57 (6): 1065–75.

Keller, Jessalynn, Kaitlynn Mendes, and Jessica Ringrose. 2016. "Speaking 'Unspeakable Things': Documenting Digital Feminist Responses to Rape Culture." *Journal of Gender Studies,* 1–15. Accessed April 15, 2017. http://dx.doi.org/10.1080/09589236 .2016.1211511.

Kelling, George L., and James Q. Wilson. 1982. "Broken Windows: The Police and Neighborhood Safety." *Atlantic Monthly,* March, 29–38.

Kelly, Brian C., Brooke E. Wells, Amy LeClair, Daniel Tracy, Jeffrey T. Parsons, and Sarit A. Golub. 2013a. "Prescription Drug Misuse Among Young Adults: Looking Across Youth Cultures." *Drug and Alcohol Review* 32 (3): 288–94.

———. 2013b. "Prevalence and Correlates of Prescription Drug Misuse Among Socially Active Young Adults." *International Journal of Drug Policy* 25: 265–76.

Kelly, Conor. 2012. "Sexism in Practice: Feminist Ethics Evaluating the Hookup Culture." *Journal of Feminist Studies in Religion* 28 (2): 27–48.

Kelly Services. 2013. "Job Searches Go Viral as Individuals Embrace Social Media." Press release, November 20. http:// ir.kellyservices.com/releasedetail.cfm? ReleaseID=808643.

Kelman, Herbert C., and V. Lee Hamilton. 1989. *Crimes of Obedience: Toward a Social Psychology of Authority and Responsibility.* New Haven, CT: Yale University Press.

Kempadoo, Kamala. 2005. "From Moral Panic to Global Justice: Changing Perspectives on Trafficking." In *Trafficking and Prostitution Reconsidered: New Perspectives on Migration, Sex Work, and Human Rights,* edited by Kamala Kempadoo with Jyoti Sanghera and Bandana Pattanaik. Boulder, CO: Paradigm.

Kempadoo, Kamala, and Jo Doezema. 1998. *Global Sex Workers: Rights, Resistance, and Redefinition.* New York: Routledge.

Kempner, Joanna. 2006. "Gendering the Migraine Market: Do Representations of Illness Matter?" *Social Science & Medicine* 63 (8): 1986–97.

Kennedy, David M. 2011. "Whither Streetwork? The Place of Outreach Workers in Community Violence Prevention." *Criminology & Public Policy* 10 (4): 1045–51.

Kennedy, Sheila, and Larry Bumpass. 2008. "Cohabitation and Children's Living Arrangements: New Estimates From the United States." *Demographic Research* 19: 1663–92.

Kenney, Shannon R., Vandana Thadani, Tehniat Ghaidarov, and Joseph W. LaBrie. 2013. "First-Year College Women's Motivations for Hooking Up: A Mixed-Methods Examination of Normative Peer Perceptions and Personal Hookup Participation." *International Journal of Sexual Health* 25 (3): 212–24.

Kenworthy, Tom. 2013. "How Two Reservoirs Have Become Billboards for What Climate Change Is Doing to the American West." ThinkProgress, August 12. http://thinkprogress.org/ climate/2013/08/12/2439931/reservoir -billboards-southwest/#.

Khan, Shamus Rahman. 2011. *Privilege: The Making of an Adolescent Elite at St. Paul's School.* Princeton, NJ: Princeton University Press.

Kids' Well-Being Indicators Clearinghouse. 2012. http://www.nyskwic.org.

Kilty, Keith M. 2009. "'Greed Is Good': The Idle Rich, the Working Poor, and Personal Responsibility." In *Family Poverty in Diverse Contexts,* edited by C. Anne Broussard and Alfred L. Joseph, 11–25. New York: Routledge.

Kilty, Keith M., and Thomas M. Meenaghan. 1977. "Drinking Status, Labeling, and Social Rejection." *Journal of Social Psychology* 102 (1): 93–104.

Kim, Susanna. 2012. "Pressure on SEC to Implement Rule Disclosing CEO to Median Worker Pay." ABC News, March 13. http:// abcnews.go.com/Business/sec-pressured -implement-ceo-worker-pay-disclosure -walmarts/story?id=15006752.

Kimmel, Michael S., and Rebecca F. Plante. 2002. "The Gender of Desire: The Sexual Fantasies of Women and Men." *Advances in Gender Research* 6: 55–78.

Kimura, A. H. 2016. *Radiation Brain Moms and Citizen Scientists: The Gender Politics of Food Contamination After Fukushima.* Durham, NC: Duke University Press.

Kinsey, Alfred C., Wardell B. Pomeroy, and Clyde E. Martin. 1998. *Sexual Behavior in the Human Male.* Bloomington: Indiana University Press. First published 1948.

Kinsey, Alfred C., Wardell B. Pomeroy, Clyde E. Martin, and Paul H. Gebhard. 1998. *Sexual Behavior in the Human Female.* Bloomington: Indiana University Press. First published 1953.

Kirsch, Irving. 2009. *The Emperor's New Drugs: Exploding the Antidepressant Myth.* London: Bodley Head.

Kirsch, Irving, Alan Scoboria, and Thomas J. Moore. 2002. "Antidepressants and Placebos: Secrets, Revelations, and Unanswered Questions." *Prevention & Treatment* 5 (1). DOI:10.1037/1522–3736.5.1.533r.

Kiss, Alexander, and Siegfried Meryn. 2001. "Effects of Sex and Gender on Psychosocial Aspects of Prostate and Breast Cancer." *British Medical Journal* 323 (7320): 1055–58.

Kitsuse, John I., and Malcolm Spector. 1973. "Toward a Sociology of Social Problems: Social Conditions, Value-Judgments, and Social Problems." *Social Problems* 20 (4): 407–19.

———. 2000. *Constructing Social Problems.* New Brunswick, NJ: Transaction.

Klein, Naomi. 2014. *This Changes Everything: Capitalism vs. The Climate.* New York: Simon & Schuster.

———. 2016. "Paris Is Good Start — But More Must Be Done." *The Boston Globe*, April 22. Accessed January 15, 2017. https://www.bostonglobe .com/opinion/columns/2016/04/21/ paris-good-start-but-more-must-done/ EDVnItEwc1mB6OQ1TGATSK/story.html.

Kleniewski, Nancy. 1997. *Cities, Change, and Conflict: A Political Economy of Urban Life.* Belmont, CA: Wadsworth.

Klinenberg, Eric. 2002. *Heat Wave: A Social Autopsy of Disaster in Chicago.* Chicago: University of Chicago Press.

Kneebone, Elizabeth, Carey Nadeau, and Alan Berube. 2011. *The Re-emergence of Concentrated Poverty: Metropolitan Trends in the 2000s.* New York: Metropolitan Policy Program, Brookings Institution. http://www.brookings.edu/~/media/ research/files/papers/2011/11/03%20 poverty%20kneebone%20nadeau%20 berube/1103_poverty_kneebone_nadeau_ berube.pdf.

Knorr-Cetina, Karin. 1992. "The Couch, the Cathedral, and the Laboratory: On the Relationship between Experiment and Laboratory in Science." In Andrew Pickering (Ed.), *Science as Practice and Culture* (pp. 113–138). Chicago: University of Chicago.

Knorr-Cetina, Karin. 1995. "Laboratory Studies: The Cultural Approach to the Study of Science." In Sheila Jasanoff, Gerald E. Markle, James C. Petersen, and Trevor Pinch (Eds.), *Handbook of Science and Technology Studies.* (pp. 140–166). Thousand Oaks, CA: Sage.

Knorr-Cetina, Karin. 1999. *Epistemic Cultures: How the Sciences Make Knowledge.* Cambridge, MA: Harvard University.

Knorr-Cetina, Karin. 1981. *The Manufacture of Knowledge: An Essay on the Constructivist and Contextual Nature of Science.* Oxford: Pergamon Press.

Kokoska, E., T. Bird, J. Robbins, S. Smith, S. Corsi, and B. Campbell. 2007. "Racial Disparities in the Management of Pediatric Appendicitis." *Journal of Surgical Research* 130 (2): 83–88.

Kollmuss, Anja, and Julian Agyeman. 2002. "Mind the Gap: Why Do People Act Environmentally and What Are the Barriers to Pro-Environmental Behavior?" *Environmental Education Research* 8 (3): 239–60.

Kolowich, Steve. 2016. "The Water Next Time: Professor Who Helped Expose Crisis in Flint Says Public Science Is Broken." *The Chronicle of Higher Education.* Retrieved February 2, 2016 from http://www .chronicle.com/article/The-Water-Next- Time-Professor/235136/

Kondilis, Elias, Stathis Giannakopoulos, Magda Gavana, Ioanna Ierodiakonou, Howard Waitzkin, and Alexis Benos. 2013. "Economic Crisis, Restrictive Policies, and the Populations' Health and Health Care: The Greek Case." *American Journal of Public Health* 103 (6): 973–79.

Korgen, Kathleen. 2002. *Crossing the Racial Divide: Close Friendships Between Black and White Americans.* Westport, CT: Praeger.

Korp, Peter. 2006. "Health on the Internet: Implications for Health Promotion." *Health Education Research* 21 (1): 78–86.

Kosanovich, Karen, and Eleni Theodossiou Sherman. 2015. "Trends in Long-Term Unemployment." U.S. Bureau of Labor Statistics, March. Accessed May 29, 2017, https://www.bls.gov/spotlight/2015/long- term-unemployment/pdf/long-term -unemployment.pdf.

Kotkin, Joel. 2012. *The Rise of Post-familialism: Humanity's Future?* Singapore: Soh Tze Min (Civil Service College).

Krafft-Ebing, Richard von. 1998. *Psychopathia Sexualis.* New York: Arcade. First published 1886.

Krase, Jerome. 2012. *Seeing Cities Change: Local Culture and Class.* Burlington, VT: Ashgate.

Kraus, Michael W., and Jacinth J. X. Tan. 2015. "Americans Overestimate Social Class Mobility." *Journal of Experimental Social Psychology* 58: 101–11.

Krebs, Christopher P., Christine H. Lindquist, Tara D. Warner, Bonnie S. Fisher, and Sandra L. Martin. 2007. "Campus Sexual Assault (CSA) Study: Final Report." Prepared for the National Institute of Justice. https://www.ncjrs.gov/pdffiles1/nij/ grants/221153.pdf.

Kreimer, Pablo, and Juan Pablo Zabala. 2007. "Chagas Disease in Argentina: Reciprocal Construction of Social and Scientific Problems." *Science Technology & Society* 12 (1): 49–72.

Kreutzer, Laura. 2012. "A Cellphone Mom Struggles to Keep in Touch." *Wall Street Journal*, April 20. http://online.wsj.com/ article/SB1000142405270230429930457 7349632055657296.html?reflink=wsj_ redirect.

Krieger, Nancy, and Stephen Sidney. 1996. "Racial Discrimination and Blood Pressure: The CARDIA Study of Young Black and White Adults." *American Journal of Public Health* 86: 1370–78.

Kristof, Nicholas D., and Sheryl WuDunn. 2009. *Half the Sky: Turning Oppression Into Opportunity for Women Worldwide.* New York: Alfred A. Knopf.

Kunkel, Dale. 2001. "Children and Television Advertising." In *Handbook of Children and the Media*, edited by Dorothy G. Singer and Jerome L. Singer, 375–94. Thousand Oaks, CA: Sage.

Kuper, Hannah, Archana Singh-Manoux, Johannes Siegrist, and Michael G. Marmot. 2002. "When Reciprocity Fails: Effort-Reward Imbalance in Relation to Coronary Heart Disease and Health Functioning Within the Whitehall II Study." *Occupational Environmental Medicine* 59: 777–84.

Kuperberg, Arielle. 2014. "Age at Co-residence, Premarital Cohabitation and Marriage Dissolution: 1985–2009." *Journal of Marriage and Family* 76 (2): 352–69.

Kutner, Lawrence, and Cheryl Olson. 2008. *Grand Theft Childhood: The Surprising Truth About Violent Video Games and What Parents Can Do.* New York: Simon & Schuster.

LaBrie, Joseph W., Justin F. Hummer, Tehniat M. Ghaidarov, Andrew Lac, and Shannon R. Kenney. 2014. "Hooking Up in the College Context: The Event-Level Effects of Alcohol Use and Partner Familiarity on Hookup Behaviors and Contentment." *The Journal of Sex Research* 51 (1): 62–73.

Lafortune, Julien, Jesse Rothstein, and Diane Whitmore Schanzenbach. 2015. "School Finance Reform and the Distribution of Student Achievement." Working Paper No 22011. Cambridge, MA: National Bureau of Economic Research.

Lafrance, Dawn E., Meika Loe, and Scott C. Brown. 2012. "'Yes Means Yes': A New Approach to Sexual Assault Prevention and Positive Sexuality Promotion." *American Journal of Sexuality Education* 7 (4): 445–60.

Lahiri-Dutt, Kuntala. 2015. "Medicalising Menstruation: A Feminist Critique of the Political Economy of Menstrual Hygiene Management in South Asia." *Gender, Place, and Culture* 22 (8): 1158–1176.

Laidler, Gita Joan. 2007. "Ice, Through Inuit Eyes: Characterizing the Importance of Sea Ice Processes, Use, and Change Around Three Nunavut Communities." Doctoral dissertation, University of Toronto.

Lambert, Megan, Elizabeth S. Perino, and Elizabeth M. Barreras. 2012. "Understanding the Barriers to Female Education in Ghana." Unpublished manuscript. Blue Kitabu Research Institute. Boston, MA.

Lambert, Tracy A., Arnold S. Kahn, and Kevin J. Apple. 2003. "Pluralistic Ignorance and Hooking Up." *Journal of Sex Research* 40: 129–34.

Lancaster, Roger N. 2011. *Sex Panic and the Punitive State.* Berkeley: University of California Press.

Langan, Patrick A., and David P. Farrington. 1998. *Crime and Justice in the United States and in England and Wales, 1981–96.* NCJ 169284. Washington, DC: U.S. Department of Justice, Bureau of Justice Statistics.

Langton, L., M. Berzofsky, C. P. Krebs, and H. Smiley-McDonald. 2012. *Victimizations Not Reported to the Police, 2006–2010.* U.S. Department of Justice, Bureau of Justice Statistics.

Lareau, Annette. 2003. *Unequal Childhoods: Class, Race, and Family Life.* Berkeley: University of California Press.

Latorre, S., K. N. Farrell, and J. Martínez-Alier. 2015. "The Commodification of Nature and Socio-Environmental Resistance in Ecuador: An Inventory of Accumulation by Dispossession Cases, 1980–2013." *Ecological Economics,* 116: 58–69.

Latour, Bruno. 1987. *Science in Action: How to Follow Scientists and Engineers Through Society.* Cambridge, MA: Harvard University Press.

Latour, Bruno, and Steve Woolgar. 1979. *Laboratory Life: The Social Construction of Scientific Facts.* Beverly Hills, CA: Sage.

Lavelle, Kristen, and Joe R. Feagin. 2006. "Hurricane Katrina: The Race and Class Debate." *Monthly Review* 58 (3): 52–66.

Law, John. 1991. *A Sociology of Monsters: Essays on Power, Technology, and Domination.* London: Routledge.

Leatherman, Janie L. 2011. *Sexual Violence and Armed Conflict.* Cambridge: Polity Press.

Lee, James. 2012. *U.S. Naturalizations: 2011.* Annual Flow Report. Washington, DC: Office of Immigration Statistics, U.S. Department of Homeland Security. http://www.dhs.gov/xlibrary/assets/statistics/publications/natz_fr_2011.pdf.

Lee, Jasmine. 2017. "Trump's Cabinet So Far Is More White and Male Than Any First Cabinet Since Reagan's." *New York Times,* March 10.

Lee, Sharon M. 1993. "Racial Classifications in the U.S. Census: 1890 to 1990." *Ethnic and Racial Studies* 16 (1): 75–94.

Lee, Valerie E. 1995. "Effects of High School Restructuring and Size on Early Gains in Achievement and Engagement." *Sociology of Education* 68 (4): 241–70.

Lee, Valerie E., and Douglas D. Ready. 2007. *Schools Within Schools: Possibilities and Pitfalls of High School Reform.* New York: Teachers College Press.

Lee, Youkyung. 2012. "South Korea: 160,000 Kids Between Age 5 and 9 Are Internet-Addicted." *Huffington Post,* November 28 (updated January 27, 2013). http://www.huffingtonpost.com/2012/11/28/south-korea-internet-addicted_n_2202371.html.

Lemert, Edwin M. 1951. *Social Pathology: A Systematic Approach to the Theory of Sociopathic Behavior.* New York: McGraw-Hill.

———. 1972. *Human Deviance, Social Problems, and Social Control.* Englewood Cliffs, NJ: Prentice-Hall.

Lemieux, Jamilah. 2016. "Not Being Petty, but I Wish bell hooks Could Find Her Way to Us." *Feministing.* Accessed April 15, 2017. http://feministing.com/2016/05/11/a-feminist-roundtable-on-bell-hooks-beyonce-and-moving-beyond-pain/.

Lemon, Bruce W., Vern L. Bengtson, and James A. Peterson. 1972. "An Exploration of the Activity Theory of Aging: Activity Types and Life Satisfaction Among In-Movers to a Retirement Community." *Journal of Gerontology* 27 (4): 511–23.

Lenski, Gerhard E. 1966. *Power and Privilege: A Theory of Social Stratification.* New York: McGraw-Hill.

Lerum, Kari. 2015. "How Popular 'Sex Trafficking' Stories Like *Abduction of Eden* Justify Bad Policy and Hurt Sex Workers." *The Society Pages.* Accessed May 1, 2017. https://thesocietypages.org/sexuality/2015/03/08/how-popular-sex-trafficking-stories-like-abduction-of-eden-justify-bad-policy-and-hurt-sex-workers/.

Letnic, M. 2000. "Dispossession, Degradation and Extinction: Environmental History in Arid Australia." *Biodiversity and Conservation* 9 (3): 295–308.

Lever, Janet, and Deanne Dolnick. 2000. "Clients and Call Girls: Seeking Sex and Intimacy." In *Sex for Sale: Prostitution, Pornography, and the Sex Industry,* edited by Ronald Weitzer, 85–101. New York: Routledge.

Levine, David I. 1998. *Working in the Twenty-First Century: Policies for Economic Growth Through Training, Opportunity, and Education.* Armonk, NY: M. E. Sharpe.

Levine, Michael P., and Kristen Harrison. 2009. "Effects of Media on Eating Disorders and Body Image." In *Media Effects: Advances in Theory and Research,* 3rd ed., edited by Jennings Bryant and Mary Beth Oliver, 490–516. New York: Routledge.

Levine, Thomas H. 2010. "What Research Tells Us About the Impact and Challenges of Smaller Learning Communities." *Peabody Journal of Education* 85 (3): 276–89.

Levintova, Marya, and Thomas Novotny. 2004. "Noncommunicable Disease Mortality in the Russian Federation: From Legislation to Policy." *Bulletin of the World Health Organization* 82 (11): 875–80.

Levitt, Steven D. 1996. "The Effect of Prison Population Size on Crime Rates: Evidence From Prison Overcrowding Litigation." *Quarterly Journal of Economics* 111 (2): 319–51.

Lewis, Melissa A., David C. Atkins, Jessica A. Blayney, David V. Dent, and Debra L. Kaysen. 2013. "What Is Hooking Up? Examining Definitions of Hooking Up in Relations to Behavior and Normative Perceptions." *Journal of Sex Research* 50 (8): 757–66.

Lewis, Oscar. 1966. "The Culture of Poverty." *Scientific American,* October, 19–25.

———. 1969. "Culture of Poverty." In *On Understanding Poverty: Perspectives From the Social Sciences,* edited by Daniel Patrick Moynihan, 187–220. New York: Basic Books.

Lichter, Daniel T., Felicia B. LeClere, and Diane K. McLaughlin. 1991. "Local Marriage Markets and the Marital Behavior of Black and White Women." *American Journal of Sociology* 96: 843–67.

Lichter, Daniel T., Diane K. McLaughlin, George Kephart, and David J. Landry. 1992. "Race and the Retreat From Marriage: A Shortage of Marriageable Men?" *American Sociological Review* 57: 781–99.

Lin, Daisy, and Bruce Hensel. 2013. "If Sexual Dysfunction Were a Virus, 'It'd Be Pandemic': Expert." NBC News, Los Angeles. http://www.nbclosangeles.com/news/local/Couples-Sexual-Problems-Health-ED-207639941.html.

Liptak, Adam. 2013. "Supreme Court Bolsters Gay Marriage With Two Major Rulings." *New York Times,* June 26. http://www.nytimes.com/2013/06/27/us/politics/supreme-court-gay-marriage.html.

Littig, Beate, and Erich Grießler. 2005. "Social Sustainability: A Catchword Between Political Pragmatism and Social Theory." *International Journal of Sustainable Development* 8 (1/2): 65–79.

Livingston, Gretchen. 2016. "Among 41 Nations, U.S. Is the Outlier When It Comes to Paid Parental Leave." Pew Research Center. Accessed May 31, 2017. http://www.pewresearch.org/fact-tank/2016/09/26/u-s-lacks-mandated-paid-parental-leave/.

Lloyd, Rachel. 2012. *Girls Like Us: Fighting for a World Where Girls Are Not for Sale, an Activist Finds Her Calling and Heals Herself.* New York: HarperPerennial.

Lofland, Lyn H. 1998. *The Public Realm: Exploring the City's Quintessential Social Territory.* New York: Aldine de Gruyter.

Lofquist, Daphne, Terry Lugaila, Martin O'Connell, and Sarah Feliz. 2012. *Households and Families: 2010.* U.S. Census Bureau, Census Brief C2010BR-14. Washington, DC: Government Printing Office. http://www.census.gov/prod/cen2010/briefs/c2010br-14.pdf.

Logan, John R., and Harvey L. Molotch. 1987. *Urban Fortunes: The Political Economy of Place.* Berkeley: University of California Press.

Lombe, Margaret, and Michael Sherraden. 2008. "Effects of Participating in an Asset-Building Intervention on Social Inclusion." *Journal of Poverty* 12 (3): 284–305.

Long, Norton E. 1958. "The Local Community as an Ecology of Games." *American Journal of Sociology* 64 (3): 251–61.

Longino, Charles F., Jr. 2005. "The Future of Ageism: Baby Boomers at the Doorstep." *Generations* 29 (3): 79–83.

Longino, Charles F., Jr., and Cary S. Kart. 1982. "Explicating Activity Theory: A Formal Replication." *Journal of Gerontology* 37 (6): 713–22.

López, Mark Hugo, and Ana Gonzalez-Barrera. 2014. "Women's College Enrollment Gains Leave Men Behind." Pew Research Center. Accessed May 16, 2017. http://www.pewresearch.org/fact-tank/2014/03/06/womens-college-enrollment-gains-leave-men-behind/.

Lopez, Nancy. 2003. *Hopeful Girls, Troubled Boys: Race and Gender Disparity in Urban Education.* New York: Routledge.

Lorber, Judith. 1993. "Believing Is Seeing: Biology as Ideology." *Gender & Society* 7 (4): 568–81.

Lorber, Judith, Anastasia Karkazis, Rebecca Jordan-Young, Georgiann Davis, and Silvia Camporesi. 2012. "Out of Bounds? A Critique of the New Policies on Hyperandrogenism in Elite Female Athletes." *The American Journal of Bioethics* 12 (7): 3–16.

Loseke, Donileen R., and Joel Best, eds. 2003. *Social Problems: Constructionist Readings.* New York: Aldine de Gruyter.

Lui, Meizhu, Barbara Robles, Betsy Leondar-Wright, Rose Brewer, and Rebecca Adamson, With United for a Fair Economy. 2006. *The Color of Wealth: The Story Behind the U.S. Racial Wealth Divide.* New York: New Press.

Lukas, J. Anthony. 1985. *Common Ground: A Turbulent Decade in the Lives of Three American Families.* New York: Alfred A. Knopf.

Luke, Nancy, Rachel E. Goldberg, Blessing U. Mberu, and Eliya M. Zulu. 2011. "Social Exchange and Sexual Behavior in Young Women's Premarital Relationships in Kenya." *Journal of Marriage and Family* 73: 1048–64.

Luna, Zakiya, and Kristin Luker. 2013. "Reproductive Justice." *Annual Review of Law and Social Science* 9: 327–52.

Luo, Michael. 2010. "At Closing Plant, Ordeal Included Heart Attacks." *New York Times,* November 24. http://www.nytimes.com/2010/02/25/us/25stress.html.

Lynch, John, George Davey Smith, Sam Harper, and Kathleen Bainbridge. 2006. "Explaining the Social Gradient in Coronary Heart Disease: Comparing Relative and Absolute Risk Approaches." *Journal of Epidemiology and Community Health* 60: 436–41.

Lynch, Michael. 1985. *Art and Artifact in Laboratory Science: A Study of Shop Work and Shop Talk in a Research Laboratory.* London: Routledge & Kegan Paul.

Lynch, Michael J. 2011. "Review of 'Wage Theft in America (Why Millions of Working Americans Are Not Getting Paid—and What We Can Do About It),' by Kim Bobo." *Contemporary Justice Review* 14 (2): 255–58.

Lyons, Christopher J., and Becky Pettit. 2011. "Compounded Disadvantage: Race, Incarceration, and Wage Growth." *Social Problems* 58 (2): 257–80.

Lyotard, Jean-François. 1984. *The Postmodern Condition: A Report on Knowledge.*

Translated by Geoff Bennington and Brian Massumi. Minneapolis: University of Minnesota Press.

Macartney, Suzanne, Alemayehu Bishaw, and Kayla Fontenot. 2013. *Poverty Rates for Selected Detailed Race and Hispanic Groups by State and Place: 2007–2011.* U.S. Census Bureau, American Community Survey Brief 11–17. Washington, DC: Government Printing Office. http://www.census.gov/prod/2013pubs/acsbr11–17.pdf.

MacDonald, John M., and Meda Chesney-Lind. 2001. "Gender Bias and Juvenile Justice Revisited: A Multiyear Analysis." *Crime & Delinquency* 47 (2): 173–95.

Macgregor, Lyn C. 2010. *Habits of the Heartland: Small-Town Life in Modern America.* Ithaca, NY: Cornell University Press.

MacKinnon, Catharine A. 2008. "The ICTR's Legacy on Sexual Violence." *New England Journal of International and Comparative Law* 14 (2): 211–20.

MacLeod, Jay. 2009. *Ain't No Makin' It: Aspirations and Attainment in a Low-Income Neighborhood*, 3rd ed. Boulder, CO: Westview Press.

MacRae, Allan, and Howard Zehr. 2004. *The Little Book of Family Group Conferences: New Zealand Style.* Intercourse, PA: Good Books.

Madden, Mary, and Lee Rainie. 2010. "Adults and Cell Phone Distractions." Pew Research Center, Internet Project, June 18. http://pewinternet.org/Reports/2010/Cell-Phone-Distractions.aspx.

Maher, Timothy. 1998. "Environmental Oppression: Who Is Targeted for Exposure?" *Journal of Black Studies* 28: 357–67.

Mahoney, Annette. 2010. "Religion in Families, 1999–2000: A Relational Spirituality Framework." *Journal of Marriage and Family* 72: 805–27.

Maines, David R., and Jeffrey C. Bridger. 1992. "Narratives, Community, and Land Use Decisions." *Social Science Journal* 29 (4): 363–80.

Malesevic, Sinisa. 2010. *The Sociology of War and Violence.* Cambridge: Cambridge University Press.

Malkus, Nat, Kathleen Mulvaney Hoyer, and Dinah Sparks. 2015. "Teaching Vacancies and Difficult-to-Staff Teaching Positions in Public Schools. Stats in Brief. NCES 2015–065." Washington, DC: National Center for Education Statistics.

Mallicoat, Stacy L. 2007. "Gendered Justice: Attributional Differences Between Males and Females in the Juvenile Courts." *Feminist Criminology* 2 (1): 4–30.

Mam, Somaly. 2009. *The Road of Lost Innocence: The True Story of a Cambodian Heroine.* New York: Spiegel & Grau.

Mamo, Laura, and Jennifer Fosket. 2009. "Scripting the Body: Pharmaceuticals and the (Re)making of Menstruation." *Signs: Journal of Women in Culture and Society* 34 (4): 925–49.

Manik, Julfikar Ali, and Jim Yardley. 2013. "Building Collapse in Bangladesh Leaves Scores Dead." *New York Times*, April 24. http://www.nytimes.com/2013/04/25/world/asia/bangladesh-building-collapse.html?_r=0.

Manning, Peter K. 2005. "The Study of Policing." *Police Quarterly* 8 (1): 23–43.

Manning, Wendy D., and Jessica A. Cohen. 2012. "Premarital Cohabitation and Marital Dissolution: An Examination of Recent Marriages." *Journal of Marriage and Family* 74: 377–87.

Manning, Wendy D., Monica Longmore, and Peggy Giordano. 2000. "The Relationship Context of Contraceptive Use at First Intercourse." *Family Planning Perspectives* 32: 104–10.

Maratea, Ray. 2008. "The e-Rise and Fall of Social Problems: The Blogosphere as a Public Arena." *Social Problems* 55 (1): 139–60.

Margo, Robert A. 1990. *Race and Schooling in the South, 1880–1950: An Economic History.* Chicago: University of Chicago Press.

Marin, Dalia. 2006. "A New International Division of Labor in Europe: Outsourcing and Offshoring to Eastern Europe." *Journal of the European Economic Association* 4 (2–3): 612–22.

Marmot, Michael G. 2006. "Health in an Unequal World." *The Lancet* 368: 2081–84.

Marmot, Michael G., Geoffrey Rose, Martin J. Shipley, and Peter J. Hamilton. 1978. "Employment Grade and Coronary Heart Disease in British Civil Servants." *Journal of Epidemiology and Community Health* 32: 244–49.

Marr, Chuck, and B. Chye-Ching Huang. 2012. *Misconceptions and Realities About Who Pays Taxes.* Washington, DC: Center on Budget and Policy Priorities. http://www.cbpp.org/files/5–26–11tax.pdf.

Marsiglio, William, and John H. Scanzoni. 1995. *Families and Friendships: Applying the Sociological Imagination.* New York: HarperCollins.

Martin, Andrew, and Andrew W. Lehren. 2012. "A Generation Hobbled by the Soaring Cost of College." *New York Times,* May 12. http://www.nytimes.com/2012/05/13/business/student-loans-weighing-down-a-generation-with-heavy-debt.html?pagewanted=all&_r=0.

Martin, Graham P., Graeme Currie, and Rachael Finn. 2009. "Reconfiguring or Reproducing Intra-professional Boundaries? Specialist Expertise, Generalist Knowledge and the 'Modernization' of the Medical Workforce." *Social Science & Medicine* 68 (7): 1191–98.

Martin, Susan Ehrlich, and Nancy C. Jurik. 1996. *Doing Justice, Doing Gender: Women in Law and Criminal Justice Occupations.* Thousand Oaks, CA: Sage.

Marx, Karl. 1844 (1978). "Economic and Philosophic Manuscripts of 1844." In *The Marx-Engels Reader, Second Edition*, edited by Robert C. Tucker,. 66–125. New York and London: W. W. Norton and Company.

Marttila, Anne-Maria. 2003. "Consuming Sex: Finnish Male Clients and Russian and Baltic Prostitution." Paper presented at the European Feminist Research Conference "Gender and Power in the New Europe," Lund University, Sweden.

Mascarenhas, Michael. 2017. *New Humanitarianism and the Crisis of Charity: Good Intentions on the Road to Help.* Bloomington, IN: Indiana University Press.

Masci, David, Anna Brown, and Jocelyn Kiley. 2017. "Five Facts About Same-Sex Marriage." Pew Research Center Fact Tank, June 26. http://www.pewresearch.org/fact-tank/2017/06/26/same-sex-marriage/

Massey, Douglas S. 1995. "The New Immigration and Ethnicity in the United States." *Population and Development Review* 21: 631–52.

Massey, Douglas S., and Nancy A. Denton. 1993. *American Apartheid: Segregation and the Making of the Underclass.* Cambridge, MA: Harvard University Press.

Massey, Douglas S., and Garvey Lundy. 2001. "Use of Black English and Racial Discrimination in Urban Housing Markets: New Methods and Findings." *Urban Affairs Review* 36 (4): 452–69.

Masters, William, and Virginia Johnson. 2010. *Human Sexual Response.* New York: Ishi Press.

Matcha, Duane A. 1997. *The Sociology of Aging: A Social Problems Perspective.* Boston: Allyn & Bacon.

———. 2011. "Crime, the Law, and Aging." In *Handbook of Sociology of Aging,* edited by Richard A. Settersten Jr. and Jacqueline L. Angel, 431–44. New York: Springer.

Matcha, Duane A., and Bonita A. Sessing-Matcha. 2007. "A Comparison of American and European Newspaper Coverage of the Elderly." *Hallym International Journal of Aging* 9 (2): 77–88.

Matchen, Quiche. 2013. "IJM Stands for 27 Hours Against Sex Trafficking." *WKU Herald,* March 26. http://wkuherald.com/news/campus_life/article_1fe4f982–9592–11e2–ba36–001a4bcf6878.html.

Mather, Mark, and Dia Adams. 2007. "The Crossover in Male-Female College Enrollment Rates." Population Reference Bureau, February. http://www.prb.org/Articles/2007/CrossoverinFemaleMaleCollegeEnrollmentRates.aspx.

Matsueda, R. L. 1988. "The Current State of Differential Association Theory." *Crime & Delinquency* 34 (3): 277–306.

Matthew Shepard Foundation. 2014. "Matthew's Story." Accessed April 17. http://www.matthewshepard.org.

Mawn, Barbara Ellen. 2011. "Children's Voices: Living With HIV." *American Journal of Maternal and Child Nursing* 36: 368–72.

Mayer-Schonberger, Viktor, and Kenneth Cukier. 2013. *Big Data: A Revolution That Will Transform How We Live, Work, and Think.* New York: Eamon Dolan/Houghton Mifflin Harcourt.

Mayo, Elton, 1933. *The Human Problems of an Industrial Civilization.* Cambridge, MA: Harvard University Press.

McCabe, Kimberly A., and Sabita Manian, eds. 2010. *Sex Trafficking: A Global Perspective.* Lanham, MD: Lexington Books.

McCall, Leslie. 2001. *Complex Inequality: Gender, Class, and Race in the New Economy.* New York: Routledge.

McChesney, Robert W. 1996. "The Payne Fund and Radio Broadcasting, 1928–1935." In *Children and the Movies: Media Influence and the Payne Fund Controversy,* edited by Garth S. Jowett, Ian C. Jarvie, and Kathryn H. Fuller, 303–35. New York: Cambridge University Press.

McCollister, K. E., M. T. French, and H. Fang, 2010. "The Cost of Crime to Society: New Crime-Specific Estimates for Policy and Program Evaluation." *Drug and Alcohol Dependence, 108* (1): 98–109.

McCombs, Maxwell E. 2004. *Setting the Agenda: The Mass Media and Public Opinion.* Cambridge, MA: Polity Press.

McCright, A. M., and R. E. Dunlap. 2011. "The Politicization of Climate Change and Polarization in the American Public's Views of Global Warming, 2001–2010." *The Sociological Quarterly, 52* (2): 155–94.

McCright, Aaron M. 2011. "Political Orientation Moderates Americans' Beliefs and Concern About Climate Change." *Climatic Change* 104 (2): 243–53.

McCright, Aaron M., and Riley E. Dunlap. 2003. "Defeating Kyoto: The Conservative Movement's Impact on U.S. Climate Change Policy." *Social Problems* 50 (3): 348–73.

———. 2010. "Anti-reflexivity: The American Conservative Movement's Success in Undermining Climate Science and Policy." *Theory, Culture & Society* 27 (2–3): 100–133.

———. 2011. "The Politicization of Climate Change and Polarization in the American Public's Views of Global Warming, 2001–2010." *The Sociological Quarterly* 52 (2): 155–94.

McCubbin, Hamilton, Anne Thompson, and Marilyn McCubbin. 1996. *Family Assessment: Resiliency, Coping, and Adaptation.* Madison: University of Wisconsin Press.

McDonald, Daniel G. 2004. "Twentieth-Century Media Effects Research." In *The Sage Handbook of Media Studies,* edited by John D. H. Downing, 183–200. Thousand Oaks, CA: Sage.

McGarvey, Robert. 2015. "8 Million Baby Boomers Are Hungry Right Now—Are You Next?" *The Street.* July 27. https://www.thestreet.com/story/13232356/1/8–million-baby-boomers-are-hungry-right-now-are-you-next.html.

McGurty, Frank, and Nathan Frandino. 2017. "Tens of Thousands in U.S. Protest Trump Immigration Order." Reuters, January 30. Accessed February 27, 2017. http://mobile.reuters.com/article/idUSKBN15D15H.

McIntosh, Peggy. 2001. "White Privilege and Male Privilege: A Persona Account of Coming to See Correspondences Through Work in Women's Studies." In *Race, Class, and Gender: An Anthology,* 4th ed., edited by Margaret L. Anderson and Patricia Hill Collins. Belmont, CA: Wadsworth.

McKibben, Bill. 2016. "Why Dakota Is the New Keystone." *New York Times,* October 28. Accessed March 1, 2017. https://www.nytimes.com/2016/10/29/opinion/why-dakota-is-the-new-keystone.html.

McKinlay, John B., and Lisa D. Marceau. 2002. "The End of the Golden Age of Doctoring." *International Journal of Health Services* 32 (2): 379–416.

McLanahan, Sara. 2011. "Family Instability and Complexity After a Nonmarital Birth: Outcomes for Children in Fragile Families." In *Social Class and Changing Families in an Unequal America,* edited by Marcia J. Carlson and Paula England, 108–33. Palo Alto, CA: Stanford University Press.

McLaughlin, Dorothy. 1998. "*Silent Spring* Revisited." *Frontline,* PBS. http://www.pbs.org/wgbh/pages/frontline/shows/nature/disrupt/sspring.html.

McNair, Brian. 2013. *Porno? Chic! How Pornography Changed the World and Made It a Better Place.* London: Routledge.

McSally, Martha E. 2011. "Defending America in Mixed Company: Gender in the U.S. Armed Forces." *Daedalus* 140 (3): 148–64.

Mead, George Herbert. 1934. *Mind, Self, and Society.* Chicago: University of Chicago Press.

Meehl, Gerald A., Francis Zwiers, Jenni Evans, Thomas Knutson, Linda Mearns, and Peter Whetton. 2000. "Trends in Extreme Weather and Climate Events: Issues Related to Modeling Extremes in Projections of Future Climate Change." *Bulletin of the American Meteorological Society* 81 (3): 427–36.

Mehli, H., L. Skuterud, A. Mosdøl, and A. Tønnessen. 2000. "The Impact of Chernobyl Fallout on the Southern Saami Reindeer Herders of Norway in 1996." *Health Physics* 79 (6): 682–90.

Mellstrom, Ulf. 2009. "The Intersection of Race, Gender, and Cultural Boundaries: Or Why Is Computer Science in Malaysia Dominated by Women?" In Wyer et al., eds., *Women, Science, and Technology: A Reader in Feminist Science Studies*, 81–100.

Melton, Heather C., and Carry Lafeve Sillito. 2012. "The Role of Gender in Officially Reported Intimate Partner Abuse." *Journal of Interpersonal Violence* 27: 1090–1111.

Merton, Robert K. 1938. "Social Structure and Anomie." *American Sociological Review* 3 (5): 672–82.

———. 1942. *The Sociology of Science: Theoretical and Empirical Investigations.* Chicago: University of Chicago Press.

———. 1968. *Social Theory and Social Structure.* New York: Simon & Schuster.

Messner, Steven F., and Richard Rosenfeld. 2013. *Crime and the American Dream,* 5th ed. Belmont, CA: Wadsworth.

Metropolitan Council. 2016. "Affordable Housing: HUD Secretary Works the Playbook." March 23. Accessed August 20, 2016. http://metrocouncil.org/News -Events/Housing/Newsletters/Affordable -housing-HUD-secretary-works-the-playbo aspx.

Meyer, John W. 1977. "The Effects of Education as an Institution." *American Journal of Sociology* 85: 55–77.

Miami Herald. 2017. "Fortunately, Trump Gives Young, Undocumented DREAMers a Reprieve—for Now." January 23. Accessed February 27, 2017. http://www .miamiherald.com/opinion/editorials/ article128334459.html.

Mickelson, Roslyn Arlin. 2003. "Gender, Bourdieu, and the Anomaly of Women's Achievement Redux." *Sociology of Education* 76 (4): 373–75.

Miller, Brian, and Mike Lapham. 2012. *The Self-Made Myth: And the Truth About How Government Helps Individuals and Businesses Succeed.* San Francisco: Berrett-Koehler.

Miller, Patricia N., Darryl W. Miller, Eithen M. McKibbin, and Gregory L. Pettys. 1999. "Stereotypes of the Elderly in Magazine Advertisements 1956–1996." *International Journal of Aging and Human Development* 49 (4): 319–37.

Miller-Young, Mireille. 2010. "Putting Hypersexuality to Work: Black Women and Illicit Eroticism in Pornography." *Sexualities* 13 (2): 219–35.

Milligan, Melinda J. 1998. "Interactional Past and Potential: The Social Construction of Place Attachment." *Symbolic Interaction* 21 (1): 1–33.

Mills, C. Wright. 1951. *White Collar: The American Middle Class.* London: Oxford University Press.

———. 1954. "Nothing to Laugh At." *New York Times,* April 25, BR20.

———. 1956. *The Power Elite.* New York: Oxford University Press.

———. 1959. *The Sociological Imagination.* New York: Oxford University Press.

———. 1961. *The Sociological Imagination.* New York: Grove Press.

———. 2000. *The Power Elite,* 2nd ed. New York: Oxford University Press.

———. 2001. *The New Men of Power: America's Labor Leaders.* Champaign: University of Illinois Press. First published 1948.

Miniño, Arialdi M., Jiaquan Xu, and Kennet D. Kochanek. 2010. *Deaths: Preliminary Data for 2008.* National Vital Statistics Reports 59, no 2. Hyattsville, MD: National Center for Health Statistics. http://www.cdc.gov/ nchs/data/nvsr/nvsr59/nvsr59_02.pdf.

Mink, Gwendolyn. 2001. "Violating Women: Rights Abuses in the Welfare Police State." *Annals of the American Academy of Political and Social Science* 577 (September): 79–93.

Minnesota Department of Human Rights. 2014. "Minnesota's New Same-Sex Marriage Law." Accessed April 17. http://www .mn.gov/mdhr/public_affairs/samesex_ marriage.html.

Minnesota for Marriage. 2012. "Why Preserving Marriage Matters." Accessed November 24. http://www.minne sotaformarriage .com/why.

Minnesotans United for All Families. 2012. "Fact Sheet." http://mnunited.org/wp-content/ uploads/2012/07/8VoteNoFacts.pdf.

Mirkin, Harris. 2009. "The Social, Political, and Legal Construction of the Concept of Child Pornography." *Journal of Homosexuality* 56 (2): 233–67.

Mishel, Lawrence, Jared Bernstein, and Heidi Shierholz. 2009. *The State of Working America, 2008–2009.* Ithaca, NY: Cornell University Press.

Mishel, Lawrence, Josh Bivens, Elise Gould, and Heidi Shierholz. 2013. *The State of Working America,* 12th ed. Ithaca, NY: Cornell University Press.

Mishel, Lawrence, Elise Gould, and Josh Bivens. 2015, "Wage Stagnation in Nine Charts." Accessed January 6, 2017. http://www.epi. org/publication/charting-wage-stagnation/.

Mitchell, Corey. 2012. "Both Sides in Marriage Battle Rake in Millions." *Star Tribune,* September 27. http://www.startribune .com/politics/statelocal/171442411.html.

Moen, Phyllis, and Patricia Roehling. 2005. *The Career Mystique: Cracks in the American Dream.* Lanham, MD: Rowman & Littlefield.

Moerman, Daniel E., and Wayne B. Jonas. 2002. "Deconstructing the Placebo Effect and Finding the Meaning Response." *Annals of Internal Medicine* 136 (6): 471–76.

Moffitt, Robert. 2008. "A Primer on U.S. Welfare Reform." *University of Wisconsin Institute for Research on Poverty Focus* 26 (1): 15–25.

Mohai, Paul, and Robin Saha. 2007. "Racial Inequality in the Distribution of Hazardous Waste: A National-Level Reassessment." *Social Problems* 54 (3): 343–70.

Mol, Arthur P. J. 2003. *Globalization and Environmental Reform: The Ecological Modernization of the Global Economy.* Cambridge, MA: MIT Press.

Mol, Arthur P. J., and Gert Spaargaren. 2000. "Ecological Modernisation Theory in Debate: A Review." *Environmental Politics* 9 (1). 17–49.

Monti, Daniel J. 1990. *Race, Redevelopment, and the New Company Town.* Albany: State University of New York Press.

———. 1999. *The American City: A Social and Cultural History.* Malden, MA: Blackwell.

———. 2013. *Engaging Strangers: Civil Rites, Civic Capitalism, and Public Order in an American City.* Lanham, MD: Fairleigh Dickinson University Press.

Monto, Martin A. 2010. "Prostitutes' Customers: Motives and Misconceptions." In *Sex for Sale: Prostitution, Pornography, and the Sex Industry,* 2nd ed., edited by Ronald Weitzer, 233–54. New York: Routledge.

Montoya, Michael J. 2011. *Making the Mexican Diabetic: Race, Science, and the Genetics of Inequality.* Berkley: University of California Press.

Moody, Harry R., and Jennifer R. Sasser. 2012. *Aging: Concepts and Controversies,* 7th ed. Thousand Oaks, CA: Sage.

Mora, Camilo, Abby G. Frazier, Ryan J. Longman, Rachel S. Dacks, Maya M. Walton, Eric J. Tong, Joseph J. Sanchez, et al. 2013. "The Projected Timing of Climate Departure From Recent Variability." *Nature* 502 (7470): 183–87.

Morath, E. 2014. "Jobs Return to Peak, but Quality Lags." *Wall Street Journal,* June 7–8, A1, A2.

Morgan, S. Philip, Erin Cumberworth, and Christopher Wimer. 2012. "Sheltering the Storm: American Families in the Great Recession." *Pathways* (Fall): 24–27.

Morgan, Steve, Paul Grootendorst, Joel Lexchin, Colleen Cunningham, and Devon Greyson. 2011. "The Cost of Drug Development: A Systematic Review. *Health Policy* 100: 4–17.

Morin, Rich. 2012. "Rising Share of Americans See Conflict Between Rich and Poor." Pew Research Center, Social and Demographic Trends, January 11. http://pewresearch .org/pubs/2167/rich-poor-social-conflict -class.

Morin, Rich, and Seth Motel. 2012. "A Third of Americans Now Say They Are in the Lower Classes." Pew Research Center, Social and Demographic Trends, September 10. http:// www.pewsocialtrends.org/files/2012/09/ the-lower-classes-final.pdf.

Morris, Allison, and Gabrielle Maxwell. 2003. "Restorative Justice in New Zealand." In *Restorative Justice and Criminal Justice: Competing or Reconcilable Paradigms,* edited by Andrew von Hirsch, Julian Roberts, Anthony E. Bottoms, Kent Roach, and Mara Schiff, 257–72. Portland, OR: Hart.

Morris, Edward W. 2007. "'Ladies' or 'Loudies'? Perceptions and Experiences of Black Girls in Classrooms." *Youth & Society* 38 (4): 490–515.

———. 2008. "'Rednecks,' 'Rutters,' and 'Rithmetic': Social Class, Masculinity, and Schooling in a Rural Context." *Gender & Society* 22 (6): 728–51.

———. 2012. *Learning the Hard Way: Masculinity, Place, and the Gender Gap in Education.* New Brunswick, NJ: Rutgers University Press.

Mortenson, Greg, and David Oliver Relin. 2006. *Three Cups of Tea: One Man's Mission to Promote Peace—One School at a Time.* New York: Penguin Books.

Moser, Charles, and Peggy J. Kleinplatz. 2005. "DSM-IV-TR and the Paraphilias:

An Argument for Removal." *Journal of Psychology and Human Sexuality* 17 (3/4): 91–109.

Mount Holyoke News. 2013. "Students Found Anti–Sex Trafficking Club on Campus." April 18. http://mountholyokenews .org/2013/04/18/students-found-anti-sex -trafficking-club-on-campus.

Mudde, Cas. 2012. *The Relationship Between Immigration and Nativism in Europe and North America.* Washington, DC: Migration Policy Institute.

Muehlenhard, Charlene L., Sharon Danoff-Burg, and Irene G. Powch. 1996. "Is Rape Sex or Violence? Conceptual Issues and Implications." In *Sex, Power, Conflict: Evolutionary and Feminist Perspectives,* edited by David M. Buss and Neil M. Malamuth, 119–37. New York: Oxford University Press.

Muhl, Charles J. 2001. "The Employment-at-Will Doctrine: Three Major Exceptions." *Monthly Labor Review,* January, 3–11. http://www.bls.gov/opub/mlr/2001/01/ art1full.pdf.

Mumford, Lewis. 1967. *The Myth of the Machine.* New York: Harcourt, Brace & World.

Muñoz, José Esteban. 2009. *Cruising Utopia: The Then and There of Queer Futurity.* New York: New York University Press.

Murdock, George Peter. 1949. *Social Structure.* New York: Macmillan.

Murphy, Sheigla, and Marsha Rosenbaum. 1999. *Pregnant Women on Drugs: Combating Stereotypes and Stigma.* New Brunswick, NJ: Rutgers University Press.

Murray, Charles. 2012. *Coming Apart: The State of White America 1960–2010.* New York: Crown Forum.

Murray, Christopher J. L., Sandeep C. Kalkarni, Catherine Michaud, Niels Tomijima, Maria T. Bulzacchelli, Terrell J. Iandiorio, and Majid Ezzati. 2006. "Eight Americas: Investigating Mortality Disparities Across Races, Counties, and Race-Counties in the United States." *Public Library of Science Medicine* 3 (9): 1513–24.

Muschert, Glenn, Brian V. Klocke, Robert Perrucci, and Jon Shefner, eds. 2016. *Agenda for Social Justice: Solutions for 2016.* Bristol: Policy Press.

Musick, Kelly, and Larry Bumpass. 2012. "Reexamining the Case for Marriage:

Union Formation and Changes in Well-Being." *Journal of Marriage and Family* 74: 1–18.

Musto, David F. 1999. *The American Disease: Origins of Narcotic Control,* 3rd ed. New York: Oxford University Press.

Mythri Speaks. 2016. "Menstruation: Rhetoric, Research, Reality." https://mythrispeaks .wordpress.com/2016/06/13/menstruation -rhetoric-research-reality/.

Nagel, Joane. 2003. *Race, Ethnicity, and Sexuality: Intimate Intersections, Forbidden Frontiers.* New York: Oxford University Press.

Naimi, Timothy S., Robert D. Brewer, Ali Mokdad, Denny Clark, Mary K. Serdula, and James S. Marks. 2003. "Binge Drinking Among US Adults." *Journal of the American Medical Association* 289 (1): 70–75.

Nakonezny, Paul A., Robert D. Shull, and Joseph Lee Rogers. 1995. "The Effect of No-Fault Divorce Law on the Divorce Rate Across the 50 States and Its Relation to Income, Education, and Religiosity." *Journal of Marriage and the Family* 57: 477–88.

Narzary, Pralip Kumar. 2013. "Sexual Exposure and Awareness of Emergency Contraceptive Pills Among Never Married." *Journal of Social and Development Sciences* 4 (4): 164–73.

National Association of Realtors. 2012. *Minneapolis–St. Paul–Bloomington Area Local Market Report, Second Quarter 2012.* Chicago: National Association of Realtors. http://www.realtor.org/sites/default/files/ reports/2012/local-market-reports-2012– q2/local-market-reports-2012–q2–mn -minneapolis.pdf.

———. 2015. "Report: Another Big Dip in Foreclosure Rates." July 14. Accessed August 20, 2016. http://realtormag.realtor .org/daily-news/2015/07/14/report -another-big-dip-in-foreclosure-rates.

National Cancer Institute. 2008. *The Role of the Media in Promoting and Reducing Tobacco Use.* Tobacco Control Monograph 19, NIH 07–6242. Bethesda, MD: U.S. Department of Health and Human Services, National Institutes of Health.

National Center for Education Statistics. 2008. "Schools and Staffing Survey." http://nces .ed.gov/surveys/sass.

———. 2012. "Trial Urban District Assessment." Nation's Report Card,

National Assessment of Educational Progress. http://nationsreportcard.gov/tuda.asp.

———. 2013. "The Nation's Report Card: Trends in Academic Progress 2012" (NCES 2013 456). Institute of Education Sciences, U.S. Department of Education, Washington, DC.

———. 2015. "Digest of Education Statistics." Accessed March 1, 2017. https://nces.ed.gov/programs/digest/2015menu_tables.asp.

———. 2016a. "Figure S3a. Difference in Average Scores of 15-Year-Old Female and Male Students on the PISA Science Literacy Scale, by Education System: 2015." Accessed March 2, 2017. https://nces.ed.gov/surveys/pisa/pisa2015/pisa2015highlights_3c.asp.

———. 2016b. "Figure M3a. Difference in average scores of 15-Year-Old Female and Male Students on the PISA Mathematics Literacy Scale, by Education System: 2015." Accessed March 2, 2017. https://nces.ed.gov/surveys/pisa/pisa2015/pisa2015highlights_5c.asp.

———. 2017. Accessed May 5, 2017. https://www.nationsreportcard.gov/reading_math_2015/#reading/gaps?grade=8.

National Center on Elder Abuse. 1999. Types of Elder Abuse in Domestic Settings. Elder Abuse Information Series, No. 1. Washington, DC: National Center on Elder Abuse.

National College Athletics Association. 2016. "Student-Athlete Participation 1981–82 to 2015–16." Accessed March 1, 2017. http://www.ncaapublications.com/productdownloads/PR1516.pdf.

National Conference of State Legislatures. 2017. "'Bathroom Bill' Legislative Tracking." Accessed September 20, 2017. http://www.ncsl.org/research/education/-bathroom-bill-legislative-tracking635951130.aspx#1.

National Drug Control Strategy: FY 2017 Budget and Performance Summary. https://obamawhitehouse.archives.gov/sites/default/files/ondcp/policy-and-research/fy2017_budget_summary-final.pdf.

National Institute on Drug Abuse. 2014. "Principles of Drug Abuse Treatment for Criminal Justice Populations: A Research-Based Guide." https://www.drugabuse.gov/publications/principles-drug-abuse-treatment-criminal-justice-populations/principles.

———. 2017a. "Abuse of Prescription (Rx) Drugs Affects Young Adults Most." http://www.drugabuse.gov/related-topics/trends-statistics/infographics/abuse-prescription-rx-drugs-affects-young-adults-most.

———. 2017b. "Trends & Statistics." https://www.drugabuse.gov/related-topics/trends-statistics#costs.

National Marriage Project. 2011. Social Indicators of Marital Health and Well-Being: Trends of the Past Five Decades. Charlottesville, VA: National Marriage Project. http://www.stateofourunions.org/2011/social_indicators.php.

National Marriage Project and the Institute for American Values. 2012. Social Indicators of Marital Health & Well-Being, Trends of the Past Five Decades in the State of Our Unions: Marriage in America 2012.

National Priorities Project. 2008. http://nationalpriorities.org.

National Public Radio. 2016. "Could You Come Up With 400 if Disaster Struck?" Accessed July 6, 2016. http://www.npr.org/2016/04/24/475432149/could-you-come-up-with-400–if-disaster-struck.

National Science Foundation. 2003. National Science Foundation Strategic Plan FY 2003–2008. https://www.nsf.gov/pubs/2004/nsf04201/FY2003-2008.pdf.

National Science Foundation. 2013. "Table 34. Highest Educational Attainment of Either Parent of Doctorate Recipients: Selected Years, 1982–2012." http://www.nsf.gov/statistics/sed/2012/pdf/tab34.pdf.

———. 2015. "Women, Minorities, and Persons With Disabilities in Science and Engineering." https://www.nsf.gov/statistics/2017/nsf17310/

National Telecommunications and Information Administration. 2013. Exploring the Digital Nation: America's Emerging Online Experience. Washington, DC: U.S. Department of Commerce. http://www.ntia.doc.gov/files/ntia/publications/exploring_the_digital_nation_-_americas_emerging_online_experience.pdf.

National Traffic Safety Administration. 2012a. Blueprint for Ending Distracted Driving. DOT HS 811 629. Washington, DC: U.S. Department of Transportation. http://www.distraction.gov/download/campaign-materials/8747–811629–060712–v5–Opt1–Web-tag.pdf.

———. 2012b. Traffic Safety Facts: 2010 Data. DOT HS 811 630. Washington, DC: U.S. Department of Transportation. http://www-nrd.nhtsa.dot.gov/Pubs/811630.pdf.

———. 2015. Traffic Safety Facts: 2015 Data. DOT HS 812 376. Washington, DC: U.S. Department of Transportation. https://crashstats.nhtsa.dot.gov/Api/Public/ViewPublication/812376.

———. 2016. Distracted Driving 2014. Traffic Safety Facts Research Note. DOT HS 812 260. April.

NBC News. 2011. "Are Immigration Laws Blocking Economic Potential?" NBC Nightly News, March 3.

Nelson, Michael. 2010. "Warrior Nation." Chronicle Review, October 29, B6–7.

Neubauer, Chuck. 2011. "Sex Trafficking in the U.S. Called 'Epidemic': 'No Class and No Child Is Immune.'" Washington Times, April 23. http://www.washingtontimes.com/news/2011/apr/23/sex-trafficking-us-called-epidemic/?page=all.

Neumark-Sztainer, Dianne, Melanie Wall, Mary Story, and Amber R. Standish. 2012. "Dieting and unhealthy weight control behaviors during adolescence: Associations with 10-year changes in body mass index." Journal of Adolescent Health 50(1): 80–86.

Neumark-Sztainer, Dianne. 2005. I'm, Like, So Fat! New York: Guilford Press.

New America Foundation. 2013. "Drone Wars Pakistan: Analysis." http://natsec.newamerica.net/drones/pakistan/analysis.

New York Times. 2009. "Support for Women on the Battlefield." New York Times/CBS News Poll, August 16. http://www.nytimes.com/imagepages/2009/08/16/us/16women_poll_ready.html.

———. 2012. "Struggling in the Suburbs." July 7. http://www.nytimes.com/2012/07/08/opinion/sunday/struggling-in-the suburbs.html.

———. 2014. "Pentagon Study Finds 50% Increase in Reports of Military Sexual Assaults." May 1. https://www.nytimes.com/2014/05/02/us/military-sex-assault-report.html?_r=0.

Newman, Katherine S. 2012. *Accordion Families: Boomerang Kids, Anxious Parents, and the Private Toll of Global Competition.* Boston: Beacon Press.

Newman, Katherine S., and Victor Tan Chen. 2007. *The Missing Class: Portraits of the Near Poor in America.* Boston: Beacon Press.

Newport, Frank. 2007. "Black or African American? 'African American' Slightly Preferred Among Those Who Have a Preference." Gallup, September 28. http://www.gallup.com/poll/28816/black-african-american.aspx.

Newton, Paula. 2013. "Canadian Teen Commits Suicide After Alleged Rape, Bullying." CNN, April 10. http://www.cnn.com/2013/04/10/justice/canada-teen-suicide/index.html.

Nickols, Sharon Y., and Robert B. Nielsen. 2011. "'So Many People Are Struggling': Developing Social Empathy Through a Poverty Simulation." *Journal of Poverty* 15 (1): 22–42.

Nicolosi, Alfredo, Edward O. Laumann, Dale B. Glasser, Edson D. Moreira, Anthony Paik, and Clive Gingell. 2004. "Sexual Behavior and Sexual Dysfunctions After Age 40: The Global Study of Sexual Attitudes and Behaviors." *Urology* 64 (5): 991–97.

Nielsen. 2012. "Television: Prime Broadcast Network TV—United States." Accessed October 22. http://www.nielsen.com/us/en/insights/top10s/television.html.

Nijman, Jan. 2000. "The Paradigmatic City." *Annals of the Association of American Geographers* 90 (1): 135–45.

Niland, Patricia, and Antonia C. Lyons. 2011. "Uncertainty in Medicine: Meanings of Menopause and Hormone Replacement Therapy in Medical Textbooks." *Social Science & Medicine* 73 (8): 1238–45.

No Mas Bebes. 2015. Directed by Renee Tajima-Pena.

Norton. 2012. *Cybercrime Report 2012.* Sunnyvale, CA: Symantec Corporation. http://us.norton.com/cybercrimereport/promo.

Norton-Taylor, Richard. 2011. "MI5 Former Chief Decries 'War on Terror.'" *Guardian,* September 2.

Oakes, Jeannie. 1985. *Keeping Track: How Schools Structure Inequality.* New Haven, CT: Yale University Press.

Oakes, Jeannie, Adam Gamoran, and Reba N. Page. 1992. "Curriculum Differentiation: Opportunities, Outcomes, and Meanings." In *Handbook of Research on Curriculum,* edited by Philip W. Jackson, 570–608. New York: Macmillan.

Oakley, Annie. 2007. "Introduction." In *Working Sex: Sex Workers Write About a Changing Industry,* edited by Annie Oakley, 7–13. Emeryville, CA: Seal Press.

ObamaCare Facts. 2013. "ObamaCare 2013: What 2013 Means for ObamaCare and Health Care Reform." http://www.obamacarefacts.com/obamacare-2013.php.

O'Brien, Eileen. 2008. *The Racial Middle: Latinos and Asian Americans Living Beyond the Racial Divide.* New York: New York University Press.

O'Brien, Eileen, and Kathleen Korgen. 2007. "It's the Message, Not the Messenger: The Declining Significance of Black-White Contact." *Sociological Inquiry* 77: 356–82.

O'Connell Davidson, Julia, and Jacqueline Sanchez Taylor. 1999. "Fantasy Islands: Exploring the Demand for Sex Tourism." In *Sun, Sex, and Gold: Tourism and Sex Work in the Caribbean,* edited by Kamala Kempadoo, 37–54. Lanham, MD: Rowman & Littlefield.

Office of National Drug Control Policy, 2016. FY 2017 Budget and Performance Summary. Companion to the National Drug Control Strategy. Washington, DC: Executive Office of the President. https://obamawhitehouse.archives.gov/sites/default/files/ondcp/policy-and-research/fy2017_budget_summary-final.pdf.

Office of the U.S. Trade Representative. 2013. "Mexico." Accessed April 27. http://www.ustr.gov/countries-regions/americas/mexico.

———. 2017. "US–Mexico Trade Facts. Accessed January 12. https://ustr.gov/countries-regions/americas/mexico.

Ogas, Ogi, and Sai Gaddam. 2012. *A Billion Wicked Thoughts: What the Internet Tells Us About Sexual Relationships.* New York: Plume.

Ogden, Cynthia L., Margaret D. Carroll, Lester R. Curtin, et al. 2010. "Prevalence of High Body Mass Index in US Children and Adolescents, 2007–2008." *Journal of the American Medical Association* 303 (3): 242–49.

Oldenburg, Ray. 1999. *The Great Good Place: Cafés, Coffee Shops, Bookstores, Bars, Hair Salons and Other Hangouts at the Heart of a Community.* New York: Da Capo Press.

Oliver, Melvin L., and Thomas M. Shapiro. 1995. *Black Wealth/White Wealth: A New Perspective on Racial Inequality.* New York: Routledge.

Olshansky, S. Jay, Toni Antonucci, Lisa Berkman, Robert H. Binstock, Axel Boersch-Supan, John T. Cacioppo, Bruce A. Carnes, Laura L. Carstensen, Linda P. Fried, Dana P. Goldman, James Jackson, Martin Kohli, John Rother, Yuhui Zheng, and John Rowe. 2012. "Differences in Life Expectancy Due to Race and Educational Differences Are Widening, and Many May Not Catch Up." *Health Affairs* 31 (8): 1803–13.

Olson, Jonathan R., James P. Marshall, H. Wallace, Goddard, and David G. Schramm. 2015. "Shared Religious Beliefs, Prayer, and Forgiveness as Predictors of Marital Satisfaction." *Family Relations* 64 (4): 519–33.

Omondi, Rose Kisia. 2003. "Gender and the Political Economy of Sex Tourism in Kenya's Coastal Resorts." Paper prepared for the international symposium/doctoral course "Feminist Perspective on Global Economic and Political Systems and Women's Struggle for Global Justice," Tromsø, Norway.

O'Neil, Shannon K. 2013. *Two Countries Indivisible: Mexico, the United States, and the Road Ahead.* Oxford: Oxford University Press.

Orcutt, James D., and J. Blake Turner. 1993. "Shocking Numbers and Graphic Accounts: Quantified Images of Drug Problems in the Print Media." *Social Problems* 40 (2): 190–206.

Organisation for Economic Co-operation and Development. 2015. Family Database. Table SF 3.1: Marriage and Divorce Rates. Accessed August 18, 2016. https://www.oecd.org/els/family/SF_3_1_Marriage_and_divorce_rates.pdf

Organisation for Economic Co-operation and Development, Program for International Student Assessment. 2009. "Mathematics, Age 15 OECD Scores."

O'Toole, James O., and Edward Lawler III. 2006. *The New American Workplace.* New York: Palgrave Macmillan.

Ott, Bryant, Nikki Blacksmith, and Ken Royal. 2008. "Job Seekers: Personal Connections Still Matter." Gallup Business Journal, May 8. http://businessjournal.gallup.com/content/106957/personal-connections-still-matter.aspx.

Ozawa, Martha N. 2004. "Social Welfare Spending on Family Benefits in the United States and Sweden: A Comparative Study." Family Relations 53 (3): 301–9.

Padilla-Walker, Laura M., Sarah M. Coyne, and Ashley M. Fraser. 2012. "Getting a High-Speed Family Connection: Associations Between Family Media Use and Family Connection." Family Relations 61: 426–40.

Pager, Devah. 2003. "Blacks and Ex-Cons Need Not Apply." Contexts 2 (4): 58–59.

Pager, Devah, Bruce Western, and Bart Bonikowski. 2009. "Discrimination in a Low-Wage Labor Market: A Field Experiment." American Sociological Review 74 (5): 777–99.

Pahl, R. E. 1970. Whose City? And Other Essays on Sociology and Planning. London: Longmans.

Panruti, Ramamurti V., Phoebe S. Liebig, and Jamuna Duvvuru. 2015. "Gerontology in India." The Gerontologist 55 (6): 894–900.

Papademetriou, Demetrios G. 2012. Rethinking National Identity in the Age of Migration. Council Statement From the 7th Plenary Meeting of the Transatlantic Council on Migration. Washington, DC: Migration Policy Institute.

Pappas, Chris. 2011. "Sex Sells, but What Else Does It Do? The American Porn Industry." In Introducing the New Sexuality Studies, 2nd ed., edited by Steven Seidman, Nancy Fischer, and Chet Meeks, 320–26. New York: Routledge.

Park, Robert E., and Ernest W. Burgess. 1924. Introduction to the Science of Sociology. Chicago: University of Chicago Press.

Park, Robert E., Ernest Burgess, and Roderick D. McKenzie. 1925. The City. Chicago: University of Chicago Press.

Parker, Kim. 2011. "The Military-Civilian Gap: Fewer Family Connections." Pew Research Center, Social and Demographic Trends, November 23. http://www.pewsocialtrends.org/2011/11/23/the-military-civilian-gap-fewer-family-connections.

———. 2012. "The Boomerang Generation: Feeling OK About Living With Mom and Dad." Pew Research Center, Social and Demographic Trends, March 15. http://www.pewsocialtrends.org/files/2012/03/PewSocialTrends-2012-BoomerangGeneration.pdf.

Parker, Kim, and Wendy Wang. 2013. Modern Parenthood: Roles of Moms and Dads Converge as They Balance Work and Family. Washington, DC: Pew Research Center. http://www.pewsocialtrends.org/files/2013/03/FINAL_modern_parenthood_03-2013.pdf.

Parreñas, Rhacel Salazar. 2005. Children of Global Migration: Transnational Families and Gendered Woes. Stanford, CA: Stanford University Press.

Parsons, Talcott. 1951. The Social System. New York: Free Press.

———. 1959. "The School Class as a Social System." Harvard Educational Review 29: 297–318.

———. 1968. "On the Concept of Value-Commitments." Social Inquiry 38: 135–60.

Parsons, Talcott, and Robert F. Bales. 1955. Family, Socialization and Interaction Process. New York: Free Press.

Pascoe, C. J. 2007. Dude, You're a Fag: Masculinity and Sexuality in High School. Berkeley: University of California Press.

Pascoe, C. J., and Jocelyn A. Hollander. 2016. "Good Guys Don't Rape: Gender, Domination, and Mobilizing Rape." Gender & Society 30 (1): 67–79.

Paternoster, Raymond, and Leeann Iovanni. 1989. "The Labeling Perspective and Delinquency: An Elaboration of the Theory and an Assessment of the Evidence." Justice Quarterly 6(3): 359–94.

Patten, Eileen. 2016. "Racial, Gender Wage Gaps Persist in U.S. Despite Some Progress." Pew Research Center Fact Tank. Accessed February 28, 2017. http://www.pewresearch.org/fact-tank/2016/07/01/racial-gender-wage-gaps-persist-in-u-s-despite-some-progress/#

Patterson, Charlotte J., and Paul D. Hastings. 2007. "Socialization in the Context of Family Diversity." In Handbook of Socialization: Theory and Research, edited by Joan E. Grusec and Paul D. Hastings, 328–51. New York: Guilford.

Paul, Pamela. 2004. "The Porn Factor." Time, January 19, 99–100.

Paull, John. 2007. "Toxic Colonialism." New Scientist, November 3, 25.

Pearlin, Leonard I., Scott Schieman, Elena M. Fazio, and Stephen C. Meersman. 2005. "Stress, Health and the Life Course: Some Conceptual Perspectives." Journal of Health and Social Behavior 46 (2): 205–19.

Peguero, Anthony A., and Amanda M. Lauck. 2008. "Older Adults and Their Vulnerabilities to the Exposure of Violence." Sociology Compass 2 (1): 62–73.

Pellow, David N., Allan Schnaiberg, and Adam S. Weinberg. 2000. "Putting the Ecological Modernisation Thesis to the Test: The Promises and Performances of Urban Recycling." In Ecological Modernisation Around the World: Perspectives and Critical Debates, edited by Arthur P. J. Mol and David A. Sonnenfeld, 109–37. London: Frank Cass.

Pencavel, John. 2007. "Unionism Viewed Internationally." In What Do Unions Do? A Twenty-Year Perspective, edited by James T. Bennett and Bruce E. Kaufman. New Brunswick, NJ: Transaction.

Pérez, Gina M. 2006. "How a Scholarship Girl Becomes a Soldier: The Militarization of Latina/o Youth in Chicago Public Schools." Identities: Global Studies in Culture and Power 13: 53–72.

Perrone, Dina. 2009. The High Life: Club Kids, Harm and Drug Policy. Boulder, CO: Lynne Rienner.

Pettit, Becky, and Jennifer L. Hook. 2009. Gendered Tradeoffs: Women, Family, and Workplace Inequality in Twenty-one Countries. New York: Russell Sage Foundation.

Pettit, Becky, and Bruce Western. 2004. "Mass Imprisonment and the Life Course: Race and Class Inequality in U.S. Incarceration." American Sociological Review 69: 151–69.

Pew Charitable Trusts. 2013. Persuading the Prescribers: Pharmaceutical Industry Marketing and Its Influence on Physicians and Patients. http://www.pewtrusts.org/en/research-and-analysis/fact-sheets/2013/11/11/persuading-the-prescribers-pharmaceutical-industry-marketing-and-its-influence-on-physicians-and-patients.

Pew Research Center. 2012. The Lost Decade of the Middle Class: Fewer, Poorer, Gloomier. Washington, DC: Pew Research

Center. http://www.pewsocialtrends.org/
files/2012/08/pew-social-trends-lost
-decade-of-the-middle-class.pdf.

———. 2016. "Racial, Gender Wage Gaps
Persist in U.S. Despite Some Progress."
http://www.pewresearch.org/fact
-tank/2016/07/01/racial-gender-wage
-gaps-persist-in-u-s-despite-some-progress/.

Pew Social Research. 2016. *Changing Attitudes
on Gay Marriage.* May 12. Accessed
August 19, 2016. http://www.pewforum
.org/2016/05/12/changing-attitudes-on
-gay-marriage/.

Pfohl, Stephen J. 1977. "The 'Discovery' of Child
Abuse." *Social Problems* 24 (3): 310–23.

Piccigallo, Jacqueline. 2008. "Men Against Rape:
Male Activists' Views Towards Campus-
Based Sexual Assault and Acquaintance
Rape." Master's thesis, University of
Delaware.

Pierce, Richard J., Jr. 1989. "Public Utility
Regulatory Takings: Should the Judiciary
Attempt to Police the Political Institutions?"
Georgetown Law Journal 77: 2031–77.

Pilon, Mary. 2010. "What's a Degree Really
Worth?" *Wall Street Journal,* February 2.
http://online.wsj.com/article/SB100014
24052748703822404575019082819966538.html.

Pincus, Fred L. 2011. *Understanding Diversity,*
2nd ed. Boulder, CO: Lynne Rienner.

Pinker, Steven. 2011. *The Better Angels of Our
Nature: Why Violence Has Declined.* New
York: Viking Press.

Pitts-Taylor, Victoria. 2016. *The Brain's Body:
Neuroscience and Corporeal Politics.*
Durham, NC: Duke University Press.

Pitzer College. 2017. "Pomona Economic
Opportunity Center." Accessed January
12, 2017. http://pitweb.pitzer.edu/cec/
community-partners/core-partners/peoc/.

Piven, Frances Fox. 2006. *Challenging Authority:
How Ordinary People Change America.*
Lanham, MD: Rowman & Littlefield.

Piven, Frances Fox, and Richard A. Cloward.
1993. *Regulating the Poor: The Functions
of Public Welfare,* updated ed. New York:
Vintage.

Plante, Rebecca F. 2006. "Hooking It Up: Sex in
the Bedroom." In *Sexualities in Context: A
Social Perspective.* Boulder, CO: Westview
Press.

Plateris, Alexander. 1973. *100 Years of
Marriage and Divorce Statistics: United
States, 1867–1967.* U.S. Department of
Health, Education, and Welfare, DHEW
Publication (HRA) 74–1902. Washington,
DC: Government Printing Office. http://
www.cdc.gov/nchs/data/series/sr_21/
sr21_024.pdf.

Polaris Project. 2017. "Sex Trafficking." Accessed
May 1, 2017. https://polarisproject.org/
sex-trafficking.

Polman, Linda. 2010. *The Crisis Caravan: What's
Wrong With Humanitarian Aid?* New York:
Macmillan.

Poortinga, Wouter. 2006. "Social Relations or
Social Capital? Individual and Community
Health Effects of Bonding Social Capital."
Social Science & Medicine 63 (1): 255–70.

Popenoe, David. 1988. *Disturbing the Nest:
Family Change and Decline in Modern
Societies.* Piscataway, NJ: Aldine
Transaction.

———. 1993. "American Family Decline,
1960–1990: A Review and Appraisal."
Journal of Marriage and the Family 55:
527–42.

———, ed. 1996. *Promises to Keep: Decline
and Renewal of Marriage in America.*
Lanham, MD: Rowman & Littlefield.

———. 2004. *War Over the Family.* Piscataway,
NJ: Transaction.

———. 2009. *Families Without Fathers:
Fathers, Marriage, and Children in Modern
Society.* Piscataway, NJ: Transaction.

Porta, Daniela, Simona Milani, Antonio
Lazzarino, Carlo A. Perucci, and Francesco
Forastiere. 2009. "Systematic Review of
Epidemiological Studies on Health Effects
Associated With Management of Solid
Waste." *Environmental Health* 8: 60.

Portes, Alejandro, and Robert D. Manning.
1986. "The Immigrant Enclave: Theory and
Empirical Examples." In *Competitive Ethnic
Relations,* edited by Susan Olzak and Joane
Nagel, 47–68. New York: Academic Press.

Portes, Alejandro, and Rubén G. Rumbaut. 2006.
Immigrant America: A Portrait, 3rd ed.
Berkeley: University of California Press.

Post, Lori A., Nancy J. Mezey, Christopher
Maxwell, and Wilma Novalés Wibert.
2002. "The Rape Tax: Tangible and
Intangible Costs of Sexual Violence."
Journal of Interpersonal Violence 17 (7):
773–82.

Pott, Larry. 2017. "Discussion Guide for
Screenings." Accessed March 22, 2017.
http://www.audrieanddaisy.com/watch
-and-discuss/discussion-guide-for
-screenings/.

Potter, Daniel. 2012. "Same-Sex Parent Families
and Children's Academic Achievement."
Journal of Marriage and the Family 74 (3):
4556–4571.

Powell, Jason L. 2006. *Social Theory and Aging.*
Lanham, MD: Rowman & Littlefield.

———. 2010. "The Power of Global Aging."
Ageing International 35: 1–14.

Prakash, Om. 2009. "The Efficacy of 'Don't Ask,
Don't Tell.'" *Joint Forces Quarterly* 55 (4):
88–94.

Pratt, Travis C., Francis T. Cullen, Christine S.
Sellers, L. Thomas Winfree Jr, Tamara D.
Madensen, Leah E. Daigle, Noelle E. Fearn
and Jacinta M. Gau. 2010. "The Empirical
Status of Social Learning Theory: A Meta-
analysis." *Justice Quarterly* 27(6): 765–802.

Preston, Julia A. 2011. "After a False Dawn,
Anxiety for Illegal Immigrant Students."
New York Times, February 8.

PricewaterhouseCoopers. 2011. *Cybercrime:
Protecting Against the Growing Threat:
Global Economic Crime Survey.* London:
PricewaterhouseCoopers. http://www.pwc
.com/en_GX/gx/economic-crime-survey/
assets/GECS_GLOBAL_REPORT.pdf.

Proctor, Bernadette D., Jessica L. Semega,
and Melissa A. Kollar. 2016. "Income
and Poverty in the United States: 2015."
Washington, DC: United States Census
Bureau, September. Accessed May 10,
2017. http://www.uah.org/wp-content/
uploads/2016/09/here.pdf.

Provine, Doris Marie. 2007. *Unequal Under the
Law: Race in the War on Drugs.* Chicago:
University of Chicago Press.

Prus, Steven G. 2011. "Comparing Social
Determinants of Self-Rated Health
Across the United States and Canada."
Social Science & Medicine 73 (1):
50–59.

Puentes, Jennifer, David Knox, and Marty E.
Zusman. 2008. "Participants in 'Friends
With Benefits' Relationships." *College
Student Journal* 42 (1): 176–80.

Pungello, Elizabeth P., Frances A. Campbell, and
W. Steven Barnett. 2006. "Poverty and
Early Childhood Educational Intervention."
University of North Carolina Center on
Poverty, Work and Opportunity, Policy Brief
Series, December 13.

Purcell, Natalie J., and Eileen L. Zurbriggen. 2013. "The Sexualization of Girls and Gendered Violence: Mapping the Connections." In *The Sexualization of Girls and Girlhood: Causes, Consequences, and Resistance,* edited by Eileen L. Zurbriggen and Tomi-Ann Roberts, 149–65. New York: Oxford University Press.

Puzzanchera, C., and W. Kang. 2013. "Easy Access to FBI Arrest Statistics 1994–2010." National Center for Juvenile Justice, Office of Juvenile Justice and Delinquency Prevention. http://www.ojjdp .gov/ojstatbb/ezaucr.

Puzzanghera, Jim. 2016, "Job Market Mystery: Where Are the Men?" *Los Angeles Times,* November 21, A-8.

Quadagno, Jill, and Jennifer Reid. 1999. "The Political Economy Perspective in Aging." In *Handbook of Theories of Aging,* edited by Vern L. Bengtson and K. Warner Schaie, 344–58. New York: Springer.

Quesnel-Vallee, Amélie, Jean-Simon Farrah, and Tania Jenkins. 2011. "Population Aging, Health Systems, and Equity: Shared Challenges for the United States and Canada." In *Handbook of Sociology of Aging,* edited by Richard A. Settersten Jr. and Jacqueline L. Angel, 563–81. New York: Springer.

Quinney, Richard. 1970. *The Social Reality of Crime.* Boston: Little, Brown.

Rahbek-Clemmensen, Jon, Emerald M. Archer, John Barr, Aaron Belkin, Mario Guerrero, Cameron Hall, and Katie E. O. Swain. 2012. "Conceptualizing the Civil-Military Gap: A Research Note." *Armed Forces and Society* 38 (4): 669–78.

Rampell, Catherine. 2009. "Money, Gender, and Job Satisfaction." *New York Times,* Economix blog, November 18. http:// economix.blogs.nytimes.com/2009/11/18/ money-gender-and-job-satisfaction.

———. 2010. "The Gender Wage Gap, Around the World." *New York Times,* Economix blog, March 9. http://economix.blogs .nytimes.com/2010/03/09/the-gender -wage-gap-around-the-world.

Rampey, B. D., R. Finnegan, M. Goodman, L. Mohadjer, T. Krenzke, J. Hogan, and S. Provasnik. 2016. "Skills of U.S. Unemployed, Young, and Older Adults in Sharper Focus: Results From the Program for the International Assessment of Adult Competencies (PIAAC) 2012/2014: First Look" (NCES 2016-039rev). U.S. Department of Education. Washington, DC: National Center for Education Statistics. http://nces.ed.gov/pubsearch.

Rape, Abuse and Incest National Network. 2016. "Victims of Sexual Violence: Statistics." Accessed March 22, 2017. https://www .rainn.org/statistics/victims-sexual -violence.

Ravetz, Jerome R. 1971. *Scientific Knowledge and Its Social Problems.* Oxford: Clarendon Press.

———. 2005. *The No-Nonsense Guide to Science.* Toronto: Between the Lines.

Ravitch, Diane. 2013. *Reign of Error: The Hoax of the Privatization Movement and the Danger to America's Public Schools.* New York: Alfred A. Knopf.

Rawls, John. 1971. *A Theory of Justice.* Cambridge, MA: Belknap Press.

Ready, Richard C. 2005. *Do Landfills Always Depress Nearby Property Values?* Rural Development Paper 27. University Park, PA: Northeast Regional Center for Rural Development. http://aese.psu.edu/nercrd/ publications/rdp/rdp27.pdf.

Reaves, Brian A. 2013. "Felony Defendants in Large Urban Counties, 2009—Statistical Tables." U.S. Department of Justice, Office of Justice Programs, Bureau of Justice Statistics. Accessed May 22, 2017. https:// www.bjs.gov/content/pub/pdf/fdluc09.pdf.

Regnerus, Mark, and Jeremy Uecker. 2011. *Premarital Sex in America: How Young Americans Meet, Mate, and Think About Marrying.* New York: Oxford University Press.

Reid, Joy-Ann. 2016. "Lemonade Is a Powerful Black Feminist Aesthetic in Its Own Right." *Feministing.* Accessed April 15, 2017. http://feministing.com/2016/05/11/a -feminist-roundtable-on-bell-hooks -beyonce-and-moving-beyond-pain/.

Reid, Julie A., Sinikka Elliott, and Gretchen R. Webber. 2011. "Casual Hookups to Formal Dates: Refining the Boundaries of the Sexual Double Standard." *Gender & Society* 25 (5): 545–68.

Reiman, Jeffrey. 2001. *The Rich Get Richer and the Poor Get Prison: Ideology, Class, and Criminal Justice,* 6th ed. Boston: Allyn & Bacon.

Reinarman, Craig, Peter D. A. Cohen, and Hendrien L. Kaal. 2004. "The Limited Relevance of Drug Policy: Cannabis in Amsterdam and in San Francisco." *American Journal of Public Health* 94 (5): 836–42.

Reinberg, Steve. 2011. "U.S. Teen Birth Rate Hits Record Low, but American Young People Are Still Having Babies at Rates Higher Than Other Rich Nations, CDC Says." *U.S. News & World Report,* April 5. http:// health.usnews.com/health-news/ family-health/brain-and-behavior/ articles/2011/04/05/us-teen-birth-rate -hits-record-low.

Reinhardt, Uwe. 2000. "Health Care for the Aging Baby Boom: Lessons From Abroad." *Journal of Economic Perspectives* 14 (2): 71–83.

Reisner, Marc. 1986. *Cadillac Desert: The American West and Its Disappearing Water.* New York: Penguin Books.

Relman, Arnold S. 1980. "The New Medical-Industrial Complex." *New England Journal of Medicine* 303: 963–70.

Reno, Virginia P., and Joni Lavery. 2005. *Options to Balance Social Security Funds Over the Next 75 Years.* Social Security Brief 18, February. Washington, DC: National Academy of Social Insurance.

Rentschler, Carrie A. 2014. "Rape Culture and the Feminist Politics of Social Media." *Girlhood Studies* 7 (1): 65–82. Accessed April 15, 2017. (file:///C:/Users/elroi .windsor/Downloads/Rape_Culture_and_ the_Feminist_Politics_o%20(2).pdf).

Reskin, Barbara, and Irene Padavic. 1994. *Women and Men at Work.* Thousand Oaks, CA: Pine Forge Press.

Rhoades, Galena K., Scott M. Stanley, and Howard J. Markman. 2009. "The Pre-engagement Cohabitation Effect: A Replication and Extension of Previous Findings." *Journal of Family Psychology* 23: 107–11.

Rhode Island Coalition Against Domestic Violence. 2000. *Domestic Violence: A Handbook for Journalists.* Warwick: Rhode Island Coalition Against Domestic Violence.

Richmond, C. A., and N. A. Ross. 2009. "The Determinants of First Nation and Inuit Health: A Critical Population Health Approach." *Health & Place* 15 (2): 403–11.

Rideout, Victoria J., Ulla G. Foehr, and Donald F. Roberts. 2010. *Generation M2: Media in the Lives of 8- to 18-Year-Olds.* Menlo Park, CA: Henry J. Kaiser Family Foundation.

Riley, Kevin M. 2010. "Suicide and the Economy." Paper available through Academia.edu. https://www.academia.edu/1963339/Suicide_and_the_Economy.

Rist, Raymond. 1977. *The Urban School: A Factory for Failure*. Cambridge, MA: MIT Press.

Ritzer, George. 1998. *The McDonaldization Thesis*. London: Sage.

Roberts, J. Timmons, and Bradley Parks. 2006. *A Climate of Injustice: Global Inequality, North–South Politics, and Climate Policy*. Cambridge, MA: MIT Press.

Robinson, B. H. 2009. "E-waste: An Assessment of Global Production and Environmental Impacts." *Science of the Total Environment* 408 (2): 183–91.

Robinson, Jennifer. 2003. "Social Classes in U.S., Britain, and Canada." Gallup, August 5. http://www.gallup.com/poll/8998/Social-Classes-US-Britain-Canada.aspx.

Roediger, David R. 1991. *The Wages of Whiteness: Race and the Making of the American Working Class*. New York: Verso.

Rogers, Chrissie, and Susie Welter. 2012. *Critical Approaches to Care: Understanding Caring Relations, Identities, and Cultures*. London: Routledge.

Romer, Daniel, Kathleen Hall Jamieson, and Sean Aday. 2003. "Television News and the Cultivation of Fear of Crime." *Journal of Communication* 53 (1): 88–104.

Romero, Mary. 2011. "Keeping Citizenship Rights White: Arizona's Racial Profiling Practices in Immigration Law Enforcement." *Law Journal for Social Justice* 1 (1): 97–113.

Roscigno, Vincent J., Diana L. Karafin, and Griff Tester. 2009. "The Complexities and Processes of Racial Housing Discrimination." *Social Problems* 56 (1): 49–69.

Rosen, Jeffrey, and Benjamin Wittes. 2011. *Constitution 3.0: Freedom and Technological Change*. Washington, DC: Brookings Institution Press.

Ross, Loretta. 2011. "Understanding Reproductive Justice." http://trustblackwomen.org/our-work/what-is-reproductive-justice/9–what-is-reproductive-justice

Ross, Loretta, and Ricky Solinger. 2017. *Reproductive Justice: An Introduction*. Berkeley, CA: University of California Press.

Ross, M. W., S. A. Månsson, and K. Daneback. 2012. "Prevalence, Severity, and Correlates of Problematic Sexual Internet Use in Swedish Men and Women." *Archives of Sexual Behavior* 41 (2): 459–66.

Rossman, Shelli B., Janine M. Zweig, Dana Kralstein, Kelli Henry, P. Mitchell Downey, and Christine Lindquist. 2011. *The Multisite Adult Drug Court Evaluation: The Drug Court Experience*, vol. 3. Washington, DC: Urban Institute.

Roth, Louise Marie, and Megan M. Henley. 2012. "Unequal Motherhood: Racial-Ethnic and Socioeconomic Disparities in Cesarean Sections in the United States." *Social Problems* 59: 207–27.

Rothstein, Richard. 2010. "How to Fix Our Schools: It's More Complicated, and More Work, Than the Klein-Rhee 'Manifesto' Wants You to Believe." *Education Digest* 76 (6): 32–37.

Rovner, Julie. 2013. "Boomer Housemates Have More Fun." *Your Health*, NPR, May 22.

Rowe, John W., and Robert L. Kahn. 1998. *Successful Aging*. New York: Pantheon Books.

Rowlingson, Karen. 2011. *Does Income Inequality Cause Health and Social Problems?* London: Joseph Rowntree Foundation.

Royster, Deirdre A. 2003. *Race and the Invisible Hand: How White Networks Exclude Black Men From Blue-Collar Jobs*. Berkeley: University of California Press.

Rozanova, Julia. 2006. "Newspaper Portrayals of Health and Illness Among Canadian Seniors: Who Ages Healthily and at What Cost?" *International Journal of Ageing and Later Life* 1 (2): 111–39.

Rudrappa, Sharmila. 2015. *Discounted Life: The Price of Global Surrogacy in India*. New York: New York University Press.

Rumburger, Russell W., and Katherine A. Larson. 1998. "Toward Explaining Differences in Educational Achievement Among Mexican American Language-Minority Students." *Sociology of Education* 71: 68–92.

Rushford, Carly, and Courtney Laird. 2012. "Join the Movement: Take Back the Date." *Colby Echo*, November 7. http://www.thecolbyecho.com/opinion/join-the-movement-take-back-the-date.

Ryan, Camille L., and Kurt Bauman. 2016. *Educational Attainment in the United States: 2015 Population Characteristics*. Washington, DC: The U.S. Census Bureau. Accessed May 5, 2017. https://www.census.gov/content/dam/Census/library/publications/2016/demo/p20–578.pdf

Ryan, William. 1976. *Blaming the Victim*, rev. ed. New York: Vintage.

Ryle, Robyn. 2012. *Questioning Gender: A Sociological Exploration*. Thousand Oaks, CA: Pine Forge Press.

Sable, Jennifer, Chris Plotts, and Lindsey Mitchell. 2010. *Characteristics of the 100 Largest Public Elementary and Secondary School Districts in the United States: 2008–09*. U.S. Department of Education, National Center for Education Statistics, NCES 2011–301. Washington, DC: Government Printing Office. http://nces.ed.gov/pubs2011/2011301.pdf.

Sadker, Myra, and David Sadker. 1994. *Failing at Fairness: How Our Schools Cheat Girls*. New York: Scribner.

Sadovnik, Alan R. 2008. *No Child Left Behind and the Reduction of the Achievement Gap: Sociological Perspectives on Federal Educational Policy*. New York: Routledge.

Saguy, Abigail C., and Rene Almeling. 2008. "Fat in the Fire? Science, the News Media, and the 'Obesity Epidemic.'" *Sociological Forum* 23 (1): 53–83.

Saguy, Abigail C., and Kjerstin Gruys. 2010. "Morality and Health: News Media Constructions of Overweight and Eating Disorders." *Social Problems* 57 (2): 231–50.

Saguy, Abigail C., Kjerstin Gruys, and Shanna Gong. 2010. "Social Problem Construction and National Context: News Reporting on 'Overweight' and 'Obesity' in the United States and France." *Social Problems* 57 (4): 586–610.

Saha, Robin, and Paul Mohai. 2005. "Historical Context and Hazardous Waste Facility Siting: Understanding Temporal Patterns in Michigan." *Social Problems* 52: 618–48.

Sampson, Robert J., and Stephen W. Raudenbush. 2004. "Seeing Disorder: Neighborhood Stigma and the Social Construction of 'Broken Windows.'" *Social Psychology Quarterly* 67 (4): 319–42.

Sampson, Robert J., Stephen W. Raudenbush, and Felton Earls. 1997. "Neighborhoods and Violent Crime: A Multilevel Study of Collective Efficacy." *Science 277* (5328): 918–24.

Sampson, Robert J., and William Julius Wilson. 1995. "Toward a Theory of Race, Crime, and Urban Inequality." In *Crime and Inequality,* edited by John Hagan and Ruth D. Peterson, 37–54. Stanford, CA: Stanford University Press.

Sanders, Stephanie A., Brandon J. Hill, William L. Yarber, Cynthia A. Graham, Richard A. Crosby, and Robin R. Milhausen. 2010. "Misclassification Bias: Diversity in Conceptualisations About Having 'Had Sex.'" *Sexual Health* 7 (1): 31–4.

Sassen, Saskia. 2001. *The Global City: New York, London, Tokyo,* 2nd ed. Princeton, NJ: Princeton University Press.

———. 2002. *Global Networks, Linked Cities* New York: Routledge.

———. 2010. *Cities in a World Economy.* Thousand Oaks, CA: Pine Forge Press.

Satterfield, Terre. 2002. *Anatomy of a Conflict: Identity, Knowledge, and Emotion in Old-Growth Forests.* Vancouver: UBC Press.

Satterthwaite, David. 2009. "The Implications of Population Growth and Urbanization for Climate Change." *Environment & Urbanization* 21 (2): 545–67.

Satterwhite, Catherine Lindsey, Elizabeth Torrone, Elissa Meites, Eileen F. Dunne, Reena Mahajan, Cheryl Bañez Ocfemia, John Su, Fujie Xu, and Hillard Weinstock. 2013. "Sexually Transmitted Infections Among US Women and Men: Prevalence and Incidence Estimates, 2008." *Sexually Transmitted Diseases* 40 (3): 187–93.

Sauder, Marylee. 2017. "Women's March on Washington Gives Voice to Sexual Assault Survivors and So Many Others." Pennsylvania Coalition Against Rape. Accessed April 15, 2017. http://www.pcar.org/blog/women%E2%80%99s-march-washington-gives-voice-sexual-assault-survivors-and-so-many-others.

Saunders, Penelope, and Gretchen Soderlund. 2003. "Threat or Opportunity? Sexuality, Gender and the Ebb and Flow of Trafficking as Discourse." *Canadian Woman Studies* 22 (3–4): 16–24.

Savage, Joanne. 2008. "The Role of Exposure to Media Violence in the Etiology of Violent Behavior: A Criminologist Weighs In." *American Behavioral Scientist* 51 (8): 1123–36.

Scanzoni, John H. 1978. *Sex Roles, Women's Work, and Marital Conflict: A Study of Family Change.* Lexington, MA: Lexington Books.

———. 1982. *Sexual Bargaining: Power Politics in the America Marriage,* 2nd ed. Chicago: University of Chicago Press.

Schalet, Amy T. 2011. *Not Under My Roof: Parents, Teens, and the Culture of Sex.* Chicago: University of Chicago Press.

Scharrer, Erica. 2008. "Media Exposure and Sensitivity to Violence in News Reports." *Journalism and Mass Communication Quarterly* 85 (2): 291–310.

Schilt, Kristen, and Elroi Windsor. 2014. "The Sexual Habitus of Transgender Men: Negotiating Sexuality Through Gender." *Journal of Homosexuality* 61 (5). 732–48.

Schilt, Kristen, and Laurel Westbrook. 2009. "Doing Gender, Doing Heteronormativity: 'Gender Normals,' Transgender People, and the Social Maintenance of Heterosexuality" *Gender & Society* 23 (4): 440–64.

Schmidt, Charles W. 2002. "e-Junk Explosion." *Environmental Health Perspectives* 110 (4): 188–94.

Schmitt, John, and Heather Boushey. 2010. *The College Conundrum: Why the Benefits of a College Education May Not Be So Clear, Especially to Men.* Washington, DC: Center for American Progress. http://www.americanprogress.org/issues/labor/report/2010/12/03/8765/the-college-conundrum.

Schnaiberg, Allan, and Kenneth Alan Gould. 1994. *Environment and Society: The Enduring Conflict.* New York: St. Martin's Press.

Schnaiberg, Allan, David N. Pellow, and Adam S. Weinberg. 2002. "The Treadmill of Production and the Environmental State." In *The Environmental State Under Pressure,* edited by Arthur P. J. Mol and Frederick H. Buttel, 15–32. London: Elsevier Science.

Schneider, Friedrich, and Dominik H. Enste. 2002. *The Shadow Economy: An International Survey.* Cambridge: Cambridge University Press.

Schneider, Joseph W. 1985. "Social Problems Theory: The Constructionist View." *Annual Review of Sociology* 11: 209–29.

Schneier, Bruce. 2010. "The Comparative Risk of Terrorism." *Wall Street Journal,* January 12.

Schor, Juliet. 2004. *Born to Buy: The Commercialized Child and the New Consumer Culture.* New York: Scribner.

Schulman, Beth. 2003. *The Betrayal of Work: How Low-Wage Jobs Fail 30 Million Americans and Their Families.* New York: The New Press.

Schultz, Steven A. 2014. "Attitudes and Beliefs Regarding Direct-to-Consumer Advertising of Pharmaceutical Drugs: An Exploratory Comparison of Physicians and Pharmaceutical Sales Representatives." *Health Marketing Quarterly* 31: 279–91.

Schulz, James H., and Robert H. Binstock. 2006. *Aging Nation: The Economics and Politics of Growing Older in America.* Baltimore: Johns Hopkins University Press.

Schwarz, Alan, and Sarah Cohen. 2013. "A.D.H.D. Seen in 11% of U.S. Children as Diagnoses Rise." *New York Times,* March 31, 2013.

Scott, Wilbur. 1990. "PTSD in DSM-III: A Case in the Politics of Diagnosis and Disease." *Social Problems* 37 (3): 294–310.

Scripps Institution of Oceanography. 2008. "Lake Mead Could Be Dry by 2021." February 12. https://scripps.ucsd.edu/news/2487.

Search Institute. 2012. *Family Assets.* Minneapolis, MN: Search Institute.

Segal, Elizabeth A. 2006. "Welfare as We *Should* Know It: Social Empathy and Welfare Reform." In *The Promise of Welfare Reform: Political Rhetoric and the Reality of Poverty in the Twenty-First Century,* edited by Keith M. Kilty and Elizabeth A. Segal, 265–74. New York: Haworth.

———. 2007. "Social Empathy: A New Paradigm to Address Poverty." *Journal of Poverty* 11 (3): 65–81.

Segal, Elizabeth A., and Keith M. Kilty. 2003. "Political Promises for Welfare Reform." *Journal of Poverty* 7 (1/2): 51–67.

Segrave, Marie, Sanja Milivojevic, and Sharon Pickering. 2009. *Sex Trafficking: International Context and Response.* New York: Taylor & Francis.

Seidman, Steven. 1996. "Introduction." In *Queer Theory/Sociology,* edited by Steven Seidman, 1–29. Malden, MA: Blackwell.

———. 2003. *The Social Construction of Sexuality.* New York: W. W. Norton.

Seltzer, Leslie J., Ashley R. Prososki, Toni E. Ziegler, and Seth D. Pollak. 2012. "Instant Messages vs. Speech: Hormones and Why We Still Need to Hear Each Other." *Evolution and Human Behavior* 33: 42–45.

Semuels, Alana. 2013. "Efficient and Exhausted." *Los Angeles Times,* April 7.

Seto, Karen C., Burak Güneralp, and Lucy R. Hutyra. 2012. "Global Forecasts of Urban Expansion to 2030 and Direct Impacts on Biodiversity and Carbon Pools." *Proceedings of the National Academy of Sciences of the United States of America* 109 (40): 16083–88.

Sewell, Kelsey K., Larissa A. McGarrity, and Donald S. Strassberg. 2016. "Sexual Behavior, Definitions of Sex, and the Role of Self-Partner Context Among Lesbian, Gay, and Bisexual Adults." *The Journal of Sex Research.* Accessed April 15, 2017. http://dx.doi.org/10.1080/00224499.2016.1249331). DOI: 10.1080/00224499.2016.1249331.

Shaefer, H. Luke, and Kathryn Edin. 2012. "Extreme Poverty in the United States, 1996 to 2011." National Poverty Center, Policy Brief 28, February. http://www.npc.umich.edu/publications/policy_briefs/brief28/policybrief28.pdf.

Shafer, Jack. 2007. "Meth Madness at Newsweek." *Slate,* January 31, http://www.slate.com/articles/news_and_politics/press_box/2005/08/meth_madness_at_newsweek.html

Shane, Scott. 2013a. "Bombings End Decade of Strikingly Few Successful Terrorism Attacks in U.S." *New York Times,* April 16.

———. 2013b. "U.S. Engaged in Torture After 9/11, Review Concludes." *New York Times,* April 16.

Shapiro, Thomas M. 2017. *Toxic Inequality: How America's Wealth Gap Destroys Mobility, Deepens the Racial Divide, and Threatens Our Future.* New York: Basic Books.

Shapiro, Thomas M., Tatjana Meschede, and Laura Sullivan. 2010. *The Racial Wealth Gap Increases Fourfold.* Research and Policy Brief, May. Waltham, MA: Institute on Assets and Social Policy. http://www.insightcced.org/uploads/CRWG/IASP-Racial-Wealth-Gap-Brief-May2010.pdf.

Sharkey, Patrick. 2007. "Survival and Death in New Orleans: An Empirical Look at the Human Impact of Katrina." *Journal of Black Studies* 37 (4): 482–501.

Shaw, Amy. 2008. "Direct-to-Consumer Advertising (DTC) of Pharmaceuticals." ProQuest Discovery Guide.

http://165.215.193.14/discoveryguides/direct/review.pdf.

Shaw, Clifford R., and Henry D. McKay. 1942. *Juvenile Delinquency and Urban Areas.* Chicago: University of Chicago Press.

Shedd, Carla. 2015. *Unequal City: Race, Schools, and Perceptions of Injustice.* New York: Russell Sage Foundation.

Shimizu, Celene Parreñas. 2007. *The Hypersexuality of Race: Performing Asian/American Women on Screen and Scene.* Stanford, CA: Stanford University Press.

Shishehbor, M. H., D. Litaker, C. E. Pothier, and M. S. Lauer. 2006. "Association of Socioeconomic Status With Functional Capacity, Heart Rate Recovery, and All-Cause Mortality." *Journal of the American Medical Association* 295 (7): 784–92.

Short, John Rennie. 2004. *Global Metropolitan: Globalizing Cities in a Capitalist World.* New York: Routledge.

Shows, Carla, and Naomi Gerstel. 2009. "Fathering, Class, and Gender: A Comparison of Physicians and Emergency Medical Technicians." *Gender & Society* 23: 161–87.

Signorielli, Nancy. 2001. "Aging on Television: The Picture in the Nineties." *Generations* 25 (3): 34–38.

Silbey, Susan. 1997. "Let Them Eat Cake: Globalization, Postmodern Colonialism, and the Possibilities of Justice." *Law and Society Review* 31: 207–35.

Silicon Valley Toxics Coalition (SVTC). 2002. *Exporting Harm: The High-Tech Trashing of Asia.* February 25, 2002. http://svtc.org/wp-content/uploads/technotrash.pdf.

Silva, Jennifer M. 2013. *Coming Up Short: Working-Class Adulthood in an Age of Uncertainty.* New York: Oxford University Press.

Simmel, Georg. 1971. *On Individuality and Social Forms.* Edited by Donald N. Levine. Chicago: University of Chicago Press.

Simmons, Cedrick-Michael. 2012. "Campus Involvement: Created Equal." E-portfolio. http://eportfolios.ithaca.edu/csimmon1/campusinvolvement/createdequal.

Simmons, Michelle. 2011. "Student Activists Push for Change." *Dickinson Magazine,* Spring. http://www.dickinson.edu/news-and-events/publications/dickinson-magazine/2011–spring/Student-Activists-Push-for-Change.

Sinkovic, Matija, Aleksandar Stulhofer, and Jasmina Bozic. 2013. "Revisiting the Association Between Pornography Use and Risky Sexual Behaviors: The Role of Early Exposure to Pornography and Sexual Sensation Seeking." *Journal of Sex Research* 50 (7): 633–41.

Sinozich, Sofi, and Lynn Langton. 2014. "Rape and Sexual Assault Victimization Among College-Age Females, 1995–2013." U.S. Department of Justice, Office of Justice Programs, Bureau of Justice Statistics. Accessed April 15, 2017. https://www.bjs.gov/content/pub/pdf/rsavcaf9513.pdf.

Sischo, Lacey, John Taylor, and Patricia Yancey Martin. 2006. "Carrying the Weight of Self-Derogation? Disordered Eating Practices as Social Deviance in Young Adults." *Deviant Behavior* 27 (1): 1–30.

Slade, Joseph W. 2001. *Pornography and Sexual Representation: A Reference Guide.* Westport, CT: Greenwood Press.

Sloan, Paul. 2007. "Getting in the Skin Game." CNN, February 13. http://money.cnn.com/magazines/business2/business2_archive/2006/11/01/8392016.

Sluka, Jeffrey. 2011. "Death From Above: UAVs and Losing Hearts and Minds." *Military Review,* May–June, 70–76.

Small, Albion W. 1903. "What Is a Sociologist?" *American Journal of Sociology* 8 (4): 468–77.

Small, Christopher, and Robert J. Nicholls. 2003. "A Global Analysis of Human Settlement in Coastal Zones." *Journal of Coastal Research* 19 (3): 584–99.

Smiler, Andrew P., and Rebecca F. Plante. 2013. "Let's Talk About Sex on Campus." *Chronicle of Higher Education,* May 20. http://chronicle.com/article/Lets-Talk-About-Sex-on-Campus/139353.

Smith, Adam. 2012. *An Inquiry Into the Nature and Causes of the Wealth of Nations.* Chicago: University of Chicago Press. First published 1776.

Smith, David A., and Michael Timberlake. 1995. "Cities in Global Matrices: Toward Mapping the World-System's City System." In *World Cities in a World-System,* edited by Paul L. Knox and Peter J. Taylor. New York: Cambridge University Press.

Smith, Jacquelyn. 2012. "The Best- and Worst-Paying Jobs for Doctors." *Forbes,* July 20. http://www.forbes.com/sites/

jacquelynsmith/2012/07/20/the-best-and -worst-paying-jobs-for-doctors-2.

———. 2013. "How Social Media Can Help (or Hurt) You in Your Job Search." *Forbes*, April 16. http://www.forbes.com/sites/ jacquelynsmith/2013/04/16/how -social-media-can-help-or-hurt-your-job -search/#9af2bb524fdb.

Smith, Janell. 2012. "Students Stand in Quad for 27 Hours to Fight Sex Trafficking." *Daily Tar Heel*, November 18. http://www.dailytarheel.com/ article/2012/11/50a9a6e7064f4.

Smith, Matthew. 2010. "Do Adults Have ADHD? A History Lesson." *British Medical Journal* 340: 939–40.

Smith, Michael D., and Christian Grov. 2011. *In the Company of Men: Inside the Lives of Male Prostitutes*. Santa Barbara, CA: Praeger.

Smith, Paul M. 2016. "June 26: An Important Anniversary in the Fight for LGBT Equality." American Constitution Society Blog. Accessed March 24, 2017. https://www .acslaw.org/acsblog/june-26–an-important -anniversary-in-the-fight-for-lgbt-equality.

Smith, Tom W., and Jaesok Son. 2013. *Trends in Public Attitudes About Sexual Morality*. Chicago: National Opinion Research Center. http://www.norc.org/PDFs/ sexmoralfinal_06–21_FINAL.PDF.

Snow, Allison A. 2005. "Genetic Modification and Gene Flow: An Overview." In *Controversies in Science and Technology: From Maize to Menopause,* edited by Daniel Lee Kleinman, Abby J. Kinchy, and Jo Handelsman, 107–18. Madison: University of Wisconsin Press.

Snow, David A., and Robert D. Benford. 1988. "Ideology, Frame Resonance, and Participant Mobilization." *International Social Movement Research* 1 (1): 197–217.

Snowden, Carisa R. 2011. *Choices Women Make: Agency in Domestic Violence, Assisted Reproduction, and Sex Work*. Minneapolis: University of Minnesota Press.

Snyder, Thomas D. 1993. "120 Years of American Education: A Statistical Portrait." National Center for Education Statistics, Institute of Education Sciences, U.S. Department of Education. Washington, DC.

Snyder, Thomas D., C. de Brey, and S. A. Dillow. 2016. *Digest of Education Statistics 2015* (NCES 2016-014). National Center for Education Statistics, Institute of Education Sciences, U.S. Department of Education. Washington, DC.

Snyder, Thomas D., and Sally A. Dillow. 2010. *Digest of Education Statistics 2009*. U.S. Department of Education, National Center for Education Statistics, NCES 2010–013. Washington, DC: Government Printing Office. http://nces.ed.gov/ pubs2010/2010013.pdf.

Society for Human Resource Management. 2012. *2012 Employee Job Satisfaction and Engagement*. Alexandria, VA: Society for Human Resource Management. http://www.shrm.org/ LegalIssues/StateandLocalResources/ StateandLocalStatutesandRegulations/ Documents/12–0537%202012_ JobSatisfaction_FNL_online.pdf.

———. 2016. *Employee Job Satisfaction and Engagement: Revitalizing a Changing Workforce*. Accessed January 12, 2017. https://www.shrm.org/hr-today/trends -and-forecasting/research-and-surveys/ pages/job-satisfaction-and-engagement -report-revitalizing-changing-workforce .aspx.

Sommer, Marni, and Murat Sahin. 2013. "Overcoming the Taboo: Advancing the Global Agenda for Menstrual Hygiene Management for Schoolgirls." *American Journal of Public Health* 103 (9): 1556–59.

Soneryd, Linda. 2007. "Deliberations on the Unknown, the Unsensed, and the Unsayable? Public Protests and the Development of Third-Generation Mobile Phones in Sweden." *Science, Technology, & Human Values* 32 (3): 287–314.

Sonnenfeld, David A., and Arthur P. J. Mol. 2002. "Globalization and the Transformation of Environmental Governance: An Introduction." *American Behavioral Scientist* 45 (9): 1318–39.

South, Scott J., and Kim M. Lloyd. 1992. "Marriage Opportunities and Family Formation: Further Implications of Imbalanced Sex Ratios." *Journal of Marriage and the Family* 54: 440–51.

Southern Nevada Water Authority. 2009. "Water Resource Plan." http://www.snwa.com/ assets/pdf/wr_plan.pdf.

Spector, Malcolm, and John I. Kitsuse. 1987. *Constructing Social Problems*. New York: Aldine de Gruyter.

Spraggins, Reneé E. 2005. *We the People: Women and Men in the United States*. Census 2000 Special Report, CENSR-20. Washington, DC: U.S. Department of Commerce. https://www.census.gov/ prod/2005pubs/censr-20.pdf.

Stacey, Judith. 2011. *Unhitched: Love, Marriage, and Family Values From West Hollywood to Western China*. New York: New York University Press.

Stacey, Judith, and Timothy J. Biblarz. 2001. "(How) Does the Sexual Orientation of Parents Matter?" *American Sociological Review* 66 (2): 159–83.

Stack, Carol. 1974. *All Our Kin: Strategies for Survival in a Black Community*. New York: Harper & Row.

Stanford Law School/NYU Law School. 2012. "Living Under Drones: Death, Injury, and Trauma to Civilians From US Drone Practices in Pakistan." September. http:// livingunderdrones.org.

Stanley, Megan, Ife Floyd, and Misha Hill. 2014. "TANF Cash Benefits Have Fallen by More Than 20 Percent in Most States and Continue to Erode." Center on Budget and Policy Priorities. Accessed May 30, 2017. http://www.cbpp.org/research/family -income-support/tanf-cash-benefits-have -fallen-by-more-than-20-percent-in -most-states.

Statistic Brain. 2017. "Elderly Abuse Statistics." http://www.statisticbrain.com/elderly -abuse-statistics.

Stedman, Lawrence C. 1987. "It's Time We Changed the Effective Schools Formula." *Phi Delta Kappan* 69 (3): 215–24.

Steele, Claude M. 1997. "A Threat in the Air: How Stereotypes Shape Intellectual Identity and Performance." *American Psychologist* 52: 613–29.

Steele, Claude M., and Joshua Aronson. 1995. "Stereotype Threat and the Intellectual Test Performance of African Americans." *Journal of Personality and Social Psychology* 69: 797–811.

Stepp, Laura Sessions. 2008. *Unhooked: How Young Women Pursue Sex, Delay Love and Lose at Both*. New York: Riverhead Trade.

Stern, Paul C. 1992. "Psychological Dimensions of Global Environmental Change." *Annual Review of Psychology* 43 (1): 269–302.

Stern, Paul C., Thomas Dietz, and Gregory A. Guagnano. 1995. "The New Ecological

Paradigm in Social-Psychological Context." *Environment & Behavior* 27 (6): 723–43.

Stern, Paul C., Thomas Dietz, and Linda Kalof. 1993. "Value Orientations, Gender, and Environmental Concern." *Environment & Behavior* 25 (5): 322–48.

Sternheimer, Karen. 2010. *Connecting Social Problems and Popular Culture*. Boulder, CO: Westview Press.

———. 2013. *Connecting Social Problems and Popular Culture*, 2nd ed. Boulder, CO: Westview Press.

Stetser, Marie C., and Robert Stillwell. 2014. "Public High School Four-Year On-Time Graduation Rates and Event Dropout Rates: School Years 2010–11 and 2011–12. First Look. NCES 2014–391."

Stewart, Phyllis L., and Cantor, Muriel G. 1982. *Varieties of Work*. Beverly Hills, CA: Sage.

Stice, Eric, and Heather E. Shaw. 1994. "Adverse Effects of the Media Portrayed Thin-Ideal on Women and Linkages to Bulimic Symptomatology." *Journal of Social and Clinical Psychology* 13: 288–308.

Stiglitz, Joseph E. 2013. "Student Debt and the Crushing of the American Dream." *New York Times*, May 12. http://opinionator .blogs.nytimes.com/2013/05/12/student -debt-and-the-crushing-of-the-american -dream.

Stiglitz, Joseph E., and Linda J. Bilmes. 2008. *The Three Trillion Dollar War: The True Cost of the Iraq Conflict*. New York: W. W. Norton.

Stinnett, Nick, and John DeFrain. 1985. *Secrets of Strong Families*. Boston: Little, Brown.

Stockholm International Peace Research Institute. 2013. "Military Expenditure." http://www.sipri.org/research/armaments/ milex.

Stockman, Farah. 2009. "Anthropologist's War Death Reverberates." *Boston Globe*, February 12.

Stoltenberg, John. 2006. "How Men Have (a) Sex." In *Reconstructing Gender: A Multicultural Approach*, 4th ed., edited by Estelle Disch, 264–74. Boston: McGraw-Hill.

Stone, Amy. 2012. *Gay Rights at the Ballot Box*. Minneapolis: University of Minnesota Press.

Storch, Eric A., Vanessa A. Milsom, Ninoska DeBraganza, Adam B. Lewin, Gary

R. Geffken, and Janet H. Silverstein. 2007. "Peer Victimization, Psychosocial Adjustment, and Physical Activity in Overweight and At-Risk-for-Overweight Youth." *Journal of Pediatric Psychology* 32 (1): 80–89.

Strawn, Kirsten. 2013. "Hooking Up: Destroying Intimacy." *The Faith Coach*, February 20. http://thefaithcoach.wordpress .com/2013/02/20/hooking-up-destroying -intimacy-1.

Strayer, David L., Frank A. Drews, and Dennis J. Crouch. 2006. "A Comparison of the Cell Phone Driver and the Drunk Driver." *Human Factors* 48 (2): 381–91.

Street, Debra, and Jeralynn Sittig Cossman. 2006. "Greatest Generation or Greedy Geezers? Social Spending Preferences and the Elderly." *Social Problems* 53 (1): 75–96.

Stull, V., M. M. Bell, and M. Ncwadi. 2016. "Environmental Apartheid: Eco-Health and Rural Marginalization in South Africa."*Journal of Rural Studies 47*: 369–80.

Subramanyam, M. A., A. V. Diez-Roux, D. A. Hickson, D. F. Sapong, M. Sims, H. A. Taylor Jr., D. R. Williams, and S. B. Wyatt. 2012. "Subjective Social Status and Psychosocial and Metabolic Risk Factors for Cardiovascular Disease Among African Americans in the Jackson Heart Study." *Social Science & Medicine* 74 (8): 1146–54.

Substance Abuse and Mental Health Services Administration. 2011. *Results From the 2010 National Survey on Drug Use and Health: Summary of National Findings*. NSDUH Series H-41, HHS Publication (SMA) 11–4658. Rockville, MD: Substance Abuse and Mental Health Services Administration.

———. 2014. *Results From the 2013 National Survey on Drug Use and Health: Summary of National Findings*. NSDUH Series H-48, HHS Publication No. (SMA) 14–4863. Rockville, MD: Substance Abuse and Mental Health Services Administration. https://www .samhsa.gov/data/sites/default/files/ NSDUHresultsPDFWHTML2013/Web/ NSDUHresults2013.htm#7.3.1.

———. 2015. *Behavioral and Health Trends in the United States: Results From the 2014 National Survey on Drug Use and Health*.

HHS Publication (SMA) 15–4927. Rockville, MD: Substance Abuse and Mental Health Services Administration.

Sue, Derald Wing. 2010. *Microaggressions in Everyday Life: Race, Gender and Sexual Orientation*. Hoboken, NJ: Wiley Press.

Sullivan, Susan Crawford. 2011. *Living Faith: Everyday Religion and Mothers in Poverty*. Chicago: University of Chicago Press.

Sutherland, Edwin H. 1947. *Principles of Criminology: A Sociological Theory of Criminal Behavior*.

Sutherland, Edwin H., and Donald R. Cressey. 1974. *Criminology*, 9th ed. Philadelphia: Lippincott.

Talen, Emily. 2000. "The Problem With Community Planning." *Journal of Planning Literature* 15 (2): 171–83.

Tan, Alexis S., and Kermit Joseph Scruggs. 1980. "Does Exposure to Comic Book Violence Lead to Aggression in Children?" *Journalism Quarterly* 57 (4): 579–83.

Tanaka, Yuki, and Marilyn Young, eds. 2009. *Bombing Civilians: A Twentieth-Century History*. New York: New Press.

Tanielian, Terri, and Lisa H. Jaycox, eds. 2008. *Invisible Wounds of War: Psychological and Cognitive Injuries, Their Consequences, and Services to Assist Recovery*. Santa Monica, CA: RAND Center for Military Health Policy Research.

Tannenbaum, F. 1938. *Crime and the Community*. New York: Colombia University Press.

Tatum, Beverly Daniel. 2003. *"Why Are All the Black Kids Sitting Together in the Cafeteria?" and Other Conversations About Race: A Psychologist Explains the Development of Racial Identity*. New York: Basic Books.

Taylor, Adam. 2016. "The Uncomfortable Question: Was the Brexit Vote Based on Racism?" *Washington Post*, June 25. Accessed February 27, 2017. https://www .washingtonpost.com/news/worldviews/ wp/2016/06/25/the-uncomfortable-question-was-the-brexit-vote-based-on-racism/?utm_term=.66d4bcdf7bac.

Taylor, Paul, Kim Parker, Richard Fry, D'Vera Cohn, Wendy Wang, Gabriel Velasco, and Daniel Dockterman. 2011. *Is College Worth It? College Presidents, Public Assess Value, Quality and Mission of Higher Education*. Washington, DC: Pew Research

Center. http://www.pewsocialtrends.org/files/2011/05/Is-College-Worth-It.pdf.

Ten Hoeve, J. E., and M. Z. Jacobson. 2012. "Worldwide Health Effects of the Fukushima Daiichi Nuclear Accident." *Energy & Environmental Science* 5 (9): 8743–57.

Tepper, Steven J. 2011. *Not Here, Not Now, Not That! Protest Over Art and Culture in America.* Chicago: University of Chicago Press.

Territo, Leonard, and George Kirkham. 2010. *International Sex Trafficking of Women and Children: Understanding the Global Epidemic.* New York: Looseleaf Law.

Thoits, Peggy A. 1995. "Stress, Coping, and Social Support Processes: Where Are We? What Next?" *Journal of Health and Social Behavior* 35 (extra issue): 53–79.

Thomas, Anna Lind. 2010. "Hooking Up on Campus: Cognitive Dissonance and Sexual Regret Among College Students." Master's thesis, California State University, Chico. Accessed April 15, 2017. http://csuchico-dspace.calstate.edu/handle/10211.4/221.

Thomas, K. J. 2015. "Delinquent Peer Influence on Offending Versatility: Can Peers Promote Specialized Delinquency?" *Criminology* 53 (2). 280–308.

Thomas, William I., and Dorothy S. Thomas. 1928. *The Child in America: Behavior Problems and Programs.* New York: Alfred A. Knopf.

Thomis, Malcolm I. 1972. *The Luddites: Machine-Breaking in Regency England.* New York: Schocken.

Thompson, Mark. 2011. "The Other 1%." *Time,* November 21. http://content.time.com/time/magazine/article/0,9171,2099152,00.html.

Thorbecke, Catherine. 2016. "Why Previously Proposed Route for Dakota Access Pipeline Was Rejected." ABC News, November 3. Accessed March 1, 2017. http://abcnews.go.com/US/previously-proposed-route-dakota-access-pipeline-rejected/story?id=43274356.

Thrasher, Frederic. 1949. "The Comics and Delinquency: Cause or Scapegoat." *Journal of Educational Sociology* 23 (4): 195–205.

Tiefer, Leonore. 2004. *Sex Is Not a Natural Act and Other Essays*, 2nd ed. Boulder, CO: Westview Press.

Tierney, Kathleen J. 2007. "From the Margins to the Mainstream? Disaster Research at the Crossroads." *Annual Review of Sociology* 33: 503–25.

Titunik, Regina F. 2008. "The Myth of the Macho Military." *Polity* 40 (2): 137–63.

Tix, Andrew P., and Patricia A. Frazier. 1998. "The Use of Religious Coping During Stressful Life Events: Main Effects, Moderation, and Mediation." *Journal of Consulting and Clinical Psychology* 66: 411–22.

Tobias, J. K., and C. A. Richmond. 2014. "That Land Means Everything to Us as Anishinaabe . . .": Environmental Dispossession and Resilience on the North Shore of Lake Superior." *Health & Place* 29: 26–33.

Tocqueville, Alexis de. 1899. *Democracy in America.* Vol. 2. Translated by H. Reeve. New York: The Colonial Press.

Tolman, Deborah. 2013. "It's Bad for Us Too: How the Sexualization of Girls Impacts the Sexuality of Boys, Men, and Women." In *The Sexualization of Girls and Girlhood: Causes, Consequences, and Resistance,* edited by Eileen L. Zurbriggen and Tomi-Ann Roberts, 84–106. New York: Oxford University Press.

Tönnies, Ferdinand. 1957. *Community and Society.* Translated and edited by Charles P. Loomis. Lansing: Michigan State University Press.

Tonry, M. 2008. "Crime and Human Rights—How Political Paranoia, Protestant Fundamentalism, and Constitutional Obsolescence Combined to Devastate Black America: The American Society of Criminology, 2007 Presidential Address." *Criminology* 46 (1): 1–34.

Toossi, Mitra. 2012. "Labor Force Projections to 20: A More Slowly Growing Workforce." *Monthly Labor Review,* January, 43–64. http://www.bls.gov/opub/mlr/2012/01/art3full.pdf.

Torry, Jack, and Jessica Wehrman. 2013. "Sen. Brown Backs Bill to Increase Social Security Benefits." *Columbus Dispatch,* November 6. http://www.dispatch.com/content/stories/local/2013/11/05/brown-backs-bill-to-increase-social-security-benefits.html.

Tough, Paul. 2008. *Whatever It Takes: Geoffrey Canada's Quest to Change Harlem and America.* Boston: Houghton Mifflin.

Tractenberg, Paul, Gary Orfield, and Greg Flaxman. 2013. *New Jersey's Apartheid and Intensely Segregated Urban Schools: Powerful Evidence of an Inefficient and Unconstitutional State Education System.* Newark, NJ: Institute on Education Law and Policy, Rutgers University. http://ielp.rutgers.edu/docs/IELP%20final%20report%20on%20apartheid%20schools%20101013.pdf.

Treviño, A. Javier. 2011. "Teaching and Learning Service Sociology." *Teaching/Learning Matters* (newsletter of the American Sociological Association's Section on Teaching and Learning in Sociology) 40 (1): 4–6.

———. 2012. "The Challenge of Service Sociology." *Social Problems* 59 (1): 2–20.

———. 2013. "On the Facilitating Actions of Service Sociology." *Journal of Applied Social Science* 7 (1): 95–109.

———. 2018. "Service Sociology and Social Problems." In *The Cambridge Handbook of Social Problems, Vol. 1,* edited by A. Javier Treviño, 133–147. New York: Cambridge University Press.

Treviño, A. Javier, and Karen M. McCormack. 2014. *Service Sociology and Academic Engagement in Social Problems.* Burlington, VT: Ashgate.

Tripicchio, G., M. Heo, L. Diewald, S. M. Noar, R. Dooley, A. Pietrobelli, K. S. Burger, and M. S. Faith. 2016. *Childhood Obesity* 12 (2): 113–118.

Truman, Jennifer L., Lynn Langton, and Michael Planty. 2013. *Criminal Victimization, 2012.* Bureau of Justice Statistics Bulletin NCJ 243389, October. Washington, DC: U.S. Department of Justice. http://www.bjs.gov/content/pub/pdf/cv12.pdf.

Truman, Jennifer L., and Rachel E. Morgan. 2016. *Criminal Victimization, 2015.* U.S. Department of Justice, Office of Justice Programs, Bureau of Justice Statistics. Accessed May 22, 2017. https://www.bjs.gov/content/pub/pdf/cv15.pdf.

Truman, Jennifer L., and Michael R. Rand. 2010. *Criminal Victimization, 2009.* Bureau of Justice Statistics Bulletin NCJ 231327, October. Washington, DC: U.S. Department of Justice. http://www.bjs.gov/content/pub/pdf/cv09.pdf.

Turkle, Sherry. 2011. *Alone Together: Why We Expect More From Technology and Less From Each Other.* New York: Basic.

Turner, Margery Austin, Stephen L. Ross, George C. Galster, and John Yinger. 2002. *Discrimination in Metropolitan Housing Markets: National Results From Phase I HDS 2000.* Washington, DC: Urban Institute, Metropolitan Housing and Communities Policy Center. http://www.urban.org/uploadedPDF/410821_Phase1_Report.pdf.

Turney, Kristin. 2015. "Liminal Men: Incarceration and Relationship Dissolution." *Social Problems* 62 (4): 499–528.

Tyson, Karolyn. 2011. *Integration Interrupted: Tracking, Black Students, and Acting White After Brown.* New York: Oxford University Press.

Uchida, Craig D. 2010. "The Development of American Police: An Historical Overview." In *Critical Issues in Policing: Contemporary Readings,* 6th ed., edited by Roger G. Dunham and Geoffrey P. Alpert, 17–36. Long Grove, IL: Waveland Press.

United Nations. 2004. "United Nations Convention Against Transnational Organized Crime and the Protocols Thereto." United Nations Office on Drugs and Crime. Accessed May 1, 2017. https://www.unodc.org/documents/treaties/UNTOC/Publications/TOC%20Convention/TOCebook-e.pdf.

———. 2006a. "Table 23. Marriages and Crude Marriage Rates, by Urban/Rural Residence: 2002–2006." In *Demographic Yearbook.* New York: United Nations. http://unstats.un.org/unsd/demographic/products/dyb/dyb2006/Table23.pdf.

———. 2006b. "Table 25. Divorces and Crude Divorce Rates, by Urban/Rural Residence: 2002–2006." In *Demographic Yearbook.* New York: United Nations. http://unstats.un.org/unsd/demographic/products/dyb/dyb2006/Table25.pdf.

———. 2009. "International Migrant Stock: The 2008 Revision." http://esa.un.org/migration/index.asp?panel=1.

———. 2010. "Water and Urbanisation." Media brief. http://www.un.org/waterforlifedecade/swm_cities_zaragoza_2010/pdf/03_water_and_urbanisation.pdf.

———. 2011. *World Population Prospects: The 2010 Revision,* 2 vols. Department of Economic and Social Affairs, Population Division. New York: United Nations.

———. 2015. "Discrimination and Violence Against Individuals Based on Their Sexual Orientation and Gender Identity." Human Rights Council, Twenty-ninth Session, Agenda Items 2 and 8. Annual Report of the United Nations High Commissioner for Human Rights and Reports of the Office of the High Commissioner and the Secretary-General. Accessed March 24, 2017. http://journalistsresource.org/wp-content/uploads/2015/06/HRC_29_23_en.docx.

———. 2016. "Marriage and Divorce." Accessed August 11, 2016. http://unstats.un.org/unsd/demographic/sconcerns/mar/mar2.htm.

United Nations, Department of Economic and Social Affairs, Population Division. 2015. "World Population Prospects: The 2015 Revision, Key Findings and Advance Tables." Working Paper No. ESA/P/WP.241.

United Nations Development Programme. 2016. "Human Development Report." http://hdr.undp.org/en/2016–report. Accessed March 2, 2017.

United Nations Educational, Scientific and Cultural Organization (UNESCO). 1986. Seville Statement on Violence. http://www.unesco.org/cpp/uk/declarations/seville.pdf.

———. 2013. "Education for All Monitoring Report: Girls' Education—The Facts." http://en.unesco.org/gem-report/sites/gem-report/files/girls-factsheet-en.pdf.

———. 2015. UNESCO Institute for Statistics. Montreal, Canada. Accessed May 8, 2017. http://data.uis.unesco.org/.

United Nations Girls' Education Initiative. 2010. "Lacking Sanitary Pads, Girls Miss School in Dadaab Refugee Camp." October 13. http://www.ungei.org/news/kenya_2922.html.

———. 2011. "UN Girls' Education Initiative Reaffirms the Need for Education to Be Central to Improving the Lives of Women and Girls." March 7. http://www.ungei.org/infobycountry/247_3065.html.

———. 2014. "Empowering Adolescent Girls in Ethiopia and Tanzania." Accessed March 25. http://www.ungei.org/tanzania_3072.html.

United Nations Human Settlements Programme. 2011. "Hot Cities: Battle-Ground for Climate Change." http://mirror.unhabitat.org/downloads/docs/E_Hot_Cities.pdf.

United Nations Office on Drugs and Crime. 2006. *2006 Global Study on Ending Violence Against Women.* Vienna: United Nations Office on Drugs and Crime.

———. 2011a. *2011 Global Study on Homicide: Trends, Context, Data.* Vienna: United Nations Office on Drugs and Crime.

———. 2011b. *Global Practices on "Harmful Practices" Against Women.* Vienna: United Nations Office on Drugs and Crime.

———. 2013. *Comprehensive Study on Cybercrime* (Draft, February). Vienna: United Nations Office on Drugs and Crime. http://www.unodc.org/documents/organized-crime/UNODC_CCPCJ_EG.4_2013/CYBERCRIME_STUDY_210213.pdf.

———. United Students Against Sweatshops. 2014. "Garment Worker Solidarity." Accessed April 16. http://usas.org/campaigns/garment-worker-solidarity.

United Nations Population Fund (UNFPA). 2016. "The State of World Population 2016."

———. 2017. "What We Do," at http://usas.org/

United States Agency for International Development (USAID). 2011. "Why Invest in Women?" http://50.usaid.gov/infographic-why-invest-in-women/usaid-women.

———. n.d. "Let Girls Learn." Fact Sheet. https://www.usaid.gov/letgirlslearn/fact-sheet.

U.S. Bureau of Justice Statistics. 2005. *State Court Sentencing of Convicted Felons.* Washington, DC: U.S. Department of Justice.

———. 2014. "Rape and Sexual Assault." Accessed March 25. http://www.bjs.gov/index.cfm?ty=tpandtid=317.

U.S. Bureau of Labor Statistics. 2010a. "National Census of Fatal Occupational Injuries in 2009 (Preliminary Results)." Press release, August 19. http://www.bls.gov/news.release/pdf/cfoi.pdf.

———. 2010b. "Workplace Injuries and Illnesses—2009." Press release, October 21. http://www.bls.gov/news.release/archives/osh_10212010.pdf.

———. 2012a. "Employment Status of the Civilian Population by Race, Sex, and Age." Accessed June 12. http://www.bls.gov/news.release/empsit.t02.htm.

———. 2012b. *Highlights of Women's Earnings in 2011.* Report 1038. Washington, DC:

U.S. Department of Labor. http://www.bls
.gov/cps/cpswom2011.pdf.

———. 2012c. *Labor Force Characteristics by Race and Ethnicity, 2011.* Report 1036. Washington, DC: U.S. Department of Labor. http://www.bls.gov/cps/cpsrace2011.pdf.

———. 2012d. "Labor Force Statistics From the Current Population Survey: Labor Force, Employment, and Unemployment Statistics by Age Group, 2012." http://www.bls.gov/cps/cpsaat03.pdf.

———. 2013a. "The Editor's Desk: Union Membership Declines in 2012." January 24. http://www.bls.gov/opub/ted/2013/ted_20130124.htm.

———. 2013b. "Employment Status of the Civilian Population by Sex and Age." Accessed April 8. http://www.bls.gov/news.release/empsit.t01.htm.

———. 2013c. "Employment Status of the Civilian Population 25 Years and Over by Educational Attainment." Accessed April 9. http://www.bls.gov/news.release/empsit.t04.htm.

———. 2013d. "Frequently Asked Questions." Accessed March 8. http://www.bls.gov/dolfaq/bls_ques23.htm.

———. 2013e. "Number of Fatal Work Injuries, 1992–2011." http://www.bls.gov/iif/oshwc/cfoi/cfch0010.pdf.

———. 2013f. "Frequently Asked Questions." http://www.bls.gov/dolfaq/bls_ques23.htm.

———. 2014a. "Labor Force Statistics From the Current Population Survey: Access to Historical Data for the Tables of the Union Membership News Release." Accessed March 26. http://www.bls.gov/cps/cpslutabs.htm.

———. 2014b. "Education Still Pays." September. Accessed May 29, 2017. https://www.bls.gov/careeroutlook/2014/data-on-display/education-still-pays.htm.

———. 2015a. "Employment by Major Industry Sector. December 8. Accessed January 3, 2017. https://www.bls.gov/emp/ep_table_201.htm.

———. 2015b. "Highlights of Women's Earnings." November. Accessed January 13, 2017. https://www.bls.gov/opub/reports/womens-earnings/archive/highlights-of-womens-earnings-in-2014.pdf.

———. 2015c. "Labor Force Characteristics by Race and Ethnicity, 2014." November.

Accessed January 13, 2017. https://www.bls.gov/opub/reports/race-and-ethnicity/archive/labor-force-characteristics-by-race-and-ethnicity-2014.pdf.

———. 2015d. "Labor Force Projections to 2024: The Labor Force Is Growing, but Slowly." Accessed January 12, 2017. https://www.bls.gov/opub/mlr/2015/article/labor-force-projections-to-2024.htm.

———. 2015e. "Median Weekly Earnings by Educational Attainment in 2014. January 23. Accessed January 12, 2017. https://www.bls.gov/opub/ted/2015/median-weekly-earnings-by-education-gender-race-and-ethnicity-in-2014.htm.

———. 2015f. "Number of Involuntary Part-Time Workers 5.8 million in October 2015." November 10, 2015. Accessed January 13, 2017. https://www.bls.gov/opub/ted/2015/number-of-involuntary-part-time-workers-5–point-8–million-in-october-2015.htm.

———. 2015g. "Employment by Major Industry Sector." December 8, 2015. Accessed 31 May 31. https://www.bls.gov/emp/ep_table_201.htm.

———. 2015h. "Women in the Labor Force" Accessed January 13, 2017. https://www.dol.gov/wb/stats/facts_over_time.htm.

———. 2016a. "Women in the Labor Force." Accessed January 13, 2017. https://www.dol.gov/wb/stats/facts_over_time.htm.

———. 2016b. "16.9 Million People Unemployed at Some Point in 2015, Down From 17.7 Million in 2014." December 23. Accessed January 12, 2017. https://www.bls.gov/opub/ted/2016/16–point-9–million-people-unemployed-at-some-point-in-2015–down-from-17–point-7–million-in-2014.htm.

———. 2016c. "Highlights of Women's Earnings in 2015." Report 1064. https://www.bls.gov/opub/reports/womens-earnings/2015/home.htm.

———. 2016d. "4,836 Fatal Work Injuries in the United States During 2015." December 21. Accessed January 12, 2017. https://www.bls.gov/opub/ted/2016/4836–fatal-work-injuries-in-the-united-states-during-2015.htm.

———. 2016e. "Duration of Unemployment in April 2016." May 10. Accessed January 11, 2017. https://www.bls.gov/opub/

ted/2016/duration-of-unemployment-in-april-2016.htm.

———. 2016f. "Employer-Reported Workplace Injuries and Illnesses—2015." October 27. Accessed January 13, 2017. https://www.bls.gov/news.release/pdf/osh.pdf.

———. 2016g. "Labor Force Characteristics From the Current Population Survey." Accessed January 13, 2017. https://www.bls.gov/cps/cpsaat37.htm.

———. 2016h. "Labor Force Characteristics by Race and Ethnicity." Accessed January 13, 2017. https://www.bls.gov/opub/reports/race-and-ethnicity/archive/labor-force-characteristics-by-race-and-ethnicity-2014.pdf.

———. 2016i. "Number of Fatal Work Injuries by Employee Status, 2003–15." Accessed January 13, 2017. https://www.bls.gov/iif/oshwc/cfoi/cfch0014.pdf.

———. 2016j. "Union Membership in the United States." September. Accessed January 13, 2017. https://www.bls.gov/spotlight/2016/union-membership-in-the-united-states/home.htm.

———. 2016k. "Usual Weekly Earnings of Wage and Salary Workers, Third Quarter." Accessed January 16, 2017. https://www.bls.gov/news.release/pdf/wkyeng.pdf.

———. 2016l. "Women's Earnings 83 Percent of Men's, but Vary by Occupation." January 15, 2016. Accessed January 12. https://www.bls.gov/opub/ted/2016/womens-earnings-83–percent-of-mens-but-vary-by-occupation.htm.

———. 2016m. "Women More Likely Than Men to Have Earned a Bachelor's Degree by Age 29. April 13. Accessed January 13, 2017. https://www.bls.gov/opub/ted/2016/women-more-likely-than-men-to-have-earned-a-bachelors-degree-by-age-29.htm.

———. 2016n. "Employer-Reported Workplace Injuries and Accidents—2015." October 27. Accessed May 30, 2017. https://www.bls.gov/news.release/pdf/osh.pdf.

———. 2016o. "National Census of Fatal Occupational Injuries in 2015." December 16. Accessed May 30, 2016. https://www.bls.gov/news.release/pdf/cfoi.pdf.

———. 2016p. "Women in the Labor Force." July. Accessed May 29, 2017. https://www.dol.gov/wb/stats/facts.

———. 2017a. "Employment Status." Table A-1. January 6. Accessed January 12. https://www.bls.gov/web/empsit/cpseea01.htm.

———. 2017b. "Labor Force Statistics From the Current Population Survey." January 6. Accessed January 11, 2017. https://www.bls.gov/cps/earnings.htm.

———. 2017c. "Databases, Tables, and Calculators." Accessed May 29, 2017. https://data.bls.gov/timeseries/LNS14000000. U.S. Bureau of Labor Statistics. 2017c. "Table 5. Employment Status of the Civilian Noninstitutional Population by Sex, Age, and Race." Accessed April 11. https://www.bls.gov/cps/cpsaat05.htm.

———. 2017d. "Table 3. Employment Status of the Civilian Noninstitutional Population by Age, Sex, and Race." Accessed April 11. https://www.bls.gov/cps/cpsaat03.htm.

———. 2017e. Table A-4. "Employment Status of the Civilian Population 25 Years and Over by Educational Attainment." May 5. Accessed May 29, 2017. https://www.bls.gov/news.release/empsit.t04.htm.

———. 2017f. "Labor Force Statistics From the Current Population Survey." April 7. Accessed May 29, 2017. https://www.bls.gov/web/empsit/cpsee_e16.htm.

———. 2017g. "Union Members Survey." January 26. Accessed May 29, 2017. https://www.bls.gov/news.release/union2.nr0.htm.

———. 2017h. "Women's Median Earnings 82 Percent of Men's in 2016." March 8. Accessed May 29, 2017. https://www.bls.gov/opub/ted/2017/womens-median-earnings-82–percent-of-mens-in-2016.htm.

U.S. Census Bureau. 2001. "Statistical Abstract of the United States." Table 117.

———. 2010. "Table UC3. Opposite Sex Unmarried Couples by Presence of Biological Children Under 18, and Age, Earnings, Education, and Race and Hispanic Origin of Both Partners: 2010." http://www.census.gov/population/www/socdemo/hh-fam/cps2010.html.

———. 2011. "American Community Survey." Tables S-1201 and S-1251.

———. 2012a. "About Families and Living Arrangements." Accessed October 19. http://www.census.gov/hhes/families/about.

———. 2012b. "Table 133. Marriages and Divorces: Number and Rate by State, 1990–2009." In Statistical Abstract of the United States: 2012. Washington, DC: Government Printing Office. http://www.census.gov/compendia/statab/2012/tables/12s0133.pdf.

———. 2012c. "Table 229. Educational Attainment by Race and Hispanic Origin: 1970 to 2010." In Statistical Abstract of the United States: 2012. Washington, DC: Government Printing Office. http://www.census.gov/compendia/statab/2012/tables/12s0230.pdf.

———. 2012d. "Table 620. Employment by Industry: 2000 to 2012." In Statistical Abstract of the United States: 2012. Washington, DC: Government Printing Office. http://www.census.gov/compendia/statab/2012/tables/12s0620.pdf.

———. 2012e. "Table 697. Money Income of Families—Median Income by Race and Hispanic Origin in Current and Constant (2009) Dollars: 1990 to 2009." In Statistical Abstract of the United States: 2012. Washington, DC: Government Printing Office. http://www.census.gov/compendia/statab/2012/tables/12s0697.pdf.

———. 2012f. "Table 699. Median Income of Families by Type of Family in Current and Constant (2009) Dollars, 1990 to 2009." In Statistical Abstract of the United States: 2012. Washington, DC: Government Printing Office. http://www.census.gov/compendia/statab/2012/tables/12s0699.pdf.

———. 2012g. "Table 1106. Motor Vehicle Occupants and Nonoccupants Killed and Injured: 1980 to 2009." In Statistical Abstract of the United States: 2012. Washington, DC: Government Printing Office. http://www.census.gov/compendia/statab/2012/tables/12s1106.pdf.

———. 2015. "American Community Survey."

———. 2016. "American Community Survey."

———. 2017. "Figure MS-2. Median Age at First Marriage: 1890 to Present." https://www.census.gov/hhes/families/data/marital.html.

U.S. Department of Commerce, Economics and Statistics Administration. 2015. July 1. Accessed May 29, 2017. http://www.esa.doc.gov/sites/default/files/temporary-help-workers-in-the-us-labor-market.pdf.

U.S. Department of Defense. 2012. Department of Defense Annual Report on Sexual Assault in the Military: Fiscal Year 2012. Washington, DC: U.S. Department of Defense. http://s3.documentcloud.org/documents/697934/pentagon-report-on-sexual-assault-in-2012.pdf.

U.S. Department of Health and Human Services. 2012. "The Center for Faith-based and Neighborhood Partnerships." Accessed November 26. http://www.hhs.gov/partnerships/index.html.

———. 2013. "2013 Poverty Guidelines." http://aspe.hhs.gov/poverty/13poverty.cfm.

———. 2015. "A Profile of Older Americans: 2015." Administration on Aging. U.S. Department of Human Services. Washington, DC.

———. 2016. Office of the Assistant Secretary for Planning and Evaluation. "Poverty Guidelines 1/25/16/." http://www.aspe.hhs.gov/poverty-guidelines.

U.S. Department of Labor. 2011. Dictionary of Occupational Titles. Washington, DC: Government Printing Office. http://www.occupationalinfo.org.

U.S. Department of State. 2007. "Trafficking in Persons Report 2007." http://www.state.gov/j/tip/rls/tiprpt/2007/index.htm.

———. 2011. "Trafficking in Persons Report 2011." http://www.state.gov/j/tip/rls/tiprpt/2011/index.htm.

———. 2014. "20 Ways You Can Help Fight Human Trafficking." Accessed March 31. http://www.state.gov/j/tip/id/help.

———. 2016. "Trafficking in Persons Report." Accessed May 1, 2017. https://www.state.gov/documents/organization/258876.pdf.

U.S. Environmental Protection Agency. 2012a. "Climate Change." Accessed May 31. http://www.epa.gov/climatechange.

———. 2012b. "Climate Change Indicators in the United States." http://www.epa.gov/climatechange/science/indicators/ghg/us-ghg-emissions.html.

U.S. Equal Employment Opportunity Commission. 2009. "Title VII of the Civil Rights Act of 1964." http://www.eeoc.gov/laws/statutes/titlevii.cfm.

U.S. Supreme Court. Obergefell v. Hodges, 14-556 U.S. (2015).

Vaes, Jeroen, Paola Paladino, and Elisa Puvia. 2011. "Are Sexualized Women Complete Human Beings? Why Men and Women

Dehumanize Sexually Objectified Women." *European Journal of Psychology* 41 (6): 774–85.

Vaidyanathan, Gayathri. 2016. "Could Sea Level Rise Swamp Cities Within a Century?" *Scientific American*, March 22. Accessed January 15, 2017. https://www .scientificamerican.com/article/could-sea -level-rise-swamp-cities-within-a-century/.

Valdés, Guadalupe. 1996. *Con Respeto: Bridging the Distances Between Culturally Diverse Families and Schools. An Ethnographic Portrait*. New York: Teachers College Press.

Van Aalst, Maarten K. 2006. "The Impacts of Climate Change on the Risk of Natural Disasters." *Disasters* 30 (1): 5–18.

Van Cleve, Nicole Gonzalez. 2016. *Crook County: Racism and Injustice in America's Largest Criminal Court*. Stanford: Stanford University Press.

Van de Water, Paul N. 2013. "Medicare Is Not 'Bankrupt': Health Reform Has Improved Program's Financing." Center on Budget and Policy Priorities, June 3. http://www .cbpp.org/cms/?fa=view&id=3532.

Van Hook, Jennifer, Susan I. Brown, and Maxwell Ndigume Kwenda. 2004. "A Decomposition of Trends in Poverty Among Children of Immigrants." *Demography* 41 (4): 649–70.

Van Ness, Daniel W., and Karen Heetderks Strong. 2010. *Restoring Justice: An introduction to Restorative Justice*, 4th ed. New Providence, NJ: LexisNexis.

Van Orden, Kimberly, and Yeates Conwell. 2011. "Suicides in Late Life." *Current Psychiatry Reports* 13 (3): 234–41.

Vandepitte, J., R. Lyerla, G. Dallabetta, F. Crabbé, M. Alary, and A. Buvé. 2006. "Estimates of the Number of Female Sex Workers in Different Regions of the World." *Sexually Transmitted Diseases* 82 (3): 18–25.

Vasquez, Jessica M. 2011. *Mexican Americans Across Generations: Immigrant Families, Racial Realities*. New York: New York University Press.

Ventola, C. Lee. 2011. "Direct-to-Consumer Pharmaceutical Advertising: Therapeutic or Toxic?" *Pharmacy and Therapeutics* 36 (10): 669–74, 681–84.

Vine, David. 2012. "Tomgram: The True Costs of Empire." December 11. http:// www.tomdispatch.com/post/1756 27/ tomgram%3A_david_vine,_the_true_ costs_of_empire.

Von Hippel, F. N. 2011. "The Radiological and Psychological Consequences of the Fukushima Daiichi Accident." *Bulletin of the Atomic Scientists* 67 (5): 27–36.

Voss, Georgina. 2012. "Treating It as a Normal Business': Researching the Pornography Industry." *Sexualities* 15 (3–4): 391–410.

Vostral, Sharra. 2008. *Under Wraps: A History of Menstrual Hygiene Technology*. Lanham, MD: Lexington Books.

Vrangalova, Zhana. 2015. "Does Casual Sex Harm College Students' Well-Being? A Longitudinal Investigation of the Role of Motivation." *Archives of Sexual Behavior* 44 (4): 945–59.

Waddan, Alex. 2010. "The US Safety Net, Inequality, and the Great Recession." *Journal of Poverty and Social Justice* 18 (3): 243–54.

Wade, Ann, and Tanya Beran. 2011. "Cyberbullying: The New Era of Bullying." *Canadian Journal of Social Psychology* 26 (1): 44–61.

Wade, Lisa. 2017. *American Hookup: The New Culture of Sex on Campus*. New York: W. W. Norton and Company.

Wade, Lisa, and Caroline Heldman. 2012. "Hooking Up and Opting Out: Negotiating Sex in the First Year of College." In *Sex for Life: From Virginity to Viagra, How Sexuality Changes Throughout Our Lives*, edited by Laura M. Carpenter and John DeLamater, 128–45. New York: New York University Press.

WAGE Project. 2012. "WAGE (Women Are Getting Even)." Accessed July 12. http:// www.wageproject.org/index.php.

Wagenaar, Hendrik, Helga Amesberger, and Sietske Altink. 2017. *Designing Prostitution Policy: Intention and Reality in Regulating the Sex Trade*. Chicago: Policy Press. Accessed May 1, 2017 (file:///C:/Users/ elroi.windsor/Downloads/627654.pdf).

Waitzkin, Howard. 2000. *The Second Sickness: Contradictions of Capitalist Health Care*. Lanham, MD: Rowman & Littlefield.

Wajcman, Judy. 2000. "Reflections on Gender and Technology Studies: In What State Is the Art?" *Social Studies of Science* 30 (3): 447–64.

Walker, Samuel, and Charles M. Katz. 2008. *The Police in America: An Introduction*, 6th ed. Boston: McGraw-Hill.

Waller, Willard. 1965. *The Sociology of Teaching*. New York: John Wiley.

Wallerstein, Immanuel. 1979. *The Capitalist World-Economy*. Cambridge: Cambridge University Press.

Walsh, Declan, and Ihsanullah Tipu Mehsud. 2013. "Civilian Deaths in Drone Strikes Cited in Report." *New York Times*, October 22, 1.

Walsh, Susan. 2014. Hooking Up Smart home page. Accessed March 28. http://www .hookingupsmart.com.

Walton, John. 1993. "Urban Sociology: The Contribution and Limits of Political Economy." *Annual Review of Sociology* 19: 301–20.

Wang, E. C., M. C. Choe, J. G. Meara, and J. A. Koempel. 2004. "Inequality of Access to Surgical Specialty Health Care: Why Children With Government-Funded Insurance Have Less Access Than Those With Private Insurance in Southern California." *Pediatrics* 114 (5): e584–90.

Wang, Wendy. 2012. "Public Says a Secure Job Is the Ticket to the Middle Class." Pew Research Center, Social and Demographic Trends. http://www.pewsocialtrends.org/ files/2012/08/Job-report-final.pdf.

Wang, Wendy, and Kim Parker. 2014. "Record Share of Americans Have Never Married." Pew Research Center, September 24. Accessed August 11, 2016. http://www .pewsocialtrends.org/2014/09/24/record -share-of-americans-have-never-married/.

Want China Times. 2012. "Over 70% of Chinese Have Had Pre-marital Sex: Survey." April 10. http://www.wantchinatimes .com/news-subclass-cnt.aspx? id=20120410000035andcid=1103.

Ward, Lester F. 1902. "Contemporary Sociology." *American Journal of Sociology* 7 (4): 475–500.

Wargo, John. 2009. *Green Intelligence: Creating Environments That Protect Human Health*. New Haven, CT: Yale University Press.

Warner, Michael. 1993. "Introduction." In *Fear of a Queer Planet: Queer Politics and Social Theory*, edited by Michael Warner, vi–xxxvi. Minneapolis: University of Minnesota Press.

Watanabe, Maiko. 2008. "Tracking in the Era of High Stakes State Accountability Reform: Case Studies of Classroom Instruction in North Carolina." *The Teachers College Record* 110 (3): 489–534.

Waters, Mary C. 1999. *Black Identities: West Indian Immigrant Dreams and American*

Realities. Cambridge, MA: Harvard University Press.

Waters, Mary C., and Tomás R. Jiménez. 2005. "Assessing Immigrant Assimilation: New Empirical and Theoretical Challenges." *Annual Review of Sociology* 31: 105–25.

Watkins, S. Craig. 2005. *Hip Hop Matters: Politics, Pop Culture, and the Struggle for the Soul of a Movement.* Boston: Beacon Press.

Weber, Max. 1958a. *From Max Weber: Essays in Sociology.* Edited by H. H. Gerth and C. Wright Mills. New York. Oxford University Press.

———. 1958b. "Bureaucracy." In *From Max Weber: Essays in Sociology,* edited by H. H. Gerth and C. Wright Mills. New York: Oxford University Press.

———. 2004. *The Protestant Ethic and the Spirit of Capitalism.* New York: Oxford University Press. First published 1904–1905.

Weil, Andrew, and Winifred Rosen. 2004. *From Chocolate to Morphine: Everything You Need to Know About Mind-Altering Drugs,* rev. ed. Boston: Houghton Mifflin.

Weinberg, Martin S., and Colin J. Williams. 2014. "Sexual Field, Erotic Habitus, and Embodiment at a Transgender Bar." In *Sexual Fields: Toward a Sociology of Collective Sexual Life,* edited by Adam Isaiah Green, 57–70. Chicago: University of Chicago Press.

Weiss, Christopher C., Brian V. Carolan, and E. Christine Baker-Smith. 2010. "Big School, Small School: (Re) Testing Assumptions About High School Size, School Engagement and Mathematics Achievement." *Journal of Youth and Adolescence* 39 (2): 163–76.

Weiss, Nicholas. 2011. "Assessment and Treatment of ADHD in Adults." *Psychiatric Annals* 41 (1): 23–31.

Weitzer, Ronald. 2007. "The Social Construction of Sex Trafficking: Ideology and Institutionalization of a Moral Crusade." *Politics and Society* 35 (3): 447–75.

———. 2012. *Legalizing Prostitution: From Illicit Vice to Lawful Business.* New York: New York University Press.

———. 2015. "Researching Prostitution and Sex Trafficking Comparatively." *Sexuality Research and Social Policy* 12 (2): 81–91.

Welsh, Wayne N., and Phillip W. Harris. 2012. *Criminal Justice Policy and Planning,* 4th ed. Waltham, MA: Elsevier.

Wertham, Fredric. 1954. *Seduction of the Innocent.* New York: Rinehart.

West, Candace, and Sarah Fenstermaker. 1993. "Power, Inequality and the Accomplishment of Gender: An Ethnomethodological View." In *Theory on Gender, Feminism on Theory,* edited by Paula England, 151–74. New York: Aldine de Gruyter.

West, Candace, and Angela Garcia. 1988. "Conversational Shift Work: A Study of Topical Transition Between Women and Men." *Social Problems* 35: 551–75.

West, Jan. 2017. "The Truth About Job Satisfaction and Friendships at Work." National Business Research Institute. Accessed May 30, 2017. https://www .nbrii.com/employee-survey-white-papers/ the-truth-about-job-satisfaction-and- friendships-at-work/.

Westbrook, Laurel, and Kristen Schilt. 2014. "Doing Gender, Determining Gender: Transgender People, Gender Panics, and the Maintenance of the Sex/Gender/ Sexuality System." *Gender & Society* 28 (1): 32–57.

Western, Bruce. 2006. *Punishment and Inequality in America.* New York: Russell Sage Foundation.

White, Kevin. 2006. *The Sage Dictionary of Health and Society.* Thousand Oaks, CA: Sage.

———. 2009. *An Introduction to the Sociology of Health and Illness.* Thousand Oaks, CA: Sage.

———. 2012. "The Body, Social Inequality and Health." In *The Routledge Handbook of Body Studies,* edited by Bryan S. Turner, 264–74. London: Routledge.

White, Merry I. 1987. *The Japanese Educational Challenge: A Commitment to Children.* New York: Free Press.

Whitehead, Harriet. 1981. "The Bow and the Burden Strap: A New Look at Institutionalized Homosexuality in Native North America." In *Sexual Meanings: The Cultural Construction of Gender and Sexuality,* edited by Sherry B. Ortner and Harriet Whitehead, 80–115. Cambridge: Cambridge University Press.

Wildeman, Christopher. 2012. "Imprisonment and Infant Mortality." *Social Problems* 59: 228–57.

Williams, Alex. 2010. "The New Math on Campus." *New York Times,* February 5.

Williams, Christine L. 1992. "The Glass Escalator: Hidden Advantages for Men in the 'Female' Professions." *Social Problems* 39 (3): 253–67.

Williams, David R., and Selina A. Mohammed. 2013. "Racism and Health I: Pathways and Scientific Evidence." *American Behavioral Scientist* 57: 1152–73.

Williams, David R., and Michelle Sternthall. 2010. "Understanding Racial-Ethnic Disparities in Health: Sociological Contributions." *Journal of Health and Social Behavior* 51 (S): S15–27.

Williamson, Celia, and Lynda M. Baker. 2009. "Women in Street-Based Prostitution: A Typology of Their Work Styles." *Qualitative Social Work* 8 (1): 27–44.

Wilson, J. Q., and G. L. Kelling. 1982. "Broken Windows." In *Critical Issues in Policing: Contemporary Readings,* 7th edition, edited by Roger G. Dunham and Geoffrey P Alpert, 455–67. Long Grove, IL: Waveland.

Wilson, Jim. 2013. "Restorative Justice Programs Take Root in Schools." *New York Times,* April 3.

Wilson, William Julius. 1978. *The Declining Significance of Race: Blacks and Changing American Institutions.* Chicago: University of Chicago Press.

———. 1987. *The Truly Disadvantaged: The Inner City, the Underclass, and Public Policy.* Chicago: University of Chicago Press.

———. 1996. *When Work Disappears: The World of the New Urban Poor.* New York: Alfred A. Knopf.

———. 2009. *More Than Just Race: Being Black and Poor in the Inner City.* New York: W. W. Norton.

Windsor, Elroi J. 2014. "Sick Sex." In *Sex Matters: The Sexuality and Society Reader,* 4th ed., edited by Mindy Stombler, Dawn M. Baunach, Wendy Simonds, Elroi J. Windsor, and Elisabeth O. Burgess, 513–20. New York: W. W. Norton.

Windsor, Liliane Cambraia, Ellen Benoit, and Eloise Dunlap. 2010. "Dimensions of Oppression in the Lives of Impoverished Black Women Who Use Drugs." *Journal of Black Studies* 41 (1): 21–39.

Wing, Steve. 2010. "Ethics for Environmental Health Research: The Case of the U.S. Nuclear Weapons Industry." *New Solutions* 20 (2): 179–87.

Wingfield, Adia Harvey. 2009. "Racializing the Glass Escalator: Reconsidering Men's Experiences With Women's Work." *Gender & Society* 23 (1): 5–26.

Wise, Tim. 2008. *White Like Me: Reflections on Race From a Privileged Son.* New York: Soft Skull Press.

Women's Sports Foundation. 2015. "Pay Inequity in Athletics." July 20. Accessed March 1, 2017. https://www.womenssportsfoundation.org/research/article-and-report/equity-issues/pay-inequity.

Wong, Kristina. 2009. "Obama on Hate Crimes Legislation Signing: 'The Bells of Freedom Ring Out a Little Louder.'" ABC News, October 28. http://abcnews.go.com/blogs/politics/2009/10/obama-on-hate-crimes-legislation-signing-the-bells-of-freedom-ring-out-a-little-louder.

Wood, Jean Elisabeth. 2006. "Variation in Sexual Violence During War." *Politics and Society* 34: 307–42.

World Commission on Environment and Development. 1987. *Our Common Future.* Oxford: Oxford University Press.

World Economic Forum. 2016. "The Global Gender Gap Report." http://reports.weforum.org/global-gender-gap-report-2010/.

World Health Organization. 2011. "Environmental and Occupational Cancers." http://www.who.int/mediacentre/factsheets/fs350/en/.

———. 2014. "Condoms for HIV Prevention." Accessed March 31. http://www.who.int/hiv/topics/condoms/en.

———. 2016a. "World Health Statistics 2016." http://www.who.int/gho/publications/world_health_statistics/2016/EN_WHS2016_AnnexB.pdf?ua=1.

———. 2016b. "WHO/Europe and Ministry of Health of Greece Expand Collaboration on Health Reform Priorities." http://www.euro.who.int/en/countries/greece/news/news/2016/09/whoeurope-and-ministry-of-health-of-greece-expand-collaboration-on-health-reform-priorities.

———. 2016c. "World Health Statistics 2016."

———. 2016d. "Violence Against Women: Intimate Partner and Sexual Violence Against Women."

World Nuclear Association. 2013. "Uranium in Niger." http://world-nuclear.org/info/Country-Profiles/Countries-G-N/Niger/#.UbTSnutYg8Y.

Worthy, Kenneth A., Richard C. Strohman, Paul R. Billings, and the Berkeley Biotechnology Working Group. 2005. "Agricultural Biotechnology Science Compromised: The Case of Quist and Chapela." In *Controversies in Science and Technology: From Maize to Menopause,* edited by Daniel Lee Kleinman, Abby J. Kinchy, and Jo Handelsman, 135–49. Madison: University of Wisconsin Press.

Xie, Yu, Michael Fang, and Kimberlee Shauman. 2015. "STEM Education." *Annual Review of Sociology* 41: 331–357.

Yablokov, Alexy V., Vassily B. Nesterenko, and Alexy V. Nesterenko. 2009. "Chernobyl: Consequences of the Catastrophe for People and the Environment." *Annals of the New York Academy of Sciences* 1181 (December). Sternthall

Yalom, Marilyn. 1997. *A History of the Breast.* New York: Ballantine Publishing Group.

Yamato, Gloria. 2001. "Something About the Subject Makes It Hard to Name." In *Race, Class, and Gender: An Anthology,* 4th ed., edited by Margaret L. Anderson and Patricia Hill Collins, 90–94. Belmont, CA: Wadsworth.

Yancey, George. 2003. *Who Is White? Latinos, Asians, and the New Black/Nonblack Divide.* Boulder, CO: Lynne Rienner.

Yang, Song. 2007. "Racial Disparities in Training, Pay-Raise Attainment, and Income." *Research in Social Stratification and Mobility* 25 (4): 323–35.

Yeager, Angela. 2012. "Survey: Health Care Providers Not Checking for Family Food Insecurity, Barriers Still Exist." Oregon State University Extension Service, July 10. http://extension.oregonstate.edu/news/release/2012/07/survey-health-care-providers-not-checking-family-food-insecurity-barriers-still-exis.

Yetman, Norman. 1999. *Majority and Minority: The Dynamic of Race and Ethnicity in American Life.* Boston: Allyn & Bacon.

Yinger, John. 1995. *Closed Doors, Opportunities Lost: The Continuing Costs of Housing Discrimination.* New York: Russell Sage Foundation.

Zaikman, Yuliana, Michael J. Marks, Tara M. Young, and Jacqueline A. Zeiber. 2016. "Gender Role Violations and the Sexual Double Standard." *Journal of Homosexuality* 63 (12): 1608–29.

Zanjari, Nasibeh, Maryam Sharifian Sani, Meimanat Hosseini Chavoshi, Hassan Rafiey, and Farahnaz Mohammadi Shahboulaghi. 2016. "Perceptions of Successful Ageing Among Iranian Elders: Insights From a Qualitative Study." *The International Journal of Aging and Human Development* 83 (4): 381–401.

Zhang, G., L. Wu, L. Zhou, W. Lu, and C. Mao. 2016. "Television Watching and Risk of Childhood Obesity: A Meta Analysis." *European Journal of Public Health* 26 (1): 13–18.

Zheng, Hui, and Linda K. George. 2012. "Rising U.S. Income Inequality and the Changing Gradient of Socioeconomic Status on Physical Functioning and Activity Limitations, 1984–2007." *Social Science & Medicine* 75 (12): 2170–82.

Zhuqing, Wang. 2012. "A Study of the Rights and Interests of the Older Persons in China." *Ageing International* 37: 386–413.

Zibbell, J., R. Hart-Malloy, J. Barry, L. Fan, and C. Flanigan. 2014. "Risk Factors for HCV Infection Among Young Adults in Rural New York Who Inject Prescription Opioid Analgesics." *American Journal of Public Health* 104 (11): 2226–32.

Zola, Irving Kenneth. 1972. "Medicine as an Institution of Social Control." *American Sociological Review* 20 (4): 487–504.

Zukin, Sharon. 1995. *The Cultures of Cities.* Malden, MA: Blackwell.

INDEX